THE BIBLE EXPOSITION COMMENTARY

VOLUME 1

THE BIBLE EXPOSITION COMMENTARY

VOLUME 1

WARREN W.
WIERSBE

VICTOR BOOKS®
A DIVISION OF SCRIPTURE PRESS PUBLICATIONS INC.
USA CANADA ENGLAND

3 4 5 6 7 8 9 10 Printing/Year 94 93 92 91 90

Recommended Dewey Decimal Classification: 220.7
Suggested Subject Headings: BIBLE, NEW TESTAMENT, COMMENTARY

Library of Congress Catalog Card Number: 89-60158
ISBN: 0-89693-659-7

VICTOR BOOKS
A division of Scripture Press
Wheaton, Illinois 60187

Contents

Foreword

It was in November 1971 that Henry Jacobsen phoned me at the Moody Church and asked me to write a book on 1 John for Scripture Press. This was a gracious gesture on his part, because the current material on 1 John had been written by Henry and he was willing to have it dropped.

Had I known then what my work load was going to be for the next eighteen years, I would have told him no. But I agreed to do the book and dutifully sent them the manuscript in the spring of 1972. My original title was *On Being a Real Christian,* but it had two strikes against it: it was too long, and there was already a book by that title.

Some anonymous Scripture Press employee, in a Title Committee meeting, said, "Why not just call it *Be Real?*" and the BE series was born. Now, twenty-three titles later, we have covered the entire New Testament, all of which are now assembled in *The Bible Exposition Commentary.* If you had told me this back in 1971, I would not have believed you!

I want to praise the Lord for His kindness and mercy to me in allowing me the privilege of ministering in this way. I can think of many of my friends who could have done a far better job in this series, but the Lord graciously led Henry to challenge me. Over the years, He has given me the strength and wisdom needed, and for this I give Him thanks.

How does a busy preacher find time to write? Much of the credit goes to my wife Betty who manages our household so well, and takes such good care of me, that I have the free time necessary for studying and writing. When I started this series, our four children were all at home. Now the New Testament BE series is ended, our children are all married, and we have seven grandchildren!

The numerous readers of the BE series have been a great source of encouragement to me, even when they have written to disagree with me! I have received letters from many parts of the world, written by people in various walks of life, and they have gladdened my heart. Unless a writer hears from his readers, his writing becomes a one-way street; and he never knows if what he wrote did anybody any good. I want to thank the pastors, missionaries, Sunday School teachers, and other students of the Word, who have been kind enough to write. We could compile a book of letters telling what God has done in the lives of people who have studied the BE series. To God be the glory!

My longtime friend and editor Jim Adair deserves special thanks for shepherding me through most of the BE books. I have worked with many different publishers and editors over the years, and I appreciate all of them; but working with Jim Adair, Lloyd Cory, Mark Sweeney, and the others on the Victor Books staff, has been a special delight. To the best of my knowledge, during all the years we have worked together, we have never had a cross word or a painful misunderstanding. Every author should be that fortunate!

As I close, there are some other people who ought to be thanked. Dr. Donald Burdick taught me New Testament at Northern Baptist Seminary and showed me how to study the Word of God. Dr. Lloyd Perry and the late Dr. Charles W. Koller both taught me how to "unlock" a Scripture passage and organize an exposition that was understandable and practical. I recommend their books on preaching to any preacher or teacher who wants to organize his or her material better.

For ten happy years, I was privileged to

pastor the Calvary Baptist Church in Covington, Kentucky, just across the river from Cincinnati. One of my happy duties was writing Bible study notes for "The Whole Bible Study Course" which was developed by the late Dr. D.B. Eastep, who pastored the church for thirty-five fruitful years. No church I have ever visited or ministered to has a greater love for the Bible or a deeper hunger for spiritual truth than the dear people at Calvary Baptist. The BE series is, in many respects, a by-product of Dr. Eastep's kindness in sharing his ministry with me, and the church's love and encouragement while I was their pastor. I honor his memory and thank God for their continued friendship and prayer support.

To you who study God's Word with me, "I commend you to God, and to the word of His grace, which is able to build you up, and to give you an inheritance among all them who are sanctified" (Acts 20:32).

Warren W. Wiersbe

MATTHEW

OUTLINE

Key theme: The King and His kingdom
Key verses: Matthew 2:2; 4:17

I. THE REVELATION OF THE KING —chapters 1–10
A. His person—1–4
B. His principles—5–7
C. His power—8–10
(Note: The message during this period of His ministry was, "The kingdom of heaven is at hand" [3:2; 4:17; 10:7].)

II. THE REBELLION AGAINST THE KING—chapters 11–13
A. His messenger rejected—11:1-19
B. His works denied—11:20-30
C. His principles refused—12:1-21
D. His person attacked—12:22-50
E. Result: the "mysteries of the kingdom"—13

III. THE RETIREMENT OF THE KING —chapters 14–20
(The Lord seeks to leave the multitudes to be alone with His disciples.)
A. Before Peter's confession—14:1–16:12
B. Peter's confession—16:13-28
(First mention of the cross—16:21)
C. After Peter's confession—17:1–20:34
(Second mention of the cross—17:22)
(Third mention of the cross—20:17-19)

IV. THE REJECTION OF THE KING—chapters 21–27
("The kingdom of God shall be taken from you," 21:43.)
A. His public presentation as King—21:1-16
B. His conflict with the rulers—21:17–23:39
C. His prophetic message—24–25
D. His suffering and death—26–27

V. THE RESURRECTION OF THE KING—chapter 28

CONTENTS

CHAPTER ONE
HERE'S GOOD NEWS!

Twenty or thirty years after Jesus had gone back to heaven, a Jewish disciple named Matthew was inspired by the Spirit of God to write a book. The finished product is what we know today as "The Gospel According to Matthew."

Nowhere in the four Gospels do we find a single recorded word that Matthew spoke. Yet in his Gospel, he gives us the words and works of Jesus Christ, "the Son of David, the Son of Abraham" (Matt. 1:1). Matthew did not write to tell us about himself. But let's get acquainted with him and the book he wrote. Then we can learn all that he wanted us to know about Jesus Christ.

The Holy Spirit used Matthew to accomplish three important tasks in the writing of his Gospel.

The Bridge-Builder: He Introduced a New Book

That book was the New Testament. If a Bible reader were to jump from Malachi into Mark, or Acts, or Romans, he would be bewildered. Matthew's Gospel is the bridge that leads us out of the Old Testament and into the New Testament.

The theme of the Old Testament is given in Genesis 5:1: "This is the book of the generations of Adam." The Old Testament gives the history of "the Adam family," and it is a sad history indeed. God created man in His own image, but man sinned—thus defiling and deforming that image. Then man brought forth children "in his own likeness, after his image" (Gen. 5:3). These children proved themselves to be sinners like their parents. No matter where you read in the Old Testament, you meet sin and sinners.

But the New Testament is, "The book of the generation of Jesus Christ" (Matt. 1:1). Jesus is the last Adam (1 Cor. 15:45), and He came to earth to save the "generations of Adam." (This includes you and me, by the way.) Through no choice of our own, we were born into the generations of Adam, and this made us sinners. But by a choice of faith, we can be born into the generation of Jesus Christ and become the children of God!

When you read the genealogy in Genesis 5, the repeated phrase *and he died* sounds like the tolling of a funeral bell. The Old Testament illustrates the truth that "the wages of sin is death" (Rom. 6:23). But when you turn to the New Testament, that first genealogy emphasizes *birth* and not death! The message of the New Testament is that "the gift of God is eternal life through Jesus Christ our Lord" (Rom. 6:23).

The Old Testament is a book of promise, while the New Testament is a book of fulfillment. (To be sure, there are many precious promises in the New Testament. But I am referring to the emphasis of each half of the Bible.) Beginning with Genesis 3:15, God promised a Redeemer; and Jesus Christ fulfilled that promise. *Fulfilled* is one of the key words in the Gospel of Matthew, used about fifteen times.

One purpose of this Gospel is to show that Jesus Christ fulfilled the Old Testament promises concerning the Messiah. His birth at Bethlehem fulfilled Isaiah 7:14 (Matt. 1:22-23). Jesus was taken to Egypt for safety, and this fulfilled Hosea 11:1 (Matt. 2:14-15). When Joseph and the family returned and decided to settle in Nazareth, this fulfilled several Old Testament prophecies (Matt. 2:22-23). Matthew used at least 129 quotations or allusions to the Old Testament in this Gospel. He wrote primarily for Jewish readers to show them that Jesus Christ was indeed their promised Messiah.

The Biographer: He Introduced a New King

None of the four Gospels is a biography in the modern sense of the word. In fact, the Apostle John doubted that a complete biography of Jesus could ever be written (John 21:25). There are many details about the earthly life of Jesus that are not given in any of the Gospels.

Each of the four Gospels has its own emphasis. Matthew's book is called, "the Gospel of the King." It was written primarily for Jewish readers. Mark's book, the Gospel of the Servant, was written to instruct Roman readers. Luke wrote mainly to the Greeks and presented Christ as the perfect "Son of man." John's appeal is universal, and his message was, "This is the Son of God." No one Gospel is able to tell the whole story as God wants us to see it. But when we put these four Gospel accounts together, we have a composite picture of the person and work of our Lord.

Being accustomed to keeping systematic records, Matthew gives us a beautifully organized account of our Lord's life and ministry. The book can be divided into ten sections in which "doing" and "teaching" alternate. Each teaching section ends with, "When Jesus had ended these sayings" or a similar transitional statement. The chapters can be divided like this:

Narrative	*Teaching*	*Transition*
1–4	5–7	7:28
8:1–9:34	9:35–10:42	11:1
11:2–12:50	13:1-52	13:53
13:53–17:27	18:1-35	19:1
19:1–23:39	24:1–25:46	26:1
26:1–28:20 (the Passion narrative)		

Matthew described Jesus as the *Doer* and the *Teacher*. He recorded at least twenty specific miracles and six major messages: the Sermon on the Mount (chaps. 5–7), the charge to the apostles (chap. 10), the parables of the kingdom (chap. 13), the lesson on forgiveness (chap. 18), the denunciation of the Pharisees (chap. 23), and the prophetic discourse on the Mount of Olives (chaps. 24–25). At least 60 percent of this book focuses on the teachings of Jesus.

Remember, Matthew focuses on the *kingdom*. In the Old Testament, the Jewish nation was God's kingdom on earth: "And you shall be unto Me a kingdom of priests, and an holy nation" (Ex. 19:6). Many people in Jesus' day were looking for the God-sent Deliverer who would release them from Roman bondage and reestablish the glorious kingdom of Israel.

The message of the kingdom of heaven was first preached by John the Baptist (Matt. 3:1-2). The Lord Jesus also preached this message from the very beginning of His ministry (Matt. 4:23). He sent out the 12 Apostles with the same proclamation (Matt. 10:1-7).

However, the Good News of the kingdom required a moral and spiritual response from the people, and not simply the acceptance of a ruler. John the Baptist called for repentance. Likewise, Jesus made it clear that He had not come to overcome Rome, but to transform the hearts and lives of those who trusted Him. Before He could enter into the glory of the kingdom, Jesus endured the suffering of the cross.

One further word about this Gospel. Matthew arranged his material in a topical order, rather than chronological. He grouped ten miracles together in chapters 8–9 instead of putting them into their historical sequence in the Gospel's narrative. Certain other events are totally omitted. By consulting a good harmony of the Gospels, you will see that, while Matthew does not contradict the other three Gospel writers, he *does* follow his own pattern.

Matthew was not only a bridge-builder who introduced a new book, the New Testament;

and a biographer who introduced a new King, Jesus Christ; but he also accomplished a third task when he wrote his book.

The Believer: He Introduced a New People

This new people, of course, was the church. Matthew is the only Gospel writer to use the word *church* (Matt. 16:18; 18:17). The Greek word translated *church* means "a called-out assembly." In the New Testament, for the most part, this word refers to a local assembly of believers. In the Old Testament, Israel was God's called-out people, beginning with the call of Abraham (Gen. 12:1ff; Deut. 7:6-8). In fact, Stephen called the nation of Israel "the church [assembly] in the wilderness" (Acts 7:38), for they were God's called-out people.

But the New Testament church is a different people, for it is composed of *both* Jews and Gentiles. In this church there were no racial distinctions (Gal. 3:28). Even though Matthew wrote primarily for the Jews, he has a "universal" element in his book that includes the Gentiles. For example, Gentile leaders came to worship the Infant Jesus (Matt. 2:1-12). Jesus performed miracles for Gentiles and even commended them for their faith (Matt. 8:5-13; 15:21-28). The Gentile Queen of Sheba was praised for her willingness to make a long journey to hear God's wisdom (Matt. 12:42). At a crisis hour in Jesus' ministry He turned to a prophecy about the Gentiles (Matt. 12:14-21). Even in the parables, Jesus indicated that the blessings which Israel refused would be shared with the Gentiles (Matt. 22:8-10; 21:40-46). The Olivet Discourse stated that the message would go "unto all nations" (Matt. 24:14); and the Lord's commission involves all nations (Matt. 28:19-20).

There were only believing Jews and believing Jewish proselytes in the church at the beginning (Acts 2–7). When the Gospel went to Samaria (Acts 8), people who were part Jewish and part Gentile came into the church. When Peter went to the household of Cornelius (Acts 10), the Gentiles became fully accepted in the church. The Conference at Jerusalem (Acts 15), settled the decision that a Gentile did not have to become a Jew before he could become a Christian.

But Matthew anticipated all of this. And when his book was read by members of the early church, both Jews and Gentiles, it helped to settle differences and create unity. Matthew made it clear that this new people, the church, must not maintain a racial or social exclusiveness. Faith in Jesus Christ makes believers "all one" in the body of Christ, the church.

Matthew's own experience with the Lord is recorded in Matthew 9:9-17; and it is a beautiful example of the grace of God. His old name was Levi, the son of Alphaeus (Mark 2:14). "Matthew" means "the gift of God." Apparently, the name was given to commemorate his conversion and his call to be a disciple.

Remember that tax collectors were among the most hated people in Jewish society. To begin with, they were traitors to their own nation because they "sold themselves" to the Romans to work for the government. Each tax collector purchased from Rome the right to gather taxes; and the more he gathered, the more he could keep. They were considered thieves as well as traitors; and their constant contacts with Gentiles made them religiously suspect, if not unclean. Jesus reflected the popular view of the publicans when He classified them with harlots and other sinners (Matt. 5:46-47; 18:17); but it was obvious that He was the "friend of publicans and sinners" (Matt. 11:19; 21:31-32).

Matthew opened his heart to Jesus Christ and became a new person. This was not an easy decision for him to make. He was a native of Capernaum, and Capernaum had rejected the Lord (Matt. 11:23). Matthew was a well-known businessman in the city, and his old friends probably persecuted him. Certainly Matthew lost a good deal of income when he left all to follow Christ.

Matthew not only opened his heart, but he also opened his home. He knew that most, if not all, of his old friends would drop him when he began to follow Jesus Christ; so Matthew took advantage of the situation and invited them to meet Jesus. He gave a great feast and invited all the other tax collectors (some of whom could have been Gentiles), and the Jewish people who were not keeping the Law ("sinners").

Of course, the Pharisees criticized Jesus for daring to eat with such a defiled group of people. They even tried to get the disciples of John the Baptist to create a disagreement (Luke 5:33). The Lord explained why He was fellowshipping with "publicans and sinners": They were spiritually sick and needed a physician. He had not come to call the righteous *because there were no righteous people.* He came to call sinners, and that included the

Pharisees. Of course, His critics did not consider themselves "spiritually sick," but they *were* just the same.

Matthew not only opened his heart and home, but he also opened his hands and worked for Christ. Alexander Whyte of Edinburgh once said that, when Matthew left his job to follow Christ, he brought his pen with him! Little did this ex-publican realize that the Holy Spirit would one day use him to write the first of the four Gospels in the New Testament.

According to tradition, Matthew ministered in Palestine for several years after the Lord's return to heaven, and then made missionary journeys to the Jews who were dispersed among the Gentiles. His work is associated with Persia, Ethiopia, and Syria, and some traditions associate him with Greece. The New Testament is silent on his life, but this we do know: Wherever the Scriptures travel in this world, the Gospel written by Matthew continues to minister to hearts.

CHAPTER TWO
THE KING'S BIRTH
Matthew 1–2

If a man suddenly appears and claims to be a king, the public immediately asks for proof. What is his background? Who pays homage to him? What credentials can he present? Anticipating these important questions, Matthew opened his book with a careful account of the birth of Jesus Christ and the events that accompanied it. He presented four facts about the King.

The Heredity of the King (Matt. 1:1-25)

Since royalty depends on heredity, it was important for Jesus to establish His rights to David's throne. Matthew gave His human heredity (Matt. 1:1-17) as well as His divine heredity (Matt. 1:18-25).

His human heredity (vv. 1-17). Genealogies were very important to the Jews, for without them they could not prove their tribal memberships or their rights to inheritances. Anyone claiming to be "the Son of David" had to be able to prove it. It is generally concluded that Matthew gave our Lord's family tree through His foster father, Joseph, while Luke gave Mary's lineage (Luke 3:23ff).

Many Bible readers skip over this list of ancient (and, in some cases, unpronounceable) names. But this "list of names" is a vital part of the Gospel record. It shows that Jesus Christ is a part of history; that all of Jewish history prepared the way for His birth. God in His providence ruled and overruled to accomplish His great purpose in bringing His Son into the world.

This genealogy also illustrates God's wonderful grace. It is most unusual to find the names of women in Jewish genealogies, since names and inheritances came through the fathers. But in this list we find references to four women from Old Testament history: Tamar (Matt. 1:3), Rahab and Ruth (Matt. 1:5), and Bathsheba "the wife of Uriah" (Matt. 1:6).

Matthew clearly omitted some names from this genealogy. Probably, he did this to give a systematic summary of three periods in Israel's history, each with fourteen generations. The numerical value of the Hebrew letters for "David" equals fourteen. Matthew probably used this approach as a memory aid to help his readers remember this difficult list.

But there were many Jewish men who could trace their family back to King David. It would take more than human pedigree to make Jesus Christ "the Son of David" and heir to David's throne. This is why the divine heredity was so important.

His divine heredity (vv. 18-25). Matthew 1:16 and 18 make it clear that Jesus Christ's birth was different from that of any other Jewish boy named in the genealogy. Matthew pointed out that Joseph did not "beget" Jesus Christ. Rather, Joseph was the "husband of Mary, of whom was born Jesus, who is called Christ." Jesus was born of an earthly mother without the need of an earthly father. This is known as the doctrine of the Virgin Birth.

Every child born into the world is a totally new creature. But Jesus Christ, being eternal God (John 1:1, 14), existed before Mary and Joseph or any of His earthly ancestors. If Jesus Christ were conceived and born just as any other baby, then He could not be God. It was necessary for Him to enter this world through an earthly mother, but not to be begotten by an earthly father. By a miracle of the Holy Spirit, Jesus was conceived in the womb of Mary, a virgin (Luke 1:26-38).

Some have raised the question that perhaps

Mary was not a virgin. They say that Matthew 1:23 should be translated "young woman." But the word translated *virgin* in this verse always means virgin and cannot be translated "young woman."

Both Mary and Joseph belonged to the house of David. The Old Testament prophecies indicated that the Messiah would be born of a woman (Gen. 3:15), of the seed of Abraham (Gen. 22:18), through the tribe of Judah (Gen. 49:10), and of the family of David (2 Sam. 7:12-13). Matthew's genealogy traced the line through Solomon, while Luke's traced it through Nathan, another one of David's sons. It is worth noting that Jesus Christ is the only Jew alive who can actually prove His claims to the throne of David! All of the other records were destroyed when the Romans took Jerusalem in A.D. 70.

To the Jewish people in that day, betrothal (engagement) was equivalent to marriage—except that the man and woman did not live together. They were called "husband and wife," and, at the end of the engagement period, the marriage was consummated. If a betrothed woman became pregnant, it was considered adultery (see Deut. 22:13-21). But Joseph did not punish or divorce Mary when he discovered she was with child, for the Lord had revealed the truth to him. All of this fulfilled Isaiah 7:14.

Before we leave this important section, we must consider the three names assigned to God's Son. The name *Jesus* means "Saviour" and comes from the Hebrew name, Joshua ("Jehovah is salvation"). There were many Jewish boys with the name Joshua (or, in the Greek, Jesus); but Mary's Boy was called "Jesus the Christ." The word *Christ* means "anointed"; it is the Greek equivalent of *Messiah.* He is "Jesus the Messiah." Jesus is His human name; Christ is His official title; and Immanuel describes who He is—"God with us." Jesus Christ is God! We find this name "Immanuel" in Isaiah 7:14 and 8:8.

The King, then, was a Jewish male who is also the divine Son of God. But, did anybody acknowledge His kingship? Yes, the magi from the East came and worshiped Him.

The Homage to the King (Matt. 2:1-12)

We must confess that we know little about these men. The word translated "wise men" (magi) refers to a group of scholars who studied the stars. Their title connects them with magic, but they were probably more like astrologers. However, their presence in the biblical record is not a divine endorsement of astrology.

God gave them a special sign, a miraculous star that announced the birth of the King. The star led them to Jerusalem where God's prophets told them that the King would be born in Bethlehem. They went to Bethlehem, and there they worshiped the Christ Child.

We do not know how many magi there were. From the three gifts listed in Matthew 2:11, some people have assumed there were three kings from the Orient, though this is not certain. But when their caravan arrived in Jerusalem, there were enough of them to trouble the whole city.

Keep in mind that these men were *Gentiles.* From the very beginning, Jesus came to be "the Saviour of the world" (John 4:42). These men were also wealthy, and they were scholars—scientists in their own right. No scholarly person who follows the light God gives him can miss worshiping at the feet of Jesus. In Jesus Christ "are hid all the treasures of wisdom and knowledge" (Col. 2:3). In Him dwells "all the fullness of the Godhead bodily" (Col. 2:9).

The magi were seeking the King, but Herod was afraid of the King and wanted to destroy Him. This was Herod the Great, called *king* by the Roman senate because of the influence of Mark Antony. Herod was a cruel and crafty man who permitted no one, not even his own family, to interfere with his rule or prevent the satisfying of his evil desires. A ruthless murderer, he had his own wife and her two brothers slain because he suspected them of treason. He was married at least nine times in order to fulfill his lusts and strengthen his political ties.

It is no surprise that Herod tried to kill Jesus, for Herod alone wanted to bear the title "King of the Jews." But there was another reason. Herod was not a full-blooded Jew; he was actually an Idumaean, a descendant of Esau. This is a picture of the old struggle between Esau and Jacob that began even before the boys were born (Gen. 25:19-34). It is the spiritual versus the carnal, the godly versus the worldly.

The magi were seeking the King; Herod was opposing the King; and the Jewish priests were ignoring the King. These priests knew the Scriptures and pointed others to the Saviour, *but they would not go to worship Him themselves!* They quoted Micah 5:2 but did not obey it. They were *five miles* from the very Son of God, yet they did not go to see Him! The Gentiles sought and found Him, but the Jews did not.

Matthew 2:9 indicates that the miraculous star was not always visible to the magi. As they started toward Bethlehem, they saw the star again; and it led them to the house where Jesus was. By now, Joseph had moved Mary and the baby from the temporary dwelling where the Lord Jesus had been born (Luke 2:7). The traditional manger scenes that assemble together the shepherds and wise men are not true to Scripture, since the magi arrived much later.

Matthew cites a second fulfilled prophecy to prove that Jesus Christ is the King (Matt. 2:5). *How* He was born was a fulfillment of prophecy, and *where* He was born was a fulfillment of prophecy. Bethlehem means "house of bread," and this was where the "Bread of Life" came to earth (John 6:48ff). Bethlehem in the Old Testament was associated with David who was a type of Jesus Christ in His suffering and glory.

Hostility against the King (Matt. 2:13-18)

A person is identified not only by his friends, but also by his enemies. Herod pretended that he wanted to worship the newborn King (Matt. 2:8), when in reality he wanted to destroy Him. God warned Joseph to take the Child and Mary and flee to Egypt. Egypt was close. There were many Jews there, and the treasures received from the magi would more than pay the expenses for traveling and living there. But there was also another prophecy to fulfill, Hosea 11:1: "I called My Son out of Egypt."

Herod's anger was evidence of his pride; he could not permit anyone to get the best of him, particularly some Gentile scholars! This led him to kill the boy babies two years of age and under who were still in Bethlehem. We must not envision hundreds of little boys being killed, for there were not that many male children of that age in a small village like Bethlehem. Even today only about 20,000 people live there. It is likely that not more than 20 children were slain. But, of course, *1* is too many!

Matthew introduced here the theme of hostility, which he focused on throughout his book. Satan is a liar and a murderer (John 8:44), as was King Herod. He lied to the magi and he murdered the babies. But even this horrendous crime of murder was the fulfillment of prophecy found in Jeremiah 31:15. In order to understand this fulfillment, we must review Jewish history.

The first mention of Bethlehem in Scripture is in connection with the death of Jacob's favorite wife, Rachel (Gen. 35:16-20). Rachel died giving birth to a son whom she named Benoni, "son of my sorrow." Jacob renamed his son Benjamin, "son of my right hand." Both of these names relate to Jesus Christ, for He was a "man of sorrows, and acquainted with grief" (Isa. 53:3), and He is now the Son of God's right hand (Acts 5:31; Heb. 1:3). Jacob put up a pillar to mark Rachel's grave which is near Bethlehem.

Jeremiah's prophecy was given about 600 years before Christ was born. It grew out of the captivity of Jerusalem. Some of the captives were taken to Ramah in Benjamin, near Jerusalem; and this reminded Jeremiah of Jacob's sorrow when Rachel died. However, now it was *Rachel* who was weeping. She represented the mothers of Israel weeping as they saw their sons going into captivity. It was as though Rachel said, "I gave my life to bear a son, and now his descendants are no more."

Jacob saw Bethlehem as a place of death, but the birth of Jesus made it a place of life! Because of His coming, there would be spiritual deliverance for Israel and, in the future, the establishment of David's throne and kingdom. Israel, "the son of my sorrow," would one day become "the son of My right hand." Jeremiah gave a promise to the nation that they would be restored to their land again (Jer. 31:16-17), and this promise was fulfilled. But he gave an even greater promise that the nation would be regathered in the future, and the kingdom established (Jer. 31:27ff). This promise shall also be fulfilled.

Very few people today think of Bethlehem as a burial place; they think of it as the birthplace of Jesus Christ. And because He died for us and rose again, we have a bright future before us. We shall live forever with Him in that glorious city where death is no more and where tears never fall.

The Humility of the King (Matt. 2:19-23)

Herod died in 4 B.C., which means that Jesus was born sometime between 6 and 5 B.C. It is impossible not to notice the parallel between Matthew 2:20 and Exodus 4:19, the call of

Moses. As God's Son, Jesus was in Egypt and was called out to go to Israel. Moses was outside Egypt, hiding for his life, and he was called to return to Egypt. But in both cases, God's program of redemption was involved. It took courage for Joseph and his family to leave Egypt, and it took courage for Moses to return to Egypt.

Archelaus was one of Herod's sons, and to him Herod had willed the title of king. However, the Jews discovered that, in spite of his promises of kindness, Archelaus was as wicked as his father. So they sent a delegation to Rome to protest his crowning. Augustus Caesar agreed with the Jews and made Archelaus an ethnarch over half of his father's kingdom. (Jesus may have had this bit of Jewish history in mind when He told the Parable of the Pounds in Luke 19:11-27.)

The whole episode is a good example of how God leads His children. Joseph knew that he and his family were no safer under the rule of Archelaus than they had been under Herod the Great. It is likely they were heading back to Bethlehem when they discovered that Archelaus was on the throne. Certainly, Joseph and Mary prayed, waited, and sought God's will. Common sense told them to be careful; faith told them to wait. In due time, God spoke to Joseph in a dream, and he took his wife and her Son to Nazareth, which had been their home earlier (Matt. 2:19-20).

But even this fulfilled prophecy! Once again, Matthew points out that every detail in the life of Jesus was foretold in the Scriptures. It is important to note that Matthew did not refer to only one prophet in Matthew 2:23, but instead says "that it might be fulfilled which was spoken by the prophets" (plural).

We will not find any specific prophecy that called Jesus a "Nazarene." The term *Nazarene* was one of reproach: "Can there any good thing come out of Nazareth?" (John 1:46) In many Old Testament prophecies, the Messiah's lowly life of rejection is mentioned; and this may be what Matthew had in mind (see Ps. 22; Isa. 53:2-3, 8). The term "Nazarene" was applied both to Jesus and His followers (Acts 24:5); and He was often called "Jesus of Nazareth" (Matt. 21:11; Mark 14:67; John 18:5, 7).

But perhaps Matthew, led by the Spirit, saw a spiritual connection between the name "Nazarene" and the Hebrew word *netzer,* which means "a branch or shoot." Several prophets apply this title to Jesus (see Isa. 4:2; 11:1; Jer. 23:5; 33:15; Zech. 3:8; 6:12-13).

Our Lord grew up in Nazareth and was identified with that city. In fact, His enemies thought He had been born there; for they said that He came from Galilee (John 7:50-52). Had they investigated the temple records, they would have discovered that He had been born in Bethlehem.

Who ever heard of a king being born in a humble village and growing up in a despised city? The humility of the King is certainly something to admire and imitate (Phil. 2:1-13).

CHAPTER THREE
THE KING'S CREDENTIALS
Matthew 3–4

Some thirty years passed between chapters 2 and 3 of Matthew, during which Jesus lived in Nazareth and worked as a carpenter (Matt. 13:55; Mark 6:3). But the time came for Him to begin His public ministry which would culminate at the cross. Was He still qualified to be King? Had anything taken place that would disqualify Him? In chapters 2 and 3, Matthew assembled the testimonies of five witnesses to the person of Jesus Christ, that He is the Son of God and the King.

John the Baptist (Matt. 3:1-15)

For over 400 years, the nation had not heard the voice of a prophet. Then John appeared and a great revival took place. Consider four facts about John.

His message (vv. 1-2, 7-10). John's preaching centered on repentance and the kingdom of heaven. The word *repent* means "to change one's mind and act on that change." John was not satisfied with regret or remorse; he wanted "fruits meet for repentance" (Matt. 3:8). There had to be evidence of a changed mind and a changed life.

All kinds of people came to hear John preach and to watch the great baptismal services he conducted. Many publicans and sinners came in sincere humility (Matt. 21:31-32), but the religious leaders refused to submit. They thought that they were good enough to please God; yet John called them a "generation of vipers." Jesus used the same language when He dealt with this self-righteous crowd (Matt. 12:34; 23:33; John 8:44).

The Pharisees were the traditionalists of their day, while the Sadducees were more liberal (see Acts 23:6-9). The wealthy Sadducees controlled the "temple business" that Jesus cleaned out. These two groups usually fought each other for control of the nation, but when it came to opposing Jesus Christ, the Pharisees and Sadducees united forces.

John's message was one of judgment. Israel had sinned and needed to repent, and the religious leaders ought to lead the way. The ax was lying at the root of the tree; and if the tree (Israel) did not bear good fruit, it would be cut down (see Luke 13:6-10). If the nation repented, the way would be prepared for the coming of the Messiah.

His authority (vv. 3-4). John fulfilled the prophecy given in Isaiah 40:3. In a spiritual sense, John was "Elijah who was to come" for he came in the "spirit and power of Elijah" (Luke 1:16-17). He even dressed as Elijah did and preached the same message of judgment (2 Kings 1:8). John was the last of the Old Testament prophets (Luke 16:16) and the greatest of them (Matt. 11:7-15; see 17:9-13).

His baptism (vv. 5-6, 11-12). The Jews baptized Gentile converts, but John was baptizing Jews! His baptism was authorized from heaven (Matt. 21:23-27); it was not something John devised or borrowed. It was a baptism of repentance, *looking forward* to the Messiah's coming (Acts 19:1-7). His baptism fulfilled two purposes: it prepared the nation for Christ and it presented Christ to the nation (John 1:31).

But John mentioned two other baptisms: a baptism of the Spirit and a baptism of fire (Matt. 3:11). The baptism of the Spirit came at Pentecost (Acts 1:5, and note that Jesus said *nothing* about fire). Today, whenever a sinner trusts Christ, he is born again and immediately baptized by the Spirit into the body of Christ, the church (1 Cor. 12:12-13). In contrast, the baptism of fire refers to the future judgment, as Matthew explains (Matt. 3:12).

His obedience (vv. 13-15). Jesus was not baptized because He was a repentant sinner. Even John tried to stop Jesus, but the Lord knew it was His Father's will. Why was Jesus baptized? First, His baptism gave approval to John's ministry. Second, He identified Himself with publicans and sinners, the very people He came to save. But mainly, His baptism pictured His future baptism on the cross (Matt. 20:22; Luke 12:50) when all the "waves and billows" of God's judgment would go over Him (Ps. 42:7; Jonah 2:3).

Thus, John the Baptist bore witness to Jesus Christ as the Son of God, and also as the Lamb of God (John 1:29). Because of John's witness, many sinners trusted Jesus Christ (John 10:39-42).

The Holy Spirit (Matt. 3:16)

The coming of the Holy Spirit like a dove identified Jesus to John (John 1:31-34), and also assured Jesus as He began His ministry that the Spirit's ministry would always be His (John 3:34). The dove is a beautiful symbol of the Spirit of God in its purity and in its ministry of peace. The first time we see a dove in Scripture is in Genesis 8:6-11. Noah sent out two birds, a raven and a dove; but only the dove came back. The raven represented the flesh; there was plenty for the raven to eat outside the ark! But the dove would not defile itself on the carcasses, so it came back to the ark. The second time the dove was released, it returned with an olive leaf, a symbol of peace. The third time, the dove did not return.

There may be another picture here. The name Jonah means "dove," and he too experienced a baptism! Jesus used Jonah as a type of Himself in death, burial, and resurrection (Matt. 12:38-40). Jonah was sent to the Gentiles, and Jesus would minister to the Gentiles.

The Father (Matt. 3:17)

On three special occasions, the Father spoke from heaven: at Christ's baptism, at the Transfiguration (Matt. 17:3), and as Christ approached the cross (John 12:27-30). In the past, God spoke *to* His Son; today He is speaking *through* His Son (Heb. 1:1-2).

The Father's statement from heaven seems to be an echo of Psalm 2:7—"The Lord hath said unto Me, 'Thou art My Son; this day have I begotten Thee.' " Acts 13:22 informs us that this "begetting" refers to His resurrection from the dead, and not to His birth at Bethlehem. This statement ties in perfectly with the Lord's baptismal experience of death, burial, and resurrection.

But the Father's statement also relates

Jesus Christ to the "Suffering Servant" prophesied in Isaiah 40–53. In Matthew 12:18, Matthew quoted from Isaiah 42:1-3, where the Messiah-Servant is called "My beloved, in whom My soul is well pleased." The Servant described in Isaiah is humble, rejected, made to suffer and die, but is also seen to come forth in victory. While the nation of Israel is seen dimly in some of these "Servant Songs," it is the Messiah, Jesus Christ, who is revealed most clearly in them. Again, we see the connection with Christ in death, burial, and resurrection.

Finally, the Father's statement approved all that Jesus had done up to that point. His "hidden years in Nazareth" were years of pleasing the Father. Certainly, the Father's commendation was a great encouragement to the Son as He started His ministry.

Satan (Matt. 4:1-11)

From the high and holy experience of blessing at the Jordan, Jesus was led into the wilderness for testing. Jesus was not tempted so that the Father could learn anything about His Son, for the Father had already given Jesus His divine approval. Jesus was tempted so that every creature in heaven, on earth, or under the earth might know that Jesus Christ is the Conqueror. He exposed Satan and his tactics, and He defeated Satan. Because of His victory, we can have victory over the tempter.

Just as the first Adam met Satan, so the Last Adam met the enemy (1 Cor. 15:45). Adam met Satan in a beautiful Garden, but Jesus met him in a terrible wilderness. Adam had everything he needed, but Jesus was hungry after forty days of fasting. Adam lost the battle and plunged humanity into sin and death. But Jesus won the battle and went on to defeat Satan in more battles, culminating in His final victory on the cross (John 12:31; Col. 2:15).

Our Lord's experience of temptation prepared Him to be our sympathetic High Priest (Heb. 2:16-18; 4:15-16). It is important to note that Jesus faced the enemy *as man,* not as the Son of God. His first word was, "*Man* shall not live by bread alone." We must not think that Jesus used His divine powers to overcome the enemy, because that is just what the enemy wanted Him to do! Jesus used the spiritual resources that are available to us today: the power of the Holy Spirit of God (Matt. 4:1), and the power of the Word of God ("It is written"). Jesus had nothing in His nature that would give Satan a foothold (John 14:30), but His temptations were real just the same. Temptation involves *the will,* and Jesus came to do the Father's will (Heb. 10:1-9).

The first temptation (vv. 1-4). This involved the love of God and the will of God. "Since You are God's beloved Son, why doesn't Your Father feed You? Why does He put You into this terrible wilderness?" This temptation sounded like Satan's words to Eve in Genesis 3! It is a subtle suggestion that our Father does not love us.

But there was another suggestion: "Use Your divine powers to meet Your own needs." When we put our physical needs ahead of our spiritual needs, we sin. When we allow circumstances to dictate our actions, instead of following God's will, we sin. Jesus could have turned the stones into bread, but He would have been exercising His powers *independently of the Father;* and He came to obey the Father (John 5:30; 6:38).

The Lord quoted Deuteronomy 8:3 to defeat Satan. Feeding on and obeying God's Word is more important than consuming physical food. In fact, *it is our food* (John 4:32-34).

The second temptation (vv. 5-7). The second temptation was even more subtle. This time Satan also used the Word of God. "So You intend to live by the Scriptures," he implied. "Then let me quote You a verse of Scripture and see if You will obey it!" Satan took the Lord Jesus to the pinnacle of the temple, probably 500 feet above the Kidron Valley. Satan then quoted from Psalm 91:11-12 where God promised to care for His own. "If You really believe the Scriptures, then jump! Let's see if the Father cares for You!"

Note carefully our Lord's reply: "It is written AGAIN" (Matt. 4:7, emphasis mine). We must never divorce one part of Scripture from another, but we must always "compare spiritual things with spiritual" (1 Cor. 2:13). We can prove almost anything by the Bible *if* we isolate texts from the contexts and turn them into pretexts. Satan had cleverly omitted the phrase "in all Thy ways" when he quoted from Psalm 91. When the child of God is in the will of God, the Father will protect him. He watches over those who are "in His ways."

Jesus replied with Deuteronomy 6:16: "Thou shalt not tempt the Lord thy God." We tempt God when we put ourselves into circumstances that force Him to work miracles on our behalf. The diabetic who refuses to take insulin and argues, "Jesus will take care of me," may be tempting the Lord. We tempt God when we try to force Him to contradict His own Word. It is important for us as believers to read *all* Scripture, and study *all* God has to say, for *all* of it is profitable for daily life (2 Tim. 3:16-17).

The third temptation (vv. 8-11). The devil offered Jesus a shortcut to His kingdom. Jesus knew that He would suffer and die before He entered into His glory (Luke 24:26; 1 Peter 1:11; 5:1). If He bowed down and worshiped Satan *just once* (this is the force of the Greek verb), He could enjoy all the glory without enduring the suffering. Satan has always wanted worship, because Satan has always wanted to be God (Isa. 14:12-14). Worshiping the creature instead of the Creator is the lie that rules our world today (Rom. 1:24-25).

There are no shortcuts to the will of God. If we want to share in the glory, we must also share in the suffering (1 Peter 5:10). As the prince of this world, Satan could offer these kingdoms to Christ (John 12:31; 14:30). But Jesus did not need Satan's offer. The Father had already promised Jesus the kingdom! "Ask of Me, and I shall give Thee the heathen [nations] for Thine inheritance" (Ps. 2:8). You find the same promise in Psalm 22:22-31, and this is the psalm of the cross.

Our Lord replied with Deuteronomy 6:13: "Thou shalt worship the Lord thy God, and Him only shalt thou serve." Satan had said nothing about service, but Jesus knew that whatever we worship, we will serve. Worship and service must go together.

Satan slunk away, a defeated foe; but he did not cease to tempt Jesus. We could translate Luke 4:13, "And when the devil had ended every possible kind of temptation, he stood off from Him until a suitable season." Through Peter, Satan again tempted Jesus to abandon the cross (Matt. 16:21-23); and through the crowd that had been fed, Satan tempted Jesus to an "easy kingdom" (John 6:15). One victory never guarantees freedom from further temptation. If anything, each victory we experience only makes Satan try harder.

Notice that Luke's account reverses the order of the second and third temptations as recorded in Matthew. The word "then" in Matthew 4:5 seems to indicate sequence. Luke only uses the simple conjunction "and" and does not say he is following a sequence. Our Lord's command at the end of the third temptation ("Get thee hence, Satan!") is proof that Matthew followed the historical order. There is no contradiction since Luke did not claim to follow the actual sequence.

After Jesus Christ had defeated Satan, He was ready to begin His ministry. No man has a right to call others to obey who has not obeyed himself. Our Lord proved Himself to be the perfect King whose sovereignty is worthy of our respect and obedience. But, true to his purpose, Matthew had one more witness to call to prove the kingship of Jesus Christ.

Christ's Ministry of Power (Matt. 4:12-15)

Matthew has already shown us that every detail of our Lord's life was controlled by the Word of God. Remember that between the end of His temptation and the statement in Matthew 4:12 comes the ministry described in John 1:19 through John 3:36. We must not think that John the Baptist was thrown into prison immediately after our Lord's temptation. Matthew wrote his book *topically* rather than chronologically. Consult a good harmony of the Gospels to study the sequence of events.

In Matthew 4:16, Matthew quoted Isaiah (see Isa. 9:1-2). The prophet wrote about people who "walked" in darkness, but by the time Matthew quoted the passage, the situation was so discouraging that the people were *sitting* in darkness! Jesus Christ brought the Light to them. He made His headquarters in Capernaum in "Galilee of the Gentiles," another reference to the universal outreach of the Gospel's message. In Galilee there was a mixed population that was somewhat despised by the racially "pure" citizens of Judea.

How did Jesus bring this Light to Galilee? We are told in Matthew 4:23: through His teaching, preaching, and healing. This emphasis is found often in the Gospel of Matthew; see 9:35; 11:4-5; 12:15; 14:34-36; 15:30; 19:2. Matthew was quite clear that He healed "all manner of sickness and all manner of disease" (Matt. 4:23). There was no case too difficult for Him!

The result of these great miracles was a tremendous *fame* for Jesus, and a great *following* of people from many areas. "Syria" refers to an area in northern Galilee. "Decapolis" means "ten cities" and was a district made up of ten cities originally built by followers of Alexander the Great. The Decapolis was in the northeastern part of Galilee. "Beyond Jordan" means Perea, the area east of the Jordan. News traveled fast, and those who had afflicted friends or family members brought them to Jesus for healing.

Matthew listed some of the "cases" in Matthew 4:24. "Diseases and torments" could cover almost any disease. Of course, our Lord often delivered people from demons. The term "lunatic" did not refer to people who were insane. Rather, it was used to describe those afflicted with epilepsy (see Matt. 17:15). *Palsy* meant "paralytic."

Miracles of healing were but a part of Christ's ministry throughout Galilee; for He also taught and preached the Word. The "light" that Isaiah promised was the Light of the Word of God, as well as the Light of His perfect life and compassionate ministry. The word *preach* in Matthew 4:17 and 23 means "to announce as a herald." Jesus proclaimed with authority the Good News that the kingdom of heaven was at hand.

The phrase *kingdom of heaven* is found thirty-two times in Matthew's Gospel. The phrase *kingdom of God* is found only five times (Matt. 6:33; 12:28; 19:24; 21:31, 43). Out of reverence for the holy name of the Lord, the Jews would not mention "God" but would substitute the word "heaven." The Prodigal Son confessed that he had sinned "against heaven," meaning, of course, against God. In many places where Matthew uses *kingdom of heaven,* the parallel passages in Mark and Luke use *kingdom of God.*

In the New Testament, the word *kingdom* means "rule, reign, authority" rather than a place or a specific realm. The phrase "kingdom of heaven" refers to the rule of God. The Jewish leaders wanted a political leader who would deliver them from Rome; but Jesus came to bring *spiritual* rule to the hearts of people. This does not deny the reality of a future kingdom as we have already noted.

But Jesus not only proclaimed the Good News and taught the people God's truth, He also called to Himself a few disciples whom He could train for the work of the kingdom. In Matthew 4:17-22 we read of the call of Peter, Andrew, James, and John, men who had already met Jesus and trusted Him (John 1:29-42). They had gone back to their fishing business, but He came and called them to give up their business and follow Him. The details of this call may be found in Mark 1:16-20 and Luke 5:1-11.

The term "fishers of men" was not new. For centuries, Greek and Roman philosophers had used it to describe the work of the man who seeks to "catch" others by teaching and persuasion. "Fishing for men" is but one of many pictures of evangelism in the Bible, and we must not limit ourselves to it. Jesus also talked about the shepherd seeking the lost sheep (Luke 15:1-7), and the workers in the harvest-field (John 4:34-38). Since these four men were involved in the fishing business, it was logical for Jesus to use this approach.

Jesus had four and possibly seven men in the band of disciples who were professional fishermen (see John 21:1-3). Why would Jesus call so many fishermen to His side? For one thing, fishermen were busy people; usually professional fishermen did not sit around doing nothing. They either sorted their catch, prepared for a catch, or mended their equipment. The Lord needs busy people who are not afraid to work.

Fishermen have to be courageous and patient people. It certainly takes patience and courage to win others to Christ. Fishermen must have skill; they must learn from others where to find the fish and how to catch them. Soul-winning demands skill too. These men had to work together, and the work of the Lord demands cooperation. But most of all, fishing demands faith: fishermen cannot see the fish and are not sure their nets will enclose them. Soul-winning requires faith and alertness too, or we will fail.

Matthew has presented to us the person of the King. Every witness affirms, "This is the Son of God, this is the King!"

CHAPTER FOUR
THE KING'S PRINCIPLES: TRUE RIGHTEOUSNESS
Matthew 5

The Sermon on the Mount is one of the most misunderstood messages that Jesus ever gave. One group says it is God's plan of salvation, that if we ever hope to go to heaven we must obey these rules. Another group calls it a "charter for world peace" and begs the nations of the earth to accept it. Still a third group tells us that the Sermon on the Mount does not apply to today, but that it will apply at some future time, perhaps during the Tribulation or the millennial kingdom.

I have always felt that Matthew 5:20 was the key to this important sermon: "For I say unto you, that except your righteousness shall exceed the righteousness of the scribes and Pharisees, ye shall in no case enter into the kingdom of heaven." The main theme is true righteousness. The religious leaders had an artificial, external righteousness based on Law. But the righteousness Jesus described is a true and vital righteousness that begins internally, in the heart. The Pharisees were concerned about the minute details of conduct, but they neglected the major matter of *character.* Conduct flows out of character.

Whatever applications the Sermon on the Mount may have to world problems, or to future events, it is certain that this sermon has definite applications for us today. Jesus gave this message to individual believers, not to the unsaved world at large. What was taught in the Sermon on the Mount is repeated in the New Testament epistles for the church today. Jesus originally gave these words to His disciples (Matt. 5:1), and they have shared them with us.

In this chapter, Jesus gave three explanations about true, spiritual righteousness.

What True Righteousness Is (Matt. 5:1-16)

Being a master Teacher, our Lord did not begin this important sermon with a negative criticism of the scribes and Pharisees. He began with a positive emphasis on righteous character and the blessings that it brings to the life of the believer. The Pharisees taught that righteousness was an external thing, a matter of obeying rules and regulations. Righteousness could be measured by praying, giving, fasting, etc. In the Beatitudes and the pictures of the believer, Jesus described Christian character that flowed from within.

Imagine how the crowd's attention was riveted on Jesus when He uttered His first word: "Blessed." (The Latin word for blessed is *beatus,* and from this comes the word *beatitude.*) This was a powerful word to those who heard Jesus that day. To them it meant "divine joy and perfect happiness." The word was not used for humans; it described the kind of joy experienced only by the gods or the dead. "Blessed" implied an inner satisfaction and sufficiency that did not depend on outward circumstances for happiness. This is what the Lord offers those who trust Him!

The Beatitudes describe the attitudes that ought to be in our lives today. Four attitudes are described here.

Our attitude toward ourselves (v. 3). To be poor in spirit means to be humble, to have a correct estimate of oneself (Rom. 12:3). It does not mean to be "poor spirited" and have no backbone at all! "Poor in spirit" is the opposite of the world's attitudes of self-praise and self-assertion. It is not a false humility that says, "I am not worth anything, I can't do anything!" It is honesty with ourselves: we know ourselves, accept ourselves, and try to be ourselves to the glory of God.

Our attitude toward our sins (vv. 4-6). We mourn over sin and despise it. We see sin the way God sees it and seek to treat it the way God does. Those who cover sin or defend sin certainly have the wrong attitude. We should not only mourn over our sins, but we should also meekly submit to God (see Luke 18:9-14; Phil. 3:1-14).

Meekness is not weakness, for both Moses and Jesus were meek men (Num. 12:3; Matt. 11:29). This word translated "meek" was used by the Greeks to describe a horse that had been broken. It refers to power under control.

Our attitude toward the Lord (vv. 7-9). We experience God's mercy when we trust Christ (Eph. 2:4-7), and He gives us a clean heart (Acts 15:9) and peace within (Rom. 5:1). But having received His mercy, we then *share* His mercy with others. We seek to keep our hearts pure that we might see God in our lives today. We become peacemakers in a troubled world and channels for God's mercy, purity, and peace.

Our attitude toward the world (vv. 10-16). It is not easy to be a dedicated Christian. Our society is not a friend to God nor to God's people. Whether we like it or not, there is *conflict* between us and the world. Why? Because we are different from the world and we have different attitudes.

As we read the Beatitudes, we find that they represent an outlook radically different from that of the world. The world praises pride, not humility. The world endorses sin, especially if you "get away with it." The world is at war with God, while God is seeking to reconcile His enemies and make them His children. We must expect to be persecuted *if* we are living as God wants us to live. But we must be sure that our suffering is not due to our own foolishness or disobedience.

How True Righteousness Comes (Matt. 5:17-20)

Certainly after the crowd heard our Lord's description of the kind of person God blesses, they said to themselves, "But we could *never* attain that kind of character. How can we have this righteousness? Where does it come from?" They wondered how His teaching related to what they had been taught all their lives. What about Moses and the Law?

In the Law of Moses, God certainly revealed His standards for holy living. The Pharisees defended the Law and sought to obey it. But Jesus said that the true righteousness that pleases God must *exceed* that of the scribes and Pharisees—and to the common people, the scribes and Pharisees were the holiest men in the community! If *they* had not attained, what hope was there for anybody else?

Jesus explained His own attitude toward the Law by describing three possible relationships.

We can seek to destroy the Law (v. 17a). The Pharisees thought Jesus was doing this. To begin with, His *authority* did not come from any of the recognized leaders or schools. Instead of teaching "from authorities" as did the scribes and Pharisees, Jesus taught *with authority.*

Not only in His authority, but also in His *activity,* Jesus seemed to defy the Law. He deliberately healed people on the Sabbath Day and paid no attention to the traditions of the Pharisees. Our Lord's *associations* also seemed contrary to the Law, for He was the friend of publicans and sinners.

Yet, it was the Pharisees who were destroying the Law! By their traditions, they robbed the people of the Word of God; and by their hypocritical lives, they disobeyed the very Law that they claimed to protect. The Pharisees thought they were *conserving* God's Word, when in reality they were *preserving* God's Word: embalming it so that it no longer had life! Their rejection of Christ when He came to earth proved that the inner truth of the Law had not penetrated their hearts.

Jesus made it clear that He had come to honor the Law and help God's people love it, learn it, and live it. He would not accept the artificial righteousness of the religious leaders. Their righteousness was only an external masquerade. Their religion was a dead ritual, not a living relationship. It was artificial; it did not reproduce itself in others in a living way. It made them proud, not humble; it led to bondage, not liberty.

We can seek to fulfill the Law (v. 17b). Jesus Christ fulfilled God's Law in every area of His life. He fulfilled it in His birth because He was "made under the Law" (Gal. 4:4). Every prescribed ritual for a Jewish boy was performed on Him by His parents. He certainly fulfilled the Law in His life, for nobody was ever able to accuse Him of sin. While He did not submit to the traditions of the scribes and Pharisees, He always did what God commanded in the Law. The Father was "well pleased" with His Son (Matt. 3:17; 17:5).

Jesus also fulfilled the Law in His teaching. It was this that brought Him into conflict with the religious leaders. When He began His ministry, Jesus found the Living Word of God encrusted with man-made traditions and interpretations. He broke away this thick crust of "religion" and brought the people back to God's Word. Then, He opened the Word to them in a new and living way—they were accustomed to the "letter" of the Law and not the inner "kernel" of life.

But it was in His death and resurrection that Jesus especially fulfilled the Law. He bore the curse of the Law (Gal. 3:13). He fulfilled the Old Testament types and ceremonies so that they no longer are required of the people of God (see Heb. 9–10). He set aside the Old Covenant and brought in the New Covenant.

Jesus did not destroy the Law by fighting it; He destroyed it by *fulfilling* it! Perhaps an illustration will make this clear. If I have an acorn, I can destroy it in one of two ways. I can put it on a rock and smash it to bits with a hammer. Or, I can plant it in the ground and let it *fulfill itself* by becoming an oak tree.

When Jesus died, He rent the veil of the temple and opened the way into the holiest (Heb. 10:19). He broke down the wall that separated the Jews and Gentiles (Eph. 2:11-13). Because the Law was fulfilled in Christ, we no longer need temples made with hands (Acts 7:48ff) or religious rituals (Col. 2:10-13).

How can we fulfill the Law? By yielding to the Holy Spirit and allowing Him to work in our lives (Rom. 8:1-3). The Holy Spirit enables us to experience the "righteousness of the law" in daily life. This does not mean we live sinlessly perfect lives, but it does mean that Christ lives out His life through us by the power of His Spirit (Gal. 2:20).

When we read the Beatitudes, we see the perfect character of Jesus Christ. While Jesus never had to mourn over His sins, since He was sinless, He was still a "man of sorrows and acquainted with grief" (Isa. 53:3). He never had to hunger and thirst after righteousness since He was the holy Son of God, but He did delight in the Father's will and find His satisfaction in doing it (John 4:34). The only way we can experience the righteousness of the Beatitudes is through the power of Christ.

We can seek to do and teach the Law (v. 19). This does not mean we major on the Old Testament and ignore the New! Second Corinthians 3 makes it clear that ours is a ministry of the *New* Covenant. But there is a proper ministry of the Law (1 Tim. 1:9ff) that is not contrary to the glorious message of God's grace. Jesus wants us to know more of the righteousness of God, obey it, and share it with others. The moral law of God has not changed. Nine of the Ten Commandments are repeated in the New Testament epistles and commanded to believers. (The exception is the Sabbath commandment, which was given as a sign to Israel, see Neh. 9:14.)

We do not obey an external Law because of fear. No, believers today obey an internal Law *and live because of love.* The Holy Spirit teaches us the Word and enables us to obey. Sin is still sin, and God still punishes sin. In fact, we in this present age are *more* responsible because we have been taught and given more!

How Righteousness Works in Daily Life (Matt. 5:21-48)

Jesus took six important Old Testament laws and interpreted them for His people in the light of the new life He came to give. He made a fundamental change without altering God's standards: He dealt with the attitudes and intents of the heart and not simply with the external action. The Pharisees said that righteousness consisted of performing certain actions, but Jesus said it centered in the attitudes of the heart.

Likewise, with sin: The Pharisees had a list of external actions that were sinful, but Jesus explained that sin came from the attitudes of the heart. Anger is murder in the heart; lust is adultery in the heart. The person who says that he "lives by the Sermon on the Mount" may not realize that the Sermon on the Mount is *more difficult* to keep than the original Ten Commandments!

Murder (vv. 21-26; Ex. 20:13). I have read that one out of every thirty-five deaths in Chicago is a murder, and that most of these murders are "crimes of passion" caused by anger among friends or relatives. Jesus did not say that anger leads to murder; He said that anger *is* murder.

There is a holy anger against sin (Eph. 4:26), but Jesus talked about an unholy anger against people. The word He used in Matthew 5:22 means "a settled anger, malice that is nursed inwardly." Jesus described a sinful experience that involved several stages. First there was *causeless anger.* This anger then exploded into *words:* "Raca—empty-headed person!" These words added fuel to the fire so that the person said, "You fool—rebel!"

Anger is such a foolish thing. It makes us destroyers instead of builders. It robs us of freedom and makes us prisoners. To hate someone is to commit murder in our hearts (1 John 3:15).

This does not mean that we should go ahead and murder someone we hate, since we have already sinned inwardly. Obviously, sinful feelings are not excuses for sinful deeds. Sinful anger robs us of fellowship with God as well as with our brothers, but it does not put us into jail as murderers. However, more than one person has become a murderer because he failed to control sinful anger.

Sinful anger must be faced honestly and must be confessed to God as sin. We must go to our brother and get the matter settled, and we must do it quickly. The longer we wait, the worse the bondage becomes! We put ourselves into a terrible prison when we refuse to be reconciled. (See Matt. 18:15-20 for additional counsel.) It has well been said that the person who refuses to forgive his brother destroys the very bridge over which he himself must walk.

Adultery (vv. 27-30; Ex. 20:14). Jesus affirmed God's law of purity, and then explained that the intent of this law was to reveal the sanctity of sex and the sinfulness of the human heart. God created sex, and God protects sex. He has the authority to regulate it and to punish those who rebel against His laws. He does not regulate sex because He wants to rob us, but rather, because He wants to bless us. Whenever God says, "No" it is that He might say "Yes."

Sexual impurity begins in the desires of the heart. Again, Jesus is not saying that lustful desires are identical to lustful deeds, and therefore a person might just as well go ahead and commit adultery. The desire and the deed are not identical, but, spiritually speaking, they are equivalent. The "look" that Jesus mentioned was not a casual glance, but a constant stare *with the purpose of lusting.* It is possible for a man to glance at a beautiful woman and know that she is beautiful, but not lust after her. The man Jesus described looked at the woman *for the purpose of feeding his inner sensual appetites* as a substitute for the act. It was not accidental; it was planned.

How do we get victory? By purifying the desires of the heart (appetite leads to action) and disciplining the actions of the body. Obviously, our Lord is not talking about literal surgery; for this would not solve the problem in the heart. The eye and the hand are usually the two "culprits" when it comes to sexual sins, so they must be disciplined. Jesus said, "Deal immediately and decisively with sin! Don't taper off—cut off!" Spiritual surgery is more important than physical surgery, for the sins of the body can lead to eternal judgment. We think of passages like Colossians 3:5 and Romans 6:13; 12:1-2; 13:14.

Divorce (vv. 31-32). Our Lord dealt with this in greater detail in Matthew 19:1-12, and we shall consider it there.

Swearing (vv. 33-37; Lev. 19:12; Deut. 23:23). This is not the sin of "cursing," but the sin of using oaths to affirm that what is said is true. The Pharisees used all kinds of tricks to sidestep the truth, and oaths were among them. They would avoid using the holy name of God, but they would come close by using the city of Jerusalem, heaven, earth, or some part of the body.

Jesus taught that our conversation should be so honest, and our character so true, that we would not need "crutches" to get people to believe us. Words depend on character, and oaths cannot compensate for a poor character. "In the multitude of words there wanteth not sin; but he that refraineth his lips is wise" (Prov. 10:19). The more words a man uses to convince us, the more suspicious we should be.

Retaliation (vv. 38-42; Lev. 24:19-22). The original law was a fair one; it kept people from forcing the offender to pay a greater price than the offense deserved. It also prevented people from taking personal revenge. Jesus replaced a law with an attitude: be willing to suffer loss yourself rather than cause another to suffer. Of course, He applied this to *personal insults,* not to groups or nations. The person who retaliates only makes himself and the offender feel worse; and the result is a settled war and not peace.

In order to "turn the other cheek," we must stay where we are and not run away. This demands both faith and love. It also means that *we* will be hurt, but it is better to be hurt on the outside than to be harmed on the inside. But it further means that *we should try to help the sinner.* We are vulnerable, because he may attack us anew; but we are also victorious, because Jesus is on our side, helping us and building our characters. Psychologists tell us that violence is born of weakness, not strength. It is the strong man who can love and suffer hurt; it is the weak man who thinks only of himself and hurts others to protect himself. He hurts others then runs away to protect himself.

Love of enemies (vv. 43-48; Lev. 19:17-18). Nowhere did the Law teach hatred for one's enemies. Passages like Exodus 23:4-5 indicate just the opposite! Jesus defined our enemies as those who curse us, hate us, and exploit us selfishly. Since Christian love is an act of the will, and not simply an emotion, He has the right to command us to love our enemies. After all, He loved us when we were His enemies (Rom. 5:10). We may show this love by blessing those who curse us, doing good to them, and praying for them. When we pray for our enemies, we find it easier to love them. It takes the "poison" out of our attitudes.

Jesus gave several reasons for this admonition. (1) This love is a mark of maturity, proving that we are *sons* of the Father, and not just little children. (2) It is Godlike. The Father shares His good things with those who oppose Him. Matthew 5:45 suggests that our love "creates a climate" of blessings that makes it easy to win our enemies and make them our friends. Love is like the sunshine and rain that the Father sends so graciously. (3) It is a testimony to others. "What do ye more than others?" is a good question. God expects us to live on a much higher plane than the lost people of the world who return good for good and evil for evil. As Christians, we must return good for evil as an investment of love.

The word *perfect* in Matthew 5:48 does not

imply *sinlessly* perfect, for that is impossible in this life (though it is a good goal to strive for). It suggests completeness, maturity, as the sons of God. The Father loves His enemies and seeks to make them His children, and we should assist Him!

CHAPTER FIVE THE KING'S PRINCIPLES: TRUE WORSHIP

Matthew 6

The true righteousness of the kingdom must be applied in the everyday activities of life. This is the emphasis in the rest of the Sermon on the Mount. Jesus related this principle to our relationships to God in worship (Matt. 6:1-18), our relationship to material things (Matt. 6:19-34), and our relationship to other people (Matt. 7:1-20).

Jesus also warned about the danger of hypocrisy (Matt. 6:2, 5, 16), the sin of using religion to cover up sin. A hypocrite is not a person who falls short of his high ideals, or who occasionally sins, because all of us experience these failures. A hypocrite *deliberately* uses religion to cover up his sins and promote his own gains. The Greek word translated *hypocrite* originally meant "an actor who wears a mask."

The righteousness of the Pharisees was insincere and dishonest. They practiced their religion for the applause of men, not for the reward of God. But true righteousness must come from within. We should test ourselves to see whether we are sincere and honest in our Christian commitment. In this chapter, Christ applied this test to four different areas of life.

Our Giving (Matt. 6:1-4)

Giving alms to the poor, praying, and fasting were important disciplines in the religion of the Pharisees. Jesus did not condemn these practices, but He did caution us to make sure that our hearts are right as we practice them. The Pharisees used almsgiving to gain favor with God and attention from men, both of which were wrong motives. No amount of giving can purchase salvation; for salvation is the gift of God (Eph. 2:8-9). And to live for the praise of men is a foolish thing because the glory of man does not last (1 Peter 1:24). It is the glory and praise of God that really counts!

Our sinful nature is so subtle that it can defile even a good thing like sharing with the poor. If our motive is to get the praise of men, then like the Pharisees, we will call attention to what we are doing. But if our motive is to serve God in love and please Him, then we will give our gifts without calling attention to them. As a result, we will grow spiritually; God will be glorified; and others will be helped. But if we give with the wrong motive, we rob ourselves of blessing and reward and rob God of glory, even though the money we share might help a needy person.

Does this mean that it is wrong to give openly? Must all giving be anonymous? Not necessarily, for everyone in the early church knew that Barnabas had given the income from the sale of his land (Acts 4:34-37). When the church members laid their money at the Apostles' feet, it was not done in secret. The difference, of course, was in the *motive* and *manner* in which it was done. A contrast is Ananias and Sapphira (Acts 5:1-11), who tried to use their gift to make people think they were more spiritual than they really were.

Our Praying (Matt. 6:5-15)

Jesus gave four instructions to guide us in our praying.

We must pray in secret before we pray in public (v. 6). It is not wrong to pray in public in the assembly (1 Tim. 2:1ff), or even when blessing food (John 6:11) or seeking God's help (John 11:41-42; Acts 27:35). But it is wrong to pray in public if we are not in the habit of praying in private. Observers may think that we are practicing prayer when we are not, and this is hypocrisy. The word translated *closet* means "a private chamber." It could refer to the store-chamber in a house. Our Lord prayed privately (Mark 1:35); so did Elisha (2 Kings 4:32ff) and Daniel (Dan. 6:10ff).

We must pray sincerely (vv. 7-8). The fact that a request is repeated does not make it a "vain repetition"; for both Jesus and Paul repeated their petitions (Matt. 26:36-46; 2 Cor. 12:7-8). A request becomes a "vain repetition" if it is only a babbling of words without a sincere heart desire to seek and do God's will. The mere reciting of memorized prayers can be vain repetition. The Gentiles had such prayers in their pagan ceremonies (see 1 Kings 18:26).

My friend Dr. Robert A. Cook has often said, "All of us have one routine prayer in our system; and once we get rid of it, then we can really start to pray!" I have noticed this, not only in my own praying, but often when I have conducted prayer meetings. With some people, praying is like putting the needle on a phonograph record *and then forgetting about it.* But God does not answer insincere prayers.

We must pray in God's will (vv. 9-13). This prayer is known familiarly as "The Lord's Prayer," but "The Disciples' Prayer" would be a more accurate title. Jesus did not give this prayer to us to be memorized and recited a given number of times. In fact, He gave this prayer *to keep us* from using vain repetitions. Jesus did not say, "Pray in these words." He said, "Pray after this manner"; that is, "Use this prayer as a pattern, not as a substitute."

The purpose of prayer is to glorify God's name, and to ask for help to accomplish His will on earth. This prayer begins with *God's* interests, not ours: God's name, God's kingdom, and God's will. Robert Law has said, "Prayer is a mighty instrument, not for getting man's will done in heaven, but for getting God's will done in earth." We have no right to ask God for anything that will dishonor His name, delay His kingdom, or disturb His will on earth.

It is worth noting that there are *no singular pronouns* in this prayer; they are all plural. It begins with "OUR Father." When we pray, we must remember that we are part of God's worldwide family of believers. We have no right to ask for ourselves anything that would harm another member of the family. If we are praying in the will of God, the answer will be a blessing to all of God's people in one way or another.

If we put God's concerns first, then we can bring our own needs. God is concerned about our needs and knows them even before we mention them (Matt. 6:8). If this is the case, then why pray? Because prayer is the God-appointed way to have these needs met (see James 4:1-3). *Prayer prepares us for the proper use of the answer.* If we know our need, and if we voice it to God, trusting Him for His provision, then we will make better use of the answer than if God forced it on us without our asking.

It is right to pray for daily physical needs, for forgiveness, and for guidance and protection from evil. "Lead us not into temptation" does not mean that God tempts His children (James 1:13-17). In this petition we are asking God to guide us so that we will not get out of His will and get involved in a situation of temptation (1 John 5:18), or even in a situation of tempting God so that He must miraculously rescue us (Matt. 4:5-7).

We must pray, having a forgiving spirit toward others (vv. 14-15). In this "appendix" to the prayer, Jesus expanded the last phrase of Matthew 6:12, "as we forgive our debtors." He later repeated this lesson to His disciples (Mark 11:19-26). He was not teaching that believers earned God's forgiveness by forgiving others; for this would be contrary to God's free grace and mercy. However, if we have truly *experienced* God's forgiveness, then we will have a readiness to forgive others (Eph. 4:32; Col. 3:13). Our Lord illustrated this principle in the Parable of the Unmerciful Servant (Matt. 18:21-35).

We have seen that true praying is a "family affair" ("Our Father"). If the members of the family are not getting along with one another, how can they claim to have a right relationship with the Father? The emphasis in 1 John 4 is that we show our love for God by loving our brothers. When we forgive each other, we are not *earning* the right to prayer; for the privilege of prayer is a part of our *sonship* (Rom. 8:15-16). Forgiveness belongs to the matter of *fellowship:* If I am not in fellowship with God, I cannot pray effectively. But fellowship with my brother helps to determine my fellowship with God; hence, forgiveness is important to prayer.

Since prayer involves glorifying God's name, hastening the coming of God's kingdom (2 Peter 3:12), and helping to accomplish God's will on earth, the one praying must not have sin in his heart. If God answered the prayers of a believer who had an unforgiving spirit, He would dishonor His own name. How could God work through such a person to get His will done on earth? If God gave him his requests, He would be encouraging sin! The important thing about prayer is not simply getting an answer, but *being the kind of person whom God can trust with an answer.*

Our Fasting (Matt. 6:16-18)
The only fast that God actually required of the Jewish people was on the annual Day of Atonement (Lev. 23:27). The Pharisees fasted each Monday and Thursday (Luke 18:12) and did so in such a way that people knew they were fasting. Their purpose, of course, was to win the praise of men. As a result, the Pharisees lost God's blessing.

It is not wrong to fast, if we do it in the right way and with the right motive. Jesus fasted (Matt. 4:3); so did the members of the early church (Acts 13:2). Fasting helps to discipline the appetites of the body (Luke 21:34) and keep our spiritual priorities straight. But fasting must never become an opportunity for temptation (1 Cor. 7:7). Simply to deprive ourselves of a natural benefit (such as food or sleep) is not *of itself* fasting. We must devote ourselves to God and worship Him. Unless there is the devotion of the heart (see Zech. 7) there is no lasting spiritual benefit.

As with giving and praying, true fasting must be done in secret; it is between the believer and God. To "make unsightly" our faces (by looking glum and asking for pity and praise) would be to destroy the very purpose of the fast. Our Lord here laid down a basic principle of spiritual living: Nothing that is truly spiritual will violate that which God has given us in nature. God usually does not tear down one good thing in order to build up another. If we have to look miserable to be considered spiritual, then there is something wrong with our views of spirituality.

Remember that *hypocrisy robs us of reality in Christian living.* We substitute reputation for character, mere words for true prayer, money for the devotion of the heart. No wonder Jesus compared the Pharisees to tombs that were whitewashed on the outside, but filthy on the inside! (Matt. 23:27-28)

But hypocrisy not only robs us of character, it also *robs us of spiritual rewards.* Instead of the eternal approval of God, we receive the shallow praise of men. We pray, but there are no answers. We fast, but the inner man shows no improvement. The spiritual life becomes hollow and lifeless. We miss the blessing of God here and now, and also lose the reward of God when Christ returns.

Hypocrisy also *robs us of spiritual influence.* The Pharisees were a negative influence; whatever they touched was defiled and destroyed. The people who admired them and obeyed the Pharisees' words thought they themselves were being helped, when in reality, they were being hurt.

The first step toward overcoming hypocrisy is to be honest with God in our secret life. We must never pray anything that we do not mean from the heart; otherwise, our prayers are simply empty words. Our motive must be to please God alone, no matter what men may say or do. We must cultivate the heart in the secret place. It has well been said, "The most important part of a Christian's life is the part that only God sees." When reputation becomes more important than character, we have become hypocrites.

Our Use of Wealth (Matt. 6:19-34)
We are accustomed to dividing life into the "spiritual" and the "material"; but Jesus made no such division. In many of His parables, He made it clear that a right attitude toward wealth is a mark of true spirituality (see Luke 12:13ff; 16:1-31). The Pharisees were covetous (Luke 16:14) and used religion to make money. If we have the true righteousness of Christ in our lives, then we will have a proper attitude toward material wealth.

Nowhere did Jesus magnify poverty or criticize the legitimate getting of wealth. God made all things, including food, clothing, and precious metals. God has declared that all things He has made are good (Gen. 1:31). God knows that we need certain things in order to live (Matt. 6:32). In fact, He has given us "richly all things to enjoy" (1 Tim. 6:17). It is not wrong to possess things, *but it is wrong for things to possess us.* The sin of idolatry is as dangerous as the sin of hypocrisy! There are many warnings in the Bible against covetousness (Ex. 20:17; Ps. 119:36; Mark 7:22; Luke 12:15ff; Eph. 5:5; Col. 3:5).

Jesus warned against the sin of living for the things of this life. He pointed out the sad consequences of covetousness and idolatry.

Enslavement (vv. 19-24). Materialism will enslave the heart (Matt. 6:19-21), the mind (Matt. 6:22-23), and the will (Matt. 6:24). We can become shackled by the material things of life, but we ought to be liberated and controlled by the Spirit of God.

If the heart loves material things, and puts earthly gain above heavenly investments, then the result can only be a tragic loss. The treasures of earth may be used for God. But if we gather material things for ourselves, we will lose them; *and we will lose our hearts with them.* Instead of spiritual enrichment, we will experience impoverishment.

What does it mean to lay up treasures in heaven? It means to use *all that we have* for the glory of God. It means to "hang loose" when it comes to the material things of life. It also means measuring life by the true riches of the kingdom and not by the false riches of this world.

Wealth not only enslaves the heart, but it also enslaves the mind (Matt. 6:22-23). God's Word often uses the eye to represent the attitudes of the mind. If the eye is properly focused on the light, the body can function properly in its movements. But if the eye is out of focus and seeing double, it results in unsteady movements. It is most difficult to make progress while trying to look in two directions at the same time.

If our aim in life is to get material gain, it will mean darkness within. But if our outlook is to serve and glorify God, there will be light within. If what should be light is really darkness, then we are being controlled by darkness; and outlook determines outcome.

Finally, materialism can enslave the will (Matt. 6:24). We cannot serve two masters simultaneously. Either Jesus Christ is our Lord, or money is our lord. It is a matter of the will. "But those who want to get rich fall into temptation and a snare" (1 Tim. 6:9). If God grants riches, and we use them for His glory, then riches are a blessing. But if we *will* to get rich, and live with that outlook, we will pay a great price for those riches.

Devaluation (vv. 25-30). Covetousness will not only cheapen our riches, but it will also cheapen *us!* We will start to become worried and anxious, and this anxiety is unnatural and unspiritual. The person who pursues money thinks that riches will solve his problems, when in reality, riches will create more problems! Material wealth gives a dangerous, false sense of security, and that feeling ends in tragedy. The birds and lilies do not fret and worry; yet they have God's wealth in ways that man cannot duplicate. All of nature depends on God, and God never fails. Only mortal man depends on money, and money always fails.

Jesus said that worry is sinful. We may dignify worry by calling it by some other name—concern, burden, a cross to bear—but the results are still the same. Instead of helping us live longer, anxiety only makes life shorter (Matt. 6:27). The Greek word translated *take no thought* literally means "to be drawn in different directions." Worry pulls us apart. Until man interferes, everything in nature works together, because all of nature trusts God. Man, however, is pulled apart because he tries to live his own life by depending on material wealth.

God feeds the birds and clothes the lilies. He will feed and clothe us. It is our "little faith" that hinders Him from working as He would. He has great blessings for us if only we will yield to Him and live for the riches that last forever.

Loss of testimony (vv. 31-33). To worry about material things is to live like the heathen! If we put God's will and God's righteousness first in our lives, He will take care of everything else. What a testimony it is to the world when a Christian dares to practice Matthew 6:33! What a tragedy it is when so many of us *fail* to practice it.

Loss of joy today (v. 34). Worrying about tomorrow does not help either tomorrow or today. If anything, it robs us of our effectiveness today—which means we will be even less effective tomorrow. Someone has said that the average person is crucifying himself between two thieves: the regrets of yesterday and the worries about tomorrow. It is right to plan for the future and even to save for the future (2 Cor. 12:14; 1 Tim. 5:8). But it is a sin to worry about the future and permit tomorrow to rob today of its blessings.

Three words in this section point the way to victory over worry: (1) *faith* (Matt. 6:30), trusting God to meet our needs; (2) *Father* (Matt. 6:32), knowing He cares for His children; and (3) *first* (Matt. 6:33), putting God's will first in our lives so that He might be glorified. If we have faith in our Father and put Him first, He will meet our needs.

Hypocrisy and anxiety are sins. If we practice the true righteousness of the kingdom, we will avoid these sins and live for God's glory.

CHAPTER SIX THE KING'S PRINCIPLES: TRUE JUDGMENT
Matthew 7

The scribes and Pharisees were guilty of exercising a false judgment about themselves, other people, and even the Lord. Their false righteousness helped to encourage this false judgment. This explains why our Lord closed this important sermon with a discussion of judgment. In it He discussed three different judgments.

Our Judgment of Ourselves (Matt. 7:1-5)

The first principle of judgment is that we begin with ourselves. Jesus did not forbid us to judge others, for careful discrimination is essential in the Christian life. Christian love is not blind (Phil. 1:9-10). The person who believes all that he hears, and accepts everyone who claims to be spiritual will experience confusion and great spiritual loss. But before we judge others, we must judge ourselves. There are several reasons for this.

We shall be judged (v. 1). The tense of the verb *judged* signifies a once-for-all final judgment. If we first judge ourselves, then we are preparing for that final judgment when we face God. The Pharisees "played God" as they condemned other people; but they never considered that God would one day judge them.

We are being judged (v. 2). The parallel passage in Luke 6:37-38 is helpful here. Not only will God judge us at the end, but people are also judging us right now; and we receive from people exactly what we give. The kind of judgment, and the measure of judgment, comes right back to us. We reap what we have sown.

We must see clearly to help others (vv. 3-5). The purpose of self-judgment is to prepare us to serve others. Christians are obligated to help each other grow in grace. When we do not judge ourselves, we not only hurt ourselves, but we also hurt those to whom we could minister. The Pharisees judged and criticized *others* to make themselves look good (Luke 18:9-14). But Christians should judge *themselves* so that they can help others look good. There is a difference!

Let's look at our Lord's illustration of this point. Jesus chose the symbol of the eye because this is one of the most sensitive areas of the human body. The picture of a man with a two-by-four stuck in his eye, trying to remove a speck of dust from another man's eye, is ridiculous indeed! If we do not honestly face up to our own sins, and confess them, we blind ourselves to ourselves; and then we cannot see clearly enough to help others. The Pharisees saw the sins of other people, but they would not look at their own sins.

In Matthew 6:22-23, Jesus used the illustration of the eye to teach us how to have a spiritual outlook on life. *We must not pass judgment on others' motives.* We should examine their actions and attitudes, but we cannot judge their motives—for only God can see their hearts. It is possible for a person to do a good work with a bad motive. It is also possible to fail in a task and yet be very sincerely motivated. When we stand before Christ at the Judgment Seat, He will examine the secrets of the heart and reward us accordingly (Rom. 2:16; Col. 3:22-25).

The image of the eye teaches us another truth: We must exercise love and tenderness when we seek to help others (Eph. 4:15). I have had extensive eye examinations, and once had surgery to remove an imbedded speck of steel; and I appreciated the tenderness of the physicians. Like eye doctors, we should minister to people we want to help with tender loving care. We can do more damage than a speck of dirt in the eye if we approach others with impatience and insensitivity.

Two extremes must be avoided in this matter of spiritual self-examination. The first is the deception of a shallow examination. Sometimes we are so sure of ourselves that we fail to examine our hearts honestly and thoroughly. A quick glance into the mirror of the Word will never reveal the true situation (James 1:22-25).

The second extreme is what I call a "perpetual autopsy." Sometimes we get so wrapped up in self-examination that we become unbalanced. But we should not look only at ourselves, or we will become discouraged and defeated. We should look by faith to Jesus Christ and let Him forgive and restore us. Satan is the accuser (Rev. 12:10), and he enjoys it when we accuse and condemn ourselves!

After we have judged ourselves honestly before God, and have removed those things that blind us, then we can help others and properly judge their works. But if we know there are sins in our lives, and we try to help others, we are hypocrites. In fact, it is possible for ministry to be a device to cover up sin! The Pharisees were guilty of this, and Jesus denounced them for it.

Our Judgment of Others (Matt. 7:6-20)

Christians must exercise discernment; for not everyone is a sheep. Some people are dogs or hogs, and some are wolves in sheep's clothing! We are the Lord's sheep, but this does not mean we should let people pull the wool over our eyes!

The reason we must judge (v. 6). As God's people, we are privileged to handle the "holy things" of the Lord. He has entrusted to us the precious truths of the Word of God (2 Cor. 4:7), and we must regard them carefully. No dedicated priest would throw meat from the altar to a filthy dog, and only a fool would give pearls to a pig. While it is true that we must carry the Gospel "to every creature" (Mark 16:15), it is also true that we must not cheapen the Gospel by a ministry that lacks discernment. Even Jesus refused to talk to Herod (Luke 23:9), and Paul refused to argue with people who resisted the Word (Acts 13:44-49).

The reason for judgment, then, is not that we might condemn others, but that we might be able to minister to them. Notice that Jesus always dealt with individuals according to their needs and their spiritual condition. He did not have a memorized speech that He used with everybody. He discussed the new birth with Nicodemus, but He spoke of living water to the Samaritan woman. When the religious leaders tried to trap Him, He refused to answer their question (Matt. 21:23-27). It is a wise Christian who first assesses the condition of a person's heart before sharing the precious pearls.

The resources God gives us (vv. 7-11). Why did our Lord discuss prayer at this point in His message? These verses seem to be an interruption, but they are not. You and I are human and fallible; we make mistakes. Only God can judge perfectly. Therefore, we must pray and seek His wisdom and direction. "If any of you lack wisdom, let him ask of God" (James 1:5).

Young King Solomon knew that he lacked the needed wisdom to judge Israel, so he prayed to God; and the Lord graciously answered (1 Kings 3:3ff). If we are to have spiritual discernment, we must keep on asking God, keep on seeking His will, keep on knocking at the door that leads to greater ministry. God meets the needs of His children.

The guiding principle (v. 12). This is the so-called "Golden Rule," one of the most misunderstood statements in the Bible. This statement is not the sum total of Christian truth, nor is it God's plan of redemption. We should no more build our theology on the Golden Rule than we should build our astronomy on "Twinkle, Twinkle Little Star."

This great truth is a principle that ought to govern our attitudes toward others. It only applies to believers, and it must be practiced in every area of life. *The person who practices the Golden Rule refuses to say or do anything that would harm himself or others.* If our judging of others is not governed by this principle, we will become proud and critical, and our own spiritual character will degenerate.

Practicing the Golden Rule releases the love of God in our lives and enables us to help others, even those who want to hurt us.

But remember that practicing the Golden Rule means paying a price. If we want God's best for ourselves and others, but others resist God's will, then they will oppose us. We are salt, and salt stings the open wound. We are light, and light exposes dirt.

The basis for judging (vv. 13-20). Since there are false prophets in the world, we must be careful of deception. But the greatest danger is *self-deception.* The scribes and Pharisees had fooled themselves into believing that they were righteous and others were sinful. It is possible for people to know the right language, believe intellectually the right doctrines, obey the right rules, and still not be saved. Jesus used two pictures to help us judge ourselves and others.

The two ways (vv. 13-14). These are, of course, the way to heaven and the way to hell. The broad way is the easy way; it is the popular way. But we must not judge spiritual profession by statistics; the majority is not always right. The fact that "everybody does it" is no proof that what they are doing is right.

Quite the contrary is true: God's people have always been a remnant, a small minority in this world. The reason is not difficult to discover: The way of life is narrow, lonely, and costly. We can walk on the broad way and keep our "baggage" of sin and worldliness. But if we enter the narrow way, we must give up those things.

Here, then, is the first test: *Did your profession of faith in Christ cost you anything?* If not, then it was not a true profession. Many people who "trust" Jesus Christ never leave the broad road with its appetites and associations. They have an easy Christianity that makes no demands on them. Yet Jesus said that the narrow way was *hard.* We cannot walk on two roads, in two different directions, at the same time.

The two trees (vv. 15-20). These show that true faith in Christ changes the life and produces fruit for God's glory. Everything in nature reproduces after its kind, and this is also true in the spiritual realm. Good fruit comes from a good tree, but bad fruit comes from a bad tree. The tree that produces rotten fruit is cut down and thrown into the fire. "Wherefore, by their fruits you shall know them" (Matt. 7:20).

The second test is this: *Did my decision for Christ change my life?* False prophets who teach false doctrine can produce only a false righteousness (see Acts 20:29). Their fruit (the results of their ministry) is false and cannot last. The prophets themselves are false; the closer we get to them, the more we see the falsity of their lives and doctrines. They magnify themselves, not Jesus Christ; and their purpose is to exploit people, not to edify them. The person who believes false doctrine, or who follows a false prophet, will never experience a changed life. Unfortunately, some people do not realize this until it is too late.

God's Judgment of Us (Matt. 7:21-29)

From picturing two ways and two trees, our Lord closed His message by picturing two builders and their houses. The two ways illustrate the *start* of the life of faith; the two trees illustrate the *growth* and results of the life of faith here and now; and the two houses illustrate the *end* of this life of faith, when God shall call everything to judgment. There are false prophets at the gate that leads to the broad way, making it easy for people to enter. But at the end of the way, there is destruction. The final test is not what we think of ourselves, or what others may think. The final test is: *What will God say?*

How can we prepare for this judgment? *By doing God's will.* Obedience to His will is the test of true faith in Christ. The test is not words, not saying "Lord, Lord," and not obeying His commands. How easy it is to learn a religious vocabulary, and even memorize Bible verses and religious songs, and yet not obey God's will. When a person is truly born again, he has the Spirit of God living within (Rom. 8:9); and the Spirit enables him to know and do the Father's will. God's love in his heart (Rom. 5:5) motivates him to obey God and serve others.

Words are not a substitute for obedience, and neither are religious works. Preaching, casting out demons, and performing miracles can be divinely inspired, but they give no assurance of salvation. It is likely that even Judas participated in some or all of these activities, and yet he was not a true believer. In the last days, Satan will use "lying wonders" to deceive people (2 Thes. 2:7-12).

We are to *hear* God's words and *do* them (see James 1:22-25). We must not stop with only hearing (or studying) His words. Our hearing must result in doing. This is what it means to build on the rock foundation. We should not confuse this symbol with the "rock" in 1 Corinthians 3:9ff. Paul founded the local church in Corinth on Jesus Christ when he preached the Gospel and won people to Christ. This is the only foundation for a local church.

The foundation in this parable is *obedience to God's Word*—obedience that is an evidence of true faith (James 2:14ff). The two men in this story had much in common. Both had desires to build a house. Both built houses that looked good and sturdy. But when the judgment came (the storm), one of the houses collapsed. What was the difference? Not the mere external looks, to be sure. The difference was in the foundation: The successful builder "dug deep" (Luke 6:48) and set his house on a solid foundation.

A false profession will last until judgment comes. Sometimes this judgment is in the form of the trials of life. Like the person who received the seed of God's Word into a shallow heart (Matt. 13:4-9), the commitment fails when the testing comes. Many people have professed faith in Christ, only to deny their faith when life becomes spiritually costly and difficult.

But the judgment illustrated here probably refers to the final judgment before God. We must not read into this parable all the doctrine that we are taught in the Epistles; for the Lord was illustrating one main point: *profession will ultimately be tested before God.* Those who have trusted Christ, and have proved their faith by their obedience will have nothing to fear. Their house is founded on the Rock, and it will stand. But those who have professed to trust Christ, yet who have not obeyed God's will, will be condemned.

How shall we test our profession of faith? By popularity? No, for there are many on the broad road to destruction. And there are many who are depending on words, saying "Lord, Lord"—but this is no assurance of salvation. Even religious activities in a church organization are no assurance. How then shall we judge ourselves and others who profess Christ as Saviour?

The two ways tell us to examine the cost of our profession. Have we paid a price to profess faith in Christ? *The two trees* tell us to investigate whether our lives have really changed. Are there godly fruits from our lives? And *the two houses* remind us that true faith in Christ will last, not only in the storms of life, but also in the final judgment.

The congregation was astonished at this sermon. Why? Because Jesus spoke with divine authority. The scribes and Pharisees spoke "from authorities," always quoting the various rabbis and experts of the Law. Jesus needed no human teacher to add authority to His words; for He spoke as the Son of God. We cannot lightly dismiss this sermon, for it is God who gave it to us! We must either bow before Him and submit to His authority, or we will be condemned.

CHAPTER SEVEN
THE KING'S POWER
Matthew 8–9

We have been introduced to the person of the King (Matt. 1–4) and the principles of the King (Matt. 5–7); and now we are ready for the power of the King. After all, if a king does not have the power to accomplish anything, what good are his credentials or his principles? In chapters 8 and 9, Matthew reported ten miracles. They are not given in chronological order, except for the last four, since Matthew followed his own approach of grouping messages or events.

Before we survey these miracles, however, we must pause to answer the obvious question: Why did our Lord perform miracles? Certainly He wanted to meet human needs. God is concerned about the temporal well-being of His creatures as well as their eternal happiness. It is wrong to separate ministry to the body and ministry to the soul, since we must minister to the whole person (see Matt. 4:23-25).

Certainly our Lord's miracles were additional credentials to prove His claim as the Messiah of Israel. "The Jews require a sign" (1 Cor. 1:22). While miracles of themselves are not proof that a man has been sent by God (even Satan can perform miracles [2 Thes. 2:9]), they do add weight to his claim, especially if his character and conduct are godly. In the case of Jesus Christ, His miracles also fulfilled Old Testament prophecies (see Isa. 29:18-19; 35:4-6). Matthew 8:17 refers us to Isaiah 53:4; and Jesus Himself in Matthew 11:1-5 referred John the Baptist to the Old Testament promises. These same "signs and wonders" would be the credentials of His followers in their ministries (Matt. 10:8; Heb. 2:1-4).

Along with His compassion and credentials, there was a third reason for miracles: His concern to reveal saving truth to people. The miracles were "sermons in action." Even Nicodemus was impressed with them (John 3:1-2). It is worth noting that five of these miracles were performed at Capernaum, and yet the city rejected Him (Matt. 11:21-23). Even the rejection by the nation of Israel fulfilled Old Testament prophecy (see John 12:37-41). Like the judgments against Egypt in Moses' day, the miracles of the Lord were judgments in Israel; for the people had to face facts and make decisions. The religious leaders decided that Jesus was working for Satan (Matt. 9:31-34; 12:24).

One thing is certain: Jesus did not perform miracles to "get a crowd." He usually avoided the crowd. Time after time, Jesus instructed those whom He had healed not to talk too much (Matt. 8:4, 18; 9:30; Luke 8:56). He did not want people trusting Him simply on the basis of spectacular deeds (see John 4:46-54). Faith must be based on His Word (Rom. 10:17).

The miracles in these chapters are recorded in three groups, with an event relating to discipleship separating the groups. Matthew did not tell his readers why he used this arrangement, but we will follow it. To help us grasp some of the spiritual lessons, I have characterized each section with a special emphasis.

Grace to the Outcasts (Matt. 8:1-22)
Lepers, Gentiles, and women were considered outcasts by many Jewish people, especially the Pharisees. Many Pharisees would pray each morning, "I give thanks that I am a man and not a woman, a Jew and not a Gentile, a free-man and not a slave."

Cleansing the leper (vv. 1-4). There were a number of afflictions that our Bible categorizes as leprosy. This dreaded infection forced the victim to live apart from others and to cry, "Unclean! Unclean!" when others approached, so they would not be defiled. That the leper ran up to Jesus and violated the code is evidence of his great faith that Jesus would heal him.

Leprosy is an illustration of sin (Isa. 1:5-6). The instructions given to the priests in Leviticus 13 help us understand the nature of sin: Sin is deeper than the skin (Lev. 13:3); it spreads (Lev. 13:8); it defiles and isolates (Lev. 13:45-46); and it is fit only for the fire (Lev. 13:52, 57).

When Jesus touched the leper, He contracted the leper's defilement; *but He also conveyed His health!* Is this not what He did for us on the cross when He was made sin for us? (2 Cor. 5:21) The leper did not question His *ability* to heal; he only wondered if He were willing. Certainly God is willing to save! He is "God our Saviour, who will have all men to be saved" (1 Tim. 2:3-4). God is "not willing that any should perish" (2 Peter 3:9).

Jesus commanded the man not to tell others but to go to the priests and have them declare him restored and fit for society. This ceremony is described in Leviticus 14 and is another beautiful picture of Christ's work for sinners. The bird slain pictures the death of Christ; the bird released pictures His resurrection. Putting the bird into the jar pictures the Incarnation, when Christ took a human body that He might die for us. The application of the blood to the ear, thumb, and toe illustrates the need for personal faith in His death. The oil on the blood reminds us of the Spirit of God, who enters the person when he trusts the Saviour.

The man did not obey Christ; he told everybody what the Lord had done! (Christ tells us to tell everybody, *and we keep quiet!*) Mark 1:45 tells us that the healed leper's witness forced Jesus to avoid the city; and yet the crowds came to Him.

The centurion's servant healed (vv. 5-13). A centurion was an officer over 100 men in the Roman army. Every centurion mentioned in the Gospels and Acts was a gentleman of high character and sense of duty, and this man was no exception. The fact that he was concerned about a lowly servant-boy indicates this. The word "palsy" indicates a kind of paralysis.

It would seem that everything about this man would prevent him from coming to Jesus. He was a professional soldier, and Jesus was a Man of peace. He was a Gentile, and Jesus was a Jew. But this soldier had one thing working for him: he was a man of great faith. This centurion understood that Jesus, like himself, was under authority. All Christ had to do was speak the word and the disease would obey Him the way a soldier obeyed his officer. It is worth noting that only those who are *under* authority have the right to *exercise* authority.

Twice in the Gospels it is recorded that Jesus marveled: here, at the *great faith* of the Gentile centurion; and in Mark 6:6, at the *great unbelief* of the Jews. Matthew recorded two "Gentile" miracles: this one, and the healing of the daughter of the Syrophoenician woman (Matt. 15:21-28). In both cases, the Lord was impressed with their great faith. This is an early indication that the Jews would not believe, but the Gentiles would. Also, in both of these miracles, our Lord healed *from a distance.* This was a reminder of the spiritual position of the Gentiles "afar off" (Eph. 2:12).

Peter's mother-in-law healed (vv. 14-17). She was in bed with a fever and Peter and Andrew told Jesus about her need when they all arrived home after the synagogue service (Mark 1:21). Women did not hold a high position in Israel, and it is doubtful that a Pharisee would have paid much attention to the need in Peter's home. Jesus healed her with a touch, and she responded by serving Him and the other men.

This seems like a "minor miracle," but the results were major; for after sundown (when the Sabbath ended), *the whole city* gathered at the door that the Lord might meet their needs (Mark 1:32-34). Blessing in the home ought to lead to blessing in the community. The change in one woman's life led to miracles in the lives of many people.

Matthew saw this as a fulfillment of Isaiah 53:4. Please note that Jesus fulfilled this prophecy *in His life* and not on the cross. He bore man's sicknesses and infirmities *during His ministry on earth.* To say that there is "healing in the Atonement," and that every believer has the "right" to claim it, is to misinterpret Scripture. First Peter 2:24 applies this same truth to the forgiving of our sins which He bore on the cross. Sin and sickness do go together (see Ps. 103:3), since sickness is a consequence of Adam's sin and also an illustration of sin. But God is not obligated to heal all sicknesses. He is obligated to save all sinners who call on Him.

First "discipleship" interlude (vv. 18-22). Because great crowds followed Jesus, and opposition had not yet begun, many would-be disciples wanted to follow Him. However, they would not pay the price. This is the first use of "Son of man" in Matthew as a name for Jesus. It comes from Daniel 7:13 and is definitely a messianic title and a claim to kingship. Matthew 8:22 might be expressed, "Let the spiritually dead bury the physically dead." Jesus was not asking the man to be disrespectful to his father (who was not yet dead), but to have the right priorities in life. It is better to preach the Gospel and give life to the spiritually dead than to wait for your father to die and bury him.

Peace to the Disturbed (Matt. 8:23–9:17)

The persons involved in these three miracles all had a need for peace, and Jesus provided that peace.

Peace in the storm (vv. 23-27). The Sea of Galilee is about thirteen miles long and eight miles wide. It was not unusual for violent storms suddenly to sweep across the water. Jesus undoubtedly knew the storm was coming, and certainly could have prevented it. But He permitted it that He might teach His disciples some lessons.

The storm came because they *obeyed* the Lord, and not because (like Jonah) they disobeyed Him. Jesus was asleep because He rested confidently in the will of His Father; and this is what the disciples should have done. Instead, they became frightened and accused Jesus of not caring! Matthew wanted his readers to contrast the "little faith" of the disciples with the "great faith" of the Gentile centurion.

Peace in a community (vv. 28-34). This dramatic incident is most revealing. It shows what *Satan* does for a man: robs him of sanity and self-control; fills him with fears; robs him of the joys of home and friends; and (if possible) condemns him to an eternity of judgment. It also reveals what *society* does for a man in need: restrains him, isolates him, threatens him, but society is unable to change him. See, then, what Jesus Christ can do for a man whose whole life—within and without—is bondage and battle. What Jesus did for these two demoniacs, He will do for anyone else who needs Him.

Christ came to them, and even braved a storm to do it. This is the grace of God! *He delivered them* by the power of His Word. *He restored them* to sanity, society, and service. The account in Mark 5:1-21 shows that one of the men asked to become a disciple of the Lord. But, instead of granting his request, Jesus sent him home to be a witness. Christian service must begin at home.

There are three prayers in this event: (1) the demons besought Jesus to send them into the swine; (2) the citizens besought Him to leave; and (3) the one man besought Him to let him follow (see Mark 5:18-20). Jesus answered the prayers of the demons and the citizens, but not the prayer of the healed man!

We can construct a "statement of faith" from the words of the demons. (Demons do have faith; see James 2:19.) They believed in the existence of God and the deity of Christ, as well as the reality of future judgment. They also believed in prayer. They knew Christ had the power to send them into the swine.

The fact that the demons destroyed 2,000 pigs is nothing compared with the fact that Jesus delivered two men from the powers of Satan. God owns everything (Ps. 50:10-11) and can do with it as He pleases. Jesus values men more than pigs or sheep (Matt. 12:12). He brought peace to these men's lives and to the community where, for a long time, they had been causing trouble.

Peace in the conscience (vv. 1-8). The Lord had shown Himself powerful over sickness and storms, but what could He do about *sin?* Palsy was a gradual paralysis. This man was unable to help himself, but fortunately he had four friends with love, faith, and hope. They brought him to Jesus and permitted nothing to stand in their way. Was the man's physical condition the result of his sin? We do not know. But we do know that Jesus dealt with the sin problem first, for this is always the greatest need.

We must not conclude from this miracle that all sickness is caused by sin, or that forgiveness automatically means physical healing. A pastor of mine often says, "God can heal every sickness *except the last one.*" More important than the healing of this man's body was the cleansing of his heart. He went home with both a sound body and a heart at peace with God. " 'There is no peace,' saith my God, 'to the wicked' " (Isa. 57:21).

Second "discipleship" interlude (vv. 9-17). We have covered the call of Matthew in the first chapter of this study. We need only to comment on the four pictures of His ministry that Jesus gave in this message. As the *Physician,* He came to bring spiritual health to sick sinners. As the *Bridegroom,* He came to give spiritual joy. The Christian life is a feast, not a funeral. The illustration of the *cloth* reminds us that He came to bring spiritual wholeness; He did not come to "patch us up" and then let us fall apart. The image of the *wineskins* teaches that He gives spiritual fullness. Jewish religion was a worn-out wineskin that would burst if filled with the new wine of the Gospel. Jesus did not come to renovate Moses or even mix Law and grace. He came with new life!

Restoration to the Broken (Matt. 9:18-38)

In this section Matthew recorded four miracles involving five persons.

A broken home (vv. 18-19, 23-26). It must have been difficult for Jairus to come to Jesus, since he was a devout Jew and the leader in the synagogue. But Jairus' love for his dying daughter compelled him to seek Jesus' help, even if the religious leaders were opposing Him. When Jairus first came to Jesus, his daughter was close to death. The delay caused by the healing of the woman gave "the last enemy" opportunity to do its work. The ruler's friends came and told him that his daughter had died.

Jesus quickly reassured the man and went with him. In fact, the delay should have helped to strengthen Jairus' faith; for he saw what the woman's meager faith had accomplished in her own life. We must learn to trust Christ and His promises no matter how we feel, no matter what others say, and no matter how the circumstances may look. The scene at home must have frightened Jairus, yet Jesus took command and raised the girl from the dead.

A broken hope (vv. 20-22). Mark 5:26 informs us that this woman had tried many physicians, but none could help her. Imagine the despair and discouragement she felt. Her hopes were shattered. Because of this hemorrhage, the woman was ceremonially unclean (Lev. 15:25ff), which only added to her hopelessness. The "hem" refers to the special tassels that the Jews wore on their garments to remind them they were God's people (Num. 15:37-41; Deut. 22:12).

It is interesting that Jairus and this woman—two opposite people—met at the feet of Jesus. Jairus was a leading Jewish man; she was an anonymous woman with no prestige or resources. He was a synagogue leader, while her affliction kept her from worship. Jairus came pleading for his daughter; the woman came with a need of her own. The girl had been healthy for 12 years, and then died; the woman had been ill for 12 years and was now made whole. Jairus' need was public—all knew it; but the woman's need was private—only Jesus understood. Both Jairus and the woman trusted Christ, and He met their needs.

Jairus may have resented the woman, because she kept Jesus from getting to his daughter before the girl died. But his real problem was not the woman, *but himself:* He needed faith in Christ. Jesus forced the woman to give her testimony (see Mark's account) both for her sake and for the sake of Jairus. The fact that God has helped others ought to encourage us to trust Him more. We ought not to be so selfish in our praying that we cannot wait on the Lord, knowing He is never late.

This woman's faith was almost superstitious; and yet Jesus honored it and healed her. People must "touch Christ" where they are able, even if they must start at the hem of His garment. The Pharisees enlarged their hems and tassels in order to appear more spiritual, but they lacked the power to heal (Matt. 23:5). Others touched the hem of Christ's garment and were also healed (Matt. 14:34-36).

When Sir James Simpson, the inventor of chloroform, was dying, a friend said to him, "You will soon be resting on His bosom." The scientist replied: "I don't know as I can do that, but I think I have hold of the hem of His garment." It is not the strength of our faith that saves us, but faith in a strong Saviour.

Broken bodies (vv. 27-34). We are not told why these men were blind. Blindness was a serious problem in the East in that day. The records state that Jesus healed at least six blind men, and each case was different. These two blind men acknowledged Christ as the Son of David (see Matt. 1:1) and persisted in following Him right into the house. (No doubt they had friends who helped guide them.) It was their faith that Christ honored. Their "Yes, Lord" was the confession that released the power for their healing and their sight was restored.

Blindness is a picture of spiritual ignorance and unbelief (Isa. 6:10; Matt. 15:14; Rom. 11:25). The sinner must be born again before he can see the things of God (John 3:3). And the believer must be careful to grow spiritually or he will damage his spiritual vision (2 Peter 1:5-9).

The final miracle in this series involved a demon (Matt. 9:32-34). While there is a difference between sicknesses and demonic workings (Matt. 10:8), the demons do have the power to cause physical afflictions. In this case, the demon made the man mute. Think of what a handicap this would be! Jesus delivered him, and the people admitted that this was a new thing in Israel.

But the religious leaders would not admit that Jesus was the Messiah. How, then, could they explain His miracles? Only by saying that His miracles were wrought in the power of the wicked one. They would repeat this charge later, and Jesus would refute it (Matt. 12:22ff). In their unbelief, the Pharisees were playing right into Satan's hands!

Third "discipleship" interlude (vv. 35-38). Not only did Jesus heal; He also taught and preached. But He could not do the work alone—He needed others to help Him. He requested that His disciples pray that God would provide the needed workers. It was not long before the disciples themselves were involved in the ministry of preaching, teaching, and healing (see Matt. 10). In the same way, when we pray as He commanded, we will see what He saw, feel what He felt, and do what He did. God will multiply our lives as we share in the great harvest that is already ripe (John 4:34-38).

CHAPTER EIGHT
THE KING'S AMBASSADORS
Matthew 10

The work of salvation could be accomplished only by Jesus Christ, and He did it alone. But the *witness* of this salvation could only be accomplished by His people, those who have trusted Him and been saved. The King needed ambassadors to carry the message—and He *still* needs them. "Whom shall I send, and who will go for Us?" (Isa. 6:8) It is not enough that we *pray* for laborers (Matt. 9:36-38). We must also make ourselves available to serve Him.

Before Jesus sent His ambassadors out to minister, He preached an "ordination sermon" to encourage and prepare them. In this sermon, the King had something to say to *all* of His servants—past, present, and future. Unless we recognize this fact, the message of this chapter will seem hopelessly confused.

Instructions for Past Apostles (Matt. 10:1-15)

A "disciple" is a learner, one who follows a teacher and learns his wisdom. Jesus had many disciples, some of whom were merely "hangers-on," and some who were truly converted (John 6:66). From this large group of followers, Jesus selected a smaller group of twelve men; and these He called "apostles." This word comes from the Greek word *apostello,* which means "to send forth with a commission." It was used by the Greeks for the personal representatives of the king, ambassadors who functioned with the king's authority. To make light of the king's envoys was to be in danger of insubordination.

A man had to meet certain qualifications to be an apostle of Jesus Christ. He must have seen the risen Christ (1 Cor. 9:1) and fellowshipped with Him (Acts 1:21-22). He had to be chosen by the Lord (Eph. 4:11). The Apostles laid the foundation of the church (Eph. 2:20) and then passed from the scene. While all believers are sent forth to represent the King (John 17:18; 20:21), no believer today can honestly claim to be an apostle; for none of us has seen the risen Christ (1 Peter 1:8).

These Apostles were given special power and authority from Christ to perform miracles. These miracles were a part of their "official credentials" (Acts 2:43; 5:12; 2 Cor. 12:12; Heb. 2:1-4). They healed the sick (and note that this included *all* kinds of diseases), cleansed the lepers, cast out demons, and even raised the dead. These four ministries paralleled the miracles that Jesus performed in Matthew 8 and 9. In a definite way, the Apostles represented the King and extended His work.

Christ's commission to these twelve men is not our commission today. He sent them only to the people of Israel. "To the Jew first" is the historic pattern, for "Salvation is of the Jews" (John 4:22). These twelve ambassadors announced the coming of the kingdom just as John the Baptist had done (Matt. 3:2) and Jesus Himself (Matt. 4:17). Sad to say, the nation rejected both Christ and His ambassadors, and the kingdom was taken from them (Matt. 21:43).

The Apostles depended on the hospitality of others as they ministered from town to town. In those days, for a town to refuse a guest was a breach of etiquette. However, the ambassadors were to remain only with those who were "worthy," those who trusted Christ and received His message of peace and forgiveness. The Apostles were not to compromise. If a town rejected their words, they were to warn the people and depart. To shake off the dust was an act of judgment (Acts 13:51).

We do not know how long this "evangelistic campaign" lasted. Jesus Himself went out to preach (see Matt. 11:1), and later the Apostles returned to Him and reported what had happened (Luke 9:10). Mark 6:7 tells us that Jesus had sent the men out in pairs, which explains why their names are listed in pairs in Matthew 10:2-4. Revelation 21:14 tells us that the names of the Apostles will be on the foundations of the heavenly walls. The name of Judas will, of course, be replaced by Matthias (Acts 1:26).

While we may learn from the spiritual principles in this paragraph, we should not apply these instructions to our lives. The Lord's commission to us includes "all the world" (Matt. 28:19-20), not just the nation of Israel. We preach the Gospel of the grace of God (Acts 20:24). Our message is, "Christ died for our sins," and not, "The kingdom of heaven is at hand." The King has come; He has already suffered, died, and risen from the dead. Now He offers His salvation to all who will believe.

Instructions for Future Disciples (Matt. 10:16-23)

The "atmosphere" of this section is different from that in the previous section. Here the Lord spoke of persecution, but we have no record that the Twelve suffered during their tour. Jesus also spoke of a ministry to the Gentiles (Matt. 10:18). The Holy Spirit had not been given, yet Jesus talked about the Spirit speaking in them (Matt. 10:20). Matthew 10:22 seems to indicate a worldwide persecution; yet the Apostles were ministering only in their own land. Finally, Matthew 10:23 speaks about the return of the Lord, which certainly moves these events into the future. It is difficult to escape the conclusion that these instructions apply to witnesses at some future time.

But, *what* time? To some degree, some of these events took place in the Book of Acts; yet Jesus Christ did not return at that time. And the ministry in Acts was not limited to "the cities of Israel" (Matt. 10:23). It seems that the period described in this section closely parallels the time of Tribulation that Jesus described in His "Olivet Discourse" (Matt. 24–25). In fact, the statement, "He that shall endure unto the end, the same shall be saved" (Matt. 10:13), is definitely a part of our Lord's prophetic discourse (Matt. 24:13; Mark 13:13). It does not refer to a person keeping himself saved, but rather enduring persecution and being faithful.

If, then, these instructions apply to that future time of Tribulation, we can easily understand why Jesus said so much about hatred and persecution. The Tribulation period will be a time of *opposition.* God's servants will be like sheep in the midst of wolves. They will need to be "tough-minded but tenderhearted." This opposition will come from organized religion (Matt. 10:17), government (Matt. 10:18), and even the family (Matt. 10:21).

While believers in scattered parts of the world are experiencing some of this persecution today, the indication is that this opposition will be worldwide. "Religion" has always persecuted true believers. Even the Apostle Paul persecuted the church when he was the unconverted Saul of Tarsus. Church history reveals that "organized religion" that has no Gospel has opposed men and women who have dared to witness boldly for Christ.

Matthew 10:18 states that *government* will

also share in this program of persecution. The prophetic Scriptures teach that, in the last days, government and religion will work together to control the world. Revelation 13 describes a time during the Tribulation period when a world ruler (the Antichrist) will force the world to worship him and his image. He will control world religion, economics, and government; and he will use all three to persecute those who stand true to Christ.

There will also be a decay of *family* love and loyalty. "Without natural affection" is one of the marks of the end times (2 Tim. 3:3). Jesus quoted Micah 7:6 to prove this point (Matt. 10:21). The three institutions which God established in this world are the home, human government, and the church. In the last days, all three of these institutions will oppose the truth instead of promote it.

But the Tribulation period will also be a time of *opportunity*. The believers will be able to witness to governors and kings (Matt. 10:18). Their enemies will try to trip them up, but the Spirit of God will teach the witnesses what to say. Believers today must not use Matthew 10:19-20 as an excuse not to study the Word in preparation for witnessing, teaching, or preaching. These verses describe an emergency situation; they are not God's regular pattern for ministry today. Even during the days of the Apostles, the Spirit gave them their messages when they faced their enemies (Acts 4:8). This unusual ministry of the Spirit will be evident during the Tribulation period.

The Tribulation will be a time of opposition and opportunity; but it will also be a time of *obligation*. The ambassadors of the King must "endure to the end" and faithfully perform their ministry, even if it costs them their lives. In spite of scourging, rejection by their families, persecution from city to city, and trials before leaders, the servants must remain true to their Lord. Their witness will be used by God to win others. Revelation 7:1-8 indicates that 144,000 Jewish witnesses will carry God's Word throughout the world during the Tribulation; and as a result, great multitudes will come to Christ (Rev. 7:9ff).

No doubt these words in Matthew 10 will become very precious and meaningful to witnesses during that time. We, today, can learn from these words, even though their primary interpretation and application are for God's servants at a future time. No matter how difficult our circumstances may be, we can turn opposition into opportunities for witness. We can trust the Spirit of God to help us remember what the Lord has taught us (John 14:26). Instead of fleeing and looking for an easier place, we can "endure to the end," knowing that God will help us and see us through.

Instructions for Present Disciples (Matt. 10:24-42)

While the truths in this section would apply to God's servants during any period of Bible history, they seem to have a special significance for the church today. The emphasis is, "Fear not!" (Matt. 10:26, 28, 31) The particular fear Christ discussed is explained in Matthew 10:32-33: the fear of confessing Christ openly before men. God has no "secret service." The public confession of faith in Christ is one evidence of true salvation (Rom. 10:9-10). Several reasons show why we must not be afraid to openly confess Christ. Let's examine these reasons that are found in Matthew 10.

Suffering is to be expected (vv. 24-25). Men persecuted Jesus Christ when He was ministering on earth, so why should we expect anything different? We are His disciples, and the disciple does not "outrank" the Master. They said that Jesus was in league with Satan (Beelzebub: lord of the dung; lord of the house); so they will say the same thing about His followers. However, we should count it a privilege to suffer *for* Him and *with* Him (Acts 5:41; Phil. 3:10).

God will bring everything to light (vv. 26-27). The enemies of Christ use secret and deceptive means to oppose the Gospel. But true believers are open and courageous in their lives and witness. We have nothing to hide. "In secret have I said nothing," said Jesus (John 18:20). False witnesses lied about Jesus during His trial, but God saw to it that the truth came out. We have nothing to fear because the Lord will one day reveal the secrets of men's hearts (Rom. 2:16) and expose them and judge them. Our task is not to please men, but to proclaim God's message. The present judgment of men does not frighten us, because we are living in the light of the future judgment of God.

We fear God alone (v. 28). All that men can do is kill the body; and, if they do, the believer's soul goes home to be with the Lord. But God is able to destroy *both* body and soul in hell! Of course, God will never condemn one of His own children (John 5:24;

Rom. 8:1). Martin Luther caught this truth when he wrote:

Let goods and kindred go,
This mortal life also;
The body they may kill:
God's truth abideth still;
His kingdom is forever.

The person who fears God alone need never fear any man or group of men. The fear of God is the fear that cancels fear.

God cares for His own (vv. 29-31). It did not cost much to purchase sparrows in the market. If we compare these verses with Luke 12:6, we discover that sparrows were so cheap that the dealer threw in an extra one! Yet the Father knows when a sparrow falls to the ground; *and the Father is there.* If God cares for sparrows in such a marvelous way, will He not also care for His own who are serving Him? He certainly will! To God, we are of greater value than many sparrows.

God is concerned about all of the details of our lives. Even the hairs of our head are numbered—not "counted" in a total, but numbered individually! God sees the sparrow fall to the ground, and God sees when a hair falls from the head of one of His children. When He protects His own, He protects them down to the individual hairs (Luke 21:18). There is no need for us to fear when God is exercising such wonderful care over us.

Christ honors those who confess Him (vv. 32-33). To confess Him means much more than to make a statement with the lips. It also means to back up that statement with the life. It is one thing to say, "Jesus Christ is Lord," and quite another thing to surrender to Him and obey His will. The walk and the talk must go together.

In heaven, Jesus has two special ministries. As our High Priest, He gives us grace to keep us from sinning. As our Advocate, He forgives and restores us when we do sin (1 John 2:1-2). The *merits* of His heavenly intercessory work do not depend on our faithfulness, for He is faithful even if we are not (2 Tim. 2:12-13). But the *benefits* of His heavenly ministry are for those who are faithful to Him. When Christ confesses us before the Father, He is securing for us the benefits of His sacrificial work on the cross. When He denies us before the Father, He is unable to share these graces with us. The fault is ours, not His.

But something else is involved. One day we shall stand before His judgment seat where the rewards will be distributed (2 Cor. 5:10; Rom. 14:10). If we have denied Him, we will lose rewards and the joy of hearing His "Well done." To be sure, anyone who denies Him on earth may be forgiven. Peter denied the Lord three times, was forgiven, and was restored.

We cannot escape conflict (vv. 34-39). Once we have identified with Jesus Christ and confessed Him, we are part of a war. We did not start the war; God declared war on Satan (Gen. 3:15). On the night our Lord was born, the angels declared, "On earth peace" (Luke 2:14). But Jesus seemed to deny this truth. "I came not to send peace, but a sword" (Matt. 10:34). Had Israel accepted Him, He would have given them peace. But the people refused Him, and the result was "a sword." Instead of there being "peace on earth," there is "peace in heaven" (Luke 19:38). He has made peace through the blood of His cross (Col. 1:20) so that men can be reconciled to God and to each other.

The only way a believer can escape conflict is to deny Christ and compromise his witness, and this would be sin. Then the believer would be at war with God and with himself. We will be misunderstood and persecuted even by those who are the closest to us; yet we must not allow this to affect our witness. It is important that we suffer for Jesus' sake, and for righteousness' sake, and not because we ourselves are difficult to live with. There is a difference between the "offense of the cross" (Gal. 5:11) and offensive Christians.

Each believer must make the decision once and for all to love Christ supremely and take up his cross and follow Christ. The love in Matthew 10:37 is the motive for the cross in Matthew 10:38. To "carry the cross" does not mean to wear a pin on our lapel or put a sticker on our automobile. It means to confess Christ and obey Him in spite of shame and suffering. It means to die to self daily. If the Lord went to a cross for us, the least we can do is carry a cross for Him.

Matthew 10:39 presents us with only two alternatives: spare your life or sacrifice your life. There is no middle ground. If we protect our own interests, we will be losers; if we die to self and live for His interests, we will be winners. Since spiritual conflict is inevitable in this world, why not die to self and let Christ win the battle *for* us and *in* us? After all, the real war is *inside*—selfishness versus sacrifice.

We can be a blessing to others (vv. 40-42). Not everyone will reject our witness. There are those who will welcome us and receive a blessing. After all, we are the ambassadors of the King! Our King will see to it that they are rewarded for what they do. When people receive us, they welcome the King; for we are His representatives. Read 2 Samuel 10 for an example of what happens when people mistreat the envoys of the King.

The blessing, however, is not automatic. It all depends on the attitude of the host. If he receives the ambassador as a prophet (a spokesman for God), then he gets one reward; if he receives him only as a righteous man, there is another reward. But even a cup of cold water, given with the right spirit, brings its own reward.

Keep in mind that the theme of this last section is discipleship, not sonship. We become the children of God through faith in Christ; we are disciples as we faithfully follow Him and obey His will. Sonship does not change, but discipleship does change as we walk with Christ. There is a great need today for faithful disciples, believers who will learn from Christ and live for Him.

This brings us to the close of the first major division of Matthew, *The Revelation of the King.* We have seen His person (Matt. 1–4), His principles (Matt. 5–7), and His power (Matt. 8–10). How will the nation respond to this revelation?

CHAPTER NINE
THE KING'S CONFLICTS
Matthew 11–12

All of the evidence had been presented. John the Baptist had introduced the King to the nation. Jesus had revealed His person, principles, and power. It was now up to the leaders of the nation to make their decision. Instead of receiving their King, they began to rebel against Him. In these two chapters four areas of rebellion are presented.

Rebellion against His Prophet (Matt. 11:1-30)

Explanation (vv. 1-15). John the Baptist was in prison in the fortress of Machaerus because he had courageously denounced the adulterous marriage of Herod Antipas and Herodias (Luke 3:19-20). It seems that the Jewish leaders would have opposed Herod and sought to free John, but they did nothing. Their attitude toward John reflected their feeling toward Jesus, for John had pointed to Jesus and honored Him.

It is not difficult to sympathize with John as he suffered in prison. He was a man of the desert, yet he was confined indoors. He was an active man, with a divine mandate to preach; yet he was silenced. He had announced judgment, and yet that judgment was slow in coming (Matt. 3:7-12). He received only partial reports of Jesus' ministry and could not see the total picture.

Our Lord's reply to John revealed both tact and tenderness. He reminded John of the Old Testament prophecies about the works of Messiah (Isa. 29:18-19; 35:4-6). John's disciples had already told him what Jesus was doing (Luke 7:18), but Jesus asked them to "show John again." John had come in the spirit and power of Elijah (Luke 1:17), and even Elijah had his days of discouragement! Jesus assured John that He was fulfilling the Father's will.

After answering John, Jesus then praised him. John was not a "popular preacher" who catered to the crowd, nor was he a reed in the wind who vacillated with every change. He was a man of conviction and courage, the greatest of the prophets. The fact that John was privileged to announce the Messiah gave him this high position. His ministry marked the climax of the Law and the Prophets.

In what sense was John "Elijah who was to come"? (Matt. 11:14) He came in the spirit and power of Elijah (Luke 1:17), and even dressed and ministered like Elijah (2 Kings 1:7-8; Matt. 3:4). Like Elijah, John had a message of judgment for the apostate nation of Israel. His ministry was prophesied (Isa. 40:3) and he fulfilled it. But Malachi 4:5 prophesied the coming of Elijah "before the coming of the great and dreadful Day of the Lord." This "Day of the Lord" is the time of Tribulation that will come on all the earth (see Matt. 24:15). But no such judgments followed the ministry of John the Baptist. Why?

John's ministry was to prepare the nation

for Jesus and to present Jesus to the nation (Luke 1:15-17; John 1:29-34). Had the people received John's witness and accepted their Messiah, John would have fulfilled the prophecies literally. Instead, they were fulfilled in a spiritual sense in the lives of those who trusted Christ. Jesus made this clear in Matthew 17:10-13. Many Bible students believe that Malachi 4:5 will be fulfilled literally when Elijah comes as one of the "two witnesses" spoken of in Revelation 11.

The common people held John in high regard (Matt. 21:26), and many of them had repented and been baptized by John. But the leaders refused to honor John, and this proved their unbelief and hardness of heart. Instead of being *childlike* and humbling themselves, the leaders were *childish* and stubborn, like children pouting because they could not have their way. The parable in Matthew 11:16-19 revealed the spiritual condition of the leaders, and unfortunately it also reveals the hearts of unbelievers today.

Condemnation (vv. 16-24). How unusual to find the word *woe* on the lips of Jesus! This word means judgment, but it also includes pity and sorrow. How tragic that these cities should treat lightly their opportunities to see and hear the Christ of God, and be saved! The Gentile cities of Tyre and Sidon, and the godless cities of Sodom and Gomorrah, would have repented had they seen the miracles that Jesus and His disciples performed. Capernaum had been "exalted to heaven" by being privileged to have the Messiah live there. Yet her greater privileges only brought greater responsibilities and greater judgment. Five of the ten miracles recorded in Matthew 8–9 were performed in Capernaum.

Invitation (vv. 25-30). Why did the religious leaders rebel against John and Jesus? Because they (the leaders) were intellectually and spiritually proud and would not become little babes in humility and honesty. There is a vast difference between the spoiled children of the parable (Matt. 11:16-19) and the submissive children of this statement of praise. The Father reveals Himself to the Son, and the Son reveals Himself and the Father to those who are willing to come to the Son in faith. These verses indicate both the sovereignty of the Father and the responsibility of the sinner. Three commands summarize this invitation.

"Come." The Pharisees all said "Do!" and tried to make the people follow Moses and the traditions. But true salvation is found only in a Person, Jesus Christ. To come to Him means to trust Him. This invitation is open to those who are exhausted and burdened down. That is exactly how the people felt under the yoke of pharisaical legalism (Matt. 23:4; Acts 15:10).

"Take." This is a deeper experience. When we come to Christ by faith, *He gives* us rest. When we take His yoke and learn, *we find* rest, that deeper rest of surrender and obedience. The first is "peace with God" (Rom. 5:1); the second is "the peace of God" (Phil. 4:6-8). To "take a yoke" in that day meant to become a disciple. When we submit to Christ, we are yoked to Him. The word "easy" means "well-fitting"; He has just the yoke that is tailor-made for our lives and needs. The burden of doing His will is not a heavy one (1 John 5:3).

"Learn." The first two commands represent a crisis as we come and yield to Christ; but this step is into a *process.* As we learn more about Him, we find a deeper peace, because we trust Him more. Life is simplified and unified around the person of Christ. This invitation is for "all"—not just the people of Israel (Matt. 10:5-6).

Rebellion against His Principles (Matt. 12:1-21)

Jesus deliberately violated the Sabbath traditions on several occasions. He had taught the people that mere external laws could never save them or make them holy; true righteousness had to come from the heart. The Hebrew word *sabat* means "repose or rest," which explains why Matthew introduced these Sabbath conflicts at this point. Jesus offers rest to all who will come to Him; there is no rest in mere religious observances.

It was lawful to satisfy your hunger from your neighbor's field (Deut. 23:24-25). But to do it on the Sabbath was a breach of the Law according to the traditions of the scribes and Pharisees; for it meant doing work. Jesus gave a threefold reply to their accusation.

He appealed to a king (vv. 3-4). The consecrated bread was to be eaten only by the priests, yet David and his soldiers ate it. Certainly the Son of David had a right to eat His Father's grain from the field! And if David broke the law and was not condemned, surely Jesus could break man's traditions and be guiltless (see 1 Sam. 21:1ff).

He appealed to the priests (vv. 5-6).

The priests had to offer a given number of sacrifices on the Sabbath (Num. 28:9-10) and yet were not condemned. In fact, their service was in obedience to the Law given by God. This suggests that man's traditions about the Sabbath were wrong, for they contradicted God's own Law.

He appealed to a prophet (v. 7). The quotation is from Hosea 6:6, one that Jesus had already quoted (Matt. 9:13). The Sabbath law was given to Israel as a mark of her relationship to God (Ex. 20:9-11; 31:13-17; Neh. 9:12-15). But it was also an act of mercy for both man and beast, to give them needed rest each week. Any religious law that is contrary to mercy and the care of nature should be looked on with suspicion. God wants mercy, not religious sacrifice. He wants love, not legalism. The Pharisees who sacrificed to obey their Sabbath laws thought they were serving God. When they accused Christ and His disciples, they thought they were defending God. How like religious legalists today!

Note that Jesus appealed to prophet, priest, and king; for He is Prophet, Priest, and King. Note too the three "greater" statements that He made: as the *Priest,* He is "greater than the temple" (Matt. 12:6); as *Prophet,* He is "greater than Jonah" (Matt. 12:41); and as *King,* He is "greater than Solomon" (Matt. 12:42).

In declaring Himself "Lord of the Sabbath," Jesus was actually affirming equality with God; for God had established the Sabbath (Gen. 2:1-3). He then proved this claim by healing the man with the paralyzed hand. It is sad that the religious leaders used this man and his handicap as a weapon to fight against Jesus. But the Lord was not afraid of their threats. Not doing good on the Sabbath Day (or any other day) is the same as doing evil. Jesus argued that if a farmer could care for his animals on the Sabbath, shouldn't we care for man, made in the image of God?

They responded to this deliberate challenge by plotting to kill Him. They had accused Him of blasphemy when He healed the paralytic (Matt. 9:1-8), and of lack of separation when He ate with Matthew's friends (Matt. 9:11-13). But this deed was even worse. He had deliberately violated the law of God! He had *worked* on the Sabbath by harvesting grain and healing a man.

Our Lord's response to their hatred was withdrawal. He did not openly fight His enemies, but fulfilled the prophecy in Isaiah 42:1-4. His enemies were but broken reeds and smoking flax. Note the double mention of the Gentiles, another hint from Matthew that Israel would reject her King and the kingdom would go to the Gentiles.

The Lord's withdrawal at this point is an anticipation of His "retirement" described in Matthew 14–20. During that time, Jesus avoided direct conflict with His enemies that He might stay on the "divine timetable" and be crucified on schedule. Also, during that time, He taught His disciples and prepared them for His crucifixion.

Rebellion against His Power (Matt. 12:22-37)

The accusation (vv. 22-24). The man that was brought to Jesus was certainly in a sad state, for he was blind, unable to speak, and possessed with a demon. Jesus delivered the man, something the Pharisees could not do. Their accusation was that He worked by the power of Satan and not by the power of God. They did not agree with Nicodemus' evaluation of His miracles (John 3:2).

The answer (vv. 25-30). Jesus pointed out that their statement was illogical and impractical. Why would Satan fight against himself? Jesus affirmed that Satan had a kingdom, for he is the god of this age (Matt. 4:8-9; John 12:31). He also stated that Satan had a "house," which seems to refer to the body of the man who was possessed (Matt. 12:43-44). If Satan casts out his own demonic helpers, then he is opposing himself, dividing his kingdom, and destroying his house.

Their accusation was also illogical from their own point of view, though they did not see it. There were Jewish exorcists (see Acts 19:13-16) who apparently were successful. By whose power did *they* cast out demons? If it was by Satan's power, they were in league with the devil! Of course, no Pharisee was about to draw that conclusion.

Jesus was able to cast out demons because He had first defeated Satan, the prince of the demons. Jesus entered Satan's kingdom, overcame his power, and claimed his spoils. His victory was through the Spirit of God ("the finger of God," Luke 11:20) and not in the power of the evil one. This means that God is Victor over Satan, and that men must decide on whose side they will stand. There can be no compromise. We are either with God or against God.

The admonition (vv. 31-37). Jesus

warned them that their words gave evidence of the evil in their hearts. The sin against the Holy Spirit is not a matter of speech; the words spoken are only "fruit" from the sinful heart. If the heart is a treasury of good, that good will overflow through the lips and do good to others. But if the heart is a treasury of evil, that evil will spill over through the lips and do harm to the person speaking and those listening.

But what is this terrible "sin against the Holy Spirit"? Can it be committed today, and, if so, how? Our Lord said that God will forgive evil words spoken against the Son, but not against the Spirit. Does this mean that the Holy Spirit is more important than Jesus Christ, God's Son? Surely not. We often hear the name of God or Jesus Christ used in blasphemy, but rarely if ever the name of the Holy Spirit. How can God forgive words spoken against His Son, and yet not forgive words spoken against the Spirit?

It appears that this situation existed *only while Christ was ministering on earth.* Jesus did not appear to be different from any other Jewish man (Isa. 53:2). To speak against Christ could be forgiven *while He was on earth.* But when the Spirit of God came at Pentecost as proof that Jesus was the Christ, and was alive, to reject the witness of the Spirit was final. The only consequence would be judgment.

When the leaders rejected John the Baptist, they were rejecting *the Father* who sent him. When they rejected Jesus, they were rejecting *the Son.* But when they rejected the ministry of the Apostles, they rejected *the Holy Spirit*—and that is the end. There is no more witness. Such rejection cannot be forgiven.

The phrase "idle word" in Matthew 12:36 means "words that accomplish nothing." If God is going to judge our "small talk," how much more will He judge our deliberate words? It is by our conversation *at unguarded moments* that we reveal our true character.

Is there an "unpardonable sin" today? Yes, the final rejection of Jesus Christ. Jesus made it clear that *all* sins can be forgiven (Matt. 12:31). Adultery, murder, blasphemy, and other sins can all be forgiven; they are not unpardonable. But God cannot forgive the rejection of His Son. It is the Spirit who bears witness to Christ (John 15:26) and who convicts the lost sinner (John 16:7-11).

Rebellion against His Person (Matt. 12:38-50)

"The Jews require a sign" (1 Cor. 1:22). To ask for a sign was evidence of unbelief: They wanted Him to *prove* that He was the Messiah. We wonder what further proof could have been given! Had they searched their own Scriptures, and sincerely examined His life, they would have concluded, "This is the Son of God!" But for Jesus to have given them a sign would have been wrong. He would have catered to their unbelief and allowed them to set the standards for faith. No matter what miracle He performed, it would not have pleased them.

Jesus gave three responses to their challenge.

He reviewed their history (vv. 39-42). The Prophet Jonah was a Jew sent to the Gentiles, and the Queen of Sheba was a Gentile who came to visit Solomon, a Jew (2 Chron. 9:1-12). Because of the bitterness between the Jews and the Gentiles, this reference to the Gentiles must have irritated the Pharisees. But we have noted other occasions when either Jesus or Matthew mentioned the Gentiles.

Jonah was a sign to the people of Nineveh because he had experienced (in the great fish) "death," burial, and resurrection. The only sign Jesus would give to His nation was death, burial, and resurrection. The messages in the first seven chapters of Acts center on the resurrection of Christ, not on His death on the cross. The Jews of that day believed that He had died, for this was the chief topic of conversation (Luke 24:18). *But they did not believe that He was alive* (Matt. 28:11-15). In Acts 2–7, the Holy Spirit gave to the nation of Israel abundant witness that Jesus was alive. This was the only sign they needed.

Jesus is greater than Jonah in many ways. He is greater in His person, for Jonah was a mere man. He was greater in His obedience, for Jonah disobeyed God and was chastened. Jesus actually died, while Jonah's "grave" was in the belly of the great fish. Jesus arose from the dead under His own power. Jonah ministered only to one city, while Jesus gave His life for the whole world. Certainly Jesus was greater in His love, for Jonah did not love the people of Nineveh—he wanted them to die. Jonah's message saved Nineveh from judgment; he was a messenger of the wrath of God. Jesus' message was that of grace and salvation. When we trust Christ, we are not only saved from judgment, but we receive eternal, abundant life.

Jesus is also greater than Solomon in His wisdom, wealth, and works. The Queen of Sheba was amazed at what she saw in Solomon's kingdom; but what we have in the kingdom of God through Christ far surpasses Solomon's glories. To sit at Christ's table and hear His words, and to share His blessings, is much more satisfying than to visit and admire the most spectacular kingdom, even that of Solomon.

The main lesson behind this history lesson is this: The citizens of Nineveh will witness against the rulers of Israel, for they repented at Jonah's preaching. The Queen of Sheba will also witness against them. She traveled a long distance to hear Solomon's wisdom, yet the Jewish leaders rejected the wisdom of Christ *who was in their very midst!* The greater the opportunity, the greater the judgment. It is a tragic feature in the history of Israel that the nation rejected their deliverers the first time, but accepted them the second time. This was true with Joseph, Moses, David, the prophets (Matt. 23:29), and Jesus Christ.

He revealed their hearts (vv. 43-45). We must connect these verses with Matthew 12:24-29. Satan's "house" is the body of the person who is possessed by the demon. It appears that the demons are restless and seek bodies in which to reside (Matt. 8:28-31). When the demon left, this man's life was changed for the better; *but his life was still empty.* When the demon returned, he brought others with him; and the man's life ended in tragedy.

The primary application is to the nation of Israel, especially that generation present when Jesus ministered on earth. The nation had been purged of the demon of idolatry which had plagued them in the Old Testament. But reformation was not enough. Reformation could cleanse, but it could not fill. The nation should have received the Saviour and been filled with spiritual life. Instead, the people rejected Him and the end was destruction.

There is a personal application. It is not enough to clean house; we must also invite in the right tenant. The Pharisees were proud of their "clean houses," *but their hearts were empty!* Mere religion, or reformation, will not save. There must be regeneration, the receiving of Christ into the heart (see Rev. 3:20). We cannot be neutral about Jesus Christ.

He rejected their honor (vv. 46-50). Even our Lord's earthly family did not fully understand Him or His ministry (John 7:1-5). Some of His friends thought He was mad (Mark 3:21). But Jesus did not want the honor that comes from people. While He was not disrespectful toward His physical family, He did emphasize the family of God.

Note His use of the word "whosoever" (Matt. 12:50). This paralleled His beautiful invitation in Matthew 11:28-30 where He encouraged all to trust Him. If the nation would not receive Him, at least individuals within the nation—and among the Gentiles—could trust Him. But what will happen to the promised kingdom?

CHAPTER TEN
THE KING'S SECRETS
Matthew 13

This chapter records the events of a crisis day in the ministry of Jesus Christ. He knew that the growing opposition of the religious leaders would lead to His crucifixion. This fact He had to explain to His disciples. But their logical question would be, "What will happen to the kingdom about which we have been preaching?" That question is answered in this series of parables. So, He first explained the truth concerning the kingdom, and then later explained to them the facts about the Cross.

Our Lord's use of parables puzzled the disciples. He had used some parables in His teaching already, but on that day He gave a series of seven interrelated parables, then added an eighth. The word *parable* means "to cast alongside." It is a story, or comparison, that is put alongside something else to help make the lesson clear. But these are not ordinary parables; Jesus called them "the mysteries of the kingdom of heaven" (Matt. 13:11). In the New Testament, a "mystery" is a spiritual truth understood only by divine revelation. It is a "sacred secret" known only to those "on the inside" who learn from the Lord and obey Him.

In this series of parables, Jesus explained the course of the Gospel in the world. If Israel had received Him as King, the blessings would have flowed out from Jerusalem to the ends of the earth. But the nation rejected Him, and God had to institute a new program on earth. During this present age, "the kingdom of heaven" is a mixture of true and false, good and bad, as pictured in these parables. It is "Christendom," professing allegiance to the King, and yet containing much that is contrary to the principles of the King.

Why did Jesus teach in parables? Two reasons were given: because of the sluggishness of the people (Matt. 13:10-17); and because it was prophesied in Psalm 78:2 (Matt. 13:34-35). Jesus did not teach in parables to confuse or condemn the people. Rather, He sought to excite their interest and arouse their curiosity. These parables would give light to those with trusting, searching hearts. But they would bring darkness to the unconcerned and unrepentant.

The seven parables describe for us the spiritual course of "the kingdom of heaven" in this present age. In them we see three stages of spiritual development.

The Beginning of the Kingdom (Matt. 13:1-9, 18-23)

The Parable of the Sower does not begin with "The kingdom of heaven is like" because it describes how the kingdom begins. It begins with the preaching of the Word, the planting of the seed in the hearts of people. When we say, "Let me plant this thought in your mind," we express the idea of this parable. The seed is God's Word; the various soils represent different kinds of hearts; and the varied results show the different responses to the Word of God. Jesus explained this parable so there is no doubt of its meaning.

Why compare God's Word to seed? Because the Word is "living and powerful" (Heb. 4:12, SCO). Unlike the words of men, the Word of God has life in it; and that life can be imparted to those who will believe. The truth of God must take root in the heart, be cultivated, and permitted to bear fruit. It is shocking to realize that three fourths of the seed did not bear fruit. Jesus did not describe an age of great harvest, but one in which the Word would be rejected. He was not impressed with the "great multitudes" that followed Him, for He knew that most of the people would not receive His Word within and bear fruit.

Fruit is the test of true salvation (Matt. 7:16). This would include holiness (Rom. 6:22), Christian character (Gal. 5:22-23), good works (Col. 1:10), winning others to Christ (Rom. 1:13), sharing what we have (Rom. 15:25-28), and praising God (Heb. 13:15). If a plant is to bear fruit, it must be rooted in soil and exposed to sunshine.

In the parable, the sun represents persecution that comes because of the Word. *Persecution helps believers grow.* But the sunshine will kill a plant with no roots. This explains why some "believers" do not last: Their faith was weak, their understanding was meager, and their decision was not sincere. It is possible to "believe" and yet not be saved (John 2:23-25). Unless there is fruit in the life, there is not saving faith in the heart.

Nineteen times in Matthew 13 we find the word "hear." The Parable of the Sower is found in the first three Gospels, and in each one, the closing admonition is different. It is important that we hear God's Word, because "Faith cometh by hearing, and hearing by the Word of God" (Rom. 10:17). Jesus said, "Who hath ears to hear" (Matt. 13:9), "Take heed *what* you hear!" (Mark 4:24), and "Take heed *how* you hear!" (Luke 8:18)

Opposition to the Kingdom (Matt. 13:24-43)

Satan opposes the kingdom by trying to snatch the Word from hearts (Matt. 13:4, 19). But when that fails, he has other ways of attacking God's work. These three parables reveal that Satan is primarily an *imitator:* He plants false Christians, he encourages a false growth, and he introduces false doctrine.

The tares—false Christians (vv. 24-30, 36-43). Satan cannot uproot the plants (true Christians), so he plants counterfeit Christians in their midst. In this parable, the good seed is not the Word of God. It represents people converted through trusting the Word. The field is not human hearts; the field is the world. Christ is sowing true believers in various places that they might bear fruit (John 12:23-26). But, wherever Christ sows a true Christian, Satan comes and sows a counterfeit.

We must beware of Satan's counterfeits. He has counterfeit Christians (2 Cor. 11:26) who believe a counterfeit Gospel (Gal. 1:6-9). He encourages a counterfeit righteousness (Rom. 10:1-3), and even has a counterfeit church (Rev. 2:9). At the end of the age, he will produce a counterfeit Christ (2 Thes. 2:1-12).

We must also stay awake to make sure that Satan's ministers do not get into the true fellowship and do damage (2 Peter 2; 1 John 4:1-6). It is when God's people go to sleep that Satan works. Our task is not to pull up the false, but to plant the true. (This does not refer to discipline within the local church.) We are not detectives but evangelists! We must oppose Satan and expose his lies. But we must also sow the Word of God and bear fruit in the place where He has planted us.

What will happen to the tares? God will gather them together and burn them. It is interesting to see that some of this "bundling" is already going on as various religious groups merge and strive for union. Spiritual unity among true Christians is one thing, but religious uniformity among mere professing Christians is quite another. It is difficult to tell the false from the true today; but at the end of the age, the angels will separate them.

The mustard seed—false growth (vv. 31-32). In the East, the mustard seed symbolizes something small and insignificant. It produces a large plant, but not a "tree" in the strictest sense. However, the plant is large enough for birds to sit in the branches.

Since Jesus did not explain this parable, we must use what He did explain in the other parables to find its meaning. The birds in the Parable of the Sower represented Satan (Matt. 13:19). Passages like Daniel 4:12 and Ezekiel 17:23 indicate that a tree is a symbol of a world power. These facts suggest that the parable teaches an abnormal growth of the kingdom of heaven, one that makes it possible for Satan to work in it. Certainly "Christendom" has become a worldwide power with a complex organization of many branches. What started in a humble manner today boasts of material possessions and political influences.

Some make this parable teach the worldwide success of the Gospel. But that would contradict what Jesus taught in the first parable. If anything, the New Testament teaches a growing decline in the ministry of the Gospel as the end of the age draws near.

The leaven—false doctrine (v. 33). The mustard seed illustrates the false *outward* expansion of the kingdom, while the leaven illustrates the *inward* development of false doctrine and false living. Throughout the Bible, leaven is a symbol of evil. It had to be removed from the Jewish homes during Passover (Ex. 12:15-19; 13:7). It was excluded from the sacrifices (Ex. 34:35), with the exception of the loaves used at the Feast of Pentecost (Lev. 23:15-21). But there the loaves symbolized Jews and Gentiles in the church, and there is sin in the church.

Jesus used leaven to picture hypocrisy (Luke 12:1), false teaching (Matt. 16:6-12), and worldly compromise (Matt. 22:16-21). Paul used leaven to picture carnality in the church (1 Cor. 5:6-8) as well as false doctrine (Gal. 5:9). Sin is like leaven (yeast): It quietly grows, it corrupts, and it "puffs up" (1 Cor. 4:18-19; 5:2; 8:1). It would seem that making the growth of the leaven a picture of the spread of the Gospel throughout the world would violate the meaning of this important symbol. It would also contradict the other parables.

Satan has worked hard to introduce false doctrine and false living into the ministry of the Word of God. From the very early days of the church, true believers have battled false doctrine and hypocrisy. How sad it is that some churches and schools that were once true to the Word have turned from the truth to fables. "Prove all things; hold fast that which is good" is sound counsel (1 Thes. 5:21).

The kingdom of heaven began with the sowing of the Word of God in the hearts of men. Much of the seed did not bear fruit; but some was fruitful. Satan opposed the work of God by sowing counterfeit Christians, by encouraging a false growth, and by introducing false doctrine. It would seem that Satan is winning! But the test is at *the end* of the age, not *during* the age.

The Outcome of the Kingdom (Matt. 13:44-50)

At the close of this age, God will have three peoples: the Jews (the hidden treasure), the church (the pearl), and the saved Gentile nations who will enter into the kingdom (the dragnet).

The hidden treasure (v. 44). The common interpretation of this parable is that the sinner finds Christ and gives up all that he possesses to gain Him and be saved. But this interpretation presents several problems. To begin with, Jesus Christ is not a hidden treasure. He is perhaps the best-known Person of history. In the second place, the sinner cannot "find Christ" for he is blind and stubborn (Rom. 3:10ff). It is the Saviour who finds the lost sinner (Luke 19:10). And no sinner could ever *purchase* salvation! Please note that the man in the parable did not purchase the treasure; he purchased *the whole field.* "The field is the world" (Matt. 13:38). Must the lost sinner purchase the world to gain Christ? Does he hide Him again?

Once again, Old Testament symbolism assists us in our interpretation. The treasure is the nation of Israel (Ex. 19:5; Ps. 135:4). That nation was placed in the world to bring glory to God, but it failed. It became a nation hidden, a treasure not being invested to produce dividends for God. Jesus Christ gave His all to purchase the whole world in order to save the nation (John 11:51). On the cross, Jesus died for the whole world; but in a special way, He died for Israel (Isa. 53:8). The nation suffered judgment and seeming destruction, but in God's sight it is "hidden" and will be revealed again in glory.

There is, then, a future for Israel. Politically, the nation was reborn on May 14, 1948. But the nation is far from what it ought to be spiritually. God sees Israel as His treasure, and one day He will establish her in her glorious kingdom.

The pearl of great price (vv. 45-46). A well-known Gospel song perpetuates the interpretation that this pearl is Jesus Christ and His salvation. But the same objections apply to this interpretation as applied to the previous parable. The sinner does not find Christ; Christ finds the sinner. No sinner is able to pay for salvation, even though he sells all that he has.

The pearl represents the church. The Bible makes a distinction between Jews, Gentiles, and the church (1 Cor. 10:32). Today, the church, the body of Christ, is composed of believing Jews and Gentiles (Eph. 2:11ff). Unlike most other gems, the pearl is a *unity*—it cannot be carved like a diamond or emerald. The church is a unity (Eph. 4:4-6), even though the professing church on earth is divided. Like a pearl, the church is the product of suffering. Christ died for the church (Eph. 5:25) and His suffering on the cross made possible her birth.

A pearl grows gradually, and the church grows gradually as the Spirit convicts and converts sinners. No one can see the making of the pearl, for it is hidden in the shell of the oyster under the waters. No one can see the growth of His church in the world. The church is among the nations today (waters in the Bible represent nations, Dan. 7:1-3; Rev. 13:1; 17:15) and one day will be revealed in its beauty.

So, in spite of Satan's subtle working in this world, Christ is forming His church. He sold all that He had to purchase His church, and nothing Satan can do will cause Him to fail. There is but one church, a pearl of great price, though there are many local churches. Not everyone who is a member of a local church belongs to the one church, the body of Christ. It is only through repentance and faith in Christ that we become a part of His church. Of course, all true believers ought to identify with a local assembly where they can worship and serve.

The net (vv. 47-50). The preaching of the Gospel in the world does not convert the world. It is like a huge dragnet that gathers all kinds of fish, some good and some bad. The professing church today has in it both true and false believers (the Parable of the Tares) and good and bad. At the end of the age, God will separate the true believers from the false and the good from the bad. When Jesus Christ returns to earth, to fight the battle of Armageddon (Rev. 19:11ff), He will separate believers and unbelievers *already on the earth.* These are living people who are not a part of the church (which was already in heaven) or Israel. These Gentiles will be dealt with in righteousness: The saved will enter into the kingdom, but the unsaved will be cast into the furnace of fire. The same idea is found in the "sheep and goats" parable (Matt. 25:31ff).

Twice in this series of parables Jesus used the phrase "the end of the world" (Matt. 13:39, 49). He was not referring to the end of this "Church Age," because the truth about the church was not shared with the disciples until later (Matt. 16:18). The "age" He referred to is the Jewish age at the close of the great Tribulation described in Matthew 24:1-31 and Revelation 6–19. We must be careful not to "read into" these passages in Matthew the truths later given through Paul and the other apostles.

When Jesus had completed this series of parables, He asked His disciples if they understood them, and they confidently replied, "Yes, Lord." Understanding involves responsibility. To explain this, the Lord added a final parable (Matt. 13:51-52) to remind them of their responsibilities.

They must be scribes who discover the truth. The scribes began as a noble group under the leadership of Ezra. Their purpose was to preserve the Law, study it, and apply its truths to daily life. Over the years, their noble cause degenerated into a routine task of preserving traditions and man-made interpretations, and adding burdens to the lives of the people (Luke 11:46-52). They were so wrapped up in the past that they ignored the present! Instead of sharing living truth from God's Word, they merchandised dead doctrines and "embalmed" traditions that could not help the people.

As believers, we do not search *after* truth, because we have truth in God's Son (John 14:6) and God's Word (John 17:17). We are taught by the Spirit of Truth (John 16:13) who is truth (1 John 5:6). We search *into* truth that we might discover more truth. We are scribes—students—who sit at the feet of Jesus and listen to His words. One joy of the Christian life is the privilege of learning God's truth from God's Word. But we must not stop there.

They must be disciples who do the truth. "Therefore every scribe who becomes a disciple of the kingdom of heaven" is a more accurate translation of Matthew 13:52. The scribe emphasizes *learning,* but the disciple emphasizes *living.* Disciples are doers of the Word (James 1:22ff), and they learn by doing.

It is difficult to keep our lives balanced. We often emphasize learning at the expense of living. Or, we may get so busy serving God that we do not take time to listen to His Word. Every scribe must be a disciple, and every disciple must be a scribe.

They must be stewards who dispense the truth. The scribes preserved the Law but did not invest it in the lives of the people. The treasure of the Law was encrusted by man's traditions. The seed was not planted so it could bear fruit. The "spiritual gold and silver" was not put to work so it could produce dividends. As Christians we should be *con*servative but not *pre*servative.

The steward guards the treasure, but he also dispenses it as it is needed. He dispenses both the old and the new. New principles and insights are based on old truths. The new cannot contradict the old because the old comes out of the new (Lev. 26:10). The new without the old is mere novelty and will not last. But the old does no good unless it is given new applications in life today. We need both.

When Jesus finished these parables, He went across the sea in a storm and delivered the demoniacs in the country of the Gadarenes. Matthew recorded this in 8:28-34. It was then that Jesus went to His hometown of Nazareth, and this event Matthew recorded in 13:53-58.

Two things amazed the people of Nazareth: the Lord's words and His works. However, they did not trust in Him, and this limited His ministry. What caused the people to doubt Him? They were too familiar with Him in a human way, for He had grown up in their midst. It was a case of knowing Him after the flesh (see 2 Cor. 5:16) and not having the spiritual discernment that God gives to those who will yield to Him (Matt. 11:25-30). These people walked by sight and not by faith.

But, if His own friends and family did not trust Him, what hope was there that the nation would believe on Him? Early in His ministry, Jesus had preached at Nazareth (Luke 4:16-31) and had been rejected; and now He was rejected again. This was His final visit to Nazareth; those villagers had no more opportunities. Jesus would be known as "Jesus of Nazareth," and His followers would be called "Nazarenes," but Nazareth would not receive Him. Matthew chose this event as a fitting close to the section "Rebellion against the King."

CHAPTER ELEVEN
THE KING'S WITHDRAWAL
Matthew 14

Chapters 14–20 I have called "The Retirement of the King." During the period of time recorded by Matthew in these chapters, Jesus often withdrew from the crowds and spent time alone with His disciples (see Matt. 14:13; 15:21, 29; 16:13; 17:1-8). There were several reasons for these withdrawals: the growing hostility of His enemies, the need for physical rest, and the need to prepare His disciples for His future death on the cross. Unfortunately, the disciples were often caught up in the excitement generated by the crowds that wanted to make Jesus their King (see John 6:15).

However, we must not think that these withdrawals, or periods of retirement from the crowds, were periods of inactivity. Often the crowds followed Jesus and He was unable to remain alone. He would unselfishly minister to their needs in spite of His own need for rest and solitude. In Matthew 14–20, we will see these three groups of people: Christ's enemies, the needy multitudes, and the disciples. As the story reaches its climax, it appears that the enemies have won; but this is not true. In the closing chapter, Matthew describes the risen King commissioning His disciples to go into all the world and share the Good News with the multitudes!

We see these same three groups of people in this chapter and our Lord's responses to them.

His Enemies: Caution (Matt. 14:1-13)

The Herod family looms large in the four Gospels and the Book of Acts, and it is easy to confuse the various rulers.

Herod the Great founded the dynasty and ruled from 37 B.C. to 4 B.C. He was not a true Jew by birth, but was an Edomite, a descendant of Esau. "He was . . . a heathen in practice, and a monster in character" (*Unger's Bible Dictionary*). He had nine wives (some say ten), and he thought nothing of slaying his own sons or wives if they got in the way of his plans. It was he who had the infants slain in Bethlehem (Matt. 2:13-18).

Herod Antipas, the Herod of this chapter, was a son of Herod the Great. His title was "tetrarch," which means "ruler over the fourth part of the kingdom." He ruled from 4 B.C. to A.D. 39, and his rule was deceptive and selfish. He loved luxury and was very ambitious to become a great ruler.

Herod Agrippa is the Herod who imprisoned Peter and killed James (Acts 12). He was a grandson of Herod the Great.

Herod Agrippa II was the Herod who tried Paul (Acts 25:13ff). He was a son of Agrippa I.

All of the Herods had Edomite blood in them, and, like their ancestor Esau, they were hostile to the Jews (Gen. 25:19ff). They practiced the Jewish religion when it helped fulfill their plans for gaining more power and wealth.

Herod Antipas was guilty of gross sin: He had eloped with Herodias, the wife of his half-brother Philip I, divorcing his own wife and sending her back to her father, the king of Petra (Lev. 18:16; 20:21). Herod listened to the voice of temptation and plunged himself into terrible sin.

But there were other voices that God sent to warn Herod.

The voice of the prophet (vv. 3-5). Boldly, John the Baptist warned Herod and called him to repent. John knew that the sin of a ruler would only pollute the land and make it easier for others to sin, and that God would judge the sinners (Mal. 3:5). We must commend John for his courage in naming sin and denouncing it. Israel was God's covenant nation, and the sins of the rulers (even though they were unbelievers) would bring the chastening of God.

Instead of listening to God's servant and obeying God's Word, Herod arrested John and imprisoned him. John was put in the fortress of Machaerus, located about four miles east of the Dead Sea. It stood 3,500 feet above sea level on a rocky ridge that was accessible from only one side.

It was Herodias, Herod's wife, who held the grudge against John (see Mark 6:19, NASB); and she influenced her husband. She plotted to have her teenage daughter perform a lascivious dance at Herod's birthday feast. Herodias knew that her husband would succumb to her daughter's charms and make some rash promise to her. She also knew that Herod would want to "save face" before his friends and officials. The plot worked, and John the Baptist was slain.

The voice of conscience (vv. 1-2). When Herod heard of the marvelous works of Jesus, he was sure that John had been raised from the dead. His conscience was troubling him, and neither his wife nor his friends could console him. The voice of conscience is a powerful voice, and it can be the voice of God to those who will listen.

Instead of heeding his conscience, Herod determined to kill Jesus just as he had killed John. Some Pharisees (probably in on the plot) warned Jesus that Herod wanted to kill Him (Luke 13:31-32). But Jesus was not disturbed by the report. The word "fox" in Luke 13:32 is feminine. Jesus said, "Go, tell that vixen." Was He perhaps referring to Herodias, the real power behind the throne?

The voice of Jesus (Luke 23:6-11). When he finally did meet Jesus, Herod found that the Son of God was *silent to him!* Herod had silenced the voice of God! "Today, if you will hear His voice, harden not your hearts" (Heb. 3:7-8).

The voice of history. Herod should have known that he could not get away with his sin. History records that Herod lost prestige and power. His armies were defeated by the Arabs, and his appeals to be made a king (urged by his wife) were refused by Emperor Caligula. Herod was banished to Gaul (France) and then Spain, where he died.

Herod is remembered as a weak ruler whose only concern was his own pleasure and position. He did not serve the people, he served himself. He has the dubious honor of being the man who killed the greatest prophet ever sent to proclaim God's Word.

What was our Lord's response to the news of John's murder? *Caution:* He quietly withdrew from that area and went to a "lonely place." He lived according to a divine timetable (see John 2:4; 7:6, 30; 8:20; 12:23, 27; 13:1; 17:1), and He did not want to deliberately provoke trouble with Herod. Because Herod's agents were all around, the Lord had to exercise wisdom and caution.

Certainly Jesus was deeply moved when He heard that John had been killed. The Jewish nation *permitted* John to be slain because they did nothing to assist him. But these same leaders would *ask* for Jesus to be slain! Jesus would never permit the Jewish rulers to forget the witness of John (Matt. 21:23ff). Because they rejected John's witness, they rejected their own Messiah and King.

The Multitudes: Compassion (Matt. 14:14-21)

Jesus and His disciples desperately needed rest (Mark 6:31); yet the needs of the multitudes touched His heart. The word translated "moved with compassion" literally means "to have one's inner being (viscera) stirred." It is stronger than sympathy. The word is used twelve times in the Gospels, and eight of these references are to Jesus Christ.

Jesus was "moved with compassion" when He saw the needy multitudes (Matt. 9:36). They were like sheep that had been lacerated from brutal fleecing—torn, exhausted, and wandering. Twice He was "moved with compassion" when He beheld the hungry multitudes without food (Matt. 14:14; 15:32). The two blind men (Matt. 20:34) and the leper (Mark 1:41) also stirred His compassion, as did the sorrow of the widow at Nain (Luke 7:13).

Jesus used this word in three of His parables. The king had compassion on his bankrupt servant and forgave him his debt; and we ought to forgive one another (Matt. 18:21-35). The Samaritan had compassion on the Jewish victim and cared for him in love (Luke 10:25-37). The father had compassion on his wayward son and ran and greeted him when he came home (Luke 15:20). If our Heavenly Father has such compassion toward us, should we not have compassion toward others?

The miracle of the feeding of the 5,000 is recorded in all four Gospels (Matt. 14:13-21; Mark 6:35-44; Luke 9:12-17; John 6:4-13). It was definitely a miracle. Those who teach that Jesus only encouraged the people to bring out their own hidden lunches have ignored the clear statements of God's Word. John 6:14 definitely calls the event a "sign" or "miracle." Would the crowd have wanted to crown Jesus King simply because He tricked them into sharing their lunches? (John 6:14-15) Not likely!

It takes little imagination to picture the embarrassing plight of the disciples. Here were more than 5,000 hungry people and they had nothing to feed them! Certainly the disciples knew that Jesus was powerful enough to meet the need, yet they did not turn to Him for help. Instead, they took inventory of their own food supply (a lad had five barley loaves and two fish) and their limited treasury. When they considered the time (evening) and the place (a desolate place), they came to the conclusion that nothing could be done to solve the problem. Their counsel to the Lord was: "Send them away!"

How like many of God's people today. For some reason, it is never the right time or place for God to work. Jesus watched His frustrated disciples as they tried to solve the problem, but "He Himself knew what He was intending to do" (John 6:6, NASB). He wanted to teach them a lesson in faith and surrender. Note the steps we must take in solving life's problems.

Start with what you have. Andrew found a lad who had a small lunch, and he brought the lad to Jesus. Was the boy willing to give up his lunch? Yes, he was! God begins where we are and uses what we have.

Give what you have to Jesus. Jesus took the simple lunch, blessed it, and shared it. The miracle of multiplication was in His hands! "Little is much if God is in it." Jesus broke the bread and gave the pieces to the disciples, and they, in turn, fed the multitudes.

Obey what He commands. The disciples had the people sit down as Jesus ordered. They took the broken pieces and distributed them, and discovered that there was plenty for everybody. As His servants, we are "distributors," not "manufacturers." If we give what we have to Him, He will bless it and give it back to us for use in feeding others.

Conserve the results. There were twelve baskets filled with pieces of bread and fish after the people had eaten all they wanted. But these pieces were carefully collected so that nothing was wasted (Mark 6:43; John 6:12). I wonder how many of the pieces the lad took back home with him? Imagine his mother's amazement when the boy told her the story!

The Apostle John recorded a sermon on "the Bread of life" that Jesus gave the next day in the synagogue in Capernaum (John 6:22ff). The people were willing to receive the physical bread, but they would not receive the living Bread—the Son of God come down from heaven. The miracle of the feeding of the 5,000 was actually a sermon in action. Jesus is the Bread of Life, and only He can satisfy the spiritual hunger in man's heart. The tragedy is, men waste their time and money on "that which is not bread" (Isa. 55:1-7). People today are making the same mistake.

Jesus still has compassion on the hungry multitudes, and He still says to His church: "Give them something to eat." How easy it is for us to send people away, to make excuses, to plead a lack of resources. Jesus asks that we give Him all that we have and let Him use it as He sees fit. A hungry world is feeding on empty substitutes while we deprive them of the Bread of Life. When we give Christ what we have, we never lose. We always end up with more blessing than when we started.

The Disciples: Care and Concern (Matt. 14:22-36)

John recorded the reason why Jesus was in such a hurry to dismiss the crowd and send the disciples back in the boat: The crowd wanted to make Jesus King (John 6:14-15). The Lord knew that their motives were not spiritual and that their purposes were out of God's will. If the disciples had stayed, they would certainly have fallen in with the plans of the crowd; for as yet, the disciples did not fully understand Christ's plans. They were guilty of arguing over "who was the greatest," and a popular uprising would have suited them perfectly.

This experience of the disciples in the storm can be an encouragement to us when we go through the storms of life. When we find ourselves in the storm, we can rest on several assurances.

"He brought me here." The storm came because they were *in* the will of God and not (like Jonah) out of the will of God. Did Jesus know that the storm was coming? Certainly! Did He deliberately direct them into the storm? Yes! They were safer in the storm in God's will than on land with the crowds out of God's will. We must never judge our security on the basis of circumstances alone.

As we read our Bibles, we discover that there are two kinds of storms: storms of *correction,* when God disciplines us; and storms of *perfection,* when God helps us to grow. Jonah was in a storm because he disobeyed God and had to be corrected. The disciples were in a storm because they obeyed Christ and had to be perfected. Jesus had tested them in a storm before, when He was in the boat with them (Matt. 8:23-27). But now He tested them by being *out of the boat.*

Many Christians have the mistaken idea that obedience to God's will produces "smooth sailing." But this is not true. "In the world you shall have tribulation," Jesus promised (John 16:33). When we find ourselves in the storm because we have obeyed the Lord, we must remember that He brought us here and He can care for us.

"He is praying for me." This entire scene is a dramatic picture of the church and the Lord today. God's people are on the sea, in the midst of a storm. Yet Jesus Christ is in heaven "making intercession for us" (Rom. 8:34). He saw the disciples and knew their plight (Mark 6:48), just as He sees us and knows our needs. He feels the burdens that we feel and knows what we are going through (Heb. 4:14-16). Jesus was praying for His disciples, that their faith would not fail.

If you knew that Jesus Christ was in the next room, praying for you, would it not give you new courage to endure the storm and do His will? Of course it would. He is not in the next room, but He *is* in heaven interceding for you. He sees your need, He knows your fears, and He is in control of the situation.

"He will come to me." Often we feel like Jesus has deserted us when we are going through the hard times of life. In the Psalms, David complained that God seemed far away and unconcerned. Yet he knew that God would ultimately rescue him. Even the great Apostle Paul got into a situation so difficult he felt "burdened excessively, beyond our strength, so that we despaired even of life" (2 Cor. 1:8, NASB).

Jesus always comes to us in the storms of life. "When you pass through the waters, I will be with you" (Isa. 43:2, NASB). He may not come at the time we think He should come, because He knows when we need Him the most. He waited until the ship was as far from land as possible, so that all human hope was gone. He was testing the disciples' faith, and this meant removing every human prop.

Why did Jesus walk on the water? To show His disciples that the very thing they feared (the sea) was only a staircase for Him to come to them. Often we fear the difficult experiences of life (such as surgery or bereavement), only to discover that these experiences bring Jesus Christ closer to us.

Why did they not recognize Jesus? Because they were not looking for Him. Had they been waiting by faith, they would have known Him immediately. Instead, they jumped to the false conclusion that the appearance was that of a ghost. Fear and faith cannot live in the same heart, for fear always blinds the eyes to the presence of the Lord.

"He will help me grow." This was the whole purpose of the storm, to help the disciples grow in their faith. After all, Jesus would one day leave them, and they would face many storms in their ministries. They had to learn to trust Him even though He was not present with them, and even though it looked as though He did not care.

Now our center of interest shifts to Peter. Before we criticize Peter for sinking, let's honor him for his magnificent demonstration of faith. He dared to be different. Anybody can sit in the boat and watch. But it takes a person of real faith to leave the boat and walk on the water.

What caused Peter to sink? His faith began to waver because he took his eyes off the Lord and began to look at the circumstances around him. "Why did you doubt?" Jesus asked him (Matt. 14:31). This word translated *doubt* carries the meaning of "standing uncertainly at two ways." Peter started out with great faith but ended up with little faith because he saw *two* ways instead of *one.*

We must give Peter credit for *knowing* that he was sinking and for crying out to the Lord for help. He cried out when he was "beginning to sink" and not when he was drowning. Perhaps this incident came to Peter's mind years later when he wrote in his first epistle: "For the eyes of the Lord are over the righteous, and His ears are open unto their prayers" (1 Peter 3:12).

This experience was difficult for Peter, but it helped him to grow in his knowledge of himself and of the Lord. The storms of life are not easy, but they *are* necessary. They teach us to trust Jesus Christ alone and to obey His Word no matter what the circumstances may be. It has well been said, "Faith is not believing in spite of evidence, but obeying in spite of consequence."

"He will see me through." If Jesus says, "Come," then that word is going to accomplish its intended purpose. Since He is the "author and finisher of our faith" (Heb. 12:2), whatever He starts, He completes. We may fail along the way, but in the end, God will succeed. Jesus and Peter walked on the water *together* and went to the ship.

Peter's experience turned out to be a blessing to the other disciples as well as to himself. When they saw the power of Jesus Christ, in conquering and calming the storm, they could only fall down and worship Him. When Jesus calmed the first storm (Matt. 8:23-27), the disciples said, "What manner of Man is this?" But now their clear testimony was, "Thou art the Son of God!"

The disciples had helped to feed 5,000 people, and then God permitted them to go through a storm. In the Book of Acts, they won 5,000 people (Acts 4:4), and then *the storm of persecution began.* No doubt Peter and the disciples recalled their storm experience with the Lord and took courage.

This miracle magnifies the kingship of Jesus Christ. In fact, when Matthew wrote Peter's request, "Bid me to come," he used a Greek word that means "the command of a king." Peter knew that Jesus Christ was King over all nature, including the wind and the waves. His word is law and the elements must obey.

The ship landed at Gennesaret, near Capernaum and Bethsaida; and there Jesus healed many people. Did these people know that He had come through a storm to meet their needs? Do *we* remember that He endured the storm of judgment to save our souls? (Ps. 42:7) He endured the storm for us that we might never face the judgment of God. We ought to imitate the disciples, bow at His feet, and acknowledge that He is King of kings and Lord of lords!

CHAPTER TWELVE
THE KING'S CONCERN
Matthew 15

As in the previous chapter, we see the Lord in conflict with His enemies (Matt. 15:1-11), teaching His own disciples (Matt. 15:12-20), and ministering to the needy multitudes (Matt. 15:21-31). This is the pattern during this period of withdrawal.

Our Lord's great concerns are *truth* and *love.* He taught the Jewish leaders the *truth* and exposed their hypocrisy, and He showed the Gentile crowds *love* as He met their needs. By studying these two concerns, we can understand the message of this chapter.

Truth: He Rejected Jewish Tradition (Matt. 15:1-20)

This dramatic event involved three requests and three replies.

The scribes and Pharisees (vv. 1-11). The fact that the scribes and Pharisees united in this attack, and came all the way from Jerusalem to speak to Jesus, indicates the seriousness of their purpose. It is likely that this committee represented the leaders of the Sanhedrin in Jerusalem.

Their accusation about "washing hands" had nothing to do with cleanliness. They were referring to the ceremonial washings of the rigidly orthodox Jews (see Mark 7:1-4). It was bad enough that Jesus and His disciples mingled with outcasts, but they did not even seek to be purified! Of course, in making this accusation, these religious leaders were forcing Jesus to deal with the very *foundation* of their religious faith. If Jesus rejected the sacred traditions of the nation, then He was a heretic!

Where did these traditions come from? They were handed down from the teachers of previous generations. These traditions were originally the "oral law" which (said the rabbis) Moses gave to the elders, and they passed down to the nation. This oral law was finally written down and became the *Mishnah.* Unfortunately, the *Mishnah* became more important and more authoritative than the original Law of Moses.

Our Lord's reply to their charge began with *an accusation* (Matt. 15:3). It was *they* who were breaking God's Law by practicing their traditions! He then proceeded with an illustration (Matt. 15:4-6), their practice of "Corban" (see Mark 7:11). The Hebrew word *Corban* means "a gift." If a Jew wanted to escape some financial responsibilities, he would declare his goods to be "Corban—a gift to God." This meant he was free from other obligations, such as caring for his parents. But in so doing, the person was losing the power of God's Word in his life, and thus hurting his character and missing God's blessing.

Jesus concluded His reply with an *application* (Matt. 15:7-11), quoting Isaiah 29:13. Jesus made it clear that obedience to tradition made a person disobedient to the Word of God; and this proved the tradition to be false. Exodus 20:12 taught a man to "honor" father and mother. But the "Corban" rule would make a person dishonor his parents, and, at the same time, disobey God.

Tradition is something *external,* while God's truth is *internal,* in the heart. People obey tradition to please men and gain status (Gal. 1:14), but we obey the Word to please God. Tradition deals with *ritual,* while God's truth deals with *reality.* Tradition brings empty words to the lips, but truth penetrates the heart and changes the life. Actually, tradition robs a person of the power of the Word of God.

Unfortunately, there are many "evangelical traditions" in churches today, man-made teachings that are often considered as authoritative as the Word of God—*even though they contradict His Word.* By obeying these traditions, Christians rob themselves of the power of God's Word.

God wants us to give Him our hearts, and not just our lip service. We *believe* in the heart (Rom. 10:9-10), *love* from the heart (Matt. 22:37), *sing* from the heart (Col. 3:16), *obey* from the heart (Rom. 6:17; Eph. 6:6), and *give* from the heart (2 Cor. 9:7). No wonder David prayed, "Create in me a clean heart, O God!" (Ps. 51:10)

Jesus declared boldly to the multitudes that sin comes from the heart, not from the diet. It is what comes out of the mouth that defiles us, not what goes in.

The disciples (vv. 12-14). The disciples were astounded by what Jesus taught about foods. After all, they had been raised good Jews (see Acts 10:14 for Peter's testimony). They knew the difference between the "clean" and "unclean" foods (Lev. 11).

But the disciples had another concern: This teaching had offended the Pharisees and was certain to create serious problems. But Jesus was not worried about the Pharisees. Neither they nor their teachings had been planted by God, and therefore would not last. While there are isolated groups that seek to maintain the traditions, for the most part, phariseeism is gone. However, the *spirit* of phariseeism (tradition, legalism, hypocrisy, externals) is still with us, what Jesus called "the leaven of the Pharisees" (Matt. 16:6).

Jesus also pointed out that the Pharisees were blind and could only lead their converts into the ditch. In Matthew 23:16, He called them "blind guides"—quite a graphic description. Why be afraid of rootless plants that are dying, or blind guides who cannot see where they are going?

Peter (vv. 15-20). Peter was not content until he had an explanation of the saying about foods. Patiently our Lord explained the lesson again. The meaning seems obvious to us, but it was astonishingly new to orthodox Jews. Whatever enters the mouth eventually goes into the stomach and comes out in human waste. Food never touches the heart. But what comes out of the mouth *begins* in the heart, and these things defile a person. Of course, *actions* are included with *words;* often actions speak louder than words.

The Lord had to repeat this lesson on foods to Peter a few years later when He was going to call him to preach to the Gentiles (Acts 10). Paul repeated it in 1 Timothy 4:3-6. He also dealt with it in Romans 14–15.

Compassion: He Responded to Gentile Needs (Matt. 15:21-39)

Not only did Jesus *teach* that no foods were unclean, but He practiced His teaching by going into Gentile territory. He left Israel and withdrew again, this time into the area of Tyre and Sidon. The Gentiles were "unclean" as far as the Jews were concerned. In fact, Jews referred to the Gentiles as "dogs." That Jesus would minister to Gentiles was no surprise (Matt. 12:17-21), though at that time, the emphasis was on ministering to Israel (Matt. 10:5-6).

The demonized (vv. 21-28). Jesus was trying to remain hidden (Mark 7:24), but somehow this Canaanite woman heard where He was and came to Him with her need. Keep in mind that our Lord responded to this woman as He did, not to destroy her faith, but to develop it. Her own replies showed that she was growing in faith and unwilling to let Him go without getting an answer. Godly Samuel Rutherford stated this principle perfectly: "It is faith's work to claim and challenge lovingkindness out of all the roughest strokes of God."

When she approached Him as "Son of David," she was definitely putting herself on Jewish ground; and this she could not do, because she was a Gentile. Of course, this title did reveal her faith in Him as the Messiah of God, for "Son of David" was a name for the Messiah (Matt. 22:42). Since she came to Him on Jewish terms, He was silent. Of course, He knew her heart, and even His silence encouraged her to continue asking.

Impatient with her persistent following and crying out, the disciples said, "Send her away!" We are not sure whether they meant, "Give her what she wants and get rid of her" or just "Get rid of her!" In either case, they were not showing much compassion for either her or her demonized daughter. Our Lord's reply in Matthew 15:24 indicates that they probably wanted Him to answer her request.

We cannot but admire the patience and persistence of this Gentile mother. "Lord, help me!" was her next plea; and this time she avoided any messianic titles. She came as a sinner needing help, and she offered no argument. In His reply, Jesus did not call her a "dog" the way the Pharisees would have addressed a Gentile. The Greek word means "a little pet dog" and not the filthy curs that ran the streets and ate the garbage. "The children" referred, of course, to the people of Israel.

Jesus was not playing games with the woman, nor was He trying to make the situation more difficult. He was drawing out of her a growing response of faith. She immediately seized on His illustration about the children's bread, *which was exactly what He wanted her to do.* We may paraphrase her reply: "It is true that we Gentiles do not sit at the table as children and eat the bread. But even the pet dogs under the table can eat some of the crumbs!" What a tremendous testimony of faith!

It was this faith that Jesus acknowledged, and immediately He healed her daughter. It is worth noting that both of the persons in the Gospel of Matthew who had "great faith" were Gentiles: this Canaanite woman and the Roman centurion (Matt. 8:5-13). In both cases, Jesus healed the one in need *from a distance.* Spiritually speaking, the Gentiles were "afar off" until Calvary, when Jesus Christ died for both Jews and Gentiles and made reconciliation possible (Eph. 2:11ff).

This woman's faith was great because she persisted in asking and trusting when everything seemed against her. Certainly her race was against her: She was a Gentile. Her sex was against her, for most Jewish rabbis paid little attention to women. It seemed that the disciples were against her, and Christ's words might have led her to believe that even *He* was against her. All of these obstacles only made her persist in asking.

The sick and handicapped (vv. 29-31). Jesus departed from the borders of Tyre and Sidon and went to the region of the Decapolis. The Decapolis included ten cities that were in a league and were authorized by the Romans to mint their own coins, run their own courts, and have their own armies. This was predominantly Gentile territory.

Jesus healed there a man who was deaf and dumb (Mark 7:31-37). Even though the Lord cautioned the man to be silent, he and his friends spread the account of the miracle abroad. This apparently caused a great crowd to gather—including people who were lame, blind, dumb, and crippled (maimed). Jesus healed these people, and the Gentiles "glorified the God of Israel."

We cannot help but marvel at the contrast between these Gentiles and the Jewish leaders who knew the Old Testament Scriptures. The Gentiles glorified Israel's God, but the Jewish leaders said that Jesus was in league with Satan (Matt. 12:22-24). Our Lord's miracles did not cause the Jewish cities to repent (Matt. 11:20ff), yet the Gentiles believed in Him. The very miracles that He performed should have convinced the Jews that He was the Messiah (Isa. 29:18-19; 35:4-6; Matt. 11:1-6). Jesus marveled at the faith of a Gentile soldier and a Gentile mother. Yet He was amazed at the unbelief of His own people (Mark 6:6).

The hungry (vv. 32-39). Critics have accused the Gospel writers of deliberately falsifying the records in order to prove that Jesus performed more miracles. They claim that the feeding of the 4,000 was merely an adaptation of the previous miracle of feeding 5,000. A careful examination of the records shows that this accusation is false and that the critics are wrong. This chart shows the differences between the two events.

Feeding 5,000	*Feeding 4,000*
Primarily Jews	Primarily Gentiles
Galilee, near Bethsaida	The Decapolis
5 loaves, 2 fish	7 loaves, "a few fish"
12 baskets over	7 baskets over
Crowd with Him 1 day	Crowd with Him 3 days
Spring of year (green grass)	Summer season
Tried to make Him King	No popular response

Since the crowd of 4,000 had been with Him three days, they had used up their own supplies of food. Our Lord's compassionate heart would not permit Him to send them on their way hungry, lest they faint along the way. The first motive for this miracle was simply the meeting of human needs. The people had already seen His miracles and glorified God, so the miracle was not for the purpose of preaching a sermon or authenticating His ministry.

However, this miracle did have a special purpose for His disciples. We are amazed that they had forgotten the miracle of the feeding of the 5,000. (Read carefully Matt. 16:6-12.) The Twelve were perplexed when they should have been saying, "Jesus is able to multiply loaves and fish, so we have no need to worry!" Of course, it may be that they thought He would not perform that kind of a miracle in Gentile territory. Or, perhaps the fact that the previous crowd had tried to make Him King would cause Jesus to avoid repeating the miracle.

As in the feeding of the 5,000, this miracle took place in His hands. As Jesus broke the bread and gave it to His disciples, the bread multiplied. Everybody ate and everybody was satisfied. Again, Jesus ordered the fragments to be collected so that nothing be wasted. The ability to perform miracles does not grant the authority to waste God's gifts.

The word translated *baskets* in Matthew 15:37 means "a large hamper." It is the same kind of basket that was used to lower Paul over the Damascus wall (Acts 9:25). The word for *basket* in Matthew 14:20 means "a wicker basket," the kind a person carried with food or other goods in it. The fact that these two different words are used is further proof that the two miracles are different.

Jesus did not preach a sermon to this crowd on "the bread of life" as He did to the Jews in Capernaum, following the feeding of the 5,000 (John 6:22ff). The facts about the Old Testament manna and the "bread of God" would have been foreign to these Gentiles. Jesus always adapted His teaching to the needs and the understanding of the people to whom He ministered.

Before leaving Matthew 15, let's review several spiritual lessons that it contains for us.

(1) The enemies of truth are often religious people who live according to man's traditions. Satan often uses "religion" to blind the minds of sinners to the simple truths of God's Word.

(2) We must beware of any religious system that gives us an excuse to sin and disobey God's Word.

(3) We must also beware of worship that comes from the lips only, and not from the heart.

(4) If we major on the inner man, the outer man will be what God wants it to be. True holiness comes from within.

(5) It is difficult to break free from tradition. There is something in us that wants to hold to the past and make no changes. Even Peter had to learn his lesson twice!

(6) We dare not limit Christ to any one nation or people. The Gospel came "to the Jew first" (Rom. 1:16), but today is for all men in all nations. "Whosoever shall call upon the name of the Lord shall be saved" (Rom. 10:13).

CHAPTER THIRTEEN
THE KING'S SURPRISE
Matthew 16

The events recorded in Matthew 16 form a dramatic turning point in our Lord's ministry. For the first time, He mentioned the church (Matt. 16:18) and openly spoke about His death on the cross (Matt. 16:21). He began to prepare the disciples for His arrest, crucifixion, and resurrection. But, as we shall see, they were slow to learn their lessons.

The theme of *faith* runs through the events in this chapter. In these events, we see four different levels of faith and how they relate to Christ.

No Faith—Tempting Christ (Matt. 16:1-4)

Their desire to silence Jesus had caused the two opposing religious parties to unite in one common effort. They were waiting for Him when He returned to Galilee. The Pharisees, of course, were the traditionalists of their day, while the Sadducees were quite liberal (see Acts 23:6-10). They united to issue a challenge to Jesus: "Show us a sign from heaven and we will believe You are the Christ."

The word translated *sign* means much more than simply a miracle or a demonstration of power. It means "a wonder by which one may recognize a person or confirm who he is."

This was the fourth time the religious leaders had asked for a sign (Matt. 12:38ff; John 2:12; 6:30). Later, they did it again (Luke 11:14ff). But miracles do not convince people of sin or give a desire for salvation (Luke 16:27-31; John 12:10-11; Acts 14:8-20). Miracles will give confirmation where there is faith, but not where there is willful unbelief.

Why did our Lord talk about the weather? To reveal to His enemies their own dishonesty and stubborn blindness. They could examine the evidence in God's world and draw valid conclusions, but they would not examine the evidence He had presented. His enemies *would not* believe, and therefore they *could not* believe (John 12:37ff). The Pharisees and Sadducees did not lack evidence; they lacked honesty and humility.

Their demand for a sign revealed the sad condition of their hearts: they were evil and adulterous. He did not accuse them of being guilty of physical adultery, but of spiritual adultery (Isa. 57; James 4:4). These men were worshiping a false god of their own manufacture, and this was spiritual adultery. Had they been worshiping the true God, they would have recognized His Son when He came.

Jesus had mentioned the sign of Jonah before (see Matt. 12:38-45). This was the sign of death, burial, and resurrection. Our Lord's crucifixion, burial, and resurrection were actually a sign to Israel that He was their Messiah. It was this sign that Peter preached about at Pentecost (Acts 2:22ff).

Matthew 16:4 records the Lord's third departure from Galilee. He departed before to avoid Herod (Matt. 14:13) and to avoid the Pharisees (Matt. 15:21). It was certainly an act of judgment.

Little Faith—Misunderstanding Christ (Matt. 16:5-12)

The disciples had but one loaf of bread with them (Mark 8:14). We are not told what happened to the many baskets of leftover food that resulted from His feeding the 4,000 just a short time before. Perhaps they gave it away. Jesus used this embarrassing event as an occasion to teach an important spiritual truth: Beware of the false teachings of the Pharisees and Sadducees.

The disciples misunderstood Him; they thought He was talking about material bread. Often in the ministry of Jesus, people misconstrued His words by interpreting them literally rather than spiritually. Nicodemus thought that Jesus was talking about an actual physical birth (John 3:4), and the Samaritan woman thought He was referring to material water from the well (John 4:11). The Jewish crowd in the synagogue thought Jesus was speaking about eating actual flesh and blood (John 6:52ff) when He was describing a spiritual experience (John 6:63).

As we noted in our study of Matthew 13, leaven was to the Jews a symbol of evil. Both the Pharisees and the Sadducees had infected the religious beliefs of Israel with false doctrine. The Pharisees were legalists who taught that only obedience to the Law and the traditions would please God and usher in His kingdom for Israel. The Sadducees were liberal in their thinking and denied that there would be such a kingdom on earth. They even denied the truth of the resurrection and the existence of angels.

Why would the Lord's mention of leaven cause the disciples to discuss their lack of bread? Possibly they were planning to purchase bread on the other side of the sea, and they thought Jesus was cautioning them not to buy unclean bread which Jews could not eat. If they had remembered how Jesus had multiplied bread on two occasions, they certainly would not have worried. Their "little faith" kept them from understanding His teaching and depending on His power to meet their needs.

"Little faith" was one of our Lord's favorite names for His disciples (Matt. 6:30; 8:26; 14:31). Of course, "little faith" is better than *no* faith. The disciples had many lessons to learn before they would graduate to "great faith."

Saving Faith—Confessing Christ (Matt. 16:13-20)

Jesus took His disciples to Gentile territory, in the region of Caesarea Philippi. They were about 120 miles from Jerusalem in the northern part of Palestine. The region was strongly identified with various religions: It had been a center for Baal worship; the Greek god Pan had shrines there; and Herod the Great had built a temple there to honor Augustus Caesar. It was in the midst of this pagan superstition that Peter confessed Jesus as the Son of God. And it was probably within sight of Caesar's temple that Jesus announced a surprise: He would not yet establish His kingdom, but He would build His church.

If anyone else asked, "Whom do men say that I am?" we would think him either mad or arrogant. But in the case of Jesus, a right confession of who He is is basic to salvation (Rom. 10:9-10; 1 John 2:18-23; 4:1-3). His person and His work go together and must never be separated. It is amazing to see how confused the public was about Jesus (John 10:19-21). Perhaps, like Herod, the people thought Jesus was John raised from the dead.

It had been prophesied that Elijah would come again (Mal. 4:5), and some thought that this prediction was fulfilled in Christ. However, Jesus did not minister as did Elijah; it was John the Baptist who came "in the spirit and power of Elias" (Luke 1:13-17). Jeremiah was the weeping prophet whose tender heart was broken at the sight of the decay of the nation. Certainly this attitude was seen in Jesus, the Man of sorrows.

One thing is clear: We can never make a true decision about Jesus Christ by taking a poll of the people. (But some people *do* get their "spiritual knowledge" this way!) The important thing is not what others say, but what do you and I personally say? The decisions of the crowd (wrong or right) can never substitute for personal decisions.

Peter had the correct response: "Thou art the Christ [the Messiah], the Son of the living God!" This confession was Peter's response to the revelation God the Father had given him. Jesus Himself explained this experience in Matthew 11:25-27. This revelation was not the result of Peter's own investigation. It came as the gracious act of God. God had hidden these things from the proud Pharisees and Sadducees and revealed them to "babes," the humble disciples.

It should be noted that there had been other confessions of faith prior to this one. Nathanael had confessed Christ as the Son of God (John 1:49), and the disciples had declared Him God's Son after He stilled the storm (Matt. 14:33). Peter had given a confession of faith when the crowds left Jesus after His sermon on the Bread of Life (John 6:68-69). In fact, when Andrew had brought his brother Simon to Jesus, it was on the basis of this belief (John 1:41).

How, then, did *this* confession differ from those that preceded it? To begin with, *Jesus explicitly asked for this confession.* It was not an emotional response from people who had seen a miracle, but the studied and sincere statement of a man who had been taught by God.

Also, Jesus *accepted this confession* and built on it to teach them new truth. It must have rejoiced His heart to hear Peter's words. The Lord knew that Peter could now be led into new steps of deeper truth and service. All of our Lord's ministry to His disciples had prepared the way for this experience. Let's look at these great words and concepts individually.

Rock. These Jewish men, steeped in Old Testament Scripture, recognized the rock as a symbol of God. "He is the Rock, His work is perfect" (Deut. 32:4). "The Lord is my Rock, and my Fortress" (Ps. 18:2). "For who is God save the Lord? Or who is a rock save our God?" (Ps. 18:31)

But let's investigate the Greek words that the Holy Spirit led Matthew to use. "Thou art *petros* [a stone], and upon this rock [*petra*—a large rock] I will build My church." Jesus had given Simon the new name of *Peter* (John 1:42) which means "a stone." The Aramaic form is *Cephas,* which also means "a stone." Everyone who believes in Jesus Christ and confesses Him as the Son and God and Saviour, is a "living stone" (1 Peter 2:5, NASB).

Jesus Christ is the foundation rock on which the church is built. The Old Testament prophets said so (Ps. 118:22; Isa. 28:16). Jesus Himself said this (Matt. 21:42), and so did Peter and the other Apostles (Acts 4:10-12). Paul also stated that the foundation for the church is Jesus Christ (1 Cor. 3:11). This foundation was laid by the Apostles and prophets as they preached Christ to the lost (1 Cor. 2:1-2; 3:11; Eph. 2:20).

In other words, when the evidence is examined, the total teaching of Scripture is that the church, God's temple (Eph. 2:19-22), is built on Jesus Christ—not on Peter. How could God build His church on a fallible man like Peter? Later, the same Peter who confessed Christ became an adversary and entertained Satan's thoughts (Matt. 16:22ff). "But that was before Peter was filled with the Spirit," some argue. Then consider Peter's doctrinal blunders recorded in Galatians 2, blunders that had to be dealt with by Paul. This event occurred *after* Peter was filled with the Spirit.

Church. This is the first occurrence of this important word in the New Testament. It is the Greek word *ekklesia* (ek-klay-SEE-uh) from which we get our English word "ecclesiastical," referring to things that pertain to the church. The literal meaning is "a called-out assembly." The word is used 114 times in the New Testament and in 90 of these references, a local church (assembly) is in view. However, in this first use of *ekklesia,* it seems likely that Jesus had the whole church in mind. He was not just building a local assembly, but a universal church composed of all who make the same confession of faith that Peter made.

The word *ekklesia* was not new to the disciples. This word was applied to the popular assembly of Greek citizens that helped to govern a city or district (Acts 19:32, 39, 41). Also, the Greek translation of the Old Testament (the Septuagint) used *ekklesia* to describe the congregation of Israel when it was gathered for religious activity (Deut. 31:30; Jud. 20:2). However, this does not mean that the Old Testament congregation of Israel was a "church" in the same sense as the churches of the New Testament. Rather, Jesus was introducing something new to His disciples.

Jesus spoke about "My church" in contrast to these other assemblies. This was to be something new and different, for in His church, Jesus Christ would unite believing Jews and Gentiles and form a new temple, a new body (Eph. 2:11–3:12). In His church, natural distinctions would be unimportant (Gal. 3:28). Jesus Christ would be the Builder of this church, the Head of this church (Eph. 1:22; Col. 1:18).

Each believer in this church is a "living stone" (1 Peter 2:5). Believers would meet in local congregations, or assemblies, to worship Christ and to serve Him; but they would also belong to a universal church, a temple being built by Christ. There is a oneness to the people of God (Eph. 4:1-6) that ought to be revealed to the world by love and unity (John 17:20-26).

Gates of hell. A better translation would be "gates of hades." Hell is the final destiny of all unsaved people after the judgment of the Great White Throne (Rev. 20:11-15). *Hades* is simply "the realm of the dead." It holds the spirits of the unsaved dead and releases them at the resurrection (Rev. 20:13; where "hell" ought to read "hades"). According to Jesus, hades is down (Matt. 11:23), and it is a prison to which He holds the keys (Rev. 1:18).

On the basis of Luke 16:19-31, some people believe that *all* the dead went to hades prior to the death and resurrection of Christ—believers to a paradise portion and unbelievers to a punishment portion. We are certain that believers today, when they die, go immediately into the presence of Christ (2 Cor. 5:6-8; Phil. 1:23).

"Gates" represent, in the Bible, authority and power. The city gate was to a Jew what city hall is to people in the Western world. Important business was transacted at the city gate (Deut. 16:18; 17:8; Ruth 4:11). "The gates of hades" then would symbolize the organized power of death and Satan. By His death and resurrection, Jesus Christ would conquer death, so that death would not be able to hold any of His people. Christ would "storm the gates" and deliver the captives! This declaration certainly is verified by 1 Corinthians 15:50ff; Hebrews 2:14-15; and other Scriptures.

Keys of the kingdom. A key is a badge of authority (Isa. 22:15, 22; Luke 11:52). "The kingdom of heaven" is *not* heaven, for no man on earth carries the keys to heaven! (All of the jokes about "St. Peter at the gate" stem from this misunderstanding. They are both unbiblical and in bad taste.) We use keys to open doors. Peter was given the privilege of opening "the door of faith" to the Jews at Pentecost (Acts 2), to the Samaritans (Acts 8:14ff), and to the Gentiles (Acts 10). But the other Apostles shared this authority (Matt. 18:18), and Paul had the privilege of "opening the door of faith" to the Gentiles outside of Palestine (Acts 14:27).

Nowhere in this passage, or in the rest of the New Testament, are we told that Peter or his successors had any special position or privilege in the church. Certainly Peter in his two epistles claimed to be nothing more than an Apostle (1 Peter 1:1), an elder (1 Peter 5:1), and a servant of Jesus Christ (2 Peter 1:1).

Binding and loosing. This was a very familiar phrase to the Jews, for their rabbis often spoke of "binding and loosing," that is, forbidding or permitting. Our Lord's statement in Matthew 16:19 referred to Peter. But His statement later in Matthew 18:18 included all of the Apostles. As the representatives of their Lord, they would exercise authority according to His Word.

The Greek verbs in Matthew 16:19 are most important. The *Expanded Translation* by Dr. Kenneth S. Wuest reads: "And whatever you bind on earth [forbid to be done], shall have been already bound . . . in heaven; and whatever you loose on earth [permit to be done], shall have already been loosed in heaven." Jesus did not say that God would obey what they did on earth, but that they should do on earth whatever God had already willed. The church does not get man's will done in heaven; it obeys God's will on earth.

The Apostles were not to share this truth about Jesus being the Son of God with other people until after His resurrection and ascension. Then the "sign of Jonah" would be completed, the Spirit would be given, and the message could be proclaimed. The nation in general, and certainly the religious leaders in particular, were not yet ready for this message. Read Peter's sermon at Pentecost and see how he proclaimed Jesus as the Christ (Acts 2).

Serving Faith—Following Christ (Matt. 16:21-28)

Having declared His person, Jesus now declared His work; for the two must go together. He would go to Jerusalem, suffer and die, and be raised from the dead. This was His first clear statement of His death, though He had hinted at this before (Matt. 12:39-40; 16:4; John 2:19; 3:14; 6:51). "And He was stating the matter plainly" (Mark 8:32, NASB).

Peter's response to this shocking statement certainly represented the feelings of the rest of the disciples: "Pity Thyself, Lord! This shall never happen to Thee!" Jesus turned His back on Peter and said, "Get behind Me, adversary! You are a stumbling block to Me!" (literal translation) Peter the "stone" who had just been blessed (Matt. 16:18) became Peter the stumbling block who was not a blessing to Jesus!

What was Peter's mistake? He was thinking like a man, for most men want to escape suffering and death. He did not have God's mind in the matter. Where do we find the mind of God? In the Word of God. Until Peter was filled with the Spirit, he had a tendency to argue with God's Word. Peter had enough faith to confess that Jesus is the Son of God, but he did not have the faith to believe that it was right for Jesus to suffer and die. Of course, Satan agreed with Peter's words, for he used the same approach to tempt Jesus in the wilderness (Matt. 4:8-10).

Today the cross is an accepted symbol of love and sacrifice. But in that day the cross was a horrible means of capital punishment. The Romans would not mention the cross in polite society. In fact, no Roman citizen could be crucified; this terrible death was reserved for their enemies. Jesus had not yet specifically stated that He would be crucified (He did this in Matt. 20:17-19). But His words that follow emphasize the cross.

He presented to the disciples two approaches to life:

deny yourself	live for yourself
take up your cross	ignore the cross
follow Christ	follow the world
lose your life for His sake	save your life for your own sake
forsake the world	gain the world
keep your soul	lose your soul
share His reward and glory	lose His reward and glory

To deny self does not mean to deny things. It means to give yourself wholly to Christ and share in His shame and death. Paul described this in Romans 12:1-2 and Philippians 3:7-10, as well as in Galatians 2:20. To take up a cross does not mean to carry burdens or have problems. (I once met a lady who told me her asthma was the cross she had to bear!) To take up the cross means to identify with Christ in His rejection, shame, suffering, and death.

But suffering always leads to glory. This is why Jesus ended this short sermon with a reference to His glorious kingdom (Matt. 16:28). This statement would be fulfilled within a week on the Mount of Transfiguration, described in the next chapter.

CHAPTER FOURTEEN THE KING'S GLORY

Matthew 17

The chapter begins with a glorious scene on a mountaintop, and ends with Peter catching a fish in order to pay his taxes. What a contrast! Yet, Jesus Christ the King is the theme of the entire chapter. The three events in this chapter give us three pictures of the King.

The King in His Glory (Matt. 17:1-13)

Matthew and Mark state that the Transfiguration took place "six days later," while Luke says "some eight days after" (Luke 9:28). There is no contradiction; Luke's statement is the Jewish equivalent of "about a week later." During that week, the disciples must have pondered and discussed what Jesus meant by His death and resurrection. No doubt they were also wondering what would happen to the Old Testament promises about the kingdom. If Jesus were going to build a church, what would happen to the promised kingdom?

The text does not name the place where this miracle took place. It was probably on Mount Hermon, which is close to Caesarea Philippi.

The Transfiguration revealed four aspects of the glory of Jesus Christ the King.

The glory of His person. As far as the record is concerned, this is the only time Jesus revealed His glory in this way while He was on the earth. The word translated *transfigured* gives us our English word "metamorphosis." A metamorphosis is a change on the outside that comes from the inside. When a caterpillar builds a cocoon and later emerges as a butterfly, it is due to the process of metamorphosis. Our Lord's glory was not *reflected* but *radiated* from within. There was a change on the outside that came from within as He allowed His essential glory to shine forth (Heb. 1:3).

Certainly this event would strengthen the faith of the disciples, particularly Peter who had so recently confessed Jesus to be the Son of God. Had Peter made his confession *after* the Transfiguration, it would not have been so meaningful. Peter believed, confessed his faith, and then received assurance (see John 11:40; Heb. 11:6).

Many years later, John recalled this event as the Spirit guided him to write: "And we beheld His glory, the glory as of the only begotten of the Father, full of grace and truth" (John 1:14). In his Gospel, John emphasized the deity of Christ and the glory of His person (John 2:11; 7:39; 11:4; 12:23; 13:31-32; 20:31).

Jesus Christ laid aside His glory when He came to earth (John 17:5). Because of His finished work on the cross, He has received back His glory and now shares it with us (John 17:22, 24). However, we do not have to wait for heaven to share in this "transfiguration glory." When we surrender ourselves to God, He will "transfigure" our minds (Rom. 12:1-2). As we yield to the Spirit of God, He changes (transfigures) us "from glory to glory" (2 Cor. 3:18). As we look into the Word of God, we see the Son of God and are transfigured by the Spirit of God into the glory of God.

The glory of His kingdom. At the close of His sermon about cross-bearing, Jesus promised that some of the disciples would see "the Son of man coming in His kingdom" (Matt. 16:28). He selected Peter, James, and John as witnesses to this event. These three friends and business partners (Luke 5:10) had been with Jesus in the home of Jairus (Luke 8:51), and they would go with Him into the Garden of Gethsemane before His crucifixion (see Matt. 26:37).

Dr. G. Campbell Morgan has pointed out that these three occasions all had to do with *death.* Jesus was teaching these three men that He was victor over death (He raised Jairus' daughter) and surrendered to death (in the Garden). The Transfiguration taught them that He was glorified in death.

The presence of Moses and Elijah was significant. Moses represented the Law and Elijah the prophets. All of the Law and Prophets point to Christ and are fulfilled in Christ (Luke 24:27; Heb. 1:1). Not one word of the Old Testament Scriptures will be unfulfilled. The promised kingdom would be established (Luke 1:32-33, 68-77). Just as the three disciples saw Jesus glorified *on earth,* so God's people would see Him in His glorious kingdom on earth (Rev. 19:11–20:6).

Peter caught this message and never forgot it. "We were eyewitnesses of His majesty. . . . And so we have the prophetic word made more sure" (see 2 Peter 1:12ff). The experience Peter had on the mount only fortified his faith in the Old Testament prophecies. The important thing is not seeing wonderful sights, but hearing God's Word. "This is My beloved Son, in whom I am well pleased; hear ye Him" (Matt. 17:5).

All who are born again belong to the kingdom of God (John 3:3-5). This is a spiritual kingdom that is separate from the material things of this world (Rom. 14:17). But one day, when Jesus returns to this earth, there will be a glorious kingdom for 1,000 years (Rev. 20:1-7) with Jesus Christ reigning as King. Those who have trusted Him shall reign on the earth with Him (Rev. 5:10).

The glory of His cross. The disciples had to learn that suffering and glory go together. Peter had opposed His going to Jerusalem to die, so Jesus had to teach him that, apart from His suffering and death, there could be no glory. Peter certainly learned the lesson, for in his first epistle he repeatedly emphasized "suffering and glory" (1 Peter 1:6-8, 11; 4:12–5:11).

Moses and Elijah talked with Jesus about His "exodus" that He would accomplish at Jerusalem (Luke 9:31). His suffering and death would not be an accident, but an accomplishment. Peter used the word *exodus* in describing his own impending death (2 Peter 1:15). For the believer, death is not a one-way street into oblivion. It is an exodus—a release—from the bondage of this life into the glorious liberty of the life in heaven.

Because Jesus died and paid the price, we have been redeemed—purchased and set free. The two Emmaus disciples had hoped that Jesus would set the nation free from Roman bondage (Luke 24:21). What He died to accomplish was not *political* freedom, but *spiritual* freedom: freedom from the world system (Gal. 1:4); freedom from a vain and empty life (1 Peter 1:18); and freedom from iniquity (Titus 2:14). Our redemption in Christ is final and permanent.

The glory of His submission. Peter could not understand why the Son of God would submit to evil men and willingly suffer. The Transfiguration was God's way of teaching Peter that Jesus is glorified when we deny ourselves, take up our cross, and follow Him. The world's philosophy is "Save yourself!" but the Christian's philosophy is "Yield yourself to God!" As He stood there in glory, Jesus proved to the three disciples that surrender always leads to glory. First the suffering, then the glory; first the cross, then the crown.

Each of the three disciples would have a need for this important truth. James would be the first of the disciples to die (Acts 12:1-2). John would be the last of the disciples to die, but he would go through severe persecution on the Isle of Patmos (Rev. 1:9). Peter would experience many occasions of suffering and would, in the end, give his life for Christ (John 21:15-19; 2 Peter 1:12).

Peter opposed the cross when Jesus first mentioned His death (Matt. 16:22ff). In the Garden, he used his sword to defend Jesus (John 18:10). In fact, even on the Mount of Transfiguration Peter tried to tell Jesus what to do. He wanted to build three booths for Jesus, Moses, and Elijah so that all of them could remain there and enjoy the glory! But the Father interrupted Peter and gave other directions: "Hear Him!" The Father will not permit His beloved Son to be put on the same level as Moses and Elijah. "Jesus only" (Matt. 17:8) is God's pattern.

As Jesus and His three disciples came down from the mountaintop, He cautioned them not to reveal what they had seen, not even to the other nine disciples. But the three men were still perplexed. They had been taught that Elijah would come first to prepare for the establishing of the kingdom. Was the presence of Elijah on the mountain the fulfillment of this prophecy? (Mal. 4:5-6)

Jesus gave a twofold answer to their question. Yes, Elijah would come as Malachi 4:5-6 promised. But spiritually speaking, Elijah already came in the person of John the Baptist (see Matt. 11:10-15; Luke 1:17). The nation permitted John to be killed, and would ask for Jesus to be slain. Yet God's program would be fulfilled in spite of the deeds of sinful leaders.

When will Elijah come to restore all things? Some people believe that Elijah will be one of the "two witnesses" whose ministry is described in Revelation 11. Others believe that the prophecy was fulfilled in the ministry of John the Baptist so that there will be no future coming of Elijah.

The King in His Power (Matt. 17:14-21)

We move from the mountain of glory to the valley of need. The sudden appearance of Jesus and the three disciples startled the multitudes (Mark 9:15). The distraught father had brought his demonized son to the nine disciples, begging them to deliver him; but they could not. The scribes had noticed their failure and were using it as a reason for argument. And while the disciples were defending themselves, and the scribes were accusing them, the demon was all but killing the helpless boy.

When we compare the Gospel accounts of this dramatic scene, we discover that this only son was indeed in great trouble and danger. Matthew recorded that the boy was an epileptic (lunatic), very ill, and suicidal, falling into the fire and the water. Mark described him as a mute, who often fell to the ground foaming at the mouth and grinding his teeth. After this display, the boy would go into a kind of *rigor mortis*. Dr. Luke said that the boy was an only son and that he would scream as he went into these convulsions. While some of these symptoms can have natural causes, this boy was at the mercy of a demon. The disciples had been helpless to do anything. No wonder the father rushed to Jesus' feet.

Our Lord's first response was one of sorrow. As He beheld the embarrassed disciples, the arguing scribes, and the needy father and son, He groaned inwardly and said, "How long shall I be with you, and put up with you?" (Luke 9:41, NASB) Their unbelief and spiritual perversity were a burden to Him. What must our Lord feel as He looks at powerless believers today?

Jesus delivered the boy and commanded the spirit never to return to him (Mark 9:25). The demon tried "one last throw" (as Spurgeon put it) so that the crowd thought the boy was dead (Mark 9:26). But Jesus raised the lad up and gave him to his father, while the crowds marveled and gave glory to God (Luke 9:43).

The nine disciples should have been able to cast out the demon. Jesus had given them this power and authority (Matt. 10:1, 8). But somehow, they had lost their power! When they asked Jesus the cause of their shameful failure, He told them: their lack of faith (Matt. 17:20), their lack of prayer (Mark 9:29), and their lack of discipline (Matt. 17:21, though this verse is not found in many manuscripts).

The nine were perhaps jealous because they had not been called to go to the mountaintop with Jesus. During the Lord's absence, they began to grow self-indulgent. They neglected prayer; their faith weakened. Then, when the crisis came, they were unprepared. Like Samson, they went out to battle without realizing that their power was gone (Jud. 16:20). From their example, we see the importance of staying spiritually healthy.

"Faith as a grain of mustard seed" suggests

not only *size* (God will honor even a little faith), but also *life* and *growth.* Faith like a mustard seed is *living* faith that is nurtured and caused to grow. Faith must be cultivated so that it grows and does even greater exploits for God (1 Thes. 3:10; 2 Thes. 1:3). Had the nine disciples been praying, disciplining themselves, and meditating on the Word, they would have been able to cast out the demon and rescue the boy.

This entire scene illustrates what Jesus will do when He leaves the glory of heaven to come to this earth. He will defeat Satan and bind him for 1,000 years (Rev. 20:1-6).

The King in His Humility (Matt. 17:22-27)

For a second time, Jesus mentioned His death and resurrection. The disciples were deeply grieved and were afraid to ask Him about it. In fact, His disciples did not believe the reports of His resurrection because they had forgotten His promises (Mark 16:14). But the enemy remembered what He said (John 2:19) and acted accordingly (Matt. 27:62-66).

What a paradox: a King too poverty-stricken to pay the annual temple tax of only a half-shekel! The unique characteristics of this miracle are worth noting.

It is recorded only by Matthew. Matthew, a former tax collector, wrote the Gospel of the King, and this miracle affirms our Lord's kingship. The kings of the earth do not take tribute from their own sons. Jesus affirmed Himself to be free from this tribute because He was the Son of the King, the Son of God. Yet, as the Son of God, He was too poor to pay even a half-shekel; and His disciples were as poor as He was. He exercised His kingship over nature to provide what was needed.

God gave Adam and Eve dominion over nature, and this included the fish in the sea (Gen. 1:26; Ps. 8:6-8). Man lost this dominion because of sin, so Peter was not able to command the fish and find the money. Jesus Christ exercised dominion over not only the fish, but also over the animals (Matt. 21:1-7) and the birds (Matt. 26:34, 74-75). What Adam lost because of his disobedience, Jesus Christ regained through His obedience (Heb. 2:6).

While today believers do not have complete dominion over nature, one day we shall reign with Christ and exercise dominion with Him. Meanwhile, God cares for His own and makes sure that all of nature is working for those who trust and obey.

It is the only miracle He performed to meet His own needs. Satan had tempted Christ to use His divine powers for Himself (Matt. 4:3-4), but He had refused. However, in this case, He did not use His power selfishly, for others were involved in this miracle. "Lest we cause them to stumble," was our Lord's explanation for the miracle. He did not want the people to be offended because He, being a Jew, did not support the temple ministry. While Jesus did not hesitate to break the man-made traditions of the Pharisees, He was careful to obey the Law of God.

As Christians, we must never use our freedom in Christ to hurt or destroy others. Technically, Jesus did not have to pay the tax; but for practical reasons, He paid it. He also included Peter so that their testimony would not be hurt.

It is the only miracle using money. Since Matthew had been a tax collector, we would expect him to be interested in this miracle. This tax had its origin in the days of Moses (Ex. 30:11ff). The original tax money was used to make the silver sockets on which the tabernacle poles were erected (Ex. 38:25-27). Subsequent taxes were used to support the ministry of the tabernacle and then the temple. The money was to be a reminder to the Jews that they had been redeemed from Egyptian slavery. We have been redeemed by the precious blood of Christ (1 Peter 1:18-19).

It is the only miracle using one fish. Jesus had multiplied the fish for Peter (Luke 5:1-11), and He would repeat that miracle (John 21:1ff). But in this case, He used only one fish. When we consider the complexity of this miracle, it amazes us. First, someone had to lose a coin in the water. Then, a fish had to take that coin in its mouth and retain it. That same fish then had to bite on Peter's hook—with an impediment in its mouth—and be caught. You cannot explain all of this in a natural way. It is too complex for an accident, and too difficult for human management.

It was performed for Peter. How the other disciples paid their taxes, we are not told. This was one of many miracles that Jesus performed for Peter. He healed Peter's mother-in-law (Mark 1:29-34), helped Peter to catch fish (Luke 5:1-11), enabled him to walk on the water (Matt. 14:22-33), healed Malchus' ear (Matt. 26:47-56), and delivered Peter from prison (Acts 12:1ff). No wonder

Peter wrote, "Casting all your care upon Him, for He cares for you" (1 Peter 5:7).

Jesus knew Peter's need and was able to meet that need. Peter thought he had the problem solved when he entered the house. But before he could tell Jesus what to do, Jesus told *him* what to do! God the Father had interrupted Peter on the mountain (Matt. 17:5), and now God the Son interrupted him in the house. If only we would let Jesus give the directions, we would see Him meet our needs for His glory.

It is the only miracle which does not have the results recorded. We would expect another verse that would read: "And Peter went to the sea, cast in a hook, and drew up a fish; and when he had opened its mouth, he found there a coin, and used it to pay the temple tax for himself and for Jesus." But Matthew 17:28 is not there. Then, how do we know that the miracle took place? *Because Jesus said it would!* "There hath not failed one word of all His good promise" (1 Kings 8:56).

We must commend Peter for his faith. The people at the seashore were accustomed to seeing Peter with a net in his hand, not a hook and line. But Peter had faith in God's Word, and God honored that faith. If we trust the King, He will meet our needs as we obey His Word.

CHAPTER FIFTEEN
THE KING'S REBUKE
Matthew 18

Why do some of God's children have such a difficult time getting along with each other? A poem I heard states the problem perfectly:

To live above, with saints we love
Will certainly be glory.
To live below, with saints we know—
Well, that's another story!

With so much division and dissension among professing Christians these days, we desperately need what Matthew 18 has to teach. Jesus rebuked His disciples for their pride and desire for worldly greatness, and He taught them the three essentials for unity and harmony among God's people.

Humility (Matt. 18:1-14)

Someone has accurately defined humility as "that grace that, when you know you have it, you've lost it!" It has well been said, "True humility is not thinking meanly of oneself; it is simply not thinking of oneself at all."

The need for humility (v. 1). "Which one of us is the greatest?" was a repeated topic of discussion among the disciples, for we find it mentioned often in the Gospel records. Recent events would have aggravated the problem, particularly with reference to Peter. After all, Peter had walked on the water, had been on the mountaintop with the Lord, and had even had his taxes paid by means of a miracle.

The fact that Jesus had been sharing with the disciples the truth about His coming suffering and death did not affect them. They were thinking only of themselves and what position they would have in His kingdom. So absorbed were the disciples in this matter that they actually *argued* with each other! (Luke 9:46)

The selfishness and disunity of God's people is a scandal to the Christian faith. What causes these problems? Pride—thinking ourselves more important than we really are. It was pride that led man into sin at the beginning (Gen. 3:5). When Christians are living for themselves and not for others, then there is bound to be conflict and division (Phil. 2:1ff).

The example of humility (vv. 2-6, 10-14). The disciples waited breathlessly for Jesus to name the greatest man among them. But He bypassed them completely and called a little child into their midst. This child was the example of true greatness.

True humility means knowing yourself, accepting yourself, and being yourself—your *best* self—to the glory of God. It means avoiding two extremes: thinking *less* of yourself than you ought to (as did Moses when God called him, Ex. 3:11ff), or thinking *more* of yourself than you ought to (Rom. 12:3). The truly humble person does not deny the gifts God has given him, but uses them to the glory of God.

An unspoiled child has the characteristics that make for humility: trust (Matt. 18:6), dependence, the desire to make others happy, an absence of boasting or selfish desire to be greater than others. By nature, all of us are rebels who want to be celebrities instead of servants. It takes a great deal of teaching for us to learn the lessons of humility.

The disciples wanted to know who was greatest *in* the kingdom. But Jesus warned them that, apart from humility, they could not even *enter* the kingdom! They had to be converted—turned around in their thinking—or they would never make it.

It seems that Jesus is, in these verses, blending two concepts: the human child as an example of humility, and the child of God no matter what his age might be. As Christians, we must not only accept the little children for Jesus' sake; but we must also receive *all* of God's children and seek to minister to them (Rom. 14:1ff). It is a serious matter to cause a child to sin or to lead him astray. It is equally as serious to cause another believer to stumble because of our poor example (Rom. 14:13ff; 1 Cor. 8:9ff). True humility thinks of others, not of self.

Jesus explained that we can have four different attitudes toward the children and, consequently, toward true humility. We can seek to *become like the children* (Matt. 18:3-4) in true humility, as to the Lord. Or, we can only *receive them* (Matt. 18:5) because Jesus told us to. If we are not careful, we will *cause them to stumble* (Matt. 18:6), and even end up *despising them* (Matt. 18:10).

It is a dangerous thing to look down on the children, because God values them highly. When we welcome a child (or a Christian believer), we welcome Christ (Matt. 18:5). The Father cares for them and the angels watch over them (Matt. 18:10). Like the good shepherd, God seeks the lost and saves them; and we must not cause them to perish. If the shepherd goes after an adult sheep, how much more important is it that he protect the lambs!

In these days of child neglect and child abuse, we need to take Christ's warning seriously. It is better to drown with a heavy millstone around one's neck, than to abuse a child and face the judgment of God (Matt. 18:6).

The cost of humility (vv. 7-9). The truly humble person helps to build up others, not to tear them down. He is a stepping-stone, not a stumbling block. Therefore, anything that makes me stumble must be removed from my life, for if it is not, I cause others to stumble. Jesus had uttered similar words in the Sermon on the Mount (Matt. 5:29-30). Paul used the eye, hand, and foot to illustrate the mutual dependence of members of the body of Christ (1 Cor. 12:14-17).

Humility begins with self-examination, and it continues with self-denial. Jesus was not suggesting that we maim our bodies, for harming our physical bodies can never change the spiritual condition of our hearts. Rather, He was instructing us to perform "spiritual surgery" on ourselves, removing anything that causes us to stumble or that causes others to stumble. The humble person lives for Jesus first and others next—he puts himself last. He is happy to deprive himself even of good things, if it will make others happy. Perhaps the best commentary on this is Philippians 2:1-18.

Honesty (Matt. 18:15-20)

We don't always practice humility. There are times when, deliberately or unconsciously, we offend others and hurt them. Even the Old Testament Law recognized "sins of ignorance" (Num. 15:22), and David prayed to be delivered from "secret faults" (Ps. 19:12), meaning "faults that are even hidden from my own eyes." What should we do when another Christian has sinned against us or caused us to stumble? Our Lord gave several instructions.

Keep the matter private. Approach the person who sinned and speak with him alone. It is possible that he does not even realize what he has done. Or, even if he did it deliberately, your own attitude of submission and love will help him to repent and apologize. Above all else, go to him with the idea of winning your brother, not winning an argument. It is possible to win the argument and lose your brother.

We must have a spirit of meekness and gentleness when we seek to restore a brother or sister (Gal. 6:1). We must not go about condemning the offender, or spreading gossip. We must lovingly seek to help him in the same way we would want him to help us if the situation were reversed. The word *restore* in Galatians 6:1 is a Greek medical word that means "to set a broken bone." Think of the patience and tenderness that requires!

Ask for help from others. If the offender refuses to make things right, then we may feel free to share the burden with one or two dependable believers. We should share the facts as we see them and ask the brethren for their prayerful counsel. After all, it may be that *we* are wrong. If the brethren feel the cause is right, then together we can go to the offender and try once again to win him. Not only can these men assist in prayer and persuasion, but they can be witnesses to the church of the truth of the conversation (Deut. 19:15; 2 Cor. 13:1).

When sin is not dealt with honestly, it always spreads. What was once a matter between two people has now grown to involve four or five people. No wonder Jesus and Paul both compared sin to leaven (yeast), because leaven spreads.

Ask the church for help. Remember, our goal is not the winning of a case but the winning of a brother. The word *gained* in Matthew 18:15 is used in 1 Corinthians 9:19-22 to refer to winning the lost; but it is also important to win the saved. This is our Lord's second mention of the church (see Matt. 16:18), and here it has the meaning of a local assembly of believers. Our Lord's disciples were raised in the Jewish synagogue, so they were familiar with congregational discipline.

What started as a private problem between two people is now out in the open for the whole church to see. Church discipline is a neglected ministry these days, yet it is taught here and in the epistles (see 1 Cor. 5; 2 Thes. 3:6-16; 2 Tim. 2:23-26; Titus 3:10). Just as children in the home need discipline, so God's children in the church need discipline. If by the time the matter comes to the whole church, the offender has not yet changed his mind and repented, then he must be disciplined. He cannot be treated as a spiritual brother, for he has forfeited that position. He can only be treated as one outside the church, not hated, but not held in close fellowship.

Keep the local church spiritual (vv. 18-20). It is important that the local assembly be at its best spiritually before it seeks to discipline a member. When a church disciplines a member, it is actually examining itself and disciplining itself. This is why our Lord added these words about authority, prayer, and fellowship. We cannot discipline others if we ourselves are not disciplined. Whatever we loose (permit) in the assembly must first have been permitted by God (see the comments on Matt. 16:19).

The church must be under the authority of God's Word. Church discipline does not refer to a group of Christian policemen throwing their weight around. Rather, it means God exercising His authority in and through a local body, to restore one of His erring children.

Not only must there be the authority of the Word, but there must also be prayer (Matt. 18:19). The word *agree* in the Greek gives us our English word "symphony." The church must agree in prayer as it seeks to discipline the erring member. It is through prayer and the Word that we ascertain the will of the Father in the matter.

Finally, there must be fellowship (Matt. 18:20). The local church must be a worshiping community, recognizing the presence of the Lord in their midst. The Holy Spirit of God can convict both the offender and the church, and He can even judge sin in the midst (Acts 5).

There is a desperate need for honesty in the church today. "Speaking the truth in love" is God's standard (Eph. 4:15). If we practice love without truth, it is hypocrisy. But if we try to have truth without love, it may be brutality. Jesus always taught the truth in love. If the truth hurts, it is because "Faithful are the wounds of a friend" (Prov. 27:6).

But keep in mind that *humility* must come before *honesty*. A proud Christian cannot speak the truth in love. He will use a brother's faults as a weapon to fight with and not as a tool to build with. The result will be only greater disharmony and disagreement.

The first internal problem of the New Testament church was dishonesty (Acts 5). Ananias and Sapphira tried to make the church members believe that they were more spiritual than they really were. They lied to themselves in thinking they could get away with the masquerade; they lied to their fellow Christians and the church leaders; and they tried to lie to the Holy Spirit. The result was judgment and death. God may not kill every hypocrite in the church today, but hypocrisy certainly helps to kill the church.

The second internal problem (Acts 6) had to do with people being neglected. The members and leaders faced this problem with truth and love, and the result was blessing. It takes both truth and love, and both must be used with humility.

Forgiveness (Matt. 18:21-35)

When we start living in an atmosphere of humility and honesty, we must take some risks and expect some dangers. Unless humility and honesty result in forgiveness, relationships cannot be mended and strengthened. Peter recognized the risks involved and asked Jesus how he should handle them in the future.

But Peter made some serious mistakes. To begin with, he lacked humility himself. He was sure his brother would sin against him, but not he against his brother! Peter's second mistake was in asking for limits and measures. Where there is love, there can be no limits or dimensions (Eph. 3:17-19). Peter thought he was showing great faith and love when he offered to forgive at least seven times. After all, the rabbis taught that three times was sufficient.

Our Lord's reply, "Until seventy times seven" (490 times) must have startled Peter. Who could keep count for that many offenses? But that was exactly the point Jesus was making: Love "keeps no record of wrongs" (1 Cor. 13:5, NIV). By the time we have forgiven a brother that many times, we are in the habit of forgiving.

But Jesus was not advising careless or shallow forgiveness. Christian love is not blind (Phil. 1:9-10). The forgiveness Christ requires is on the basis of the instructions He gave in Matthew 18:15-20. If a brother is guilty of a repeated sin, no doubt he would find strength and power to conquer that sin through the encouragement of his loving and forgiving brethren. If we condemn a brother, we bring out the worst in him. But if we create an atmosphere of love and forgiveness, we can help God bring out the best in him.

The parable illustrates the power of forgiveness. It is important to note that *this parable is not about salvation,* for salvation is wholly of grace and is unconditionally given. To make God's forgiveness a temporary thing is to violate the very truth of Scripture (Rom. 5:8; Eph. 2:8-9; Titus 3:3-7). The parable deals with forgiveness between *brothers,* not between lost sinners and God. The emphasis in this chapter is on brother forgiving brother (Matt. 18:15, 21).

The main character in this parable went through three stages in his experience of forgiveness.

He was a debtor (vv. 23-27). This man had been stealing funds from the king and, when the books were audited, his crime was discovered. The total tax levy in Palestine was about 800 talents a year, so you can see how dishonest this man was. In terms of today's buying power, this was probably equivalent to over $10 million.

But this man actually thought he could get out of the debt. He told the king that, given enough time, he could pay it back. We detect two sins here: pride and a lack of sincere repentance. The man was not ashamed because he stole the money; he was ashamed because he got caught. And he actually thought he was big enough to earn the money to repay the king's account. In the economy of that day, a man would have had to work twenty years to earn one talent.

His case was hopeless, except for one thing: The king was a man of compassion. He assumed the loss and forgave the servant. This meant that the man was free and that he and his family would not be thrown into a debtor's prison. The servant did not deserve this forgiveness; it was purely an act of love and mercy on the part of the master.

He was a creditor (vv. 28-30). The servant left the presence of the king and went and found a fellow servant who owed him 100 pence. The average worker earned one penny a day, so this debt was insignificant compared to what the servant had owed the king. Instead of sharing with his friend the joy of his own release, the servant mistreated his friend and demanded that he pay the debt. The debtor used the same approach as the servant: "Have patience with me and I will pay you all of it!" But the unjust servant was unwilling to grant to others what he wanted others to grant to him.

Perhaps he had the *legal* right to throw the man in prison, but he did not have the *moral* right. He had been forgiven himself—should he not forgive his fellow servant? He and his family had been spared the shame and suffering of prison. Should he not spare his friend?

He became a prisoner (vv. 31-34). The king originally delivered him from prison, but the servant put himself back in. The servant exercised justice and cast his friend into prison. "So you want to live by justice?" asked the king. "Then you shall have justice! Throw the wicked servant in prison and torment him! I will do to him as he has done to others." (There is no suggestion that the entire family was sentenced. After all, it was the father who abused the other servant and ignored the king's kindness.)

The world's worst prison is the prison of an unforgiving heart. If we refuse to forgive others, then we are only imprisoning ourselves and causing our own torment. Some of the most miserable people I have met in my ministry have been people who would not forgive others. They lived only to imagine ways to punish these people who had wronged them. But they were really only punishing themselves.

What was wrong with this man? The same

thing that is wrong with many professing Christians: They have *received* forgiveness, but they have not really *experienced* forgiveness deep in their hearts. Therefore, they are unable to *share* forgiveness with those who have wronged them. If we live only according to justice, always seeking to get what is ours, we will put ourselves into prison. But if we live according to forgiveness, sharing with others what God has shared with us, then we will enjoy freedom and joy. Peter asked for a just measuring rod; Jesus told him to practice forgiveness and forget the measuring rod.

Our Lord's warning is serious. He did not say that God *saves* only those who forgive others. The theme of this parable is forgiveness between brothers, not salvation for lost sinners. Jesus warned us that God cannot forgive us *if we do not have humble and repentant hearts.* We reveal the true condition of our hearts by the way we treat others. When our hearts are humble and repentant, we will gladly forgive our brothers. But where there is pride and a desire for revenge, there can be no true repentance; and this means God cannot forgive.

In other words, it is not enough to *receive* God's forgiveness, or even the forgiveness of others. We must *experience* that forgiveness in our hearts so that it humbles us and makes us gentle and forgiving toward others. The servant in the parable did not have a deep experience of forgiveness and humility. *He was simply glad to be "off the hook."* He had never really repented.

"And be you kind one to another, tenderhearted, forgiving one another, even as God for Christ's sake hath forgiven you" (Eph. 4:32). "Forbearing one another, and forgiving one another, if any man have a quarrel against any: even as Christ forgave you, so also do you" (Col. 3:13).

CHAPTER SIXTEEN
THE KING'S INSTRUCTIONS
Matthew 19:1-15

The King's "retirement" from the crowds was about to come to an end. But the attacks of the enemy would grow more intense, culminating in His arrest and crucifixion. The religious leaders had already tried to ensnare Him with questions about the Sabbath and signs, and they had failed. They tried again, this time with a most controversial issue—divorce.

This subject is both important and controversial today. The divorce rate continues to climb (at this writing, one divorce for every 1.8 marriages), and divorce has invaded even the homes of Christian leaders. Someone has commented that couples "are married for better or for worse, but not for long." We need to examine again what Jesus taught about this subject. He explained four different laws relating to marriage and divorce.

The Original Creation Law (Matt. 19:3-6)

Instead of going back to Deuteronomy, Jesus went back to Genesis. What God did when He established the first marriage teaches us *positively* what He had in mind for a man and a woman. If we build a marriage after God's ideal pattern, we will not have to worry about divorce laws.

The reasons for marriage. The only thing that was not "good" about Creation was the fact that the man was alone (Gen. 2:18). The woman was created to meet this need. Adam could not find fellowship with the animals. He needed a companion who was equal to him and with whom he could find fulfillment. God's answer to this need was Eve.

Marriage makes possible the continuation of the race. "Be fruitful, and multiply" was God's mandate to the first married couple (Gen. 1:28). From the beginning it was God's command that sex be practiced in the commitment of marriage. Outside of marriage, sex becomes a destructive force; but within the loving commitment of marriage, sex can be creative and constructive.

Marriage is one way to avoid sexual sins

(1 Cor. 7:1-6). Of course, a man should not marry simply to legalize lust! If he is lustful outside of marriage, he will no doubt be lustful after he is married. He should not think that getting married will solve all of his personal problems with lust. But marriage is God's appointed way for a man and a woman to share the physical joys of sex.

Paul used marriage as an illustration of the intimate relationship between Christ and the church (Eph. 5:22-23). Just as Eve was taken from the side of Adam (Gen. 2:21), so the church was born from the suffering and death of Christ on the cross. Christ loves His church, nourishes it with His Word, cleanses it, and cares for it. Christ's relationship to His church is the example for all husbands to follow.

The characteristics of marriage. By going back to the original Edenic Law, Jesus reminded His listeners of the true characteristics of marriage. If we remember these characteristics, we will better know how to build a happy and enduring marriage.

It is a divinely appointed union. God established marriage, and therefore only God can control its character and laws. No court of law can change what God has established.

It is a physical union. The man and woman become "one flesh." While it is important that a husband and wife be of one mind and heart, the basic union in marriage is physical. If a man and woman became "one spirit" in marriage, then death would not dissolve the marriage; for the spirit never dies. Even if a man and woman disagree, are "incompatible," and cannot get along, they are still married; for the union is a physical one.

It is a permanent union. God's original design was that one man and one woman spend one life together. God's original Law knows nothing of "trial marriages." God's Law requires that the husband and wife enter into marriage without reservations.

It is a union between one man and one woman. God did not create two men and one woman, two women and one man, two men, or two women. "Group marriages," "gay marriages," and other variations are contrary to the will of God, no matter what some psychologists and jurists may say.

The Seventh Commandment (Matt. 5:27-30)

While Jesus did not refer to the seventh commandment in this discussion, He did quote it in the Sermon on the Mount (Matt. 5:27-32). Let's examine what He said.

Jesus and the New Testament writers affirm the authority of "Thou shalt not commit adultery" (Ex. 20:14). While the word *fornication* seems to cover many kinds of sexual sins (see Mark 7:21; Rom. 1:29; 1 Cor. 6:13), *adultery* involves only married people. When a married person has intercourse with someone other than his or her mate, that is adultery. God has declared that it is wrong and it is sin. There are numerous warnings in the New Testament against sexual sins, including adultery (Acts 15:20; 1 Cor. 6:15-18; Gal. 5:19ff; Eph. 4:17ff; 5:3-12; Col. 3:5; 1 Thes. 4:3-7; Heb. 13:4).

This commandment affirms the sanctity of sex. God created it, God protects it, and God punishes when His law is violated. Nine of the Ten Commandments are repeated in the New Testament for us to heed. (The Sabbath commandment was given only to Israel and does not apply to the church today.) We must not think that because we are "under grace" we can flaunt God's Law and get away with it. "Fornicators and adulterers God will judge" (Heb. 13:4, NASB).

However, Jesus went much deeper in His discussion of adultery. He showed that this can be a sin of the heart as well as a sin of the body. It is not enough simply to control the body; we must also control the inner thoughts and desires. To look at a woman *for the purpose of lusting after her* is to commit adultery in the heart. This does not mean that we cannot admire a beautiful person or picture; for it is possible to do that and not sin. It is when we look *with the intention* of satisfying lustful desires, that we commit adultery in the heart.

A sanctified sex life begins with the inner desires. Jesus singled out the eye and the hand, because seeing and feeling are usually the first steps toward sexual sin. Of course, He did not command us to perform *physical* surgery, since He was clearly dealing with the *inner* desires. He commanded us to deal drastically with sin, to remove from our lives anything that would pamper our wrong desires. We must "hunger and thirst after righteousness."

Jesus did not alter the original Edenic Law of marriage, nor did He annul the seventh commandment. What He taught was based solidly on God's creation and God's moral law.

The Mosaic Law of Divorce (Matt. 19:7-8)

Like many people who "argue religion," these Pharisees were not interested in discovering truth. They were interested only in defending themselves and what they believed. This was why they asked about the Jewish law of divorce recorded in Deuteronomy 24:1-4.

I suggest you read this important passage in the *New American Standard Bible* to distinguish the tenses of the verbs. This translation makes it clear that Moses gave *only one commandment:* The divorced wife could not return to her first husband if she was put away by a second husband. *Moses did not command divorce;* he permitted it. He commanded that the husband give his ex-wife a legal bill of divorcement. But the wife could not return to her first husband after being remarried and divorced.

What a wise law this was. To begin with, the husband would think twice before hastily putting away his wife, since he could not get her back again. Furthermore, it would have taken time to find a scribe (not everyone could write legal documents), and during that time the two estranged people might have been reconciled. The Pharisees were interpreting Moses' Law as though it were a commandment. Jesus made it clear that Moses was only giving *permission* for divorce.

But what did Moses mean by *some uncleanness in her?* The Hebrew means "some matter of nakedness," but this need not refer to sexual sin. That phrase is the equivalent of "some shameful thing" (see Gen. 2:25; 3:7, 10). It is the interpretation of this phrase that divided the two schools of Rabbi Hillel and Rabbi Shammai, famous first-century Jewish scholars. Hillel took a very lax view and said that the husband could divorce his wife for almost any reason, while Shammai took the stricter view and said Moses was speaking only about sexual sin. No matter which side Jesus took, He would surely offend somebody.

There were several laws of marriage given to the Jews, and we must examine them in order to get some perspective. For example, if a man married a woman and discovered that she was not a virgin, he could expose her sin and have her stoned (Deut. 22:13-21). Of course, he had to have proof; and if he did not, he was fined and had to live with the woman all of his life. This law was as much a protection to the woman as to the man.

If a man suspected his wife of unfaithfulness, he followed the procedure outlined in Numbers 5:11ff. We cannot follow that procedure today (which certainly included elements of divine judgment) since there is no priesthood or tabernacle.

Remember that the Law of Moses demanded *the death penalty* for those who committed adultery (Lev. 20:10; Deut. 22:22). Our Lord's enemies appealed to this law when they tried to trap Him (John 8:1). While we have no record in the Old Testament that anyone was stoned for committing adultery, this was the divine law. The experience of Joseph (Matt. 1:18-25) indicates that the Jews used divorce rather than stoning in dealing with an adulterous wife.

Why did God command that the adulterer or adulteress be stoned to death? Certainly as an example to warn the people, for adultery undermines the very fabric of society and the home. There must be commitment in marriage, and faithfulness to each other and to God, if there is to be stability in society and in the church. God had to preserve Israel because the promised Saviour would come through that nation. God opposed divorce in Israel because it weakened the nation and threatened the birth of the Messiah (see Mal. 2:10-16).

But there was another reason for capital punishment: This left the other party free to marry again. Death breaks the marriage bond, since marriage is a physical union (Rom. 7:1-3). It was important that families be continued in Israel that they might protect their inheritance (Num. 36).

We must note one final fact before leaving this section: The divorce that Moses permitted in Deuteronomy 24 *actually severed the original marriage relationship.* God permitted the woman to marry again, and her second marriage was not considered adulterous. The second man she married was called a "husband" and not an adulterer. This explains how the woman of Samaria could have had five *husbands,* and yet be living with a man not her husband (John 4:16-18). Apparently all five of those marriages had been legal and scriptural.

This means that scriptural divorce does sever the marriage relationship. *Man* cannot break this relationship by his laws, but *God can break it.* The same God who gives the laws that join people together can also give laws to put them asunder. God can do it, but man cannot.

Finally, Jesus made it clear that this Mosaic Law of divorce was a concession on God's part. God's original law of marriage left no room for divorce, but that law was laid down before man had sinned. Rather than have two people living together in constant conflict, with one or both of them seeking fulfillment elsewhere and thus commit sin, God permitted divorce. *This divorce included the right to remarriage.* The Pharisees did not ask about remarriage, for this was no problem. They accepted the fact that the parties would seek other mates, and this was allowed by Moses.

Our Lord's Law of Marriage (Matt. 19:9-12; 5:31-32)

When Jesus said "And I say unto you," He was claiming to be God; for only God can establish or alter the laws of marriage. He declared that marriage was a permanent union that could only be broken by sexual sin. The word *fornication* in the New Testament covers many kinds of sexual sins. The definition of fornication as "sexual sin between two unmarried persons" would not apply here, for Jesus was talking about married persons. Are we to believe that the 23,000 men who committed fornication under the enticement of Baalam (Num. 25) were all unmarried men? Was the admonition of Acts 15:20, 29 sent only to single church members?

Marriage is a permanent physical union that can be broken only by a physical cause: death or sexual sin. (I would take it that homosexuality and bestiality would qualify.) Man cannot break the union, but God can. Under the Old Testament Law, the sinner was stoned to death. But the church today does not bear the sword (Rom. 13:1-4). Were adultery and fornication more serious under the Law than the same sins are today? Of course not! If anything, such sins are even worse today in the light of the full revelation of God's grace and holiness that we now have in Jesus Christ.

The conclusion seems to be that divorce in the New Testament is the equivalent of death in the Old Testament: It permitted the innocent party freedom to remarry.

Notice that our Lord's new law of marriage and divorce was based on the three previous laws. From the Edenic Law He took the principle that marriage was a physical union that could only be broken by a physical cause, and that only God could permit the breaking of the union. From the seventh commandment He took the principle that sexual sin did indeed break the marriage union. From the Mosaic Law of divorce He took the principle that God could ordain divorce and effectively break the marriage union, and that the freed party could remarry and not be guilty of adultery.

Our Lord's teaching is that there is only one scriptural basis for divorce, and that is sexual sin (fornication). If two people are divorced on any other basis, and marry other mates, they are committing adultery.

Jesus did not teach that the offended mate *had* to get a divorce. Certainly there can be forgiveness, patient healing, and a restoration of the broken relationship. This would be the Christian approach to the problem. But, sad to say, because of the hardness of our hearts, it is sometimes impossible to heal the wounds and save the marriage. Divorce is the *final* option, not the first option.

Happy marriages are not accidents. They are the result of commitment, love, mutual understanding, sacrifice, and hard work. If a husband and wife are fulfilling their marriage vows, they will enjoy a growing relationship that will satisfy them and keep them true to each other. Except for the possibility of sudden temptation, no husband or wife would think of a relationship with another person, so long as their relationship at home is growing and satisfying. And the pure love of a husband or wife is a great protection against even sudden temptation.

The disciples' response to Christ's teaching showed that they disagreed with Him. "If there is no way to get out of a bad marriage, then you are better off staying single!" was their argument. Jesus did not want them to consider divorce as an "out" because then they would not have a serious attitude toward marriage.

In Matthew 19:12, Jesus made it clear that each man (and woman) must consider God's will concerning marriage. Some people should not get married because of physical or emotional problems from birth. Others should not get married because of their responsibilities in society; they have been "made eunuchs by man." An only child who must care for aged parents might be an example of this category. Some, like the Apostle Paul, stay single that they might better serve the Lord (1 Cor. 7:7).

It is fitting that our Lord's teaching about marriage should be followed by His blessing of the children for children are the happy heritage of those who are married. Jesus did not look on the children as a curse or a burden.

"Two shall become one flesh" is fulfilled in the birth of children, and the love of the parents is deepened and matured as it is shared with others in the home.

The parents brought the children to Jesus that He might bless them. There is no thought here of baptism or even of salvation. Children who have not reached the age of accountability (Isa. 7:16) are surely covered by the death of Christ (Rom. 5:17-21). Children are born sinners (Ps. 51:5); but if they die before they are accountable, they are regenerated and taken to heaven (2 Sam. 12:23; Ps. 23:6).

The children were certainly privileged to have Jesus take them in His arms and pray for them. Our practice of baby dedication today seeks to follow this example. How happy those children are whose parents are married in the will of God, and who are seeking to obey God, and who bring them to Jesus for His blessing.

CHAPTER SEVENTEEN
THE KING'S DEMANDS
Matthew 19:16–20:34

We cannot follow the King without paying a price. After all, He went to the cross for us! Have we the right to escape sacrifice and suffering? In this section, our Lord explains the rightful demands that He makes on those who want to trust Him and be His disciples.

We Must Love Christ Supremely (Matt. 19:16-26)

Each of the first three Gospels records this event. When we combine the facts, we learn that this man was rich, young, and a ruler—probably the ruler of a synagogue. We can certainly commend this young man for coming publicly to Christ and asking about external matters. He seemed to have no ulterior motive and was willing to listen and learn. Sadly, he made the wrong decision.

The event seems to develop around several important questions.

"What good thing shall I do, that I may have eternal life?" (vv. 16-17) The man was obviously sincere, though his approach to salvation was centered on works and not faith. But this was to be expected among the Jews of that day. However, in spite of his position in society, his morality, and his religion, he felt a definite need for something more.

But our Lord's reply did not focus on salvation. He forced the young man to think seriously about the word *good* that he had used in addressing Jesus. "Only God is good," Jesus said. "Do you believe that I am good and therefore that I am God?" If Jesus is only one of many religious teachers in history, then His words carry no more weight than the pronouncements of any other religious leader. But if Jesus is good, then He is God, and we had better heed what He says.

Why did Jesus bring up the commandments? Did He actually teach that people receive eternal life by obeying God's Law? If anyone *could* keep the commandments, he certainly would enter into life. But no one can keep God's Law perfectly. "Therefore by the deeds of the Law there shall no flesh be justified in His sight: for by the Law is the knowledge of sin" (Rom. 3:20). Jesus did not introduce the Law to show the young man how to be saved, but to show him that *he needed to be saved.* The Law is a mirror that reveals what we are (James 1:22ff).

"Which commandments?" (vv. 18-19) Was the young man being evasive? I don't think so. But he was making a mistake, for one part of God's Law cannot be separated from another part. To classify God's laws into "lesser" and "greater" is to miss the whole purpose of the Law. "For whosoever shall keep the whole Law, and yet offend in one point, he is guilty of all" (James 2:10). The Law represents the authority of God, and to disobey what we may think is a minor law is still to rebel against His authority.

Of course, the young man thought only of external obedience. He forgot about the attitudes of the heart. Jesus had taught in the Sermon on the Mount that hatred was the moral equivalent of murder, and that lust was the equivalent of adultery. We rejoice that this young man had such good manners and morals. But we regret that he did not see his sin, repent, and trust Christ.

The one commandment that especially applied to him, Jesus did not quote: "Thou shalt not covet" (Ex. 20:17). The young man should have pondered *all* of the commandments and not just the ones that Jesus quoted.

Was he looking for easy discipleship? Was he being dishonest with himself? I believe that his testimony was sincere, *as far as he knew*. But he did not permit the light of the Word to penetrate deeply enough. Jesus felt a sudden love for this young man (Mark 10:21), so He continued to try to help him.

"What lack I yet?" (vv. 20-22) Nowhere in the Bible are we taught that a sinner is saved by selling his goods and giving the money away. Jesus never told Nicodemus to do this, or any other sinner whose story is recorded in the Gospels. Jesus knew that this man was covetous; he loved material wealth. By asking him to sell his goods, Jesus was forcing him to examine his own heart and determine his priorities. With all of his commendable qualities, the young man still did not truly love God with *all* of his heart. Possessions were his god. He was unable to obey the command, "Go and sell . . . come and follow."

The young man went away grieved, but he could have gone away in great joy and peace. We cannot love and serve two masters (Matt. 6:24ff). We can be sure that, apart from Christ, even the material possessions of life give no lasting joy or pleasure. It is good to have the things money can buy provided we do not lose the things that money cannot buy. Unless this rich ruler eventually turned to Christ, he died without salvation, one of the "richest" men in the cemetery.

"Who then can be saved?" (vv. 23-26) The Jewish people of that day believed that riches were an evidence of God's blessing. They based this on the promises God gave the Jewish nation at the beginning of their history. It is true that God *did* promise material blessing if they obeyed, and material loss if they disobeyed (see Deut. 26–28). But in the infancy of the race, the only way God could teach them was through rewards and punishments. We teach young children in the same manner.

However, the highest kind of obedience is not based on a desire for reward or the fear of punishment. It is motivated by love. In His life and His teaching, Jesus tried to show the people that the inner spiritual blessings are far more important than the material gains. God sees the heart, and God wants to build character. Salvation is the gift of God in response to man's faith. Material riches are not a guarantee that God is pleased with a man.

The disciples, being good Jews, were amazed at the Lord's statement about riches. Their question reflected their theology: "If a rich man cannot be saved, what hope is there for the rest of us?" Of course, Jesus did not say that the *possessing* of wealth kept a man from the kingdom. Some manuscripts of Mark 10:24 read, "How hard it is for those who trust in riches to enter the kingdom of God." This is certainly the import of our Lord's teaching. Abraham was a very wealthy man, yet he was a man of great faith. It is good to possess wealth *if* wealth does not possess you.

We cannot follow the King and live for worldly wealth. We cannot serve God and money. The love of money is the root of all kinds of evil (1 Tim. 6:6-10). Jesus Christ demands of all who will follow Him that they love Him supremely.

We Must Obey Him Unreservedly (Matt. 19:27–20:16)

Peter was quick to see the contrast between the wealthy ruler and poor disciples. "We have forsaken all, and followed Thee; what shall we have therefore?" Jesus gave them a marvelous promise of rewards in this life and in the next. They would even share thrones when He established His kingdom. Whatever good things they had forsaken for His sake would be returned to them a hundredfold. In other words, they were not making sacrifices—they were making investments. But not all of the dividends would be received in this life.

However, Jesus detected in Peter's question the possibility of a wrong motive for service. This was why He added the warning that some who were first in their own eyes would be last in the judgment, and some who were last would end up first. This truth was amplified in the Parable of the Workers in the Vineyard.

This parable has nothing to do with salvation. The penny (a day's wages in that time) does not represent salvation, for nobody works for his salvation. Nor is the parable talking about rewards, for we are not all going to receive the same reward. "And every man shall receive his own reward according to his own labor" (1 Cor. 3:8).

The parable is emphasizing *a right attitude in service*. It is important to note that there were actually two kinds of workers hired that day: those who wanted a contract and agreed to work for a penny a day, and those who had no contract and agreed to take whatever the owner thought was right. The first laborers that he hired insisted on a contract.

This explains why the householder paid the workers as he did: He wanted those who were hired first (who insisted on a contract) to see how much he paid the workers who were hired later. It was one way the owner could show those workers how really generous he was.

Put yourself in the place of those workers who were hired first but paid last. They each expected to get a penny, because that was what they agreed to accept. But imagine their surprise when they saw the laborers who were hired *last* each receiving a penny! This meant their own wages should have been twelve pennies each!

But the 3 o'clock workers also received a penny—for only three hours of work. The men last in line quickly recalculated their wages: four pennies for the day's work. When the men hired at noon also were paid a penny, this cut the salary of the contract workers considerably, for now they would earn only two pennies.

But the owner gave them one penny each. Of course, they complained! But they had no argument, because *they had agreed to work for a penny.* They received what they asked for. Had they trusted the goodness of the owner, they would have received far more. But they insisted on a contract.

The lesson for Christ's disciples is obvious. We should not serve Him because we want to receive an expected reward, and we should not insist on knowing what we will get. God is infinitely generous and gracious and will always give us better than we deserve.

Now we can understand the perils that were hidden in Peter's question in Matthew 19:27. For one thing, we must not "suppose" (Matt. 20:10) that we will get something more if we really do not deserve it. It is possible to do the Father's work and yet not do His will from the heart (Eph. 6:6). If we serve Him only for the benefits (temporal and eternal), then we will miss the best blessings He has for us. We must trust Him unreservedly and believe that He will always give what is best.

There is the danger of pride. "What shall we have?" asked Peter. This parable warned him, "How do you know you will have anything?" Beware of overconfidence when it comes to the rewards God will give, for those first in their own eyes (and in the eyes of others) may end up last! Likewise, do not get discouraged; for those who consider themselves "unprofitable servants" may end up first.

Beware of the danger of watching other workers and measuring yourself by them. "Judge nothing before the time," Paul warns in 1 Corinthians 4:5. We see the worker and the work, but God sees the heart.

Finally, we must beware of criticizing God and feeling that we have been left out. Had the early morning workers trusted the owner and not asked for an agreement, the owner would have given them much more. He was generous, but they would not trust him. They did not rejoice that others received more; instead, they were jealous and complained. The goodness of the owner did not lead them to repentance (Rom. 2:4). It revealed the true character of their hearts: They were selfish! Whenever we find a complaining servant, we know he has not fully yielded to the master's will.

We Must Glorify Him Completely (Matt. 20:17-34)

For the third time, Jesus announced His arrest, crucifixion, and resurrection (see Matt. 16:21; 17:22). In the previous announcements, He had not specified how He would die. But now He clearly mentioned the cross. He also clearly mentioned His resurrection, but the message did not penetrate the disciples' hearts.

In contrast to this announcement of suffering and death, we have the request of James and John and their mother, Salome. Jesus spoke about a cross, but they were interested in a crown. They wanted reserved seats on special thrones! We get the impression that the mother, Salome, was the real inspiration behind this request, and that she was interested in promoting her sons.

Before we criticize what they did, let's notice some commendable features in this event. For one thing, they *did* believe in prayer, and they dared to believe the promise Jesus had given about sitting on thrones (Matt. 19:28). The word "regeneration" in that verse means "new birth," and refers to the new world over which Jesus and His followers will reign when He returns to earth. It must have taken faith on their part to believe He would establish these thrones, because He had just told them that He was going to die.

But there were several things wrong with

their request. To begin with, it was born in ignorance. "Ye know not what ye ask," Jesus replied. Little did Salome realize that the path to the throne is a difficult one. James was the first of the disciples to be martyred, and John had to endure hard days on the Isle of Patmos. These three believers wanted *their* will, not God's will, and they wanted it *their* way.

Another factor was their lack of heavenly direction. They were thinking like *the world:* James and John wanted to "lord it over" the other disciples the way the unsaved Gentile rulers lorded it over their subjects. Their request was *fleshly* (sensual), because they were selfishly asking for glory for themselves, not for the Lord. No doubt they felt relieved that they had gotten to Jesus with this request before Peter did!

Finally, the request was not only of the world and the flesh, but it was of *the devil.* It was motivated by pride. Satan had sought a throne (Isa. 14:12-15) and had been cast down. Satan had offered Jesus a throne and had been refused (Matt. 4:8-11). Satan magnifies *the end* (a throne) but not *the means* to that end. Jesus warned Salome and her sons that the special thrones were available to those who were worthy of them. There are no shortcuts in the kingdom of God.

The result of this request was "indignation" on the part of the other disciples—probably because they had not thought of it first! The wisdom from above always leads to peace; the wisdom of this world leads to war (James 3:13–4:3). Selfishness will only result in dissension and division.

This disagreement gave Jesus the opportunity to teach a practical lesson on leadership. In His kingdom, we must not follow the examples of the world. Our example is Jesus, not some corporation president or wealthy celebrity. Jesus came as a servant; therefore, we should serve one another. He came to give His life; therefore, we should give our lives in service to Him and others.

The word *minister* in Matthew 20:26 means "a servant." Our English word "deacon" comes from it. The word *servant* in Matthew 20:27 means "a slave." Not every servant was a slave, but every slave was a servant. It is sad to note in the church today that we have many celebrities, but very few servants. There are many who want to "exercise authority" (Matt. 20:25), but few who want to take the towel and basin and wash feet.

The key to greatness is not found in position or power, but in character. We get a throne by paying with our lives, not by praying with our lips. We must identify with Jesus Christ in His service and suffering, for even He could not reach the throne except by way of the cross. The best commentary on this is Philippians 2:1-18.

To improve our praying we must improve our serving. If we are serving Him and others, then we will not be praying selfishly. If we honestly can say, "Speak, Lord, for Thy servant heareth," then He will say to us, "Speak, servant, for thy Lord heareth." If our prayers do not make us better servants, then there is something wrong with them.

Do our prayers make us easier to live with? The two disciples prayed selfishly and threw the fellowship into an uproar! Do our prayers make us more like Jesus Christ? *Do our prayers cost us anything?* Prayer in the will of God does not mean escape; it means involvement. If our prayers do not bring us nearer to the cross, they are out of God's will.

Salome learned her lesson. When Jesus was crucified, she was standing near the cross (John 19:25, "his mother's sister") and sharing in His sorrow and pain. She did not see two thrones on either side of her Lord—she saw two thieves on two crosses. And she heard Jesus give her son, John, to His mother Mary. Salome's selfishness was rebuked, and she meekly accepted it.

The closing event of Matthew 20 is the healing of Bartimaeus and his friend, both of whom were blind (see Mark 10:46-52). Here Jesus put into practice what He had just taught the disciples. He became a servant to two rejected blind beggars. The crowds around Jesus tried to silence the two men. After all, what claim did they have on the great Teacher? But Jesus had compassion on them and healed them. He was the servant even of beggars.

This chapter contains some hard things for us to receive and practice. If we love the things of this world, we cannot love God supremely. If we are not yielded completely to His will, we cannot obey Him unreservedly. If we seek glory for ourselves, or if we compare ourselves with other believers, then we cannot glorify Him.

We cannot acknowledge Jesus as our King unless we love Him supremely, obey Him unreservedly, and glorify Him completely. But if we do these things, we will share in His life and joy, and one day reign with Him!

CHAPTER EIGHTEEN THE KING'S JUDGMENTS

Matthew 21:1–22:14

We now enter the fourth major section of Matthew's Gospel, "The Rejection of the King." In this section (Matt. 21:1–22:14), the Lord Jesus revealed the sins of Israel and explained why the religious leaders rejected Him and His message.

Spiritual Blindness (Matt. 21:1-11)

Since it was Passover, there were probably about 2 million people in and around Jerusalem. This was the only time in His ministry that Jesus actually planned and promoted a public demonstration. Up to this time, He had cautioned people not to tell who He was, and He had deliberately avoided public scenes.

Why did Jesus plan this demonstration? For one thing, He was obeying the Word and fulfilling the prophecy recorded in Zechariah 9:9. This prophecy could apply only to Jesus Christ, for He is the only One with credentials that prove He is Israel's King. We usually do not associate the lowly donkey with kingship, but this was the royal animal of Jewish monarchs (1 Kings 2:32ff). There were actually two animals involved, the mother and the colt (foal). Jesus sat on the colt with the mother walking beside.

By comparing Matthew's quotation with the original prophecy in Zechariah, we discover some interesting facts. Zechariah's prophecy opens with, "Rejoice greatly" but Matthew omitted this phrase. When Jesus approached the city, He wept! How could He (or the people) rejoice when judgment was coming?

Mathew also omitted "He is just, and having salvation." Our Lord's coming to Jerusalem was an act of mercy and grace, not an act of justice or judgment. He did have salvation for them, but they refused to accept it (John 1:11). The next time Israel sees the King, He will ride in great power and glory (Rev. 19:11ff).

This colt had never been ridden (Mark 11:2), yet he meekly bore his burden. The presence of the mother helped, of course. But keep in mind that his rider was the King who has "dominion over . . . all sheep and oxen, yea, and the beasts of the field" (Ps. 8:6-7). The fact that Jesus rode this beast and kept him in control is another evidence of His kingship.

There was a second reason for this public presentation: It forced the Jewish leaders to act. When they saw the spontaneous demonstration of the people, they concluded that Jesus had to be destroyed (see John 12:19). The prophetic Scriptures required that the Lamb of god be crucified on Passover. This demonstration of Christ's popularity incited the rulers to act.

The people acclaimed Jesus as their King both by their words and their deeds. They shouted *Hosanna* which means, "Save now!" They were quoting from Psalm 118:25-26, and this psalm is definitely messianic in character. Later that week, Jesus Himself would refer to this psalm and apply it to Himself (Ps. 118:22-23; Matt. 21:42).

Keep in mind that this Passover crowd was composed of at least three groups: the Jews who lived in Jerusalem, the crowd from Galilee, and the people who saw Jesus raise Lazarus from the dead (John 12:17-18). Sharing the news of this miracle undoubtedly helped to draw such a large crowd. The people wanted to see this miracle-worker for themselves.

But the Jews still did not recognize Jesus as their King. What caused Israel's spiritual blindness? For one thing, their religious leaders had robbed them of the truth of their own Word and had substituted man-made traditions (Luke 11:52). The leaders were not interested in truth; they were concerned only with protecting their own interests (John 11:47-53). "We have no king but Caesar!" was their confession of willful blindness. Even our Lord's miracles did not convince them. And the longer they resisted the truth, the blinder they became (John 12:35ff).

Hypocrisy (Matt. 21:12-22)

Jesus performed two acts of judgment: He cleansed the temple, and He cursed a fig tree. Both acts were contrary to His usual manner of ministry, for He did not come to earth to judge, but to save (John 3:17). Both of these acts revealed the hypocrisy of Israel: The temple was a den of thieves, and the nation (symbolized by the fig tree) was without fruit. Inward corruption and outward fruitlessness were evidences of their hypocrisy.

Cleansing the temple (vv. 12-16).

Jesus had opened His ministry with a similar act (John 2:13-25). Now, three years later, the temple was defiled again by the "religious business" of the leaders. They had turned the court of the Gentiles into a place where foreign Jews could exchange money and purchase sacrifices. What had begun as a service and convenience for visitors from other lands soon turned into a lucrative business. The dealers charged exorbitant prices and no one could compete with them or oppose them. Historians tell us that Annas, the former high priest, was the manager of this enterprise, assisted by his sons.

The purpose of the court of the Gentiles in the temple was to give the "outcasts" an opportunity to enter the temple and learn from Israel about the true God. But the presence of this "religious market" turned many sensitive Gentiles away from the witness of Israel. The court of the Gentiles was used for mercenary business, not missionary business.

When Jesus called the temple "My house," He was affirming that He is God. When He called it "My house of prayer," He was quoting Isaiah 56:7. The entire 56th chapter of Isaiah denounces the unfaithful leaders of Israel. The phrase "den of robbers" comes from Jeremiah 7:11 and is part of a long sermon that Jeremiah delivered in the gate of the temple, rebuking the people for the same sins that Jesus saw and judged in His day.

Why did Jesus call the temple "a den of thieves"? Because the place where thieves hide is called a den. The religious leaders, and some of the people, were using the temple and the Jewish religion to cover up their sins.

What does God want in His house? God wants *prayer* among His people (1 Tim. 2:1ff), for true prayer is an evidence of our dependence on God and our faith in His Word. He also wants *people* being helped (Matt. 21:14). The needy should feel welcome and should find the kind of help they need. There should be *power* in God's house, the power of God working to change people. *Praise* is another feature of God's house (Matt. 21:15-16). Here Jesus quoted from Psalm 8:2.

Cursing the tree (vv. 17-22). That Jesus would curse a tree may surprise us. The same power that killed the tree could also have given it new life and fruit. Jesus certainly would not hold a tree morally responsible for being fruitless.

When we consider the time and place of this event, we understand it better. Jesus was near Jerusalem in the last week of His public ministry to His people. The fig tree symbolized the nation of Israel (Jer. 8:13; Hosea 9:10, 16; Luke 13:6-9). Just as this tree had leaves but no fruit, so Israel had a show of religion but no practical experience of faith resulting in godly living. Jesus was not angry at the tree. Rather, He used this tree to teach several lessons to His disciples.

God wants to produce fruit in the lives of His people. Fruit is the product of life. The presence of leaves usually indicates the presence of fruit, but this was not the case. In the Parable of the Fig Tree (Luke 13:6-9), the gardener was given more time to care for the tree; but now the time was up. This tree was taking up space and doing no good.

While we can make a personal application of this event, the main interpretation has to do with Israel. The time of judgment had come. The sentence was pronounced by the Judge, but it would not be executed for about forty years. Then Rome would come and destroy the city and temple and scatter the people.

Jesus used this event to teach His disciples a practical lesson about faith and prayer. The temple was supposed to be a "house of prayer," and the nation was to be a believing people. But both of these essentials were missing. We too must beware of the peril of fruitlessness.

Disobedience to the Word (Matt. 21:23–22:14)

This series of three parables grew out of the demand of the chief priests and elders for Jesus to explain what authority He had for cleansing the temple. As the custodians of the spiritual life of the nation, they had the right to ask this question. But we are amazed at their ignorance. Jesus had given them three years of ministry, and they still would not face the facts. They wanted more evidence.

In taking them back to the ministry of John, Jesus was not trying to avoid the issue. John had prepared the way for Jesus. Had the rulers received John's ministry, they would have received Jesus. Instead, the leaders permitted Herod to arrest John and then to kill him. If they would not accept the authority of John, they would not accept the authority of Jesus; for both John and Jesus were sent by God.

It is a basic principle of Christian living that we cannot learn new truth if we disobey what God has already told us. "If any man is willing to do His will, he shall know of the teaching, whether it is of God" (John 7:17, NASB). The religious rulers had rejected the truth preached by John, and therefore Jesus could not impart new truth. Both He and John were under the same authority.

They rejected God the Father (vv. 23-32). The vineyard, of course, speaks of the nation of Israel (Ps. 80:8-16; Isa. 5). The two sons represent the two classes of people in that nation: the self-righteous religious people, and the publicans and sinners. When John came ministering, the religious crowd showed great interest in his work, but they would not repent and humble themselves and be baptized (Matt. 3:7-12; John 1:19-28). The nonreligious crowd, however, confessed their sins and obeyed John's words and were baptized.

The leaders committed two sins: They would not believe John's message and they would not repent of their sins. Of course, the leaders felt that they had no need to repent (Luke 18:9-14). But when they saw what repentance did for the publicans and sinners, they should have been convinced that John's message was true and salvation was real. Again and again, the religious rulers rejected the clear evidence God gave them.

Their rejection of John was actually a rejection of the Father who had sent him. But God is gracious, and instead of sending judgment, He sent His Son. This leads to the next parable.

They rejected the Son (vv. 33-46). We are still at the vineyard. This parable is based on Isaiah 5:1-7, and in it Jesus reminded the Jews of God's goodness to them as a nation. God delivered them from Egypt and planted them in a rich land of milk and honey. He gave them material and spiritual blessings and asked only that they bear fruit for His glory. From time to time, God sent His servants (the prophets) to the people to receive the fruit. But the people mistreated the servants, and even killed some of them.

What should the householder do? He could have sent his armies to destroy these wicked men. But instead he sent his own son to them. The reference, of course, is to Jesus Christ, the Son of God. He is "the Heir" (Heb. 1:2). Instead of receiving and honoring the son, the men cast him out of the vineyard and killed him. Jesus was crucified "outside the gate" (Heb. 13:12-13, NASB), rejected by His own nation.

The people listening to the parable were caught up in the drama and did not realize that they passed sentence on themselves. Jesus quoted Psalm 118:22-23 to explain that He was that Son and the religious leaders were the husbandmen (Matt. 21:45). The crowds had quoted from Psalm 118:26 when they had welcomed Jesus into the city, so this Scripture was fresh in the minds of the rulers.

Often in the Old Testament, God is referred to as a rock or a stone (Deut. 32:4, 18, 30-31; Ps. 18:2, 31, 46). The stone is also a messianic title. To Israel, Jesus was a stumbling stone (Isa. 8:14-15; Rom. 9:32-33; 1 Cor. 1:23). Israel rejected the Messiah, but in His death and resurrection He created the church. To the church, Jesus is the foundation stone, the head of the corner (Eph. 2:20-22; 1 Peter 2:4-5). At the end of the age, Jesus will come as the smiting stone (Dan. 2:34), destroy Gentile kingdoms, and establish His own glorious kingdom.

Of course, the Jewish leaders knew the messianic import of the Scripture Jesus quoted. They were the *builders* who rejected the stone (Acts 4:11). What were the consequences? For one thing, the kingdom would be taken from Israel and given to another nation, the church (1 Peter 2:9, and note the context, 1 Peter 2:6-10). Those who would attack this stone would be "pulverized"; those whom Christ judges will be crushed to bits.

They rejected the Holy Spirit (vv. 1-14). This parable must not be confused with the Parable of the Great Supper (Luke 14:16-24) even though they have elements in common. Again we meet the Father and the Son; and the Son is alive (in spite of what the husbandmen did) and has a bride. The suggestion is that the Lord Jesus and His church are depicted (Eph. 5:22-33). The period described in this parable must be after His resurrection and ascension and the coming of the Holy Spirit.

The Father is still inviting the people of Israel to come, in spite of what they did to His Son. When we study the first seven chapters of Acts, we discover that the message is going out to none but Jews (Acts 2:5, 10, 14, 22, 36; 3:25; 6:7). "To the Jew first" was God's plan (Acts 3:26; Rom. 1:16). How did the nation's leaders respond to the ministry of the Holy Spirit through the Apostles? They rejected the Word and persecuted the church. The same rulers who permitted John to be killed, and who asked for Jesus to be killed, themselves killed Stephen! Later, Herod killed James (Acts 12:1ff).

How did the king in the parable respond to the way the people treated his servants? He became angry and sent his armies to destroy them and their city. He then turned to other people and invited them to come to the feast. This is a picture of God's dealing with Israel. They rejected the Father when they refused to obey John the Baptist's preaching. Israel rejected the Son when they arrested Him and crucified Him. In His grace and patience, God sent other witnesses. The Holy Spirit came on the early believers and they witnessed with great power that Jesus was alive and the nation could be saved (Acts 2:32-36; 3:19-26). The miracles they did were proof that God was at work in and through them.

But Israel also rejected the Holy Spirit! This was Stephen's indictment against the nation: "You do always resist the Holy Ghost" (Acts 7:51). With the stoning of Stephen, God's patience with Israel began to end, though He delayed the judgment for almost forty years. In Acts 8 we read that the message went to the Samaritans, and in Acts 10 we read that it even went to the Gentiles.

This final rejection is, to me, the awful "blasphemy against the Holy Spirit" that Jesus spoke about in Matthew 12:22-32. This was a national sin, committed by Israel. When they rejected John, they rejected the Father who sent him; but there remained the ministry of the Son. When they rejected the Son, *they were forgiven* because of their ignorance (Luke 23:34; Acts 3:17). No sinner *today* can be forgiven for rejecting Christ, for this rejection is what condemns the soul (John 3:16-22).

But there remained the ministry of the Holy Spirit. The Spirit came on the church at Pentecost, and the Apostles performed great signs and wonders (Acts 2:43; Heb. 2:1-4). The rulers rejected the witness of the Spirit, *and this brought final judgment.* They had rejected the Father, the Son, and the Spirit, and there were no more opportunities left.

This "sin against the Holy Spirit" cannot be committed today in the same way as Israel committed it, because the situation is different. The Spirit of God is bearing witness through the Word to the person and work of Jesus Christ. It is the Spirit who convinces the world of sin (John 16:7-11). The Spirit can be resisted by unbelievers (Acts 7:51), but nobody knows that crisis hour (if there is one) when the Spirit stops dealing with a lost sinner.

Matthew 22:11-14 seems like an appendix to the parable, but it is vitally important. The wedding garment was provided by the host so that everybody was properly attired and the poor did not feel conspicuous. Salvation is personal and individual. We must accept what God gives to us—the righteousness of Christ—and not try to make it on our own. Since these parables had a definite *national* emphasis, this *personal* emphasis at the end was most important.

The nation's leaders were guilty of spiritual blindness, hypocrisy, and deliberate disobedience to the Word. Instead of accepting this indictment from Jesus, and repenting, they decided to attack Him and argue with Him. The result: judgment. We should be careful not to follow their example of disobedience.

CHAPTER NINETEEN THE KING'S DEFENSE

Matthew 22:15-46

On Tuesday of Passover week, our Lord's enemies tried to trap Him by using a series of "loaded" questions. These men were still smarting from the treatment they had received in the series of parables He had given. He had exposed their evil intentions and warned them that they were only asking for judgment. The religious leaders did not enjoy being humiliated before the crowds. They were wholeheartedly bent on destroying Jesus, and they hoped to trap Him into saying something that would permit them to arrest Him.

But there was another reason for the questions, one that His enemies did not realize. Jesus was going to die as the Lamb of God, and it was necessary for the lamb to be examined before Passover (Ex. 12:3-6). If any blemish whatsoever was found on the lamb, it could not be sacrificed. Jesus was examined publicly by His enemies, and they could find no fault in Him.

Of course, this personal interchange between our Lord and the religious leaders was also an opportunity for them to believe and be saved. In fact, one Pharisee came very close to the kingdom (Mark 12:32-34). Even at the last minute, there is hope for the lost sinner, if he will receive the truth, repent, and believe.

There are four questions involved in this public discussion, three of them from the enemy, and one from Jesus Christ.

A Political Question about Taxes (Matt. 22:15-22)

The Pharisees and the Herodians were enemies; but their common foe brought them together. The Pharisees opposed the Roman poll tax for several reasons: (1) They did not want to submit to a Gentile power; (2) Caesar was revered as a god; and (3) they had better uses for the money than to give it to Rome. Since the Herodians were the party supporting Herod, they were in favor of the tax. After all, Herod's authority was given to him by Caesar; and Herod would have had a difficult time staying in power without Rome's support.

Palestine was an occupied nation, and the Jews had no special love for their conquerors. Every tax the poor people had to pay was another reminder that they were not free. The Zealots, an "underground" organization of fanatical Jews, often staged protests against Rome. They would oppose any Roman tax.

It is easy to see why the Pharisees and Herodians chose the poll tax as the bait for their trap. It appeared that no matter which side Jesus took, He would create problems for Himself and His ministry. If He opposed the tax, He would be in trouble with Rome. If He approved the tax, He would be in trouble with the Jews.

Jesus immediately saw through their scheme. He knew that their real purpose was not to get an answer to a question, but to try to trap Him. They were only acting a part, and this made them hypocrites. On this basis alone, He could have refused to answer them. But He knew the people around Him would not understand. Here was an opportunity for Him to silence His enemies and, at the same time, teach the people an important spiritual truth.

Each ruler minted his own coins and put his own image on them. The "penny" (denarius) had Caesar's image on it, so it belonged to Caesar. "Give back to Caesar what belongs to Caesar," was His reply. "And give back to God what belongs to God." In this simple, but profound reply, Jesus taught several important truths.

Christians must honor and obey rulers. This is taught elsewhere in the New Testament (Rom. 13; 1 Peter 2:13-17; 1 Tim. 2:1ff). Christians have a dual citizenship, in heaven (Phil. 3:20) and on earth. We must respect our earthly rulers (or elected leaders), obey the law, pay taxes, and pray for all who are in authority.

Christians must honor and obey God. Caesar was not God. While governments cannot enforce religion (Acts 5:29), neither should they restrict freedom of worship. The best citizen honors his country because he worships God.

Man bears God's image and owes God his all. Caesar's image was on the coin; God's image is on man (Gen. 1:26-27). Sin has marred that image, but through Jesus Christ, it can be restored (Eph. 4:24; Col. 3:10).

The relationship between religion and government is personal and individual. It is right for the people of God to serve in government (remember Daniel and Joseph). But it is wrong for government to control the church, or for the church to control government.

A Doctrinal Question about the Resurrection (Matt. 22:23-33)

In spite of the fact that the Pharisees and Herodians had been worsted, the Sadducees entered the field and tried *their* attack. Keep in mind that this group accepted only the authority of the five Books of Moses. The Sadducees did not believe in a spirit world or in the doctrine of the resurrection (Acts 23:8). They had often challenged the Pharisees to prove the doctrine of the resurrection from Moses, but the Pharisees were not too successful with their arguments.

The Sadducees' hypothetical illustration was based on the Jewish law of "levirate marriage" from Deuteronomy 25:5-10. (The word *levirate* comes form the Latin word *levir* which means "a husband's brother." It has nothing to do with the tribe of Levi.) The purpose of this custom was to preserve a man's name should he die without a male heir. In a nation like Israel, where family inheritance was a major thing, it was important that each home have an heir. It was considered a disgrace for a man to refuse to raise up a family for his dead brother.

The Sadducees based their disbelief of the resurrection on the fact that no woman could have seven husbands in the future life. Like many people today, they conceived of the future life as an extension of their present life—only better.

But Jesus told them that they were ignorant. They did not know the Scriptures, nor did they know the power of God, which inferred that they really did not know God. There will be no need for marriage in the next life because there will be no death. Therefore it will not be necessary to bear children to replace those who die.

Jesus did *not* say that we would be angels when we are glorified in heaven. He said we would be *"as* the angels" in that we would be sexless and not married or given in marriage. The foolish stories we hear and the cartoons we see about people dying and becoming angels are certainly unbiblical.

Our Lord was not content to refute the Sadducees' foolish views about the future life. He also wanted to answer their claim that there was no resurrection; *and He did it by referring to Moses!* He knew that Moses was the only authority they would accept. He reminded them of Exodus 3:6 where God said to Moses, "I am the God of Abraham, and the God of Isaac, and the God of Jacob." He did not say, "I *was* the God of Abraham," for that would mean that Abraham was no more. By saying "I am," the Lord made it clear that these three men of faith were *at that time alive.* And by repeating "the God of," the Lord was saying that He knew them and loved them personally and individually.

It is a dangerous thing to speculate about the future life. We must rest on the authority of the Word of God, for only there do we have truth that answers man's questions about the future. The Bible does not tell us everything about the future life, but it does encourage and enlighten us. Jesus answered the foolish, ignorant Sadducees so completely that they were "muzzled" (the word *silence* in Matt. 22:34). Even the crowds were astonished and amazed at His answer.

An Ethical Question about the Law (Matt. 22:34-40)

The Pharisees probably enjoyed the embarrassment of their enemies, the Sadducees. One of their number showed respect for the Lord and His answer (Mark 12:28) and asked a question of his own: "Teacher, which is the great commandment in the Law?" (Matt. 22:36, NASB) We have every reason to believe that he asked the question in sincerity and with a humble attitude.

This was not a new question, for the scribes had been debating it for centuries. They had documented 613 commandments in the Law, 248 positive and 365 negative. No person could ever hope to know and fully obey all of these commandments. So, to make it easier, the experts divided the commandments into "heavy" (important) and "light" (unimportant). A person could major on the "heavy commandments" and not worry about the trivial ones.

The fallacy behind this approach is obvious: You need only break *one law,* heavy or light, to be guilty before God. "For whosoever shall keep the whole Law, and yet offend in one point, he is guilty of all" (James 2:10).

Jesus quoted the "Shema" (Deut. 6:4), a statement of faith that was recited daily by every orthodox Jew. (The word *Shema* comes from the Hebrew word which means "to hear.") The confession of faith begins with, "Hear, O Israel!") The greatest commandment is to love God with all that we are and have—heart, soul, mind, strength, possessions, service. To love God is not to "have good feelings about Him," for true love involves the will as well as the heart. Where there is love, there will be service and obedience.

But love for God cannot be divorced from love for one's neighbor; so Jesus also quoted Leviticus 19:18 and put it on the same level as the Shema. All of the Law and the Prophets hang on *both* of these commandments. We might add that the teachings of the Epistles in the New Testament agree with this statement. If a man really loves God, he must also love his brother and his neighbor (1 John 3:10-18; 4:7-21).

If we have a right relationship with God, we will have no problems with His commandments. Love is the basis for obedience. In fact, all of the Law is summed up in love (Rom. 13:8-10). If we love God, we will love our neighbor; and if we love our neighbor, we will not want to do anything to harm him.

But Jesus had a deeper meaning to convey in this marvelous answer. The Jews were afraid of idolatry. When Jesus claimed to be God, they opposed Him because they could not believe it was right to worship a creature. Jesus received worship and did not rebuke those who honored Him. Was this idolatry? No, because He is God! But if the Law commands us to love God *and our neighbor,* then it would not be wrong for the Jews to love

Jesus. Instead, they were plotting to kill Him. He had said to them one day, "If God were your Father, you would love Me" (John 8:42). They accepted the authority of the Law, yet they refused to obey it in their lives.

The scribe who had asked the original question seemed to be an honest and sincere man. Not all of the Pharisees were hypocrites. He publicly agreed with Jesus (Mark 12:32-33). This must have given his fellow Pharisees a fright. Jesus discerned that the man's heart was sincere, and He commended him for his intelligence and honesty. Did the man ever get all the way into the kingdom, when he was so very near? We trust so.

Jesus had now answered three difficult questions. He had dealt with the relationship between religion and government, between this life and the next life, and between God and our neighbors. These are fundamental relationships, and we cannot ignore our Lord's teachings. But there is a question more fundamental than these, and Jesus asked it of His enemies.

A Personal Question about the Messiah (Matt. 22:41-46)

Jesus did not phrase this question as He had when He asked His disciples, "Whom say you that I am?" (Matt. 16:15) These men who had been arguing with Him were not sympathetic with His cause, nor were they honest in their assessment of His credentials. Jesus had to take an indirect approach with His enemies. He made this sound like another theological question, when in reality it was the most important *personal* question they would ever face.

"Whose Son is the Messiah?" He asked them. As trained experts in the Law, they knew the answer: "He is the Son of David." Had they been asked, they could have referred to numbers of Old Testament Scriptures, including 2 Samuel 7:12-13; Psalm 78:68-72; and Micah 5:2. Once they had given this answer, Jesus asked a second question, this time quoting from Psalm 110:1—"The LORD [Jehovah] said unto my Lord [Hebrew "Adonai"], 'Sit Thou at My right hand, until I make Thine enemies Thy footstool.' "

Every orthodox Jewish scholar interpreted this to refer to the Messiah. Only the Messiah could sit at the right hand of Jehovah God. Jesus believed in the inspiration and accuracy of the Old Testament Scriptures, for He said that David spoke these words "in the Spirit" (Matt. 22:43, NASB). Nobody dared to question the accuracy or the authority of the text.

"If Messiah is David's Son," Jesus asked, "then how could Messiah also be David's Lord?" There is only one answer to this question. As God, Messiah is David's Lord; as man, He is David's Son. He is both "the root and the offspring of David" (Rev. 22:16). Psalm 110:1 teaches the deity and the humanity of Messiah. He is David's Lord and He is David's Son.

When He was ministering on earth, Jesus often accepted the messianic title "Son of David" (see Matt. 9:27; 12:23; 15:22; 20:30-31; 21:9, 15). The rulers had heard the multitudes proclaim Him as "Son of David" when He rode into Jerusalem. The fact that He accepted this title is evidence that Jesus knew Himself to be the Messiah, the Son of God. As God, He was David's Lord; but as man, He was David's Son, for He was born into the family of David (Matt. 1:1, 20).

The scholars in that day were confused about the Messiah. They saw two pictures of Messiah in the Old Testament and could not reconcile them. One picture showed a Suffering Servant, the other a conquering and reigning Monarch. Were there two Messiahs? How could God's servant suffer and die? (see 1 Peter 1:10-12)

Had they listened to what Jesus said, they would have learned that there was only one Messiah, but that He would be both human and divine. He would suffer and die as a sacrifice for sins. He would then rise from the dead in triumph, and one day return to defeat His enemies. However, these religious leaders had their own ideas, and they did not want to change. If they had accepted His teaching, then they would also have to accept Him as the Messiah; and this they were unwilling to do.

The result of this day of dialogue was silence on the part of His enemies. They dared not ask Jesus any more questions, not because they had believed the truth, but because they were afraid to face the truth. "For they did not have courage to question Him any longer about anything" (Luke 20:40, NASB). But neither did they have courage to face the truth and act on it.

Making a decision about Jesus Christ is a matter of life or death. The evidence is there for all to examine. We can examine it defensively and miss the truth. Or we can examine it honestly and humbly, and discover the truth, believe, and be saved. The religious leaders were so blinded by tradition, position, and selfish pride that they could not—and *would* not—see the truth and receive it.

We dare not make the same mistake today.

CHAPTER TWENTY
THE KING'S DENUNCIATION
Matthew 23

This was our Lord's last public message. It is a scathing denunciation of false religion that paraded under the guise of truth. Some of the common people no doubt were shocked at His words, for they considered the Pharisees to be righteous.

Perhaps we should remind ourselves that not all of the Pharisees were hypocrites. There were about 6,000 Pharisees in that day, with many more who were "followers" but not full members of the group. Most of the Pharisees were middle-class businessmen and no doubt they were sincere in their quest for truth and holiness. The name "Pharisees" came from a word that means "to separate." The Pharisees were separated from the Gentiles, the "unclean" Jews who did not practice the Law ("publicans and sinners," Luke 15:1-2), and from any who opposed the tradition that governed their lives.

Among the Pharisees were a few members who sought for true spiritual religion. Nicodemus (John 3; 7:50-53), Joseph of Arimathea (John 19:38ff), and the unnamed man mentioned in Mark 12:32-34, come to mind. Even Gamaliel showed a great deal of tolerance toward the newly formed church (Acts 5:34ff). But for the most part, the Pharisees used their religion to promote themselves and their material gain. No wonder Jesus denounced them. Note the three divisions in this message.

Explanation to the Crowd (Matt. 23:1-12)

In this section, Jesus explained the basic flaws of pharisaical religion.

They had a false concept of righteousness (vv. 2-3). To begin with, they had assumed an authority not their own. "The scribes and the Pharisees *have seated themselves* in Moses' seat" is the literal translation. There is no record in the Scriptures that God assigned any authority to this group. Their only authority was the Word of God. Therefore, the people were to obey whatever the Pharisees taught *from the Word.* But the people were not to obey the traditions and the man-made rules of the Pharisees.

To the Pharisee, righteousness meant outward conformity to the Law of God. They ignored the inward condition of the heart. Religion consisted in obeying numerous rules that goverened every detail of life, including what you did with the spices in your cupboard (Matt. 23:23-24). The Pharisees were careful to say the right words and follow the right ceremonies, but they did not *inwardly* obey the Law. God desired truth in the inward parts (Ps. 51:6). To preach one thing and practice another is only hypocrisy.

They had a false concept of ministry (v. 4). To them, ministry meant handing down laws to the people and adding to their burdens. In other words, the Pharisees were harder on others than they were on themselves. Jesus came to lighten men's burdens (Matt. 11:28-30), but legalistic religion always seeks to make burdens heavier. Jesus never asks us to do anything that He has not first done. The Pharisees commanded, but they did not participate. They were hypocritical religious dictators, not spiritual leaders.

They had a false concept of greatness (vv. 5-12). To them, success meant recognition by men and praise from men. They were not concerned about the approval of God. They used their religion to attract attention, not to glorify God (Matt. 5:16). This even meant using religious ornaments to display their piety. "Phylacteries" were small leather boxes into which the Pharisees placed portions of the Scriptures. They wore these boxes on their foreheads and arms, in literal obedience to Deuteronomy 6:8 and 11:18. They also increased the size of their "tassels" on the hems of their garments (Num. 15:38; see Matt. 9:20).

The Pharisees also thought that *position* was a mark of greatness, so they sought the best seats in the synagogue and at the public dinners. Where a man sits bears no relationship to what a man is. Albert Einstein wrote,

"Try not to become a man of success, but rather try to become a man of value."

They also thought that *titles of honor* were a mark of greatness. The title "rabbi" means "my great one" and was coveted by the religious leaders. (Today religious leaders covet honorary doctor's degrees.) Jesus forbad His disciples to use the title *rabbi* because all of them were brothers, and Jesus alone was their Teacher ("Master" in Matt. 23:8). There is a spiritual equality among the children of God, under the lordship of Jesus Christ.

Jesus also forbad them to use the title *father* with reference to spiritual things. Certainly it is not wrong to call one's biological father by that name, but it is wrong to use it when addressing a spiritual leader. Paul referred to himself as a "spiritual father" because he had begotten people through the Gospel (1 Cor. 4:15). But he did not ask them to use that term when addressing him.

A third title that was forbidden was *master* (Matt. 23:10), which means "guide, instructor, leader." This is not the same word that is translated "Master" in Matthew 23:8 in the *King James Version.* That word means "teacher," while this one means "one who goes before and guides." Perhaps a modern equivalent would be "authority." God has placed spiritual leaders in the church, but they must not replace God in our lives. A true spiritual leader directs his people into freedom and a closer fellowship with Christ, not into bondage to his ideas and beliefs.

True greatness is found in serving others, not in forcing others to serve us (John 3:30; 13:12-17). True greatness is not manufactured; it can only come from God as we obey Him. If we exalt ourselves, God will humble us. But if we humble ourselves, in due time God will exalt us (1 Peter 5:6).

Denunciation of the Pharisees (Matt. 23:13-36)

We must not read this series of denunciations with the idea that Jesus lost His temper and was bitterly angry. Certainly He was angry at their sins, and what those sins were doing to the people. But His attitude was one of painful sorrow that the Pharisees were blinded to God's truth and to their own sins.

Perhaps the best way to deal with these eight "woes" is to contrast them with the eight beatitudes found in Matthew 5:1-12. In the Sermon on the Mount the Lord described true righteousness; here He described a false righteousness.

Entering the kingdom—shutting up the kingdom (v. 13; 5:3). The poor in spirit enter the kingdom, but the proud in spirit keep themselves out and even keep others out. The Greek verb indicates people trying to get in who cannot. It is bad enough to keep yourself out of the kingdom, but worse when you stand in the way of others. By teaching man-made traditions instead of God's truth, they "took away the key of knowledge" and closed the door to salvation (Luke 11:52).

Mourners comforted—destroyers condemned (v. 14; 5:4). While this verse is not in some manuscripts of Matthew, it is found in Mark 12:40 and Luke 20:47. Instead of mourning over their own sins, and mourning with needy widows, the Pharisees took advantage of people in order to rob them. They used their religion as a "cloak of covetousness" (1 Thes. 2:5).

Meek inherit the earth—proud send souls to hell (v. 15; 5:5). A proselyte is a convert to a cause. The Pharisees were out to win others to their legalistic system, yet they could not introduce these people to the living God. Instead of saving souls, the Pharisees were condemning souls!

A "child of hell" is the equivalent of "child of the devil," which is what Jesus called the Pharisees (Matt. 12:34; 23:33; John 8:44). A "child of the devil" is a person who has rejected God's way of salvation (righteousness through faith in Christ). This person parades his own self-righteousness through whatever religious system he belongs to. The convert usually shows more zeal than his leader, and this "double devotion" only produces double condemnation. How tragic that people can think they are going to heaven, when actually they are going to hell!

Hungering for holiness—greedy for gain (vv. 16-22; 5:6). "Blind guides" is a perfect description, one that must have brought a smile to the lips of the listeners. Jesus had used it before (Matt. 15:14). The Pharisees were blind to the true values of life. Their priorities were confused. They would take an oath and use some sacred object to substantiate that oath—the gold in the temple, for example, or the gift on the altar. But they would not swear by the temple itself or the altar. It was the temple that sanctified the gold and the altar that sanctified the gift. They were leaving God out of their priorities.

Jesus knew that the Pharisees wanted both

the gold and the gifts on the altar. This is why the Pharisees practiced "Corban"—anything dedicated to God could not be used for others (Matt. 15:1-9; Mark 7:10-13). These men were not seeking for the righteousness of God; they were greedy for gain. They worked out a "religious system" that permitted them to rob God and others and still maintain their reputations.

Obtaining mercy—rejecting mercy (vv. 23-24; 5:7). The Pharisees majored on minors. They had rules for every minute area of life, while at the same time they forgot about the important things. It is usually the case that legalists are sticklers for details, but blind to great principles. This crowd thought nothing of condemning an innocent man, yet they were afraid to enter Pilate's judgment hall lest they be defiled (John 18:28).

There is no question that the Old Testament Law required tithing (Lev. 27:30; Deut. 14:22ff). Abraham had practiced tithing long before the Law was given (Gen. 14:20), and Jacob followed his grandfather's example (Gen. 28:20-22). The principles of Christian giving under grace are given in 2 Corinthians 8–9. We are not content simply to give a tithe (10 percent), but we also want to bring offerings to the Lord out of hearts filled with love.

Justice, mercy, and faithfulness are the important qualities God is seeking. Obeying the rules is no substitute. While it is good to pay attention to details, we must never lose our sense of priorities in spiritual matters. Jesus did not condemn the practice of tithing. But He did condemn those who allowed their legalistic scruples to keep them from developing true Christian character.

Pure in heart—defiled in heart (vv. 25-28; 5:8). Jesus used two illustrations: the cup and platter, and the sepulcher. They both stated the same truth: it is possible to be clean on the outside and at the same time defiled on the inside. Imagine using dishes that were defiled! Whatever you put into the dish or cup would also become defiled. The Pharisees were careful to keep the outside very clean, because that was the part that men would see; and they wanted the praise of men. But God sees the heart (1 Sam. 16:7). When God looked within, He saw "greed and self-indulgence" (Matt. 23:25, NIV).

Jewish people were careful not to touch dead bodies or anything relating to the dead, because this would make them ceremonially unclean (Num. 19:11ff). They would whitewash the tombs lest someone accidentally get defiled, and this was done especially at Passover season. What a graphic picture of the hypocrite: white on the outside, but filled with defilement and death on the inside!

"Blessed are the pure in heart," was our Lord's promise. "Watch over your heart with all diligence, for from it flow the springs of life" (Prov. 4:23, NASB). D.L. Moody used to say, "If I take care of my character, my reputation will take care of itself." The Pharisees lived for reputation, not character.

Peacemakers and persecuted are God's children—persecutors are the devil's children (vv. 29-33; 5:9-12). When Jesus called the Pharisees "serpents . . . generation of vipers," He was identifying them with Satan who is the serpent (Gen. 3:1ff). In His Parable of the Tares, Jesus made it clear that *Satan has a family* (Matt. 13:38). Satan is a murderer and a liar (John 8:44), and his children follow his example. The Pharisees were liars (Matt. 23:30) and murderers (Matt. 23:34).

It was traditional for the Pharisees to build, improve, and embellish the tombs of the martyrs. But it was "their fathers" who killed the martyrs! Not their biological fathers, of course, but their "spiritual fathers"—the hypocrites of the past ages.

There have always been counterfeit believers in the world, starting with Cain (Gen. 4:1-15; 1 John 3:10-15). The Pharisees and their kind are guilty of all the righteous blood shed in the name of "religion." The first martyr recorded in Old Testament Scripture was Abel (Gen. 4), and the last one recorded was the Prophet Zechariah (2 Chron. 24:20-22—the Hebrew Bible ends with 2 Chronicles, not Malachi).

What will be the result of this long history of murders? Terrible judgment! "This generation" (the "generation of vipers," Matt. 23:33) would taste the wrath of God when the cup of iniquity was full (Gen. 15:16; Matt. 23:32). Some of this judgment came when Jerusalem was destroyed, and the rest will be meted out in eternity.

As we review these tragic *woes* from the lips of our Lord, we can see why the Pharisees were His enemies. He emphasized the inner man; they were concerned with externals. He taught a spiritual life based on principles, while the Pharisees majored on rules and regulations. Jesus measured spirituality in terms of character, while the Pharisees measured it in terms of religious activities and conformity to external laws. Jesus taught humility and sacrificial service; but the Pharisees were proud and used people to accomplish their own purposes. The holy life of Jesus exposed their artificial piety and shallow religion. Instead of coming out of the darkness, the Pharisees tried to put out the Light; and they failed.

Lamentation over Jerusalem (Matt. 23:37-39)

Jesus spoke these words of lamentation as a sincere expression of His love for Jersualem, and His grief over the many opportunities for salvation that they had passed by. "Jerusalem" refers to the entire nation of Israel. The nation's leaders had been guilty of repeated crimes as they rejected God's messengers, and even killed some of them. But in His grace, Jesus came to gather the people and save them.

"I would have . . . ye would not" summarizes the tragedy of final rejection of the truth. There is no argument here about divine sovereignty and human responsibility, for both are included. God could not force His salvation on the people; neither could He change the consequences of their stubborn rejection. "You will not come to Me that you may have life" (John 5:40).

The image of the mother bird gathering and covering her brood is a familiar one. Moses used it in his farewell sermon (Deut. 32:11). It is a picture of love, tender care, and a willingness to die to protect others. Jesus did die for the sins of the world, including the nation of Israel: but "His own received Him not" (John 1:11).

"Your house" probably means both the temple and the city, both of which would be destroyed in A.D. 70 by invading Roman armies. The temple was "My house" in Matthew 21:13, but now it has been abandoned and left empty. Jesus left both the temple and the city and went out to the Mount of Olives (Matt. 24:1-3).

Yet, Jesus left the nation with a promise: He would one day return, the nation would see Him and say, "Blessed be He that cometh in the name of the Lord!" This is a quotation from Psalm 118:26, that great messianic psalm that was quoted so many times in His last week of ministry. The crowds had used those words on Palm Sunday (Matt. 21:9).

When would this promise be fulfilled? At the end of the age when Jesus Christ returns to earth to deliver Israel and defeat their enemies (Zech. 12; Rom. 11:25-27). The fact that Israel rejected the King would not hinder God's great plan of redemption. Instead of establishing His glorious kingdom on earth, Jesus would build His church (Matt. 16:18; Eph. 2:11-22). When that work is finished, He will return and take His church to heaven (1 Thes. 4:13-18). Then there will be a time of judgment on earth ("the Day of the Lord," "the time of Jacob's trouble"), at the end of which He will return to deliver Israel.

We cannot read this severe denunciation without marveling at the patience and goodness of the Lord. No nation has been blessed like Israel, and yet no nation has sinned against God's goodness as has Israel. They have been the channel of God's blessing to the world, for "salvation is of the Jews" (John 4:22). Yet they have suffered greatly in this world.

Jesus was born a Jew, and He loved His nation. We who are Gentiles ought to thank God for the Jews, for they gave us the witness of the one true God, they gave us the Bible, and they gave us Jesus Christ the Saviour. Like Jesus, we ought to love the Jews, seek to win them, pray for the peace of Jerusalem, and encourage them every way we can.

CHAPTER TWENTY-ONE THE KING'S RETURN—PART 1

Matthew 24:1-44

The Olivet Discourse grew out of some questions the disciples asked when Jesus told them that the temple would one day be destroyed. First, they wanted to know *when*. This answer is not recorded in Matthew but is given in Luke 21:20-24. Second, they asked about the sign of Christ's return. This is answered in Matthew 24:29-44. In their final question, they asked about the sign of the end of the age. Christ's reply is in Matthew 24:4-8.

We must keep in mind that the "atmosphere" of this discourse is *Jewish*. Jesus talked about Judea (Matt. 24:16), the Sabbath (Matt. 24:20), and the prophecies of Daniel concerning the Jewish people (Matt. 24:15). The full truth about the Rapture of the church (1 Cor. 15:51ff; 1 Thes. 4:13-18) had not yet been revealed, for it was a mystery (Eph. 3:1-12).

Matthew 24:1-44 indicates that our Lord was discussing events that will take place on earth during the time of Tribulation. (See Matt. 24:8, where "birth-pangs" are a symbol of the Tribulation; and see also Matt. 24:21, 29). After the church has been suddenly taken out of the world, there will be a period of "peace and safety" (1 Thes. 5:1-4) followed by a time of terrible suffering. Many Bible scholars believe this period will last seven years (Dan. 9:24-27). It is this period of "Tribulation" that Jesus described in the Olivet Discourse. At the end of that period, Jesus will return to the earth, defeat His foes, and establish the promised kingdom.

In the section before us, Jesus explained three different periods in the time of the Tribulation.

The Beginning of the Tribulation (Matt. 24:4-14)

The events described in this section are "the beginning of birth-pangs" (Matt. 24:8). The image of a woman in travail is a picture of the Tribulation period (Isa. 13:6-11; 1 Thes. 5:5). Let's consider some of the significant events that will occur at the beginning of this period.

Religious deception (vv. 4-5). The Jews have often been led astray by false prophets and false christs. The rider on the white horse in Revelation 6:1-2 is the Antichrist, that final world dictator who will lead the nations astray. He will begin his career as a peacemaker, signing a covenant with Israel to protect her from her enemies (Dan. 9:27). Israel will welcome this man as their great benefactor (John 5:43).

Wars (v. 6). Note that wars are not a sign of the end. There have always been wars in the world, and will be until the very end. Wars of themselves do not announce the end of the age or the coming of the Lord.

Famines (v. 7a). War and famine usually go together. Revelation 6:6 suggests terribly high prices for staple foods, for a "penny" was a day's wages.

Death (vv. 7b-8). Earthquakes help to create famines, and both help to cause epidemics that take many lives.

Martyrs (v. 9). Christians have always been hated by the world, but here we have an acceleration of persecutions and murders. All nations will be involved. This certainly was not true in the history of the early church.

Worldwide chaos (vv. 10-13). Those who once were true to each other will betray each other. This suggests that marriages, homes, and nations will be torn asunder because of lack of loyalty. Lawlessness will abound (Matt. 24:12), for even the law enforcement agencies will not be able to keep the peace.

Matthew 24:13 has nothing to do with personal salvation in this present age of grace. "The end" does not mean the end of this life; it refers to the end of the age (Matt. 24:14). Those believers on earth during this terrible period, who endure in their faith, will be saved when the Lord comes at the end and delivers them.

Worldwide preaching (v. 14). Revelation 7:1-8 teaches that God will choose and seal 144,000 Jewish evangelists who will carry the kingdom message to the ends of the earth. This verse does not teach that the Gospel of God's grace must be spread to every nation today before Jesus can return for His church. It is the Lord's return *at the end of the age* that is in view here.

The Middle of the Tribulation (Matt. 24:15-22)

The midpoint of the Tribulation period is most important, for at that time an event will take place that was prophesied centuries ago by Daniel (Dan. 9:24-27). Please notice that this prophecy concerns only the Jews and the city of Jerusalem ("thy people and . . . thy holy city," Dan. 9:24). To apply it to the church or to any other people or place is to misinterpret God's Word.

The prophecy involves seventy weeks, and the Hebrew word "week" means "a week of years," or seven years. Seventy sevens would equal 490 years. But this period of 490 years is broken up into three parts:

(1) During seven weeks (49 years) the city of Jerusalem would be rebuilt and the worship reestablished.

(2) After 63 weeks (434 years) Messiah would come to Jerusalem and die for the sins of the world.

(3) The prince will make an agreement with

the Jews for one week (seven years) to protect them from their enemies.

The decree to rebuild Jerusalem was given in 445 B.C. by Cyrus (2 Chron. 36:22-23; Ezra 1). The city was rebuilt in troubled times. Sir Robert Anderson in his classic book *The Coming Prince* (Kregel, 1975) has proved that there were exactly 482 prophetic years (of 360 days each) between the giving of the decree and the day that Jesus rode into Jerusalem as the King.

But we must account for the remaining "week" of seven years. Where does it fit in? Note that the same city that was rebuilt will also be destroyed "by the people of the prince that shall come" (Dan. 9:26), that is, the Romans. ("The prince that shall come" is a name for the Antichrist.) This event took place in A.D. 70. But the Jewish nation would be spared and the city restored again. For at some future date, the prince that shall come (Antichrist) will make a covenant with the Jews *for seven years.* This is where the missing "week" fits in. He will agree to protect them from their enemies and permit them to rebuild their temple. (Dan. 9:27 talks about a restoration of the sacrifices, and this would demand a temple.)

The logical place for this seven-year period is after the Rapture of the church. "The time of Jacob's trouble," the Tribulation period, will be seven years long. Second Thessalonians 2:1-12 indicates that the Antichrist cannot be revealed until the *restrainer* is taken out of the midst. That restrainer is the Holy Spirit in the church. Once the church is out of the world, then Satan can produce his masterpiece, the Antichrist.

He will make the agreement for seven years, but after three-and-one-half years ("in the midst of the week") he will break that agreement. He will then move into the Jewish temple himself and proclaim that he is God (2 Thes. 2:3-4; Rev. 13).

The Antichrist will cause a living statue of himself to be put into the temple, and his associate (the false prophet, Rev. 20:10) will cause the whole earth to worship it. Satan has always wanted the world's worship, and in the middle of the Tribulation he will begin to receive it (Matt. 4:8-11). Jesus called this statue "the abomination of desolation" (Dan. 9:27; Matt. 24:15).

An interesting parenthesis occurs at the end of Matthew 24:15—"whoso readeth, let him understand." This statement indicates that what Jesus was teaching would have greater significance for people reading Matthew's Gospel in the latter days. By reading the Prophet Daniel and the words of Jesus, these believers will understand the events and know what to do. This is another evidence that the Olivet Discourse applies to people during the Tribulation period.

Prophetic scholars have speculated as to why the Antichrist would break his covenant with the Jews after three-and-one-half years. It has been suggested that the invasion of Israel by Russia, prophesied in Ezekiel 38–39, would occur at that point. Certainly Israel will be at ease and dwelling in safety at that time, for she will be protected by the Antichrist (Ezek. 38:11). At that time, he will be the ruler of a ten-nation alliance, "The United States of Europe" (Rev. 17:12-13). Russia, of course, will be soundly beaten, not by Israel, but by Almighty God. When the Antichrist sees that his great enemy, Russia, has been beaten, he will take advantage of the opportunity and move into Israel, breaking his covenant and taking over the temple.

The readers of this prophecy in the latter days will know what to do: Get out of Judea! These instructions are similar to those given in Luke 21:20ff, but they refer to a different time period. Luke's instructions apply to the siege of Jerusalem in A.D. 70, and the "sign" was the gathering of the armies around the city. Matthew's instructions apply to Jewish believers in the middle of the Tribulation, and the "sign" is the desecration of the temple by the image of the Antichrist. Those who have confused those two "sign events" have ended up believing that Jesus Christ returned in A.D. 70!

This entire paragraph relates only to Jews, for no Christian believer would worry about breaking a Sabbath law. This event ushers in "the Great Tribulation," the last half of Daniel's seventieth week, when the judgments of God will be hurled on the earth. During the first three-and-one-half years of the Tribulation, the judgments were natural: wars, famines, earthquakes, etc. But during the last half, the judgments will be supernatural and devastating.

During this period, God will care for His elect (Matt. 24:22), referring to Jews and Gentiles who believe and are converted. "The elect" here does not refer to the church since the church will have been raptured at least three-and-one-half years previously.

The End of the Tribulation (Matt. 24:23-44)

World conditions will be so terrible that men will wonder if any relief will come, and this will give false christs opportunities to deceive many. Satan is capable of performing "lying wonders" (2 Thes. 2:9-12; Rev. 13:13-14). The fact that a religious leader performs miracles is no assurance that he has come from God. Many Jews will be deceived, for "the Jews require a sign" (1 Cor. 1:22). Jesus performed true signs in His Father's name, and the nation rejected Him (John 12:37ff). Satan's miracles they will accept.

Matthew 24:27 indicates that the return of Jesus to the earth will be sudden, like a stroke of lightning. The event that precedes His return is the gathering of the Gentile nations at Armageddon (Rev. 16:13-16; 19:11ff). The eagles flying around the carcass picture the awful carnage that will result from this great battle (Rev. 19:17-19). The cosmic changes mentioned in Matthew 24:29 precede the return of Jesus Christ to the earth.

We are not told what "the sign of the Son of man in heaven" is, but the people on earth at that time will recognize it. When Jesus comes for the church, He will come in the air and His people will be caught up to meet Him in the air (1 Thes. 4:17). But our Lord's second coming at the end of the Tribulation will be a great public event, with every eye seeing Him (Rev. 1:7).

This event will have special meaning for Israel. Jesus will return at that hour when Israel is about to be defeated by the Gentile armies (Zech. 12). He will rescue His people, and they will see Him and recognize that He is their Messiah (Zech. 12:9-14). There will be a national repentance, national cleansing, and national restoration under the gracious leadership of their Messiah.

We must not confuse the trumpet of Matthew 24:31 with the "trump of God" mentioned in 1 Thessalonians 4:16. "His elect" in Matthew 24:31 refers to people on earth, Jews and Gentiles, who have trusted Christ and been saved. In the Old Testament, Israel's movements were announced by trumpet signals (Num. 10; Joel 2:1ff). Israel has been a scattered people for many centuries. The angels will gather Israel with trumpets just as the priests did in Old Testament times (Lev. 23:23-25).

Scholars of prophecy do not agree on all the details of future events. But the following summary is a fair representation of what many prophetic scholars believe as to the order of events:

1. The Rapture of the church (1 Cor. 15:51-58; 1 Thes. 4:13-18). This can occur at any time.
2. The leader of the ten European nations makes a seven-year agreement with Israel (Dan. 9:26-27).
3. After three-and-one-half years, he breaks the agreement (Dan. 9:27).
4. He moves to Jerusalem and sets up his image in the temple (2 Thes. 2:3-4; Rev. 13).
5. The Antichrist begins to control the world and forces all people to worship and obey him. At this time God sends great tribulation upon the earth (Matt. 24:21).
6. The nations gather at Armageddon to fight the Antichrist and Israel, but see the sign of Christ's coming and unite to fight Him (Zech. 12; Rev. 13:13-14; 19:11ff).
7. Jesus returns to the earth, defeats His enemies, is received by the Jews, and establishes His kingdom on earth (Rev. 19:11ff; Zech. 12:7–13:1). He will reign on earth for 1,000 years (Rev. 20:1-5).

The purpose of prophecy is not to entertain the curious, but to encourage the consecrated. Jesus closed this section of His discourse with three practical admonitions, built around three illustrations: a fig tree, Noah, and a thief in the night. Matthew 24:36 makes it clear that no one will know the day or the hour of the Lord's coming. But they can be aware of the movements of events and not be caught by surprise.

The fig tree (vv. 32-35). Luke 21:29 reads, "Behold the fig tree and all the trees" (NASB). The fig tree in the Bible is often a picture of Israel (Hosea 9:10; Luke 13:6-10); and the other trees would picture the nations of the world. Perhaps our Lord was suggesting that increased nationalism will be one of the signs of the end times. Certainly future events cast their shadows before them. "And when these things *begin* to come to pass" (Luke 21:28, italics mine) suggests that a sign need not be full-blown before it is important to God's people.

The budding of the trees indicates that summer is near. The beginning of these signs indicates that the Lord's coming is near. The generation alive on earth at that time will see these events take place. Our generation sees a foreshadowing of these signs. We do not look for signs as such; we look for the Saviour

(Phil. 3:20). Jesus can come for His church at *any* time.

The days of Noah (vv. 36-42). Here the emphasis is on the fact that the people did not know *the day* when judgment would strike. Noah and his family in the ark are a picture of God's miraculous preservation of Israel during the awful time of the Tribulation. (Enoch is a picture of the church which is raptured before the Tribulation—Gen. 5:21-24; Heb. 11:5; 1 Thes. 1:10; 5:1-10.)

What kept the people from listening to Noah's message and obeying? The common interests of life—eating, drinking, marrying, giving in marriage. They lost the *best* by living for the *good.* It is a dangerous thing to get so absorbed in the pursuits of life that we forget Jesus is coming.

The verb "taken" in Matthew 24:39-41 means "taken away in judgment." *Do not apply these verses to the Rapture of the church* when believers are caught up in the air to meet the Lord. During the Tribulation, a division will take place: Some people will perish in judgment (be taken away), while others will remain to enter into the kingdom. The use of "took them all away" in Matthew 24:39 makes this clear.

The thief in the night (vv. 42-44). Jesus used Noah to warn that men will not know *the day,* and He used the picture of the burglar to warn that they will not know *the hour.* After the Rapture of the church, there will be a time of peace and safety on earth (1 Thes. 5:1ff). Then suddenly God's judgments will fall (2 Peter 3:10ff).

People alive on earth during the Tribulation period will be able, from the Scriptures, to tell the drift of events; but they will not be able to calculate the exact day or hour of Christ's return. Added to this is the fact that the days will be "shortened . . . for the elect's sake" (Matt. 24:22). This may mean fewer days of tribulation, or it may mean fewer hours so that the people on earth suffer a bit less (Rev. 8:12).

When we combine the exhortations found in these three pictures, we end up with: "Know that He is near! Watch therefore! Be ye also ready!" Believers alive during that period of history will certainly find great comfort in the promises of the Word of God.

While the interpretation of this section relates to Israel during the Tribulation, we may apply the Word to our own hearts. We do not know when our Lord will return for His church. Therefore, we must be alert, watchful, and faithful. Jesus dealt with this in detail in the next section of the Olivet Discourse (Matt. 24:45–25:30).

How grateful we ought to be that God has not appointed us to wrath, but to obtain salvation when Jesus Christ appears. He has saved us from the wrath to come (1 Thes. 1:10; 5:9-10). As the people of God, we will certainly go through tribulation (John 16:33; Acts 14:22), but not *the* Tribulation.

CHAPTER TWENTY-TWO THE KING'S RETURN—PART 2

Matthew 24:45–25:46

We noted that the "atmosphere" of the first section of the Olivet Discourse was definitely Jewish. A careful reading of this section indicates that the "atmosphere" has changed. Jesus had been describing the sign-events of the Tribulation period, and had named one judgment after another, culminating in His return to earth. But in this section, the emphasis is on *the Lord delaying His return* (Matt. 24:48; 25:5, 19).

It seems reasonable to assign Matthew 24:45–25:30 to our present age of the church, during which time it appears that the Lord is delaying His return (2 Peter 3). The closing section (Matt. 25:31-46) describes the judgment the Lord will execute when He returns to earth. In general, the teachings in the Olivet Discourse relate to the Jews (Matt. 24:4-44), the professing church (Matt. 24:45–25:30), and the Gentile nations (Matt. 25:31-46). This corresponds with the threefold division of mankind mentioned by Paul in 1 Corinthians 10:32. We have already studied in detail our Lord's coming as it relates to Israel, so let us look at it in the two remaining relationships.

Christ's Coming and the Professing Church (Matt. 24:45–25:30)

We must not be surprised that our Lord suddenly changed from discussing His return as it relates to Israel to His return as it relates to the church. It is not uncommon in Scripture for a speaker or writer to change emphasis right in the middle of a sentence. For example, the entire Church Age occurs in the time period between the words *given* and *and* in Isaiah 9:6. A similar "leap" is seen in Isaiah 61:2, where the Church Age takes place in the period between the "year of the Lord" and the "day of vengeance."

In the section devoted to Israel, Jesus described primarily the outward events of the period; in this section, He described inward attitudes. While everyone who has trusted Jesus Christ as Saviour is going to heaven (John 3:16-18; 17:24), not every believer is ready to meet the Lord.

When Jesus Christ returns and takes His church to heaven, He will sit on His judgment seat and judge His own people (Rom. 14:10-12; 2 Cor. 5:8-11). He will not judge our sins, because these have already been judged on the cross (Rom. 8:1-4). But He will judge our works and will give rewards to those who have earned them (1 Cor. 3:9-15). These parables suggest that Jesus will judge three different groups of professed believers.

Obedient and disobedient servants (vv. 45-51). God's people on earth are called a household (Gal. 6:10; Eph. 2:19). God has put servants over each household to feed the members. This suggests to us the local church family with its spiritual leaders. The purpose of spiritual leadership is that the leaders feed the people, not that the people feed the leaders! The Apostle Peter caught this truth and emphasized it in his first letter (1 Peter 5:1-4).

It is a serious thing to be a pastor or other officer in a local church. We must take care that our motives are right and that we serve Christ and His people in love. Both in word and deed, we must lead the family in the right way (Heb. 13:7-8). The members of the family should submit to spiritual leadership, because one day both people and leaders will face the Judgment Seat of Christ (Heb. 13:17).

The servant's task is not to be popular, but to be obedient. He must feed the family the food that it needs, when it needs it. He should bring out of his "spiritual cupboard" things new and old (Matt. 13:52). Some Bible teachers, in their search for something new and exciting, forget the nutrition of the old truths of the Word. But other ministers are so wrapped up in the old that they fail to discover the new insights and new applications of the old truths. The new grows out of the old, and the old is made more meaningful by the new.

If the spiritual leader is obediently doing his job when the Lord returns, he shall be rewarded. But if that leader is not doing his job when the Lord returns, he will be dealt with in a severe way. I prefer to translate Matthew 24:51: "And shall punish him severely and appoint him his portion with the hypocrites." (Even in that day of despotic rule, it would be unthinkable for a master to cut his servant in half.) The whole picture is one of pain and loss. This does not suggest punitive measures at the Judgment Seat of Christ, because there we will have glorified bodies. But it does suggest loss of reward and loss of opportunity.

Jesus did not amplify the truth here, but from other Scriptures we learn that one reward for obedient service will be ministry in the kingdom that He will establish on earth (Luke 19:11ff). The reward for obedient service is the capacity for greater service. Not to have a place of ministry in His kingdom would, to me, be a tremendous loss.

What caused this servant's downfall? *Something went wrong in his heart:* He ceased to expect his Lord to return (Matt. 24:48). He lived like the world and mistreated his fellow servants. Whenever God's servants cannot work together, it is often because somebody has forgotten that the Lord will return. Looking for His appearing, and loving His appearing, should motivate us to be faithful and loving (1 Thes. 2:19-20; 1 John 2:28).

Wise and foolish witnesses (vv. 1-13). A wedding in that day had two parts. First, the bridegroom and his friends would go from his house to claim the bride from her parents. Then the bride and groom would return to the groom's house for the marriage feast. The suggestion here is that the groom has already claimed his bride and is now on his way back home. However, we must not press the image of the church as a bride too far, because much of this truth was not revealed until the ministry of Paul (Eph. 5:22ff).

The church has known for 2,000 years that Jesus is coming again, and yet many believers have become lethargic and drowsy. They are no longer excited about the soon-coming of the Lord. As a result, there is little effective witness given that the Lord is returning.

The oil for burning reminds us of the special oil used in the tabernacle services (Ex. 27:20-21). Oil is usually a symbol of the Spirit of

God, but I wonder if this particular oil is not also a symbol of the Word of God. The church should be "holding forth the word of life" in this dark and wicked world (Phil. 2:12-16). We need to keep the word of His patience (Rev. 3:10) and keep witnessing of the return of Jesus Christ.

When the bridegroom and bride appeared, half of the bridesmaids were unable to light their lamps because they had no oil. "Our lamps are going out!" they cried. The bridesmaids who had oil were able to light their lamps and keep them shining bright. It was they who entered into the wedding feast and not the foolish girls who had no oil. This suggests that not every professing Christian will enter heaven, for some really have not trusted Jesus Christ sincerely. Without the Spirit of God and the Word of God, there can be no true salvation.

Jesus ended this parable with the warning He had uttered before: "Watch" (Matt. 24:42; 25:13). This does not mean standing on a mountaintop gazing at the heavens (Acts 1:9-11). It means "to stay awake and be alert" (Matt. 26:38-41).

Profitable and unprofitable servants (vv. 14-30). This parable must not be confused with the Parable of the Pounds (Luke 19:11-27) though the two parables do have similarities. Please note that each servant in this parable was given money (a talent was worth about twenty years' wages) according to his ability. The man with much ability was given five talents; the man with average ability received two talents; the man with minimal ability received one talent.

The talents represent opportunities to use our abilities. If five talents were given to a person with minimal ability, he would be destroyed by the heavy responsibility. But if only one talent were given to a man of great ability, he would be disgraced and degraded. God assigns work and opportunity according to ability. We are living in the period of time between Matthew 25:18 and 19. We have been assigned our ministries according to the abilities and gifts God has given us. It is our privilege to serve the Lord and multiply His goods.

The three servants fell into two categories: faithful and unfaithful. The faithful servants took their talents and put them to work for their Lord. The unfaithful servant hid his talent in the earth. Instead of using his opportunities, he buried them! He did not purposely do evil. But by doing nothing, he was committing sin and robbing his Lord of service and increase.

The two men who put their money to work each received the same commendation (Matt. 25:21, 23). It was not the *portion* but the *proportion* that made the difference. They started as servants, but their Lord promoted them to rulers. They were faithful with a few things, so the Lord trusted them with many things. They had worked and toiled, and now they entered into joy. Their faithfulness gave each of them a capacity for greater service and responsibility.

The third servant was unfaithful and therefore was unrewarded. Because this man was afraid he might fail, he never tried to succeed. He feared life and his responsibilities. This paralyzed him with anxiety, so he buried the talent to protect it. The least he could have done was put the money in a bank and collect some interest. There was no real risk in that.

What we do not use for the Lord, we are in danger of losing. The master reprimanded the unfaithful, unprofitable servant, and then took his talent from him. The man with the most talents received the extra talent.

Some feel that this unprofitable servant was not a true believer. But it seems that he *was* a true servant, even though he proved to be unprofitable. The "outer darkness" of Matthew 25:30 need not refer to hell, even though that is often the case in the Gospels (Matt. 8:12; 22:13). It is dangerous to build theology on parables, for parables illustrate truth in vivid ways. The man was dealt with by the Lord, he lost his opportunity for service, and he gained no praise or reward. To me, that is outer darkness.

It is possible that the one-talent man thought that his one talent was not really very important. He did not have five talents, or even two. Why worry about one? *Because he was appointed as a steward by the Lord.* Were it not for the one-talent people in our world, very little would get accomplished. His one talent could have increased to two and brought glory to his master.

These three parables encourage us to love His appearing, look for His appearing, and labor faithfully until He comes. We should be watching, witnessing, and working. We may not be successful in the eyes of men, or even popular with others. But if we are faithful and profitable, we shall receive our reward.

Christ's Coming and the Gentile Nations (Matt. 25:31-46)

This section explains to us how Jesus Christ will judge the Gentile nations. The word *nations* in Matthew 25:32 means "Gentiles," and it is in the neuter gender in the Greek. The word *them* in that same verse is in the masculine. This means that the nations will be gathered before Jesus Christ, but He will judge them as *individuals*. This will not be a judgment of groups (Germany, Italy, Japan, etc.) but of individuals within these nations.

We must not confuse this judgment with the Great White Throne Judgment described in Revelation 20:11-15. Some scholars merge both passages and call this "the general judgment." The Bible knows nothing of a "general judgment." This judgment takes place on earth immediately after the Battle of Armageddon. The White Throne Judgment takes place in space somewhere ("the earth and the heaven fled away," Rev. 20:11). The judgment here in Matthew 25 takes place *before* the kingdom is established on earth, for the saved are told to "inherit the kingdom" (Matt. 25:34). The White Throne Judgment will take place *after* the 1,000-year reign of Christ (Rev. 20:7ff).

There is another error we must avoid. We must not force this passage to teach salvation by good works. A superficial reading would give the impression that helping one's neighbor is sufficient to earn salvation and go to heaven. But this is not the message of this passage. Nobody at any time in the history of the world was ever saved by good works.

The Old Testament saints were saved by faith (Heb. 11); the New Testament saints were saved by faith in Jesus Christ (Eph. 2:8-10). People today are saved the same way. The gospel of "do good" is not a scriptural message. It is right for *believers* to do good (Gal. 6:10; Heb. 13:16), but this is not the way unbelievers can be saved.

If we keep in mind the three groups in the account, it will help to solve this problem: There were sheep, goats, and brethren. Who are these people that the King dares to call "My brethren"? It seems likely that they are the believing Jews from the Tribulation period. These are people who will hear the message of the 144,000 and trust Jesus Christ. Since these believing Jews will not receive the "mark of the beast" (Rev. 13:16-17), they will be unable to buy or sell. How, then, can they survive? Through the loving care of the Gentiles who have trusted Christ and who care for His brethren.

The interesting thing about this judgment is that the *sheep* individuals are surprised at what they hear. They will not remember having seen the Lord Jesus Christ and ministering to His needs. But just as they lovingly ministered to the believing Jews, they did it to Christ. Their motive was not reward, but sacrificial love. In fact, these Gentiles took their own lives in their hands when they welcomed the homeless Jews and cared for them. "He that receiveth you receiveth Me," Jesus said to His disciples (Matt. 10:40); and surely this would also apply to His brethren.

The individuals designated *goats* were judged because they did not trust Jesus Christ and give evidence of that faith by caring for His brethren. They apparently received the mark of the beast and took care of themselves and their own, but they had no time for the Jewish remnant that was suffering on earth (Rev. 12:17). There are sins of omission as well as sins of commission (James 4:17). Not doing good is the moral equivalent of doing evil.

When we compare the two judicial sentences (Matt. 25:34, 41), we discover some interesting truths. To being with, the sheep were blessed of the Father; but it does not say that the goats were "cursed of the Father." The sheep *inherit* the kingdom, and inheritance is based on birth. Because they had been born again through faith, they inherited the kingdom.

This kingdom was prepared for these saved individuals, but Matthew 25:41 does not state that the everlasting fire was prepared for the goats. It was prepared for the devil and his angels (Rev. 20:10). God never prepared hell for people. There is no evidence from Scripture that God predestines people to go to hell. If sinners listen to Satan, and follow his ways, they will end up where he ends up—in the torments of hell. There are only two eternal destinies: everlasting punishment for those who reject Christ or eternal life for those who trust Him.

The sheep will be ushered into the kingdom to share in Christ's glory. The church will be reigning with Christ, and Israel will enjoy the fulfillment of the promises made through the prophets. All of creation will share in the glorious liberty of God's children (Rom. 8:19-21). Jesus Christ will rule from David's throne in Jerusalem (Luke 1:30-33), and peace will reign for 1,000 years (Isa. 11).

As we look back over the Olivet Discourse, we should review several facts. To begin with, God is not finished with the people of Israel. Jesus made it clear in this sermon that Israel would be purified and brought to faith in the Messiah. God has not cast away His people (Rom. 11:1ff).

Second, the Old Testament promises of the kingdom will be fulfilled. The Tribulation period will be a very difficult time for people on the earth. But it will be "travail" in preparation for the birth of the kingdom. The suffering will lead to glory.

Third, God is going to judge this world. He is not sending cataclysmic judgments today because this is a day of grace when His message is, "Be you reconciled to God" (2 Cor. 5:14ff). The heavens are silent because man's sins have already been judged at the Cross. God has spoken once and for all through His Son, and He will not speak to this earth again until He sends His judgments during the Tribulation.

Fourth, we as Christians and members of His church are not looking for signs. "The Jews require a sign" (1 Cor. 1:22). There will be no signs given prior to the sudden return of Christ in the air for His church. However, as we see some of these Tribulation signs *beginning* ("When these things begin to take place," Luke 21:28, NASB), we feel that the end is not far away. It seems that international tensions and problems are increasing to the point where the world will cry out for a dictator, and Satan will have his candidate ready.

Finally, no matter what view of prophecy we take, we know that Jesus is coming again. As Christians, we must be alert and ready. We must not waste our opportunities. We may not have a great deal of ability or a great many gifts, but we can still be faithful in the calling He has given us.

CHAPTER TWENTY-THREE
THE KING'S PREPARATION
Matthew 26:1-56

Events were now moving to a climax. The King was preparing to suffer and die. This preparation was in three stages and at three different locations. As we examine these stages, we can see the growing conflict between Christ and the enemy.

At Bethany: Worship versus Waste (Matt. 26:1-16)

Matthew does not claim to give us a chronological account of the events of the last week. At this point he inserted a flashback to describe the feast in Bethany and the beautiful act that Mary performed. The religious leaders were meeting to plot against Jesus, but His friends were meeting to show their love and devotion to Him. Also, by joining these two accounts, Matthew showed the connection between Mary's worship and Judas' betrayal. It was after the feast in Bethany that Judas went to the priests and offered his help (Mark 14:10-11). The Lord's rebuke triggered Judas' response.

The feast at Bethany took place "six days before the Passover" (John 12:1) in the house of Simon the leper. Apparently he had been healed by the Lord Jesus. There were at least seventeen people at this dinner: Simon, Mary, Martha, Lazarus, Jesus, and the 12 Apostles. True to her character as the "doer" in the family, Martha did the serving (Luke 10:38-42). The three key persons in this event are Mary, Judas, and Jesus.

Mary (v. 7). Only John identifies this woman as Mary, sister of Martha and Lazarus. She is found only three times in the Gospels, and in each instance she is at the feet of Jesus. She sat at His feet and listened to the Word (Luke 10:38-42); she came to His feet in sorrow after the death of Lazarus (John 11:28-32); and she worshiped at His feet when she anointed Him with the ointment (John 12:1ff). Mary was a deeply spiritual woman. She found at His feet her blessing, she brought to His feet her burdens, and she gave at His feet her best.

When we combine the Gospel records, we learn that she anointed both His head and His feet, and wiped His feet with her hair. A woman's hair is her glory (1 Cor. 11:15). She surrendered her glory to the Lord and worshiped Him with the precious gift that she brought. It was an act of love and devotion that brought fragrance to the whole house.

Because she had listened to His word, Mary knew that soon Jesus would die and be buried. She also knew that His body would not need the traditional care given to the dead because His body would not see corruption (Ps. 16:10; Acts 2:22-28). Instead of anointing His body *after* His death, she did so *before* His death. It was an act of faith and love.

Judas (vv. 8-9). The disciples did not know the true character of Judas. His criticism of Mary sounded so "spiritual" that they joined him in attacking her. We know the real reason Judas wanted the ointment sold: The money would go into the treasury and he would be able to use it (John 12:6).

Judas is a tragic figure. He was called to be one of Christ's disciples and was named an apostle along with the others (Mark 3:13-19). He received power to heal (Matt. 10:1-4), and he probably used this power. It is not the power to do miracles that is proof of salvation (Matt. 7:21-29), but obedience to God's Word.

In spite of his affiliation with the band of disciples, and his association with Christ, Judas was not a true believe. When Jesus washed the disciples' feet, He made it clear that one of them (Judas) was not cleansed (John 13:10-11). Like many professing Christians today, Judas was "in" the group of believers but not "of" them.

Notice that every time Mary sought to do something for Jesus, she was misunderstood. Her sister Martha misunderstood her when Mary sat at Jesus' feet to hear Him teach the Word. Judas and the other disciples misunderstood her when she anointed Jesus. Her friends and neighbors misunderstood her when she came out of the house to meet Jesus after Lazarus had been buried (John 11:28-31). When we give Jesus Christ first place in our lives, we can expect to be misunderstood and criticized by those who claim to follow Him.

Why did Judas follow Jesus for three years, listen to His Word, share His ministry, and then turn traitor? One thing is certain: Judas was not the victim of circumstances or the passive tool of providence. It was prophesied that one of Messiah's close associates would betray Him, (Pss. 41:9; 55:12-14), but this fact does not relieve Judas of responsibility. We must not make him a martyr because he fulfilled this prophecy.

While we can never fully understand the mind and heart of Judas, we do know that he had every opportunity to be saved. He was often warned by Jesus: in the Upper Room, Jesus even washed Judas' feet. Probably, Judas saw in Jesus the hope for Israel's political freedom. If Jesus established His kingdom, Judas, as treasurer, would have had an important position. When Jesus repeatedly refused to become a political Messiah, Judas turned against Him. Satan found a willing tool in Judas. Satan put the ideas into Judas' mind (John 13:2) and then entered into Judas to use him to betray Jesus to the enemy (John 13:27).

Judas' life is a warning to those who pretend to serve Christ but whose hearts are far from God. He is also a warning to those who waste their opportunities and their lives. "Why this waste?" asked Judas when he saw that expensive ointment poured out on Jesus. Yet Judas wasted his opportunities, his life, and his soul! Jesus called him *son of perdition* (John 17:12) which literally means "son of waste."

Jesus (vv. 10-16). He immediately came to the defense of Mary, for He always protects His own. He rebuked Judas and the other disciples and praised Mary for her loving act of devotion. *Nothing given to Jesus in love is ever wasted.* Her act of worship not only brought joy to the heart of Jesus and fragrance to the house, but also blessing to the whole world. Her devotion encourages us to love and serve Christ with our very best. Such service brings blessings to others that perhaps we will know nothing about until we see Him.

Jesus did not criticize the disciples because they were concerned about the poor. He was concerned about the poor, and we should be too. He was cautioning them against missing their opportunity to worship Him. They would always have opportunities to help the poor. But they would not always have the opportunity to worship at His feet and prepare Him for burial.

In the Upper Room: Faithfulness versus Betrayal (Matt. 26:17-30)

Preparation for Passover (vv. 17-19). It was necessary to purchase and prepare the materials needed for the Passover feast. It was also necessary to find a place in crowded Jerusalem where the feast could be held. Jesus sent Peter and John to make these important preparations (Luke 22:8). They were to follow a man who was carrying a pitcher of water and he would show them a large upper room. It would be most unusual for a *man* to be carrying the water, for this was usually done by the women.

Peter and John would have had to secure the bread and bitter herbs, as well as the wine, for the feast. They would have had to find a perfect lamb, and then have had the lamb slain in the court of the temple and the blood put on the altar. The lamb would be roasted whole, and then the feast would be ready.

Announcement of a betrayer (vv. 20-25). Up to the very end, the disciples did not realize that one of their own number, Judas, was the traitor. They did not see any difference in the way Jesus treated Judas, which is remarkable testimony to our Lord's patience and love. It was during the Passover feast, as they were eating, that Jesus announced the presence of a traitor. The disciples looked at one another, wondering who the traitor might be. Then they asked Jesus, "It is not I, is it?" The construction of the question indicates they expected *No* as the answer.

Judas was reclining to our Lord's left; this was a place of honor at a feast. (This may explain why the disciples *again* started arguing over who was the greatest. See Luke 22:24-30.) John was reclining at our Lord's right, and thus was able to rest on His breast (John 13:23). It was an act of friendship to eat bread together, especially bread that had been dipped into the dish of herbs. It was also an honor to be given a morsel of bread by your host. Jesus gave the bread to Judas (Ps. 41:9), and Judas accepted it *knowing full well that he was betraying his Lord.* For Jesus, giving the bread was a gracious act of hospitality; for Judas, accepting the bread was an evil act of treachery.

Matthew 26:24 presents both the human and the divine sides of this event. From the divine point of view, Judas' treachery was predicted in Scripture and was part of the plan of God. But from the human point of view, Judas was guilty of a base crime and was completely responsible for what he did. Divine sovereignty and human responsibility are not in conflict, even though we may not be able to understand how they work together to fulfill God's will.

After Judas took the morsel of bread, Satan entered into him (John 13:27). He then went out to keep his promise to the religious leaders in delivering Jesus into their hands; and even then, the other disciples did not know what he was doing. "He went immediately out; and it was night" (John 13:30). For Judas, it is still night.

Institution of the Lord's Supper (vv. 26-30). It was after Judas had left the room that Jesus instituted something new, the Lord's Supper (1 Cor. 11:23-34). He took wo elements from the Passover feast, the unleavened bread and the cup, and He used these to picture His own death. The broken bread pictured His body given for the sins of the world. The "fruit of the vine" (Matt. 26:29) pictured His blood, shed for the remission of sins. The text does not indicate that anything special or mysterious happened to these two elements. They remained bread and the "fruit of the vine" but they now conveyed a deeper meaning: the body and the blood of Jesus Christ.

The Lord's Supper reminds us to *look ahead* for Christ's return. We will observe this supper until He comes (1 Cor. 11:26). The Passover pointed ahead to the Lamb of God who would take away the sins of the world (John 1:29). The Lord's Supper announces that this great work has been accomplished.

In Matthew 26:29, Jesus added the note of future glory in the kingdom. Jesus did eat bread, fish, and honey after His resurrection (Luke 24:41-43; John 21:9-15). But there is no record that He drank the fruit of the vine. Even as He faced the rejection of His nation and the suffering of the cross, He was looking ahead to the kingdom that would be established because of His sacrifice. There were traditionally four cups drunk at the Passover feast, each cup relating to one of the four promises in Exodus 6:6-7. Jesus instituted the Lord's Supper between the third and fourth cups.

The hymn that Jesus and His disciples sang before they left the Upper Room was part of the traditional Hallel, Psalms 116–118. Read those psalms in the light of Christ's death and resurrection and see how they take on new meaning. Imagine our Lord being able to sing praises to God in the face of rejection, suffering, and death.

Gethsemane: Submission versus Resistance (Matt. 26:31-56)

At the Mount of Olives was a private garden which Jesus often had used as a retreat (John 18:2). *Gethsemane* means "oil press," a significant name in the light of our Lord's agony in that Garden.

The disciples' failure announced (vv. 31-35). This announcement was probably made as the band of men made their way to the Garden. We usually point to Peter as the one who had failed the Lord, but *all* of the disciples were involved. Jesus referred to Zechariah 13:7 in warning His disciples, but He also added a word of promise: He would rise again and meet them in Galilee. Unfortunately, the men paid little attention to the promise of His resurrection. On Resurrection Day, the angels reminded them of the meeting in Galilee (Matt. 28:7, 10).

When Peter disagreed with the Lord, this was the beginning of his sin of denying the Lord. Peter was unwilling to apply the word "all" to himself. Instead of reassuring Peter, the Lord gave him a personal warning: He would deny Christ three times! Peter thought he was *better* than the other men, and Jesus told him he would be even more cowardly than the others.

Peter's response was to deny Christ's word even more fervently, and the other disciples joined in this protest. Had Peter listened to the word and obeyed it, he would not have denied his Lord three times.

Jesus' surrender accomplished (vv. 36-46). He left eight of the disciples at the entrance to the Garden, while He and Peter, James, and John went further into the Garden. This was the third time He had taken these three men with Him. They were with Him on the Mount of Transfiguration (Matt. 17:1ff) and in the home of Jairus where He raised Jairus' daughter from the dead (Luke 8:49ff). He wanted them to watch and pray. He was entering into a difficult time, and the presence of His disciples would be an encouragement to Him.

We must not think that it was the fear of death that made our Lord so agonize in the Garden. He did not fear death, but faced it with courage and peace. He was about to "drink the cup" that His Father had prepared for Him, and this meant bearing on His body the sins of the world (John 18:11; 1 Peter 2:24). Many godly people have been arrested, beaten, and slain because of their faith. But only Jesus experienced being made sin and a curse for mankind (2 Cor. 5:21; Gal. 3:13). The Father has never forsaken any of His own, yet He forsook His Son (Matt. 27:46). This was the cup that Jesus willingly drank for us.

Jesus was not wrestling with God's will or resisting God's will. He was yielding Himself to God's will. As perfect Man, He felt the awful burden of sin, and His holy soul was repelled by it. Yet as the Son of God, He knew that this was His mission in the world. The mystery of His humanity and deity is seen vividly in this scene.

Peter and his fellow disciples had promised to be faithful to death, *and yet they went to sleep!* They needed to pray for themselves, because danger was around the corner. And how much it would have meant to their Lord if they had watched and prayed with Him. They had failed, but their Lord had succeeded.

The arrest achieved (vv. 47-56). Jesus knew that Judas and the arresting officers were near, so He awakened the sleeping disciples and prepared them for what was coming. The fact that this band of soldiers and temple guards carried weapons and lanterns shows that Judas did not really understand Jesus. Judas thought they would have to search for Him in the Garden and fight off His disciples in order to arrest Him. But Jesus came to them and calmly surrendered. It would not even have been necessary for Judas to betray Jesus with a kiss, for Jesus told the soldiers who He was.

It is tragic to see how Judas cheapened everything that he touched. His name means *praise* (Gen. 29:35), yet who would name a son "Judas" today? He used the kiss as a weapon, not as a sign of affection. In that day, it was customary for disciples to kiss their teacher. But in this case, it was not a mark of submission or respect. The Greek verbs indicate that Judas kissed Jesus repeatedly.

At this point, some of the other disciples asked, "Shall we strike with the sword?" When He was with them in the Upper Room, Jesus had talked to them about swords (Luke 22:31-38). Jesus was preparing them for a different kind of life. They would need to use whatever means He provided for their care and safety. They would be in a hostile world, and He would not always perform miracles to help them.

The problem was, the disciples misunderstood what He taught them. As usual, they took Him literally. " 'Lord, look, here are two swords.' And He said to them, 'It is enough' " (Luke 22:38, NASB). Peter had argued with the Word, denied the Word, and disobeyed the Word (when he went to sleep). Now he ran ahead of the Word. In his zeal to help Jesus, Peter cut off Malchus' ear with a sword. He did not wait for the Lord to tell him what to do, but (like Moses in Egypt, Ex. 2:11-15) Peter rushed ahead and trusted the arm of flesh. Had Jesus not healed the ear of Malchus, there probably would have been *four* crosses on Calvary!

The fact that the guards had not arrested Him in the temple indicates that there was a divine timetable controlling His life. These things were not happening by accident, but by appointment. It was all part of God's plan, yet evil men were responsible for the deed. "This Man, delivered up by the predetermined plan and foreknowledge of God, you nailed to a cross by the hands of godless men and put Him to death" (Acts 2:23, NASB).

Of course, they had no right to arrest Jesus. He had broken no laws, He had committed no crimes. They were treating Him like a common thief—and yet it was *Judas* who was the thief! The disciples who bravely promised to deliver Him deserted Him. "Behold, the hour cometh, yea, is now come, that you shall be scattered, every man to his own, and shall leave Me alone; and yet I am not alone, because the Father is with Me" (John 16:32). Later, even the Father would leave Him!

Each of us must decide: Will it be the sword or the cup? Will I resist God's will or submit to God's will? The cup usually involves suffering, but that suffering ultimately leads to glory. We need not fear the cup, for it has been prepared by the Father especially for us. He knows how much we can take, and He mixes the contents in wisdom and love.

CHAPTER TWENTY-FOUR THE KING'S TRIAL

Matthew 26:57–27:26

After Jesus was arrested, He was taken to the house of Annas, the former high priest who was the father-in-law of Caiaphas, the high priest (John 18:13ff). Annas, a shrewd politican, was something of a "godfather" in the temple establishment. Jesus then was taken to Caiaphas and, in the morning, to the meeting of the Sanhedrin. They turned Him over to Pilate who tried to put Him under Herod's jurisdiction (Luke 23:6-12). But Herod sent Him back to Pilate.

Matthew centered his attention on four persons who were involved in the trial and suffering of the Lord.

Caiaphas (Matt. 26:57-68)

According to Old Testament Law, the high priest was to serve until death. But when the Romans took over the nation of Israel, they made the high priesthood an appointed office. This way they could be certain of having a religious leader who would cooperate with their policies. Annas served as high priest from A.D. 6 to A.D. 15, and five of his sons, as well as Caiaphas his son-in-law succeeded him. Caiaphas was high priest from A.D. 18–36, but Annas was still a power behind the throne (see Luke 3:2).

Both Annas and Caiaphas were Sadducees, which meant they did not believe in the resurrection, the spirit world, or the authority of any of the Old Testament except the five Books of Moses. It was the high priestly family that managed the "temple business' which Jesus had overthrown twice during His ministry. Of course, these men were most happy to lay hands on their enemy. Caiaphas had already made it clear that he intended to sacrifice Jesus in order to save the nation (John 11:47-54).

The high priest hastily assembled the Sanhedrin, composed of the chief priests, the elders, and the scribes (Mark 14:53). While the men were gathering, Caiaphas and his assistants were seeking for witnesses to testify against the prisoner. They had already determined that He was guilty, but they wanted to go through the motions of a legal trial.

Since no honest witnesses could be found (which in itself proves our Lord's innocence), the leaders arranged for false witnesses to testify. The Law of Moses warned against false witnesses (Deut. 19:15-21), but even the religious leaders twisted God's Word to accomplish their selfish purposes. That there were *two* witnesses fulfilled the letter of the Law. But that they deliberately lied broke both the letter and the spirit of the Law. These witnesses cited a statement Jesus had made early in His ministry: "Destroy this temple, and in three days I will raise it up" (John 2:19). It was a serious matter to speak against the temple; this very charge later led to the death of Stephen (Acts 6:12-14; 7:45-50).

When confronted with this charge, Jesus remained silent. This was a fulfillment of Isaiah 53:7. Jesus could not deny that He made the statement, and yet neither could He explain the spiritual meaning of the statement to this group of worldly minded men. In His attitude toward His enemies, Jesus set an example for us to follow (1 Peter 2:18-23).

When Caiaphas saw that the false charges were not incriminating Jesus, he took another approach. He put Jesus under oath. In our day of repeated perjury and carelessness with the truth, we cannot appreciate the solemn importance that the Jews gave to oaths. This, of course, was according to their Law (Ex. 20:7; Lev. 19:12; Num. 30:2). Caiaphas knew that Jesus claimed to be the Son of God (John 10:30-33), so he put Him under oath to declare this. The clever priest knew that Jesus could not avoid replying.

Jesus *did* affirm that He is the Son of God. He applied to Himself Psalm 110:1 and Daniel 7:13, both of which are messianic passages. In these two quotations, Jesus predicted His resurrection and ascension and His return in glory. This would mean salvation to those who trust Him, but for Caiaphas it would mean condemnation.

Without even considering the evidence, Caiaphas passed the sentence. The treatment given Jesus after the verdict had been reached was certainly illegal and inhumane. Of course, all of this only revealed the wickedness of the priest's heart. At the same time, it fulfilled the messianic prophecies (Isa. 50:6).

Peter (Matt. 26:69-75)

Peter has been criticized for following "afar off" (Matt. 26:58); but that was not his mistake. His mistake was that he followed at all. He was supposed to get out! Jesus had warned Peter that he would deny Him. Jesus had also quoted Zechariah 13:7 which states that the "sheep shall be scattered." Finally, Jesus had expressly commanded the disciples not to follow: "Let these go their way" (John 18:8-9). If Peter had listened to the word and obeyed it, he would never have failed the Lord in such a humiliating way.

The Apostle John was also a part of this failure, for he had followed with Peter and gotten both of them entrance into the high priest's house (John 18:15-16). Jesus had warned them to "watch and pray" lest they enter into temptation (Matt. 26:41). But they had gone to sleep instead. Consequently, they entered into temptation, and Peter fell.

Peter's denial of Christ was the climax of a series of failures. When the Lord first warned Peter that he would be tested by Satan, Peter affirmed his faith and his ability to remain true to the Lord. In pride, Peter argued with the Word of God! He even dared to compare himself to the other disciples and affirmed that, though they might fall, *he* would remain true.

The fact that Peter was standing by the enemy's fire, warming himself, indicates how defeated he was. The denial was even more humiliating because two of the interrogators were servant girls. The third challenge came from a man, one of the bystanders; but Peter failed again. This man was a relative of Malchus, the man Peter had wounded (John 18:26). So Peter's impulsive deed caught up with him even after Jesus had repaired the damage.

Mark's account of this event indicates that the cock would crow twice (Mark 14:30). After the third denial, the cock crowed for the second time (Mark 14:72). This means that the first cock-crowing was a warning to Peter, and he should have left the scene immediately. The third denial and the second cock-crow climaxed the test, and Peter had failed.

The crowing of the cock reminded Peter of the word of Jesus. Had Peter remembered and obeyed the word, he would never have denied his Lord. It was at that time that Jesus turned and looked at Peter (Luke 22:61), and that look of love broke the apostle's heart. Peter went out and wept bitterly.

After His resurrection, Jesus met privately with Peter and restored him to his discipleship (Mark 16:7; 1 Cor. 15:5). Jesus also restored him publicly (John 21:15-19). Peter learned some important lessons during that difficult experience. He learned to pay attention to the Word, to watch and pray, and to put no confidence in his own strength.

Judas (Matt. 27:1-10)

The Jewish council reconvened in the morning and delivered the official verdict against Jesus, so that people could not say that their hastily called night meeting was unlawful. Now *all* were able to attend. It is likely that Nicodemus and Joseph of Arimathea either did not attend or abstained from voting (John 19:38-42). But the Jews did not have the authority to exercise capital punishment (John 18:31), so the prisoner went to Pilate, the Roman procurator. Only he could sentence the prisoner to death.

At this point, Judas returned to the scene. He witnessed the official trial and sentencing of Jesus and realized that He was condemned to die. Judas' response was one of remorse and regret. The Greek word translated "repented himself" in Matthew 27:3 indicates, not a sorrow for sin that leads to a change of mind and action, but a regret at being caught, a remorse that leads to despair. Peter truly repented, and Jesus restored him. But Judas did not repent, and this led him to suicide.

Judas had sold Jesus for the price of a slave (Ex. 21:32). In desperation, he threw the money on the temple floor and left. The Law would not permit the use of this kind of *tainted* money for temple purposes (Deut. 23:18). The leaders were careful to observe the Law even while they were guilty of breaking it. They used the money to buy a "potter's field" where Jewish strangers who died could be buried properly.

Acts 1:18-19 adds to our understanding of the event. Judas went off by himself, brooded over his terrible crime, and finally hanged himself. Apparently his body was not discovered for some days, because it became bloated and his bowels gushed out. Perhaps the tree limb on which he was hanging also broke and helped to cause this.

Acts 1:18 does not say that Judas committed suicide in the field that the priests bought with the money. That act would have defiled the land and the priests would never have purchased it. Matthew 27:7 states that the priests bought a field; Acts 1:18 states that the money Judas acquired was used to buy it. Judas could not have purchased a field with that money because he gave the money back to the priests. The priests called the cemetery "the field of blood" because it was purchased with "blood money." Judas' suicide added more "blood" to the name, since it was he who contributed the money.

But, why did Matthew relate this event to a prophecy in Jeremiah, when the prophecy is found in Zechariah 11:12-13? One possible solution is that his prophecy was *spoken* by Jeremiah (note Matt. 27:9) and became a part of the Jewish oral tradition. It was later *written* by Zechariah. The Prophet Jeremiah definitely was involved in the purchase of a field (Jer. 32:6ff), and also with a potter's house (Jer. 18:1ff), and a burial ground (Jer. 19:1-12). Matthew may have been referring to these general facts as background for the specific prophecy written by Zechariah.

Pilate (Matt. 27:11-6)

Pontius Pilate was the sixth Roman procurator to serve in Judea. He was not liked by the Jews because he did things that deliberately violated their Law and provoked them. He was not above killing people to accomplish his purposes (Luke 13:1). Pilate's position was always rather precarious because of his bad relationship with Israel and because of Rome's changing policy with the Jews.

The Jewish leaders accused Jesus of three crimes. They claimed that He was guilty of misleading the nation, forbidding the paying of taxes, and claiming to be a king (Luke 23:2). These were definitely political charges, the kind that a Roman governor could handle. Pilate focused on the third charge—that Jesus claimed to be a king—because this was a definite threat to Rome. If he could deal with this "revolutionary" properly, Pilate could please the Jews and impress the Emperor at the same time.

"Are You the King of the Jews?" Pilate asked. Jesus gave him a clear reply: "It is as you say." However, Jesus then asked Pilate a question about his question (John 18:34-37). Was Pilate thinking of "kingship" in the Roman sense? If so, then Jesus is not that kind of a king. Jesus explained to the governor that His kingdom was not of this world, that He had no armies, that His followers did not fight. Rather, His kingdom was a reign of truth.

This conversation convinced Pilate that Jesus was not a dangerous revolutionary. "I find no fault in Him," was Pilate's decision. But the Jewish rulers were insistent that Pilate condemn Jesus. They repeated their charges and, as they enlarged on them, mentioned that Jesus was from Galilee. When Pilate heard that, he saw a way out of his dilemma, since Galilee was under Herod's jurisdiction. It is possible that Herod was displeased with Pilate because Pilate had slain some of Herod's citizens (Luke 13:1). This would have been an opportunity for Pilate to become reconciled to Herod.

Matthew did not record the trial held before Herod Antipas (Luke 23:6-12). Herod was the one who had murdered John the Baptist and had threatened to kill Jesus (Luke 13:31-32). Jesus was silent before Herod, for Herod had silenced the voice of God. All the king could do was mock Jesus and send Him back to Pilate. If Pilate had hoped to get rid of the problem, he was disappointed. However, this maneuver did patch up the quarrel between the two rulers.

Pilate wanted to solve the problem but not make any definite decision about Jesus. As a Roman governor, he was pledged to uphold the law. But as a politician, he knew he had to get along with the people. Every decision Pilate made forced him to make another decision, until he was the prisoner of his own evasions. He questioned Jesus further, but He made no reply.

Pilate had one more scheme: He would follow the tradition of releasing a prisoner. Instead of selecting some unknown prisoner, Pilate deliberately chose the most notorious prisoner he had, Barabbas. This man was a robber (John 18:40) and a murderer (Mark 15:7). Pilate reasoned that the crowd would reject Barabbas and ask for Jesus to be released, for who wants a convicted murderer and robber turned loose into society?

But Pilate was wrong. In spite of the fact that Jesus had ministered by healing the sick and even raising the dead, the people rejected Him and chose a murderer to be released. Pilate realized that a riot was in the making, and he could not afford to let this happen. The very thing the rulers wanted to prevent—a riot at Passover season (Matt. 26:5)—they engineered themselves in order to force Pilate to act. The governor *did* act, purely out of expediency and not on the basis of integrity. He released a guilty man and condemned an innocent Man, and that innocent Man is the Son of God.

Pilate took three steps in an attempt to exonerate himself. First, he washed his hands and declared that he was innocent of any guilt. Second, he stated clearly that Jesus was a just person, that is, not worthy of death. Third, he offered to punish Jesus and then release Him, but the rulers would accept no compromise. Finally, the religious rulers used the one weapon against which Pilate had no defense: "If you release this Man, you are no friend of Caesar; everyone who makes himself out to be a king opposes Caesar" (John 19:12, NASB). At this, Pilate capitulated, had Jesus scourged, and delivered Him to be crucified.

Since the Jews could not execute criminals, it was necessary for the Roman officials to assist; and Pilate issued the order. Of course, all of this was in fulfillment of prophecy. The Jews did not crucify; they used stoning to execute criminals. Psalm 22, written by a Jew, is a vivid picture of crucifixion. "They pierced my hands and my feet" (Ps. 22:16). Jesus was made a curse for us, for "cursed is everyone who hangs on a tree" (Deut. 21:23; Gal. 3:13). But still God was at work in fulfilling His divine purposes.

Pilate knew what was right, but refused to do anything about it. He was "willing to please the people" (Mark 15:15). Judas yielded to *the devil* in his great sin (John 13:2, 27); Peter yielded to *the flesh* when he denied his Lord; but Pilate yielded to *the world* and listened to the crowd. Pilate looked for the easy way, not the right way. He has gone down in history as the man who condemned Jesus.

CHAPTER TWENTY-FIVE THE KING'S SUFFERING AND DEATH

Matthew 27:27-66

Matthew and the other Gospel writers recorded the historical facts of our Lord's suffering and death. It remained for the writers of the New Testament Epistles to explain the theological meaning of this event. History states that "Christ died," but theology explains, "Christ died for our sins" (1 Cor. 15:3). Let's consider the various kinds of suffering that our Lord endured that day.

Mocked by the Soldiers (Matt. 27:27-30)

The official indictment against Jesus was that He claimed to be the King of the Jews (Matt. 27:37). The soldiers took advantage of this accusation and paid "homage" to the king. It was a cruel way to treat an innocent prisoner who had already been scourged. But Pilate did nothing to restrain them. He was glad to get the prisoner off of his hands.

First, the soldiers disrobed Jesus and dressed Him in an old "soldier's cloak." Imagine attiring the Prince of Peace (Isa. 9:6) in a discarded military uniform! Matthew described the robe as *scarlet,* while Mark used the word *purple.* There is no contradiction; "reddish-purple" would be a good description of an old faded garment. Imagine how our Lord must have felt when this robe was thrown on His bleeding body.

A king must have a crown, so they wove together the thorny twigs of a plant, and pushed it on His head. They gave Him a reed as a scepter, and then bowed before Him, saying, "Hail, King of the Jews!" They repeated this mock homage not realizing that the One they were mocking was indeed King of kings and Lord of lords.

Then they did something that no subject would ever do to his king: They spat on Him and hit Him with the reed. While some of the soldiers were bowing before Him, others were hitting Him on the head or spitting on Him (Isa. 50:6). Jesus took all of this humiliation and pain without speaking or fighting back (1 Peter 2:18ff). His submission was not a sign of weakness; it was a sign of strength.

Crucified (Matt. 27:31-38)

Crucifixion was the most shameful and painful way to execute a criminal. Jesus did not simply die; He died "even the death of a cross" (Phil. 2:8). Roman citizens ordinarily were not crucified. In fact, crucifixion was never mentioned in polite society, so degrading was this form of capital punishment.

Jesus was led outside the city to the place of execution (Heb. 13:12-13). It was required that the prisoner carry his own cross (or at least the crossbeam), and that he wear a placard around his neck announcing his crime. That placard was then hung over his head on the cross for all to see.

While the record does not state so expressly, it appears that Jesus was unable to carry the cross, and this was slowing down the progress of the group. When we remember that He had been awake all night, scourged, and abused by the soldiers, we can conclude that He was exhausted. Jesus started out bearing His cross (John 19:17). Mark 15:22 says, "And they bring Him to Golgotha" (literal translation). This suggests that the soldiers had to assist Jesus in the procession, for the word "bring" has the meaning of "to carry, to bear."

There was to be no delay in this execution. The Passover was about to be celebrated, and the Jewish leaders did not want their holy day desecrated by the dead bodies of criminals (John 19:31). In order to hasten the procession, the soldiers drafted a visitor to Jerusalem, Simon from Cyrene. He had come to Jerusalem to celebrate Passover, and now he was humiliated by being forced to carry the cross of an unknown criminal! Roman soldiers had the authority to draft citizens (Matt. 5:41).

Mark referred to Simon as though the people reading his Gospel would recognize him: "the father of Alexander and Rufus" (Mark 15:21). Apparently these two sons were well-known members of the church. It seems likely that this humiliating experience resulted in Simon's conversion as well as in the conversion of his family. Simon came to Jerusalem to sacrifice his Passover lamb, and he met the Lamb of God who was sacrificed for him.

It was customary to give a narcotic drink to those about to be crucified, for this would help to ease the pain. Jesus refused this drink; He did the will of God in complete control of His faculties. Also this act fulfilled Psalm 69:21.

It was customary for the soldiers to share the loot at an execution. This was a fulfillment of Psalm 22:18. After they had finished gambling for His clothing (John 19:23-25), they sat down and "guarded Him there" (Matt. 27:36). After all, this Jesus was known to be a miracle-worker. Nobody knew how many followers He had, and perhaps they were even then preparing to rescue Him. He had one man in His band of disciples who had been a Zealot (Matt. 10:4—"Simon the Zealot"), and that fanatical group stopped at nothing when it came to opposing Roman authority.

By combining the Gospel records, we arrive at the full accusation that was put over His head: "This is Jesus of Nazareth the King of the Jews." The Jewish rulers did not approve of what Pilate wrote, but for once the governor did not vascillate (John 19:21-22). In one sense, this title proved to be the first

"Gospel tract" ever written. It announced to one of the thieves crucified with Him that He was the Saviour and a King. He dared to believe this message and asked Jesus to save him!

Mocked by Jews (Matt. 27:39-44)

Jesus was not executed in a quiet building, away from the city's noise and activity. He was executed on a public highway, on a day when perhaps hundreds of people were traveling. The fact that His indictment was written in three languages—Greek, Hebrew, and Latin—indicates that a cosmopolitan crowd passed by Golgotha, "the place of the skull." This in itself was humiliating, for the passersby could stare and shout bitter mockery at the victims. Again, this mockery from the crowd had been predicted (Ps. 22:6-8).

It was bad enough that the common rabble mocked Him, but even the Jewish leaders joined the attack. They reminded Him of His promise to rebuild the temple in three days (Matt. 26:61; John 2:19). "If You can do that, You can come down from the cross and prove to us that You are God's Son!" In reality, it was the fact that He *stayed* on the cross that proved His divine sonship.

The Jewish rulers mocked His claim to be the Saviour. "He saved others; He cannot save Himself" (Matt. 27:42, NASB). He *had* saved others. But if He saved Himself, then nobody else could be saved! He did not come to save His life, but to give it as a ransom for sinners.

Rejected by the Father (Matt. 27:45-56)

Jesus was crucified at 9 o'clock in the morning; and from 9 until noon, He hung in the light. But at noon, a miraculous darkness covered the land. This was not a sandstorm or an eclipse, as some liberal writers have suggested. It was a heaven-sent darkness that lasted for three hours. It was as though all of creation was sympathizing with the Creator. There were three days of darkness in Egypt before Passover (Ex. 10:21-23); and there were three hours of darkness before the Lamb of God died for the sins of the world.

Jesus had spoken at least three times before this darkness fell. While they were crucifying Him, He repeatedly prayed, "Father, forgive them, for they know not what they do" (Luke 23:34). He had spoken to the repentant thief and assured him a place in paradise (Luke 23:39-43). He had also given His mother into the care of His beloved disciple, John (John 19:18-27). But when the darkness came, Jesus was silent for three hours.

After three hours, the darkness left. Then Jesus cried, "My God, My God, why hast Thou forsaken Me?" This was a direct quotation from Psalm 22:1. It was during the time of darkness that Jesus had been made sin for us (2 Cor. 5:21). He had been forsaken by the Father! That darkness was a symbol of the judgment that He endured when He was "made a curse" for us (Gal. 3:13). Psalm 22:2 suggests a period of light and a period of darkness; and Psalm 22:3 emphasizes the holiness of God. How could a holy God look with favor on His Son who had become sin?

Jesus spoke these words in Hebrew, and the spectators did not understand Him. They thought He was calling for Elijah to help Him. Had they listened carefully and consulted Psalm 22 in its entirety, they would have understood the truth.

In rapid succession, the Lord spoke three more times. He said, "I thirst" (John 19:28); and this fulfilled Psalm 69:21. Someone took pity on Him and moistened His lips with some sour wine. The others waited to see if perhaps Elijah would come to His rescue.

Then Jesus shouted, "It is finished! Father, into Thy hands I commit My spirit!" The fact that Jesus shouted with a loud voice indicates that He was in complete control of His faculties. Then He voluntarily yielded up His spirit and died.

Though He was "crucified through weakness" (2 Cor. 13:4), He exercised wonderful power when He died. Three miracles took place simultaneously: The veil of the temple was torn in two from top to bottom; an earthquake opened many graves; some saints arose from the dead. The rending of the veil symbolized the wonderful truth that the way was now open to God (Heb. 10:14-26). There was no more need of temples, priests, altars, or sacrifices. Jesus had finished the work of salvation on the cross.

The earthquake reminds us of what happened at Mount Sinai when God gave the Law to Moses (Ex. 19:16ff). The earthquake at Calvary signified that the demands of the Law had been met and the curse of the Law forever abolished (Heb. 12:18-24). The torn veil indicates that He conquered sin; the earthquake suggests that He conquered the Law and fulfilled it; and the resurrections prove that He defeated death.

We are not told who these saints were; they were simply believers who had died. The *King James Version* suggests that they did not come out of the graves until *after* His resurrection; the *New American Standard Bible* agrees with this. It is difficult to believe that they were given life on Friday afternoon and yet remained in their tombs until Sunday. The *New International Version* suggests that these saints were resurrected immediately and came out of their tombs, but that they did not visit in Jerusalem until after Jesus had been raised from the dead. It is not likely that many Jews would be in the cemetery on Passover, since they might be defiled by the dead. These resurrections could have taken place with nobody finding out at that time.

The result of all of this was the testimony of the centurion and those watching. "Truly this was the Son of God." Did this indicate saving faith? Not necessarily. But certainly it indicated hearts that were open to the truth.

The only disciple at the cross when Jesus died was John (John 19:35). But many women were watching from a distance, undoubtedly those who had assisted Him in His ministry (Luke 8:2). Three women were named: Mary Magdalene, who had been delivered of seven demons (Luke 8:2); Mary, the mother of James and Joses, who also was at the tomb on Resurrection morning (Matt. 28:1; Mark 16:1); and Salome, the mother of James and John. Salome had asked Jesus for special thrones for her sons. We wonder how she felt as she saw Him hanging on a cross.

His Guarded Tomb (Matt. 27:57-66)

Were it not for the intervention of Jospeh of Arimathea and Nicodemus (John 19:38), the body of Jesus might not have had a decent burial. Joseph and Nicodemus had come to believe in Jesus, even though they had not openly testified of their faith. God kept them hidden, as it were, that they might care for the body of Jesus. Since Joseph was a rich man, and he prepared the new tomb, he helped in the fulfillment of prophecy, Isaiah 53:9—"He was assigned a grave with the wicked, and with the rich in His death" (NIV).

It is not likely that Joseph prepared that tomb for himself. He was a wealthy man and certainly would not want to be buried so near a place of execution. He prepared that tomb for Jesus, and he selected a site near Golgotha so that he and Nicodemus could bury Christ's body quickly. Joseph and Nicodemus could very well have been in the garden waiting for Jesus to die. When they took Him from the cross, they defiled themselves and were not able to eat the Passover. But, what difference did it make? They had found the Lamb of God!

In contrast to the loving care given by Jesus' friends, notice the plottings and maneuvering of the Jewish leaders. The disciples had forgotten that Jesus promised to rise from the dead on the third day, but His enemies remembered. Pilate permitted the leaders to set a guard at the tomb. This guard put an official Roman seal on the stone. All of this was of God, for now it was impossible for anyone—friend or foe—to steal the body. Without realizing it, the Jewish leaders and the Roman government joined forces to help prove the resurrection of Jesus Christ.

CHAPTER TWENTY-SIX THE KING'S VICTORY

Matthew 28

If anything proves the kingship of Jesus Christ, it is His resurrection from the dead. The final chapter in Matthew's Gospel is a record of victory. It is a thrilling fact that believers today share in that victory.

Notice the various stages in the experience of the believers with reference to His resurrection.

They Thought He Was Dead (Matt. 28:1)

The women who had lingered at the cross came early to the tomb, bringing spices that they might anoint His body. They thought He was dead. In fact, they wondered how they would move the huge stone that blocked the entrance to the tomb (Mark 16:3). It is remarkable that they did not believe in His resurrection when He had taught this truth repeatedly (Matt. 16:21; 17:23; 20:19; 26:32).

We must never underestimate the importance of the resurrection of Jesus Christ. The world believes that Jesus died, but the world does not believe that He arose from the dead.

Peter's message at Pentecost emphasized the Resurrection. In fact, it is emphasized throughout the Book of Acts. What is the significance of the Resurrection?

It proves that Jesus is God's Son. Jesus stated that He had authority to lay down His life and to take it up again (John 10:17-18).

It verifies the truth of Scripture. Both in the Old Testament and in the teaching of Jesus, His resurrection is clearly taught (see Pss. 16:10; 110:1). If Jesus had not come out of the tomb, then these Scriptures would not be true.

It assures our own future resurrection. Because Jesus died and rose again, we shall one day be raised to be like Him (1 Thes. 4:13-18). In fact, the entire structure of the Christian faith rests on the foundation of the Resurrection. If we do away with His resurrection, we have no hope.

It is the proof of a future judgment. "Because He hath appointed a day, in the which He will judge the world in righteousness by that man who He hath ordained; whereof He hath given assurance unto all men, in that He hath raised Him from the dead" (Acts 17:31).

It is the basis for Christ's heavenly priesthood. Because He lives by the power of an endless life, He is able to save us "to the uttermost" (Heb. 7:23-28). He lives to intercede for us.

It gives power for Christian living. We cannot live for God by our own strength. It is only as His resurrection power works in and through us that we can do His will and glorify His name (see Rom. 6:4).

It assures our future inheritance. Because we have a living hope, we can experience hopeful living. A dead hope grows weaker and weaker before it eventually dies. But because Jesus Christ is alive, we have a glorious future (see 1 Peter 1:3-5).

Whenever God's people gather on the Lord's Day they bear witness that Jesus is alive and that the church has received spiritual blessings. When the followers of the Lord gathered that first Lord's Day, they were discourged and defeated.

They Heard He Was Alive (Matt. 28:2-8)

"And behold, a severe earthquake had occurred" (Matt. 28:2, NASB). Two angels had appeared (Luke 24:4) and one of them had rolled the stone away from the door. Of course, the soldiers on duty were greatly frightened by this sudden demonstration of supernatural power. The stone was not rolled away to permit Jesus to come out, for He had already left the tomb. It was rolled back so that the people could see for themselves that the tomb was empty.

One of the angels spoke to the women and calmed their fears. "He is not here! Come, and see!" Keep in mind that these women, as well as the disciples, did not expect Jesus to be alive.

What did they see in the tomb? The graveclothes lying on the stone shelf, still wrapped in the shape of the body (John 20:5-7). Jesus had passed through the graveclothes and left them behind as evidence that He was alive. They lay there like an empty cocoon. There was no sign of struggle, the graveclothes were not in disarray. Even the napkin (which had been wrapped around His face) was folded carefully in a place by itself.

We cannot examine this evidence in the same way the believers did that first Easter Sunday. But we do have the evidence of the Word of God. Jesus was not held by the bonds of death (Acts 2:24). He had promised to arise from the dead, and His Word was never broken.

The remarkable change in the early believers is another proof of His resurrection. One day they were discouraged and hiding in defeat. The next day they were declaring His resurrection and walking in joyful victory. In fact, they were willing to die for the truth of the Resurrection. If all of this were a manufactured tale, it could never have changed their lives or enabled them to lay down their lives as martyrs.

There were over 500 witnesses who saw Jesus alive at one time (1 Cor. 15:3-8). These appearances of the risen Christ were of such a nature that they could not be explained as hallucinations or self-deception. The people who saw Him were surprised. It would have been impossible for over 500 people to suffer hallucinations at the same time. Even the Apostle Paul, who was an enemy of the church, saw the risen Christ; that experience transformed his life (Acts 9).

The existence of the church, the New Testament, and the Lord's Day add further proof that Jesus is alive. For centuries, the Jews had been God's people, and they had honored the seventh day, the Sabbath. Then a change took place: Jews and Gentiles united in the church and became God's people; they met on the first day of the week, the Lord's Day. The New Testament is a lie if Jesus is dead, for every part of it points to a risen Christ.

Of course, Christians have experienced His resurrection power in their own lives. While the inward, subjective experience *alone* would not prove our Lord's historic resurrection, when combined with the other evidences, it adds great weight to the case. Still it is possible for people to be self-deluded. "Believers" in all kinds of cults will claim their way is true because of what they have experienced. But Christians have the weight of church history, Scripture, and dependable witnesses to back up their own personal experiences of faith.

"Come and see!" was followed by "Go and tell!" We must not keep the Resurrection news to ourselves. The angel sent the women to tell (of all people) Christ's own disciples. They should have been expecting the news, but instead, they questioned it even when they heard it.

They Met the Living Christ Personally (Matt. 28:9-15)

It is when we are obeying God's Word that He comes to us. Jesus had already appeared to Mary Magdalene in the garden (John 20:11-18; Mark 16:9). Notice that our Lord's first two Resurrection appearances were to believing women. These faithful women were not only the last to leave Calvary, but they were also the first to come to the tomb. Their devotion to Jesus was rewarded.

"All hail!" can be translated, *Grace.* What a marvelous greeting for the Resurrection Day! The women fell at His feet, took hold of Him, and worshiped Him. There must have been some fear in their hearts, for He immediately assured them with His typical, "Be not afraid!"

Not only had the angel commissioned them, but the Lord also commissioned them. The phrase "My brethren" revealed the intimate relationship between Christ and His followers. Jesus had spoken similar words to Mary Magdalene earlier that morning (John 20:17). Jesus reinforced the instructions of the angel that the disciples meet Him in Galilee (see Matt. 28:7). In the Garden, Jesus had told His disciples that He would rise from the dead and meet them in Galilee; but they had forgotten (Matt. 26:31-32).

While the believers were worshiping the living Christ, the unbelievers were plotting to destroy the witness of the resurrection of Jesus Christ. By now, some of the soldiers had realized that they were in a desperate plight. The Roman seal had been broken, the stone had been rolled away, and the body was not in the tomb. For a Roman soldier to fail in his duty was an offense punishable by death (Acts 12:19; 16:27-28). But the soldiers were shrewd: They did not report to Pilate or to their superior officers; they reported to the Jewish chief priests. They knew that these men were as anxious to cover up the miracle as were the soldiers themselves! Between the chief priests, the elders, and the soldiers, they put together a story that would explain the empty tomb: The body was stolen.

By examining this story, we see that it actually *proves* the resurrection of Jesus Christ. If Jesus' body was stolen, then it was taken either by His friends or His enemies. His friends could not have done it since they had left the scene and were convinced that Jesus was dead. His enemies would not steal His body because belief in His resurrection was what they were trying to prevent. They would have defeated their own purposes if they had removed His body. And, if they had taken it, why did they not produce it and silence the witness of the early church?

Anyone who stole the body would have taken the body *in the graveclothes.* Yet the empty graveclothes were left in the tomb in an orderly manner. This was hardly the scene of a grave robbery.

The religious leaders had given money to Judas to betray Jesus. They also gave money to the soldiers to say that the body had been stolen. These Romans would have demanded a large price, for their lives were at stake. If their superiors heard that these soldiers had failed, they could have been executed. Even if the story got to Pilate, he was not likely to do much about it. He was sure that Jesus was dead (Mark 15:43-45), and that was all that mattered to him. The disappearance of Jesus' body created no problems for Pilate.

Mark Twain once wrote that a lie can go around the world while truth is still lacing up her boots. There is something in human nature that makes it easy for people to believe lies. It was not until the coming of the Spirit at Pentecost, and the powerful witness of the Apostles, that the Jews in Jerusalem discovered the truth: Jesus Christ is alive! Any sincere person who studies this evidence with an open heart will conclude that the resurrection of Jesus Christ is a historic fact that cannot be refuted.

Our Lord also appeared to the two Emmaus disciples that day (Luke 24:13-32), and also to the ten disciples in the Upper Room in Jerusalem (John 20:19-25). A week later, He appeared to the eleven disciples and dealt with Thomas' unbelief (John 20:19-25). On that first Easter Sunday, Jesus also made a special appearance to Peter (Luke 24:33-35; 1 Cor. 15:5).

That day began with the disciples and the women thinking Jesus was dead. Then they were told that He was alive. Following that announcement, they met Him personally. There was one more stage in their experience.

They Shared the Good News with Others (Matt. 28:16-20)

Some Bible scholars equate this "mountain meeting" in Galilee with the appearance of the Lord to "more than 500 brethren at one time" (1 Cor. 15:6). The fact that some of the people present doubted His resurrection would suggest that more than the eleven Apostles were present, for these men were now confirmed believers. Our Lord's ascension did not take place at this time, but later, after He had ministered to His disciples in Jerusalem (Luke 24:44-53).

Matthew 28:18-20 is usually called "the Great Commission," though this statement is no greater than that in any of the other Gospels, nor is it the last statement Jesus made before He returned to heaven. However, this declaration does apply to us as believers, so we should understand the factors that are involved.

An authority (v. 18). In this verse, the word *power* means "authority," the right to use power. The entire Gospel of Matthew stresses the authority of Jesus Christ. There was authority to His teaching (Matt. 7:29). He exercised authority in healing (Matt. 8:1-13), and even in forgiving sins (Matt. 9:6). He had authority over Satan, and He delegated that authority to His Apostles (Matt. 10:1). At the close of his Gospel, Matthew made it clear that Jesus has ALL authority.

Since Jesus Christ today has all authority, we may obey Him without fear. No matter where He leads us, no matter what circumstances we face, He is in control. By His death and resurrection, Jesus defeated all enemies and won for Himself all authority.

Christianity is a missionary faith. The very nature of God demands this, for God is love and God is not willing that any should perish (2 Peter 3:9). Our Lord's death on the cross was for the whole world. If we are the children of God and share His nature, then we will want to tell the good news to the lost world.

When we read the Book of Acts, we see that the early church operated on the basis of the Lord's sovereign authority. They ministered in His name. They depended on His power and guidance. They did not face a lost world on the basis of their own authority, but on the authority of Jesus Christ.

An activity (vv. 19-20a). The Greek verb translated *go* is actually not a command but a present participle (going). The only command in the entire Great Commission is "make disciples" ("teach all nations"). Jesus said, "While you are going, make disciples of all the nations." No matter where we are, we should be witnesses for Jesus Christ and seek to win others to Him (Acts 11:19-21).

The term "disciples" was the most popular name for the early believers. Being a disciple meant more than being a convert or a church member. *Apprentice* might be an equivalent term. A disciple attached himself to a teacher, identified with him, learned from him, and lived with him. He learned, not simply by listening, but also by doing. Our Lord called twelve disciples and taught them so that they might be able to teach others (Mark 3:13ff).

A disciple, then, is one who has believed on Jesus Christ and expressed this faith by being baptized. He remains in the fellowship of the believers that he might be taught the truths of the faith (Acts 2:41-47). He is then able to go out and win others and teach them. This was the pattern of the New Testament church (2 Tim. 2:1-2).

In many respects, we have departed from this pattern. In most churches, the congregation pays the pastor to preach, win the lost, and build up the saved—while the church members function as cheerleaders (if they are enthusiastic) or spectators. The "converts" are won, baptized, and given the right hand of fellowship, then they join the other spectators. How much faster our churches would grow, and how much stronger and happier our church members would be, if each one were discipling another believer. The only way a local church can "be fruitful and multiply" (instead of growing by "additions") is with a systematic discipleship program. This is the responsibility of *every* believer, and not just a small group who have been "called to go."

Jesus had opened the minds of His disciples to understand the Scriptures (Luke 24:44-45). They knew what He wanted them to teach to their own converts. It is not enough to win people to the Saviour; we must also teach them the Word of God. This is also a part of the Great Commission.

An ability (v. 20b). Jesus is not only "in the midst" when His people gather together (Matt. 18:20), but He is also present with them as they scatter into the world to witness. Had He remained on earth, Jesus could not have fulfilled this promise. It was when the Spirit came that Jesus could be with His people no matter where they were.

Dr. G. Campbell Morgan told about an experience in his life that involved this statement. Early in his Christian life, Morgan used to visit several ladies once a week to read the Bible to them. When he came to the end of Matthew's Gospel, Morgan read, "Lo, I am with you always, even unto the end of this age." He added, "Isn't that a wonderful promise?" One of the ladies quickly replied, "Young man, that is not a promise—it is a fact!"

There are no conditions for us to meet, or even to believe; for *Jesus Christ is with us.* Paul discovered this to be true when he was seeking to establish a church in the difficult city of Corinth. Obeying this commission, Paul came to the city (Acts 18:1), won people to Christ and baptized them (Acts 18:8) and taught them the word (Acts 18:11). When the going was tough, Paul had a special visit from the Lord: "Be not afraid . . . for I am with thee" (Acts 18:9-10).

The phrase "the end of the age" indicates that our Lord has a plan; He is the Lord of history. As the churches follow His leading and obey His Word, they fulfill His purposes in the world. It will all come to a climax one day; meanwhile, we must all be faithful.

MARK

OUTLINE

Key theme: Jesus Christ the servant
Key verse: Mark 10:45

I. THE PRESENTATION OF THE SERVANT—1:1-13

II. THE SERVANT'S MINISTRY IN GALILEE—1:14–9:50
A. Period of popularity—1:14–6:29
B. Period of withdrawal—6:30–9:32
C. Period of completion—9:33-50

III. THE SERVANT'S JOURNEY TO JERUSALEM—chapter 10

IV. THE SERVANT'S MINISTRY IN JERUSALEM—chapters 11–16
A. Public teaching and controversy—11:1–12:44
B. Private teaching and ministry—13:1–14:31
C. Arrest, trial, and crucifixion—14:32–15:47
D. Resurrection and ascension—16

CONTENTS

CHAPTER ONE
GOD'S SERVANT IS HERE!
Mark 1

"The Gospel is neither a discussion nor a debate," said Dr. Paul S. Rees. "It is an announcement!"

Mark wasted no time giving that announcement, for it is found in the opening words of his book. Matthew, who wrote primarily for the Jews, opened his book with a genealogy. After all, he had to prove to his readers that Jesus Christ is indeed the rightful Heir to David's throne. Since Luke focused mainly on the sympathetic ministry of the Son of man, he devoted the early chapters of his book to a record of the Saviour's birth. Luke emphasized Christ's humanity, for he knew that his Greek readers would identify with the perfect Babe who grew up to be the perfect Man.

John's Gospel begins with a statement about eternity! Why? Because John wrote to prove to the whole world that Jesus Christ of Nazareth is the Son of God (John 20:31). The *subject* of John's Gospel is the deity of Christ, but the *object* of his Gospel is to encourage his readers to believe on this Saviour and receive the gift of eternal life.

Where does Mark's Gospel fit in? Mark wrote for the Romans, and his theme is *Jesus Christ the Servant.* If we had to pick a "key verse" in this Gospel, it would be Mark 10:45—"For even the Son of man came not to be ministered unto, but to minister, and to give His life a ransom for many."

The fact that Mark wrote with the Romans in mind helps us understand his style and approach. The emphasis in this Gospel is on *activity.* Mark describes Jesus as He busily moves from place to place and meets the physical and spiritual needs of all kinds of people. One of Mark's favorite words is "straightway," meaning "immediately." He uses it forty-one times. Mark does not record many of our Lord's sermons because his emphasis is on what Jesus did rather than what Jesus said. He reveals Jesus as God's Servant, sent to minister to suffering people and to die for the sins of the world. Mark gives us no account of our Lord's birth, nor does he record a genealogy, unnecessary in regard to a servant.

In this opening chapter, Mark shares three important facts about God's Servant.

The Servant's Identity (Mark 1:1-11)

How does Mark identify this Servant? He records the testimonies of several dependable witnesses to assure us that Jesus is all that He claims to be.

John Mark, the author of the book, is the first witness (v. 1). He states boldly that Jesus Christ is the Son of God. It is likely that Mark was an eyewitness of some of the events that he wrote about. He lived in Jerusalem with his mother, Mary; and their home was a meeting place for believers in the city (Acts 12:1-19). Several scholars believe that Mark was the young man described in Mark 14:51-52. Since Peter called Mark "my son" (1 Peter 5:13), it is probable that it was Peter who led Mark to faith in Jesus Christ. Church tradition states that Mark was "Peter's interpreter," so that the Gospel of Mark reflects the personal experiences and witness of Simon Peter.

The word *gospel* simply means "the good news." To the Romans, Mark's special target audience, *gospel* meant "joyful news about the emperor." The "Gospel of Jesus Christ" is the Good News that God's Son has come into the world and died for our sins. It is the Good News that our sins can be forgiven, that we can belong to the family of God and one day go to live with God in heaven. It is the announcement of victory over sin, death, and hell (1 Cor. 15:1-8, 51-52; Gal. 1:1-9).

The second witness is that of the prophets (vv. 2-3). Mark cites two quotations from the Old Testament prophets, Malachi 3:1 and Isaiah 40:3 (note also Ex. 23:20). The words *messenger* and *voice* refer to John the Baptist, the prophet God sent to prepare the way for His Son (Matt. 3; Luke 3:1-18; John 1:19-34). In ancient times, before a king visited any part of his realm, a messenger was sent before him to prepare the way. This included both repairing the roads and preparing the people. By calling the nation to repentance, John the Baptist prepared the way for the Lord Jesus Christ. Isaiah and Malachi join voices in declaring that Jesus Christ is the Lord, Jehovah God.

John the Baptist is the next witness (vv. 4-8). Jesus called him the greatest of the prophets (Matt. 11:1-15). In his dress, manner of life, and message of repentance, John identified with Elijah (2 Kings 1:8; Mal. 4:5; Matt. 17:10-13; and note Luke 1:13-17). The "wilderness" where John ministered is the rugged wasteland along the western shore of the Dead Sea. John was telling the people symbolically that they were in a "spiritual wilderness" far worse than the physical wilderness which their ancestors had endured for forty years. John called the people to leave their spiritual wilderness, trust their "Joshua" (Jesus), and enter into their inheritance.

John was careful to magnify Jesus and not himself (see John 3:25-30). John would baptize repentant sinners in water, but "the coming One" would baptize them with the Spirit (Acts 1:4-5). This did not mean that John's baptism was unauthorized (see Matt. 21:23-27), or that water baptism would one day be replaced by Spirit baptism (see Matt. 28:19-20). Rather, John's message and baptism were *preparation* so that the people would be ready to meet and trust the Messiah, Jesus Christ. Our Lord's Apostles were no doubt baptized by John (see John 4:1-2 and Acts 1:21-26).

The Father and the Holy Spirit are Mark's final witnesses to the identity of God's Servant (vv. 9-11). When Jesus was baptized, the Spirit came on Him as a dove, and the Father spoke from heaven and identified His beloved Son. The people who were there did not hear the voice or see the dove, but Jesus and John did (see John 1:29-34). The word *beloved* not only declares affection, but it also carries the meaning of "the only one." The Father's announcement from heaven reminds us of Psalm 2:7 and Isaiah 42:1.

You will want to note these references in Mark's Gospel to Jesus Christ as the Son of God—Mark 1:1, 11; 3:11; 5:7; 9:7; 12:1-11; 13:32; 14:61-62; and 15:39. Mark did not write his book about just any Jewish servant. He wrote his book about the very Son of God who came from heaven to die for the sins of the world.

Yes, Jesus is the Servant—but He is a most unusual Servant. After all, it is the servant who prepares the way for others and announces their arrival. But *others* prepared the way for Jesus and announced that He had come! Even heaven itself took note of Him! This Servant is God the Son.

The Servant's Authority (Mark 1:12-28)

We expect a servant to be *under authority* and to *take* orders, but God's Servant *exercises* authority and *gives* orders—even to demons—and His orders are obeyed. In this section, Mark describes three scenes that reveal our Lord's authority as the Servant of God.

Scene one—His temptation (vv. 12-13). Mark does not give as full an account of the Temptation as do Matthew (4:1-11) and Luke (4:1-13); but Mark adds some vivid details that the others omit. The Spirit "driveth Him" into the wilderness. This is a strong word that Mark used eleven times to describe the casting out of demons. It is *impelled* in the *New American* and *sent* in the *New International.* It does not suggest that our Lord was either unwilling or afraid to face Satan. Rather, it is Mark's way of showing the intensity of the experience. No time was spent basking in the glory of the heavenly voice or the presence of the heavenly dove. The Servant had a task to perform and He immediately went to do it.

In concise form, Mark presents us with two symbolic pictures. Our Lord's forty *days* in the wilderness remind us of Israel's forty *years* in the wilderness. Israel failed when they were tested, but our Lord succeeded victoriously. Having triumphed over the enemy, Jesus could now go forth and call a new people who would enter into their spiritual inheritance. Since the name *Jesus* is the Greek form of "Joshua," we can see the parallel.

The second picture is that of the "last Adam" (1 Cor. 15:45). The first Adam was tested in a beautiful Garden and failed; but Jesus was tempted in a dangerous wilderness and won the victory. Adam lost his "dominion" over Creation because of his sin (Gen. 1:28; Ps. 8), but in Christ, that dominion has been restored for all who trust Him (Heb. 2:6-8). Jesus was with the wild beasts and they did not harm Him. He gave a demonstration of that future time of peace and righteousness, when the Lord shall return and establish His kingdom (Isa. 11:9; 35:9). Indeed, He is a Servant with authority!

Scene two—His preaching (vv. 14-22). If ever a man spoke God's truth with authority, it was Jesus Christ (see Matt. 7:28-29). It has been said that the scribes spoke *from* authorities but that Jesus spoke *with authority.* Mark was not recording here the beginning of our Lord's ministry, since He had already ministered in other places (John 1:35–4:4). He is telling us why Jesus left Judea and came to Galilee: Herod had arrested John the Baptist, and wisdom dictated that Jesus relocate. By the way, it was during this journey that Jesus talked with the Samaritan woman (John 4:1-45).

Our Lord's message was the Gospel of the kingdom of God, or "the Gospel of God" as some texts read. No doubt most of the Jews read "political revolution" into the phrase "kingdom of God," but that was not what Jesus had in mind at all. His kingdom has to do with His reign in the lives of His people; it is a spiritual realm and not a political organization. The only way to enter God's kingdom is by believing the Good News and being born again (John 3:1-7).

The Gospel is called "the Gospel of God" because it comes from God and brings us to God. It is "the Gospel of the kingdom" because faith in the Saviour brings you into His kingdom. It is the "Gospel of Jesus Christ" because He is the heart of it; without His life, death, and resurrection, there would be no Good News. Paul called it "the Gospel of the grace of God" (Acts 20:24) because there can be no salvation apart from grace (Eph. 2:8-9). There is only one Gospel (Gal. 1:1-9), and it centers in what Jesus Christ did for us on the cross (1 Cor. 15:1-11).

Jesus preached that people should repent (change their minds) and believe (see Acts 20:21). Repentance alone is not enough to save us, even though God expects believers to turn from their sins. We must also put positive faith in Jesus Christ and believe His promise of salvation. Repentance without faith could become remorse, and remorse can destroy people who carry a burden of guilt (see Matt. 27:3-5; 2 Cor. 7:8-10).

Because Jesus preached with authority, He was able to call men from their regular occupations and make them His disciples. Who else could interrupt four fishermen at their work and challenge them to leave their nets and follow Him? Several months before, Jesus had already met Peter, Andrew, James, and John; and they had come to trust Him (see John 1:35-49). This was not their initial call to faith and salvation; it was an initial call to discipleship. The fact that Zebedee had hired servants suggests that his fishing business was successful and that he was a man of means. It also assures us that James and John did not mistreat their father when they heeded Christ's call. With the help of his servants, Zebedee could still manage the business.

Jesus did not invent the term "fishers of men." In that day, it was a common description of philosophers and other teachers who "captured men's minds" through teaching and persuasion. They would "bait the hook" with their teachings and "catch" disciples. It is likely that as many as seven of our Lord's disciples were fishermen (John 21:1-3). Surely the good qualities of successful fishermen would make for success in the difficult ministry of winning lost souls: courage, the ability to work together, patience, energy, stamina, faith, and tenacity. Professional fishermen simply could not afford to be quitters or complainers!

Jesus ministered not only in the open air but also in the synagogues. The Jewish synagogues developed during the nation's exile when the people were in Babylon after the temple had been destroyed. Wherever there were ten Jewish men above the age of twelve, a synagogue could be organized. The synagogue was not a place of sacrifice—that was done at the temple—but of reading the Scriptures, praying and worshiping God. The services were led, not by priests, but by laymen; and the ministry was supervised by a board of elders which was presided over by a "ruler" (Mark 5:22). It was customary to ask visiting rabbis to read the Scriptures and teach, which explains why Jesus had such freedom to minister in the synagogues. The Apostle Paul also took advantage of this privilege (Acts 13:14-16; 14:1; 17:1-4).

Our Lord had set up His headquarters in Capernaum, possibly in or near the home of Peter and Andrew (Mark 1:29). You may see the remains of a Capernaum synagogue when you visit the Holy Land today, but it is not the one in which Jesus worshiped. The people assembled for services on the Sabbath as well as on Mondays and Thursdays. Being a faithful Jew, Jesus honored the Sabbath by going to the synagogue; and when He taught the Word, the people were astonished at His authority.

You will discover as you read Mark's Gospel that he delights in recording the emotional responses of people. The congregation in the synagogue was "astonished" at His teaching and "amazed" at His healing powers (Mark 1:27; also note 2:12; 5:20, 42; 6:2, 51; 7:37; 10:26; 11:18). You even find Mark recording our Lord's amazement at the unbelief of the people in Nazareth (Mark 6:6). There is certainly nothing monotonous about this narrative!

Scene three—His command (vv. 23-28). We wonder how many synagogue services that man had attended without revealing that he was demonized. It took the presence of the Son of God to expose the demon; and Jesus not only exposed him, but He also commanded him to keep quiet about His identity and to depart from the man. The Saviour did not want, nor did He need, the assistance of Satan and his army to tell people who He is (see Acts 16:16-24).

The demon certainly knew exactly who Jesus is (see Acts 19:13-17) and that he had nothing in common with Him. The demon's use of plural pronouns shows how closely he was identified with the man through whom he was speaking. The demon clearly identified Christ's humanity ("Jesus of Nazareth") as well as His deity ("the Holy One of God"). He also confessed great fear that Jesus might judge him and send him to the pit. There are people today just like this demonized man: in a religious meeting, able to tell who Jesus is, and even trembling with fear of judgment—yet lost! (see James 2:19)

"Hold thy peace!" literally means "Be muzzled!" Jesus would use the same words when stilling the storm (Mark 4:39). The demon tried one last convulsive attack, but then had to submit to the authority of God's Servant and come out of the man. The people in the synagogue were amazed and afraid. They realized that something new had appeared on the scene—a new doctrine and a new power. Our Lord's *words* and *works* must always go together (John 3:2). The people kept on talking about both, and the fame of Jesus began to spread. Our Lord did not encourage this kind of public excitement lest it create problems with both the Jews and the Romans. The Jews would want to follow Him only because of His power to heal them, and the Romans would think He was a Jewish insurrectionist trying to overthrow the government. This explains why Jesus so often told people to keep quiet (Mark 1:44; 3:12; 5:43; 7:36-37; 8:26, 30; 9:9). The fact that they did not obey created problems for Him.

The Servant's Sympathy (Mark 1:29-45)

Two miracles of healing are described in this section, both of which reveal the compassion of the Saviour for those in need. In fact, so great was His love for the needy that the Saviour ministered to great crowds of people after the Sabbath had ended, when it was lawful for them to come for help. It would appear that God's Servant was at the beck and call of all kinds of people, including demoniacs and lepers; and He lovingly ministered to them all.

Jesus and the four disciples left the synagogue and went to Peter and Andrew's house for their Sabbath meal. Perhaps Peter was a bit apologetic because his wife had to care for her sick mother and was unable to entertain them in the usual manner. We do not know about the other disciples, but we do know that Peter was a married man (Mark 1:30).

Peter and Andrew not only brought their friends James and John home with them from the service, but they also brought the Lord home. That is a good example for us to follow: don't leave Jesus at the church—take Him home with you and let Him share your blessings and your burdens. What a privilege it was for Peter and his family to have the very Son of God as guest in their humble home. Before long, the Guest became the Host, just as one day the Passenger in Peter's boat would become the Captain (Luke 5:1-11).

By faith, the men told Jesus about the sick woman, no doubt expecting Him to heal her. That is exactly what He did! The fever left her immediately, and she was able to go to the kitchen and serve the Sabbath meal. If you have ever had a bad fever, then you know how painful and uncomfortable it is. You also know that after the fever leaves you, it takes time for you to regain your strength. But not so in this case! She was able to serve the Lord immediately. And isn't service to our Lord one of the best ways to thank Him for all He has done for us?

What was the result of this miracle? When the Sabbath ended at sundown, the whole city showed up at Peter's door! They brought their sick and afflicted, and the Lord (who was no doubt weary) healed them all. The Greek verb indicates that they "kept on bringing" people to Him, so that He must have gone to sleep at a very late hour. Note in Mark 1:32 the clear distinction made between the diseased and the demonized. While Satan can cause physical affliction, not all sickness is caused by demonic power.

Late hours did not keep Jesus from His appointed meeting with His Father early the next morning. Read Isaiah 50:4 for a prophetic description of God's righteous Servant as He meets the Father morning by morning. What an example for us to follow! It is no surprise that Jesus had such authority and power when His prayer life was so disciplined (see Mark 9:28-29; 6:46; 14:32-38).

However, the crowds wanted to see Jesus

again, not to hear His word, but to experience His healing and see Him perform miracles. Peter was surprised that Jesus did not hasten to meet the crowds but instead left for other towns where He might preach the Gospel. Peter did not realize the shallowness of the crowds, their unbelief, and their lack of appetite for the Word of God. Jesus said it was more important for Him to preach the Gospel in other places than to stay there and heal the sick. He did not permit popular acclaim to change His priorities.

Perhaps we can understand our Lord's concern for a feverish woman, but that He would meet *and touch* a leper is somewhat beyond our understanding. Lepers were supposed to keep their distance and warn everyone that they were coming, lest others would be defiled (Lev. 13:45-46). This man knew that Jesus was *able* to heal him, but he was not sure the Master was *willing* to heal him. Lost sinners today have the same unnecessary concern, for God has made it abundantly clear that He is not willing that sinners perish (2 Peter 3:9) and that He is willing that all men be saved (1 Tim. 2:4).

When you read the "tests" for leprosy described in Leviticus 13, you can see how the disease is a picture of sin. Like sin, leprosy is deeper than the skin (Lev. 13:3); it spreads (Lev. 13:5-8); it defiles and isolates (Lev. 13:44-46); and it renders things fit only for the fire (Lev. 13:47-59). Anyone who has never trusted the Saviour is spiritually in worse shape than this man was physically.

Jesus had compassion on the man (note Mark 6:34; 8:2; 9:22) and healed him. He did it with His touch and with His Word. No doubt this was the first loving touch this leper had felt in a long time. As with the fever, so with the leprosy: it was gone instantly!

For reasons already stated, Jesus commanded the man not to tell everybody. He was to go to the priests and follow the instructions given in Leviticus 14, so that he might be declared clean and received back into the social and religious life of the community. However, the man disobeyed orders. Jesus told this man to keep quiet, and yet he told everybody. Jesus commands us to tell everybody—and we keep quiet! The crowds that came to get help from Jesus created a serious problem for Him and probably hindered Him from teaching the Word as He intended to do (Mark 1:38).

The ceremony described in Leviticus 14 presents a beautiful picture in type of the work of redemption. The two birds represent two different aspects of our Lord's ministry: His incarnation and death (the bird put into the jar and then killed), and His resurrection and ascension (the bird stained with the blood and then set free). The blood was applied to the man's right ear (God's Word), right thumb (God's work), and right great toe (God's walk). Then the oil was put on the blood, symbolizing the Holy Spirit of God. The Holy Spirit cannot come on human flesh until first the blood has been applied.

We should learn some important spiritual lessons from this chapter. To begin with, if the Son of God came as a servant, then being a servant is the highest of all callings. We are never more like the Lord Jesus than when we are serving others. Second, God shares His authority with His servants. Only those who are *under* authority have the right to *exercise* authority. Finally, if you are going to be a servant, be sure you have compassion; because people will come to you for help and rarely ask if it is convenient!

Yet, what a privilege it is to follow in the steps of Jesus Christ and meet the needs of others by being one of God's compassionate servants.

CHAPTER TWO
WHAT THE SERVANT OFFERS YOU
Mark 2:1–3:12

With amazing speed the news spread that a miracle-working Teacher had come to Capernaum; and wherever our Lord went, great crowds gathered. They wanted to see Him heal the sick and cast out demons. Had they been interested in His message of the Gospel, these multitudes would have been an encouragement to Jesus; but He knew that most of them were shallow in their thinking and blind to their own needs. Often the Lord found it necessary to leave the city and go out into the wilderness to pray (Luke 5:15-16). Every servant of God should follow His example and take time away from people in order to meet the Father and be refreshed and revitalized through prayer.

Now the time had come for Jesus to demonstrate to the people what His ministry was all about. After all, He had come to do much more than relieve the afflictions of the sick and the demonized. Those miracles were wonderful, but there was something greater for the people to experience—they could enter into the kingdom of God! They needed to understand the spiritual lessons that lay behind the physical miracles He was performing.

In this section, our Lord makes it clear that He came to bring to all who would trust Him three wonderful gifts: forgiveness (Mark 2:1-12), fulfillment (Mark 2:13-22), and freedom (Mark 2:23–3:12).

Forgiveness (Mark 2:1-12)

Whether this event took place in His own house ("He was at home," NASB), or Peter's house, is not made clear. Since hospitality is one of the basic laws of the East, the people of Capernaum did not wait for an invitation but simply came to the house in droves. This meant that some of the truly needy people could not get close enough to Jesus to receive His help. However, four friends of a palsied man decided to lower their friend through the roof, trusting that Jesus would heal him; and Jesus did. This miracle of healing gave our Lord the opportunity to teach an important lesson about forgiveness.

Consider this scene through the eyes of the Lord Jesus. When He *looked up,* He saw the four men on the roof with their sick friend. Houses had flat roofs which were usually accessible by means of an outside stairway. It would not be difficult to remove the tiles, laths, and grass that comprised the roof and make an opening large enough to fit their friend through on his mat.

We must admire several characteristics of these men, qualities that ought to mark us as "fishers of men." For one thing, they were deeply concerned about their friend and wanted to see him helped. They had the faith to believe that Jesus could and would meet his need. They did not simply "pray about it," but they put some feet to their prayers; and they did not permit the difficult circumstances to discourage them. They worked together and dared to do something different, and Jesus rewarded their efforts. How easy it would have been for them to say, "Well, there is no sense trying to get to Jesus today! Maybe we can come back tomorrow."

When our Lord *looked down,* He saw the palsied man lying on his mat; and immediately Jesus went to the heart of the man's problem—sin. Not all sickness is caused by sin (see John 9:1-3), but evidently this man's condition was the result of his disobedience to God. Even before He healed the man's body, Jesus spoke peace to the man's heart and announced that his sins were forgiven! Forgiveness is the greatest miracle that Jesus ever performs. It meets the greatest need; it costs the greatest price; and it brings the greatest blessing and the most lasting results.

Then Jesus *looked around* and saw the critics who had come to spy on Him (see Luke 5:17). These religious leaders certainly had every right to investigate the ministry of this new teacher, since the religious life of the nation was under their supervision (Deut. 13). But they should have come with open minds and hearts, seeking truth, instead of with critical minds, seeking heresy. Some of the negative attitude that had been present in Judea (John 4:1-4) had now invaded Galilee, and this was the beginning of the official opposition that ultimately led to our Lord's arrest and death. He was now so popular that the Jewish leaders dared not ignore Him. In fact, they must have arrived early for the meeting, because they were right at the scene of action! Or perhaps Jesus graciously gave them front row seats.

When the Lord *looked within,* He saw the critical spirit in their hearts and knew that they were accusing Him of blasphemy. After all, only God *can* forgive sins; and Jesus had just told the paralytic that his sins were forgiven. Jesus was claiming to be God!

But the next instant, He *proved* Himself to be God by reading their hearts and telling them what they were thinking (see John 2:25; Heb. 3:13). Since they wanted to "reason" about things, He gave them something to ponder: Which is easier, to heal the man or to tell him he is forgiven? Obviously, it is easier to say, "Your sins are forgiven!" *because nobody can prove whether or not the forgiveness really took place.* So, to back up His words, Jesus immediately healed the man and sent him home. The healing of the man's body was but an illustration and demonstration of the healing of his soul (Ps. 103:3). The scribes and Pharisees, of course, could neither heal the man nor forgive his sins; so they were caught in their own trap and condemned by their own thoughts.

Jesus affirmed His deity not only by forgiving the man's sins and healing his body, but also by applying to Himself the title "Son of man." This title is used fourteen times in Mark's Gospel, and twelve of these references are found after Mark 8:29 when Peter confessed Jesus as the Christ of God (Mark 2:10, 28; 8:31, 38; 9:9, 12, 31; 10:33, 45; 13:26, 34; 14:21, 41, 62). It was definitely a messianic title (Dan. 7:13-14) and the Jews would have interpreted it that way. Jesus used this title about eighty times in the Gospels.

Suppose the religious leaders had opened their hearts to the truth that day, what could they have learned? For one thing, they could have learned that sin is like sickness and that forgiveness is like having your health restored. This was not a new truth, for the Old Testament Scriptures had said the same thing (Ps. 103:3; Isa. 1:5-6, 16-20); but now it had been demonstrated before their very eyes. They also could have learned that Jesus Christ of Nazareth is indeed the Saviour with authority to forgive sins—and their own sins could have been forgiven! What an opportunity they missed when they came to the meeting with a critical spirit instead of with a repentant heart!

Fulfillment (Mark 2:13-22)

It soon became evident that Jesus was deliberately associating Himself with the outcasts of Jewish society. He even called a tax collector to become one of His disciples! We do not know that Levi was a dishonest man, though most of the tax collectors were; but the fact that he worked for Herod Antipas and the Romans was enough to disgrace him among loyal Jews. However, when Jesus called him, Levi did not argue or delay. He got up and followed Jesus, even though he knew that Rome would never give him back his job. He burned his bridges ("And he left everything behind"—Luke 5:28, NASB), received a new name ("Matthew, the gift of God"), and enthusiastically invited some of his "sinner" friends to meet the Lord Jesus. These were Jewish people like himself who did not follow the Law or appear to have much interest in things religious. It was exactly the kind of people Jesus wanted to reach.

Of course, the critics had to be there; but our Lord used their questions to teach the guests about Himself and the spiritual work He came to do. He explained His mission by using three interesting comparisons.

The Physician (vv. 16-17). Jesus did not consider these people "rejects," even though they had been excommunicated by the religious leaders. Matthew's friends were *patients* who needed a physician, and Jesus was that Physician. We have already seen that sin may be compared to sickness and forgiveness to having your health restored. Now we see that our Saviour may be compared to a physician: He comes to us in our need; He makes a perfect diagnosis; He provides a final and complete cure; and *He pays the bill!* What a physician!

But there are three kinds of "patients" whom Jesus cannot heal of their sin sickness: (1) those who do not know about Him; (2) those who know about Him but refuse to trust Him; and (3) those who will not admit that they need Him. The scribes and Pharisees were in that third category, as are all self-righteous sinners today. Unless we admit that we are sinners, deserving of God's judgment, we cannot be saved. Jesus saves only sinners (Luke 19:10).

In Jesus' day, as in the days of the prophets, there were those who claimed to bring spiritual healing to the people, but whose remedies were ineffective. Jeremiah rebuked the priests and false prophets of his day because they were worthless physicians who gave only a false hope to the nation. "They have healed also the hurt of the daughter of my people slightly, saying, 'Peace, peace'; when there is no peace" (Jer. 6:14; 8:11). They applied their weak medicines to the surface symptoms and did not get down deep into the basic problem—the sinful heart (Jer. 17:9). We must beware of such worthless physicians today.

The Bridegroom (vv. 18-20). While the first question they asked had to do with the kind of company Jesus was keeping, their second question raised the issue of why Jesus was having such a good time with these people at the table. His conduct, to them, seemed inappropriate. John the Baptist was an austere man, somewhat of a recluse; but Jesus accepted invitations to meals, played with the children, and enjoyed social gatherings (Matt. 11:16-19). No doubt John's disciples were a bit scandalized to see Jesus at a party, and the pious disciples of the Pharisees (see Matt. 23:15) were quick to join them in their perplexity.

Jesus had already made it clear that He came to convert the sinners, not to compliment the self-righteous. Now He told them that he had come to bring gladness, not sadness. Thanks to the legalism imposed by the scribes and Pharisees, the Jewish religion had become a burdensome thing. The poor people were weighed down by rules and regulations that were impossible to obey (Matt. 23:4). "Life is not supposed to be a funeral!" Jesus told them. "God wants life to be a wedding feast! I am the Bridegroom and these people are My wedding guests. Are not wedding guests supposed to have a good time?"

The Jews knew that marriage was one of the pictures used in the Old Testament to help explain Israel's relationship to the Lord. They had been "married to Jehovah" and they belonged only to Him (Isa. 54:5; Jer. 31:32). When the nation turned to foreign gods, as they often did, they committed "spiritual adultery." They were unfaithful to their Husband, and they had to be disciplined. The major theme of Hosea is God's love for His adulterous wife and His desire to restore the nation to His favor once again.

John the Baptist had already announced that Jesus was the Bridegroom (John 3:29), and our Lord had performed His first miracle at a joyous marriage feast (John 2:1-11). Now He was inviting people to come to the wedding! After all, becoming a Christian is not unlike entering into the marriage relationship (see Rom. 7:4—"that ye should be married to another"). Two people are not married just because they know each other, or even because they have strong feelings about each other. In order to be married, they must commit themselves to each other and make this commitment known. In most societies, the man and woman publicly affirm this commitment when each says, "I do!"

Salvation from sin involves much more than a person knowing about Christ, or even having "good feelings" toward Christ. Salvation comes when the sinner commits himself or herself to Jesus Christ and says, "I do!" Then the believer immediately enters into the joys of this spiritual marriage relationship: bearing His name; sharing His wealth and power; enjoying His love and protection; and one day living in His glorious home in heaven. When you are "married to Christ," life becomes a wedding feast, in spite of trials and difficulties.

Mark 2:20 is a hint of our Lord's anticipated death, resurrection, and return to heaven. It is unlikely that His disciples, at that early stage in their training, even understood what He meant. However, Jesus was not suggesting that His absence from earth would mean that His followers would have to replace the feast with a funeral! He was only pointing out that occasional fasting would be proper at a future time, but that joyful celebration should be the normal experience of believers.

The garment and the wineskins (vv. 21-22). Jesus taught two important lessons about His ministry: (1) He came to save sinners, not to call the religious; and (2) He came to bring gladness and not sadness. The third lesson is this: He came to introduce the new, not to patch up the old.

The religious leaders were impressed with our Lord's teaching, and perhaps they would have been happy to make some of His ideas a part of their own religious tradition. They were hoping for some kind of compromise that would retain the best of pharisaic Judaism and the best of what Christ had to offer. But Jesus exposed the folly of that approach. It would be like tearing patches from a new unshrunk garment and sewing them on an old garment. You would ruin the new garment; and when the old garment was washed, the patches would shrink, rip away, and ruin that garment too (note Luke 5:36-39). Or, it would be like putting new unfermented wine in old brittle wineskins. As soon as the wine began to ferment and the gases formed, the old skins would burst—and you would lose both the wine and the skins.

Jesus came to usher in the new, not to unite with the old. The Mosaic economy was decaying, getting old, and ready to vanish away (Heb. 8:13). Jesus would establish a New Covenant in His blood (Luke 22:19-20). The Law would be written on human hearts, not on stones (2 Cor. 3:1-3; Heb. 10:15-18); and the indwelling Holy Spirit would enable God's people to fulfill the righteousness of the Law (Rom. 8:1-4).

By using this illustration, Jesus refuted once and for all the popular idea of a compromising "world religion." Well-meaning but spiritually blind leaders have suggested that we take "the best" from each religion, blend it with what is "best" in the Christian faith, and thus manufacture a synthetic faith that would be acceptable to everybody. But the Christian faith is *exclusive* in character; it will not accept any other faith as its equal or its superior. "There is none other name under heaven, given among men, whereby we must be saved" (Acts 4:12).

Salvation is not a partial patching up of one's life; it is a whole new robe of righteousness (Isa. 61:10; 2 Cor. 5:21). The Christian life is not a mixing of the old and the new; rather, it is a fulfillment of the old in the new. There are two ways to destroy a thing: you can smash it, or you can permit it to fulfill itself. An acorn, for example, can be smashed with a hammer, or it can be planted and allowed to grow into an oak. In both instances, the destruction of the acorn is accomplished; but in the second instance, the acorn is destroyed by being fulfilled.

Jesus fulfilled the prophecies, types, and demands of the Law of Moses. The Law was ended at Calvary when the perfect sacrifice was once offered for the sins of the world (Heb. 8–10). When you trust Jesus Christ, you become part of a new creation (2 Cor. 5:17), and there are always new experiences of grace and glory. How tragic when people hold on to dead religious tradition when they could lay hold of living spiritual truth. Why cherish the shadows when the reality has come? (Heb. 10:1ff) In Jesus Christ we have the fulfillment of all that God promised (2 Cor. 1:20).

Freedom (Mark 2:23–3:12)

The Sabbath was cherished by the Jews as a sacred institution. God gave the people of Israel the Sabbath after they came out of Egypt (Ex. 20:8-11; Neh. 9:14), and it was a special sign between Israel and Jehovah (Ex. 31:13-17). There is no record in Scripture that God ever gave the Sabbath to any other nation. So, when Jesus began openly to violate the Sabbath traditions, it was like declaring war against the religious establishment. He began His campaign by healing a man who had been sick for thirty-eight years (John 5), and then followed with the events recorded in this section.

Jewish tradition stated that there were thirty-nine acts that were strictly forbidden on the Sabbath. Moses had prohibited work on the Sabbath, but he did not give many specifics (Ex. 20:10). It was wrong to kindle a fire for cooking (Ex. 35:3), gather fuel (Num. 15:32ff), carry burdens (Jer. 17:21ff), or transact business (Neh. 10:31; 13:15, 19). But Jewish tradition went into great detail and even informed the people how far they could travel on the Sabbath (200 cubits, based on Josh. 3:4). In short, the Sabbath Day had become a crushing burden, a symbol of the galling religious bondage that had captured the nation.

After healing the man at the Pool of Bethesda, our Lord's next act of "Sabbath defiance" was to walk through the fields on the Sabbath and permit His disciples to pluck the grain, rub it between their hands, and eat it. It was not illegal for a hungry person to take some of his neighbor's fruit or grain, provided he did not fill a vessel or use a harvesting implement (Deut. 23:24-25). However, that was not what upset the Pharisees. What upset them was that the disciples had worked on the Sabbath Day!

When you read Matthew's account of this event, you note that Jesus gave three arguments to defend His disciples: what David did (Matt. 12:3-4), what the priests did (Matt. 12:5-6), and what the Prophet Hosea said (Matt. 12:7-8). Mark's Roman readers would not be interested in Jewish prophets and priests, so Mark focused on David whom the Romans would recognize as a great hero and king. The argument is reasonable: if a hungry king and his men were permitted to eat the holy bread from the tabernacle (1 Sam. 21:1-6), then it was right for the Lord of the Sabbath to permit His men to eat the grain from His fields. David broke a definite law given by Moses, for the showbread was for the priests only (Lev. 24:5-9); but the disciples had violated only a man-made tradition. God is surely more concerned with meeting the needs of people than He is with protecting religious tradition. The Pharisees had their priorities confused.

Did Jesus make a mistake when He mentioned Abiathar as the high priest? The record in 1 Samuel 21 names Abimelech, the father of Abiathar (1 Sam. 22:20), as high priest; so our Lord's words appear to be a contradiction. They are not. It is possible that father and son each had both names (1 Chron. 18:16 and 24:6; 1 Sam. 22:20 and 2 Sam. 8:17). Also it is likely that our Lord used "Abiathar" to refer to the Old Testament *passage* about Abiathar rather than to the man. This is the way the Jews identified sections of the Word since their manuscripts did not have chapters and verses such as we have today in our Bibles (see Mark 12:26).

On that same Sabbath Day, Jesus went into the synagogue to worship; and while He was there, He deliberately healed a man. Certainly He could have waited one more day, but once again He wanted to challenge the pharisaical legalistic traditions. This time the Pharisees (Luke 6:7) were expecting Him to heal, so they kept their eyes wide open. Our Lord's questions in Mark 3:4 were never answered by His enemies. Since *evil* is at work every day, including the Sabbath Day, why should *good* not be at work as well? Death is always at work, but that should not hinder us from seeking to save life.

Jesus could see "the hardening of their hearts" (literal translation), and their sin made Him angry. Our Lord never became angry at the publicans and sinners, but He did express anger toward the self-righteous Pharisees (Matt. 23). They would rather protect their traditions than see a man healed! The man, of course, knew little about this spiritual conflict. He simply obeyed our Lord's command, stretched out his hand, and was healed.

So incensed were the Pharisees over what Jesus had done that they united with the Herodians and started making plans to arrest Jesus and destroy Him. The Herodians were not a religious party; they were a group of Jews who were sympathetic to King Herod and supported his rule. Most of the Jews despised Herod and obeyed his laws reluctantly; so it was surprising that the Pharisees, who were strict Jews, would join themselves with these disloyal politicians. But it was a common enemy—Jesus—that brought the two groups together.

In response to this united opposition, Jesus simply withdrew from there; but He could not prevent the great crowds from following Him. These crowds were dangerous to His cause, of course, because they were not spiritually motivated; and the authorities could accuse Him of leading a popular revolt against the Romans. Yet Jesus received the people, healed the sick, and delivered the demonized. Once again, He warned the demons not to reveal who He is (Mark 1:23-26).

Our Lord had now reached a crisis in His ministry. Great crowds were following Him, but their interest was not in things spiritual. The religious leaders wanted to destroy Him, and even some of Herod's friends were getting involved. His next step would be to spend a night in prayer (Luke 6:12), call twelve men to assist Him as His Apostles, and preach a sermon—The Sermon on the Mount—explaining the spiritual basis of His kingdom.

He offered them forgiveness, fulfillment, and freedom; but they refused His offer.

Have *you* accepted His offer?

CHAPTER THREE
THE SERVANT, THE CROWDS, AND THE KINGDOM
Mark 3:13–4:34

No matter where He went, God's Servant was thronged by excited crowds (Mark 3:7-9, 20, 32; 4:1). Had Jesus been a "celebrity" and not a servant, He would have catered to the crowds and tried to please them (see Matt. 11:7-15). Instead, He withdrew from the crowds and began to minister especially to His disciples. Jesus knew that most of the people who pushed to get near Him were shallow and insincere, but His disciples did not know this. Lest they take all of this "success" seriously, Jesus had to teach these men the truth about the crowds and the kingdom. In this section, we see our Lord's three responses to the pressure of the crowd.

He Founded a New Nation (Mark 3:13-19)

The number of the disciples is significant because there were twelve tribes in the nation of Israel. In Genesis, God started with Jacob's twelve sons, and in Exodus, He built them into a mighty nation. Israel was chosen to bring the Messiah into the world so that through Him all the nations of the earth could be blessed (Gen. 12:1-3). However, the nation of Israel was now spiritually decayed and ready to reject her own Messiah. God had to establish "a holy nation, a peculiar [purchased] people" (1 Peter 2:9), and the 12 Apostles were the nucleus of this new "spiritual" nation (Matt. 21:43).

Jesus spent all night in prayer before choosing these twelve men (Luke 6:12). When He selected them, He had three purposes in mind: (1) training them by personal example and teaching, (2) sending them out to preach the Gospel, and (3) giving them authority to heal and cast out demons (see Mark 1:14-15, 38-39; 6:7-13). These twelve men would thus be able to continue His work when He returned to the Father, and they would also be able to train others to carry on the ministry after them (2 Tim. 2:2).

In the New Testament, you will find three other lists of the names of the twelve disciples: Matthew 10:2-4; Luke 6:14-16; and Acts 1:13. Luke tells us that Jesus gave them the special name "apostles." A disciple is one who learns by doing; our modern equivalent might be "an apprentice." An "apostle" is one who is sent on official service with a commission. Jesus had many disciples but only 12 Apostles, His special "ambassadors."

When you compare the lists, it appears that the names are arranged in pairs: Peter and Andrew; James and John; Philip and Bartholomew (Nathanael [John 1:45]); Thomas and Matthew (Levi); James, the son of Alphaeus, and Thaddaeus (Judas, son of James, not Iscariot [John 14:22]); Simon the Zealot and Judas Iscariot. Since Jesus sent His Apostles out two by two, this was a logical way to list them (Mark 6:7).

Simon's name was changed to Peter, "the rock" (John 1:40-42); and Levi's was changed to Matthew, "the gift of God." James and John were given the nicknames, "Boanerges—the sons of thunder." We commonly think of John as the apostle of love, but he certainly did not begin with that kind of reputation, nor did James his brother (Mark 9:38-41; 10:35-39; Luke 9:54-55). It is encouraging to see what Jesus was able to do with such a diversified group of unlikely candidates for Christian service. There is still hope for us!

Mark defined the Hebrew word *Boanerges* because he was writing for Roman readers. In his Gospel you will find several of these "special notes for Gentiles" (Mark 5:41; 7:11, 34; 11:9; 14:36; 15:22, 34). The word *Canaanite* in Mark 3:18 has nothing to do with national or racial origin. It is the Hebrew word *cananaean,* which comes from a word that means "to be jealous, to be zealous." The Zealots were a group of Jewish extremists organized to overthrow Rome; and they used every means available to advance their cause. The historian Josephus called them "daggermen." It would be interesting to know how Simon the Zealot responded when he first met Matthew, a former employee of Rome.

If you consult a harmony of the Gospels, you will see that between Mark 3:19 and 20, Jesus preached the Sermon on the Mount (Matt. 5–7) and participated in the events described in Luke 7:1–8:3. Mark's Gospel does not include that famous sermon because his emphasis is on what Jesus did rather than what Jesus said.

He Established a New Family (Mark 3:20-21, 31-35)

Our Lord's friends were sure that Jesus was confused, and possibly deranged! The great crowds they saw following Him, and the amazing reports they heard about Him, convinced them that He desperately needed help. He simply was not living a normal life, so His friends came to Capernaum to "take charge of Him." Then his mother and "brethren" (Mark 6:3) traveled thirty miles from Nazareth to plead with Him to come home and get some rest, but even they were unable to get near Him. This is the only place in the Gospel of Mark where Mary is seen, and her venture was a failure.

History reveals that God's servants are usually misjudged by their contemporaries, and often misunderstood by their families. D.L. Moody was called "Crazy Moody" by many people in Chicago, and even the great Apostle Paul was called mad (Acts 26:24-25). Emily Dickinson wrote:

> Much madness is divinest sense
> To a discerning eye;
> Much sense the starkest madness.
> 'Tis the majority
> In this, as all, prevails.
> Assent, and you are sane;
> Demur—you're straightway dangerous,
> And handled with a chain.

Our Lord was not being rude to His family when He remained in the house and did not try to see them. He knew that their motives were right but their purpose was definitely wrong. If Jesus had yielded to His family, He would have played right into the hands of the opposition. The religious leaders would have said, "See, He agreed with His family—He needs help! Don't take Jesus of Nazareth too seriously." Instead of giving in, He used this crisis as an opportunity to teach a spiritual lesson: His "family" is made up of all those who do the will of God. Our Lord's half brothers were not believers (John 7:1-5) and Jesus felt closer to the believing publicans and sinners than He did to James, Joses, Judah, and Simon, His half-brothers.

Our Lord was not suggesting that believers ignore or abandon their families in order to serve God, but only that they put God's will above everything else in life. Our love for God should be so great that our love for family would seem like hatred in comparison (Luke

14:26). Certainly it is God's will that we care for our families and provide for them (see 1 Tim. 5:8), but we must not permit even our dearest loved ones to influence us away from the will of God. When you consider the importance of the family in the Jewish society, you can imagine how radical Christ's words must have sounded to those who heard them.

How does one enter into the family of God? By means of a new birth, a spiritual birth from above (John 3:1-7; 1 Peter 1:22-25). When the sinner trusts Jesus Christ as Saviour, he experiences this new birth and enters into God's family. He shares God's divine nature (2 Peter 1:3-4) and can call God "Father" (Rom. 8:15-16). This spiritual birth is not something that we accomplish for ourselves, nor can others do it for us (John 1:11-13). It is God's work of grace; all we can do is believe and receive (Eph. 2:8-9).

He Announced a New Kingdom (Mark 3:22-30; 4:1-34)

The crowds hoped that Jesus would deliver the nation and defeat Rome. Instead, He called twelve ordinary men and founded a "new nation," a spiritual nation whose citizens had their names written down in heaven (Luke 10:20; Phil. 3:20). The crowds wanted Jesus to behave like a loyal Jew and honor His family, but Jesus established a "new family" made up of all those who trusted Him and did the will of God. The crowds also expected Him to restore the kingdom and bring back Israel's lost glory; but His response was to announce a new kingdom, a spiritual kingdom.

"Kingdom" is a key word in this section (Mark 3:24; 4:11, 26, 30). John the Baptist had announced that the arrival of the King was near and he had warned the people to prepare to meet Him (Mark 1:1-8). Jesus took up John's message and preached the Good News of the kingdom and the necessity for sinners to repent and believe (Mark 1:14-15). But what is this kingdom like? If the Lord was not going to restore Israel and set up a political kingdom, what kind of kingdom was He planning to establish?

At this point, Mark introduced a new word—*parables* (see Mark 3:23; 4:2, 10-11, 13, 33-34). Jesus explained the kingdom, not by giving a lecture on theology, but by painting pictures that captured the attention of the people and forced them to use their imaginations and think. Our English word *parable* comes from two Greek words that mean "to cast alongside" (*para*—alongside; *ballo*—to throw or cast). A parable is a story or figure placed alongside a teaching to help us understand its meaning. It is much more than "an earthly story with a heavenly meaning," and it certainly is not an "illustration" such as a preacher would use in a sermon. A true parable gets the listener deeply involved and compels that listener to make a personal decision about God's truth and his or her life. So penetrating and personal are parables that, after they heard several of them, the religious leaders wanted to kill the Lord Jesus! (see Matt. 21:45-46)

A parable begins innocently as *a picture* that arrests our attention and arouses our interest. But as we study the picture, it becomes *a mirror* in which we suddenly see ourselves. If we continue to look by faith, the mirror becomes *a window* through which we see God and His truth. How we respond to that truth will determine what further truth God will teach us.

Why did Jesus teach in parables? His disciples asked Him that very question (Mark 4:10-12; and see Matt. 13:10-17). A careful study of His reply reveals that Jesus used parables both to hide the truth and to reveal it. The crowd did not judge the parables; the parables judged the crowd. The careless listener, who thought he knew everything, would hear only a story that he did not really understand; and the result in his life would be judgment (see Matt. 11:25-30). The sincere listener, with a desire to know God's truth, would ponder the parable, confess his ignorance, submit to the Lord, and then begin to understand the spiritual lesson Jesus wanted to teach.

Jesus placed a great deal of importance on *the hearing of the Word of God.* In one form or another, the word *hear* is used thirteen times in Mark 4:1-34. Obviously, our Lord was speaking, not about physical hearing, but about hearing with spiritual discernment. To "hear" the Word of God means to understand it and obey it (see James 1:22-25).

Our Lord gave several parables to help the people (and that included His disciples) understand the nature of His kingdom.

The strong man (vv. 22-30). Jesus healed a demoniac who was both blind and dumb (Matt. 12:22-24), and the scribes and Pharisees used this miracle as an opportunity to attack Him. The crowd was saying, "Perhaps this Man is indeed the Son of David, the

Messiah." But the religious leaders said, "No, He is in league with Beelzebub! It is Satan's power that is at work in Him, not God's power."

"Beelzebub" (or "Beelzebul") is a name for the devil, and it means "master of the house." Jesus picked up on this meaning and gave a parable about a strong man guarding his house. To plunder the house, one must first overcome the strong man.

Jesus exposed both their bad theology and their faulty logic. If it was by the power of Satan that He had cast out the demon, then Satan was actually fighting against himself! This meant that Satan's house and kingdom were divided and therefore on the verge of collapse. Satan had been guarding that man carefully because the devil does not want to lose any of his territory. The fact that Jesus delivered the man was proof that He was stronger than Satan and that Satan could not stop Him.

Jesus did much more than answer their false accusation. He went on to explain the seriousness of what they had said. After all, our words reveal what is hidden in our hearts (Matt. 12:35), and what is in our hearts determines our character, conduct, and destiny. We sometimes say, "Talk is cheap!" But in reality, what we say can be very costly. Jesus warned the Jewish religious leaders that they were in danger of committing an eternal and unforgivable sin (Matt. 12:32).

When you ask people, "What is the unpardonable sin?" they usually reply, "It is blaspheming the Holy Spirit" or "It is the sin of attributing to the devil the works of the Holy Spirit." Historically speaking, these statements are true; but they do not really answer the question. How do we *today* blaspheme the Spirit of God? What miracles is the Holy Spirit performing *today* that might be carelessly or even deliberately attributed to Satan? Must a person see a miracle in order to commit this terrible sin?

Jesus made it clear that God would forgive *all* sin and *all* blasphemy, *including blasphemy against the very Son of God Himself!* (Matt. 12:32) Does this mean that God the Son is less important than the Holy Spirit? Why would a sin against God the Son be forgivable and yet a sin against the Holy Spirit be unforgivable?

The answer lies in the nature of God and in His patient dealings with the nation of Israel. God the Father sent John the Baptist to prepare the nation for the coming of their Messiah. Many of the common people responded to John's call and repented (Matt. 21:32), but the religious leaders *permitted* John to be arrested and eventually killed. God the Son came as promised and called the nation to trust Him, but those same religious leaders *asked for* Jesus to be killed. On the cross, our Lord prayed, "Father, forgive them, for they know not what they do" (Luke 23:34).

The Holy Spirit came at Pentecost and demonstrated God's power in many convicting ways. How did those same religious leaders respond? By arresting the Apostles, ordering them to keep silent, and then *killing Stephen themselves!* Stephen told them what their sin was: "Ye do always resist the Holy Ghost" (Acts 7:51). They had sinned against the Father and the Son, but had been graciously forgiven. When they sinned against the Holy Spirit, they had reached "the end of the line" and there could be no more forgiveness.

People today cannot commit the "unpardonable sin" in the same way the Jewish religious leaders did when Jesus was ministering on earth. The only sin today that God cannot forgive is rejection of His Son (John 3:16-21, 31). When the Spirit of God convicts the sinner and reveals the Saviour, the sinner may resist the Spirit and reject the witness of the Word of God, but that does not mean he has forfeited all his opportunities to be saved. If he will repent and believe, God can still forgive him. Even if the sinner so hardens his heart that he seems to be insensitive to the pleadings of God, so long as there is life, there is hope. Only God knows if and when any "deadline" has been crossed. You and I must never despair of any sinner (1 Tim. 2:4; 2 Peter 3:9).

The sower and the soils (vv. 1-20). This parable helped the disciples understand why Jesus was not impressed by the large crowds that followed Him. He knew that most of them would never produce fruit from changed lives, because the Word He was teaching them was like seed falling into poor soil.

The seed represents God's Word (Luke 8:11) and the sower is the servant of God who shares that Word with others (see 1 Cor. 3:5-9). The human heart is like soil: it must be prepared to receive the seed before that seed can take root and produce a harvest. Like seed, the Word is alive and able to produce spiritual fruit, but the seed must be planted and cultivated before that harvest will come.

As in that day, so today, there are four kinds of hearts and they respond to God's message in four different ways. The *hard heart* (Mark 4:4, 15) resists the Word of God and makes it easy for Satan (the birds) to snatch it away. Soil becomes hard when too many feet tread on it. Those who recklessly "open their hearts" to all kinds of people and influences are in danger of developing hard hearts (see Prov. 4:23). Hard hearts must be "plowed up" before they can receive the seed, and this can be a painful experience (Jer. 4:3; Hosea 10:12).

The shallow heart (vv. 5-6, 16-17). This heart is like thin soil on a rock, very typical to Palestine. Since there is no depth, whatever is planted cannot last because it has no roots. This represents the "emotional hearer" who joyfully accepts God's Word but does not really understand the price that must be paid to become a genuine Christian. There may be great enthusiasm for several days or weeks; but when persecution and difficulties begin, the enthusiasm wanes and the joy disappears. It is easy for fallen human nature to counterfeit "religious feelings" and give a professed Christian a feeling of false confidence.

The crowded heart (vv. 7, 18-19). This heart pictures the person who receives the Word but does not truly repent and remove the "weeds" out of his or her heart. This hearer has too many different kinds of "seeds" growing in the soil—worldly cares, a desire for riches, a lust for things—and the good seed of the Word has no room in which to grow. To change the image, this person wants to walk the "broad way" and the "narrow way" at the same time (Matt. 7:13-14); and it cannot be done.

The fruitful heart (vv. 8, 20). This heart pictures the true believer, because fruit—a changed life—is the evidence of true salvation (2 Cor. 5:17; Gal. 5:19-23). The other three hearts produced no fruit, so we conclude that they belong to persons who have never been born again. Not all true believers are equally as productive; but from every genuine Christian's life, there will be some evidence of spiritual fruit.

Each of the three fruitless hearts is influenced by a different enemy: the hard heart—the devil himself snatches the seed; the shallow heart—the flesh counterfeits religious feelings; the crowded heart—the things of the world smother the growth and prevent a harvest. These are the three great enemies of the Christian: the world, the flesh, and the devil (Eph. 2:1-3).

The lamp (vv. 21-25). In this parable, our Lord used a common object (a lamp) in a familiar scene (a home). The lamp was a clay dish filled with oil, with a wick put into the oil. In order to give light, the lamp had to "use itself up"; and the oil had to be replenished. If the lamp was not lit, or if it was covered up, it did the home no good.

The Apostles were like that lamp: they were called to shed God's light and reveal His truth. But they could not "give out" without first "taking in"; hence, the admonition of Mark 4:24-25. The more we hear the Word of God, the better we are able to share it with others. The moment we think that we know it all, what we think we know will be taken from us. We must take heed *what* we hear (Mark 4:24) as well as take heed *how* we hear (Luke 8:18). Our spiritual hearing determines how much we have to give to others. There is no sense trying to "cover things up" because God will one day reveal all things.

The seed growing (vv. 26-34). The first parable reminds us that we cannot make the seed grow; in fact, we cannot even explain *how* it grows. There is a mystery to the growth of the seed and the development of the harvest. It takes a good deal of faith to be a farmer, and also a good deal of patience. In the Parable of the Sower and the Soils, the Lord suggested that much of the seed scattered would fall on unproductive soil. This fact could discourage His workers; so, in this parable, He reassured them "in due season we shall reap if we faint not" (Gal. 6:9).

The second parable gave the disciples both warning and encouragement. The encouragement was that, from very small beginnings, the kingdom would eventually grow in size and in influence. While a mustard seed is not the smallest seed in the world, it was probably the smallest seed that the Jews sowed in their gardens. It was a traditional symbol of that which is tiny. Our Lord began with 12 Apostles. Later, there were as many as 500 believers (1 Cor. 15:6). Peter won 3,000 at Pentecost; and throughout the Book of Acts, that number steadily increased (Acts 4:4; 5:14; 6:1, 7). In spite of the sins and weaknesses of the church, the message has been carried to other nations; and one day, saints from *every* nation shall worship before His throne (Rev. 5:9).

But the growth of the seed is only one part

of the story; we must also account for the birds in the branches. In the Parable of the Sower and Soils, the birds stood for Satan, who snatches the seed (Mark 4:15). If we are to be consistent in our interpretation, we must take this into consideration, for both parables were taught on the same day. The growth of the kingdom will not result in the conversion of the world. In fact, some of the growth will give opportunity for Satan to get in and go to work! There was Judas in the disciple band, and Ananias and Sapphira were in fellowship with the Jerusalem church (Acts 5:1-11). Simon Magus was part of the church in Samaria (Acts 8:1-24), and Satan's ministers boldly invaded the Corinthian church (2 Cor. 11:13-15). The bigger the net, the greater the possibility of catching both good and bad fish (Matt. 13:47-50).

Through faith in Jesus Christ, we become citizens of the heavenly nation, children in God's family, and subjects of the King of kings and Lord of lords. What a privilege it is to know the Lord Jesus Christ!

CHAPTER FOUR THE SERVANT CONQUERS!

Mark 4:35–5:43

God's Servant, Jesus Christ, is the Master of every situation and the Conqueror of every enemy. If we trust Him and follow His orders, we need never be afraid. *Victory* is the major theme that binds this long section together. Mark recorded four miracles that Jesus performed, and each miracle announces even to us today the defeat of an enemy.

Victory over Danger (Mark 4:35-41)

"The same day" refers to the day on which Jesus gave the "parables of the kingdom." He had been teaching His disciples the Word and now He would give them a practical test to see how much they had really learned. After all, the hearing of God's Word is intended to produce faith (Rom. 10:17); and faith must always be tested. It is not enough for us merely to learn a lesson or be able to repeat a teaching. We must also be able to practice that lesson by faith, and that is one reason why God permits trials to come to our lives.

Did Jesus know that the storm was coming? Of course He did! The storm was a part of that day's curriculum. It would help the disciples understand a lesson that they did not even know they needed to learn: Jesus can be trusted in the storms of life. Many people have the idea that storms come to their lives only when they have disobeyed God, but this is not always the case. Jonah ended up in a storm because of his disobedience, but the disciples got into a storm because of their *obedience* to the Lord.

The geographic location of the Sea of Galilee is such that sudden violent storms are not unusual. While crossing this very sea one summer afternoon, I asked an Israeli tour guide if he had ever been in such a storm. "I certainly have!" he replied, throwing up his hands and shaking his head. "And I never want to be in one like it again!"

The storm described here must have been especially fierce if it frightened experienced fishermen like the disciples. There were at least three good reasons why none of the men in the ship should have been disturbed, even though the situation appeared to be threatening.

To begin with, they had His promise that they were going to the other side (Mark 4:35). His commandments are always His enablements and nothing can hinder the working out of His plans. He did not promise an easy trip, but He did promise a guaranteed arrival at their destination.

Second, the Lord Himself was with them, so what was there to fear? They had already seen His power demonstrated in His miracles, so they should have had complete confidence that He could handle the situation. For some reason, the disciples did not yet understand that He was indeed the Master of every situation.

Finally, they could see that Jesus was perfectly at peace, even in the midst of the storm. This fact alone should have encouraged them. Jesus was in God's will and knew that the Father would care for Him, so He took a nap. Jonah slept during a storm because he had a false sense of security, even though he was running from God. Jesus slept in the storm because He was truly secure in God's will. "I will both lay me down in peace, and sleep, for Thou, Lord, only makest me dwell in safety" (Ps. 4:8).

How often in the trials of life we are prone to imitate the faithless disciples and cry out, "Lord, don't You care?" Of course, He cares! He arose and rebuked the storm, and immediately there was a great calm. But Jesus did not stop with the calming of the elements, for the greatest danger was not the wind or the waves: it was the unbelief in the hearts of the disciples. Our greatest problems are within us, not around us. This explains why Jesus gently rebuked them and called them "men of little faith." They had heard Him teach the Word and had even seen Him perform miracles, and yet they still had no faith. It was their unbelief that caused their fear, and their fear made them question whether Jesus really cared. We must beware of "an evil heart of unbelief" (Heb. 3:12).

This was only one of many lessons Jesus would teach His disciples in the familiar environs of the Sea of Galilee, and each lesson would reveal some wonderful new truth about the Lord Jesus. They already knew that He had the authority to forgive sins, to cast out demons, and to heal diseases. Now they discovered that He even had authority over the wind and the sea. This meant that they had no reason ever again to be afraid, for their Lord was in constant control of every situation.

Victory over Demons (Mark 5:1-20)

When Jesus and the disciples landed on the other side, they encountered two demoniacs, one of whom was especially vocal (see Matt. 8:28). This entire scene seems very unreal to us who live in so-called "modern civilization," but it would not be unreal on many mission fields. In fact, some Bible teachers believe that demon possession is becoming even more prevalent in today's "modern society."

We see in this scene three different forces at work: Satan, society, and the Saviour. These same three forces are still at work in our world, trying to control the lives of people.

First, we see what *Satan* can do to people. Satan is a thief whose ultimate purpose is to destroy (John 10:10; and see Rev. 9:11). We are not told how the demons entered these men and took control, but possibly it was the result of their yielding to sin. Demons are "unclean spirits" and can easily get a foothold in the lives of people who cultivate sinful practices.

Because they yielded to Satan, the thief, these two men lost everything! They lost their homes and the fellowship of their families and friends. They lost their decency as they ran around in the tombs naked. They lost their self-control and lived like wild animals, screaming, cutting themselves, and frightening the citizens. They lost their peace and their purpose for living, and they would have remained in that plight had Jesus not come through a storm to rescue them.

Never underestimate the destructive power of Satan. He is our enemy and would destroy all of us if he could. Like a roaring lion, he seeks to devour us (1 Peter 5:8-9). It is Satan who is at work in the lives of unbelievers, making them "children of disobedience" (Eph. 2:1-3). The two men in the Gerasene graveyard were no doubt extreme examples of what Satan can do to people, but what they reveal is enough to make us want to resist Satan and have nothing to do with him.

The second force at work on these men was *society,* but society was not able to accomplish very much. About all that society can do for problem people is to isolate them, put them under guard and, if necessary, bind them (Luke 8:29). Often these men had been chained, but the demons had given them strength to break the chains. Even the attempts to tame these men had failed. With all of its wonderful scientific achievements, society still cannot cope with the problems caused by Satan and sin. While we thank God that society does offer a limited amount of restraint and protection, we must confess that society cannot permanently solve these problems and deliver Satan's terrorized victims.

This brings us to the third force, that of *the Saviour.* What did Jesus Christ do for these men? To begin with, He graciously came to them in love, and even went through a storm to do it. Some think that the storm itself may have been satanic in origin, since Jesus used the same words to calm the sea as He did to cast out demons (compare Mark 1:25 and 4:39). Perhaps Satan was trying to destroy Jesus, or at least prevent Him from coming to the men who needed Him. But nothing could stop the Lord from coming to that graveyard and bringing deliverance to those men.

Not only did Jesus come to them, but He spoke to them and permitted them to speak to Him. The citizens of that area avoided the two demoniacs, but Jesus treated them with love and respect. He came to seek and to save that which was lost (Luke 19:10).

It is interesting to note that, as the demons spoke through the man, they confessed what they really believed. Demons have faith and even tremble because of what they believe (James 2:19); but neither their faith nor their fear can save them. Demons believe that Jesus is the Son of God and that He has authority over them. They believe in the reality of judgment and that one day they will be cast into hell (see Matt. 8:29). This is more than many religious people believe today!

Nowhere does the Bible explain either the psychology or the physiology of demon possession. The man who spoke to Jesus was under the control of *a legion* of demons, and a Roman legion could consist of as many as 6,000 men! It is frightening to think of the horrors this man experienced day and night as thousands of unclean spirits tormented him. No doubt the other demonized man experienced his share of agony too.

Satan tried to destroy these men, but Jesus came to deliver them. By the power of His Word, He cast out the demons and set the men free. Demons even believe in prayer, for they begged Jesus not to send them into the abyss, the place of torment (Mark 5:7; Luke 8:31). It is encouraging to note that the demons did not know what Jesus planned to do. This suggests that Satan can know God's plans only if God reveals them. In fact, there is no evidence in Scripture that Satan can read the mind of a believer, let alone the mind of God.

Mark 5 tells of three requests: the demons requested that Jesus send them into the pigs (Mark 5:12); the citizens requested that Jesus leave the area (Mark 5:17); and one of the former demoniacs requested that Jesus allow him to follow Him (Mark 5:18). Our Lord granted the first two requests but not the third one.

Did Jesus have the right to destroy 2,000 pigs and possibly put their owners out of business? If these men were Jews, then they had no right to be raising and selling unclean pigs anyway. However, this was Gentile territory, so the owners were probably Gentiles.

Certainly, Jesus was free to send the demons wherever He desired—into the abyss, into the swine, or to any other place that He chose. Then why send them into the swine? For one thing, by doing it that way, Jesus gave proof to all the spectators that a miracle of deliverance had really taken place. The destruction of the pigs also gave assurance to the two men that the unclean spirits were actually gone. But more than anything else, the drowning of the 2,000 swine was a vivid object lesson to this Christ-rejecting crowd that, to Satan, a pig is as good as a man! In fact, Satan will make a man into a pig! The Lord was warning the citizens against the powers of sin and Satan. It was a dramatic sermon before their very eyes: "The wages of sin is death!"

The swineherds did not want to be blamed for the loss of the pigs, so they immediately ran to tell the owners what had happened. When the owners arrived at the scene, they were afraid as they beheld the dramatic changes that had taken place in the two men. Instead of running around naked, the men were clothed, seated, and in their right minds. They were new creatures! (2 Cor. 5:17)

Why would the owners ask Jesus to leave? Why not ask Him to stay and perform similar cures for others who were also in need? The owners had one main interest—business—and they were afraid that if Jesus remained any longer, He would do even more "damage" to the local economy! Our Lord does not stay where He is not wanted, so He left. What an opportunity these people missed!

Why did Jesus not permit the healed demoniac to follow Him? The man's request was certainly motivated by love for the Lord Jesus, and what a testimony he had! But Jesus knew that the man's place was in his own home, with his loved ones, where he could bear witness to the Saviour. After all, effective Christian living must begin at home where people know us the best. If we honor God there, then we can consider offering ourselves for service elsewhere. This man became one of the earliest missionaries to the Gentiles. Jesus had to leave, but the man remained and bore faithful witness to the grace and power of Jesus Christ. We trust that many of those Gentiles believed on the Saviour through his witness.

Victory over Disease (Mark 5:21-34)

One crowd sighed with relief as they saw Jesus leave, but another crowd was waiting to welcome Him when He returned home to Capernaum. In that latter crowd stood two people who were especially anxious to see Him—Jairus, a man with a dying daughter; and an anonymous woman suffering from an incurable disease. It was Jairus who approached Jesus first, but it was the woman who was first helped; so we shall begin with her.

The contrast between these two needy people is striking and reveals the wideness of Christ's love and mercy. Jairus was an important synagogue officer, and the woman was an anonymous "nobody"; yet Jesus welcomed and helped both of them. Jairus was about to lose a daughter who had given him twelve years of happiness (Mark 5:42), and the woman was about to lose an affliction that had brought her twelve years of sorrow. Being a synagogue officer, Jairus was no doubt wealthy; but his wealth could not save his dying daughter. The woman was already bankrupt! She had given the doctors all of her money, and yet none of them could cure her. Both Jairus and the poor woman found the answers to their needs at the feet of Jesus (Mark 5:22 and 33).

The woman had a hemorrhage that was apparently incurable and was slowly destroying her. One can only imagine the pain and emotional pressure that sapped her strength day after day. When you consider her many disappointments with the doctors and the poverty it brought her, you wonder how she endured as long as she did. But there was one added burden: according to the Law, she was ceremonially unclean, which greatly restricted both her religious and her social life (Lev. 15:19ff). What a burden she carried!

However, she let nothing stand in her way as she pushed through the crowd and came to Jesus. She could have used any number of excuses to convince herself to stay away from Him. She might have said: "I'm not important enough to ask Jesus for help!" or "Look, He's going with Jairus, so I won't bother Him now." She could have argued that nothing else had helped her, so why try again? Or she might have concluded that it was not right to come to Jesus as a last resort, after visiting all those physicians. However, she laid aside all arguments and excuses and came by faith to Jesus.

What kind of faith did she have? It was weak, timid, and perhaps somewhat superstitious. She kept saying to herself that she had to touch His clothes in order to be healed (see Mark 3:10; 6:56). She had heard reports of others being healed by Jesus (Mark 5:27), so she made this one great attempt to get through to the Saviour. She was not disappointed: Jesus honored her faith, weak as it was, and healed her body.

There is a good lesson here for all of us. Not everybody has the same degree of faith, but Jesus responds to faith no matter how feeble it might be. When we believe, He shares His power with us and something happens in our lives. There were many others in that crowd who were close to Jesus and even pressing against Him, but they experienced no miracles. Why? Because they did not have faith. It is one thing to throng Him and quite something else to trust Him.

The woman planned to slip away and get lost in the crowd, but Jesus turned and stopped her. Tenderly, He elicited from her a wonderful testimony of what the Lord had done for her. Why did Jesus deal with her publicly? Why did He not simply permit her to remain anonymous and go her way?

For one thing, He did it for her own sake. He wanted to be to her something more than a healer: He wanted to be her Saviour and Friend as well. He wanted her to look into His face, feel His tenderness, and hear His loving words of assurance. By the time He finished speaking to her, she experienced something more than physical healing. He called her "daughter" and sent her on her way with a benediction of peace (Mark 5:34). To "be made whole" meant much more than receiving mere physical healing. Jesus had given her spiritual healing as well!

He dealt with her publicly not only for her sake, but also for the sake of Jairus. His daughter was close to death, and he needed all the encouragement he could get. It was bad enough that the crowd was impeding their progress, but now this woman had to interfere and stop Jesus! When one of Jairus' friends arrived and announced that the girl had died, no doubt Jairus felt that the end had come. The Lord's words to the woman about faith and peace must have encouraged Jairus as much as they encouraged her.

Finally, Jesus dealt with her publicly that she might have the opportunity to share her testimony and glorify the Lord. "Let the redeemed of the Lord say so, whom He hath redeemed from the hand of the enemy. . . . He sent His word, and healed them. . . . Oh, that men would praise the Lord for His goodness, and for His wonderful works to the children of men!" (Ps. 107:2, 20-21) No doubt some people in that crowd heard her words and trusted in the Saviour; and when she arrived home, she already knew what it meant to witness for Christ.

Victory over Death (Mark 5:35-43)

It was not easy for Jairus to come to Jesus publicly and ask for His help. The religious leaders who were opposed to Jesus would certainly not approve, nor would some of the other synagogue leaders. The things that Jesus had done and taught in the synagogues had aroused the anger of the scribes and Pharisees, some of whom were probably Jairus' friends. But Jairus was desperate, as many people are when they come to Jesus. He would rather lose his friends and save his beloved daughter.

It is beautiful to watch Jesus deal with Jairus and lead him to joyful victory. Throughout this entire event, it was our Lord's *words* that made the difference. Consider the three statements that He made.

The word of faith (v. 36). At this point, Jairus had to believe either his friend or the Lord Jesus. No doubt all of his being responded with convulsive sorrow when he heard that his beloved daughter was dead. But Jesus assured him, "Be not afraid, go on believing" (literal translation). In other words, "You had a certain amount of faith when you came to Me, and your faith was helped when you saw what I did for that woman. Don't quit! Keep on believing!"

It was easier for Jairus to trust the Lord while his daughter was still alive, and while Jesus was still walking with him to his house. But when Jesus stopped to heal the woman, and when the friend came with the bad news, Jairus just about lost his faith. Let's not be too hard on him. We have probably given way to doubts when circumstances and feelings have overwhelmed us. Sometimes God has delayed and we have wondered why. That is when we need that special "word of faith" from the Lord, and we receive it as we spend time in His Word.

The word of hope (v. 39). When Jesus and Jairus arrived at the house, they saw and heard the professional Jewish mourners who were always summoned when a death occurred. It was traditional for them to wail loudly, to weep, and to lead the family and friends in lamentation. The presence of the mourners in the home is proof that the girl was actually dead, for the family would not have called them if there had been even the slightest hope that the girl was still alive.

"The child is not dead but sleeps!" were our Lord's words of hope to Jairus and his wife. To the believer, death is only sleep; for the body rests until the moment of resurrection (1 Thes. 4:13-18). The spirit does not sleep; for in death, the spirit of the believer leaves the body (James 2:26) and goes to be with Christ (Phil. 1:20-23). It is the body that sleeps, awaiting the return of the Lord and the resurrection (1 Cor. 15:51-58). This truth is a great encouragement to all of us who have had Christian loved ones and friends depart in death. It is His word of hope to us.

The word of love and power (v. 41). Unbelief laughs at God's Word, but faith lays hold of it and experiences the power of God. Jesus did not make a spectacle of this miracle. He was sensitive to the feelings of the parents and grieved by the scornful attitude of the mourners. *Talitha cumi* is Aramaic for "Little girl, get up!" Jesus added, "I say unto thee" (with the emphasis on the *I*), because it was by His authority that her spirit returned to her body (Luke 8:55). The words were not some magic formula that anybody might use to raise the dead.

The girl not only came back to life, but was also healed of her sickness, for she was able to get out of bed and walk around. Always the loving Physician, Jesus instructed the astounded parents to give her some food lest she have a relapse. Divine miracles never replace commonsense human care; otherwise, we are tempting God.

As with previous miracles, Jesus told the witnesses to keep quiet (Mark 1:44; 3:12). Perhaps the word got out from the mourners that the girl had been "in a coma" and had not actually been dead. According to them, there had not been a miracle after all! However, there had been witnesses to the miracle. The Law required only two or three witnesses for confirmation of truth (Deut. 17:6; 19:15), but for this miracle there were *five* witnesses! We have reason to conclude that Jairus and his wife became believers in Jesus Christ, though there is no further mention of them in the Gospel record. All her life, the daughter was a witness to the power of Jesus Christ.

Yes, God's Servant is the conqueror over danger, demons, disease, and death. This series of miracles illustrates how Jesus met and helped all kinds of people, from His own disciples to a pair of demoniacs; and it assures us that He is able to help us today.

This does not mean that God *always* must rescue His people from danger (see Acts 12) or heal every affliction (see 2 Cor. 12:1-10); but it does mean that He holds the ultimate authority and that we need never fear. We are "more than conquerors through Him who loved us" (Rom. 8:37).

CHAPTER FIVE
WILL ANYONE TRUST GOD'S SERVANT?
Mark 6:1-56

Charles Darwin said that *belief* was "the most complete of all distinctions between man and the lower animals." If this observation is true, it suggests that lack of faith on man's part puts him on the same level as the animals! Agnostic orator Col. Robert Ingersoll took a different point of view, for he once described a believer as "a songless bird in a cage." You would probably agree that his words better describe an *un*believer!

One of the central themes in this section of Mark's Gospel is the unbelief of people who came into contact with God's Servant. All of these people had every reason to trust Jesus Christ, yet all of them failed to do so, including His own disciples! As you study this chapter, keep in mind the solemn admonition of Hebrews 3:12, "Take heed, brethren, lest there be in any of you an evil heart of unbelief, in departing from the living God." God takes unbelief seriously, and so should we.

The Unbelief of His Acquaintances (Mark 6:1-6)

Jesus returned to Nazareth where a year before He had been rejected by the people and evicted from the synagogue (Luke 4:16-30). It was certainly an act of grace on His part to give the people another opportunity to hear His Word, believe, and be saved; and yet their hearts were still hard. This time, they did not evict Him: they simply did not take Him seriously.

Our Lord's reputation had once again preceded Him, so He was permitted to teach in the synagogue. Keep in mind that He was ministering to people who knew Him well, because Nazareth was His "hometown." However, these acquaintances had no spiritual perception at all. In fact, Jesus reminded them of what He had told them at that first dramatic visit, that a prophet is without honor in his own country and among his own people (Mark 6:4; Luke 4:24; John 4:44).

Two things astonished these people: His mighty works and His wonderful wisdom. Actually, Jesus did not do any mighty works while He was there, so the people must have been referring to the reports they had heard about His miracles (see Mark 1:28, 45; 3:7-8; 5:20-21). In fact, their unbelief hindered Jesus from having a greater ministry among them.

What was their problem? Why were they unable to trust Him and experience the wonders of His power and grace as had others? *They thought that they really knew Him.* After all, He had been their neighbor for nearly thirty years, they had seen Him at work in the carpenter's shop, and He appeared to be just another Nazarene. He was a "commoner" and the people saw no reason to commit themselves to Him!

"Familiarity breeds contempt" is a well-known maxim that goes all the way back to Publius the Syrian, who lived in 2 B.C. Aesop wrote a fable to illustrate it. In Aesop's fable, a fox had never before seen a lion, and when he first met the king of the beasts, the fox was nearly frightened to death. At their second meeting, the fox was not frightened quite as much; and the third time he met the lion, the fox went up and chatted with him! "And so it is," Aesop concluded, "that familiarity makes even the most frightening things seem quite harmless."

The maxim, however, must be taken with a grain of salt. For example, can you imagine a loving husband and wife thinking less of each other because they know each other so well? Or two dear friends starting to despise each other because their friendship has deepened over the years? Phillips Brooks said it best: "Familiarity breeds contempt, only with contemptible things or among contemptible people." The contempt shown by the Nazarenes said nothing about Jesus Christ, but it said a great deal about them!

A tourist, eager to see everything in the art gallery, fled from picture to picture, scarcely noticing what was in the frames. "I didn't see anything very special here," he said to one of the guards as he left. "Sir," the guard replied, "it is not the pictures that are on trial here—it is the visitors."

A carpenter was a respected artisan in that day, but nobody expected a carpenter to do miracles or teach profound truths in the synagogue. Where did He get all this power and wisdom? From God or from Satan? (see Mark 3:22) And why did His brothers and sisters not possess this same power and wisdom? Even more, why did His brothers and sisters not believe in Him? The people who called Him "the son of Mary" were actually insulting Him; because in that day you identified a man by calling him the son of his father, not the son of his mother.

The people of Nazareth were "offended at Him," which literally means "they stumbled over Him." The Greek word gives us our English word *scandalize.* Kenneth Wuest wrote in his book *Wuest's Word Studies* (Eerdmans), "They could not explain Him, so they rejected Him." Jesus was certainly a "stone of stumbling" to them because of their unbelief (Isa. 8:14; Rom. 9:32-33; 1 Peter 2:8).

Twice in the Gospel record you find Jesus marveling. As this passage reveals, He marveled at the unbelief of the Jews, and He marveled at the great faith of a Roman centurion, a Gentile (Luke 7:9). Instead of remaining at Nazareth, Jesus departed and made another circuit of the towns and villages in Galilee. His heart was broken as He saw the desperate plight of the people (Matt. 9:35-38), so He decided to send out His disciples to minister with His authority and power.

The Unbelief of His Enemies (Mark 6:7-29)

When the Lord originally called the 12 Apostles, His purpose was to teach and train them so that they might assist Him and eventually be able to take His place when He returned to the Father (Mark 3:13-15). Before sending them out, He reaffirmed their authority to heal and to cast out demons (Mark 6:7); and He gave them some pointed instructions (see Matt. 10 for a more detailed account of this sermon).

He told them to take what they already owned and not go out and buy special equipment for their itinerant travels. They were not to be loaded down with extra baggage. (You cannot miss the note of urgency in this "commissioning sermon.") Jesus wanted them to be adequately supplied, but not to the point of ceasing to live by faith. The word *bag* means "a beggar's bag." They were definitely not to beg for either food or money.

As they ministered from place to place, they would encounter both hospitality and hostility, both friends and enemies. He cautioned them to stay at one house in each community and not to "pick and choose" when it came to their food and accommodations. After all, they were there to be profitable servants, not pampered guests. If a house or a village did not receive them, they had His permission to declare God's judgment on those people. It was customary for the Jews to shake the dust off their feet whenever they left Gentile territory, but for Jews to do this to their fellow Jews would be something new (Luke 10:10-11; Acts 13:51).

The word translated "send" in Mark 6:7 is *apostello* in the Greek and gives us our English word *apostle.* It means "to send someone with a special commission to represent another and to accomplish his work." Jesus gave these twelve men both the apostolic authority and the divine ability to do the job He sent them to do. They were not "on their own"; they represented Him in all that they did and said.

We noted before (Mark 3:16-19) that a comparison of the lists of the Apostles' names reveals that the names are given in several pairs: Peter and Andrew, James and John, Philip and Bartholomew, etc. Jesus sent them out in pairs because it is always easier and safer for servants to travel and work together. "Two are better than one" (Ecc. 4:9), and the Law, as previously observed, required two witnesses to verify a matter (Deut. 17:6; 19:15; 2 Cor. 13:1). They would not only help each other; they would also learn from each other.

The men went out and did what Jesus told them to do. It is remarkable that a band of ordinary men could go out in this way to represent Almighty God, and that they could demonstrate their authority by performing miracles. God's commandments always include His enablements (2 Cor. 3:5-6). They proclaimed the Good News of the kingdom, called on sinners to repent, and healed many who were sick (Mark 6:12-13; Luke 9:6).

The reports of Christ's ministry, augmented by that of His disciples (Luke 9:7), even reached into the palace of Herod Antipas. Mark called Him "King," which is what Herod wanted to be called; but in reality, godless Herod was only a tetrarch, the ruler of a fourth part of the nation. When Herod the Great died, the Romans divided his territory among his three sons; and Antipas was made tetrarch of Perea and Galilee.

Herod Antipas had married the daughter of King Aretas IV and then had divorced her so he could marry Herodias, the wife of his half brother, Herod Philip. It was a wicked alliance that was contrary to the Law of Moses (Lev. 18:16; 20:21), and the fearless John the Baptist had denounced the king for his sins. When Herod heard about the wonderful works of Jesus, he was sure that John the Baptist had come back from the dead to haunt him and condemn him! Herod's conscience was bothering him, but he was unwilling to face his sins honestly and repent.

At this point, Mark shifted into a flashback to explain how John the Baptist had been cruelly and unjustly arrested and slain. Even in this brief account, we sense the tension in the palace, for Herod feared John, privately listened to him preach, and was in a state of perplexity over what he should do. "Queen" Herodias, on the other hand, hated John, wanted to kill him, and patiently waited for the most convenient time. In their evil character and lawless deeds, these two remind us of Ahab and Jezebel (1 Kings 18–21).

The "strategic day" came (Mark 6:21, NASB) for Herodias to put her plan into action: the celebration of Herod's birthday. Royal feasts were extravagant both in their display of wealth and in their provision for pleasure. The Jews would not have permitted a woman to dance before a group of men, and most Gentile mothers would have forbidden a daughter to do what the daughter of Herodias did. (History informs us that the girl's name was Salome.) But the girl was a part of the mother's plan to get rid of John the Baptist, and Salome played her part well.

When Herod heard the girl's macabre request, he was "greatly distressed" (see Mark 14:34, where the same verb is used of Jesus); but he had to be true to his promise or lose face before a group of influential people. The word *oath* in Mark 6:26 is actually in the plural—"for his many oaths' sake"—because Herod had repeatedly declared his desire to reward the girl for her performance. This was one way he had of impressing his guests, but it backfired. Herod had not been courageous enough to obey John's word, but now he had to obey his own word! The result was the death of an innocent man.

It is remarkable that there is no evidence that any of the Jewish leaders did anything to rescue John the Baptist after he had been arrested. The common people considered John a prophet sent from God, but the religious leaders did not obey John's message (Mark 11:27-33). John's death was the first of three notable violent deaths in the history of Israel. The other two are the crucifixion of Christ and the stoning of Stephen (Acts 7). For the significance of these events, review the comments on Mark 3:22-30. Herod had feared that John's messages would stir up a revolt among the people, something he wanted to avoid. Also, he wanted to please his wife, even though it meant the murdering of a godly man.

John's disciples were permitted to take the body of their leader and bury it, and then they went to tell Jesus what had happened (Matt. 14:12). No doubt the report of John's death deeply stirred our Lord, for He knew that one day His own life would be laid down.

We meet Herod Antipas one more time in the Gospels, when he "tried" Jesus and hoped to see the Lord perform a miracle (Luke 23:6-12). Jesus would not even speak to this adulterer and murderer, let alone please him by doing a miracle! Jesus called Herod a "fox" (Luke 13:31-35), an apt description of this crafty man. In A.D. 39, Herod Agrippa (Acts 12:1), nephew of Herod Antipas, denounced his uncle to the Roman emperor, and Antipas was deposed and sent into exile. "For what shall it profit a man, if he shall gain the whole world, and lose his own soul?" (Mark 8:36)

The Unbelief of His Disciples (Mark 6:30-56)

Jesus took His disciples to a secluded place so that they might rest after their labors. He wanted to discuss their ministry with them and prepare them for their next mission. As Vance Havner has said, "If you don't come apart and rest, you will come apart." Even God's Servant-Son needed time to rest, fellowship with His friends, and find renewal from the Father.

Another factor was the growing opposition of both the political and the religious leaders. Herod's murder of John the Baptist was evidence enough that the "climate" was now changing and that Jesus and His disciples had to be careful. In the next chapter, we shall encounter the hostility of the Jewish religious leaders, and, of course, the political enthusiasm of the crowds was always a problem (John 6:15ff). The best thing to do was to get away.

But the overzealous crowds would not

leave Him alone. They followed Him to the area near Bethsaida, hoping to see Him perform some miraculous cures (Luke 9:10-11; John 6:1ff). In spite of the interruption to His plans, the Lord welcomed them, taught them the Word, and healed those who were afflicted. Having experienced interruptions many times in my own life and ministry, I marvel at His patience and grace! What an example for us to follow!

Mark recorded two miracles that Jesus performed.

The feeding of the 5,000 (vv. 33-44). Jesus sent the 12 Apostles out to minister because He had compassion on the needy multitudes (Matt. 9:36-38). This time, the needy multitudes came to them—and the disciples wanted to send them away! As yet, they had not learned to look at life through the eyes of their Master. To them, the crowds were a problem, perhaps even a nuisance, but to Jesus, they were as sheep without a shepherd.

When D.L. Moody was building his great Sunday School in Chicago, children came to him from everywhere. They often passed by other churches and Sunday Schools to be with Mr. Moody. When asked why he walked so far to attend Moody's Sunday School, one boy replied, "Because they love a fella over there!" The children could tell the difference.

The disciples had two suggestions for solving the problem: either send the people away to find their own food, or raise enough money to buy a bit of bread for everybody. As far as the disciples were concerned, they were in the wrong place at the wrong time, and nothing could be done! With that kind of approach, they would have made ideal committee members! Someone has defined a committee as a group of people who individually can do nothing and collectively decide that nothing can be done.

Jesus looked at the situation, not as a problem, but as an opportunity to trust the Father and glorify His name. An effective leader is someone who sees potential in problems and is willing to act by faith. Acting on the basis of human wisdom, His disciples saw the problem but not the potential. How many times God's people have complained, "If we only had enough money, we could do something!" Two hundred pence (denarii) would be the equivalent of a year's wages for the average laborer! The first step is not to measure *our* resources, but to determine God's will and trust Him to meet the need.

It was Andrew who found the lad with the lunch (John 6:8-9). The Lord had the people sit down in organized groups on the green grass (see Pss. 23:2; 78:19), quite a contrast to Herod's glittering sensual feast. Jesus took the little lunch, blessed it, broke it, and gave it to the disciples to distribute to the hungry people. The miracle took place in His hands, not in theirs; for whatever we give to Him, He can bless and multiply. We are not manufacturers; we are only distributors.

John tells us that Jesus used this miracle as the basis for a sermon on "the bread of life" (John 6:22ff). After all, He did not perform miracles just to meet human needs, though that was important. He wanted each miracle to be a revelation of Himself, a sermon in action. For the most part, the people were amazed at the miracles, appreciated the help He gave them, but failed to get the spiritual message (John 12:37). They wanted the gift but not the Giver, the enjoyment of physical blessings but not the enrichment of spiritual blessings.

The stilling of the storm (vv. 45-56). A number of miracles were involved in this event: Jesus walking on the water, Peter walking on the water (Mark did not record this; see Matt. 14:28-32), Jesus stilling the storm, and the boat arriving on shore the instant Jesus entered it (John 6:21). It was certainly a "night of wonders" for the Twelve!

Why did Jesus compel His disciples to leave? Because the crowd was getting restless, and there was danger they might start a popular uprising to make Jesus King (John 6:14-15). The Twelve were not ready to face this kind of test, because their ideas of the kingdom were still too national and political.

There was a second reason: He wanted to teach them a lesson on faith that would help prepare them for the work that lay ahead of them after He was gone. The disciples had just completed a very successful mission, healing the sick and preaching the Gospel. They had shared in the miraculous feeding of 5,000 people. They were on a "spiritual high" and this in itself was dangerous. It is good to be on the mountaintop if you don't get careless and step off a cliff.

Spiritual blessings must be balanced with burdens and battles; otherwise, we may become pampered children instead of mature sons and daughters. On a previous occasion, Jesus had led His disciples into a storm following an exciting day of teaching (Mark 4:35-41). Now, after a time of miraculous ministry, He again led them into a storm. In the Book of Acts, it is interesting to note that the "storm" of official persecution began after the disciples had won 5,000 people to Christ (Acts 4:1-4). Perhaps while they were in confinement, the Apostles recalled the storm that followed the feeding of the 5,000, and they must have encouraged themselves with the assurance that Jesus would come to them and see them through.

Each new experience of testing demands of us more faith and courage. In that first storm experience, the disciples had Jesus in the boat with them; but this time, He was on the mountain praying for them. He was teaching them to live by faith. (For that matter, even when He was in the ship with them, they were still afraid!) The scene illustrates the situation of God's people today: We are in the midst of this stormy world, toiling and seemingly ready to sink, but He is in glory interceding for us. When the hour seems the darkest, He will come to us—and we will reach shore!

The waves that frightened the disciples (including the fishermen in the group) were only stairsteps to bring the Lord Jesus to them. He waited until their situation was so desperate that they could do nothing to help themselves. But why did He act as though He would pass them by? Because He wanted them to recognize Him, trust Him, and invite Him into the ship. They did not recognize Him, but instead screamed with fear because they thought He was a ghost!

Jesus reassured them with His word: "Take courage; it is I, do not be afraid" (Mark 6:50, NASB). At this point, Peter asked Jesus to let him walk on the water; but Mark omits this detail. Tradition says that Mark wrote as Peter's spokesman, so perhaps Peter was reticent to include this experience lest it give people the wrong impression. It is easy to criticize Peter for sinking—but have you ever gotten out of the boat yourself?

The disciples had failed their test because they lacked spiritual insight and receptive hearts. The miracle of the loaves and fishes had made no lasting impression on them. After all, if Jesus could multiply food and feed thousands of people, then surely He could protect them in the storm. Even a disciple of Jesus Christ can develop a hard heart if he fails to respond to the spiritual lessons that must be learned in the course of life and ministry.

As you review these two miracles, you see that Jesus Christ brings *provision* and *protection.* "The Lord is my shepherd; I shall not want. . . . I will fear no evil" (Ps. 23:1, 4). If we trust Him, we will always have sufficiency and security, no matter what the situation might be. The important thing is that we trust Him.

Mark closed this section on a positive note as he described the people who brought their sick for Jesus to heal. These people had faith and their faith was rewarded. This scene is in contrast to that in Nazareth where very few were healed because the people lacked faith.

"And this is the victory that overcomes the world, even our faith" (1 John 5:4). Trust the Servant! He never fails.

CHAPTER SIX THE SERVANT-TEACHER

Mark 7:1–8:26

Throughout his Gospel, Mark's emphasis is primarily on what Jesus did. However, in this section of our study you will find Mark recording some of the important *teachings* of the Lord. Mark also describes His ministry among the Gentiles, which would be of special interest to Roman readers. We see in this section three ministries of Jesus, the Servant-Teacher.

Teaching the Jews (Mark 7:1-23)

There are four stages in this drama, and the first is *accusation* (Mark 7:1-5). The Jewish religious leaders were now openly hostile toward the Lord and His ministry. It was not unusual for them to follow Him from place to place simply to watch for something to criticize. In this case, they accused the disciples of failing to practice the Jewish ceremonial washing. These washings had nothing to do with personal hygiene, nor were they commanded in the Law. They were a part of the tradition that the scribes and Pharisees had given to the people to add to their burdens (Matt. 23:4).

Our Lord had already violated their Sabbath traditions (Mark 2:23–3:5), so the Jews were eager to accuse Him when they saw the disciples eat "with defiled hands." Why would such a seemingly trivial matter upset these religious leaders? Why would they feel compelled to defend their ceremonial washings? For one thing, these leaders resented it when our Lord openly flaunted their authority. After all, these practices had been handed down from the fathers and carried with them the authority of the ages! The Jews called tradition "the fence of the Law." It was not the Law that protected the tradition, but the tradition that protected the Law!

But something much more important was involved. Whenever the Jews practiced these washings, they declared that they were "special" and that other people were "unclean"! If a Jew went to the marketplace to buy food, he might be "defiled" by a Gentile or (God forbid!) a Samaritan. This tradition had begun centuries before to remind the Jews that they were God's elect people and therefore had to keep themselves separated. However, a good reminder had gradually degenerated into an empty ritual, and the result was pride and religious isolation.

These washings not only indicated a wrong attitude toward people, but they also conveyed a wrong idea of the nature of sin and personal holiness. Jesus made it clear in the Sermon on the Mount that true holiness is a matter of inward affection and attitude and not just outward actions and associations. The pious Pharisees thought they were holy because they obeyed the Law and avoided external defilement. Jesus taught that a person who obeys the Law externally can still break the Law *in his heart,* and that external "defilement" has little connection with the condition of the inner person.

So the conflict was not only between God's truth and man's tradition, but also between two divergent views of sin and holiness. This confrontation was no incidental skirmish; it got to the very heart of true religious faith. Each new generation must engage in a similar conflict, for human nature is prone to hold on to worn-out man-made traditions and ignore or disobey the living Word of God. It is true that some traditions are helpful as reminders of our rich heritage, or as "cement" to bind generations, but we must constantly beware lest tradition take the place of truth. It does us good to examine our church traditions in the light of God's Word and to be courageous enough to make changes. (Note that the word *tradition* in 2 Thes. 2:15 refers to the body of doctrinal truth "handed down" from the Apostles to leaders in the church. See also 2 Tim. 2:2.)

The next stage can be labeled *condemnation* (Mark 7:6-13) as Jesus defended His disciples and exposed the hypocrisy of their accusers. The first thing He did was to quote from the Prophet Isaiah (Isa. 29:13), and then He brought in the Law of Moses (Ex. 20:12; 21:17; Lev. 20:9). How could the Pharisees argue with the Law and the Prophets?

In defending their tradition, the Pharisees eroded their own characters and also the character of the Word of God. They were hypocrites, "playactors," whose religious worship was practiced in vain. True worship must come from the heart, and it must be directed by God's truth, not man's personal ideas. What a tragedy that religious people would ignorantly practice their religion and become the worse for doing it!

But they were not only destroying their character; they were also destroying the influence and authority of the very Word of God that they claimed to be defending. Note the tragic sequence: teaching their doctrines as God's Word (Mark 7:7); laying aside God's Word (Mark 7:8); rejecting God's Word (Mark 7:9); finally, robbing God's Word of its power (Mark 7:13). People who revere man-made traditions above the Word of God eventually lose the power of God's Word in their lives. No matter how devout they may appear, their hearts are far from God.

History reveals that the Jewish religious leaders came to honor their traditions far above the Word of God. Rabbi Eleazer said, "He who expounds the Scriptures in opposition to the tradition has no share in the world to come." The *Mishna,* a collection of Jewish traditions in the *Talmud,* records, "It is a greater offense to teach anything contrary to the voice of the Rabbis than to contradict Scripture itself." But before we criticize our Jewish friends, perhaps we should examine what influence "the church fathers" are having in our own Christian churches. We also may be guilty of replacing God's truth with man's traditions.

Once He had exposed their hypocrisy, Jesus then turned to the Law of Moses and indicted them for breaking the fifth commandment. They had an ingenious way of breaking the Law and not feeling guilty. Instead of using their wealth to support their parents, the Pharisees dedicated that wealth to God ("Corban" = "an offering, a gift"; see Num. 30) and claimed that the wealth could now be used only for "spiritual purposes." However, they continued to get the benefit of that wealth, even though it technically belonged to God. These men claimed to love God, but they had no love for their parents!

The third stage is *declaration* (Mark 7:14-16). Jesus announced to the whole crowd that the source of holy living is from within, not from without. Actually, He was declaring null and void the entire Mosaic system of "clean and unclean" foods; but at that time, He did not explain this radical truth to the crowd. Later, He did explain it in private to His own disciples.

But this declaration was surely understood by His enemies. They realized that He was breaking down one of the "walls" that separated the Jews from the Gentiles. Of course, the Law itself was not set aside until Jesus died on the cross (Eph. 2:14-15; Col. 2:14), but the principle Jesus announced had been true throughout the ages. In every period of history, true holiness has always been a matter of the heart, a right relationship with God by faith. Ceremonial purity was a matter of external obedience to a law as evidence of that faith (Ps. 51:6, 10, 16-17). Moses made it clear in Deuteronomy that God wanted love and obedience to come from the heart, and not be merely outward obedience to rules (note Deut. 6:4-5; 10:12; 30:6, 20).

Our Lord's *explanation* (Mark 7:17-23) was given privately to His disciples when they asked Him "concerning the parable." His explanation seems obvious to us, but we must remember that these twelve men had been brought up under the strict Jewish dietary code that categorized all foods as either "clean" or "unclean" (Lev. 11). In fact, Acts 10:14 suggests that Peter kept a kosher household for years even after he had heard this truth. It is not easy to change our religious traditions.

The human heart is sinful and produces all manner of evil desires, thoughts, and actions, everything from murder to envy ("an evil eye"). Jesus had no illusions about human nature, as do some liberal theologians and humanistic teachers today. He realized that man is a sinner, unable to control or change his own nature; *and that is why Jesus came to earth—to die for lost sinners.*

The Jewish dietary laws were given by God to teach His chosen people to make a difference between what was clean and what was unclean. (No doubt there were also some practical reasons involved, such as sanitation and health.) To disobey these laws was a matter of ceremonial defilement, and that was an external matter. Food *ends up* in the stomach, but sin *begins* in the heart. The food we eat is digested and the waste evacuated, but sin remains and it produces defilement and death.

This dramatic lesson on "truth vs. tradition" could only irritate the Jewish religious leaders more and make them want to silence Jesus. This increased opposition was the reason why He departed from the crowded places and took His disciples into Gentile territory.

Before we leave this section, however, it might be good for us to contrast man's traditions and God's truth.

Man's traditions	*God's truth*
Outward forms—bondage	Inward faith—liberty
Trifling rules	Fundamental principles
Outward piety	True inward holiness
Neglect, replace the Word	Exalts the Word of God

Helping the Gentiles (Mark 7:24–8:9)

Mark records three miracles that Jesus performed as He ministered to the Gentiles in the region of Tyre and Sidon. This is the only recorded instance of our Lord actually leaving Palestine. He was practicing what he had just taught the disciples: there is no difference between Jews and Gentiles, for all are sinners and need the Saviour.

Casting out a demon (vv. 24-30). Of the thirty-five recorded miracles in the Gospels, four directly involve women: the healing of Peter's mother-in-law (Mark 1:30-31); the raising of the widow's son (Luke 7:11-17); the raising of Lazarus (John 11); and the casting out of the demon as recorded here.

Jesus came to this area (about forty miles from Capernaum) so that He might have some privacy, but a concerned mother discovered He was there and came to Him for help. There were many obstacles in her way, yet she overcame them all by faith and got what she needed.

To begin with, her nationality was against her: she was a Gentile and Jesus was a Jew. Besides that, she was a woman, and society in that day was dominated by the men. Satan was against her, for one of his demons had taken control in her daughter's life. The disciples were against her; they wanted Jesus to send her away and let Him (and them) have some rest. For a time, it looked as though even Jesus was against her! It was not an easy situation, and yet she triumphed because of her great faith.

Samuel Rutherford, the saintly Scottish minister who suffered greatly for Christ, once wrote to a friend: "It is faith's work to claim and challenge loving-kindnesses out of all the roughest strokes of God." That is exactly what this Gentile mother did, and we today have much that we can learn from her about faith.

When she first asked Him for help, Jesus did not even answer her! Encouraged by His silence, the disciples urged Him to send her away. When Jesus did speak, it was not to the woman but to the disciples; and His words seem to exclude her completely: "I am not sent but unto the lost sheep of the house of Israel" (Matt. 15:24). However, none of these barriers stopped her from pressing on with her plea.

The first time she cried for help, the mother addressed Jesus as "Son of David," a Jewish title; but the next time she cried out for help, she simply said, "Lord, help me" (Matt. 15:25). It was then that Jesus spoke about feeding the children (Israel) first and not throwing their food to "the little pet puppies." Jesus was not calling the Gentiles "dirty scavenger dogs" as did many of the proud Jews; He was giving her hope, and she took hold of it.

Her reply revealed that faith had triumphed. She did not deny the special place of the "children" (Jews) in God's plan, nor did she want to usurp it. All she wanted were a few crumbs of blessing from the table; for, after all, "Salvation is of the Jews" (John 4:22). It must have rejoiced His heart when she took *His very words* and used them as a basis for her plea! She accepted her place, she believed His Word, and she persisted in her plea; and Jesus not only met her need, but commended her for her faith.

It is significant that the two times in the Gospel record when Jesus commended "great faith," He was responding to the faith of Gentiles and not Jews: this Syrophoenician woman and the Roman centurion (Matt. 8:5-13). It is also worth noting that in both situations, Jesus healed *at a distance,* suggesting the spiritual distance between Jews and Gentiles at that time (Eph. 2:11-22). Finally, the people of Tyre and Sidon were not known for their faith (Matt. 11:21-22), yet this woman dared to believe that Jesus could deliver her daughter.

Great faith is faith that takes God at His Word and will not let go until God meets the need. Great faith can lay hold of even the slightest encouragement and turn it into a fulfilled promise. "Lord, increase our faith."

Healing a deaf man (vv. 31-37). The region of Decapolis ("ten cities") was also Gentile territory, but before Jesus left the region, the people were glorifying the God of Israel (Matt. 15:30-31). The man they brought to Jesus was handicapped both by deafness and an impediment in his speech, and Jesus healed him. This miracle is recorded only by Mark and would be especially appreciated by his Roman readers, since the "ten cities" region was like a "Rome away from Rome."

Jesus took the man away from the crowd so that the healing would be private and the man would not become a public attraction. Since the man was deaf, he could not hear our Lord's words, but he could feel Jesus' fingers in his ear and the touch on his tongue; and this would encourage the man's faith. The "sigh" was an inward groan, our Lord's compassionate response to the pain and sorrow sin has brought into the world. It was also a prayer to the Father on behalf of the handicapped man. (The same word is used in connection with prayer in Rom. 8:23, and the noun in Rom. 8:26.)

Ephphatha is an Aramaic word that means "be opened, be released." The man did not hear Jesus speak, but the creation heard the command of the Creator, and the man was healed. Both the tongue and the ears functioned normally again. In spite of our Lord's strict command for the people to keep quiet about the miracles, they told the news everywhere (see Mark 1:34, 44; 3:12; 5:43); and this resulted in a large crowd gathering and bringing people who were ill or handicapped. Even though Jesus was trying to enjoy some rest, He took time to heal them all. The result? These Gentiles "glorified the God of Israel" (Matt. 15:31).

Feeding the 4,000 (vv. 1-9). Those who

try to find contradictions in the Bible often confuse this miracle with the feeding of the 5,000 which is recorded in all four Gospels. Only Matthew and Mark record this event, and it is not difficult to distinguish it from the other miracle of the multiplying of bread and fish. The first miracle took place in Galilee, near Bethsaida, and involved predominantly Jews. This miracle took place near Decapolis and involved mostly Gentiles. In the first miracle, Jesus started with five loaves and two fish, while here He had seven loaves "and a few fish." The 5,000 had been with Him one day, but the 4,000 had been with him three days. Twelve baskets of fragments were left over after the 5,000 were fed, but only seven baskets after the 4,000 were fed. There were even two different kinds of baskets used: for the 5,000, small wicker lunch baskets (*kophinos*); for the 4,000, large hampers, big enough to hold a man (*spuris,* see Acts 9:25).

Once again, we are encouraged by our Lord's compassion and His complete control over the situation. However, we are discouraged by the blindness and unbelief of the disciples. Had they completely forgotten the previous miracle? Let's not be too hard on them. How many times have *we* forgotten the mercies of the Lord? We need to remind ourselves that Jesus Christ is still the same and has the solution to every problem. All we need do is trust Him, give Him our all, and obey.

Warning the Disciples (Mark 8:10-26)

Jesus and the disciples crossed to the western side of the Sea of Galilee where they were met by the Pharisees who were still angry at Him because of His earlier indictment of their hypocrisy (Mark 7:1-23). This time they tempted Him to prove His divine authority by giving them a sign from heaven. They did not want an earthly miracle, such as the healing of a sick person. They wanted Him to do something spectacular, like bring fire from heaven or bread from heaven (John 6:30-31). This would prove He was indeed sent from God.

Our Lord's response was one of deep grief and disappointment (see Mark 7:34). How tragic that the religious leaders of God's chosen people should be so hardhearted and spiritually blind! Their desire for a sign from heaven was but another evidence of their unbelief, for faith does not ask for signs. True faith takes God at His Word and is satisfied with the inward witness of the Spirit.

Since Mark was writing primarily for Gentile readers, he did not include our Lord's words concerning the sign of the Prophet Jonah (Matt. 16:4; and see Matt. 12:38-41). What is "the sign of Jonah"? Death, burial, and resurrection. The proof that Jesus is what He claimed to be is the fact of His own death, burial, and resurrection (Acts 2:22-36; 3:12-26).

Jesus left them and crossed to the east side of the Sea of Galilee, and en route taught His disciples an important spiritual lesson. It appears that they were almost as blind as the Pharisees! The men were having a private discussion about their food supply, because somebody had forgotten to pack bread. Who was to blame?

It must have grieved Jesus that His handpicked helpers were so spiritually obtuse. The fact that He had multiplied bread on two occasions and fed over 10,000 people had apparently made little impression on them! Why worry and argue over one loaf of bread when you have Jesus in the boat with you? Their minds were dull, their hearts were hard (see Mark 6:52), their eyes were blind, and their ears were deaf (see Mark 4:11-12).

God's people often have a tendency to forget His blessings (Ps. 103:1-2). He meets our needs, but then when the next problem arises, we complain or become frightened. As long as we are with Him, we can be sure He will care for us. It would do us all good to pause occasionally and remind ourselves of His goodness and faithfulness.

But the main lesson had to do with *leaven* (yeast) and not with bread. In the Bible, leaven is consistently a symbol of evil. Each Passover season, the Jews had to remove all leaven from their dwellings (Ex. 12:18-20), and leaven was not allowed with the offerings (Ex. 23:18; 34:25; Lev. 2:11; 6:17). Evil, like leaven, is small and hidden, but it spreads and soon infects the whole (Gal. 5:9).

The Bible uses leaven as a picture of false doctrine (Gal. 5:1-9), unjudged sin in the church (1 Cor. 5), and hypocrisy (Luke 12:1). In this context, Jesus warned them about the teaching (false doctrine) of the Pharisees and the followers of Herod. The Pharisees "said but they did not"; in other words, they practiced and encouraged hypocrisy (note Mark 7:6). The Herodians were a worldly group who catered to Herod, accepted the Roman way of life, and saw in Herod and his rule the promised kingdom for the Jewish nation. If this false teaching got into the hearts and minds of the disciples, it would infect them and pollute the truth Jesus had given them to proclaim about Himself and His kingdom.

We can never be too careful about detecting and avoiding false doctrine. Only a small deviation from the Word may get into an individual or a church, but before long it will grow and infect everything. Our Lord did not often say "Beware!" but when He did it was important!

In this section, Mark recorded two miracles that are not found in the other Gospels: the healing of the deaf man who had a speech impediment (Mark 7:31-37), and the healing of the blind man outside Bethsaida (Mark 8:22-26). Perhaps we can see in these two men illustrations of the disciples' spiritual condition described in Mark 8:18! Jewish readers would connect these two miracles with the messianic promises in Isaiah 35.

In both these situations, friends brought the men to Jesus; and in both situations, Jesus led the men away from the crowds. In fact, in the latter case, He took the man *outside the city*. Why? Probably because the city of Bethsaida had already been judged because of its unbelief (Matt. 11:21-24). No more evidence would be given to them.

The unique thing about this miracle of healing is that it occurred *gradually* and not instantly. The Gospels record the healing of at least seven blind men, and they show that our Lord used a variety of approaches. Perhaps it was the atmosphere of unbelief in Bethsaida that hindered Him (see Mark 6:5-6), or it may have been the spiritual condition of the man himself. For some reason not given, the man was not ready for instant sight, so Jesus restored him gradually. The fact that the man recognized men and trees suggests that he had not been born blind but had been blinded by accident or disease.

The man was not from Bethsaida, for Jesus sent him home and cautioned him not to enter that town. Now that he had been healed, why go to unbelieving Bethsaida where Jesus had been rejected? His job was to go home and spread the Good News of the kingdom, and to demonstrate its power by showing others what Jesus had done for him (see Mark 2:11; 5:34; 10:52). Should he not give another opportunity to the people in Bethsaida? Perhaps they would believe if they heard how Jesus had restored his sight. No, Bethsaida had been given adequate evidence, but still had refused to believe. It is a dangerous thing for anybody to reject the message of God and harden his or her heart in unbelief.

The disciples learned some valuable lessons on this trip, lessons that they would need to remember and apply in later years of ministry. We today need to learn these same lessons: (1) don't seek after signs, but live by faith in His Word; (2) trust Jesus to meet needs; (3) avoid the leaven of false doctrine; (4) let Jesus work as He wills, and expect variety in His working.

Mark recorded the events of some busy days in the ministry of God's Servant! Next he will take us "behind the scenes" as the Servant instructs His disciples and prepares them for His death on the cross.

CHAPTER SEVEN
THE SERVANT'S SECRETS
Mark 8:27–9:50

A secret has been defined as "something you tell one person at a time." From time to time, Jesus shared special "secrets" with His disciples, and three of them are given here. Believers today need to understand and apply these spiritual secrets if their own lives are to be all that God wants them to be.

Suffering Leads to Glory (Mark 8:27–9:13)

Jesus had been preparing His disciples for this private meeting at which He intended to reveal to them what would happen to Him at Jerusalem. He had given hints along the way, but now He would explain matters to them more fully. For the site, He selected Caesarea Philippi, a town about twenty-five miles north of Bethsaida, sitting at the foot of beautiful Mt. Hermon. The town was named after Augustus Caesar and Herod Philip, and it contained a marble temple dedicated to Augustus. It was a place dedicated to the glory of Rome, and that glory is now gone, but the glory of Jesus Christ remains and will go on eternally.

Confession (vv. 27-30). If you were to go around asking your friends, "What do people say about me?" they would take it as an evidence of pride. What difference does it really make what people think or say about us? We are not that important! But what people believe and say about Jesus Christ *is* important, for He is the Son of God and the only Saviour of sinners.

Your confession concerning Jesus Christ is a matter of life or death (John 8:21, 24; 1 John 2:22-27; 4:1-3). The citizens of Caesarea Philippi would say, "Caesar is lord!" That confession might identify them as loyal Roman citizens, but it could never save them from their sins and from eternal hell. The only confession that saves us is "Jesus is Lord!" (1 Cor. 12:1-3) when that confession comes from a heart that truly believes in Him (Rom. 10:9-10).

It is remarkable the number of different opinions the people held about Jesus, though the same situation probably exists today. That some thought He was John the Baptist is especially perplexing, since John and Jesus had been seen publicly together. They were quite different in personality and ministry (Matt. 11:16-19), so it seems strange that the people would confuse them.

John the Baptist came "in the spirit and power of Elijah" (Luke 1:17), in a ministry of judgment, whereas Jesus came in a spirit of meekness and service. John performed no miracles (John 10:41), but Jesus was a miracle-worker. John even dressed like the Prophet Elijah (2 Kings 1:8; Mark 1:6). How could the people confuse the two?

Some said that Jesus was one of the prophets, perhaps Jeremiah (Matt. 16:14). Jeremiah was "the weeping prophet," and Jesus was a Man of sorrows; so there is a definite parallel. Jeremiah called the people to true repentance from the heart, and so did Jesus. Both men were misunderstood and rejected by their own people, both condemned the false religious leaders and the hypocritical worship in the temple, and both were persecuted by those in authority.

In His words and His works, Jesus gave every evidence to the people that He was the Son of God, the Messiah, and yet they did not get the message. Instead of diligently seeking for the truth, the people listened to popular opinion and followed it, just as many people do today. They had opinions instead of convictions, and this is what led them astray. Elbert Hubbard defined public opinion as "the judgment of the incapable many, opposed to that of the discerning few." Thank God for the discerning few!

Peter's confession was bold and uncompromising, just as ours should be: "Thou art the Christ, the Son of the living God!" (Matt. 16:16) The word *Christ* means "the Anointed One, the promised Messiah." Prophets, priests, and kings were all anointed when installed in their offices, and our Lord holds all three offices.

Why did Jesus warn them to keep quiet about Him? For one thing, the disciples themselves still had much to learn about Him and what it truly meant to follow Him. The religious leaders of the nation had already made up their minds about Him, and to proclaim Him as Messiah now would only upset God's plans. The common people wanted to see His miracles, but they had little desire to submit to His message. To announce Him as Messiah might well result in a political uprising that would only do harm.

Confusion (vv. 31-38). Now that they had confessed their faith in Christ (but see John 6:66-71), the disciples were ready for the "secret" Jesus wanted to share with them: He was going with them to Jerusalem where He would die on a cross. From this point on, Mark will focus on their journey to Jerusalem and the emphasis will be on Jesus' approaching death and resurrection (Mark 9:30-32; 10:32-34).

This announcement stunned the disciples. If He is indeed the Christ of God, as they had confessed, then why would He be rejected by the religious leaders? Why would these leaders crucify Him? Did not the Old Testament Scriptures promise that Messiah would defeat all their enemies and establish a glorious kingdom for Israel? There was something wrong somewhere and the disciples were confused.

True to character, it was Peter who expressed their concern. One minute Peter was led by God to confess his faith in Jesus Christ (Matt. 16:17), and the next minute he was thinking like an unbelieving man and expressing the thoughts of Satan! This is a warning to us that when we argue with God's Word, we open the door for Satan's lies. Peter began rebuking his Master, and Mark used the same word that describes our Lord's rebuking of the demons (Mark 1:25; 3:12).

Peter's protest was born out of his ignorance of God's will and his deep love for his Lord. One minute Peter was a "rock," and the next minute he was a stumbling block! Dr. G. Campbell Morgan said, "The man who loves Jesus, but who shuns God's method, is a stumbling block to Him." Peter did not yet understand the relationship between suffering and glory. He would eventually learn this lesson and would even emphasize it in his first epistle (note 1 Peter 1:6-8; 4:13–5:10).

Note, however, that when Jesus rebuked Peter, He also "looked on His disciples," because they agreed with Peter's assessment of the situation! Steeped in Jewish traditional interpretation, they were unable to understand how their Messiah could ever suffer and die. To be sure, some of the prophets had written about Messiah's sufferings, but much more had been written about Messiah's glory. Some of the rabbis even taught that there would be *two* Messiahs, one who would suffer and one who would reign (see 1 Peter 1:10-12). No wonder the disciples were confused.

But the problem was more than theological; it was very practical. Jesus had called these men to follow Him, and they knew that whatever happened to Him would happen to them. If there was a cross in *His* future, there would be one in *their* future as well. That would be reason enough to disagree with Him! In spite of their devotion to Him, the disciples were still ignorant of the true relationship between the cross and the crown. They were following Satan's philosophy (glory without suffering) instead of God's philosophy (suffering transformed into glory). Which philosophy you accept will determine how you live and how you serve.

Mark 8:34 indicates that, though Jesus and His disciples had met in private, the crowds were not far away. Jesus summoned the people and taught them what He taught His own disciples: *there is a price to pay for true discipleship.* He knew that the crowds were following Him only because of the miracles, and that most of the people were unwilling to pay the price to become true disciples.

Jesus laid down three conditions for true discipleship: (1) we must surrender ourselves completely to Him; (2) we must identify with Him in suffering and death; and (3) we must follow Him obediently, wherever He leads. If we live for ourselves, we will lose ourselves, but if we lose ourselves for His sake and the Gospel's, we will find ourselves.

Denying self is not the same as self-denial. We practice self-denial when, for a good purpose, we occasionally give up things or activities. But we deny self when we surrender ourselves to Christ and determine to obey His will. This once-for-all dedication is followed by a daily "dying to self" as we take up the cross and follow Him. From the human point of view, we are losing ourselves, but from the divine perspective, we are finding ourselves. When we live for Christ, we become more like Him, and this brings out our own unique individuality.

But note the motivation for true discipleship: "for My sake and the Gospel's" (Mark 8:35). To lose yourself is not an act of desperation; it is an act of devotion. But we do not stop there: personal devotion should lead to practical duty, the sharing of the Gospel with a lost world. "For My sake" could lead to selfish religious isolationism, so it must be balanced with "and the Gospel's." Because we live for Him, we live for others.

Discipleship is a matter of profit and loss, a question of whether we will *waste* our lives or *invest* our lives. Note the severe warning Jesus gives us here: once we have spent our lives, we cannot buy them back! Remember, He was instructing His *disciples,* men who had already confessed Him as the Son of God. He was not telling them how to be saved and go to heaven, but how to save their lives and make the most of their opportunities on earth. "Losing your soul" is the equivalent of wasting your life, missing the great opportunities God gives you to make your life count. You may "gain the whole world" and be a success in the eyes of men, and yet have nothing to show for your life when you stand before God. If that happens, though you did own the whole world, it would not be a sufficient price to give to God to buy another chance at life.

Is there any reward for the person who is a true disciple? Yes, there is: he becomes more like Jesus Christ and one day shares in His glory. Satan promises you glory, but in the end, you receive suffering. God promises you suffering, but in the end, that suffering is transformed into glory. If we acknowledge Christ and live for Him, He will one day acknowledge us and share His glory with us.

Confirmation (vv. 1-8). It takes faith to accept and practice this lesson on discipleship, so six days later, the Lord gave a dazzling proof that God indeed does transform suffering into glory. (Luke's "about eight days" is inclusive of the day of the lesson and the day of the glory, Luke 9:28.) He took Peter, James, and John to the top of a mountain (it may have been Mt. Hermon), and there He revealed His glory. This event was a vivid confirmation of His words as recorded in Mark

8:38 as well as a demonstration of the glory of the future kingdom (Mark 9:1; John 1:14; 2 Peter 1:12-21). The message was clear: first the suffering, then the glory.

Moses represented the Law and Elijah the Prophets, both of which find their fulfillment in Jesus Christ (Luke 24:25-27; Heb. 1:1-2). Moses had died and his body was buried, but Elijah had been raptured to heaven (2 Kings 2:11). When Jesus returns, He will raise the bodies of the saints who died and will rapture the living saints (1 Thes. 4:13-18). Jesus will one day establish His glorious kingdom and fulfill the many promises made through the prophets. Christ's sufferings and death would not *prevent* God from establishing His kingdom; rather, by solving the sin problem in God's world, the cross would help to make the kingdom possible.

The word *transfigured* describes a change on the outside that comes from the inside. It is the opposite of "masquerade," which is an outward change that does not come from within. Jesus allowed His glory to radiate through His whole being, and the mountaintop became a holy of holies! As you meditate on this event, keep in mind that He has shared this glory with us and promised us a glorious home forever (John 17:22-24). According to Romans 12:1-2 and 2 Corinthians 3:18, believers today can experience this same transfiguration glory.

The three disciples had gone to sleep while Jesus was praying (Luke 9:29, 32), a failure they would repeat in the Garden of Gethsemane (Mark 14:32-42). They almost missed seeing Moses and Elijah and Jesus in His glory! Peter's suggestion reflects again human thinking and not divine wisdom. How wonderful it would be to stay on the mountaintop and bask in His glory! But discipleship means denying self, taking up a cross, and following Him; and you cannot do that and selfishly stay on the mount of glory. There are needs to be met in the valley below. If we want to share the glory of Christ on the mountaintop, we must be willing to follow Him into the sufferings of the valley below.

The Father interrupted Peter's speech and focused their attention, not on the vision, but on the Word of God: "Hear Him!" The memory of visions will fade, but the unchanging Word abides forever. The glorious vision was not an end in itself; it was God's way of confirming the Word (see 2 Peter 1:12-21). Discipleship is not built on spectacular visions but on the inspired, unchanging Word of God. Nor do we put Moses, Elijah, and Jesus on the same level, as Peter hinted. It is "Jesus only"—His Word, His will, His kingdom, and His glory.

The three men were not allowed to tell the other nine what they had seen on the mount. No doubt their explanation after His resurrection brought great encouragement to the believers who themselves would experience suffering and death for His sake.

Correction (vv. 11-13). The disciples now understood God's plan much better, but they were still confused about the coming of Elijah to prepare the way for the Messiah. They knew the prophecies in Malachi 3:1 and 4:5-6, and that their teachers expected these prophecies to be fulfilled before the Messiah appeared (John 1:21). Had Elijah already come and they missed him, or was he yet to come? Perhaps the appearing of Elijah on the mount was the fulfillment of the prophecy.

Jesus made two facts clear. First, for those who had trusted in Him, this "Elijah" was John the Baptist, for John had indeed prepared the way before Him. John had denied that he was Elijah come from the dead (John 1:21, 25), but he did minister in the "spirit and power of Elijah" (Luke 1:16-17). Second, there would be a future coming of Elijah, just as Malachi had predicted (Matt. 17:11), before the time of Great Tribulation. Some students connect this with Revelation 11:2-12. The nation did not accept John's ministry. Had they received John, he would have served as the "Elijah" God sent; and they also would have received Jesus. Instead, they rejected both men and allowed them to be slain.

Power Comes from Faith (Mark 9:14-29)

The Christian life is "a land of hills and valleys" (Deut. 11:11). In one day, a disciple can move from the glory of heaven to the attacks of hell. When our Lord and His three friends returned to the other nine disciples, they found them involved in a dual problem: they were unable to deliver a boy from demonic control, and the scribes were debating with them and perhaps even taunting them because of their failure. As always, it was Jesus who stepped in to solve the problem.

The boy was both deaf and dumb (Mark 9:17, 25), and the demon was doing his best to destroy him. Imagine what it would be like for that father to try to care for the boy and protect him! Jesus had given His disciples authority to cast out demons (Mark 6:7, 13), and yet their ministry to the boy was ineffective. No wonder the Lord was grieved with them! How often He must be grieved with us when we fail to use the spiritual resources He has graciously given to His people!

Since the disciples had failed, the desperate father was not even sure that Jesus could succeed; hence his statement, "If you can do anything" (Mark 9:22, NASB). However, the father was honest enough to admit his own unbelief and to ask the Lord to help him and his son. Jesus did cast out the demon and restore the boy to his father.

The main lesson of this miracle is the power of faith to overcome the enemy (Mark 9:19, 23-24; and see Matt. 17:20). Why had the nine disciples failed? Because they had been careless in their personal spiritual walk and had neglected prayer and fasting (Mark 9:29). The authority that Jesus had given them was effective only if exercised by faith, but faith must be cultivated through spiritual discipline and devotion. It may be that the absence of their Lord, or His taking the three disciples with Him and leaving them behind, had dampened their spiritual fervor and diminished their faith. Not only did their failure embarrass them, but it also robbed the Lord of glory and gave the enemy opportunity to criticize. It is our faith in Him that glorifies God (Rom. 4:20).

Service Leads to Honor (Mark 9:30-50)

Jesus was still leading His disciples to Jerusalem, and as they went, He reminded them of what would happen to Him there. Note that He also reminded them of His resurrection, but they were unable to understand what He was saying (see Matt. 17:9). They were "exceedingly sorry" ("deeply grieved," Matt. 17:23, NASB).

However, they were not grieved enough to set aside their personal dispute over which of them was the greatest! After they heard what Jesus had said about His own suffering and death, you would think they would have forgotten their own selfish plans and concentrated on Him. Perhaps the fact that Peter, James, and John had gone on the mount with Jesus had added some fuel to the fires of competition.

To teach them (and us) a lesson on honor, Jesus set a child before them and explained that the way to be first is to be last, and the way to be last is to be the servant of all. The unspoiled child is an example of submission and humility. A child knows he is a child and acts like a child, and that is his secret of attracting love and care. The child who tries to impress us by acting like an adult does not get the same attention.

True humility means knowing yourself, accepting yourself, being yourself—your *best* self—and giving of yourself for others. The world's philosophy is that you are "great" if others are working for you, but Christ's message is that greatness comes from our serving others. Since the words "child" and "servant" are the same in the Aramaic language, it is easy to see why Jesus connected the two. If we have the heart of a child, we will have little difficulty being servants; and if we have the attitude of servants, we will welcome the children as the representatives of Jesus Christ and the Father.

At this point, John felt it necessary to defend the disciples (Mark 9:38-41) by pointing out their zeal. Imagine telling a man to stop casting out demons when the nine disciples had failed to deliver the deaf and dumb boy from Satan's power! To use the name of Jesus is the same as working under His authority, so the men had no right to stop the man. "To his own master he stands or falls" (Rom. 14:4).

Mark 9:40 should be compared with Matthew 12:30, "He that is not with Me is against Me." Both statements declare the impossibility of neutrality when it comes to our relationship with Jesus Christ. Since we cannot be neutral, if we are not for Him, we must be against Him; if we are not against Him, we must be for Him. The anonymous exorcist was bringing glory to His name, so he had to be *for* the Saviour and not against Him.

But it is not necessary to perform great miracles to prove our love for Christ. When we lovingly receive a child or compassionately share a cup of cold water, we are giving evidence that we have the humble heart of a servant. After all, we are serving Christ, and that is the highest service in the world (Matt. 25:31-46).

Jesus did not treat John's statement lightly; in fact, He went on to explain the danger of causing others to stumble and therefore stop serving the Lord (Mark 9:42-50). "These little ones" refers to all God's children who follow Christ and seek to serve Him. The way believers treat others in the family of God is a serious thing, and God wants us to "have peace one with another" (Mark 9:50). The disciples did not get along with each other, nor did they get along with other believers!

This solemn message about hell carries a warning to all of us to deal drastically with sin. Whatever in our lives makes us stumble, and therefore causes others to stumble, must be removed as if by surgery. The hand, foot, and eye would be considered valuable parts of the body, yet they must be removed if they are causing sin. Of course, the Lord is not commanding literal physical surgery, since He had already made it clear that sin comes from the heart (Mark 7:20-23). What He is teaching is that sin is to the inner person what a cancerous tumor is to the body, and it must be dealt with drastically.

Some people are shocked to hear from the lips of Jesus such frightening words about hell (see Isa. 66:24). Jesus believed in a place called hell, a place of eternal torment and righteous punishment (see Luke 16:19ff). After an army chaplain told his men that he did not believe in hell, some of them suggested that his services were not needed. After all, if there is no hell, then why worry about death? But if there is a hell, then the chaplain was leading them astray! Either way, they would be better off without him!

The word translated "hell" is *gehenna.* It comes from a Hebrew phrase "the valley [*ge*] of Hinnon," referring to an actual valley outside Jerusalem where wicked King Ahaz worshiped Molech, the fire god, and even sacrificed his children in the fire (2 Chron. 28:1-3; Jer. 7:31; 32:35).

Some manuscripts do not have Isaiah 66:24 quoted in Mark 9:44 and 46, but the statement is quoted in verse 48, and that one verse is sufficient. Hell is not temporary; it is forever (see Rev. 20:10). How essential it is for sinners to trust Jesus Christ and be delivered from eternal hell, and how important it is for believers to get the message out to a lost world!

"But isn't that too great a sacrifice to ask from us?" someone might argue. "To deal that drastically with sin would cost us too much!" In Mark 9:49-50, Jesus used the concept of "living sacrifices" to illustrate His point (see Rom. 12:1-2). The sacrifice ends up on the altar and is consumed by the fire. Would you rather endure the fires of hell as a lost sinner or the purifying fires of God as a sacrifice for His glory? Remember, Satan promises you glory now, but the pain comes later. Jesus calls us to suffering now, and then we will enjoy the glory.

The Jews were not allowed to put leaven or honey on their sacrifices, but they were required to use salt (Lev. 2:11, 13). Salt speaks of purity and preservation. It was used in Old Testament days in the establishing of covenants. The disciples were God's salt (Matt. 5:13), but they were in danger of losing their flavor and becoming worthless. Our salt today is purified and does not lose its taste; but the salt of that day contained impurities and could lose its flavor. Once you have lost that precious Christian character, how will you restore it?

Instead of rebuking others, the disciples should have been examining their own hearts! It is easy to lose our "saltiness" and become useless to God. Christians will experience the fire of trials and persecutions (1 Peter 1:6-7; 4:12) and they need to stand together, no matter who is the greatest! Commitment and character are the essentials, if we are to glorify Him and have peace with each other.

The three lessons Jesus taught in this section are basic to Christian living today. If we are yielded to Him, then suffering will lead to glory, faith will produce power, and our sacrificial service will lead to honor. In spite of his impetuousness and occasional mistakes, Peter got the message and wrote: "But the God of all grace, who hath called us unto His eternal glory by Christ Jesus, after you have suffered awhile, make you perfect, establish, strengthen, settle you. To Him be glory and dominion forever and ever" (1 Peter 5:10).

CHAPTER EIGHT
THE SERVANT'S PARADOXES
Mark 10

As a master Teacher, our Lord used many different approaches in sharing God's Word: symbols, miracles, types, parables, proverbs, and paradoxes. A paradox is a statement that seems to contradict itself and yet expresses a valid truth or principle. "When I am weak, then am

I strong" is a paradox (2 Cor. 12:10; also see 2 Cor. 6:8-10). There are times when the best way to state a truth is by means of paradox; and this chapter describes our Lord doing just that. He could have preached long sermons; but instead, He gave us these five important lessons that can be expressed in five succinct, paradoxical statements.

Two Shall Be One (Mark 10:1-12)

Jesus completed His ministry in Galilee, left Capernaum, and came to the Trans-Jordan area, still on His way to the city of Jerusalem (Mark 10:32). This district was ruled by Herod Antipas, which may explain why the Pharisees tried to trap Him by asking a question about divorce. After all, John the Baptist had been slain because he preached against Herod's adulterous marriage (Mark 6:14-29).

But there was more than politics involved in their trick question, because divorce was a very controversial subject among the Jewish rabbis. No matter what answer Jesus gave, He would be sure to displease somebody, and this might give opportunity to arrest Him. The verbs indicate that the Pharisees "kept asking Him," as though they hoped to provoke Him to say something incriminating.

In that day there were two conflicting views on divorce, and which view you espoused depended on how you interpreted the phrase *some uncleanness* in Deuteronomy 24:1-4. The followers of Rabbi Hillel were quite lenient in their interpretation and permitted a man to divorce his wife for any reason, even the burning of his food. But the school of Rabbi Shimmai was much more strict and taught that the critical words *some uncleanness* referred only to premarital sin. If a newly married husband discovered that his wife was not a virgin, then he could put her away.

As He usually did, Jesus ignored the current debates and focused attention on the Word of God, in this case, the Law of Moses in Deuteronomy 24:1-4. As you study this passage, it is important to note two facts. First, it was *the man* who divorced the wife, not the wife who divorced the husband; for women did not have this right in Israel. (Roman women did have the right of divorce.) Second, the official "bill of divorcement" was given to the wife to declare her status and to assure any prospective husband that she was indeed free to remarry. Apart from the giving of this document, the only other requirement was that the woman not return to her first husband if her second husband divorced her. Among the Jews, the question was not, "May a divorced woman marry again?" because remarriage was permitted and even expected. The big question was, "What are the legal grounds for a man to divorce his wife?"

The Law of Moses did not give adultery as grounds for divorce; for, in Israel, the adulterer and adulteress were stoned to death (Deut. 22:22; Lev. 20:10; also see John 8:1-11). Whatever Moses meant by "some uncleanness" in Deuteronomy 24:1, it could not have been adultery.

Jesus explained that Moses gave the divorce law because of the sinfulness of the human heart. The law protected the wife by restraining the husband from impulsively divorcing her and abusing her like an unwanted piece of furniture, instead of treating her like a human being. Without a bill of divorcement, a woman could easily become a social outcast and be treated like a harlot. No man would want to marry her, and she would be left defenseless and destitute.

By giving this commandment to Israel, God was not putting His approval on divorce or even encouraging it. Rather, He was seeking to restrain it and make it more difficult for men to dismiss their wives. He put sufficient regulations around divorce so that the wives would not become victims of their husbands' whims.

The Lord then took them back beyond Moses to the record of the original Creation (Gen. 1:27; 2:21-25). After all, in the beginning, it was *God* who established marriage; and He has the right to make the rules. According to Scripture, marriage is between a man and a woman, not two men or two women; and the relationship is sacred and permanent. It is the most intimate union in the human race, for the two become one flesh. This is not true of a father and son or a mother and daughter, but it is true of a man and wife.

While the spiritual element is vitally important in marriage, the emphasis here is that marriage is a *physical* union: the two become one *flesh,* not one spirit. Since marriage is a physical union, only a physical cause can break it—either death (Rom. 7:1-3) or fornication (Matt. 5:32; 19:9). Mark did not include the "exception clause" found in Matthew, but neither did he say that death breaks the marriage union.

Privately, the Lord further explained the matter to His questioning disciples, who by now were convinced that it was a dangerous thing to get married. To remarry after divorce, *other than one granted on the grounds of fornication,* would make the person guilty of committing adultery, and this is a serious thing. Note that Jesus included the women in His warning, which certainly elevated their status in society and gave them equality of responsibility with the men. The rabbis would not have gone this far.

Mark 10:9 warns us that *man* cannot separate those who have been united in marriage, *but God can.* Since He established marriage, He has the right to lay down the rules. A divorce may be legal according to our laws and yet not be right in the eyes of God. He expects married people to practice commitment to each other (Mark 10:7) and to remain true to each other. Too many people view divorce as "an easy way out," and do not take seriously their vows of commitment to each other and to the Lord.

Adults Shall Be as Children (Mark 10:13-16)

First marriage, then children; the sequence is logical. Unlike many "moderns" today, the Jews of that day looked on children as a blessing and not a burden, a rich treasure from God and not a liability (Pss. 127–128). To be without children brought a couple both sorrow and disgrace.

It was customary for parents to bring their children to the rabbis for a blessing, and so it was reasonable that they would bring the little ones to Jesus. Some were infants in arms (Luke 18:15), while others were young children able to walk; and He welcomed them all.

Why would the disciples rebuke the people and try to keep the children away from Jesus? (See Matt. 15:23 and Mark 6:36 for other instances of the disciples' seeming hardness of heart.) They probably thought they were doing Him a favor by helping Him protect His time and conserve His strength. In other words, *they did not consider the children to be important!* Their attitude was strange, because Jesus had already taught them to receive the children in His name and to be careful not to cause any of them to stumble (Mark 9:36ff). Once again, they forgot what He had taught them.

The phrase *much displeased* is too tame. Our Lord actually became indignant as He openly rebuked His disciples for standing in the way. Then He announced that the children were better kingdom examples than were the adults. We tell the children to behave like adults, but Jesus tells the adults to model themselves after the children!

In what ways are children a pattern? In their humble dependence on others, their receptivity, their acceptance of themselves and their position in life. Of course, Jesus was speaking about an unspoiled child, not one who was trying to act like an adult. A child enjoys much but can explain very little. Children live by faith. By faith they accept their lot, trusting others to care for them and see them through.

We enter God's kingdom by faith, like little children: helpless, unable to save ourselves, totally dependent on the mercy and grace of God. We enjoy God's kingdom by faith, believing that the Father loves us and will care for our daily needs. What does a child do when he or she has a hurt or a problem? Take it to Father and Mother! What an example for us to follow in our relationship with our Heavenly Father! Yes, God wants us to be childlike, but not childish!

There is no suggestion here that Jesus baptized these children, for Jesus did not even baptize adults (John 4:1-2). If the disciples had been accustomed to baptizing infants, they certainly would not have turned the people away. Jesus took these precious little ones in His loving arms and blessed them—and what a blessing that must have been!

The First Shall Be Last (Mark 10:17-31)

Of all the people who ever came to the feet of Jesus, this man is the only one who went away worse than he came. And yet he had so much in his favor! He was a young man (Matt. 19:22) with great potential. He was respected by others, for he held some ruling office, perhaps in a local court (Luke 18:18). Certainly he had manners and morals, and there was enough desire in his heart for spiritual things that he ran up to Jesus and bowed at His feet. In every way, he was an ideal young man; and when Jesus beheld him, He loved him.

With all of his fine qualities, the young man was very superficial in his views of spiritual things. He certainly had a shallow view of salvation, for he thought that he could *do something* to earn or merit eternal life. This was a common belief in that day among the Jews (John 6:28), and it is very common today. Most unsaved people think that God will one day add up their good works and their bad works; and if their good works exceed their bad works, they will get into heaven.

Behind this good-works approach to salvation is a superficial view of sin, man, the Bible, Jesus Christ, and salvation. Sin is rebellion against the holy God. It is not simply an action; it is an inward attitude that exalts man and defies God. Did this young man actually think that he could do a few religious works and settle his account with the holy God?

The young man had a superficial view of Jesus Christ. He called Him "Good Master" (Teacher), but we get the impression that he was trying to flatter the Lord; for the Jewish rabbis did not allow the word *good* to be applied to them. Only God was good, and the word must be reserved for Him alone. Jesus was not denying that He was God; rather, He was affirming it. He just wanted to be sure that the young man really knew what he was saying and that he was willing to accept the responsibilities involved.

This explains why Jesus pointed the young man to the Law of Moses: He wanted him to see himself as a sinner bowed before the holy God. We cannot be saved from sin by keeping the Law (Gal. 2:16-21; Eph. 2:8-10). The Law is a mirror that shows us how dirty we are, but the mirror cannot wash us. One purpose of the Law is to bring the sinner to Christ (Gal. 3:24), which is what it did in this man's case. The Law can bring the sinner to Christ, but the Law cannot make the sinner like Christ. Only grace can do that.

The young ruler did not see himself as a condemned sinner before the holy God. He had a superficial view of the Law of God, for he measured obedience only by external actions and not by inward attitudes. As far as his actions were concerned, he was blameless (see Phil. 3:6); but his inward attitudes were not blameless, because he was covetous. He may have kept some of the commandments, but the last commandment caught him: "Thou shalt not covet!" Covetousness is a terrible sin; it is subtle and difficult to detect, and yet it can cause a person to break all the other commandments. "For the love of money is a root of all sorts of evil" (1 Tim. 6:10, NASB).

Looking at this young man, you would conclude that he had everything, but Jesus said that one thing was lacking: *a living faith in God.* Money was his god: he trusted it, worshiped it, and got his fulfillment from it. His morality and good manners only concealed a covetous heart.

Our Lord's directions in Mark 10:21 are not to be applied to everyone who wants to become a disciple, because Jesus was addressing the specific needs of the rich young ruler. The man was rich, so Jesus told him to liquidate his estate and give the money to the poor. The man was a ruler, so Jesus told him to take up a cross and follow Him which would be a humbling experience. Jesus offered this man the gift of eternal life, but he turned it down. It is difficult to receive a gift when your fist is clenched around money and the things money can buy. The Greek word translated "grieved" gives the picture of storm clouds gathering. The man walked out of the sunshine and into a storm! He wanted to get salvation on his terms, and he was disappointed.

The disciples were shocked at the Lord's declaration about wealth, because most Jews thought that the possession of great wealth was the evidence of God's special blessing. Many people today still cling to this error, in spite of the message of Job, the example of Christ and the Apostles, and the clear teaching of the New Testament. In the case of this young man, his wealth *robbed him* of God's greatest blessing, eternal life. Today, wealth continues to make rich people poor and the first last (see 1 Cor. 1:26-31).

Money is a marvelous servant but a terrible master. If you possess money, be grateful and use it for God's glory; but if money possesses you, beware! It is good to have the things that money can buy, provided you don't lose the things that money cannot buy. The deceitfulness of riches had so choked the soil of this young man's heart that he was unable to receive the good seed of the Word and be saved (Matt. 13:22). What a bitter harvest he would reap one day!

However, Peter's response indicated that there were a few problems in his own heart. "What then will there be for us?" (Matt. 19:27, NASB) This statement reveals a rather commercial view of the Christian life: "We have given up everything for the Lord; now, what will we get in return?" Contrast Peter's words with those of the three Hebrew men in Daniel 3:16-18, and with Peter's later testimony in Acts 3:6. He certainly came a long way from "What will I get?" to "What I have, I will give!"

Jesus assured His disciples that no one who follows Him will ever lose what is really important, either in this life or in the life to come. God will reward each one. However, we must be sure our motives are right: "For My sake and the Gospel's" (see Mark 8:35). The well-known Christian industrialist of a decade ago, R.J. LeTourneau, used to say, "If you give because it pays, it won't pay!" If we sacrifice only to get a reward, that reward will never come.

Note that Jesus also promised "persecutions." He had already told His disciples what both the Jews and Gentiles would do to Him in Jerusalem, and now He informed them that they would have their share of persecution. God balances blessings with battles, developing mature sons and daughters.

To the general public, the rich ruler stood first and the poor disciples stood last. But God saw things from the perspective of eternity—and the first became last while the last became first! Those who are first in their own eyes will be last in God's eyes, but those who are last in their own eyes will be rewarded as first! What an encouragement for true disciples!

Servants Shall Be Rulers (Mark 10:32-45)

The destination was still Jerusalem, and Jesus was still leading the way. As Mark wrote his account of the Saviour's journey to Calvary, he must have meditated much on the great "Servant Songs" in Isaiah 42–53. "For the Lord God will help me; therefore shall I not be confounded: therefore I have set my face like a flint, and I know that I shall not be ashamed" (Isa. 50:7). We cannot but admire the courage of God's Servant as He made His way to Calvary, and we should adore Him all the more because He did it for us.

We must try to understand the bewilderment and fear of His followers, for this was a difficult experience for them and not at all what they had planned or expected. Each new announcement of His death only added to their perplexity. In the first two announcements (Mark 8:31; 9:31), Jesus had told them *what* would occur; but now He told them *where* His passion will take place—in the Holy City of Jerusalem! In this third announcement, He also included the part that the Gentiles would play in His trial and death, and for the fourth time, He promised that He would rise again (note Mark 9:9). He told His disciples the truth, but they were in no condition to understand it.

In the light of our Lord's announcement of His death, we are embarrassed and ashamed to read of James and John asking for thrones. How could they and their mother (Matt. 20:20-21) be so callous and selfish? Peter had responded to the first announcement by arguing with Jesus; after the second announcement, the disciples responded by arguing among themselves over who was the greatest (Mark 9:30-34). These men seemed blind to the meaning of the Cross.

Actually, Salome and her two sons were claiming the promise Jesus had given that, in the future kingdom, the disciples would sit on twelve thrones with the Lord Jesus. (See Matt. 19:28. Since Mark was writing especially for the Gentiles, he did not include this promise.) It took a great deal of faith on their part to claim the promise, especially since Jesus had just reminded them of His impending death. The three of them were in agreement (Matt. 18:19), and they had His Word to encourage them, so there was no reason why Jesus should not grant their request.

Except for one thing: they were praying selfishly, and God does not answer selfish prayers (James 4:2-3). If He does, it is only that He might discipline us and teach us how to pray in His will (Ps. 106:15; 1 John 5:14-15). James, John, and Salome did not realize that *it costs something to get answers to prayer.* For Jesus to grant their request, He would have to suffer and die. Why should He pay such a great price just so they could enjoy free thrones? Is that the way to glorify God?

Jesus compared His approaching suffering and death to the drinking of a cup (Mark 14:32-36) and the experiencing of a baptism (Luke 12:50; also see Pss. 41:7; 69:2, 15). It would be a devastating experience—and yet James and John said they were able to go through it with Jesus! Little did they realize what they were saying, for in later years they would indeed have their share of the baptism and the cup. James would be the first of the disciples to be martyred (Acts 12:1-2), and John would experience great persecution.

Because their prayer was motivated by earthly wisdom, not heavenly wisdom, James and John aroused the anger of the other disciples and brought disunity to the group (see James 3:13–4:1). No doubt the men were unhappy because they had not thought of asking first! Once again, Jesus tried to teach them what it means to be an "important person" in the kingdom of God (see Mark 9:33-37).

Like many people today, the disciples were making the mistake of following the wrong examples. Instead of modeling themselves after Jesus, they were admiring the glory and authority of the Roman rulers, men who loved position and authority. While there is nothing wrong with aspiring to greatness, we must be careful how we define "greatness" and why we want to achieve it. Jesus said, "Whoever wishes to become great among you shall be your servant; and whoever wishes to be first among you shall be slave of all" (Mark 10:43-44, NASB).

God's pattern in Scripture is that a person must first be a servant before God promotes him or her to be a ruler. This was true of Joseph, Moses, Joshua, David, Timothy, and even our Lord Himself (Phil. 2:1-11). Unless we know how to obey orders, we do not have the right to give orders. Before a person exercises authority, he or she must know what it means to be under authority. If Jesus Christ followed this pattern in accomplishing the great work of redemption, then surely there is no other pattern for us to follow.

The Poor Become Rich (Mark 10:46-52)
A large crowd of Passover pilgrims followed Jesus and His disciples to Jericho, about eighteen miles from Jerusalem. There were actually two cities named Jericho: the old city in ruins, and the new city a mile away where Herod the Great and his successors built a lavish winter palace. This may help explain the seeming contradiction between Mark 10:46 and Luke 18:35.

There were two blind beggars sitting by the road (Matt. 20:30), one of whom was named Bartimaeus. Both Mark and Luke focused attention on him since he was the more vocal of the two. The beggars heard that Jesus of Nazareth, the Healer, was passing by; they did their best to get His attention so that they might receive His merciful help and be healed.

At first, the crowd tried to silence them, but when Jesus stopped and called for the men, the crowd encouraged them! Desperate people do not permit the crowd to keep them from Jesus (see Mark 5:25-34). Bartimaeus threw off his garment so it would not trip him, and he hastened to the Master. No doubt some of the pilgrims or disciples helped him.

"What do you want Me to do for you?" seems like a strange question to ask a blind man. (It was the same question He had asked James, John, and Salome, Mark 10:36.) But Jesus wanted to give the man opportunity to express himself and give evidence of his own faith. What did he really believe Jesus *could* do for him?

When Bartimaeus called Jesus "Lord," he used the title *Rabboni,* meaning "my Master." The only other person in the Gospels who used it was Mary (John 20:16). The beggar had twice called him "Son of David," a national messianic title, but "Rabboni" was an expression of personal faith.

Matthew tells us that Jesus was moved with compassion and touched their eyes (Matt. 20:34), and immediately they were healed. Out of gratitude to Jesus, the men joined the pilgrim band and started toward Jerusalem, following Jesus. This is the last healing miracle recorded in Mark, and it certainly fits into Mark's "Servant" theme. We see Jesus Christ, God's Suffering Servant, on His way to the cross, and yet He stops to serve two blind beggars! What love, what mercy, and what grace!

CHAPTER NINE
THE SERVANT IN JERUSALEM
Mark 11:1–12:44

Jerusalem at Passover season was the delight of the Jews and the despair of the Romans. Thousands of devout Jews from all over the world arrived in the Holy City, their hearts filled with excitement and nationalistic fervor. The population of Jerusalem more than tripled during the feast, making it necessary for the Roman military units to be on special alert. They lived with the possibility that some enthusiastic Jewish Zealot might try to kill a Roman official or incite a riot, and there was always potential for disputes among the various Jewish religious groups.

Into this situation came God's Servant with less than a week remaining before He would be crucified outside the city walls. In this section, we see God's Servant ministering in three different official roles.

The Servant-King (Mark 11:1-11)
On the road Jesus took, a traveler would arrive first at Bethany and then come to

Bethphage, about two miles from Jerusalem. The elevation at this point is about 2,600 feet, and from it you have a breathtaking view of the Holy City. The Lord was about to do something He had never done before, something He had repeatedly cautioned others not to do for Him: He was going to permit His followers to give a public demonstration in His honor.

Jesus sent two of His disciples to Bethphage to get the colt that He needed for the event. Most people today think of a donkey as nothing but a humble beast of burden, but in that day, it was looked on as an animal fit for a king to use (1 Kings 1:33). Our Lord needed this beast so that He might fulfill the messianic prophecy found in Zechariah 9:9. Mark does not quote this verse or refer to it because he was writing primarily for Gentile readers.

In fulfilling this prophecy, Jesus accomplished two purposes: (1) He declared Himself to be Israel's King and Messiah; and (2) He deliberately challenged the religious leaders. This set in motion the official plot that led to His arrest, trial, and crucifixion. The Jewish leaders had decided not to arrest Him during the feast, but God had determined otherwise. The Lamb of God must die at Passover.

Many patriotic Jews from the crowd of pilgrims eagerly joined the procession that proclaimed Jesus as the King, the Son of David come in the name of the Lord. The visitors from Galilee were most prominent in the procession, along with the people who had witnessed the raising of Lazarus from the dead (John 12:12-18). You sometimes hear it said that the same people who cried "Hosanna!" on Palm Sunday ended up crying "Crucify Him!" on Good Friday, but this is not true. The crowd that wanted Him crucified came predominantly from Judea and Jerusalem, whereas the Galilean Jews were sympathetic with Jesus and His ministry.

When welcoming a king, it was customary for people to lay their outer garments on the road, and then add festal branches (2 Kings 9:13). The shout "Hosanna!" means "Save now!" and comes from Psalm 118:25-26. Of course, Jesus knew that the people were quoting from a messianic psalm (relate Ps. 118:22-23 with Matt. 21:42-44 and Acts 4:11), but He allowed them to go right ahead and shout. He was openly affirming His kingship as the Son of David.

What were the Romans thinking as they watched this festive demonstration? After all, the Romans were experts at parades and official public events. We call this event "the Triumphal Entry," but no Roman would have used that term. An official "Roman Triumph" was indeed something to behold! When a Roman general came back to Rome after a complete conquest of an enemy, he was welcomed home with an elaborate official parade. In the parade he would exhibit his trophies of war and the illustrious prisoners he had captured. The victorious general rode in a golden chariot, priests burned incense in his honor, and the people shouted his name and praised him. The procession ended at the arena where the people were entertained by watching the captives fight with the wild beasts. That was a "Roman Triumph."

Our Lord's "triumphal entry" was nothing like that, but it was a triumph just the same. He was God's anointed King and Saviour, but His conquest would be spiritual and not military. A Roman general had to kill at least 5,000 enemy soldiers to merit a Triumph; but in a few weeks, the Gospel would "conquer" some 5,000 Jews and transform their lives (Acts 4:4). Christ's "triumph" would be the victory of love over hatred, truth over error, and life over death.

After looking into the temple area, where He would return the next day, Jesus left the city and spent the night in Bethany, where it was safer and quieter. No doubt He spent time in prayer with His disciples, seeking to prepare them for the difficult week that lay ahead.

The Servant-Judge (Mark 11:12-26)

Our Lord's condemning of the tree and cleansing of the temple were both symbolic acts that illustrated the sad spiritual condition of the nation of Israel. In spite of its many privileges and opportunities, Israel was outwardly fruitless (the tree) and inwardly corrupt (the temple). It was unusual for Jesus to act in judgment (John 3:17), yet there comes a time when this is the only thing God can do (John 12:35-41).

Cursing the fig tree (vv. 12-14, 20-26). The fig tree produces leaves in March or April and then starts to bear fruit in June, with another crop in August and possibly a third crop in December. The presence of leaves could mean the presence of fruit, even though that fruit was "left over" from the previous season. It is significant that in this instance

Jesus did not have special knowledge to guide Him; He had to go to the tree and examine things for Himself.

If He had power to kill the tree, why didn't He use that power to restore the tree and make it produce fruit? Apart from the drowning of the pigs (Mark 5:13), this is the only instance of our Lord using His miraculous power to destroy something in nature. He did it because He wanted to teach us two important lessons.

First, there is a lesson on *failure:* Israel had failed to be fruitful for God. In the Old Testament, the fig tree is associated with the nation of Israel (Jer. 8:13; Hosea 9:10; Nahum 3:12). Like the fig tree our Lord cursed, Israel had "nothing but leaves." Note that the tree dried up "from the roots" (Mark 11:20). Three years before, John the Baptist had put the ax to the roots of the tree (Matt. 3:10), but the religious leaders would not heed his message. Whenever an individual or a group "dries up" spiritually, it is usually from the roots.

The disciples would probably connect this miracle with the parable which Jesus gave some months before (Luke 13:1-9), and they would see in the miracle a vivid picture of God's judgment on Israel. They might also recall Micah 7:1-6 where the prophet declares that God is seeking "the first ripe fruit" from His people. Christ is still seeking fruit from His people, and for us to be fruitless is sin (John 15:16). We must carefully cultivate our spiritual roots and not settle for "leaves."

Jesus also used this miracle to teach us a lesson on *faith.* The next morning, when the disciples noticed the dead tree, Jesus said, "Have faith in God," meaning, "Constantly be trusting God; live in an attitude of dependence on Him." In Jewish imagery, a mountain signifies something strong and immovable, a problem that stands in the way (Zech. 4:7). We can move these mountains only by trusting God.

Of course, this is not the only lesson Jesus ever gave on prayer; and we must be careful not to isolate it from the rest of Scripture. Prayer must be in the will of God (1 John 5:14-15), and the one praying must be abiding in the love of God (John 15:7-14). Prayer is not an emergency measure that we turn to when we have a problem. Real prayer is a part of our constant communion with God and worship of God.

Nor should we interpret Mark 11:24 to mean, "If you pray hard enough and *really believe,* God is obligated to answer your prayers, no matter what you ask." That kind of faith is not faith in God; rather, it is nothing but faith in faith, or faith in feelings. True faith in God is based on His Word (John 15:7; Rom. 10:17), and His Word reveals His will to us. It has well been said that the purpose of prayer is not to get man's will done in heaven, but to get God's will done on earth.

True prayer involves forgiveness as well as faith. I must be in fellowship with both my Father in heaven and my brethren on earth if God is to answer my prayers (see Matt. 5:21-26; 6:14-15; 18:15-35). The first word in "The Lord's Prayer" is *our—"Our* Father which art in heaven" and not "My Father which art in heaven." Though Christians may pray in private, no Christian ever prays alone; for all of God's people are part of a worldwide family that unites to seek God's blessing (Eph. 3:14-15). Prayer draws us together.

We do not earn God's blessing by forgiving one another. Our forgiving spirit is one evidence that our hearts are right with God and that we want to obey His will, and this makes it possible for the Father to hear us and to answer prayer (Ps. 66:18). Faith works by love (Gal. 5:6). If I have faith in God, I will also have love for my brother.

Cleansing the temple (vv. 15-19). Jesus had cleansed the temple during His first Passover visit (John 2:13-22), but the results had been temporary. It was not long before the religious leaders permitted the money changers and the merchants to return. The priests received their share of the profits, and, after all, these services were a convenience to the Jews who traveled to Jerusalem to worship. Suppose a foreign Jew carried his own sacrifice with him and then discovered that it was rejected because of some blemish? The money rates were always changing, so the men who exchanged foreign currency were doing the visitors a favor, even though the merchants were making a generous profit. It was easy for them to rationalize the whole enterprise.

This "religious market" was set up in the court of the Gentiles, the one place where the Jews should have been busy doing serious missionary work. If a Gentile visited the temple and saw what the Jews were doing *in the name of the true God,* he would never want to believe what they taught. The Jews might not have permitted idols of wood and stone in their temple, but there were idols there just the same. The court of the Gentiles should have been a place for praying, but it was instead a place for preying and paying.

Mark especially mentioned the people who sold doves. The dove was one of the few sacrifices that the poor people could afford (Lev. 14:22). It was the sacrifice Joseph and Mary brought when they dedicated Jesus in the temple (Luke 2:24). Even the poor people were victimized by the merchants in the temple, and this in itself must have grieved the Lord Jesus, for He was always sensitive to the poor (see Mark 12:41-44).

Jesus quoted two Scriptures to defend what He did—Isaiah 56:7 and Jeremiah 7:11. At the same time, He exposed the sins of the religious leaders. The Jews looked on the temple primarily as a place of sacrifice, but Jesus saw it as a place of prayer. True prayer is in itself a sacrifice to God (Ps. 141:1-2). Jesus had a spiritual view of the Jewish religion, while the leaders promoted a traditional view that was cluttered with rules and regulations.

Campbell Morgan points out that "a den of thieves" is the place to which thieves run *when they want to hide.* The chief priests and scribes were using the temple and its religious services to "cover up" their sin and hypocrisy. Both Isaiah (Isa. 1:10-17) and Jeremiah (Jer. 7:1-16) had warned the people of their day that the presence of the physical temple was no guarantee of blessing from God. It was what the people did in the temple *from their hearts* that was really important. The nation had not heeded the warning of the prophets, nor would they heed our Lord's warning.

When the scribes and chief priests heard the report of our Lord's activities, they kept seeking some way to arrest Him (see Mark 14:1-2). Judas would solve the problem for them. Before we quickly condemn the Jewish religious leaders for their sins, we should examine our own ministries to see if perhaps we are making merchandise of the Gospel. Do the outsiders in our community think of our church buildings as houses of prayer? Are all nations welcomed there? Do we as church members flee to church on Sundays in an attempt to cover up our sins? Do we "go to church" in order to maintain our reputation or to worship and glorify God? If the Lord Jesus were to show up in our house of worship, what changes would He make?

The Servant-Prophet (Mark 11:27–12:44)

In the days that followed, the representatives of the religious and political establishment descended on Jesus as He ministered in the temple, trying their best to trip Him up with their questions. He answered four questions, and then He asked them a question that silenced them for good.

A question of authority (11:27–12:12). As the official guardians of the Law, the members of the Sanhedrin had both the right and the responsibility to investigate anyone who claimed to be sent by God; and that included Jesus (see Deut. 18:15-22). However, these men did not have open minds or sincere motives. They were not seeking truth; they were looking for evidence to use to destroy Him (Mark 11:18). Jesus knew what they were doing, so He countered their question with another question and exposed their hypocrisy.

Why take them all the way back to John the Baptist? For a very good reason: God does not teach us new truth if we have rejected the truth He has already revealed. This basic principle is expressed in John 7:17: "If any man is willing to do His will, he shall know of the teaching, whether it is of God, or whether I speak from Myself" (NASB). "Obedience is the organ of spiritual knowledge," said the British preacher F.W. Robertson. The Jewish religious leaders had not accepted what John had taught, so why should God say anything more to them? Had they obeyed John's message, they would have gladly submitted to Christ's authority, for John came to present the Messiah to the nation.

The Jewish leaders were caught in a dilemma of their own making. They were not asking "What is true?" or "What is right?" but "What is safe?" This is always the approach of the hypocrite and the crowd-pleaser. It certainly was not the approach of either Jesus (Mark 12:14) or John the Baptist (Matt. 11:7-10). Jesus did not refuse to answer their question; He only refused to accept and endorse their hypocrisy. He was not being evasive; He was being honest.

Before they had opportunity to escape, He told them a parable that revealed *where their sins were leading them.* They had already permitted John the Baptist to be killed, but soon they would ask for the crucifixion of God's Son!

The vineyard was a familiar image of Israel

(Ps. 80:8-16; Isa. 5:1-7). According to Leviticus 19:23-25, a farmer would not use the fruit until the fifth year, though we are not sure the Jews were obeying this regulation at that time. In order to retain his legal rights to the property, the owner had to receive produce from the tenants, even if it was only some of the vegetables that grew between the rows of trees or vines. This explains why the tenants refused to give him anything: they wanted to claim the vineyard for themselves. It also explains why the owner continued to send agents to them; it was purely a question of authority and ownership.

If Mark 12:2-5 covers the three years when the fruit was not used, then it was in the fourth year that the beloved Son was sent. *This is the year when the fruit was devoted to the Lord* (Lev. 19:24), and it makes the sending of the Son even more meaningful. If the tenants could do away with the heir, they would have a clear claim to the property; so they cast him out (see Heb. 13:12-13) and killed him. They wanted to preserve their own position and were willing even to kill to accomplish their evil purpose (John 11:47-53).

Jesus then asked, "What shall, therefore, the lord of the vineyard do?" The leaders answered the question first and thereby condemned themselves (Matt. 21:41), and then Jesus repeated their answer as a solemn verdict from the Judge. But before they could appeal the case, He quoted what they knew was a messianic prophecy, Psalm 118:22-23. We met this same psalm at His triumphal entry (Mark 11:9-10). "The Stone" was a well-known symbol for the Messiah (Ex. 17:6; Dan. 2:34; Zech. 4:7; Rom. 9:32-33; 1 Cor. 10:4; and 1 Peter 2:6-8). The Servant-Judge announced a double verdict: they had not only rejected the Son, but they had also refused the Stone! There could be only one consequence—judgment (Matt. 22:1-14).

A question of responsibility (vv. 13-17). A common threat forced two enemies to unite, the Pharisees and the Herodians. The Herodians supported the family of Herod as well as the Romans who gave them the authority to rule. The Pharisees, however, considered the Herod clan to be the evil usurpers of the throne of David; for, after all, Herod was an Edomite and not a Jew. The Pharisees also opposed the poll tax that the Romans had inflicted on Judea, and they resented the very presence of Rome in their land.

Their temporary alliance was a subtle trap, for no matter how Jesus replied to their question, He was in trouble with either Rome or Herod! But Jesus moved the discussion from politics to principle and caught the hypocrites in their own trap. We might state our Lord's reply something like this:

"Caesar's image is on his coins, so they must be minted by his authority. The fact that you possess these coins and use them indicates that you think they are worth something. Therefore, you are already accepting Caesar's authority, or you would not use his money! But don't forget that you were created in the image of God and therefore must live under God's authority as well."

I once carried on a brief correspondence with a man who objected to my interpretation of Romans 13. He said that all government was of the devil and that Christians must not bow to the authority of "the powers that be." I pointed out to him that even his use of the United States mail service was an acceptance of governmental authority. The money he spent buying the paper and stamps also came from the "powers that be." For that matter, the very freedom he had to express himself was a right guaranteed by—the government!

The word translated "render" in Mark 12:17 means "to pay a debt, to pay back." Jesus looked on taxes as the citizens' debt to the government in return for the services performed. Today those services would include, among other things, fire and police protection, national defense, the salaries of the officials who manage the affairs of state, special programs for the poor and underprivileged, etc. The individual Christian citizen might not agree with the way all of his tax money is used, and he can express himself with his voice and his vote, but he must accept the fact that God has established human government for our good (Rom. 13; 1 Tim. 2:1-6; 1 Peter 2:13-17). Even if we cannot respect the people in office, we must respect the office.

A question about eternity (vv. 18-27). This is the only place in Mark where the Sadducees are mentioned. This group accepted only the Law of Moses as their religious authority; so, if a doctrine could not be defended from the first five books of the Old Testament, they would not accept it. They did not believe in the existence of the soul, life after death, resurrection, final judgment, angels, or demons (see Acts 23:8). Most of the Sadducees were priests and were wealthy. They considered themselves the "religious aristocrats" of Judaism and tended to look down on everybody else.

They brought a hypothetical question to Jesus, based on the law of marriage given in Deuteronomy 25:7-10. This woman had a series of seven husbands during her lifetime, all brothers, and all of whom had died. "If there is such a thing as a future resurrection," they argued, "then she must spend eternity with seven husbands!" It seemed a perfect argument, as most arguments are that are based on hypothetical situations.

The Sadducees thought that they were smart, but Jesus soon revealed their ignorance of two things: the power of God and the truth of Scripture. Resurrection is not the restoration of life as we know it; it is the entrance into a new life that is different. The same God who created the angels and gave them their nature is able to give us the new bodies we will need for new life in heaven (1 Cor. 15:38ff). Jesus did not say that we would become angels or be like the angels in everything, for God's children are higher than the angels (John 17:22-24; 1 John 3:1-2). He said that in our resurrection bodies, we would be sexless like the angels; and therefore marriage would no longer exist. In the eternal state, where our new bodies are perfect and there is no death, there will be no need for marriage, procreation, and the continuance of the race.

The Sadducees were also ignorant of the Scriptures. They claimed to accept the authority of Moses, but they failed to notice that Moses taught the continuation of life after death. Once again, our Lord went back to Scripture (note Mark 2:25; 10:19; 12:10), in this case to the passage about the burning bush (Ex. 3). God did not tell Moses that He *was* (past tense) the God of Abraham, Isaac, and Jacob. He said, "I am the God of Abraham, and the God of Isaac, and the God of Jacob." The patriarchs were *alive* when God spoke those words to Moses; therefore, Moses does teach that there is life after death.

A question of priority (vv. 28-34). The next challenger was a scribe who was also a Pharisee (see Matt. 22:34-35). The scribes had determined that the Jews were obligated to obey 613 precepts in the Law, 365 negative precepts and 248 positive. One of their favorite exercises was discussing which of these divine commandments was the greatest.

The Lord quoted Deuteronomy 4:4-5, the great confession of faith that even today pious Jews recite each morning and evening. It is called "The Shema" from the first word of the confession which means "hear." Then He quoted Leviticus 19:18 which emphasizes love for one's neighbor. Jesus made love the most important thing in life, because "love is the fulfilling of the Law" (Rom. 13:8-10). If we love God, we will experience His love within and will express that love to others. We do not live by rules but by relationships, a loving relationship to God that enables us to have a loving relationship with others.

When he started this conversation, the scribe was only the tool of the Pharisees who were trying to get evidence against Jesus (note Matt. 22:35). But after he heard our Lord's answer, the scribe stood and dared to commend the Lord for His reply. The Word had spoken to the man's heart and he was beginning to get a deeper spiritual understanding of the faith he thought he understood. Even the Old Testament Scriptures taught that there was more to the Jewish religion than offering sacrifices and keeping laws (see 1 Sam. 15:22; Pss. 51:16-17; 141:1-2; Jer. 7:22-23; Hosea 6:6; Micah 6:6-8).

What does it mean when a person is "not far from the kingdom of God"? It means he or she is facing truth honestly and is not interested in defending a "party line" or even personal prejudices. It means the person is testing his or her faith by what the Word of God says and not by what some religious group demands. People close to the kingdom have the courage to stand up for what is true even if they lose some friends and make some new enemies.

A question of identity (vv. 35-37). Now it was our Lord's turn to ask the questions, and He focused on the most important question of all: Who is the Messiah? "What think ye of Christ? Whose Son is He?" (Matt. 22:42) This is a far more important question than the ones His enemies had asked Him, for if we are wrong about Jesus Christ, we are wrong about salvation. This means we end up condemning our own souls (John 3:16-21; 8:24; 1 John 2:18-23).

Jesus quoted Psalm 110:1 and asked them to explain how David's son could also be David's Lord. The Jews believed that the Messiah would be David's son (John 7:41-42), but the only way David's son could also be David's Lord would be if Messiah were *God come in human flesh.* The answer, of course, is our Lord's miraculous conception and virgin birth (Isa. 7:14; Matt. 1:18-25; Luke 1:26-38).

This section closes with two warnings from the Lord: a warning against the pride of the scribes (Mark 12:38-40) and against the pride of the rich (Mark 12:41-44). If a person is "important" only because of the uniform he wears, the title he bears, or the office he holds, then his "importance" is artificial. It is *character* that makes a person valuable, and nobody can give you character: you must develop it yourself as you walk with God.

There were thirteen trumpet-shaped chests around the walls of the court of the women, and here the people dropped in their offerings. The rich made a big production out of their giving (see Matt. 6:1-4), but Jesus rejected them and their gifts. It is not the *portion* but the *proportion* that is important: the rich gave out of their abundance, but the poor widow gave all that she had. For the rich, their gifts were a small contribution, but for the widow, her gift was true consecration of her whole life.

Pride of living and pride of giving are sins we must avoid at all cost. How tragic that the leaders depended on a religious system that shortly would pass off the scene. How wonderful that the common people gladly listened to Jesus and obeyed His Word.

In which group are you?

CHAPTER TEN THE SERVANT UNVEILS THE FUTURE

Mark 13

The Jews were proud of their temple, in spite of the fact that it was built by the Herod family in order to placate the Jews. Jesus had already given His estimate of the temple (Mark 11:15-17), but His disciples were fascinated by the magnificence of the structure. Imagine how shocked they were when Jesus informed them that the building they admired so much would one day be demolished. The Jewish leaders had defiled it; Jesus would depart from it and leave it desolate (Matt. 23:38); the Romans would destroy it.

Once away from the crowds, Jesus' disciples asked Him when this momentous event would take place and what would happen to indicate it was soon to occur. Their questions revealed that their understanding of prophecy was still quite confused. They thought that the destruction of the temple coincided with the end of the age and the return of their Lord (Matt. 24:3). But their questions gave Jesus the opportunity to deliver a prophetic message that is generally called "The Olivet Discourse" (Matt. 24–25; Luke 21:5-36).

As we study this important sermon, we must follow some practical guidelines. To begin with, we must study this discourse in the light of the rest of Scripture, especially the Book of Daniel. The prophetic Scriptures harmonize if we consider all that God has revealed.

Second, we must see the practical application of the discourse. Jesus did not preach this sermon to satisfy the curiosity of His disciples, or even to straighten out their confused thinking. At least four times He said "Take heed!" (Mark 13:5, 9, 23, 33) and He closed the address with the admonition, "Watch!" While studying this address can help us better understand future events, we must not make the mistake of setting dates! (Mark 13:32)

Third, as we study, we must keep in mind the "Jewish atmosphere" of the discourse. The Olivet Discourse grew out of some questions asked of a Jewish rabbi by four Jewish men, about the future of the Jewish temple. The warnings about "false Christs" would especially concern Jews (Mark 13:5-6, 21-22), as would the warning about Jewish courts and trials (Mark 13:9). The Jews would especially appreciate the reference to "Daniel the prophet" and the admonition to flee from Judea (Mark 13:14).

Finally, we must remember that this chapter describes a period of time known as "the Tribulation" (Mark 13:19, 24; also see Matt. 24:21, 29). The Old Testament prophets wrote about this period and called it "the time of Jacob's trouble" (Jer. 30:7), a time of wrath (Zeph. 1:15-18), and a time of indignation and punishment (Isa. 26:20-21). As we shall see, it is Daniel the prophet who gives us the "key," resulting in a better understanding of the sequence of events.

In Mark 13, Jesus described three stages in this Tribulation period: (1) the beginning (Mark 13:5-13), (2) the middle (Mark 13:14-

18), and (3) the events that lead to the end (Mark 13:19-27). He then closed with two parables that urge believers to watch and take heed (Mark 13:28-37). Matthew's Gospel is more detailed but has the same basic outline: the beginning of sorrows (Matt. 24:4-14), the middle of the Tribulation (Matt. 24:15-28), the end (Matt. 24:29-31), closing parabolic application (Matt. 24:32-44).

I must point out that it is the conviction of many students of prophecy that believers in this present age of the church will be raptured by Christ and taken to heaven *before the Tribulation begins* (1 Thes. 4:13–5:11; Rev. 3:10-11). At the close of the Tribulation, they will return to earth with Christ and reign with Him (Rev. 19:11–20:6). I agree with this interpretation, but I do not make it a test of orthodoxy or spirituality.

The First Half of the Tribulation (Mark 13:5-13)

The key statement is at the end of Mark 13:8: "These are the beginnings of sorrows." The word translated "sorrows" means "birth pangs," suggesting that the world at that time will be like a woman in travail (see Isa. 13:6-8; Jer. 4:31; 6:24; 13:21; 22:20-23; 1 Thes. 5:3). The birth pangs will come suddenly, build up gradually, and lead to a time of terrible sorrow and tribulation for the whole world.

"Don't be deceived." Jesus listed the things that must *not* be taken as the "signs" of His coming. Rather, they are indications that the Tribulation "birth pangs" are just beginning. These signs are: the success of false Christs (Mark 13:5-6), nations in conflict (Mark 13:7-8a), natural disturbances (Mark 13:8b), and religious persecutions (Mark 13:9-13). They have been always been with us, but since these events are compared to "birth pangs," our Lord may be saying that *an acceleration of these things* would be significant.

False messiahs. The pages of history are filled with the tragic stories of false messiahs, false prophets, and their enthusiastic but deluded disciples. Jesus warned about false prophets (Matt. 7:15-20), as did Paul (Acts 20:28-31), and John (1 John 4:1-6). There is something in human nature that loves a lie and refuses to believe the costly lessons of the past. Mark Twain said that a lie runs around the world while Truth is putting on her shoes! How easy it is for spiritually blind people to follow popular leaders and gullibly accept their simple but erroneous solutions for the problems of life. Jesus warned His disciples not to be deceived by these imposters, and that warning holds good today.

Political conflicts. He also warned them not to be disturbed by political conflicts among the nations. The Roman Empire had enjoyed a measure of peace for many years, but it would not last. As the empire decayed and nationalism developed, it was inevitable that nations would come into conflict. The "Pax Romana" would be gone forever.

Natural disasters. War often leaves famine in its wake (2 Kings 25:2-3; Ezek. 6:11). Famine is also caused by man's abuse of the environment, or it can be sent by God as a judgment (1 Kings 17:1). There have always been earthquakes, and some are evidences of God's wrath (Rev. 6:12; 8:5; 11:13; 16:18). Since natural disasters have many causes, it is dangerous to dogmatically make them "the signs of the times."

"Don't be discouraged!" Not only were the believers to take heed and avoid the deceivers, but they were also to *take heed to themselves* (Mark 13:9-13). Why? Because they would face increasing opposition and persecution from sources both official (Mark 13:9-11) and personal (Mark 13:12-13). It was important that the believers use these experiences as opportunities to witness for Jesus Christ. Persecution would begin in the local Jewish courts, but it would move to the higher courts where governors and kings would be involved. You see a similar development recorded in the Book of Acts (Acts 4–5; 7; 12; 16; 21–28).

But persecution would only result in proclamation! The believers would suffer *for His sake* and in that way declare His Gospel. "We multiply whenever we are mown down by you," said Tertullian to his persecutors. "The blood of Christians is seed!" While I do not think that taking the Gospel to all nations (Mark 13:10) is a *condition* for our Lord's return, it is certainly Christ's commission to His people (Matt. 28:19-20). The "end" here means "the end of the age," the Tribulation period.

It would not be easy for these "common people" to face courts, governors, and kings; but Jesus assured them that the Holy Spirit would minister through them whenever they had opportunity to witness (Mark 13:11). This passage should not be used as an excuse or a crutch for poorly prepared preachers. It is an encouragement for all believers who sincerely want to witness for Christ and honor Him (John 14:26; Acts 4:8). If we are walking in the Spirit, we will have no trouble bearing witness for Christ when the opportunities arrive (John 15:26-27).

We can understand official persecution, but why would friends and family members create problems for believers? (see Micah 7:4ff; John 15:18-27) You would think that Jewish families in particular would be loyal to each other. But the Christian faith was looked on as heresy and blasphemy by both the Jews and the Gentiles. Twice daily, orthodox Jews affirmed, "Hear, O Israel! The Lord our God is one Lord!" (Deut. 6:4) The Jew who said "Jesus is Lord!" blasphemed and was worthy of death. Rome expected its citizens to declare "Caesar is lord!" or suffer the consequences. Thus, families and friends would be torn between their loyalty to their "ancient faith" and their nation, and their devotion to loved ones.

The real cause for persecution is stated in Mark 13:13, "for My name's sake." If we identify with Jesus Christ, we can expect the world to treat us the way it treated Him (John 15:20ff). You can belong to all sorts of weird religious groups today and not suffer much opposition from family and friends, but the minute you bring the name of Jesus into the picture, and share the Gospel, somebody will start to oppose you. His name is still hated.

Do not interpret Mark 13:13 as a condition for salvation, for it applies primarily to witnesses during the Tribulation. In any period a person lives, if he is truly born again, God will love him (John 13:1; Rom. 8:35-38) and keep him (John 10:27-29; Rom. 8:29-34). Since "the end" in Mark 13:7 means "the end of the age," that is likely what it means in Mark 13:13. During the Tribulation, the true believers will prove their faith by their faithfulness. They will not give in to the godless pressures of false religion (Rev. 13).

The Middle of the Tribulation (Mark 13:14-18)

The phrase "abomination of desolation" comes from the Book of Daniel and refers to the idolatrous pollution of the Jewish temple by the Gentiles. To the Jews, all idolatry is an abomination (Deut. 29:17; 2 Kings 16:3). The Jewish temple was defiled in 167 B.C. by the Syrian king Antiochus IV (also called "Epiphanes," meaning "illustrious") when he poured swine's blood on the altar. This event was predicted in Daniel 11:31. The temple was also defiled by the Romans in A.D. 70 when they captured and destroyed the city of Jerusalem. However, these events were but anticipations of the final "abomination of desolation" prophesied in Daniel 9:27 and 12:11.

In order to understand Daniel 9:24-27, we must remember that the Jewish calendar is built on a series of sevens. The seventh day of the week is the Sabbath, and the seventh week after Passover brings Pentecost. The seventh month brings the Feast of Trumpets, the Day of Atonement, and the Feast of Booths. The seventh year is a Sabbatical year, and after seven Sabbatical years comes the Year of Jubilee.

Daniel saw seventy weeks, or periods of seven years, divinely determined for the Jews and for their Holy City, Jerusalem. This period of 490 years began with the decree of Artaxerxes in 445 B.C. permitting the Jews to return to their land and rebuild Jerusalem (Ezra 1:1-4). Why must the city be restored? Because 483 years later (7 x 69), Messiah would come to the city and give His life for sinners.

Now we must do some simple calculating. Most historians agree that Jesus was born in 5 B.C.; for Herod the Great was still living at the time, and he died in March, 4 B.C. If our Lord died at about the age of 33, that would take us to A.D. 27 or 28, and this would be 483 years after 445 B.C. when the decree was given!

We have accounted for 483 of Daniel's 490 years, but what about the remaining 7 years? Daniel 9:27 assigns them to the Tribulation period that we are now studying. (Note that Dan. 9:26 also predicts the destruction of Jerusalem—by the Romans, commentators conclude—but these two events must not be confused.) "The time of Jacob's trouble" will last seven years.

But what signals the beginning of this awful seven-year period? The signing of a covenant between the nation of Israel and "the prince that shall come" (Dan. 9:26). This "prince" is the coming world dictator that we usually call "the Antichrist." In the Book of Revelation, he is called "the Beast" (Rev. 13–14). He will agree to protect Israel from her many enemies for seven years, and will even allow the Jews to rebuild their temple and restore their ancient liturgy and sacrifices. The Jews rejected their true Messiah but will accept a false messiah (John 5:43). However, after three and a half years, Antichrist will break this covenant, invade the temple, set up his own image, and force the world to worship Satan (see 2 Thes. 2:1-12; Rev. 13). This is Daniel's "abomination of desolation," and it will usher in the last half of the Tribulation period, a time known as "the Great Tribulation" (Matt. 24:21). Note in Mark 13:14 that Mark's parenthesis is for *readers* at a future time, not *hearers* when Jesus gave this message. This message will have special meaning to them as they see these events taking place.

Jesus gave a special warning to the Jewish believers in Jerusalem and Judea: "Get out as fast as you can!" This same warning applied when Rome attacked Jerusalem in A.D. 70. (See Luke 21:20-24, and remember that Daniel 9:26 predicted the invasion.) What happened in A.D. 70 foreshadowed what will happen in the middle of the Tribulation. Dr. Harry Rimmer used to say, "Coming events cast their shadows before. Straight ahead lies yesterday!" The warnings in Mark 13:14-18 do not apply to believers today, but they do remind us that God's people in every age must know the prophetic Word and be prepared to obey God at any time.

The Last Half of the Tribulation (Mark 13:19-27)

In the Book of Revelation, the last half of the Tribulation is called "the wrath of God" (Rev. 14:10, 19; 15:1, 7; 16:1, 19; 19:15). During this time, God will judge the world and prepare Israel for the coming of her Messiah. It will be a time of intensive judgment such as the world has never seen or will ever see again. In it, God will be working out His purposes and setting the stage for the coming of the Conqueror (Rev. 19:11ff).

Even in the midst of His wrath, God remembers mercy (Hab. 3:2); and for the sake of His elect, He shortens the days of the Tribulation. (The "elect" refers to Israel and the Gentiles who believe during the Tribulation. See Rev. 14.) To "shorten the days" means that He limits them to the three and a half years already determined and stops on time.

Satanic deception will continue to the very end, and false Christs and false prophets will lead people astray. In fact, they will even do miracles (Matt. 7:21-23; 2 Thes. 2:9-12; Rev. 13:13-14). So deceptive will be these miracles that even the elect will be tempted to believe their lies. Of themselves, miracles are not a proof of divine calling and approval (Deut. 13:1-5). The final test is the Word of God.

The Tribulation period will climax with the appearing of terrifying signs in the heavens and worldwide chaos on the earth (Luke 21:25-26). These signs, which have been predicted by the prophets (Isa. 13:10; 34:4; Joel 2:10; 3:15), will prepare the way for the coming of Jesus Christ to the earth. It will be a revelation of His great glory (see Dan. 7:13-14; Mark 8:38) as He comes to establish His rule on the earth (Acts 1:11; Rev. 1:7).

Mark 13:27 describes the regathering of Israel from the nations to which they have been scattered throughout the world (Deut. 30:3-6; Isa. 11:12; Jer. 31:7-9). They will see their Messiah and trust Him, and the nation will be created in holiness and glory (Zech. 12:9–13:1; 14:4-11). That there is a glorious future for Israel is stated by Paul in Romans 11.

Jesus did not want His disciples to get so involved in the prophecies of the future that they would neglect the responsibilities of the present; so He closed the Olivet Discourse with two parables. (Matt. 25 adds three other parables—the bridesmaids, the talents, and the sheep and goats.) Note that the first parable (Mark 13:28-31) emphasizes knowing that His coming is near, while the second parable emphasizes *not knowing* the time of His return. Is this a contradiction? No, because they were addressed to two different groups of people—the first, to the Tribulation saints, and the second, to all believers of every age.

The fig tree has a special association with the nation of Israel (see Mark 11:12-14, but note that Luke 21:29 adds "and all the trees"). Most of the trees in Palestine are evergreens and do not change dramatically with the seasons. Not so the fig tree; it is one of the latest to leaf out in spring, so its shoots are an indication that summer is indeed near.

As Christian believers today, we are not looking for "signs" of His coming; we are looking for Him! But people living during the Tribulation will be able to watch these things occur and will know that His coming is near. This assurance will help them to endure (Mark 13:13) and to be good witnesses.

We think of a "generation" as a body of people living at the same time in history. But to what "generation" was Jesus referring in Mark 13:30? Not the generation then living in Judea, because they did not see "all these things" actually take place. Perhaps He meant the generation living during the Tribulation period. But since the Tribulation covers only seven years, why refer to an entire generation? For that matter, several different generations live together during every period of history.

The Greek word translated "generation" can also mean "race, stock, family." On several occasions, Jesus used it to refer to the Jewish nation (Mark 8:12, 38; 9:19); and that is probably how He used it in Mark 13:30. The chosen nation, God's elect, would be preserved to the very end; and God would fulfill His promises to them. His Word will never fail (Josh. 21:45; 1 Kings 8:56; Matt. 24:35). We as believers do not depend on signs; we depend on His unchanging Word, the "sure word of prophecy" (2 Peter 1:19-21).

The Parable of the Fig Tree cautions Tribulation saints to watch and to know the "signs of the times." But the Parable of the Householder warns *all of us today* (Mark 13:37) to be alert, because we do not know when He will return to take us to heaven (1 Cor. 15:51-52). Like the householder in the story, before our Lord went from us back to heaven, He gave each of us work to do. He expects us to be faithful while He is gone and to be working when He returns. "Take heed, watch and pray" is His admonition.

To "watch" means to be alert, to stay at one's best, to stay awake. (The English name "Gregory" comes from this Greek word translated "watch.") Why must we stay alert? Because nobody knows when Jesus Christ will return. When He was on earth in His humiliation, Jesus did not know the day or hour of His coming again. Even the angels do not know. The unsaved world scoffs at us because we continue to cling to this "blessed hope," but He will return as He promised (2 Peter 3). Our task is to be faithful and to be busy, not to speculate or debate about the hidden details of prophecy.

Watchfulness has nothing to do with going to heaven. It is purely a matter of pleasing Him, hearing His loving commendation, and receiving His reward (Matt. 25:14-30). There is no suggestion here that, when He returns, Jesus will take only the faithful to heaven and leave the others on earth to suffer the Tribulation. His family is one, and He is now preparing a home for all of them, even the least worthy (John 14:1-6). We go to heaven because of His grace, not because of our faithfulness or good works (Eph. 2:8-10).

The Christians who read Mark's Gospel eventually had to face intense persecution from Rome (1 Peter 4:12ff), and this particular message must have brought comfort and strength to them. After all, if God is able to help His people witness during the Great Tribulation, the worst persecution of all, then surely He could strengthen the saints in the Roman Empire as they faced their fiery trial.

While Christians today will not experience the terrible sufferings described in this chapter, we will have our share of persecution and tribulation in this world before the Lord returns (John 16:33; Acts 14:22). But the warnings of this message in Mark 13 may be applied to our own lives: "Take heed that you are not deceived" (Mark 13:5, 23); "Take heed that you do not become discouraged and quit" (Mark 13:9); "Take heed, watch and pray" (Mark 13:33).

"And what I say unto you, I say unto all, 'Watch' " (Mark 13:37).

CHAPTER ELEVEN THE SERVANT SUFFERS

Mark 14:1–15:20

While thousands of Passover pilgrims were preparing for the joys of the feast, Jesus was preparing for the ordeal of His trial and crucifixion. Just as He had steadfastly set His face to go to Jerusalem (Luke 9:51), so He steadfastly set His heart to do the Father's will. The Servant was "obedient unto death, even the death of the cross" (Phil. 2:8).

Follow His footsteps during the days and hours of the last week, and you will be amazed to see the responses of various people to the Lord Jesus Christ.

In Bethany—Adored (Mark 14:1-11)

This event took place six days before Passover, which would put it on the Friday before the Triumphal Entry (John 12:1). By placing this story between the accounts of the plot to arrest Jesus, Mark contrasted the treachery of Judas and the leaders with the love and loyalty of Mary. The ugliness of their sins makes the beauty of her sacrifice even more meaningful.

Neither Mark nor Matthew names the woman, but John tells us that it was Mary of Bethany, the sister of Martha and Lazarus (John 11:1-2). Mary is found three times in the Gospel story; and each time, she is at the feet of Jesus (Luke 10:38-42; John 11:31-32; 12:1-8). Mary had a close fellowship with the Lord as she sat at His feet and listened to His Word. She is a good model for all of us to follow.

Mary's anointing of the Lord must not be confused with a similar event recorded in Luke 7:36-50. The unnamed woman in the house of Simon the Pharisee was a converted harlot who expressed her love to Christ because of His gracious forgiveness of her many sins. In the house of Simon the (healed) leper, Mary expressed her love to Christ because He was going to the cross to die for her. She prepared His body for burial as she anointed His head (Mark 14:3) and His feet (John 12:3). She showed her love for Jesus while He was still alive.

It was an expensive offering that she gave to the Lord. Spikenard was imported from India, and a whole jar would have cost the equivalent of a common worker's annual income. Mary gave lavishly and lovingly. She was not ashamed to show her love for Christ openly.

There were three consequences to her act of worship. First, the house was filled with the beautiful fragrance of the ointment (John 12:3; also note 2 Cor. 2:15-16). There is always a "spiritual fragrance" in that home where Jesus Christ is loved and worshiped.

Second, the disciples, led by Judas, criticized Mary for wasting her money! It sounded so pious for Judas to talk about the poor, when in reality he wanted the money for himself! (John 12:4-6) Even in the Upper Room, six days later, the disciples still thought Judas was concerned about helping the poor (John 13:21-30). It is interesting that the word translated "waste" in Mark 14:4 is translated "perdition" in John 17:12 *and applied to Judas!* Judas criticized Mary for "wasting money," but he wasted his entire life!

Third, Jesus commended Mary and accepted her gracious gift. He knew the heart of Judas and understood why the other disciples followed his bad example. He also knew Mary's heart and quickly defended her (Rom. 8:33-39). No matter what others may say about our worship and service, the most important thing is that we please the Lord. The fact that others misunderstand and criticize us should not keep us from showing our love to Christ. Our concern should be His approval alone.

When Mary gave her best at the feet of Jesus, she started a "wave of blessing" that has been going on ever since. She was a blessing to Jesus as she shared her love, and she was a blessing to her home as the fragrance spread. Were it not for Mary, her village, Bethany, would probably have been forgotten. The account of her deed was a blessing to the early church that heard about it and, because of the records in three of the Gospels, Mary has been a blessing to the whole world—and still is! The Lord's prediction has certainly been fulfilled.

Mary gave her best in faith and love; Judas gave his worst in unbelief and hatred. He solved the problem of how the Jewish leaders could arrest Jesus without causing a riot during the feast. He sold his Master for the price of a slave (see Ex. 21:32), the basest act of treachery in history.

In the Upper Room—Betrayed (Mark 14:12-26)

The Passover lamb was selected on the tenth day of the month Nisan (our March–April), examined for blemishes, and then slain on the fourteenth day of the month (Ex. 12:3-6). The lamb had to be slain in the temple precincts and the supper eaten within the Jerusalem city limits. For the Jews, the Passover feast was the memorial of a past victory, but Jesus would institute a new supper that would be the memorial of His death.

Peter and John saw to it that the supper was prepared (Luke 22:8). It would not be difficult to locate the man carrying the jar of water because the women usually performed this task. Was this man John Mark's father? Did Jesus eat the Passover in an upper room in John Mark's home? These are fascinating speculations, but we have no evidence that can confirm them. However, we do know that John Mark's home was a center for Christian fellowship in Jerusalem (Acts 12:12).

The original Passover feast consisted of the roasted lamb, the unleavened bread, and the dish of bitter herbs (Ex. 12:8-20). The lamb reminded the Jews of the blood that was applied to the doorposts in Egypt to keep the angel of death from slaying their firstborn. The bread reminded them of their haste in leaving Egypt (Ex. 12:39), and the bitter herbs spoke of their suffering as Pharaoh's slaves. At sometime in the centuries that followed, the Jews had added to the ceremony the drinking of four cups of wine diluted with water.

Since for the Jews the new day began with sundown, it would be Friday when Jesus and His disciples met in the Upper Room. This was His last Passover, and on that day, He would fulfill the Passover by dying on the cross as the spotless Lamb of God (John 1:29; 1 Cor. 5:7; 1 Peter 2:21-24).

Between Mark 14:17 and 18 are details of the washing of the disciples' feet and the lesson on humility (John 13:1-20). Following that lesson, Jesus became deeply troubled and announced that one of the disciples was a traitor. This announcement stunned all the disciples except Judas, who knew that Jesus was speaking about him. Until the very end, Jesus hid from the other disciples the identity of His betrayer, for He wanted to give Judas every opportunity to turn from sin. He even washed Judas' feet! Had Peter known the truth about Judas, he might have been tempted to kill him.

Some people try to defend Judas by arguing that he betrayed Jesus in order to force Him into revealing His power and setting up the Jewish kingdom. Others say that he was nothing but a servant who obediently fulfilled God's Word. Judas was neither a martyr nor a robot. He was a responsible human being who made his own decisions but, in so doing, fulfilled the Word of God. He must not be made into either a hero ("After all, somebody had to betray Jesus!") or a helpless victim of merciless predestination. Judas was lost for the same reason millions are lost today: he did not repent of his sins and believe on Jesus Christ (John 6:64-71; 13:10-11). If you have never been born again, one day you will wish you had not been born at all.

None of the other disciples really thought himself to be the traitor, for their questions imply a negative answer: "It is not I, is it?" The men had often debated over which of them was the greatest, but now they were discussing which of them was the vilest. To make matters worse, Jesus said that His betrayer had even eaten bread with Him at the table! In the East, to break bread with someone means to enter into a pact of friendship and mutual trust. It would be an act of the basest treachery to break bread and then betray your host. However, even this was the fulfillment of the Word of God (Ps. 41:9).

Judas was sitting in the place of honor at our Lord's left, while John was reclining to His right (John 13:23). When Jesus gave Judas the bread dipped in the herbs, it was the gracious act of a host to a special guest. Even this did not break Judas' heart, for after Judas took the morsel, Satan possessed him. Judas left the Upper Room to go to make the final arrangements to arrest the Lord Jesus. But even then the disciples did not know the truth about Judas (John 13:27-30); and they would not find out the truth until they met him later in the Garden of Gethsemane.

After Judas left the scene, Jesus instituted what Christians commonly call "the Lord's Supper" or "the Eucharist." (The word *Eucharist* comes from a Greek word which means "to give thanks.") Before the cup, Jesus took one of the unleavened loaves, blessed it, broke it, and told the men, "This is My body." He then took the Passover cup, blessed it, and gave it to them, saying, "This is My blood" (see 1 Cor. 11:23-26).

Bread and wine were two common items that were used at practically every meal, but Jesus gave them a wonderful new meaning. When Jesus said, "This is My body," and, "This is My blood," He did not transform either the bread or the wine into anything different. When the disciples ate the bread, it was still bread; when they drank the wine, it was still wine. However, the Lord gave a new meaning to the bread and the wine, so that, from that hour, they would serve as memorials of His death.

What, then, did Jesus accomplish by His death? On the cross, Jesus fulfilled the Old Covenant and established a New Covenant (Heb. 9–10). The Old Covenant was ratified with the blood of animal sacrifices, but the New Covenant was ratified by the blood of God's Son. The New Covenant in His blood would do what the Old Covenant sacrifices could not do—take away sin and cleanse the heart and conscience of the believer. We are not saved from our sins by participating in a religious ceremony, but by trusting Jesus Christ as our Saviour.

Our Lord's command was, "This do in remembrance of Me" (1 Cor. 11:24-25). The word translated "remembrance" means much more than "in memory of," for you can do something in memory of a dead person—yet Jesus is alive! The word carries the idea of a present participation in a past event. Because

Jesus is alive, as we celebrate the Lord's Supper, by faith we have communion with Him (1 Cor. 10:16-17). This is not some "magical" experience produced by the bread and cup. It is a spiritual experience that comes through our discerning of Christ and the meaning of the Supper (1 Cor. 11:27-34).

The last thing Jesus and His disciples did in the Upper Room was to sing the traditional Passover hymn based on Psalms 115–118. Imagine our Lord *singing* when the cross was only a few hours away!

In the Garden—Forsaken (Mark 14:27-52)

On the way to the Garden of Gethsemane ("oil press"), Jesus warned the disciples that they would all forsake Him; but He then assured them that He would meet them again in Galilee after His resurrection. He even quoted Zechariah 13:7—"Smite the shepherd, and the sheep shall be scattered"—to back up His warning. Their minds and hearts were unable to receive and retain His words, for three days later, they did not believe the reports of His resurrection! And the angel had to give them a special reminder to meet Him in Galilee (Mark 16:6-7). Had they listened to His word and believed it, they would have saved themselves a great deal of anxiety; and Peter would not have denied the Lord.

The quotation from Zechariah told the disciples what to do when the Jews arrested Jesus: *scatter!* In fact, at the very time of His arrest, Jesus said, "Let these [disciples] go their way" (John 18:8). In other words, "Men, get out of here!" I have read eloquent sermons blaming Peter for "following afar off," but they completely miss the point. He was not supposed to follow at all! Had he obeyed the Lord, he would not have attacked a man with his sword or denied the Lord three times.

Peter seemed to have a difficult time applying Jesus' commands to himself. The other men might forsake Jesus, but Peter would stand true and, if necessary, go with Him to prison and to death. Of course, the other disciples echoed Peter's boast; so he was not the only self-confident one in the group. In the end, all of them failed.

When about to experience great suffering, most people want to have someone with them, to help share the burden. Often in my pastoral ministry, I have sat with people at the hospital, waiting for the surgeon to come with a report. Being perfectly human, Jesus wanted companionship as He faced the cross, and He selected Peter, James, and John, the same men who had accompanied Him to the home of Jairus (Mark 5:37) and to the Mount of Transfiguration (Mark 9:2). These three experiences parallel Philippians 3:10: "That I may know Him [Mount of Transfiguration], and the power of His resurrection [home of Jairus], and the fellowship of His sufferings [Garden of Gethsemane]."

Our Lord's struggle in the Garden can be understood only in the light of what would happen to Him on the cross: He would be made sin for us (2 Cor. 5:21) and bear the curse of the Law (Gal. 3:13). It was not the physical suffering that almost overwhelmed Him with "anguish and sorrow," but the contemplation of being forsaken by His Father (Mark 15:34). This was "the cup" that He would drink (John 18:11). According to Hebrews 5:7-9, He asked to be saved, not "from death" but *out of death;* that is, raised from the dead; and the Father granted His request.

Abba is an Aramaic word that means "papa" or "daddy." It reveals the intimate relationship between our Lord and His Father. While believers today would probably not use that term in public, it does belong to us because we belong to Him (Rom. 8:15; Gal. 4:6). Note that Jesus did not tell the Father what to do; He had perfect confidence in God's will. Three times He prayed about the matter, and each time He yielded to the Father's will in loving surrender.

What were the three disciples doing? Sleeping! And Peter had vowed that he would die with his Lord—yet he could not even watch with Him! How gently Jesus rebuked the disciples and warned them. "Watch and pray" is an admonition that is often repeated in Scripture (Neh. 4:9; Mark 13:33; Eph. 6:18; Col. 4:2). It means, "Be alert as you pray! Keep your spiritual eyes open, for the enemy is near!"

The third time our Lord returned to the sleeping men, He said, "Are you still sleeping and taking your rest? It is enough; the hour has come" (Mark 14:41, NASB). It was the hour of His sacrifice, when He would die for the sins of the world. At that moment, Judas and the temple guards arrived to arrest Jesus, and Judas kissed Jesus repeatedly as the sign that He was the one to arrest. What hypocrisy!

The fact that Judas brought such a large group of armed men is evidence that neither he nor the religious leaders really understood Jesus. They thought that Jesus would try to escape, or that His followers would put up a fight, or that perhaps He might do a miracle. Our Lord's words in Mark 14:49 were proof that He was in control, for they could have arrested Him many times earlier, except that His hour had not yet come.

Peter did a foolish thing by attacking Malchus (John 18:10), for we do not fight spiritual battles with physical weapons (2 Cor. 10:3-5). He used the wrong weapon, at the wrong time, for the wrong purpose, with the wrong motive. Had Jesus not healed Malchus, Peter would have been arrested as well; and there might have been four crosses on Calvary.

At this point, the disciples forsook Jesus and fled, and so did an unknown young man who came into the Garden and witnessed the arrest. Was this John Mark? We do not know, but since the Gospel of Mark is the only one of the four Gospels that records this event, the author could well have been writing about himself. If the Upper Room was in the home of John Mark, then perhaps Judas led the soldiers there first. John Mark may have hastily put on an outer garment and followed the mob to the Garden. The soldiers may have even tried to arrest him, so he fled.

The disciples were scattered and the Servant was now alone, "and yet I am not alone, because the Father is with Me" (John 16:32). Soon, even the Father would forsake Him!

In the High Priest's Palace—Rejected (Mark 14:53-72)

Both the Jewish trial and the Roman trial were in three stages. The Jewish trial was opened by Annas, the former high priest (John 18:13-24). It then moved to the full council to hear witnesses (Mark 14:53-65), and then to an early morning session for the final vote of condemnation (Mark 15:1). Jesus was then sent to Pilate (Mark 15:1-5; John 18:28-38), who sent Him to Herod (Luke 23:6-12), who returned Him to Pilate (Mark 15:6-15; John 18:39–19:6). Pilate yielded to the cry of the mob and delivered Jesus to be crucified.

By the time the soldiers arrived at the palace of the high priest, Peter and John, heedless of the Lord's repeated warnings, followed the mob and even went into the courtyard. Jesus that night had sweat "as it were great drops of blood" (Luke 22:44), but Peter was cold and sat by the enemy fire! The two disciples could not witness the actual trial, but at least they were near enough to see the outcome (Matt. 26:58; John 18:15).

After questioning and insulting Jesus, Annas sent Jesus bound to his son-in-law Caiaphas, the high priest. The Sanhedrin was assembled and the witnesses were ready. It was necessary to have at least two witnesses before the accused could be declared guilty and worthy of death (Deut. 17:6). Many witnesses testified against Jesus, but since they did not agree, their testimony was invalid. How tragic that a group of religious leaders would encourage people to lie, and during a special holy season!

Throughout this time of false accusation, our Lord said nothing (Isa. 53:7; 1 Peter 2:23). But when the high priest put Him under oath, Jesus had to reply, and He testified clearly that he was indeed the Son of God. The title "Son of man" is messianic (Dan. 7:13), and the members of the council knew exactly what Jesus was saying: He was claiming to be God come in human flesh! This claim, of course, was blasphemy to the Jews, and they declared Him guilty and worthy of death. Since it was irregular for the Sanhedrin to vote on capital cases at night, the council met again early the next morning and gave the official sentence (Mark 15:1).

While the Lord was being mocked and abused, Peter was in the courtyard below, trying to escape detection. Had he heeded the Lord's warnings, he would have avoided walking into temptation and denying his Master three times. He is a warning to all of us, for, after all, if an apostle who walked with Christ denied his Lord, what might we do in similar circumstances? The Roman believers who read Mark's Gospel no doubt learned from this account, for they would soon be entering the furnace of persecution themselves.

First, one of the high priest's servant girls spoke to Peter, and he denied knowing anything about Jesus. Then the cock crowed. Another servant girl pointed Peter out to some of the bystanders, and again Peter denied knowing Jesus. Finally, a man accused him of being one of the disciples, and some of the bystanders joined in; but Peter vehemently denied knowing Jesus, and even put himself under a curse. Then the cock crowed for the second time and the Lord's prediction was fulfilled (see Mark 14:30).

However, it was not the crowing of the cock that convicted Peter; it was the remembering of Christ's words. It is always the Word that penetrates the heart and brings about true repentance. Peter pondered what Jesus had said and what he himself had done; and then Jesus, on His way to Pilate's hall, turned and looked at Peter. It was a look of love, to be sure, but *injured* love (Luke 22:61). His heart broken, Peter went out quickly and wept bitterly.

Before we judge Peter too severely, we need to examine our own lives. How many times have we denied the Lord and lost opportunities to share the Gospel with others? Do we, like Peter, talk when we should listen, argue when we should obey, sleep when we should pray, and fight when we should submit? Peter at least was sorry for his sins and wept over them, and the Lord did forgive him. After His resurrection, Jesus had a private meeting with Peter (Luke 24:34); then Jesus helped Peter make a public confession when He met the disciples in Galilee (John 21).

In Pilate's Hall—Condemned (Mark 15:1-20)

As soon as their early morning meeting was over, and the verdict officially recorded, the Jewish leaders delivered Jesus to the Roman governor, Pontius Pilate. The governor usually resided at Caesarea, but it was his custom to be in Jerusalem each year for the feast. His presence pleased some of the Jews, and he could be on hand if any problems arose among the thousands of people crowded into Jerusalem. Roman governors held court early in the morning, so he was quite prepared when they brought the prisoner to him.

The Jewish council had to convince Pilate that Jesus was guilty of a capital crime and therefore worthy of death (John 18:31-32). In spite of their political corruption, many Roman officials had an appreciation for justice and tried to deal fairly with prisoners. Furthermore, Pilate had no great love for the Jews and was not about to do them any favors. He knew that the Jewish leaders were not interested in seeing justice done; what they really wanted was vengeance (Mark 15:10).

John gives us the most details of the Roman trial, and when you combine the Gospel records, you discover that Pilate repeatedly stated that he found no fault in Jesus (John 18:38; Luke 23:14; John 19:4; Luke 23:22; Matt. 27:24). His problem was that he lacked the courage to stand for what he believed. He wanted to avoid a riot (Matt. 27:24), so he was "willing to content the people" (Mark 15:15). Pilate did not ask, "Is it right?" Instead, he asked, "Is it safe? Is it popular?"

The council had only one capital crime that they might be able to present to Pilate: Jesus claimed to be a king and He stirred up the people. They tried to pass Him off as a dangerous revolutionary who was undermining the authority of Rome. As Pilate questioned Jesus, the Lord said nothing, but the chief priests kept accusing Him and trying to wear down the governor's resistance.

Pilate thought he could avoid making a decision by sending Jesus to Herod, the ruler of Galilee (Luke 23:6-12), but Herod only sent Jesus back after mocking Him. Then the governor offered the people a choice—Jesus the Nazarene, or Barabbas, the murderer and insurrectionist—thinking that surely sanity would prevail and they would ask to have Jesus released. But the chief priests had prepared the crowd carefully (Mark 15:11), and they asked for Barabbas to be set free and Jesus to be crucified.

The governor then tried a third ruse: he had Jesus scourged, hoping that the sight of the suffering prisoner would somehow arouse their pity (Mark 15:15; John 19:1ff). But the plan did not work. The governor gave in and delivered Jesus to be crucified.

Then followed the disgraceful mockery by the soldiers, as they beat Him, spat on Him, and bowed in mock homage. Roman soldiers would certainly laugh at a Jew who claimed to be a king! "We have no king but Caesar!" (John 19:12-15) Our Lord quietly suffered and did not fight back, a lesson that Mark's readers would need to learn as they faced official persecution (1 Peter 2:21-24).

But men had not yet done their worst to God's Son. Now they would lead Him outside the city and nail Him to a cross, and the Servant would die for the sins of the very people who were crucifying Him.

CHAPTER TWELVE
THE SERVANT FINISHES HIS WORK
Mark 15:21–16:20

Cecil Rhodes devoted his life to British expansion in South Africa, plus making a fortune in diamonds. He was not yet fifty years old when he died, and his last words were, "So little done, so much to do."

"I have glorified Thee on the earth," Jesus said to His Father; "I have finished the work which Thou gavest Me to do" (John 17:4). It would be wonderful if all of us could give that same kind of report when we get to the end of life's journey. To know that we have accomplished His work and glorified His name would certainly make us look back with thanksgiving and ahead with excitement and anticipation.

The four events described in this final section of Mark give us the climax of the Gospel story and the historical basis for the message of the Gospel (1 Cor. 15:1-8).

The Servant's Death (Mark 15:21-41)

Three specific hours are mentioned in this section of Mark: the third (Mark 15:25), the sixth (Mark 15:33), and the ninth (Mark 15:33-34). The Jews reckoned time from 6 A.M. to 6 P.M., so this means that the third hour was 9 A.M., the sixth hour noon, and the ninth hour 3 P.M. Mark followed the Jewish system, whereas the Apostle John used Roman time in his Gospel. This means that "the sixth hour" in John 19:14 is 6 A.M.

The third hour (15:21-32). According to law, the guilty victim had to carry his cross, or at least the cross beam, to the place of execution, and Jesus was no exception. He left Pilate's hall bearing His cross (John 19:16-17), but He could not continue; so the soldiers "drafted" Simon of Cyrene to carry the cross for Him. Roman officers had the privilege of "impressing" men for service, and the way they used this privilege irritated the Jews (Matt. 5:41).

When you consider all that our Lord had endured since His arrest, it is not surprising that His strength failed. Indeed, "He could have called 10,000 angels," yet He willingly bore the suffering on our behalf. There was a higher purpose behind this act: the victim carried the cross because he had been found guilty, *but our Lord was not guilty.* We are the guilty ones, and Simon carried that cross on our behalf. Simon Peter boasted that he would go with Jesus to prison and to death (Luke 22:33), but it was Simon of Cyrene, not Simon Peter, who came to the aid of the Master.

In one of his folksy letters to his mother, Harry Truman wrote, "I went to the White House to see the President and discovered I was the President." Simon had come to Jerusalem to celebrate the Passover (Acts 2:10; 6:9), and he ended up meeting the Passover Lamb! We have good reason to believe that Simon trusted the Saviour and went home and led his two sons to the Lord. No doubt many of Mark's Roman readers knew Alexander and Rufus (Rom. 16:13), and perhaps they had even known Simon.

Golgotha is a Hebrew word that means "skull," though nowhere does the text explain why the place bore that name. Visitors to the Holy Land today are shown "Gordon's Calvary," which does have the appearance of a skull, but guides also point out another possible site in the Church of the Holy Sepulchre. We do not know the exact place where our Lord was crucified, nor is it important that we know. He was crucified outside the city walls, the place of rejection (Heb. 13:12-13); and He died for the sins of the world.

It was customary for the victims to be given a narcotic potion that would help deaden the pain (Prov. 31:6), but our Lord refused it. For one thing, He wanted to be in full possession of His faculties as He did the Father's will and accomplished the work of redemption. He would enter fully into His sufferings on our behalf and take no short cuts. He refused the cup of sympathy so that He might better drink the cup of iniquity (Matt. 26:36-43). What an example for us to follow as we do God's will and share "the fellowship of His sufferings" (Phil. 3:10).

None of the Gospel writers gives us a description of crucifixion, nor is one necessary. Their aim is not to arouse our pity but to assure our faith. Many of their readers had probably witnessed crucifixions, so any details would have been unnecessary. Crucifixion was such a detestable thing that it was not mentioned in decent society, any more than today we would discuss the gas chamber or the electric chair. Suffice it to say, crucifixion is one of the most horrible forms of death ever devised by man. Read Psalm 22 for a description of some of our Lord's agonies as He hung on the cross.

The victim usually wore a placard that declared his offense. Pilate wrote the one that Jesus wore and that was later hung above Him on the cross: "This is Jesus of Nazareth, the King of the Jews." The Jewish leaders protested, but Pilate for once stood his ground (John 19:19-22). It may be that the message of this sign first aroused the hopes of the repentant thief (Luke 23:39-43). He may have reasoned: "If His name is Jesus, then He is a Saviour. If He is from Nazareth, then He would identify with rejected people (John 1:46). If He has a kingdom, then perhaps there is room for me!"

The soldiers at the execution were not only doing their duty, but they were also fulfilling prophecy as they gambled for our Lord's garments (Ps. 22:18). The fact that the innocent Son of God was placed between two guilty criminals also fulfilled prophecy (Isa. 53:12; and see Luke 22:37). The word used for "thieves" is rendered *robber* in John 18:40 in reference to Barabbas, so perhaps these two men had been members of his rebel band.

It seems incredible that the religious leaders so hated Jesus that they even went out to Golgotha to mock Him. Thomas Carlyle called ridicule "the language of the devil," and in this case, that definition is certainly true. The idle spectators who passed by were only too eager to follow the bad example of their leaders, so enduring mockery was added to the sufferings of our Lord. They mocked Him as Prophet (Mark 15:29), as Saviour (Mark 15:31), and as King (Mark 15:32). It is possible that their sarcastic "He saved others!" may have encouraged the one thief to trust Him. The thief may have reasoned, "If He saved others, then He can save me!" So God uses even the wrath of man to praise Him (Ps. 76:10).

The sixth hour (v. 33). At noon, a miraculous darkness came over the land, and all creation sympathized with the Creator as He suffered. This was indeed a miracle and not some natural phenomenon, such as a sand storm or an eclipse. It would not be possible to have an eclipse during full moon at Passover. By means of this darkness, God was saying something to the people.

For one thing, the Jews would certainly think about the first Passover. The ninth plague in Egypt was a three-day darkness, followed by the last plague, the death of the firstborn (Ex. 10:22–11:9). The darkness at Calvary was an announcement that God's Firstborn and Beloved Son, the Lamb of God, was giving His life for the sins of the world. It was also an announcement that judgment was coming and men had better be prepared.

The ninth hour (vv. 34-41). Our Lord made seven statements from the cross, three of them before the darkness came: "Father, forgive them, for they know not what they do" (Luke 23:34); "Today shalt thou be with Me in paradise" (Luke 23:43); and "Woman, behold thy son! . . . Behold thy mother!" (John 19:26-27) When the darkness came, there was silence on His cross, for it was then that He was made sin for us (2 Cor. 5:21).

At the ninth hour, Jesus expressed the agony of His soul when He cried out from the cross, "My God, My God, why hast Thou forsaken Me?" (see Ps. 22:1) The darkness symbolized the judgment Jesus experienced when the Father forsook Him. As was so often the case, the people did not understand His words; they thought He was calling for Elijah the prophet. There was not only darkness over the land, but there was darkness in the minds and hearts of the people (2 Cor. 4:3-6; John 3:16-21; 12:35-41).

Then Jesus said, "I thirst" (John 19:28), and the kind act of the soldier in giving Jesus a sip of vinegar (see Ps. 69:21) assisted Him in uttering two more wonderful statements: "It is finished!" (John 19:30) and "Father, into Thy hands I commit My spirit" (Luke 23:46; and see Ps. 31:5). Jesus was not murdered; He willingly laid down His life for us (John 10:11, 15, 17-18). He was not a martyr; He was a willing sacrifice for the sins of the world.

Two remarkable events occurred at His death: there was an earthquake (Matt. 27:51), and the veil in the temple was torn in two. The veil had separated man from God, but now, through His death, Jesus had opened for the whole world a "new and living way" (Heb. 10:12-22; also see John 14:6). There had been an earthquake at Sinai when the Law was given (Ex. 19:16-18), but now the Law was fulfilled in Jesus Christ and its curse removed (Rom. 10:4; Gal. 3:10-14). Through His sacrifice, Jesus had purchased not only freedom from the Law, but also freedom from the entire sacrificial system.

It is thrilling to read the witness of the Roman centurion, especially when you consider that his words could have gotten him into trouble with both the Jews and the Romans. That Jesus Christ is the Son of God is one of Mark's important themes (Mark 1:1, 11; 3:11; 5:7; 9:7; 14:61-62). This makes His servanthood even more wonderful (Phil. 2:1-11).

It is touching to see how the women stood near the cross until the very end. John had also been there, but he had taken Mary, our Lord's mother, to his own home where he could care for her (John 19:25-27). Faithful women were the last at the cross on Friday and the first at the tomb on Sunday. What a contrast to the disciples who had boasted that they would die for Him! The church of Jesus Christ owes much to the sacrifice and devotion of believing women.

The Servant's Burial (Mark 15:42-47)

The Jews recognized two evenings: "early evening," from 3 to 6 o'clock, and "evening," after 6 o'clock, when the new day would begin. This explains how both Matthew (27:57) and Mark could call late Friday afternoon "evening." It was important that the place of execution be quickly cleared, because the Jewish Sabbath was about to begin, and that Sabbath was a "high day" because of the Passover (John 19:31).

God had a wealthy member of the Sanhedrin, Joseph of Arimathea, ready to take care of the body of Jesus (Matt. 27:57). He was assisted by Nicodemus, also a member of the council (John 19:38-42). We must not think that these two men suddenly decided to bury Jesus, because what they did demanded much preparation.

To begin with, Joseph had to prepare the tomb in a garden near the place where Jesus died. This tomb was probably not for Joseph himself, since a wealthy man would not likely choose to be buried near a place of execution. The men also had to obtain a large quantity of spices (John 19:39), and this could not be done when the shops were closed for Passover. And all of this had to be done without the council's knowledge.

It seems evident that God prepared these two men and directed them in their activities. Nicodemus had come to Jesus privately (John 3) and had even defended Him before the council (John 7:45-53). I believe that Joseph and Nicodemus searched the Scriptures together and discovered, led by the Spirit, that the Lamb would die at Passover. It is possible that they were hiding in the new tomb when Jesus died. It was a simple matter for Joseph to go to Pilate for permission to take the body, and for Nicodemus to guard the body until the official release was given. Had these men not acted boldly, the body of Jesus might have been disposed of like rubbish.

It was important that His body be prepared for burial so that the empty graveclothes could be left behind in the tomb (John 20:1-10). Also, the way He was buried fulfilled prophecy (Isa. 53:9). The fact that He was buried is proof that Jesus actually died on the cross, for the Roman officials would not have released the body without proof that Jesus was dead.

The Servant's Resurrection (Mark 16:1-18)

Jesus Christ was "delivered for our offenses, and was raised again for our justification" (Rom. 4:25). A dead Saviour cannot save anybody. The resurrection of Jesus Christ from the dead is as much a part of the Gospel message as His sacrificial death on the cross (1 Cor. 15:1-8). In fact, in the Book of Acts, the church gave witness primarily to the Resurrection (Acts 1:22; 4:2, 33).

The Resurrection proves that Jesus Christ is what He claimed to be, the very Son of God (Rom. 1:4). He had told His disciples that He would be raised from the dead, but they had not grasped the meaning of this truth (Mark 9:9-10, 31; 10:34). Even the women who came early to the tomb did not expect to see Him alive. In fact, they had purchased spices to complete the anointing that Joseph and Nicodemus had so hastily begun.

When you combine the accounts in the Gospels, you arrive at the following probable order of Resurrection appearances on that first day of the week: (1) to Mary Magdalene (John 20:11-18 and Mark 16:9-11), (2) to the other women (Matt. 28:9-10), (3) to Peter (Luke 24:34 and 1 Cor. 15:5), (4) to the two men going to Emmaus (Mark 16:12 and Luke 24:13-32), and (5) to ten of the disciples in the Upper Room (Mark 16:14 and John 20:19-25).

It was still dark when Mary Magdalene, Mary the mother of James, Salome, and Joanna (Luke 24:10) started out for the tomb (John 20:1); and they arrived at early dawn (Luke 24:1). Their first surprise was finding the stone already rolled away from the door (Matt. 28:2-4) so that they were able to enter into the tomb. The second surprise was meeting two angels in the tomb (Luke 24:4; Mark focused on only one angel); and the third surprise was hearing the message they delivered. No wonder the women were amazed!

The message was that Jesus was not there: He had risen from the dead, and He was going before them into Galilee where He would meet them. The women were the first messengers of the glorious Resurrection message! Note that there was a special word of encouragement for Peter (Mark 16:7), and keep in mind that Mark wrote his Gospel with Peter's assistance.

Mary Magdalene ran to tell Peter and John what she had discovered (John 20:2-10), and then she lingered at the tomb after they left. It was then that Jesus appeared to her (John 20:11-18). From her conversation with Jesus, it seems that Mary did not fully grasp what the angels had said, but she was the first believer to see the risen Christ. Mark 16:8 may give the idea that all the women fled, but Mark 16:9 states that Mary met Jesus personally.

After He appeared to Mary, Jesus met the other women as they were on their way to report their conversation with Jesus to the disciples (Matt. 28:9-10). Initially, the women were both joyful and afraid, but after they met the risen Christ, they found the disciples and shared the good news (Matt. 28:8). It is one thing to hear the message and quite something else to meet the risen Lord personally. When you meet Him, you have something to share with others.

The emphasis in Mark 16:9-14 is on the unbelief of the disciples who were mourning and weeping instead of rejoicing at the good news. Was it because they were prejudiced against the witness of the women? Perhaps, for the testimony of a woman was not accepted in a Jewish court. But even when the two Emmaus disciples gave their witness, not everybody believed. Compare Mark 16:13 with Luke 24:33-35. Apparently there was division in the Upper Room until Jesus Himself appeared.

But when He did appear, He reproached them for their unbelief which was caused by their hardness of heart (see Mark 6:52; 8:17). He was making it clear that the witnesses of His resurrection could and should be trusted. The phrase "the Eleven" in Mark 16:14 simply means "the Apostles," because there were only ten of them together at that time, since Thomas was absent (John 20:19-25).

Before His ascension forty days later, the Lord gave several commissions to His followers (Matt. 28:18-20; Luke 24:47-49; John 20:21; 21:15-17; Acts 1:4-8). The one Mark gives probably is a part of the Great Commission that Jesus gave on a mountain in Galilee (Matt. 28:16-20).

In this commission, Jesus pointed out our message and our ministry, and then backed it up with the miraculous credentials that only He could give. The message is the Gospel, the Good News of salvation through faith in Jesus Christ. The ministry is to share this message with the whole world.

A superficial reading of Mark 16:15-16 would suggest that sinners must be baptized to be saved, but this misinterpretation disappears when you note that the emphasis is on *believing*. If a person does not believe, he is condemned, even if he has been baptized (see John 3:16-18, 36). It was expected in the early church that believers would be baptized (Acts 2:41; 10:44-48).

When God sent Moses to challenge Pharaoh in Egypt, He gave him special miracles to perform as his divine credentials, proving that he was sent from God (Ex. 4:1-9). This was also true of some of the prophets (1 Kings 18; 2 Kings 2:14-25). The Apostles were also given special "signs" that enforced their message (Acts 19:11-12; 2 Cor. 12:12; Heb. 2:3-4). Of themselves, miracles do not prove that a person has been sent by God, for the message must also be true to God's Word (see 2 Thes. 2; Rev. 13).

Most of the signs listed here did take place in the days of the Apostles and are recorded in the Book of Acts. The closest thing we have to taking up serpents is Paul's experience on Malta (Acts 28:3-6), but we have no biblical record of anyone drinking poison and surviving. No doubt God has performed many wonders for His own that we know nothing about, but we shall learn about them in heaven.

It is tragic when well-meaning but untaught people claim these signs for themselves and then die because of snake bites or poison. Of course, the excuse is given that they did not have enough faith! But whatever is not of faith is sin (Rom. 14:23); therefore, they should not have done it in the first place.

The person who takes up serpents just to prove his or her faith is yielding to the very temptation Satan presented to Jesus on the pinnacle of the temple (Matt. 4:5-7): "Cast Yourself down and see if God will take care of

You," Satan said in effect. He wants us to "show off" our faith and force God to perform unnecessary miracles. Jesus refused to tempt God, and we should follow His example. Yes, God cares for His children when, in His will, they are in dangerous places; but He is not obligated to care for us when we foolishly get out of His will. We are called to live by faith, not by chance, and to trust God, not tempt Him.

The Servant's Ascension (Mark 16:19-20)

In a remarkable way, the Gospel of Mark parallels the great "Servant passage" in Philippians 2.

He came as a Servant (Phil. 2:1-7)—
Mark 1–13
He died on a cross (Phil. 2:8)—
Mark 14–15
He was exalted to glory (Phil. 2:9)—
Mark 16

Both Paul and Mark emphasize the need for God's people to get the message out to all nations (Mark 16:15-16; Phil. 2:10-11), and there is the added assurance that God is at work in and through them (Mark 16:19-20; Phil. 2:12-13).

Our Lord's ascension marked the completion of His earthly ministry and the beginning of His new ministry in heaven as High Priest and Advocate for His people (Heb. 7–10; 1 John 2:1-3). The "right hand of God" is the place of honor and authority (Ps. 110:1; 1 Peter 3:22). Our Lord is like Melchizedek, King of Righteousness and King of Peace (Gen. 14:17-19; Heb. 7:2).

One of His heavenly ministries is that of enabling His people to do His will (Heb. 13:20-21). It is fitting that the Gospel of the Servant should end with this reference to work, just as it is fitting for Matthew, the Gospel of the King, to end with a reference to His great authority. By His Holy Spirit, the Lord wants to work *in* us (Phil. 2:12-13), *with* us (Mark 16:20), and *for* us (Rom. 8:28).

The Apostles and Prophets laid the foundation for the church (Eph. 2:20), so their work is finished and the apostolic signs have ceased. But the Lord's working has not ceased, and He is still working in and through His people to save a lost world. His Servant-Son Jesus returned to heaven, but He still has His people on earth who can be His servants, if they will.

What a privilege to have the Lord working with us!

What an opportunity and obligation we have to carry the Gospel to the whole world!

"For even the Son of man came not to be ministered unto, but to minister, and to give His life a ransom for many" (Mark 10:45).

Are you serving—or are you expecting others to serve you?

LUKE

OUTLINE

Key theme: Our Lord's journeys as the Son of man
Key verse: Luke 19:10

I. **JOURNEY FROM HEAVEN TO EARTH—1:5–4:13**
   A. Birth announcements—1:5-56
   B. The babies are born—1:57–2:20
   C. Jesus' childhood and youth—2:21-52
   D. Jesus' baptism and temptation—3:1–4:13

II. **THE JOURNEY THROUGHOUT GALILEE—4:14–9:17**

III. **THE JOURNEY TO JERUSALEM—9:18–19:27**

IV. **THE MINISTRY IN JERUSALEM—19:28–24:53**

CONTENTS

CHAPTER ONE
HEAR THE GOOD NEWS!
Luke 1

If ever a man wrote a book filled with good news for everybody, Dr. Luke is that man. His key message is, "For the Son of man is come to seek and to save that which was lost" (Luke 19:10). He presents Jesus Christ as the compassionate Son of man, who came to live among sinners, love them, help them, and die for them.

In this Gospel you meet individuals as well as crowds, women and children as well as men, poor people as well as rich people, and sinners along with saints. It's a book with a message for *everybody,* because Luke's emphasis is on the universality of Jesus Christ and His salvation: "good tidings of great joy, which shall be to all people" (Luke 2:10).

Dr. Luke is named only three times in the New Testament: in Colossians 4:14; 2 Timothy 4:11; and Philemon 24. He wrote Acts (compare Luke 1:1-4 with Acts 1:1) and traveled with Paul (note the "we" sections in Acts 16:10-17; 20:4-15; 21:1-18, and 27:1–28:16). He was probably a Gentile (compare Colossians 4:11 and 14) and was trained as a physician. No wonder he began his book with detailed accounts of the births of two important babies! No wonder he emphasized Christ's sympathy for hurting people! He wrote with the mind of a careful historian and with the heart of a loving physician.

The Gospel of Luke was written for Theophilus ("lover of God"), probably a Roman official who had trusted Christ and now needed to be established in the faith. It's also possible that Theophilus was a seeker after truth who was being taught the Christian message, because the word translated *instructed* in Luke 1:4 gives us our English word *catechumen,* "someone who is being taught the basics of Christianity."

The life and message of Christ were so important that many books had already been written about Him, but not everything in them could be trusted. Luke wrote his Gospel so that his readers might have an accurate and orderly narrative of the life, ministry, and message of Jesus Christ. Luke had carefully researched his material, interviewed eyewitnesses, and listened to those who had ministered the Word. Most important, he had the guidance of the Holy Spirit. The phrase *from the very first* (Gk. *anothen)* can be translated "from above," as it is in John 3:31 and 19:11. It speaks of the inspiration of the Spirit of God on the message that Luke wrote.

In this first chapter, Luke tells us how God's wonderful news came to different people and how they responded to it. You will discover four different responses.

Unbelief (Luke 1:5-25)

It was indeed a dark day for the nation of Israel. The people had heard no prophetic Word from God for 400 years, not since Malachi had promised the coming of Elijah (Mal. 4:5-6). The spiritual leaders were shackled by tradition and, in some instances, corruption; and their king, Herod the Great, was a tyrant. He had nine (some say ten) wives, one of whom he had executed for no apparent reason. But no matter how dark the day, God always has His devoted and obedient people.

A faithful priest (vv. 5-7). Zacharias ("Jehovah has remembered") and Elizabeth ("God is my oath") were a godly couple who both belonged to the priestly line. The priests were divided into twenty-four courses (1 Chron. 24), and each priest served in the temple two weeks out of the year. In spite of the godlessness around them, Zacharias and Elizabeth were faithful to obey the Word of God and live blamelessly.

Their only sorrow was that they had no family, and they made this a matter of constant prayer. Little did they know that God would answer their prayers and give them, not a priest, but a prophet! And no ordinary prophet, for their son would be the herald of the coming King!

A fearful priest (vv. 8-17). The priests on duty drew lots to see which ministries they would perform, and Zacharias was chosen to offer incense in the holy place. This was a high honor that was permitted to a priest but once in a lifetime. The incense was offered daily before the morning sacrifice and after the evening sacrifice, about 3 o'clock in the afternoon. It was probably the evening offering that was assigned to Zacharias.

You have probably noticed that God often speaks to His people and calls them while they are busy doing their daily tasks. Both Moses and David were caring for sheep, and Gideon was threshing wheat. Peter and his partners were mending nets when Jesus called them. It is difficult to steer a car when the engine is not running. When we get busy, God starts to direct us.

Luke mentions angels twenty-three times in his Gospel. There are innumerable angels (Rev. 5:11), only two of which are actually named in Scripture: Michael (Dan. 10:13, 21; 12:1; Jude 9; Rev. 12:7) and Gabriel (Dan. 8:16; 9:21; Luke 1:19, 26). When Gabriel appeared by the altar, Zacharias was frightened, for the angel's appearance could have meant divine judgment.

"Fear not" is a repeated statement in the Gospel of Luke (1:13, 30; 2:10; 5:10; 8:50; 12:7, 32). Imagine how excited Zacharias must have been when he heard that he and Elizabeth were to have a son! "Rejoicing" is another key theme in Luke, mentioned at least nineteen times. Good news brings joy!

Gabriel instructed him to name his son John ("Jehovah is gracious") and to dedicate the boy to God to be a Nazarite all of his life (Num. 6:1-21). He would be filled with the Spirit before birth (Luke 1:41) and would be God's prophet to present His Son to the people of Israel (see John 1:15-34). God would use John's ministry to turn many people back to the Lord, just as Isaiah had promised (Isa. 40:1-5).

A faithless priest (vv. 18-22). You would think that the presence of an angel and the announcement of God's Word would encourage Zacharias' faith, but they did not. Instead of looking to God by faith, the priest looked at himself and his wife and decided that the birth of a son was impossible. He wanted some assurance beyond the plain word of Gabriel, God's messenger, perhaps a sign from God.

This, of course, was unbelief, and unbelief is something God does not accept. Zacharias was really questioning God's ability to fulfill His own Word! Had he forgotten what God did for Abraham and Sarah? (Gen. 18:9-15; Rom. 4:18-25) Did he think that his physical limitations would hinder Almighty God? But before we criticize Zacharias too much, we should examine ourselves and see how strong our own faith is.

Faith is blessed, but unbelief is judged; and Zacharias was struck dumb (and possibly deaf, Luke 1:62) until the Word was fulfilled. "I believed, and therefore have I spoken" (2 Cor. 4:13). Zacharias did not believe; therefore he could not speak. When he left the holy place, he was unable to give the priestly benediction to the people (Num. 6:22-27) or even tell them what he had seen. Indeed, God had given him a very personal "sign" that he would have to live with for the next nine months.

A favored priest (vv. 23-25). Zacharias must have had a difficult time completing his week of ministry, not only because of his handicap, but also because of his excitement. He could hardly wait to return "to the hill country" (Luke 1:39) where he lived, to tell his wife the good news.

God kept His promise and Elizabeth conceived a son in her old age. "There is nothing too hard for the Lord" (Jer. 32:17). Apparently the amazement and curiosity of the people forced her to hide herself even as she praised the Lord for His mercy. Not only was she to have a son, but the birth of her son was evidence that *the Messiah was coming!* These were exciting days indeed!

Faith (Luke 1:26-38)

In the sixth month of Elizabeth's pregnancy, Gabriel brought a second birth announcement, this time to a young virgin in Nazareth named Mary. At least there was variety in his assignments: an old man, a young woman; a priest, a descendent of David, the king; the temple, a common home; Jerusalem, Nazareth; unbelief, faith.

The people in Judah disdained the Jews in Galilee and claimed they were not "kosher" because of their contacts with the Gentiles there (Matt. 4:15). They especially despised the people from Nazareth (John 1:45-46). But

God in His grace chose a girl from Nazareth in Galilee to be the mother of the promised Messiah!

When it comes to Mary, people tend to go to one of two extremes. They either magnify her so much that Jesus takes second place (Luke 1:32), or they ignore her and fail to give her the esteem she deserves (Luke 1:48). Elizabeth, filled with the Spirit, called her "the mother of my Lord" (Luke 1:43); and that is reason enough to honor her.

What do we know about Mary? She was a Jewess of the tribe of Judah, a descendant of David, and a virgin (Isa. 7:14). She was engaged to a carpenter in Nazareth named Joseph (Matt. 13:55), and apparently both of them were poor (Lev. 12:8; Luke 2:24). Among the Jews at that time, engagement was almost as binding as marriage and could be broken only by divorce. In fact, the man and the woman were called "husband" and "wife" even before the marriage took place (compare Matt. 1:19 and Luke 2:5). Since Jewish girls married young, it is likely that Mary was a teenager when the angel appeared to her.

Mary's surprise (vv. 26-33). When you consider Gabriel's greeting, you can well understand why Mary was perplexed and afraid: "Greetings, you who are highly favored! The Lord is with you!" (The phrase *Blessed art thou among women* is not found here in many Greek manuscripts. You find it in Luke 1:42.) Why would an angel come to greet *her?* In what way was she "highly favored" ("greatly graced") by God? How was God with her?

Mary's response reveals her humility and honesty before God. She certainly never expected to see an angel and receive special favors from heaven. There was nothing unique about her that such things should happen. If she had been different from other Jewish girls, as some theologians claim she was, then she might have said, "Well, it's about time! I've been expecting you!" No, all of this was a surprise to her.

Gabriel then gave her the good news: she would become the mother of the promised Messiah whom she would name *Jesus* ("Jehovah is salvation"; see Matt. 1:21). Note that Gabriel affirmed both the deity and the humanity of Jesus. As Mary's son, He would be human; as Son of the Highest (Luke 1:32), He would be the Son of God (Luke 1:35). "For unto us a Child is born [His humanity], unto us a Son is given [His deity]" (Isa. 9:6). The emphasis is on the greatness of the Son (cf. Luke 1:15), not the greatness of the mother.

But He would also be a King, inherit David's throne, and reign over Israel forever! If we interpret literally what Gabriel said in Luke 1:30-31, then we should also interpret literally what he said in Luke 1:32-33. He was referring to God's covenant with David (2 Sam. 7) and His kingdom promises to the people of Israel (Isa. 9:1-7; 11–12; 61; 66; Jer. 33).

Jesus came to earth to be the Saviour of the world, but He also came to fulfill the promises God made to the Jewish fathers (Rom. 15:14). Today, Jesus is enthroned in heaven (Acts 2:29-36), but it is not on *David's* throne. One day Jesus will return and establish His righteous kingdom on earth, and then these promises will be fulfilled.

Mary's surrender (vv. 34-48). Mary knew *what* would happen, but she did not know *how* it would happen. Her question in Luke 1:34 was not an evidence of unbelief (cf. Luke 1:18); rather, it was an expression of faith. She believed the promise, but she did not understand the performance. How could a virgin give birth to a child?

First, Gabriel explained that this would be a miracle, the work of the Holy Spirit of God. Joseph, her betrothed, would not be the father of the child (Matt. 1:18-25), even though Jesus would be legally identified as the son of Joseph (Luke 3:23; 4:22; John 1:45; 6:42). It's possible that some people thought Mary had been unfaithful to Joseph and that Jesus was "born of fornication" (John 8:41). This was a part of the pain that Mary had to bear all her life (Luke 2:35).

Gabriel was careful to point out that the Baby would be a "holy thing" and would not share the sinful human nature of man. Jesus knew no sin (2 Cor. 5:21), He did no sin (1 Peter 2:22), and He had no sin (1 John 3:5). His body was prepared for Him by the Spirit of God (Heb. 10:5) who "overshadowed" Mary. That word is applied to the presence of God in the holy of holies in the Jewish tabernacle and temple (Ex. 40:35). Mary's womb became a holy of holies for the Son of God!

The angel ended his message by giving Mary a word of encouragement: her aged relative Elizabeth was with child, proving that "with God nothing shall be impossible." God gave a similar word to Abraham when He announced the birth of Isaac (Gen. 18:14). That our God can do anything is the witness of many, including Job (Job 42:2), Jeremiah (Jer. 32:17), and even our Lord Jesus (Matt. 19:26). I personally like the translation of this verse found in the 1901 *American Standard Version:* "For no word of God shall be void of power." God accomplishes His purposes through the power of His Word (Ps. 33:9).

Mary's believing response was to surrender herself to God as His willing servant. She experienced the grace of God (Luke 1:30) and believed the Word of God, and therefore she could be used by the Spirit to accomplish the will of God. A "handmaid" was the lowest kind of female servant, which shows how much Mary trusted God. She belonged totally to the Lord, body (Luke 1:38), soul (Luke 1:46), and spirit (Luke 1:47). What an example for us to follow! (Rom. 12:1-2)

Joy (Luke 1:39-56)

Now that Mary knew she was to become a mother, and that her kinswoman Elizabeth would give birth in three months, she wanted to see Elizabeth so they could rejoice together. "Joy" is the major theme of this section as you see three persons rejoicing in the Lord.

The joy of Elizabeth (vv. 39-45). As Mary entered the house, Elizabeth heard her greeting, was filled with the Spirit, and was told by the Lord why Mary was there. The one word that filled her lips was "blessed." Note that she did not say that Mary was blessed *above* women but *among* women, and certainly this is true. While we don't want to ascribe to Mary that which only belongs to God, neither do we want to minimize her place in the plan of God.

The thing that Elizabeth emphasized was Mary's *faith*: "Blessed is she that believed" (Luke 1:45). We are saved "by grace . . . through faith" (Eph. 2:8-9). Because Mary believed the Word of God, she experienced the power of God.

The joy of the unborn son, John (vv. 41, 44). This was probably the time when he was filled with the Spirit as the angel had promised (Luke 1:15). Even before his birth, John rejoiced in Jesus Christ, just as he did during his earthly ministry (John 3:29-30). As John the Baptist, he would have the great privilege of introducing the Messiah to the Jewish nation.

The joy of Mary (vv. 46-56). Hers was a joy that compelled her to lift her voice in a hymn of praise. The fullness of the Spirit should lead to joyful praise in our lives (Eph. 5:18-20), and so should the fullness of the Word (Col. 3:16-17). Mary's song contains quotations from and references to the Old Testament Scriptures, especially the Psalms and the song of Hannah in 1 Samuel 2:1-10. Mary hid God's Word in her heart and turned it into a song.

This song is called "The Magnificat" because the Latin version of Luke 1:46 is *Magnificat anima mea Dominum.* Her great desire was to magnify the Lord, not herself. She used the phrase "He hath" eight times as she recounted what God had done for three recipients of His blessing.

What God did for Mary (vv. 46-49). To begin with, God had saved her (Luke 1:47), which indicates that Mary was a sinner like all of us and needed to trust the Lord for her eternal salvation. Not only had He saved her, but He had also chosen her to be the mother of the Messiah (Luke 1:48). He had "regarded" her, which means He was mindful of her and looked with favor on her. No doubt there were others who could have been chosen, but God chose her! The Lord had indeed showered His grace on her (see 1 Cor. 1:26-28).

Not only was God mindful of her, but He was also mighty for her, working on her behalf (Luke 1:49). Mary would have no problem singing "Great Things He Hath Done!" (see Luke 8:39; 1 Sam. 12:24; 2 Sam. 7:21-23; and Ps. 126:2-3) Because she believed God and yielded to His will, He performed a miracle in her life and used her to bring the Saviour into the world.

What God did for us (vv. 50-53). In the second stanza of her song, Mary included *all* of God's people who fear Him from generation to generation. We have all received His mercy and experienced His help. Mary named three specific groups to whom God had been merciful: the helpless (Luke 1:51), the humble (Luke 1:52), and the hungry (Luke 1:53).

The common people of that day were almost helpless when it came to justice and civil rights. They were often hungry, downtrodden, and discouraged (Luke 4:16-19), and there was no way for them to "fight the system." A secret society of patriotic Jewish extremists called "the zealots" used violent means to oppose Rome, but their activities made matters only worse.

Mary saw the Lord turning everything upside down: the weak dethrone the mighty, the humble scatter the proud, the nobodies are exalted, the hungry are filled, and the rich end up poor! The grace of God works contrary to the thoughts and ways of this world system (1 Cor. 1:26-28). The church is something like that band of men that gathered around David (1 Sam. 22:2).

What God did for Israel (vv. 54-55). "He shall save His people from their sins" (Matt. 1:21). In spite of Israel's destitute condition, the nation was still God's servant and He would help the people fulfill His purposes. God was on Israel's side! He would remember His mercy and keep His promises (Ps. 98:1-3; also see Gen. 12:1-3; 17:19; 22:18; 26:4; 28:14). Were it not for Israel, Jesus Christ could not have been born into the world.

Mary stayed with Elizabeth until John was born, and then she returned to Nazareth. By then, it was clear that she was pregnant, and no doubt the tongues began to wag. After all, she had been away from home for three months; and why, people were likely asking, had she left in such a hurry? It was then that God gave the good news to Joseph and instructed him what to do (Matt. 1:18-25).

Praise (Luke 1:57-80)

God's blessing was resting abundantly on Zacharias and Elizabeth. He sent them a baby boy, just as He promised; and they named him "John" just as God had instructed. The Jews looked on children as a gift from God and a "heritage from the Lord" (Pss. 127:3-5; 128:1-3), and rightly so, for they are. Israel would not follow the practices of their pagan neighbors by aborting or abandoning their children. When you consider that 1½ million babies are aborted each year in the United States alone, you can see how far we have drifted from the laws of God.

"The greatest forces in the world are not the earthquakes and the thunderbolts," said Dr. E.T. Sullivan. "The greatest forces in the world are babies."

Traditionally, a baby boy would be named after his father or someone else in the family; so the relatives and neighbors were shocked when Elizabeth insisted on the name *John.* Zacharias wrote "His name is John" on a tablet, and that settled it! Immediately God opened the old priest's mouth, and he sang a hymn that gives us four beautiful pictures of what the coming of Jesus Christ to earth really means.

The opening of a prison door (v. 68). The word *redeem* means "to set free by paying a price." It can refer to the releasing of a prisoner or the liberating of a slave. Jesus Christ came to earth to bring "deliverance to the captives" (Luke 4:18), salvation to people in bondage to sin and death. Certainly we are unable to set ourselves free; only Christ could pay the price necessary for our redemption (Eph. 1:7; 1 Peter 1:18-21).

The winning of a battle (vv. 69-75). In Scripture, a horn symbolizes power and victory (1 Kings 22:11; Ps. 89:17, 24). The picture here is that of an army about to be taken captive, but then help arrives and the enemy is defeated. In the previous picture, the captives were set free; but in this picture, the enemy is defeated *so that he cannot capture more prisoners.* It means total victory for the people of God.

The word *salvation* (Luke 1:69, 71) carries the meaning of "health and soundness." No matter what the condition of the captives, their Redeemer brings spiritual soundness. When you trust Jesus Christ as Saviour, you are delivered from Satan's power, moved into God's kingdom, redeemed, and forgiven (Col. 1:12-14).

Where did the Redeemer come from? He came from the house of David (Luke 1:69), who himself was a great conqueror. God had promised that the Saviour would be a Jew (Gen. 12:1-3), from the tribe of Judah (Gen. 49:10), from the family of David (2 Sam. 7:12-16), born in David's city, Bethlehem (Micah 5:2). Both Mary (Luke 1:27) and Joseph (Matt. 1:20) belonged to David's line. The coming of the Redeemer was inherent in the covenants God made with His people (Luke 1:72), and it was promised by the prophets (Luke 1:70).

Note that the results of this victory are sanctity and service (Luke 1:74-75). He sets us free, not to do our own will, because that would be bondage, but to do His will and enjoy His freedom.

The canceling of a debt (vv. 76-77). *Remission* means "to send away, to dismiss, as a debt." All of us are in debt to God because we have broken His law and failed to live up to His standards (Luke 7:40-50). Furthermore, all of us are spiritually bankrupt, unable to pay our debt. But Jesus came and paid the debt for us (Ps. 103:12; John 1:29).

The dawning of a new day (vv. 78-79). *Dayspring* means "sunrise." The people were sitting in darkness and death, and distress gripped them when Jesus came; but He brought light, life, and peace. It was the dawn of a new day because of the tender mercies of God (see Matt. 4:16).

The old priest had not said anything for nine months, but he certainly compensated for his silence when he sang this song of praise to God! And how joyful he was that his son was chosen by God to prepare the way for the Messiah (Isa. 40:1-3; Mal. 3:1). John was "prophet of the Highest" (Luke 1:76), introducing to Israel "the Son of the Highest" (Luke 1:32) who was conceived in Mary's womb by "the power of the Highest" (Luke 1:35).

Instead of enjoying a comfortable life as a priest, John lived in the wilderness, disciplining himself physically and spiritually, waiting for the day when God would send him out to prepare Israel for the arrival of the Messiah. People like Simeon and Anna (Luke 2:25-38) had been waiting for this day for many years, and soon it would come.

God calls us today to believe His Good News. Those who believe it experience His joy and want to express their praise to Him. It is not enough for us to say that Jesus is *a* Saviour, or even *the* Saviour. With Mary, we must say, "My spirit hath rejoiced in God *my* Saviour" (Luke 1:47, italics mine).

CHAPTER TWO
THE LORD IS COME!
Luke 2

Luke 2 may well be the most familiar and beloved portion in Luke's Gospel. My wife and I still read the first twenty verses together each Christmas Eve, just as we did when our children were growing up. The story is old, but it is ever new; and God's people never tire of it.

Dr. Luke gives us three glimpses into the early years of the Lord Jesus Christ.

The Newborn Baby (Luke 2:1-20)

"As weak as a baby!" is a common expression that could not be applied to the Baby Jesus in the manger. While He was as weak as any other baby humanly speaking, He was also the center of power as far as heaven was concerned.

His birth drew Mary and Joseph to Bethlehem (vv. 1-7). Augustus Caesar was ruling, but God was in charge, for He used Caesar's edict to move Mary and Joseph eighty miles from Nazareth to Bethlehem to fulfill His Word. Rome took a census every fourteen years for both military and tax purposes, and each Jewish male had to return to the city of his fathers to record his name, occupation, property, and family.

When Mary said "Be it unto me according to Thy word" (Luke 1:38), it meant that from then on, her life would be a part of the fulfillment of divine prophecy. God had promised that the Saviour would be a human, not an angel (Gen. 3:15; Heb. 2:16), and a Jew, not a Gentile (Gen. 12:1-3; Num. 24:17). He would be from the tribe of Judah (Gen. 49:10), and the family of David (2 Sam. 7:1-17), born of a virgin (Isa. 7:14) in Bethlehem, the city of David (Micah 5:2).

All of this occurred just as the Scriptures said, and Caesar unknowingly played an important part. A.T. Pierson used to say, "History is His story," and President James A. Garfield called history "the unrolled scroll of prophecy." If God's Word controls our lives, then the events of history only help us fulfill the will of God. "I am watching over My word to perform it," promises the Lord (Jer. 1:12, NASB).

Mary and Joseph were already husband and wife but since they did not consummate the marriage until after Jesus was born, she is called his "espoused wife" (Matt. 1:18-25). The journey must have been very trying for her, but she rejoiced in doing the will of God, and she was no doubt glad to get away from the wagging tongues in Nazareth.

Mothers in that day wrapped their infants in long bands of cloth to give the limbs strength and protection. The word translated "manger" (Luke 2:7, 12, 16) is translated "stall" in Luke 13:15, and can mean either a feeding trough or an enclosure for animals. You see ancient stone troughs even today as you travel in the Holy Land, and it is probable that such a trough cradled the Infant Jesus. Many scholars believe that our Lord was born in a cave where animals were sheltered and not in a wooden shed such as you see in modern manger scenes.

Bethlehem means "house of bread," the ideal birthplace for the Bread of Life (John 6:35).

Its rich historic heritage included the death of Rachel and the birth of Benjamin (Gen. 35:16-20; also see Matt. 2:16-18), the marriage of Ruth, and the exploits of David. It is worth noting that the name *Benjamin* means "son of my right hand," and the name *David* means "beloved." Both of these names apply to our Lord, for He is the Beloved Son (Luke 3:22) at God's right hand (Ps. 110:1).

His birth drew the angels from heaven (vv. 8-14). How amazed the angels must have been when they saw the Creator born as a creature, the Word coming as a speechless baby. The best commentary on this is 2 Corinthians 8:9, and the best response from our hearts is wonder and worship. "Great is the mystery of godliness: God was manifest in the flesh" (1 Tim. 3:16).

The first announcement of the Messiah's birth was given by an angel to some anonymous shepherds. Why shepherds? Why not to priests or scribes? By visiting the shepherds, the angel revealed the grace of God toward mankind. Shepherds were really outcasts in Israel. Their work not only made them ceremonially unclean, but it kept them away from the temple for weeks at a time so that they could not be made clean. God does not call the rich and mighty; He calls the poor and the lowly (Luke 1:51-53; 1 Cor. 1:26-29).

The Messiah came to be both the Good Shepherd (John 10) and the Lamb of God sacrificed for the sins of the world (John 1:29). Perhaps these shepherds were caring for the flocks that would provide sacrifices for the temple services. It was fitting that the good news about God's Shepherd and Lamb be given first to humble shepherds.

Shepherds are not easily fooled. They are practical men of the world who have little to do with fantasy. If they said that they saw angels and went and found the Messiah, then you could believe them. God selected hard-working men to be the first witnesses that His Son had come into the world.

First, one angel appeared (Gabriel?) and gave the glad announcement; and then a chorus of angels joined him and gave an anthem of praise. For the first time in centuries, the glory of God returned to earth. If brave shepherds were afraid at what they saw and heard, then you can be sure it was real!

"Fear not!" is one of the key themes of the Christmas story (Luke 1:13, 30, 74; and see Matt. 1:20). Literally the angel said, "I announce to you good news, a great joy which shall be to all the people." He used the word which means "to preach the Good News," a word Luke uses often in both his Gospel and in the Book of Acts. We see here Luke's emphasis on a worldwide Gospel: the Good News is for everybody, not just the Jews.

What was the Good News? Not that God had sent a soldier or a judge or a reformer, but that He had sent a Saviour to meet man's greatest need. It was a message of peace to a world that had known much war. The famous "Pax Romana" (Roman Peace) had been in effect since 27 B.C. but the absence of war doesn't guarantee the presence of peace.

The Stoic philosopher Epictetus said, "While the emperor may give peace from war on land and sea, he is unable to give peace from passion, grief, and envy. He cannot give peace of heart for which man yearns more than even for outward peace."

The Jewish word *shalom* (peace) means much more than a truce in the battles of life. It means well-being, health, prosperity, security, soundness, and completeness. It has to do more with character than circumstances. Life was difficult at that time just as it is today. Taxes were high, unemployment was high, morals were slipping lower, and the military state was in control. Roman law, Greek philosophy, and even Jewish religion could not meet the needs of men's hearts. Then, God sent His Son!

The angels praised God at Creation (Job 38:7), and now they praised Him at the beginning of the new creation. The whole purpose of the plan of salvation is "glory to God" (see Eph. 1:6, 12, 14). God's glory had dwelt in the tabernacle (Ex. 40:34) and in the temple (2 Chron. 7:1-3), but had departed because of the nation's sin (1 Sam. 4:21; Ezek. 8:4; 9:3; 10:4, 18; 11:22-23). Now God's glory was returning to earth in the person of His Son (John 1:14). That lowly manger was a holy of holies because Jesus was there!

His birth drew the shepherds from the fields (vv. 15-20). The phrase "even unto Bethlehem" suggests that these men were located some distance away, but they were willing to make the trip in order to see the newborn Messiah. Certainly they arranged for others to care for their flocks while they hastened to Bethlehem. Halford Luccock called this "the first Christmas rush," but it was certainly different from the Christmas rushes we see today!

The verb *found* in Luke 2:16 means "found

after a search." The shepherds knew what to look for: a newborn Baby wrapped in swaddling clothes and lying in a manger. And they found Him! They worshiped Him and marveled at God's grace and goodness and the miracle He had wrought for them.

These shepherds are good examples for us to imitate today. They received by faith the message God sent them and then responded with immediate obedience. After finding the Baby, they reported the good news to others, "glorifying and praising God." *They took the place of the angels!* (Luke 2:13-14) Then they humbly returned to their duties, new men going back to the same old job.

For some reason, shepherds were not permitted to testify in court, but God used some humble shepherds to be the first human witnesses that prophecy had been fulfilled and the Messiah had been born. The angels have never experienced the grace of God, so they can't bear witness as we can. Telling others about the Saviour is a solemn obligation as well as a great privilege, and we who are believers must be faithful.

The Child (Luke 2:21-38)

Dr. Luke now tells us about three important meetings in the temple in Jerusalem: the child Jesus met Moses (Luke 2:20-24), Simeon (Luke 2:25-35), and Anna (Luke 2:36-38).

Moses (vv. 21-24). Note that the word *law* is used five times in Luke 2:21-40. Though He came to deliver His people from the bondage of the Law, Jesus was "made under the Law" and obeyed its commands (Gal. 4:1-7). He did not come to destroy the Law but to fulfill it (Matt. 5:17-18).

Jesus' parents obeyed the Law first by having the child circumcised when He was eight days old. This was the sign and seal of the covenant that God made with Abraham (Gen. 17), and it was required of every Jewish male who wanted to practice the faith. The Jews were proud to be God's covenant people, and they scornfully called the Gentiles "the uncircumcision" (Eph. 2:11-12). It is unfortunate that circumcision became an empty ritual for many Jews, because it proclaimed an important spiritual truth (Deut. 10:15-20; Rom. 2:28-29).

"His circumcision was His first suffering for us," said the late Donald Grey Barnhouse, a Philadelphia minister and author. It symbolized the work the Saviour did on the cross in dealing with our sin nature (Gal. 6:15; Phil. 3:1-3; Col. 2:10-11). In obedience to the Lord, Mary and Joseph gave Him the name *Jesus,* which means "Jehovah is salvation" (Matt. 1:21).

But circumcision was only the beginning. When the child was forty days old, Mary and Joseph had to come to the temple for the purification rites described in Leviticus 12. They also had to "redeem" the boy since He was Mary's firstborn (Ex. 13:1-12). They had to pay five shekels to redeem the Redeemer who would one day redeem us with His precious blood (1 Peter 1:18-19). Their humble sacrifice would suggest that they were too poor to bring a lamb (2 Cor. 8:9). But He was the Lamb!

Our Lord's relationship to the Law is an important part of His saving ministry. He was made under the Law (Gal. 4:4); and though He rejected man's religious traditions, He obeyed God's Law perfectly (John 8:46). He bore the curse of the Law for us (Gal. 3:13) and set us free from bondage (Gal. 5:1).

Simeon (vv. 25-35). Simeon and Anna, like Zacharias and Elizabeth, were a part of the faithful Jewish remnant that eagerly looked for their Messiah (Mal. 3:16). Because of his readiness and eagerness to die (Luke 2:29), Simeon is usually pictured as a very old man, but nothing in Scripture supports this. Tradition says he was 113 years old, but it is only tradition.

"The consolation of Israel" means the messianic hope. One of the traditional Jewish prayers is, "May I see the consolation of Israel!" That prayer was answered for Simeon when he saw Jesus Christ in the temple. He was a man who was led by the Spirit of God, taught by the Word of God, and obedient to the will of God; and therefore he was privileged to see the salvation of God. How important it is for people to see God's salvation, Jesus Christ, before they see death.

In Luke 2:29-32 we find Simeon's response to seeing Jesus. This is the fifth and last of the "Christmas songs" in Luke. (Elizabeth, 1:42-45; Mary, 1:46-56; Zacharias, 1:67-79; the angels, 2:13-14). It is first of all a *worship* hymn as he blesses God for keeping His promise and sending the Messiah. He joyfully praises God that he has been privileged to see the Lord's Christ.

But his song is also a *salvation* hymn: "For mine eyes have seen Thy salvation" (Luke 2:30). Now he is ready to die! The word *depart* in the Greek has several meanings, and each of them tells us something about the death of a Christian. It means to release a prisoner, to untie a ship and set sail, to take down a tent (see 2 Cor. 5:1-8), and to unyoke a beast of burden (see Matt. 11:28-30). God's people are not afraid of death because it only frees us from the burdens of this life and leads into the blessings of the next life.

Simeon's song is a *missionary* hymn, which is something unusual for a devout Jew standing in the temple. He sees this great salvation going out to the Gentiles! Jesus has restored the glory to Israel and brought the light to the Gentiles so that all people can be saved (see Luke 2:10). Remember that the compassion of Christ for the whole world is one of Luke's major themes.

Then Simeon stopped praising and started prophesying (Luke 2:34-35), and in his message used three important images: the stone, the sign, and the sword.

The stone is an important Old Testament image of God (Gen. 49:24; Pss. 18:2; 71:3; Deut. 32:31). Messiah would be a "rejected cornerstone" (Ps. 118:22; Luke 20:17-18; Acts 4:11), and the nation of Israel would stumble over Him (Isa. 8:14; Rom. 9:32). Because of Jesus Christ, many in Israel would fall in conviction and then rise in salvation. (Simeon seems to be speaking about one group, not two.) Even today, God's people Israel stumble over the Cross (1 Cor. 1:23) and do not understand that Jesus is their Rock (1 Peter 2:1-6).

The word *sign* means "a miracle," not so much as a demonstration of power but as a revelation of divine truth. Our Lord's miracles in John's Gospel are called "signs" because they reveal special truths about Him (John 20:30-31). Jesus Christ is God's miracle; and yet, instead of admiring Him, the people attacked Him and spoke against Him. His birth was a miracle, yet they slandered it (John 8:41). They said His miracles were done in the power of Satan (Matt. 12:22-24) and that His character was questionable (John 8:48, 52; 9:16, 24). They slandered His death (Ps. 22:6-8; Matt. 27:39-44) and lied about His resurrection (Matt. 27:62-66). Today, people are even speaking against His coming again (2 Peter 3).

But the way people speak about Jesus Christ is evidence of what is in their hearts. He is not only the "salvation stone" and the "judgment stone" (Dan. 2:34, 45), but He is also the "touchstone" that exposes what people are really like. "What think ye of Christ?" (Matt. 22:42) is still the most important question for anybody to answer (1 John 4:1-3).

The image of the sword was for Mary alone, and it spoke of the suffering and sorrow she would bear as the mother of the Messiah. (This suggests that Joseph was dead when Jesus began His ministry thirty years later, or Joseph would have been included.) The Greek word means a large sword such as Goliath used (1 Sam. 17:51), and the verb means "constantly keep on piercing."

During our Lord's life and ministry, Mary did experience more and more sorrow until one day she stood by His cross and saw Him suffer and die (John 19:25-27). However, without minimizing her devotion, Mary's personal pain must not in any way be made a part of Christ's redemptive work. Only He could die for the sins of the world (1 Tim. 2:5-6).

How much did Mary and Joseph understand of God's great plan for this miracle Child? We don't know, but we do know that Mary stored up all these things and pondered them (Luke 2:19, 51). The word means "to put things together"; Mary sought for some pattern that would help her understand God's will. There were times when Mary misunderstood Him (Mark 3:31-35), and this would add to her suffering. The last time you find Mary named in Scripture, she is in the Upper Room, praying with the other believers (Acts 1:14).

Anna (vv. 36-38). Her name means "grace," and she was a godly widow of great age. There are forty-three references to women in Luke's Gospel, and of the twelve widows mentioned in the Bible, Luke has three (Luke 2:36-40; 7:11-15; 21:1-4; and note 18:1-8). It isn't difficult to see the heart of a physician in Luke's presentation.

Widows didn't have an easy time in that day; often they were neglected and exploited in spite of the commandment of the Law (Ex. 22:21-22; Deut. 10:17-18; 14:29; Isa. 1:17). Anna devoted herself to "serving God by worship" through fastings and prayers. She moved from the tribe of Asher and remained in the temple, waiting for the appearing of God's promised Messiah (see 1 Tim. 5:3-16).

God's timing is always perfect. Anna came up just as Simeon was praising the Lord for the Child Jesus, so she joined in the song! I would like to have heard these elderly people singing in the temple! Their praise was inspired by the Spirit of God, and God accepted it. But Anna did much more than sing; she also spread the Good News among the other faithful members of "the remnant" who were waiting for the redemption of Israel. The excitement began to spread as more and more people heard the Good News.

Anna was a prophetess, which meant she had a special gift of declaring and interpreting God's message. Other prophetesses in Scripture are Miriam (Ex. 15:20), Deborah (Jud. 4:4), Hulduh (2 Kings 22:14), Noadiah (Neh. 6:14), and the wife of Isaiah (Isa. 8:3). The evangelist Philip had four daughters who were prophetesses (Acts 21:8-9).

The Youth (Luke 2:39-52)

Having obeyed the Law in everything, Mary and Joseph returned to Nazareth, which would be our Lord's home until He started His official ministry. There were many Jewish men with the name *Jesus* (Joshua), so He would be known as "Jesus of Nazareth" (Acts 2:22); and His followers would be called "Nazarenes" (Acts 24:5; see Matt. 2:23). His enemies used the name scornfully and Pilate even hung it on the cross (Matt. 21:11), but Jesus was not ashamed to use it when He spoke from heaven (Acts 22:8). That which men scorned (John 1:46), Jesus Christ took to heaven and made glorious!

What did Jesus do during the "hidden years" at Nazareth? Dr. Luke reports that the lad developed physically, mentally, socially, and spiritually (Luke 2:40, 52). In His incarnation, the Son of God set aside the independent use of His own divine attributes and submitted Himself wholly to the Father (Phil. 2:1-11). There are deep mysteries here that no one can fully understand or explain, but we have no problem accepting them by faith.

Jesus did not perform any miracles as a Boy, traditions notwithstanding, because the turning of water into wine was the beginning of His miracles (John 2:1-11). He worked with Joseph in the carpenter shop (Matt. 13:55; Mark 6:3) and apparently ran the business after Joseph died. Joseph and Mary had other children during those years (Matt. 13:55-56; John 7:1-10), for the "until" of Matthew 1:25 indicates that the couple eventually had normal marital relations.

Luke gives us only one story from our Lord's youthful years. Joseph and Mary were devout Jews who observed Passover in Jerusalem every year. Three times a year the Jewish men were required to go to Jerusalem to worship (Deut. 16:16), but not all of them could afford to do so. If they chose one feast, it was usually the Passover; and they tried to take their family with them, for it was the most important feast on the Jewish calendar.

People traveled to the feasts in caravans, the women and children leading the way and setting the pace, and the men and young men following behind. Relatives and whole villages often traveled together and kept an eye on each other's children. At the age of twelve, Jesus could easily have gone from one group to another and not been missed. Joseph would think Jesus was with Mary and the other children, while Mary would suppose He was with Joseph and the men, or perhaps with one of their relatives.

They had gone a day's journey from Jerusalem when they discovered that Jesus was missing. It took a day to return to the city and another day for them to find Him. During those three days, Joseph and Mary had been "greatly distressed" (Luke 2:48, "sorrowing"). This word is used to describe Paul's concern for lost Israel (Rom. 9:2) as well as the pain of lost souls in hades (Luke 16:24-25).

It is worth noting that Luke's phrase "Joseph and His mother" (Luke 2:43) suggests the Virgin Birth, while the phrase "Thy father and I" (Luke 2:48) indicates that Joseph was accepted as the legal father of Jesus (see Luke 3:23). To use Luke 2:48 to disprove the Virgin Birth is stretching a point.

Whether Jesus had spent the entire time in the temple, we don't know. It certainly would have been safe there and the Heavenly Father was watching over Him. We do know that when Joseph and Mary found Him, He was in the midst of the teachers, asking them questions and listening to their answers; and the teachers were amazed at both His questions and His answers.

Mary's loving rebuke brought a respectful but astonished reply from Jesus: "Why is it that you were looking for Me? Did you not know that I had to be in My Father's house?" (Luke 2:49, NASB) It can also be translated "in the things of My Father" (NASB margin), but the idea is the same. Jesus was affirming His divine sonship and His mission to do the will of the Father.

The word *must* was often on our Lord's lips: "I must preach" (Luke 4:43); "The Son of man must suffer" (Luke 9:22); the Son of man "must be lifted up" (John 3:14). Even at the age of twelve, Jesus was moved by a divine compulsion to do the Father's will.

Since Jesus "increased in wisdom" (Luke

2:52), we wonder how much He understood God's divine plan at that time. We must not assume that at the age of twelve He was omniscient. Certainly He grew in His comprehension of those mysteries as He communed with His Father and was taught by the Spirit.

One thing is sure: Joseph and Mary didn't understand! This was a part of the pain from "the sword" that Simeon had promised her (Luke 2:35), and no doubt it happened again and again as the boy matured. Years later, during His ministry, our Lord's family didn't understand Him (Luke 8:19-21; John 7:1-5).

Jesus is a wonderful example for all young people to follow. He grew in a balanced way (Luke 2:52) without neglecting any part of life, and His priority was to do the will of His Father (see Matt. 6:33). He knew how to listen (Luke 2:46) and how to ask the right questions. He learned how to work, and He was obedient to His parents.

The Boy Jesus grew up in a large family, in a despised city, nurtured by parents who were probably poor. The Jewish religion was at an all-time low, the Roman government was in control, and society was in a state of fear and change. Yet when Jesus emerged from Nazareth, eighteen years later, the Father was able to say of Him, "Thou art My beloved Son; in Thee I am well pleased" (Luke 3:22).

May the Father be able to say that about us!

CHAPTER THREE
THIS IS THE SON OF GOD!
Luke 3–4

"If Socrates would enter the room, we should rise and do him honor," said Napoleon Bonaparte. "But if Jesus Christ came into the room, we should fall down on our knees and worship Him."

Dr. Luke would have agreed with the famous French general, for in these two chapters, he makes it clear that Jesus Christ of Nazareth is indeed the Son of God. Notice the witnesses that he presents, all of whom declare that Jesus is God's Son.

John the Baptist (Luke 3:1-20)

When he came (vv. 1-2). When John the Baptist appeared on the scene, no prophetic voice had been heard in Israel for 400 years. His coming was a part of God's perfect timing, for everything that relates to God's Son is always on schedule (Gal. 4:4; John 2:4; 13:1). The fifteenth year of Tiberius Caesar was A.D. 28/29.

Luke named seven different men in Luke 3:1-2, including a Roman emperor, a governor, three tetrarchs (rulers over a fourth part of an area), and two Jewish high priests. But God's Word was not sent to any of them! Instead, the message of God came to John the Baptist, a humble Jewish prophet.

How he came (v. 3). Resembling the Prophet Elijah in manner and dress (Luke 1:17; Matt. 3:4; 2 Kings 1:8), John came to the area near the Jordan River, preaching and baptizing. He announced the arrival of the kingdom of heaven (Matt. 3:3) and urged the people to repent. Centuries before, Israel had crossed the Jordan (a national baptism) to claim their Promised Land. Now God summoned them to turn from sin and enter His spiritual kingdom.

Keep in mind that John did much more than preach against sin; he also proclaimed the Gospel. The word *preached* in Luke 3:18 gives us the English word *evangelize* ("to preach the Good News"). John introduced Jesus as the Lamb of God (John 1:29) and told people to trust in Him. John was only the best man at the wedding: Jesus was the Bridegroom (John 3:25-30). John rejoiced at the opportunity of introducing people to the Saviour, and then getting out of the way.

A unique feature about John's ministry was baptism (Luke 20:1-8; John 1:25-28). Baptism was nothing new to the people, for the Jews baptized Gentile proselytes. But John baptized *Jews,* and this was unusual. Acts 19:1-5 explains that John's baptism *looked forward* to the coming of the Messiah, while Christian baptism *looks back* to the finished work of Christ.

But there was something even beyond John's baptism, and that was the baptism that the Messiah would administer (Luke 3:16). He would baptize believers with the Holy Spirit, and this began at Pentecost (Acts 1:5; 2:1ff). Today, the moment a sinner trusts Christ, he or she is baptized by the Spirit into the body of Christ (1 Cor. 12:13).

What is the "baptism of fire"? It does not

refer to the "tongues of fire" at Pentecost, for tongues over a person's head could hardly be called a "baptism." John's use of the symbol of "fire" in Luke 3:9 and 17 indicates that he is talking about *judgment* and not blessing. In A.D. 70 the nation experienced a baptism of fire when Titus and the Roman armies destroyed Jerusalem and scattered the people. All unbelievers will experience a baptism of judgment in the lake of fire (Rev. 20:11-15).

Why he came (vv. 4-20). The illustrations used in the chapter help us understand the ministry God gave to John.

To begin with, John the Baptist was *a voice* "crying in the wilderness" (Luke 3:4; also see Isa. 40:1-5 and John 1:23). He was like the herald who went before the royal procession to make sure the roads were ready for the king. Spiritually speaking, the nation of Israel was living in a "wilderness" of unbelief, and the roads to spiritual reality were twisted and in disrepair. The corruption of the priesthood (instead of one, there were *two* high priests!) and the legalistic hypocrisy of the scribes and Pharisees had weakened the nation spiritually. The people desperately needed to hear a voice from God, and John was that faithful voice.

It was John's task to prepare the nation for the Messiah and then present the Messiah to them (Luke 1:16-17, 76-77; John 1:6-8, 15-34). He rebuked their sins and announced God's salvation, for without conviction there can be no conversion.

John is also compared to *a farmer* who chops down useless trees (Luke 3:9) and who winnows the grain to separate the wheat from the chaff (Luke 3:17). Like some "religious sinners" today, many of the Jews thought they were destined for heaven simply because they were descendants of Abraham (see John 8:31-34; Rom. 4:12-17; Gal. 3:26-29). John reminded them that God gets to the *root* of things and is not impressed with religious profession that does not produce fruit. In the last judgment, the true believers (wheat) will be gathered by God, while the lost sinners (chaff) will be burned in the fire.

In Luke 3:7, John pictured the self-righteous sinners as snakes that slithered out of the grass because a fire was coming! Jesus compared the Pharisees to vipers (Matt. 23:33) because their self-righteousness and unbelief made them the children of the devil (John 8:44-45; Rev. 20:2). How tragic that the religious leaders refused to obey John's message and submit to his baptism (Luke 20:1-8). They not only failed to enter the kingdom themselves, but their bad example and false teaching kept other people from entering.

John the Baptist was also *a teacher* (Luke 3:12). He not only preached publicly, but he also had a personal ministry to the people, telling them how to practice their new faith (Luke 3:10-14). He told them not to be selfish but to share their blessings with others (see Acts 2:44-45; 4:32-37).

Even the tax collectors came to John for counsel. These men were despised by their fellow Jews because they worked for the Romans and usually extorted money from the people. Luke emphasized the fact that Jesus was the friend of tax collectors (Luke 5:27ff; 15:1-2; 19:1-10). John did not tell them to quit their jobs but to do their work honestly.

Likewise, the soldiers were not condemned for their vocation. Rather, John told them to refrain from using their authority to get personal gain. These were probably Jewish soldiers attached to the temple or to the court of one of the Jewish rulers. It was not likely that Roman soldiers would ask a Jewish prophet for counsel.

John was faithful in his ministry to prepare the hearts of the people and then to present their Messiah to them. He clearly stated that Jesus was "the Lord" (Luke 3:4) and the Son of God (John 1:34). Because John rebuked Herod Antipas for his adulterous marriage to Herodias, he was imprisoned by the king and finally beheaded. However, he had faithfully finished his God-given assignment and prepared the people to meet the Messiah, the Son of God.

The Father and the Spirit (Luke 3:21-38)

One day, after all the others had been baptized, Jesus presented Himself for baptism at the Jordan; and John at first refused to comply (Matt. 3:13-15). He knew that Jesus of Nazareth was the perfect Son of God who had no need to repent of sin. Why then was the sinless Son of God baptized?

To begin with, in His baptism He identified with the sinners that He came to save. Also, His baptism was the official start of His ministry (Acts 1:21-22; 10:37-38). He was "about thirty years of age" (Luke 3:23), and the Jewish Levites began their work at age thirty (see

Num. 4:3, 35). But our Lord's words tell us the main reason for His baptism: "for in this way it is fitting for Us to fulfill all righteousness" (Matt. 3:15, NASB). In what way? In the way pictured by His baptism in the Jordan. Many Bible scholars agree that New Testament baptism was by immersion, which is a picture of death, burial, and resurrection. *Our Lord's baptism in water was a picture of His work of redemption* (Matt. 20:22; Luke 12:50). It was through His baptism of suffering on the cross that God "fulfilled all righteousness." (The "Us" in Matthew 3:15 does not mean John and Jesus. It means the Father, the Son, and the Spirit.)

When our Lord came up from the water, the Father spoke from heaven and identified Him as the beloved Son of God, and the Spirit visibly came upon Jesus in the form of a dove. Those who deny the Trinity have a difficult time explaining this event.

This is the first of three recorded occasions when the Father spoke from heaven. The second was when Jesus was transfigured (Luke 9:28-36), and the third was during His last week before the cross (John 12:28).

Only Luke mentions that Jesus was praying, and this was only one of many occasions (Luke 5:16; 6:12; 9:18, 28-29; 11:1; 23:34, 46). As the perfect Son of man, Jesus depended on His Father to meet His needs, and that was why He prayed.

Luke interrupted his narrative at this point to give us a genealogy of Jesus. Matthew's genealogy (Matt. 1:1-17) begins with Abraham and moves forward to Jesus, while Luke's begins with Jesus and moves backward to Adam. Matthew gives us the genealogy of Joseph, the legal foster-father of Jesus, while Luke gives us the genealogy of His mother Mary. Luke 3:23 can be translated: "When He began His ministry, Jesus was about thirty years old (being supposedly the son of Joseph), the son of Heli [an ancestor of Mary]." Mary herself would not be mentioned because it was unusual for women to be named in the official genealogies, though Matthew names four of them (Matt. 1:3, 5, 16).

By putting the genealogy here, Luke reminded his readers that the Son of God was also the Son of man, born into this world, identified with the needs and problems of mankind. And, since Joseph and Mary were both in David's line, these genealogies prove that Jesus of Nazareth has the legal right to David's throne (Luke 1:32-33).

Satan (Luke 4:1-13)

Even the enemy must admit that Jesus is the Son of God. "If Thou be the Son of God" (Luke 4:3, 9) is not a supposition but an affirmation. It means "in view of the fact that You are the Son of God" (WUEST). In fact, the fact of His deity was the basis for the first of the three temptations. "Since You are the Son of God," Satan argued, "why be hungry? You can change stones into bread!" Satan wanted Jesus to disobey the Father's will by using His divine power for His own purposes.

Why was Jesus tempted? For one thing, it was proof that the Father's approval was deserved (Luke 4:22). Jesus is indeed the "beloved Son" who always does whatever pleases His Father (John 8:29). Also, in His temptation, Jesus exposed the tactics of the enemy and revealed to us how we can overcome when we are tempted. This experience helped prepare our Lord for His present ministry as our sympathetic High Priest, and we may come to Him for the help we need to overcome the tempter (Heb. 2:16-18; 4:14-16). The first Adam was tempted in a beautiful Garden and failed. The Last Adam was tempted in a dangerous wilderness (Mark 1:13) and succeeded.

We have at our disposal the same spiritual resources that Jesus used when He faced and defeated Satan: prayer (Luke 3:22), the Father's love (Luke 3:23), the power of the Spirit (Luke 4:1), and the Word of God ("It is written"). Plus, we have in heaven the interceding Saviour who has defeated the enemy completely. Satan tempts us to bring out the worst in us, but God can use these difficult experiences to put the best into us. Temptation is Satan's weapon to defeat us, but it can become God's tool to build us (see James 1:1-8, 13-17).

In the first temptation, Satan suggested that there must be something wrong with the Father's love since His "beloved Son" was hungry. In years past Israel hungered in the wilderness, and God sent them bread from heaven; so surely Jesus could use His divine power to feed Himself and save His life. Satan subtly used this same approach on Eve: "God is holding out on you! Why can't you eat of *every* tree in the Garden? If He really loved you, He would share everything with you!"

But the test was even more subtle than that, for Satan was asking Jesus to *separate the physical from the spiritual.* In the Christian life, eating is a spiritual activity, and we can use even our daily food to glorify God (Rom. 14:20-21; 1 Cor. 10:31). Whenever we label different spheres of our lives "physical," "material," "financial," or "spiritual," we are bound to leave God out of areas where He rightfully belongs. Christ must be first in *everything,* or He is first in nothing (Matt. 6:33). It is better to be hungry in the will of God than satisfied out of the will of God.

When our Lord quoted Deuteronomy 8:3, He put the emphasis on the word *man.* As the eternal Son of God, He had *power* to do anything; but as the humble Son of man, He had *authority* to do only that which the Father willed. (Note carefully John 5:17, 30; 8:28; 10:17-18; 15:10, 15.) As the Servant, Jesus did not use His divine attributes for selfish purposes (Phil. 2:5-8). Because He was man, He hungered; but He trusted the Father to meet His needs in His own time and His own way.

You and I need bread for the body (Matt. 6:11), but we must not live by physical bread alone. We also need food for the inner person to satisfy our spiritual needs. This food is the Word of God (Ps. 119:103; Jer. 15:16; 1 Peter 2:2). What digestion is to the body, meditation is to the soul. As we read the Word and meditate on it, we receive spiritual health and strength for the inner person, and this enables us to obey the will of God.

We do not know why Luke reversed the second and third temptations, but since he did not claim to record the events in order, he is not contradicting Matthew 4:1-11. The word *then* in Matthew 4:5 indicates that Matthew's order is the correct one. We do seem to have in Luke's order a parallel to 1 John 2:16: the lust of the flesh (stones into bread), the lust of the eyes (the world's kingdoms and glory), and the pride of life (jump from the pinnacle of the temple); but it's doubtful that Luke had this in mind.

The Father had already promised to give the Son all the kingdoms of the world (Ps. 2:7-8), but first the Son had to suffer and die (John 12:23-33; Rev. 5:8-10). The suffering must come first, then the glory (Luke 24:25-27). The adversary offered Jesus these same kingdoms if He would *once* worship him, and this would eliminate the necessity of His going to the cross (note Matt. 16:21-23). Satan has always wanted to take God's place and receive worship (Isa. 14:13-14).

As the prince of this world, Satan has a certain amount of delegated authority from God (John 12:31; 14:30). One day he will share this authority with the Antichrist, the man of sin, who will rule the world for a brief time (Rev. 13). Satan's offer to Christ was valid, but his terms were unacceptable; and the Saviour refused.

Again, Jesus quoted God's Word, this time Deuteronomy 6:13. Satan had said nothing about *service,* but Jesus knew that whatever we worship, we will serve. Service to the Lord is true freedom, but service to Satan is terrible bondage. God's pattern is to start with suffering and end with glory (1 Peter 5:10), while Satan's pattern is to start with glory and end with suffering. Satan wants us to sacrifice the eternal for the temporary and take the "easy way."

There are no "shortcuts" in the Christian life, and there is no easy way to spiritual victory and maturity. If the perfect Son of God had to hang on a tree before He could sit on the throne, then His disciples should not expect an easier way of life (see Luke 9:22-26; Acts 24:22).

Satan questioned the Father's love when he tempted Jesus to turn stones into bread. He questioned His hope when he offered Jesus the world's kingdoms this side of the Cross (see Heb. 12:1-3). Satan questioned the Father's faithfulness when he asked Jesus to jump from the temple and prove that the Father would keep His promise (Ps. 91:11-12). Thus, the enemy attacked the three basic virtues of the Christian life—faith, hope, and love.

The pinnacle was probably a high point at the southeast corner of the temple, far above the Kidron Valley. Satan can tempt us even in the Holy City at the highest part of the holy temple! Following the example of Jesus, Satan decided to quote Scripture, and he selected Psalm 91:11-12. Of course, he misquoted the promise and besides he omitted "in all thy ways."

When a child of God is in the will of God, he can claim the Father's protection and care. But if he willfully gets into trouble and expects God to rescue him, then he is tempting God. (For an example of this, see Ex. 17:1-7.) We tempt God when we "force" Him (or dare Him) to act contrary to His Word. It is a dangerous thing to try God's patience, even though He is indeed long-suffering and gracious.

Our Lord's reply was, "on the other hand, it is written" (Matt. 4:7, NASB); and He quoted Deuteronomy 6:16. *Jesus balanced Scripture with Scripture to get the total expression of God's will.* If you isolate verses from their contexts, or passages from the total revelation of Scripture, you can prove almost anything from the Bible. Almost every false cult claims to be based on the teachings of the Bible. When we get our orders from God by picking out verses from here and there in the Bible, we are not living by faith. We are living by chance and tempting the Lord. "For whatever is not of faith is sin" (Rom. 14:23), and "faith comes by hearing, and hearing by the Word of God" (Rom. 10:17, NKJV).

Jesus came out of the wilderness a victor, but Satan did not give up. He watched for other opportunities to tempt the Saviour away from the Father's will. "Let us be as watchful after the victory as before the battle," said Andrew Bonar; and he was right.

The Scriptures (Luke 4:14-30)

The events recorded in John 1:19-4:45 took place at this time, but Matthew, Mark, and Luke did not record them. They moved right into the Lord's ministry in Galilee, and Luke alone reports His visit to His hometown of Nazareth. By now, the news had spread widely about the miracle-worker from Nazareth; so His family, friends, and neighbors were anxious to see and hear Him.

It was our Lord's custom to attend public worship, a custom His followers should imitate today (Heb. 10:24-25). He might have argued that the "religious system" was corrupt, or that He didn't need the instruction; but instead, He made His way on the Sabbath to the place of prayer.

A typical synagogue service opened with an invocation for God's blessing and then the recitation of the traditional Hebrew confession of faith (Deut. 6:4-9; 11:13-21). This was followed by prayer and the prescribed readings from the Law and from the Prophets, with the reader paraphrasing the Hebrew Scriptures in Aramaic.

This was followed by a brief sermon given by one of the men of the congregation or perhaps by a visiting rabbi (see Acts 13:14-16). If a priest was present, the service closed with a benediction. Otherwise, one of the laymen prayed and the meeting was dismissed.

Jesus was asked to read the Scripture text and to give the sermon. The passage He read included Isaiah 61:1-2, and He selected it for His "text." The Jewish rabbis interpreted this passage to refer to the Messiah, and the people in the synagogue knew it. You can imagine how shocked they were when Jesus boldly said that it was written about Him and that He had come to usher in the "acceptable year of the Lord."

The reference here is the "Year of Jubliee" described in Leviticus 25. Every seventh year was a "Sabbatical year" for the nation, when the land was allowed to rest; and every fiftieth year (after seven Sabbaticals) was set apart as the "Year of Jubilee." The main purpose of this special year was the balancing of the economic system: slaves were set free and returned to their families, property that was sold reverted to the original owners, and all debts were canceled. The land lay fallow as man and beast rested and rejoiced in the Lord.

Jesus applied all of this to His own ministry, not in a political or economic sense, but in a physical and spiritual sense. He had certainly brought Good News of salvation to bankrupt sinners and healing to brokenhearted and rejected people. He had delivered many from blindness and from bondage to demons and disease. Indeed, it was a spiritual "Year of Jubilee" for the nation of Israel!

The problem was that His listeners would not believe in Him. They saw Him only as the son of Mary and Joseph, the Boy they had watched grow up in their own city. Furthermore, they wanted Him to perform in Nazareth the same miracles He had done in Capernaum, but He refused. That's the meaning of the phrase, "Physician, heal thyself." Do a miracle!

At first, they admired the way He taught, but it didn't take long for their admiration to turn into antagonism. Why? *Because Jesus began to remind them of God's goodness to the Gentiles!* The Prophet Elijah bypassed all the Jewish widows and helped a Gentile widow in Sidon (1 Kings 17:8-16), and his successor Elisha healed a Gentile leper from Syria (2 Kings 5:1-15). Our Lord's message of grace was a blow to the proud Jewish exclusivism of the congregation, and they would not repent. Imagine this hometown Boy saying that Jews had to be saved by grace just like the pagan Gentiles!

The congregation was so angry, they took action to kill Jesus! St. Augustine said, "They love truth when it enlightens them, but hate truth when it accuses them." That applies well to many congregations today, people who want "gracious words" (Luke 4:22) but who don't want to face the truth (see John 1:17).

In spite of the unbelief of the people in Nazareth, the Scriptures declared that Jesus of Nazareth is God's Son, the Messiah sent to fulfill His promises. The people who do not want Him and who reject "the acceptable year of the Lord" will one day face "the day of vengeance of our God" (Isa. 61:2). How significant that Jesus stopped reading at that very place!

The Demons (Luke 4:31-44)

Jesus left Nazareth and set up His headquarters in Capernaum (Matt. 4:13-16), the home of Peter, Andrew, James, and John. He taught regularly in the synagogue and astonished the people by the authority of His message (see Matt. 7:28-29). He further astonished them by His authority over the demons.

Why would a demonized man attend the synagogue? Did he know Jesus would be there? Our Lord did not want the demons to bear witness to Him, so He told them to be still and He cast them out. Of course, the demons know that Jesus is the Son of God (Luke 4:34, 41); and knowing this, they tremble (James 2:19).

After the service, Jesus went to Peter's house, and there He healed Peter's mother-in-law. (Dr. Luke noted that she had a "great fever.") At sundown, when the Sabbath had ended and healing was permissible, a host of people brought their sick and afflicted to Peter's house and asked Jesus to help them. Again, He silenced the demons who confessed Him to be the Son of God.

The Lord must have been weary after such a demanding day, and yet He was up early the next morning to pray (Mark 1:35). It was in prayer that He found His strength and power for service, and so must we.

CHAPTER FOUR
THE DIFFERENCE JESUS MAKES
Luke 5

Jesus was concerned about individuals. He preached to great crowds, but His message was always to the individual; and He took time to help people personally. His purpose was to transform them and then send them out to share His message of forgiveness with others. Luke describes in this chapter our Lord's meetings with four individuals and the changes they experienced because they trusted Him.

From Failure to Success (Luke 5:1-11)

This event is not parallel to the one described in Matthew 4:18-22 and Mark 1:16-20. In those accounts, Peter and Andrew were busy fishing, but in this account they had fished all night and caught nothing and were washing their nets. (If nets are not washed and stretched out to dry, they rot and break.) Jesus had enlisted Peter, Andrew, James, and John earlier, and they had traveled with Him in Capernaum and Galilee (Mark 1:21-39), but then they went back to their trade. Now He would call them to a life of full-time discipleship.

It is possible that at least seven of the disciples were fishermen (John 21:1-3). Consider the fact that fishermen generally have the qualities that make for success in serving the Lord. It takes courage and daring, patience and determination to work on the seas; and it also takes a great deal of faith. Fishermen must be willing to work together (they used nets, not hooks) and help one another. They must develop the skills necessary to get the job done quickly and efficiently.

If I had fished all night and caught nothing, I would probably be *selling* my nets, not washing them to get ready to go out again! But true fishermen don't quit. Peter kept on working while Jesus used his ship as a platform from which to address the huge crowd on the shore. "Every pulpit is a fishing boat," said Dr. J. Vernon McGee, "a place to give out the Word of God and attempt to catch fish."

But there was another side to this request:

Peter was a "captive audience" as he sat in the ship listening to the Word of God. "So then faith comes by hearing, and hearing by the Word of God" (Rom. 10:17, NKJV). In a short time, Peter would have to exercise faith, and Jesus was preparing him. First He said, "Thrust out a little"; and then, when Peter was ready, He commanded, "Launch out into the deep." If Peter had not obeyed the first seemingly insignificant command, he would never have participated in a miracle.

Peter must have been surprised when Jesus took command of the ship and its crew. After all, Jesus was a carpenter by trade (Mark 6:3), and what do carpenters know about fishing? It was a well-known fact that, in the Sea of Galilee, you caught fish at night in the shallow water, not in the daytime in the deep water. What Jesus asked Peter to do was contrary to all of his training and experience, but Peter obeyed. The key was his faith in the Word of God: "Nevertheless, at Thy word" (Luke 5:5).

The word translated "Master" (Luke 5:5) is used only by Luke and it has a variety of meanings, all of which speak of authority: chief commander, magistrate, governor of a city, and president of a college. Peter was willing to submit to the authority of Jesus, even though he did not understand all that the Lord was doing. And remember, a great crowd was watching from the shore.

How people respond to success is one indication of their true character. Instead of claiming the valuable catch for themselves, Peter and Andrew called their partners to share it. We are not reservoirs, but channels of blessing, to share with others what God has graciously given to us.

From Sickness to Health (Luke 5:12-16)

Here was a man who *needed to be changed,* for he was a leper. Among the Jews, several skin diseases were classified as leprosy, including our modern Hansen's disease. In spite of modern medical advances, an estimated 10 million people around the world have leprosy. One form of leprosy attacks the nerves so that the victim cannot feel pain. Infection easily sets in, and this leads to degeneration of the tissues. The limb becomes deformed and eventually falls off.

It was the task of the Jewish priest to examine people to determine whether they were lepers (Lev. 13). Infected people were isolated and could not return to normal society until declared "cleansed." Leprosy was used by Isaiah as a picture of sin (Isa. 1:4-6), and the detailed instructions in Leviticus 13–14 would suggest that more was involved in the procedure than maintaining public health.

Like sin, leprosy is deeper than the skin (Lev. 13:3) and cannot be helped by mere "surface" measures (see Jer. 6:14). Like sin, leprosy spreads (Lev. 13:7-8); and as it spreads, it defiles (Lev. 13:44-45). Because of his defilement, a leprous person had to be isolated outside the camp (Lev. 13:46), and lost sinners one day will be isolated in hell. People with leprosy were looked on as "dead" (Num. 12:12), and garments infected with leprosy were fit only for the fire (Lev. 13:52). How important it is for lost sinners to trust Jesus Christ and get rid of their "leprosy"!

This man not only needed to be changed, but *he wanted to be changed.* Lepers were required to keep their distance, but he was so determined that he broke the Law and approached the Lord Jesus personally. Throughout his Gospel, Luke makes it clear that Jesus was the Friend of the outcast, and they could come to Him for help. The man humbled himself before the Lord and asked for mercy.

By the grace and power of God, this man *was changed!* In fact, Jesus even touched the man, which meant that He became unclean Himself. This is a beautiful picture of what Jesus has done for lost sinners: He became sin for us that we might be made clean (2 Cor. 5:21; 1 Peter 2:24). Jesus is not only willing to save (1 Tim. 2:4; 2 Peter 3:9), but He is also able to save (Heb. 7:25); and He can do it now (2 Cor. 6:2).

Jesus encouraged the man to see the priest and to obey the rules for restoration given in Leviticus 14. The ceremony is a picture of the work of Jesus Christ in His incarnation, His death, and His resurrection. All of this was done over running water, a symbol of the Holy Spirit of God. This sacrifice reminds us that Jesus had to die for us in order to deliver us from our sins.

Jesus instructed the man not to reveal who had healed him, but the cleansed leper became an enthusiastic witness for the Lord. (Jesus commands us to tell everybody, and we keep quiet!) Because of this witness, great multitudes came to Jesus for help, and He graciously ministered to them. But Jesus was not impressed by these great crowds, for He knew that most of the people wanted only His healing power and not His salvation. He often left the crowds and slipped away into a quiet place to pray and seek the Father's help. That's a good example for all of God's servants to follow.

From Guilt to Forgiveness (Luke 5:17-26)

Jesus returned to Capernaum, possibly to Peter's house, and the crowd gathered to see Him heal and to hear Him teach. But a new element was added: some of the official religious leaders from Jerusalem were present to investigate what He was doing. They had every right to do this since it was the responsibility of the elders to prevent false prophets from leading the people astray (Deut. 13; 18:15-22). They had interrogated John the Baptist (John 1:19-34) and now they would examine Jesus of Nazareth.

Since this is the first time the scribes and Pharisees are mentioned in Luke's Gospel, it would be good for us to get acquainted with them. The word *Pharisee* comes from a Hebrew word that means "to divide, to separate." The scribes and Pharisees probably developed out of the ministry of Ezra, the priest, who taught the Jewish people to obey the Law of Moses and be separate from the heathen nations around them (Ezra 9–10; Neh. 8–9). The great desire of the scribes and Pharisees was to understand and magnify God's Law and apply it in their daily lives.

However, the movement soon became quite legalistic and its leaders laid so many burdens on the people that it was impossible to "serve the Lord with gladness" (Ps. 100:2). Furthermore, many of the Pharisees were hypocrites and did not practice what they preached (see Matt. 15:1-20; 23:1-36). In the Sermon on the Mount (Matt. 5–7), Jesus exposed the shallowness of pharisaical religion. He explained that true righteousness is a matter of the heart and not external religious practices alone.

The scribes and Pharisees picked a good time to attend one of our Lord's meetings, because God's power was present in a special way and Jesus would heal a man with palsy. If leprosy illustrates the corruption and defilement of sin, then palsy is a picture of the paralysis that sin produces in a life. But Jesus would do more than heal the man; He would also forgive his sins and teach the crowd a lesson in forgiveness.

The paralytic was unable to come to Jesus himself, but he was fortunate enough to have four friends who were able to get him to Jesus. These four men are examples of how friends ought to minister to one another and help needy sinners come to the Saviour.

To begin with, they had faith that Jesus would heal him (Luke 5:20); and it is faith that God honors. Their love for the man united them in their efforts so that nothing discouraged them, not even the crowd at the door. (How tragic it is when spectators stand in the way of people who want to meet Jesus. Zaccheus would have this problem. See Luke 19:3.) When they could not get in at the door, they went on the roof, removed the tiling, and lowered the man on his mat right in front of the Lord!

Jesus could have simply healed the man and sent him home, but instead, He used the opportunity to teach a lesson about sin and forgiveness. Certainly it was easier to say to the man, "Your sins be forgiven!" than it was to say, "Rise up and walk!" Why? *Because nobody could prove whether or not his sins really were forgiven!* Jesus took the harder approach and healed the man's body, something everybody in the house could witness.

Was the man's affliction the result of his sin? We do not know, but it is probable (see John 5:1-14). The healing of his body was an outward evidence of the spiritual healing within. Jesus astounded the religious leaders by claiming to have authority both to heal the body and to forgive sins. The people had already acknowledged His authority to teach and to cast out demons (Luke 4:32, 36), but now He claimed authority to forgive sins as well. The scribes and Pharisees could not deny the miracle of healing, but they considered His claim to forgive sins nothing less than blasphemy, for only God can forgive sins. For making that kind of statement, Jesus could be stoned, because He was claiming to be God.

In Luke 5:24, we have the first recorded use of the title Son of man in Luke's Gospel, where it is found twenty-three times. Our Lord's listeners were familiar with this title. It was used of the Prophet Ezekiel over eighty times, and Daniel applied it to the Messiah (Dan. 7:13, 18). "Son of man" was our Lord's favorite name for Himself; this title is found at least eighty-two times in the Gospel record. Occasionally He used the title "Son of God" (Matt. 27:43; Luke 22:70; John 5:25; 9:35; 10:36; 11:4), but "Son of man" was used more. Certainly the Jewish people caught the messianic character of this title, but it also identified Him with the people He came to save (Luke 19:10). Like Ezekiel, the Old Testament "son of man," Jesus "sat where they sat" (Ezek. 3:15).

The healing was immediate and the people glorified God. But even more than receiving healing, the man experienced forgiveness and the start of a whole new life. Our Lord's miracles not only demonstrated His deity and His compassion for needy people, but they also revealed important spiritual lessons about salvation. They were "object lessons" to teach spiritually blind people what God could do for them if only they would believe in His Son.

From the Old to the New (Luke 5:27-39)

When Jesus called Levi, He accomplished three things: He saved a lost soul; He added a new disciple to His band; and He created an opportunity to explain His ministry to Levi's friends and to the scribes and Pharisees. This event probably took place shortly after Jesus healed the palsied man, for the "official committee" was still there (Luke 5:17). And it is likely that Jesus at this time gave Levi his new name—"Matthew, the gift of God" (Luke 6:15; see also Matt. 9:9).

Matthew sat at the toll booth and levied duty on the merchandise that was brought through. Since the tax rates were not always clear, it was easy for an unscrupulous man to make extra money for himself. But even if a tax collector served honestly, the Jews still despised him for defiling himself by working for the Gentiles. John the Baptist had made it clear that there was nothing innately sinful in collecting taxes (Luke 3:12-13), and we have no evidence that Matthew was a thief. But to the Jews, Levi was a sinner, and Jesus was suspect for having anything to do with him and his sinner friends.

We wonder how much Matthew knew about Jesus. Our Lord's friendship with Peter and his partners would put Him in touch with the businessmen of Capernaum, and certainly Matthew had heard Jesus preach by the seaside. Matthew instantly obeyed the Lord's call, left everything, and followed Jesus. He was so overjoyed at his salvation experience that he invited many of his friends to rejoice with him (see Luke 15:6, 9, 23).

The scribes and Pharisees criticized Jesus because they did not understand either His message or His ministry. Jesus simply did not fit into their traditional religious life. It is unfortunate when leaders resist change and refuse to try to understand the new things that God is doing. In order to help them understand, Jesus gave four illustrations of what He was doing.

The Physician (vv. 31-32). The scribes and Pharisees saw Matthew and his friends as condemned sinners, but Jesus saw them as spiritually sick "patients" who needed the help of a physician. In fact, He had illustrated this when He cleansed the leper and healed the paralytic. Sin is like a disease: it starts in a small and hidden way; it grows secretly; it saps our strength; and if it is not cured, it kills. It is tragic when sickness kills the body, but it is even more tragic when sin condemns the soul to hell.

The scribes and Pharisees were quick to diagnose the needs of others, but they were blind to their own needs, for they were sinners like everyone else. They appeared righteous on the outside but were corrupt within (Matt. 23:25-28). They may not have been "prodigal sons" who were guilty of sins of the flesh, but they were certainly "elder brothers" who were guilty of sins of the spirit (Luke 15:11-32; 2 Cor. 7:1).

As I was writing this chapter, I received a phone call from a woman in Canada who disagreed with my radio ministry and repeatedly condemned "the judgmental fundamentalists." I tried to reason with her from the Word, but she would not accept it. According to her, there was no hell and I had no right to preach about it. As I quoted Scripture to her, she hung up; all I could do was pause to pray for her, and I did it with a heavy heart.

The first step toward healing sin sickness is admitting that we have a need and that we must do something about it. False prophets give a false diagnosis that leads to a false hope (Jer. 6:14); but the servant of God tells the truth about sin, death, and hell, and offers the only remedy: faith in Jesus Christ. The religion of the scribes and Pharisees could offer no hope to Matthew's friends, but Jesus could.

What a wonderful Physician Jesus is! He comes to us in love; He calls us; He saves us when we trust Him; *and He "pays the bill."* His diagnosis is always accurate and His cure is perfect and complete. No wonder Matthew was so happy and wanted to share the Good News with his friends!

The Bridegroom (vv. 33-35). The scribes and Pharisees were not only upset at the disciples' friends, but also at their obvious joy as they fellowshipped with Jesus and the guests. We get the impression that the Pharisees experienced little if any joy in the practice of their religion (see Matt. 6:16; Luke 15:25-32). Jesus was "a Man of Sorrows" (Isa. 53:3), but He was also filled with joy (Luke 10:21; John 15:11; 17:13).

Jewish weddings lasted a week and were times of great joy and celebration. By using this image, Jesus was saying to His critics, "I came to make life a wedding feast, not a funeral. If you know the Bridegroom, then you can share His joy." He said that one day He would be "taken away," which suggested rejection and death; but meanwhile, there was good reason for joy, for sinners were coming to repentance.

Fasting is found often in the Old Testament, but nowhere is it commanded in the New Testament. However, the example of the prophets and the early church is certainly significant for believers today. Our Lord's words in Matthew 6:16-18 assume that we will fast ("when," not "if"), and passages like Acts 13:1-3 and 14:23 indicate that fasting was a practice of the early church (see also 1 Cor. 7:5; 2 Cor. 6:5; 11:27).

The garment (v. 36). Jesus did not come to patch up the old; He came to give the new. The Pharisees would admit that Judaism was not all it could be, and perhaps they hoped that Jesus would work with them in reviving the old religion. But Jesus showed the foolishness of this approach by contrasting two garments, an old one and a new one. If you take a patch from a new garment and sew it to an old garment, you ruin both of them. The new garment has a hole in it, and the old garment has a patch that does not match and that will tear away when the garment is washed.

In Scripture, garments are sometimes used to picture character and conduct (Col. 3:8-17). Isaiah wrote about a "robe of righteousness" (Isa. 61:10; see also 2 Cor. 5:21), and he warned against our trusting our own good works for salvation (Isa. 64:6). Many people have a "patchwork" religion of their own making, instead of trusting Christ for the robe of salvation that He gives by grace.

The wineskins (vv. 37-39). If unfermented wine is put into brittle old wineskins, the gas will burst the skins and both the skins and the wine will be lost. The new life of the Spirit could not be forced into the old wineskins of Judaism. Jesus was revealing that the ancient Jewish religion was getting old and would soon be replaced (see Heb. 8:13). Most of the Jews preferred the old and refused the new. It was not until A.D. 70, when the Romans destroyed Jerusalem and the temple, and scattered the people, that the Jewish religion *as described in the Law* came to an end. Today, the Jews do not have a priesthood, a temple, or an altar; so they cannot practice their religion as their ancestors did (see Hosea 3:4).

The things in the ceremonial Law were fulfilled by Jesus Christ, so there is no need today for sacrifices, priests, temples, and ceremonies. All of God's people are priests who bring spiritual sacrifices to the Lord (1 Peter 2:5, 9). The tables of Law have been replaced by the tables of the human heart, where God's Spirit is writing the Word and making us like Jesus Christ (2 Cor. 3:1-3, 18).

Jesus Christ still offers "all things new" (Rev. 21:5). As the Physician, He offers sinners new life and spiritual health. As the Bridegroom, He brings new love and joy. He gives us the robe of righteousness and the wine of the Spirit (Eph. 5:18; also see Acts 2:13). Life is a feast, not a famine or a funeral; and Jesus Christ is the only one who can make that kind of a difference in our lives.

CHAPTER FIVE
SO WHAT'S NEW? EVERYTHING!
Luke 6

For over a year, Jesus ministered as a popular itinerant Teacher and Healer, and multitudes followed Him. But now the time had come for Him to "organize" His followers and declare just what His kingdom was all about.

In this chapter, we see the Lord Jesus establishing three new spiritual entities to replace that which was now "worn out" in the Jewish religion: a new Sabbath, a new nation, and a new blessing in the new spiritual kingdom.

A New Sabbath (Luke 6:1-11)

The sanctity of the seventh day was a distinctive part of the Jewish faith. God gave Israel the Sabbath law at Sinai (Neh. 9:13-14) and made it a sign between Him and the nation (Ex. 20:8-11; 31:12-17). The word *Sabbath* means "rest" and is linked with God's cessation of work after the six days of Creation (Gen. 2:2-3). Some of the rabbis taught that Messiah could not come until Israel had perfectly kept the Sabbath, so obeying this law was very important both personally and nationally.

To call Sunday "the Sabbath" is to confuse the first day and the seventh day and what each signifies. The Sabbath is a reminder of the completion of "the old Creation," while the Lord's Day is a reminder of our Lord's finished work in "the new Creation" (2 Cor. 5:21; Eph. 2:10; 4:24). The Sabbath speaks of rest *after* work and relates to the Law, while the Lord's Day speaks of rest *before* work and relates to grace. The Lord's Day commemorates the resurrection of Jesus Christ from the dead as well as the coming of the Holy Spirit and the "birthday" of the church (Acts 2).

The early church met on the first day of the week (Acts 20:7; 1 Cor. 16:1-2). However, some Jewish believers kept the Sabbath, and this sometimes led to division. Paul addressed this problem in Romans 14:1–15:13 where he gave principles to promote both liberty and unity in the church. But Paul always made it clear that *observing special days had nothing to do with salvation* (Gal. 4:1-11; Col. 2:8-17). We are not saved from sin by faith in Christ *plus* keeping the Sabbath. We are saved by faith in Christ alone.

By their strict and oppressive rules, the Pharisees and scribes had turned the Sabbath Day into a burden instead of the blessing God meant it to be, and Jesus challenged both their doctrine and their authority. He had announced a new "Year of Jubilee" (Luke 4:19), and now He would declare a new Sabbath. He had already healed a lame man on the Sabbath, and the religious leaders had determined to kill Him (John 5:18; also note John 5:16). Now He was to violate their Sabbath laws on two more occasions.

In the field (vv. 1-5). It was lawful for a Jew to eat from a neighbor's vineyard, orchard, or field, provided he did not fill a container or use a harvesting implement (Deut. 23:24-25). The disciples were hungry, so they picked the heads of wheat, rubbed them in their hands, and ate them. But in so doing, according to the rabbis, they broke the Sabbath law, because they were harvesting, winnowing, and preparing food!

Always alert for something to criticize, some of the Pharisees asked Jesus why He permitted His disciples to violate the Sabbath laws. This was His second offense, and they were sure they had a case against Him. How tragic that their slavish devotion to religious rules blinded them to the true ministry of the Law as well as the very presence of the Lord who gave them the Law.

Jesus did not argue with them; instead, He took them right to the Word of God (1 Sam. 21:1-6). The "showbread" was comprised of twelve loaves, one for each tribe in Israel; and it stood on the table in the holy place in the tabernacle and then in the temple (Ex. 25:23-30; Lev. 24:5-9). Fresh bread was put on the table each Sabbath, and only the priests were allowed to eat the loaves.

But David and his men ate the loaves, and what Jew would condemn Israel's great king? "He was God's anointed!" they might argue, *but that was exactly what Jesus claimed for Himself* (Luke 4:18). Not only was He God's Anointed, but He was also the Lord of the Sabbath! When Jesus made that statement, He was claiming to be Jehovah God, because it was the Lord who established the Sabbath. If Jesus Christ is indeed Lord of the Sabbath, then He is free to do *on* it and *with* it whatever He pleases. The Pharisees did not miss His meaning, you can be sure.

God is more concerned about meeting human needs than He is about protecting religious rules. Better that David and his men receive strength to serve God than that they perish only for the sake of a temporary law. God desires compassion, not sacrifice (Matt. 12:7, quoting Hosea 6:6). The Pharisees, of course, had a different view of the Law (Matt. 23:23).

In the synagogue (vv. 6-11). The Pharisees knew that it was our Lord's practice to be in the synagogue on the Sabbath, so they were there to watch Him and to gather more evidence against Him. Did they know that the handicapped man would also be there? Did they "plant" him there? We do not know, and Jesus probably did not care. His compassionate heart responded to the man's need, and He healed him. Jesus could have waited a few hours until the Sabbath was over, or He could have healed the man in private, but He did it openly and immediately. It was a deliberate violation of the Sabbath traditions.

Our Lord's defense in the field was based

on the Old Testament Scriptures, but His defense in the synagogue was based on *the nature of God's Sabbath law.* God gave that law to help people, not to hurt them. "The Sabbath was made for man, and not man for the Sabbath" (Mark 2:27). Every man in the synagogue would rescue a sheep on the Sabbath, so why not rescue a man made in the image of God? (Matt. 12:11-12) The scribes and Pharisees had turned God's gift into a heavy yoke that nobody could bear (Acts 15:10; Gal. 5:1).

This miracle illustrates the power of faith in God's Word. Jesus commanded the man to do the very thing he could not do, and yet *he did it!* "For no word from God shall be void of power" (Luke 1:37, ASV). God's commandments are always God's enablements.

The scribes and Pharisees were filled with fury. It certainly did not do them any good to worship God in the synagogue that morning. So angry were they that they even joined forces with the Herodians (the Jews who supported Herod) in a plot to kill Jesus (Mark 3:6). Jesus knew their thoughts (Matt. 12:15; Luke 6:8); so He merely withdrew to the Sea of Galilee, ministered to the multitudes, and then went up to a mountain alone to pray.

Jesus gives a spiritual "Sabbath rest" that is in the heart all the time (Matt. 11:28-30). Unlike the galling yoke of the Law, the yoke that Jesus gives is "well-fitting," and His "burden is light." When the sinner trusts the Saviour, he has peace with God because his sins are forgiven and he is reconciled to God (Rom. 5:1-11). As the believer yields to Christ in daily experience, he enjoys "the peace of God" in his heart and mind (Phil. 4:6-7).

A New Nation (Luke 6:12-19)

Jesus spent the whole night in prayer, for He was about to call His 12 Apostles from among the many disciples who were following Him. A *disciple* is a learner, an apprentice; while an *apostle* is a chosen messenger sent with a special commission. Jesus had many disciples (see Luke 10:1) but only twelve handpicked Apostles.

Why did He pray all night? For one thing, He knew that opposition against Him was growing and would finally result in His crucifixion; so He prayed for strength as He faced the path ahead. Also, He wanted the Father's guidance as He selected His 12 Apostles, for the future of the church rested with them. Keep in mind that one of the Twelve would betray Him, *and Jesus knew who he was from the beginning* (John 6:64). Our Lord had real human emotions (Luke 22:41-44; Heb. 5:7-8), and it was through prayer that He made this difficult choice.

The names of the Apostles are also given in Matthew 10:1-4; Mark 3:16-19; Acts 1:13 (minus Judas). In all the lists, Peter is named first and, except in Acts 1:13, Judas is named last. The Judas in Acts 1:13 is Judas the brother [more likely "the son"] of James, who is also called Thaddeus in Mark 3:18. It was not unusual for one man to have two or more names.

Simon received the name *Peter* (stone) when Andrew brought him to Jesus (John 1:40-42). Bartholomew is the same as Nathanael (John 1:45-49). The other Simon in the group was nicknamed "Zelotes," which can mean one of two things. It may mean that he belonged to a group of fanatical Jewish patriots known as "the Zealots," whose purpose was to deliver Israel from the tyranny of Rome. They used every means at hand, including terror and assassination, to accomplish their purposes. Or, perhaps the word *Zelotes* translates from the Hebrew word *qanna* which means "jealous for God, zealous for God's honor." (It is transliterated in Matt. 10:4 as "Simon the Canaanite" [*qanna*].) Whether Simon was known for his zeal to honor God, or his membership in a subversive organization, we cannot be sure—possibly both.

Nor are we sure of the origin of the word *Iscariot.* It probably means "man [*ish* in Hebrew] of Kerioth," a town in southern Judah (Josh. 15:25). Some connect it with the Aramaic word *seqar* which means "falsehood." Thus, "Judas the false one." The geographical explanation is probably right.

What an interesting group of men! They illustrate what Paul wrote in 1 Corinthians 1:26-29, and they are an encouragement to us today. After all, if God could use them, can He not use us? Perhaps seven of them were fishermen (see John 21:1-3), one was a tax collector, and the other four are anonymous as far as their vocations are concerned. They were ordinary men; their personalities were different; yet Jesus called them to be with Him, to learn from Him, and to go out to represent Him (Mark 3:14).

Why 12 Apostles? Because there were twelve tribes in Israel, and Jesus was forming the nucleus for a new nation (see Matt. 21:43; 1 Peter 2:9). The first Christians were Jews because the Gospel came "to the Jew first" (Acts 13:46; Rom. 1:16). Later, the Gentiles were added to the church through the witness of the scattered Jewish believers (Acts 11:19ff) and the ministry of Paul, apostle to the Gentiles. In the church, there is no difference between Jew and Gentile; we are "all one in Christ Jesus" (Gal. 3:28).

It is significant that after Jesus called His 12 Apostles, and before He preached this great sermon, He took time to heal many needy people. This was a demonstration of both His power and His compassion. It was also a reminder to His newly appointed assistants that their job was to share His love and power with a needy world. It is estimated that there were 300 million people in the world in Jesus' day, while there are over 5 billion today, four fifths of them in the less-developed nations. What a challenge to the church!

A New Blessing (Luke 6:20-49)

This sermon is probably a shorter version of what we call "The Sermon on the Mount" (Matt. 5–7), though some fine evangelical scholars believe these were two different events. If they are the same event, the fact that Matthew locates it on a mountain (Matt. 5:1), while Luke puts it "in the plain" (Luke 6:17), creates no problem. Dr. D.A. Carson points out that the Greek word translated "plain" can mean "a plateau in a mountainous region" (*Exegetical Fallacies,* Baker, p. 43).

Jesus went "into the hill country" with His disciples. After a night of prayer, He came down to a level place, ordained the Twelve, ministered to the sick, and then preached this sermon. It was His description of what it means to have a life of "blessing."

To most Jewish people, the word "blessing" evoked images of a long life, wealth, a large, healthy family, a full barn, and defeated enemies. God's covenant with Israel did include such material and physical blessings (Deut. 28; Job 1:1-12; Prov. 3:1-10), for this was how God taught and disciplined them. After all, they were "little children" in the faith, and we teach children by means of rewards and punishments. With the coming of Jesus, Israel's childhood period ended, and the people had to mature in their understanding of God's ways (Gal. 4:1-6).

Jesus was preaching to His disciples as well as to the multitudes (Luke 6:27, 47), for even the Twelve had to unlearn many things before they could effectively serve Him. Furthermore, they had left everything to follow Jesus (Luke 5:11, 28), and no doubt were asking themselves, "What is in store for us?" (see Matt. 19:27) The Lord explained in this sermon that the truly blessed life comes not from *getting,* or from *doing,* but from *being.* The emphasis is on Godlike character.

This sermon is not "the Gospel" and nobody goes to heaven by "following the Sermon on the Mount." Dead sinners cannot obey the living God; they must first be born again and receive God's life (John 3:1-7, 36).

Nor is this sermon a "constitution" for the kingdom God will one day establish on earth (Matt. 20:21; Luke 22:30). The Sermon on the Mount applies to life today and describes the kind of godly character we should have as believers in this world. Certainly our Lord describes a life situation quite unlike that of the glorious kingdom, including hunger, tears, persecution, and false teachers.

What Jesus did was to focus on *attitudes:* our attitude toward circumstances (Luke 6:20-26), people (Luke 6:27-38), ourselves (Luke 6:39-45), and God (Luke 6:46-49). He emphasized four essentials for true happiness: faith in God, love toward others, honesty with ourselves, and obedience toward God.

Circumstances (vv. 20-26). Life was difficult for the people of that day and there was not much hope their circumstances would be improved. Like people today, many of them thought that happiness came from having great possessions, or holding an exalted position, or enjoying the pleasures and popularity that money can buy. Imagine how surprised they were when they heard Jesus describe happiness in terms *just the opposite of what they expected!* They discovered that what they needed most was not a change in circumstances but a change in their relationship to God and in their outlook on life.

Jesus was not teaching that poverty, hunger, persecution, and tears were blessings *in themselves.* If that were true, He would never have done all He did to alleviate the sufferings of others. Rather, Jesus was describing the *inner attitudes* we must have if we are to experience the blessedness of the Christian life. We should certainly do what we can to help others in a material way (James 2:15-17; 1 John 3:16-18), but we must remember that no amount of "things" can substitute for a personal relationship with God.

Matthew's account makes this clear: "Blessed are the poor *in spirit.* . . . Blessed are they which do hunger and thirst *after righteousness*" (Matt. 5:3, 6, italics mine). Jesus was not glorifying material poverty; rather, He was calling for that brokenness of heart that confesses spiritual poverty within (Luke 18:9-14; Phil. 3:4-14). The humble person is the only kind the Lord can save (Isa. 57:15; 66:2; 1 Peter 5:6). If you compare "The Beatitudes" with Isaiah 61:1-3 and Luke 4:18, you will see that our Lord's emphasis was on the condition of the heart and not the outward circumstances. Mary expressed this same insight in her song of praise (Luke 1:46-55).

Jesus Himself would experience the persecution described in Luke 6:22, and so would His disciples. How can we rejoice when men attack us? By remembering that it is a privilege to suffer for His sake (Phil. 3:10). When they treat us the way they treated Him, it is evidence that we are starting to live as He lived, and that is a compliment. All of the saints of the ages were treated this way, so we are in good company! Furthermore, God promises a special reward for all those who are faithful to Him; so the best is yet to come!

The four "woes" all share a common truth: you take what you want from life and you pay for it. If you want immediate wealth, fullness, laughter, and popularity, you can get it; but there is a price to pay: *that is all you will get.* Jesus did not say that these things were wrong. He said that *being satisfied with them is its own judgment.*

H.H. Farmer wrote that "to Jesus the terrible thing about having wrong values in life and pursuing wrong things is not that you are doomed to bitter disappointment, but that you are *not;* not that you do not achieve what you want, but that you *do*" (*Things Not Seen,* Nishbet [London], p. 96). When people are satisfied with the lesser things of life, the good instead of the best, then their successes add up only as failures. These people are spiritually bankrupt and do not realize it.

Life is built on character, and character is built on decisions. But decisions are based on values, *and values must be accepted by faith.* Moses made his life-changing decisions on the basis of values that other people thought were foolish (Heb. 11:24-29), but God honored his faith. The Christian enjoys all that God gives him (1 Tim. 6:17) because he lives "with eternity's values in view."

People (vv. 27-38). Jesus assumed that anybody who lived for eternal values would get into trouble with the world's crowd. Christians are the "salt of the earth" and "the light of the world" (Matt. 5:13-16), and sometimes the salt stings and the light exposes sin. Sinners show their hatred by avoiding us or rejecting us (Luke 6:22), insulting us (Luke 6:28), physically abusing us (Luke 6:29), and suing us (Luke 6:30). This is something we must expect (Phil. 1:29; 2 Tim. 3:12).

How should we treat our enemies? We must love them, do them good, and pray for them. Hatred only breeds more hatred, "for man's anger does not bring about the righteous life that God desires" (James 1:20, NIV). This cannot be done in our own strength, but it can be done through the power of the Holy Spirit (Rom. 5:5; Gal. 5:22-23).

We must not look at these admonitions as a series of rules to be obeyed. They describe an attitude of heart that expresses itself positively when others are negative, and generously when others are selfish, all to the glory of God. It is an inner disposition, not a legal duty. We must have wisdom to know when to turn the other cheek and when to claim our rights (John 18:22-23; Acts 16:35-40). Even Christian love must exercise discernment (Phil. 1:9-11).

Two principles stand out: we must treat others as we would want to be treated (Luke 6:31), which assumes we want the very best spiritually for ourselves; and we must imitate our Father in heaven and be merciful (Luke 6:36). The important thing is not that we are vindicated before our enemies but that we become more like God in our character (Luke 6:35). This is the greatest reward anyone can receive, far greater than riches, food, laughter, or popularity (Luke 6:24-26). Those things will one day vanish, but character will last for eternity. We must believe Matthew 6:33 and practice it in the power of the Spirit.

Luke 6:37-38 reminds us that we reap what we sow and in the amount that we sow. If we judge others, we will ourselves be judged. If we forgive, we shall be forgiven, but if we condemn, we shall be condemned (see Matt. 18:21-35). He was not talking about eternal judgment but the way we are treated in this life. If we live to give, God will see to it that we receive; but if we live only to get, God will see to it that we lose. This principle applies not only to our giving of money, but also to the giving of ourselves in ministry to others.

Self (vv. 39-45). The four striking figures in this section teach us some important lessons about ministry. To begin with, as His disciples, we must be sure that we see clearly enough to guide others in their spiritual walk. While there are blind people who have a keen sense of direction, it is not likely any of them will be hired as airplane pilots or wilderness guides. Jesus was referring primarily to the Pharisees who were leading the people astray (Matt. 15:14; 23:16). If we see ourselves as excellent guides, but do not realize our blindness, we will only lead people into the ditch (see Rom. 2:17-22).

Luke 6:40 reminds us that we cannot lead others where we have not been ourselves, nor can we be all that our Master is. In fact, the more we strive to be like Him, the more we realize how far short we fall. This is a warning against pride, for nothing blinds a person like pride.

Continuing the image of "the eye," Jesus taught that we must be able to see clearly enough to help our brother see better. It certainly is not wrong to help a brother get a painful speck of dirt out of his eye, *provided we can see what we are doing.* The crowd must have laughed out loud when Jesus described an "eye doctor" with *a plank* in his eye, performing surgery on a patient with *a speck* in his eye!

The emphasis here is on being honest with ourselves and not becoming hypocrites. It is easy to try to help a brother with his faults *just so we can cover up our own sins!* People who are constantly criticizing others are usually guilty of something worse in their own lives.

The illustration of the tree reminds us that fruit is always true to character. An apple tree produces apples, not oranges; and a good person produces good fruit, not evil. Believers do sin, but the witness of their words and works is consistently good to the glory of God. In terms of ministry, servants of God who are faithful will reproduce themselves in people who are in turn true to the Lord (2 Tim. 2:2).

The last image, the treasury, teaches us that what comes out of the lips depends on what is inside the heart. The human heart is like a treasury, and what we speak reveals what is there. A man who apologized for swearing by saying, "It really wasn't in me!" heard a friend say, "It had to be in you or it couldn't have come out of you!"

We must be honest with ourselves and admit the blind spots in our lives, the obstacles that blur our vision, and the areas within that must be corrected. Then we can be used of the Lord to minister to others and not lead them astray.

God (vv. 46-49). Our Lord's emphasis here is on obedience. It is not enough merely to hear His Word and call Him "Lord." We must also obey what He commands us to do. All of us are builders and we must be careful to build wisely. To "build on the rock" simply means to obey what God commands in His Word. To "build on the sand" means to give Christ lip service, but not obey His will. It may look as if we are building a strong house, but if it has no foundation, it cannot last. The storm here is not the last judgment but the tests of life that come to every professing Christian. Not everybody who professes to know the Lord has had a real experience of salvation. They may have been active in church and other religious organizations, but if they are not saved by faith, they have no foundation to their lives. When difficulties come, instead of glorifying the Lord, they desert Him; and their house of testimony collapses.

Nobody can really call Jesus Christ "Lord" except by the Holy Spirit of God (Rom. 8:16; 1 Cor. 12:3). If Christ is in our hearts, then our mouths must confess Him to others (Rom. 10:9-10). If we are "rooted and built up in Him" (Col. 2:7), then our fruits will be good and our house will withstand the storms. We may have our faults and failures, but the steady witness of our lives will point to Christ and honor Him.

This is the "new blessing" that Jesus offered His nation and that He offers us today. We can experience the "heavenly happiness" and true blessedness which only He can give. The basis for all of this is personal saving faith in the Lord Jesus Christ, for, as Dr. H.A. Ironside once said, "We cannot live the life until first we possess it."

CHAPTER SIX COMPASSION IN ACTION

Luke 7

Compassion has been defined as "your pain in my heart." What pain our Lord must have felt as He ministered from place to place! In this chapter alone, Jesus is confronted with the miseries of a dying servant, a grieving widow, a perplexed prophet, and a repentant sinner; and He helped them all. If a "hardship committee" had been asked to decide which of these persons was "deserving," we wonder who would have been chosen.

Jesus helped them all, because compassion does not measure: it ministers. Bernard of Clairvaux said, "Justice seeks out only the *merits* of the case, but pity only regards the *need.*" It was compassion, not justice, that motivated the Great Physician who came "not to call the righteous, but sinners to repentance" (Luke 5:32). Let's meet these four hurting people and see our Lord's responses to their needs.

The Servant: His Response to Faith (Luke 7:1-10)

In the Gospels and the Book of Acts, Roman centurions are presented as quality men of character, and this one is a sterling example. The Jewish elders had little love for the Romans in general and Roman soldiers in particular, and yet the elders commended this officer to Jesus. He loved the Jewish people in Capernaum and even built them a synagogue. He loved his servant and did not want him to die. This centurion was not a Stoic who insulated himself from the pain of others. He had a heart of concern, even for his lowly servant boy who was dying from a paralyzing disease (Matt. 8:6).

Matthew's condensed report (Matt. 8:5-13) does not contradict Luke's fuller account. The centurion's friends represented him to Jesus and then represented Jesus to him. When a newscaster reports that the President or the Prime Minister said something to Congress or Parliament, this does not necessarily mean that the message was delivered by them in person. It was probably delivered by one of their official representatives, but the message would be received as from the President or Prime Minister personally.

We are impressed not only with this man's great love, but also his great humility. Imagine a Roman officer telling a poor Jewish rabbi that he was unworthy to have Him enter his house! The Romans were not known for displaying humility, especially before their Jewish subjects.

But the characteristic that most impressed Jesus was the man's faith. Twice in the Gospel record we are told that Jesus marveled. Here in Capernaum, He marveled at the faith of a Gentile; and in Nazareth, He marveled at the unbelief of the Jews (Mark 6:6). The only other person Jesus commended for having "great faith" was a Gentile woman whose daughter He delivered from a demon (Matt. 15:28). It is worth noting that in both of these instances, Jesus healed *at a distance* (see Ps. 107:20; Eph. 2:11-13).

The centurion's faith certainly was remarkable. After all, he was a Gentile whose background was pagan. He was a Roman soldier, trained to be self-sufficient, and we have no evidence that he had ever heard Jesus preach. Perhaps he heard about Jesus' healing power from the nobleman whose son Jesus had healed, also at a distance (John 4:46-54). His soldiers may also have brought him reports of the miracles Jesus had performed, for the Romans kept close touch with the events in Jewish life.

The important word in Luke 7:8 is "also." (It should be in Matt. 8:9 as well, but the KJV omits it for some reason. The NASB has "too" in both places.) The officer saw a parallel between the way he commanded his soldiers and the way Jesus commanded diseases. Both the centurion and Jesus were under authority, and because they were under authority, they had the right to exercise authority. *All they had to do was say the word and things happened.* What tremendous faith this man exhibited! No wonder Jesus marveled.

If this Roman, with very little spiritual instruction, had that kind of faith in God's Word, how much greater *our* faith ought to be! We have an entire Bible to read and study, as well as nearly 2,000 years of church history to encourage us, and yet we are guilty of "no faith" (Mark 4:40) or "little faith" (Matt. 14:31). Our prayer ought to be, "Lord, increase our faith!" (Luke 17:5)

The Widow: Jesus' Response to Despair (Luke 7:11-17)

Nain was about twenty-five miles from Capernaum, a good day's journey away, yet Jesus went there even though He was not *requested* to come. Since the Jews buried their dead the same day (Deut. 21:23; Acts 5:5-10), it is likely that Jesus and His disciples arrived at the city gate late in the afternoon of the day the boy died. Four special meetings took place at the city gate that day.

Two crowds met. We can only marvel at the providence of God when we see Jesus meet that funeral procession just as it was heading for the burial ground. He lived on a divine timetable as He obeyed the will of His Father (John 11:9; 13:1). The sympathetic Saviour always gives help when we need it most (Heb. 4:16).

What a contrast between the crowd that was following Jesus and the crowd following the widow and her dead son. Jesus and His disciples were rejoicing in the blessing of the Lord, but the widow and her friends were lamenting the death of her only son. Jesus was heading for the city while the mourners were heading for the cemetery.

Spiritually speaking, each of us is in one of these two crowds. If you have trusted Christ, you are going to the city (Heb. 11:10, 13-16; 12:22). If you are "dead in sin," you are already in the cemetery and under the condemnation of God (John 3:36; Eph. 2:1-3). You need to trust Jesus Christ and be raised from the dead (John 5:24; Eph. 2:4-10).

Two only sons met. One was alive but destined to die, the other dead but destined to live. The term *only begotten* as applied to Jesus means "unique," "the only one of its kind." Jesus is not a "son" in the same sense that I am, having been brought into existence by conception and birth. Since Jesus is eternal God, He has always existed. The title *Son of God* declares Christ's divine nature and His relationship to the Father, to whom the Son has willingly subjected Himself from all eternity. All the Persons of the Godhead are equal, but in the "economy" of the Trinity, each has a specific place to fill and task to fulfill.

Two sufferers met. Jesus, "the Man of Sorrows," could easily identify with the widow's heartache. Not only was she in sorrow, but she was now left alone in a society that did not have resources to care for widows. What would happen to her? Jesus felt the pain that sin and death have brought into this world, and He did something about it.

Two enemies met. Jesus faced death, "the last enemy" (1 Cor. 15:26). When you consider the pain and grief that it causes in this world, death is indeed an enemy, and only Jesus Christ can give us victory (see 1 Cor. 15:51-58; Heb. 2:14-15). Jesus had only to speak the word and the boy was raised to life and health.

The boy gave two evidences of life: he sat up and he spoke. He was lying on an open stretcher, not in a closed coffin; so it was easy for him to sit up. We are not told what he said, but it must have been interesting! What an act of tenderness it was for Jesus to take the boy and give him to his rejoicing mother. The whole scene reminds us of what will happen when the Lord returns, and we are reunited with our loved ones who have gone to glory (1 Thes. 4:13-18).

The response of the people was to glorify God and identify Jesus with the Prophet the Jews had been waiting for (Deut. 18:15; John 1:21; Acts 3:22-23). It did not take long for the report of this miracle to spread. People were even more enthusiastic to see Jesus, and great crowds followed Him (Luke 8:4, 19, 42).

John the Baptist: His Response to Doubt (Luke 7:18-35)

Confusion (vv. 18-20). John had been in prison some months (Luke 3:19-20), but he knew what Jesus was doing because his own disciples kept him informed. It must have been difficult for this man, accustomed to a wilderness life, to be confined in a prison. The physical and emotional strain were no doubt great, and the long days of waiting did not make it easier. The Jewish leaders did nothing to intercede for John, and it seemed that even Jesus was doing nothing for him. If He came to set the prisoners free (Luke 4:18), then John the Baptist was a candidate!

It is not unusual for great spiritual leaders to have their days of doubt and uncertainty. Moses was ready to quit on one occasion (Num. 11:10-15), and so were Elijah (1 Kings 19) and Jeremiah (Jer. 20:7-9, 14-18); and even Paul knew the meaning of despair (2 Cor. 1:8-9).

There is a difference between doubt and unbelief. Doubt is a matter of the mind: we cannot understand what God is doing or why He is doing it. Unbelief is a matter of the will: we refuse to believe God's Word and obey what He tells us to do. "Doubt is not always a sign that a man is wrong," said Oswald Chambers; "it may be a sign that he is thinking." In John's case, his inquiry was not born of willful unbelief, but of doubt nourished by physical and emotional strain.

You and I can look back at the ministry of Christ and understand what He was doing, but John did not have that advantage. John had announced judgment, but Jesus was doing deeds of love and mercy. John had promised that the kingdom was at hand, but there was no evidence of it so far. He had presented Jesus as "the Lamb of God" (John 1:29), so John must have understood something about Jesus' sacrifice; yet how did this sacrifice relate to the promised kingdom for Israel? He was perplexed about God's plan and his place in it. But let's not judge him harshly, for even the prophets were perplexed about some of these things (1 Peter 1:10-12).

Confirmation (vv. 21-23). Jesus did not give the two men a lecture on theology or prophecy. Instead, He invited them to watch as He healed many people of many different afflictions. Certainly these were His credentials as the promised Messiah (Isa. 29:18-19; 35:4-6; 42:1-7). He had not established a political kingdom, but the kingdom of God was there in power.

The Greek word translated "offended" gives us our English word *scandalize,* and it referred originally to the "bait stick" in a trap. John was in danger of being trapped because of his concern about what Jesus was *not* doing. He was stumbling over his Lord and His ministry. Jesus gently told him to have faith, for his Lord knew what He was doing.

There are many people today who criticize the church for not "changing the world" and solving the economic, political, and social problems of society. What they forget is that God changes His world by changing individual people. History shows that the church has often led the way in humanitarian service and reform, but the church's main job is to bring lost sinners to the Saviour. Everything else is a by-product of that. Proclaiming the Gospel must always be the church's first priority.

Commendation (vv. 24-30). What we think of ourselves, or what others think of us, is not as important as what God thinks. Jesus waited until the messengers had departed and then He publicly commended John for his ministry. At the same time, He exposed the sinful hearts of those who rejected John's ministry.

John the Baptist was not a *compromiser,* a reed blowing in the wind (note Eph. 4:14); nor was he a popular *celebrity,* enjoying the friendship of great people and the pleasures of wealth. John did not waver or weaken, no matter what people did to him. John was not only a prophet, but he was a prophet whose ministry was prophesied! (see Isa. 40:3 and Mal. 3:1) The last of the Old Testament prophets, John had the great privilege as God's messenger of introducing the Messiah to Israel.

How is the least person in the kingdom of God greater than John? In position, not in character or ministry. John was the herald of the King, announcing the kingdom; believers today are children of the kingdom and the friends of the King (John 15:15). John's ministry was a turning point in both the nation's history and in God's plan of redemption (Luke 16:16).

Luke 7:29-30 are the words of Jesus, not an explanation from Luke (see Matt. 21:32). They answer the question some of the people were asking, "If John is such a great prophet, why is he in prison?" The answer is: because of the willful unbelief of the religious leaders. The common people accepted John's message and were baptized by him as proof of their repentance. They "justified God," which means they agreed with what God said about them (Ps. 51:4). But the religious leaders justified themselves (Luke 16:15), not God, and rejected John and his message.

Condemnation (vv. 31-35). Jesus compared that generation to people who were childish, not childlike, and nothing pleased them. He was probably referring to the scribes and Pharisees in particular. John was an individual who declared a stern message of judgment, and they said, "He has a demon!" Jesus mingled with the people and preached a gracious message of salvation, and they said, "He's a glutton, a winebibber, and a friend of publicans and sinners!" They wanted neither the funeral nor the wedding, because nothing pleased them.

People who want to avoid the truth about themselves can always find something in the preacher to criticize. This is one way they "justify themselves." But God's wisdom is not frustrated by the arguments of the "wise and prudent." *It is demonstrated in the changed lives of those who believe.* This is how true wisdom is "justified."

A Sinful Woman: His Response to Love (Luke 7:36-50)

Jesus not only accepted hospitality from the publicans and sinners but also from the Pharisees. They needed the Word of God too, whether they realized it or not. We trust that Simon's invitation was a sincere one and that he did not have some ulterior motive for having Jesus in his home. If he did, his plan backfired, because he ended up learning more about himself than he cared to know!

The repentant woman (vv. 36-38). It was customary in that day for outsiders to hover around during banquets so they could watch the "important people" and hear the conversation. Since everything was open, they could even enter the banquet hall and speak to a guest. This explains how this woman had access to Jesus. He was not behind locked doors. In that day women were not invited to banquets.

Jewish rabbis did not speak to women in public, nor did they eat with them in public. A woman of this type would not be welcomed in the house of Simon the Pharisee. Her sins are not named, but we get the impression she was a woman of the streets with a bad reputation.

Do not confuse this event with a similar one involving Mary of Bethany (John 12:1-8), and do not identify this woman with Mary Magdalene (Mark 16:9; Luke 8:2) as many continue to do.

The woman admitted she was a sinner and gave evidence that she was a *repentant* sinner. If you check a harmony of the Gospels, you will discover that just before this event, Jesus had given the gracious invitation, "Come unto Me . . . and I will give you rest" (Matt. 11:28-30). Perhaps that was when the woman turned from her sin and trusted the Saviour. Her tears, her humble attitude, and her expensive gift all spoke of a changed heart.

The critical host (vv. 39-43). Simon was embarrassed, both for himself and for his guests. People had been saying that Jesus was a great Prophet (Luke 7:16), but He certainly was not exhibiting much prophetic discernment if He allowed a sinful woman to anoint His feet! He must be a fraud.

Simon's real problem was *blindness*: he could not see himself, the woman, or the Lord Jesus. It was easy for him to say, "*She* is a sinner!" but impossible for him to say, "I am also a sinner!" (see Luke 18:9-14) Jesus proved that He was indeed a prophet by reading Simon's thoughts and revealing his needs.

The parable does not deal with the *amount* of sin in a person's life but the *awareness* of that sin in his heart. How much sin must a person commit to be a sinner? Simon and the woman were both sinners. Simon was guilty of sins of the spirit, especially pride, while the woman was guilty of sins of the flesh (see 2 Cor. 7:1). Her sins were known, while Simon's sins were hidden to everyone except God. *And both of them were bankrupt and could not pay their debt to God.* Simon was just as spiritually bankrupt as the woman, only he did not realize it.

Forgiveness is a gift of God's grace; the debt was paid in full by Jesus Christ (Eph. 1:7; 1 Peter 1:18-19). The word *frankly* means "graciously and freely." The woman accepted God's free offer of salvation and expressed her love openly. Simon rejected that offer and remained unforgiven. He was not only blind to himself, but he was blind to the woman and to his honored guest!

The forgiving Saviour (vv. 44-50). The woman was guilty of sins of commission, but Simon was guilty of sins of omission. He had not been a gracious host to the Lord Jesus. (For a contrast, see Abraham in Gen. 18:1-8.) Everything that Simon neglected to do, the woman did—and she did it better!

There are two errors we must avoid as we interpret our Lord's words. First, we must not conclude that this woman was saved by her tears and her gift. Jesus made it clear that it was *her faith* alone that saved her (Luke 7:50), for no amount of good works can pay for salvation (Titus 3:4-7).

Nor should we think that lost sinners are saved by love, either God's love for them or their love for God. God loves the whole world (John 3:16), yet the whole world is not saved. "For by grace you have been saved through faith, and that not of yourselves; it is the gift of God, not of works, lest anyone should boast" (Eph. 2:8-9, NKJV). Grace is love that pays a price, and that price was the death of the Son of God on the cross.

Jesus did not reject either the woman's tears or her gift of ointment, because her works were the evidence of her faith. "Faith without works is dead" (see James 2:14-26). We are not saved by faith plus works; we are saved by a faith that leads to works. This anonymous woman illustrates the truth of Galatians 5:6, "The only thing that counts is faith expressing itself through love" (NIV).

How did the woman know that her sins were forgiven? *Jesus told her.* How do we know today that we have been forgiven? *God tells us so in His Word.* Here are just a few verses to consider: Isaiah 1:18; 43:25-26; 55:6-7; Acts 13:38-39; Romans 4:7-8; Ephesians 4:32; and Hebrews 8:12. Once you understand the meaning of God's grace you have no trouble receiving His free and full forgiveness and rejoicing in it.

Of course, the legalistic critics at the dinner were shocked when Jesus said, "Her sins, which are many, are forgiven." By saying this, Jesus was claiming to be God! (see Luke 5:21) But He *is* God, and He died for the sins that she committed. His words of forgiveness were not cheap words; they cost Him dearly on the cross.

How was this woman saved? She repented of her sins and put her faith in Jesus Christ. How did she know she was truly forgiven? She had the assurance of His word. What was the proof of her salvation? Her love for Christ expressed in sacrificial devotion to Him. For the first time in her life, she had peace with God (Luke 7:50). Literally it reads, "Go *into* peace," for she had moved out of the sphere of enmity toward God and was now enjoying peace with God (Rom. 5:1; 8:7-8).

When Jesus healed the centurion's servant, it was a great miracle. An even greater miracle was His raising the widow's son from the dead. But in this chapter, the greatest miracle of all was His saving this woman from her sins and making her a new person. The miracle of salvation has to be the greatest miracle of all, for it meets the greatest need, brings the greatest results (and they last forever), and cost the greatest price.

Simon was blind to the woman and blind to himself. He saw her past, but Jesus saw her future. I wonder how many rejected sinners have found salvation through the testimony of this woman in Luke's Gospel. She encourages us to believe that Jesus can take any sinner and make him or her into a child of God.

But God's forgiveness is not automatic; we can reject His grace if we will. In 1830, a man named George Wilson was arrested for mail theft, the penalty for which was hanging. After a time, President Andrew Jackson gave Wilson a pardon *but he refused to accept it!* The authorities were puzzled: should Wilson be freed or hanged?

They consulted Chief Justice John Marshall, who handed down this decision: "A pardon is a slip of paper, the value of which is determined by the acceptance of the person to be pardoned. If it is refused, it is no pardon. George Wilson must be hanged."

If you have never accepted God's pardon, now is the time to believe and be saved.

CHAPTER SEVEN LESSONS ABOUT FAITH

Luke 8

One of the major themes in Luke 8 is how to get faith and use it in the everyday experiences of life. In the first section, Jesus laid the foundation by teaching His disciples that faith comes through receiving the Word of God into an understanding heart. In the second part, He put them through a series of "examinations" to see how much they had really learned. Most of us enjoy Bible study, but we wish we could avoid the examinations that often follow the lessons! However, it is in the tests of life that faith really grows and we get closer to Christ.

The cynical American editor H.L. Mencken defined faith as "an illogical belief in the occurrence of the impossible," and Mark Twain said (through one of his characters) that faith is "believin' what you know ain't so." Of course, these men are describing superstition, not faith; for the faith of a Christian rests on solid foundations.

Everybody lives by faith in something or someone. The difference between the Christian believer and the unsaved person is not that one has faith and the other does not. They *both* have faith. The difference is in *the object of their faith,* for faith is only as good as the object. The Christian believer has put his faith in Jesus Christ, and he bases that faith on the Word of God.

Teaching: Hearing God's Word (Luke 8:1-21)

The Lord continued His itinerant ministry in Galilee, assisted by His disciples and partially supported by some godly women. It was not unusual for Jewish rabbis to receive gifts from grateful people, and these women had certainly benefited from Jesus' ministry. The New Testament church leaders were supported by gifts from friends (2 Tim. 1:16-18) and from churches (Phil. 4:15-17), and Paul supported himself by his own labor (2 Thes. 3:6-10).

The word *hear* is used nine times in this section. It means much more than simply listening to words. "Hearing" means listening with spiritual understanding and receptivity. "So then faith comes by hearing, and hearing by the Word of God" (Rom. 10:17). With this in mind, we can understand the three admonitions Jesus gave His followers.

Hear and receive the Word (vv. 4-15). Initially, the Sower is Jesus Christ, but the sower represents any of God's people who share the Word of God (John 4:35-38). The seed is the Word of God, for, like seed, the Word has life and power (Heb. 4:12) and can produce spiritual fruit (Gal. 5:22-23). But the seed can do nothing until it is planted (John 12:24). When a person hears and understands the Word, then the seed is planted in the heart. What happens after that depends on the nature of the soil.

Jesus called this parable "The Parable of the Sower" (Matt. 13:18), but it could also be called "The Parable of the Soils." The seed without the soil is fruitless, and the soil without the seed is almost useless. The human heart is like soil: if it is prepared properly, it can receive the seed of the Word of God and produce a fruitful harvest.

Jesus described four different kinds of hearts, three of which did not produce any fruit. The proof of salvation is *fruit* and not merely hearing the Word or making a profession of faith in Christ. Jesus had already made that clear in His "Sermon on the Mount" (Luke 6:43-49; also note Matt. 7:20).

The hard soil (vv. 5, 12). This soil represents the person who hears the Word but immediately allows the devil to snatch the seed away. How did the heart become hard? The "wayside" was the path that ran through the common field, separating the plots; and the foot traffic hardened the soil. Whatever goes into the ear or eye finally enters the heart, so be careful who is allowed to "walk on your heart."

The shallow soil (vv. 6, 13). This soil illustrates the emotional hearer who quickly responds to the message, but his interest wanes and he does not continue (see John 8:31-32). In many parts of the Holy Land you find a substratum of limestone covered with a thin layer of soil. The shoot can grow up, but the roots cannot go down, and the sun withers the rootless plant. The sun represents the testing that comes to all professing believers to prove their faith. Sun is good for plants *if they have roots.* Persecution can deepen the roots of a true Christian, but it only exposes the shallowness of the false Christian.

The crowded soil (vv. 7, 14). This soil illustrates the person who does not repent and "weed out" the things that hinder the harvest. There is enough soil so the roots can go down, but not enough room for the plant to grow up and produce fruit. The plant is crowded out and the fruit is choked. "Cares, riches, and the pleasures of this life" are like weeds in a garden that keep the soil from being fruitful. The person with the "crowded heart" comes closest to salvation, but he still does not bring forth "fruit to perfection."

The good soil (vv. 8, 15). This soil alone is fruitful. It illustrates the individual who hears the Word, understands it, receives it within, is truly saved, and proves it by patiently producing fruit (see 1 Thes. 2:13; 1 Peter 1:22-25). Not everybody produces the same amount of fruit (Matt. 13:8), but all true believers will produce some fruit as evidence of spiritual life. That fruit may include winning others to Christ (Rom. 1:13), money given to God's work (Rom. 15:25-28), good works (Col. 1:10), Christian character (Gal. 5:22-23), and praise to the Lord (Heb. 13:15).

This parable shows that Jesus was not impressed by the great crowds that followed Him. He knew that most of the people did not really "hear" the Word and receive it in their hearts. He gave this story to encourage the disciples in their future ministry, and to encourage us today. When you consider how much teaching, preaching, and witnessing goes on in the course of a month or a year, you wonder why there is such a small harvest. The fault does not lie with the sower or the seed. The problem is with the soil. The human heart will not submit to God, repent and receive the Word, and be saved.

"Faith comes first to the hearing ear, not to the cogitating mind," said A.W. Tozer, the much-quoted pastor and author. Faith is not a matter of IQ or education; it is a matter of humbly preparing the heart to receive God's truth (James 1:19-21). The wise and prudent are blind to truths that are easy for the babes to understand (Matt. 11:20-26).

Hear and share the Word (vv. 16-18). The disciples were perplexed because Jesus taught in parables, so they asked Him for an explanation (Luke 8:9-10; also see Matt. 13:10-17). His reply seems to suggest that He used parables in order to *hide* the truth from the crowds, but just the opposite is true, and Luke 8:16-18 makes that clear. His teaching is a light that must be allowed to shine so that sinners may be saved.

The word *parable* means "to cast alongside." A parable is a story that teaches something new by putting the truth alongside something familiar. The people knew about seeds and soil, so the Parable of the Sower interested them. Those who were indifferent or proud would shrug it off. Our Lord's parables aroused the interest of the concerned.

A parable starts off as a *picture* that is familiar to the listeners. But as you carefully consider the picture, it becomes a *mirror* in which you see yourself, and many people do not like to see themselves. This explains why some of our Lord's listeners became angry when they heard His parables, and even tried to kill Him. But if we see ourselves as needy sinners and ask for help, then the mirror becomes a *window* through which we see God and His grace. To understand a parable and benefit from it demands honesty and humility on our part, and many of our Lord's hearers lacked both.

It is a serious thing to hear and understand the Word of God, because this puts on us the obligation to share that Word with others. Everyone who receives the seed then becomes a sower, a light-bearer, and a transmitter of God's truth (see 1 Thes. 1:5-8). If we keep it to ourselves, we will lose it; but if we share it, we will receive more.

Hear and obey the Word (vv. 19-21). Our Lord's mother, Mary, and His half brothers (Matt. 13:55-56; Acts 1:14) were worried about Jesus and wanted to talk with Him. Some of His friends had already said that He was out of His mind (Mark 3:21), and perhaps His family agreed with them. Jesus took this as an opportunity to teach another spiritual lesson: being a part of His spiritual family is much more important than any human relationship and is based on obedience to the Word of God. It is not enough to "hear" the Word of God; we must also "keep it" (Luke 8:15).

In one of my radio series, I emphasized the importance of *doing* the Word of God, putting it into practice in daily life (James 1:22-25). I warned listeners that it is easy to think we are "spiritual" because we listen to one preacher after another, take notes, mark our Bibles, *but never really practice what we learn.* We are only fooling ourselves.

A listener wrote that my words had made her angry, but then she faced up to the fact that she was indeed guilty of being an "auditor" and not a doer of the Word. She began to listen to fewer radio preachers, to listen more carefully, and to practice what she heard. "This new approach to Bible study has transformed me!" she wrote. "The Bible has become a new Book to me and my life has changed!"

As His disciples, we must take heed *what we hear* (Mark 4:24) and *how we hear* (Luke 8:18), because God will hold us accountable. Listening to the wrong things, or listening to the right things with the wrong attitude, will rob us of truth and blessing. If we are faithful to receive the Word and share it, God will give us more; but if we fail to let our light shine, we will lose what we have. It is a solemn thing to hear the Word of God.

Testing: Heeding God's Word (Luke 8:22-56)

By the time the Lord had finished giving "the Parables of the Kingdom" (Matt. 13:1-52), the disciples must have felt like postgraduate students in the School of Faith! They now understood mysteries that were hidden from the scribes and rabbis and even from the Old Testament prophets. What they did not realize (and we are so like them!) is that *faith must be tested before it can be trusted.* It is one thing to learn a new spiritual truth, but quite something else to practice that truth in the everyday experiences of life.

Satan does not care how much Bible truth we learn so long as we do not live it. Truth that is only in the head is purely academic and never will get into the heart until it is practiced by the will. "Doing the will of God from the heart" is what God wants from His children (Eph. 6:6). Satan knows that academic truth is not dangerous, but *active* truth is.

Watch the Lord Jesus Christ as He meets four challenges to faith and comes forth the Victor. His people face these same challenges today and can also overcome by faith.

Dangerous circumstances (vv. 22-25). Jesus was weary from a long day of teaching and went to sleep as the ship left Capernaum for the opposite shore. But before He did, He gave them a word of command that was also a word of promise: they were going to the opposite shore. This word should have encouraged and strengthened the disciples during the storm, but their faith was still small (Matt. 8:26).

While our tour group was sailing from Tiberias to Capernaum, I asked our guide if he had even been in a storm on the Sea of Galilee. His eyes opened wide and he said, "Yes, and I hope it never happens to me again!" The situation is such that sudden squalls occur as winds from the mountains funnel to the lake located 600 feet below sea level. When the cold air and warm air meet in this natural basin, a storm is sure to develop.

The disciples were afraid, *but Jesus was not!* He kept on sleeping, confident that His Father was completely in control (Ps. 89:8-9). The disciples became so frightened that they awakened Him and begged Him to rescue them. The title *Master* is the same one Peter used in Luke 5:5. Of course, their problem was not the storm around them but the unbelief within them. Actually, their unbelief was more dangerous than the storm!

The word *rebuked* was used by Jesus when dealing with demons (Luke 4:35, 41; 9:42). It is possible that Satan was behind this severe storm, attempting to destroy Jesus or at least hinder Him from reaching the demonized men at Gadara. But Jesus calmed both the wind and the sea by simply speaking the word. Usually after the winds die down, the waves remain rough for hours; but in this instance, everything became calm immediately and stayed that way (Ps. 148:8).

The disciples failed this test of faith because they did not lay hold of His word that He was going to the other side. It has well been said that faith is not believing in spite of circumstances; it is obeying in spite of feelings and consequences. The disciples looked around and saw danger, and looked within and saw fear; but they failed to look up by faith and see God. Faith and fear cannot dwell together in the same heart.

A woman said to D.L. Moody, "I have found a wonderful promise!" and she quoted Psalm 56:3, "What time I am afraid, I will trust in Thee."

"Let me give you a better one," said Moody; and he quoted Isaiah 12:2, "Behold God is my salvation; I will trust and not be afraid."

Satan (vv. 26-39). Two demonized men met Jesus when He landed at Gadara (Matt. 8:28), but one of them was the more forward and did all the speaking. Both were pitiful cases: naked, living in the tombs, violent, dangerous, a menace to the area, and controlled by a legion of demons. (A Roman legion could have as many as 6,000 men!) Satan is the thief (John 10:10) who robs his people of everything good and then tries to destroy them. No amount of man-made authority or restraint can control or change the devil's servants. Their only hope is in the Saviour.

Demons have faith (James 2:19), but it is not saving faith. They believe that Jesus Christ is the Son of God with authority to command them. They believe in a future judgment (Matt. 8:29) and in the existence of a place of torment to which Jesus could send them ("the abyss," Luke 8:31). They also believe in prayer, for the demons begged Jesus not to send them to the abyss. They asked to be sent into the pigs, and Jesus granted their request.

Did Jesus have the right to permit the legion of demons to destroy a herd of 2,000 swine and perhaps put the owners out of business? God owns everything (see Ps. 50:10-11) and can dispose of it as He pleases. Furthermore, these two men were worth far more than many pigs (see Matt. 12:12). The community should have thanked Jesus for ridding their neighborhood of these two menaces, but instead, *they begged Him to leave!*

What a transformation in these two men! You would have expected the people who saw the miracle to ask Jesus to stay and heal others who were sick and afflicted. Apparently money was more important to them than mercy, and they asked Jesus to leave.

The one former demoniac kept pleading with Jesus to be allowed to travel with Him and help Him. What a noble desire from a newly converted man! He had more spiritual discernment than all the other citizens put together. The man was not yet ready to become a disciple, but he could serve Jesus as a witness, starting at home among his Gentile relatives and friends. Jesus did not want Jews who had been healed to say too much about it, but it was safe for the Gentiles to tell others what Jesus had done for them, and that is what he did.

Sickness (vv. 40-48). When Jesus returned to Capernaum, the people welcomed Him, particularly a man and a woman who each had heavy burdens to share with Jesus. The contrast here is interesting, for it shows the variety of people who came to Jesus for help. The man's name is given (Jairus) but the woman is anonymous. Jairus was a wealthy leading citizen, but the woman was a lowly person who had spent all her money trying to get well. Here was a man interceding for his child and a woman hoping to get help for herself, and both came to the feet of Jesus. Jairus had been blessed with twelve years of joy with his daughter, and now might lose her, while the woman had experienced twelve years of misery because of her affliction, and now she was hoping to get well.

This woman had a hidden need, a burden she had lived with for twelve long years. It affected her physically and made life difficult. But it also affected her spiritually, because the hemorrhage made her ceremonially defiled and unable to participate in the religious life of the nation (Lev. 15:19-22). She was defiled, destitute, discouraged, and desperate; but she came to Jesus and her need was met.

Her faith was almost superstitious, but the Lord honored it. She knew that He had healed others and she wanted Him to heal her. She could have used many excuses—the crowd was pressing around Him; nothing had worked for twelve years; it was not right to come to Jesus as a last resort; she was not an important person; He was on His way to heal Jairus' daughter—but she allowed nothing to stand in her way.

Jewish men wore tassels of blue twisted cords on the corners of their outer garments, as a reminder that they were to obey God's commandments (Num. 15:37-40; Deut. 22:12). The Pharisees went to extremes in obeying this rule to impress people with their sanctity (Matt. 23:5). Why the woman chose to touch this part of His garment, we do not know, but Jesus knew somebody with faith had touched Him and had been healed by His power. The healing was immediate and complete.

Why did the Lord ask her to give witness publicly? Was this not an embarrassment to her? Not in the least. To begin with, this public confession was for her sake. It was an opportunity for her to confess Christ and glorify God. Had she stolen away in the crowd, she would not have met Jesus personally or heard His words of assurance and comfort (Luke 8:48).

But her confession was also an encouragement to Jairus, who would soon hear that his daughter had died. (Perhaps he wanted to blame the woman for the delay!) The woman's twelve years of trial were ended, and the same Christ who helped her would help Jairus. She was a testimony to the power of faith. True, she did not exercise "great faith," but Christ honored it and healed her body.

Finally, her witness was a rebuke to the multitude. You can be a part of the crowd and never get any blessing from being near Jesus! It is one thing to "press Him" and another thing to "touch Him" by faith. We may not have strong faith, but we do have a strong Saviour, and He responds even to a touch at the hem of His garment.

When the inventor of chloroform, Sir James Simpson, was dying, a friend said to him, "You will soon be resting on His bosom." Simpson humbly replied, "I don't know as I can do that, but I think I have hold of the hem of His garment."

Death (vv. 49-56). The ruler of a synagogue was the elder in charge of the public services and the care of the facilities. He saw to it that people were appointed to pray, read the Scriptures, and give the sermon. He presided over the elders of the synagogue and was usually a man of reputation and wealth. It took a great deal of humility and courage for Jairus to approach Jesus and ask His help, for by this time the Jewish religious leaders were plotting to kill Him.

When Jairus left home, his daughter was so sick she was ready to die. By the time Jesus got away from the crowd to go with him, the girl had died. Jairus' friends thought that Jesus could help only living people, so they advised Jairus to drop the matter and come home. But Jesus encouraged the distraught father with a word of hope.

The scene at the home would have discouraged anybody! The professional mourners were already there, weeping and wailing; and a crowd of friends and neighbors had gathered. Jewish people in that day lost no time or energy in showing and sharing their grief. The body of the deceased would be buried that same day, after being washed and anointed.

Jesus took command of the situation and told the crowd to stop weeping because the girl was not dead but asleep. Of course she was dead, for her spirit had left her body (compare Luke 8:55 with James 2:26); but to Jesus, death was only sleep. This image is often used in the New Testament to describe the death of believers (John 11:11-14; Acts 7:59-60; 1 Cor. 15:51; 1 Thes. 4:13-18). Sleep is a normal experience that we do not fear, and we should not fear death. It is the body that sleeps, not the spirit, for the spirit of the believer goes to be with Christ (Phil. 1:20-24; 2 Cor. 5:6-8). At the resurrection, the body will be "awakened" and glorified, and God's people will share the image of Christ (1 John 3:1-2).

The mourners laughed at Jesus because they knew the girl was dead and that death was final. But they failed to realize that Jesus is "the resurrection and the life" (John 11:25-26). Had He not raised the widow's son from the dead? Did He not tell John the Baptist that the dead were being raised? (Luke 7:22) Apparently the mourners did not believe these reports and thought Jesus was a fool.

So He put them all out! This situation was much too tender and special for Him to allow dozens of unbelieving spectators to watch. He took the parents and three of His disciples, Peter, James, and John; and together they entered the room where the little girl lay dead.

He took her by the hand and spoke in Aramaic, "Talitha cumi! Little girl, arise!" (Peter would one day say "Tabitha cumi!"—Acts 9:40.) This was not a magic formula but a word of command from the Lord of life and death (Rev. 1:17-18). Her spirit returned to her body and she arose and began to walk around the room! Jesus told them to give her something to eat, for it is likely that during her illness she had eaten little or nothing. Jesus also instructed them not to spread the news, but still the word got around (Matt. 9:26).

Resurrection is a picture of the way Jesus Christ saves lost sinners and raises them from spiritual death (John 5:24; Eph. 2:1-10). The Gospels record three such resurrections, though Jesus probably performed more. In each instance, the person raised gave evidence of life. The widow's son began to speak (Luke 7:15), Jairus' daughter walked and ate food, and Lazarus was loosed from the graveclothes (John 11:44). When a lost sinner is raised from the dead, you can tell it by his speech, his walk, his appetite, and his "change of clothes" (Col. 3:1ff). You cannot hide life!

Peter, James, and John accompanied Jesus on three special occasions; and this was the first. The second was on the Mount of Transfiguration (Luke 9:28ff), and the third was in the Garden of Gethsemane (Mark 14:33ff). Campbell Morgan has pointed out that each of these events has something to do with death and that the three disciples learned from these experiences some valuable lessons about Jesus and death.

In the home of Jairus, they learned that Jesus is victorious over death. On the Mount of Transfiguration, they discovered that He would be glorified in His death; and in the Garden, they saw that He was surrendered to death. James was the first of the Twelve to die (Acts 12:1-2), John the last to die, and Peter's death was predicted by Jesus (John 21:18-19; 2 Peter 1:13-21). All three men needed these lessons, and we need them today.

CHAPTER EIGHT A MANY-SIDED MINISTRY

Luke 9

It was an exasperating evening. I was studying and writing, and the phone was ringing every half hour. Had the calls been from friends, I would have enjoyed taking a break and chatting, but they came from people wanting to sell me everything from dance tickets to investments. By the time I got to bed that night, I had just about decided to get an unlisted number and start protecting my privacy.

At 11 o'clock, a man phoned who was contemplating committing suicide; and with the Lord's help, I was able to encourage him to get a new grip on life. When I hung up, I gave thanks that I did not have an unlisted number. As I lay down to go back to sleep, I thought of the Lord Jesus and the kind of schedule He must have had. He was available to all kinds of people at all times, and He did not turn anyone away. He probably would not have had an unlisted number.

In this chapter, Dr. Luke described the busy life of the compassionate Son of man as He performed four ministries.

Sending (Luke 9:1-11)

The commission (vv. 1-6). The Twelve had been ordained some months before (Luke 6:13-16) and had been traveling with Jesus as

His helpers. Now He was going to send them out in pairs (Mark 6:7) to have their own ministry and to put into practice what they had learned. This was their "solo flight."

But before He sent them out, He gave them the equipment needed to get the job done, as well as the instructions to follow. The parallel passage in Matthew 10 reveals that the Twelve were sent only to the people of Israel (Matt. 10:5-6). Luke does not mention this since he wrote primarily for the Gentiles and emphasized the worldwide outreach of the Gospel.

Power is the ability to accomplish a task, and *authority* is the right to do it, and Jesus gave both to His Apostles. They were able to cast out demons and heal the sick, but the most important ministry He gave them was that of preaching the Gospel. The word *preach* in Luke 9:6 describes a herald proclaiming a message from the king, and in Luke 9:6 it means "to preach the Good News." They were heralds of the Good News!

The Apostles' ability to heal was a special gift that authenticated their ministry (see Rom. 15:18-19; 2 Cor. 12:12; Heb. 2:1-4). Miracles were one evidence that the Lord had sent them and was working through them (Mark 16:20). Today we test a person's ministry by the truth of the Word of God (1 John 2:18-29; 4:1-6). Miracles alone are not proof that a person is truly sent of God, for Satan can enable his false ministers to do amazing things (Matt. 24:24; 2 Cor. 11:13-15; 2 Thes. 2:9-10).

Jesus told the Apostles what to take on their journey, with an emphasis on urgency and simplicity. They were not to take a "begging bag" along but were to trust God to open up homes for their hospitality. Matthew 10:11-15 tells how they were to select these homes. If they were refused, they should shake off the dust from their feet, a familiar act performed by orthodox Jews whenever they left Gentile territory (see Luke 10:10-11; Acts 13:51).

The confusion (vv. 7-9). When the disciples left, Jesus also departed and ministered for a time in Galilee (Matt. 11:1); and together they attracted a great deal of attention. In fact, their work was even discussed in the highest levels of government! Herod Antipas (Luke 3:1) was a son of Herod the Great and the man who had John the Baptist killed (Matt. 14:1-12; Luke 3:19-20).

Who was this miracle worker? John the Baptist had done no miracles (John 10:41), but that might change if he were raised from the dead. The Jews expected Elijah to come, so perhaps the prophecy was being fulfilled (see Mal. 4:5; Matt. 11:10-14; 17:11-13; Luke 1:17). Herod's conscience was no doubt convicting him, and he was wondering if perhaps God had sent John back to judge him.

Herod kept trying to see Jesus; but Jesus, unlike some modern "religious celebrities," did not make it a point to go out of His way to mingle with the high and mighty. Jesus called the evil king a "fox" and was not intimidated by his threats (Luke 13:31-32). When Herod and Jesus did finally meet, the king hoped to see a miracle, but the Son of God did nothing and said nothing to him. Evil King Herod had silenced God's voice to him (Luke 23:6-12).

The conclusion (vv. 10-11). The Apostles returned and gave a glowing report of their ministry, and Jesus suggested that they all take some time off for rest (Mark 6:30-32). As the popular speaker Vance Havner used to say, "If we don't come apart and rest, we'll just come apart." Their mission of preaching and healing had been demanding and they all needed time alone for physical and spiritual renewal. This is a good example for busy (and sometimes overworked) Christian workers to imitate.

Attracted by the signs Jesus was doing, the crowds would not leave Him alone, but followed Him from the cities. When Jesus and the Twelve landed, the crowd was already there to meet them, and Jesus had compassion on them and ministered to them (Matt. 14:13-14). The Son of man could not even take a day off!

Feeding (Luke 9:12-17)

Our Lord was not the kind of person who could teach the Word and then say to hungry people, "Depart in peace, be ye warm and filled" (James 2:16). The disciples were only too eager to see the crowd leave (Luke 18:15; see Matt. 15:23). They had not yet caught the compassion of Christ and the burden He had for the multitudes, but one day they would.

When you combine all four accounts of this miracle, you find that Jesus first asked Philip where they could buy enough bread to feed such a great crowd. (There could well have been 10,000 people there.) He was only testing Philip, "for He Himself knew what He was intending to do" (John 6:6, NASB). In the crisis hours of life, when your resources are low and your responsibilities are great, it is good to remember that God already has the problem solved.

Jesus started with what they had, a few loaves and fishes that were generously donated by a lad found by Andrew (John 6:8-9). Did Andrew know the boy? Or did the boy offer his little lunch without being asked? Before we ask God to do the impossible, let's start with the possible and give Him what we have. And while we are at it, let's give thanks for mothers who give their sons something to give to Jesus.

The Lord looked up to heaven, the source of our daily bread (Matt. 6:11), gave thanks, and blessed the food; and then He multiplied the few loaves and fishes. Jesus was the "producer" and His disciples were the "distributors." The amazing thing is that *everybody* was served and satisfied, and there were twelve baskets of leftovers, one for each of the disciples. Jesus takes good care of His servants.

This miracle was more than an act of mercy for hungry people, though that was important. It was also a sign of our Lord's messiahship and an illustration of God's gracious provision for man's salvation. The next day, Jesus preached a sermon on "the bread of life" and urged the people to receive Him just as they had received the bread (John 6:22-59). But the people were more interested in their stomachs than their souls, and completely missed the spiritual impact of the miracle. Their desire was to make Jesus King so He could give them bread for the rest of their lives! (John 6:14-15)

After Jesus returned to heaven, the disciples must often have been encouraged by remembering this miracle. It teaches us to have compassion, to look on problems as opportunities for God to work, and to give Him all that we have and trust Him to meet the needs. If we do all we can, He will step in and do the rest. "Let God's promises shine on your problems," said Corrie Ten Boom, and that is good counsel for us.

Teaching (Luke 9:18-36)

In Luke's Gospel, the feeding of the 5,000 marks the end of what is called the "Great Galilean Ministry" (Luke 4:14–9:17). Jesus now begins His journey to Jerusalem (see Luke 9:51; 13:22; 17:11; 18:31; and 19:11, 28). This would be a time of relative retirement with His disciples as He prepared them for what lay ahead. There is a parallel between this account and the account in Acts of Paul's last journey to Jerusalem. In both books we have "a tale of two cities": in Luke, from Nazareth to Jerusalem; and in Acts, from Jerusalem to Rome.

In this section, you see Jesus teaching them three basic lessons about His person, His sacrifice, and His kingdom.

His person (vv. 18-21). If any of us asked our friends what people were saying about us, it would be an evidence of pride, but not so with Jesus Christ. People had better know who He is, because what we think about Jesus determines our eternal destiny (John 8:24; 1 John 4:1-3). It is impossible to be wrong about Jesus and right with God.

Jesus had prayed all night before choosing His disciples (Luke 6:12-13), and now He prayed before asking for their personal confession of faith. The crowd would have its opinions (see Luke 9:7-8), but His disciples must have convictions. Peter was the spokesman for the group and gave a clear witness to the deity of Jesus Christ. This was the second time that he confessed Christ publicly (John 6:68-69). Except for Judas (John 6:70-71), all of the Twelve had faith in Jesus Christ.

Jesus commanded them (the word means "an order from a military officer") not to spread this truth openly. To begin with, the message of His messiahship could not be divorced from the fact of His death and resurrection, and He was now going to teach this to the Twelve. They had a difficult time grasping this new lesson and did not really understand it until after He was raised from the dead (Luke 24:44-48). The Jewish people saw Jesus primarily as a healer and a potential deliverer. If the Apostles began preaching that He was indeed the Messiah, it might cause a popular uprising against Rome.

His sacrifice (vv. 22-26). Jesus had already given a number of "hints" about His sacrificial death, but now He began to teach this truth clearly to His disciples. John the Baptist had presented Him as the "Lamb of God" (John 1:29), and Jesus had predicted the "destruction" of the temple of His body (John 2:19). When He compared Himself to the serpent in the wilderness (John 3:14) and to Jonah (Matt. 12:38-40), Jesus was making statements about His suffering and death.

This is the first of three statements in Luke about His coming passion in Jerusalem (Luke 9:43-45; 18:31-34). It is clear that the Twelve did not understand, partly because of their unbelief and immaturity, and partly because it was "hidden" from them by God. Jesus taught them as they were able to receive the truth (John 16:12). It must have shocked the men to hear that their own religious leaders would kill their Master.

But Jesus did not stop with a private announcement of His own death. He also made a public declaration about a cross for *every* disciple. In his Gospel, Matthew tells us that this was necessary because of Peter's desire to protect Jesus from suffering (Matt. 16:22ff). Keep in mind that Jesus is talking about *discipleship* and not *sonship*. We are not saved from our sins because we take up a cross and follow Jesus, but because we trust the Saviour who died on the cross for our sins. After we become children of God, then we become disciples.

The closest contemporary word to "disciple" is probably "apprentice." A disciple is more than a student who learns lessons by means of lectures and books. He is one who learns by living and working with his teacher in a daily "hands on" experience. Too many Christians are content to be listeners who gain a lot of knowledge but who have never put that knowledge into practice.

In the Roman world, the cross was a symbol of shame, guilt, suffering, and rejection. There could be no more despicable way to die. Crucifixion was not mentioned in polite conversation, and the people would no more think of wearing crosses on their person than we would think of wearing gold or silver electric chairs. Jesus laid down the stern requirements for discipleship. We must first say no to ourselves—not simply to pleasures or possessions, but to *self*—and then take up *our* cross and follow Christ daily. This means to be identified with Him in surrender, suffering, and sacrifice. You cannot crucify yourself; you can only yield your body (Rom. 12:1-2) and let God do the rest.

Of course, this kind of life seems foolish to the world; but to the Christian, it is wisdom. To save your life is to lose it, and how can you ever get it back again? But to give your life to Christ is to save it and to live it in fullness. If a person owned the whole world, he would still be too poor to buy back a lost life.

Discipleship is a daily discipline: we follow Jesus a step at a time, a day at a time. A weary cleaning woman said to a friend of mine, "The trouble with life is that it's so daily!" But she was wrong. One of the *best* things about life is that we can take it a day at a time (Deut. 33:25).

Our motive should be to glorify Christ. Anyone who is ashamed of Christ will never take up a cross and follow Him. But if we are ashamed of Him now, He will be ashamed of us when He comes again (Mark 8:38; 2 Tim. 2:11-13) and we will be ashamed before Him (1 John 2:28).

His kingdom (vv. 27-36). As far as the Gospel record is concerned, the Transfiguration was the only occasion during Christ's earthly ministry when He revealed the glory of His person. Luke did not use the word *transfigure* but he described the same scene (Matt. 17:2; Mark 9:2). The word means "a change in appearance that comes from within," and it gives us the English word *metamorphosis.*

What were the reasons behind this event? For one thing, it was God's seal of approval to Peter's confession of faith that Jesus is the Son of God (John 1:14). It was also the Father's way of encouraging the Son as He began to make His way to Jerusalem. The Father had spoken at the baptism (Luke 3:22) and would speak again during that final week of the Son's earthly ministry (John 12:23-28). Beyond the suffering of the cross would be the glory of the throne, a lesson that Peter emphasized in his first epistle (1 Peter 4:12–5:4).

Our Lord's own words in Luke 9:27 indicate that the event was a demonstration (or illustration) of the promised kingdom of God. This seems logical, for the disciples were confused about the kingdom because of Jesus' words about the cross. (We must not be too hard on them because the prophets were also confused—1 Peter 1:10-12.) Jesus was reassuring them that the Old Testament prophecies would be fulfilled, but first He had to suffer before He could enter into His glory (note especially 2 Peter 1:12-21).

But there is also a practical lesson here, for we can have a spiritual "transfiguration" experience each day as we walk with the Lord. Romans 12:1-2 and 2 Corinthians 3:18 tell us how. As we surrender body, mind, and will, the Lord transforms us from within so that we are not conformed to the world. As we behold Him in the Word (the mirror), we are "transfigured" by the Spirit "from glory to glory." The theological name for this experience is *sanctification,* the process by which we become more like the Lord Jesus Christ, which is the Father's goal for each of His children (Rom. 8:19; 1 John 3:2). Note that our Lord was once again praying, which suggests that prayer is one of the keys to a transformed life.

Peter, James, and John had accompanied Jesus when He raised Jairus' daughter from the dead (Luke 8:51ff), and they would accompany Him when He prayed in the Garden (Matt. 26:36-46). These three occasions remind me of Philippians 3:10, "That I may know Him [the Transfiguration], and the power of His resurrection [raising the girl], and the fellowship of His sufferings [in the Garden]."

This may well have been the greatest "Bible conference" ever held on earth! Even apart from the great glory that was involved, here you certainly had the greatest speakers: Moses, the Law; Elijah, the Prophets; and Jesus, who came to fulfill the Law and the Prophets. You had the greatest topic: Jesus' "decease" (the Greek is *exodus*) that He would accomplish at Jerusalem. Moses had led Israel out of bondage to Egypt, and Elijah had delivered them from bondage to false gods; but Jesus would die to set *a sinful world* free from bondage to sin and death (Gal. 1:4; Col. 1:13; Heb. 2:14-15).

And while all of this was going on, the three privileged disciples were sleeping! (They would repeat this failure in the Garden.) Peter's suggestion reminds us of the Jewish "Feast of Booths" that in the Bible is related to the future kingdom (Lev. 23:33-44; Zech. 14:16-21). Peter wanted Jesus to hold on to the glory *apart from the suffering*, but this is not God's plan.

The Father interrupted Peter by bathing the scene in a cloud of glory (Ex. 13:21-22; 40:35, 38) and speaking out of the cloud. (Peter would one day be interrupted by the Son [Matt. 17:24-27] and by the Spirit [Acts 10:44].) These arresting words from heaven remind us of Deuteronomy 18:15; Psalm 2:7; and Isaiah 42:1. When the cloud was gone, Elijah and Moses were also gone.

As wonderful as these experiences are, they are not the basis for a consistent Christian life. That can come only through the Word of God. Experiences come and go, but the Word remains. Our recollection of past experiences will fade, but God's Word never changes. The farther we get from these events, the less impact they make on our lives. That was why the Father said, "Hear Him!" and why Peter made this same emphasis on the Word in his report (2 Peter 1:12-21). Our own personal "transfiguration" comes from inner renewal (Rom. 12:1-2), and that comes from the Word (2 Cor. 3:18).

Enduring (Luke 9:37-62)

"How long shall I stay with you and put up with you?" (Luke 9:41, NIV) You might expect that lament to come from an overworked kindergarten teacher, or an impatient army drill instructor, but it was made by the sinless Son of God! We are prone to forget how long-suffering our Lord had to be while He was ministering on earth, especially with His own disciples.

When you analyze this section of Luke's Gospel, you can better understand why Jesus spoke those words: *He was grieved over the failures of His followers.* He had given His Apostles authority over Satan, yet they were too weak to cast out a demon (Luke 9:37-45). In feeding the 5,000, Jesus gave them an example of compassion, yet they persisted in manifesting selfishness and lack of love (Luke 9:46-56). He taught clearly what it meant to follow Him, yet the volunteers turned out to be "me first" disciples (Luke 9:57-62). No wonder He was grieved!

Lack of power (vv. 37-45). We dare not stay on the glorious mountaintop when there are battles to fight in the valley below. Here was another "only child" needing the help of the Lord (Luke 7:12; 8:42), and even more so because His own disciples had failed. They had the power and the authority (Luke 9:1) but they did not have the success. Why?

When you study all three reports (Matt. 17; Mark 9), you discover what was lacking in their lives. First on the list was *faith* (Matt. 17:19-20); they were part of an unbelieving generation and had lost the confidence that they needed in order to use their power. But *prayer* and *fasting* were also lacking (Mark 9:29), which indicates that the nine men had allowed their devotional disciplines to erode during their Lord's brief absence. No matter what spiritual gifts we may have, their exercise is never automatic.

The devil tried one last throw (a wrestling term in the Greek), but Jesus rebuked the demon and cast him out. The Lord lovingly gave the boy back to his father (see Luke 7:15) and then took the Twelve aside for another lesson about the cross. After all, it was at the cross that Jesus would give Satan that final blow of defeat (John 12:31-32; Col. 2:15).

Lack of love (vv. 46-56). The disciples did not have much love for each other, or they would not have argued over who was the greatest (Luke 9:46-48). Perhaps this debate started because of envy (three of the disciples had been with Jesus on the mount), or because of pride (the other nine had failed to cast out the demon). Also, just before this, Jesus had paid Peter's temple tax for him (Matt. 17:24-27); and this may have aroused some envy.

In His kingdom, the example of greatness is a little child—helpless, dependent, without status, living by faith. The only thing worse than a child trying to act like an adult is an adult acting like a child! There is a great difference between being childlike and childish! (see 1 Cor. 13:4-5; 14:20)

They also showed a lack of love for believers outside their own group (Luke 9:49-50). This is what we would expect from a "son of thunder"! (Mark 3:17) Perhaps John was trying to impress Jesus with his zeal for protecting His name, but the Lord was not impressed. Believers who think that their group is the only group God recognizes and blesses are in for a shock when they get to heaven.

Nor did the Apostles love their enemies (Luke 9:51-56). James and John had seen the Prophet Elijah on the mount, so they thought they might imitate him and call down fire from heaven! (2 Kings 1) The Samaritans and Jews had been enemies for centuries (2 Kings 17:24-41), so it was understandable that this village would reject Jesus as He traveled toward Jerusalem (John 4:9, 20). Jesus rebuked their vengeful spirit and simply went to another village (Matt. 5:37-48). Later, Samaria would be reached with the Gospel (Acts 8).

Lack of discipline (vv. 57-62). Three men could have become disciples, but they would not meet the conditions that Jesus laid down. The first man was a scribe (Matt. 8:19) who volunteered to go until he heard the cost: he had to deny himself. Apparently he was accustomed to a comfortable home.

The second man was called by Jesus (what an honor!), but he was rejected because he would not take up the cross and die to self. He was worried about somebody else's funeral when he should have been planning his own! Jesus is not suggesting here that we dishonor our parents, but only that we not permit our love for family to weaken our love for the Lord. We should love Christ so much that our love for family would look like hatred in comparison (Luke 14:26).

The third man also volunteered, but he could not follow Christ because he was looking back instead of ahead. There is nothing wrong with a loving farewell (1 Kings 19:19-21), but if it gets in the way of obedience, it becomes sin. Jesus saw that this man's heart was not wholly with Him, but that he would be plowing and looking back (see Gen. 19:17, 26; Phil. 3:13-14).

No wonder the laborers are few! (Luke 10:2)

It would appear that what Jesus taught His disciples and the multitudes had done them little good. They lacked power, love, and discipline, and they grieved His heart. If we today lack these spiritual essentials, we can never truly be His disciples, but they are available to us from the Lord. "For God did not give us a spirit of timidity, but of power, of love and of self-discipline" (2 Tim. 1:7, NIV).

Are we a joy to Jesus Christ, or are we breaking His heart?

CHAPTER NINE
WHAT IN THE WORLD DOES A CHRISTIAN DO?
Luke 10

The three scenes in Luke 10 illustrate the threefold ministry of every Christian believer, and they answer the question, "What in the world does a Christian do?"

To begin with, we are the Lord's *ambassadors,* sent to represent Him in this world (Luke 10:1-24). We are also *neighbors,* looking for opportunities to show mercy in the name of Christ (Luke 10:25-37). But at the heart of all our ministry is devotion to Christ, so we must be *worshipers* who take time to listen to His Word and commune with Him (Luke 10:38-42).

Whether we are in the harvest field, on the highway, or in the home, our highest privilege and our greatest joy is to do the will of God.

Ambassadors: Representing the Lord (Luke 10:1-24)

This event should not be confused with the sending out of the Twelve (Matt. 10; Luke 9:1-11). There are similarities in the charges given, but this is to be expected since both groups were sent by the same Master to do the same basic job. The 12 Apostles ministered throughout Galilee, but these men were sent into Judea, and the men in this chapter are not called Apostles. They were anonymous disciples.

Why is this event recorded only by Luke, and why did Jesus select seventy men instead of some other number? (Some texts say seventy-two, and the textual evidence is about even.) Just as the Twelve were associated in number with the twelve sons of Jacob and the twelve tribes of Israel, so the Seventy may be associated with the seventy nations listed in Genesis 10. Luke's emphasis is on the universality of the Gospel message, so it seems reasonable that he would be led by the Holy Spirit to include this event. It was a symbolic way of saying, "Jesus wants the message spread to all nations."

Explanation (vv. 1-12). These men were not called "apostles," but they were still "sent *[apostello]* with a commission" to represent the Lord. They were therefore truly ambassadors of the King. Not only were they sent *by* Him, but they were also sent *before* Him to prepare the way for His coming. Their calling was certainly a dignified one.

It was also a difficult calling (Luke 10:2). Harvesting is hard work, even when there are many people helping you, but these men were sent into a vast field with very few workers to help them reap a great harvest. Instead of praying for an easier job, they were to pray for more laborers to join them, and we today need to pray that same prayer. (Please note that it is *laborers,* not spectators, who pray for more laborers! Too many Christians are praying for somebody else to do a job they are unwilling to do themselves.)

Their calling was a dangerous one. As they invaded enemy territory (Luke 10:17), they would be like "lambs among wolves" (Luke 10:3). But as long as they relied on the Lord, they would win the battle. "Any man who takes Jesus Christ seriously becomes the target of the devil," Vance Havner often told audiences. "Most church members do not give Satan enough trouble to arouse his opposition."

It would require discipline and faith for them to do the job (Luke 10:4-8). There was an urgency about the work, and the Lord did not want them to be overburdened with extra supplies or be delayed on the road by elaborate Eastern greetings. They had to trust God to provide homes and food for them, and they were not to be embarrassed to accept hospitality. After all, they were laboring for the Lord and bringing blessing into the home, and "the laborer is worthy of his hire" (Luke 10:7; see also 1 Cor. 9:14; 1 Tim. 5:18).

They were ambassadors of peace, bringing healing to the sick, deliverance to the possessed, and the Good News of salvation to lost sinners. Like Joshua's army of old, they first proclaimed peace to the cities. If a city rejected the offer of peace, then it chose judgment (Deut. 20:10-18). It is a serious thing to reject the ambassadors God sends.

It is important to note that the special power that Jesus gave to His Apostles (Luke 9:1) and to the Seventy is not ours to claim today. These two preaching missions were very special ministries, and God did not promise to duplicate them in our age. Our Lord's commission to us emphasizes the proclamation of the message, not the performing of miracles (Matt. 28:19-20; Luke 24:46-49).

Denunciation (vv. 13-16). This seems like harsh language from the lips of the Son of God, but we dare not ignore it or try to explain it away. He named three ancient cities that had been judged by God—Sodom (Gen. 19), and Tyre and Sidon (Ezek. 26–28; Isa. 23)—and used them to warn three cities of His day: Chorazin, Bethsaida, and Capernaum. These three cities had been given more privileges than the three ancient cities, and therefore they had more responsibility. If Sodom, Tyre, and Sidon were destroyed, how could Chorazin, Bethsaida, and Capernaum escape?

To hear Christ's ambassadors means to hear Him, and to despise His representatives means to despise Him. "As My Father hath sent Me, even so send I you" (John 20:21; see also 2 Cor. 5:18-21). The way a nation treats an ambassador is the way it treats the government the ambassador represents. For an interesting illustration of this truth, read 2 Samuel 10.

Jubilation (vv. 17-24). There is a threefold joy here: the joy of service (Luke 10:17-19), the joy of salvation (Luke 10:20), and the joy of sovereignty (Luke 10:21-24).

We can well understand the joy of the Seventy as they returned to report their victories to Jesus. He had given them power and authority to heal, to cast out demons, and to preach the Word, and they were successful! In the midst of their great joy, they were careful to give God the glory ("in Thy name").

They had seen individual victories from city to city, but Jesus saw these victories as part of a war that dethroned and defeated Satan (note Isa. 14:4-23; John 12:31-32; and Rev. 12:8-9). As believers, we are weak in ourselves, but we can be "strong in the Lord, and in the power of His might" (Eph. 6:10ff). Each victory is important to the Lord, no matter how insignificant it may seem in our eyes. Satan will not finally be judged until Jesus casts him into the lake of fire (Rev. 20:10), but God's people can today claim Christ's Calvary victory by faith (Col. 2:15).

But the enemy will not give up! Satan would certainly attack Christ's servants and seek to destroy them. That is why our Lord added the words of encouragement in Luke 10:19. He assured them that their authority was not gone now that the preaching mission had ended, and that they could safely tread on the "old serpent" without fear (Gen. 3:15; Rev. 12:9).

The Lord cautioned them not to "go on rejoicing" over their victories but to rejoice because their names had been written in heaven. (The verb means "they have been written and they stand written." It is a statement of assurance. See Phil. 4:3; Rev. 20:12-15.) As wonderful as their miracles were, the greatest miracle of all is still the salvation of a lost soul. The Greek word translated "written" means "to inscribe formally and solemnly." It was used for the signing of a will, a marriage document, or a peace treaty, and also for the enrolling of a citizen. The perfect tense in the Greek means "it stands written."

But our highest joy is not found in service or even in our salvation, but in being submitted to the sovereign will of the Heavenly Father, for this is the foundation for both service and salvation. Here we see God the Son rejoicing through God the Holy Spirit because of the will of God the Father! "I delight to do Thy will, O my God" (Ps. 40:8).

Jesus was not rejoicing because sinners were blind to God's truth, for God is "not willing that any should perish" (2 Peter 3:9). He rejoiced because *the understanding of that truth* did not depend on natural abilities or education. If that were the case, most of the people in the world would be shut out of the kingdom. When the Twelve and the Seventy were preaching, they did not see the "wise and learned" humbling themselves to receive God's truth and grace, but they saw the "common people" trusting the Word (Luke 7:29-30; 1 Cor. 1:26-29). In His sovereign will, God has ordained that sinners must humble themselves before they can be lifted up (James 4:6; 1 Peter 5:6).

Christ's ambassadors were indeed privileged people. They were able to see and hear things that the greatest saints in the Old Testament ages yearned to see and hear but could not. The Messiah was at work, and they were a part of His work!

Neighbors: Imitating the Lord (Luke 10:25-37)

It was expected that rabbis would discuss theological matters in public, and the question this scribe (lawyer) asked was one that was often debated by the Jews. It was a good question asked with a bad motive, because the lawyer hoped to trap our Lord. However, Jesus trapped the lawyer!

Our Lord sent the man back to the Law, not because the Law saves us (Gal. 2:16, 21; 3:21), but because the Law shows us that we need to be saved. There can be no real conversion without conviction, and the Law is what God uses to convict sinners (Rom. 3:20).

The scribe gave the right answer, but he would not apply it personally to himself and admit his own lack of love for both God and his neighbor. So, instead of *being justified* by throwing himself on the mercy of God (Luke 18:9-14), he tried to *justify himself* and wriggle out of his predicament. He used the old debating tactic, "Define your terms! What do you mean by 'neighbor'? Who is my neighbor?"

Jesus did not say that this story was a parable, so it could well be the report of an actual occurrence. For Jesus to tell a story that made the Jews look bad and the Samaritans look good would either be dangerous or self-defeating. "You just made that up!" they could say. "We all know that nothing like that would ever happen!" So it is possible that some of His listeners, including the lawyer, knew that such a thing had really happened. Either way, the account is realistic.

The worst thing we can do with any parable, especially this one, is turn it into an allegory and make everything stand for something. The victim becomes the lost sinner who is half dead (alive physically, dead spiritually), helplessly left on the road of life. The priest and Levite represent the Law and the sacrifices, neither of which can save the sinner.

The Samaritan is Jesus Christ who saves the man, pays the bill, and promises to come again. The inn stands for the local church where believers are cared for, and the "two pence" are the two ordinances, baptism and Communion. If you take this approach to Scripture, you can make the Bible say almost anything you please, and you are sure to miss the messages God wants you to get.

The road from Jerusalem down to Jericho was indeed a dangerous one. Since the temple workers used it so much, you would have thought the Jews or Romans would have taken steps to make it safe. It is much easier to maintain a religious system than it is to improve the neighborhood.

Most of us can think up excuses for the priest and Levite as they ignored the victim. (Maybe we have used them ourselves!) The priest had been serving God at the temple all week and was anxious to get home. Perhaps the bandits were still lurking in the vicinity and using the victim as "bait." Why take a chance? Anyway, it was not his fault that the man was attacked. The road was busy, so somebody else was bound to come along and help the man. The priest left it to the Levite, and then the Levite did what the priest did—nothing! Such is the power of the bad example of a religious man.

By using a Samaritan as the hero, Jesus disarmed the Jews, for the Jews and Samaritans were enemies (John 4:9; 8:48). It was not a Jew helping a Samaritan but a Samaritan helping a Jew *who had been ignored by his fellow Jews!* The Samaritan loved those who hated him, risked his own life, spent his own money (two days' wages for a laborer), and was never publicly rewarded or honored as far as we know.

What the Samaritan did helps us better understand what it means to "show mercy" (Luke 10:37), and it also illustrates the ministry of Jesus Christ. The Samaritan identified with the needs of the stranger and had compassion on him. There was no logical reason why he should rearrange his plans and spend his money just to help an "enemy" in need, but mercy does not need reasons. Being an expert in the Law, the scribe certainly knew that God required His people to show mercy, even to strangers and enemies (Ex. 23:4-5; Lev. 19:33-34; Micah 6:8).

See how wisely Jesus "turned the tables" on the lawyer. Trying to evade responsibility, the man asked, "Who is my neighbor?" But Jesus asked, "Which of these three men was neighbor to the victim?" The big question is, "To whom can I be a neighbor?" and this has nothing to do with geography, citizenship, or race. Wherever people need us, there we can be neighbors and, like Jesus Christ, show mercy.

The lawyer wanted to discuss "neighbor" in a general way, but Jesus forced him to consider a specific man in need. How easy it is for us to talk about abstract ideals and fail to help solve concrete problems. We can discuss things like "poverty" and "job opportunities" and yet never personally help feed a hungry family or help somebody find a job.

Of course, the lawyer wanted to make the issue somewhat complex and philosophical, but Jesus made it simple and practical. He moved it from *duty* to *love,* from *debating* to *doing.* To be sure, our Lord was not condemning discussions or debates; He was only warning us not to use these things as excuses for doing nothing. Committees are not always committed!

One of my favorite D.L. Moody stories illustrates this point. Attending a convention in Indianapolis, Mr. Moody asked singer Ira Sankey to meet him at 6 o'clock one evening at a certain street corner. When Sankey arrived, Mr. Moody put him on a box and asked him to sing, and it was not long before a crowd gathered. Moody spoke briefly, inviting the crowd to follow him to the nearby opera house. Before long, the auditorium was filled, and the evangelist preached the Gospel to the spiritually hungry people.

When the delegates to the convention started to arrive, Moody stopped preaching and said, "Now we must close as the brethren of the convention wish to come and to discuss the question, 'How to Reach the Masses.' " *Touché!*

We may read this passage and think only of "the high cost of caring," but it is far more costly *not* to care. The priest and the Levite lost far more by their neglect than the Samaritan did by his concern. They lost the opportunity to become better men and good stewards of what God had given them. They could have been a good influence in a bad world, but they chose to be a bad influence. *The Samaritan's one deed of mercy has inspired sacrificial ministry all over the world.* Never say that such ministry is wasted! God sees to it that no act of loving service in Christ's name is ever lost.

It all depends on your outlook. To the thieves, this traveling Jew was a victim to exploit, so they attacked him. To the priest and Levite, he was a nuisance to avoid, so they ignored him. But to the Samaritan, he was a neighbor to love and help, so he took care of him. What Jesus said to the lawyer, He says to us: "Go and *keep on doing it* likewise" (literal translation).

Worshipers: Listening to the Lord (Luke 10:38-42)

Worship is at the heart of all that we are and all that we do in the Christian life. It is important that we be busy ambassadors, taking the message of the Gospel to lost souls. It is also essential to be merciful Samaritans, seeking to help exploited and hurting people who need God's mercy. But before we can represent Christ as we should, or imitate Him in our caring ministry, we must spend time with Him and learn from Him. We must "take time to be holy."

Mary of Bethany is seen three times in the Gospel record, and on each occasion, she is in the same place: at the feet of Jesus. She sat at His feet and listened to His Word (Luke 10:39), fell at His feet and shared her woe (John 11:32), and came to His feet and poured out her worship (John 12:3). It is interesting to note that in each of these instances, there is some kind of fragrance: in Luke 10, it is food; in John 11, it is death (John 11:39); and in John 12, it is perfume.

Mary and Martha are often contrasted as though each believer must make a choice: be a *worker* like Martha or a *worshiper* like Mary. Certainly our personalities and gifts are different, but that does not mean that the Christian life is an either/or situation. Charles Welsey said it perfectly in one of his hymns:

> Faithful to my Lord's commands,
> I still would choose the better part;
> Serve with careful Martha's hands,
> And loving Mary's heart.

It seems evident that the Lord wants each of us to imitate Mary in our worship and Martha in our work. Blessed are the balanced!

Consider Martha's situation. She received Jesus into her home *and then neglected Him as she prepared an elaborate meal that He did not need!* Certainly a meal was in order, but what we do *with* Christ is far more important than what we do *for* Christ. Again, it is not an either/or situation; it is a matter of balance. Mary had done her share of the work in the kitchen and then had gone to "feed" on the Lord's teachings. Martha felt neglected after Mary left the kitchen, and she began to complain and to suggest that neither the Lord nor Mary really cared!

Few things are as damaging to the Christian life as trying to work for Christ without taking time to commune with Christ. "For without Me ye can do nothing" (John 15:5). Mary chose the better part, the part that could not be taken from her. She knew that she could not live "by bread alone" (Matt. 4:4).

Whenever we criticize others and pity ourselves because we feel overworked, we had better take time to examine our lives. Perhaps in all of our busyness, we have been ignoring the Lord. Martha's problem was not that she had too much work to do, but that she allowed her work to distract her and pull her apart. She was trying to serve two masters! If serving Christ makes us difficult to live with, then something is terribly wrong with our service!

The key is to have the right priorities: Jesus Christ first, then others, then ourselves. It is vitally important that we spend time "at the feet of Jesus" every single day, letting Him share His Word with us. *The most important part of the Christian life is the part that only God sees.* Unless we meet Christ personally and privately each day, we will soon end up like Martha: busy but not blessed.

Often in my pastoral ministry, I have asked people with serious problems, "Tell me about your devotional life." The usual response has been an embarrassed look, a bowed head, and the quiet confession, "I stopped reading my Bible and praying a long time ago." And they wondered why they had problems!

According to John 12:1-2, Martha must have learned her lesson, for she prepared a feast for Jesus, the Twelve, and her brother and sister—that's fifteen people—*and did not utter one word of complaint!* She had God's peace in her heart because she had learned to sit at the feet of Jesus.

We are ambassadors, neighbors, and worshipers, these three; and the greatest of these is worshipers.

CHAPTER TEN
LEARNING LIFE'S LESSONS
Luke 11

Our Lord's teaching in Luke 11 grew out of a prayer meeting, a miracle, and an invitation to dinner. Jesus used these occasions to give instructions about four important topics: prayer, Satan, spiritual opportunity, and hypocrisy. It is important that we today understand these topics and apply these truths to our own lives.

Prayer (Luke 11:1-13)

The priority of prayer (v. 1). We usually think of John the Baptist as a prophet and martyr, and yet our Lord's disciples remembered him as a man of prayer. John was a "miracle baby," filled with the Holy Spirit before he was born, and yet he had to pray. He was privileged to introduce the Messiah to Israel, and yet he had to pray. Jesus said that John was the greatest of the prophets (Luke 7:28), and yet John had to depend on prayer. If prayer was that vital to a man who had these many advantages, how much more important it ought to be to us who do not have these advantages!

John's disciples had to pray and Jesus' disciples wanted to learn better how to pray. They did not ask the Master to teach them how to preach or do great signs; they asked Him to teach them to pray. We today sometimes think that we would be better Christians if only we had been with Jesus when He was on earth, but this is not likely. The disciples were with Him and yet they failed many times! They could perform miracles, and yet they wanted to learn to pray.

But the greatest argument for the priority of prayer is the fact that our Lord was a Man of prayer. Thus far we have seen that He prayed at His baptism (Luke 3:21), before He chose the Twelve (Luke 6:12), when the crowds increased (Luke 5:16), before He asked the Twelve for their confession of faith (Luke 9:18), and at His Transfiguration (Luke 9:29). The disciples knew that He often prayed alone (Mark 1:35), and they wanted to learn from Him this secret of spiritual power and wisdom.

If Jesus Christ, the perfect Son of God, had to depend on prayer during "the days of His flesh" (Heb. 5:7), then how much more do you and I need to pray! Effective prayer is the provision for every need and the solution for every problem.

Pattern for prayer (vv. 2-4). We call this "The Lord's Prayer," not because Jesus prayed it (He never had to ask for forgiveness), but because Jesus taught it. There is nothing wrong with praying this prayer personally or as part of a congregation, so long as we do it from a believing heart that is sincere and submitted. How easy it is to "recite" these words and not really mean them, but that can happen even when we sing and preach! The fault lies with us, not with this prayer.

This is a "pattern prayer," given to guide us in our own praying (see Matt. 6:9-15 for the parallel). It teaches us that true prayer depends on a spiritual relationship with God that enables us to call Him "Father," and this can come only through faith in Jesus Christ (Rom. 8:14-17; Gal. 4:1-7).

Lyndon Johnson's press secretary, Bill Moyers, was saying grace at a staff lunch, and the President shouted, "Speak up, Bill! I can't hear a thing!" Moyers quietly replied, "I wasn't addressing you, Mr. President." It is good to remind ourselves that when we pray, we talk to God.

True prayer also involves *responsibilities:* honoring God's kingdom and doing God's will (Luke 11:2). It has well been said that the purpose of prayer is not to get man's will done in heaven, but to get God's will done on earth. Prayer is not telling God what we want and then selfishly enjoying it. Prayer is asking God to use us to accomplish *what He wants* so that His name is glorified, His kingdom is extended and strengthened, and His will is done. I must test all of my personal requests by these overruling concerns if I expect God to hear and answer my prayers.

It is important for Christians to know the Word of God, for there we discover the will of God. We must never separate prayer and the Word (John 15:7). During my ministry, I have seen professing Christians disobey God and defend themselves by saying, "I prayed about it and God said it was all right!" This includes a girl who married an unsaved man (2 Cor. 6:14-18), a fellow living with a girl who was not his wife (1 Thes. 4:1-8), and a preacher who started his own church because all the other churches were wrong and only he had true "spiritual insight" (Phil. 2:1-16).

Once we are secure in our relationship with God and His will, then we can bring our *requests* to Him (Luke 11:3-4). We can ask Him to provide our needs (not our greeds!) for today, to forgive us for what we have done yesterday, and to lead us in the future. All of our needs may be included in these three requests: material and physical provision, moral and spiritual perfection, and divine protection and direction. If we pray this way, we can be sure of praying in God's will.

Persistence in prayer (vv. 5-8). In this parable, Jesus did not say that God is like this grouchy neighbor. In fact, He said just the opposite. If a tired and selfish neighbor finally meets the needs of a bothersome friend, how much more will a loving Heavenly Father meet the needs of His own dear children! He is arguing from the lesser to the greater.

We have already seen that prayer is based on *sonship* ("Our Father"), not on friendship; but Jesus used friendship to illustrate persistence in prayer. God the Father is not like this neighbor, for He never sleeps, never gets impatient or irritable, is always generous, and delights in meeting the needs of His children. The friend at the door had to keep on knocking in order to get what he needed, but God is quick to respond to His children's cries (Luke 18:1-8).

The argument is clear: If persistence finally paid off as a man beat on the door of a reluctant friend, how much more would persistence bring blessing as we pray to a loving Heavenly Father! After all, we are the children *in the house with Him!*

The word translated "importunity" means "shamelessness" or "avoidance of shame." It can refer to the man at the door who was not ashamed to wake up his friend, but it can also refer to the friend in the house. Hospitality to strangers is a basic law in the East (Gen. 18:1ff). If a person refused to entertain a guest, he brought disgrace on the whole village and the neighbors would have nothing to do with him. The man in the house knew this and did not want to embarrass himself, his family, or his village; so he got up and met the need.

Why does our Father in heaven answer prayer? Not just to meet the needs of His children, but to meet them in such a way that it brings glory to His name. "Hallowed be Thy name." *When God's people pray, God's reputation is at stake.* The way He takes care of His children is a witness to the world that He can be trusted. Phillips Brooks said that prayer is not overcoming God's reluctance; it is laying hold of His highest willingness. Persistence in prayer is not an attempt to change God's mind ("Thy will be done") but to get ourselves to the place where He can trust us with the answer.

Promises for prayer (vv. 9-13). The tenses of the verbs are important here: "Keep on asking . . . keep on seeking . . . keep on knocking." In other words, *don't come to God only in the midnight emergencies, but keep in constant communion with your Father.* Jesus called this "abiding" (John 15:1ff), and Paul exhorted, "Pray without ceasing" (1 Thes. 5:17). As we pray, God will either answer or show us why He cannot answer. Then it is up to us to do whatever is necessary in our lives so that the Father can trust us with the answer.

Note that the lesson closes with an emphasis on God as Father (Luke 11:11-13). Because He knows us and loves us, *we never need to be afraid of the answers that He gives.* Again, Jesus argued from the lesser to the greater: if an earthly father gives what is best to his children, surely the Father in heaven will do even more. This even includes "the good things of the Holy Spirit" (compare Luke 11:13 with Matt. 7:11), blessings that in the Old Testament were reserved only for a special few.

Satan (Luke 11:14-28)

Accusation (vv. 14-16). This is the third miracle of deliverance our Lord performed that elicited from His enemies the accusation that He was in league with Satan (see Matt. 9:32-34; 12:22-37). Instead of rejoicing that God had sent a Redeemer, the religious leaders were rebelling against the truth of God's Word and seeking to discredit Christ's work and character. Imagine people being so blind that they could not distinguish a work of God from a work of Satan!

"Beelzebub" was one of the names of the Philistine god Baal (2 Kings 1:1-3); it means "lord of flies." A variant is "Beelzebul" which means "lord of the dwelling" and ties in with Christ's illustrations in Luke 11:18-26. The Jews often used this name when referring to Satan.

The request in Luke 11:16 was a part of the accusation. "If you are really working for

God," they were saying in effect, "prove it by giving us a sign from heaven, not just a miracle on earth." They were tempting God, which is a dangerous thing to do.

Refutation (vv. 17-22). Jesus answered their charges with three arguments. First, their accusation was illogical. Why would Satan fight against himself and divide his own kingdom? (Note that Jesus believed in a real devil who has a kingdom that is strong and united. See Eph. 2:1-3; 6:10ff.) Second, their charges were self-incriminating: by what power were the Jews casting out demons? How do their works differ from Christ's works? On the contrary, Christ's miracles show that the kingdom of *God* is present, not the kingdom of *Satan!*

Finally, their accusation was really an admission of His power, for He could not defeat Satan unless He were stronger than Satan. Jesus pictured Satan as a strong man in armor, guarding his palace and his goods. But Jesus invaded Satan's territory, destroyed his armor and weapons, and claimed his spoils! (see John 12:31-33; Col. 2:15; 1 John 3:8) Our Lord has "led captivity captive" (Eph. 4:8) and set the prisoners free (Luke 4:18). Though he is permitted limited authority, Satan is a defeated enemy.

Application (vv. 23-28). It is impossible to be neutral in this spiritual war (Luke 11:23; also see 9:50), for neutrality means standing against Him. There are two spiritual forces at work in the world, and we must choose between them. Satan is scattering and destroying, but Jesus Christ is gathering and building. We must make a choice, and if we choose to make *no* choice, we are really choosing against Him.

Jesus illustrated the danger of neutrality by telling the story of the man and the demon. The man's body was the demon's "house" (Luke 11:24, and note vv. 17 and 21). For some unknown reason, the demonic tenant decided to leave his "house" and go elsewhere. The man's condition improved immediately, *but the man did not invite God to come and dwell within.* In other words, the man remained neutral. What happened? The demon returned with seven other demons worse than himself, and the man's condition was abominable.

"Neutrality in religion is always cowardice," wrote Oswald Chambers. "God turns the cowardice of a desired neutrality into terror."

Taking sides with Jesus means much more than saying the right things, like the woman who cried, "Blessed is the womb that bore You, and the breasts which nursed You" (Luke 11:27, NKJV). She was certainly sincere, but that was not enough. *We take sides with Jesus Christ when we hear His Word and obey it* (see Luke 6:46-49; 8:19-21).

Opportunity (Luke 11:29-36)

Because He knew what was in their hearts, Jesus was not impressed by the big crowds, but the disciples were. In order to keep the Twelve from being swayed by "success," Jesus gave them some insights into what was really happening as they ministered the Word. He used three illustrations to show the seriousness of spiritual opportunities.

Jonah (vv. 29-30, 32). The leaders kept asking Jesus for a sign to prove that He was the Messiah. The only sign He promised was "the sign of Jonah the prophet," which is *death, burial, and resurrection.* It is the resurrection of our Lord that proves He is the Messiah, the Son of God (Rom. 1:4), and this is what Peter preached to Israel on the Day of Pentecost (Acts 2:22ff). The witness of the early church was centered on Christ's resurrection (Acts 1:22; 3:15; 5:30-32; 13:32-33). Jonah was a living miracle and so is our Lord Jesus Christ.

Solomon (v. 31). The emphasis here is on the wisdom of a king, not the works of a prophet. The Queen of Sheba traveled many miles to hear the wisdom of Solomon (1 Kings 10), but here was the very Son of God *in their midst,* and the Jews would not believe His words! Even if Jesus had performed a sign, it would not have changed their hearts. They needed the living wisdom of God, but they were content with their stale religious tradition.

The important thing about these illustrations is that *they involved Gentiles.* When Jonah preached to the Gentiles in Nineveh, they repented and were spared. When a Gentile queen heard Solomon's wisdom, she marveled and believed. If, with all their privileges, the Jews did not repent, then the people of Nineveh and the Queen of Sheba would bear witness against them in the last judgment. The Lord gave Israel so many opportunities, yet they would not believe (Luke 13:34-35; John 12:35-41).

Light (vv. 33-36). The third illustration was from daily life, not from history, and was one Jesus had used before (Matt. 6:22-23).

God's Word is a light that shines in this dark world (Ps. 119:105; Prov. 6:23). But it is not enough that the light be shining *externally*; it must enter our lives before it can do any good. "The entrance of Thy words giveth light; it giveth understanding unto the simple" (Ps. 119:130). The brightest sun cannot enable a blind man to see.

When we trust Jesus Christ, our eyes are opened, the light shines in, and we become children of light (John 8:12; 2 Cor. 4:3-6; Eph. 5:8-14). The important thing is that we take advantage of the light and have a *single outlook of faith*. If we keep one eye on the things of God and the other eye on the world (1 John 2:16), the light will turn into darkness! There is no "twilight living" for the Christian, for God demands total submission and obedience (Luke 11:23).

Three men in the Bible illustrate this truth. They began in the light and ended up in the darkness because they were double-minded. The name *Samson* probably means "sunny," yet he ended up a blind slave in a dark dungeon because he yielded to the "lust of the flesh" (Jud. 16). Lot began as a pilgrim with his uncle Abraham. He ended as a drunk in a cave, committing incest (Gen. 19:30-38), because he yielded to "the lust of the eyes" (Gen. 13:10-11). Lot wanted to serve two masters and look in two directions!

King Saul began his reign as a humble leader but his pride led him to a witch's cave (1 Sam. 28), and he died of suicide on the field of battle (1 Sam. 31). His sin was "the pride of life"; he would not humble himself and obey the will of God.

Each of us is controlled either by light or darkness. The frightening thing is that some people have so hardened themselves against the Lord that *they cannot tell the difference!* They think they are following the light when, in reality, they are following the darkness. The scribes and Pharisees claimed to "see the light" as they studied the Law, but they were living in the darkness (see John 12:35-50).

Hypocrisy (Luke 11:37-54)

At this stage in Christ's ministry, when the religious leaders were bent on destroying Him, why would a Pharisee invite Him to his home for a meal? If he had been sincerely seeking truth, he would have talked with our Lord privately. It seems obvious that he was looking for an opportunity to accuse Jesus, and he thought he had it when Jesus did not practice the ceremonial washing before eating (Mark 7:2-3). Knowing what the host was thinking, Jesus responded by giving a "spiritual analysis" of the Pharisees.

He exposed their folly (vv. 37-41). The basic error of the Pharisees was thinking that righteousness was only a matter of external actions, and they minimized internal attitudes. They were very careful to keep the outside clean, but they ignored the wickedness within. They seemed to forget that the same God who created the outside also created the inside, the "inner person" that also needs cleansing (Ps. 51:6, 10).

The Pharisees boasted of their giving (Matt. 6:1-4; Luke 18:11-12), but they did not give *what was within* to the Lord. The way to make the *outside* pure is to make the *inside* pure (Luke 11:41). Kenneth Wuest translates this verse, "Rather, the things which are inside give as alms, and behold, all things are clean to you" (WUEST). The way to clean up a dirty vocabulary is not to brush your teeth but to cleanse your heart.

He denounced their sins (vv. 42-52). These six "woes" parallel the "woes" in Matthew 23. Jesus started with the sins of the Pharisees (Luke 11:42-44) and then turned to the sins of the scribes, for it was their interpretations of the Law that formed the basis for the whole pharisaical system (Luke 11:45-52).

The first three "woes" denounce the Pharisees for their *wrong priorities*. They were careful about tithing even the tiny leaves and seeds from the herbs, but they forgot about important things like justice and love (Micah 6:7-8). They majored on the minors! Jesus did not say they should stop tithing but that they should put their religious activities into proper perspective.

They also put *reputation* above *character*. They thought that sitting in the right seats and being acknowledged by the right people would make them spiritual. Reputation is what people think we are; character is what God knows we are.

The comparison in Luke 11:44 must have infuriated the host and the other Pharisees who were present. The Jews had to be especially careful about ceremonial defilement from dead bodies (Num. 19:11-22; note especially v. 16), so they made sure the graves were carefully marked. But the Pharisees were like *unmarked graves* that did not look like graves at all! This meant that they were *unconsciously defiling others when they thought they were helping them become holier!* Instead of helping people, the Pharisees were harming them.

The scribes felt the sting of our Lord's words and tried to defend themselves. Jesus used three vivid illustrations in answering them: burdens, tombs, and keys.

The scribes were good at adding to the burdens of the people, but they had no heart for helping them carry those burdens. What a tragedy when "ministers" of God's Word create more problems for people who already have problems enough! A pastor friend of mine prays daily, "Lord, help me today not to add to anybody's problems." Jesus had these "religious burdens" in mind when He gave the gracious invitation recorded in Matthew 11:28-30.

The scribes were also good at "embalming" the past and honoring the prophets who had been martyred by the religious establishment *to which they belonged.* Both Bible history and church history reveal that true servants of God are usually rejected by the people who most need their ministry, but the next generation will come along and honor these people. The Pharisees were like "hidden graves," but the scribes built elaborate tombs!

The first recorded martyrdom in the Old Testament is that of Abel, and the last is that of Zechariah (see Gen. 4:1-15; 2 Chron. 24:20-27, and remember that 2 Chron. is the last book in the Hebrew Bible). Jesus did not suggest that the scribes and Pharisees were *personally* responsible for killing the Old Testament prophets. Rather, He was affirming that *people just like the scribes and Pharisees* did these terrible things to God's servants. Their ultimate crime would be the crucifixion of the Son of God.

Finally, the scribes were guilty of robbing the common people of the knowledge of the Word of God. It was bad enough that they would not enter the kingdom themselves, but they were hindering others from going in! It is a serious thing to teach God's Word and not everyone is supposed to do it (James 3:1). Unfortunately, what some people call "Bible study" is too often just a group of unprepared people exchanging their ignorance.

But there is another side to this: the scribes convinced the people that nobody could understand and explain the Law except the trained and authorized teachers. We have some of that arrogant attitude showing itself today. Teachers who overemphasize the Bible languages give people the impression that the Holy Spirit cannot teach anyone who does not know Greek and Hebrew. There are so many "study Bibles" these days (and many of them are helpful) that you wonder if a student can learn anything from a simple text Bible. We must not despise true Christian scholarship, but we must also keep things in balance.

Jesus is the key to the Scriptures (Luke 24:44-48). When you take away that key, you cannot understand what God has written. As helpful and necessary as theological studies are, the most important requirements for Bible study are a yielded heart and an obedient will. Some of the best Bible teachers I have known in my own ministry were men and women who learned the truth of God's Word on their knees and on the battlefield of life. They were Spirit-taught, not man-taught.

He aroused their anger (vv. 53-54). Hypocrites do not want their sins exposed; it hurts their reputation. Instead of opposing the Lord, these men should have been seeking His mercy. They deliberately began to attack Him with "catch questions" in hopes they could trap Him in some heresy and then arrest Him. What a disgraceful way to treat the Son of God.

But there are religious systems today that are very much like the system defended by the scribes and Pharisees. The leaders interpret and apply the Word for the followers and you are not permitted to ask embarrassing questions or raise objections. The leaders exploit the people and do little or nothing to ease their burdens. Worst of all, the leaders use the system to cover up their own sins. God's truth should set us free, but these groups only lead people into more and more bondage.

God has given teachers to His church (Eph. 4:11), and we should listen to them. But we should also test what we hear by the Scriptures to make sure they are teaching the truth (1 Thes. 5:19-21), and we should not permit anyone to bring us into bondage and exploit us (2 Cor. 11:20).

It is a privilege to have the light of the Word of God and the privilege of prayer. The enemy wants to rob us of the blessings of spiritual growth and freedom. His plan is to substitute hypocrisy for reality and to encourage us to be more concerned about the outside than the inside: reputation and not character.

So serious is this danger that Jesus will have more to say about it in Luke 12. Meanwhile, let us beware!

CHAPTER ELEVEN
BELIEVER, BEWARE!
Luke 12

Our Lord's disciples may not have realized it, but they were in great danger. For one thing, they were surrounded by immense crowds of people whose major concern was not to hear spiritual truth but to see Jesus do a miracle or meet some personal need. At the same time, the scribes and Pharisees were plotting against Jesus and trying to get Him out of the way. The snare of popularity and the fear of man has brought ruin to more than one servant of God.

In Luke 12, Luke recorded five warnings from our Lord. Four of these warnings must be heeded by God's people today if we are to be faithful disciples; and the fifth warning should be heeded by a lost world.

Beware of Hypocrisy (Luke 12:1-12)

The word *hypocrite* comes from a Greek word that means "an actor," "one who plays a part." There are hypocrites in every walk of life, people who try to impress others in order to hide their real selves. In the Christian life, a hypocrite is somebody who tries to appear more spiritual than he or she really is. These people know that they are pretending, and they hope they will not be found out. Their Christian life is only a shallow masquerade.

It is easy to see why Jesus gave this warning at this particular time. The disciples might be tempted either to gain popularity by pleasing the crowds, or avoid trouble by pleasing the scribes and Pharisees. All of us want people to like us, and it seems such an easy thing to "act the part" that others want to see.

How can we keep hypocrisy out of our lives?

We must understand what hypocrisy really is (v. 1). Jesus compared it to leaven (yeast), something that every Jew would associate with evil. (See Ex. 12:15-20. Paul also used leaven to symbolize sin. See 1 Cor. 5:6-8; Gal. 5:9.) Like yeast, hypocrisy begins very small but grows quickly and quietly. As it grows, it infects the whole person. Hypocrisy does to the ego what yeast does to bread dough: it puffs it up (see 1 Cor. 4:6, 18-19; 5:2). Soon pride takes over and the person's character deteriorates rapidly.

If we want to keep hypocrisy out of our lives, we must avoid that first bit of "leaven." Once we start to pretend, the process goes on quickly; and the longer we wait, the worse it gets. Sir Walter Scott wrote:

> O what a tangled web we weave
> When first we practice to deceive.

Hypocrisy is foolish and futile (vv. 2-3). Why? Because nothing can really be hidden. Jesus referred here primarily to His own teachings, but the principle applies to other areas of life. The Twelve might be tempted to cover or compromise the truth so that neither the crowds nor the Pharisees would be offended (see Luke 8:16-18; 11:33). God's truth is like light, not leaven, and it must not be hidden. The lies of the hypocrite will one day be revealed, so why go on pretending? Let your light shine!

We must understand what causes hypocrisy (vv. 4-7). Jesus mentioned "fear" five times in these verses, so He is teaching us that a basic cause of hypocrisy is *the fear of man.* When we are afraid of what others may say about us or do to us, then we try to impress them in order to gain their approval. If necessary, we will even lie to accomplish our purposes, and this is hypocrisy. Unfortunately, many of the scribes and Pharisees were more concerned about reputation than character, what people *thought* about them than what God *knew* about them. The fear of man always brings a snare (Prov. 29:25), and Jesus wanted His disciples to avoid that snare.

The remedy for hypocrisy is to forget about what people may say and do and *fear God alone.* The fear of God is the fear that conquers all other fears, for the person who truly fears God need fear nothing else. All that men can do is kill the body, but God can condemn the soul! Since He is the final Judge, and He judges for eternity, it is logical that we put the fear of God ahead of everything else. Our God knows us and cares for us. He cares for the sparrows, and we are of more value than they; so what do we have to fear from men?

We must confess Christ openly (vv. 8-9). Once we have done this, we will have an easier time living the truth and avoiding hypocrisy. How can we fear men when we know Jesus Christ is confessing us before the Father in heaven? It is not important that men praise our names on earth, but it is important that God acknowledges us in heaven (see 2 Tim. 2:8-14).

We must depend on the Holy Spirit (vv. 10-12). Jesus appears to be contradicting Himself. In Luke 12:8-9, He demands that we openly confess Him, but in Luke 12:10, He says we can speak against Him and be forgiven. However, if we speak against the Spirit, there is no forgiveness! Does this mean that the Holy Spirit is more important than the Son of God?

Note that this statement is connected with the ministry of the Spirit in and through the Apostles (Luke 12:11-12). The Jewish nation rejected *God the Father* when they refused to obey John the Baptist and repent, for John was sent by the Father. They rejected *God the Son* when they asked Pilate to crucify Him. But that sin could be forgiven because there was still the ministry of the Spirit.

God did not judge the nation immediately. Instead, Jesus prayed for them as He hanged on the cross (Luke 23:34; see also Acts 3:17). Then God sent the Holy Spirit who ministered through the Apostles and other believers in the church. *This was the last opportunity for the nation, and they failed by rejecting the witness of the Spirit* (Acts 7:51). Luke 12:11-12 was fulfilled during the first chapters of Acts when the message went "to the Jew first" (Acts 3:26; 13:46; Rom. 1:16). Israel's third "national sin" was the stoning of Stephen (Acts 7), after which the message went out to the Samaritans (Acts 8), and then the Gentiles (Acts 10). Note that Stephen said, "You always resist the Holy Spirit" (Acts 7:51).

I do not believe that the "sin against the Holy Spirit" is committed by people today as it was by Israel centuries ago. I believe that the only "unpardonable sin" today is the final rejection of Jesus Christ (John 3:36). The Spirit of God witnesses through the Word, and it is possible for sinners to reject that witness and resist the Spirit. But the Spirit bears witness to Christ (John 16:7-15); so the way people treat the Spirit is the way they treat the Son of God.

Beware of Covetousness (Luke 12:13-21)

At this point, a man in the crowd interrupted Jesus and asked Him to solve a family problem. Rabbis were expected to help settle legal matters, but Jesus refused to get involved. Why? Because He knew that no answer He gave would solve the *real* problem, which was covetousness in the hearts of the two brothers. (The "you" in Luke 12:14 is plural.) As long as both men were greedy, *no* settlement would be satisfactory. Their greatest need was to have their hearts changed. Like too many people today, they wanted Jesus to serve them but not to save them.

Covetousness is an unquenchable thirst for getting more and more of something we think we need in order to be truly satisfied. It may be a thirst for money or the things that money can buy, or even a thirst for position and power. Jesus made it clear that true life does not depend on an abundance of possessions. He did not deny that we have certain basic needs (Matt. 6:32; 1 Tim. 6:17). He only affirmed that we will not make life richer by acquiring *more* of these things.

Mark Twain once defined "civilization" as "a limitless multiplication of unnecessary necessities," and he was right. In fact, many Christians are infected with covetousness and do not know it. They think that Paul's admonition in 1 Timothy 6 applies only to the "rich and famous." Measured by the living standards of the rest of the world, most believers in America are indeed wealthy people.

Jesus told this parable to reveal the dangers that lurk in a covetous heart. As you read it, test your own responses to this farmer's various experiences.

How do you respond to the wealthy farmer's *dilemma?* Here was a man who had a problem with too much wealth! If we say, "I certainly wish I had that problem!" we may be revealing covetousness in our hearts. If suddenly you inherited a great deal of wealth, would it create a problem for you? Or would you simply praise God and ask Him what He wanted you to do with it?

There are perils to prosperity (Prov. 30:7-9). Wealth can choke the Word of God (Matt. 13:22), create snares and temptations (1 Tim. 6:6-10, 17-19), and give you a false sense of security. People say that money does not satisfy, but it does satisfy *if you want to live on that level.* People who are satisfied only with the things that money can buy are in great danger of losing the things that money cannot buy.

This farmer saw his wealth as an opportunity to please himself. He had no thoughts of others or of God.

How do you respond to the *decisions* of the rich man? Are you saying, "Now that is shrewd business! Save and have it ready for the future!" But Jesus saw selfishness in all that this man did (note the eleven personal pronouns), and He said the man was a fool. The world's philosophy is "Take care of Number One!" But Jesus does not endorse that philosophy.

There is certainly nothing wrong with following good business principles, or even with saving for the future (1 Tim. 5:8). Jesus does not encourage waste (John 6:12). But neither does He encourage selfishness motivated by covetousness.

How do you respond to the farmer's *desires?* Are you saying, "This is the life! The man has success, satisfaction, and security! What more could he want?" But Jesus did not see this farmer enjoying life; He saw him facing death! Wealth cannot keep us alive when our time comes to die, nor can it buy back the opportunities we missed while we were thinking of ourselves and ignoring God and others.

Jesus made it clear that true life does not come from an abundance of things, nor do true success or security. This man had a false view of both life and death. He thought that life came from accumulating things, and that death was far away. On March 11, 1856, Henry David Thoreau wrote in his journal, "That man is the richest whose pleasures are cheapest." He also said, "A man is rich in proportion to the number of things which he can afford to let alone."

Finally, how do you respond to the *death* of the boastful farmer? We are prone to say, "Too bad this fellow died just when he had everything going for him! How tragic that he could not finish his great plans." But the greatest tragedy is not what the man left behind but what lay *before* him: eternity without God! The man lived without God and died without God, and his wealth was but an incident in his life. God is not impressed with our money.

What does it mean to be "rich toward God"? It means to acknowledge gratefully that everything we have comes from God, and then make an effort to use what He gives us for the good of others and the glory of God. Wealth can be *enjoyed* and *employed* at the same time if our purpose is to honor God (1 Tim. 6:10ff). To be rich toward God means spiritual enrichment, not just personal enjoyment. How tragic when people are rich in this world but poor in the next! (see Matt. 6:19-34)

Beware of Worrying (Luke 12:22-34)

The rich farmer worried because he had too much, but the disciples might be tempted to worry because they did not have enough! They had given up all they had in order to follow Christ. They were living by faith, and faith is always tested.

Worry is destructive. The word translated "anxious" in Luke 12:22 means "to be torn apart," and the phrase "doubtful mind" (Luke 12:29) means "to be held in suspense." It is the picture of a ship being tossed in a storm. Our English word *worry* comes from an old Anglo-Saxon word that means "to strangle." "Worry does not empty tomorrow of its sorrow," said Corrie Ten Boom; "it empties today of its strength."

Worry is also deceptive. It gives us a false view of life, of itself, and of God. Worry convinces us that life is made up of what we eat and what we wear. We get so concerned about *the means* that we totally forget about *the end,* which is to glorify God (Matt. 6:33). There is a great difference between making a living and making a life.

Worry blinds us to the world around us and the way God cares for His creation. God makes the flowers beautiful, and He even feeds the unclean ravens who have no ability to sow or reap. He ought to be able to care for men *to whom He has given the ability to work.* Jesus was not suggesting that we sit around and let God feed us, for the birds themselves work hard to stay alive. Rather, He encourages us to trust Him and cooperate with Him in using the abilities and opportunities that He gives us (2 Thes. 3:6-15).

But worry even blinds us to itself. We can get to the place where we actually think that worry accomplishes good things in our lives! In Luke 12:25, Jesus pointed out that our worries do not add one extra minute to our lives (Ps. 39:5) or one extra inch to our height. The rich farmer's fretting certainly did not lengthen his life! Instead of adding to our lives, our worries take away from our lives. People can worry themselves into the hospital or into the grave!

Once again, Jesus argued from the lesser to the greater. If God feeds the birds, He will surely feed His children. If He beautifies the plants that grow up one day and are cut down the next, surely He will clothe His own people. The problem is not His little power, for He can do anything; the problem is our little faith.

Worry is deformative. It keeps us from growing and it makes us like the unsaved in the world (Luke 12:30). In short, worry is unchristian; worry is a sin. How can we witness to a lost world and encourage them to put faith in Jesus Christ if we ourselves are doubting God and worrying? Is it not inconsistent to preach faith and yet not practice it? The late chaplain of the United States Senate, Peter Marshall, once prayed "that ulcers would not become the badge of our faith." Too often they are!

How do we win over worry? The first step is to realize that *God knows our needs,* so we can trust Him to meet them. We are sheep in His little flock, children in His family, and servants in His kingdom; and He will see to it that our needs are fully met. It is His *pleasure* to give us His kingdom, so will He not give us everything that we need? (see Rom. 8:32)

But God's pleasures and our treasures must go together. We must look at earth from heaven's point of view and make sure that we put God's kingdom first in everything. The main question is, "Where is your heart?" If our hearts are fixed on the transient things of earth, then we will always worry. But if we are fixed on the eternal, then God's peace will guard our minds and hearts (Phil. 4:6-9). We must "hang loose" when it comes to this world's goods, and be willing even to sell what we have in order to help others (Acts 2:44-45; 4:34-35). It is not wrong to own things so long as things do not own us.

Beware of Carelessness (Luke 12:35-53)

Jesus shifted the emphasis from being worried about the present to being watchful about the future. The themes in Luke 12 all go together, for one of the best ways to conquer hypocrisy, covetousness, and worry is to look for the Lord's return. When you are "living in the future tense," it is difficult for the things of the world to ensnare you. In this section, Jesus explained how we can be ready for His return.

Waiting and watching (vv. 35-40). Jewish weddings were held at night, and a bridegroom's servants would have to wait for their master to come home with his bride. The new husband would certainly not want to be kept waiting at the door with his bride! But the servants had to be sure they were ready to go to work, with their robes tucked under their girdles so they were free to move (see 1 Peter 1:13ff).

But the remarkable thing in this story is that the master serves the servants! In Jewish weddings, the bride was treated like a queen and the groom like a king; so you would not expect the "king" to minister to his staff. Our King will minister to His faithful servants when He greets us at His return, and He will reward us for our faithfulness.

To "watch" means to be alert, to be ready, not to be caught by surprise. That is the attitude we must have toward the second coming of Jesus Christ. His coming will be like that of a thief: unannounced and unexpected (Matt. 24:43; 1 Thes. 5:2; Rev. 16:15). We must be ready!

The saintly Presbyterian pastor Robert Murray McCheyne sometimes asked people, "Do you believe that Jesus is coming today?" If they replied in the negative, he would say, "Then you had better be ready, for He is coming at an hour when you think not!"

Working (vv. 41-48). Lest we get the idea that watching and waiting are all that He requires, Jesus added this parable to encourage us to be working when He comes. The Apostles had a special responsibility to feed God's household, His church; but each of us has some work to do in this world, assigned to us by the Lord. Our responsibility is to be faithful when He comes. We may not appear successful in our own eyes, or in the eyes of others; but that is not important. The thing God wants is faithfulness (1 Cor. 4:2).

Once a believer starts to think his Master is *not* coming back, his life begins to deteriorate. Our relationship with others depends on our relationship to the Lord; so if we stop looking for Him, we will stop loving His people. The motive for Christian life and service must be a desire to please the Lord and be found faithful at His return.

I do not think that Luke 12:46 teaches that unfaithful believers lose their salvation, because our going to heaven depends on faith in Jesus Christ and not good works (Eph. 2:8-10; 2 Tim. 2:11-13). The phrase "cut him in sunder" means "cut him off, separate him"; and "unbelievers" can also be translated "unfaithful." Our Lord will separate the faithful believers from the unfaithful; He will reward the faithful, but the unfaithful servants will lose their rewards (1 Cor. 3:13-15).

God's judgment will be fair. It will be based on what the servants know of God's will. This is not to suggest that the more ignorant we are, the easier time we will have at the Judgment Seat of Christ! We are admonished to know God's will (Rom. 12:2; Col. 1:9) and to grow in our knowledge of Jesus Christ (2 Peter 3:18). Jesus is stating a general principle: the more we have from God, the greater our accountability before God.

Warring (vv. 49-53). As we wait, watch, and work, we will not have an easy time, because we are aliens in enemy territory. The images Jesus used—fire, baptism, division—speak of opposition and conflict. To the Jews, fire was a symbol of judgment; and our Lord's coming into this world did bring judgment (John 9:39-41).

Our Lord's "baptism" in Luke 12:50 refers to His suffering and death, which was pictured by His baptism in the Jordan. (See Ps. 42:7 and Jonah 2:3, and note His reference to Jonah in Luke 11:29-30.) The Apostles certainly received a baptism of suffering as they witnessed for Christ after Pentecost.

Luke opened his book announcing "peace on earth" (Luke 2:14), but now he has the Lord seemingly contradicting this promise. Jesus does give peace to those who trust Him (Rom. 5:1), but often their confession of faith becomes a declaration of war among their family and friends. Jesus is a cause of division (see John 7:12, 43; 9:16; 10:19). But even if there is not "peace on earth," there is "peace in heaven" (Luke 19:38) because of the finished work of Jesus Christ on the cross.

After instructing His disciples, Jesus turned and gave a final warning to the people around Him.

Beware of Spiritual Dullness (Luke 12:54-59)

Jesus used two illustrations to impress on the crowds the importance of discernment and diligence in spiritual matters. First, He talked about the weather, and then He talked about a lawsuit.

Discernment (vv. 54-57). If people were as discerning about spiritual things as they are about the weather, they would be better off! The crowd could predict a storm, but it could not foresee the coming judgment. It knew that the temperature was about to change, but it could not interpret the "signs of the times." The Jewish nation had the prophetic Scriptures for centuries and should have known what God was doing, but their religious leaders led them astray.

How tragic that men today can predict the movements of the heavenly bodies, split atoms, and even put men on the moon; but they are blind to what God is doing in the world. They know how to get to the stars, but they do not know how to get to heaven! Our educated world possesses a great deal of scientific knowledge but not much spiritual wisdom.

Diligence (vv. 58-59). Anyone will do whatever is necessary to stay out of prison, but how many people will apply that same concern and diligence to stay out of hell? If lawyers and judges would examine God's Word as diligently as they examine their law books, they will gain a wisdom that the law cannot give.

The nation of Israel was marching to judgment, and the Judge was Almighty God, yet they would not seek for terms of peace (Luke 13:34-35). Jesus knew that the Roman armies would come to destroy the city and the temple (Luke 19:41-44), but He could not convince the people to repent. Their debt was mounting up and they would pay the last mite.

We must apply these truths to our own lives personally. If we knew a storm was coming, we would prepare for it. If we knew the officer was coming to take us to court, we would get a lawyer and try to settle the case out of court. The storm of God's wrath is coming, and the Judge is already standing before the door (James 5:9).

"Behold, now is the accepted time; behold, now is the day of salvation" (2 Cor. 6:2).

CHAPTER TWELVE QUESTIONS AND ANSWERS

Luke 13

A Jewish student asked his teacher, "Rabbi, why is it that when I ask you a question, you always reply by asking me another question?"

The rabbi replied, "So why shouldn't I?"

As Jesus continued His journey toward Jerusalem, He encountered four situations involving questions that had to be answered. "To question a wise man is the beginning of wisdom," says a German proverb. Not everyone who questioned the Lord did so from a right motive, but that did not stop Jesus from teaching them what they needed to know. As you study His replies in Luke 13, you can learn more about Him and His ministry, and also more about living the Christian life so as to please Him.

A Political Question about Justice (Luke 13:1-9)

Pontius Pilate, the Roman governor, did not get along with the Jews because he was insensitive to their religious convictions. For example, he brought the official Roman ensigns into Jerusalem and infuriated the Jews who resented having Caesar's image in the Holy City. Pilate threatened to kill the protestors *and they were willing to die!* Seeing their determination, the governor relented and moved the ensigns to Caesarea, but that did not stop the hostilities.

The atrocity mentioned in Luke 13:1 may have taken place when Pilate "appropriated" money from the temple treasury to help finance an aqueduct. A large crowd of angry Jews gathered in protest; so Pilate had soldiers *in civilian clothes* mingle with the mob. Using concealed weapons, the soldiers killed a number of innocent and unarmed Jews, and this only added to the Jews' hatred for their governor.

Since Jesus was going up to Jerusalem, anything He said about Pilate was sure to get there before Him. If He ignored the issue, the crowd would accuse Him of being pro-Roman and disloyal to His people. If He defended the Jews and accused Pilate, He would be in trouble with the Romans, and the Jewish leaders would have a good excuse to get Him arrested.

Our Lord moved the whole issue to a higher level and avoided politics completely. Instead of discussing *Pilate's* sins, He dealt with the sins of the people questioning Him. He answered their question by asking a question!

To begin with, He made it clear that human tragedies are not always divine punishments and that it is wrong for us to "play God" and pass judgment. Job's friends made this mistake when they said that Job's afflictions were evidence that he was a sinner. If we take that approach to tragedy, then we will have a hard time explaining the sufferings of the Prophets and Apostles, and even of our Lord Himself.

"How would you explain the deaths of the people on whom the tower in Siloam fell?" He asked. "That was not the fault of Pilate. Was it God's fault? Shall we blame Him? The eighteen who were killed were just doing their job, yet they died. They were not protesting or creating trouble."

When the blind English poet John Milton was old and obscure, he was visited one day by Charles II, son of the king that the Puritans had beheaded. "Your blindness is a judgment from God for the part you took against my father," said the king. Milton replied, "If I have lost my *sight* through God's judgment, what can you say of your father who lost his *head?*"

Jesus went on to show the logical conclusion of their argument: if God *does* punish sinners in this way, then they themselves had better repent because all men are sinners! The question is not, "Why did these people die?" but, "What right do you have to live?" None of us is sinless, so we had all better get prepared.

It is easier to talk about other people's deaths than it is to face our own sin and possible death. The American publishing tycoon William Randolph Hearst would not permit anyone to mention death in his presence, *yet he died.* I asked a friend of mine what the death rate was in his city, and he replied, "One apiece." Then he added, "People are dying who never died before."

According to Leviticus 19:23-25, fruit from newly planted trees was not eaten the first three years, and the fourth year the crops belonged to the Lord. A farmer would not get any figs for himself until the fifth year, but this man had now been waiting for *seven* years! No wonder he wanted to cut down the fruitless tree!

The parable has an application to individuals and to the nation of Israel. God is gracious and long-suffering toward people (2 Peter 3:9) and does more than enough to encourage us to repent and bear fruit (Matt. 3:7-10). He has had every right to cut us down, but in His mercy, He has spared us. Yet we must not presume upon the kindness and long-suffering of the Lord, for the day of judgment will finally come.

But the tree also reminds us of God's special goodness to Israel (Isa. 5:1-7; Rom. 9:1-5) and His patience with them. God waited three years during our Lord's earthly ministry, but the nation did not produce fruit. He then waited about forty years more before He allowed the Roman armies to destroy Jerusalem and the temple; and during those years, the church gave to the nation a powerful witness of the Gospel message. Finally, the tree was cut down.

It is significant that the parable was "open-ended," so that the listeners had to supply the conclusion. (The Book of Jonah is another example of this approach.) Did the tree bear fruit? Did the special care accomplish anything? Was the tree spared or cut down? We have no way to know the answers to these questions, *but we can answer as far as our own lives are concerned!* Again, the question is not "What happened to the tree?" but "What will happen to *me?*"

God is seeking fruit. He will accept no substitutes, and the time to repent is NOW. The next time you hear about a tragedy that claims many lives, ask yourself, "Am I just taking up space, or am I bearing fruit to God's glory?"

A Legal Question about the Sabbath (Luke 13:10-21)

Liberation (vv. 10-13). If I had been crippled for eighteen years, I wonder if I would be faithful to worship God week after week in the synagogue? Surely this woman had prayed and asked God for help, and yet she was not delivered. However, God's seeming unconcern did not cause her to become bitter or resentful. There she was in the synagogue.

Ever sensitive to the needs of others, Jesus saw the woman and called her to come forward. It may have seemed heartless to the congregation for Him to do this and expose her handicap publicly (see Matt. 12:13), but He knew what He was doing. For one thing, Satan was in the synagogue and He wanted to expose him and defeat him. But He also wanted the woman to help Him teach the people an important lesson about freedom.

Not only does Satan bow people down, but so do sin (Ps. 38:6), sorrow (Ps. 42:5), and suffering (Ps. 44:25). Jesus Christ is the only One who can set the prisoner free. He spoke the word, laid His hands on her, and she was healed and gave glory to God! That was a synagogue service the people never forgot.

Indignation (v. 14). Instead of rejoicing and giving God the glory, the ruler of the synagogue (see Luke 8:41) became very angry. He did not have the courage to express his anger to Jesus, so he scolded the congregation! But the more you ponder his tirade, the more laughable it becomes. Suppose they *did* bring their sick to be healed; who would heal them? Did *he* have that kind of power; and, if he did, why had he not used it to help people before? What a cowardly hypocrite!

The bondage of the ruler of the synagogue was worse than that of the woman. Her bondage affected only her body, but his bondage shackled his mind and heart. He was so bound and blinded by tradition that he ended up opposing the Son of God! Elbert Hubbard called tradition "a clock that tells us what time it was." The ruler of the synagogue could not "discern this time" (Luke 13:12:56) and he stood condemned.

Vindication (vv. 15-17). Jesus could have healed this woman on any other day of the week. After all, she had been bound for eighteen painful years, and one more day would have made little difference. But He deliberately chose the Sabbath Day because He wanted to teach a lesson about freedom. Note the repetition of the word "loose" (Luke 13:12, 15-16).

First, the Lord defended the woman and rebuked the ruler of the synagogue. Jesus reminded him that he treated his animals far better than he treated this poor woman. This indictment included the people in the congregation as well. Our Lord was arguing from the lesser to the greater: if God permits people to help their thirsty animals on the Sabbath, would He not want us to care for needy people made in the image of God? Any tradition that keeps us from helping others is not from God. In fact, it is easy to use tradition as an excuse for not caring for others.

Jesus said that the woman was a "daughter of Abraham," referring to her spiritual condition and not her physical birth (Luke 19:9; Gal. 3:7). All the Jewish women present would have been "daughters of Abraham." Does this mean that she was a converted person *before* the Lord healed her? If so, then she is the only *believer* in the New Testament who was physically afflicted because of demonic attack. (We are not sure what Paul's "thorn in the flesh" was or exactly how Satan used it to buffet Paul. See 2 Cor. 12.)

Perhaps it is a matter of semantics, but I prefer to speak of demonic work in believers as "demon oppression" rather than "demon possession." In fact, the Greek word is "demonized," so we need not think of "possession" in spatial terms. Certainly Satan can and does attack the bodies and minds of God's people. Some satanic oppression could last for many years until someone detects that Satan is at work. Not all sickness is caused by demons (Luke 6:17-19), so we must not blame everything on Satan.

There were people in the congregation who hoped to use this Sabbath violation to accuse Jesus, but He left them so ashamed that they said nothing. The lesson that He taught was clear: Satan puts people into bondage, but true freedom comes from trusting Christ. The Sabbath that God wants to give us is a "heart rest" that comes through His grace and not from obeying traditions (Matt. 11:28-30).

The parables in Luke 13:18-21 were probably spoken to the congregation just before Jesus and the Twelve departed from the synagogue. He had used these parables before and the disciples understood them (Matt. 13:31-33, 51). Some see in them a picture of the visible outward growth of the kingdom (the mustard seed) and the invisible inward influence of the kingdom (the leaven). By using these parables, Jesus was saying, "You Jewish religious leaders may hold to your dead traditions and oppose the truth, but God's living kingdom will still increase. Satan will be defeated!"

But, we must keep two other considerations in mind. First, Jesus had already used leaven as a picture of evil (Luke 12:1), and He was not likely to contradict Himself. Second, the context of Matthew 13 indicates opposition and seeming defeat for God's kingdom, not worldwide conquest. Yes, there will be ultimate victory; but meanwhile, much of the seed sown will bear no fruit, Satan will sow counterfeits, and the net will catch all kinds of fish, good and bad. I cannot find either in church history or in contemporary reports any proof that the kingdom of God has "permeated the whole world." In view of the population increase, we are losing ground!

The Jews knew their Scriptures and recognized the images that Jesus used. Leaven represented evil (Ex. 12:14-20), and a mighty tree pictured a great world kingdom (Ezek. 17:22-24; 31:3-9; Dan. 4:20-22). A mustard seed produces a shrub, not a great tree. The kingdom would be infected with false teaching (Gal. 5:1-9), and the small seed ("little flock," Luke 12:32) would grow into an organization that would be a home for Satan. (The birds represent the evil one, Matt. 13:19.) The professing church today fits both descriptions.

A Theological Question about Salvation (Luke 13:22-30)

The events recorded in John 9–10 fit between Luke 13:21 and 22. Note in John 10:40-42 that Jesus then left Judea and went beyond the Jordan into Perea. The events of Luke 13:22–17:10 took place in Perea as the Lord gradually moved toward Jerusalem.

The scribes often discussed the question of how many people would be saved, and somebody asked Jesus to give His thoughts on the issue. As with the question about Pilate, Jesus immediately made the matter personal. "The question is not how many will be saved, but whether or not *you* will be saved! Get that settled first, and then we can discuss what you can do to help get others saved."

I sometimes receive "theological letters" from radio listeners who want to argue about predestination, election, and other difficult doctrines. When I reply, I usually ask them about their prayer life, their witnessing, and their work in the local church. That often ends the correspondence. Too many professed Christians want to discuss these profound doctrines, but they do not want to put them into practice by seeking to win people to Jesus Christ! D.L. Moody prayed, "Lord, save the elect, and then elect some more!"

"Many . . . will seek to enter in, and shall not be able" (Luke 13:24). Why? The parable tells us why, and it focuses primarily on the Jewish people of that day. However, it has a personal application to all of us today.

Jesus pictured the kingdom as a great feast, with the patriarchs and prophets as honored guests (Luke 13:28). But many of the people who were invited waited too long to respond; and, when they arrived at the banquet hall, it was too late and the door was shut (see Matt. 22:1-14; Luke 14:15-24).

But why did they wait so long? The parable suggests several reasons. To begin with, salvation is not easy; the sinner must enter a narrow gate and walk a narrow way (Luke 13:24; also see 9:23ff). The world's crowd is on the easy way, the way that leads to destruction (Matt. 7:13-14), and it is much easier to walk with them.

Another reason for their delay was their false sense of security. Jesus had been among them; they had even eaten with Him and enjoyed His fellowship, *yet they had never trusted Him.* God gave the nation many privileges and opportunities, but they wasted them (see Luke 10:13-16). God is long-suffering; however, there comes a time when even God shuts the door.

Pride also played a big part: they would not humble themselves before God. In their own eyes, they were first, but in God's eyes, they were last—*and the Gentiles would come and take their place!* (see Matt. 21:43) Imagine the "unclean Gentile dogs" sitting at the feast with Abraham, Isaac, and Jacob, while the unbelieving Jews were outside!

These people were lost because they depended on their ancient religion to save them; but Jesus saw them as "workers of iniquity," not doers of righteousness (Isa. 64:4; Titus 1:16). It takes more than reverence for tradition to get into God's kingdom!

But the major reason was given by Jesus Himself: "Ye would not" (Luke 13:34). Their minds had been instructed by the Word (Luke 13:26), and their hearts had been stirred by His mighty works, but their wills were stubborn and would not submit to Him. *This is the deadly consequence of delay.* The longer sinners wait, the harder their hearts become. "Today, if you will hear His voice, do not harden your hearts" (Heb. 4:7).

The Spanish composer Manuel de Falla was notorious for not answering his mail. When he heard that a friend had died, the composer said, "What a pity! He died before I answered his letter, which he sent me five years ago!"

When sinners fail to answer *God's* invitation to His feast, *they are the ones who die.* They are "thrust out" of the joys of the kingdom and are punished with "weeping and gnashing of teeth" (Luke 13:28). It is a picture of people who are overwhelmed with regret because they see how foolish they were to delay; but, alas, it is too late. One of the agonies of hell will be the remembrance of opportunities wasted.

What is the answer? "Strive to enter in at the narrow gate!" (Luke 13:24) The word *strive* comes from the sports arena and describes an athlete giving his best to win the contest. Our English word *agonize* comes from this word. If people today would put as much effort into things spiritual as they do things athletic, they would be much better off.

A Personal Question about Danger (Luke 13:31-35)

Jesus was in Perea, which was ruled by Herod Antipas, son of Herod the Great. The Pharisees wanted to get Jesus back into Judea where the religious leaders could watch Him and ultimately trap Him, so they tried to frighten Him away.

Herod had been perplexed by our Lord's ministry and was afraid that John the Baptist, whom he murdered, had come back from the dead (Luke 9:7-9). In fact, at one point, Herod wanted to meet Jesus so he could see Him perform a miracle! (Luke 23:8) But it appears that Herod's heart was getting harder, for now he threatened to kill Jesus. The warning the Pharisees gave (Luke 13:31) was undoubtedly true or Jesus would not have answered as He did.

Our Lord was not afraid of danger. He followed a "divine timetable" and nothing could harm Him. He was doing the will of God according to the Father's schedule (see John 2:4; 7:30; 8:20; 13:1; 17:1). It had been decreed from eternity that the Son of God would be crucified in Jerusalem at the Passover (1 Peter 1:20; Rev. 13:8), and even Herod Antipas could not hinder the purposes of God. Quite the contrary, our Lord's enemies only helped *fulfill* the will of God (Acts 2:23; 3:13-18).

Jesus used a bit of "holy sarcasm" in His reply. He compared Herod to a fox, an animal that was not held in high esteem by the Jews (Neh. 4:3). Known for its cunning, the fox was an apt illustration of the crafty Herod. Jesus had work to do and He would accomplish it. After all, Jesus walked in the light (John 9:4; 11:9-10), and foxes went hunting in the darkness!

But Jesus also had a word to say about His nation: "It cannot be that a prophet perish out of Jerusalem" (Luke 13:33). This parallels what He had said to the scribes and Pharisees in Luke 11:47-51. The nation not only rejected God's loving invitation to His feast, but they even killed the servants who brought them the invitation! (see Acts 13:27)

Our Lord's heart was grieved as He saw the unbelief and rebellion around Him, and He broke out in a lamentation over the sad plight of the Jewish nation. It was a sob of anguish, not an expression of anger. His compassionate heart was broken.

The image of the hen and her chicks would be a familiar one to an agricultural people like the Jews (see Ps. 91:4). Some of the Old Testament references to "wings" refer to the wings of the cherubim in the holy of holies in the tabernacle or temple (see Ex. 25:20; Ruth 2:12; Pss. 36:7-8; 61:4). The hen gathers her chicks when she sees danger is coming. The

Pharisees told Jesus that He was in danger, when in reality *they* were in danger!

In this lament, Jesus was addressing the whole nation and not just the Pharisees who had tried to provoke Him. The people had been given many opportunities to repent and be saved, but they had refused to heed His call. "House" refers both to the "family" of Jacob ("the house of Israel") and to the temple ("the house of God"), both of which would be "left desolate." The city and temple were destroyed and the people were scattered.

But there is a future for Israel. The time will come when their Messiah will return and be recognized and received by the people. They will say, "Blessed is He that cometh in the name of the Lord" (Luke 13:35; also see Ps. 118:26). Some of the people would use these words at His "triumphal entry" (Luke 19:38), but they will not have their fulfillment until His coming in glory (see Zech. 12:10; 14:4ff; Matt. 24:30-31).

Israel's house has been left desolate. The nation has no king or priest, no temple or sacrifice (Hosea 3:4-5). But the nation has God's promise that she has not been forsaken (Rom. 11:1ff). There can be no peace on earth until the Prince of Peace (Isa. 9:6) is seated on David's throne (Isa. 11:1ff).

Pray for the peace of Jerusalem! (Ps. 122:6)

Strive to enter in at the narrow gate!

CHAPTER THIRTEEN THE MAN WHO CAME TO DINNER

Luke 14

Sabbath Day hospitality was an important part of Jewish life, so it was not unusual for Jesus to be invited to a home for a meal after the weekly synagogue service. Sometimes the host invited Him sincerely because he wanted to learn more of God's truth. But many times Jesus was asked to dine only so His enemies could watch Him and find something to criticize and condemn. That was the case on the occasion described in Luke 14 when a leader of the Pharisees invited Jesus to dinner.

Jesus was fully aware of what was in men's hearts (John 2:24-25), so He was never caught off guard. In fact, instead of hosts or guests judging Jesus, it was Jesus who passed judgment on them when they least expected it. Indeed, in this respect, He was a dangerous person to sit with at a meal or to follow on the road! In Luke 14, we see Jesus dealing with five different kinds of people and exposing what was false in their lives and their thinking.

The Pharisees: False Piety (Luke 14:1-6)

Instead of bringing them to repentance, Jesus' severe denunciation of the Pharisees and scribes (Luke 11:39-52) only provoked them to retaliation, and they plotted against Him. The Pharisee who invited Jesus to his home for dinner also invited a man afflicted with dropsy. This is a painful disease in which, because of kidney trouble, a heart ailment, or liver disease, the tissues fill with water. How heartless of the Pharisees to "use" this man as a tool to accomplish their wicked plan, but if we do not love the Lord, neither will we love our neighbor. Their heartless treatment of the man was far worse than our Lord's "lawless" behavior on the Sabbath.

This afflicted man would not have been invited to such an important dinner were it not that the Pharisees wanted to use him as "bait" to catch Jesus. They knew that Jesus could not be in the presence of human suffering very long without doing something about it. If He ignored the afflicted man, then He was without compassion; but if He healed him, then He was openly violating the Sabbath and they could accuse Him. They put the dropsied man right in front of the Master so He could not avoid him, and then they waited for the trap to spring.

Keep in mind that Jesus had already "violated" their Sabbath traditions on at least seven different occasions. On the Sabbath Day, He had cast out a demon (Luke 4:31-37), healed a fever (Luke 4:38-39), allowed His disciples to pluck grain (Luke 6:1-5), healed a lame man (John 5:1-9), healed a man with a paralyzed hand (Luke 6:6-10), delivered a crippled woman who was afflicted by a demon (Luke 13:10-17), and healed a man born blind (John 9). Why our Lord's enemies thought that one more bit of evidence was necessary, we do not know, but we do know that their whole scheme backfired.

When Jesus asked what their convictions were about the Sabbath Day, He used on them the weapon they had forged for Him. To begin with, they couldn't heal anybody on *any* day, and everybody knew it. But even more, if the Pharisees said that nobody should be healed on the Sabbath, the people would consider them heartless; if they gave permission for healing, their associates would consider them lawless. The dilemma was now theirs, not the Lord's, and they needed a way to escape. As they did on more than one occasion, the scribes and Pharisees evaded the issue by saying nothing.

Jesus healed the man and let him go, knowing that the Pharisee's house was not the safest place for him. Instead of providing evidence against *Jesus,* the man provided evidence against the *Pharisees,* for he was "exhibit A" of the healing power of the Lord Jesus Christ.

The Lord knew too much about this legalistic crowd to let them escape. He knew that on the Sabbath Day they would deliver their farm animals from danger, so why not permit Him to deliver a man who was made in the likeness of God? Seemingly, they were suggesting that animals were more important than people. (It is tragic that some people even today have more love for their pets than they do for their family members, their neighbors, or even for a lost world.)

Jesus exposed the false piety of the Pharisees and the scribes. They claimed to be defending God's Sabbath laws, when in reality they were denying God by the way they abused people and accused the Saviour. There is a big difference between protecting God's truth and promoting man's traditions.

The Guests: False Popularity (Luke 14:7-11)

Experts in management tell us that most people wear an invisible sign that reads, "Please make me feel important"; if we heed that sign, we can succeed in human relations. On the other hand, if we say or do things that make others feel insignificant, we will fail. Then people will respond by becoming angry and resentful, because everybody wants to be noticed and made to feel important.

In Jesus' day, as today, there were "status symbols" that helped people enhance and protect their high standing in society. If you were invited to the "right homes" and if you were seated in the "right places," then people would know how important you really were. The emphasis was on reputation, not character. It was more important to sit in the right places than to live the right kind of life.

In New Testament times, the closer you sat to the host, the higher you stood on the social ladder and the more attention (and invitations) you would receive from others. Naturally, many people rushed to the "head table" when the doors were opened because they wanted to be important.

This kind of attitude betrays a false view of success. "Try not to become a man of success," said Albert Einstein, "but try to become a man of value." While there may be some exceptions, it is usually true that valuable people are eventually recognized and appropriately honored. Success that comes only from self-promotion is temporary, and you may be embarrassed as you are asked to move down (Prov. 25:6-7).

When Jesus advised the guests to take the lowest places, He was not giving them a "gimmick" that guaranteed promotion. The false humility that takes the lowest place is just as hateful to God as the pride that takes the highest place. God is not impressed by our status in society or in the church. He is not influenced by what people say or think about us, because He sees the thoughts and motives of the heart (1 Sam. 16:7). God still humbles the proud and exalts the humble (James 4:6).

British essayist Francis Bacon compared fame to a river that easily carried "things light and swollen" but that drowned "things weighty and solid." It is interesting to scan old editions of encyclopedias and see how many "famous people" are "forgotten people" today.

Humility is a fundamental grace in the Christian life, and yet it is elusive; if you know you have it, you have lost it! It has well been said that humility is not thinking meanly of ourselves; it is simply not thinking of ourselves at all. Jesus is the greatest example of humility, and we would do well to ask the Holy Spirit to enable us to imitate Him (Phil. 2:1-16).

The Host: False Hospitality (Luke 14:12-14)

Jesus knew that the host had invited his guests for two reasons: (1) to pay them back because they had invited him to past feasts, or (2) to put them under his debt so that they would invite him to future feasts. Such hospitality was not an expression of love and grace but rather an evidence of pride and selfishness. He was "buying" recognition.

Jesus does not prohibit us from entertaining family and friends, but He warns us against entertaining *only* family and friends exclusively and habitually. That kind of "fellowship" quickly degenerates into a "mutual admiration society" in which each one tries to outdo the others and no one dares to break the cycle. Sad to say, too much church social life fits this description.

Our motive for sharing must be the praise of God and not the applause of men, the eternal reward in heaven and not the temporary recognition on earth. A pastor friend of mine used to remind me, "You can't get your reward twice!" and he was right (see Matt. 6:1-18). On the day of judgment, many who today are first in the eyes of men will be last in God's eyes, and many who are last in the eyes of men will be first in the eyes of God (Luke 13:30).

In our Lord's time, it was not considered proper to ask poor people and handicapped people to public banquets. (The women were not invited either!) But Jesus commanded us to put these needy people at the top of our guest list *because they cannot pay us back.* If our hearts are right, God will see to it that we are properly rewarded, though getting a reward must not be the motive for our generosity. When we serve others from unselfish hearts, we are laying up treasures in heaven (Matt. 6:20) and becoming "rich toward God" (Luke 12:21).

Our modern world is very competitive, and it is easy for God's people to become more concerned about profit and loss than they are about sacrifice and service. "What will *I* get out of it?" may easily become life's most important question (Matt. 19:27ff). We must strive to maintain the unselfish attitude that Jesus had and share what we have with others.

The Jews: False Security (Luke 14:15-24)

When Jesus mentioned "the resurrection of the just," one of the guests became excited and said, "Blessed is he that shall eat bread in the kingdom of God!" The Jewish people pictured their future kingdom as a great feast with Abraham, Isaac, Jacob, and the prophets as the honored guests (Luke 13:28; see Isa. 25:6). This anonymous guest was confident that he would one day be at the "kingdom feast" with them! Jesus responded by telling him a parable that revealed the sad consequences of false confidence.

In Jesus' day when you invited guests to a dinner, you told them the day but not the exact hour of the meal. A host had to know how many guests were coming so he could butcher the right amount of animals and prepare sufficient food. Just before the feast was to begin, the host sent his servants to each of the guests to tell them the banquet was ready and they should come (see Es. 5:8; 6:14). In other words, *each of the guests in this parable had already agreed to attend the banquet.* The host expected them to be there.

But instead of eagerly coming to the feast, all of the guests insulted the host by refusing to attend, and they all gave very feeble excuses to defend their change in plans.

The first guest begged off because he had to "go and see" a piece of real estate he had purchased. In the East, the purchasing of property is often a long and complicated process, and the man would have had many opportunities to examine the land he was buying. Anybody who purchases land that he has never examined is certainly taking a chance. Since most banquets were held in the evening, the man had little daylight left even for a cursory investigation.

The second man had also made a purchase—ten oxen that he was anxious to prove. Again, who would purchase that many animals without first testing them? Not many customers in our modern world would buy a used car that they had not taken out for a "test drive." Furthermore, how could this man really put these oxen to the test when it was so late in the day? His statement "I go to prove them!" suggests that he was already on his way to the farm when the servant came with the final call to the dinner.

The third guest really had no excuse at all. Since they involved so much elaborate preparation, Jewish weddings were never surprises, so this man knew well in advance that he was taking a wife. That being the case, he should not have agreed to attend the feast in the first place. Since only Jewish men were invited to banquets, the host did not expect the wife to come anyway. Having a new wife could have kept the man from the battlefield (Deut. 24:5) but not from the festive board.

Of course, these were only excuses. I think it was Billy Sunday who defined an excuse as "the skin of a reason stuffed with a lie." The person who is good at excuses is usually not good at anything else. These three guests actually expected to get another invitation in the future, *but that invitation never came.*

Having prepared a great dinner for many guests, the host did not want all that food to go to waste, so he sent his servant out to gather a crowd and bring them to the banquet hall. What kind of men would be found in the streets and lanes of the city or in the highways and hedges? The outcasts, the loiterers, the homeless, the undesireables, *the kind of people that Jesus came to save* (Luke 15:1-2; 19:10). There might even be some Gentiles in the crowd!

These men may have had only one reason for refusing the kind invitation: they were unprepared to attend such a fine dinner. So, the servant constrained them to accept (see 2 Cor. 5:20). They had no excuses. The poor could not afford to buy oxen; the blind could not go to examine real estate; and the poor, maimed, lame, and blind were usually not given in marriage. This crowd would be hungry and lonely and only too happy to accept an invitation to a free banquet.

Not only did the host get other people to take the places assigned to the invited guests, but he also *shut the door so that the excuse-makers could not change their minds and come in* (see Luke 13:22-30). In fact, the host was angry. We rarely think of God expressing judicial anger against those who reject His gracious invitations, but verses like Isaiah 55:6 and Proverbs 1:24-33 give a solemn warning that we not treat His calls lightly.

This parable had a special message for the proud Jewish people who were so sure they would "eat bread in the kingdom of God." Within a few short years, the Gospel would be rejected by the official religious leaders, and the message would go out to the Samaritans (Acts 8) and then to the Gentiles (Acts 10; 13ff).

But the message of this parable applies to all lost sinners today. God still says, "All things are now ready. Come!" Nothing more need be done for the salvation of your soul, for Jesus Christ finished the work of redemption when He died for you on the cross and arose from the dead. The feast has been spread, the invitation is free, and you are invited to come.

People today make the same mistake that the people in the parable made: they delay in responding to the invitation *because they settle for second best.* There is certainly nothing wrong with owning a farm, examining purchases, or spending an evening with your wife. But if these *good* things keep you from enjoying the *best* things, then they become *bad* things. The excuse-makers were actually successful people in the eyes of their friends, but they were failures in the eyes of Jesus Christ.

The Christian life is a feast, not a funeral, and all are invited to come. Each of us as believers must herald abroad the message, "Come, for all things are now ready!" God wants to see His house filled, and "yet there is room." He wants us to go home (Mark 5:19), go into the streets and lanes (Luke 14:21), go into the highways and hedges (Luke 14:23), and go into all the world (Mark 16:15) with the Gospel of Jesus Christ.

This parable was the text of the last sermon D.L. Moody preached, "Excuses." It was given on November 23, 1899 in the Civic Auditorium in Kansas City, and Moody was a sick man as he preached. "I must have souls in Kansas City," he told the students at his school in Chicago. "Never, never have I wanted so much to lead men and women to Christ as I do this time!"

There was a throbbing in his chest, and he had to hold to the organ to keep from falling, but Moody bravely preached the Gospel; and some fifty people responded to trust Christ. The next day, Moody left for home, and a month later he died. Up to the very end, Moody was "compelling them to come in."

The Multitudes: False Expectancy (Luke 14:25-35)

When Jesus left the Pharisee's house, great crowds followed Him, but He was not impressed by their enthusiasm. He knew that most of those in the crowd were not the least bit interested in spiritual things. Some wanted only to see miracles, others heard that He fed the hungry, and a few hoped He would overthrow Rome and establish David's promised kingdom. They were expecting the wrong things.

Jesus turned to the multitude and preached a sermon that deliberately thinned out the ranks. He made it clear that, when it comes to personal discipleship, He is more interested in *quality* than *quantity.* In the matter of saving lost souls, He wants His house to be filled (Luke 14:23); but in the matter of personal discipleship, He wants only those who are willing to pay the price.

A "disciple" is a learner, one who attaches himself or herself to a teacher in order to learn a trade or a subject. Perhaps our nearest modern equivalent is "apprentice," one who learns by watching and by doing. The word *disciple* was the most common name for the followers of Jesus Christ and is used 264 times in the Gospels and the Book of Acts.

Jesus seems to make a distinction between salvation and discipleship. Salvation is open to all who will come by faith, while discipleship is for believers willing to pay a price. Salvation means coming to the cross and trusting Jesus Christ, while discipleship means carrying the cross and following Jesus Christ. Jesus wants as many sinners saved as possible ("that My house may be filled"), but He cautions us not to take discipleship lightly; and in the three parables He gave, He made it clear that there is a price to pay.

To begin with, we must love Christ supremely, even more than we love our own flesh and blood (Luke 14:26-27). The word *hate* does not suggest positive antagonism but rather "to love less" (see Gen. 29:30-31; Mal. 1:2-3; and Matt. 10:37). Our love for Christ must be so strong that all other love is like hatred in comparison. In fact, we must hate our own lives and be willing to bear the cross after Him.

What does it mean to "carry the cross"? It means daily identification with Christ in shame, suffering, and surrender to God's will. It means death to self, to our own plans and ambitions, and a willingness to serve Him as He directs (John 12:23-28). A "cross" is something we willingly accept from God as part of His will for our lives. The Christian who called his noisy neighbors the "cross" he had to bear certainly did not understand the meaning of dying to self.

Jesus gave three parables to explain why He makes such costly demands on His followers: the man building a tower, the king fighting a war, and the salt losing its flavor. The usual interpretation is that believers are represented by the man building the tower and the king fighting the war, and we had better "count the cost" before we start, lest we start and not be able to finish. But I agree with Campbell Morgan that the builder and the king represent not the believer but Jesus Christ. *He is the One who must "count the cost" to see whether we are the kind of material He can use to build the church and battle the enemy.* He cannot get the job done with halfhearted followers who will not pay the price.

As I write this chapter, I can look up and see on my library shelves hundreds of volumes of Christian biographies and autobiographies, the stories of godly men and women who made great contributions to the building of the church and the battle against the enemy. They were willing to pay the price, and God blessed them and used them. They were people with "salt" in their character.

Jesus had already told His disciples that they were "the salt of the earth" (Matt. 5:13). When the sinner trusts Jesus Christ as Saviour, a miracle takes place and "clay" is turned into "salt." Salt was a valued item in that day; in fact, part of a soldier's pay was given in salt. (The words *salt* and *salary* are related; hence, the saying, "He's not worth his salt.")

Salt is a preservative, and God's people in this world are helping to retard the growth of evil and decay. Salt is also a purifying agent, an antiseptic that makes things cleaner. It may sting when it touches the wound, but it helps to kill infection. Salt gives flavor to things and, most of all, makes people thirsty. By our character and conduct, we ought to make others thirsty for the Lord Jesus Christ and the salvation that He alone can give.

Our modern salt is pure and does not lose its flavor, but the salt in Jesus' day was impure and could lose its flavor, especially if it came in contact with earth. Once the saltiness was gone, there was no way to restore it, and the salt was thrown out into the street to be walked on. When a disciple loses his Christian character, he is "good for nothing" and will eventually be "walked on" by others and bring disgrace to Christ.

Discipleship is serious business. If we are not true disciples, then Jesus cannot build the tower and fight the war. "There is always an *if* in connection with discipleship," wrote Oswald Chambers, "and it implies that we need not [be disciples] unless we like. There is never any compulsion; Jesus does not coerce us. There is only one way of being a disciple, and that is by being devoted to Jesus."

If we tell Jesus that we want to take up our cross and follow Him as His disciples, then He wants us to know exactly what we are getting into. He wants no false expectancy, no illusions, no bargains. He wants to use us as stones for building His church, soldiers for battling His enemies, and salt for bettering His world; *and He is looking for quality.*

After all, He was on His way to Jerusalem when He spoke these words, and look what happened to Him there! He does not ask us to do anything for Him that He has not already done for us.

To some, Jesus says, "You cannot be My disciples!" Why? Because they will not forsake all for Him, bear shame and reproach for Him, and let their love for Him control them.

And they are the losers.

Will *you* be His disciple?

CHAPTER FOURTEEN THE JOYS OF SALVATION

Luke 15

When D.L. Moody was directing his Sunday School in Chicago, one boy walked several miles to attend; and somebody asked him, "Why don't you go to a Sunday School closer to home?"

His reply might have been used by the publicans and sinners in Jesus' day: "Because they love a feller over there."

It is significant that Jesus *attracted* sinners while the Pharisees *repelled* them. (What does this say about some of our churches today?) Lost sinners came to Jesus, not because He catered to them or compromised His message, but because He cared for them. He understood their needs and tried to help them, while the Pharisees criticized them and kept their distance (see Luke 18:9-14). The Pharisees had a knowledge of the Old Testament Law and a desire for personal purity, yet they had no love for lost souls.

Three words summarize the message of this chapter: *lost, found,* and *rejoice.* Jesus spoke these parables to answer the accusations of the Pharisees and scribes who were scandalized at His behavior. It was bad enough that Jesus *welcomed* these outcasts and taught them, but He went so far as to *eat with them!* The Jewish religious leaders did not yet understand that the Son of man had "come to seek and to save that which was lost" (Luke 19:10). Even more, they were still blind to the fact that *they themselves were among the lost.*

This chapter makes it clear that there is one message of salvation: God welcomes and forgives repentant sinners. But these parables also reveal that there are *two aspects to this salvation.* There is *God's* part: the shepherd seeks the lost sheep, and the woman searches for the lost coin. But there is also *man's* part in salvation, for the wayward son willingly repented and returned home. To emphasize but one aspect is to give a false view of salvation, for both the sovereignty of God and the responsibility of man must be considered (see John 6:37; 2 Thes. 2:13-14).

Since one of the major themes of this chapter is joy, let's consider the three different joys that are involved in salvation. C.S. Lewis wrote, "Joy is the serious business of heaven," and it is a joy in which you and I can share.

The Joy of Finding (Luke 15:1-10)

The story about the lost sheep would touch the hearts of the men and boys in the crowd, and the women and girls would appreciate the story about the coin that was lost from the wedding necklace. Jesus sought to reach everybody's heart.

The lost sheep (vv. 3-7). The sheep was lost because of foolishness. Sheep have a tendency to go astray, and that is why they need a shepherd (Isa. 53:6; 1 Peter 2:25). The scribes and Pharisees had no problem seeing the publicans and sinners as "lost sheep," but they would not apply that image to themselves! And yet the prophet made it clear that all of us have sinned and gone astray, and that includes religious people.

The shepherd was responsible for each sheep; if one was missing, the shepherd had to pay for it unless he could prove that it was killed by a predator (see Gen. 31:38-39; Ex. 22:10-13; Amos 3:12). This explains why he would leave the flock with the other shepherds, go and search for the missing animal, and then rejoice when he found it. Not to find the lost sheep meant money out of his own pocket, plus the disgrace of being known as a careless shepherd.

By leaving the ninety-nine sheep, the shepherd was not saying they were unimportant to him. They were safe but the lost sheep was in danger. The fact that the shepherd would go after *one* sheep is proof that each animal was dear to him. Jesus was not suggesting that the scribes and Pharisees were not in need of salvation, for they certainly were. We must not make every part of the parable mean something, otherwise we will turn it into an allegory and distort the message.

There is a fourfold joy expressed when a lost sinner comes to the Saviour. Though nothing is said in the story about how the sheep felt, there is certainly joy in the heart of the *person found.* Both Scripture (Acts 3:8; 8:39) and our own personal experience verify the joy of salvation.

But there is also the joy of the person who does the finding. Whenever you assist in leading a lost soul to faith in Christ, you experience a wonderful joy within. Others join with us in rejoicing as we share the good news of a new child of God in the family, and there is also joy in heaven (Luke 15:7, 10). The angels know better than we do what we are saved *from* and *to,* and they rejoice with us.

The lost coin (vv. 8-10). The sheep was lost because of its foolishness, but the coin was lost because of the carelessness of another. It is a sobering thought that our carelessness *at home* could result in a soul being lost.

When a Jewish girl married, she began to wear a headband of ten silver coins to signify that she was now a wife. It was the Jewish version of our modern wedding ring, and it would be considered a calamity for her to lose one of those coins. Palestinian houses were dark, so she had to light a lamp and search until she found the lost coin; and we can imagine her joy at finding it.

We must not press parabolic images too far, but it is worth noting that the coin would have on it the image of the ruler (Luke 20:19-25). The lost sinner bears the image of God, even though that image has been marred by sin. When a lost sinner is "found," God begins to restore that divine image through the power of the Spirit; and one day, the believer will be like Jesus Christ (Rom. 8:29; 2 Cor. 3:18; Col. 3:10; 1 John 3:1-2).

These two parables help us understand something of what it means to be lost. To begin with, it means being *out of place.* Sheep belong with the flock, coins belong on the chain, and lost sinners belong in fellowship with God. But to be lost also means *being out of service.* A lost sheep is of no value to the shepherd, a lost coin has no value to the owner, and a lost sinner cannot experience the enriching fulfillment God has for him in Jesus Christ.

But to turn this around, to be "found" (saved) means that you are back in place (reconciled to God), back in service (life has a purpose), and out of danger. No wonder the shepherd and the woman rejoiced and invited their friends to rejoice with them!

It is easy for us today to read these two parables and take their message for granted, but the people who first heard them must have been shocked. *Jesus was saying that God actually searches for lost sinners!* No wonder the scribes and Pharisees were offended, for there was no place in their legalistic theology for a God like that. They had forgotten that God had sought out Adam and Eve when they had sinned and hidden from God (Gen. 3:8-9). In spite of their supposed knowledge of Scripture, the scribes and Pharisees forgot that God was like a father who pitied his wayward children (Ps. 103:8-14).

There are few joys that match the joy of finding the lost and bringing them to the Saviour. "The church has nothing to do but to save souls," said John Wesley, the founder of Methodism. "Therefore, spend and be spent in this work."

The Joy of Returning (Luke 15:11-24)

We call this story "The Parable of the Prodigal Son" (the word *prodigal* means "wasteful"), but it could also be called "The Parable of the Loving Father," for it emphasizes the graciousness of the father more than the sinfulness of the son. Unlike the shepherd and the woman in the previous parables, the father did not go out to seek the son, but it was the memory of his father's goodness that brought the boy to repentance and forgiveness (see Rom. 2:4). Note in the story the three experiences of the younger son.

Rebellion—he went to the far country (vv. 11-16). According to Jewish law, an elder son received twice as much as the other sons (Deut. 21:17), and a father could distribute his wealth during his lifetime if he wished. It was perfectly legal for the younger son to ask for his share of the estate and even to sell it, but it was certainly not a very loving thing on his part. It was as though he were saying to his father, "I wish you were dead!" Thomas Huxley said, "A man's worst difficulties begin when he is able to do just as he likes." How true!

We are always heading for trouble whenever we value things more than people, pleasure more than duty, and distant scenes more than the blessings we have right at home. Jesus once warned two disputing brothers, "Take heed and beware of covetousness!" (Luke 12:15) Why? Because the covetous person can never be satisfied, no matter how much he acquires, and a dissatisfied heart leads to a disappointed life. The prodigal learned the hard way that you cannot enjoy the things money can buy if you ignore the things money cannot buy.

"The far country" is not necessarily a distant place to which we must travel, because "the far country" exists first of all *in our hearts.* The younger son dreamed of "enjoying" his freedom far from home and away from his father and older brother. If the sheep was lost through foolishness and the coin through carelessness, then the son was lost because of willfulness. He wanted to have his own way so he rebelled against his own father and broke his father's heart.

But life in the far country was not what he expected. His resources ran out, his friends left him, a famine came, and the boy was forced to do for a stranger what he would not do for his own father—go to work! This scene in the drama is our Lord's way of emphasizing what sin really does in the lives of those who reject the Father's will. Sin promises freedom, but it only brings slavery (John 8:34); it promises success, but brings failure; it promises life, but "the wages of sin is death" (Rom. 6:23). The boy thought he would "find himself," but he only lost himself! When God is left out of our lives, enjoyment becomes enslavement.

Repentance—he came to himself (vv. 17-19). To "repent" means "to change one's mind," and that is exactly what the young man did as he cared for the pigs. (What a job for a Jewish boy!) He "came to himself," which suggests that up to this point he had not really "been himself." There is an "insanity" in sin that seems to paralyze the image of God within us and liberate the "animal" inside. Students of Shakespeare like to contrast two quotations that describe this contradiction in man's nature.

> What a piece of work is a man! How noble in reason! how infinite in faculty! in form, in moving, how express and admirable! in action how like an angel! in apprehension how like a god!
>
> (*Hamlet,* II, ii)

> When he is best, he is a little worse than a man; and when he is worst, he is little better than a beast.
>
> (*The Merchant of Venice,* I, ii)

The young man changed his mind about himself and his situation, and he admitted that he was a sinner. He confessed that his father was a generous man and that service at home was far better than "freedom" in the far country. It is God's goodness, not just man's badness, that leads us to repentance (Rom. 2:4). If the boy had thought only about himself—his hunger, his homesickness, his loneliness—he would have despaired. But his painful circumstances helped him to see his father in a new way, and this brought him hope. If his father was so good to *servants,* maybe he would be willing to forgive a *son.*

Had he stopped there, the boy would have experienced only regret or remorse (2 Cor. 7:10), but true repentance involves the will as well as the mind and the emotions—"I will arise . . . I will go . . . I will say. . . ." Our resolutions may be noble, but unless we act on them, they can never of themselves bring about any permanent good. If repentance is truly the work of God (Acts 11:18), then the sinner will obey God and put saving faith in Jesus Christ (Acts 20:21).

Rejoicing—he came to the father (vv. 20-24). Here Jesus answered the accusations of the scribes and Pharisees (Luke 15:2), for the father not only ran to welcome his son, but he honored the boy's homecoming by preparing a great feast and inviting the village to attend. The father never did permit the younger son to finish his confession; he interrupted him, forgave him, and ordered the celebration to begin!

Of course, the father pictures to us the attitude of our Heavenly Father toward sinners who repent: He is rich in His mercy and grace, and great in His love toward them (Eph. 2:1-10). All of this is possible because of the sacrifice of His Son on the cross. No matter what some preachers (and singers) claim, we are not saved by God's love; God loves the whole world, and the whole world is not saved. We are saved by God's grace, and grace is *love that pays a price.*

In the East, old men do not run; yet the father ran to meet his son. Why? One obvious reason was his love for him and his desire to show that love. But there is something else involved. This wayward son had brought disgrace to his family and village and, according to Deuteronomy 21:18-21, he should have been stoned to death. *If the neighbors had started to stone him, they would have hit the father who was embracing him!* What a picture of what Jesus did for us on the cross!

Everything the younger son had hoped to find in the far country, he discovered back home: clothes, jewelry, friends, joyful celebration, love, and assurance for the future. What made the difference? Instead of saying, "Father, *give* me!" he said, "Father, *make* me!" He was willing to be a servant! Of course, the father did not ask him to "earn" his forgiveness, because no amount of good works can save us from our sins (Eph. 2:8-10; Titus 3:3-7). In the far country, the prodigal learned the meaning of misery; but back home, he discovered the meaning of mercy.

The ring was a sign of sonship, and the "best robe" (no doubt the father's) was proof of his acceptance back into the family (see Gen. 41:42; Isa. 61:10; 2 Cor. 5:21). Servants did not wear rings, shoes, or expensive garments. The feast was the father's way of showing his joy and sharing it with others. Had the boy been dealt with according to the Law, there would have been a funeral, not a feast. What a beautiful illustration of Psalm 103:10-14!

It is interesting to consider the father's description of his son's experience: he was dead, and was now alive; he was lost, and now was found. This is the spiritual experience of every lost sinner who comes to the Father through faith in Jesus Christ (John 5:24; Eph. 2:1-10). Note the parallels between the prodigal's coming to the father and our coming to the Father through Christ (John 14:6):

The Prodigal	*Jesus Christ*
He was lost (v. 24)	"I am the way"
He was ignorant (v. 17)	"I am the truth"
He was dead (v. 24)	"I am the life"

There is only one way to come to the Father, and that is through faith in Jesus Christ. Have you come home?

The Joy of Forgiving (Luke 15:25-32)

At this point in the parable, the scribes and Pharisees felt confident that they had escaped our Lord's judgment, for He had centered His attention on the publicans and sinners, pictured by the prodigal son. But Jesus continued the story and introduced the elder brother, who is a clear illustration of the scribes and Pharisees. The publicans and sinners were guilty of the obvious sins of the flesh, but the Pharisees and scribes were guilty of sins of the spirit (2 Cor. 7:1). Their outward actions may have been blameless, but their inward attitudes were abominable (see Matt. 23:25-28).

We must admit that the elder brother had some virtues that are commendable. He worked hard and always obeyed his father. He never brought disgrace either to the home or to the village, and apparently he had enough friends so that he could have planned an enjoyable party (Luke 15:29). He seems like a good solid citizen and, compared to his younger brother, almost a saint.

However, important as obedience and diligence are, they are not the only tests of character. Jesus taught that the two greatest commandments are to love God and to love others (Luke 10:25-28), but the elder brother broke both of these divine commandments. He did not love God (represented in the story by the father), and he did not love his brother. The elder brother would not forgive his brother who wasted the family inheritance and disgraced the family name. But neither would he forgive his father who had graciously forgiven the young man those very sins!

When you examine the sins of the elder brother, you can easily understand why he pictures the scribes and Pharisees. To begin with, he was *self-righteous.* He openly announced the sins of his brother, but he could not see his own sins (see Luke 18:9-14). The Pharisees defined sin primarily in terms of outward actions, not inward attitudes. They completely missed the message of the Sermon on the Mount and its emphasis on inward attitudes and holiness of heart (Matt. 5–7).

Pride was another one of his failings. Just think, he had served his father all those years and had *never* disobeyed his will! What a testimony! But his heart was not in his work, and he was always dreaming of throwing a big party at which he and his friends could enjoy themselves. He was only a drudge. Like the Prophet Jonah, the elder brother did God's will *but not from the heart* (Jonah 4; Eph. 6:6). He was a hard worker and a faithful worker—qualities to be commended—but his work was not a "labor of love" that would please his father.

You cannot help but notice his *unconcern for his missing brother.* Imagine having to be told that his brother had come home! The father watched for the younger son day after day and finally saw him afar off, but the elder brother did not know his brother was home until one of the servants told him.

Even though he knew it would make his father happy, the elder brother did not want his younger brother to come home. Why should he share his estate with somebody who had wasted his own inheritance? Why should he even share the father's love with somebody who had brought shame to the family and the village? Reports of the prodigal's lifestyle only made the elder brother look good, and perhaps this would make the father love his obedient son even more. No doubt about it—the arrival of the younger son was a threat to the older son.

Perhaps the most disturbing thing about the elder son was his fierce *anger.* He was angry at both his father and his brother and would not go into the house and share in the joyful celebration.

Anger is a normal emotion and it need not be sinful. "Be ye angry, and sin not" (Eph. 4:26, quoting Ps. 4:4). Moses, David, the prophets, and our Lord Jesus displayed holy anger at sin, and so should we today. The Puritan preacher Thomas Fuller said that anger was one of the "sinews of the soul." Aristotle gave good advice when he wrote: "Anybody can become angry. That is easy. But to be angry with the right person and to the right degree and at the right time and for the right purpose and in the right way—that is not within everybody's power and is not easy."

The elder brother was angry with his father because his father had given the younger son the feast that the elder brother had always wanted. "You never gave me so much as a goat," he said to his father, "but you killed for him the valuable fatted calf!" The elder brother's dreams were all shattered because the father had forgiven the prodigal.

Of course the elder brother was angry at his younger brother for getting all that attention and receiving the father's special gifts. As far as the elder brother was concerned, *the younger brother deserved none of it.* Had he been faithful? No! Had he obeyed the father? No! Then why should he be treated with such kindness and love?

The Pharisees had a religion of good works. By their fasting, studying, praying, and giving, they hoped to earn blessings from God and merit eternal life. They knew little or nothing about the grace of God. However, it was not what they did, but what they did not do, that alienated them from God (see Matt. 23:23-24). When they saw Jesus receiving and forgiving irreligious people, they rebelled against it. Even more, they failed to see that *they themselves also needed the Saviour.*

The same father who ran to meet the prodigal came out of the house of feasting to plead with the older son. How gracious and condescending our Father is, and how patient He is with our weaknesses! The father explained that he would have been willing to host a feast for the older boy and his friends, but the boy had never asked him. Furthermore, ever since the division of the estate, the elder brother owned everything, and he could use it as he pleased.

The elder brother refused to go in; he stayed outside and pouted. He missed the joy of forgiving his brother and restoring the broken fellowship, the joy of pleasing his father and uniting the family again. How strange that the elder brother could speak peaceably to a servant boy, but he could not speak peaceably to his brother or father!

If we are out of fellowship with God, we cannot be in fellowship with our brothers and sisters and, conversely, if we harbor an unforgiving attitude toward others, we cannot be in communion with God (see Matt. 5:21-26; 1 John 4:18-21). When they show true repentance, we must forgive those who sin, and we should seek to restore them in grace and humility (Matt. 18:15-35; Gal. 6:1-5; Eph. 4:32).

The father had the last word, so we do not know how the story ended. (See Jonah 4 for a parallel narrative.) We do know that the scribes and Pharisees continued to oppose Jesus and separate themselves from His followers, and that their leaders eventually brought about our Lord's arrest and death. In spite of the Father's pleading, they would not come in.

Everybody in this chapter experienced joy except the elder brother. The shepherd, the woman, and their friends all experienced the joy of finding. The younger son experienced the joy of returning and being received by a loving, gracious father. The father experienced the joy of receiving his son back safe and sound. But the elder brother would not forgive his brother, so he had no joy. He could have repented and attended the feast, but he refused; so he stayed outside and suffered.

In my years of preaching and pastoral ministry, I have met elder brothers (and sisters!) who have preferred nursing their anger to enjoying the fellowship of God and God's people. Because they will not forgive, they have alienated themselves from the church and even from their family; they are sure that everyone else is wrong and they alone are right. They can talk loudly about the sins of others, but they are blind to their own sins.

"I never forgive!" General Oglethorpe said to John Wesley, to which Wesley replied, "Then, sir, I hope you never sin."

Don't stand outside! Come in and enjoy the feast!

CHAPTER FIFTEEN THE RIGHT AND WRONG OF RICHES

Luke 16

The *Wall Street Journal* quoted an anonymous wit who defined *money* as "an article which may be used as a universal passport to everywhere except heaven, and as a universal provider for everything except happiness." The writer might have added that money is also a provoker of covetousness and competition, a wonderful servant but a terrible master. The love of money is still "a root of all kinds of evil" (1 Tim. 6:10, NKJV) and has helped fill our world with corruption and lust (1 Peter 1:4).

When you read our Lord's sermons and parables, you are struck with the fact that He had a great deal to say about material wealth. He ministered to people who, for the most part, were poor and who thought that acquiring more wealth was the solution to all their problems. Jesus was not blind to the needs of the poor, and by His example and teaching, He encouraged His followers to share what they had with others. The early church was a fellowship of people who willingly shared their possessions with the less fortunate (Acts 2:44-47; 4:33-37).

In His portrait of the prodigal and the elder brother, Jesus described two opposite philosophies of life. Prior to his repentance, the prodigal *wasted* his life, but his elder brother only *spent* his life as a faithful drudge. Both attitudes are wrong, for the Christian approach to life is that we should *invest* our lives for the good of others and the glory of God. This chapter emphasizes that truth: life is a stewardship, and we must use our God-given opportunities faithfully. One day we must give an account to the Lord of what we have done with all He has given to us, so we had better heed what Jesus says in this chapter about the right and wrong use of wealth.

Neither of the two accounts in this chapter is called a parable either by Jesus or by Luke, so it is likely that our Lord was describing actual happenings. However, whether they are actual events or only parables, the spiritual values are the same.

The Right Use of Wealth (Luke 16:1-13)

A foolish steward (vv. 1-2). A steward is someone who manages another's wealth. He does not own that wealth himself, but he has the privilege of enjoying it and using it for the profit of his master. The most important thing about a steward is that he serve his master faithfully (1 Cor. 4:2). When he looks at the riches around him, the steward must remember that they belong to his master, not to him personally, and that they must be used in a way that will please and profit the master.

This particular steward *forgot* that he was a steward and began to act as if he were the owner. He became a "prodigal steward" who wasted his master's wealth. His master heard about it and immediately asked for an inventory of his goods and an audit of his books. He also fired his steward.

Before we judge this man too severely, let's examine our own lives to see how faithful we have been as stewards of what God has given to us. To begin with, we are stewards of the *material wealth* that we have, whether much or little; and we will one day have to answer to God for the way we have acquired it and used it.

Christian stewardship goes beyond paying God a tithe of our income and then using the remainder as we please. True stewardship means that we thank God for *all* that we have (Deut. 8:11-18) and use it as He directs. Giving God 10 percent of our income is a good way to begin our faithful stewardship, but we must remember that God should control what we do with the remaining 90 percent as well.

We are also stewards of *our time* (Eph. 5:15-17). The phrase "redeeming the time" comes from the business world and means "buying up the opportunity." Time is eternity, minted into precious minutes and handed to us to use either wisely or carelessly. The main lesson of this narrative is that the steward, as dishonest as he was, used his opportunity wisely and prepared for the future. Life ceased to be "enjoyment" and became "investment."

Christians are stewards of the *gifts and abilities* God has given them (1 Peter 4:10), and we must use those gifts and abilities to serve others. The thief says, "What's yours is mine—I'll take it!" The selfish man says, "What's mine is mine—I'll keep it!" But the Christian must say, "What's mine is a gift from God—I'll share it!" We are stewards and we must use our abilities to win the lost, encourage the saints, and meet the needs of hurting people.

Finally, God's people are stewards of the Gospel (1 Thes. 2:4). God has committed the treasure of His truth to us (2 Cor. 4:7), and we must guard this treasure (1 Tim. 6:20) and invest it in the lives of others (2 Tim. 2:2). The enemy wants to rob the church of this treasure (Jude 3-4), and we must be alert and courageous.

Like this steward, we will one day have to give an account of our stewardship (Rom. 14:10-12; 2 Cor. 5:10ff). If we have been faithful, the Lord will give us His commendation and reward (Matt. 25:21; 1 Cor. 4:5); but if we have not been faithful, we will lose those blessings, even though we will be saved and enter heaven (1 Cor. 3:13-15).

Vance Havner often said, "God called us to play the game, not keep the score." If we are faithful stewards, God will reward us generously, and that reward will bring glory to His name.

A wise steward (vv. 3-8). The steward knew he would lose his job. He could not change the past, but he could prepare for the future. How? By making friends of his master's creditors so that they would take him in when his master threw him out. He gave each of them a generous discount, provided they paid up immediately, and they were only too glad to cooperate. Even his master complimented him on his clever plan (Luke 16:8).

Jesus did not commend the steward for robbing his master or for encouraging others to be dishonest. *Jesus commended the man for his wise use of opportunity.* "The children of this world" are experts at seizing opportunities for making money and friends and getting ahead. God's people should take heed and be just as wise when it comes to managing the spiritual affairs of life. "The children of this world" are wiser only "in their generation"; they see the things of time, but not the things of eternity. Because the child of God lives "with eternity's values in view," he should be able to make far better use of his opportunities.

The application (vv. 9-13). Jesus gave three admonitions, based on the experience of the steward.

First, He admonishes us to *use our opportunities wisely* (Luke 16:9). One of these days, life will end, and we will not be able to earn or use money. Therefore, while we have the opportunity, we must invest our money in "making friends" for the Lord. This means winning people to Christ who will one day welcome us to heaven. Our lives and our resources will one day end, so it behooves us to use them wisely.

It is tragic to see how God's wealth is being wasted by Christians who live as though Jesus never died and judgment is never coming. The old couplet is certainly true:

> The only difference between men and boys
> Is that men buy more expensive toys.

The heritage of the past must be used wisely in the present to guarantee spiritual dividends in the future. All of us should want to meet people in heaven who trusted Christ because we helped to pay the bill for Gospel witness around the world, starting at home. Thoreau wrote that a man is wealthy in proportion to the number of things he can afford to do without, and he was right. I once heard the late Jacob Stam pray, "Lord, the only thing we know about sacrifice is how to spell the word." I wonder if today some of us can even spell the word!

Our Lord's second admonition is *be faithful in the way you use your material wealth* (Luke 16:10-12). He makes it clear that you cannot divorce the "spiritual" from the "material." Notice the contrasts:

The material	*The spiritual*
the god "Mammon"	the true God
that which is least	that which is much
false riches	true riches
that which is another's	that which is yours

Why is our Lord so concerned about the way we use money? Because money is not neutral; it is basically evil ("the mammon of unrighteousness"), and only God can sanctify it and use it for good. It is significant that both Paul and Peter called money "filthy lucre" (1 Tim. 3:3, 8; Titus 1:7, 11; 1 Peter 5:2). Apparently by its very nature, money defiles and debases those who love it and let it control their lives. "We cannot safely use mammon," writes Richard Foster, "until we are absolutely clear that we are dealing, not just with mammon, but with unrighteous mammon" (*Money, Sex and Power,* Harper & Row, p. 57).

People who are unfaithful in the way they use money are also unfaithful in the way they use the "true riches" of God's kingdom. We cannot be orthodox in our theology and at the same time heretical in the way we use money. God will not commit His true riches to individuals or ministries that waste money and will not give an honest accounting to the people who have supported them. When it came to money, Paul was very careful that everything was honest "not only in the sight of the Lord, but also in the sight of men" (2 Cor. 8:21).

Finally, the Lord admonishes us to *be wholly devoted to God and single-minded* (Luke 16:13; and see Matt. 6:19-24). We cannot love or serve two masters, anymore than we can walk in two directions at one time. If we choose to serve money, then we cannot serve God. If we choose to serve God, then we will not serve money. Jesus is demanding *integrity,* total devotion to God that puts Him first in everything (Matt. 6:33).

If God is our Master, then money will be our servant, and we will use our resources in the will of God. But if God is not our Master, then *we will become the servants of money,* and money is a terrible master! We will start *wasting* our lives instead of *investing* them, and we will one day find ourselves "friendless" as we enter the gates of glory.

Henry Fielding wrote, "Make money your god and it will plague you like the devil!" Jesus said, "Make money your servant and use today's opportunities as investments in tomorrow's dividends." Be a wise steward! There are souls to win to the Saviour, and our money can help get the job done.

The Wrong Use of Money (Luke 16:14-31)

Jesus had been speaking primarily to His disciples, but the Pharisees had been listening, and their response was anything but spiritual. They sneered at Him! (The Greek word means "to turn up one's nose.") In spite of their strict religious practices, they loved money and cultivated values that were godless. They professed to trust God, but they measured life by wealth and possessions, the same as the unbelieving worldly crowd. *Far too many professed Christians today are making the same mistake.* With their lips, they honor the Lord; but with their wealth, they live like the world.

The Pharisees needed to stop "drifting" with the crowd and start "pressing into the kingdom" as many others were doing. The Pharisees had rejected the ministry of John the Baptist and permitted him to be killed, even though they knew he was God's prophet. They were also rejecting the ministry of Jesus Christ and would ultimately ask Pilate to have Him crucified. When your life is controlled by the love of money, you open the door to every kind of sin.

The Law and the Prophets were "until John," for John introduced the Saviour to the nation and announced the arrival of the kingdom. But that did not mean that the Law was discredited or destroyed, for in Jesus Christ, the Law has been fulfilled (Matt. 5:17-20). The Pharisees prided themselves in their faithful obedience to the Law of Moses, but they did not receive the Saviour of whom Moses wrote!

Why did Jesus talk about divorce and remarriage when His basic discussion was about covetousness? The scribes and Pharisees were divided on this question, and perhaps they wanted to provoke Jesus into an argument, but He thwarted their plans. (In most marriages and divorces, money is involved, so the topic was not completely foreign to the discussion.) Some of the Jews were very lax in their views of divorce and remarriage, while others were very strict. Jesus had spoken about this subject before, so it was not a new teaching (Matt. 5:31-32).

Having silenced the sneering Pharisees,

Jesus then gave them a vivid description of what would happen to them if they continued in their covetousness and unbelief. The account focuses on an anonymous rich man and a beggar named Lazarus ("God is my help"), and it warns us against covetousness by presenting several contrasts.

A contrast in life (vv. 19-21). This man was indeed rich if he could afford daily to wear expensive clothes and host splendid feasts. The one word that best describes his lifestyle is "flamboyant." He was definitely among "the rich and famous," and other people admired and envied him.

Why is one man wealthy and another man poor? Had the Jewish people obeyed God's commandments concerning the Sabbatical Year and the Year of Jubilee, there would have been little or no poverty in the land, for the wealth and real estate could not have fallen into the hands of a few wealthy people (see Lev. 25, and note Ex. 23:11; Deut. 14:28-29). The Old Testament prophets denounced the rich for amassing great estates and exploiting the widows and the poor (Isa. 3:15; 10:2; Amos 2:6; 4:1; 5:11-12; 8:4-6; Hab. 2:9-13). In Jesus' day, Palestine was under the rule of Rome, and life was very difficult for the common people.

Lazarus was sick and possibly crippled, because he was "laid" at the rich man's gate daily (see Acts 3:1-2). The only attention he got was from the dogs! The rich man could easily have assisted Lazarus, but he ignored him and went on enjoying his recognition and his riches. Life was comfortable for him and he felt secure.

The rich man obviously had no concept of stewardship, or he would have used part of his wealth to help Lazarus. It is a mystery why he even allowed the beggar to camp at his front door. Perhaps he thought that providing a place for the man was ministry enough, and it may be that some of his wealthy guests occasionally gave Lazarus alms. Did any of them ever recall what the Old Testament had to say about the care of the poor, such as Proverbs 14:21; 19:17; 21:13; or 28:27?

A contrast in death (v. 22). "The rich and poor meet together; the Lord is the Maker of them all" (Prov. 22:2). As John Donne said, death is the "great leveler." The rich man died in spite of his wealth (Ps. 49:6-9) and "was buried," no doubt with an expensive funeral. But when Lazarus died, he was carried to Abraham's bosom. What a difference! Perhaps the beggar's body did not even have a decent burial, though the Jews were usually compassionate in such cases. Lazarus certainly did not have the traditional Jewish funeral, with its paid mourners, costly spices, and elaborate tomb. After Lazarus' body was taken away, the neighbors probably said, "Well, we're glad he's not around anymore!"

Death takes place when the spirit leaves the body (James 2:26). But death is not the end; it is the beginning of a whole new existence in another world. For the Christian, death means to be present with the Lord (2 Cor. 5:1-8; Phil. 1:21). For the unbeliever, death means to be away from God's presence and in torment.

A contrast in eternity (vv. 23-31). The *King James Version* uses the word *hell* in Luke 16:23, but the Greek word is not "hell" but "hades." It is the temporary realm of the dead as they await the judgment. The permanent place of punishment for the lost is "hell," the lake of fire. One day, death will give up the bodies and hades will give up the souls (Rev. 20:13, where "hell" should be "hades"), and the lost will stand before Christ in judgment (Rev. 20:10-15).

From our Lord's description, we learn that hades had two sections: a paradise portion called "Abraham's bosom," and a punishment portion. It is believed by many theologians that our Lord emptied the paradise part of hades when He arose from the dead and returned to the Father (John 20:17; Eph. 4:8-10). We know that today "paradise" is in heaven, where Jesus reigns in glory (Luke 23:43; 2 Cor. 12:1-4). There is no indication in Scripture that souls in heaven can communicate with people in hades or with people on earth.

This narrative refutes so-called "soul sleep," for both the rich man and Lazarus were conscious, one enjoying comfort and the other suffering torment. It is a solemn thing to ponder one's eternal destiny and realize the reality of divine punishment.

C.S. Lewis was told about a gravestone inscription that read: "Here lies an atheist—all dressed up and no place to go." Lewis quietly replied, "I bet he wishes that were so!"

The interesting thing is that, in hades, the rich man began to pray! First, he prayed for himself, that Abraham would have mercy on him and allow Lazarus to bring him some comfort (Luke 16:23-26). Even a drop of cool water would be welcomed. What a change from his sumptuous feasts when slaves ran to do his bidding!

The word *torment* is used four times in this account, and it speaks of definite pain. This is the same word that is used for the doom feared by the evil spirits (Mark 5:7) and the judgments God will send on an unrepentant world (Rev. 9:5; 11:10; 20:10). If hell is the permanent prison of the damned, then hades is the temporary jail, and the suffering in both is very real.

People ask, "How can a loving God even permit such a place as hell to exist, let alone send people there?" But in asking that question, they reveal that they do not understand either the love of God or the wickedness of sin. God's love is a *holy* love ("God is light," 1 John 1:5), not a shallow sentiment, and sin is rebellion against a holy and loving God. God does not "send people to hell." They send themselves there by refusing to heed His call and believe on His Son. The "unbelieving" are named second on the list of the people who go to hell, even before the murderers and the liars (Rev. 21:8; also see John 3:18-21, 36).

Abraham gave two reasons why Lazarus could not bring the comfort that was requested: the character of the rich man and the character of the eternal state. The rich man had lived for the "good things" of earth, and had experienced abundant temporal blessings. He had his reward (Matt. 6:2, 5, 16). He had determined his own destiny by leaving God out of his life, and now neither his character nor his destiny could be changed. Lazarus could not leave his place of comfort and make even a brief visit to the place of torment.

Then the rich man prayed for his brothers (Luke 16:27-31). He did not say, "I'm glad my brothers will also come here. We'll have a wonderful time together!" Occasionally you hear a lost person say, "Well, I don't mind if I go to hell. I'll have a lot of company!" *But there is no friendship or "company" in hell!* Hell is a place of torment and loneliness. It is not an eternal New Year's Eve party at which sinners have a good time doing what they used to do on earth.

Luke 16:28 suggests that Lazarus had testified to the rich man and probably to his brothers, but none of them had taken his witness seriously. But now, Lazarus' testimony is very important! The brothers knew that Lazarus had died, so if the beggar appeared to them, they would be frightened and would listen to his witness. *People in hades have a concern for the lost, but they cannot do anything about it.*

Abraham explained that only one thing could prevent the five men from eventually joining their brother: they needed to hear the Word of God and respond to it by faith. Moses and the Prophets tell sinners how to repent and be saved, and the Jews heard them read every Sabbath in the synagogue. Though miracles can attest to the authority of the preacher, they cannot produce either conviction or conversion in the hearts of the lost. Faith that is based solely on miracles is not saving faith (John 2:23-25). A man named Lazarus *did* come back from the dead, *and some of the people wanted to kill him!* (see John 11:43-57; 12:10) Those who claim that there can be no effective evangelism without "signs and wonders" need to ponder this passage and also John 10:41-42.

In the rich man's lifetime, God had spoken to him in many ways. God had permitted him to have riches, yet he did not repent (Rom. 2:4-5). Lazarus had witnessed to the rich man, and so had the Old Testament Scriptures that were familiar to the Jews, but his heart remained unbelieving. The fact that Lazarus died first was a strong witness to the rich man, a reminder that one day he would also die, but even a death at his very doorstep did not melt the man's heart.

In spite of the fact that he was in torment in hades, the rich man did not change; he was still self-centered. He prayed, but it was for *his* comfort and the safety of *his* family. He was not concerned about other lost sinners; his only concern was his five brothers. He argued with God instead of submitting to His will. This indicates that the punishment of lost sinners is not remedial; it does not improve them. Hades and hell are not hospitals for the sick; they are prisons for the condemned.

Dr. Luke does not tell us how the covetous Pharisees responded to this account. They certainly knew Moses and the Prophets, and this meant even greater responsibility—*and greater condemnation* (John 12:35-41).

We must remind ourselves that the rich man was not condemned because he was rich, nor was Lazarus saved because he was poor. Abraham was a very wealthy man, yet he was not in torment in hades. The rich man trusted in his riches and did not trust in the Lord.

"The safest road to hell," wrote C.S. Lewis, "is the gradual one—the gentle slope, soft underfoot, without sudden turnings, without milestones, without signposts."

"For what shall it profit a man, if he shall gain the whole world, and lose his own soul?" (Mark 8:36)

Jesus asked that question.

What is your answer?

CHAPTER SIXTEEN THINGS THAT REALLY MATTER

Luke 17

As Jesus made His way to Jerusalem, He continued to teach His disciples and prepare them for what He would suffer there. But He was also preparing them for the time when He would no longer be with them and they would be ministering to others in His place. It was a critical period in their lives.

In this chapter, Luke recorded lessons that Jesus gave His disciples about some of the essentials of the Christian life: forgiveness (Luke 17:1-6), faithfulness (Luke 17:7-10), thankfulness (Luke 17:11-19), and preparedness (Luke 17:20-37).

Forgiveness (Luke 17:1-6)

After Jesus warned the Pharisees about the sin of loving money (Luke 16:14-31), He then turned to His disciples to warn them about possible sins in their lives, for occasions to stumble ("offenses") are an unfortunate part of life. After all, we are all sinners living in a sinful world. But we must take heed not to cause others to stumble, for it is a serious thing to sin against a fellow believer and tempt him or her to sin (Rom. 14:13; 1 Cor. 10:32; 1 John 2:10).

By "these little ones" (Luke 17:2), Jesus was referring not only to children but also to young believers who were learning how to follow the Lord (Matt. 18:1-6; Luke 10:21). Since Luke 17:1-10 is part of a context that begins with Luke 15:1, "little ones" would include the publicans and sinners who had come to believe in Jesus Christ. The Pharisees had criticized Jesus, and this might well have caused these new believers to stumble. So serious is this sin that a person would be better off cast alive into the sea, never to be seen again, than to deliberately cause others to stumble and sin.

But suppose *you* are not the one who does the sinning. Suppose another believer sins against you. Jesus anticipated this question in Luke 17:3-4 and instructed us what to do. First, we must have a personal concern for each other and obey His warning, "Take heed to yourselves." This means that we should lovingly watch over each other and do all we can to keep one another from sinning.

If a brother or sister does sin against us, we should give a private loving rebuke. Our tendency might be to feel hurt down inside, nurse a grudge, and then tell others what happened to us, but this is the wrong approach (see Matt. 18:15-20). "Speaking the truth in love" (Eph. 4:15) is the first step toward solving personal differences.

Our aim is not to embarrass or hurt the offender, but to encourage him or her to repent (Gal. 6:1). If the offender does repent, then we must forgive (Eph. 4:32; and see Matt. 5:43-48). In fact, we must be *in the habit of forgiving,* for others might sin against us seven times a day—or even seventy times seven! (Matt. 18:21ff) No one is likely to commit that much sin in one day, but this use of hyperbole emphasized the point Jesus was making: do not enumerate the sins of others, for love "keeps no record of wrongs" (1 Cor. 13:4-6). We should always be ready to forgive others, for one day we may want them to forgive us!

We might have expected the disciples to respond with the prayer, "Increase our love!" Certainly love is a key element in forgiveness, but faith is even more important. *It takes living faith to obey these instructions and forgive others.* Our obedience in forgiving others shows that we are trusting God to take care of the consequences, handle the possible misunderstandings, and work everything out for our good and His glory.

Mature Christians understand that forgiveness is not a cheap exchange of words, the way squabbling children often flippantly say "I'm sorry" to each other. True forgiveness always involves pain; somebody has been hurt and there is a price to pay in healing the wound. Love *motivates* us to forgive, but faith *activates* that forgiveness so that God can use it to work blessings in the lives of His people.

Our Lord's image of the mustard seed conveys the idea of life and growth. The mustard seed is very small, but it has life in it and, therefore, it can grow and produce fruit (Mark 4:30-32). If our faith is a *living* faith (James 2:14-26), it will grow and enable us to obey God's commands. "Commit thy way unto the Lord; trust also in Him; and He shall bring it to pass" (Ps. 37:5). Forgiveness is a test of both our faith and our love.

Human nature being what it is, there will always be offenses that can easily become opportunities for sin. God's people must get into the habit of facing these offenses honestly and lovingly, and forgiving others when they repent. The Anglican pastor and poet George Herbert wrote, "He who cannot forgive breaks the bridge over which he himself must pass."

Faithfulness (Luke 17:7-10)

The introductory word *but* indicates that Jesus was now going to balance one lesson with another. There was a danger that the Twelve might get so carried away with transplanting trees that they would ignore the everyday responsibilities of life! Faith that does not result in faithfulness will not accomplish God's work. It is good to have faith to do the *difficult* (Luke 17:1-3) and the *impossible* (Luke 17:4-6), but it is essential that we have faith to do even the *routine tasks* our Master has committed to us. Privileges must always be balanced with responsibilities.

The servant in the story was evidently a "jack-of-all-trades," for he was responsible for farming, shepherding, and cooking. It was not unusual for people with only modest means to hire at least one servant, but Jesus described a situation which in that day was unthinkable: a master ministering to his servant! In fact, He introduced the story with a phrase that means, "Can any of you imagine. . . ?" Their answer had to be, "No, we cannot imagine such a thing!"

Jesus had already discussed His relationship to His servants *and had promised to serve them if they were faithful* (Luke 12:35-38). He Himself was among them as a servant (Luke 22:27), even though He was Master of all. This story emphasizes faithfulness to duty no matter what the demands might be, and the argument is from the lesser to the greater. If a common servant is faithful to obey the orders of his master who does not reward (thank) him, how much more ought Christ's disciples obey their loving Master, who has promised to reward them graciously!

A faithful servant should not expect any special reward, since he did only what he was told to do. The word translated "unprofitable" means "without need"—that is, "nobody owes us anything." The servant was indeed profitable; after all, he cared for his master's fields, flocks, and food. The statement means, "My master does not owe me anything extra." *The fact that Jesus will reward His servants is wholly a matter of God's grace.* We do not deserve anything because we have obeyed Him and served Him.

As His servants, we must beware lest we have the wrong attitude toward our duties. There are two extremes to avoid: merely doing our duty in a slavish way *because we have to,* or doing our duty *because we hope to gain a reward.* Christian industrialist R.G. LeTourneau used to say, "If you give because it pays, *it won't pay.*" This principle also applies to service. Both extremes are seen in the attitudes of the elder brother (Luke 15:25-32) who was miserably obedient, always hoping that his father would let him have a party with his friends.

What then is the proper attitude for Christian service? "Doing the will of God from the heart" (Eph. 6:6). "If you love Me, keep My commandments" (John 14:15, NKJV). To the person who is born again, "His commandments are not grievous" (1 John 5:3). Serving Him is a delight, not just a duty, and we obey Him because we love Him. "I delight to do Thy will, O my God: yea, Thy law is within my heart" (Ps. 40:8).

Thankfulness (Luke 17:11-19)

Between Luke 17:10 and 11, the events of John 11 occurred as the Lord Jesus made His way to Jerusalem. At the border of Samaria and Judea, Jesus healed ten lepers at one time, and the fact that the miracle involved a Samaritan made it even more significant (see Luke 10:30-37). Jesus used this event to teach a lesson about gratitude to God.

The account begins with *ten unclean men* (Luke 17:11-13), all of whom were lepers (see the comments on Luke 5:12-15). The Jews and Samaritans would not normally live together, but misery loves company and all ten were outcasts. What difference does birth make if you are experiencing a living death? But these men had hope, for Jesus was there, and they cried out for mercy. The word translated "master" is the same one Peter used (Luke 5:5) and means "chief commander." They knew that Jesus was totally in command of even disease and death, and they trusted Him to help them.

The account continues by referring to *nine ungrateful men* (Luke 17:17). Jesus commanded the men to go show themselves to the priest, which in itself was an act of faith, for they had not yet been cured. When they turned to obey, they were completely healed, for their obedience was evidence of their faith (see 2 Kings 5:1-14).

You would have expected all ten men to run to Jesus and thank Him for a new start in life, but only one did so—and he was not even a Jew. How grateful the men should have been for the providence of God that brought Jesus into their area, for the love that caused Him to pay attention to them and their need, and for the grace and power of God that brought about their healing. They should have formed an impromptu men's chorus and sung Psalm 103 together!

But before we judge them too harshly, what is our own "GQ"—"Gratitude Quotient"? How often do we take our blessings for granted and fail to thank the Lord? "Oh that men would praise the Lord for His goodness, and for His wonderful works to the children of men!" (Ps. 107:8, 15, 21, 31) Too often we are content to enjoy the gift but we forget the Giver. We are quick to pray but slow to praise.

The next time you sing "Now Thank We All Our God," try to remember that Martin Rinkhart wrote it during the Thirty Years' War when his pastoral duties were most difficult. He conducted as many as forty funerals a day, including that of his own wife; yet he wrote those beautiful words as a table grace for his family. In spite of war and plague around him and sorrow within him, he was able to give thanks to the Lord from a grateful heart.

Luke's account closes with *one unusual man* (Luke 17:15-19). The Samaritan shouted "Glory to God!" and fell at Jesus' feet to praise Him and give thanks. It would have been logical for him to have followed the other men and gone to the temple, but he first came to the Lord Jesus with his sacrifice of praise (Ps. 107:22; Heb. 13:15). This pleased the Lord more than all the sacrifices the other men offered, even though they were obeying the Law (Ps. 51:15-17). Instead of *going to* the priest, the Samaritan *became* a priest, and he built his altar at the feet of Jesus (read Ps. 116:12-19).

By coming to Jesus, the man received something greater than physical healing: he was also saved from his sins. Jesus said, "Your faith has saved you" (literal translation), the same words He spoke to the repentant woman who anointed His feet (Luke 7:50). The Samaritan's nine friends were declared clean by the priest, but he was declared *saved* by the Son of God! While it is wonderful to experience the miracle of physical healing, it is even more wonderful to experience the miracle of eternal salvation.

Every child of God should cultivate the grace of gratitude. It not only opens the heart to further blessings but glorifies and pleases the Father. An unthankful heart is fertile soil for all kinds of sins (Rom. 1:21ff).

Preparedness (Luke 17:20-37)

The Jewish people lived in an excited atmosphere of expectancy, particularly at the Passover season when they commemorated their deliverance from Egypt. They longed for another Moses who would deliver them from their bondage. Some had hoped that John the Baptist would be the deliverer, and then the attention focused on Jesus (John 6:15). The fact that He was going to Jerusalem excited them all the more (Luke 19:11). Perhaps He would establish the promised kingdom!

The Pharisees were the custodians of the Law (Matt. 23:2-3), so they had the right to ask Jesus when He thought the kingdom of God would appear. It was customary for Jewish teachers to discuss these subjects publicly, and Jesus gave them a satisfactory answer. However, He reserved His detailed lessons for His disciples.

The word translated "observation" (Luke 17:20) is used only here in the New Testament and means in classical Greek "to observe the future by signs." It carries the idea of spying, lying in wait, and even scientific investigation. The point Jesus made was that God's kingdom would not come with great "outward show" so that people could predict its arrival and plot its progress.

The Pharisees' question was legitimate, but it was also tragic; for Jesus had been ministering among them for some three years, and these men were still in spiritual darkness. They did not understand who Jesus was or what He was seeking to accomplish. Their views of the kingdom were political, not spiritual; Jewish, not universal. Jesus did not deny that there would be a future earthly kingdom, but He did emphasize the importance of the *spiritual* kingdom that could be entered only by the new birth (John 3:1-8).

The statement "the kingdom of God is within you" has challenged Bible translators and interpreters for centuries, and many explanations have been given. One thing we can be sure of is that He was not telling the unbelieving Pharisees that they had the kingdom of God in their hearts!

The Greek preposition can mean "within," "among," or "in the midst of." Jesus was saying, "Don't look for the kingdom 'out there' unless it is first in your own heart" (see Rom. 14:17). At the same time, He may also have been saying, "The fact that I am here in your midst is what is important, for I am the King. How can you enter the kingdom if you reject the King?" (see Luke 19:38-40) The Pharisees were preoccupied with the great events of the future but were ignoring the opportunities of the present (Luke 12:54-57).

Having answered the Pharisees, Jesus then turned to His disciples to instruct them about the coming of the kingdom. He warned them not to become so obsessed with His return that they ended up doing nothing else but trying to track Him down. This is a good warning to believers who do nothing but study prophecy. Certainly we should look for His return and long to see Him come, but at the same time, we should be busy doing His work when He comes (note Acts 1:6-11).

To begin with, His coming will affect the whole world, so it is foolish for anyone to follow false prophets who say "He is here!" or "He is there!" Furthermore, His coming will be as sudden as a flash of lightning (Matt. 24:27, 30). While a study of the prophetic Scriptures will help us understand the general characteristics of the time of His coming, we cannot know the day or the hour (Matt. 25:13; Luke 12:40, 46). It is futile to investigate signs and try to calculate the day of His coming.

Jesus then used two Old Testament events to illustrate the certainty and the suddenness of His coming: the Flood (Gen. 6–8) and the destruction of Sodom (Gen. 19). In both examples, the people of the world were caught unprepared as they engaged in their everyday activities of eating and drinking, marrying, buying, and selling. Noah witnessed to his generation in the years preceding the Flood (2 Peter 2:5), but his preaching did not convert them. Noah and his wife, his three sons, and their wives—only eight people—were saved from destruction because they entered the ark. Peter saw this as an illustration of the salvation Christians have through faith in Jesus Christ (1 Peter 3:18-22).

Both Noah and Lot lived in days of religious compromise and moral declension, not unlike our present time. During "the days of Noah," population growth was significant (Gen. 6:1), lawlessness was on the increase (Gen. 6:5), and the earth was given over to violence (Gen. 6:11, 13). In Lot's day, the unnatural lusts of Sodom and Gomorrah were so abhorrent to God that He completely destroyed the cities. Only Lot, two of his daughters, and his wife (who later was destroyed) were saved from the terrible judgment.

Luke 17:30-36 describes what will occur when Jesus Christ returns in judgment to defeat His enemies and establish His kingdom on earth (Rev. 19:11–20:6). Believers in every age of the church can take warning from these verses, but they apply in a special way to Israel at the end of the age (see Matt. 24:29-44). When Jesus comes for His church and takes it to heaven, it will happen "in a moment, in the twinkling of an eye" (1 Cor. 15:52). Nobody taking part in the rapture of the church need worry about being on a housetop or in a field and wanting to get something out of the house! However, when the Lord returns *to the earth,* His coming will first be preceded by a "sign" in heaven (Matt. 24:30-31), and some people might try to hurry home to rescue something. "Remember Lot's wife!"

The verb *taken* in Luke 17:34-36 does not mean "taken to heaven" but "taken away in judgment" (Matt. 24:36-41). The person "left" is a believer who enters into the kingdom. Noah and his family were "left" to enjoy a new beginning, while the whole population of the earth was "taken" in the Flood. In spite of their sins, Lot and his daughters were "left" while the people in Sodom and Gomorrah were "taken" when the fire and brimstone destroyed the cities.

The fact that it is night in Luke 17:34 but day in Luke 17:35-36 indicates that the whole world will be involved in the return of Jesus Christ in glory. "Behold, He cometh with clouds; and every eye shall see Him" (Rev. 1:7).

Three times the disciples had heard Jesus talk about people being "taken" and "left," so they asked Him a most logical question: "Where, Lord?" Our Lord's reply has the sound of a familiar proverb: "Just as the eagles [and vultures, Matt. 24:28] gather at a corpse, so the lost will be gathered together for judgment." The description of the last battle in Revelation 19:17-21 certainly parallels the image of carrion-eating birds gorging themselves on flesh.

In other words, when the Lord Jesus returns to judge His enemies, there will be a separation of the saved and the lost. Whether it be day or night, whether people are working or sleeping, the separation and judgment will come. Those who are saved will be left to enter the glorious kingdom, while those who are lost will be taken away in judgment.

Even though the primary interpretation of these verses is for Israel in the end times, they do emphasize for the church the importance of being ready when Jesus returns. We must not be like Lot's wife whose heart was so in Sodom that she looked back in spite of the angels' warning (Gen. 19:17, 26). There are many professed Christians today whose plans would be interrupted if Jesus returned! (note 1 Thes. 5:1-11) Our Lord's warning in Luke 17:33 finds parallels in Matthew 10:39; Luke 9:24; and John 12:25, and is a fundamental principle of the Christian life. The only way to save your life is to lose it for the sake of Christ and the Gospel.

Jesus pictured civilization as a "rotting corpse" that would one day be ripe for judgment. The discerning believer sees evidence of this on every hand and realizes that the "days of Noah" and the "days of Lot" are soon on us. Our Lord can return for His church at any time, so we are not looking for signs; but we do know that "coming events cast their shadows before." As we see many of these things begin to come to pass (Luke 21:28), we know that His return is nearing.

Are we looking for His return, and do we really want to see Him come?

CHAPTER SEVENTEEN
PEOPLE TO MEET, LESSONS TO LEARN
Luke 18

Lord Chesterfield, the English statesman, wrote, "Learning . . . is only to be acquired by reading men, and studying all the various editions of them."

He was referring to "the knowledge of the world," but what he said applies to *spiritual* knowledge as well. Much can be learned from reading the "book of humanity," whether in daily life, history, biography, or even fiction.

There are several "editions" of mankind introduced in this chapter, and each one has a spiritual lesson to teach us. Being a compassionate physician, Dr. Luke wrote about widows and politicians, Pharisees and publicans, little children and adults, rich men and beggars. From this colorful cast of characters, I have selected four "editions" for us to "read." The lessons they teach us are important.

A Demanding Widow (Luke 18:1-8)

Luke mentions widows more than do all the other Gospel writers combined (Luke 2:37-38; 4:25-26; 7:11-17; 18:1-8; 20:45-47; 21:1-4). In that day, widows usually had a difficult time making ends meet, in spite of the care God instructed His people to give them (Ex. 22:22-24; Deut. 14:28-29; 16:9-15; Ps. 146:9; Isa. 1:17, 23; Jer. 7:6). The early church was serious about the care of Christian widows (Acts 6:1; 1 Tim. 5:3-10; James 1:27), a good example for us to follow today.

As you study this parable, try to see it in its Eastern setting. The "courtroom" was not a fine building but a tent that was moved from place to place as the judge covered his circuit. The judge, not the law, set the agenda; and he sat regally in the tent, surrounded by his assistants. Anybody could watch the proceedings from the outside, but only those who were approved and accepted could have their cases tried. This usually meant bribing one of the assistants so that he would call the judge's attention to the case.

The widow had three obstacles to overcome. First, being a woman she, therefore, had little standing before the law. In the Palestinian society of our Lord's day, women did not go to court. Since she was a widow, she had no husband to stand with her in court. Finally, she was poor and could not pay a bribe even if she wanted to. No wonder poor widows did not always get the protection the law was supposed to afford them!

Now that we understand something of the setting of this parable, we can better understand what Jesus was teaching. Basically, He was encouraging His disciples to pray, and He did this by presenting three contrasts.

Praying contrasted with fainting (v. 1). If we don't pray, we will faint; it's as simple as that! The word *faint* describes a believer who loses heart and gets so discouraged that he or she wants to quit. I can recall two occasions when I have fainted physically, and it is the most helpless feeling I have ever experienced. I felt myself "going," but I couldn't seem to do a thing about it!

There is a connection between what our Lord said in Luke 18:1 and His statement in Luke 17:37. If society is like a rotting corpse, then the "atmosphere" in which we live is being slowly polluted, and this is bound to affect our spiritual lives. But when we pray, we draw on the "pure air" of heaven, and this keeps us from fainting.

But what does it mean "always to pray" or to "pray without ceasing"? (1 Thes. 5:17) It certainly doesn't mean that we should constantly be repeating prayers, because Jesus warned against that kind of praying (Matt. 6:5-15). Rather, it means to make prayer as natural to us as our regular breathing. Unless we are sick or smothering, we rarely think about our breathing; we just do it. Likewise with prayer—it should be the natural habit of our lives, the "atmosphere" in which we constantly live.

Prayer is much more than the words of our lips; it is the desires of our hearts, *and our hearts are constantly "desiring" before Him,* even if we never speak a word. So, to "pray without ceasing" means to have such holy desires in our hearts, in the will of God, that we are constantly in loving communion with the Father, petitioning Him for His blessing.

Take your choice: do you want to pray—or faint?

The widow contrasted with God's elect (vv. 2-5). Jesus did not say that God's people are like this woman; in fact, He said just the opposite. Because we are *not* like her, we should be encouraged in our praying. He argued from the lesser to the greater: "If a poor widow got what she deserved from a selfish judge, how much more will God's children receive what is right from a loving Heavenly Father!"

Consider the contrasts. To begin with, the woman was a stranger, *but we are the children of God,* and God cares for His children (Luke 11:13). The widow had no access to the judge, but God's children have an open access into His presence and may come at any time to get the help they need (Eph. 2:18; 3:12; Heb. 4:14-16; 10:19-22).

The woman had no friend at court to help get her case on the docket. All she could do was walk around outside the tent and make a nuisance of herself as she shouted at the judge. But when Christian believers pray, they have in heaven a Saviour who is Advocate (1 John 2:1) and High Priest (Heb. 2:17-18), who constantly represents them before the throne of God.

When we pray, we can open the Word and claim the many promises of God, but the widow had no promises that she could claim as she tried to convince the judge to hear her case. We not only have God's unfailing promises, but we also have the Holy Spirit, who assists us in our praying (Rom. 8:26-27).

Perhaps the greatest contrast is that the widow came to a court of law, but God's children come to a throne of grace (Heb. 4:14-16). She pled out of her poverty, but we have all of God's riches available to us to meet our every need (Phil. 4:19). The point is clear: if we fail to pray, our condition spiritually will be just like that of the poor widow. That should encourage us to pray!

The judge contrasted with the Father (vv. 6-8). Unless you see that Jesus is pointing out contrasts, you will get the idea that God must be "argued" or "bribed" into answering prayer! God is *not* like this judge; for God is a loving Father, who is attentive to our every cry, generous in His gifts, concerned about our needs, and ready to answer when we call. The only reason the judge helped the widow was because he was afraid she would "weary" him, which literally means "give me a black eye"—i.e., ruin his reputation. God answers prayer for His glory and for our good, and He is not vexed when we come.

How, then, do we explain *delays* in answers to prayer, especially when Jesus said that God would "avenge [give them justice] speedily"? (Luke 18:8) Remember that God's delays are not the delays of inactivity but of preparation. God is always answering prayer, otherwise Romans 8:28 could not be in the Bible. God works in all things at all times, causing all things to work together to accomplish His purposes. The moment we send Him a request that is in His will (see 1 John 5:14-15), God begins to work. We may not see it now, but one day the answer will come.

The question in Luke 18:8 ties in with what Jesus taught in Luke 17:22-37: "Shall He find [that kind of] faith on the earth?" The end times will not be days of great faith. Eight people were saved in Noah's day, and only four out of Sodom (and one of them perished on the way). Passages like 1 Timothy 4 and 2 Timothy 3 paint a dark picture of the last days.

A Deluded Pharisee (Luke 18:9-17)

Throughout His public ministry, Jesus exposed the self-righteousness and unbelief of the Pharisees (see Luke 11:39-54). He pictured them as debtors too bankrupt to pay what they owed God (Luke 7:40-50), guests fighting for the best seats (Luke 14:7-14), and sons proud of their obedience but unconcerned about the needs of others (Luke 15:25-32). The sad thing is that the Pharisees were completely deluded and thought they were right and Jesus was wrong. This is illustrated in this parable.

The Pharisee was deluded about prayer, for he prayed with himself and told God (and anybody else listening) how good he was. The Pharisees used prayer as a means of getting public recognition and not as a spiritual exercise to glorify God (Matt. 6:5; 23:14).

He was deluded about himself, for he thought he was accepted by God because of what he did or what he did not do. The Jews were required to fast only once a year, on the Day of Atonement (Lev. 16:29), but he fasted twice a week. He tithed everything that came into his possession, even the tiny herbs from his garden (Matt. 23:23).

He was deluded about the publican who was also in the temple praying. The Pharisee thought that the publican was a great sinner, but the publican went home justified by God while the proud Pharisee went home only self-satisfied. To be "justified" means to be declared righteous by God on the basis of the sacrifice of Jesus Christ on the cross (Rom. 3:19–4:25).

The publican repeatedly smote his breast, for he knew where his greatest problem was, and he called to God for mercy. The publican knew the enormity of his sins, but the Pharisee was blissfully ignorant of his own heart. The Pharisee's pride condemned him, but the publican's humble faith saved him (see Luke 14:11 and Isa. 57:15). It is the prodigal son and elder brother over again (Luke 15:11ff).

In contrast to the proud Pharisee are the children who were brought to Jesus (Luke 18:15-17). It was customary for the Jews to bring little children to the rabbis to receive their special blessing, so it is strange that the disciples would stand in the way. Perhaps they thought Jesus was weary and needed rest, or they may have decided that He was not really interested in children. How wrong they were!

However, this was not the first time the disciples had attempted to "get rid of" people. They wanted to send the crowd away hungry, but Jesus fed them (Matt. 14:15ff); and they tried to stop the Canaanite woman from asking Jesus to heal her daughter (Matt. 15:21ff), but Jesus answered her prayer. The Twelve did not yet have the compassion of their Master, but it would come in due time.

Jesus wants us to be *childlike* but not *childish.* An unspoiled child illustrates humility, faith, and dependence. A child has a sense of wonder that makes life exciting. The only way to enter God's kingdom is to become like a child and be born again (John 3). If the proud Pharisee had become like a child, he too would have gone home justified.

A Dishonest Youth (Luke 18:18-34)

The rich young ruler (Matt. 19:20) may be the only man in the Gospels who came to the feet of Jesus and went away in worse condition than when he came. And yet he had so much in his favor! He was moral and religious, earnest and sincere, and probably would have qualified for membership in the average church. Yet he refused to follow Jesus Christ and instead went his own way in great sorrow.

What was wrong with him? In a word: *dishonesty.* In spite of the fact that he came to the right Person, asked the right question, and received the right answer, *he made the wrong decision.* Why? Because he was not honest with God or with himself. Therefore, he would not do what he was commanded to do. He was a superficial young man who said one thing but did another. Consider the areas in which he was dishonest.

His view of Christ (vv. 18-19). The rabbis were called "Master" (Teacher), but it was most unusual for a rabbi to be called "good." The Jews reserved the word *good* for God (Pss. 25:8; 34:8; 86:5; 106:1). This explains why our Lord asked the young man what he meant, for if he really believed that Jesus was "good," *then he had to confess that Jesus was God.* By asking this question, our Lord was not denying His deity but affirming it. He was testing the young man to see if he really understood what he had just said.

His subsequent behavior proved that the young ruler did not believe that Jesus Christ was God. If he really thought he was in the presence of Almighty God, why did he argue politely about the Law, brag about his character, and then refuse to obey the Word? Surely he knew that God sees the heart and knows all things!

His view of sin (vv. 20-21). He also had a superficial view of his own sin. No doubt the young man sincerely tried to keep the Law; in fact, this may have been what brought him to the feet of Jesus (Gal. 3:24). Jesus did not quote the Law to him as a means of salvation, because obedience to the Law does not save us. He held the Law before the young man as a mirror to reveal his sins (Rom. 3:19-20; Gal. 2:21; 3:21).

But the young man looked into the mirror and would not see the stains and blemishes in his life. When Jesus quoted from the second table of the Law, He did not quote the last commandment, "Thou shalt not covet" (Ex. 20:17). Jesus knew the young man's heart, so instead of preaching to him about covetousness, He asked him to do something that a covetous person would not do.

Nobody is saved by giving all his wealth to the poor, but nobody can be saved who will not repent of his sins and turn away from them. This young man was possessed by the love of money and he would not let go.

His view of salvation (vv. 22-34). The young man thought that eternal life came to those who "did something" (Luke 18:18), which was a typical Jewish conviction (Luke 18:9-12). But when Jesus gave him something to do, he refused to obey! He wanted salvation on his terms, not God's, so he turned and went away in great sorrow.

The disciples were shocked when Jesus announced that it was difficult for rich people to be saved. They were Jews and the Jews believed that riches were a mark of God's blessing. "If rich people can't be saved," they reasoned, "what hope is there for the rest of us?" John D. Rockefeller would have agreed with them, for he once said that riches were "a gift from heaven signifying, 'This is My beloved son, in whom I am well pleased.' "

It is not possessing riches that keeps people out of heaven, for Abraham, David, and Solomon were wealthy men. It is *being possessed* by riches and *trusting* them that makes salvation difficult for the wealthy. Wealth gives people a false sense of success and security, and when people are satisfied with themselves, they feel no need for God.

Peter's comment in Luke 18:28 suggests that he had a rather commercial view of discipleship: "What then will there be for us?" (Matt. 19:27, NASB) Jesus promised all of them ("you" in Luke 18:29 is plural) blessings in this life and reward in the life to come, but then He balanced His words with another announcement about His impending suffering and death. How could Peter be thinking about personal gain when his Lord was going to Jerusalem to be crucified?

The rich young ruler is a warning to people who want a Christian faith that does not change their values or upset their lifestyle. Jesus does not command every seeking sinner to sell everything and give to the poor, but He does put His finger of conviction on any area in our lives about which we are dishonest.

A Determined Beggar (Luke 18:35-43)

Matthew tells us that there were *two* blind beggars who met Jesus as He *left* Jericho (Matt. 20:29-30), but Luke introduces us to one blind beggar, Bartimaeus, who called out as Jesus *approached* Jericho. There were two Jerichos, the old ruined city and the new one built by Herod the Great, and they stood about a mile apart. The two men, one of whom was more outspoken, were sitting at the entrance to the new city, so there is no contradiction (note Mark 10:46).

In that day, blindness was a common affliction for which there was no cure, and all a blind person could do was beg. These two men had not been born blind, for their prayer was to "regain" their sight (Luke 18:41, NASB, and note Matt. 20:34, NASB). They persisted in crying out to the Lord, in spite of the obstacles in their way: their inability to see Jesus, the opposition of the crowd, and our Lord's delay in responding to them. They were not going to let Jesus pass them without first pleading for mercy.

The fact that they addressed Him as "Son of David," a messianic title, indicates that these two Jewish beggars knew that Jesus could give sight to the blind (Isa. 35:5; and see Luke 4:18). Jesus responded to their faith and healed them, and what a change took place! They went from darkness to light, from begging to following Jesus, and from crying to praising the Lord. They joined the pilgrim crowd going to Jerusalem and lifted their voices in praising the Lord.

The contrast is obvious between these two beggars and the rich young ruler (Luke 18:18-27). The beggars were poor, yet they became rich, while the young man was rich and became eternally poor. The beggars claimed no special merit and openly admitted their need, while the young man lied about himself and bragged about his character. The young man would not believe, so he went away from Jesus very sad; but the two beggars believed in Jesus and followed Him with songs of praise. "He hath filled the hungry with good things; and the rich He hath sent empty away" (Luke 1:53).

The "human editions" we have "read" in this chapter encourage us to put our faith in Jesus Christ, no matter what others may say or do. The widow was not discouraged by the indifferent attitude of the judge, nor the publican by the hypocritical attitude of the Pharisee. The parents brought their little ones to Jesus in spite of the selfish attitude of the Apostles, and the blind men came to Jesus even though the crowd told them to keep quiet and stay put. Jesus always responds to faith and rewards those who believe.

But the rich young ruler stands as a warning to all who depend on character to save them from sin. This young man shows us how close a person may come to salvation and yet turn away in unbelief. John Bunyan closed his *Pilgrim's Progress* with the warning, "Then I saw that there was a way to hell, even from the gates of heaven, as well as from the City of Destruction." Heed that warning today!

CHAPTER EIGHTEEN JERUSALEM AT LAST!

Luke 19

When Christopher Columbus made his voyage west in 1492, he kept two log books, one of which contained falsified information. He wanted his men to believe that they were closer to land than they really were. Apparently Columbus felt that the morale of the crew was more important than the integrity of the captain.

As Jesus journeyed to Jerusalem, He told His disciples what would happen there, but they could not grasp what their Lord was saying (Luke 18:31-34). Some of the people in the crowd thought He was going to Jerusalem to deliver Israel from Roman bondage and usher in the kingdom of God. Still others followed Him just to see the next miracle He would perform.

In this chapter, Dr. Luke focuses on who Jesus really is as he presents Him in a threefold ministry.

The Saviour Who Seeks the Lost (Luke 19:1-10)

The name *Zaccheus* means "righteous one," but this supervisor of tax collectors was not living up to his name. Certainly the Jewish religious community in Jericho would not have considered him righteous, for he not only collected taxes from his own people but also worked for the unclean Gentiles! And publicans were notorious for collecting more taxes than required; the more money they collected, the more income they enjoyed (Luke 3:12-13). Though Zaccheus was a renegade in the eyes of the Jews, he was a precious lost sinner in the eyes of Jesus.

It is interesting to see the changes Zaccheus experienced that day, all because Jesus visited Jericho.

A man became a child (vv. 2-4). In the East, it is unusual for a man to run, especially a wealthy government official; yet Zaccheus ran down the street like a little boy following a parade. And he even climbed a tree! Curiosity is certainly characteristic of most children, and Zaccheus was motivated by curiosity that day.

John Calvin wrote, "Curiosity and simplicity are a sort of preparation for faith." This is often the case, and it was certainly true of Zaccheus. Why the big crowd? Who is this Jesus of Nazareth they are following? What am I missing?

Jesus said, "Whosoever shall not receive the kingdom of God like a little child shall in no way enter therein" (Luke 18:17). Perhaps more than anything else, it is pride that keeps many "successful" people from trusting Jesus Christ.

A seeking man became found (v. 5). Zaccheus thought he was seeking Jesus (Luke 19:3), but Jesus was seeking him! (Luke 19:10) By nature, the lost sinner does not seek the Saviour (Rom. 3:11). When our first parents sinned, they hid from God, but God came and sought them (Gen. 3:1-10). When Jesus was ministering on earth, He sought out the lost; and today the Holy Spirit, through the church, is searching for lost sinners.

We do not know how God had worked in the heart of Zaccheus to prepare him for this meeting with Jesus. Was Levi, the former publican (Luke 5:27-39), one of his friends? Had he told Zaccheus about Jesus? Was he praying for Zaccheus? Had Zaccheus become weary of wealth and started yearning for something better? We cannot answer these questions, but we can rejoice that a seeking Saviour will always find a sinner who is looking for a new beginning.

A small man became big (vv. 7-8). It was not Zaccheus' fault that he was "little of stature" and could not see over the crowd. He did what he could to overcome his handicap by putting aside his dignity and climbing a tree. In a spiritual sense, all of us are "little of stature," for "all have sinned and come short of the glory of God" (Rom. 3:23). No one measures up to God's high standards; we are all "too little" to enter into heaven.

The tragedy is, many lost sinners think they are "big." They measure themselves by man's standards—money, position, authority, popularity—things that are an "abomination in the sight of God" (Luke 16:15). They think they have everything when really they have nothing (Rev. 3:17).

Zaccheus trusted Jesus Christ and became a true "son of Abraham," meaning, of course, a child of faith (Rom. 4:12; Gal. 3:7). That is as big as you can get!

A poor man became rich (vv. 9-10). The people thought Zaccheus was a wealthy man, but actually he was only a bankrupt sinner who needed to receive God's gift of eternal life, the most expensive gift in the world. This is the only instance in the four Gospels of Jesus inviting Himself to someone's home, and it illustrates the words of Revelation 3:20.

Zaccheus was not saved because he promised to do good works. He was saved because he responded by faith to Christ's gracious word to him. Having trusted the Saviour, he then gave evidence of his faith by promising to make restitution to those he had wronged. Saving faith is more than pious words and devout feelings. It creates a living union with Christ that results in a changed life (James 2:14-26).

Under the Mosaic Law, if a thief voluntarily confessed his crime, he had to restore what he took, add one fifth to it, and bring a trespass offering to the Lord (Lev. 6:1-7). If he stole something he could not restore, he had to repay fourfold (Ex. 22:1); and if he was caught with the goods, he had to repay double (Ex. 22:4). Zaccheus did not quibble over the terms of the Law; he offered to pay the highest price because his heart had truly been changed.

The child of God is born rich, for he shares "every spiritual blessing" in Jesus Christ (Eph. 1:3). We have the riches of God's mercy and grace (Eph. 1:7; 2:4) as well as the riches of His glory (Phil. 4:19) and wisdom (Rom. 11:33). These are "unsearchable riches" that can never be fully understood or completely exhausted (Eph. 3:8).

The host became the guest (v. 6). Jesus invited Himself to Zaccheus' house, and Zaccheus received Him joyfully. *Joy* is one of the key themes in the Gospel of Luke, and the word is found over twenty times in one form or another. The experience of salvation certainly ought to produce joy in the believer's heart.

Zaccheus became the guest in his own house, for Jesus was now his Master. He was ready to obey the Lord and do whatever was necessary to establish a genuine testimony before the people. To be sure, the people criticized Jesus for visiting in a publican's house (Luke 5:27-32), but the Lord paid no attention to their words. The critics also needed to be saved, but there is no evidence that they trusted Jesus.

When a day begins, you never know how it will end. For Zaccheus, that day ended in joyful fellowship with the Son of God, for he was now a changed man with a new life. Jesus is still seeking the lost and yearning to save them. Has He found you?

The Master Who Rewards the Faithful (Luke 19:11-27)

Passover season was always an emotionally charged time for the Jews, because it reminded them of their deliverance from the slavery of Egypt. This annual celebration aggravated the misery of their bondage to Rome and made them yearn all the more for a deliverer. Of course, there were subversive groups like the Zealots who used commando tactics against Rome, and politicians like the Herodians who compromised with Rome, but most of the Jews rejected those approaches. They wanted God to fulfill the Old Testament prophecies and send them their promised King.

Jesus knew that many of the people in the crowd were hoping to see Him establish the kingdom, so He gave this parable to clarify things. Many of the people who listened no doubt connected it with an event in Jewish history that had occurred many years before. When Herod the Great died in 4 B.C., he left Judea to his son Archelaus, who had to go to Rome to have the inheritance approved. Not wanting Archelaus as their ruler, the Jews sent fifty men to argue their case before Augustus Caesar, who did ratify the inheritance without giving Archelaus the title of "king."

Jesus explained that the kingdom would not come until a future time, but that His servants had better be faithful now to do the job assigned to them. In the parable, you see three different responses to the Master.

Faithful obedience (vv. 16-19, 24). Each of the servants received an amount of money equal to three months' wages for a laboring man, so you can figure out its buying power today. *Occupy* means "do business, put my money to work." They could give the money to investors and earn interest, or purchase goods and sell them for a profit. The important thing was that they give back to their master more than he had given to them. How they did it was up to them, so long as it was legal and profitable.

We are given a report on only three of the ten servants, and the first two proved to be successful. The first servant brought ten pounds more, the second brought five pounds more, and both were rewarded accordingly. These men did their job faithfully even though they were promised no rewards and had no assurance that their master would even return, let alone secure the kingdom that he sought.

The Parable of the Talents (Matt. 25:14-30) is similar to the Parable of the Pounds, but their lessons must not be confused. In this parable, each of the ten servants received the same amount but different rewards, while in the Parable of the Talents, the servants received different amounts but the same reward, the approval and joy of the Lord (Matt. 25:21).

The Parable of the Talents teaches us to be faithful to use our different gifts as God gives us opportunities to serve. Some people have a great deal of ability, so God gives them greater opportunity. The important thing is not how much ability you have but how faithful you are to use what you have for the Lord. The person with the least ability, if he or she is faithful, will receive the same reward as the most gifted church leader.

In the Parable of the Pounds, each servant has the same deposit, which probably represents the message of the Gospel (1 Thes. 2:4; 1 Tim. 1:11; 6:20). Our gifts and abilities are different, but our job is the same: to share the Word of God so that it multiplies and fills the world (1 Thes. 1:8; 2 Thes. 3:1). Only 120 believers met together on the Day of Pentecost (Acts 1:15), but before that day ended, there were 3,000 more (Acts 2:41). And before long, there were 5,000 believers (Acts 4:4). In time, the Jewish leaders accused the disciples of "filling Jerusalem" with the message! (Acts 5:28)

When it comes to witnessing, all believers start on the same level, so the reward is according to faithfulness and achievement. The faithful servants were rewarded by being made *rulers* of various cities. The reward for faithful work is always—more work! But what a compliment to be entrusted with the management of so many cities! How we serve the Lord today will help determine our reward and ministry when He comes to establish His kingdom on earth. Faithfulness now is preparation for blessed service then.

Unfaithful disobedience (vv. 20-23). At least one of the ten men did not obey his master and as a result lost even the pound that the master gave him. It is a basic principle of the Christian life that wasted opportunity means loss of reward *and possibly loss of the privilege of service.* If we do not use the gifts God gives us under His direction, why should we even have them? Somebody else can make better use of the gifts to the glory of God (see Matt. 13:12 and Luke 8:18).

"It is always so," wrote Charles Haddon Spurgeon; "the gracious and faithful man obtains more grace and more means of usefulness, while the unfaithful man sinks lower and lower and grows worse and worse. We must either make progress or else lose what we have attained. There is no such thing as standing still in religion."

This servant was unfaithful because his heart was not right toward his master. He saw his master as a hard man who was demanding and unfair. The servant had no love for his master; in fact, he feared him and dreaded to displease him. Rather than lose the pound and incur his master's anger, he guarded it so that he would at least have something to give the master if he returned and asked for a reckoning.

It is sad when a Christian is motivated by slavish fear instead of loving faith. While there is a proper "fear of the Lord" that should be in every Christian's heart, that "fear" should be the respect of a loving child and not the dread of a frightened slave. "Nothing twists and deforms the soul more than a low or unworthy conception of God," wrote Dr. A.W. Tozer. How important it is that we do the will of God from our hearts (Eph. 6:6).

Outright rebellion (vv. 14-27). The "citizens" or "enemies" are mentioned at the beginning and the ending and are an important part of the story, for most of the people in the crowd that day were in that category. Jesus was near Jerusalem, and in a few days He would hear the mob shout, "We have no king but Caesar!" (John 19:15) In other words, "We will not have this Man to reign over us!"

God was gracious to Israel and gave the nation nearly forty years of grace before judgment fell (Luke 19:41-44). But we must be careful to see in this a warning to all who reject Jesus Christ—Jew or Gentile—for during this time while He is away in heaven, Jesus Christ is calling men everywhere to repent and submit to Him.

The faithful servants obeyed because they trusted their master and wanted to please him. The unfaithful servant disobeyed because he feared his master. But these citizens rebelled because they hated their king (Luke 19:14). Jesus quoted Psalm 69:4 and told His disciples, "They hated Me without a cause" (John 15:25).

We are living today in the period between Luke 19:14 and 15 when our Master is absent but will return according to His promise. We have been given a task to perform, and we must be faithful until He comes. What will the King say to us when He returns? Will His words mean reward, rebuke, or possibly retribution? "Moreover it is required in stewards, that a man be found faithful" (1 Cor. 4:2).

The King Who Offers Peace (Luke 19:28-48)

The traditional calendar for the events of our Lord's last week of ministry looks like this:

Sunday—Triumphal Entry into Jerusalem
Monday—Cleansing the temple
Tuesday—Controversies with the Jewish leaders
Wednesday—Apparently a day of rest
Thursday—Preparation for Passover
Friday—Trial and Crucifixion
Saturday—Jesus rests in the tomb
Sunday—Jesus raised from the dead

Keep in mind that the Jewish day went from sundown to sundown, so that our Thursday evening would be their Friday, the Day of Passover.

Preparation (vv. 28-36). The owners of the donkey and the colt were disciples of the Lord and had everything ready for Him. The plan was executed quietly because the Jewish leaders had let it be known that anyone confessing Christ would be excommunicated (John 9:22). The fact that the rulers planned to kill Jesus made it even more important that the owners be protected (John 7:1, 19, 25; 8:37; 11:47-57).

We think of the donkey as a lowly animal, but to the Jew it was a beast fit for a king (1 Kings 1:33, 44). Jesus rode the colt (Luke 19:35) while the mother walked along with it. The fact that the colt had never been ridden and yet submitted to Jesus indicates our Lord's sovereignty over His creation. The laying of garments on the animals and on the road and the waving and spreading of branches were all part of a traditional Jewish reception for royalty.

Celebration (vv. 37-40). This is the only time that Jesus permitted a public demonstration on His behalf, and He did so for at least two reasons. First, He was fulfilling prophecy and presenting Himself as Israel's king (Zech. 9:9). How much of this the crowd really understood we cannot tell, even though they responded by quoting their praises from a messianic psalm (Ps. 118:25-26). No doubt many of the Passover pilgrims thought that Jesus would now get rid of the Roman invaders and establish the glorious kingdom.

The second reason for this demonstration was to force the Jewish religious leaders to act. They had hoped to arrest Him *after* the Passover (Matt. 26:3-5), but God had ordained that His Son be slain *on* Passover as the "Lamb of God, who taketh away the sin of the world" (John 1:29; and see 1 Cor. 5:7). Every previous attempt to arrest Jesus had failed because "His hour had not yet come" (John 7:30; 8:20; also see John 13:1; 17:1). When they saw this great public celebration, the leaders knew that they had to act, and the willing cooperation of Judas solved their problem for them (Matt. 26:14-16).

The theme of the celebration was *peace.* Dr. Luke opened his Gospel with the angel's announcement of "peace on earth" (Luke 2:14), but now the theme was "peace in heaven." Because the King was rejected, there could be no peace on earth. Instead, there would be constant bitter conflict between the kingdom of God and the kingdom of evil (Luke 12:49-53). There would be no peace on earth but, thanks to Christ's work on the cross, there is "peace with God" in heaven (Rom. 5:1; Col. 1:20). The appeal today is, "Be ye reconciled to God!" (2 Cor. 5:17-21)

Lamentation (vv. 41-44). While the crowd was rejoicing, Jesus was weeping! This is the second occasion on which our Lord wept openly, the first being at the tomb of Lazarus (John 11:35). There He wept quietly, but here He uttered a loud lamentation like one mourning over the dead. In this, He was like the Prophet Jeremiah who wept bitterly over the destruction of Jerusalem (Jer. 9:lff; see also the Book of Lamentations). Jonah looked on Nineveh and hoped it would be destroyed (Jonah 4), while Jesus looked at Jerusalem and wept because it had destroyed itself.

No matter where Jesus looked, He found cause for weeping. If He looked *back,* He saw how the nation had wasted its opportunities and been ignorant of their "time of visitation." If He looked *within,* He saw spiritual ignorance and blindness in the hearts of the people. They should have known who He was, for God had given them His Word and sent His messengers to prepare the way.

As He looked *around,* Jesus saw religious activity that accomplished very little. The temple had become a den of thieves, and the religious leaders were out to kill Him. The city was filled with pilgrims celebrating a festival, but the hearts of the people were heavy with sin and life's burdens.

As Jesus looked *ahead,* He wept as He saw the terrible judgment that was coming to the nation, the city, and the temple. In A.D. 70, the Romans would come and, after a siege of 143 days, kill 600,000 Jews, take thousands more captive, and then destroy the temple and the city. Why did all of this happen? Because the people did not know that God had visited them! "He came unto His own, and His own received Him not" (John 1:11). "We will not have this man to reign over us!" (Luke 19:14)

Denunciation (vv. 45-48). Jesus lodged in Bethany that night (Matt. 21:17) and came into the city early the next morning. It was then that He cursed the fig tree (Mark 11:12-14) and cleansed the temple for the second time. (See John 2:13-22 for the record of the first cleansing of the temple.)

The court of the Gentiles was the only place in the temple that was available to the Gentiles. There the Jews could witness to their "pagan" neighbors and tell them about the one true and living God. But instead of being devoted to evangelism, the area was used for a "religious marketplace" where Jews from other lands could exchange money and purchase approved sacrifices. The priests managed this business and made a good profit from it.

Instead of *praying* for the people, the priests were *preying* on the people! The temple was not a "house of prayer" (Isa. 56:7); it was a "den of thieves" (Jer. 7:11). Campbell Morgan reminds us that a "den of thieves" is a place where thieves *run to hide* after they have committed their wicked deeds. The religious leaders were using the services of the holy temple to cover up their sins (see Isa. 1:1-20). But before we condemn them too harshly, have we ever gone to church and participated in religious worship just to give people the impression that we were godly?

Jesus remained in the temple and used it as a gathering place for those who needed help. He healed many who were sick and afflicted, and He taught the people the Word of God. The hypocritical religious leaders tried to destroy Him, but His hour had not yet come and they could not touch Him. In the days that followed, they argued with Him and tried to catch Him in His words (Luke 20), but they failed. When His hour came, He would surrender to them and they would crucify Him.

The courageous Son of God had set His face like a flint and come to Jerusalem. During His last week of ministry, He would courageously face His enemies and then bravely go to the cross to die for the sins of the world.

He still summons us to *be courageous!*

CHAPTER NINETEEN
ISSUES AND ANSWERS
Luke 20

Jesus had already told the Twelve to expect conflict and suffering when they arrived in the Holy City. "The Son of man must suffer many things, and be rejected of the elders and chief priests and scribes, and be slain, and be raised the third day" (Luke 9:22). Jesus knew fully what was coming, and He was not afraid.

In this chapter, you meet the three groups of religious leaders (Luke 20:1) and witness their conflict with Jesus. They challenged Him because He had cleansed the temple and called them "thieves." They tried to catch Him in His words so they could trump up some charge against Him and have Him arrested as an enemy of the state.

But there was more to this series of questions than mere guile. The word translated "rejected" in Luke 9:22 (and also Luke 20:17) means "to reject after investigation." It was required that the Jews carefully examine the Passover lambs from the tenth day to the fourteenth day to make sure they had no blemishes (Ex. 12:1-6). Jesus Christ, the Lamb of God (John 1:29), was watched and tested by His enemies during that final week; and yet in spite of what they saw and learned, they rejected Him.

However, *Jesus was also examining them!* For as they questioned Him, He questioned them, and their responses revealed the ignorance, hatred, and unbelief of their hearts.

Our Lord's questions centered on four different men.

A Question about John the Baptist (Luke 20:1-19)

The cleansing of the temple was a dramatic event that both captured the attention of the people and aroused the anger of the religious establishment. The fact that Jesus daily made the temple His headquarters for ministry only made the members of the Sanhedrin more indignant, so they decided to question Him. "What authority do You have to do these things?" they asked. "And if You do have authority, who gave it to You?"

Authority is important for the success of any social, political, or religious organization; without authority, you have confusion. The chief priests claimed their authority from Moses, for the Law set the tribe of Levi apart to serve in the sanctuary. The scribes were students of the Law and claimed their authority from the rabbis whose interpretations they studied. The elders of Israel were the leaders of the families and clans, chosen usually for their experience and wisdom. All of these men were sure of their authority and were not afraid to confront Jesus.

They wanted to push our Lord into a dilemma so that no matter how He answered, He would be in trouble. If He said that He had *no* authority, then He was in trouble with the Jews for invading their temple and acting like a prophet. If He said that His authority came from God, then He would be in trouble with the Romans who were always alert to would-be messiahs, especially during Passover season (see Acts 5:34-39; 21:37-39).

Note our Lord's wise approach as He turned things around and put them completely on the defensive. First, *He asked a question* (Luke 20:3-8); then *He gave a parable* (Luke 20:9-16); and finally, *He quoted a prophecy* (Luke 20:17-18). In each of these approaches, He revealed the sins of the nation of Israel.

Their past rejection (vv. 3-8). Jesus took them back to John the Baptist for two reasons. First, John had pointed to Jesus and introduced Him to the nation (John 1:15-34), so their rejection of John was actually a rejection of the Lord Jesus Christ. Second, it is a spiritual principle that if we disobey truth we already know, God cannot reveal new truth to us (see John 7:14-17). Why answer their question when they had refused to submit to John's message?

Now it was the religious leaders who were in the dilemma! No matter what answer they gave, they were in trouble, so they decided to "play dumb" and not answer at all. They were deceitful in asking the question and dishonest in the way they avoided answering it. Even if Jesus *had* given them an answer, *their hearts were not prepared to receive it.* If they had disobeyed God's message given by John the Baptist (Luke 7:24-30), they would disobey the message given by God's Son. That was the theme of the parable Jesus told.

Their present rebellion (vv. 9-16). These men knew the Scriptures and recognized that Jesus was speaking about the "vineyard" of Israel (Ps. 80:8ff; Isa. 5:1-7). God the Father blessed the nation abundantly and gave the Jews a land that was rich and pleasant. All He asked was that they obey His statutes and give Him the "spiritual harvest" He deserved.

Instead of being grateful for their blessings and joyfully giving the Lord His due, the nation proceeded to rob God and reject His messengers (see Neh. 9:26; Jer. 7:25-26; 25:4). God was patient and sent them one servant after another, but they refused to obey (Matt. 23:29-39). Finally, He sent His beloved Son (Luke 3:22) and they killed Him. In this story, Jesus gave His own death announcement.

Under Jewish law, any man could lay claim to ownerless property. The tenants may have concluded that the owner was dead; otherwise he would have come himself. If they killed the son, then they could claim the vineyard for themselves. *This is exactly the way the religious leaders were thinking as they stood there before Jesus!* (see John 11:47-54)

Their future ruin (vv. 17-18). Jesus fixed a steady gaze on them and quoted Psalm 118:22. The rulers knew that this was a messianic psalm, and they had heard it shouted by the crowd when Jesus rode into the city (compare Luke 19:38 with Ps. 118:26). By applying this verse to Himself, Jesus was clearly claiming to be the Messiah. The "builders," of course, were the Jewish religious leaders (Acts 4:11).

In the Old Testament, the "stone" is a familiar symbol of God and of the promised Messiah (see Gen. 49:24; Ex. 17:6; 33:22; Deut. 32:4, 15, 30-31; Isa. 8:14; 28:16; 1 Cor. 10:4). Because the Jews did not believe, they stumbled over Him and were judged. Those who trust Jesus Christ find Him to be the foundation stone and the chief cornerstone of the church (1 Cor. 3:11; Eph. 2:20).

But Jesus also referred to Daniel 2:34-35, 44-45, where the Messiah is pictured as a "smiting stone" that crushes all that gets in its way. He was warning the Sanhedrin that they would only destroy themselves if they condemned Him. The same principle applies today, and unbelievers should carefully heed His warning.

When the rulers rejected John the Baptist, they sinned against the Father who sent Him. When they crucified Jesus, they sinned against the Son. Jesus had told them that they could sin against Him and still be forgiven, but when they sinned against the Holy Spirit, there could be no forgiveness (Matt. 12:24-37). Why? *Because that was the end of God's witness to the nation.* This is the so-called "unpardonable sin," and it was committed by the Jewish leaders when they finally rejected the witness of the Spirit of God through the Apostles. The evidence of their rejection was the stoning of Stephen (Acts 7:51-60). Then the Gospel went from the Jews to the Samaritans (Acts 8) and then to the Gentiles (Acts 10).

In this parable, Jesus illustrated the insidious nature of sin: *the more we sin, the worse it becomes.* The tenants started off beating some of the servants and wounding others, but they ended up becoming murderers! The Jewish leaders *permitted* John the Baptist to be killed, they *asked* for Jesus to be crucified, and then *they themselves stoned Stephen.* They sinned against the Father and the Son and the Holy Spirit, and that was the end of God's witness to them.

It is a serious thing to reject the message of God and the messengers of God (see John 12:35-43; Heb. 2:1-4).

A Question about Caesar (Luke 20:20-26)

Jesus knew that the men who questioned Him were spies sent by the Pharisees and the Herodians (Mark 12:13), but He patiently listened and replied. These two groups were usually fighting each other, but now they had a common enemy, and this brought them together. They wanted to discuss taxes and Roman authority, hoping to provoke Jesus into offending either the Jews ("Pay the poll tax!") or the Romans ("Don't pay the poll tax!"). But Jesus lifted the discussion to a much higher level and forced the spies to think about the relationship between the kingdom of God and the kingdoms of men.

Governmental authority is instituted by God and must be respected (Prov. 8:15; Dan.

2:21, 37-38; Rom. 13; 1 Peter 2:11-17). Yes, our citizenship is in heaven (Phil. 3:20), and we are strangers and pilgrims on earth, but that does not mean we should ignore our earthly responsibilities. Human government is essential to a safe and orderly society, for man is a sinner and must be kept under control.

Jesus was not suggesting that we divide our loyalties between God and government. Since "the powers that be are ordained of God" (Rom. 13:1), *we live as good citizens when we obey the authorities for the Lord's sake.* When obedience to God conflicts with obedience to man, then we must put God first (Acts 4:19-20; 5:29), but we must do it in a manner that is honorable and loving. Even if we cannot respect the people in office, *we must respect the office.* The counsel that Jeremiah gave to the Jewish exiles in Babylon is a good one for God's "strangers and pilgrims" to follow today (Jer. 29:4-7): "Seek the peace of the city!"

Caesar's image and name were on the coins, so it was basically *his* currency. To pay the poll tax meant simply to give Caesar back that which belonged to him. God's image is stamped on us; therefore, He has the right to command our lives as citizens in His kingdom. We should seek to be such good citizens that God will be glorified and the unsaved will be attracted to the Gospel and want to become Christians (1 Peter 2:9-12; 3:8-17).

It is unfortunate that some Christians have the mistaken idea that the more obnoxious they are as citizens, the more they please God and witness for Christ. We must never violate our conscience, but we should seek to be peacemakers and not troublemakers. Daniel is an example to follow (Dan. 1).

A Question about Moses (Luke 20:27-40)

Next in line were the Sadducees with a hypothetical question based on the Jewish law of "levirate marriage" (Gen. 38; Deut. 25:5-10). The word *levirate* comes from the Latin *levir,* which means "a husband's brother." The Sadducees accepted as Scripture only the Five Books of Moses, and they did not believe in angels, spirits, or the resurrection of the dead (Acts 23:8). They claimed that Moses did not write about any of these doctrines. The priestly party in Israel was composed of Sadducees, which explains why the priests opposed the Apostles' preaching of the Resurrection (Acts 4:1-2) and why they wanted to kill Lazarus, who was raised from the dead (John 12:10-11).

Jesus pointed out that His opponents were wrong and that their question revealed assumptions that limited God's power and denied God's Word. Resurrection is not reconstruction; it is the miraculous granting of a new body that has continuity with the old body but not identity. Paul compared our present body to a planted seed and the future resurrection body to the glorious flower and fruit (1 Cor. 15:35-50). Our Lord's resurrection body was the same as before His death and yet different! His friends recognized Him and even felt Him; He could eat food and yet He could also walk through closed doors, change His appearance, and vanish suddenly.

The future life with God is not a mere continuation of the present life only on "a higher scale." We will maintain our identities and know each other, but there will be no more death—hence, no need for marriage and procreation. Christians do not become angels. In heaven we will share the image of Jesus Christ and be much higher than the angels (1 John 3:2). Angels appear in Scripture as men, but they are spirit beings without sexuality. It is in this regard that we will be like them; there will be no marriage or childbearing in heaven.

Is not God powerful enough to raise the dead and give them new bodies suited to their new environment? If today He can give different bodies to the various things in creation, why can He not give people new bodies at the resurrection? (1 Cor. 15:35-44) In their attempt to be "rational," the Sadducees denied the very power of God!

But Jesus went beyond logic and referred them to the Word of God, particularly what happened to Moses as recorded in Exodus 3. There God identified Himself with Abraham, Isaac, and Jacob, and thus affirmed that these three patriarchs were very much alive. But if they were alive, then they were "out of the body," for they had died (James 2:26). There must be a real world of spirit beings or Moses would not have written these words. (By the way, Moses also affirmed the existence of angels: Gen. 19:1, 15; 28:12; 32:1.)

But Jesus said that Exodus 3:6, 15-16 taught not only the truth of life after death but also the reality of the resurrection. In what way? Not by direct statement but by inference. God is the God of the whole person—spirit, soul, and body (1 Thes. 5:23)—because

He created the whole person. He does not simply "save our souls" and ignore the rest of our being. Inherent in the very nature of God's creative act is His concern for the total person. Hence, He will not keep us disembodied spirits forever but will give us glorious bodies to match our heavenly perfection.

Another factor is God's covenental relationship with the patriarchs. He made promises of earthly blessing to them and their descendants, but He cannot fulfill these promises if His people are going to live forever only as disembodied spirits. Can there be a glorious new heaven and earth but no corporeal glory for the people of God?

Jesus affirmed what the Sadducees denied: the existence of angels, the reality of life after death, and the hope of a future resurrection—and He did it with only one passage from Moses! Of course, He could have referred to other passages that teach a future resurrection, but He met His adversaries on their own ground (see Job 14:14; 19:25-27; Pss. 16:9-10; 17:15; Isa. 26:19; Ezek. 37; Dan. 12:2).

A Question about David (Luke 20:41-44)

While the Pharisees were still gathered together, Jesus asked them a final question: "What do you think about the Christ? Whose Son is He?" (Matt. 22:41-42, NKJV) This is the *key* question for every generation and each individual, for our salvation and eternal destiny are dependent on what we think about Christ (1 John 2:21-25; 4:1-6; 5:1).

Of course, they knew the expected reply: "The Son of David." They based this on such verses as 2 Samuel 7:13-14; Isaiah 11:1; and Jeremiah 23:5. God had ordained that the Messiah should come from the family of David and be born in David's city, Bethlehem (Micah 5:2). The fact that the Jewish people identified Jesus with Nazareth, not Bethlehem, indicates that they had not really looked into the facts connected with His birth (John 7:40-53).

Jesus then referred them to Psalm 110, which is quoted in the New Testament more than any other psalm. The Jewish religious leaders in that day identified Psalm 110 as a prophetic psalm and said that David was speaking of the Messiah. But if the Messiah is David's *Lord,* how can He be David's *son?* Here was an enigma for them to solve!

The only explanation is that Messiah must be both God and man. As eternal God, Messiah is David's Lord, but as man, He is David's son (Rom. 1:3; 9:4-5; Acts 2:32-36; 13:22-23).

On Palm Sunday, the multitudes had acclaimed Jesus as the Son of David, and He had not rebuked them (Matt. 21:9; Mark 11:10). By applying Psalm 110:1 to Himself, Jesus claimed to be Israel's promised Messiah, the Son of God.

Then why did the Pharisees not believe in Him? Because their minds were made up, their hearts were hardened, and their eyes were blind (John 12:37-50). They did not have the courage to confess the truth, and they persecuted those who did affirm faith in Jesus Christ. Christ's question silenced His enemies (Matt. 22:46) and ended their public challenges, but they would not admit defeat.

Because of their hypocrisy and dishonesty, the scribes and Pharisees were dangerous to have around, so Jesus warned the people about them (Luke 20:45-47; see Matt. 23). Men see the outside, but God sees the heart (1 Sam. 16:7; Heb. 4:12).

These religious leaders did not desire personal holiness; they wanted public recognition. Therefore, they wore special garments, expected special titles and greetings, and looked for special seats at public gatherings.

There is a double tragedy here. First of all, their deliberate hypocrisy was only a cover-up that enabled them to fool people and exploit them. Of all rackets, religious rackets are the worst. The religious leaders had turned the temple of God into a den of thieves and religious devotion into playacting. The general public actually thought that their leaders were godly men, when in reality they were defiling and destroying souls (Matt. 23:13-36).

The second tragedy is that they rejected their own Messiah and voted to crucify Him. They led the nation into ruin because they would not admit their sins and confess Jesus Christ. Keep in mind that these men were "experts" in the Bible, yet they did not apply its truths to their own lives. Their religion was a matter of external observance, not internal transformation.

At this point, according to Matthew (Matt. 23:37-39), Jesus once again uttered a lamentation over the blind unbelief of the nation and their unwillingness to trust in Him.

He had given them many opportunities, but they had wasted them.

Now it was too late.

This same tragedy is reenacted today. This is why the Holy Spirit warns, "Today, if you will hear His voice, do not harden your hearts" (Heb. 3:7-8, NKJV).

"How often I wanted to . . . but you were not willing!" (Matt. 23:37, NKJV)

CHAPTER TWENTY
QUESTIONS ABOUT TOMORROW
Luke 21

Now it was the disciples' turn to ask the questions!

It all started with the arrival in the temple of a poor widow with an offering for the Lord (Luke 21:1-4). Compared to the gifts of the rich men, her two copper coins seemed insignificant, but Jesus said that she gave more than all the others combined. "The widow's mite" does not represent *the least* we can give, but *the most,* our very all. When we sing, "Take my silver and my gold/ Not a mite will I withhold," we are telling God that everything we have belongs to Him.

When it comes to our giving, God sees more than the *portion;* He also sees the *proportion.* Men see *what is given,* but God sees *what is left,* and by that He measures the gift and the condition of our hearts. Winston Churchill said, "We make a living by what we get, but we make a life by what we give." He may have learned that from Jesus (Luke 6:38) or perhaps from Paul (2 Cor. 8:1-15).

The temple was a beautiful structure, embellished with many costly decorations that a poor widow could never give, and the disciples mentioned this to Jesus. But our Lord was not impressed. He told them that the day would come when the beautiful Jewish temple would be demolished (Luke 21:5-6). He had already announced that the city would be destroyed (Luke 19:41-44), but now He specifically mentioned the destruction of the temple.

Jesus left the temple and went to the Mount of Olives, and there Peter, James, and John asked Him three questions: (1) When would the temple be destroyed? (2) What would be the sign of His coming? (3) What would be the sign of the end of the age? (see Mark 13:3-4; Matt. 24:3) The disciples thought that these three events would occur at the same time, but Jesus explained things differently. Actually, the temple would be destroyed first, and then there would be a long period of time before He would return and establish His kingdom on earth (see Luke 19:11-27).

Our Lord's reply comprises what we call "The Olivet Discourse," the greatest prophetic sermon He ever preached. It is recorded in greater detail in Matthew 24–25 and Mark 13, and you will want to compare the three passages. Since Luke wrote with the Gentile reader in mind, he omitted some of the strong Jewish elements of the sermon while retaining the essential truths that we must consider and apply.

Keep in mind that this was a message given to Jews by a Jew about the future of the Jewish nation. Though there are definite applications to God's people today, the emphasis is on Jerusalem, the Jews, and the temple. Our Lord was not discussing His coming for the church, for that can occur at any time and no signs need precede it (1 Cor. 15:51-58; 1 Thes. 4:13-18). "For the Jews require a sign" (1 Cor. 1:22); the church looks for a Saviour (Phil. 3:20-21).

The sermon focuses on a period in God's program called "the Tribulation" when God will pour out His wrath on the nations of the world. Many Bible students believe that the Tribulation will begin after the Lord comes *in the air* and takes His church to heaven (1 Thes. 4:13-5:11). It will climax with the return of Jesus Christ *to the earth,* at which time He will defeat His foes and establish His kingdom (Rev. 19:1–20:6).

It is helpful to see the development of the sermon as a whole, so here is a suggested outline:

The first half of the Tribulation
(Matt. 24:4-14; Mark 13:5-13; Luke 21:8-19)
The middle of the Tribulation
(Matt. 24:15-28; Mark 13:14-18; note Dan. 9:24-27)
The last half of the Tribulation
(Matt. 24:29-31; Mark 13:19-27; Luke 21:25-27)
Closing admonitions
(Matt. 24:32–25:51; Mark 13:28-37; Luke 21:28-36)

Jesus answered the disciples' questions by

discussing four topics relating to the future of the nation of Israel.

The Description of the Age (Luke 21:8-19)

The characteristics Jesus stated can be seen in *every* age of the church, for from the beginning there have been counterfeit messiahs, national and international upheavals, and religious persecution. But these things will *increase and intensify* as the time of Jesus' coming draws near. Thomas Campbell, British poet and educator, said that "coming events cast their shadows before" and he was right.

There will be *religious delusion* (Luke 21:8), and even God's people will be in danger of being deceived. Satan is a counterfeiter who for centuries has led people astray by deceiving their minds and blinding their hearts (2 Cor. 4:1-6; 11:1-4, 13-15). Israel was often seduced into sin by false prophets, and the church has had its share of false teachers (2 Peter 2).

Most people are naturally concerned about the future, especially when world events are threatening; therefore, religious racketeers can prey on them and take advantage of them. In every age, there are those who either claim to be the Christ or claim to know when He will return. These false prophets often "use" the Scriptures to "prove" the accuracy of their predictions, in spite of the fact that Jesus clearly stated that nobody knows the time of His return (Matt. 24:36-44).

"Be not deceived!" is our Lord's admonition, and we must take it to heart. The only sure way to keep our balance in a deceptive world is to know the Scriptures and obey what God tells us to do (2 Peter 3:17-18). It is foolish and hurtful to become so obsessed with Bible prophecy that we start to neglect the practical things of the Christian life. Blessed are the balanced!

There will also be *international distress* (Luke 21:9-11). I have a friend who has been keeping track of the earthquakes that have occurred in recent years. Another prophetic student has a list of all the wars and attempted invasions. Both have overlooked the fact that Jesus said that wars, earthquakes, pestilences, and famines *by themselves* are not signs of His soon return. These things have been going on throughout the history of the world.

However, during the first half of the Tribulation, these events will multiply and intensify. Matthew 24:1-14 lists them in detail, and if you compare Revelation 6, you will see the parallel:

Events	*Matthew*	*Revelation*
false Christs	24:4-5	6:1-2
wars	24:6	6:3-4
famines	24:7a	6:5-6
death	24:7b-8	6:7-8
martyrs	24:9	6:9-11
worldwide chaos	24:10-13	6:12-17

In fact, most of Revelation 6–19, describes the Tribulation period in detail and follows the outline of Matthew 24: (1) first half of the Tribulation, chapters 6–9; (2) middle of the Tribulation, chapters 10–14; (3) last half of the Tribulation, chapters 15–19.

Our Lord's admonition to His people is, "Don't be terrified!" These things must come to pass; there is nothing anyone can do to prevent them. This does not mean that God's people are submitting to blind fate; rather, it means they are yielding to the plan of a loving Father who works all things "after the counsel of His own will" (Eph. 1:11).

Finally, there will be *religious persecution,* both official (Luke 21:12-15) and personal (Luke 21:16-19). Of course, there has been religious persecution ever since Cain killed Abel (Matt. 23:34-36; and see Acts 4:1ff; 5:17ff; 6:9ff; 8:1ff). Jesus promised that His people would suffer (John 15:18–16:4, 32-33), and that promise holds true today (2 Tim. 3:12). But the persecution in the end times will be much more severe and many will give their lives for Christ.

Notice the encouragements Jesus gives to all who suffer persecution. To begin with, we must remember that when we are persecuted, we suffer *for His name's sake* (Luke 21:12), and this is a high honor (Acts 5:41). It is not important what people say about our names, but it is important that the name of Christ be glorified.

Second, times of suffering provide opportunities for witness (Luke 21:13-15). The Apostles made good use of the witness stand when they were arrested and taken before the council (Acts 4–5), and Christ's servants and martyrs down through the centuries have followed their example. The English word *martyr* comes from the Greek word *martus* which means "a witness" (see 1 Peter 3:13-17).

Because of official persecution, God's witnesses will stand before important people; and when that happens, they must not panic, for

God will give them the words to speak. This promise is not an excuse for lazy preachers or Sunday School teachers who do not want to study! Rather, it is an assurance to faithful witnesses that God will always give them the words they need when they need them.

Not only will the saints endure official persecution from the government, but there will also be opposition from family and friends. Relatives will even follow in the footsteps of Judas and betray their Christian loved ones to be killed. Hatred, arrest, and death will be the lot of many of God's children during the Tribulation.

But they must not despair, for God is in control. Not a hair on their head can perish apart from His sovereign will (Matt. 10:28-31). Knowing this, they can have endurance and be able to face the challenge with faith and courage.

While many Christians today enjoy freedom from official persecution, or even family opposition, there are others who suffer greatly for their faith, and what our Lord said here is an encouragement to them. A friend of mine ministered in Eastern Europe, and a believer in Poland said to him, "We are praying for you Christians in the Western world *because you have it too easy.* The Lord must help you not to compromise."

Remember, the things Jesus described here are not signs of His soon return, because they have been going on for centuries. However, as the coming of the Lord draws near, these things will multiply and intensify. No matter what our views may be of the coming of the Lord, we all need to heed His three admonitions: "Don't be deceived! Don't be afraid! Don't worry!"

The Destruction of the Temple (Luke 21:20-24)

This paragraph is peculiar to Luke; there is no parallel in Matthew or Mark, in spite of the similar language in Matthew 24:16-21 and Mark 13:14-17. However, it is clear that both Matthew and Mark were referring to events in the middle of the Tribulation when "the abomination of desolation" would be set up in the Jewish temple and the Antichrist (the world ruler) would begin to persecute Israel (Dan. 9:24-27; Rev. 13). Jesus warned the people to flee and go into hiding, for "great tribulation" was about to fall.

Luke's account refers not to a distant event to occur during the Tribulation but to the destruction of Jerusalem by Titus and the Roman army in A.D. 70, just forty years from that time (see Luke 19:41-44). This terrible event was in many respects a "dress rehearsal" for what will happen when Satan vents his anger on Israel and the believing Gentiles during the last half of the Tribulation (Rev. 12:7-17). The Jewish historian Josephus claimed that nearly a million people were killed by the Romans, and over 100,000 taken captive, when Titus captured the city.

This was not the first time Jerusalem would be "trodden down of the Gentiles," for the Babylonians had destroyed the city in 586 B.C. when "the times of the Gentiles" began. This significant period in God's plan will end when Jesus Christ returns to the earth, destroys all Gentile power, and sets up His own righteous kingdom (Dan. 2:34-36, 44-45; Rev. 19:11ff).

Believers today who are looking for their Lord's return should not apply Luke 21:20-24 to their own situation. Jesus was talking about Jerusalem in A.D. 70. In Matthew 24:15-28 and Mark 13:14-23, He was speaking about Israel's situation at the middle of the Tribulation. Since our Lord's coming for the church will take place "in the twinkling of an eye" (1 Cor. 15:52), no one will have time to go back home for a coat; nor will we have to worry about traveling on the Sabbath or caring for nursing babies.

Thus far in His message, our Lord has told the disciples when the temple would be destroyed and what signs would point to the end of the age. Now He tells them about His own coming at the end of the Tribulation period.

The Return of the Lord (Luke 21:25-28)

Revelation 15–19 describes the frightening judgment signs that God will send on the earth during the last half of the "time of Jacob's trouble" (Jer. 30:7). When these things occur, it will be evidence that the Lord's coming is drawing near. The image of "waves roaring" describes nations rising and falling like waves in a storm (Ps. 46:1-6; Rev. 17:15). It will be an awesome time, and the population of the earth will tremble with fear, but men will not repent of their sins and turn to God by faith (Rev. 9:20-21; 16:9-11).

Matthew 24:29 informs us that the sun and moon will be darkened and the stars will fall (Isa. 13:10; 34:4; Joel 2:10, 31; 3:15). Matthew 24:30 states that "the sign of the Son of man" will appear in heaven. We do not know what this "sign" is, but it will produce fear among the nations of the earth. However, then Jesus Christ will appear, and every eye will see Him (Rev. 1:7). The nation of Israel will at last recognize their Messiah, repent, believe, and be saved (Zech. 12:10-14; and see Mark 14:61-62).

These awesome signs will bring terror to the lost people of the world, but hope to those who have trusted the Lord during the Tribulation period (Rev. 7), for these believers know that the Lord's coming will be soon. Believers today look for the Saviour, not signs. However, as we see "coming events casting their shadows," we believe that the Lord's return is near.

Christ's appearing will be sudden, glorious, and with great power (Luke 21:27). The image here is taken from Daniel 7:13-14, a messianic passage that must have been familiar to the disciples. The angels promised that Jesus would return to earth in the same way He departed (Acts 1:9-11), and He will (Rev. 1:7).

There are those who ignore and even ridicule the doctrine of the return of Christ. After all, the church has been waiting for the Lord for 2,000 years, and He has not returned yet! Peter answered that accusation in 2 Peter 3. He pointed out that God keeps His promises whether we believe them or not, and that God measures time differently from the way men measure it. Furthermore, the reason He waits is so that *unsaved sinners may repent, be saved, and be ready when Jesus comes.* While His seeming delay is a trial to the church, it is an opportunity for the lost.

Having answered their questions, the Lord then "applied" the message to their hearts by giving them two closing admonitions: "Know!" and "Watch!"

The Responsibilities of the Believers (Luke 21:29-38)

In the Bible, the fig tree is often an image of Israel (Hosea 9:10; Luke 13:6-10). Some students interpret this parable to mean that the emergence of the State of Israel on May 15, 1948 was the "sign" that the Lord would soon return. Surely it is a significant thing that Israel is now a free nation after so many centuries of political bondage. But Luke added "and all the trees" (Luke 21:29), suggesting that more than one nation is involved. Perhaps Jesus was saying that *the rise of nationalism around the world* is the thing to watch. In recent years we have certainly seen the growth of nationalism and the emerging of new nations, and this may be a "sign" that the coming of the Lord is near.

However, the basic idea here is that of *knowing what is going on.* As the budding of the trees indicates that summer is near, so the occurring of these signs indicates that the Lord's return is near (see Luke 12:54-57 for a similar passage). The important thing is that the believer *knows* that God is keeping His promises and that His Word will not fail (Josh. 23:14).

To what "generation" does Luke 21:32 apply? Some who doubt that Jesus will literally return say that this statement applies to the generation of the Apostles, so that "the coming of the Lord" was either the coming of the Spirit at Pentecost (Acts 2) or the destruction of Jerusalem in A.D. 70. *But none of the signs Jesus mentioned took place before or during those events.* Nor did they climax with the deliverance of Israel and the establishing of the kingdom.

Jesus was probably referring to the generation that would be alive on earth at the time all these things take place. He was not suggesting that it would take a whole generation to accomplish these things, for they will occur with swiftness once they begin. The Greek word translated "generation" can also mean "race" and could refer to the people of Israel. Jesus used it that way in Mark 8:12, 38; 9:19. Jesus was assuring the disciples that, in spite of all the difficulties Israel would endure, the nation would be protected by God and not be destroyed. Satan has wanted to destroy the nation of Israel, but he will not succeed.

His first admonition was "Know!" and His second was "Watch!" (Luke 21:34-36) Both admonitions apply to God's people in every age, though they will have a special meaning for the Jews of the Tribulation period. "Watch!" does not mean to stand around looking for signs. It means, "Be awake! Be alert! Don't get caught unprepared!" This admonition carries a warning for us today, because it is so easy for us to "get weighted down" with the cares of this life and the temptations of the world and the flesh (see Luke 12:35-48).

During difficult times, it is easy to give up and start living like the unsaved world; and believers during the Tribulation period will face that temptation. They must "watch and pray" and resist the temptations around them, for they want to be ready when their Lord returns.

Luke 21:36 refers primarily to believers standing before the Lord at the judgment when He returns to earth to establish His kingdom (Matt. 25:31-46). The sheep will enter into the kingdom while the goats will be cast out. While some of God's people will die during the Tribulation judgments and persecutions, some will "escape" and see Jesus Christ when He returns in glory.

If believers during that *difficult* age will be tempted to yield to the world and the flesh, Christians in this present age of comfort and affluence must face even greater dangers. We today do not know when our Lord will return, and it behooves us to be faithful and to be ready.

"I'm not looking for signs," said the late Vance Havner; "I'm listening for a sound."

The sound of the trumpet! The shout of the archangel!

"Even so, come, Lord Jesus!" (Rev. 22:20)

CHAPTER TWENTY-ONE
IN THE UPPER ROOM
Luke 22:1-38

Jesus had "steadfastly set His face to go to Jerusalem" (Luke 9:51), knowing full well what would happen to Him there; and now those events were about to occur. They were appointments, not accidents, for they had been determined by the Father and written centuries ago in the Old Testament Scriptures (Luke 24:26-27). We cannot but admire our Saviour and love Him more as we see Him courageously enter into this time of suffering and eventual death. We must remember that He did it for us.

The Passover supper in the Upper Room gives us the focus for our present study.

Before the Supper: Preparation (Luke 22:1-13)

Passover, Pentecost, and Tabernacles were the three most important feasts on the Jewish calendar (Lev. 23); and all the Jewish men were expected to go to Jerusalem each year to celebrate (Deut. 16:16). The Feast of Passover commemorated the deliverance of Israel from Egypt, and it was a time for both remembering and rejoicing (Ex. 11–12). Thousands of excited pilgrims crowded in and around Jerusalem during that week, causing the Romans to always be nervous about possible uprisings. Passover had strong political overtones, and it was the ideal time for some would-be messiah to attempt to overthrow Rome. This explains why King Herod and Pontius Pilate, the Roman governor, were in Jerusalem instead of being at Tiberius and Caesarea respectively. They wanted to help keep the peace.

The religious leaders prepared for a crime (vv. 1-6). It is incredible that these men perpetrated history's greatest crime during Israel's holiest festival. During Passover, the Jews were expected to remove all leaven (yeast) from their houses (Ex. 12:15) as a reminder that their ancestors left Egypt in haste and had to eat unleavened bread. Jesus had warned His disciples about the "leaven of the Pharisees, which is hypocrisy" (Luke 12:1; also see Matt. 16:6; 1 Cor. 5:1-8), and now we see this hypocrisy at work.

The religious leaders had cleansed their homes but not their hearts (see Matt. 23:25-28). For a long time now, they had wanted to arrest Jesus and get Him out of the way, but they had not been able to work out a safe plan that would protect them from the people. Judas solved their problem for them. He guaranteed to deliver Jesus to them privately so there would be no uproar from the people. The last thing the Jewish Sanhedrin wanted was a messianic uprising at Passover season (see Luke 19:11).

Judas was motivated and energized by Satan (John 13:2, 27), for he never was a true believer in Jesus Christ. His sins had never been cleansed by the Lord (John 13:10-11), and he had never believed and received eternal life (John 6:64-71). Yet none of the other Apostles had the least suspicion that Judas was a traitor. We have every reason to believe that Judas had been given the same authority as the other men and that he had preached the same message and performed the same miracles. It shows how close a person can come to God's kingdom and still be lost (Matt. 7:21-29).

Why did Judas betray the Lord Jesus? We know that he was a thief (John 12:4-6) and that money played a part in his terrible deed. But thirty pieces of silver was not a large payment for such a great crime, and there had to be something more involved. It is possible that Judas saw in Jesus the salvation of the Jewish nation and, therefore, he followed Him because he hoped to hold an office in the kingdom. Keep in mind that the Twelve often argued over who was the greatest in the kingdom, and Judas, the treasurer, surely participated in those important discussions.

When Judas understood that Jesus would not establish the kingdom but rather would surrender to the authorities, he turned against Him in bitter retaliation. The "leaven" in his life grew quietly and secretly until it produced "malice and wickedness" (1 Cor. 5:6-8). When you cooperate with Satan, you pay dearly, and Judas ended up destroying himself (Matt. 27:3-5). Satan is a liar and a murderer (John 8:44), and he reproduced himself perfectly in Judas.

Jesus prepared for the Passover (vv. 7-13). The way our Lord arranged for the Passover feast indicates that He knew there were plots afoot. Until the disciples arrived at the Upper Room, only Jesus and Peter and John had known where the feast would be held. Had Judas known, he might have been tempted to inform the authorities.

Peter and John would have no trouble locating the man with the water pitcher, because men rarely carried pitchers of water. This was the task of the women. Like the men who owned the ass and colt (Luke 19:28-34), this anonymous man was a disciple of Jesus who made his house available to the Master for His last Passover.

Peter and John would purchase an approved lamb and take it to the temple to be slain. Then they would take the lamb and the other elements of the supper to the house where they planned to meet, and there the lamb would be roasted. The table would be furnished with wine, unleavened bread, and the paste of bitter herbs that reminded the Jews of their long and bitter bondage in Egypt (see Ex. 12:1-28).

There is a chronological question here that must be addressed or it will appear that the Gospel writers are contradicting each other. According to John 18:28, the Jewish leaders had not yet eaten the Passover, and the day Jesus was tried and condemned was "the preparation of the Passover" (John 19:14). But our Lord and His disciples had already eaten the Passover!

In their excellent *Harmony of the Gospels* (Harper & Row), Robert Thomas and Stanley Gundry suggest a possible solution to the dilemma (pp. 320–23). The Jews at that time reckoned days in one of two ways: from sunset to sunset or from sunrise to sunrise. The first approach was traditionally Jewish (Gen. 1:5) while the second was Roman, though it had biblical precedent (see Gen. 8:22).

If Matthew, Mark, and Luke used the Jewish reckoning, and John the Roman, then there is no contradiction. There was an "overlapping" of days that permitted both groups to celebrate on the same *date* but a different *day*. The temple priests permitted the Jews to bring their lambs for sacrifice either the earlier or the later time. Apparently the Jewish leaders followed the Roman form of reckoning (John 18:28) while Jesus and the disciples followed the Jewish form. Our Lord was crucified on Passover at the time when the lambs were being slain, becoming a fulfillment of Old Testament type.

During the Supper: Revelation (Luke 22:14-16, 21-38)

The disciples did not know what to expect as they met in the Upper Room, but it turned out to be an evening of painful revelation. Jesus, the Host of the supper, met them with the traditional kiss of peace (He kissed Judas!), and then the men reclined around the table, Judas at our Lord's left and John at His right (John 13:23).

Jesus revealed His love (vv. 14-16). He did this by what He *said* and by what He *did*. He told His friends that He had a great desire to share this last Passover with them before He suffered. Passover commemorated the Exodus of Israel from Egypt centuries before, but He would accomplish a greater "exodus" on the cross. He would purchase redemption from sin for a world of lost sinners (Luke 9:31).

Then He arose, girded Himself with a towel, and washed the disciples' feet, including Judas' (John 13:1-20). Later that evening, the Twelve would argue over which of them was the greatest, so this lesson on humility and service did not penetrate their hearts. Perhaps Peter had this scene in mind when years later he admonished his readers to "be clothed with humility" (1 Peter 5:5; and see Phil. 2:1-11).

Our Lord's words in Luke 22:16 indicate that there would be no more Passover on God's calendar. The next feast would be the great "kingdom feast" when He would return to establish His rule on earth (Luke 22:28-30;

13:24-30; Matt. 8:11-12). He saw beyond the suffering to the glory, beyond the cross to the crown; and in His love, He reached out to include His friends.

Jesus revealed the presence of treachery (vv. 21-23). He had already hinted to His disciples that one of their number was not truly with Him (John 6:66-71), but now He openly spoke about a traitor in their midst. However, He did not do this just for the sake of the disciples, but more for the sake of Judas. Jesus had kissed Judas and washed his feet, and now He was giving Judas another opportunity to repent. It is most significant that Jesus did not openly identify Judas as the traitor but protected him until the very end.

If Jesus knew that Judas would betray Him, why did He choose him in the first place? And, if *somebody* had to betray the Lord, why condemn Judas? After all, he simply did God's will and fulfilled the Old Testament prophecy (see Pss. 41:9; 55:12-14; compare Pss. 69:25 and 109:8 with Acts 1:15-20).

Before He chose His 12 Apostles, Jesus spent a whole night in prayer (Luke 6:12-16), so we must believe that it was the Father's will that Judas be among them (John 8:29). But the selection of Judas did not seal his fate; rather, it gave him opportunity to watch the Lord Jesus closely, believe, and be saved. God in His sovereignty had determined that His Son would be betrayed by a friend, *but divine foreknowledge does not destroy human responsibility or accountability.* Judas made each decision freely and would be judged accordingly, even though he still fulfilled the decree of God (Acts 2:23).

The fact that the disciples were puzzled by this strange announcement reveals that they did not know Judas' true character, their own hearts ("Which of us could do such a terrible thing?"), or the prophecies in the psalms. Nor did they remember the Lord's statements that He would be betrayed into the hands of the enemy (Matt. 17:22; 20:18). If Peter had fully understood what was happening, he might have used his sword on Judas!

Much about Judas remains a mystery to us, and we must not speculate too much. Judas is certainly a witness to the sinlessness of Jesus Christ, for if anybody could have given witness against Him, it was Judas. However, the authorities had to find false witnesses in order to build their case against Jesus. Judas admitted that he had "betrayed innocent blood" (Matt. 27:4).

At this point, Judas left the Upper Room to go to the religious leaders and get ready for the arrest of Jesus in the Garden. Judas went out "and it was night" (John 13:30), for he was obeying the prince of darkness (Luke 22:53). Alas, for Judas, *it is still night and always will be night!*

Jesus revealed the disciples' worldliness (vv. 24-30). This was not the first time the disciples had committed this sin (Matt. 20:20-28; Mark 9:33-37; Luke 9:46-48), but in the light of what their Lord had said and done that evening, this latest exhibition was inexcusable. Perhaps the argument grew out of their speculating over who would betray Him, or there may have been some jealousy over the way they had been seated at the table. When you are interested in promoting yourself, it doesn't take much to start an argument.

Jesus had to explain that they were thinking like the unsaved Gentiles and not like God's children. The Romans in particular vied for honors and did all they could, legally and illegally, to win promotion and recognition, but they are not the examples for us to follow. As in all things, Jesus is our example, and He has completely reversed the measure of true greatness.

True greatness means to be like Jesus, and that means being a servant to others. A servant does not argue over who is the greatest, because he knows that he is the least, and he accepts this from the hand of God. Since all Christians are to be servants, there is no reason for us to compete with one another for honors and recognition. It is too bad that this competitive spirit is so strong in the church today as people promote themselves and their ministries as "the greatest."

Jesus closed this lesson on servanthood by reminding them of their future reward in the kingdom (Luke 22:28-30). In spite of their weaknesses and failures, the disciples had stood by Jesus during His earthly ministry, and God would honor them for their faithfulness. We should not mind being servants today, for we shall sit on thrones in the future kingdom! For that matter, our faithful service today is preparing us for the rewards we shall receive. Jesus has set the example: first the cross, then the crown.

Jesus revealed Peter's denial (vv. 31-38). It is interesting that this word of warning followed the dispute over who was the greatest! Imagine how the disciples must have felt when they heard that not only would one of their number betray Him, but that their spokesman and leader would publicly deny Him! If a strong man like Peter was going to fail the Lord, what hope was there for the rest of them?

The word *you* in Luke 22:31 is plural; Satan asked to have all the disciples so he might sift them like wheat. These men had been with Jesus in His trials (Luke 22:28), and He would not forsake them in their trials. This was both a warning and an encouragement to Peter and the other men, and our Lord's prayers were answered. Peter's courage failed but not his faith; he was restored to fellowship with Christ and was greatly used to strengthen God's people.

Peter's self-confident boasting is a warning to us that none of us really knows his own heart (Jer. 17:9) and that we can fail *in the point of our greatest strength.* Abraham's greatest strength was his faith, and yet his faith failed him when he went down to Egypt and lied about Sarah (Gen. 12:10–13:4). Moses' strength was in his meekness (Num. 12:3), yet he lost his temper, spoke rashly with his lips, and was not allowed to enter Canaan (Num. 20). Peter was a brave man, but his courage failed him and he denied his Lord three times. "Therefore let him who thinks he stands take heed lest he fall" (1 Cor. 10:12, NKJV).

The word *converted* in Luke 22:32 means "turned around." Peter was already a *saved* man, but he would soon start going in the wrong direction and would have to be turned around. He would not lose the gift of eternal life, but he would disobey the Lord and jeopardize his discipleship. Actually, all of the disciples would forsake Jesus, but Peter would also deny Him. It is a humbling lesson for all of us.

Our Lord's counsel in Luke 22:35-38 was not fully understood by the disciples, because they interpreted what He said quite literally. Peter's use of the sword in the Garden is evidence of this (Luke 22:49-51). The point He was making was this: "You are now moving into a whole new situation. If they arrest Me, they will one day arrest you. If they treat Me like a common criminal (Isa. 53:12), they will do the same to you; so, be prepared!"

During their ministry with Jesus, the disciples had been sent out with special authority, and they were treated with respect and appreciation (Luke 9:1ff; 10:1ff). At that time, Jesus was still a very popular rabbi, and the authorities were not able to attack His disciples. But now "His hour had come" and the situation would change radically. Today, God's people are aliens in enemy territory, and we must use our faith and sanctified common sense as we serve the Lord. This is a good warning to zealous people who foolishly get themselves into tight spots and then expect God to perform miracles for them. The Apostle Paul knew how to use the "sword" of human government to protect him and the Gospel (Acts 16:35-40; 21:37-40; 25:11; Rom. 13).

Their words, "Here are two swords!" must have grieved the Lord, for they indicated that the disciples had missed the meaning of His words. Did they think that He needed their protection or that He would now overthrow Rome and establish the kingdom? "It is enough!" means "Don't say anything more about the matter" (Deut. 3:26). His kingdom does not advance by means of men's swords (John 18:36-37) but by the power of God's truth, the Word of God that is sharper than any human sword (Eph. 6:17; Heb. 4:12).

After the Supper: Commemoration (Luke 22:17-20)

It was when the Passover meal was drawing to a close (Matt. 26:25; Luke 22:20) that Jesus instituted the ordinance that the church calls "The Communion" (1 Cor. 10:16), or "The Lord's Supper" (1 Cor. 11:20), or "The Eucharist," from the Greek word which means "to give thanks."

The Passover feast opened with a prayer of thanksgiving, followed by the drinking of the first of four cups of wine. (The wine was diluted with water and was not intoxicating.)

Next they ate the bitter herbs and sang Psalms 113–114. Then they drank the second cup of wine and began eating the lamb and the unleavened bread. After drinking the third cup of wine, they sang Psalms 115–118; and then the fourth cup was passed among them. It is likely that between the third and fourth cups of wine, Jesus instituted the Supper.

Paul gave the order of the Supper in 1 Corinthians 11:23-26. First, Jesus broke a piece from the unleavened loaf, gave thanks, and shared it with the disciples, saying that it represented His body which was given for them. He then gave thanks for the cup and shared it, saying that it represented His blood. It was a simple observance that used the basic elements of a humble Jewish meal. Jesus sanctified the simple things of life and used them to convey profound spiritual truths.

Jesus stated one of the purposes for the Supper: "in remembrance of Me" (1 Cor. 11:24-25). It is a memorial feast to remind the believer that Jesus Christ gave His body and blood for the redemption of the world. There is no suggestion in the accounts of the Supper that anything "miraculous" took place when Jesus blessed the bread and the cup. The bread remained bread and the wine remained wine, and the physical act of receiving the elements did not do anything special to the eleven disciples. When we partake, we identify ourselves with His body and blood (1 Cor. 10:16), but there is no suggestion here that we receive His body and blood.

A second purpose for the supper is the proclaiming of His death until He returns (1 Cor. 11:26). The Supper encourages us to *look back* with love and adoration to what He did for us on the cross and to *look forward* with hope and anticipation to His coming again. Since we must be careful not to come to the Lord's table with known sin in our lives, the Supper should also be an occasion for *looking within,* examining our hearts, and confessing our sins (1 Cor. 11:27-32).

A third blessing from the Supper is the reminder of the unity of the church: we are "one loaf" (1 Cor. 10:17). It is "The *Lord's* Supper" and is not the exclusive property of any Christian denomination. Whenever we share in the Supper, we are identifying with Christians everywhere and are reminded of our obligation to "keep the unity of the Spirit in the bond of peace" (Eph. 4:3).

For us to receive a spiritual blessing from the Supper, it takes more than mere physical participation. We must also be able to "discern the body" (1 Cor. 11:29), that is, see the spiritual truths that are inherent in the bread and the cup. This spiritual discernment comes through the Spirit using the Word. The Holy Spirit makes all of this real to us as we wait before the Lord at the table.

Following the instituting of the Supper, Jesus taught His disciples many of the basic truths they desperately needed to know in order to have effective ministries in a hostile world (John 14–16). He prayed for His disciples (John 17); then they sang a hymn and departed from the Upper Room for the Garden of Gethsemane. Judas knew they would go there and he would have the arresting officers all prepared.

As you review this passage, you cannot help but be impressed with the calmness and courage of the Saviour. It is He who is in control, not Satan or Judas or the Sanhedrin. It is He who encourages the Apostles! And He is able even to sing a hymn before He goes out to die on a cross! Isaac Watts has best expressed what our response should be:

> Love so amazing, so divine,
> Demands my soul, my life, my all.

CHAPTER TWENTY-TWO
THE NIGHT THEY ARRESTED GOD
Luke 22:39-71

Perhaps the best way to grasp the spiritual lessons behind the tragic events of that night is to focus on the *symbols* that appear in the narrative. The Bible is a picture book as well as a book of history and biography, and these pictures can say a great deal to us. In this passage, there are six symbols that can help us better understand our Lord's suffering and death. They are: a lonely Garden, a costly cup, a hypocritical kiss, a useless sword, a crowing cock, and a glorious throne.

A Lonely Garden (Luke 22:39)

The Son of man left the Upper Room and went with His disciples to the Garden of Gethsemane on the Mount of Olives. This was His customary place of retirement when in Jerusalem (Luke 21:37). Knowing that the Lord would be there (John 18:1-2), Judas led his band of Roman soldiers and temple guards into the Garden to arrest Jesus, who willingly yielded Himself into their hands.

But why a Garden? Human history began in a Garden (Gen. 2:7-25) and so did human sin (Gen. 3). For the redeemed, the whole story will climax in a "garden city" where there will be no sin (Rev. 21:1–22:7). But between the Garden where man failed and the Garden where God reigns is Gethsemane, the Garden where Jesus accepted the cup from the Father's hand.

John informs us that when Jesus went to

the Garden, He crossed the Kidron brook (John 18:1). John may have had in mind King David's experience when he left Jerusalem and fled from his son Absalom (2 Sam. 15; and note especially v. 23). Both David and Jesus were throneless kings, accompanied by their closest friends and rejected by their own people. The name *Kidron* means "murky, dark," and *Gethsemane* means "olive press." Surely these names are significant.

Guides in modern Jerusalem can take visitors to four different sites that lay claim to being the ancient Garden of Gethsemane. Perhaps the most widely accepted one, and surely the most popular, is outside the east wall of Jerusalem near the Church of All Nations. The olive trees there are indeed very old, but it is not likely that they go back as far as the time of Christ since the Romans destroyed all the trees in their invasion of Judea in A.D. 70.

The geographical location of the Garden of Gethsemane is not as important as the spiritual message that we receive from what Jesus did there when He accepted "the cup" from His Father's hand. The first Adam rebelled in the Garden of Eden and brought sin and death into the world, but the Last Adam (1 Cor. 15:45) submitted in the Garden of Gethsemane and brought life and salvation for all who will believe.

A Costly Cup (Luke 22:40-46)

Jesus left eight of His disciples somewhere in the Garden and took Peter, James, and John with Him to a private place to pray (Mark 14:32-33). This is the third time He has shared a special occasion with these three men. The first was when Jesus raised Jairus' daughter from the dead (Luke 8:41-56), and the second was when He was transfigured before them (Luke 9:28-36). There must be a spiritual message here.

Dr. G. Campbell Morgan, the British expositor, has pointed out that each of these occasions had something to do with death. In Jairus' house, Jesus proved Himself to be victorious over death; and on the Mount of Transfiguration, He was glorified through death. (He and Moses and Elijah were talking about His "exodus" in Jerusalem [Luke 9:31].) Here in the Garden, Jesus was surrendered to death. Since James was the first of the apostles to die (Acts 12:1-2), John the last to die, and Peter experienced great persecution and eventually was crucified, these three lessons were very practical for their own lives.

Jesus is the Son of God and knew full well that He would be raised from the dead, and yet His soul experienced agony as He anticipated what lay before Him. In the hours ahead, He would be humiliated and abused, and suffer shame and pain on the cross. But even more, He would be made sin for us and separated from His Father. He called this solemn experience "drinking the cup." (For parallel uses of this image, see Pss. 73:10; 75:8; Isa. 51:17, 22; Jer. 25:15-28.)

A comparison of the Gospel accounts reveals that Jesus prayed three times about the cup and returned three times to the disciples, only to find them asleep. How little they realized the testing and danger that lay before them! And how much it would have meant to Jesus to have had their prayer support as He faced Calvary! (see Heb. 5:7-8)

Dr. Luke is the only Gospel writer who mentions "sweat . . . like great drops of blood." His use of the word *like* may suggest that the sweat merely fell to the ground like clots of blood. But there is a rare physical phenomenon known as *hematidrosis,* in which, under great emotional stress, the tiny blood vessels rupture in the sweat glands and produce a mixture of blood and sweat. The first Adam sinned in a Garden and was condemned to living by the sweat of his brow (Gen. 3:19). Jesus, the Last Adam, obeyed the Father in a Garden and conquered Adam's sin (Rom. 5:12-21).

Luke is also the only writer to mention the ministry of the angel (Luke 22:43). In fact, both the Gospel of Luke and the Book of Acts give angels a prominent place in the work of the Lord. Angels could not come to die for our sins, but they could strengthen our Saviour as He courageously accepted the cup from His Father's hand. Dr. George Morrison said, "Every life has its Gethsemane, and every Gethsemane has its angel." What an encouragement to God's people when they wrestle and pray about difficult and costly decisions!

A Hypocritical Kiss (Luke 22:47-48)

Someone has defined "kiss" as "the contraction of the mouth due to the enlargement of the heart." But not all kisses are born out of a loving heart, for kisses can also be deceitful. In the case of Judas, his kiss was the basest kind of hypocrisy and treachery.

It was customary in that day for disciples to greet their teachers with a loving and respectful kiss. Judas used the kiss as a sign to tell the arresting officers who Jesus was (Matt. 26:48-49). Jesus had taught in the temple day after day, and yet the temple guards could not recognize Him!

The presence of such a large group of armed soldiers shows how little Judas really knew about the Lord Jesus. Did he think that Jesus would try to run away or perhaps hide somewhere in the Garden? Judas must have expected Jesus and the disciples to resist arrest; otherwise he would not have enlisted so much help. Perhaps he feared that Jesus might perform a miracle, but even if He did, what can a group of armed men do against the power of Almighty God?

Judas was deceitful; he was a liar just like Satan who entered into him (John 8:44; 13:27). He defiled almost everything that he touched: his name (*Judah* = "praise"), the disciple band (Luke 6:13-16), gifts given to Christ (John 12:1-8), and the kiss. He even invaded a private prayer meeting, defiled it with his presence, and betrayed the Saviour *with a kiss.* "Faithful are the wounds of a friend, but the kisses of an enemy are deceitful" (Prov. 27:6).

A Useless Sword (Luke 22:49-53)

The disciples remembered (and misunderstood) His words about the sword (Luke 22:35-38), so they asked Him if now was the time to make use of their two swords. Without waiting for the answer, Peter rushed ahead and attacked a man who turned out to be Malchus, a servant to the high priest (John 18:10, 26-27).

Why did Peter do this? For one thing, he had to back up the boastful words he had spoken in the Upper Room (Luke 22:33) and again on the way to the Garden (Matt. 26:30-35). Peter had been sleeping when he should have been praying, talking when he should have been listening, and boasting when he should have been fearing. Now he was fighting when he should have been surrendering!

Peter made a number of serious mistakes when he attacked Malchus with his sword. To begin with, Peter was fighting the wrong enemy with the wrong weapon. Our enemies are not flesh and blood, and they cannot be defeated with ordinary weapons (2 Cor. 10:3-6; Eph. 6:10-18). In His wilderness temptations, Jesus defeated Satan with the Word of God (Matt. 4:1-11), and that is the weapon we must use (Eph. 6:17; Heb. 4:12).

Peter also revealed the wrong attitude and trusted the wrong energy. While Jesus was surrendering, Peter was busy declaring war! And he was depending on "the arm of flesh." His whole approach to the situation was not at all Christlike (John 18:36) and stands as a good warning to us today. The lost world may act this way, but it is not the way God's servants should act (Matt. 12:19; 2 Tim. 2:24).

It is just like Jesus to act in grace when others are acting in malice (Ps. 103:10). He showed grace to Peter by rebuking his presumptuous sin and repairing the damage he had done. He showed grace to Malchus, a lowly slave, by healing his ear, and He showed grace to the whole world by willingly yielding Himself to the mob and going to Calvary. He did not come to judge but to save (Luke 19:10; John 3:17).

Our Lord's last miracle before the cross was not a big flashy thing that attracted attention. It is likely that very few of the men who were there that night even knew what Peter and Jesus had done. Jesus could have summoned twelve legions of angels (Matt. 26:53), one legion (6,000 soldiers) for each of the eleven disciples and one for Himself, but He did not. Instead of performing some spectacular feat, He lovingly healed the ear of an obscure slave and then presented His hands to be bound.

Each of us must decide whether we will go through life *pretending,* like Judas; or *fighting,* like Peter; or *yielding to God's perfect will,* like Jesus. Will it be the kiss, the sword, or the cup?

A Crowing Cock (Luke 22:54-62)

Our Lord endured six different "trials" before He was condemned to be crucified, three before the Jews and three before the Roman authorities. First, He was taken to Annas, the former high priest who was an influential man in the nation and retained his former title (John 18:12-13). Annas sent Jesus to Caiaphas, his son-in-law, who was the official high priest (Matt. 26:57). Finally, at daybreak, He was tried before the Sanhedrin and found guilty (Luke 22:66-71).

The Jews did not have the right of capital punishment (John 18:31-32), so they had to take Jesus to the Roman authorities to get Him crucified. First, they took Him to Pilate (Luke 23:1-4), who tried to avoid a decision by sending Him to Herod (Luke 23:6-12), who sent Him back to Pilate! (Luke 23:13-25)

When Pilate saw that he could not escape making a decision, he gave the Sanhedrin what they asked for and condemned Jesus to die on a Roman cross.

It was during the second Jewish "trial," the one before Caiaphas, that Peter in the courtyard denied his Lord three times. How did it happen? To begin with, Peter did not take the Lord's warnings seriously (Matt. 26:33-35; Luke 22:31-34), nor did he "watch and pray" as Jesus had instructed in the Garden (Mark 14:37-38). For all of his courage and zeal, the Apostle Peter was totally unprepared for Satan's attacks.

Jesus was led out of the Garden, and "Peter followed afar off" (Luke 22:54). This was the next step toward his defeat. In spite of all the sermons that have been delivered on this text, criticizing him for walking at a distance, *Peter was not intended to follow at all.* The "sheep" were supposed to scatter and then meet Jesus later in Galilee (Matt. 26:31). In fact, when He was arrested, Jesus said to the guards, "Let these [disciples] go their way" (John 18:8-9), a clear signal that they were not to follow Him.

Peter and John followed the mob and gained entrance into the courtyard of Caiaphas' house (John 18:15-16). It was a cold night (though Jesus had been sweating!), and Peter first *stood* by the fire (John 18:18) and then *sat down* with the servants and officers (Luke 22:55). Sitting there in enemy territory (Ps. 1:1), Peter was an easy target. While he was thinking only of his own comfort, his Master was being abused by the soldiers (Luke 22:63-65).

First, it was one of the high priest's servant girls who challenged Peter. She accused him of being with Jesus and of being one of His disciples. Peter lied and said, "Woman, I am not one of His disciples! I don't know Him and I don't know what you are talking about!" He left the fire and went out to the porch (Matt. 26:71), and the cock crowed the first time (Mark 14:68). This in itself should have warned him to get out, but he lingered.

Peter could not escape notice, and a second servant girl told the bystanders, "This man was with Jesus of Nazareth! He is one of them!" For a second time, Peter lied and said, "I am not! I don't know the Man!"

The bystanders were not convinced, especially when one of Malchus' relatives showed up and asked, "Didn't I see you in the Garden with Him?" Others joined in and said, "Surely you are one of them, because the way you talk gives you away. You talk like a Galilean." (The Galileans had a distinctive dialect.) At this point Peter used an oath and said, "I don't know the Man! I don't know what you are talking about!" It was then that the cock crowed for the second time and the Lord's prediction was fulfilled (Mark 14:30).

At that moment, Jesus, being led away to the next trial, turned and looked at Peter; and His look broke Peter's heart. While the bystanders were watching Jesus, Peter slipped out and went off and wept bitterly. It is to Peter's credit that all the Lord had to do was *look* at him to bring him to the place of repentance.

For one cock to crow at the right time while the other birds in the city remained silent was certainly a miracle. But the crowing of the cock was much more than a miracle that fulfilled our Lord's words; it was also a special message to Peter, a message that helped to restore him to fellowship again. What encouragements did the crowing of the cock give to the Apostle Peter?

First, it was an assurance to him that Jesus Christ was still in control of things even though He was a prisoner, bound and seemingly helpless before His captors. Peter could recall witnessing his Lord's authority over the fish, the winds, and the waves, and even over disease and death. No matter how dark the hour was for Peter, Jesus was still in control!

Second, the crowing of the cock assured Peter that he could be forgiven. Peter had not been paying close attention to the Word of God. He had argued with it, disobeyed it, and even run ahead of it, but now he "remembered the word of the Lord" (Luke 22:61), and this brought him hope. Why? Because with the word of warning was also a promise of restoration! Peter would be converted and strengthen his brethren (Luke 22:32).

Finally, the miracle of the cock told Peter that a new day was dawning, for after all, that is what the rooster's call means each day. It was not a new day for Judas or for the enemies of the Lord, but it was a new day for Peter as he repented and wept bitterly. "A broken and a contrite heart, O God, thou wilt not despise" (Ps. 51:17). On Resurrection morning, the angel sent a special message to encourage Peter (Mark 16:7), and the Lord Himself appeared to Peter that day and restored him to fellowship (Luke 24:34).

Each one of us, at one time or another, will

fail the Lord and then hear (in one way or another) "the crowing of the cock." Satan will tell us that we are finished, that our future has been destroyed, but that is not God's message to us. It was certainly not the end for Peter! His restoration was so complete that he was able to say to the Jews, "But you denied the Holy One and the Just!" (Acts 3:14, NKJV) Peter did not have 1 John 1:9 to read, but he did experience it in his own heart.

A Glorious Throne (Luke 22:63-71)
Jesus had not yet officially been declared guilty, and yet the soldiers were permitted to mock Him and abuse Him. Here they mocked His claim to being a Prophet; later they would mock His claim to being a King (John 19:1-3). But their mockery, sinful as it was, actually fulfilled Christ's own promise (Matt. 20:19). He is an example to us of how we should behave when sinners ridicule us and our faith (see 1 Peter 2:18-25).

It is generally believed that the Jewish council could not vote on capital offenses at night; so the chief priests, scribes, and elders had to assemble again as soon as it was day. Whether this ruling was in force in our Lord's day, we are not sure, but it does explain the early morning meeting of the Sanhedrin.

This was the climax of the religious trial, and the key issue was, "Is Jesus of Nazareth the Christ of God?" They were sure His claims were false and that He was guilty of blasphemy, and the penalty for blasphemy was death (Lev. 24:10-16).

Jesus knew the hearts of His accusers, their unbelief, and intellectual dishonesty (Luke 20:1-8). It was futile to preach a sermon or enter into a debate. They had already rejected the evidence He had given them (John 12:37-43), and more truth would only have increased their responsibility and their judgment (John 9:39-41).

Our Lord called Himself "Son of man," a messianic title found in Daniel 7:13-14. He also claimed to have the right to sit "on the right hand of the power of God" (Luke 22:69), a clear reference to Psalm 110:1, another messianic passage. It was this verse that He quoted earlier that week in His debate with the religious leaders (Luke 20:41-44). Jesus saw beyond the sufferings of the cross to the glories of the throne (Phil. 2:1-11; Heb. 12:2).

That our Lord is seated at the right hand of the Father is a truth that is often repeated in the New Testament (Heb. 1:3; 8:1; 10:12; 12:2; 1 Peter 3:22; Acts 2:33; 5:31; 7:55-56; Rom. 8:34; Eph. 1:20; Col. 3:1). This is the place of honor, authority, and power; and by claiming this honor, Jesus was claiming to be God.

Only Luke records the direct question in Luke 22:70 and our Lord's direct answer, which literally was: "You say that I am." They would use this testimony later when they brought Him to Pilate (John 19:7). Some liberal theologians say that Jesus never claimed to be God, and we wonder what they do with this official trial? The Jewish religious leaders knew what Jesus was talking about, and this is why they condemned Him for blasphemy.

The "religious trial" was now over. The next step was to put Him through a civil trial and convince the Roman governor that Jesus of Nazareth was a criminal worthy of death. The Son of God was to be crucified, and only the Romans could do that.

Referring to the Jewish authorities, William Stalker wrote in *The Trial and Death of Jesus Christ:* "It may be said that they walked according to their light; but the light that was in them was darkness."

"None so blind as those that will not see," wrote Matthew Henry, the noted Bible commentator.

"While you have the light, believe in the light, that you may become sons of light" (John 12:36, NKJV).

CHAPTER TWENTY-THREE
CONDEMNED AND CRUCIFIED
Luke 23

The trial and death of Jesus Christ revealed both the wicked heart of man and the gracious heart of God. When men were doing their worst, God was giving His best. "But where sin abounded, grace did much more abound" (Rom. 5:20). Jesus was not crucified because evil men decided to get Him out of the way. His crucifixion was "by the determinate counsel and foreknowledge of God" (Acts 2:23), an appointment made from eternity (1 Peter 1:20; Rev. 13:8).

As you study this chapter, notice the six encounters our Lord experienced during those critical hours.

Jesus and Pilate (Luke 23:1-25)

Pontius Pilate served as governor of Judea from A.D. 26 to A.D. 36, at which time he was recalled to Rome and then passed out of official Roman history. He was hated by the orthodox Jews and never really understood them. Once he aroused their fury by putting up pagan Roman banners in the Jewish temple, and he was not beneath sending armed spies into the temple to silence Jewish protesters (Luke 13:1-3).

In his handling of the trial of Jesus, the governor proved to be indecisive. The Gospel of John records seven different moves that Pilate made as he went *out* to meet the people and then went *in* to question Jesus (John 18:29, 33, 38; 19:1, 4, 9, 13). He kept looking for a loophole, but he found none. Pilate has gone down in history as the man who tried Jesus Christ, three times declared Him not guilty, and yet crucified Him just the same.

Pilate affirming (vv. 1-5). Roman officials were usually up early and at their duties, but Pilate was probably surprised that morning to learn that he had a capital case on his hands, and on Passover at that. The Jewish leaders knew that their religious laws meant nothing to a Roman official, so they emphasized the political aspects of their indictment against Jesus. There were three charges: He perverted the nation, opposed paying the poll tax to Caesar, and claimed to be a king.

Pilate privately interrogated Jesus about His kingship because that was the crucial issue, and he concluded that He was guilty of no crime. Three times during the trial, Pilate clearly affirmed the innocence of Jesus (Luke 23:4, 14, 22). Dr. Luke reported three other witnesses besides Pilate who also said, "Not guilty!": King Herod (Luke 23:15), one of the malefactors (Luke 23:40-43), and a Roman centurion (Luke 23:47).

Pilate deferring (vv. 6-12). The Jews rejected his verdict and began to accuse Jesus all the more. When they mentioned Galilee, Pilate, astute politician that he was, immediately saw an opportunity to get Jesus off his hands. He sent Him to Herod Antipas, ruler of Galilee, the man who had murdered John the Baptist, who was anxious to see Jesus (Luke 9:7-9). Perhaps the wily king could find some way to please the Jews.

Herod must have been shocked and perhaps nervous when the guards brought Jesus in, but the more he questioned Him, the bolder he became. Perhaps Jesus might even entertain the king with a miracle! In spite of the king's persistent interrogation and the Jews' vehement accusations, Jesus said nothing. *Herod had silenced the voice of God.* It was not Herod who was judging Jesus; it was Jesus who was judging Herod.

The king finally became so bold as to mock Jesus and permit his soldiers to dress Him in "an elegant robe," the kind that was worn by Roman candidates for office. Herod did not issue an official verdict about Jesus (Luke 23:15), but it was clear that he did not find Him guilty of any crime worthy of death (Luke 23:15).

The only thing accomplished by this maneuver was the mending of a broken friendship. Herod was grateful to Pilate for helping him to see Jesus and for honoring him by seeking his counsel. The fact that Herod sent Jesus back to Pilate without issuing a verdict could be interpreted as, "Since we are not in Galilee, Pilate, you have the authority to act, and I will not interfere. Jesus is *your* prisoner, not mine. I know you will do the right thing." Finally, the fact that the two men met over a common threat (or enemy) helped them to put aside their differences and become friends again.

Pilate bargaining (vv. 13-23). He met the Jewish leaders and announced for the second time that he did not find Jesus guilty of the charges they had made against Him. The fact that Herod backed Pilate's decision would not have impressed the Jews very much, because they despised Herod almost as much as they despised the Romans.

Since it was customary at Passover for the governor to release a prisoner, Pilate offered the Jews a compromise: he would chastise Jesus and let Him go. He had another prisoner on hand, Barabbas, but Pilate was sure the Jews would not want him to be released. After all, Barabbas was a robber (John 18:40), a murderer, and an insurrectionist (Luke 23:19). He may have been a leader of the Jewish Zealots who at that time was working for the overthrow of Rome.

We must not think that the general populace of the city was gathered before Pilate and crying out for the blood of Jesus, though a curious crowd no doubt gathered. It was primarily the official religious leaders of the nation, the chief priests in particular (Luke 23:23), who shouted Pilate down and told him to crucify Jesus. To say that the people who cried "Hosanna!" on Palm Sunday ended up crying "Crucify Him!" on Good Friday is not completely accurate.

Pilate yielding (vv. 24-25). Pilate realized that his mishandling of the situation had almost caused a riot, and a Jewish uprising was the last thing he wanted during Passover. So, he called for water and washed his hands before the crowd, affirming his innocence (Matt. 27:24-25). He was a compromiser who was "willing to content the people" (Mark 15:15). Barabbas was released and Jesus was condemned to die on a Roman cross.

Pilate was a complex character. He openly said that Jesus was innocent, yet he permitted Him to be beaten and condemned Him to die. He carefully questioned Jesus and even trembled at His answers, but the truth of the Word did not make a difference in his decisions. He wanted to be popular and not right; he was more concerned about reputation than he was character. If Herod had silenced the voice of God, then Pilate smothered the voice of God. He had his opportunity and wasted it.

Jesus and Simon (Luke 23:26)

It was a part of the prisoner's humiliation that he carry his own cross to the place of execution, so when Jesus left Pilate's hall, He was carrying either the cross or the crossbeam (John 19:17). Apparently, He was unable to go on, for the soldiers had to "draft" Simon of Cyrene to carry the cross for Him. (This was a legal Roman procedure. See Matt. 5:41.) When you consider all that Jesus had endured since His arrest in the Garden, it is not difficult to imagine Him falling under the load. But there is something more involved: carrying the cross was a sign of guilt, *and our Lord was not guilty!*

Thousands of Jews came to Jerusalem from other nations to celebrate the feasts (Acts 2:5-11), and Simon was among them. He had traveled over 800 miles from Africa to celebrate Passover, and now he was being humiliated on a most holy day! What would he say to his family when he got home?

What looked to Simon like a catastrophe turned out to be a wonderful opportunity, for it brought him in contact with Jesus Christ. (By the way, where was the *other* Simon—Simon Peter—who had promised Jesus to go with Him to prison and to death?) Simon may have come into the city to attend the 9 A.M. prayer meeting in the temple, but the soldiers rearranged his schedule for him.

We have good reason to believe that Simon was converted because of this encounter with Jesus. Mark identified him as "the father of Alexander and Rufus" (Mark 15:21), two men that Mark assumed his Roman readers would know. A Christian named Rufus was greeted by Paul in Romans 16:13, and it is possible that he was the son of Simon of Cyrene. Apparently Simon and his two sons became well-known Christians who were held in honor in the church.

Before Simon met Jesus, he had religion and devotion; but after he met Jesus, he had reality and salvation. He did both a physical and spiritual "about face" that morning, and it transformed his life. God can still use unexpected and difficult situations, even humiliating situations, to bring people to the Saviour.

Jesus and the Jerusalem Women (Luke 23:27-31)

Public executions drew crowds of spectators, and one involving Jesus would especially attract attention. Add to this the fact that Jerusalem was crowded with pilgrims, and it is not difficult to believe that a "great multitude" was following the condemned man to Calvary.

In that crowd was a group of women who openly wept and lamented as they sympathized with Jesus and contemplated the terrible spiritual condition of their nation. It has been pointed out that, as far as the Gospel records are concerned, no woman was ever an enemy of Jesus. Nor was Jesus ever the enemy of womankind. His example, His teachings, and most of all, His redemption have done much to dignify and elevate women. The news of His birth was shared with a Jewish maiden, His death was witnessed by grieving women, and the good news of His resurrection was announced first to a woman who had been demon-possessed.

Jesus appreciated their sympathy and used it to teach them and us an important lesson. While they were weeping over the injustice of *one man's death,* He was looking ahead and grieving over the terrible destruction of *the entire nation,* a judgment that was wholly justified (see Luke 19:41-44). Alas, it would be the women and children who would suffer the most, a fact supported by history. The Romans attempted to starve the Jews into submission; and hungry men, defending their city, took food from their suffering wives and children and even killed and ate their own flesh and blood.

The nation of Israel was like a "green tree" during the years when Jesus was on earth. It was a time of blessing and opportunity, and it should have been a time of fruitfulness. But the nation rejected Him and became like a "dry tree," fit only for the fire. Jesus often would have gathered His people together, but they would not. In condemning Him, they only condemned themselves.

We might paraphrase His words: "If the Roman authorities do this to One who is innocent, what will they do to you who are guilty? When the day of judgment arrives, can there be any escape for you?"

Jesus and the Malefactors (Luke 23:32-43)

It had been prophesied that the Suffering Servant would be "numbered with the transgressors" (Isa. 53:12; Luke 22:37), and two criminals were crucified with Jesus, men who were robbers (Matt. 27:38). The Greek word means "one who uses violence to rob openly," in contrast to the thief who secretly enters a house and steals. These two men may have been guilty of armed robbery involving murder.

The name *Calvary* comes from the Latin *calvaria* which means "a skull." (The Greek is *kranion,* which gives us the English word *cranium,* and the Aramaic word is *Golgotha.*) The name is not explained in the New Testament. The site may have resembled a skull, as does "Gordon's Calvary" near the Damascus Gate in Jerusalem. Or perhaps the name simply grew out of the ugly facts of execution.

Our Lord was crucified about 9 A.M. and remained on the cross until 3 P.M.; and from noon to 3 P.M., there was darkness over all the land (Mark 15:25, 33). Jesus spoke seven times during those six terrible hours:

1. "Father, forgive them" (Luke 23:34).
2. "Today shalt thou be with Me in paradise" (Luke 23:43).
3. "Woman, behold thy son" (John 19:25-27).
   [Three hours of darkness; Jesus is silent]
4. "Why hast Thou forsaken Me?" (Matt. 27:46)
5. "I thirst" (John 19:28).
6. "It is finished!" (John 19:30)
7. "Father, into Thy hands" (Luke 23:46).

Luke recorded only three of these seven statements, the first, the second, and the last. Our Lord's prayer for His enemies, and His ministry to a repentant thief, fit in well with Luke's purpose to show Jesus Christ as the sympathetic Son of man who cared for the needy.

While they were nailing Him to the cross, He repeatedly prayed, "Father, forgive them; for they know not what they do" (Luke 23:34). Not only was He practicing what He taught (Luke 6:27-28), but He was fulfilling prophecy and making "intercession for the transgressors" (Isa. 53:12).

We must not infer from His prayer that ignorance is a basis for forgiveness, or that those who sinned against Jesus were automatically forgiven because He prayed. Certainly both the Jews and the Romans were ignorant of the *enormity* of their sin, but that could not absolve them. The Law provided a sacrifice for sins committed ignorantly, but there was no sacrifice for deliberate presumptuous sin (Ex. 21:14; Num. 15:27-31; Ps. 51:16-17). Our Lord's intercession postponed God's judgment on the nation for almost forty years, giving them additional opportunities to be saved (Acts 3:17-19).

It was providential that Jesus was crucified *between* the two thieves, for this gave both of them equal access to the Saviour. Both could read Pilate's superscription, "This is Jesus of Nazareth the King of the Jews," and both could watch Him as He graciously gave His life for the sins of the world.

The one thief imitated the mockery of the religious leaders and asked Jesus to rescue him from the cross, but the other thief had different ideas. He may have reasoned, "If this Man is indeed the Christ, and if He has a kingdom, and if He has saved others, then He can meet my greatest need which is salvation from sin. I am not ready to die!" It took courage for this thief to defy the influence of his friend and the mockery of the crowd, and it took faith for him to trust a dying King! When you consider all that he had to overcome, the faith of this thief is astounding.

The man was saved wholly by grace; it was the gift of God (Eph. 2:8-9). He did not deserve it and he could not earn it. His salvation was personal and secure, guaranteed by the word of Jesus Christ. The man hoped for some kind of help in the future, but Jesus gave him forgiveness that very day, and he died and went with Jesus to paradise (2 Cor. 12:1-4).

It should be noted that the people at Calvary fulfilled Old Testament prophecy in what they did: gambling for our Lord's clothing (Ps. 22:18), mocking Him (Ps. 22:6-8), and offering Him vinegar to drink (Ps. 69:21). God was still on the throne and His Word was still in control.

Jesus and the Father (Luke 23:44-49)

We must keep in mind that what our Lord accomplished on the cross was an eternal transaction that involved Him and the Father. He did not die as a martyr who had failed in a lost cause. Nor was He only an example for people to follow. Isaiah 53 makes it clear that Jesus did not die for His own sins, because He had none; He died for our sins. He made His soul an offering for sin (Isa. 53:4-6, 10-12).

The three hours of darkness was a miracle. It was not an eclipse, because that would have been impossible during the Passover season when there is a full moon. It was a God-sent darkness that shrouded the cross as the Son of God was made sin for us (2 Cor. 5:21). It was as though all nature was sympathizing with the Creator as He suffered and died. When Israel was in Egypt, three days of darkness preceded the first Passover (Ex. 10:21ff). When Jesus was on the cross, three hours of darkness preceded the death of God's Lamb for the sins of the world (John 1:29).

Both Matthew 27:45-46 and Mark 15:33-34 record our Lord's cry at the close of the darkness, a Hebrew quotation from Psalm 22:1, "My God, My God, why hast Thou forsaken Me?" What this abandonment was and how Jesus felt it are not explained to us, but certainly it involves the fact that He became sin for us.

Our Lord cried with a loud voice, "It is finished!" (John 19:30) a declaration of victory. He had finished the work the Father gave Him to do (John 17:4). The work of redemption was completed, the types and prophecies were fulfilled (Heb. 9:24ff), and the Saviour could now rest.

He then addressed His Father in the final statement from the cross, "Father, into Thy hands I commend My spirit" (Ps. 31:5). This was actually a bedtime prayer used by Jewish children, and it tells us how our Lord died: confidently, willingly (John 10:17-18), and victoriously. Those who know Jesus as their Saviour may die with the same confidence and assurance (2 Cor. 5:1-8; Phil. 1:20-23).

When our Lord released His spirit, the veil of the temple was torn in two "from the top to the bottom" (Mark 15:38). This miracle announced to the priests and people that the way into God's presence was open for all who would come to Him by faith through Jesus Christ (Heb. 9:1–10:25). No more do sinners need earthly temples, altars, sacrifices, or priests, for all had now been fulfilled in the finished work of the Son of God.

Luke recorded three responses to the events of the last moments of Christ's death. The centurion who was in charge of the execution testified, "Certainly this was a righteous [innocent] man, the Son of God" (Mark 15:39; Luke 23:47). He was greatly impressed by the darkness, the earthquake (Matt. 27:54), and certainly the way Jesus suffered and died. He must have been shocked when Jesus shouted and then instantly died, for victims of crucifixion often lingered for days and did not have the strength to speak.

The people who came to "see the spectacle" began to drift away one by one, some of them beating their breasts as they felt their guilt (Luke 18:13). Were these people believers? Probably not. They were spectators who were attracted to the execution, but certainly they saw and heard enough to convict them of their own sins.

Finally, our Lord's friends were there, including the women who followed Jesus (Luke 8:1-3; 24:22). It is significant that the women were the last at the cross and the first at the tomb on Easter morning.

Jesus and Joseph of Arimathea (Luke 23:50-56)

Joseph and his friend Nicodemus (John 19:38-42) were both members of the Jewish council, but they had not been present to vote against Jesus. Mark 14:64 states that the whole council condemned Him, and that could not have happened if Joseph and Nicodemus had been there.

It is likely that Joseph and Nicodemus had learned from the Old Testament Scriptures how Jesus would die, so they agreed to take care of His burial. The new tomb was likely

Joseph's, prepared in a garden near Golgotha but not for himself; it was for Jesus. No rich man would prepare his own burial place so near a place of execution and so far from his own home. The two men could well have been hiding in the tomb while Jesus was on the cross, waiting for that moment when He would yield up His life. They would have the spices and the winding sheets all prepared, for they would probably not be able to go shopping for these items on Passover.

When Jesus died, Joseph immediately went to Pilate for permission to have the body, and Nicodemus stayed at Calvary to keep watch. They tenderly took Jesus from the cross, quickly carried Him to the garden, washed the body, and wrapped it with the spices. It was a temporary burial; they would return after the Sabbath to do the job properly. When they laid Jesus into the new tomb, they fulfilled Isaiah 53:9, and they kept the Romans from throwing His body on the garbage dump outside the city. Condemned criminals lost the right to proper burial, but God saw to it that His Son's body was buried with dignity and love.

It was important that the body be buried properly, for God would raise Jesus from the dead. If there were any doubt about His death or burial, that could affect the message and the ministry of the Gospel (1 Cor. 15:1-8).

When after six days God finished the work of the "old Creation," He rested (Gen. 2:1-3). After six hours, our Lord finished the work of the "new Creation" (2 Cor. 5:17), and He rested on the Sabbath in Joseph's tomb.

But that was not the end of the story.

He would rise again!

CHAPTER TWENTY-FOUR
THE SON OF MAN TRIUMPHS!
Luke 24

"Christianity is in its very essence a resurrection religion," says Dr. John Stott. "The concept of resurrection lies at its heart. If you remove it, Christianity is destroyed."

The resurrection of Jesus Christ affirms to us that He is indeed the Son of God, just as He claimed to be (Rom. 1:4). It also proves that His sacrifice for sin has been accepted and that the work of salvation is completed (Rom. 4:24-25). Those who trust Him can "walk in newness of life" because He is alive and imparts His power to them (Rom. 6:4; Gal. 2:20). Our Lord's resurrection also declares to us that He is the Judge who will come one day and judge the world (Acts 17:30-31).

It is no surprise, then, that Satan has attacked the truth of the Resurrection. The first lie that he spawned was that the disciples came and stole Christ's body (Matt. 28:11-15), but it is difficult to imagine how they could have done this. To begin with, the tomb was carefully guarded (Matt. 27:61-66); and it would have been next to impossible for the frightened Apostles to overpower the soldiers, open the tomb, and secure the body. But the biggest obstacle is the fact that the Apostles themselves *did not believe that He would be resurrected!* Why, then, would they steal His body and try to perpetrate a hoax?

A second lie is that Jesus did not really die on the cross but only swooned, and when He was put into the cool tomb, He revived. But Pilate carefully checked with the centurion to see whether Jesus was dead (Mark 15:44), and the Roman soldiers who broke the legs of the two thieves knew that Jesus had died (John 19:31-34). Furthermore, how could a "cool tomb" transform Christ's body so that He could appear and disappear and walk through closed doors?

The message of the Gospel rests on the death of Jesus Christ *and His resurrection* (1 Cor. 15:1-8). The Apostles were sent out as witnesses of His resurrection (Acts 1:22), and the emphasis in the Book of Acts is on the resurrection of Jesus Christ.

This explains why Luke climaxed his book with a report of some of the appearances of Jesus after He had been raised from the dead. He first appeared to Mary Magdalene (John 20:11-18), then to the "other women" (Matt. 28:9-10), and then to the two men on the way to Emmaus (Luke 24:13-22). At some time, He also appeared to Peter (Luke 24:34) and to His half brother James (1 Cor. 15:7).

That evening, He appeared to the Apostles (Luke 24:36-43), but Thomas was not with them (John 20:19-25). A week later, He appeared to the Apostles again, especially for the sake of Thomas (John 20:26-31). He appeared to seven of the Apostles when they were fishing at the Sea of Galilee (John 21). He appeared several times to the Apostles before His ascension, teaching them and preparing them for their ministry (Acts 1:1-12).

When the believers discovered that Jesus was alive, it made a tremendous difference in their lives.

Perplexed Hearts: He Opens the Tomb (Luke 24:1-12)

We do not know at what time Jesus arose from the dead on the first day of the week, but it must have been very early. The earthquake and the angel (Matt. 28:2-4) opened the tomb, not to let Jesus out but to let the witnesses in. "Come and see, go and tell!" is the Easter mandate for the church.

Mary Magdalene had been especially helped by Jesus and was devoted to Him (Luke 8:2). She had lingered at the cross (Mark 15:47), and then she was first at the tomb. With her were Mary the mother of James; Joanna; and other devout women (Luke 24:10), hoping to finish preparing their Lord's body for burial. It was a sad labor of love that was transformed into gladness when they discovered that Jesus was alive.

"Who will roll the stone away?" was their main concern. The Roman soldiers would not break the Roman seal, especially for a group of mourning Jewish women. But God had solved the problem for them; the tomb was open *and there was no body to prepare!*

At this point two angels appeared on the scene. Matthew 28:2 and Mark 16:5 mention only one of the two, the one who gave the message to the women. There was a kind rebuke in his message as he reminded them of their bad memories! More than once, Jesus had told His followers that He would suffer and die and be raised from the dead (Matt. 16:21; 17:22-23; 20:17-19; Luke 9:22, 44; 18:31-34). How sad it is when God's people forget His Word and live defeated lives. Today, the Spirit of God assists us to remember His Word (John 14:26).

Obedient to their commission, the women ran to tell the disciples the good news, but the men did not believe them! (According to Mark 16:14, Jesus later rebuked them for their unbelief.) Mary Magdalene asked Peter and John to come to examine the tomb (John 20:1-10), and they too saw the proof that Jesus was not there. However, all that the evidence said was that the body was gone and that apparently there had been no violence.

As Mary lingered by the tomb weeping, Jesus Himself appeared to her (John 20:11-18). It is one thing to see the empty tomb and the empty graveclothes, but quite something else to meet the risen Christ. We today cannot see the evidence in the tomb, but we do have the testimony of the witnesses found in the inspired Word of God. And we can live out our faith in Jesus Christ and know *personally* that He is alive in us (Gal. 2:20).

Keep in mind that these women did not expect to see Jesus alive. They had forgotten His resurrection promises and went to the tomb only to finish anointing His body. To say that they had hallucinations and only thought they saw Jesus is to fly in the face of the evidence. And would this many people hallucinate about the same thing at the same time? Not likely. They became excited witnesses, even to their leaders, that Jesus Christ is alive!

Discouraged Hearts: He Opens Their Eyes (Luke 24:13-35)

Emmaus was a small village eight miles northwest of Jerusalem. The two men walking from Jerusalem to Emmaus were discouraged disciples who had no reason to be discouraged. They had heard the reports of the women that the tomb was empty and that Jesus was alive, but they did not believe them. They had hoped that Jesus would redeem Israel (Luke 24:21), but their hopes had been shattered. We get the impression that these men were discouraged and disappointed because God did not do what they wanted Him to do. They saw the glory of the kingdom, but they failed to understand the suffering.

Jesus graciously walked with them and listened to their "animated heated conversation" (Luke 24:17, WUEST). No doubt they were quoting various Old Testament prophecies and trying to remember what Jesus had taught, but they were unable to put it all together and come up with an explanation that made sense. Was He a failure or a success? Why did He have to die? Was there a future for the nation?

There is a touch of humor in Luke 24:19 when Jesus asked, "What things?" *He had been at the heart of all that had happened in Jerusalem, and now He was asking them to tell Him what occurred!* How patient our Lord is with us as He listens to us tell Him what He already knows (Rom. 8:34). But we may come "boldly" ("with freedom of speech") to His throne and pour out our hearts to Him, and He will help us (Ps. 62:8; Heb. 4:16).

The longer Cleopas talked, the more he indicted himself and his friend for their unbelief. What more evidence could they want? Witnesses (including Apostles) had seen the tomb empty. Angels had announced that Jesus was alive. Witnesses had seen Him alive and heard Him speak. The proof was there!

"Faith comes by hearing, and hearing by the word of God" (Rom. 10:17, NKJV). This explains why Jesus opened the Word to these two men as the three of them walked to Emmaus. Their real problem was not in their heads but in their hearts (see Luke 24:25 and 32, and note v. 38). They could have discussed the subject for days and never arrived at a satisfactory answer. What they needed was a fresh understanding of the Word of God, and Jesus gave that understanding to them. He opened the Scriptures and then opened their eyes, and they realized that Jesus was not only alive *but right there with them!*

What was their basic problem? They did not believe all that the prophets had written about the Messiah. That was the problem with most of the Jews in that day: they saw Messiah as a conquering Redeemer, but they did not see Him as a Suffering Servant. As they read the Old Testament, they saw the glory but not the suffering, the crown but not the cross. The teachers in that day were not unlike some of the "success preachers" today, blind to the *total* message of the Bible.

That was some Bible conference, and I wish I could have been there! Imagine the greatest Teacher explaining the greatest themes from the greatest Book and bringing the greatest blessings to men's lives: eyes open to see Him, hearts open to receive the Word, and lips open to tell others what Jesus said to them!

Perhaps Jesus started at Genesis 3:15, the first promise of the Redeemer, and traced that promise through the Scriptures. He may have lingered at Genesis 22, which tells of Abraham placing his only beloved son on the altar. Surely He touched on Passover, the levitical sacrifices, the tabernacle ceremonies, the Day of Atonement, the serpent in the wilderness, the Suffering Servant in Isaiah 53, and the prophetic messages of Psalms 22 and 69. *The key to understanding the Bible is to see Jesus Christ on every page.* He did not teach them only doctrine or prophecy; He taught "the things concerning Himself" (Luke 24:27).

These men had talked to Jesus and listened to Jesus, and when He made as though He would go on alone, they asked Jesus to come home with them. *They had been won by the Word of God,* and they did not even know who the Stranger was. All they knew was that their hearts were "burning" within them, and they wanted the blessing to last.

The more we receive the Word of God, the more we will want to fellowship with the God of the Word. The hymn writer expressed it perfectly: "Beyond the sacred page/I seek Thee, Lord." Understanding Bible knowledge can lead to a "big head" (1 Cor. 8:1), but receiving Bible truth and walking with the Saviour will lead to a burning heart.

Jesus opened the Scriptures to them, and then He opened their eyes so that they recognized Him. *Now they knew for themselves that Jesus was alive.* They had the evidence of the open tomb, the angels, the witnesses, the Scriptures and now their own personal experience with the Lord. The fact that Jesus vanished did not mean that He abandoned them, for He was with them even though they could not see Him; and they would see Him again.

The best evidence that we have understood the Bible and met the living Christ is that we have something exciting to share with others. The two men immediately left Emmaus and returned to Jerusalem to tell the believers that they had met Jesus. But when they arrived, the apostles and the others *told them* that Jesus was alive and had appeared to Peter! What a difference it would make in our church services if everybody who gathered came to tell about meeting the living Christ! If our services are "dead" it is probably because we are not really walking with and listening to the living Saviour.

The "breaking of bread" (Luke 24:30, 35) refers to a meal and not to the Lord's Supper. As far as we know, the Apostles were the only ones Jesus had instructed about the Lord's Supper; and it was not likely that our Lord would celebrate it at this time. Jesus revealed Himself to them during a common meal, and that is often how He works. We must learn to see Him in the everyday things of life. However, as we do celebrate the Lord's Supper from time to time, we want Jesus to reveal Himself to us in a new way, and we must not be satisfied with anything less.

Troubled Hearts: He Opens Their Minds (Luke 24:36-46)

So many exciting things had happened that day and so much was unexplained that ten of the Apostles, plus other believers, met together that evening and shared their witness with one another. While Cleopas and his friend were telling their story, *Jesus Himself appeared in the room!* And the doors were shut! (John 20:19)

You would have expected the believers to heave a great sigh of relief and sing a hymn of praise, but instead they became terrified, frightened, and troubled (Luke 24:37-38). They thought a ghost had appeared! It all happened so suddenly that they were totally unprepared, even though several of them had already seen the risen Christ. Mark 16:14 suggests that the condition of their hearts had something to do with the expression of their fears.

Jesus sought to calm them. The first thing He did was to give them His blessing: "Peace be unto you!" He even repeated the blessing (John 20:19-21). "The God of peace" had raised Jesus from the dead, and there was nothing for them to fear (Heb. 13:20-21). Because of His sacrifice on the cross, men and women could now have peace with God (Rom. 5:1) and enjoy the peace of God (Phil. 4:6-7).

The next thing He did to calm them was to show them His wounded hands and feet (Ps. 22:16) and assure them that He was not a ghost. Songwriters sometimes mention His "scars," but the record says nothing about "scars." The "prints" of Calvary were on His glorified body (John 20:24-29), and they are still there (Rev. 5:6, 9, 12). It has well been said that the only work of man now in heaven is the marks of Calvary on the body of the exalted Saviour.

Jesus even ate some honey and fish to prove to His doubting followers that He was indeed alive and real, and He even invited them to *feel* His body (Luke 24:39; 1 John 1:1). With our limited knowledge, we cannot explain how a human body can be solid flesh and bones and still pass through closed doors and appear and disappear, or how it can be glorified and still carry the marks of the cross. We do know that we shall one day be like Him and share His glory (1 John 3:1-2).

Luke 24:41 describes a perplexing emotion: "they believed not for joy." It was just too good to be true! Jacob had this same feeling when he got the news that Joseph was alive (Gen. 45:26-28), and the nation of Israel experienced it when God gave them a great deliverance (Ps. 126:1-3). Jesus had told His disciples that they would rejoice when they saw Him again, and the promise was fulfilled (John 16:22).

The final source of peace and assurance is the Word of God, so our Lord "opened their understanding" of the Old Testament Scriptures, just as He had done with the Emmaus disciples. After all, the believers were not being sent into the world to share their own personal experiences but to share the truths of the Word of God. We today cannot touch and feel the Lord Jesus, nor is it necessary that we do so; but we can rest our faith on the Word of God (1 John 1:1-5).

Jesus not only enabled them to understand the Law, the Prophets, and the Psalms, but He also reminded them of what He had taught them, and He explained how it all fit together. Now they began to understand the necessity for His suffering and death and how the Cross related to the promise of the kingdom (see 1 Peter 1:10-12). What a privilege it was for them to listen to Jesus expound the Word!

Joyful Hearts: He Opens Their Lips (Luke 24:47-53)

But privilege always brings responsibility; they were to be witnesses of all that He had said and done (Acts 1:8). A witness is somebody who sincerely tells what he has seen and heard (Acts 4:20), and the word *witness* is used in one way or another twenty-nine times in the Book of Acts. As Christians, we are not judges or prosecuting attorneys sent to condemn the world. We are witnesses who point to Jesus Christ and tell lost sinners how to be saved.

How could a group of common people ever hope to fulfill that kind of a commission? God promised to provide the power (Luke 24:49; Acts 1:8), and He did. On the Day of Pentecost, the Holy Spirit came upon the church and empowered them to preach the Word (Acts 2). After Pentecost, the Spirit continued to fill them with great power (see Acts 4:33).

Witnessing is not something that we do for the Lord; it is something that He does through us, *if* we are filled with the Holy Spirit. There is a great difference between a "sales talk" and a Spirit-empowered witness. "People do not come to Christ at the end of an argument," said Vance Havner. "Simon Peter came to Jesus because Andrew went after him with a testimony." We go forth in the authority of His name, in the power of His spirit, heralding His Gospel of His grace.

Luke 24:50-52 should be compared with Mark 16:19-20 and Acts 1:9-12. For some reason, our Lord's ascension is not given the prominence in the church that it deserves. Think of what it meant to Him to return to heaven and sit on the throne of glory! (John 17:5, 11) His ascension is proof that He has conquered every enemy and that He reigns supremely "far above all" (Eph. 1:18-23).

In heaven today, our Lord ministers as our High Priest (Heb. 7:25) and our Advocate (1 John 2:1). As High Priest, He gives us the grace we need to face testing and temptation (Heb. 4:14-16); and if we fail, as Advocate He forgives and restores us when we confess our sins (1 John 1:6-10). As the glorified Head of the church, Jesus Christ is equipping His people to live for Him and serve Him in this present world (Eph. 4:7-16; Heb. 13:20-21). Through the Word of God and prayer, He is ministering to us by His Spirit and making us more like Himself.

Of course, He is also preparing in heaven a home for His people (John 14:1-6), and one day He will return and take us to be with Him forever.

The last thing our Lord did was to bless His people, and the first thing they did was to worship Him! The two always go together, for as we truly worship Him, He will share His blessings. He not only opened their lips to witness, but He also opened their lips to worship and praise Him!

Dr. Luke opened his Gospel with a scene in the temple (Luke 1:8ff), and he closed his Gospel the same way (Luke 24:53). But what a contrast between the unbelieving, silent priest and the trusting, joyful saints! Luke has explained how Jesus went to Jerusalem and accomplished the work of redemption. His book begins and ends in Jerusalem. But his next book, The Acts of the Apostles, would explain how that Gospel traveled from Jerusalem to Rome!

Is the Gospel going out to the ends of the earth from your Jerusalem?

JOHN

OUTLINE

Key theme: Jesus is the Christ; believe and live!
Key verse: John 20:31

I. **OPPORTUNITY—1:15–6:71**
He presents Himself to:
A. His disciples—1:19–2:12
B. The Jews—2:13–3:36
C. The Samaritans—4:1-54
D. The Jewish leaders—5:1-47
E. The multitudes—6:1-71

II. **OPPOSITION—chapters 7–12**
There is conflict with the Jewish leaders over:
A. Moses—7:1–8:11
B. Abraham—8:12–59
C. Who Messiah is—9:1–10:42
D. His miraculous power—11:1–12:36
E. They would not believe on Him—12:37-50

III. **OUTCOME—chapters 13–21**
A. The faith of the disciples—13–17
B. The unbelief of the Jews—18–19
C. The victory of Christ—20–21

CONTENTS

CHAPTER ONE
GOD IS HERE!
John 1

"But will God indeed dwell on the earth?" asked Solomon as he dedicated the temple (1 Kings 8:27). A good question, indeed! God's glory had dwelt in the tabernacle (Ex. 40:34), and in the temple (1 Kings 8:10-11); but that glory had departed from disobedient Israel (Ezek. 9:3; 10:4, 18; 11:22-23).

Then a marvelous thing happened: the glory of God came to His people again, in the person of His Son, Jesus Christ. The writers of the four Gospels have given us "snapshots" of our Lord's life on earth, for no complete biography could ever be written (John 21:25). Matthew wrote with his fellow Jews in mind and emphasized that Jesus of Nazareth had fulfilled the Old Testament prophecies. Mark wrote for the busy Romans. Whereas Matthew emphasized the King, Mark presented the Servant, ministering to needy people. Luke wrote his Gospel for the Greeks and introduced them to the sympathetic Son of man.

But it was given to John, the beloved disciple, to write a book for both Jews and Gentiles, presenting Jesus as the Son of God. We know that John had Gentiles in mind as well as Jews, because he often "interpreted" Jewish words or customs for his readers (John 1:38, 41-42; 5:2; 9:7; 19:13, 17; 20:16). His emphasis to the Jews was that Jesus not only fulfilled the Old Testament prophecies, but He also fulfilled the *types.* Jesus is the Lamb of God (John 1:29) and the Ladder from heaven to earth (John 1:51; and see Gen. 28). He is the New Temple (John 2:19-21), and He gives a new birth (John 3:4ff). He is the serpent lifted up (John 3:14) and the Bread of God that came down from heaven (John 6:35ff).

Whereas the first three Gospels major on describing *events* in the life of Christ, John emphasized the *meaning* of these events. For example, all four Gospels record the feeding of the 5,000 but only John records Jesus' sermon on "The Bread of Life" which followed that miracle when He interpreted it for the people.

But there is one major theme that runs throughout John's Gospel: Jesus Christ is the Son of God, and if you commit yourself to Him, He will give you eternal life (John 20:31). In this first chapter, John recorded seven names and titles of Jesus that identify Him as eternal God.

The Word (John 1:1-3, 14)

Much as our words reveal to others our hearts and minds, so Jesus Christ is God's "Word" to reveal His heart and mind to us. "He that hath seen Me hath seen the Father" (John 14:9). A word is composed of letters, and Jesus Christ is "Alpha and Omega" (Rev. 1:11), the first and last letters of the Greek alphabet. According to Hebrews 1:1-3, Jesus Christ is God's *last* Word to mankind, for He is the climax of divine revelation.

Jesus Christ is the eternal Word (vv. 1-2). He existed in the beginning, not because He had a beginning as a creature, but because He is eternal. He *is* God and He was *with* God. "Before Abraham was, I am" (John 8:58).

Jesus Christ is the creative Word (v. 3). There is certainly a parallel between John 1:1 and Genesis 1:1, the "new creation" and the "old creation." God created the worlds through His word: "And God said, 'Let there be. . . .' " / "For He spake, and it was done; He commanded, and it stood fast" (Ps. 33:9). God created all things through Jesus Christ (Col. 1:16), which means that Jesus is not a created being. He is eternal God.

The verb *was made* is perfect tense in the

Greek, which means a "completed act." Creation is finished. It is not a process still going on, even though God is certainly at work in His creation (John 5:17). Creation is not a process; it is a finished product.

Jesus Christ is the incarnate Word (v. 14). He was not a phantom or a spirit when He ministered on earth, nor was His body a mere illusion. John and the other disciples each had a personal experience that convinced them of the reality of the body of Jesus (1 John 1:1-2). Even though John's emphasis is the deity of Christ, he makes it clear that the Son of God came *in the flesh* and was subject to the sinless infirmities of human nature.

In his Gospel, John points out that Jesus was weary (John 4:6) and thirsty (John 4:7). He groaned within (John 11:33) and openly wept (John 11:35). On the cross, He thirsted (John 19:28), died (John 19:30), and bled (John 19:34). After His resurrection, He proved to Thomas and the other disciples that He still had a real body (John 20:24-29), howbeit, a glorified body.

How was the "Word made flesh"? By the miracle of the Virgin Birth (Isa. 7:14; Matt. 1:18-25; Luke 1:26-38). He took on Himself sinless human nature and identified with us in every aspect of life from birth to death. "The Word" was not an abstract concept of philosophy, but a real Person who could be seen, touched, and heard. Christianity is Christ, and Christ is God.

The revelation of God's glory is an important theme in the Gospel. Jesus revealed God's glory in His person, His works, and His words. John recorded seven wonderful signs (miracles) that openly declared the glory of God (John 2:11). The glory of the Old Covenant of Law was a fading glory, but the glory of the New Covenant in Christ is an increasing glory (see 2 Cor. 3). The Law could reveal sin, but it could never remove sin. Jesus Christ came with *fullness* of grace and truth, and this fullness is available to all who will trust Him (John 1:16).

The Light (John 1:4-13)

Life is a key theme in John's Gospel; it is used thirty-six times. What are the essentials for human life? There are at least four: light (if the sun went out, everything would die), air, water, and food. Jesus is all of these! He is the Light of life and the Light of the world (John 8:12). He is the "Sun of righteousness" (Mal. 4:2). By His Holy Spirit, He gives us the "breath of life" (John 3:8; 20:22), as well as the Water of life (John 4:10, 13-14; 7:37-39). Finally, Jesus is the Living Bread of Life that came down from heaven (John 6:35ff). He not only has life and gives life, but He *is* life (John 14:6).

Light and darkness are recurring themes in John's Gospel. God is light (1 John 1:5) while Satan is "the power of darkness" (Luke 22:53). People love either the light or the darkness, and this love controls their actions (John 3:16-19). Those who believe on Christ are the "sons of light" (John 12:35-36). Just as the first Creation began with "Let there be light!" so the New Creation begins with the entrance of light into the heart of the believer (2 Cor. 4:3-6). The coming of Jesus Christ into the world was the dawning of a new day for sinful man (Luke 1:78-79).

You would think that blind sinners would welcome the light, but such is not always the case. The coming of the true light brought conflict as the powers of darkness opposed it. A literal translation of John 1:5 reads, "And the light keeps on shining in the darkness, and the darkness has not overcome it or understood it." The Greek verb can mean "to overcome" or "to grasp, to understand." Throughout the Gospel of John, you will see both attitudes revealed: people will not understand what the Lord is saying and doing and, as a result, they will oppose Him. John 7–12 records the growth of that opposition, which ultimately led to the crucifixion of Christ.

Whenever Jesus taught a spiritual truth, His listeners interpreted it in a material or physical way. The light was unable to penetrate the darkness in their minds. This was true when He spoke about the temple of His body (John 2:19-21), the new birth (John 3:4), the living water (John 4:11), eating His flesh (John 6:51ff), spiritual freedom (John 8:30-36), death as sleep (John 11:11-13), and many other spiritual truths. Satan strives to keep people in the darkness, because darkness means death and hell, while light means life and heaven.

This fact helps explain the ministry of John the Baptist (John 1:6-8). John was sent as a witness to Jesus Christ, to tell people that the Light had come into the world. The nation of Israel, in spite of all its spiritual advantages, was blind to their own Messiah! The word *witness* is a key word in this book; John uses the noun fourteen times and the verb thirty-three times. John the Baptist was one of many people who bore witness to Jesus, "This is the Son of God!" Alas, John the Baptist was martyred and the Jewish leaders did nothing to prevent it.

Why did the nation reject Jesus Christ? Because they "knew Him not." They were spiritually ignorant. Jesus is the "true Light"—the original of which every other light is a copy—but the Jews were content with the copies. They had Moses and the Law, the temple and the sacrifices; but they did not comprehend that these "lights" pointed to the true Light who was the fulfillment, the completion, of the Old Testament religion.

As you study John's Gospel, you will find Jesus teaching the people that He is the fulfillment of all that was typified in the Law. It was not enough to be born a Jew; they had to be born again, born from above (John 3). He deliberately performed two miracles on the Sabbath to teach them that He had a new rest to give them (John 5; 9). He was the satisfying manna (John 6) and the life-giving Water (John 7:37-39). He is the Shepherd of a new flock (John 10:16), and He is a new Vine (John 15). But the people were so shackled by religious tradition that they could not understand spiritual truth. Jesus came to His own world that He had created, but His own people, Israel, could not understand Him and would not receive Him.

They saw His works and heard His words. They observed His perfect life. He gave them every opportunity to grasp the truth, believe, and be saved. Jesus is the way, but they would not walk with Him (John 6:66-71). He is the truth, but they would not believe Him (John 12:37ff). He is the life, and they crucified Him!

But sinners today need not commit those same blunders. John 1:12-13 gives us the marvelous promise of God that anyone who receives Christ will be born again and enter the family of God! John says more about this new birth in John 3, but he points out here that it is a spiritual birth from God, not a physical birth that depends on human nature.

The Light is still shining! Have you *personally* received the Light and become a child of God?

The Son of God (John 1:15-28, 49)

John the Baptist is one of the most important persons in the New Testament. He is mentioned at least eighty-nine times. John had the special privilege of introducing Jesus to the nation of Israel. He also had the difficult task of preparing the nation to receive their Messiah. He called them to repent of their sins and to prove that repentance by being baptized and then living changed lives.

John summarized what John the Baptist had to say about Jesus Christ (John 1:15-18). First, *He is eternal* (John 1:15). John the Baptist was actually born six months before Jesus (Luke 1:36); so in this statement he is referring to our Lord's preexistence, not His birth date. Jesus existed before John the Baptist was ever conceived.

Jesus Christ has *fullness of grace and truth* (John 1:16-17). Grace is God's favor and kindness bestowed on those who do not deserve it and cannot earn it. If God dealt with us only according to truth, none of us would survive; but He deals with us on the basis of grace *and* truth. Jesus Christ, in His life, death, and resurrection, met all the demands of the Law; now God is free to share fullness of grace with those who trust Christ. Grace without truth would be deceitful, and truth without grace would be condemning.

In John 1:17, John did not suggest that there was no grace under the Law of Moses, because there was. Each sacrifice was an expression of the grace of God. The Law also revealed God's truth. But in Jesus Christ, grace and truth reach their fullness; and this fullness is available to us. We are saved by grace (Eph. 2:8-9), but we also live by grace (1 Cor. 15:10) and depend on God's grace in all that we do. We can receive one grace after another, for "He giveth more grace" (James 4:6). In John 1:17, John hinted that a whole new order had come in, replacing the Mosaic system.

Finally, *Jesus Christ reveals God to us* (John 1:18). As to His essence, God is invisible (1 Tim. 1:17; Heb. 11:27). Man can see God revealed in nature (Ps. 19:1-6; Rom. 1:20) and in His mighty works in history; but he cannot see God Himself. Jesus Christ reveals God to us, for He is "the image of the invisible God" (Col. 1:15) and "the express image of His person" (Heb. 1:3). The word translated "declared" gives us our English word *exegesis,* which means "to explain, to unfold, to lead the way." Jesus Christ explains God to us and interprets Him for us. We simply cannot understand God apart from knowing His Son, Jesus Christ.

The word *Son* is used for the first time in John's Gospel as a title for Jesus Christ (John

1:18). The phrase "only-begotten" means "unique, the only one of its kind." It does not suggest that there was a time when the Son was not, and then the Father brought Him into being. Jesus Christ is eternal God; He has always existed.

At least nine times in John's Gospel, Jesus is called "the Son of God" (John 1:34, 49; 3:18; 5:25; 10:36; 11:4, 27; 19:7; 20:31). You will recall that John had as his purpose in writing to convince us that Jesus is the Son of God (John 20:31). At least nineteen times, Jesus is referred to as "the Son." He is not only the Son of God, but He is God the Son. Even the demons admitted this (Mark 3:11; Luke 4:41).

John the Baptist is one of six persons named in the Gospel of John who gave witness that Jesus is God. The others are Nathanael (John 1:49), Peter (John 6:69), the blind man who was healed (John 9:35-38), Martha (John 11:27), and Thomas (John 20:28). If you add our Lord Himself (John 5:25; 10:36), then you have seven clear witnesses.

John gave the record of four days in the life of John the Baptist, Jesus, and the first disciples. He continues this sequence in John 2 and presents, as it were, a "week" in the "new creation" that parallels the Creation week in Genesis 1.

On the first day (John 1:19-24), a committee from the Jewish religious leaders interrogated John the Baptist. These men had every right to investigate John and his ministry, since they were the custodians and guardians of the faith. They asked him several questions and he clearly answered them.

"Who are you?" was a logical question. Was he the promised Messiah? Was he the Prophet Elijah who was supposed to come before the Messiah appeared? (Mal. 4:5) Great crowds had gathered to hear John, and many people had been baptized. Though John did no miracles (John 10:41), it was possible the people thought that he was the promised Messiah.

John denied being either Elijah or the Messiah. (In one sense, he was the promised Elijah. See Matt. 17:10-13.) John had nothing to say about himself because he was sent to talk about Jesus! Jesus is the Word; John was but "a voice"—and you cannot see a voice! John pointed back to Isaiah's prophecy (Isa. 40:1-3) and affirmed that he was the fulfillment.

Having ascertained who John was, the committee then asked what he was doing. "Why are you baptizing?" John got his authority to baptize, not from men, but from heaven, because he was commissioned by God (Matt. 21:23-32). The Jewish religious leaders in that day baptized Gentiles who wanted to adopt the Jewish faith; *but John baptized Jews!*

John explained that his baptism was in water, but that the Messiah would come and baptize with a spiritual baptism. Again, John made it clear that he was not establishing a new religion or seeking to exalt himself. He was pointing people to the Saviour, the Son of God (John 1:34). We shall learn later that it was through baptism that Jesus Christ would be presented to the people of Israel.

Lamb of God (John 1:29-34)

This is the second day of the week that the Apostle John recorded, and no doubt some of the same committee members were present to hear John the Baptist's message. This time, he called Jesus "the Lamb of God," a title he would repeat the next day (John 1:35-36). In one sense, the message of the Bible can be summed up in this title. The question in the Old Testament is, "Where is the lamb?" (Gen. 22:7) In the four Gospels, the emphasis is "Behold the Lamb of God!" Here He is! After you have trusted Him, you sing with the heavenly choir, "Worthy is the Lamb!" (Rev. 5:12)

The people of Israel were familiar with lambs for the sacrifices. At Passover, each family had to have a lamb; and during the year, two lambs a day were sacrificed at the temple altar, plus all the other lambs brought for personal sacrifices. Those lambs were brought by men to men, but here is God's Lamb, given by God to men! Those lambs could not take away sin, but the Lamb of God can take away sin. Those lambs were for Israel alone, but this Lamb would shed His blood for the whole world!

What does John's baptism have to do with Jesus as the Lamb of God? It is generally agreed by scholars of all denominations that, in the New Testament, baptism was by immersion. It pictured death, burial, and resurrection. When John the Baptist baptized Jesus, Jesus and John were picturing the "baptism" Jesus would endure *on the cross* when He would die as the sacrificial Lamb of God (Isa. 53:7; Luke 12:50). It would be through death, burial, and resurrection that the Lamb of God would "fulfill all righteousness" (Matt. 3:15).

Perhaps John was mistaken. Perhaps John was not sure that Jesus of Nazareth was the

Lamb of God or the Son of God. But the Father made it clear to John just who Jesus is by sending the Spirit like a dove to light on Him. What a beautiful picture of the Trinity!

The Messiah (John 1:35-42)

This is now the third day in the sequence. The seventh day included the wedding at Cana (John 2:1); and since Jewish weddings traditionally were on Wednesdays, it would make this third day the Sabbath Day. But it was not a day of rest for either John the Baptist or Jesus, for John was preaching and Jesus was gathering disciples.

The two disciples of John who followed Jesus were John, the writer of the Gospel, and his friend Andrew. John the Baptist was happy when people left him to follow Jesus, because his ministry focused on Jesus. "He must increase, but I must decrease" (John 3:30).

When Jesus asked them, "What are you seeking?" He was forcing them to define their purposes and goals. Were they looking for a revolutionary leader to overthrow Rome? Then they had better join the Zealots! Little did Andrew and John realize that day how their lives would be transformed by the Son of God.

"Where are You dwelling?" may have suggested, "If You are too busy now, we can visit later." But Jesus invited them to spend the day with Him (it was 10 A.M.) and no doubt He told them something of His mission, revealed their own hearts to them, and answered their questions. They were both so impressed that they found their brothers and brought them to Jesus. Andrew found Simon and John brought James. Indeed, they *were* their brothers' keepers! (Gen. 4:9) Whenever you find Andrew in John's Gospel, he is bringing somebody to Jesus: his brother, the lad with the loaves and fishes (John 6:8), and the Greeks who wanted to see Jesus (John 12:20-21). No sermons from Andrew are recorded, but he certainly preached great sermons by his actions as a personal soul winner!

"We have found the Messiah!" was the witness Andrew gave to Simon. *Messiah* is a Hebrew word that means "anointed," and the Greek equivalent is "Christ." To the Jews, it was the same as "Son of God" (see Matt. 26:63-64; Mark 14:61-62; Luke 22:67-70). In the Old Testament, prophets, priests, and kings were anointed and thereby set apart for special service. Kings were especially called "God's anointed" (1 Sam. 26:11; Ps. 89:20); so, when the Jews spoke about their Messiah, they were thinking of the king who would come to deliver them and establish the kingdom.

There was some confusion among the Jewish teachers as to what the Messiah would do. Some saw Him as a suffering sacrifice (as in Isa. 53), while others saw a splendid king (as in Isa. 9 and 11). Jesus had to explain even to His own followers that the cross had to come before the crown, that He must suffer before He could enter into His glory (Luke 24:13-35). Whether or not Jesus was indeed the Messiah was a crucial problem that challenged the Jews in that day (John 7:26, 40-44; 9:22; 10:24).

Simon's interview with Jesus changed his life. It also gave him a new name—*Peter* in the Greek, *Cephas* in the Aramaic that Jesus spoke—both of which mean "a rock." It took a great deal of work for Jesus to transform weak Simon into a rock, but He did it! "Thou art . . . thou shalt be" is a great encouragement to all who trust Christ. Truly, He gives us the "power to become" (John 1:12).

It is worth noting that Andrew and John trusted Christ through the faithful preaching of John the Baptist. Peter and James came to Christ because of the compassionate personal work of their brothers. Later on, Jesus would win Philip personally; and then Philip would witness to Nathanael and bring him to Jesus. Each man's experience is different, because God uses various means to bring sinners to the Saviour. The important thing is that we trust Christ and then seek to bring others to Him.

The King of Israel (John 1:43-49)

Jesus called Philip personally and Philip trusted Him and followed Him. We do not know what kind of heart preparation Philip experienced, for usually God prepares a person before He calls him. We do know that Philip proved his faith by seeking to share it with his friend Nathanael.

John 21:2 suggests that at least seven of our Lord's disciples were fishermen, including Nathanael. Fishermen are courageous and stick to the job, no matter how difficult it may be. But Nathanael started out a doubter: he did not believe that anything worthwhile could come out of Nazareth. Our Lord was born in Bethlehem, but He grew up in Nazareth and bore that stigma (Matt. 2:19-23). To be called "a Nazarene" (Acts 24:5) meant to be looked down on and rejected.

When Nathanael hesitated and argued, Philip adopted our Lord's own words: "Come and see" (John 1:39). Later on, Jesus would invite, "Come and drink!" (John 7:37) and, "Come and dine!" (John 21:12) "Come" is the great invitation of God's grace.

When Nathanael came to Jesus, he discovered that the Lord already knew all about him! What a shock! By calling him "an Israelite in whom is no guile," Jesus was certainly referring to Jacob, the ancestor of the Jews, a man who used guile to trick his brother, his father, and his father-in-law. Jacob's name was changed to "Israel, a prince with God." The reference to "Jacob's ladder" in John 1:51 confirms this.

When Jesus revealed His knowledge of Nathanael, where he had been and what he had been doing, this was enough to convince the man that Jesus indeed was "the Son of God, the King of Israel." His experience was like that of the Samaritan woman at the well. "When He [Messiah] is come, He will tell us all things. . . . Come, see a man who told me all things that ever I did" (John 4:25, 29). The revealing of the human heart should also take place in the ministry of local churches (1 Cor. 14:23-35).

When Philip witnessed to Nathanael, the evidence he gave was Moses and the Prophets (John 1:45). Perhaps Jesus gave Philip a "quick course" in the Old Testament messianic prophecies, as He did with the Emmaus disciples (Luke 24:13ff). It is always good to tie our personal witness to the Word of God.

"King of Israel" would be a title similar to "Messiah, anointed One," for the kings were always God's anointed (see Ps. 2, especially vv. 2, 6-7). At one point in His ministry, the crowds wanted to make Jesus King, but He refused them (John 6:15ff). He did present Himself as King (John 12:10ff), and He affirmed to Pilate that He was born a King (John 18:33-37).

Some students believe that Nathanael and Bartholomew are the same person. John never mentions Bartholomew in his Gospel, but the other three writers name Bartholomew and not Nathanael. Philip is linked with Bartholomew in the lists of names (Matt. 10:3; Mark 3:18; Luke 6:14), so it is possible that the two men were "paired off" and served together. It was not unusual in that day for one man to have two different names.

The Son of Man (John 1:50-51)

"Son of man" was one of our Lord's favorite titles for Himself; it is used eighty-three times in the Gospels and at least thirteen times in John. The title speaks of both the deity and humanity of Jesus. The vision in Daniel 7:13 presents the "Son of man" in a definite messianic setting; and Jesus used the title in the same way (Matt. 26:64).

As Son of man, Jesus is the "living link" between heaven and earth. This explains His reference to "Jacob's ladder" in Genesis 28. Jacob the fugitive thought he was alone, but God had sent the angels to guard and guide him. Christ is God's "ladder" between heaven and earth. "No man cometh to the Father, but by Me" (John 14:6). Often in this Gospel, you will find Jesus reminding people that He came down from heaven. The Jewish people knew that "Son of man" was a name for their Messiah (John 12:34).

At the close of that fourth day, Jesus had six believing men who were His disciples. They did not immediately "forsake all and follow Him"; that was to come later. But they had trusted Him and experienced His power. In the three years that lay ahead, they would grow in their faith, learn more about Jesus, and one day take His place on the earth so that the Word might be carried to all mankind.

Jesus of Nazareth is God come in the flesh. When Philip called Him "the son of Joseph," he was not denying Jesus' virgin birth or divine nature. That was merely His legal identification, for a Jewish person was identified according to who his father was (John 6:42). The witness of this entire chapter is clear: Jesus of Nazareth is God come in the flesh!

God is here!

CHAPTER TWO
LEARNING ABOUT JESUS
John 2

The six disciples who now trusted Jesus started on their lifelong walk with Him and from the beginning began to learn more about Him. We who read the Gospel record in its entirety are prone to take these events for granted; but to the disciples, each day and each new event brought marvels that were difficult to understand. In this chapter alone, John recorded three wonderful revelations of Jesus Christ.

His Glory (John 2:1-12)

"The third day" means three days after the call of Nathanael (John 1:45-51). Since that was the fourth day of the week recorded in John (John 1:19, 29, 35, 43), the wedding took place on "the seventh day" of this "new creation week." Throughout his Gospel, John makes it clear that Jesus was on a divine schedule, obeying the will of the Father.

Jewish tradition required that virgins be married on a Wednesday, while widows were married on a Thursday. Being the "seventh day" of John's special week, Jesus would be expected to rest, just as God rested on the seventh day (Gen. 2:1-3). But sin had interrupted God's Sabbath rest, and it was necessary for both the Father and the Son to work (John 5:17; 9:4). In fact, John recorded two specific miracles that Jesus deliberately performed on Sabbath days (John 5; 9).

At this wedding, we see Jesus in three different roles: the Guest, the Son, and the Host.

Jesus the Guest (vv. 1-2). Our Lord was not a recluse, as was John the Baptist (Matt. 11:16-19). He accepted invitations to social events, even though His enemies used this practice to accuse Him (Luke 15:1-2). Our Lord entered into the normal experiences of life and sanctified them by His presence. Wise is that couple who invite Jesus to their wedding!

He was accompanied by His mother and His six disciples. Perhaps it was the addition of seven more people that helped create the crisis; but it must have been a small wedding feast if this were the case. We have reason to believe that our Lord's earthly family was not prosperous, and it is likely that their friends were not wealthy people. Perhaps the shortage of wine was related to a low-budget feast.

Were Jesus and His disciples invited because of Mary, or because of Nathanael? (John 21:2) Our Lord was not yet well known; He had performed no miracles as yet. It was not likely that He was invited because the people knew who He was. It was probably His relationship with Mary that brought about the invitation.

Jesus the Son (vv. 3-5). Since Jewish wedding feasts lasted a week, it was necessary for the groom to have adequate provisions. For one thing, it would be embarrassing to run out of either food or wine; and a family guilty of such gaucherie could actually be fined! So, to run out of wine could be costly both financially and socially.

Why did Mary approach Jesus about the problem? Did she actually expect Him to do something special to meet the need? Certainly she knew who He was, even though she did not declare this wonderful truth to others. She must have been very close to either the bride or the bridegroom to have such a personal concern for the success of the festivities, or even to know that the supply of wine was depleted. Perhaps Mary was assisting in the preparation and serving of the meal.

Mary did not tell Jesus what to do; she simply reported the problem. (Compare the message of Mary and Martha to Jesus, when Lazarus was sick—John 11:3.) Jesus' reply seems a bit abrupt, and even harsh; but such is not the case. "Woman" was a polite way to address her (John 19:26; 20:13), and His statement merely means, "Why are you getting Me involved in this matter?" He was making it clear to His mother that He was no longer under her supervision (it is likely that Joseph was dead), but that from now on, He would be doing what the Father wanted Him to do. There had been a hint of this some years before (Luke 2:40-52).

At this point, John introduced one of the key elements of his record, the idea of "the hour." Jesus lived on a "heavenly timetable," marked out for Him by the Father. (See John 7:30; 8:20; 12:23; 13:1; 17:1; and note also the words of Jesus as recorded in John 11:9-10.) As you study John's Gospel, you will observe how this concept of "the hour" is developed.

Mary's words to the servants reveal that she was willing to let her Son do whatever He pleased, and that she trusted Him to do what was right. It would be wise for all of us to obey what she said! It is worth noting that it was Jesus, not Mary, who took command and solved the problem; and that Mary pointed, not to herself, but to Jesus.

Jesus the Host (vv. 6-12). Our Lord's first miracle was not a spectacular event that everybody witnessed. Mary, the disciples, and the servants knew what had happened; but nobody else at the feast had any idea that a miracle had taken place. His first miracle was a quiet event at a wedding in contrast to His last miracle recorded by John (John 11), a public event after a funeral.

Each of the six stone waterpots could contain about twenty gallons each. However, we are not told that all of the available water in the jars turned into wine. Only that which the servants drew out and served was transformed into wine. The quality of this new wine was so superior that the man in charge of the banquet highly praised it and, of course, the groom's family basked in the glory of the compliments.

The fact that this was "the beginning of miracles" automatically declares as false the stories about the miracles performed by Jesus when He was an Infant or a young Child. They are nothing but superstitious fables and ought to be rejected by anyone who accepts the authority of the Bible.

The miracle did something for His disciples. It revealed His glory (John 1:14) and gave them a stronger foundation for their faith. Though miracles *alone* are insufficient evidence for declaring Jesus to be the Son of God (2 Thes. 2:9-10), the cumulative effect of miracle after miracle should certainly convince them of His deity. The disciples had to begin somewhere, and over the months, their faith deepened as they got to know Jesus better.

But there is certainly more to this miracle than simply meeting a human need and saving a family from social embarrassment. The Gospel of John, unlike the other three Gospels, seeks to share the *inner meaning*—the spiritual significance—of our Lord's works, so that each miracle is a "sermon in action." We must be careful not to "spiritualize" these events so that they lose their historical moorings; but, at the same time, we must not be so shackled to history that we are blind to (as A.T. Pierson used to say) "His story."

To begin with, the word John used in his book is not *dunamis,* which emphasizes power, but *sēmeion,* which means "a sign." What is a sign? Something that points beyond itself to something greater. It was not enough for people to believe in Jesus' works; they had to believe in Him and in the Father who sent Him (John 5:14-24). This explains why Jesus often added a sermon to the miracle and in that sermon interpreted the sign. In John 5, the healing of the paralytic on the Sabbath opened the way for a message on His deity, "the Lord of the Sabbath." The feeding of the 5,000 (John 6) led naturally into a sermon on the Bread of Life.

If our Lord had preached a sermon after He turned the water into wine, what might He have said? For one thing, He likely would have told the people that the world's joy always runs out and cannot be regained, but the joy He gives is ever new and ever satisfying. (In the Scriptures, wine is a symbol of joy. See Jud. 9:13 and Ps. 104:15.) The world offers the best at the first, and then, once you are "hooked," things start to get worse. But Jesus continues to offer that which is best until we one day enjoy the finest blessings in the eternal kingdom (Luke 22:18).

But our Lord would certainly have a special message here for His people, Israel. In the Old Testament, the nation is pictured as "married" to God and unfaithful to her marriage covenant (Isa. 54:5; Jer. 31:32; Hosea 2:2ff). The wine ran out, and all Israel had left were six empty waterpots! They held water for *external* washings, but they could provide nothing for internal cleaning and joy. In this miracle, our Lord brought fullness where there was emptiness, joy where there was disappointment, and something *internal* for that which was only external (water for ceremonial washings).

When John mentioned "the third day" (John 2:1), he may have been giving us a hint of our Lord's resurrection. All of these blessings are possible because of His sacrifice on the cross and His resurrection from the dead (John 2:19).

Interestingly Moses' first miracle was a plague—turning water into blood (Ex. 7:19ff), which speaks of judgment. Our Lord's first miracle spoke of grace.

This miracle also presents a practical lesson in service for God. The water turned into wine because the servants cooperated with

Jesus and obeyed His commands. Several of the signs in John's Gospel involve the cooperation of man and God: the feeding of the 5,000 (John 6), the healing of the man born blind (John 9), and the raising of Lazarus (John 11). Whether we pass out bread, wash away mud, or roll away the stone, we are assisting Him in performing a miracle.

It is significant that the servants knew the source of this special wine (John 2:9). When Jesus healed the nobleman's son (John 4:46-54), it was the servants who were in on the secret. We are not just His servants; we are also His friends, and we know what He is doing (John 15:15).

Wine was the normal drink of the people in that day, and we must not use this miracle as an argument for the use of alcoholic beverages today. A man given to drink once said to me, "After all, Jesus turned water into wine!"

My reply was, "If you use Jesus as your example for drinking, why don't you follow His example in everything else?" Then I read Luke 22:18 to him. This verse clearly states that, in heaven now, Jesus is a teetotaler!

Sincere Christians of our day consider such verses as 1 Corinthians 8:9; 10:23, 31 before concluding that the use of alcoholic beverages is a wise thing today. I am reminded of the story of the drunken coal miner who was converted and became a vocal witness for Christ. One of his friends tried to trap him by asking, "Do you believe that Jesus turned water into wine?"

"I certainly do!" the believer replied. "In my home, He has turned wine into furniture, decent clothes, and food for my children!"

Finally, it is worth noting that the Jews always diluted the wine with water, usually to the proportion of three parts water to one part wine. While the Bible does not command total abstinence, it certainly *magnifies* it and definitely warns against drunkenness.

His Zeal (John 2:12-22)

Jesus, His family, and His disciples remained in Capernaum a few days, and then He went to Jerusalem for the Passover feast. Each Jewish man was required to attend three annual feasts at the Holy City: Passover, Pentecost, and Tabernacles (Deut. 16:16). The feasts mentioned in the Gospel of John are Passover (John 2:13; 6:4; 12:1), Tabernacles (John 7:2), and Dedication (John 10:22). The unnamed feast in John 5:1 may have been Purim (Es. 9:26, 31).

Though He deliberately violated the man-made religious traditions of the Pharisees, our Lord obeyed the statutes of the Law and was faithful to uphold the Law. In His life and death, He fulfilled the Law so that, today, believers are not burdened by that "yoke of bondage" (Acts 15:10).

Jesus revealed His zeal for God first of all by *cleansing the temple* (John 2:13-17). The priests had established a lucrative business of exchanging foreign money for Jewish currency, and also selling the animals needed for the sacrifices. No doubt, this "religious market" began as a convenience for the Jews who came long distances to worship in the temple; but in due time the "convenience" became a business, not a ministry. The tragedy is that this business was carried on in the court of the Gentiles in the temple, the place where the Jews should have been meeting the Gentiles and telling them about the one true God. Any Gentile searching for truth would not likely find it among the religious merchants in the temple.

Our Lord suddenly appeared in the temple and cleaned house! He was careful not to destroy anyone's property (He did not release the doves, for example); but He made it clear that He was in command. The temple was His Father's house, and He would not have the religious leaders pollute it with their money-making enterprises.

The condition of the temple was a vivid indication of the spiritual condition of the nation. Their religion was a dull routine, presided over by worldly minded men whose main desire was to exercise authority and get rich. Not only had the wine run out at the wedding feast but the glory had departed from the temple.

When they saw His courageous zeal, the disciples remembered Psalm 69:9, "The zeal of [for] Thine house hath eaten me up." Psalm 69 is definitely a messianic psalm that is quoted several times in the New Testament: Psalm 69:4 (John 15:25); Psalm 69:8 (John 7:3-5); Psalm 69:9 (John 2:17; Rom. 15:3); Psalm 69:21 (Matt. 27:34, 48); and Psalm 69:22 (Rom. 11:9-10).

There was still a godly remnant in Israel who loved God and revered His temple (Luke 1:5-22; 2:25-38), but most religious leaders were false shepherds who exploited the people. When Jesus cleansed the temple, He "declared war" on the hypocritical religious leaders (Matt. 23), and this ultimately led to His death. Indeed, His zeal for God's house *did* eat Him up!

He also revealed His zeal by *giving His life* (John 2:18-22). It was logical for the religious leaders to ask Him to show the source of His authority. After all, they were the guardians of the Jewish faith, and they had a right to test any new prophet who appeared. "The Jews require a sign" (1 Cor. 1:22). Often, during His ministry, the leaders asked Jesus to give them a sign; and He refused to do so, *except* for the sign of Jonah (Matt. 12:39ff). The "sign of Jonah" is death, burial, and resurrection.

Jesus used the image of the temple to convey this truth. "Destroy this temple [My body], and in three days I will raise it up" (John 2:19). Being spiritually blind, those who heard misunderstood what He was saying. Throughout the Gospel of John, you will find people misunderstanding *spiritual* truth and interpreting in material or physical terms (John 3:4; 4:11; 6:52). Herod's temple was started in 20 B.C. and not completed until A.D. 64. How could one man "raise it up" in three days?

This statement was, of course, a prediction of His own death and resurrection; and His disciples remembered it after He was raised from the dead. But His enemies also remembered it and used it at His trial (Matt. 26:59-61); and some of the people mocked Him with it when He was dying on the cross (Matt. 27:40).

In writing this Gospel, John included a number of vivid pictures of the death of the Saviour. The first is the slaying of the Lamb in John 1:29, indicating that His death would be that of a substitute for sinners. The destroying of the temple is the second picture (John 2:19), suggesting a violent death that would end in victorious resurrection.

The third picture is that of the serpent lifted up (John 3:14), a reference to Numbers 21:5-9. The Saviour would be made sin for us (1 Peter 2:24). His death would be voluntary (John 10:11-18): the Shepherd would lay down His life for the sheep. Finally, the planting of the seed (John 12:20-25) teaches that His death would produce fruit to the glory of God. His death and burial would look like failure, but in the end, God would bring victory.

The temple was an important element of the Jewish faith, for in it God was supposed to dwell. All of the ceremonies and sacrifices of the Jewish religion centered in the temple. When Jesus suggested that their precious building would be destroyed, their angry reaction was predictable. After all, if *His* body is the temple, then the Jewish temple would be needed no more. In this cryptic statement, our Lord actually predicted the end of the Jewish religious system.

But that was one of the purposes John had in mind when he wrote his Gospel: the legal system has ended, and "grace and truth" have come through Jesus Christ. He is the new sacrifice (John 1:29) and the new temple (John 2:19). John will tell us later, that the new worship will depend on inward integrity, not outward geography (John 4:19-24).

His Knowledge (John 2:23-25)

While in Jerusalem for the Passover, Jesus performed miracles that are not given in detail in any of the Gospels. It must have been these signs that especially attracted Nicodemus (John 3:2). Because of the miracles, many people professed to believe in Him; but Jesus did not accept their profession. No matter what the people themselves said, or others said about them, He did not accept human testimony. Why? Because, being God, He knew what was in each person's heart and mind.

The words *believed* in John 2:23 and *commit* in John 2:24 are the same Greek word. These people believed in Jesus, but He did not believe in them! They were "unsaved believers"! It was one thing to respond to a miracle but quite something else to commit oneself to Jesus Christ and continue in His Word (John 8:30-31).

John was not discrediting the importance of our Lord's signs, because he wrote his book to record these signs and to encourage his readers to trust Jesus Christ and receive eternal life (John 20:30-31). However, throughout the book, John makes it clear that it takes more than believing in miracles for a person to be saved. Seeing the signs and believing in them would be a great beginning; in fact, even the disciples started that way and had to grow in their faith (compare John 2:11 and v. 22).

Throughout the Gospel of John, you see the Jewish people divided over the meaning of these miracles (John 9:16; 11:45-46). The same miracles that attracted Nicodemus to Jesus caused some of the other religious leaders to want to kill Him! They even asserted that His miracles were done in the power of Satan! Our Lord's miracles were testimonies

(John 5:36), giving evidence of His divine sonship; but they were also *tests,* exposing the hearts of the people (John 12:37ff). The same events that opened some eyes only made other eyes that much more blind (John 9:39-41).

It is important to see that Jesus tied His miracles to the truth of His message. He knew that the human heart is attracted to the sensational. The 5,000 that He fed wanted to make Him King—until He preached a sermon on the Bread of Life, and then they left Him in droves! "Grace and truth came by Jesus Christ" (John 1:17). In grace, Jesus fed the hungry; in truth, He taught the Word. The people wanted the physical food but not the spiritual truth, so they abandoned Him.

"He knew what was in man" is a statement that is proved several times in John's Gospel. Jesus knew the character of Simon (John 1:42). He knew what Nathanael was like (John 1:46ff), and He told the Samaritan woman "all things" that she had ever done (John 4:29). He knew that the Jewish leaders did not have God's love in their hearts (John 5:42), and that one of His disciples was not truly a believer (John 6:64). He saw the repentance in the heart of the adulteress (John 8:10-11) and the murder in the hearts of His enemies (John 8:40ff). Several times in the Upper Room message, Jesus revealed to His disciples their own inner feelings and questions.

As you follow our Lord's ministry in John's Gospel, you see Him moving gradually out of the bright light of popularity and into the dark shadows of rejection. At the beginning, it was easy for people to follow the crowd and watch His miracles. But then, His words began to penetrate hearts, with conviction following; and conviction leads either to conversion or opposition. It is impossible to be neutral. People had to decide, and most of them decided against Him.

Yes, Jesus knows the human heart. "Except ye see signs and wonders, ye will not believe" (John 4:48). People who want His works but not His Word can never share His life. "Seeing is believing" is not the Christian approach (John 11:40; 20:29). First we believe; then we see. Miracles can only lead us to the Word (John 5:36-38), and the Word generates saving faith (Rom. 10:17).

Our Lord's accurate knowledge of the human heart is another evidence of His deity, for only God can see the inner person. This brief paragraph prepares us for the important interview with Nicodemus recorded in the next chapter. Note the repetition of the word *man* from John 2:25 to 3:1. Nicodemus wanted to learn more about Jesus, but he ended up learning more about himself!

CHAPTER THREE
A MATTER OF LIFE AND DEATH
John 3

Not only was Benjamin Franklin a great statesman and inventor, but he was also a great correspondent and received letters from famous people from all over the world. One day he received what could well have been the most important letter ever to come to his desk. It was from the well-known British preacher George Whitefield.

"I find that you grow more and more famous in the learned world," Whitefield wrote. "As you have made such progress in investigating the mysteries of electricity, I now humbly urge you to give diligent heed to the mystery of the new birth. It is a most important and interesting study and, when mastered, will richly repay you for your pains."

The new birth is one of the key topics in John 3. In addition, in this chapter we see Jesus Christ in three different roles: the Teacher (John 3:1-21), the Bridegroom (John 3:22-30), and the Witness (John 3:31-36).

Jesus Christ the Teacher (John 3:1-21)

We have already noted the connection between John 2:23-25 and 3:1. Nicodemus was initially attracted to Jesus because of the miracles He did. He wanted to know more about Jesus and the doctrines that He taught. Nicodemus himself was "*the* teacher of the Jews" (John 3:10, literal translation) and he had great respect for the Teacher from Galilee.

Nicodemus was a Pharisee, which meant he lived by the strictest possible religious rules. Not all of the Pharisees were hypocrites (as one may infer from Jesus' comments recorded in Matt. 23), and evidence indicates that

Nicodemus was deeply sincere in his quest for truth. He came to Jesus by night, not because he was afraid of being seen, but most likely because he wanted to have a quiet uninterrupted conversation with the new Teacher "come from God." The fact that Nicodemus used the plural pronoun "we," and Jesus responded with the plural "ye" (John 3:7) may indicate that Nicodemus was representing the religious leaders. He was a man of high moral character, deep religious hunger, and yet profound spiritual blindness.

In order to instruct Nicodemus in the basics of salvation, our Lord used four quite different illustrations.

Birth (vv. 1-7). Our Lord began with that which was familiar, birth being a universal experience. The word translated "again" also means "from above." Though all human beings have experienced natural birth on earth, if they expect to go to heaven, they must experience a supernatural spiritual birth from above.

Once again,. we meet with the blindness of sinners: this well-educated religious leader, Nicodemus, did not understand what the Saviour was talking about! Jesus was speaking about a spiritual birth, but Nicodemus thought only of a physical birth. The situation is no different today. When you talk with people about being born again, they often begin to discuss their family's religious heritage, their church membership, religious ceremonies, and so on.

Being a patient teacher, our Lord picked up on Nicodemus' words and further explained the new birth. To be "born of water" is to be born physically ("enter a second time into his mother's womb") but to be born again means to be born of the Spirit. Just as there are two parents for physical birth, so there are two "parents" for spiritual birth: the Spirit of God (John 3:5) and the Word of God (James 1:18; 1 Peter 1:23-25). The Spirit of God takes the Word of God and, when the sinner believes, imparts the life of God.

Jesus was not teaching that the new birth comes through water baptism. In the New Testament, baptism is connected with *death,* not birth; and no amount of physical water can effect a spiritual change in a person. The emphasis in John 3:14-21 is on *believing,* because salvation comes through faith (Eph. 2:8-9). The evidence of salvation is the witness of the Spirit within (Rom. 8:9), and the Spirit enters your life when you believe (Acts 10:43-48; Eph. 1:13-14).

Water baptism is certainly a part of our obedience to Christ and our witness for Christ (Matt. 28:18-20; Acts 2:41). But it must not be made an essential for salvation; otherwise, none of the Old Testament saints was ever saved, nor was the thief on the cross (Luke 23:39-43). In every age, there has been but one way of salvation—faith in God's promise—though the *outward evidence* of that faith has changed from age to age.

Human birth involves travail (John 16:21), and so does the birth from above. Our Saviour had to travail on the cross so that we might become members of the family of God (Isa. 53:11). Concerned believers have to travail in prayer and witness as they seek to lead sinners to Christ (1 Cor. 4:15; Gal. 4:19).

The child inherits the nature of the parents, and so does the child of God. We become "partakers of the divine nature" (2 Peter 1:4). Nature determines appetite, which explains why the Christian has an appetite for the things of God (1 Peter 2:2-3). He has no desire to go back to the foul things of the world that once appealed to him (2 Peter 2:20-22). He feeds on the Word of God and grows into spiritual maturity (Heb. 5:11-14).

Of course, birth involves life; and spiritual birth from above involves *God's* life. John uses the word *life* thirty-six times in his Gospel. The opposite of life is death, and the person who has not believed on Jesus Christ does not have God's life, eternal life, abundant life. *You do not manufacture Christians any more than you manufacture babies!* The only way to enter God's family is through the new birth (John 1:11-13).

Birth involves a future, and we are "born again to a living hope" (1 Peter 1:3, NASB). A newborn baby cannot be arrested because he or she has no past! When you are born again into God's family, your sins are forgiven and forgotten, and your future is bright with a living hope.

Nicodemus must have had a surprised and yet bewildered look on his face, for the Lord had to say, "You must not be surprised that I told you that all of you must be born again" (John 3:7, PH). But Nicodemus was born a Jew! He was a part of God's covenant people! (Rom. 9:4-5) Certainly his birth was better than that of a Gentile or a Samaritan! And his life was exemplary, for he was a faithful Pharisee! He could well understand Jesus telling the *Romans* that they had to be born again, but certainly not the *Jews!*

The wind (vv. 8-13). It is likely that the evening wind was blowing just then as Nicodemus and Jesus sat on the housetop conversing. The word *wind* in both Hebrew and Greek can also be translated "spirit." One of the symbols of the Spirit of God in the Bible is the wind or breath (Job 33:4; John 20:22; Acts 2:2). Like the wind, the Spirit is invisible but powerful; and you cannot explain or predict the movements of the wind.

When Jesus used this symbol, Nicodemus should have readily remembered Ezekiel 37:1-14. The prophet saw a valley full of dead bones; but when he prophesied to the wind, the Spirit came and gave the bones life. Again, it was the combination of the Spirit of God and the Word of God that gave life. The nation of Israel (including Nicodemus and his fellow council members) was dead and hopeless; but in spite of the morality and religion of the people, they needed the life of the Spirit.

The new birth from above is a necessity ("Ye must be born again"), but it is also a mystery. Everyone who is born of the Spirit is like the wind: you cannot fully explain or predict either the wind or the child of God! For that matter, human birth is still a mystery, in spite of all that we know about anatomy and physiology. Each new life is exciting and different.

Nicodemus came "by night," and he was still in the dark! He could not understand the new birth even after Jesus had explained it to him. Our Lord stated clearly that Nicodemus' knowledge of the Old Testament should have given him the light he needed (John 3:10). Alas, "the teacher of the Jews" knew the *facts* recorded in the Scriptures, but he could not understand the *truths.*

What was the problem? For one thing, the religious leaders would not submit to the authority of Christ's witness (John 3:11). We will see this "authority conflict" increase as we continue in our studies. The religious leaders claimed to believe Moses, yet they could not believe Jesus (John 5:37-47). The Pharisees were more concerned about the praise of men than the praise of God (John 12:37-50).

"I have used earthly illustrations," said Jesus, "and you cannot understand. If I began to share the deep spiritual truths, you still would not believe" (John 3:12).

The serpent on the pole (vv. 14-18). The story in Numbers 21:4-9 was certainly familiar to Nicodemus. It is a story of sin, for the nation rebelled against God and had to be punished. God sent fiery serpents that bit the people so that many died. It is also a story of grace, for Moses interceded for the people and God provided a remedy. He told Moses to make a brass serpent and lift it up on a pole for all to see. Any stricken person who looked at the serpent would immediately be healed. So, it is also a story of faith: when the people looked by faith, they were saved.

The verb *lifted up* has a dual meaning: to be crucified (John 8:28; 12:32-34) and to be glorified and exalted. In his Gospel, John points out that our Lord's crucifixion was actually the means of His glorification (John 12:23ff). The cross was not the end of His glory; it was the means of His glory (Acts 2:33).

Much as the serpent was lifted up on that pole, so the Son of God would be lifted up on a cross. Why? To save us from sin and death. In the camp of Israel, the solution to the "serpent problem" was not in killing the serpents, making medicine, pretending they were not there, passing antiserpent laws, or climbing the pole. The answer was in looking by faith at the uplifted serpent.

The whole world has been bitten by sin, and "the wages of sin is death" (Rom. 6:23). God sent His Son to die, not only for Israel, but for a whole world. How is a person born from above? How is he or she saved from eternal perishing? By believing on Jesus Christ; by looking to Him in faith.

On January 6, 1850, a snowstorm almost crippled the city of Colchester, England; and a teenage boy was unable to get to the church he usually attended. So he made his way to a nearby Primitive Methodist chapel, where an ill-prepared layman was substituting for the absent preacher. His text was Isaiah 45:22—"Look unto Me, and be ye saved, all the ends of the earth." For many months this young teenager had been miserable and under deep conviction; but though he had been reared in church (both his father and grandfather were preachers), he did not have the assurance of salvation.

The unprepared substitute minister did not have much to say, so he kept repeating the text. "A man need not go to college to learn to look," he shouted. "Anyone can look—a child can look!" About that time, he saw the visitor sitting to one side, and he pointed at him and said, "Young man, you look very miserable. Young man, look to Jesus Christ!"

The young man did look by faith, and that was how the great preacher Charles Haddon Spurgeon was converted.

The difference between perishing and living, and between condemnation and salvation, is faith in Jesus Christ. Jesus could well have come to this world as a Judge and destroyed every rebellious sinner; but in love, He came to this world as our Saviour, *and He died for us on the cross!* He became the "uplifted serpent." The serpent in Moses' day brought physical life to dying Jews; but Jesus Christ gives eternal life to anyone who trusts Him. He has salvation for a whole world!

Light and darkness (vv. 19-21). This is one of the major images used in this Gospel (John 1:4-13). Why will sinners not come into the "light of life"? Because they love the darkness! They want to persist in their evil deeds, and this keeps them from coming to the light; for the closer the sinner gets to the light, the more his sins are exposed. It is not "intellectual problems" that keep people from trusting Christ; it is the moral and spiritual blindness that keeps them loving the darkness and hating the light.

Please note that Nicodemus finally did "come to the light." He was in the "midnight of confusion" (John 3:1-21), but eventually he came out into the "sunlight of confession" when he identified with Christ at Calvary (John 19:38-42). He realized that the uplifted Saviour was indeed the Son of God.

Jesus the Bridegroom (John 3:22-30)

Until John the Baptist was arrested by Herod and put into prison, his ministry overlapped that of the Lord Jesus. John did not want anyone to follow him; his ministry was to point to the Lamb of God and urge people to trust Him. But when two popular preachers are involved in similar work, it is easy for both friends and enemies to get caught up in competition and comparison.

It appears that some of John's disciples started the argument. It began on doctrinal grounds—the matter of purifying—but soon moved to personal grounds. In John 3:25, some manuscripts read "a Jew" instead of "the Jews." Could this unnamed Jew have possibly been Nicodemus? We cannot say, but it is a possibility.

The matter of purifying was important to the Jews (Mark 7:1-23). Under the Old Testament Law, it was necessary for them to keep themselves ceremonially clean if they were to serve God and please Him. Unfortunately, the Pharisees added so many extra traditions to the Law that the observing of it became a burden.

Without realizing it, John's disciples were putting him into a situation of competing against the Lord Jesus! "All men come to Him!" (John 3:26) sounds like a wail of despair. It is interesting to note that four of the greatest men in the Bible faced this problem of comparison and competition: Moses (Num. 11:26-30), John the Baptist (John 3:26-30), Jesus (Luke 9:46-50), and Paul (Phil. 1:15-18). A leader often suffers more from his zealous disciples than from his critics!

How did John the Baptist handle this controversy? To begin with, he stated a conviction: all ministry and blessing come from God, so there can be no competition (John 3:27). Paul would have agreed with this (1 Cor. 3:1-9; 4:1-7). Our gifts and opportunities come from God, and He alone must get the glory.

Then John used a beautiful illustration. He compared Jesus to the bridegroom and himself only to the best man (John 3:29). Once the bridegroom and bride had been brought together, the work of the best man was completed. What a foolish thing it would be for the best man to try to "upstage" the bridegroom and take his place. John's joy was to hear the voice of the Bridegroom and know that He had claimed His bride.

Even before his birth, John the Baptist rejoiced in the Lord (Luke 1:44). John was content to be the voice announcing Jesus to be the Word (John 1:23). Jesus was the Light, and John the Baptist was the witness pointing to the Light (John 1:6-8).

Often press releases and book reviews cross my desk, along with conference folders; and at times I am perturbed by what I read. Very few speakers and writers are ordinary people. They are "world travelers" or "noted lecturers" who have addressed "huge audiences." They are always in "great demand," and their ministries are described in such ways that they make the Apostle Paul a midget by comparison.

A Presbyterian pastor in Melbourne, Australia introduced J. Hudson Taylor by using many superlatives, especially the word *great.* Taylor stepped to the pulpit and quietly said, "Dear friends, I am the little servant of an illustrious Master." If John the Baptist in heaven heard that statement, he must have shouted "Hallelujah!"

The image of the Bridegroom would have been significant to the Jewish people, for Jehovah had a "marriage covenant" with the nation (Isa. 54:5; 62:4ff; Jer. 2:2; 3:20; Ezek. 16:8; Hosea 2:19ff). Alas, Israel had been unfaithful to her vows, and God had to put her away temporarily. Today, God is calling out a people for His name, the church, the bride of Christ (2 Cor. 11:1-3; Eph. 5:22-33). One day the Bridegroom will come to claim His bride and take her to her home in heaven (Rev. 19:6-9; 21:9ff).

The word *must* is used in three significant ways in this chapter. There is the "must" of the sinner (John 3:7), the "must" of the Saviour (John 3:14), and the "must" of the servant (John 3:30).

Jesus the Witness (John 3:31-36)

Bible scholars do not agree as to who is speaking in John 3:31-36, John the apostle or John the Baptist. For that matter, some students believe that John 3:16-21 came from the Apostle John and not the Lord Jesus. There were no quotation marks in early manuscripts, but since all Scripture is inspired, it really makes little difference who said the words.

The emphasis in this paragraph is on witness ("testimony"), one of the key subjects in John's Gospel. The Greek word translated "witness" or "testimony" is used forty-seven times. John bore witness to Jesus (John 1:7; 5:33), but Jesus was also a witness to the truth. Why should we heed His witness? For several reasons.

He came from heaven (v. 31). He was not simply called from heaven, or empowered by heaven; He *came* from heaven. It was this claim that the Jews disputed, because they knew it was His claim that He was God (John 6:38-42). John the Baptist certainly was not "from above," nor did he claim to be. No earthly messenger of God came "from above." Only Jesus Christ can make that claim and prove it to be true.

Since Jesus came from heaven, He represents the Father; and to reject His witness is to reject the Father (John 5:23). We know that His witness is true because He is the true God. We can trust it and rely on it.

It comes from Him firsthand (vv. 32-33). He shares what He has seen and heard from the Father (John 8:38). Those who receive His witness *and act on it* know by personal experience that His witness is true (John 7:17). Our Lord's teachings are not to be studied intellectually, separated from everyday life. It is when we obey His Word and put it into practice that we see its truth and experience its power.

The Father has authorized His Son (vv. 34-35). God sent Him (another key theme in John's Gospel); God gave Him the Word; God gave Him the Spirit; and God gave Him all things (John 13:3). What a commissioning! To reject the Son's witness is to rebel against the highest authority in the universe.

We usually think of God's love for a lost world (John 3:16), but John reminds us of the Father's love for His Son. Jesus is the Father's "beloved Son" (Matt. 3:17; Mark 1:11; Luke 3:22). Because the Father loves the Son, He has given Him all things, and He shows Him all things (John 5:20). It is a love that can hold nothing back.

Therefore, when we receive His witness, we share in His love and His wealth. To reject Christ's witness is to sin against love and light. No wonder our Lord wept over the city of Jerusalem (Matt. 23:37-39). They had rejected His witness—both His messages and His miracles—and their rejection led to judgment.

We might escape the wrath of God (v. 36). This is the only place in any of John's epistles or his Gospel that he uses the word *wrath.* (He uses it six times in the Book of Revelation.) This verse parallels John 3:18 and makes it clear that there can be no neutrality when it comes to the witness of Jesus Christ: we either trust Him or we reject Him.

"Everlasting life" does not simply mean eternity in heaven. The believer possesses that life right now! It is the life of God in the believer. The opposite of eternal life is eternal death, the wrath of God. A person does not have to die and go to hell to be under the wrath of God. "He that believeth not is condemned already" (John 3:18). The verdict has already been given, but the sentence has not yet been executed. Why? Because God is patient and long-suffering, and continues to call sinners to repentance (2 Peter 3:9).

As you review John 3, you can see that the Apostle John is emphasizing a personal relationship with Jesus Christ.

It is a *living relationship* that begins with the new birth, the birth from above. When we receive Jesus Christ into our lives, we share His very life and become children in the family of God.

It is also a *loving relationship,* for He is the Bridegroom and we are a part of the bride. Like John the Baptist, we desire that Jesus Christ increase as we decrease. He must receive all the honor and glory.

It is a *learning relationship,* for He is the faithful Witness who shares God's truth with us. What a delight it is to receive His Word, meditate on it, and make it part of our very lives.

But we must never forget the cost of these blessings. For us to be born into God's family, Jesus Christ had to die. For us to enter into the loving relationship of salvation, He had to endure the hatred and condemnation of men. He had to be lifted up on the cross so that we might experience forgiveness and eternal life.

May we never take this for granted!

"He must increase, but I must decrease" (John 3:30).

CHAPTER FOUR
THE BAD SAMARITAN
John 4

In John 4, our Lord ministers to a variety of people: the sinful Samaritan woman, His own disciples, the many Samaritans who trusted in Him, and finally, a nobleman and his household. What did these have in common? *Faith* in Jesus Christ. John was fulfilling the purpose of his Gospel in showing his readers how various kinds and classes of people came to believe in Jesus as the Son of God.

Let's meet these various persons and discover how their faith began, how it grew, and what it did for them and for others.

The Samaritan Woman (John 4:1-30)

Because the Pharisees were trying to incite competition between Jesus and John the Baptist (John 3:25-30), Jesus left Judea and started north for Galilee. He could have taken one of three possible routes: along the coast, across the Jordan and up through Perea, or straight through Samaria. Orthodox Jews avoided Samaria because there was a longstanding, deep-seated hatred between them and the Samaritans.

The Samaritans were a mixed race, part Jew and part Gentile, that grew out of the Assyrian captivity of the ten northern tribes in 727 B.C. Rejected by the Jews because they could not prove their genealogy, the Samaritans established their own temple and religious services on Mt. Gerizim. This only fanned the fires of prejudice. So intense was their dislike of the Samaritans that some of the Pharisees prayed that no Samaritan would be raised in the resurrection! When His enemies wanted to call Jesus an insulting name, they called Him a Samaritan (John 8:48).

Because He was on a divinely appointed schedule, it was necessary that Jesus go through Samaria. Why? Because He would meet a woman there and lead her into saving faith, the kind of true faith that would affect an entire village. Our Lord was no respecter of persons. Earlier, He counseled a moral Jewish man (John 3), and now He would witness to an immoral Samaritan woman!

He arrived at Jacob's well at 6 o'clock in the evening, the usual time for women to come for water. The disciples went to the nearby town for food while Jesus deliberately waited at the well. He was weary, hungry, and thirsty. John not only presents Jesus as the Son of God but also as true man. Our Lord entered into all the normal experiences of our lives and is able to identify with us in each of them.

As you read our Lord's interview with this woman, notice how her knowledge of Jesus increases until she acknowledges that He is the Christ. There were four stages in this experience.

He is "a Jew" (vv. 7-10). In that day, it was not considered proper for any man, especially a rabbi, to speak in public to a strange woman (John 4:27). But our Lord set social customs aside because a soul's eternal salvation was at stake. It certainly surprised her when He asked for a drink of water. She surmised that He was a Jewish rabbi, and perhaps she tried to "read between the lines" to find another meaning to His request. What was He *really* seeking?

The information in John's parenthesis at the end of John 4:9 was for the benefit of his Gentile readers. Since the disciples had gone into the city to purchase food, it is obvious that the Jews did have *some* "dealings" with the Samaritans; so John was not trying to exaggerate. The phrase can be translated "ask no favors from the Samaritans" or "use no vessels in common with the Samaritans." Why would Jesus, a Jew, want to use her "polluted" vessel to get a drink of water?

Of course, our Lord's request was simply a way to open the conversation and share with her the truth about "living water." Whenever He witnessed to people, Jesus did not use a "sales talk" that He adapted to meet every situation. To Nicodemus, He spoke about new birth; but to this woman, He spoke about living water.

Jesus pointed out to her that she was ignorant of three important facts: Who He was, what He had to offer, and how she could receive it. Here was eternal God speaking to her, offering her eternal life! The Samaritans were as blind as the Jews (John 1:26). But our Lord's words had aroused her interest, so she pursued the conversation.

"Greater than Jacob" (vv. 11-15). Jesus was speaking about spiritual water, but she interpreted His words to mean literal water. Again, we see how easily people confuse the material and the spiritual. Furthermore, this woman was concerned about *how* He would obtain this water, instead of simply asking Him to give her a drink of it.

Of course Jesus *is* greater than Jacob—and greater than the well itself! To paraphrase His reply: "Whosoever *continues to drink* of this material water (or anything the world has to offer) will thirst again. But whosoever *takes one drink* of the water I give will never thirst again!" (see John 4:13-14) How true it is that the things of this world never completely satisfy. In hell today, people are crying, "I thirst!"

We have noted before that *life* is one of John's key concepts. He uses the word at least thirty-six times. Campbell Morgan has pointed out that mankind needs air, water, and food in order to have life. (We might also add that he needs light.) All of these are provided in Jesus Christ. He provides the "breath" (Spirit) of God (John 3:8; 20:22). He is the Bread of Life (John 6:48) and the Light of Life (John 1:4-5), and He gives us the water of life.

The woman's immediate response was to ask for this gift, but she did not know what she was saying. The seed of the Word fell on shallow soil, and the shoots that sprang up had no root (Matt. 13:20-21). She had made progress, but she still had a long way to go; so Jesus patiently dealt with her.

"A prophet" (vv. 16-24). The only way to prepare the soil of the heart for the seed is to plow it up with conviction. That was why Jesus told her to go get her husband: He forced her to admit her sin. There can be no conversion without conviction. There must first be conviction and repentance, and then there can be saving faith. Jesus had aroused her mind and stirred her emotions, but He also had to touch her conscience, and that meant dealing with her sin.

"I have no husband" was the shortest statement she made during the entire conversation! Why? Because now she was under conviction and her "mouth was stopped" (Rom. 3:19). But this was the best thing that could have happened to her!

However, instead of listening to Jesus, she tried to get Him on a "detour" by discussing the differences between the Jewish and the Samaritan religions. It is much more comfortable to discuss religion than to face one's sins! However, Jesus once again revealed her spiritual ignorance: she did not know who to worship, where to worship, or how to worship! He made it clear that all religions are not equally acceptable before God, that some worshipers act in ignorance and unbelief.

The only faith that God will accept is that which came through the Jews. The Bible is of Jewish origin, and our Saviour was a Jew. The first Christians were Jews. A religious worker in an airport told me that the world's deliverer came from Korea, but Jesus said, "Salvation is of the Jews." Only those who have the indwelling Holy Spirit, and who obey the truth, can worship God acceptably.

It was a devastating statement to say that worship would no longer be limited to the Jewish temple. This ties in with John 2:19-21 and also Stephen's statement in Acts 7:48-50. John's Gospel clearly reveals that there is a new sacrifice (John 1:29), a new temple (John 2:19-21; 4:20-24), a new birth (John 3:1-7), and a new water (John 4:11). Jews reading this Gospel should realize that God has established in Jesus Christ a whole new economy. The Old Covenant Law has been fulfilled and set aside.

"The Christ" (vv. 25-30). In spite of her ignorance, there was one truth this woman did know: the Messiah was coming and would reveal the secrets of hearts. Where did she learn this truth? We do not know, but that seed had lain buried in her heart until that very hour, and now it was going to bear fruit. Our Lord's response to her statement was, literally: "I that speak to thee, I am!" He dared to utter the holy name of God!

At this point, the woman put her faith in Jesus Christ and was converted. Immediately she wanted to share her faith with others, so she went into the village and told the men she had met the Christ. When you consider how little spiritual truth this woman knew, her zeal and witness put us to shame. But God used her simple testimony, and many of the people came out to the well to meet Jesus. The rabbis said, "It is better that the words of the Law be burned than be delivered to a woman!" But Jesus did not agree with that narrow prejudice.

Why did she leave her waterpot when she hurried into the city? For one thing, she had the living water within and was now satisfied. Also, she intended to come back; and perhaps in the interim, the disciples and Jesus could use the vessel to satisfy their thirst. Gone were the racial barriers and battles that had existed before! They were all one in faith and love!

This woman did not come to faith in Christ immediately. Jesus was patient with her, and in this, He sets a good example for us in our own personal work. Certainly she was the least likely prospect for salvation, yet God used her to win almost an entire village!

The Disciples (John 4:31-38)

When the disciples returned from obtaining food, they were shocked that Jesus was conversing with a woman, and especially a Samaritan; but they did not interrupt. They were learning that their Master knew what He was doing and did not need their counsel. But, after the woman left, they urged Jesus to share the meal with them, because they knew that He was hungry.

"I have food to eat that ye know not of" was His reply and, as usual, they did not understand it. They thought He was speaking of literal food, and they wondered where He got it. Then He explained that doing the Father's will—in this case, leading the woman to salvation—was true nourishment for His soul. The disciples were satisfied with bread, but He was satisfied with accomplishing the Father's work.

"Seek your life's nourishment in your life's work," said Phillips Brooks. The will of God ought to be a source of strength and satisfaction to the child of God, just as if he sat down to a sumptuous feast. If what we are doing tears us down instead of builds us up, then we may well question whether it is the will of God for us.

Our Lord did not look on the Father's will as a heavy burden or a distasteful task. He viewed His work as the very nourishment of His soul. Doing the Father's will fed Him and satisfied Him inwardly. "I delight to do Thy will, O my God; yea, Thy Law is within my heart" (Ps. 40:8). The Samaritan woman was now doing the Father's will and finding excitement and enrichment in it.

Jesus then changed the image from that of food to that of the harvest, which is the source of the food. He quoted the familiar Jewish proverb about waiting for the harvest, and then pointed to the villagers even then coming out to the well to meet Him, thanks to the witness of the woman. The disciples went into the village to get food for themselves, but they did no evangelizing. The woman took their place!

The image of the harvest is a familiar one in the Bible and is often applied to the ministry of winning lost souls. Both the Parable of the Sower and the Parable of the Tares (Matt. 13:1-30) relate to this theme, and Paul used it in his letters (Rom. 1:13; 1 Cor. 3:6-9; Gal. 6:9). We plant the seed of God's Word in the hearts of people who hear it, and we seek to cultivate that seed by our love and prayers. In due time, that seed may bear fruit to the glory of God.

No doubt the disciples had said, as they approached the city of Sychar, "There can be no harvest here! These people despise us Jews and would have no use for our message." But just the opposite was true: the harvest was ready and only needed faithful workers to claim it. For some reason, when it comes to witnessing for Christ, it is always the wrong time and the wrong place! It takes faith to sow the seed, and we must do it even when the circumstances look discouraging. Read Ecclesiastes 11:4 and take it to heart!

There is no competition in the Lord's harvest. Each of us has an assigned task and we are all a part of each other's labors (1 Cor. 3:6-9). One sows, one reaps; but each worker gets his honest reward for the work he has done.

John 4:38 indicates that others had labored in Samaria and had prepared the way for this harvest. We do not know who these faithful workers were, nor do we need to know; for God will reward them. Perhaps some of these people had heard John the Baptist preach, or perhaps some of John's followers had reached into this difficult field. Some archeologists have located "Aenon near Salim" where John baptized (John 3:23) near the biblical Shechem, which is close to Sychar and Jacob's well. If this is the case, then John the Baptist prepared the soil and planted the seed, and Jesus and the disciples reaped the harvest. Of course, the woman herself planted some of the seed through her witness to the men.

The disciples were learning a valuable lesson that would encourage them in the years to come. They were not alone in the work of the Lord, and they must never look on any opportunity for witness as wasted time and energy. It takes faith to plow the soil and plant the seed, but God has promised a harvest (Ps. 126:5-6; Gal. 6:9). In a few years, Peter and John would participate in another harvest among the Samaritans (Acts 8:5-25). Those who sow may not see the harvest, but those who reap will see it and give thanks for the faithful labors of the sowers.

The Greek word translated "labor" in John 4:38 is translated "wearied" in John 4:6. Sowing, cultivating, and harvesting are difficult tasks, not only in the physical realm, but also in the spiritual. There is no place in the harvest for lazy people. The work is too difficult and the laborers are too few.

The Samaritans (John 4:39-42)

Many of the Samaritans believed because of the testimony of the woman, and then many more believed when they heard Jesus personally. So excited were they about Him that they begged Him to stay with them; and He stayed for two days. During that short time, His word produced fruit in their lives.

It is important that new converts be grounded in the Word—the Bible. These Samaritans began their spiritual walk by trusting in what the woman said, but they soon learned to trust the Word taught by the Saviour. Theirs was no "secondhand" salvation. They knew that they were saved because they had believed His message. "Now we know!" was their happy testimony.

You would have thought that these Samaritans would have been narrow in their faith, seeing Jesus as the Saviour of the Jews and the Samaritans. But they declared that He was "the Saviour of the world" (John 4:42). They had been converted only a few days, but they already had a missionary vision! In fact, their vision was wider than that of the Apostles!

It is interesting to trace our Lord's movements that brought Him to Samaria. He was in Jerusalem (John 2:23) and then came into Judea (John 3:22). From Judea He went into Samaria (John 4:4), and the Samaritans declared Him to be "the Saviour of the world." This is a perfect parallel to Acts 1:8—"And ye shall be witnesses unto Me both in Jerusalem, and in all Judea, and in Samaria, and unto the uttermost part of the earth." Our Lord has set the example. If we follow, He will give us the harvest.

This unnamed Samaritan woman was a fruitful believer: she bore fruit ("many believed"), more fruit ("many more believed"), and today continues to bear "much fruit" to the glory of God (see John 15:1-5). Nobody knows how many lost sinners have come to the Saviour because of the witness of this woman recorded in John 4.

The Nobleman (John 4:43-54)

Our Lord continued His journey to Galilee (John 4:3) and came again to Cana. Galilee was known as *"Galil ha goyim*—Galilee of the Gentiles." Apparently Jesus had detected in Judea (His own country) the increasing hostility of the religious leaders, though the real opposition would not yet appear for some months. Our Lord was really never identified with Judea even though He had been born in Bethlehem. He was known as the Prophet from Galilee (Matt. 21:11; John 7:52). Jesus knew that the public response to His ministry in Jerusalem had been insincere and shallow (John 2:23-25), and that it was not honoring to Him at all.

Why did Jesus return to Cana? Perhaps He wanted to cultivate the "seed" He had planted there when He attended the wedding feast. Nathanael came from Cana, so perhaps there was a personal reason for this visit. Jesus was met at Cana by a nobleman from Capernaum, some twenty miles away. The man had heard about His miracles and came all that distance to intercede for his son who was dying. The first miracle at Cana came at the request of His mother (John 2:1-5), and this second miracle at Cana at the request of a father (John 4:47).

Was this man a Jew or a Gentile? We do not know. Nor do we know his exact position in the government. He may have been a member of Herod's court; but whatever his national or social standing, he was clearly at his wit's end and desperately needed the help of the Saviour. He "kept beseeching Him" to travel to Capernaum to heal his son.

John 4:48 was not a rebuke of this nobleman. Rather, it was our Lord's lament at the spiritual condition of the people in general, both in Judea and Galilee. "Seeing is believing" has always been the "pragmatic" philosophy of the lost world, even the religious world. The nobleman believed that Jesus could heal his son, but he made two mistakes in his thinking: that Jesus had to go to Capernaum to save the lad, and that if the boy died meanwhile, it was too late.

We must admire this man's faith. Jesus simply said, "Go thy way; thy son liveth" (John 4:50). And the man believed Jesus and started to return home! Both the Samaritan woman and this anonymous nobleman must have rejoiced the heart of Jesus as they believed the word and acted on it.

The boy was healed the instant Jesus spoke those words; so the man's servants started out to find him so they could share the good news. (Again, it is the servants who know what is going on. See John 2:9; 15:15.) The boy had been healed at the seventh hour, which, in Roman time, would be 7 o'clock in the evening. The father certainly would not have traveled at night, for that would have been dangerous; nor would the servants have taken that risk. The father's faith was so strong that he was willing to delay going home, even though his heart yearned to see his beloved son.

When the father and the servants met the next day, their report confirmed his faith. Note that the father thought the healing would be gradual ("began to improve"); but the servants reported a complete, instant recovery.

This man began with *crisis faith*. He was about to lose his son and he had no other recourse but the Lord Jesus Christ. Many people came to Jesus with their crises, and He did not turn them away. The nobleman's crisis faith became *confident* faith: he believed the Word and had peace in his heart. He was even able to delay his trip home, knowing that the boy was out of danger.

His confident faith became *confirmed* faith. Indeed, the boy had been completely healed! And the healing took place at the very time when Jesus spoke the Word. It was this fact that made a believer out of the nobleman and his household. He believed that Jesus was the Christ, the Son of God; and he shared this faith with his family. He had *contagious* faith and shared his experience with others.

This is one of several miracles that Jesus performed "at a distance." He healed the centurion's servant from a distance (Matt. 8:5-13, and note that he too lived in Capernaum), and He healed the daughter of the Canaanite woman in the same manner (Matt. 15:21-28). These two were Gentiles and, spiritually speaking, were "at a distance" (Eph. 2:12-13). Perhaps this nobleman was also a Gentile. We do not know.

John 4:54 does not state that this healing was the second miracle that Jesus ever performed, for that would contradict John 2:23 and 3:2. This was the second miracle He performed *in Cana of Galilee* (see John 2:1, 11). He certainly gave those people special privileges.

But we must note that both miracles were "private" rather than public. Mary, the disciples, and the servants knew where the excellent wine had come from, but the guests did not. (Of course, it is possible that the servants told the story to others.) The nobleman's son was healed at Capernaum, not Cana; but news traveled rapidly in those days and certainly the word got out.

Jesus' first miracle at the wedding revealed His power over *time*. The Father is always making water into wine, but He takes a season or two to finish the work. Jesus made the wine instantly. In this sense, our Lord's miracles were only *instantaneous* copies of what the Father is always doing. "My Father worketh hitherto, and I work" (John 5:17). The Father is constantly multiplying bread, season after season, but the Son multiplied it instantly.

In the second recorded miracle, Jesus showed His power over *space*. He was not limited simply because He was in Cana and the sick boy was in Capernaum. The fact that the father believed the word and did not know the results until the next day is evidence that he had confident faith. He trusted the word that Jesus spoke, and so should we.

CHAPTER FIVE
THE MAN WHO WAS EQUAL WITH GOD
John 5

Our Lord's first two miracles recorded by John were somewhat private in nature. The servants and the disciples knew that He transformed the water into wine, and the servants and the nobleman's family knew that He had healed the sick son. The miracle recorded in John 5 was not only public, but it was performed on the Sabbath Day and incited the opposition of the religious leaders. We see here the beginning of "official persecution" against the Saviour.

There are three exciting "acts" in this drama.

The Cure (John 5:1-15)

When you visit St. Anne's Church in Jerusalem, they will show you the deep excavation that has revealed the ancient Pool of Bethesda. The Hebrew name *Bethesda* has been spelled various ways and given differing meanings. Some say it means "house of mercy" or "house of grace," but others say it means "place of the two outpourings." There is historical and archeological evidence that two adjacent pools of water served this area in ancient times.

The pool is situated near the northeast corner of the Old City, close to the Sheep Gate (Neh. 3:1; 12:39). Perhaps John saw some spiritual significance to this location, for he had already told his readers that Jesus Christ is "the Lamb of God" (John 1:29).

We do not know which feast Jesus was observing when He went to Jerusalem, and it is not important that we know. His main purpose for going was not to maintain a religious tradition but to heal a man and use the miracle as the basis for a message to the people. The miracle illustrated what He said in John 5:24—the power of His Word and the gift of life.

While it is true that some manuscripts omit the end of John 5:3 and all of verse 4, it is also true that the event (and the man's words in John 5:7) would make little sense if these words are eliminated. Why would anybody, especially a man sick for so many years, remain in one place if nothing special were occurring? You would think that after thirty-eight years of nothing happening to *anybody,* the man would go elsewhere and stop hoping! It seems wisest for us to accept the fact that something extraordinary kept all these handicapped people at this pool, hoping for a cure.

John described these people as "impotent, blind, lame, paralyzed." What havoc sin has wrought in this world! But the healing of these infirmities was one of the prophesied ministries of the Messiah (Isa. 35:3-6). Had the religious leaders known their own Scriptures, they would have recognized their Redeemer; but they were spiritually blind.

No matter how you look at this miracle, it is an illustration of the grace of God. It was grace that brought Jesus to the Pool of Bethesda, for who would want to mingle with a crowd of helpless people! Jesus did not heal all of them; He singled out one man and healed him. The fact that Jesus came to the man, spoke to him, healed him, and then met him later in the temple is proof of His wonderful grace and mercy.

John noted that the man had been ill for thirty-eight years. Perhaps he saw in this a picture of his own Jewish nation that had wandered in the wilderness for thirty-eight years (Deut. 2:14). Spiritually speaking, Israel was a nation of impotent people, waiting hopelessly for something to happen.

Jesus knew about the man (see John 2:23-24) and asked him if he wanted to be healed. You would think that the man would have responded with an enthusiastic, "Yes! I want to be healed!" But, instead, he began to give excuses! He had been in that sad condition for so long that his will was as paralyzed as his body. But if you compare John 5:6 with verse 40, you will see that Jesus had a spiritual lesson in mind as well. Indeed, this man did illustrate the tragic spiritual state of the nation.

The Lord healed him through the power of His spoken word. He commanded the man to do the very thing he was unable to do, but in His command was the power of fulfillment (see Mark 3:5; Heb. 4:12). The cure was immediate and certainly some of the many people at the pool must have witnessed it. Jesus did not pause to heal anyone else; instead, He "moved away" (John 5:13) so as not to create a problem. (The Greek word means "to dodge.")

The miracle would have caused no problem except that it occurred on the Sabbath Day. Our Lord certainly could have come a day earlier, or even waited a day; but He wanted to get the attention of the religious leaders. Later, He would deliberately heal a blind man on the Sabbath (John 9:1-14). The scribes had listed thirty-nine tasks that were prohibited on the Sabbath, and carrying a burden was one of them. Instead of rejoicing at the wonderful deliverance of the man, the religious leaders condemned him for carrying his bed and thereby breaking the law.

It is not easy to understand the relationship between this man and Jesus. There is no evidence that he believed on Christ and was converted, yet we cannot say that he was opposed to the Saviour. In fact, he did not even know who it was that healed him until Jesus met him in the temple. No doubt the man went there to give thanks to God and to offer the appropriate sacrifices. It seems strange that the man did not actively seek a closer relationship with the One who healed him, but more than one person has gratefully accepted the gift and ignored the Giver.

Did the man "inform" on Jesus because of fear? We do not know. The Jewish leaders at least turned from him and aimed their accusations at Jesus Christ; and, unlike the healed blind man in John 9, this man was not excommunicated. The Lord's words (John 5:14) suggest that the man's physical plight had been the result of sin; but Jesus did not say that the man's sins had been forgiven as He did in dealing with the sick man lowered through the roof (see Mark 2:1-12). It is possible to experience an exciting miracle and still not be saved and go to heaven!

The Controversy (John 5:16-18)

The Jewish leaders did not prosecute the man who was healed, even though he had broken the law; but they did begin to persecute the Lord Jesus. As the guardians of the faith, the members of the Jewish Sanhedrin (the religious ruling council) had the responsibility of investigating new preachers and teachers who appeared in the land, lest some false prophet come along and lead the people astray. They had looked into the ministry of John the Baptist (John 1:19ff) and more recently had been scrutinizing the ministry of Jesus.

Jesus had healed a demoniac on the Sabbath (Luke 4:31-37), so the Sanhedrin was already suspicious. In the days following the miracle recorded in John 5, Jesus would defend His disciples for picking grain on the Sabbath (Matt. 12:1-8), and would heal a man's withered hand on the Sabbath (Matt. 12:9-14). He deliberately challenged the legalistic traditions of the scribes and Pharisees. They had taken the Sabbath—God's gift to man—and had transformed it into a prison house of regulations and restrictions.

When they confronted Jesus with His unlawful conduct, He simply replied that He was doing only what His Father was doing! God's Sabbath rest had been broken by man's sin (see Gen. 3); and ever since the fall of man, God has been seeking lost sinners and saving them. But when Jesus said "My Father" instead of the usual "our Father," used by the Jews, He claimed to be equal with God.

The Jewish leaders instantly understood His claim, and they changed their accusation from that of Sabbath-breaking to blasphemy, because Jesus claimed to be God. Liberal theologians who say that Jesus never claimed to be God have a difficult time with this passage.

Of course, the penalty for such blasphemy was death. It is here that the "official persecution" of Jesus began, culminating in His crucifixion. In the days that followed, our Lord often confronted His enemies with their evil desire to kill Him (John 7:19, 25; 8:37, 59). They hated Him without a cause (John 15:18-25). They ignored the good deeds that He performed for the helpless and hopeless, and centered their attention on destroying Him.

Jesus made Himself equal with God because He is God. This is the theme of John's Gospel. The Jewish leaders could not disprove His claims, so they tried to destroy Him and get Him out of the way. Both in His crucifixion and His resurrection, Jesus openly affirmed His deity and turned His enemies' weapons against them.

British writer George MacDonald pointed out that John 5:17 gives us a profound insight into our Lord's miracles. Jesus did *instantly* what the Father is always doing slowly. For example, in nature, as mentioned earlier, the Father is slowly turning water into wine; but Jesus did it instantly. Through the powers in nature, the Father is healing broken bodies; but Jesus healed them immediately. Nature is repeatedly multiplying bread, from sowing to harvest; but Jesus multiplied it instantly in His own hands.

The Claims (John 5:19-47)

In response to their accusations, Jesus made three significant claims that proved His sonship.

He claimed to be equal with God (vv. 19-23). Instead of denying their accusation, He endorsed it! If today a man made this kind of a claim, we would conclude that he was joking or mentally disturbed. Jesus was certainly not insane, and there is every evidence that He was deadly serious when He spoke these words. Either He is what He claims to be, or He is a liar; and if He is a liar, how do you explain all the good He has done in the lives of needy people? Nobody wants to trust a liar; Jesus' disciples were willing to die for Him.

Jesus claimed to be one with His Father in *His works*. If healing a man on the Sabbath was a sin, then the Father was to blame! Jesus did nothing "of Himself " but only that which the Father was doing. The Father and the Son worked together, doing the same deeds in the same way. "I and the Father are One" (John 10:30).

When our Lord came to earth as man, He submitted Himself to the Father in everything. "Lo, I come to do Thy will, O God" (Heb. 10:9). He veiled His glory and laid aside the independent exercise of His divine attributes. In the wilderness, Satan tempted Him to use His divine powers for Himself; but He refused to act independently. He was totally dependent on the Father and the power of the Holy Spirit of God.

Not only did the Father show the Son His works and enable Him to do them, but the Father also shared His love (John 5:20). The first three Gospels open with the Father calling Jesus "My beloved Son," and John echoed this statement in John 3:35. We usually think of the Father's love for the lost world, as in John 3:16; but we must also remember the Father's love for His dear Son.

Because the Father loves the Son, the Father shows Him His works. The blind religious leaders could not see what Jesus was doing, because they did not know the Father or the Son. In fact, even greater works were in the Father's plan, works that would cause them to marvel. Perhaps He had in mind the healing of Lazarus; for in John 5:21, He mentioned the raising of the dead.

For Jesus to claim to have power to raise the dead was a blasphemous thing in the eyes of the Jewish leaders; they gave that power to God alone. They said that Jehovah held the three great keys: the key to open the heavens and give rain (Deut. 28:12); the key to open the womb and give conception (Gen. 30:22); and the key to open the grave and raise the dead (Ezek. 37:13). As far as the Gospel records are concerned, Jesus had not yet raised anyone from the dead; so to make this claim was to invite even more opposition.

John 5:21 certainly can mean much more than the physical raising of people from the dead, for certainly Jesus was referring to His gift of spiritual life to the spiritually dead. He amplified this truth further as recorded in John 5:24-29.

So, Jesus claimed to be equal with the Father in His works, but He also claimed to be equal with the Father in *executing judgment* (John 5:22). To the orthodox Jew, Jehovah God was "the Judge of all the earth" (Gen. 18:25); and no one dared to apply that august title to himself. But Jesus did! By claiming to be the Judge, He claimed to be God. "Because He [God] hath appointed a day in the which He will judge the world in righteousness by that Man whom He hath ordained" (Acts 17:31).

Our Lord claimed equality in another area, namely, *equal honor with the Father* (John 5:23). The fact that He is the appointed Judge should cause men to honor Him. What a tremendous claim: if you do not honor the Son, you are not honoring the Father! The "religious" people who say that they worship God, but who deny the deity of Christ, have neither the Father nor the Son! Apart from Jesus Christ, we cannot know the Father, worship the Father, or serve the Father.

He claimed to have authority to raise the dead (vv. 24-29). For a second time, Jesus introduced His words with the solemn "verily, verily" (see John 5:19, 24-25). More than twenty times in John's Gospel you will find Jesus using this solemn form of address. It is as though He was saying, "Pay attention to this! What I am about to say is important!"

In this fascinating paragraph, Jesus spoke about four different resurrections. He described the resurrection of lost sinners into eternal life (see John 5:24-25; Eph. 2:1-10). The lost sinner is as lifeless and helpless as a corpse. No matter how an undertaker may prepare a corpse, it is still dead; and no corpse is "deader" than any other corpse. If you are dead, you are dead! The lost sinner is helpless to save himself and he certainly cannot give himself life.

How are dead sinners raised from the dead? By hearing God's Word and believing on God's Son. Jesus healed the paralyzed man at the pool by His word (John 5:8). Each time He raised somebody from the dead, He spoke the word (Luke 7:11-17; 8:49-56; John 11:41-44). His Word is "living and powerful" (Heb. 4:12) and can raise sinners from spiritual death. "Everlasting life" means that they can never die spiritually again, nor can they ever come into judgment (Rom. 8:1). To hear His Word and believe means salvation; to reject His Word means condemnation (John 12:48).

The second resurrection mentioned is the resurrection of our Lord Himself (John 5:26). Our life is derived, but His life is original, "in Himself." "In Him was life" (John 1:4). The grave could not hold Him because He is "the Prince of Life" (Acts 2:24; 3:15). Jesus laid down His life and then took it up again (John 10:17-18). Because He has life in Himself, He can share that life with all who will trust Him.

The third resurrection named is the future resurrection of life, when believers are raised from the dead (John 5:28-29a). This wonderful truth is explained in 1 Thessalonians 4:13-18 and 1 Corinthians 15. Keep in mind that resurrection is not reconstruction. It does not imply that God "puts the pieces back together again." The resurrection body is a new body, a glorified body, suited to the new heavenly environment. Death is not the end for the believer, nor will he live in heaven as a disembodied spirit. God saves the whole person, and this includes the body (Rom. 8:23; Phil. 3:20-21). This resurrection of life will take place when Jesus Christ returns in the air and calls His people to Himself.

The fourth resurrection He mentioned is the resurrection of condemnation (John 5:29b). This resurrection involves only the lost, and it will take place just before Jesus Christ ushers in the new heaven and the new earth (Rev. 20:11-15). What an awesome event that will be, when the dead "small and great" stand before Jesus Christ! The Father has committed all judgment to the Son (John 5:22) and has given Him the authority to execute judgment (John 5:27). Today Jesus Christ is the Saviour, but one day He shall sit as the Judge.

The title "Son of man" used in John 5:27 refers to Daniel 7:13-14 and is a definite messianic title. It is used twelve times in John's Gospel and over eighty times in all four Gospels. The Jews would know this title from their reading of the Book of Daniel; and they would know that, by using it, Jesus was claiming to be the Messiah, and the Judge.

Believers will be given resurrection bodies so that they might reign with Christ in glory. Unbelievers will be given resurrection bodies—but not glorified bodies—that they might be judged and then suffer punishment in those bodies. Bodies that were used for sin will suffer the consequences of that sin.

The fact that Jesus has the authority to raise the dead is proof that He is equal with the Father, and therefore He is God.

He claimed that there are valid witnesses who support His claim to deity (vv. 30-47). The word *witness* is a key word in John's Gospel; it is used forty-seven times. Jesus did bear witness to Himself, but He knew they would not accept it; so He called in three other witnesses.

The first was John the Baptist (John 5:30-35), whom the religious leaders had interrogated carefully (John 1:15ff). In fact, at the very end of His ministry, our Lord pointed the rulers back to the witness of John the Baptist (Matt. 21:23-27). John knew who Jesus was and faithfully declared what he knew to the people of Israel. John told the people that Jesus was the Lord (John 1:23), the Lamb of God (John 1:29, 36), and the Son of God (John 1:34).

John was a "burning and a shining lamp" (Jesus is the Light, John 8:12), and the Jewish people were excited about his ministry. However, their enthusiasm cooled; and nobody lifted a finger to try to deliver John when he was arrested by Herod. The leaders looked on John as a "local celebrity" (Matt. 11:7-8), but they did not want to receive his message of repentance. The publicans and sinners accepted John's message and were converted, but the religious leaders refused to submit (Matt. 21:28-32).

Whenever God raises up a spiritual leader who commands attention, there is always the danger of attracting people who want to bask in his popularity but not submit to his authority. A "mixed multitude" followed Moses and Israel out of Egypt, people who were impressed with the miracles but not yielded to the Lord. The prophets and Apostles, as well as the great leaders in church history, all had to put up with shallow people who followed the crowd but refused to obey the truth. We have them in churches today.

Our Lord's second witness was the witness of His miracles (John 5:36). You will remember that John selected seven of these "signs" to include in his Gospel as proof that

Jesus is the Son of God (John 20:30-31). Jesus made it clear that His works were the works of the Father (John 5:17-20; 14:10). Even Nicodemus had to admit that our Lord's miracles identified Him as "sent from God" (John 3:2).

But the Bible also records miracles performed by ordinary men, such as Moses, Elijah, and Paul. Do these miracles prove that they are also sent of God? Yes, they do (see Heb. 2:3-4), but none of these men ever claimed to be the very Son of God. No servant of God able to perform God's mighty works would ever claim to be God Himself. The fact that Jesus made this claim, backed up by His mighty works and perfect life, is evidence that His claim is true.

Jesus indicated that the Father gave Him a specific ministry to finish while He was here on earth. "I have finished the work which Thou gavest Me to do" (John 17:4). He was not only on a divine timetable, but He followed a divine agenda. He had specific works to accomplish in the Father's will.

Since the Old Testament Law required the testimony of two or three witnesses (Num. 35:30; Deut. 17:6), the Lord met that requirement by giving three trustworthy witnesses.

The third and final witness our Lord summoned was *the Word of the Father* (John 5:37-47). The Jewish people highly revered the written Word of God, particularly the Law that was given through Moses. Moses heard God's voice and saw God's glory; but we have that same voice and glory in the inspired Word of God (see 2 Peter 1:12-21). The Old Testament Scriptures bear witness to Jesus Christ, yet the people who received and preserved that Word were blind to their own Messiah. Why?

For one thing, they did not permit that Word to generate faith in their hearts (John 5:38). John 5:39 is probably a statement of fact and not a command and could be rendered: "Ye search the Scriptures, for in them ye think ye have eternal life." The Jewish scribes sought to know the Word of God, but they did not know the God of the Word! They counted the very letters of the text, but they missed the spiritual truths that the text contained.

Because of my radio ministry, I often receive letters from people who disagree with my interpretations or applications of Scripture; and sometimes these letters are quite angry. (I will not quote here the language I have seen in letters from professed Christians!) It is unfortunate when our "study" of the Bible makes us arrogant and militant instead of humble and anxious to serve others, even those who disagree with us. The mark of true Bible study is not knowledge that puffs up, but love that builds up (1 Cor. 8:1).

So, there was something wrong with *the minds* of these Jewish leaders: they did not see Christ in their own Scriptures (see 2 Cor. 3:14-18; 4:3-6). But there was also something wrong with their *wills:* they would not trust in the Saviour. Because they did not have the Word in their hearts, they did not want Christ in their hearts. They were religious and self-righteous, but they were not saved.

These leaders had a third problem, and this was the lack of love in their *hearts.* "Ye have not the love of God in you" (John 5:42). This means the experience of God's love for them as well as their expression of love for God. They claimed to love God, but their attitude toward Jesus Christ proved that their love was counterfeit.

Their attitude toward God's Word hindered their faith, but so also did their attitude toward themselves and one another. The Pharisees enjoyed being honored by men (see Matt. 23:1-12) and they did not seek for the honor that comes from God alone. They did not honor the Son (John 5:23) because He did not honor them! Because they rejected the true Son of God who came in the Father's name, they would one day accept a false messiah, the Antichrist, who would come in his own name (John 5:43; and see 2 Thes. 2; Rev. 13). If we reject that which is true, we will ultimately receive that which is false.

Our Lord closed this penetrating sermon by warning the Jewish leaders that Moses, whom they honored, would be their judge, not their savior. The very Scriptures that they used to defend their religion would one day bear witness against them. The Jews *knew* what Moses wrote, but they did not really *believe* what he wrote. It is one thing to have the Word in our hands or our heads, but quite another thing to have it in our hearts. Jesus is the Word made flesh (John 1:14), and the written Word bears witness to the Incarnate Word. "And beginning at Moses and all the prophets, He expounded unto them in all the Scriptures the things concerning Himself" (Luke 24:27).

The witness of John the Baptist, the witness of the divine miracles, and the witness of the Word of God all unite to declare that Jesus Christ is indeed One with the Father and the very Son of God.

Our Lord was not intimidated by the accusations of the religious leaders. If you check a harmony of the Gospels, you will see that after the events recorded in John 5, Jesus deliberately violated the Sabbath again! He permitted His disciples to pick grain on the Sabbath, and He healed a man with a withered hand (Matt. 12:1-14). These events probably took place in Galilee, but the news would certainly reach the leaders in Jerusalem and Judea.

The healing of the man on the Sabbath would come up again (John 7:21-23). The leaders would persist in protecting tradition instead of understanding truth (see Mark 7:1-13). But before we judge them, perhaps we ought to examine our own lives and churches. Are we permitting religious tradition to blind us to the truth of God's Word? Are we so involved in "Bible study" that we fail to see Jesus Christ in the Word? Does our knowledge of the Bible give us a "big head" or a "burning heart"?

CHAPTER SIX
JESUS LOSES HIS CROWD
John 6

Since John's Gospel is selective (John 20:30-31), he does not record events in the life of Jesus that do not help him fulfill his purpose. Between the healing of the paralytic (John 5) and the feeding of the 5,000, you have many events taking place, some of which are mentioned in Luke 6:1–9:10 and Mark 3:1–6:30. During this period our Lord preached "the Sermon on the Mount" (Matt. 5–7) and gave the parables of the kingdom (Matt. 13).

The feeding of the 5,000 was a miracle of such magnitude that it is recorded in all four Gospels. A great multitude had been following Jesus for several days, listening to His teaching and beholding His miracles. Jesus had tried to "get away" to rest, but the needs of the crowd pressed on Him (Mark 6:31-34). Because of His compassion, He ministered to the multitude in three different ways.

Jesus Feeds the Multitude (John 6:1-14)
The problem, of course, was how to meet the needs of such a vast crowd of people. Four solutions were proposed.

First, the disciples suggested that Jesus send the people away (Mark 6:35-36). Get rid of the problem (see Matt. 15:23). But Jesus knew that the hungry people would faint on the way if somebody did not feed them. It was evening (Matt. 14:15), and that was no time for travel.

The second solution came from Philip in response to our Lord's "test question" (John 6:5): raise enough money to buy food for the people. Philip "counted the cost" and decided they would need the equivalent of 200 days' wages! And even that would not provide bread enough to satisfy the hunger of all the men, women, and children (Matt. 14:21). Too often, we think that money is the answer to every need. Of course, Jesus was simply testing the strength of Philip's faith.

The third solution came from Andrew, but he was not quite sure how the problem would be solved. He found a little boy who had a small lunch: two little fish and five barley cakes. Once again, Andrew is busy bringing somebody to Jesus (see John 1:40-42; 12:20-22). We do not know how Andrew met this lad, but we are glad he did! Though Andrew does not have a prominent place in the Gospels, he was apparently a "people person" who helped solve problems.

The fourth solution came from our Lord, and it was the true solution. He took the little boy's lunch, blessed it, broke it, handed it out to His disciples, and they fed the whole crowd! The miracle took place in the hands of the Saviour, not in the hands of the disciples. He multiplied the food; they only had the joyful privilege of passing it out. Not only were the people fed and satisfied, but the disciples salvaged twelve baskets of fragments for future use. The Lord wasted nothing.

The practical lesson is clear: whenever there is a need, give all that you have to Jesus and let Him do the rest. Begin with what you have, but be sure you give it all to Him. That little lad is to be commended for sharing his lunch with Christ, and his mother is to be commended for giving him something to give to Jesus. The gift of that little snack meant as much to Jesus as the pouring out of the expensive ointment (John 12:1ff).

But did Jesus really perform a miracle? Perhaps the generosity of the boy only embarrassed the other people so that they brought out their hidden lunches and shared them all around. Nonsense! Jesus knows the hearts of men (John 2:24; 6:61, 64, 70) and He declared that the people were hungry. Surely He would have known of the existence of hidden food! Furthermore, the people themselves declared that this was a miracle and even wanted to crown Him King! (John 6:14-16) Had this event been only the result of mass psychology, the crowd would not have responded that way. John would never have selected this as one of the "signs" if it were not an authentic miracle.

It is significant that twice John mentioned the fact that Jesus gave thanks (John 6:11, 23). Matthew, Mark, and Luke all state that Jesus looked up to heaven when He gave thanks. By that act, He reminded the hungry people that God is the source of all good and needful gifts. This is a good lesson for us: instead of complaining about what we do not have, we should give thanks to God for what we do have, and He will make it go farther.

Jesus Leaves the Multitude (John 6:15-21)

Jesus compelled the disciples to get into the boat (Matt. 14:22; Mark 6:45) because He knew they were in danger. The crowd was now aroused and there was a movement to make Him King. Of course, some of the disciples would have rejoiced at the opportunity to become famous and powerful! Judas would have become treasurer of the kingdom, and perhaps Peter would have been named prime minister! But this was not in the plan of God, and Jesus broke up the meeting immediately. Certainly the Roman government would have stepped in had a movement begun.

Did Jesus know that a storm was coming? Of course. Then why did He deliberately send His friends into danger? Quite the opposite is true: He was rescuing them from greater danger, the danger of being swept along by a fanatical crowd. But there was another reason for that storm: the Lord has to balance our lives; otherwise we will become proud and then fall. The disciples had experienced great joy in being part of a thrilling miracle. Now they had to face a storm and learn to trust the Lord more. The feeding of the 5,000 was the lesson, but the storm was the examination after the lesson.

Sometimes we are caught in a storm because we have disobeyed the Lord. Jonah is a good example. But sometimes the storm comes because we have *obeyed* the Lord. When that happens, we can be sure that our Saviour will pray for us, come to us, and deliver us. In writing the account of this event years later, perhaps John saw in it a picture of Christ and His church. Christ is in heaven interceding for us, but we are in the midst of the storms of life, trying to reach the shore. One day, He will come for us and we shall reach the port safely, the storms all past.

Actually, there were several miracles involved in this event. Jesus walked on the water, and so did Peter (Matt. 14:28-32). Jesus stilled the storm, and instantly the boat was on the other shore. Of course, all of this happened at night so that only Jesus and His disciples knew what had occurred. Jesus had led His people into the green pastures (John 6:10), and now He brought them into the still waters (Ps. 23:2). What a wonderful Shepherd He is!

As you read the Gospel records, note that our Lord was never impressed by the great crowds. He knew that their motives were not pure and that most of them followed Him in order to watch His miracles of healing. "Bread and circuses" was Rome's formula for keeping the people happy, and people today are satisfied with that kind of diet. Give them food and entertainment and they are happy. Rome set aside ninety-three days each year for public games at government expense. It was cheaper to entertain the crowds than to fight them or jail them.

We must never be deceived by the "popularity" of Jesus Christ among certain kinds of people today. Very few want Him as Saviour and Lord. Many want Him only as Healer or Provider, or the One who rescues them from problems they have made for themselves. "And ye will not come to Me, that ye might have life" (John 5:40).

Jesus Teaches the Multitude (John 6:22-71)

The purpose of the sign was that He might preach the sermon. Again, it was a ministry of "grace and truth" (John 1:17). In grace, our Lord fed the hungry people; but in truth, He gave them the Word of God. They wanted the food but they did not want the truth; and, in the end, most of them abandoned Jesus and refused to walk with Him. He lost His crowd with one sermon!

The next day began with a mystery: how did Jesus get to Capernaum? The crowd saw the disciples embark to go across the Sea of Galilee to Capernaum, and then the men were lost in the storm. The crowd also saw Jesus leave the place and go by Himself to a mountain. But the next morning, here were Jesus and His disciples *together* in Capernaum! Certainly He had not walked around the lake, and there was no evidence that He had taken another boat. Other boats had arrived, no doubt driven in by the storm; but Jesus had not been in any of them.

No doubt some of the people who had been fed simply went away to their homes, while others stayed to see what Jesus would do next. Our Lord's sermon probably began outdoors, and then the discussion moved into the synagogue (John 6:59). It would be impossible for a huge crowd to participate in the synagogue service, though the overflow could remain outside and hear what was being said.

This sermon on "the bread of life" is actually a dialogue between Christ and the people, especially the religious leaders ("the Jews"). We see four responses of the crowd to the Lord Jesus in John 6: seeking (vv. 22-40), murmuring (vv. 41-51), striving (vv. 52-59), and departing (vv. 60-71).

Seeking (vv. 22-40). The disciples may have been impressed that so many people stayed through a storm in order to seek their Master, but Jesus was not impressed. He knows the human heart. He knew that the people originally followed Him because of His miracles (John 6:2), but now their motive was to get fed! Even if they were attracted only by the miracles, at least there was still a possibility they might be saved. After all, that is where Nicodemus started (John 3:1-2). But now their interest had degenerated to the level of food.

Jesus pointed out that there are two kinds of food: food for the body, which is necessary but not the most important; and food for the inner man, the spirit, which is essential. What the people needed was not food but *life*, and life is a gift. Food only *sustains* life, but Jesus *gives* eternal life. The words of Isaiah come to mind: "Why do you spend money for what is not bread, and your wages for what does not satisfy?" (Isa. 55:2, NASB)

The people picked up the word *labor* and misinterpreted it to mean they had to *work* for salvation. They completely missed the word *give*. Steeped in legalistic religion, they thought they had to "do something" to merit eternal life. Jesus made it clear that only one "work" was necessary—to believe on the Saviour. When a person believes on Christ, he is not performing a good work that earns him salvation. There is certainly no credit in believing, for it is what God does *in response to our faith* that is important (see Eph. 2:8-10).

The crowd began by seeking Christ, but then started to seek a sign from Him. "For the Jews require a sign" (1 Cor. 1:22). The rabbis taught that, when Messiah came, He would duplicate the miracle of the manna (see Ex. 16). If Jesus was truly sent by God (see John 6:29, 38, 57), then let Him prove it by causing manna to fall from heaven. They wanted to "see and believe." But faith that is based on signs alone, and not on the truth of the Word, can lead a person astray; for even Satan is able to perform "lying wonders" (2 Thes. 2:8-10). Note also John 2:18-25; 4:48.

The quotation in John 6:31 is from Psalm 78:24, a psalm that records the unbelief and rebellion of the nation of Israel.

In His reply, our Lord sought to deepen the people's understanding of the truth. It was *God,* not Moses, who gave the manna; so they must take their eyes off Moses and focus them on God. Also, God *gave* the manna in the past, but the Father is *now giving* the true bread in the person of Jesus Christ. The past event is finished, but the present spiritual experience goes on!

Then Jesus clearly identified what the bread is: He is the true Living Bread that came down from heaven. But He came, not only for Israel but for the whole world. And He came, not just to *sustain* life, but to *give* life! Seven times in this sermon, our Lord referred to His "coming down from heaven" (John 6:33, 38, 41-42, 50-51, 58), a statement that declared Him to be God. The Old Testament manna was but a type of the "true bread," the Lord Jesus Christ.

This dialogue began with the crowd seeking Christ and then seeking a sign, but listeners soon began to seek the "true bread" that Jesus talked about. However, like the woman of Samaria, they were not ready for salvation (see John 4:15). She wanted the living water so she would not have to keep going to the well. The crowd wanted the bread so they would not have to toil to maintain life. People today still want Jesus Christ only for the benefits He is able to give.

In His reply to their impetuous request, Jesus used two key words that often appear in this sermon: *come* and *believe.* To come to Jesus means to believe on Him, and to believe on Him means to come to Him. Believing is not merely an intellectual thing, giving mental assent to some doctrine. It means to come to Christ and yield yourself to Him. At the close of His sermon, Jesus illustrated *coming* and *believing* by speaking about *eating* and *drinking.* To come to Christ and believe on Him means to receive Him within, just as you receive food and drink.

John 6:35 contains the first of seven great I AM statements recorded by John, statements that are found nowhere else in the Gospels. (For the other six, see John 8:12; 10:7-9, 11-14; 11:25-26; 14:6; 15:1, 5.) God revealed Himself to Moses by the name I AM (Jehovah) (Ex. 3:14). God is the self-existent One who "is, and . . . was, and . . . is to come" (Rev. 1:8). When Jesus used the name I AM, He was definitely claiming to be God.

John 6:37-40 contains Jesus' explanation of the process of personal salvation. These are among the most profound words He ever spoke, and we cannot hope to plumb their depths completely. He explained that salvation involves both divine sovereignty and human responsibility. The Father *gives* men and women to the Son (John 6:37, 39; 17:2, 6, 9, 11-12, 24), but these men and women must *come* to Him, that is, *believe* on Him. He assured them that nobody who came to Him would ever be lost but would be raised at the last day. Even death cannot rob us of salvation! (In regard to the "last day," see John 6:40, 44, 54. Jesus was referring to His return and the final events that climax God's program for mankind.)

From our human and limited perspective, we cannot see how divine sovereignty and human responsibility can work together; but from God's perspective, there is no conflict. When a church member asked Charles Spurgeon how he reconciled these two, he replied, "I never try to reconcile friends." It is the Father's will that sinners be saved (1 Tim. 2:4; 2 Peter 3:9) and that those who trust Christ be secure in their salvation. Believers receive eternal life and Jesus can never lose them.

Murmuring (vv. 41-51). Our Lord's statement "For I came down from heaven" (John 6:38), disturbed the religious leaders, for they knew it was a claim of deity. They thought they knew Jesus, who He was and where He came from (see Matt. 13:53-58; John 7:40-43). Jesus, of course, was the *legal* son of Joseph but not his natural son, for He was born of a virgin (Luke 1:34-38). The leaders identified Jesus with Nazareth in Galilee, not Bethlehem in Judea; and they thought that Joseph was His natural father. Had they investigated the matter, they would have learned who Jesus really is.

Even in the days of Moses, the Jews were known for their murmuring (Ex. 15:24; 17:3; Num. 14:2). Perhaps the leaders and some of the crowd had now moved into the synagogue to continue the discussion. The main issue was, "Where did He come from?" Five times Jesus used the phrase "came down from heaven," but they would not accept it.

Jesus further explained how the sinner can come to God: it is through the truth of the Word (John 6:44-45). The Father draws the sinner by His Word. Jesus quoted Isaiah 54:13 (or perhaps Jer. 31:33-34) to prove His point: "And they shall all be taught of God." It is through the teaching of the Word that God draws people to the Saviour. (Note John 5:24 and its emphasis on hearing the Word.) The sinner hears, learns, and comes as the Father draws him. A mystery? Yes! A blessed reality? Yes!

This was basically the same message He gave after He had healed the paralytic (see John 5:37-40). The crowd wanted to *see* something, but their real need was to *learn* something. It is by the Word that we "see" God and receive the faith to come to Christ and trust Him (Rom. 10:17).

When Jesus called Himself "the Living Bread," He was not claiming to be exactly like the manna. *He was claiming to be even greater!* The manna only *sustained life* for the Jews, but Jesus *gives life* to the whole world. The Jews ate the daily manna and eventually died; but when you receive Jesus Christ within, you live forever. When God gave the manna, He gave only a gift; but when Jesus came, He gave Himself. There was no cost to God in sending the manna each day, but He gave His Son at great cost. The Jews had to eat the manna every day, but the sinner who trusts Christ *once* is given eternal life.

It is not difficult to see in the manna a picture of our Lord Jesus Christ. The manna was a mysterious thing to the Jews; in fact, the word *manna* means "What is it?" (see Ex. 16:15) Jesus was a mystery to those who saw Him. The manna came at night from heaven, and Jesus came to this earth when sinners were in moral and spiritual darkness. The manna was small (His humility), round (His eternality), and white (His purity). It was sweet to the taste (Ps. 34:8) and it met the needs of the people adequately.

The manna was given to a rebellious people; it was the gracious gift of God. All they had to do was stoop and pick it up. If they failed to pick it up, *they walked on it.* The Lord is not far from any sinner. All the sinner has to do is humble himself and take the gift that God offers.

Jesus closed this part of His message by referring to His *flesh,* a word that will be used six more times before the dialogue is concluded. John 6:51 is a declaration that the Son of God will give Himself as a sacrifice "for the life of the world." The substitutionary death of Jesus Christ is a key doctrine in John's Gospel. Jesus would die for the world (John 3:16; 6:51), for His sheep (John 10:11, 15), for the nation (John 11:50-52), and for His friends (John 15:12). Paul made it personal, and so should we: "Who loved me, and gave Himself for me" (Gal. 2:20). We must not limit the work of Christ on the cross. He is the sacrifice not for our sins only, but also for the sins of the whole world (1 John 2:2).

Striving (vv. 52-59). The word striving means "to fight and quarrel." Being orthodox Jews, the listeners knew the divine prohibition against eating human flesh or any kind of blood (Gen. 9:3-4; Lev. 17:10-16; 19:26). Here we have another example in John's Gospel of the people misunderstanding a spiritual truth by treating it literally (see John 2:19-21; 3:4; 4:11). All Jesus said was, "Just as you take food and drink within your body and it becomes a part of you, so you must receive Me within your innermost being so that I can give you life."

Some interpreters tell us that Jesus was speaking about the Lord's Supper, and that we eat His flesh and drink His blood when we partake of the elements at the table, the bread and the cup. I do not believe that Jesus had the Communion (or eucharist) in mind when He spoke these words.

For one thing, why would He discuss the Lord's Supper with a group of disagreeable unbelievers? He had not even shared that truth with His own disciples! Why would He cast this precious pearl before the swine?

Second, He made it clear that He was not speaking in literal terms (John 6:63). He was using a human analogy to convey a spiritual truth, just as He did with Nicodemus and the Samaritan woman.

Third, Jesus made it plain that this eating and drinking were *absolutely essential* for eternal life. He made no exceptions. If, then, He was speaking about a church ordinance (or sacrament), then everybody who has never shared in that experience is spiritually dead and is going to hell. This would include all the Old Testament saints, the thief on the cross, and a host of people who have trusted Christ in emergency situations (hospitals, accidents, foxholes, etc.). I personally cannot believe that our gracious God has excluded from salvation all who cannot participate in a church ceremony.

Another factor is the tense of the Greek verbs in John 6:50-51, and 53. It is the aorist tense which signifies a once-for-all action. The Communion service is a repeated thing; in fact, it is likely that the early church observed the Lord's Supper daily (Acts 2:46).

It is significant that the word *flesh* is never used in any of the reports of the Lord's Supper, either in the Gospels or in 1 Corinthians 11:23-34. The word used is "body."

If a person holds that our Lord was speaking about the Communion service, then he must believe that somehow the two elements, the bread and the fruit of the vine, turn into the very body and blood of Christ; for He said, "So he that eateth *Me,* even he shall live by *Me*" (John 6:57, italics mine). How does this "miracle" take place? What is the secret of accomplishing it? Why is it not apparent?

Our Lord's messages recorded in the Gospel of John are filled with symbolism and imagery. To take them literally is to make the same mistake the people made who first heard them.

Departing (vv. 60-71). Our Lord's teaching was not hard to understand but hard to accept once you understood it. The Jewish religious leaders both misunderstood His words and rejected them. They were "offended" by what He taught. (The Greek word is "scandalized.") They stumbled over the fact that He claimed to come down from heaven. They also stumbled over the idea that they had to eat His flesh and drink His blood in order to be saved. But if they stumbled over these two matters, what would they do if they saw Him ascend back into heaven? (John 6:62)

Jesus explained that His language was figurative and spiritual, not literal. There is no salvation in "flesh." In fact, the New Testament has nothing good to say about "the flesh." There is nothing good in it (Rom. 7:18) and we must not have confidence in it (Phil. 3:3).

How, then, do we "eat His flesh and drink His blood"? *Through the Word.* "The words that I speak unto you, they are spirit and they are life" (John 6:63). "And the Word became flesh" (John 1:14). Our Lord said the same thing: "He that heareth My word and believeth on Him that sent Me, hath everlasting life" (John 5:24). The scribes who knew Jeremiah 31:31-34 would have understood the concept of receiving God's Word into one's inner being.

The result of this message was the loss of most of our Lord's disciples. They went back to the old life, the old religion, and the old hopeless situation. Jesus Christ is "the way" (John 14:6), but they would not walk with Him. This was no surprise to the Lord, because He knows the hearts of all people.

When Jesus asked His 12 Apostles if they planned to desert Him too, it was Peter who spoke up and declared their faith. Where else could they go? "Thou hast the words of eternal life." Peter got the message! He knew that Jesus was speaking about *the Word* and not about literal flesh and blood.

Peter was one of several people who declared their belief that Jesus is the Son of God (see John 1:34, 49; 3:18; 5:25; 9:35; 10:36; 11:4, 27; 19:7; 20:31). The only mistake he made was to bear witness for the entire group. Peter was sure that *all* of the Apostles were believers, which shows how convincing Judas was. Even Peter did not know that Judas was an unbeliever!

The preaching of the Word of God always leads to a sifting of the hearts of the listeners. God draws sinners to the Saviour through the power of truth, His Word. Those who reject the Word will reject the Saviour. Those who receive the Word will receive the Saviour and experience the new birth, eternal life.

Do you feel your need because there is a spiritual hunger within? Are you willing to admit that need and come to the Saviour? If you will, He will save you and satisfy you *forever!*

CHAPTER SEVEN
FEAST FIGHT
John 7

The Feast of Tabernacles looked back to Israel's journey through the wilderness, and looked forward to the promised kingdom of Messiah. The Jews lived in booths made of branches to remind them of God's providential care of the nation for nearly forty years (Lev. 23:33-44).

Following the Feast of Trumpets and the solemn Day of Atonement, Tabernacles was a festive time for the people. The temple area was illumined by large candlesticks that reminded the people of the guiding pillar of fire; and each day the priests would carry water from the Pool of Siloam and pour it out from a golden vessel, reminding the Jews of the miraculous provision of water from the rock.

The feast may have been a jubilant time for the people, but it was a difficult time for Jesus, for it marked the beginning of open and militant opposition to Him and His ministry. Ever since He had healed the paralytic on the Sabbath Day, Jesus had been targeted by the Jewish leaders who wanted to kill Him (John 7:1, 19-20, 25, 30, 32, 44; and note 8:37, 40). He remained in Galilee, where He would be safer, but He could not remain in Galilee and also observe the feast.

John 7 has three time divisions: before the feast (vv. 1-10), in the midst of the feast (vv. 11-36), and on the last day of the feast (vv. 37-52). The responses during each of those periods can be characterized by three words: disbelief, debate, and division.

Before the Feast: Disbelief (John 7:1-10)

Mary bore other children, with Joseph as their natural father (Matt. 13:55-56; Mark 6:1-6); so Jesus would have been their half brother. It seems incredible that His brothers could have lived with Him all those years and not realized the uniqueness of His person. Certainly they knew about His miracles (see John 7:3-4) since everybody else did. Having been in the closest contact with Him, they had the best opportunity to watch Him and test Him; yet they were still unbelievers.

Here were men going up to a religious feast, yet rejecting their own Messiah! How easy it is to follow tradition and miss eternal truth. The publicans and sinners were rejoicing at His message, but His own half brothers were making fun of Him.

These men certainly had the world's point of view: if you want to get a following, use your opportunities to do something spectacular. Jerusalem would be crowded with pilgrims and this would give Jesus the ideal "platform" to present Himself and win disciples. No doubt the brothers knew that the multitude of disciples had deserted Jesus (John 6:66). This was His opportunity to recoup His losses. Satan had offered a similar suggestion three years before (Matt. 4:1ff).

Jesus had already turned down the crowd's offer to make Him King (John 6:15), and He was not about to yield to them in any way. Celebrities might ride to success on the applause of the crowd, but God's servants know better. By doing miracles during the feast, at the "official city," Jesus could muster a crowd, reveal Himself as Messiah, and overcome the enemy. The suggestion, of course, came from hearts and minds blinded by unbelief. This unbelief had been prophesied in Psalm 69:8—"I am become a stranger unto My brethren, and an alien unto My mother's children." (Since Jesus was not Joseph's natural son, He could not say "My father's children.")

It was not the right time for Jesus to show Himself to the world (John 14:22ff). One day He shall return, and "every eye shall see Him" (Rev. 1:7). We have noticed that our Lord lived on a "divine timetable" that was marked out by the Father (John 2:4; 7:6, 8, 30; 8:20; 12:23; 13:1; 17:1).

Jesus was exercising caution because He knew that the Jewish leaders wanted to kill Him. Though they were "religious" leaders, they were a part of "the world" that hated Jesus because He exposed their evil works. By His character and His ministry, He revealed the shallowness and emptiness of their futile religious system; He called the people back to the reality of life in God. History reveals that the "religious system" often persecutes the very prophets of God who are sent to save it!

Some manuscripts do not have the word *yet* in John 7:8, but its absence does not alter the thrust of the statement. Jesus was certainly not lying or being evasive; rather, He was exercising sensible caution. Suppose He told His brothers His plans, and they told somebody else? Could the information possibly get to the leaders? "I am going to the feast when the right time comes," is what He said. After His family had gone, Jesus went to Jerusalem "under cover," so as not to call attention to Himself.

In our Lord's actions, we see a beautiful illustration of divine sovereignty and human responsibility. The Father had a plan for His Son, and nothing could spoil that plan. Jesus did not tempt the Father by rushing to the feast, nor did He lag behind when the proper time had come for Him to attend the feast. It requires spiritual discernment to know God's timing.

In the Midst of the Feast: Debate (John 7:11-36)

Note that this public debate about the Lord Jesus involved three different groups of people. First, of course, were the Jewish leaders ("the Jews") who lived in Jerusalem and were attached to the temple ministry. This would include the Pharisees and the chief priests (most of whom were Sadducees) as well as the scribes. These men differed theologically, but they agreed on one thing: their opposition to Jesus Christ and their determination to get rid of Him. The exceptions would be Nicodemus and Joseph of Arimathea (John 19:38-42).

The second group would be "the people" (John 7:12, 20, 31-32). This would be the festival crowd that had come to Jerusalem to worship. Many of them would not be influenced by the attitude of the religious leaders at Jerusalem. You will note in John 7:20 that "the people" were amazed that anybody would want to kill Jesus! They were not up to date on all the gossip in the city and had to learn the hard way that Jesus was considered a lawbreaker by the officials.

The third group was composed of the Jews who resided in Jerusalem (John 7:25). They, of course, would have likely sided with the religious leaders.

The debate began before Jesus even arrived at the city, and it centered on *His character* (John 7:11-13). The religious leaders "kept seeking" Jesus, while the crowd kept arguing whether He was a good man or a deceiver. He would have to be one or the other, because a truly good man would not deceive anybody. Yes, Jesus is either what He claims to be, or He is a liar.

But when Jesus began to teach openly in the temple, the debate shifted to *His doctrine*

(John 7:14-19). Character and doctrine go together, of course. It would be foolish to trust the teachings of a liar! The Jews were amazed at what He taught because He did not have any credentials from their approved rabbinical schools. But since He lacked this "proper accreditation," His enemies said that His teachings were nothing but private opinions and not worth much. It has often been said that Jesus taught with authority, while the scribes and Pharisees taught from authorities, quoting all the famous rabbis.

Jesus explained that His doctrine came from the Father. He had already made it clear that He and the Father were one in the works that He performed (John 5:17) and in the judgment that He executed (John 5:30). Now He claimed that His teachings also came from the Father, and He would make that astounding claim again (John 8:26, 38). When I teach the Word of God, I can claim authority for the Bible but not for all of my interpretations of the Bible. Jesus rightly could claim absolute authority for everything that He taught!

But does not *every* religious teacher make a similar claim? How, then, can we know that Jesus is teaching us the truth? *By obeying what He tells us to do.* God's Word proves itself true to those who will sincerely do it. The British preacher F.W. Robertson said that "obedience is the organ of spiritual knowledge." John 7:17 literally reads, "If any man is willing to do His [God's] will, he shall know." This explains why the Jewish leaders did not understand Jesus' teachings: they had stubborn wills and would not submit to Him (John 5:40).

Is our Lord suggesting here a "pragmatic test" for divine truth? Is He saying, "Try it! If it works, it must be true!" and thus suggesting that if it does not work it must be false? This kind of a test would lead to confusion, for almost any cultist could say, "I tried what the cult teaches, and it works!"

No, our Lord's statement goes much deeper. He was not suggesting a shallow "taste test" but rather the deep personal commitment of the person to truth. The Jews depended on education and authorities and received their doctrine secondhand, but Jesus insisted that we experience the authority of truth *personally.* The Jewish leaders were attempting to *kill Jesus,* yet at the same time they claimed to understand God's truth and obey it. This proves that an enlightened and educated mind is no guarantee of a pure heart or a sanctified will. Some of the world's worst criminals have been highly intelligent and well-educated people.

Satan offered Adam and Eve knowledge, but it was knowledge based on disobedience (Gen. 3:5). Jesus offered knowledge as the result of obedience: first the yoke of responsibility, then the joy of knowing God's truth. Dr. G. Campbell Morgan said it perfectly: "When men are wholly, completely consecrated to the will of God and want to do that above everything else, then they find out that Christ's teaching is divine, that it is the teaching of God."

If we really seek God's will, then we will not worry over who gets the glory. All truth is God's truth and God alone deserves the glory for what He has taught us. No teacher or preacher can take the credit for what only can come from God. If he does go after the glory, then it is proof that his teaching is self-generated and not received from God. This is the origin of many cults and church splits: somebody "invents" a doctrine, takes credit for it, and uses it to divide God's people.

The first "debate" was with the Jews: but the visitors to the city entered into the discussion (John 7:20). Jesus had boldly announced that the leaders wanted to kill Him because He had violated the Sabbath and then claimed to be God (see John 5:10-18). The orthodox Jews broke the Sabbath laws when they had their sons circumcised on the Sabbath, so why could He not heal a man on the Sabbath? "Why go ye about to kill Me?"

The visitors, of course, did not know that their leaders were out to kill Jesus; so they challenged His statement. But their reply contained a serious accusation—that Jesus had a demon. This was not a new accusation, for the leaders had said it before (Matt. 9:32ff; 10:25; 11:18-19; 12:24ff). "You must be crazy to think that anybody wants to kill You!"

Our Lord used the very Law of Moses to refute the enemy's argument; but He knew that they would not give in. Why? Because their standard of judgment was not honest. They evaluated things on the basis of superficial examination of the facts. They judged on the basis of "seems" and not "is." Unfortunately, too many people make that same mistake today. John 7:24 is the opposite of verse 17, where Jesus called for sincere devotion to truth.

The residents of Jerusalem entered the conversation (John 7:25). They knew that the rulers wanted to kill Jesus, and they were amazed that He was teaching openly and getting away with it! Perhaps the rulers had been convinced that indeed He is the Messiah, sent from God! Then why were they not worshiping Him and leading others to worship Him?

Their question (John 7:25) suggested a negative answer: "No, the rulers do not believe that He is the Christ, do they?" They were able to defend their conclusion with logic:

1. Nobody knows where the Christ comes from.
2. We know where Jesus of Nazareth came from.
3. Conclusion: Jesus cannot be the Messiah.

Once again, the people could not see the truth because they were blinded by what they thought were dependable facts. Jesus had met this same kind of resistance in the synagogue in Capernaum (John 6:42ff). Even the learned teachers—the "expert builders"—would not be able to identify the Chief Cornerstone, even though they had studied the God-given "blueprints" for centuries! (Acts 4:11)

At this point, our Lord raised His voice so that everybody could hear (note also John 7:37). He was probably speaking in a tone revealing irony: "Yes, you think you know Me and where I came from! But really, you do not!" Then He explained why they did not know Him: *they did not know the Father!* This was a serious accusation to make against an orthodox Jew, for the Jews prided themselves in knowing the true God, the God of Israel.

But Jesus went even further: He boldly asserted that He not only knew the Father, but was sent by Him! He was once again claiming to be God! He was not simply *born* into this world like any other human; He was *sent* to earth by the Father. This means that He existed before He was born on the earth.

This was certainly a crisis hour in His ministry, and some of the leaders tried to have Him arrested; but "His hour was not yet come." Many of the pilgrims put their faith in Him. It was a faith based on miracles, but at least it was a beginning (see John 2:23; 6:2, 26). Nicodemus first became interested in Jesus because of His miracles (John 3:1-2), and eventually he openly professed faith in Christ.

The Pharisees and chief priests, who presided over the Jewish religious establishment, resented the fact that the people were trusting in Jesus. Apparently these "believers" were not afraid to tell what they had done (John 7:13, 32). This time, the rulers sent members of the temple guard to arrest Jesus, but it was Jesus who "arrested" them! He warned them that they had but "a little while" to hear the truth, believe, and be saved (see John 12:35ff). It was not Jesus who was in danger, but those who wanted to arrest Him!

As in previous messages, the people misunderstood what Jesus was saying. Within six months, Jesus would go back to the Father in heaven, and the unsaved Jews would not be able to follow Him. What a contrast between "where I am, there ye cannot come" (John 7:34) and "that where I am, there ye may be also"! (John 14:3)

Had these men been willing to do God's will, they would have known the truth. Soon it would be too late.

The End of the Feast: Division (John 7:37-52)

The last day of the feast would be the seventh day, a very special day on which the priests would march seven times around the altar, chanting Psalm 118:25. It would be the last time they would draw the water and pour it out. No doubt just as they were pouring out the water, symbolic of the water Moses drew from the rock, Jesus stood and shouted His great invitation to thirsty sinners.

It has been pointed out that this "great day," the twenty-first of the seventh month, is the same date on which the Prophet Haggai made a special prediction about the temple (Hag. 2:1-9). While the ultimate fulfillment must await the return of Christ to this earth, certainly there was a partial fulfillment when Jesus came to the temple. Haggai 2:6-7 is quoted in Hebrews 12:26-29 as applying to the return of the Lord.

Jesus was referring to the experience of Israel recorded in Exodus 17:1-7. That water was but a picture of the Spirit of God. Believers would not only drink the living water, but they would become channels of living water to bless a thirsty world! The "artesian well" that He promised in John 4:14 has now become a flowing river! While there are no specific prophetic Scriptures that indicate "rivers of water" flowing from the believer, there are a number of verses that parallel this thought: Isaiah 12:3; 15; 32:2; 44:3; and 58:11; and Zechariah 14:8. Note that Zechariah 14:16ff speaks about the future Feast of Tabernacles, when the Lord is King.

Water for drinking is one of the symbols of

the Holy Spirit in the Bible. (Water for washing is a symbol of the Word of God; see John 15:3 and Eph. 5:26.) Just as water satisfies thirst and produces fruitfulness, so the Spirit of God satisfies the inner person and enables us to bear fruit. At the feast, the Jews were reenacting a tradition that could never satisfy the heart. Jesus offered them living water and eternal satisfaction!

What was the result of this declaration and invitation? The people were divided: some defended Him and some wanted to arrest Him. Is He a "good man" or "a deceiver"? (John 7:12) Is He "the Christ"? (John 7:31) Is He the promised "Prophet"? (John 7:40; Deut. 18:15) If only they had honestly examined the evidence, they would have discovered that, indeed, He was the Christ, the Son of God. They identified Jesus with Galilee (John 1:45-46; 7:52) when in reality He was born in Bethlehem (see John 6:42 for similar reasoning).

The temple officers returned to the Jewish council meeting empty-handed. It certainly should have been relatively easy for them to arrest Jesus, yet they failed to do so. What stopped them? "Never man spoke like this Man!" was their defense. In other words, "This Jesus is more than a man! No mere man speaks as He does!" They were "arrested" by the Word of God, spoken by the Son of God.

Again, the leaders refused to face facts honestly but passed judgment on the basis of their prejudices and their superficial examination of the facts. It is much easier to label people (and *libel* people!) than to listen to the facts they present. "So some of the people have believed on Jesus! So what? These common people know nothing about the Law anyway! Have any *important* people—like ourselves—believed on Him? Of course not!" They would use a similar argument to try to discredit the witness of the blind man that Jesus healed (John 9:34).

We should not be surprised when "the intelligentsia" refuses to trust Jesus Christ, or when religious leaders reject Him. God has hidden His truth from "the wise and prudent" and revealed it to "spiritual babes," the humble people who will yield to Him (Matt. 11:25-27). Paul was a very intelligent rabbi when God saved him, yet he had to be "knocked down" before he would acknowledge that Jesus Christ was the resurrected Son of God. Read 1 Corinthians 1:26-31 to learn Paul's explanation for the difficulty of winning "smart religious people" to the Saviour.

No doubt the rulers would have sent the guard out again, but Nicodemus spoke up. This man is found three times in John's Gospel, and each time he is identified as the one "who came to Jesus by night" (see John 3:1-2; 19:39). No doubt Nicodemus had been doing a great deal of thinking and studying since that first interview with Jesus, and he was not afraid to take his stand for truth.

Nicodemus was sure that the council was not giving Jesus an honest hearing. The rulers had already passed judgment and were trying to arrest Him before He had even been given a fair and lawful trial! Perhaps Nicodemus had in mind such Old Testament Scriptures as Exodus 23:1 and Deuteronomy 1:16-17; 19:15-21.

What did Nicodemus want them to consider about Jesus? His Word and His works. It was Jesus the Teacher and the miracle worker who had attracted Nicodemus' interest in the first place (John 3:2). In fact, Jesus had pointed to His works as proof of His deity (John 5:32); and He repeatedly urged the people to pay attention to His words. The two go together, for the miracles point to the messages, and the messages interpret the spiritual meaning of the miracles.

You can hear the sarcasm and disdain in the reply of the rulers: "Are you a lowly and despised Galilean too?" They refused to admit that Nicodemus was right in asking for a fair trial, but the only way they could answer him was by means of ridicule. This is an ancient debate trick: when you cannot answer the argument, attack the speaker.

They challenged Nicodemus to search the prophecies to see if he could find any statement that a prophet would come out of Galilee. Of course, Jonah was from Galilee; and Jesus said that Jonah was a picture of Himself in death, burial, and resurrection (Matt. 12:38-41). Perhaps Nicodemus read Isaiah 9:1-2 (see Matt. 4:12-16) and began to trace the great messianic prophecies in the Old Testament. If he did, then he became convinced that Jesus of Nazareth was the very Son of God.

You cannot help but feel sorry for the people described in this chapter, people who responded to Jesus in the wrong ways. His half brothers responded with disbelief; various people responded with debate; and the result was division. Had they willingly received the truth, and had they acted with sincere obedience, they would have ended up at the feet of

Jesus, confessing Him as Messiah and Son of God.

But people *today* commit the same blunder and permit their prejudices and superficial evaluations to blind them to the truth.

Don't let it happen to you!

CHAPTER EIGHT
CONTRASTS AND CONFLICTS
John 8

Is the story of the woman taken in adultery a part of Scripture? If it is, where does it belong in the Gospel record? John 7:53–8:11 is not found in some of the ancient manuscripts; where it is found, it is not always in this location in John's Gospel. Most scholars seem to agree that the passage is a part of inspired Scripture ("a fragment of authentic Gospel material," says Dr. F.F. Bruce) regardless of where it is placed.

To many of us, the story fits right here! In fact, the development of the entire chapter can easily be seen to grow out of this striking event in the temple. Our Lord's declaration on His being the Light of the world (John 8:12) certainly fits, and so do His words about true and false judgment (John 8:15-16, 26). The repeated phrase "die in your sins" (John 8:21, 24) would clearly relate to the judgment of the woman; and the fact that the chapter ends with an attempt to stone Jesus shows a perfect parallel to the opening story. The transition from John 7:52 to 8:12 would be too abrupt without a transitional section.

Our Lord found Himself again in conflict with the Jewish religious leaders; but this time, they set a trap, hoping to get enough evidence to arrest Jesus and get Him out of the way. However, their plot failed; but a controversy followed. In this chapter we see a series of contrasts that reveal the graciousness of Christ and the wickedness of man.

Grace and Law (John 8:11)

The Feast of Tabernacles had ended, but Jesus took advantage of the opportunity to minister to the pilgrims in the temple. During the feast, word had quickly spread that Jesus was not only attending but openly teaching in the temple (see Luke 21:37). He taught in the court of the women at the place where the treasury was situated (John 8:20). The scribes and Pharisees knew where He would be, so they hatched their plot together.

They would not be likely to catch a couple in the "very act" of adultery; so we wonder if the man (who never was indicted!) was part of the scheme. The Law required that *both* guilty parties be stoned (Lev. 20:10; Deut. 22:22) and not just the woman. It does seem suspicious that the man went free. The scribes and Pharisees handled the matter in a brutal fashion, even in the way they interrupted the Lord's teaching and pushed the woman into the midst of the crowd.

The Jewish leaders, of course, were trying to pin Jesus on the horns of a dilemma. If He said, "Yes, the woman must be stoned!" then what would happen to His reputation as the "friend of publicans and sinners"? The common people would no doubt have abandoned Him and would never have accepted His gracious message of forgiveness.

But, if He said, "No, the woman should not be stoned!" then He was openly breaking the Law and subject to arrest. On more than one occasion, the religious leaders had tried to pit Jesus against Moses, and now they seemed to have the perfect challenge (see John 5:39-47; 6:32ff; 7:40ff).

Instead of passing judgment on the woman, Jesus passed judgment on the judges! No doubt He was indignant at the way they treated the woman. He was also concerned that such hypocrites should condemn another person and not judge themselves. We do not know what He wrote on the dirt floor of the temple. Was He simply reminding them that the Ten Commandments had been originally written "by the finger of God" (Ex. 31:18), and that He is God? Or was He perhaps reminding them of the warning in Jeremiah 17:13?

It was required by Jewish Law that the accusers cast the first stones (Deut. 17:7). Jesus was not asking that sinless men judge the woman, for He was the only sinless Person present. If our judges today had to be perfect, judicial benches would be empty. He was referring to *the particular sin of the woman,* a sin that can be committed in the heart as well as with the body (Matt. 5:27-30). Convicted by their own consciences, the accusers quietly left the scene, and Jesus was left alone with the woman. He forgave her and warned her to sin no more (John 5:14).

We must not misinterpret this event to mean that Jesus was "easy on sin" or that He contradicted the Law. For Jesus to forgive this woman meant that He had to one day die for her sins. Forgiveness is free but it is not cheap. Furthermore, Jesus perfectly fulfilled the Law so that no one could justly accuse Him of opposing its teachings or weakening its power. By applying the Law to the woman *and not to themselves,* the Jewish leaders were violating both the letter and the spirit of the Law—and they thought they were defending Moses!

The Law was given to reveal sin (Rom. 3:20), and we must be condemned by the Law before we can be cleansed by God's grace. Law and grace do not compete with each other; they complement each other. Nobody was ever saved by keeping the Law, but nobody was ever saved by grace who was not *first* indicted by the Law. There must be conviction before there can be conversion.

Nor is Christ's gracious forgiveness an excuse to sin. "Go, and sin no more!" was our Lord's counsel. "But there is forgiveness with Thee, that Thou mayest be feared" (Ps. 130:4). Certainly the experience of gracious forgiveness would motivate the penitent sinner to live a holy and obedient life to the glory of God.

Light and Darkness (John 8:12-20)

This second great I AM statement certainly fits into the context of the first eleven verses of John 8. Perhaps the sun was then appearing (John 8:2) so that Jesus was comparing Himself to the rising sun. But this would mean He was once again claiming to be God, for to the Jew, the sun was a symbol of Jehovah God (Ps. 84:11; Mal. 4:2). There is, for our universe, only one sun; and it is the center and the source of life. So there is but one God who is the center of all and the source of all life (John 1:4). "God is light" (1 John 1:5); and wherever the light shines, it reveals man's wickedness (Eph. 5:8-14).

Our Lord's I AM statement was also related to the Feast of Tabernacles, during which the huge candelabra were lighted in the temple at night to remind the people of the pillar of fire that had guided Israel in their wilderness journey. In fact, John has combined three "wilderness images": the manna (John 6), the water from the rock (John 7), and the pillar of fire (John 8).

To "follow" the Lord Jesus means to believe on Him, to trust Him; and the results are *life* and *light* for the believer. The unsaved are walking in darkness because they love darkness (John 3:17ff). One of the major messages in this Gospel is that the spiritual light is now shining, but people cannot comprehend it—and they try to put it out (John 1:4-5).

Not all of the Jewish leaders had left the group, and others had no doubt come along after the woman left. As usual, they debated with Jesus. This time, they accused Him of bearing witness to Himself by claiming to be the Light of the world; and Jewish courts would not permit a person to bear witness to himself.

But light *has to* bear witness to itself! The only people who cannot see the light are *blind* people!

I recall the first time I flew at night. I was fascinated by the changing textures of colored lights in the cities below me. When our plane left the New York area and headed out into the night, I was amazed that I could see pinpoints of light miles away. Then I understood why it was necessary to have blackouts during the war; for the enemy pilots could see the smallest evidence of light and thus find the target. Light bears witness to itself; it tells you it is there.

Perhaps the Pharisees were quoting our Lord's own words (see John 5:31ff); but He quickly refuted *their* argument. One of the key words in this section is *witness;* it is used seven times. Jesus made it clear that their witness was not dependable because their judgment was faulty. They judged on the basis of externals, mere human judgment, but He judged on the basis of spiritual knowledge. The way they judged the woman taken in adultery proved that they neither understood the Law nor their own sinful hearts.

Since they wanted to use the Law to condemn the woman and trap the Saviour, Jesus also used the Law to answer them. He quoted a principle found in Deuteronomy 17:6 and 19:15, as well as Numbers 35:30, that the testimony of two men was required to validate a judgment. Jesus had those two testimonies: *He* gave witness and so did *His Father.* We have seen from John 5:37-47 that the witness of the Father is found in the Word of God.

How tragic that these experts in the Law did not even know their own Messiah as He stood before them! They claimed to know the Law of God, but they did not know the God of the Law. They did not have His Word abiding in their hearts (John 5:38), nor did they experience His love (John 5:42). They did not know the Father, and therefore did not know the Son.

Jesus never really answered their question, "Where is Thy Father?" The word *father* is used twenty-one times in this chapter, so Jesus did not avoid the issue but faced it honestly. He knew that their "father" was not God—but the devil! These men were religious, and yet they were the children of the devil!

Their further attempts to arrest Jesus were again thwarted by the Father, for it was not yet our Lord's hour when He should give His life. When the servant of God is in the will of God, he can have courage and peace as he does his duty.

Life and Death (John 8:21-30)

Jesus had already mentioned His leaving them (John 7:34), but the Jews had misunderstood what He said. Once again, He warned them: He would leave them, they would not be able to follow Him, and they would die in their sins! They were wasting their God-given opportunities by arguing with Him instead of trusting Him; and one day soon, their opportunities would end.

Once again, the people misunderstood His teaching. They thought He was planning to kill Himself! Suicide was an abhorrent thing to a Jew, for the Jews were taught to honor all life. If Jesus committed suicide, then He would go to a place of judgment; and this, they reasoned, was why they could not follow Him.

Actually, just the opposite was true: it was *they* who were going to the place of judgment! Jesus was returning to His Father in heaven, and nobody can go there who has not trusted the Saviour. The reason Jesus and the Jewish leaders were going to different destinations was because they had different *origins:* Jesus came from heaven, but they belonged to the earth. Jesus was *in* the world, but He did not belong to the world (see John 17:14-16).

The true believer has his citizenship in heaven (Luke 10:20; Phil. 3:20-21). His affection and attention are fixed heavenward. But the unsaved belong to this world; in fact, Jesus called them "the children of this world" (Luke 16:8). Since they have not trusted Christ and had their sins forgiven, their destiny is to die in their sins. The Christian dies "in the Lord" because he lives "in the Lord" (Rev. 14:13); but the unbeliever dies in his sins because he lives in his sins.

It seems incredible that these religious "experts" should ask, "Who are You?" He had given them every evidence that He is the Son of God, yet they had deliberately rejected the evidence. Our Lord's reply may be expressed, "I am exactly what I said!" In other words, "Why should I teach you *new* things, or give you *new* proof, when you have not honestly considered the witness I have already given?"

Jesus boldly made several claims to deity (John 8:26). He said He would judge, and judgment (to the Jews) belonged only to God. He claimed to be sent by God, and He claimed to have heard from God the things that He taught. How did the religious leaders respond to these clear affirmations of deity? They did not understand! God reveals His truth to the "babes" and not to the "wise and prudent" (Luke 10:21).

Now Jesus spoke about His own death, when He would be "lifted up" on the cross (John 3:14; 12:32). The word translated "lifted up" has a dual meaning: "lifted up in crucifixion," and "lifted up in exaltation and glorification." Jesus often combined the two, for He saw His crucifixion in terms of glory and not just suffering (John 12:23; 13:30-31; 17:1). This same combination of "suffering and glory" is repeated in Peter's first letter.

It would be in His death, burial, resurrection, and ascension that Jesus would be revealed to the Jewish nation. This was the message Peter preached at Pentecost (Acts 2), not only the death of Jesus but also His resurrection and exaltation to glory. Even a Roman soldier, beholding the events at Golgotha would confess, "Truly this Man was the Son of God" (Mark 15:39). The early church, following the example of their Lord (Luke 24:25-27), would show from the Old Testament prophecies both the sufferings and the glory of the Messiah.

Jesus made two more stupendous claims: not only was He sent by the Father, but the Father was with Him because He always did what pleased the Father (John 8:29). No doubt, His enemies reacted violently to these words: but some of the listeners put their faith in Him. Whether this was true saving faith or not (see John 2:23-25), we cannot tell; but our Lord's words to them would indicate that they knew what they were doing.

Salvation is a matter of life or death. People who live in their sins and reject the Saviour must die in their sins. There is no alternative. We either receive salvation by grace or experience condemnation under God's Law. We either walk in the light and have eternal life, or walk in the darkness and experience eternal death. There is a fourth contrast.

Freedom and Bondage (John 8:31-47)

What listeners are represented by the pronoun "they" in John 8:33? In the previous verses, Jesus addressed the "believers" mentioned in John 8:30, and He warned them that continuance in the Word—discipleship—was proof of true salvation. When we obey His Word, we grow in spiritual knowledge; and as we grow in spiritual knowledge, we grow in freedom from sin. Life leads to learning, and learning leads to liberty.

It is not likely that the pronoun *they* refers to these new believers, for they would probably not argue with their Saviour! If John 8:37 is any guide, "they" probably refers to the same unbelieving Jewish leaders who had opposed Jesus throughout this conversation (John 8:13, 19, 22, 25). As before, they did not understand His message. Jesus was speaking about true spiritual freedom, freedom from sin, but they were thinking about political freedom.

Their claim that Abraham's descendants had never been in bondage was certainly a false one that was refuted by the very record in the Old Testament Scriptures. The Jews had been enslaved by seven mighty nations, as recorded in the Book of Judges. The ten Northern tribes had been carried away captive by Assyria, and the two Southern tribes had gone into seventy years of captivity in Babylon. And at that very hour, the Jews were under the iron heel of Rome! How difficult it is for proud religious people to admit their failings and their needs!

Jesus explained that the difference between spiritual freedom and bondage is a matter of whether one is a son or a servant. The servant may live in the house, but he is not a part of the family; and he cannot be guaranteed a future. (Jesus may have had Isaac and Ishmael in mind here; see Gen. 21.) "Whosoever keeps on practicing sin [literal translation] is the servant of sin." These religious leaders would not only *die* in their sins (John 8:21, 24), but they were right then *living* in bondage to sin!

How can slaves of sin be set free? Only by the Son. How does He do it? Through the power of His Word. Note the emphasis on the Word in John 8:38-47, and He had already told them, "The truth shall make you free" (John 8:32). They would not "make room" for His Word in their hearts.

In the rest of this section, you see the debate centering around the word *father.* Jesus identified Himself with the Father in heaven, but He identified them with the father from hell, Satan. Of course, the Jews claimed Abraham as their father (Luke 3:8ff), but Jesus made a careful distinction between "Abraham's seed" (physical descendants) and "Abraham's children" (spiritual descendants because of personal faith; Gal. 3:6-14).

These Jewish leaders, who claimed to belong to Abraham, were very unlike Abraham. For one thing, they wanted to kill Jesus; Abraham was the "friend of God" and fellowshipped with Him in love (Isa. 41:8). Abraham listened to God's truth and obeyed it, but these religious leaders rejected the truth.

Nature is determined by birth, and birth is determined by paternity. If God is your Father, then you share God's nature (2 Peter 1:1-4); but if Satan is your father, then you share in his evil nature. Our Lord did not say that *every* lost sinner is a "child of the devil," though every lost sinner is certainly a child of wrath and disobedience (Eph. 2:1-3). Both here and in the Parable of the Tares (Matt. 13:24-32, 36-43), Jesus said that the Pharisees and other "counterfeit" believers were the children of the devil. Satan is an imitator (2 Cor. 11:13-15), and he gives his children a false righteousness that can never gain them entrance into heaven (Rom. 10:1-4).

What were the characteristics of these religious leaders who belonged to the devil? For one thing, they rejected the truth (John 8:40) and tried to kill Jesus because He spoke the truth. They did not love God (John 8:42) nor could they understand what Jesus taught (John 8:43, 47). Satan's children may be well versed in their religious traditions, but they have no understanding of the Word of God.

Satan is a liar and a murderer. He lied to our first parents ("Yea, hath God said?") and engineered their deaths. Cain was a child of the devil (1 John 3:12), for he was both a liar and a murderer. He killed his brother Abel and then lied about it (Gen. 4). Is it any wonder that these religious leaders lied about

Jesus, hired false witnesses, and then had Him killed?

The worst bondage is the kind that the prisoner himself does not recognize. He thinks he is free, yet he is really a slave. The Pharisees and other religious leaders thought that they were free, but they were actually enslaved in terrible spiritual bondage to sin and Satan. They would not face the truth, and yet it was the truth alone that could set them free.

Honor and Dishonor (John 8:48-59)

The leaders could not refute our Lord's statements, so they attacked His person. Some students think that the leaders' statement in John 8:41—"We are not born of fornication"—was a slur on our Lord's own birth and character. After all, Mary was with child before she and Joseph were married. But the personal attacks in John 8:48 are quite obvious. For a Jew to be called a Samaritan was the grossest of insults, and then to be called a demon-possessed person only added further insult.

Note that Jesus did not even dignify the racial slur with an answer. (No doubt there was also in this the suggestion that, like the Samaritans, Jesus was a heretic.) They were dishonoring Him, but He was honoring the Father. You will recall that He made it clear that it was impossible to honor the Father without honoring the Son (John 5:23). They were seeking their own glory (see John 5:41-44), but He was seeking the glory that belongs to God alone. Tradition-centered religion, without Christ, is often a "mutual admiration society" for people who want the praise of men.

Jesus had warned them that they would die in their sins because of their unbelief, and now He invited them to trust His Word and "never see death" (John 8:51). He had said this before in His synagogue sermon (John 6:39-40, 44, 54). Once again, the leaders lacked the spiritual insight to understand what He was saying. Abraham was dead, yet he was a godly man; and the faithful prophets were also dead. This kind of talk only convinced them the more that He had a demon! (John 7:20)

By claiming to be the Lord of death, He was claiming to be God (John 5:21-29). This was not an honor He made for Himself; the Father gave it to Him. In fact, Abraham (whom they claimed as their father) saw His day and rejoiced! Instead of rejoicing, they were revolting and trying to kill Him.

How did Abraham "see" our Lord's day, that is, His life and ministry on earth? The same way he saw the future city: by faith (Heb. 11:10, 13-16). God did not give Abraham some special vision of our Lord's life and ministry, but He did give him the spiritual perception to "see" these future events. Certainly Abraham saw the birth of the Messiah in the miraculous birth of his own son, Isaac. He certainly saw Calvary when he offered Isaac to God (Gen. 22). In the priestly ministry of Melchizedek (Gen. 14:17-24), Abraham could see the heavenly priesthood of the Lord. In the marriage of Isaac, Abraham could see a picture of the marriage of the Lamb (Gen. 24).

His statement found in John 8:58 can be translated, "Before Abraham came into being, I AM." Again, this was another affirmation of His divine sonship; and the Jewish leaders received it as such. He had once again made Himself equal with God (John 5:18), and this was the sin of blasphemy, worthy of death (Lev. 24:16). Jesus was divinely protected and simply walked away. His hour had not yet come. We cannot help but admire His courage as He presented the truth and invited blind religious men to trust Him and be set free.

The most difficult people to win to the Saviour are those who do not realize that they have a need. They are under the condemnation of God, yet they trust their religion to save them. They are walking in the darkness and not following the light of life. They are sharing a "living death" because of their bondage to sin; and, in spite of their religious deeds, they are dishonoring the Father and the Son. These are the people who crucified Jesus Christ, and Jesus called them the children of the devil.

Whose child are you? Is God your Father because you have received Jesus Christ into your life? (John 1:12-13) Or is Satan your father because you are depending on a counterfeit righteousness, a "works righteousness," not the righteousness that comes through faith in Jesus Christ?

If God is your Father, then heaven is your home. If He is not your Father, then hell is your destiny.

It is truly a matter of life or death!

CHAPTER NINE
THE BLIND MAN CALLS THEIR BLUFF
John 9

Our Lord performed miracles in order to meet human needs. But He also used those miracles as a "launching pad" for a message conveying spiritual truth. Finally, His miracles were His "credentials" to prove that He was indeed the Messiah. "The blind receive their sight" was one such messianic miracle (Matt. 11:5), and we see it demonstrated in this chapter. Jesus used this miracle as the basis for a short sermon on spiritual blindness (John 9:39-41) and a longer sermon on true and false shepherds (John 10:1-18).

I am told that in the United States somebody goes blind every twenty minutes. The man we meet in this chapter was *born* blind; he had never seen the beauty of God's creation or the faces of his loved ones. When Jesus arrived on the scene, everything changed, and the man was made to see. However, the greatest miracle was not the opening of his eyes but the opening of his heart to the Saviour. It cost him everything to confess Jesus as the Son of God, but he was willing to do it.

The easiest way to grasp the message of this chapter is to note the stages in this man's growing understanding of who Jesus is.

"A Man Called Jesus" (John 9:1-12)

About the only thing a blind man could do in that day was beg, and that is what this man was doing when Jesus passed by (John 9:8). No doubt there were many blind people who would have rejoiced to be healed, but Jesus selected this man (see Luke 4:25-27). Apparently the man and his parents were well known in the community. It was on the Sabbath when Jesus healed the man (John 9:14), so that once again He was upsetting and deliberately challenging the religious leaders (John 5:9ff).

The disciples did not look at the man as an object of mercy but rather as a subject for a theological discussion. It is much easier to discuss an abstract subject like "sin" than it is to minister to a concrete need in the life of a person. The disciples were sure that the man's congenital blindness was caused by sin, either his own or his parents', but Jesus disagreed with them.

In the final analysis, *all* physical problems are the result of our fall in Adam, for his disobedience brought sin and death into the world (Rom. 5:12ff). But afterward, to blame a specific disability on a specific sin committed by specific persons is certainly beyond any man's ability or authority. Only God knows why babies are born with handicaps, and only God can turn those handicaps into something that will bring good to the people and glory to His name.

Certainly both the man and his parents had at some time committed sin, but Jesus did not see their sin as the cause of the man's blindness. Nor did He suggest that God deliberately made the man blind so that, years later, Jesus could perform a miracle. Since there is no punctuation in the original manuscripts, we are free to read John 9:3-4 this way:

> Neither has this man sinned nor his parents. But that the works of God should be made manifest in him, I must work the works of Him that sent Me, while it is day.

Our Lord's method of healing was unique: He put clay on the man's eyes and told him to go wash. Once Jesus healed two blind men by merely touching their eyes (Matt. 9:27-31), and He healed another blind man by putting spittle on his eyes (Mark 8:22-26). Though the healing power was the same, our Lord varied His methods lest people focus on the *manner* of healing and miss the *message* in the healing.

There were at least two reasons for our Lord's use of the clay. For one thing, it was a picture of the *Incarnation.* God made the first man out of the dust, and God sent His Son as a real Man. Note the emphasis on the meaning of "Siloam"—"sent." And relate this to John 9:4, "The works of Him that sent Me" (see also John 3:17, 34; 5:36; 7:29; 8:18, 42). Jesus gave a little illustration of His own coming to earth, sent by the Father.

The second reason for the clay was *irritation;* it encouraged the man to believe and obey! If you have ever had an irritation in your eyes, you know how quickly you seek *irrigation* to cleanse it out! You might compare this "irritation" to the convicting work of the Holy

Spirit as He uses God's Law to bring the lost sinner under judgment.

But the illumination now led to a problem in *identification:* was this really the blind beggar, and who caused him to see? Throughout the rest of John 9, a growing conflict takes place around these two questions. The religious leaders did not want to face the fact that Jesus had healed the man, or even that the man had been healed!

Four times in this chapter people asked, "How were you healed?" (John 9:10, 15, 19, 26) First the neighbors asked the man, and then the Pharisees asked him. Not satisfied with his reply, the Pharisees then asked the man's parents and then gave the son one final interrogation. All of this looked very official and efficient, but it was really a most evasive maneuver on the part of both the people and the leaders. The Pharisees wanted to get rid of the evidence, and the people were afraid to speak the truth!

They were all asking the wrong question! They should not have asked "How?" but "Who?" (Simply rearrange the letters!) But we are so prone to ask "How?" We want to understand the mechanics of a miracle instead of simply trusting the Saviour, who alone can perform the miracle. Nicodemus wanted to know how he could reenter his mother's womb (John 3:4, 9). "How can this man give us His flesh to eat?" (John 6:52) Understanding the process, even if we could, is no guarantee that we have experienced the miracle.

When asked to describe his experience, the man simply told what had happened. All he knew about the person who had done the miracle was that He was "a man called Jesus." He had not seen our Lord, of course; but he had heard His voice. Not only was the beggar ignorant of Jesus' identity, but he did not know where Jesus had gone. At this point, the man has been healed, but he has not been saved. The light had dawned, but it would grow brighter until he saw the face of the Lord and worshiped Him (see Prov. 4:18).

At least twelve times in the Gospel of John, Jesus is called "a man" (see John 4:29; 5:12; 8:40; 9:11, 24; 10:33; 11:47, 50; 18:14, 17, 29; 19:5). John's emphasis is that Jesus Christ is God, but the apostle balances it beautifully by reminding us that Jesus is also true man. The Incarnation was not an illusion (1 John 1:1-4).

"A Prophet" (John 9:13-23)

Since the Pharisees were the custodians of the faith, it was right that the healed man be brought to them for investigation. The fact that they studied this miracle in such detail is only further proof that Jesus did indeed heal the man. Since the man was *born* blind, the miracle was even greater, for blindness caused by sickness or injury might suddenly go away. Our Lord's miracles can bear careful scrutiny by His enemies.

But Jesus' act of deliberately healing the man on the Sabbath Day caused the Pharisees great concern. It was illegal to work on the Sabbath; and by making the clay, applying the clay, and healing the man, Jesus had performed three unlawful "works." The Pharisees should have been praising God for a miracle; instead, they sought evidence to prosecute Jesus.

When people refuse to face evidence honestly, but in fear evade the issue (see John 9:22), then it is impossible to come to a united conclusion. Once again, Jesus was the cause of division (John 9:16; also see 7:12, 43). The religious leaders were judging on the basis of one thing: nobody who breaks the Sabbath could possibly be a true prophet of God. They were "one-issue" thinkers, not unlike some religious people today. The Pharisees did not realize that Jesus was offering the people something greater than the Sabbath—the true spiritual rest that comes from God (Matt. 11:28-30).

But the beggar was not intimidated by the threats of the Pharisees. When asked who he thought Jesus was, the man boldly said, "He is a prophet!" (Note John 4:19 for a parallel.) Some of the Old Testament prophets, such as Moses, Elijah, and Elisha, did perform miracles. The Jewish people would look on their prophets as men of God who could do wonderful things by the power of God.

But the religious leaders did not want to see Jesus given that kind of high designation. "This man is not of God!" (John 9:16) Perhaps they could discredit the miracle. If so, then they could convince the people that Jesus had plotted the whole thing and was really deceiving the people. He had craftily "switched" beggars so that the sighted man was not the man who had been known as the blind beggar.

The best way to get that kind of evidence would be to interrogate the parents of the beggar, so they called them in and asked them two questions: (1) "Is this your son?" And (2)

"If he is, how does he now see?" If they refused to answer either question, they were in trouble; or if they answered with replies contrary to what the leaders wanted, they were in trouble. What a dilemma!

They answered the first question honestly: he was their son and he had been born blind. They answered the second question evasively: they did not know how he was healed or who healed him. They then used the old-fashioned tactic called "passing the buck" by suggesting that the Pharisees ask the man himself. After all, he was of age!

What lay behind all of this questioning and these furtive replies? *The fear of people.* We met it at the Feast of Tabernacles (John 7:13), and we shall meet it again at our Lord's last Passover (John 12:42). These people were seeking the honor of men and not the honor that comes from God (John 5:44). To be sure, it was a serious thing to be excommunicated from the synagogue, but it was far more serious to reject the truth and be lost forever. "The fear of man brings a snare" (Prov. 29:25, NASB). The Pharisees were trying to trap Jesus, and the parents were trying to avoid a trap; but all of them were only ensnaring themselves! The parents should have heeded the counsel of Isaiah 51:7 and 12.

The Pharisees could present a "good case" for their position. After all, they did have the Law of Moses as well as centuries of Jewish tradition. What they failed to understand was that Jesus Christ had fulfilled all of this ceremonial law and was now bringing in something new. In Moses, you have preparation; but in Jesus Christ, you have consummation (see John 1:17).

"A Man of God" (John 9:24-34)

Anxious to settle the case, the Pharisees did call the man in; and this time, they put him under oath. "Give God the praise" is a form of Jewish "swearing in" at court (see Josh. 7:19).

But the "judges" prejudiced everybody from the start! "We know that this Man is a sinner!" They were warning the witness that he had better cooperate with the court, or he might be excommunicated. But the beggar was made of sturdier stuff than to be intimidated. He had experienced a miracle, and he was not afraid to tell them what had happened.

He did not debate the character of Jesus Christ, because that was beyond his knowledge and experience. But one thing he did know: now he could see. His testimony (John 9:25) reminds me of Psalm 27. Read that psalm in the light of this chapter, from the viewpoint of the healed beggar, and see how meaningful it becomes.

For the fourth time, the question is asked, "How did He open your eyes?" (see John 9:10, 15, 19, and 26) I can imagine the man getting quite impatient at this point. After all, he had been blind all his life, and there was so much now to see. He certainly did not want to spend much longer in a synagogue court, looking at angry faces and answering the same questions!

We admire the boldness of the man in asking those irate Pharisees if they wanted to follow Jesus! The man expected a negative answer, but he was courageous even to ask it. Unable to refute the evidence, the judges began to revile the witness; and once again Moses is brought into the picture (John 5:46). The Pharisees were cautious men who would consider themselves conservatives, when in reality they were "preservatives." A true conservative takes the best of the past and uses it, but he is also aware of the new things that God is doing. The new grows out of the old (Matt. 13:52). A "preservative" simply embalms the past and preserves it. He is against change and resists the new things that God is doing. Had the Pharisees really understood Moses, they would have known who Jesus was and what He was doing.

The leaders were sure about Moses, but they were not sure about Jesus. They did not know where He came from. He had already told them that He had come from heaven, sent by the Father (John 6:33, 38, 41-42, 50-51). They were sure that He was the natural son of Mary and Joseph, and that He was from the city of Nazareth (John 6:42; 7:41-42). They were judging "after the flesh" (John 8:15) and not exercising spiritual discernment.

It seemed incredible to the healed man that the Pharisees would not know this Man who had opened his eyes! How many people were going around Jerusalem, opening the eyes of blind people? Instead of investigating the miracle, these religious leaders should have been investigating the One who did the miracle and learning from Him. The "experts" were rejecting the Stone that was sent to them (Acts 4:11).

The beggar then gave the "experts" a lesson in practical theology. Perhaps he had Psalm 66:18 in mind: "If I regard iniquity in my heart, the Lord will not hear me." The leaders called Jesus a sinner (John 9:24), yet Jesus was used of God to open the blind man's eyes.

He added another telling argument: Jesus healed a man *born* blind. Never, to their knowledge, had this occurred before. So, God not only heard Jesus, but He enabled Him to give the man sight. How, then, could Jesus be a sinner?

Religious bigots do not want to face either evidence or logic. Their minds are made up. Had the Pharisees honestly considered the facts, they would have seen that Jesus is the Son of God, and they could have trusted Him and been saved.

Again, the leaders reviled the man and told him he was born in sin. However, he would not *die* in his sins (see John 8:21, 24); because before this chapter ends, the beggar will come to faith in Jesus Christ. All of us are born in sin (Ps. 51:5), but we need not live in sin (Col. 3:6-7) or die in our sins. Faith in Jesus Christ redeems us from sin and gives us a life of joyful liberty.

The religious leaders officially excommunicated this man from the local synagogue. This meant that the man was cut off from friends and family and looked on by the Jews as a "publican and sinner." But Jesus came for the "outcasts" and never let them down.

"The Son of God" (John 9:35-41)

The Good Shepherd always cares for His sheep. Jesus knew that the man had been excommunicated, so He found him and revealed Himself to him. Remember, the man knew our Lord's voice, but he had never seen His face.

The man now reached the climax of his knowledge of Jesus Christ and his faith in Him. It is not enough to believe that He is "a man called Jesus," or even "a prophet" or "a man of God." "Whosoever believeth that Jesus is the Christ is born of God" (1 John 5:1). John wrote his Gospel to prove that Jesus is the Son of God, and to present to his readers the testimonies of people who met Jesus and affirmed that He is God's Son. This beggar is one such witness.

Jesus identified Himself as the Son of God (see John 9:35; also 5:25), and the beggar believed and was saved (John 9:38). "My sheep hear My voice" (John 10:27). He did not "see and believe"; he *heard* and believed. Not only did he trust the Saviour, but he worshiped Him. If Jesus Christ is not God, then why did He accept worship? Peter, Paul, and Barnabas certainly didn't accept worship (see Acts 10:25-26; 14:11-15).

John the Baptist affirmed that Jesus is the Son of God (John 1:34) and so did Nathanael (John 1:49). Jesus stated that He is the Son of God (John 5:25; 9:35), and Peter also affirmed it (John 6:69). Now the healed blind beggar has joined this group of witnesses.

Wherever Jesus went, some of the Pharisees tried to be present so they could catch Him in something He said or did. Seeing them, Jesus closed this episode by preaching a brief but penetrating sermon on spiritual blindness.

John 9:39 does not contradict John 3:16-17. The *reason* for our Lord's coming was salvation, but the *result* of His coming was condemnation of those who would not believe. The same sun that brings beauty out of the seeds also exposes the vermin hiding under the rocks. The religious leaders were blind and would not admit it; therefore, the light of truth only made them blinder. The beggar admitted his need, and he received both physical and spiritual sight. No one is so blind as he who will not see, the one who thinks he has "all truth" and there is nothing more for him to learn (John 9:28, 34).

The listening Pharisees heard what Jesus said and it disturbed them. "Are we blind also?" they asked, expecting a negative answer. Jesus had already called them "blind leaders of the blind" (Matt. 15:14), so they had their answer. They were blinded by their pride, their self-righteousness, their tradition, and their false interpretation of the Word of God.

Our Lord's reply was a paradox. "If you were blind, you would be better off. But you claim to see. Therefore, you are guilty!" Blindness would at least be an excuse for not knowing what was going on. But they *did* know what was going on. Jesus had performed many miracles and the religious leaders ignored the evidence to make a right decision.

Jesus is the Light of the world (John 8:12; 9:5). The only people who cannot see the light are blind people and those who refuse to look, those who make themselves blind. The beggar was physically blind and spiritually blind, yet both his eyes and his heart were opened. Why? Because he listened to the Word, believed it, obeyed, and experienced the grace of God. The Pharisees had good physical vision, but they were blind spiritually. Had they listened to the Word and sincerely considered the evidence, they too would have believed on Jesus Christ and been born again.

In what sense did the Pharisees "see"? They saw the change in the blind beggar and could not deny that he had been healed. They saw the mighty works that Jesus performed. Even Nicodemus, one of their number, was impressed with the Lord's miracles (John 3:2). If they had examined the evidence with honesty, they would have seen the truth clearly. "If any man wills to do His [God's] will, he shall know of the doctrine" (John 7:17, literal translation). "And ye will not come to Me, that ye might have life" (John 5:40).

John 10 is actually a continuation of our Lord's ministry to the Pharisees. The healing of the blind beggar is the background (John 10:21). In fact, the word translated "cast out" in John 9:35 is translated "puts forth" in John 10:4. The beggar was cast out of the synagogue but taken by the Good Shepherd and added to His flock! The emphasis in John 10 is on Jesus Christ, the Good and True Shepherd, as opposed to the Pharisees who were false shepherds.

We never meet this healed beggar again, but surely the man followed Jesus closely and was among those who witnessed for Him. We hope that he was able to win his fearful parents to the Lord. While being excommunicated from the synagogue was certainly a painful experience for him, he certainly found in his fellowship with Jesus Christ much more spiritual help and encouragement than he could ever have found in the Jewish traditions.

Even today, there are people who must choose between Christ and family, or Christ and their traditional religion.

This blind beggar made the right choice, even though the cost was great.

"The path of the just is as the shining light, that shineth more and more unto the perfect day" (Prov. 4:18).

CHAPTER TEN
THE GOOD SHEPHERD AND HIS SHEEP
John 10

Perhaps you remember the "Candid Camera" TV program that took place at an exclusive prep school where all of the students were well above average. The "Candid Camera" people posed as career consultants who were going to advise these brilliant young men concerning the careers that would be best suited to them, on the basis of "tests" and "interviews" that seemed (to the students) quite authentic.

One young man eagerly awaited the "counselor's" verdict. Surely the adviser would tell the boy to be a college president or a bank president, or perhaps a research scientist. But, no, the "counselor" had other ideas. You should have seen the look on the boy's face when the "counselor" said:

"Son, after evaluating your tests and interview, I've decided that the best job for you is—a shepherd."

The student did not know whether to laugh or cry. After all, who in his right mind would want to be a shepherd? Why devote your life to "stupid sheep" who do not seem to have sense enough to find their way home?

John 10 focuses on the image of sheep, sheepfolds, and shepherds. It is a rural and Eastern image, to be sure; but it is an image that can say a great deal to us today, even in our urban industrialized world. Paul used this image when admonishing the spiritual leaders in the church at Ephesus (Acts 20:28ff). The truths that cluster around the image of the shepherd and the sheep are found throughout the Bible, and they are important to us today. The symbols that Jesus used help us understand who He is and what He wants to do for us.

Perhaps the easiest way to approach this somewhat complex chapter of John's Gospel is to note the three declarations that Jesus made about Himself.

"I Am the Door" (John 10:1-10)
This sermon grew out of our Lord's confrontation with Jewish leaders, following the excommunication of the beggar (John 9). He had

briefly spoken to them about light and darkness, but now He changed the image to that of the shepherd and the sheep. Why? Because to the Jewish mind, a "shepherd" was any kind of leader, spiritual or political. People looked on the king and prophets as shepherds. Israel was privileged to be "the flock of the Lord" (Ps. 100:3). For background, read Isaiah 56:9-12; Jeremiah 23:1-4; 25:32-38; Ezekiel 34; and Zechariah 11.

Jesus opened His sermon with *a familiar illustration* (John 10:1-6), one that every listener would understand. The sheepfold was usually an enclosure made of rocks, with an opening for the door. The shepherd (or a porter) would guard the flock, or flocks, at night by lying across the opening. It was not unusual for several flocks to be sheltered together in the same fold. In the morning, the shepherds would come, call their sheep, and assemble their own flocks. Each sheep recognized his own master's voice.

The true shepherd comes in through the door, and the porter recognizes him. The thieves and robbers could never enter through the door, so they have to climb over the wall and enter the fold through deception. But even if they did get in, they would never get the sheep to follow them, for the sheep follow only the voice of their own shepherd. The false shepherds can never *lead* the sheep, so they must *steal* them away.

It is clear that the listeners did not understand what Jesus said or why He said it. (The word translated "parable" means "a dark saying, a proverb." Our Lord's teaching in John 10 is not like the parables recorded in the other Gospels.) The occasion for this lesson was the excommunication of the beggar from the synagogue (John 9:34). The false shepherds did not care for this man; instead, they mistreated him and threw him out. But Jesus, the Shepherd, came to him and took him in (John 9:35-38).

It is unfortunate that John 10:1 is often used to teach that the sheepfold is heaven, and that those who try to get in by any way other than Christ are destined to fail. While the teaching is true (Acts 4:12), it is not based on this verse. Jesus made it clear that the fold is the nation of Israel (John 10:16). The Gentiles are the "other sheep" not of the fold of Israel.

When Jesus came to the nation of Israel, He came the appointed way, just as the Scriptures promised. Every true shepherd must be called of God and sent by God. If he truly speaks God's Word, the sheep will "hear his voice" and not be afraid to follow him. The true shepherd will love the sheep and care for them.

Since the people did not understand His symbolic language, Jesus followed the illustration with an *application* (John 10:7-10). Twice He said, "I am the Door." He is the Door of the sheepfold and makes it possible for the sheep to *leave* the fold (the religion of Judaism) and to *enter* His flock. The Pharisees *threw* the beggar out of the synagogue, but Jesus *led* him out of Judaism and into the flock of God!

But the Shepherd does not stop with leading the sheep out; He also leads them *in.* They become a part of the "one flock" (not "fold") which is His church. He is the Door of salvation (John 10:9). Those who trust Him enter into the Lord's flock and fold, and they have the wonderful privilege of going "in and out" and finding pasture. When you keep in mind that the shepherd actually was the "door" of the fold, this image becomes very real.

As the Door, Jesus delivers sinners from bondage and leads them into freedom. They have salvation! This word "saved" means "delivered safe and sound." It was used to say that a person had recovered from severe illness, come through a bad storm, survived a war, or was acquitted at court. Some modern preachers want to do away with an "old-fashioned" word like "saved," but Jesus used it!

Jesus was referring primarily to the religious leaders of that day (John 10:8). He was not condemning every prophet or servant of God who ever ministered before He came to earth. The statement "are thieves and robbers" (not "were") makes it clear that He had the present religious leaders in mind. They were not true shepherds nor did they have the approval of God on their ministry. They did not love the sheep, but instead exploited them and abused them. The beggar was a good example of what the "thieves and robbers" could do.

It is clear in the Gospel record that the religious rulers of Israel were interested only in providing for themselves and protecting themselves. The Pharisees were covetous (Luke 16:14) and even took advantage of the poor widows (Mark 12:40). They turned God's temple into a den of thieves (Matt. 21:13), and they plotted to kill Jesus so that Rome would not take away their privileges (John 11:49-53).

The True Shepherd came to save the sheep, but the false shepherds take advantage of the sheep and exploit them. Behind these false shepherds is "the thief" (John 10:10), probably a reference to Satan. The thief wants to steal the sheep from the fold, slaughter them, and destroy them. We shall see later that the sheep are safe in the hands of the Shepherd and the Father (John 10:27-29).

When you go through "the Door," you receive life and you are saved. As you go "in and out," you enjoy *abundant* life in the rich pastures of the Lord. His sheep enjoy fullness and freedom. Jesus not only gave His life *for* us, but He gives His life *to* us right now!

The emphasis in this first section is on "the door." Our Lord then shifted the emphasis to "the shepherd" and made a second declaration.

"I Am the Good Shepherd" (John 10:11-21)

This is the fourth of our Lord's I AM statements in John's Gospel (John 6:35; 8:12; 10:9). Certainly in making this statement, He is contrasting Himself to the false shepherds who were in charge of the Jewish religion of that day. He had already called them "thieves and robbers," and now He would describe them as "hirelings."

The word translated "good" means "intrinsically good, beautiful, fair." It describes that which is the ideal, the model that others may safely imitate. Our Lord's goodness was inherent in His nature. To call Him "good" is the same as calling Him "God" (Mark 10:17-18).

Some of the greatest people named in the Bible were shepherds by occupation: Abel, the patriarchs, Moses, and David, to name a few. Even today in the Holy Land, you may see shepherds leading flocks and revealing how intimately they know each sheep, its individual traits, and its special needs. Keep in mind that Jewish shepherds did not tend the sheep in order to slaughter them, unless they were used for sacrifice. Shepherds tended them that the sheep might give wool, milk, and lambs.

Jesus pointed out four special ministries that He performs as the Good Shepherd.

He dies for the sheep (vv. 11-13). Under the old dispensation, the sheep died for the shepherd; but now the Good Shepherd dies for the sheep! Five times in this sermon, Jesus clearly affirmed the sacrificial nature of His death (John 10:11, 15, 17-18). He did not die as a martyr, killed by men; He died as a substitute, willingly laying down His life for us.

The fact that Jesus said that He died "for the sheep" must not be isolated from the rest of biblical teaching about the Cross. He also died for the nation Israel (John 11:50-52) and for the world (John 6:51). While the blood of Jesus Christ is *sufficient* for the salvation of the world, it is *efficient* only for those who will believe.

Jesus contrasted Himself to the hireling who watches over the sheep only because he is paid to do so. But when there is danger, the hireling runs away, while the true shepherd stays and cares for the flock. The key phrase is "whose own the sheep are not." The Good Shepherd *purchases the sheep* and they are His because He died for them. They belong to Him, and He cares for them. By nature, sheep are stupid and prone to get into danger; and they need a shepherd to care for them.

Throughout the Bible, God's people are compared to sheep; and the comparison is a good one. Sheep are clean animals, unlike pigs and dogs (2 Peter 2:20-22). They are defenseless and need the care of the shepherd (Ps. 23). They are, to use Wesley's phrase, "prone to wander," and must often be searched for and brought back to the fold (Luke 15:3-7). Sheep are peaceful animals, useful to the shepherd. In these, and other ways, they picture those who have trusted Jesus Christ and are a part of God's flock.

The Pharisees, in contrast to good shepherds, had no loving concern for the beggar, so they put him out of the synagogue. Jesus found him and cared for him.

He knows His sheep (vv. 14-15). In the Gospel of John, the word *know* means much more than intellectual awareness. It speaks of an intimate relationship between God and His people (see John 17:3). The Eastern shepherd knows his sheep personally and therefore knows best how to minister to them.

To begin with, our Lord knows our names (see John 10:3). He knew Simon (John 1:42) and even gave him a new name. He called Zaccheus by name (Luke 19:5); and when He spoke Mary's name in the garden, she recognized her Shepherd (John 20:16). If you have ever had your identity "lost" in a maze of computer operations, then you can appreciate the comforting fact that the Good Shepherd knows each of His sheep by name.

He also knows our natures. While all sheep

are alike in their essential nature, each sheep has its own distinctive characteristics; and the loving shepherd recognizes these traits. One sheep may be afraid of high places, another of dark shadows. A faithful shepherd will consider these special needs as he tends the flock.

Have you ever noticed how different the 12 Apostles were from one another? Peter was impulsive and outspoken, while Thomas was hesitant and doubting. Andrew was a "people person" who was always bringing somebody to Jesus, while Judas wanted to "use" people in order to get their money for himself. Jesus knew each of the men personally, and He knew exactly how to deal with them.

Because He knows our natures, He also knows our needs. Often, *we* do not even know our own needs! Psalm 23 is a beautiful poetic description of how the Good Shepherd cares for His sheep. In the pastures, by the waters, and even through the valleys, the sheep need not fear, because the shepherd is caring for them and meeting their needs. If you connect Psalm 23:1 and 6, you get the main theme of the poem: "I shall not want . . . all the days of my life."

As the shepherd cares for the sheep, the sheep get to know their shepherd better. The Good Shepherd knows His sheep and His sheep know Him. They get to know Him better by listening to His voice (the Word) and experiencing His daily care. As the sheep follow the Shepherd, they learn to love and to trust Him. He loves "His own" (John 13:1) and He shows that love in the way He cares for them.

The Good Shepherd brings other sheep into the flock (v. 16). The "fold" is Judaism (John 10:1), but there is another fold—the Gentiles who are outside the covenants of Israel (Eph. 2:11ff). In our Lord's early ministry, He concentrated on the "lost sheep of the house of Israel" (Matt. 10:5-6; 15:24-27). The people converted at Pentecost were Jews and Jewish proselytes (Acts 2:5, 14), but the church was not to remain a "Jewish flock." Peter took the Gospel to the Gentiles (Acts 10–11), and Paul carried the message to the Gentiles in the far reaches of the Roman Empire (Acts 13:1ff).

The phrase "one fold" should read "one flock." There is but one flock, the people of God who belong to the Good Shepherd. God has His people all over this world (see Acts 18:1-11), and He will call them and gather them together.

The missionary message of the Gospel of John is obvious: "For God so loved the world" (John 3:16). Jesus Himself defied custom and witnessed to a Samaritan woman. He refused to defend the exclusivist approach of the Jewish religious leaders. He died for a lost world, and His desire is that His people reach a lost world with the message of eternal life.

The Good Shepherd takes up His life again (vv. 17-21). His voluntary death was followed by His victorious resurrection. From the human point of view, it appeared that Jesus was executed; but from the divine point of view, He laid down His life willingly. When Jesus cried on the cross, "It is finished!" He then voluntarily yielded up His spirit to the Father (John 19:30). Three days later, He voluntarily took up His life again and arose from the dead. The Father gave Him this authority in love.

Sometimes the Scriptures teach that it was the Father who raised the Son (Acts 2:32; Rom. 6:4; Heb. 13:20). Here, the Son stated that He had authority to take up His life again. Both are true, for the Father and the Son worked together in perfect harmony (John 5:17, 19). In a previous sermon, Jesus had hinted that He had power to raise Himself from the dead (John 5:26). Of course, this was a claim that the Jews would protest; because it was tantamount to saying "I am God!"

How did the listeners respond to this message? "There was a division therefore again among the Jews" (John 10:19). Note that word *again* (John 7:43; 9:16). The old accusation that Jesus was a demoniac was hurled at Him again (John 7:20; 8:48, 52). People will do almost anything to avoid facing the truth!

Since Jesus Christ is "the Door," we would expect a division, because a door shuts some people in and others out! He is the Good Shepherd, and the shepherd must separate the sheep from the goats. It is impossible to be neutral about Jesus Christ; for, what we believe about Him is a matter of life or death (John 8:24).

His third declaration was the most startling of all.

"I Am the Son of God" (John 10:22-42)

The events in this section occurred about two and a half months after those described in John 10:1-21. John put them together because in both messages, Jesus used the imagery of the shepherd and the sheep.

The encounter (vv. 22-24). The "Feast

of the Dedication" (Hanukkah, "the feast of lights") takes place in December, near the time of the Christian Christmas celebration. The feast commemorates the rededication of the temple by Judas Maccabeus in 164 B.C., after it had been desecrated by the Romans. This historical fact may bear a relationship to the words of Jesus in John 10:36, for He had been set apart (dedicated) by the Father and sent into the world. The Jewish leaders were celebrating a great event in history yet passing by a great opportunity right in their own temple!

The leaders surrounded Jesus in the temple so that He had to stop and listen to them. They had decided that it was time for a "showdown" and they did not want Him to evade the issue any longer. "How long are You going to hold us in suspense?" they kept saying to Him. "Tell us plainly—are You the Messiah?"

The explanation (vv. 25-42). Jesus reminded them of what He had already taught them. He emphasized the witness of His *words* ("I told you") and His *works* (see John 5:17ff, and 7:14ff for similar replies).

But our Lord went much deeper in His explanation this time, for He revealed to the Jewish leaders *why* they did not understand His words or grasp the significance of His works: they were not His sheep. From the human standpoint, we become His sheep by believing; but from the divine standpoint, we believe because we are His sheep. There is a mystery here that we cannot fathom or explain, but we can accept it and rejoice (Rom. 11:33-36). God has His sheep and He knows who they are. They will hear His voice and respond.

The lost sinner who hears God's Word knows nothing about divine election. He hears only that Christ died for the sins of the world, and that he may receive the gift of eternal life by trusting the Saviour. When He trusts the Saviour, he becomes a member of God's family and a sheep in the flock. Then he learns that he was "chosen . . . in Him [Christ] before the foundation of the world" (Eph. 1:4). He also learns that each saved sinner is the Father's "love gift" to His Son (see John 10:29; 17:2, 6, 9, 11-12, 24).

In the Bible, divine election and human responsibility are perfectly balanced; and what God has joined together, we must not put asunder.

Jesus went on to explain that His sheep are secure in His hand and in the Father's hand. "They shall never perish" is His promise (John 3:16; 6:39; 17:12; 18:9). The false shepherds bring destruction (John 10:10, same Greek word); but the Good Shepherd sees to it that His sheep shall never perish.

The security of God's sheep is assured here in several ways. First, by definition—we have "eternal life," and that cannot be conditional and still be eternal. Second, this life is a gift, not something that we earn or merit. If we were not saved by our own good works, but by His grace, then we cannot be lost by our "bad works" (Rom. 11:6). But most important, Jesus gave us His promise that His sheep do not perish, and that His promise cannot be broken.

It is important to keep in mind that Jesus was talking about sheep—true believers—and not counterfeits. The dog and the pig will go back into sin (2 Peter 2:20-22); but the sheep, being a clean animal, will follow the Shepherd into the green pastures. The false professor will talk about his faith and even his works, but he will never make it into heaven (Matt. 7:13-29). Most of us know people who professed to be saved and then went back into sin, but their doing so only proved that they never really trusted Christ to begin with. Jesus did not promise security to anyone but His true sheep.

As you review our Lord's teaching about His ministry as the Good Shepherd, you note that He has a threefold relationship to His sheep. He has a *loving* relationship because He died for the sheep, as well as a *living* relationship because He cares for the sheep. It is also a *lasting* relationship, for He keeps His sheep and not a one is lost.

Our Lord made a statement that He knew would startle His enemies and give them more reason to oppose Him (John 10:30). It was the "plain answer" that the religious leaders had asked for. "I and My Father are One" is as clear a statement of His deity as you will find anywhere in Scripture. This was even stronger than His statement that He had come down from heaven (John 6) or that He existed before Abraham ever lived (John 8:58).

The word *One* does not suggest that the Father and the Son are identical persons. Rather, it means that they are one in essence: the Father is God and the Son is God, but the Father is not the Son and the Son is not the Father. He is speaking about unity, not identity. (See John 17:21-24 for similar language.)

The Jewish leaders understood clearly what He was saying! Some modern liberal theologians would water down our Lord's statement, but the people who heard it knew exactly what He was saying: "I am God!" (Note John 10:33.) To speak this way, of course, was blasphemy; and according to Jewish belief, blasphemy had to be punished by being put to death (see Lev. 24:16; Num. 15:30ff; Deut. 21:22).

Our Lord used Psalm 82:6 to refute their accusation and halt their actions. The picture in Psalm 82 is that of a court, where God has assembled the judges of the earth, to warn them that they too will one day be judged. The Hebrew word *elohim* can be translated as "god" or as "judges," as in Exodus 21:6 and 22:8-9. It is also one of the Old Testament names for God. The Jewish rulers certainly knew their own language and they knew that Jesus was speaking the truth. If God called human judges "gods," then why should they stone Him for applying the same title to Himself?

John 10:36 is crucial because it gives a double affirmation of the deity of Christ. First, the Father sanctified (set apart) the Son and sent Him into the world, and second, Jesus stated boldly, "I am the Son of God" (see John 5:25). He gave them the "plain answer" they asked for, but they would not believe it!

Could they have believed? Jesus *invited* them, urged them, to believe, if only on the basis of His miracles (John 10:37-38). If they would believe the miracles, then they would know the Father, and that would open the way for them to know the Son and believe on Him. It was simply a matter of examining the evidence honestly and being willing to accept the truth.

Once again, they tried to arrest Him (see John 7:44; 8:59), but He escaped and left the area completely. He did not return to Jerusalem until "Palm Sunday," when He presented Himself as Israel's King.

John the Baptist had ministered at Bethabara (John 1:28), but we are not sure where this was. It was on the other side of the Jordan River, perhaps eighteen to twenty miles from Jerusalem. Some maps put it almost directly across from Jerusalem, just east of Jericho.

Why did Jesus go there? For one thing, it was a safe retreat; the Jewish religious leaders were not likely to follow Him there. Also, it was a good place to prepare for His final week of public ministry when He would lay down His life for the sheep. As He remembered His own baptism by John, and all that He had experienced at that time (Matt. 3:13-17; John 1:20-34), it must have fortified Him for the suffering that He knew He must endure.

The common people continued to seek Jesus, and He continued to minister to them. It is worth noting that John the Baptist's witness was still bearing fruit long after he was dead! His witness to Jesus Christ led many to trust the Saviour. John was not a miracle worker, but he was a faithful witness who pointed to Jesus Christ. "He must increase, but I must decrease" (John 3:30).

Have you responded personally to our Lord's three great declarations recorded in this chapter?

He is the Door. Have you "entered in" by faith so that you are saved?

He is the Good Shepherd. Have you heard His voice and trusted Him? After all, He laid down His life for you!

He is the Son of God. Do you believe that? Have you given yourself to Him and received eternal life?

Remember His stern warning: "If ye believe not that I am He, ye shall die in your sins" (John 8:24).

CHAPTER ELEVEN
THE LAST MIRACLE—THE LAST ENEMY
John 11

The raising of Lazarus from the dead was not our Lord's last miracle before the Cross, but it was certainly His greatest and the one that aroused the most response both from His friends and His enemies. John selected this miracle as the seventh in the series recorded in his book because it was really the climactic miracle of our Lord's earthly ministry. He had raised others from the dead, but Lazarus had been in the grave four days. It was a miracle that could not be denied or avoided by the Jewish leaders.

If Jesus Christ can do nothing about death, then whatever else He can do amounts to nothing. "If in this life only we have hope in Christ, we are of all men most miserable" (1 Cor. 15:19). Death is man's last enemy (1 Cor. 15:26), but Jesus Christ has defeated this horrible enemy totally and permanently.

The emphasis in John 11 is on faith; you find some form of the word *believe* at least eight times in this account. Another theme is "the glory of God" (John 11:4, 40). In what Jesus said and did, He sought to strengthen the faith of three groups of people.

The Disciples (John 11:1-16)

We sometimes think of the disciples as "supersaints," but such was not the case. They often failed their Lord, and He was constantly seeking to increase their faith. After all, one day He would leave them and they would have the responsibility of carrying on the ministry. If their faith was weak, their work could never be strong.

Jesus was at Bethabara, about twenty miles from Bethany (John 1:28; 10:40). One day, a messenger arrived with the sad news that our Lord's dear friend Lazarus was sick. If the man had traveled quickly, without any delay, he could have made the trip in one day. Jesus sent him back the next day with the encouraging message recorded in John 11:4. Then Jesus waited two more days before He left for Bethany; and by the time He and His disciples arrived, Lazarus had been dead for four days. This means that Lazarus had died *the very day* the messenger left to contact Jesus!

The schedule of events would look something like this, allowing one day for travel:

Day 1—The messenger comes to Jesus (Lazarus dies).
Day 2—The messenger returns to Bethany.
Day 3—Jesus waits another day, then departs.
Day 4—Jesus arrives in Bethany.

When the messenger arrived back home, he would find Lazarus already dead. What would his message convey to the grieving sisters now that their brother was already dead and buried? Jesus was urging them to believe His word no matter how discouraging the circumstances might appear.

No doubt the disciples were perplexed about several matters. First of all, if Jesus loved Lazarus so much, why did He permit him to get sick? Even more, why did He delay to go to the sisters? For that matter, could He not have healed Lazarus at a distance, as He did the nobleman's son? (John 4:43-54) The record makes it clear that there was a strong love relationship between Jesus and this family (John 11:3, 5, 36); yet our Lord's behavior seems to contradict this love.

God's love for His own is not a pampering love; it is a perfecting love. The fact that He loves us, and we love Him is no guarantee that we will be sheltered from the problems and pains of life. After all, the Father loves His Son: and yet the Father permitted His beloved Son to drink the cup of sorrow and experience the shame and pain of the Cross. We must never think that love and suffering are imcompatible. Certainly they unite in Jesus Christ.

Jesus could have prevented Lazarus' sickness or even healed it from where He was; but He chose not to. He saw in this sickness an opportunity to glorify the Father. It is not important that we Christians are comfortable, but it is important that we glorify God in all that we do.

In their "prayer" to Jesus, the two sisters did not tell Him what to do. They simply informed Him that there was a need, and they reminded Him of His love for Lazarus. They knew that it was dangerous for Jesus to return to Judea because the Jewish leaders were out to destroy Him. Perhaps they hoped that He would "speak the word" and their brother would be restored to health.

Our Lord's message to the sisters did not say that their brother would not die. It promised only that death would not be the *ultimate* result, for the ultimate result would be the glory of God. (Note that once again, Jesus called Himself "the Son of God.") He wanted them to lay hold of this promise; in fact, He reminded Martha of this message when she balked at having the tomb opened (John 11:40).

When we find ourselves confronted by disease, disappointment, delay, and even death, our only encouragement is the Word of God. We must live by faith and not by sight. Their situation seemed hopeless, yet the sisters knew that Jesus was the Master of every situation. The promise in Psalm 50:15 finds a parallel here: "And call upon Me in the day of trouble: I will deliver thee, and thou shalt glorify Me."

What about our Lord's delay? He was not waiting for Lazarus to die, for he was already dead. Jesus lived on a divine timetable (John 11:9) and He was waiting for the Father to tell Him when to go to Bethany. The fact that the man had been dead four days gave greater authenticity to the miracle and greater opportunity for people to believe, including His own disciples (see John 11:15).

When our Lord announced that He was returning to Judea, His disciples were alarmed, because they knew how dangerous it would be. (Bethany is only about two miles from Jerusalem.) But Jesus was willing to lay down His life for His friends (John 15:13). He knew that His return to Judea and the miracle of raising Lazarus would precipitate His own arrest and death.

The Lord calmed their fears by reminding them that He was on the Father's schedule, and that nothing could harm them. As we have seen, this is an important theme in the Gospel of John (John 2:4; 7:6, 8, 30; 8:20; 12:23; 13:1; 17:1). But the disciples not only misunderstood the schedule, they also misunderstood the reason for the visit. They thought that, if Lazarus was sleeping, he was getting better! It was another example of their inability to grasp spiritual truth. "If he is sleeping, he must be improving—so let's not bother to go to Bethany!"

Then He told them openly that Lazarus was dead. (Death for the believer is compared to sleep. See Acts 7:60; 1 Cor. 15:51; 1 Thes. 4:13-18.) He did not say He was glad that His friend died, but that He was glad He had not been there; for now He could reveal to His disciples His mighty power. The result would be glory to God and the strengthening of their faith.

If Thomas' attitude was any indication, the faith of the disciples certainly needed strengthening! The name Thomas means "twin" in the Aramaic language; the Greek equivalent is Didymus. We do not know whose twin he was, but there are times when *all of us* seem to be his twin when we consider our unbelief and depressed feelings! It was Thomas who demanded evidence before he would accept the truth of our Lord's resurrection (John 20:24-28).

Thomas was a doubting man, but we must confess that he was a devoted man: he was willing to go with Jesus into danger and risk his own life. We may not admire his faith, but we can certainly applaud his loyalty and courage.

The Sisters (John 11:17-40)

Jesus was concerned not only about the faith of His own disciples, but also about the faith of Mary and Martha (John 11:26, 40). Each experience of suffering and trial ought to increase our faith, but this kind of spiritual growth is not automatic. We must respond positively to the ministry of the Word and the Spirit of God. Jesus had sent a promise to the two sisters (John 11:4), and now He would discover how they had received it.

The event recorded in Luke 10:38-42 makes it clear that Mary and Martha were quite different in their personalities. Martha was the worker, the active one, while Mary was the contemplative one who sat at the feet of Jesus and listened to His word. Jesus did not condemn Martha's service, but He did rebuke her for being "torn apart" by so many things. She needed to have priorities and center her activities on the things that God would approve. As an old Wesley hymn puts it, we need to have a balanced life:

> Faithful to my Lord's commands,
> I still would choose the better part:
> Serve with careful Martha's hands
> And loving Mary's heart.

We would expect Martha to rush out to meet Jesus while Mary sat in the house, weeping with her friends. Since Mary later echoed Martha's words of greeting (John 11:32), it is likely that the sisters often said these words to each other as they waited for Jesus to arrive. While there may have been a tinge of disappointment in the statement, there was also evidence of faith, for nobody ever died in the presence of Jesus Christ. "If" is such a big word! How futile it is to imagine what might have been, if—!

Martha was quick to affirm her faith in Jesus Christ (John 11:22), and Jesus responded to that faith by promising her that her brother would rise again. He was thinking of the immediate situation, but she interpreted His words to mean the future resurrection in the last day (Dan. 12:2-3; John 5:28-29). Here is another instance in John's Gospel of people lacking spiritual perception and being unable to understand the words of Jesus.

Our Lord's reply is the fifth of the I AM

statements. It is important to note that Jesus did not deny what Martha said about the future resurrection. The resurrection of the human body is a cardinal doctrine in the orthodox Jewish faith. But in His great I AM statement, our Lord completely transformed the doctrine of the resurrection and, in so doing, brought great comfort to Martha's heart.

To begin with, He brought the doctrine of the resurrection out of the shadows and into the light. The Old Testament revelation about death and resurrection is not clear or complete; it is, as it were, "in the shadows." In fact, there are some passages in Psalms and Ecclesiastes that almost make one believe that death is the end and there is no hope beyond the grave. False teachers like to use these passages to support their heretical teachings, but they ignore (or misinterpret) the clear teachings found in the New Testament. After all, it was not David or Solomon who "brought life and immortality to light through the Gospel" (2 Tim. 1:10), but Jesus Christ!

By His teaching, His miracles, and His own resurrection, Jesus clearly taught the resurrection of the human body. He has declared once for all that death is real, that there is life after death, and that the body will one day be raised by the power of God.

He transformed this doctrine in a second way: He took it out of a book and put it into a person, Himself. "I am the resurrection and the life"! (John 11:25) While we thank God for what the Bible teaches (and all Martha had was the Old Testament), we realize that we are saved by the Redeemer, Jesus Christ, and not by a doctrine written in a book. When we know Him by faith, we need not fear the shadow of death.

When you are sick, you want a doctor and not a medical book or a formula. When you are being sued, you want a lawyer and not a law book. Likewise, when you face your last enemy, death, you want the Saviour and not a doctrine written in a book. In Jesus Christ, every doctrine is made personal (1 Cor. 1:30). When you belong to Him, you have all that you ever will need in life, death, time, or eternity!

But perhaps the greatest transformation Jesus performed was to move the doctrine of the resurrection out of the future and into the present. Martha was looking to the future, knowing that Lazarus would rise again and she would see him. Her friends were looking to the past and saying, "He could have prevented Lazarus from dying!" (John 11:37) But Jesus tried to center their attention on the *present:* wherever He is, God's resurrection power is available *now* (Rom. 6:4; Gal. 2:20; Phil. 3:10).

Jesus affirmed that believers would one day be raised from the dead (John 11:25). Then He immediately revealed the added truth that some believers would never die (and it is a double negative, "never never die!") (John 11:26). How is this possible? The answer is found in 1 Thessalonians 4:13, 18. When Jesus Christ returns in the air to take His people home, those who are alive at His coming shall never die. They shall be changed and caught up to meet Him in the air!

Martha did not hesitate to affirm her faith. She used three different titles for Jesus: Lord, Christ (Messiah), and Son of God. The words "I believe" are in the perfect tense, indicating a fixed and settled faith. "I have believed and I will continue to believe!"

Our Lord dealt with Martha's faith; now He had to help Mary. Why did Martha call Mary "secretly"? Possibly because of the danger involved: they knew that the Jewish leaders were out to arrest Jesus. When Mary arose to go to meet Jesus, her friends misunderstood her actions and thought she was going to the tomb to weep. They wanted to weep with her, so they followed along. Imagine their surprise when they met Jesus!

Mary is found three times in the Gospel record, and each time she is at the feet of Jesus (Luke 10:39; John 11:32; 12:3). She sat at His feet and listened to His word; she fell at His feet and poured out her sorrow; and she came to His feet to give Him her praise and worship. Mary's only recorded words in the Gospels are given in John 11:32, and they echo what Martha had already said (John 11:21).

Mary did not say much because she was overcome with sorrow and began to weep. Her friends joined in the weeping, as Jewish people are accustomed to do. The word used means "a loud weeping, a lamentation." Our Lord's response was to groan within and "be moved with indignation." At what was He indignant? At the ravages of sin in the world that He had created. Death is an enemy, and Satan uses the fear of death as a terrible weapon (Heb. 2:14-18). No wonder Jesus was indignant!

The mystery of our Lord's incarnation is seen by His question in John 11:34. Jesus knew that Lazarus had died (John 11:11), but He had to ask where he was buried. Our Lord never used His divine powers when normal human means would suffice.

"Jesus wept" is the shortest and yet the deepest verse in Scripture. His was a silent weeping (the Greek word is used nowhere else in the New Testament) and not the loud lamentation of the mourners. But why did He weep at all? After all, He knew that He would raise Lazarus from the dead (John 11:11).

Our Lord's weeping reveals the humanity of the Saviour. He has entered into all of our experiences and knows how we feel. In fact, being the perfect God-Man, Jesus experienced these things in a deeper way than we do. His tears also assure us of His sympathy; He is indeed "a Man of sorrows and acquainted with grief" (Isa. 53:3). Today, He is our merciful and faithful High Priest, and we may come to the throne of grace and find all the gracious help that we need (Heb. 4:14-16).

We see in His tears the tragedy of sin but also the glory of heaven. Perhaps Jesus was weeping *for* Lazarus, as well as *with* the sisters, because He knew He was calling His friend from heaven and back into a wicked world where he would one day have to die again. Jesus had come down from heaven; He knew what Lazarus was leaving behind.

The spectators saw in His tears an evidence of His love. But some of them said, "If Jesus loved Lazarus so much, why did He not prevent his death?" Perhaps they were thinking, "Jesus is weeping because He was unable to do anything. They are tears of deep regret." In other words, *nobody present really expected a miracle!* For this reason, nobody could accuse Jesus of "plotting" this event and being in collusion with the two sisters and their friends. Even the disciples did not believe that Jesus would raise Lazarus from the dead!

The one person who declared her faith was Martha (John 11:27), and she failed at the last minute. "Open the tomb? By now he smells!" Jesus gently reminded her of the message He had sent at least three days before (John 11:4), and He urged her to believe it. True faith relies on God's promises and thereby releases God's power. Martha relented, and the stone was rolled away.

The Jews (John 11:41-57)

The emphasis from this point on was on the faith of the spectators, the people who had come to comfort Mary and Martha. Jesus paused to pray (John 11:41; also see 6:11) and thanked the Father that the prayer had already been heard. When had He prayed? Probably when He received the message that His friend was sick (John 11:4). The Father then told Him what the plan was, and Jesus obeyed the Father's will. His prayer now was for the sake of the unbelieving spectators, that they might know that God had sent Him.

A quaint Puritan writer said that if Jesus had not named Lazarus when He shouted, He would have emptied the whole cemetery! Jesus called *Lazarus* and raised him from the dead. Since Lazarus was bound, he could not walk to the door of the tomb; so God's power must have carried him along. It was an unquestioned miracle that even the most hostile spectator could not deny.

The experience of Lazarus is a good illustration of what happens to a sinner when he trusts the Saviour (Eph. 2:1-10). Lazarus was dead, and all sinners are dead. He was decayed, because death and decay go together. All lost people are spiritually dead, but some are more "decayed" than others. No one can be "more dead" than another.

Lazarus was raised from the dead by the power of God, and all who trust Christ have been given new life and lifted out of the graveyard of sin (see John 5:24). Lazarus was set free from the graveclothes (see Col. 3:1ff) and given new liberty. You find him seated with Christ at the table (John 12:2), and all believers are "seated with Christ" in heavenly places (Eph. 2:6), enjoying spiritual food and fellowship.

Because of the great change in Lazarus, many people desired to see him; and his "living witness" was used by God to bring people to salvation (John 12:9-11). There are no recorded words of Lazarus in the Gospels, but his daily walk is enough to convince people that Jesus is the Son of God. Because of his effective witness, Lazarus was persecuted by the religious leaders who wanted to kill him and get rid of the evidence.

As with the previous miracles, the people were divided in their response. Some did believe and on "Palm Sunday" gave witness of the miracle Jesus had performed (John 12:17-18). But others immediately went to the religious leaders and reported what had happened in Bethany. These "informers" were so near the kingdom, yet there is no evidence that they believed. If the heart will not yield to truth, then the grace of God cannot bring salvation. These people could have experienced a spiritual resurrection in their own lives!

It was necessary that the Jewish council (Sanhedrin) meet and discuss what to do with Jesus. They were not seeking after truth; they were seeking for ways to protect their own selfish interests. If He gathered too many followers, He might get the attention of the Roman authorities; and this could hurt the Jewish cause.

The high priest, Caiaphas, was a Sadducee, not a Pharisee (Acts 23:6-10); but the two factions could always get together to fight a common enemy. Unknown to himself and to the council, Caiaphas uttered a divine prophecy: Jesus would die for the nation so that the nation would not perish. "For the transgression of My people was He stricken" (Isa. 53:8). True to his vision of a worldwide family of God, John added his inspired explanation: Jesus would die not only for the Jews, but for all of God's children who would be gathered together in one heavenly family. (Note John 4:42 and 10:16.)

The official decision that day was that Jesus must die (see Matt. 12:14; Luke 19:47; John 5:18; 7:1, 19-20, 25). The leaders thought that *they* were in control of the situation, but it was God who was working out His predetermined plan (Acts 2:23). Originally, they wanted to wait until after the Passover, but God had decreed otherwise.

Jesus withdrew to Ephraim, about fifteen miles north of Jerusalem; and there He remained in quiet retirement with His disciples. The crowd was gathering in Jerusalem for the Passover feast, and the pilgrims were wondering if Jesus would attend the feast even though He was in danger. He was now on the "wanted" list, because the council had made it known that anyone who knew where Jesus was must report it to the officials.

John 11 reveals the deity of Jesus Christ and the utter depravity of the human heart. The rich man in hades had argued, "If one went unto them from the dead, they will repent" (Luke 16:30). Lazarus came back from the dead, and the officials wanted to kill him! Miracles certainly reveal the power of God, but of themselves they cannot communicate the grace of God.

The stage had been set for the greatest drama in history, during which man would do his worst and God would give His best.

CHAPTER TWELVE
CHRIST AND THE CRISIS
John 12

John 12 records the second major crisis in the ministry of our Lord as seen by John the apostle. The first occurred when many of His disciples would no longer walk with Him (John 6:66), even though He is "the way" (John 14:6). In this chapter, John tells us that many would not believe in Him (John 12:37ff), even though He is "the truth." The third crisis will come in John 19: even though He is "the life," the leaders crucified Him.

John opened his book by telling us that Jesus "came unto His own [world], and His own [people] received Him not" (John 1:11). In the first twelve chapters, John presented one witness after another, and one proof after another, to convince us that Jesus is indeed the Christ, the Son of God. All of this evidence was seen firsthand by the leaders of the nation, and yet they rejected His claims. Having been rejected by "His own" nation, Jesus then retired with "His own" disciples (John 13:1) whom He loved to the uttermost.

We see in John 12, the Lord Jesus Christ as He relates to four different groups of people, and there are lessons that we can learn as we study this section.

Jesus and His Friends (John 12:1-11)

Our Lord knew that the Jewish leaders were out to arrest Him and kill Him (John 11:53, 57), but He still returned to Bethany, only two miles from the very citadel of His enemies. Why? So that He might spend a quiet time with His dear friends Mary, Martha, and Lazarus. True to their personalities, Martha busily served and Mary worshiped at the feet of Jesus (see Luke 10:38-42).

The account of Mary's anointing of her Lord is found also in Matthew 26:6-13 and Mark 14:3-9. But it must not be confused with the account given in Luke 7:36-50, where a former harlot anointed Jesus in the house of Simon the Pharisee. Mary was a virtuous woman, and she anointed Jesus in the house of Simon the (former) leper (Mark 14:3). The Luke 7 event took place in Galilee, while the account we are now considering occurred in Judea. The fact that there are two "Simons" involved should not surprise us, for Simon was a common name in that day.

When you combine all three accounts, you learn that Mary anointed both His head and His feet. It was an act of pure love on her part, for she knew her Lord was about to endure suffering and death. Because she sat at Jesus' feet and listened to Him speak, she knew what He was going to do. It is significant that Mary of Bethany was not one of the women who went to the tomb to anoint the body of Jesus (Mark 16:1).

In a sense, Mary was showing her devotion to Jesus *before* it was too late. She was "giving the roses" while He was yet alive, and not bringing them to the funeral! Her act of love and worship was public, spontaneous, sacrificial, lavish, personal, and unembarrassed. Jesus called it "a good work" (Matt. 26:10; Mark 14:6) and both commended her and defended her.

It would have required a year's wages from a common laborer to purchase that ointment. Like David, Mary would not give to the Lord that which cost her nothing (2 Sam. 24:24). Her beautiful act of worship brought a fragrance to the very house in which they were dining, and the blessing of her deed has spread around the world (Matt. 26:13; Mark 14:9). Little did Mary realize that night that her love for Christ would be a blessing to believers around the world for centuries to come!

When she came to the feet of Jesus, Mary took the place of a slave. When she undid her hair (something Jewish women did not do in public), she humbled herself and laid her glory at His feet (see 1 Cor. 11:15). Of course, she was misunderstood and criticized; but that is what usually happens when somebody gives his or her best to the Lord.

It was Judas who started the criticism, and, sad to say, the other disciples took it up. They did not know that Judas was a devil (John 12:70), and they admired him for his concern for the poor. After all, he was the treasurer; and especially at Passover season, he would want to share with those who were less fortunate (see John 13:21-30). Until the very end, the disciples believed that Judas was a devoted follower of the Lord.

John 12:4 records Judas' first words found anywhere in the four Gospels. His last words are found in Matthew 27:4. Judas was a thief and was in the habit of stealing money from the money box that he carried. (The Greek word translated "bag" meant originally a small case in which mouthpieces were kept for wind instruments. Then it came to mean any small box, and especially a money box. The Greek version of the Old Testament uses this word in 2 Chron. 24:8-10 for King Joash's money chest.) No doubt Judas had already decided to abandon Jesus, and he wanted to get what he could out of what he considered a bad situation. Perhaps he had hoped that Jesus would defeat Rome and set up the kingdom; in which case, Judas would have been treasurer of the kingdom!

What Mary did was a blessing to Jesus and a blessing to her own life. She was also a blessing to the home, filling it with fragrance (see Phil. 4:18); and today, she is a blessing to the church around the world. Her one act of devotion in the little village of Bethany still sends "ripples of blessing."

But not so Judas! We call our daughters "Mary," but no parent would call a son "Judas." His very name is listed in the dictionary as a synonym for treachery. Mary and Judas are seen in contrast in Proverbs 10:7—"The memory of the just is blessed, but the name of the wicked shall rot." "A good name is better than precious ointment," says Ecclesiastes 7:1; and Mary had both.

Matthew 26:14 gives the impression that immediately after this rebuke, Judas went to the priests and bargained to deliver Jesus into their hands. But it is likely that the events recorded in Matthew 21–25 took place first. No doubt the Lord's rebuke of Judas at Bethany played an important part in his decision actually to betray Jesus. Also, the fact that Jesus once again openly announced His death would motivate Judas to escape while the opportunity was there.

As we look at this event, we see some "representative people" who are examples to us. Martha represents *work* as she served the dinner she had prepared for the Lord. This was just as much a "fragrant offering" as was Mary's ointment (see Heb. 13:16). Mary represents *worship,* and Lazarus represents *witness* (John 11:9-11). People went to Bethany just to be able to see this man who had been raised from the dead!

As mentioned we have no recorded words from Lazarus in the New Testament, but his miraculous life was an effective witness for Jesus Christ. (In contrast, John the Baptist did no miracles, yet his words brought people to Jesus. See John 10:40-42.) We today ought to "walk in newness of life" (Rom. 6:4) because we have been "raised from the dead" (Eph. 2:1-10; Col. 3:1ff). Actually, the Christian life ought to be a beautiful balance of worship, work, and witness.

But the fact that Lazarus was a walking miracle put him into a place of danger: the Jewish leaders wanted to kill *him* as well as Jesus! Our Lord was right when He called them children of the devil, for they were murderers indeed (John 8:42-44). They threw the healed blind man out of the synagogue rather than permit him to bear witness to Christ every Sabbath, and they tried to put Lazarus back into the tomb because he was leading people to faith in Christ. If you will not accept the evidence, you must try to get rid of it!

This quiet evening of fellowship—in spite of the cruel way the disciples treated Mary—must have brought special encouragement and strength to the Saviour's heart as He faced the demands of that last week before the Cross. We should examine our own hearts and homes to ask whether we are bringing joy to His heart by our worship, work, and witness.

Jesus and the Passover Pilgrims (John 12:12-19)

John shifted the scene from a quiet dinner in Bethany to a noisy public parade in Jerusalem. All four Gospels record this event and their accounts should be compared. This was the only "public demonstration" that our Lord allowed while He was ministering on earth. His purpose was to fulfill the Old Testament prophecy (Zech. 9:9). The result was a growing animosity on the part of the religious leaders, leading eventually to the crucifixion of the Saviour.

There were three different groups in the crowd that day: (1) the Passover visitors from outside Judea (John 12:12, 18); (2) the local people who had witnessed the raising of Lazarus (John 12:17); and (3) the religious leaders who were greatly concerned about what Jesus might do at the feast (John 12:19). At each of the different feasts, the people were in keen expectation, wondering if Jesus would be there and what He would do. It looked as though Jesus was actually seeking to incite a revolution and establish Himself as King, but that was not what He had in mind.

What did this event mean to Jesus? For one thing, it was a part of His obedience to the Father's will. The Prophet Zechariah (Zech. 9:9) prophesied that the Messiah would enter Jerusalem in that manner, and He fulfilled the prophecy. "Daughter of Zion" is another name for the city of Jerusalem (Jer. 4:31; Lam. 2:4, 8, 10). Certainly Jesus was openly announcing to the people that He indeed is the King of Israel (John 1:49), the promised Messiah. No doubt many of the pilgrims hoped that *now* He would defeat the Romans and set the nation of Israel free.

What did this demonstration mean to the Romans? Nothing is recorded about the Roman viewpoint, but it is certain that they kept a close watch that day. During the annual Passover feast, it was not uncommon for some of the Jewish nationalists to try to arouse the people; and perhaps they thought this parade was that kind of an event. I imagine that some of the Roman soldiers must have smiled at the "Triumphal Entry," because it was nothing like their own "Roman triumph" celebrations in the city of Rome.

Whenever a Roman general was victorious on foreign soil, killing at least 5,000 of the enemy, and gaining new territory, he was given a "Roman triumph" when he returned to the city. It was the Roman equivalent of the American "ticker-tape parade," only with much more splendor. The victor would be permitted to display the trophies he had won and the enemy leaders he had captured. The parade ended at the arena where some of the captives entertained the people by fighting wild beasts. Compared to a "Roman triumph," our Lord's entry into Jerusalem was nothing.

What did the "Triumphal Entry" mean to the people of Israel? The pilgrims welcomed Jesus, spread their garments before Him, and waved palm branches as symbols of peace and victory (Rev. 7:9). They quoted from Psalm 118:26, which is a messianic psalm; and they proclaimed Him the "King of Israel." But while they were doing this, Jesus was weeping! (Luke 19:37-44)

The name *Jerusalem* means "city of peace" or "foundation of peace"; and the people were hoping that Jesus would bring them the peace that they needed. However, He wept because He saw what lay ahead of the nation—war, suffering, destruction, and a scattered people. At His birth, the angels announced "peace on earth" (Luke 2:13-14); but in His ministry Jesus announced "war on earth" (Luke 12:51ff). It is significant that the crowds shouted "peace in heaven" (Luke 19:38), because that is the only place where there is peace today!

The nation had wasted its opportunities; their leaders did not know the time of God's visitation. They were ignorant of their own Scriptures. The next time Israel sees the King, the scene will be radically different! (Rev. 19:11ff) He will come in glory, not in humility; and the armies of heaven will accompany Him. It will be a scene of victory as He comes to defeat His enemies and establish His kingdom.

It is a repeated theme in Scripture that there can be no glory unless first there is suffering. Jesus knew that He must die on the cross before He could enter into His glory (Luke 24:26). The Jewish theologians were not clear in their minds concerning the sufferings of the Messiah and the glorious kingdom that the prophets announced. Some teachers held that there were two Messiahs, one who would suffer and one who would reign. Even our Lord's own disciples were not clear as to what was going on (see John 11:16).

How did the Jewish leaders respond to the "Triumphal Entry" of the Lord? As they watched the great crowd gather and honor Jesus, the Pharisees were quite sure that Jesus had won the day. They were anticipating some kind of general revolt during the Passover season. Perhaps Jesus would perform a great miracle and in that way capture the minds and hearts of the restless people. How little they really understood the mind and heart of the Master! What they did not realize was that Jesus was "forcing their hand" so that the Sanhedrin would act *during the feast.* The Lamb of God had to give His life when the Passover lambs were being slain.

The statement, "Behold, the world is gone after Him!" (John 12:19) was both an exaggeration and a prophecy. In the next section, we meet some visitors from outside Israel.

Jesus and the Gentile Visitors (John 12:20-36)

Following His entry into Jerusalem, our Lord cleansed the temple for the second time. He quoted Isaiah 56:7 and Jeremiah 7:11, "Is it not written, 'My house shall be called of all nations the house of prayer'? But ye have made it a den of thieves" (Mark 11:17). Perhaps these Greeks heard that word and were encouraged by it.

One of John's major themes is that Jesus is the Saviour of the world, not simply the Redeemer of Israel. He is the Lamb of God who takes away the sin of the world (John 1:29). "For God so loved the world" (John 3:16). The Samaritans rightly identified Him as "the Saviour of the world" (John 4:42). He gave His life for the world and He gives life *to* the world (John 6:33). He is the Light of the world (John 8:12). The universal emphasis of John's Gospel is too obvious to miss. Jesus will bring the "other sheep" who are outside the Jewish fold (John 10:16; and see 11:51-52).

The original text indicates that these Greeks "were accustomed to come and worship at the feast." They were not curious visitors or one-time investigators. No doubt they were "God-fearers," Gentiles who attended the Jewish synagogue and sought the truth, but who had not yet become proselytes. Gentiles came to see Jesus when He was a young child (Matt. 2), and now Gentiles came to see Him just before His death.

These men "kept asking" Philip for the privilege of an interview with Jesus. Philip finally told Andrew (who was often bringing people to Jesus), and Andrew gave the request to the Lord. No doubt there were many people who wanted private interviews with the Lord, but they were afraid of the Pharisees (John 9:22). Being from out of the country, the Gentile visitors either did not know about the danger, or did not fear the consequences.

We can commend these Greeks for wanting to see Jesus. The Jews would say, "We would see a sign!" (Matt. 12:38; 1 Cor. 1:22) but these men said, "We would see [have an interview with] Jesus." There is no record that Jesus did talk with these men, but the message that He gave in response contains truths that all of us need.

The central theme of this message is the glory of God (John 12:23, 28). We would have expected Jesus to say, "The hour is come, that the Son of man should be crucified." But Jesus saw beyond the cross to the glory that would follow (see Luke 24:26; Heb. 12:2). In fact, the glory of God is an important theme in the remaining chapters of John's Gospel (see John 13:31-32; 14:13; 17:1, 4-5, 22, 24).

Jesus used the image of a seed to illustrate the great spiritual truth that there can be no glory without suffering, no fruitful life without death, no victory without surrender. Of itself, a seed is weak and useless; but when it is planted, it "dies" and becomes fruitful.

There is both beauty and bounty when a seed "dies" and fulfills its purpose. If a seed could talk, it would no doubt complain about being put into the cold, dark earth. But the only way it can achieve its goal is by being planted.

God's children are like seeds. They are small and insignificant, but they have life in them, God's life. However, that life can never be fulfilled unless we yield ourselves to God and permit Him to "plant us." We must die to self so that we may live unto God (Rom. 6; Gal. 2:20). The only way to have a fruitful life is to follow Jesus Christ in death, burial, and resurrection.

In these words, Jesus challenges us today to surrender our lives to Him. Note the contrasts: loneliness or fruitfulness; losing your life or keeping your life; serving self or serving Christ; pleasing self or receiving God's honor.

I read about some Christians who visited a remote mission station to see how the ministry was going. As they watched the dedicated missionary team at work, they were impressed with their ministry, but admitted that they missed "civilization."

"You certainly have buried yourself out here!" one of the visitors exclaimed.

"We haven't buried ourselves," the missionary replied. "We were planted!"

Our Lord knew that He was facing suffering and death, and His humanity responded to this ordeal. His soul was troubled, not because He was questioning the Father's will, but because He was fully conscious of all that the Cross involved. Note that Jesus did not say, "What shall I do?" because He knew what He was ordained to do. He said, "What shall I say?" In the hour of suffering and surrender, there are only two prayers we can pray, either "Father, save me!" or "Father, glorify Thy name!"

In one of my radio messages, I made the statement, "God does not expect us to be comfortable, but He does expect us to be conformable." No sooner had the program ended than my office phone rang and an anonymous listener wanted to argue with me about that statement.

"Conformable to what?" the voice thundered. "Haven't you read Romans 12:2—'Be not conformed to this world'?"

"Sure I've read Romans 12:2," I replied. "Have you read Romans 8:29? God has predestined us 'to be conformed to the image of His Son.' "

After a long pause (I was glad he was paying the phone bill), he grunted and said, "OK."

Comfortable or *conformable:* that is the question. If we are looking for comfortable lives, then we will protect our plans and desires, save our lives, and never be planted. But if we yield our lives and let God plant us, we will never be alone but will have the joy of being fruitful to the glory of God. "If any man [Jew or Greek] serve Me, let him follow Me." This is the equivalent of Matthew 10:39 and Mark 8:36.

The prayer, "Father, glorify Thy name!" received a reply from heaven! God the Father spoke to His Son and gave Him a double assurance: the Son's past life and ministry had glorified the Father, and the Son's future suffering and death would glorify the Father. It is significant that the Father spoke to the Son at the beginning of the Son's ministry (Matt. 3:17), as the Son began His journey to Jerusalem (Matt. 17:5), and now as the Son entered the last days before the Cross. God always gives that word of assurance to those who willingly suffer for His sake.

The people heard a sound but did not know the message that had been conveyed. Yet if the voice was for their sakes and they could not understand it, what good was it? In that the voice assured Jesus, who was to die for their sakes, the voice was for their good. They heard Him pray and they heard a sound from heaven in response to that prayer. That should have convinced them that Jesus was in touch with the Father. We might translate John 12:30, "That voice came more for your sake than for Mine."

Jesus then openly spoke about the Cross. It was an hour of judgment for the world and for Satan, the prince of the world. The death of Jesus Christ would seem like a victory for the wicked world, but it would really be a judgment of the world. On the cross, Jesus would defeat Satan and his world system (Gal. 6:14). Even though he is permitted to go to and fro on the earth, Satan is a defeated enemy. As we serve the Lord, we overcome the wicked one (Luke 10:17-19). One day Satan shall be cast out of heaven (Rev. 12:10), and eventually he will be judged and imprisoned forever (Rev. 20:10).

We have met the phrase "lifted up" before (John 3:14; 8:28). Its basic meaning is *crucifixion* (note John 12:33), but it also carries the idea of *glorification.* "Behold, My servant will prosper, He will be high and lifted up, and greatly exalted" (Isa. 52:13, NASB). The Son of man was *glorified* by being *crucified!*

The phrase "all men" does not suggest universal salvation. It means "all people without distinction," that is, Jews and Gentiles. He does not force them; He draws them (see John 6:44-45). He was "lifted up" that men might find the way (John 12:32), know the truth (John 8:28), and receive the life (John 3:14). The cross reminds us that God loves a whole world and that the task of the church is to take the Gospel to the whole world.

The people did not understand what He was teaching. They knew that "Son of man" was a title for Messiah, but they could not understand why Messiah would be crucified! Did not the Old Testament teach that the Messiah would live forever? (See Pss. 72:17; 89:36; 110:4; Isa. 9:7.)

But that was no time to be discussing the fine points of theology! It was an hour of crisis (see John 12:31, where the Greek word *krisis* means judgment) and an hour of opportunity. The light was shining and they had better take advantage of their opportunity to be saved! We have met this image of light and darkness before (John 1:4-9; 3:17-20; 8:12; 9:39-41). By a simple step of faith, these people could have passed out of spiritual darkness and into the light of salvation.

This marked the end of our Lord's public ministry as far as John's record is concerned. Jesus departed and hid Himself. It was judgment on the nation that saw His miracles, heard His messages, and scrutinized His ministry, and yet refused to believe on Him.

Jesus and Unbelieving Jews (John 12:37-49)

The key word in this section is *believe;* it is used eight times. First, John explained the unbelief of the people. They *would not* believe (John 12:37-38, with a quotation from Isa. 53:1); they *could not* believe (John 12:39); and they *should not* believe (John 12:40-41, with a quotation from Isa. 6:9-10).

In spite of all the clear evidence that was presented to them, the nation would not believe. The "arm of the Lord" had been revealed to them in great power, yet they closed their eyes to the truth. They had heard the message ("report") and seen the miracles, and yet would not believe.

When a person starts to resist the light, something begins to change within him; and he comes to the place where he cannot believe. There is "judicial blindness" that God permits to come over the eyes of people who do not take the truth seriously. (This quotation is found in a number of places in the New Testament. See Matt. 13:14-15; Mark 4:12; Luke 8:10; Acts 28:25-27; Rom. 11:8.) It is a serious thing to treat God's truth lightly, for a person could well miss his opportunity to be saved. "Seek ye the Lord while He may be found, call ye upon Him while He is near" (Isa. 55:6).

There were those who would not believe, and there were those who would not openly confess Christ even though they had believed (John 12:42-43). Nicodemus and Joseph of Arimathea belonged to this group initially, but eventually came out openly in their confession of Christ (John 19:38ff). In the early church, there were numbers of Pharisees (Acts 15:5) and even priests (Acts 6:7). It was the old struggle between the glory of God and the praise of men (John 12:25-26). It was a costly thing to be excommunicated (John 9:22), and these "secret believers" wanted the best of both worlds. Note John 5:44 in this regard.

In John 12:44-50 we have our Lord's last message before He "hid Himself" from the people. Again, the emphasis was on faith. A number of the basic themes in John's Gospel run through this message: God sent the Son; to see the Son means to see the Father; Jesus is the Light of the world; His words are the very words of God; faith in Him brings salvation; to reject Him is to face eternal judgment. In fact, the very Word that He spoke will judge those who have rejected it and Him!

It is an awesome thought that the unbeliever will face at the judgment every bit of Scripture he has ever read or heard. The very Word that he rejects becomes his judge! Why? Because the written Word points to the Living Word, Jesus Christ (John 1:14).

Many people reject the truth simply because of the fear of man (John 12:42-43). Among those who will be in hell are "the fearful" (Rev. 21:8). Better to fear God and go to heaven than to fear men and go to hell!

The word *judge* is repeated four times in the closing words of this message, and a solemn word it is. Jesus did not come to judge; He came to save (John 3:18; 8:15). But if the sinner will not trust the Saviour, the Saviour must become the Judge. The sinner is actually passing judgment on himself, not on the Lord!

As you have studied these twelve chapters of the Gospel of John, you have seen Jesus

Christ in His life, His ministry, His miracles, His message, and His desire to save lost sinners.

You have considered the evidence. Have you come to the conviction that Jesus Christ is indeed the Son of God, the Saviour of the world?

Have *you* trusted Him and received everlasting life?

"While you have the light, believe in the light, that you may become sons of light" (John 12:36, NKJV).

CHAPTER THIRTEEN THE SOVEREIGN SERVANT

John 13:1-35

Three times in my ministry I have had to deliver "farewell messages" to congregations I had served, and it is not an easy thing to do. I may not have succeeded, but my purpose was always to prepare them for the future. This included warning as well as instruction. They would call a new pastor and enter into a new phase of ministry, and I wanted them to be at their best.

John 13–17 is our Lord's "farewell message" to His beloved disciples, climaxing with His intercessory prayer for them and for us. Other farewell addresses in Scripture were delivered by Moses (Deut. 31–33), Joshua (Josh. 23–24), and Paul (Acts 20). However, Jesus added a significant "action section" to His message when He washed His disciples' feet. It was an object lesson they would never forget.

In this passage, we see our Lord in a fourfold relationship: to His Heavenly Father (John 13:1-5), to Simon Peter (John 13:6-11), to all of the disciples (John 13:12-17), and to Judas (John 13:18-35). In each of these sections of John's Gospel, you will discover a special message, a spiritual truth to help you in your own Christian life.

Humility: Jesus and the Father (John 13:1-5)

Jesus had entered Jerusalem on Sunday, and on Monday had cleansed the temple. Tuesday was a day of conflict as the religious leaders sought to trip Him up and get evidence to arrest Him. These events are recorded in Matthew 21–25. Wednesday was probably a day of rest, but on Thursday He met in the Upper Room with His disciples in order to observe Passover.

The emphasis in John 13:1-3 is on *what our Lord knew,* and in John 13:4-5 on *what our Lord did.*

Jesus knew that "His hour was come." More than any of the Gospel writers, John emphasized the fact that Jesus lived on a "heavenly timetable" as He did the Father's will. Note the development of this theme:

2:4—"Mine hour is not yet come."
7:30—"His hour was not yet come."
8:20—"His hour was not yet come."
12:23—"The hour is come that the Son of man should be glorified."
13:1—"Jesus knew that His hour was come."
17:1—"Father, the hour is come."

What was this divinely appointed "hour"? It was the time when He would be glorified through His death, resurrection, and ascension. From the human point of view, it meant suffering; but from the divine point of view, it meant glory. He would soon leave this world and return to the Father who sent Him, Jesus having finished His work on earth (John 17:4). When the servant of God is in the will of God, he is immortal until his work is done. They could not even arrest Jesus, let alone kill Him, until the right hour had arrived.

Jesus also knew that Judas would betray Him. Judas is mentioned eight times in John's Gospel, more than in any of the other Gospels. Satan had entered into Judas (Luke 22:3), and now he would give him the necessary thought to bring about the arrest and crucifixion of the Son of God. The word translated "put" in John 13:2 literally means "to throw." It reminds us of the fiery darts of the wicked one (Eph. 6:16). Judas was an unbeliever (John 6:64-71), so he did not have a "shield of faith" to use to ward off Satan's attacks.

Finally, Jesus knew that the Father had given Him all things (John 13:3). This statement parallels John 3:35, and it also reminds us of Matthew 11:27. Even in His humiliation, our

Lord had all things through His Father. He was poor and yet He was rich. Because Jesus knew who He was, where He came from, what He had, and where He was going, He was complete master of the situation. You and I as believers know that we have been born of God, that we are one day going to God, and that in Christ we have all things; therefore, we ought to be able to follow our Lord's example and serve others.

What Jesus knew helped determine *what Jesus did* (John 13:4-5). The disciples must have been shocked when they saw their Master rise from supper, lay aside His outer garments, wrap a towel around His waist, take a basin of water, and wash their feet. Jewish servants did not wash their masters' feet, though Gentile slaves might do it. It was a menial task, and yet Jesus did it! As a special mark of affection, a host or hostess might wash a guest's feet, but it was not standard operating procedure in most homes.

Jesus knew that there was a competitive spirit in the hearts of His disciples. In fact, within a few minutes, the men were disputing over which of them was the greatest (Luke 22:24-30). He gave them an unforgettable lesson in humility, and by His actions rebuked their selfishness and pride. The more you think about this scene, the more profound it becomes. It is certainly an illustration of what Paul wrote years later in Philippians 2:1-16. Peter must have recalled the event when he wrote his first epistle and urged his readers to "be clothed with humility" (1 Peter 5:5).

Too often we confuse "the poor in spirit" (Matt. 5:3) with the "poor-spirited," and true humility with timidity and inferiority. The British literary giant Samuel Johnson was once asked to prepare a funeral sermon for a girl who had died, and he asked what her special virtues were. He was told that she was kind to her inferiors. Johnson replied that this was commendable, but that it would be difficult to determine who her inferiors were!

The Father had put all things into the Son's hands, *yet Jesus picked up a towel and a basin!* His humility was not born of poverty, but of riches. He was rich, yet He became poor (2 Cor. 8:9). A Malay proverb says, "The fuller the ear is of rice-grain, the lower it bends."

It is remarkable how the Gospel of John reveals the humility of our Lord even while magnifying His deity: "The Son can do nothing of Himself" (John 5:19, 30). "For I came down from heaven, not to do Mine own will" (John 6:38). "My doctrine is not Mine" (John 7:16). "And I seek not Mine own glory" (John 8:50). "The word which ye hear is not Mine" (John 14:24). His ultimate expression of humility was His death on the cross.

Jesus was the Sovereign, yet He took the place of a servant. He had all things in His hands, yet He picked up a towel. He was Lord and Master, yet He served His followers. It has well been said that humility is not thinking meanly of yourself; it is simply not thinking of yourself at all. True humility grows out of our relationship with the Father. If our desire is to know and do the Father's will so that we might glorify His name, then we will experience the joy of following Christ's example and serving others.

We today, just like the disciples that night, desperately need this lesson on humility. The church is filled with a worldly spirit of competition and criticism as believers vie with one another to see who is the greatest. We are growing in knowledge, but not in grace (see 2 Peter 3:18). "Humility is the only soil in which the graces root," wrote Andrew Murray. "The lack of humility is the sufficient explanation of every defect and failure."

Jesus served His disciples because of His humility and because of His love. Contrast John 13:1 with 1:11 and 3:16: Jesus came "unto His own [world], and His own [people] received him not." "For God so loved the world." In the Upper Room, Jesus ministered in love to His own disciples, and they received Him and what He had to say. The Greek text says, "He loved them to the uttermost."

Holiness: Jesus and Peter (John 13:6-11)

As Peter watched the Lord wash his friends' feet, he became more and more disturbed and could not understand what He was doing. As you read the life of Christ in the Gospels, you cannot help but notice how Peter often spoke impulsively out of his ignorance and had to be corrected by Jesus. Peter opposed Jesus going to the cross (Matt. 16:21-23), and he tried to manage our Lord's affairs at the Transfiguration (Matt. 17:1-8). He expressed the faith of the disciples (John 6:66-71) without realizing that one of the number was a traitor.

The word translated "wash" in John 13:5-6, 8, 12, and 14 is *niptō* and means "to wash a part of the body." But the word translated "washed" in John 13:10 is *louō* and means "to bathe all over." The distinction is important, for Jesus was trying to teach His disciples the importance of a holy walk.

When the sinner trusts the Saviour, he is "bathed all over" and his sins are washed away and forgiven (see 1 Cor. 6:9-11; Titus 3:3-7; and Rev. 1:5). "And their sins and iniquities will I remember no more" (Heb. 10:17). However, as the believer walks in this world, it is easy to become defiled. He does not need to be bathed all over again; he simply needs to have that defilement cleansed away. God promises to cleanse us when we confess our sins to Him (1 John 1:9).

But why is it so important that we "keep our feet clean"? Because if we are defiled, we cannot have communion with our Lord. "If I wash thee not, thou hast no part with Me" (John 13:8). The word translated "part" is *meros,* and it carries the meaning here of "participation, having a share in someone or something." When God "bathes us all over" in salvation, He brings about our *union* with Christ; and that is a settled relationship that cannot change. (The verb *wash* in John 13:10 is in the perfect tense. It is settled once and for all.) However, our *communion* with Christ depends on our keeping ourselves "unspotted from the world" (James 1:27). If we permit unconfessed sin in our lives, we hinder our walk with the Lord; and that is when we need to have our feet washed.

This basic truth of Christian living is beautifully illustrated in the Old Testament priesthood. When the priest was consecrated, he was bathed all over (Ex. 29:4), and that experience was never repeated. However, during his daily ministry, he became defiled; so it was necessary that he wash his hands and feet at the brass laver in the courtyard (Ex. 30:18-21). Only then could he enter the holy place and trim the lamps, eat the holy bread, or burn the incense.

The Lord cleanses us through the blood of Christ, that is, His work on the cross (1 John 1:5-10), and through the application of His Word to our lives (Ps. 119:9; John 15:3; Eph. 5:25-26). The "water of the Word" can keep our hearts and minds clean so that we will avoid the pollutions of this world. But if we do sin, we have a loving Advocate in glory who will hear our prayers of confession and forgive us (1 John 2:1-2).

Peter did not understand what his Lord was doing; but instead of waiting for an explanation, he impulsively tried to tell the Lord what to do. There is a strong double negative in John 13:8. The Greek scholar Kenneth Wuest translated Peter's statement, "You shall by no means wash my feet, no, never" (WUEST). Peter really meant it! Then when he discovered that to refuse the Lord would mean to lose the Lord's fellowship, he went in the opposite direction and asked for a complete bath!

We can learn an important lesson from Peter: don't question the Lord's will or work, and don't try to change it. He knows what He is doing. Peter had a difficult time accepting Christ's ministry to him *because Peter was not yet ready to minister to the other disciples.* It takes humility and grace to serve others, but it also takes humility and grace to allow others to serve us. The beautiful thing about a submissive spirit is that it can both give and receive to the glory of God.

John was careful to point out that Peter and Judas were in a different relationship with Jesus. Yes, Jesus washed Judas' feet! But it did Judas no good because he had not been bathed all over. Some people teach that Judas was a saved man who sinned away his salvation, but that is not what Jesus said. Our Lord made it very clear that Judas had never been cleansed from his sins and was an unbeliever (John 6:64-71).

It is a wonderful thing to deepen your fellowship with the Lord. The important thing is to be honest with Him and with ourselves and keep our feet clean.

Happiness: Jesus and the Disciples (John 13:12-17)

John 13:17 is the key—"If ye know these things, happy are ye if ye do them." The sequence is important: humbleness, holiness, then happiness. Aristotle defined happiness as "good fortune joined to virtue . . . a life that is both agreeable and secure." That might do for a philosopher, but it will never do for a Christian believer! Happiness is the by-product of a life that is lived in the will of God. When we humbly serve others, walk in God's paths of holiness, and do what He tells us, then we will enjoy happiness.

Jesus asked the disciples if they understood what He had done, and it is not likely that they did. So, He explained it: He had given them a lesson in humble service, an example for them to follow. The world thinks that happiness is the result of others serving us, but real joy comes when we serve others in the name of Christ. The world is constantly pursuing happiness, but that is like chasing a shadow: it is always just beyond your reach.

Jesus was their Master, so He had every right to command their service. Instead, He served them! He gave them an example of true Christian ministry. On more than one occasion during the previous three years, He had taught them lessons about humility and service; but now He had demonstrated the lesson to them. Perhaps the disciples remembered His lesson about the child (Matt. 18:1-6), or the rebuke He gave James and John when they asked for thrones (Matt. 20:20-28). Now it was all starting to fall into place.

The servant (slave) is not greater than his master; so, if the master becomes a slave, where does that put the slave? *On the same level as the master!* By becoming a servant, our Lord did not push us down: He lifted us up! He dignified sacrifice and service. You must keep in mind that the Romans had no use for humility, and the Greeks despised manual labor. Jesus combined these two when He washed the disciples' feet.

The world asks, "How many people work for you?" but the Lord asks, "For how many people do you work?" When I was ministering at a conference in Kenya, an African believer shared one of their proverbs with me: "The chief is servant of all." How true it is that we need leaders who will serve and servants who will lead. G.K. Chesterton said that a really great man is one who makes others feel great, and Jesus did this with His disciples *by teaching them to serve.*

However, it is not enough just to *know* this truth; we must put it into practice. James 1:22-27 makes it clear that the blessing comes in the *doing* of the Word, not the hearing. Wuest translates the last phrase in James 1:25, "This man shall be prospered spiritually in his doing." Even studying this section in John's Gospel can stir us emotionally or enlighten us intellectually; but it cannot bless us spiritually until we do what Jesus told us to do. This is the only way to lasting happiness.

Be sure to keep these lessons in their proper sequence: humbleness, holiness, happiness. Submit to the Father, keep your life clean, and serve others. This is God's formula for true spiritual joy.

Hypocrisy: Jesus and Judas (John 13:18-35)

A dark shadow now fell across the scene as Jesus dealt with Judas, the traitor. It is important to note that Judas was not a true believer; he was a hypocrite. He had never believed in Jesus (John 6:64-71), he had not been bathed all over (John 13:10-11), and he had not been among the chosen ones whom the Father gave to the Son (John 13:18 and 17:12). How close a person can come to salvation and yet be lost forever! Judas was even the treasurer of the group (John 12:6) and was certainly held in high regard by his fellow disciples.

At that hour, Jesus had two great concerns: to fulfill the Word of God (John 13:18-30) and to magnify the glory of God (John 13:31-35).

The Scripture Jesus quoted was Psalm 41:9—"Yea, mine own familiar friend, in whom I trusted, which did eat of my bread, hath lifted up his heel against me." When David wrote the psalm, he was probably referring to his counselor Ahithophel, who turned traitor and joined Absalom's rebellion (see 2 Sam. 15–17). It is significant that both Judas and Ahithophel committed suicide by hanging themselves (2 Sam. 17:23; Matt. 27:3-10; Acts 1:18). However, Judas did not commit suicide in order to fulfill biblical prophecy, for that would make God the author of his sin. Judas was responsible for his own decisions, and those decisions fulfilled God's Word.

Jesus was concerned that Judas' treachery would not weaken His disciples' faith. This is why He related it to the Word of God: when the disciples saw all of this fulfilled, it would make their faith stronger (see John 8:28). Judas had been disloyal, but He expected them to be loyal to Him and His cause. After all, He was God the Son sent by God the Father. They were Christ's chosen representatives; to receive them would be the same as receiving the Father and the Son. What a privilege, to be ambassadors of the King!

The remarkable thing is that the others at the table with Jesus did not know that Judas was an unbeliever and a traitor. Up to the very hour of his treachery, Judas was protected by the Saviour whom he betrayed. Had Jesus openly revealed what He knew about Judas, it is likely that the men would have turned on him. Remember what Peter did to Malchus when soldiers came to take Jesus!

From the very beginning, Jesus knew what Judas would do (John 6:64), but He did not compel him to do it. Judas was exposed to the same spiritual privileges as the other disciples, yet they did him no good. The same sun that melts the ice only hardens the clay. In spite of all that our Lord said about money, and all of His warning about covetousness, Judas continued to be a thief and steal from the treasury. In spite of all our Lord's warning about unbelief, Judas persisted in his rejection. *Jesus even washed Judas' feet!* Yet his hard heart did not yield.

Jesus had spoken before about a traitor (John 6:70), but the disciples did not take it to heart. Now when He spoke openly about it at the table, His disciples were perplexed.

Peter signaled to John, who was the closest to Jesus at the table, and asked him to find out who the traitor was. The Lord's reply to John was certainly not heard by all the men; in fact, they were carrying on discussions among themselves about who the traitor might be (Luke 22:23). When Jesus gave the bread to Judas, it was interpreted as an act of love and honor. In fact, Judas was seated at the place of honor, so our Lord's actions were seen in that light: He was bestowing a special honor on Judas. No wonder, after Judas left the room, the disciples got into an argument over who was the greatest (Luke 22:24-30).

John was no doubt stunned by this revelation, but before he could say or do anything, Jesus had sent Judas on his way. Even though Satan had entered Judas, it was Jesus who was in charge. He lived on the timetable given to Him by the Father, and He wanted to fulfill what was written in the Word. Since Judas was the treasurer, it was logical for the disciples to conclude that he had been sent on a special mission by the Lord. Judas had hypocritically expressed an interest in the poor (John 12:4-6), so perhaps he was on an errand of mercy to help the poor.

Keep in mind that Judas knew what he was doing and that he did it deliberately. He had already met with the Jewish religious leaders and agreed to lead them to Jesus in such a way that there would not be any public disturbance (Luke 21:37–22:6). He heard Jesus say, "Woe unto that man by whom the Son of man is betrayed! It had been good for that man if he had not been born!" (Matt. 26:24) Yet, he persisted in his unbelief and treachery.

John's little phrase "and it was night" carries a tremendous impact when you remember that *light* and *darkness* are important spiritual images in his Gospel. Jesus is the Light of the world (John 8:12), but Judas rejected Jesus and went out into darkness; and for Judas, *it is still night!* Those who do evil hate the light (John 3:18-21). Our Lord's warning in John 12:25-26 went unheeded by Judas—and it goes unheeded by lost sinners today, people who will go where Judas went unless they repent and trust the Saviour.

The instant Judas was gone, the atmosphere was cleared, and Jesus began to instruct His disciples and prepare them for His crucifixion and His ultimate return to heaven. It was after Judas' departure that He instituted the Lord's Supper, something that Judas as an unbeliever certainly could not share. Judas was out in the night, controlled by the prince of darkness, Satan; but Jesus was in the light, sharing love and truth with His beloved disciples. What a contrast!

The theme now changes to the glory of God (John 13:31-35). From the human perspective, the death of Christ was a dastardly deed involving unspeakable suffering and humiliation; but from the divine perspective it was the revelation of the glory of God. "The hour is come that the Son of man should be glorified" (John 12:23). Twelve times in this Gospel, the title "Son of man" appears, and this one in John 12:31 is the final instance. Daniel 7:13 identifies this title as messianic, and Jesus sometimes used it this way (Matt. 26:64).

What did it mean for Jesus to glorify the Father? He tells us in His prayer: "I have glorified Thee on the earth; I have finished the work which Thou gavest Me to do" (John 17:4). This is the way all of us glorify God, by faithfully doing what He calls us to do. In our Lord's case, the Father's will was that the Son die for lost sinners, be raised from the dead, and then ascend to heaven. The Son glorified the Father and the Father glorified the Son (John 17:1, 5).

There would come a time when the Son would be glorified in these disciples (John 17:10), but they could not follow Him at that time. Peter boasted that he would follow the Lord even to death (Luke 22:33), but unfortunately ended up denying Him three times.

Jesus had said to the Jews on two occasions that they would seek Him but not be able to find Him or follow Him (John 7:33-36; 8:21-24). Note that He did not tell His disciples that they would not be able to find Him, but He did say that to the unbelieving Jews. One day the believing disciples would go to be with Him (John 14:1-3), and they would also see Him after His resurrection. But during this time of His suffering and death, it was important that they not try to follow Him.

I have heard eloquent sermons about the sin of Peter who "followed afar off" (Luke 22:54), and the emphasis was that he should have followed nearer. The simple fact is that he should not have followed at all! The statement in John 13:33 is proof enough, and when you add Matthew 26:31 (quoted from Zech. 13:7) and our Lord's words in John 18:8, the evidence is conclusive. Because Peter disregarded this warning, he got into trouble.

The disciples' responsibility was to love one another just as Christ had loved them. They would certainly need this love in the hours to follow, when their Master would be taken from them and their brave spokesman, Peter, would fail Him and them. In fact, all of them would fail, and the only thing that would bring them together would be their love for Christ and for each other.

The word *love* is used only twelve times in John 1–12, but in John 13–21 it is used forty-four times! It is a key word in Christ's farewell sermon to His disciples, as well as a burden in His High Priestly Prayer (John 17:26). The word *new* does not mean "new in time," because love has been important to God's people even from Old Testament times (see Lev. 19:18). It means "new in experience, fresh." It is the opposite of "worn out." Love would take on a new meaning and power because of the death of Christ on the cross (John 15:13). With the coming of the Holy Spirit, love would have a new power in their lives.

This section begins and ends with love: Jesus' love for His own (John 13:1) and the disciples' love for one another. It is love that is the true evidence that we belong to Jesus Christ. The church leader Tertullian (A.D. 155–220) quoted the pagans as saying of the Christians, "See how they love one another?" And how do we evidence that love? By doing what Jesus did: laying down our lives for the brethren (1 John 3:16). And the way to start is by getting down and washing one another's feet in sacrificial service.

CHAPTER FOURTEEN
HEART TROUBLE
John 13:36–14:31

This section opens and closes with our Lord's loving admonition, "Let not your heart be troubled" (John 14:1, 27). We are not surprised that the Apostles were troubled. After all, Jesus had announced that one of them was a traitor, and then He warned Peter that he was going to deny his Lord three times. Self-confident Peter was certain that he could not only follow his Lord, but even die with Him and for Him. Alas, Peter did not know his own heart, nor do we really know *our* hearts, except for one thing: our hearts easily become troubled.

Perhaps the heaviest blow of all was the realization that Jesus was going to leave them (John 13:33). Where was He going? Could they go with Him? How could they get where He was going? These were some of the perplexing questions that tumbled around in their minds and hearts and were tossed back and forth in their conversation at the table.

How did Jesus calm their troubled hearts? By giving them six wonderful assurances to lay hold of, assurances that we today may claim and thus enjoy untroubled hearts. If you are a believer in Jesus Christ, you may claim every single one of these assurances.

You Are Going to Heaven (John 13:36–14:6)

Jesus did not rebuke Peter for asking Him where He was going, but His reply was somewhat cryptic. One day Peter would "follow" Jesus to the cross (John 21:18-19; 2 Peter 1:12-15), and then he would follow Him to heaven. Tradition tells us that Peter was crucified, though he asked to be crucified head-downward because he did not feel worthy to die as his Master died.

Just as Peter was beginning to feel like a hero, Jesus announced that he himself would soon become a casualty. The message not only shocked Peter, but it also stunned the rest of the disciples. After all, if brave Peter denied the Lord, what hope was there for the rest of them? It was then that Jesus gave His message to calm their troubled hearts.

According to Jesus, heaven is a real place. It is not a product of religious imagination or the result of a psyched-up mentality, looking for "pie in the sky by and by." Heaven is the place where God dwells and where Jesus sits today at the right hand of the Father. Heaven is described as a kingdom (2 Peter 1:11), an inheritance (1 Peter 1:4), a country (Heb. 11:16), a city (Heb. 11:16), and a home (John 14:2).

The word *Father* is used fifty-three times in John 13–17. Heaven is "My Father's house," according to the Son of God. It is "home" for God's children! Some years ago, a London newspaper held a contest to determine the best definition of "home." The winning entry was, "Home is the place where you are treated the best and complain the most." The poet Robert Frost said that home is the place that, when you arrive there, they have to take you in. A good definition!

The Greek word *monē* is translated "mansions" in John 14:2 and "abode" in John 14:23. It simply means "rooms, abiding places," so we must not think in terms of manor houses. It is unfortunate that some unbiblical songs have perpetuated the error that faithful Christians will have lovely mansions in glory, while worldly saints will have to be content with little cottages or even shacks. Jesus Christ is now preparing places for all true believers, and each place will be beautiful. When He was here on earth, Jesus was a carpenter (Mark 6:3). Now that He has returned to glory, He is building a church on earth and a home for that church in heaven.

John 14:3 is a clear promise of our Lord's return for His people. Some will go to heaven through the valley of the shadow of death, but those who are alive when Jesus returns will *never* see death (John 11:25-26). They will be changed to be like Christ and will go to heaven (1 Thes. 4:13-18).

Since heaven is the Father's house, it must be a place of love and joy. When the Apostle John tried to describe heaven, he almost ran out of symbols and comparisons! (Rev. 21–22) Finally, he listed the things that would not be there: death, sorrow, crying, pain, night, etc. What a wonderful home it will be—and we will enjoy it forever!

Thomas' question revealed his keen desire to be with Jesus (see John 11:16), and this meant that he had to know where the Master was going and how he himself would get there. The Lord made it clear that He was going to the Father, and that He was the only way to the Father. Heaven is a real place, a loving place, and an exclusive place. Not everybody is going to heaven, but rather only those who have trusted Jesus Christ (see Acts 4:12; 1 Tim. 2:4-6).

Jesus does not simply teach the way or point the way; *He is the way.* In fact, "the Way" was one of the early names for the Christian faith (Acts 9:2; 19:9, 23; 22:4; 24:14, 22). Our Lord's statement, "No man cometh unto the Father but by Me," wipes away any other proposed way to heaven—good works, religious ceremonies, costly gifts, etc. There is only one way, and that way is Jesus Christ.

How would this assurance of going to heaven help to calm the disciples' troubled hearts? Dr. James M. Gray put it beautifully in a song he wrote years ago: "Who could mind the journey, when the road leads home?" The assurance of a heavenly home at the end of life's road enables us to bear joyfully with the obstacles and battles along the way. It was this assurance that even encouraged our Lord, "who for the joy that was set before Him endured the cross" (Heb. 12:2). Paul had this truth in mind when he wrote, "For I reckon that the sufferings of this present time are not worthy to be compared with the glory which shall be revealed in us" (Rom. 8:18).

You Know the Father Right Now (John 14:7-11)

We do not have to wait until we enter heaven to get to know the Father. We can know Him today and receive from Him the spiritual resources we need to keep going when the days are difficult.

What does it mean to "know the Father"? The word *know* is used 141 times in John's Gospel, but it does not always carry the same meaning. In fact, there are four different "levels" of *knowing* according to John. The lowest level is simply knowing a fact. The next level is to understand the truth behind that fact. However, you can know the fact and know the truth behind it and still be lost in your sins. The third level introduces *relationship;* "to know" means "to believe in a person and become related to him or her." This is the way "know" is used in John 17:3. In fact, in Scripture, "to know" is used of the most intimate relationship between man and wife (Gen. 4:1).

The fourth use of "know" means "to have a deeper relationship with a person, a deeper communion." It was this level Paul was referring to when he wrote, "That I may know

Him" (Phil. 3:10). Jesus will describe this deeper relationship in John 14:19-23, so we will save any further comment until we deal with that section.

When Jesus said that knowing Him and seeing Him was the same as knowing and seeing the Father, He was claiming to be God. From now on, they would understand more and more about the Father, even though Jesus was leaving them.

I appreciate Philip's desire to know the Father. He had come a long way since that day Jesus found him and called him (John 1:43-45). The burning desire of every believer ought to be to know God better. We read and study the Word of God so that we might better know the God of the Word.

The Greek construction of the question in John 14:10 indicates that the Lord expected a yes answer from Philip: he *did* believe that Jesus was in the Father and the Father in Him. That being the case, Philip should have realized that the words of Jesus, as well as His works, came from the Father and revealed the Father. Believers today have not seen the Lord Jesus in the flesh (1 Peter 1:8), but we do see Him and His works in the Word. The emphasis throughout John's Gospel is that you cannot separate Christ's words and works, for both come from the Father and reveal the Father.

The "believe" in John 14:10 is singular, for Jesus was addressing Philip; but in John 14:11, it is plural and He addresses all of the disciples. The tense of both is "go on believing." Let your faith grow!

Four hundred years before Christ was born, the Greek philosopher Plato wrote, "To find out the Father and Maker of all this universe is a hard task, and when we have found Him, to speak of Him to all men is impossible." But Plato was wrong! We *can* know the Father and Maker of the universe, for Jesus Christ revealed Him to us. Why should our hearts be troubled when the Creator and Governor of the universe is *our own Father?*

The very Lord of heaven and earth is our Father (Luke 10:21). There is no need for us to have troubled hearts, for He is in control.

Of course, it is not the believer *himself* who does these "greater things"; it is God working in and through the believer: "The Lord working with them" (Mark 16:20). "For it is God which worketh in you" (Phil. 2:13). Faith and works must always go together, for it is faith that releases the power of God in our lives.

You Have the Privilege of Prayer (John 14:12-15)

"Why pray when you can worry?" asks a plaque that I have seen in many homes. One of the best remedies for a troubled heart is prayer.

"O what peace we often forfeit,
O what needless pain we bear;
All because we do not carry
Everything to God in prayer."

However, if God is going to answer our prayers and give us peace in our hearts, there are certain conditions that we must meet. In fact, the meeting of these conditions is a blessing in itself!

We must pray in faith (v. 12). This is a promise for us to claim, and the claiming of it demands faith. The double "verily" assures us that this is a solemn announcement. The fact that Jesus did return to the Father is an encouragement, for there He is interceding for us. He will have more to say about this intercessory work later in His discourse.

The "greater works [things]" would apply initially to the Apostles who were given the power to perform special miracles as the credentials of their office (Rom. 15:18-19; Heb. 2:3-4). These miracles were not greater in *quality,* for "the servant is not greater than his lord" (John 13:16), but rather in scope and quantity. Peter preached one sermon and 3,000 sinners were converted in one day! The fact that ordinary people performed these signs made them even more wonderful and brought great glory to God (Acts 5:13-16).

Both love and obedience are part of effective prayer. "If I regard [see and approve] iniquity in my heart, the Lord will not hear me" (Ps. 66:18).

We do not obey the Lord simply because we want our prayers answered, somewhat like the attitude of a child just before Christmas. We obey Him because we love Him; and the more we obey Him, the more we experience His love. To "keep" His commandments means to value them, treasure them, guard them, and do them. "I have esteemed the words of His mouth more than my necessary food" (Job 23:12).

Believing prayer is wonderful medicine to soothe a troubled heart. Meditate on Philippians 4:6-7—and then put it into practice!

We must pray in Christ's name (vv. 13-14). This is not a "magic formula" that we automatically attach to our prayer requests, guaranteeing that God will answer. To ask anything of the Father, in the name of Jesus, means that we ask what Jesus would ask, what would please Him, and what would bring Him glory by furthering His work. When a friend says to you, "You may use my name!" he is handing you a great privilege as well as a tremendous responsibility.

The "whatsoever" in John 14:13 is qualified by all that God has revealed in His Word about prayer; likewise, the "anything" in John 14:14. God is not giving us *carte blanche;* "in My name" is the controlling element. To know God's name means to know His nature, what He is, and what He wants to do. God answers prayer in order to honor His name; therefore, prayer must be in His will (1 John 5:14-15). The first request in "The Lord's Prayer" is, "Hallowed be Thy name" (Matt. 6:9). Any request that does not glorify God's name should not be asked in His name.

We must pray in loving obedience (v. 15). When you love someone, you honor his or her name; and you would never use that name in a demeaning manner. *Love* is an important theme in the Gospel of John; it is used as a verb or noun a total of fifty-six times.

We Have the Holy Spirit (John 14:16-18)

Jesus had a great deal to say about the Holy Spirit in His Upper Room message, for apart from the help of the Spirit of God, we cannot live the Christian life as God would have us live it. We must know who the Holy Spirit is, what He does, and how He does it.

The Holy Spirit is given two special names by our Lord: "another Comforter" and "the Spirit of truth." The Greek word translated "Comforter" is *paraklētos* and it is used only by John (14:16, 26; 15:26; 16:7; 1 John 2:1). It means "called alongside to assist." The Holy Spirit does not work instead of us, or in spite of us, but in us and through us.

Our English word *comfort* comes from two Latin words meaning "with strength." We usually think of "comfort" as soothing someone, consoling him or her; and to some extent this is true. But true comfort strengthens us to face life bravely and keep on going. It does not rob us of responsibility or make it easy for us to give up. Some translations call the Holy Spirit "the Encourager," and this is a good choice of words. *Paraklētos* is translated "Advocate" in 1 John 2:1. An "advocate" is one who represents you at court and stands at your side to plead your case.

As "the Spirit of Truth," the Holy Spirit is related to Jesus, the Truth, and the Word of God, which of itself is the truth (John 14:6; 17:17). The Spirit inspired the Word and also illumines the Word so we may understand it. Later on in this message, Jesus will explain the teaching ministry of the Holy Spirit. Since He is the "Spirit of Truth," the Holy Spirit cannot lie or be associated with lies. He never leads us to do anything contrary to the Word of God, for again God's Word is truth.

If we want the Holy Spirit to work in our lives, we must seek to glorify Christ; and we must make much of the Word of God. When you compare Ephesians 5:18–6:9 with Colossians 3:16–4:1, you will see that both passages describe the same kind of Christian life—joyful, thankful, and submissive. To be filled with the Spirit is the same as to be controlled by the Word. The Spirit of Truth uses the Word of truth to guide us into the will and the work of God.

The Holy Spirit abides in the believer. He is a gift from the Father in answer to the prayer of the Son. During His earthly ministry, Jesus had guided, guarded, and taught His disciples; but now He was going to leave them. The Spirit of God would come to them *and dwell in them,* taking the place of their Master. Jesus called the Spirit "another Comforter," and the Greek word translated "another" means "another of the same kind." The Spirit of God is not different from the Son of God, for both are God. The Spirit of God had dwelt *with* the disciples in the person of Jesus Christ. Now He would dwell *in* them.

Of course, the Spirit of God had been on earth before. He empowered men and women in the Old Testament to accomplish God's work. However, during the Old Testament Age, the Spirit of God would come on people and then leave them. God's Spirit departed from King Saul (1 Sam. 16:14; 18:12); and David, when confessing his sin, asked that the Spirit not be taken from him (Ps. 51:11). When the Holy Spirit was given at Pentecost, He was given to God's people to remain with them forever. Even though we may grieve the Spirit, He will not leave us.

The way we treat the Holy Spirit is the way we treat the Lord Jesus Christ. The believer's body is the temple of the Spirit (1 Cor. 6:19-20), so what he or she does with that body affects the indwelling Holy Spirit. The Spirit wrote the Word of God, and the way we treat the Bible is the way we treat the Spirit of God and the Son of God.

The world cannot receive the Spirit because the world lives "by sight" and not by faith. Furthermore, the world does not know Jesus Christ; and you cannot have knowledge of the Spirit apart from the Son. The presence of the Spirit in this world is actually an indictment against the world, for the world rejected Jesus Christ.

The word translated "comfortless" in John 14:18 means "orphans." We are not alone, abandoned, helpless, and hopeless! Wherever we go, the Spirit is with us, so why should we feel like orphans? There is no need to have a troubled heart when you have the very Spirit of God dwelling within you!

We Enjoy the Father's Love (John 14:19-24)

"The love of God is shed abroad in our hearts by the Holy Spirit which is given unto us" (Rom. 5:5). Orphans feel unwanted and unloved, but our Father shares His love with us. Jesus explained a threefold manifestation of God's love.

There was a past manifestation to the disciples (vv. 19-20). John 14:19 focuses on His resurrection and post-resurrection appearances to His disciples and other believers. The last time the world saw Jesus was when Joseph and Nicodemus took Him from the cross and buried Him. The next time the world sees Him, He will come in power and great glory to judge lost sinners.

John 14:20 centers especially on the coming of the Spirit at Pentecost and the oneness of the believers with their Lord. Jesus returned to heaven as the exalted Head of the church (Eph. 1:19-23); then He sent the Spirit so that the members of the body would be joined to their Head in a living union. Believers today, of course, did not see Jesus after His resurrection or in His ascension, but we are united to Him by the indwelling Holy Spirit.

There is a present manifestation of Himself to believers (vv. 21, 23-24). Note the repetition of the word *love.* If we treasure His Word and obey it, then the Father and the Son will share Their love with us and make Their home in us. The word translated "abode" in John 14:23 means "make our home" and is related to "mansions" in John 14:2.

When the sinner trusts Christ, he is born again and the Spirit immediately enters his body and bears witness that he is a child of God. The Spirit is resident and will not depart. But as the believer yields to the Father, loves the Word, prays, and obeys, there is a deeper relationship with the Father, Son, and Spirit. Salvation means we are going to heaven, but submission means that heaven comes to us!

This truth is illustrated in the experiences of Abraham and Lot, recorded in Genesis 18 and 19. When Jesus and the two angels visited Abraham's tent, they felt right at home. They even enjoyed a meal, and Jesus had a private talk with Abraham. But our Lord did not go to Sodom to visit Lot, because He did not feel at home there. Instead, He sent the two angels.

Our experience with God ought to go deeper and deeper, and it will as we yield to the Spirit of Truth and permit Him to teach us and guide us. If we love God and obey Him, He will manifest His love to us in a deeper way each day.

There will be a future manifestation when Jesus Christ returns (v. 19). Judas (not Iscariot) recalled that Jesus had said He would not manifest Himself to the world (John 14:22). But this seemed to contradict other statements He had made, such as recorded in Matthew 24:30. His question was, "What has come to pass that You are no longer going to reveal Yourself to the world?" Has there been a change in the divine plan?

Jesus had been rejected by His own people, so He could not manifest Himself to them. In fact, it was an act of mercy that He did not manifest Himself to the world, because that would have meant judgment. He has revealed Himself to His church and left the church in the world to be a witness of God's love. He is patiently waiting, still giving lost sinners opportunity to repent and be saved (2 Peter 3:1-10). One day He will return (Rev. 1:7) and the world will behold Him.

One of the best ways to ease a troubled heart is to bathe it in the love of God. When you feel like an "orphan," let the Spirit of God reveal God's love to you in a deeper way. Charles Spurgeon said, "Little faith will take your soul to heaven, but great faith will bring heaven to your soul." Your heart can become a "heaven on earth" as you commune with the Lord and worship Him.

You Have His Gift of Peace (John 14:25-31)

Shalom—peace—is a precious word to the Jewish people. It means much more than just the absence of war or distress. *Shalom* means wholeness, completeness, health, security, even prosperity in the best sense. When you are enjoying God's peace, there is joy and contentment. But God's peace is not like the "peace" that the world offers.

The world bases its peace on its *resources,* while God's peace depends on *relationships.* To be right with God means to enjoy the peace of God. The world depends on personal ability, but the Christian depends on spiritual adequacy in Christ. In the world, peace is something you hope for or work for; but to the Christian, peace is God's wonderful gift, received by faith. Unsaved people enjoy peace when there is an absence of trouble; Christians enjoy peace *in spite of trials* because of the presence of power, the Holy Spirit.

People in the world walk by sight and depend on the externals, but Christians walk by faith and depend on the eternals. The Spirit of God teaches us the Word and guides us (not drags us!) into the truth. He also reminds us of what He has taught us so that we can depend on God's Word in the difficult times of life. The Spirit uses the Word to give us His peace (John 14:27), His love (John 15:9-10), and His joy (John 15:11). If that does not calm a troubled heart, nothing will!

Again, Jesus assured them that they would see Him again (John 14:28). Why rejoice because He returned to the Father? Because His return made possible His wonderful intercessory ministry on our behalf, our great High Priest in heaven (Heb. 2:17-18; 4:14-16). We have the Spirit within us, the Saviour above us, and the Word before us! What tremendous resources for peace!

In John 14:30-31, the Lord named two of our great spiritual enemies—the world and the devil. Jesus overcame the world and the devil (John 12:31), and the devil has no claim on Him. There is no point in Jesus Christ where the devil can get a foothold. Since we are "in Christ," Satan can get no foothold in the believer's life, unless we permit it. Neither Satan nor the world can trouble our hearts if we are yielded to the "peace of God" through the Holy Spirit.

When Jesus said "My Father is greater than I" (John 14:28), He was not denying His own deity or His equality with God, for then He would have been contradicting Himself (John 10:30). When Jesus was here on earth, He was necessarily limited by having a human body. He voluntarily laid aside the independent exercise of His divine attributes and submitted Himself to the Father. In that sense, the Father was greater than the Son. Of course, when the Son returned to heaven, all He had laid aside was restored once again (John 17:1, 5).

Jesus showed His love for the Father (and for the world) by voluntarily going to the cross. He did not hide or flee. He willingly laid down His life. He and the disciples may have left the Upper Room at this point (John 14:31) so that what Jesus said from that point on was spoken on the way to the Garden. Or, they may have arisen from the table and lingered awhile as He instructed them. We can easily imagine the allegory of the vine being given as they walked that night through the vineyards.

His own perfect peace assures us that He alone can give true peace. Jesus was always the Master of the situation, and He enables us to take control of our lives as we surrender to Him and receive His legacy of peace.

CHAPTER FIFTEEN RELATIONSHIPS AND RESPONSIBILITIES

John 15:1-17

This is the seventh and last of the "I AM" statements of Christ recorded in the Gospel of John. However, Jesus did not stop with this image, but went on to use the picture of "the friend." These two pictures of the believer—branches and friends—reveal both our privileges and our responsibilities. As *branches,* we have the privilege of sharing His life, and the responsibility of abiding. As *friends,* we have the privilege of knowing His will, and the responsibility of obeying.

Branches—We Must Abide (John 15:1-11)

The cultivation of vineyards was important to the life and economy of Israel. A golden vine adorned Herod's temple. When our Lord used this image, He was not introducing something new; it was familiar to every Jew. There are four elements in this allegory that we must understand to benefit from His teaching.

The vine. There are actually three different vines found in Scripture. The *past* vine was the nation of Israel (see Ps. 80:8-19; Isa. 5:1-7; Jer. 2:21; Ezek. 19:10-14; and Hosea 10:1). In an act of wonderful grace, God "transplanted" Israel into Canaan and gave the nation every possible benefit. "What could have been done more to My vineyard, that I have not done in it?" God asked (Isa. 5:4). If ever a nation had everything it needed to succeed, it was Israel.

But the vine produced wild grapes! Instead of practicing justice, it practiced oppression; instead of producing righteousness, it produced unrighteousness and cries of distress from the victims. God had to deal with the nation Israel and chasten it, but even that did not produce lasting results. When God's own Son came to the vineyard, they cast Him out and killed Him (Matt. 21:33-46).

There is also a *future* vine, "the vine of the earth" described in Revelation 14:14-20. This is the Gentile world system ripening for God's judgment. Believers are branches in "the vine of heaven," but the unsaved are branches in "the vine of the earth." The unsaved depend on this world for their sustenance and satisfaction, while believers depend on Jesus Christ. The "vine of the earth" will be cut down and destroyed when Jesus Christ returns.

The *present* Vine is our Lord Jesus Christ, and, of course, the vine includes the branches. He is the "true Vine," that is, "the original of which all other vines are a copy." As Christians, we do not live on substitutes! The symbolism of the Vine and branches is similar to that of the Head and the body: we have a living relationship to Christ and belong to Him.

When we lived in Chicago, we had a small grape arbor in our backyard; but what we cultivated was nothing like what is even today cultivated in the Holy Land. Ours was a very fragile plant and it was easy to break off a branch. The vines I saw in the Holy Land were large and strong, and it was next to impossible for anyone to break off a mature branch *without injuring the vine itself.* Our union with Christ is a *living* union, so we may bear fruit; a *loving* union, so that we may enjoy Him; and a *lasting* union, so that we need not be afraid.

The branches. Of itself, a branch is weak and useless. It is good for either bearing or burning, but not for building (read Ezek. 15). The branch cannot produce its own life; it must draw that life from the vine. It is our communion with Christ through the Spirit that makes possible the bearing of the fruit.

Many of the images of Christ and the believer given in Scripture emphasize this important concept of *union and communion:* the body and its members (1 Cor. 12), the bride and the Bridegroom (Eph. 5:25-33), the sheep and the Shepherd (John 10). A member of the body cut off from the body would die. The marriage creates the union, but it takes daily love and devotion to maintain the communion. The shepherd brings the sheep into the flock, but the sheep must follow the shepherd in order to have protection and provision.

The sooner we as believers discover that we are but branches, the better we will relate to the Lord; for we will know our own weakness and confess our need for His strength.

The key word is *abide;* it is used eleven times in John 15:1-11 ("continue" in John 15:9 and "remain" in John 15:11). What does it mean to "abide"? It means to keep in fellowship with Christ so that His life can work in and through us to produce fruit. This certainly involves the Word of God and the confession of sin so that nothing hinders our communion with Him (John 15:3). It also involves obeying Him because we love Him (John 15:9-10).

How can we tell when we are "abiding in Christ"? Is there a special feeling? No, but there are special evidences that appear and they are unmistakably clear. For one thing, when you are abiding in Christ, you produce fruit (John 15:2). What that "fruit" is, we will discuss later. Also, you experience the Father's "pruning" so that you will bear more fruit (John 15:2). The believer who is abiding in Christ has his prayers answered (John 15:7) and experiences a deepening love for Christ and for other believers (John 15:9, 12-13). He also experiences joy (John 15:11).

This abiding relationship is natural to the branch and the vine, but it must be cultivated in the Christian life. It is not automatic. Abiding in Christ demands worship, meditation on God's Word, prayer, sacrifice, and service—but what a joyful experience it is! Once you have begun to cultivate this deeper communion with Christ, you have no desire to return to the shallow life of the careless Christian.

The vinedresser. The vinedresser is in charge of caring for the vines, and Jesus said that this is the work of His Father. It is He who "purges" or prunes the branches so they will produce more fruit. Note the progression here: no fruit (John 15:2), fruit, more fruit, much fruit (John 15:5, 8). Many Christians pray that God will make them more fruitful, but they do not enjoy the pruning process that follows!

The vinedresser prunes the branches in two ways: he cuts away dead wood that can breed disease and insects, and he cuts away living tissue so that the life of the vine will not be so dissipated that the quality of the crop will be jeopardized. In fact, the vinedresser will even cut away whole bunches of grapes so that the rest of the crop will be of higher quality. God wants both quantity and quality.

This pruning process is the most important part of the whole enterprise, and the people who do it must be carefully trained or they can destroy an entire crop. Some vineyards invest two or three years in training the "pruners" so they know where to cut, how much to cut, and even at what angle to make the cut.

The greatest judgment God could bring to a believer would be to let him alone, let him have his own way. Because God loves us, He "prunes" us and encourages us to bear more fruit for His glory. If the branches could speak, they would confess that the pruning process hurts; but they would also rejoice that they will be able to produce more and better fruit.

Your Heavenly Father is never nearer to you than when He is pruning you. Sometimes He cuts away the dead wood that might cause trouble; but often He cuts off the living tissue that is robbing you of spiritual vigor. Pruning does not simply mean spiritual surgery that removes what is bad. It can also mean cutting away the good and the better so that we might enjoy the best. Yes, pruning hurts, but it also helps. We may not enjoy it, but we need it.

How does the Father prune us? Sometimes He simply uses the Word to convict and cleanse us. (The word translated "purge" in John 15:2 is the same as "clean" in John 13:10. See Eph. 5:26-27.) Sometimes He must chasten us (Heb. 12:1-11). At the time, it hurts when He removes something precious from us; but as the "spiritual crop" is produced, we see that the Father knew what He was doing.

The more we abide in Christ, the more fruit we bear; and the more fruit we bear, the more the Father has to prune us so that the quality keeps up with the quantity. Left to itself, the branch might produce many clusters, but they will be inferior in quality. God is glorified by a bigger crop that is also a *better* crop.

The fruit. The word *results* is often heard in conversations among Christian workers, but this is not actually a Bible concept. A machine can produce results, and so can a robot, but it takes *a living organism* to produce fruit. It takes time and cultivation to produce fruit; a good crop does not come overnight.

We must remember that the branches do not eat the fruit: others do. We are not producing fruit to please ourselves but to serve others. We should be the kind of people who "feed" others by our words and our works. "The lips of the righteous feed many" (Prov. 10:21).

Several different kinds of spiritual fruit are named in the Bible. We bear fruit when we win others to Christ (Rom. 1:13). We are a part of the harvest (John 4:35-38). As we grow in holiness and obedience, we are bearing fruit (Rom. 6:22). Paul considered Christian giving to be fruit from a dedicated life (Rom. 15:28). "The fruit of the Spirit" (Gal. 5:22-23) is the kind of Christian character that glorifies God and makes Christ real to others. Even our good works, our service, grow out of our abiding life (Col. 1:10). The praise that comes from our hearts and lips is actually fruit to the glory of God (Heb. 13:15).

Many of these things could be counterfeited by the flesh, but the deception would eventually be detected, for real spiritual fruit has in it *the seeds for more fruit.* Man-made results are dead and cannot reproduce themselves, but Spirit-produced fruit will go on reproducing from one life to another. There will be fruit—more fruit—much fruit.

A true branch, united with the vine, will always bear fruit. Not every branch bears a bumper crop, just as not every field has a bumper harvest (Matt. 13:8, 23), but there is always fruit where there is life. If there is no fruit, the branch is worthless and it is cast away and burned. I do not believe our Lord is teaching here that true believers can lose their salvation, for this would contradict what He taught in John 6:37 and 10:27-30. It is unwise to build a theological doctrine on a parable or allegory. Jesus was teaching one main truth—

the fruitful life of the believer—and we must not press the details too much. Just as an unfruitful branch is useless, so an unfruitful believer is useless; and both must be dealt with. It is a tragic thing for a once-fruitful believer to backslide and lose his privilege of fellowship and service. If anything, John 15:6 describes divine discipline rather than eternal destiny. "There is [for believers] a sin unto death" (1 John 5:16).

Our Lord had spoken about peace (John 14:27); now He mentions love and joy (John 15:9-11). Love, joy, and peace are the first three "fruit of the Spirit" named in Galatians 5:22-23. Our abiding in Christ certainly ought to produce His love, joy, and peace in our hearts. Because we love Him, we keep His commandments; and, as we keep His commandments, we abide in His love and experience it in a deeper way.

Several times in John's Gospel you will find Jesus speaking about the Father's love for Him. We so emphasize God's love for the world and the church that we forget that the Father loves the Son. Because the Father does love the Son, He has put all things into the Son's hand (John 3:35) and has revealed all things to the Son (John 5:20). The Father loved the Son before the foundation of the world (John 17:24); He loved the Son when the Son died on the cross (John 10:17). The amazing thing is believers today can experience personally that same love! Jesus prayed "that the love with which Thou hast loved Me may be in them [the disciples and believers today]" (John 17:26).

As branches in the Vine, we have the privilege of abiding and the responsibility of bearing fruit. Now we turn to the second picture, that of *friends.*

Friends—We Must Obey (John 15:12-17)

Most of us have many acquaintances but very few friends, and even some of our friends may prove unfriendly or even unfaithful. What about Judas? "Yes, mine own familiar friend, in whom I trusted, which did eat of my bread, hath lifted up his heel against me" (Ps. 41:9). Even a devoted friend may fail us when we need him most. Peter, James, and John went to sleep in the Garden when they should have been praying; and Peter even denied the Lord three times. Our friendship to each other and to the Lord is not perfect, but His friendship to us is perfect.

However, we must not interpret this word *friend* in a limited way, because the Greek word means "a friend at court." It describes that "inner circle" around a king or emperor. (In John 3:29, it refers to the "best man" at a wedding.) The "friends of the king" would be close to him and know his secrets, but they would also be subject to him and have to obey his commands. There is thus no conflict between being a friend and being a servant.

The perfect illustration of this in Scripture is Abraham, "the friend of God" (2 Chron. 20:7; Isa. 41:8; James 2:23), who was also the servant of God (Gen. 26:24). In Genesis 18, our Lord and two angels came to visit Abraham as they were on their way to investigate the sin of Sodom. Even though Abraham was nearly 100 years old, he interrupted his noonday rest, greeted the visitors, saw to their comfort, and fed them a lovely meal. In the first fifteen verses of this chapter, Abraham is on the move; and twice he refers to himself as a servant (Gen. 18:3, 5). Note that this old man "hastened" and "ran" and encouraged others to perform their work quickly, a perfect example of a servant. Nor did Abraham sit and eat with them. Like a true servant, he stood nearby, ready to do their bidding.

In the last half of the chapter, the atmosphere changes, and Abraham is quietly standing still, communing with the Lord. He is still a servant, but now he is being a friend. "Shall I hide from Abraham that which I do?" the Lord asked. As a friend of God, Abraham shared God's secrets.

It is this kind of a relationship that Jesus described when He called His disciples "friends." It was certainly a relationship of *love,* both for Him and for each other. The "friends of the King" could not compete with each other for attention or promotion. They were a part of the "inner circle," not to promote themselves, but to serve their King. What a rebuke this must have been to the selfish disciples who often argued over who was the greatest!

How is it possible for Jesus to *command* us to love one another? Can true love be commanded? You must keep in mind that Christian love is not basically a "feeling"; it is an act of the will. The proof of our love is not in our feelings but in our actions, even to the extent of laying down our lives for Christ and for one another (1 John 3:16). Jesus laid down His life for both His friends and His enemies! (Rom.

5:10) While the emotions are certainly involved, real Christian love is an act of the will. It means treating others the way God treats us.

So, our friendship with Christ involves love and obedience. But it also involves knowledge: He "lets us in on" His plans. Indeed, He is our Master (John 13:13, 16), but He does not treat us as servants. He treats us as friends, *if* we do what He commands. Abraham was God's friend because he obeyed God (Gen. 18:19). If we have friendship with the world, we then experience enmity with God (James 4:1-4). Lot in Sodom was not called God's friend, even though Lot was a saved man (2 Peter 2:7). God told Abraham what He planned to do to the cities of the plain, and Abraham was able to intercede for Lot and his family.

It is interesting to note that, in John's Gospel, it was the servants who knew what was going on! The servants at the wedding feast in Cana knew where the wine came from (John 2:9), and the nobleman's servants knew when the son was healed (John 4:51-53).

One of the greatest privileges we have as His friends is that of learning to know God better and "getting in on" God's secrets. I can never forget the impact on my own heart when I heard Dr. Oswald Sanders say to the Back to the Bible staff, "Each of us is as close to God as we choose to be." We are His friends, and we ought to be near the throne, listening to His Word, enjoying His intimacy, and obeying His commandments.

One day while he was a fugitive, David was near Bethlehem, his home city, and he longed for a drink of water from the well by the gate. Three of his mighty men were close enough to David to hear his sigh, and they risked their lives to bring their king the water that he wanted (2 Sam. 23:15-17). That is what it means to be a friend of the king.

In John 14:16, Jesus reminded the men that they had this privileged position only because of His grace. They did not choose Him; He chose them! He chose them out of the world (John 14:19) and ordained them to do His will. Again, we find this important word *fruit.* As branches, we share His life and bear fruit; and as friends, we share His love and bear fruit. As branches, we are pruned by the Father; as friends, we are instructed by the Son, and His Word controls our lives.

The word *ordained* simply means "appointed." It refers to the act of setting someone apart for special service. We have graciously been chosen and set apart by the Lord in order to go into the world and bear fruit. He has sent us into the world (John 17:18) as His personal ambassadors to tell others about the King and His great salvation. When we witness to others and win them to Christ, this is bringing forth fruit to the glory of God.

As I mentioned before, the evidence of true sonship, discipleship (John 15:8), and friendship (John 15:15) is *fruit.* "Wherefore by their fruits ye shall know them" (Matt. 7:20). Where there is true fruit, it remains; man-made "results" eventually disappear. Fruit has in it the seed for more fruit, so the process goes on and on. Whatever is born of the Spirit of God has the mark of eternity on it, and it will last.

Once again, Jesus brought up the privilege of prayer. The friends of the king certainly speak to their sovereign and share their burdens and needs with him. In the days of monarchies, it was considered a very special honor to be invited to speak to the king or queen; yet the friends of Jesus Christ can speak to Him at any time. The throne of grace is always available to them.

John 15:15-16 summarize for us what it means to be a friend of the King of kings. It is a humbling experience, for He chose us and we did not choose Him. We must keep this in mind lest we become proud and presumptuous. It means that we keep our ears open and listen to what He says to us. "Hast thou heard the secret of God?" (Job 15:8) "The secret of the Lord is with them that fear Him; and He will show them His covenant" (Ps. 25:14). We must be attentive and alert.

But the purpose for all of this is that we might obey Him and get His work done. The King has tasks that must be performed; and if we love Him, we will obey His commands. We will seek to bear fruit that will please Him and glorify the Father. Our joy should be to please Him.

Jesus closed this part of His message by reminding them (and us) of the most important commandment of all: love one another. There are dozens of "one another" statements in the New Testament, but all of them are summarized in "love one another." Jesus had already given this commandment to the Eleven (John 13:34-35), and now He has repeated it twice (John 15:12, 17). It will be stated in one way or another many more times in the New Testament letters, especially by John in his first epistle. The friends of the King must not only love Him, but also one another. What joy it brings to His heart when He sees His friends loving one another and working together to obey His commands.

This study began in the vineyard and ended in the throne room! The next study will take us to the battlefield where we experience the hatred of the lost world. If we are not abiding as branches and obeying as friends, we will never be able to face the opposition of the world. If we do not love one another, how can we ever hope to love lost men and women in the world? If we are not marching together as the friends of the King, we will never present a united front to the enemy.

"Without Me, ye can do nothing" (John 15:5).

We are not simply handicapped or hindered. We are hopelessly paralyzed! We can do *nothing!*

But if we abide in Him, if we stay close to the throne, we can do *anything* that He commands us to do!

What a privilege—and what a responsibility!

CHAPTER SIXTEEN
WHAT IN THE WORLD IS THE SPIRIT DOING?
John 15:18–16:16

This long section—John 15:18–16:16—is tied together by two important themes: the opposition of the world against the church, and the ministry of the Spirit to and through the church. Our Lord had been talking about love (John 15:9-13, 17), but now He is talking about *hatred;* and He used the word seven times. It seems incredible that anyone would hate Jesus Christ and His people, but that is exactly what the situation is today; *and some of that hatred comes from religious people.* In a few hours, the religious leaders of Israel would be condemning their Messiah and crying out for His blood.

Our Lord had openly taught His disciples that one day persecution would come. He mentioned it in the Sermon on the Mount (Matt. 5:10-12, 44) and in His "commissioning sermon" when He sent out the disciples to minister (Matt. 10:16-23). In His sermon denouncing the Pharisees, Jesus openly said that they would persecute and kill God's servants (Matt. 23:34-35); and there was a similar warning given in His prophetic message on Mt. Olivet (Mark 13:9-13).

Throughout the Gospel of John, it is evident that the religious establishment not only opposed Jesus, but even sought to kill Him (John 5:16; 7:19, 25; 8:37, 59; 9:22; also note 11:8). As He continued His ministry, there was a tide of resentment, then hatred, and then open opposition against Him. So, the disciples should not have been surprised when Jesus brought up the subject of persecution, for they had heard Him warn them and they had seen Him face men's hatred during His ministry.

Until the Lord returns, or until we die, we must live in this hostile world and face continued opposition. How can we do it? What is the secret of victory? It is the presence and power of the Holy Spirit of God in our lives. This is the key section in the Upper Room message about the Holy Spirit and His ministry.

Before we study this passage and see the threefold ministry of the Spirit to the church in the world, we must pause to remind ourselves just who the Holy Spirit is. The Holy Spirit of God is a Person; Jesus referred to the Spirit as "He" and not "it." The Holy Spirit has a mind (Rom. 8:27), a will (1 Cor. 12:11), and emotional feelings (Gal. 5:22-23).

In John 15:26 all three Persons of the Godhead are mentioned: Jesus the Son will send the Spirit from the Father. Because the Holy Spirit is a Person, and is God, it means that the Christian has God indwelling his body! If we did not have the Holy Spirit within, we would not be able to serve the Lord in this present evil world. We are to walk in the Spirit (Gal. 5:16), worship in the Spirit (Phil. 3:3), and witness in the Spirit (Acts 1:8).

Christians can stand and withstand in the midst of the world's hatred because of the special ministries of the Holy Spirit.

The Spirit as Comforter Encourages the Church (John 15:18–16:4)

We should begin by clarifying what Jesus means by "the world," because the term is used in Scripture in at least three different ways. It can mean *the created world* ("the world was made by Him"—John 1:10), the world of *humanity* ("For God so loved the world"—John 3:16), or *society apart from God and opposed to God.* We sometimes use the phrase "the world system" to define this special meaning.

For example, when you listen to the radio news, you may hear the announcer say, "And now the news from the world of sports!" Obviously, "the world of sports" is not a special country or planet where everybody lives who is connected in some way with sports. "The world of sports" refers to all the organizations, people, plans, activities, philosophies, etc. that are a part of sports. Some of these things are visible and some are invisible, but all of them are organized around one thing—sports.

"The world" from a Christian point of view involves all the people, plans, organizations, activities, philosophies, values, etc. that belong to society without God. Some of these things may be very cultural; others may be very corrupt; but all of them have their origins in the heart and mind of sinful man and promote what sinful man wants to enjoy and accomplish. As Christians, we must be careful not to love the world (1 John 2:15-17) or be conformed to the world (Rom. 12:1-2).

Jesus pulls no punches when He tells His disciples that their situation in the world will be serious and even dangerous. Note the progress in the world's opposition: hatred (John 15:18-19), persecution (John 15:20), excommunication, and even death (John 16:2). You can trace these stages of resistance as you read the Book of Acts.

Why does the world system, including the "religious world," hate the Christian, the one who believes on Jesus Christ and seeks to follow Him? Jesus gave several reasons.

We are identified with Christ (vv. 18, 20). If they hated Him, they will also hate those of us who are identified with Him. In John 15:20, Jesus quoted the statement He had made earlier (John 13:16), and the logic of it is clear. He is the Master; we are the servants. He is greater than we are, so He must receive the praise and glory. But the world will not give Him praise and glory! The world hates Him, and therefore the world must hate us. If with all of His greatness and perfection, Jesus does not escape persecution, what hope is there for us with our imperfections?

This principle is seen in some of the other images of the relationship between Christ and His own. He is the Shepherd and we are the sheep; and when they attack the Shepherd, it affects the sheep (Matt. 26:31). He is the Master (Teacher) and we are the disciples, the learners. But it is encouraging to know that when God's people are persecuted, our Lord enters into their suffering, for He is the Head of the body and we are the members. "Saul, Saul, why persecutest thou Me?" (Acts 9:4) Anything that the enemy can do to us has already been done to Jesus Christ, and He is "with us" as we suffer.

We do not belong to the world (v. 19). When we trusted Christ, we moved into a new spiritual position: we are now "in Christ" and "out of the world." To be sure, we are *in* the world physically, but not *of* the world spiritually. Now that we are "partakers of the heavenly calling" (Heb. 3:1) we are no longer interested in the treasures or pleasures of sin in this world. This does not mean that we are isolated from reality or insulated from the world's needs, so "heavenly minded that we are no earthly good." Rather, it means that we look at the things of earth from heaven's point of view.

The world system functions on the basis of conformity. As long as a person follows the fads and fashions and accepts the values of the world, he or she will "get along." But the Christian refuses to be "conformed to this world" (Rom. 12:2). The believer is a "new creation" (2 Cor. 5:17) and no longer wants to live the "old life" (1 Peter 4:1-4). We are the light of the world and the salt of the earth (Matt. 5:13-16), but a dark world does not want light and a decaying world does not want salt! In other words, the believer is not just "out of step"; he is out of place! (See John 17:14, 16, and 1 John 4:5.)

The world is spiritually ignorant and blind (v. 21). If you had asked the religious leaders in Jerusalem if they knew the God they were seeking to defend, they would have said, "Of course we know Him! Israel has known the true God for centuries!" But Jesus said that they *did not* know the Father and, therefore, they could not know the Son (see John 16:3). The religious leaders knew a great deal about Jehovah God and could quote chapter and verse to defend their doctrines, but they did not personally know God.

This was not a new theme for our Lord to discuss, because He had mentioned it before to the religious leaders who opposed Him. "Ye neither know Me, nor My Father; if ye had known Me, ye should have known My Father also" (John 8:19). "Yet ye have not known Him; but I know Him" (John 8:55). Jesus had taught them the Word and had demonstrated His deity in miraculous signs and a godly walk; and yet the religious leaders of the nation were blind to His identity: "The world knew Him not" (John 1:10).

The religious world today claims to know God, but it does not want to bow the knee to Jesus Christ as the Son of God and the only Saviour of the world. Satan has blinded their minds (2 Cor. 4:3-4) and sin has blinded their hearts (Eph. 4:17-19). Like Saul of Tarsus, they are so convinced that their "religion" and "righteousness" are satisfactory that *in the name of that religion* they persecute God's people!

The world will not be honest about its own sin (vv. 22-24; 16:1-4). Once again, Jesus emphasized His words and His works. We have seen this emphasis throughout the Gospel of John (3:2; 5:36-38; 10:24-27; 14:10-11). The people had no excuse ("cloak") for their sin. They had seen His works and heard His word, but they would not admit the truth. All of the evidence had been presented, but they were not honest enough to receive it and act on it.

This statement is parallel to what Jesus told the Pharisees after He had healed the blind man (John 9:39-41). They had to admit that Jesus had healed the man born blind, but they would not follow the evidence to its logical conclusion and put *their* trust in Him. Jesus told them that they were the ones who were blind! But since they admitted that they had seen a miracle, this made their sin even worse. They were not sinning in ignorance; they were sinning against a flood of light. Why? Because that light revealed their own sin and they did not want to face their sin honestly. Their attitude was similar to that described in 2 Peter 3:5—"For this they *willingly* are ignorant" (italics mine).

How does the Holy Spirit encourage believers when they are experiencing the hatred and opposition of the world? It is primarily through the Word of God. For one thing, the Spirit reminds us that this opposition is clearly expressed by various writers in the Scriptures. In John 15:25, Jesus quoted Psalms 35:19 and 69:4. The Word assured Him that the hatred of the world was not because of anything He had done to deliberately incite such opposition. We today can turn to passages like Philippians 1:28-30; 2 Timothy 2:9-12; Hebrews 12:3-4; and 1 Peter 4:12ff. We also have the encouraging words of our Lord found in the Gospels.

The Spirit also witnesses to us and through us during times of persecution (John 15:26-27). He reminds us that what we are experiencing is "the fellowship of His [Christ's] sufferings" (Phil. 3:10) and that it is a privilege to bear reproach for His name. (Read *carefully* 1 Peter 4:12-19.)

Times of persecution have always been for the church times of proclamation and witness. We must be "ready always to give an answer" when unsaved people attack us (1 Peter 3:15). The Spirit witnesses to us so that we can witness to the world (Mark 13:11). Apart from the power of the Spirit of God, we cannot give a clear witness for Christ (Acts 1:8).

There is no reason for the believer to stumble ("be offended," John 16:1) when the world stokes up the furnace of persecution. He should expect persecution, if only because his Lord told him it was coming. (Note especially John 13:19 and 14:29 where the Lord warned His disciples in advance.) Furthermore, they must not stumble when this persecution comes from religious people who actually think they are serving God. The word translated "service" in John 16:2 means "priestly service." This statement is certainly a description of Saul of Tarsus, who thought he was serving God by destroying the church (see Acts 7:57-8:3; 22:3-4; and 26:9-12).

It is tragic when "religious" people persecute and murder in the name of God. While it is true that "the blood of the martyrs is the seed of the church" (Tertullian), it is also true that their blood is the stain on the pages of history.

The Spirit as Reprover Witnesses through the Church (John 16:5-11)

For three years, Jesus had been with them to protect them from attack; but now He was about to leave them. He had told them this earlier in the evening (John 13:33), and Peter had asked Him where He was going (John 13:36). However, Peter's question revealed more concern about *himself* than about the Lord Jesus! Also, his question centered on the immediate, not the ultimate. It was necessary for Jesus to explain why it was important *for them* that He return to the Father.

The major reason, of course, is that the Holy Spirit might come to empower the church for life and witness. Also, the ascended Saviour would be able to intercede for His people at the heavenly throne of grace. With all of their faults, the disciples dearly loved their Master; and it was difficult for them to grasp these new truths.

It is important to note that the Spirit comes *to the church* and not to the world. This means that He works in and through the church. The Holy Spirit does not minister in a vacuum. Just as the Son of God had to have a body in order to do His work on earth, so the Spirit of God needs a body to accomplish His ministries; and that body is the church. Our bodies are His tools and temples, and He wants to use us to glorify Christ and to witness to a lost world.

Sometimes we hear people pray, "Lord, send Your Spirit to speak to the lost! May the Spirit go from heart to heart." Such praying is no doubt sincere, but is it biblical? The Spirit does not "float" in some ghostly way up and down the rows of a church building, seeking to win the lost. The Holy Spirit works through the people in whom He lives. When the Holy Spirit came at Pentecost, He empowered Peter to preach; and the preaching of the Word brought conviction to those who heard.

The key word here is *reprove* (John 16:8). It is a legal word that means "to bring to light, to expose, to refute, to convict and convince." It could be translated "pronounce the verdict." The world may think that it is judging Christians, but it is the Christians who are passing judgment on the world as they witness to Jesus Christ! Believers are the witnesses, the Holy Spirit is the "prosecuting attorney," and the unsaved are the guilty prisoners. However, the purpose of this indictment is not to condemn but to bring salvation.

The Holy Spirit convicts the world of one particular sin, the sin of *unbelief.* The law of God and the conscience of man will convict the sinner of his *sins* (plural) specifically; but it is the work of the Spirit, through the witness of the believers, to expose the unbelief of the lost world. After all, it is unbelief that condemns the lost sinner (John 3:18-21), not the committing of individual sins. A person could "clean up his life" and quit his or her bad habits and still be lost and go to hell.

The Spirit also convicts the sinner of *righteousness,* not *un*righteousness. Whose righteousness? The righteousness of Jesus Christ, the perfect Lamb of God. The world would not receive the Son of God (John 1:10), so He has returned to the Father. When He was here on earth, He was accused by men of being a blasphemer, a lawbreaker, a deceiver, and even a demoniac. The Spirit of God reveals the Saviour in the Word and in this way glorifies Him (John 16:13-14). The Spirit also reveals Christ in the lives of believers. The world cannot receive or see the Spirit of God, but they can see what He does as they watch the lives of dedicated believers.

The Spirit convicts the lost sinner of *judgment.* Do not confuse this statement with Acts 24:25 ("of righteousness, temperance, and judgment to come"). Jesus was referring to His judgment of Satan that was effected by His death on the cross (John 12:31). Satan is the prince of this world, but he is a defeated prince. Satan has already been judged and the verdict announced. All that must take place is the executing of the sentence, and that will occur when Jesus returns.

When a lost sinner is truly under conviction, he will see the folly and evil of unbelief; he will confess that he does not measure up to the righteousness of Christ; and he will realize that he is under condemnation because he belongs to the world and the devil (Eph. 2:1-3). The only person who can rescue him from such a horrible situation is Jesus Christ, the Son of God. There can be no conversion without conviction, and there can be no conviction apart from the Spirit of God using the Word of God and the witness of the child of God.

Witnessing is a great privilege, but it is also a serious responsibility. It is a matter of life or death! How we need to depend on the Holy Spirit to guide us to the right persons, give us the right words, and enable us patiently to glorify Jesus Christ.

The Spirit as Teacher Guides the Church (John 16:12-15)

Our Lord was always careful to give His disciples the right amount of truth at the best time. This is always the mark of a great teacher. The Holy Spirit is our Teacher today, and He follows that same principle: He teaches us the truths we need to know, when we need them, and when we are ready to receive them.

When you compare John 14:26 with 16:13, you see the wonderful way that God arranged for the writing of the New Testament Scriptures. The Spirit would remind them of what Jesus had taught them; this gives us the four Gospels. The Spirit would also "guide" them into all truth; and this would result in the epistles. "He will show you things to come" refers to the prophetic Scriptures, especially the Book of Revelation.

It is essential that we see that the work of the Spirit of God is never divorced from Jesus Christ or the Word of God. "He shall testify of Me" (John 15:26); "He shall glorify Me" (John 16:14). People who claim that the Spirit of God led them to do things contrary to the example of Christ or the teaching of the Word are mistaken and are being led astray by Satan. Jesus is the truth (John 14:6), and the Word is truth (John 17:17), and the Holy Spirit is "the Spirit of Truth." Where the Holy Spirit is at work, there must be truth.

The phrase "He [the Spirit] shall not speak of Himself" (John 16:13) does not mean that the Spirit never refers to Himself, for when He wrote the Bible, the Spirit often mentioned Himself. Rather, it means that He does not speak apart from the Father and the Son; He does not "manufacture" a different message. You have the entire Godhead mentioned in John 16:13, because the Spirit of God does not ignore either the Father or the Son. They work harmoniously together.

The teaching of the Spirit through the Apostles was not different from the teaching of the Spirit through Jesus Christ. Some theologians like to contrast the "Christianity of Christ" with the "Christianity of Paul." They claim that Paul "ruined" Christianity by making it so theological and complicating the "simple message" of Jesus Christ. What a sad interpretation this is. What Jesus said in John 14:26 and 16:13 completely refutes this false teaching. The same Holy Spirit communicated the truths found in the four Gospels, the epistles, and the Book of Revelation; and He also wrote the history and doctrine found in Acts.

It is the ministry of the Spirit to enrich us with the treasures of God's truth. He enlightens us with God's truth and enriches us with God's treasures. The Word of God is a rich mine of gold, silver, and precious jewels (Prov. 3:13-15; 8:10-21). What a joy it is to have the Spirit illumine His Word.

We do not study the Word of God in order to "argue religion" with people, or to show off our grasp of spiritual things. We study the Word to see Jesus Christ, to know God better, to glorify Him in our lives. As we witness in this hostile world, the Spirit uses the Word He has taught us; and we share Jesus Christ with the lost. It is our job to witness; it is the Spirit's job to convict.

Perhaps some of us need to quit acting like prosecuting attorneys—or judges—so that the Spirit can use us as faithful witnesses.

CHAPTER SEVENTEEN
LET THERE BE JOY!
John 16:16-33

This section—John 16:16-33—concludes the Upper Room Discourse and deals primarily with the emotions of the disciples. They were sorrowing, they were confused about some of Jesus' teaching, and they were afraid. It is an encouragement to me to know that the disciples were real men with real problems, yet the Lord was able to use them. We sometimes get the false impression that these men were different from us, especially endowed with spiritual knowledge and courage; but such was not the case. They were human!

One of the recurring themes in this section is *joy* (John 16:20-22, 24, 33). The Eleven were certainly not experiencing much joy that night! But what Jesus said to them eventually made a difference in their lives, just as it can make a difference in our lives today. Tenderly and patiently, our Lord explained how His people can have joy in their lives.

There Is a Principle to Grasp (John 16:16-22)

The principle is simply this: God brings joy to our lives, not by substitution, but by transformation. His illustration of the woman giving birth makes this clear. *The same baby that caused the pain also caused the joy.* In birth, God does not substitute something else to relieve the mother's pain. Instead, He uses what is there already but transforms it.

Every parent knows what it is like to have an unhappy child because a toy is broken or a playmate has gone home. The parent can do one of two things: substitute something else for the broken toy or absent friend, or transform the situation into a new experience for the unhappy child. If Mother always gets a new toy for the child each time a toy is broken, that child will grow up expecting every problem to be solved by substitution. If Mother always phones another playmate and invites him or her over, the child will grow up expecting people to come to his rescue whenever there is a crisis. The result either way is a spoiled child who will not be able to cope with reality.

The way of substitution for solving problems is the way of immaturity. The way of transformation is the way of faith and maturity. We cannot mature emotionally or spiritually if somebody is always replacing our broken toys.

Jesus did not say that the mother's sorrow (pain) was replaced by joy, but that the sorrow was transformed into joy. The same baby that caused the pain also caused the joy! And so it is in the Christian life: God takes seemingly impossible situations, adds the miracle of His grace, and transforms trial into triumph and sorrow into joy. "The Lord thy God turned the curse into a blessing" (Deut. 23:5; see Neh. 13:2).

Joseph's brothers sold him as a slave, and Potiphar put him into prison as a criminal; but God transformed that hopeless situation of defeat into victory. Egypt's persecution of Israel only caused them to multiply and prosper the more. King Saul's murderous pursuit of David only made him more a man of God and helped produce the psalms that encourage our hearts today. Even Jesus took the cross, a symbol of defeat and shame, and transformed it into a symbol of victory and glory.

Now that we understand this principle, we can better understand the problems and questions of the disciples.

In John 16:16, Jesus announced that in a little while, they would not see Him; then, in a little while, they would see Him. It was a deliberately puzzling statement (John 16:25, He spoke in proverbs ["dark sayings"]) and the disciples did not understand. This also encourages me as I study my Bible and find statements that I cannot understand. Even the disciples had their hours of spiritual ignorance!

What did Jesus mean? Possibly He was talking about the soon-to-occur events in connection with His death and resurrection. After His burial, they would not see Him for a little while; but then He would rise from the dead and they would see Him again. He had told them on previous occasions that He would rise from the dead after three days, but His words did not sink into their minds and hearts.

However, I think that Jesus was speaking primarily about His return to the Father ("Because I go to the Father"—John 16:16). This ties in with John 16:10—"Because I go to My Father, and ye see Me no more." The disciples did not live to see the return of Christ, but they did die and see Him when they arrived in glory. In comparison to eternity, the time that the church has been awaiting the Lord's return has really been but "a little while" (see 2 Cor. 4:16-18). In fact, the phrase "a little while" is used in this very sense in Hebrews 10:37—"For yet a little while, and He that shall come will come, and will not tarry."

Instead of asking Jesus to explain His words, the men began to discuss it among themselves, almost as though they were embarrassed to admit their ignorance. However, you do not get very far by exchanging your ignorance! It is when we come to the Lord and ask for His help that we learn the important lessons of life.

Egypt was glad when Israel departed (Ps. 105:38), and the world was glad when Jesus Christ moved off the scene. Both the religious and political leaders of that day expected to see the early believers die out and the "Christian movement" disappear; but such was not the case. Jesus sent His Holy Spirit to His church, and the church is carrying the Word of His grace to the ends of the earth. The early believers even rejoiced when they were persecuted (Acts 5:41).

To the mother experiencing birth pains, every minute may seem an hour. Our concept of time changes with our feelings. Thirty minutes in the dentist chair may seem like hours, while hours fishing or dining with friends may seem like a very short time. The mother feels as though the birth is taking a long time, when really it may be only "a little while." When the baby has been born, pain is forgotten as joy fills her heart.

The world today does not want Jesus Christ or His church. The world is rejoicing while we are suffering, longing for our Lord to return. In fact, all of creation is suffering "birth pangs" because of sin, awaiting His return (Rom. 8:22). When the Bridegroom is away, the bride mourns (Matt. 9:15). But, in "a little while" He shall return and we shall go with Him to heaven to enjoy the Father's house.

While the immediate application may have been to the sorrowing hearts of the disciples, the ultimate application is to all of God's people as they await the coming of Jesus Christ. To us, it seems like a long wait; but God does not measure time as we do (see 2 Peter 3). But while we are waiting, we must deal with our trials and hurts on the basis of *transformation* and not *substitution,* if we expect to mature in the Christian life.

There Is a Promise to Believe (John 16:23-28)

The central theme of this paragraph is prayer: "Ask, and ye shall receive, that your joy may be full" (John 16:24). It is important to note that the text uses two different words for "ask," although they can be used interchangeably. The word used in John 16:19, 23a, and 26 means "to ask a question" or "to ask a request." It is used when someone makes a request of someone equal. The word translated "ask" in John 16:23b, 24, and 26b ("pray") means "to request something of a superior." This latter word was never used by Jesus in His prayer life because He is equal to the Father. We come as inferiors to God, asking for His blessing; but He came as the very Son of God, equal with the Father.

In John 16:23, what period of time did Jesus mean by "in that day"? I think He was referring to the time after the coming of the Spirit. He promised them in John 16:22 that He would see them again, and He kept His promise. He spent forty days with them after His resurrection, teaching them clearly the truths they needed to know in order to take His place and minister on earth (Acts 1:3ff). "That day" cannot refer to the day of His return for His church, because there is no evidence in Scripture that we shall pray to Him after we get to heaven.

Jesus knew that they wanted to ask Him a question (John 16:19). He assured them that a day would soon come when they would not ask Him questions. Instead, they would pray to the Father and He would meet their needs. This was the promise that they desperately needed to believe: that the Father loved them and would hear their requests and meet their needs. While Jesus was on earth, He met all the needs of His disciples. Now He would return to the Father, but the Father would meet their needs. Here is the wonderful promise and privilege of prayer.

Our Lord had mentioned prayer many times in His ministry, and He had set the example for prayer in His own life. He was indeed a man of prayer. In His Upper Room message, Jesus emphasized prayer (John 14:12-14; 15:7, 16; 16:23-26). He made it clear that believing prayer is one of the secrets of a fruitful Christian life.

In John 16:25-27, Jesus explained that there would be a new situation because of His resurrection and ascension, and because of the coming of the Holy Spirit. He would no longer speak to them in terms that demanded spiritual insight for their understanding. He would speak to them plainly and reveal the Father to them. There in the Upper Room, He had used a number of symbolic images to get His message across: the washing of their feet, the "Father's house," the vine and branches, and the birth of a baby. In the days that followed, these images would become clearer to the disciples as they would be taught by the Spirit of God.

The purpose of Bible study is not simply to understand profound truths, but to get to know the Father better. "I will show you plainly of the Father" (John 16:25). If our reading and Bible study falls short of this, it does more harm than good.

There would be not only a new situation in teaching, but also a new situation in their praying. He had already intimated this in John 16:23. Jesus would return to heaven to be with the Father, and there He would minister as our High Priest, making intercession for us (Rom. 8:34; Heb. 7:25). He would also minister as our Advocate (1 John 2:1). As our High Priest, Jesus gives us grace to keep us from sinning. As our Advocate, He restores us when we confess our sins. His ministry in heaven makes possible our ministry of witness on earth, through the power of the Spirit.

When you read the Book of Acts, you discover that the early church depended on prayer. They believed the promises of God and asked God for what they needed. It would do all of God's people good if they reviewed regularly what Jesus taught about prayer in this Upper Room Discourse. There is indeed joy in praying and in receiving answers to prayer. There is joy in meeting the conditions Jesus has laid down for successful praying. I think it was George Müller who said that true prayer was not overcoming God's reluctance, but overcoming God's willingness.

There is joy in prayer, and there is joy in realizing the principle of *transformation.* Jesus shared a third kind of joy, the joy of sharing His victory over the world.

There Is a Position to Claim (John 16:29-33)

In John 16:29-30, the disciples suddenly moved out of their spiritual stupor and made a tremendous affirmation of faith. First, they claimed to understand what He had been teaching them, though this claim was probably presumptuous, as their subsequent actions proved. They seemed unable to grasp the meaning of His promised resurrection. They were bewildered even after His resurrection as to the future of Israel (Acts 1:6ff). I am not criticizing them, because we today have just as many blind spots when it comes to understanding His Word. All I am suggesting is that their affirmation was a bit presumptuous.

They not only affirmed their understanding, but they also affirmed their faith and assurance. "Now we are sure . . . by this we believe." It was quite a statement of faith, and I believe the Lord accepted it. In His prayer recorded in the next chapter, Jesus told the Father about His disciples and reported on their spiritual condition (John 17:6-8). Certainly He knew their weaknesses, but He was quick to approve their growing evidences of faith and assurance.

But it is possible to have faith, understanding, and assurance *and still fail the Lord.* Unless we practice that faith, apply that understanding, and rest on that assurance, we will fail when the time of testing comes. That is what happened to the disciples, and Jesus warned them that it would happen.

He had already warned Peter that he would deny Him, but now He warned the entire band of disciples that they would all forsake Him. John does not quote the Old Testament prophecy (Zech. 13:7); it is quoted in Matthew 26:31. This statement from the Lord should have been a warning to Peter not to follow Jesus when He was arrested. "Let these go their way!" was our Lord's word in the Garden (John 18:8). He knew that it was not safe for them to tarry.

Jesus has promised never to leave us alone (Matt. 28:20; Heb. 13:5); yet His own disciples left Him alone. Peter, James, and John went into the Garden with Him, but then fell asleep. Jesus knew that the Father would be with Him. "I am not alone, but I and the Father that sent Me" (John 8:16). "And He that sent Me is with Me. The Father hath not left Me alone" (John 8:29). What an encouragement it was to the Son to know that He was doing the Father's will and that He could depend on the Father's help.

At one point, however, Jesus did feel the absence of the Father: "My God, My God, why hast Thou forsaken Me?" (Matt. 27:46; Ps. 22:1) When He was made sin for us, He was separated from the Father. He was alone that we might never be alone. He was forsaken that we might never be forsaken.

John 16:33 is the summary and climax of the Upper Room message. Why did He give this message? So that the disciples might have peace in a world of tribulation. Note the contrast between "in Me" and "in the world." In Christ there is peace; in the world there is tribulation. This is the position we need to claim: we are *in Christ,* and therefore we can overcome the world and all of its hatred.

George Morrison defined peace as "the possession of adequate resources." In Jesus Christ, we have all the resources that we need. But peace depends also on appropriate relationships, because spiritual resources depend on spiritual relationships. "In Me" is the key. In ourselves, we have nothing; but "in Christ" we have all that we need.

Every believer is either *overcome* or an *overcomer.* "And this is the victory that overcometh the world, even our faith" (1 John 5:4). The world wants to overcome us; this is why Satan uses the world to persecute and pressure believers. The world wants us to conform; it does not want us to be different. When we yield ourselves to Christ and trust Him, He enables us to be overcomers. We must claim our spiritual position in Christ and believe Him for victory.

"Be of good cheer!" is one of our Lord's repeated statements of encouragement. Literally it means, "Cheer up!" There is the "good cheer" of His pardon (Matt. 9:1-8), His power (Matt. 9:18-22), and His presence (Matt. 14:22-27). Here in John 16:33, He announces the "good cheer" of His victory over the world. We are overcomers because He has first overcome for us.

As we review this section, we can see how these three explanations our Lord gave all fit together. He revealed a wonderful principle—God transforms sorrow into joy. But this principle will not work in our lives unless we believe His promise and pray. God has ordained that His work is accomplished through believing prayer. But we will not be able to pray effectively if we do not claim our position as conquerors in Jesus Christ.

But John 16:33 is also a preface to His great High Priestly Prayer. He had taught them the Word; now He would pray for them. The Word and prayer must always go together (Acts 6:4). He used the word *world* nineteen times in this prayer, for in it He shows us how to overcome the world. He Himself was facing the hatred of the world *and the devil,* yet He would be able to endure the suffering and win the victory.

There is joy when we permit God to transform sorrow into joy. There is joy when God answers prayer. There is joy when we overcome the world.

Let there be joy!

CHAPTER EIGHTEEN THE PRAYER OF THE OVERCOMER

John 17

Most scholars who have sought to harmonize the accounts in the four Gospels have the Lord Jesus praying the prayer of John 17 in the Upper Room after He had finished His instructions to the disciples. Then He and the disciples sang the traditional Passover psalms, left the Upper Room, and headed for the Garden of Gethsemane where Jesus had been accustomed to meet with them and pray (see Matthew 26:30-46 and Mark 14:26-42).

Whether He prayed it in the Upper Room or en route to the Garden, this much is sure: it is the greatest prayer ever prayed on earth and the greatest prayer recorded anywhere in Scripture. John 17 is certainly the "holy of holies" of the Gospel record, and we must approach this chapter in a spirit of humility and worship. To think that we are privileged to listen in as God the Son converses with His Father just as He is about to give His life as a ransom for sinners!

No matter what events occurred later that evening, this prayer makes it clear that Jesus was and is the Overcomer. He was not a "victim"; He was and is the Victor! "Be of good cheer," He had encouraged His disciples; "I have overcome the world" (John 16:33). The word *world* is used nineteen times in this prayer, so it is easy to see the connection between the prayer and John 16:33. If you and I will understand and apply the truths revealed in this profound prayer, it will enable us to be overcomers too.

The progression of thought in this prayer is not difficult to discover. Jesus first prayed for Himself and told the Father that His work on earth had been finished (John 17:1-5). Then He prayed for His disciples, that the Father would *keep them* and *sanctify them* (John 17:6-19). He closed His prayer by praying for you and me and the whole church, that we might be unified in Him and one day share His glory (John 17:20-26).

Why did Jesus pray this prayer? Certainly He was preparing Himself for the sufferings that lay ahead. As He contemplated the glory that the Father promised Him, He would receive new strength for His sacrifice (Heb. 12:1-3). But He also had His disciples in mind (John 17:13). What an encouragement this prayer should have been to them! He prayed about their security, their joy, their unity, and their future glory! He also prayed it for us today, so that we would know all that He has done for us and given to us, and all that He will do for us when we get to heaven.

In this prayer, our Lord declares four wonderful privileges we have as His children, privileges that help to make us overcomers.

We Share His Life (John 17:1-5)

Our Lord began this prayer by praying for Himself, but in praying for Himself, He was also praying for us. "A prayer for self is not by any means necessarily a selfish prayer," wrote Dr. R.A. Torrey, and an examination of Bible prayers shows that this is true. Our Lord's burden was the glory of God, and this glory would be realized in His finished work on the cross. The servant of God has every right to ask his Father for the help needed to glorify His name. "Hallowed be Thy name" is the first petition in the Lord's Prayer (Matt. 6:9), and it is the first emphasis in this prayer.

"Father, the hour is come," reminds us of the many times in John's Gospel when "the hour" is mentioned, beginning at John 2:4. Jesus had lived on a "divine timetable" while on earth and He knew He was in the will of the Father. "My times are in Thy hand" (Ps. 31:15).

The important word *glory* is used five times in these verses, and we must carefully distinguish the various "glories" that Jesus mentions. In John 17:5, He referred to His preincarnate glory with the Father, the glory that He laid aside when He came to earth to be born, to serve, to suffer, and to die. In John 17:4, He reported to the Father that His life and ministry on earth had glorified Him, because He (Jesus) had finished the work the Father gave Him to do. In John 17:1 and 5, our Lord asked that His preincarnate glory be given to Him again, so that the Son might glorify the Father in His return to heaven.

The word *glory* is used eight times in this prayer, so it is an important theme. He glorified the Father in His miracles (John 2:11; 11:40), to be sure; but He brought the greatest glory to the Father through His sufferings and death (see John 12:23-25; 13:31-32). From the human point of view, Calvary was a revolting display of man's sin; but from the divine point of view, the cross revealed and magnified the grace and glory of God. Jesus anticipated His return to heaven when He said, "I have finished the work which Thou gavest Me to do" (John 17:4). This "work" included His messages and miracles on earth (John 5:17-19), the training of the disciples for future service, and most of all, His sacrifice on the cross (Heb. 9:24-28; 10:11-18).

It is on the basis of this "finished work" that we as believers have the gift of eternal life (John 17:2-3). The word *give* is used in one form or another in this prayer at least seventeen times. Seven times Jesus states that believers are the Father's gift to His Son (John 17:2, 6, 9, 11-12, 24). We are accustomed to thinking of Jesus as the Father's love gift to us (John 3:16), but the Lord affirms that believers are the Father's "love gift" to His beloved Son!

"Eternal [everlasting] life" is an important theme in John's Gospel; it is mentioned at least seventeen times. Eternal life is God's free gift to those who believe on His Son (John 3:15-16, 36; 6:47; 10:28). The Father gave His Son the authority to give eternal life to those whom the Father gave to the Son. From the human viewpoint, we receive the gift of eternal life when we believe on Jesus Christ. But from the divine viewpoint, we have already been given to the Son in divine election. This is a mystery that the human mind cannot fully understand or explain; we must accept it by faith.

What is "eternal life"? It is knowing God personally. Not just knowing *about* Him, but having a personal relationship with Him through faith in Jesus Christ. We cannot know the Father apart from the Son (John 14:6-11). It is not enough simply to "believe in God"; this will never save a lost soul from eternal hell. "The devils [demons] also believe, and tremble" (James 2:19). Our Lord's debate with the Jewish leaders (John 8:12ff) makes it clear that people may be devoutly religious and still not know God. Eternal life is not something we earn by character or conduct; it is a gift we receive by admitting we are sinners, repenting, and believing on Jesus Christ and Jesus Christ alone.

The Father answered His Son's request and gave Him the glory. There is in heaven today a glorified Man, the God-Man, Jesus Christ! Because He has been glorified in heaven, sinners can be saved on earth. Anyone who trusts Jesus Christ will receive the gift of eternal life.

Because we share His life, we are overcomers; for we also share His victory! "For whatsoever is born of God overcometh the world; and this is the victory that overcometh the world, even our faith" (1 John 5:4). When you were born the first time, you were born "in Adam" and were a loser. When you are born again through faith in Christ, you are born a winner!

Satan has tried to obscure the precious truth of the finished work of Jesus Christ, because he knows it is a basis for spiritual victory. "And they overcame him [Satan] by the blood of the Lamb" (Rev. 12:11). Don't let Satan rob you of your overcoming power through Christ's finished work.

We Know His Name (John 17:6-12)

Christ has given His own eternal life (John 17:2), but He has also given them the revelation of the Father's name (John 17:6). The Old Testament Jew knew his God as "Jehovah," the great I AM (Ex. 3:11-14). Jesus took this sacred name "I AM" and made it meaningful to His disciples: "I am the Bread of Life" (John 6:35); "I am the Light of the world" (John 8:12); "I am the Good Shepherd" (John 10:11); etc. In other words, Jesus revealed the Father's gracious name by showing His disciples that He was everything they needed.

But the Father's name includes much more than this, for Jesus also taught His disciples that God—the great I AM—was their Heavenly Father. The word *Father* is used 53 times in John 13–17, and 122 times in John's Gospel! In His messages to the Jews, Jesus made it clear that the Father sent Him, that He was equal to the Father, and that His words and works came from the Father. It was a clear claim to Deity, but they refused to believe.

In the Bible, "name" refers to "nature," because names so often were given to reveal something special about the nature of the person bearing the name. Jacob was a schemer, and his name comes from a Hebrew root that means "to take by the heel," i.e., to trip up, to deceive (Gen. 25:26). The name *Isaac* means "laughter" (Gen. 21:6) because he brought joy to Abraham and Sarah. Even the name Jesus reveals that He is the Saviour (Matt. 1:21).

"I have manifested Thy name" means "I have revealed the nature of God." One of the ministries of the Son was to declare the Father (John 1:18). The Greek word translated "declared" means, "to unfold, to lead, to show the way." Jesus did not instantly reveal the Father in a blaze of blinding glory, because His disciples could not have endured that kind of experience. Gradually, by His words and His deeds, He revealed to them the nature of God, as they were able to bear it (John 16:12).

The emphasis in this section is on the safety of the believer; God keeps His own (John 17:11-12). Our safety depends on the nature of God, not our own character or conduct. When He was on earth, Jesus kept His disciples and they could depend on Him. "I kept them in Thy name" (John 17:12). If the limited Saviour, in a human body, could keep His own while He was on earth, should He not be able to keep them now that He is glorified in heaven? He and the Father, together with the Holy Spirit, are surely able to guard and secure God's people!

Furthermore, God's people are the Father's gift to His Son. Would the Father present His Son with a gift that would not last? The disciples had belonged to the Father by creation and by covenant (they were Jews), but now they belonged to the Son. How precious we are in His sight! How He watches over us and even now prays for us! Whenever you feel as though the Lord has forgotten you, or that His love seems far away, read Romans 8:28-39—and rejoice!

Our security rests in another fact: we are here to glorify Him (John 17:10). With all of their failures and faults, the disciples still receive this word of commendation: "I am glorified in them." Would it bring glory to God if one of His own, who trusted in the Saviour, did not make it to heaven? Certainly not! This was Moses' argument when the nation of Israel sinned: "Wherefore should the Egyptians speak, and say, 'For mischief did He bring them out, to slay them in the mountains, and to consume them from the face of the earth?' " (Ex. 32:12) Certainly God knows all things, so why save them at all if He knows they will fail along the way? Whatever God starts, He finishes (Phil. 1:6).

God has provided the divine resources for us to glorify Him and be faithful. We have His Word (John 17:7-8), and His Word reveals to us all that we have in Jesus Christ. The Word gives us faith and assurance. We have the Son of God interceding for us (John 17:9; Rom. 8:34; Heb. 4:14-16). Since the Father always answers the prayers of His Son (John 11:41-42), this intercessory ministry helps to keep us safe and secure.

We also have the fellowship of the church: "that they may be one, as we are" (John 17:11). The New Testament knows nothing of isolated believers; wherever you find saints, you find them in fellowship. Why? Because God's people need each other. Jesus opened His Upper Room message by washing the disciples' feet and teaching them to minister to one another. In the hours that would follow, these men (including confident Peter!) would discover how weak they were and how much they needed each other's encouragement.

The believer, then, is secure in Christ for many reasons: the very nature of God, the nature of salvation, the glory of God, and the intercessory ministry of Christ. But what about Judas? Was he secure? How did he fall? Why did Jesus not keep him safe? For the simple reason that *Judas was never one of Christ's own.* Jesus faithfully kept all that the Father gave to Him, but Judas had never been given to Him by the Father. Judas was not a believer (John 6:64-71); he had never been cleansed (John 13:11); he had not been among the chosen (John 13:18); he had never been given to Christ (John 18:8-9).

No, Judas is not an example of a believer who "lost his salvation." He is an example of an unbeliever who *pretended to have salvation* but was finally exposed as a fraud. Jesus keeps all whom the Father gives to Him (John 10:26-30).

We are overcomers because we share His life. There is a third privilege that enables us to overcome.

We Have His Word (John 17:13-19)

"I have given them Thy Word" (John 17:14, and see v. 8). The Word of God is the gift of God to us. The Father gave the words to His

Son (John 17:8), and the Son gave them to His disciples who, in turn, have passed them along to us as they were inspired by the Spirit (2 Tim. 3:16; 2 Peter 1:20-21). The Word is divine in origin, a precious gift from heaven. We must never take God's Word for granted, for those who are overcomers know the Word and how to use it in daily life.

How does the Word of God enable us to overcome the world? To begin with, *it gives us joy* (John 17:13); and this inward joy gives us the strength to overcome (Neh. 8:10). We commonly think of Jesus Christ as "a man of sorrows" (Isa. 53:3), and indeed He was; but He was also a person of deep abiding joy. John 17:13 is the very heart of this prayer, *and its theme is joy!*

Jesus had referred to His joy already (John 15:11) and had explained that joy comes by transformation and not substitution (John 16:20-22). Joy also comes from answered prayer (John 16:23-24). Now He made it clear that joy comes from the Word also. The believer does not find his joy in the world but in the Word. Like John the Baptist, we should rejoice greatly when we hear the Bridegroom's voice! (John 3:29)

We must never picture Jesus going around with a long face and a melancholy disposition. He was a man of joy and He revealed that joy to others. His joy was not the fleeting levity of a sinful world but the abiding enjoyment of the Father and the Word. He did not depend on outward circumstances but on inward spiritual resources that were hidden from the world. This is the kind of joy He wants us to have, and we can have it through His Word. "Thy word was unto me the joy and rejoicing of mine heart" (Jer. 15:16). "I have rejoiced in the way of Thy testimonies, as much as in all riches" (Ps. 119:14). "I rejoice at Thy word, as one that findeth great spoil" (Ps. 119:162).

The Word not only imparts the joy of the Lord, but it also *assures us of His love* (John 17:14). The world hates us, but we are able to confront this hatred with God's own love, a love imparted to us by the Spirit through the Word. The world hates us because we do not belong to its system (John 15:18-19) and will not be conformed to its practices and standards (Rom. 12:2). The Word reveals to us what the world is really like; the Word exposes the world's deceptions and dangerous devices.

The world competes for the Father's love (1 John 2:15-17), but the Word of God enables us to enjoy the Father's love. One of the first steps toward a worldly life is the neglect of the Word of God. D.L. Moody wrote in the front of his Bible, "This book will keep you from sin or sin will keep you from this book." Just as the pillar of fire was darkness to the Egyptians but light to Israel, so God's Word is our light in this dark world, but the world cannot understand the things of God (Ex. 14:20; 1 Cor. 2:12-16).

The Word of God not only brings us God's joy and love, but it also imparts God's power for holy living (John 17:15-17). The burden of our Lord's prayer in John 17:6-12 was *security,* but here it is *sanctity,* practical holy living to the glory of God. We are *in* the world but not *of* the world, and we must not live *like* the world. Sometimes we think it would be easier if we were "out of the world," but this is not true. Wherever we go, we take our own sinful self with us, and the powers of darkness will follow us. I have met people who have gone into "spiritual isolation" in order to become more holy, only to discover that it does not always work.

True sanctification (being set apart for God) comes through the ministry of the Word of God. "Now ye are clean through the word which I have spoken unto you" (John 15:3). When you were saved, you were set apart for God. As you grow in your faith, you are more and more experiencing sanctification. You love sin less and you love God more. You want to serve Him and be a blessing to others. All of this comes through the Word.

God's truth has been given to us in three "editions": His Word is truth (John 17:17); His Son is the truth (John 14:6); and His Spirit is the truth (1 John 5:6). We need all three if we are to experience true sanctification, a sanctification that touches every part of our inner person. With the mind, we *learn* God's truth through the Word. With the heart, we *love* God's truth, His Son. With the will, we yield to the Spirit and *live* God's truth day by day. It takes all three for a balanced experience of sanctification.

It is not enough merely to study the Bible and learn a great deal of doctrinal truth. We must also love Jesus Christ more as we learn all that He is and all He has done for us. Learning and loving should lead to living, allowing the Spirit of God to enable us to obey His Word. This is how we glorify Him in this present evil world.

The Word gives us joy, love, and power to

live a holy life. It also gives us what we need to serve Him as witnesses in this world (John 17:18-19). Sanctification is not for the purpose of selfish enjoyment or boasting; it is so that we might represent Christ in this world and win others to Him. Jesus set Himself apart for us, and now He has set us apart for Him. The Father sent Him into the world, and now He sends us into the world. We are people "under orders" and we had better obey! Jesus is now "set apart" in heaven, praying for us, that our witness will bear fruit as many repent of their sins and turn to the Lord.

How can we be overcome by the world when we have the Word of God to enlighten us, enable us, and encourage us?

We Share His Glory (John 17:20-26)

Here our Lord focuses our attention on the future. He begins to pray for us who live today, for the whole church throughout all ages. He has already prayed about security and sanctity; now the burden of His prayer is *unity*. He is concerned that His people experience a spiritual unity that is like the oneness of the Father and the Son. Christians may belong to different fellowships, but they all belong to the Lord and to each other.

The disciples had often exhibited a spirit of selfishness, competition, and disunity; and this must have broken the Saviour's heart. I wonder how He feels when He sees the condition of the church today! The Puritan preacher Thomas Brooks wrote: "Discord and division become no Christian. For wolves to worry the lambs is no wonder, but for one lamb to worry another, this is unnatural and monstrous."

What is the basis for true Christian unity? The person and work of Jesus Christ and His glory (John 17:2-5). He has already given His glory to us, and He promises that we will further experience that glory when we get to heaven! All true believers have God's glory within, no matter what they may look like on the outside. Christian harmony is not based on the externals of the flesh but the internals and eternals of the Spirit in the inner person. We must look beyond the elements of our first birth—race, color, abilities, etc.—and build our fellowship on the essentials of our new birth.

We already possess His glory within (John 17:22, and note Rom. 8:29), and one day we shall behold His glory in heaven (John 17:24). As we grow in the Lord, the glory within begins to grow and to reveal itself in what we say and do and the way we say and do it. People do not see us and glorify us; they see the Lord and glorify Him (Matt. 5:16; 1 Cor. 6:19-20).

One of the things that most impresses the world is the way Christians love each other and live together in harmony. It is this witness that our Lord wants in the world "that the world may believe that Thou hast sent Me" (John 17:21). The lost world cannot see God, but they can see Christians; and what they see in us is what they will believe about God. If they see love and unity, they will believe that God is love. If they see hatred and division, they will reject the message of the Gospel.

Jesus has assured us that some will believe because of our witness (John 17:20), but we must make sure that our witness is true and loving. Some Christians are prosecuting attorneys and judges instead of faithful witnesses, and this only turns lost sinners away from the Saviour.

There is every reason why believers should love one another and live in unity. We trust the same Saviour and share the same glory. We will one day enjoy the same heaven! We belong to the same Father and seek to do the same work, witnessing to a lost world that Jesus Christ alone saves from sin. We believe the same truth, even though we may have different views of minor doctrinal matters; and we follow the same example that Jesus set for His people, to live a holy life. Yes, believers do have their differences; but we have much more in common, and this should encourage us to love one another and promote true spiritual unity.

I have often used John 17:24 as a text for funeral meditations. How do we know that Christians go to heaven? Because of the price that Jesus paid (1 Thes. 5:9-10), and the promise that Jesus made (John 14:1-6), and the prayer that Jesus prayed (John 17:24). The Father always answers His Son's prayers, so we know that believers who die do go to heaven to behold the glory of God.

In John 17:25-26, there are no petitions. Jesus simply reported to His Father about the ministry in the world, and He made several declarations that are important to us. He declared that the world does not know the Father, but that we believers know Him because the Son has revealed the Father to us. The world certainly has many opportunities to get to know the Father, but it prefers to go on in blindness and hardness of heart. Our task as Christians is to bear witness to the lost world and share God's saving message.

He also declares the importance of truth and love in the church. Believers know God's name (nature) and even share in that divine nature. Jesus makes it clear that *truth* and *love* must go together (see Eph. 4:15). It has well been said that truth without love is brutality, but love without truth is hypocrisy. The mind grows by taking in truth, but the heart grows by giving out in love. Knowledge alone can lead to pride (1 Cor. 8:1), and love alone can lead to wrong decisions (see Phil. 1:9-10). Christian love must not be blind!

As you review this prayer, you see the spiritual priorities that were in the Saviour's heart: the glory of God; the sanctity of God's people; the unity of the church; the ministry of sharing the Gospel with a lost world. We today would be wise to focus on these same priorities.

One day, each of us will have to give an account of his or her ministry. It is a solemn thought that we shall stand before the Judgment Seat of Christ and give our "final report."

I trust that we will be able to say, "I have glorified Thee on the earth; I have finished the work which Thou gavest me to do" (John 17:4).

CHAPTER NINETEEN
GUILT AND GRACE IN THE GARDEN
John 18:1-27

The private ministry of our Lord with His disciples has now ended, and the public drama of redemption is about to begin. Man will do his worst, and God will respond with His very best. "But where sin abounded, grace did much more abound" (Rom. 5:20).

Perhaps the best way to see the truths in John 18:1-27, and grasp the lessons they convey, is to pay attention to the symbolism that is involved. John's Gospel is saturated with symbols, some more obvious than others; and these symbols convey some important spiritual truths. There are five such symbols in this section.

The Garden—Obedience (John 18:1)
The Kidron Valley is located east of Jerusalem, between the city wall and the Mount of Olives; and the Garden of Gethsemane is on the western slope of Olivet. Jesus often went to this Garden with His disciples, no doubt to rest, meditate, and pray (Luke 22:39). Jerusalem was filled with pilgrims attending the Passover, and Jesus would want to get away from the crowded city to a private place. He knew that Judas would come for Him there, and He was ready.

Human history began in a Garden (Gen. 2:8ff), and the first sin of man was committed in that Garden. The first Adam disobeyed God and was cast out of the Garden, but the Last Adam (1 Cor. 15:45) was obedient as He went into the Garden of Gethsemane. In a Garden, the first Adam brought sin and death to mankind; but Jesus, by His obedience, brought righteousness and life to all who will trust Him. He was "obedient unto death, even the death of the cross" (Phil. 2:8).

History will one day end in another garden, the heavenly city that John describes in Revelation 21 and 22. In that garden, there will be no more death and no more curse. The river of the water of life will flow ceaselessly and the tree of life will produce bountiful fruit. Eden was the Garden of disobedience and sin; Gethsemane was the Garden of obedience and submission; and heaven shall be the eternal garden of delight and satisfaction, to the glory of God.

The name *Gethsemane* means "oil press." Even today there are ancient olive trees in Gethsemane, though certainly not the ones that were there in Jesus' day. The olives would be picked and put into the press for their oil. What a picture of suffering! So our Lord would go through the "oil press" and the "winepress" (Isa. 63:3) and taste our judgment for us.

The Brook Kidron is also significant. The name means "dusky, gloomy," referring to the dark waters that were often stained by the blood from the temple sacrifices. Our Lord and His disciples were about to go through "dark waters," and Jesus would experience the "waves and billows" of God's wrath (Ps. 42:7; also note Jonah 2:3).

The Kidron had special historical significance, for King David crossed the Kidron when he was rejected by his nation and betrayed by his own son, Absalom (2 Sam. 15; also note John 18:23). Jesus had been rejected by His people and at that very moment was being betrayed by one of His own disciples! It is interesting that David's treacherous counselor Ahithophel hanged himself (2 Sam. 17:23), and David's treacherous son Absalom was caught in a tree and killed while hanging there (2 Sam. 18:9-17). Judas, of course, went out and hanged himself (Matt. 27:3-10).

Jesus fully knew what lay before Him, yet He went to the Garden in obedience to the Father's will. He left eight of the men near the entrance, and took Peter, James, and John and went to another part of the Garden to pray (Matt. 26:36-46; Mark 14:32-42). His human soul longed for the kind of encouragement and companionship they could give Him at this critical hour; but, alas, they went to sleep! It was easy for the men to boast about their devotion to Christ, but when the test came, they failed miserably. Before we judge them too severely, however, we had better examine our own hearts.

The Kiss—Treachery (John 18:2-9)

Judas had lived with the Lord Jesus for perhaps three years, and had listened to Him teach; yet he knew very little about Him. The traitor actually brought a company of temple guards, armed with swords and clubs! (Matt. 26:55) Just think of the privileges Judas despised and the opportunities he wasted! The word *band* in John 18:3 could be translated "cohort." A Roman cohort was a tenth of a legion, and this would be 600 men! It is not likely that Judas brought that many to the Garden, but apparently a full cohort was made available to him had he needed it. Did he not realize that the Lamb of God would meekly submit and that there would be no need to battle?

Jesus was in full control; He knew what would happen (see John 13:1, 3, 11; 16:19). Judas expected some kind of deception, so he arranged to identify Jesus by kissing Him (Matt. 26:48-49). But Jesus shocked both Judas and the arresting officers by boldly presenting Himself to them. He had nothing to fear and nothing to hide; He would *willingly* lay down His life for His sheep. Furthermore, by surrendering to the officers, Jesus helped to protect His disciples. He kept them safe not only spiritually (John 17:11-12) but also physically.

Why did the arresting soldiers draw back and fall to the ground when Jesus told them, "I am He"? The Jews present would be struck by His "I AM" statement, an affirmation of Deity. The Romans, who were in the majority, would be struck by His bearing, for it was obvious that He was in command. It was an emotionally charged situation, and we do not know what Judas had told them about Jesus to help prepare them for this confrontation. The Jewish leaders had tried to have Jesus arrested before and always without success. The band was prepared for conflict, and when they met with surrender and calm, they were overwhelmed.

Perhaps it was a manifestation of divine power, or an exhibition of the majesty of Jesus Christ. "When the wicked, even mine enemies and my foes, came upon me to eat up my flesh, they stumbled and fell" (Ps. 27:2).

Judas' kiss, which was given repeatedly to the Lord, was certainly one of the basest acts of treachery recorded anywhere in sacred or secular history. In that day, a kiss was a sign of affection and devotion. Members of the family kissed each other in meeting and in parting, but Judas was not a member of God's family. Disciples greeted a rabbi by kissing him; it was a sign of devotion and obedience. But Judas was not truly a disciple of Jesus Christ, though he belonged to the disciple band. In the Garden, Judas stood with the enemy, not with Jesus' friends!

When people today pretend to know and love the Lord, they are committing the sin of Judas. It is bad enough to betray Christ, but to do it with *a kiss,* a sign of affection, is the basest treachery of all. It was born in the pit of hell.

The Sword—Rebellion (John 18:10)

All of the disciples had courageously affirmed their devotion to Christ (Matt. 26:35), and Peter decided to prove it; so he quickly drew out a small sword and started to fight! He certainly misunderstood what Jesus had said about swords earlier that evening (Luke 22:35-38). He had warned them that from now on the situation would change, and men would treat them as transgressors. He was not suggesting that they use material swords to fight spiritual battles, but that they get a new mind-set and expect opposition and even danger. He had provided for them and protected them while He was with them on earth, but now He was returning to the Father. They would have to depend on the Holy Spirit and exercise wisdom. Peter apparently took His words literally and thought he was supposed to declare war!

Peter's sword symbolizes rebellion against the will of God. Peter should have known that Jesus would be arrested and that He would willingly surrender to His enemies (Matt. 16:21ff; 17:22-23; 20:17-19). Peter made every mistake possible! He fought the wrong enemy, used the wrong weapon, had the wrong motive, and accomplished the wrong result! He was openly resisting the will of God and hindering the work that Jesus came to accomplish! While we admire his courage and sincerity, it was certainly a demonstration of zeal without knowledge.

Why did Peter fail so miserably? For one thing, he had argued with the Lord when Jesus warned him that he would deny his Master that very night. Peter had slept when he should have been praying, and he talked when he should have been listening. He imitated the very enemies who came to arrest Jesus, for they too were armed with swords. Peter would discover that the sword of the Spirit is the weapon God's servants use in fighting their spiritual battles (Heb. 4:12; Eph. 6:17). He would use that sword at Pentecost and "slay" 3,000 souls!

Jesus did not need Peter's protection. He could have summoned legions of angels had He wanted to be delivered (Matt. 26:52-54). Luke tells us that Jesus healed Malchus' ear (John 22:51), which was certainly an act of grace on His part. It was gracious from Peter's point of view; for had He not healed Malchus, Peter might have been arrested and crucified! Peter was acting like one of the Jewish "zealots" and not like a disciple of Jesus Christ.

But it was also an act of grace toward Malchus. After all, he was only a servant; and why worry about what happens to a servant? He was also an enemy, standing with the men who came to arrest Jesus; so he ought to suffer! Is it possible that Malchus had actually laid hold of Jesus? We do not know; but if he did, he laid hands on the holy Son of God. However, our Lord did not judge Malchus, though he was a sinner deserving the wrath of God. Instead, He healed him! It was our Lord's last public miracle before the cross.

Keep in mind that this miracle reveals His grace toward us. If Jesus had the power to stun an armed mob and heal a severed ear, He could have saved Himself from arrest, trial, and death. *But He willingly submitted!* And He did it for us!

It is a sad thing when well-meaning but ignorant Christians take up the sword to "defend" the Lord Jesus Christ. Peter hurt Malchus, something no believer should do. Peter hurt the testimony of Christ and gave the false impression that His disciples hate their enemies and try to destroy them. (Note our Lord's reply to Pilate in John 18:36.)

The Cup—Submission (John 18:11-14)

Peter had a sword in his hand, but our Lord had a cup in His hand. Peter was resisting God's will but the Saviour was accepting God's will. Earlier, Jesus had prayed, "O My Father, if it be possible, let this cup pass from Me; nevertheless, not as I will, but as Thou wilt" (Matt. 26:39). The cup represented the suffering He would endure and the separation from the Father that He would experience on the cross. He prayed this prayer three times, evidence that His whole being was sensitive to the price He would pay for our salvation. His holy soul must have been stirred to the depths when He contemplated being made sin!

The drinking of a cup is often used in Scripture to illustrate experiencing suffering and sorrow. When Babylon captured Jerusalem, the city had "drunken the dregs of the cup of trembling" (Isa. 51:17). Jeremiah pictured God's wrath against the nations as the pouring out of a cup (Jer. 25:15-28). There is also a cup of consolation (Jer. 16:7) and the overflowing cup of joy (Ps. 23:5).

Jesus had compared His own sufferings to the drinking of a cup and the experiencing of a baptism (Matt. 20:22-23). When He instituted the supper, He compared the cup to His blood, shed for the remission of sins (Matt. 26:27-28). The image was a familiar one to His disciples, and it is not an unfamiliar image today. To "drink the cup" means to go through with a difficult experience; and "not my cup of tea" means saying no to a certain course of action. The fact that some trophies are designed like cups suggests that winners have been through demanding experiences and had to "swallow a lot."

Jesus was able to accept the cup because it was mixed by the Father and given to Him from the Father's hand. He did not resist the Father's will, because He came to do the Father's will and finish the work the Father gave

Him to do. "I delight to do Thy will, O my God: yea, Thy law is within my heart" (Ps. 40:8). Since the Father had mixed and measured the contents of the cup, Jesus knew He had nothing to fear.

This is a good lesson to us: we need never fear the cups that the Father hands to us. To begin with, our Saviour has already drunk the cup before us, and we are only following in His steps. We need never fear what is in the cup because the Father has prepared it for us in love. If we ask for bread, He will never give us a stone; and the cup He prepares will never contain anything that will harm us. We may suffer pain and heartbreak, but He will eventually transform that suffering into glory.

Jesus deliberately gave Himself to His enemies. They bound Him and led Him to the house of Annas, which was not too far away. Annas had served as high priest until he was deposed by the Romans; now his son-in-law Caiaphas was the high priest. God had ordained that one man should serve as high priest for a lifetime, so it is easy to see that the Jewish religious establishment was in sad condition. It is generally believed that the high priest's family was in charge of the temple "business," and the fact that Jesus twice cleansed the temple must have aroused their anger against Him.

The "trial" before Annas was more like an informal hearing. It was illegal and it was brutal. Imagine a guard being allowed to strike a prisoner! Imagine a man not holding an office interrogating a prisoner!

Annas, of course, was looking for some kind of evidence on which to base an accusation that would lead to a verdict of capital punishment. What doctrine was Jesus teaching? Was it subversive? Jesus told him to ask the people who listened to Him, because He had said nothing secretly. In fact, Annas himself could have come and listened!

What about our Lord's disciples? Were they organized to overthrow the government? Did not one of them use his sword in the Garden? Jesus was careful to say nothing about His disciples. Think of it: while Peter was in the courtyard denying his Lord, Jesus was on trial protecting Peter!

Jewish law demanded that witnesses be called before a prisoner was questioned. Annas defied this law, and eventually the council hired *false* witnesses. Jesus knew His rights ("bear witness of the evil"—John 18:23), but He did not insist on them. He is an example to us when we suffer wrongfully (1 Peter 2:19-25; 4:12-19).

The Fire—Denial (John 18:15-27)

Jesus had predicted that Peter would deny Him three times (Matt. 26:34; John 13:38), but that he would be restored to fellowship and service (Luke 22:32). Peter followed the crowd when he should have been fleeing (John 18:8; and see Matt. 26:30-32). Had he gone his way, he would never have denied the Lord. While we certainly admire his love and courage, we cannot agree with his actions; for he walked right into temptation. This is what Jesus warned him about in the Garden (Matt. 26:41).

We do not know who the other disciple was who went with Peter into the courtyard of the home of the high priest. It was probably John, though it is difficult to understand how a fisherman could be acquainted with the high priest and his household. Was this "other disciple" possibly Nicodemus or Joseph of Arimathea? They would certainly have access to this home.

As you watch Peter, you see him gradually moving into the place of temptation and sin; and his actions parallel the description in Psalm 1:1. First, Peter walked "in the counsel of the ungodly" when he followed Jesus and went into the high priest's courtyard. Peter should have followed the counsel of Jesus and gotten out of there in a hurry! Then, Peter *stood* with the enemy by the fire (John 18:16, 18); and before long, he *sat* with the enemy (Luke 22:55). It was now too late and within a short time, he would deny his Lord three times.

First, a servant girl asked, "Art not thou also one of this Man's disciples?" The Greek text indicates that she expected a negative answer, and that is what she got! Peter denied Christ by denying that he belonged to the band of disciples.

Peter remained by the fire, so it is no wonder that he was approached again. (That same night, Jesus had been perspiring as He had prayed in the Garden!) Another servant girl asked the same question, again expecting a negative reply. The pronoun *they* in John 18:25 suggests that others in the circle around the fire took up the question and one by one hurled it at Peter.

The third question came from one of Malchus' relatives! The Greek construction indicates that he expected an *affirmative* answer:

"I saw you in the Garden with Jesus, didn't I? Yes, I did!" After all, this man had gotten a good look at Peter because he was probably standing with Malchus when Jesus was arrested. Some of the bystanders took up the discussion (Matt. 26:73; Mark 14:70) so that Peter may have been surrounded by challengers.

At that point, Peter's resistance broke down completely. He began to "curse and swear" (Matt. 26:74). This does not mean that Peter let loose a volley of blasphemies, but rather that he put himself under a curse in order to emphasize his statement. He was on trial, so he put himself under an oath to convince his accusers that he was telling the truth.

It was at that point that the cock began to crow (John 18:27) just as Jesus had predicted (Matt. 26:34). There were four "watches": evening (6-9 P.M.), midnight (9-12), cockcrowing (12 midnight to 3 A.M.), and morning (3-6 A.M.) (see Mark 13:35). The crowing of the cock reminded Peter of the Lord's words, and he went out and wept bitterly.

The crowing of the cock was assurance to Peter that Jesus was totally in control of the situation, even though He was bound and being harassed by the authorities. By controlling one bird, Jesus affirmed His sovereignty. According to Genesis 1:26, God gave man authority over the fish, the fowl, and the animals. Peter had seen Jesus exercise authority over the fish (Matt. 17:24-27; Luke 5:1-11) and the animals (Matt. 21:1-11); but now he recognized His authority over the birds.

But the cockcrowing was also an invitation to repentance. "When thou art converted, strengthen thy brethren" (Luke 22:32). Luke tells us that Jesus turned and looked at Peter (Luke 22:61), and this look of love broke Peter's heart. Peter had been a witness of Christ's sufferings (1 Peter 5:1), and by his own denials he added to those sufferings.

Keep in mind that the crowing of the cock was the announcement of the dawning of a new day! "Weeping may endure for a night, but joy cometh in the morning" (Ps. 30:5). It is worthwhile to contrast Peter and Judas. Peter wept over his sins and repented, while Judas admitted his sins but never really repented. Judas experienced remorse, not repentance. When Judas went out from the Upper Room, "it was night" (John 13:30); but when Peter went out to weep bitterly, there was the dawning of a new day. It is the contrast between godly sorrow that leads to true repentance, and the sorrow of the world (regret and remorse) that leads to death (2 Cor. 7:9-10). We will discover that Jesus restored Peter (John 21) and enabled him to serve with great power and blessing.

In the Garden that night, you would find both guilt and grace. Peter was guilty of resisting God's will. Judas was guilty of the basest kind of treachery. The mob was guilty of rejecting the Son of God and treating Him as though He were the lowest kind of criminal.

But Jesus was gracious! Like King David, He crossed the Kidron, fully conscious that Judas was betraying Him. He went into the Garden of Gethsemane surrendered to the Father's will. He healed Malchus' ear. He protected His disciples. He yielded Himself into the hands of sinners that He might suffer and die for us.

"Love so amazing, so divine,
Demands my soul, my life, my all!"

What is in your hand today—the sword, or the cup?

CHAPTER TWENTY
"SUFFERED UNDER PONTIUS PILATE"
John 18:28–19:16

Long before the Jewish leaders had Jesus arrested in the Garden, they had determined to kill Him (John 11:47-54). However, the Jewish council did not have the right to execute prisoners; so it was necessary to get the cooperation and approval of Rome. This meant a visit to the Roman procurator, Pontius Pilate.

There were three stages in both the Jewish "trial" and the Roman "trial." After His arrest, Jesus was taken to the home of Annas and there interrogated informally (John 18:12-14, 19-23). Annas hoped to get information that would implicate Jesus as an enemy of the state. He wanted to prove that both His doctrine and His disciples were anti-Roman, for then He would be worthy of death.

Stage two of the Jewish trial took place before Caiaphas and whatever members of the Sanhedrin the high priest could assemble at that hour of the night (Matt. 26:57-68; Mark 14:53-65). When Jesus confessed clearly that He was the Christ, the council found Him guilty of blasphemy and therefore, according to their law, worthy of death. However, it was necessary for the council to meet early the next morning and give their verdict, since it was not considered legal to try capital cases at night. So, stage three of the Jewish trial took place as early as possible, and the leaders condemned Jesus to death (Matt. 27:1; Luke 22:66-71).

The three stages of the Roman trial were: the first appearance before Pilate (John 18:28-38), the appearance before Herod (Luke 23:6-12), and the second appearance before Pilate (John 18:39–19:16; and see Matt. 27:15-26; Mark 15:6-15; and Luke 23:13-25). As you can see, the Apostle John records only the interrogations by Annas and Pilate, and mentions Caiaphas only in passing. He focuses primarily on the Roman trial. By the time he wrote this Gospel, the Jewish nation had been scattered by Rome, Jerusalem had been destroyed, and Roman power was all that really mattered.

Pontius Pilate was in office from A.D. 26–36 and was not greatly liked by the Jews. He could be ruthless when he wanted to be (see Luke 13:1-2), but he also understood the Jewish power structures and knew how to use them. His handling of the trial of Jesus reveals an indecisive man, a weak man, a compromising man. Rome's motto was, "Let justice be done though the heavens fall!" Pilate was not concerned about justice; his only concern was to protect himself, his job, and Rome. Alas, he failed in all three!

As you read John's account, you see Pilate seeking to find some "loophole" that would please both sides. He was afraid of the crowd, but then he grew more and more afraid of the prisoner! At least three times he announced that Jesus was not guilty of any crime (Luke 23:14; John 19:4; Luke 23:22; John 19:6). Yet he refused to release Him!

The Roman "trial," conducted by Pilate, revolved around four key questions.

"What Is the Accusation?" (John 18:28-32)

As soon as the Sanhedrin had voted to condemn Jesus, the officers took Him to the palace where Pilate was living during the Passover season. It was customary for the Roman governor to be in Jerusalem during Passover in case there were any outbursts of Jewish nationalism. The religious leaders did not hesitate to condemn an innocent man, but they were careful not to be defiled by walking on Gentile ground! It would be tragic to be ceremonially defiled during the seven days of Passover!

It was logical for Pilate to ask for the official accusation. Instead of stating the charges clearly, the Jewish leaders "beat around the bush" and probably made the astute politician suspicious. Luke 23:2 lists three "official charges": (1) He led the nation astray; (2) He opposed paying tribute to Caesar; and (3) He claimed to be the Jewish Messiah and King.

Pilate was not anxious to get involved in a Jewish court case, especially at Passover; so he tried to evade the issue. After all, if the prisoner was creating problems for the Jews, let the Jews try Him under their own law. Rome had permitted the Jews to retain a certain amount of jurisdiction, especially in matters relating to their religious laws and customs. (See Acts 18:12-16 for another example.)

But had the Jews *alone* judged Jesus and found Him guilty, He would have been killed by stoning; and God had determined that the Son would be crucified (see John 3:14; 8:28; 12:32-33). Jesus was to bear the curse of the law and become a curse for us; and in order to do this, He had to hang on a tree (Deut. 21:22-23; Gal. 3:13). The fact that the Romans allowed the Jews to stone Stephen to death indicates that Rome was lenient with the Sanhedrin on some capital cases (Acts 7:57-60).

When you seriously consider the three accusations against Jesus, you quickly see that they were completely unsupportable. For one thing, He had not "subverted" the nation, either politically or religiously. Of course, He had publicly denounced the Pharisees and their hypocritical religious system, but He was not the first one—or the only one—to do that. Jesus had blessed the nation and brought them new hope. The fact that some of the militant Jews saw in Him a potential King (John 6:15) was not our Lord's fault, and He fled from all such political demonstrations.

As for opposing paying tribute to Caesar, *He taught just the opposite!* "Render therefore unto Caesar the things which are Caesar's," He said, "and unto God the things that are God's" (Matt. 22:21).

He did claim to be King but not in a political sense. Even His own disciples did not fully understand these truths until after His resurrection (Acts 1:1-8). It is no wonder the common people sometimes misunderstood Him (Luke 19:11). Of course, the Jewish religious leaders were groping for any piece of evidence they could find on which they could build a case; and they were even willing to secure false witnesses!

"Are You the King of the Jews?" (John 18:33-38)

The question asking Jesus if He was King of the Jews is recorded by each of the Gospel writers. As Roman governor, Pilate would certainly be interested in the claims of any king. Messianic expectations always ran high at Passover season, and it would be easy for a Jewish pretender to incite the people into a riot or a rebellion against Rome. Pilate no doubt felt himself on safe ground when he asked about Christ's kingship.

However, he was not prepared for His answer. "It is as you say" (Matt. 27:11, NASB). But then Jesus added a question of His own: "Are you saying this on your own initiative, or did others tell you about Me?" (John 18:34, NASB) What was our Lord really asking? "What kind of a king do you have in mind? A Roman king or a Jewish king? A political king or a spiritual king?" Jesus was not evading the issue; He was forcing Pilate to clarify the matter *for his own sake.* After all, it was not Jesus that was on trial; it was Pilate!

If Pilate had a Roman king in mind, then Jesus could be considered a rebel. If the governor was thinking about a Jewish kind of king, then political matters could be set aside. It is interesting that Pilate called Jesus "king" at least four times during the trial, and even used that title for the placard he hung on the cross (John 18:39; 19:3, 14-15, 19).

Pilate's reply to Jesus showed what the Romans thought of the Jews: "Am I a Jew?" No doubt there was an obvious note of disdain and sarcasm in his voice. Jesus was not a prisoner because Pilate had arrested him, but because His own nation's leaders had arrested Him! Where there is smoke there must be fire; so Pilate asked, "What have You done?"

Graciously, Jesus consented to explain Himself and His kingdom. Yes, He admitted that He is a King; but His kingdom (reign) does not come from the authority of the world. The Jews were under Roman authority, and Pilate was under the authority of the emperor; but Jesus derived His authority from God. His kingdom is spiritual, in the hearts of His followers; and He does not depend on worldly or fleshly means to advance His cause. If His kingdom were from the world, by now His followers would have assembled an army and fought to release Him.

Jesus did not say that He had no kingdom in this world, or that He would never rule on earth. He does have a kingdom in this world, wherever there are people who have trusted Him and yielded to His sovereignty. One day He shall return and establish a righteous kingdom on earth (Dan. 7:13-28). Pilate's concern was the source of this kingdom: where did Jesus derive His authority?

In John 18:37, Jesus explained who He is and what kind of kingdom belonged to Him. Pilate probably did not grasp the significance of these profound words, but we today can discern some of the meaning Jesus had in mind. He was "born," which indicates His humanity; but He also "came into the world," which indicates His deity. The fact that Jesus came "into the world" means that He had existed before His birth at Bethlehem; and this is an important and repeated truth in John's Gospel (John 1:9-10; 3:17, 19; 9:39; 10:36; 12:46; 16:28; 17:18).

But Jesus not only told Pilate of His origin; He also explained His ministry: to bear witness unto the truth. His was a spiritual kingdom of truth; and He won people to His cause, not through force, but through conviction and persuasion. He spoke the truth of God's Word, and all who were His people would respond to His call (see John 8:47; 10:27). Rome's weapon was the sword; but our Lord's weapon was the truth of God, the sword of the Spirit (Eph. 6:17).

We do not know with what attitude Pilate asked his now-famous question, "What is truth?" In his classic essay "Of Truth," Francis Bacon wrote, " 'What is Truth?' said jesting Pilate; and would not stay for an answer." But we are not certain that Pilate was jesting. Perhaps he was sincere. For centuries, Roman and Greek philosophers had discussed and debated this very question and had come to no settled conclusions. Whether Pilate was sneering or sighing as he asked the question, we do not know; so it would be unwise to pass judgment.

At least he had the courage to face the crowd and declare his verdict: "I find in Him no fault at all." But he did not get the response he desired, for the chief priests and elders only began to accuse Jesus all the more! (see Matt. 27:12-14) Jesus was silent before His accusers (1 Peter 2:21-23) and this silence amazed Pilate. Could this King not even defend Himself? If He did not speak, how could anyone secure any evidence? Pilate faced a dilemma.

But the chief priests and elders solved his problem when they shouted that Jesus had stirred up the people even in Galilee (Luke 23:5). Galilee! That was Herod's responsibility, so why not send the prisoner to Herod, who was also in Jerusalem for the feast? Between John 18:38 and 39 you have the events recorded in Luke 23:6-12. Pilate's maneuver did not solve his problem, because Herod sent Jesus back! All that it accomplished was the healing of the breach between these two rulers. Pilate still had to deal with Jesus and the Jews.

"Shall I Release the King of the Jews?" (John 18:39–19:7)

The fact that Herod had found nothing worthy of death in Jesus encouraged Pilate to confront the Jewish leaders and seek to release the prisoner. He summoned the chief priests and rulers and told them that he found no guilt in Jesus, that Herod had found no guilt in Jesus, and that the next step would be to punish Jesus and release Him. The Jews had already made it clear that they wanted Jesus to die (John 18:31), but Pilate was feebly trying to do the noble thing.

Hoping to strengthen this suggestion, Pilate offered to bargain with the Jewish leaders. It was a custom at Passover for the governor to release a prisoner and please the Jews; so, why not release Jesus? Or, he could release Barabbas; but why would the Jews want Barabbas set free? After all, he was a robber (John 18:40), a notorious prisoner (Matt. 27:16), an insurrectionist and a murderer (Luke 23:19). Who would want *that* kind of a prisoner turned loose?

Incredible as it seems, the crowd asked for Barabbas! The people were persuaded by the chief priests and elders (Matt. 27:20) whose religious convictions did not motivate them toward justice and equity. National feelings always increased during Passover, and a vote *for* Barabbas was a vote *against* Rome. Even though Jesus had been a popular figure among the people, many of them no doubt were disappointed that He had not led a popular uprising to overthrow Rome. Perhaps they had even hoped that His "triumphal entry" a few days before would be the start of Jewish liberation.

There is no explaining how a mob chooses its heroes. No doubt many of the Jews admired Barabbas for his cunning and courage, and they rejoiced that he was fighting Rome. Had they honestly compared and contrasted the two "candidates," the people would have had to vote for Jesus Christ. But when a mob is manipulated by crafty leaders, in an atmosphere of patriotic fervor, it loses itself and starts to think with its feelings instead of its brains. Their condemning vote said nothing about the Son of God, but it said a great deal about them.

Never at a loss for an idea, Pilate tried a new approach—sympathy. The crowd had cried "Crucify Him!" (Mark 15:14) but perhaps they would be placated if Jesus were scourged. What man could behold a scourged prisoner and still want the victim crucified? The scourge was a leather whip, knotted and weighted with pieces of metal or bone; and many a prisoner never survived the whipping. It pains us to think that the sinless Son of God was subjected to such cruelty. He was innocent, yet He was treated as though He were guilty; and He did it for us. He was slapped in the face before Annas (John 18:22), and spat on and beaten before Caiaphas and the council (Matt. 26:67). Pilate scourged Him and the soldiers smote Him (John 19:1-3); and before they led Him to Calvary, the soldiers mocked Him and beat Him with a rod (Mark 15:19). How much He suffered for us!

Pilate had called Him "King of the Jews" (John 18:39), so the soldiers decided that the "king" should have a crown and a robe. The Jews had mocked His claim to being a Prophet (Matt. 26:67-68), and now the Gentiles mocked His claim to being a King. The verb tenses in the Greek text in John 19:3 indicate that the soldiers *repeatedly* came to Him, mocked Him, and beat Him with their hands. The forces of hell were having a heyday in Pilate's hall.

Sin had brought thorns and thistles into the

world (Gen. 3:17-19), so it was only fitting that the Creator wear a crown of thorns as He bore the sins of the world on the cross. The very metal He had created and placed in the ground was used to make nails to pound through His hands and feet.

For the third time, Pilate went out to face the people (John 18:29, 38; 19:4), this time bringing Jesus with him. Surely the sight of this scourged and humiliated prisoner would arouse some pity in their hearts; but it did not. For the second time, Pilate declared that he found no fault in Jesus, but his words only aroused their hateful passions more. "Behold the man!" carries the idea, "Look at this poor fellow! Hasn't He suffered enough? Take pity on Him and let me release Him." It was a noble effort on Pilate's part, but it failed.

The failure of Pilate's plan teaches us an important lesson: it takes more than human sentiment to bring the lost sinner to salvation. There is a view of the Atonement called "the moral influence theory" that would fit right into the governor's approach. It states that the realization of our Lord's sufferings moves the heart of the sinner so that he turns from sin and begins to love God. It is purely subjective and has no bearing on the holiness of God or the importance of satisfying divine justice.

If any crowd should have been moved by pity, it was the Jewish crowd that waited on Pilate. What nation has suffered more than the Jews? Here was one of their own, a Jewish prophet, suffering unjustly at the hands of the Romans, and the Jews did not repent or even show any touch of pity! If sinners who actually saw Christ in His suffering did not repent, what hope is there for people twenty centuries later who only read about His agonies?

The cross involves much more than an exhibition of innocent suffering. On that cross, the Son of God paid the price for the sins of the world and thereby declared the love of God and defended the holiness and justice of God. We are not saved by feeling pity for Jesus. We are saved by repenting of our sins and trusting Jesus, the sinless Substitute. "If Christ was not actually doing something by His death," wrote Dr. Leon Morris, "then we are confronted with a piece of showmanship, nothing more."

This does not mean that it is wrong for the believer to contemplate the cross and meditate on Christ's sufferings. The familiar hymn "When I Survey the Wond'rous Cross" helps us realize afresh the price that Jesus paid for us, but we must not confuse sentimentality with true spiritual emotion. It is one thing to shed tears during a church service and quite something else to sacrifice, suffer, and serve after the meeting has ended. We do not simply contemplate the cross; we carry it.

For the third time, Pilate announced, "I find no fault in Him!" The crowd might well have shouted, "Then why did you have Him scourged?" Pilate's actions belied his words. He was a weak-willed man who, like many politicians, hoped to find a happy compromise that would please everybody. The Chinese teacher Confucius defined "cowardice" as "to know what is right and not do it."

The religious leaders were not at a loss for a powerful reply: "We have a law, and by our law He ought to die, because He made Himself the Son of God" (John 19:7). This statement is not found in the other Gospels (but see Matt. 26:63-64); however, it fits right into John's purpose in writing his Gospel (John 20:31).

"Where Are You From?" (John 19:8-16)

The Romans and Greeks had numerous myths about the gods coming to earth as men (note Acts 14:8-13), so it is likely that Pilate responded to the phrase "Son of God" with these stories in mind. Already the governor had been impressed by the words and demeanor of our Lord; he had never met a prisoner like Him before. Was He indeed a god come to earth? Did He have supernatural powers? No wonder Pilate was starting to be afraid! Also, Pilate's wife had sent him a strange message that he should have nothing to do with Jesus (Matt. 27:19). Jesus had even come into her dreams!

Why did Jesus not answer Pilate's question? Because He had already answered it (John 18:36-37). It is a basic spiritual principle that God does not reveal new truth to us if we fail to act on the truth we already know. Furthermore, Pilate had already made it clear that he was not personally interested in spiritual truth. All he was concerned about was maintaining peace in Jerusalem as he tried to expedite the trial of Jesus of Nazareth. Pilate did not deserve an answer!

Fear and anger often go together. When we are afraid we are weak, we go the other extreme and try to appear strong. This is what Pilate did as he reminded Jesus of his Roman authority. But his statement did not demonstrate his power; it demonstrated his weakness. For if he had the authority to release Jesus, *why did he not do it?* He condemned himself with his own boastful words.

Of course, our Lord's silence before both Herod and Pilate was a fulfillment of Isaiah 53:7. Peter later used this as an example for suffering Christians to follow (1 Peter 2:18-23).

John 19:11 records our Lord's last words to Pilate, words that reveal His faith in the Father and His surrender to His will (see 1 Peter 2:23; 4:19). All authority comes from God (Rom. 13:1ff). Jesus was able to surrender to Rome and the Jews because He was first of all yielded to God. Pilate was boasting about his authority (John 19:10), but Jesus reminded him that his so-called authority was only delegated to him from God. One day God would call him to account for the way he had used his privileges and responsibilities.

To whom was Jesus referring when He said "he that delivered Me up unto thee"? Certainly not God, because God does not and cannot sin. Jesus was referring to Caiaphas, the corrupt high priest who had long before determined that Jesus must die (John 11:47-54). Caiaphas knew the Scriptures and had been given every opportunity to examine the evidence. He had willfully closed his eyes and hardened his heart. He had seen to it that Jesus was not given a fair trial. It was his associates who were inciting the mob to cry, "Let Him be crucified!" Pilate was a spiritually blind pagan, but Caiaphas was a Jew who had a knowledge of Scripture. Therefore, it was Caiaphas, not Pilate, who had the greater sin.

What a dilemma Pilate was in! How would he go about investigating the claim that Jesus was "the Son of God"? And there was no evidence that He was a troublemaker or a seditionist. In a final burst of courage, Pilate tried to release Jesus. John does not tell us what steps Pilate took (the Greek text says "he kept seeking to release Him"), but they all failed. In fact, the crowd started to accuse *Pilate* of being a traitor to Caesar! This was too much for the governor, so he gave his official verdict and delivered Jesus to be crucified. Matthew tells us that Pilate washed his hands before the crowd (Matt. 27:24), but this did not cleanse his heart. Alas, it was Pilate who was on trial, not Jesus!

It is likely that John used Roman time, so that "the sixth hour" would have been 6 A.M. Mark tells us that Jesus was crucified "the third hour," which, in Jewish reckoning, would have been 9 A.M. Since John wrote "*about* the sixth hour," we need not try to figure out why it took three hours to get Jesus from Pilate's hall to Calvary.

The "preparation" refers to the preparation for the Sabbath (see John 19:31) which would begin at sundown that day (Friday). Being the Passover Sabbath, it was an especially holy day. The religious leaders were more concerned about their traditions than they were knowing the truth and obeying the will of God. On a high and holy day, they crucified their own Messiah, Jesus the Son of God!

The crowd had the last word: "We have no king but Caesar!" "We will not have this man to reign over us!" (Luke 19:14) Well-meaning preachers have often said that the crowd that on Palm Sunday shouted "Hosannah!" turned right around and shouted "Crucify Him!" on Good Friday. However, it was two different crowds. The Palm Sunday crowd came primarily from Galilee where Jesus was very popular. The crowd at Pilate's hall was from Judea and Jerusalem where the religious leaders were very much in control. If the Galilean disciples had had their way, they would have revolted and delivered Jesus!

From the human standpoint, the trial of Jesus was the greatest crime and tragedy in history. From the divine viewpoint, it was the fulfillment of prophecy and the accomplishment of the will of God. The fact that God had planned all of this did not absolve the participants of their responsibility. In fact, at Pentecost, Peter put both ideas together in one statement! (Acts 2:23)

When Israel asked to have a king, and God gave them Saul, the nation rejected God the Father (1 Sam. 8:5-7). When they asked for Barabbas, they rejected God the Son. Today, they are rejecting the pleading of God the Holy Spirit (Acts 7:51; Rom. 10:21). Yet there will come a day when they shall see their King, believe, and be saved (Zech. 12:10-11; Matt. 24:30; Rev. 1:7).

Both the nation and the governor were on trial, and both failed miserably.

May we not fail!

CHAPTER TWENTY-ONE "EVEN THE DEATH OF THE CROSS"

John 19:17-42

The Apostle's Creed states it without embellishment: "He was crucified, dead, and buried." These three events are described in John 19:17-42, momentous events that we should understand not only from the historical point of view but also from the doctrinal. *What* happened is important; *why* it happened is also important, if you hope to go to heaven.

Crucified (John 19:17-27)

Pilate delivered Jesus to the chief priests; and they, with the help of the Roman soldiers, took Jesus to be crucified. "It was the most cruel and shameful of all punishments," said the Roman statesman-philosopher Cicero. "Let it never come near the body of a Roman citizen; nay, not even near his thoughts or eyes or ears."

Crucifixion probably had its origin among the Persians and Phoenicians, but it was the Romans who made special use of it. No Roman citizen could be crucified, though there were exceptions. This mode of capital punishment was reserved for the lowest kind of criminals, particularly those who promoted insurrection. Today, we think of the cross as a symbol of glory and victory; but in Pilate's day, the cross stood for the basest kind of rejection, shame, and suffering. It was Jesus who made the difference.

It was customary for the criminal to carry his cross, or at least the crossbeam, from the hall of judgment to the place of execution. Jesus began the mile-long walk carrying His cross, but He was relieved by Simon of Cyrene whom the Roman soldiers "drafted" to do the job. We do not know why Jesus was relieved of this burden; the Scriptures are silent. Was He too weak from the scourgings to carry the load? Was His weakness holding back the procession at a time when the Jews were anxious to get it over with so they could celebrate their Passover Sabbath? One thing is sure: the bearing of the cross was a mark of guilt; *and Jesus was not guilty* (see Mark 15:20-21 and Rom. 16:13).

It was also required that the criminal wear a placard announcing his crime. The only announcement recorded in the Gospels is the one that Pilate wrote: "This is Jesus of Nazareth the King of the Jews." The chief priests protested the title, but Pilate refused to change it. It was his final thrust against the Jewish religious establishment. He knew that the priests and elders envied Jesus and wanted to destroy Him (Matt. 27:18). A shrewd politician like Pilate well understood the workings of the Jewish religious establishment. He knew that his placard would insult and embarrass them, and that is exactly what he wanted.

The fact that this title was written in Hebrew (Aramaic), Greek, and Latin is significant. For one thing, it shows that our Lord was crucified in a place where many peoples and nations met, a cosmopolitan place. Hebrew is the language of religion, Greek of philosophy, and Latin of law; and all three combined to crucify the Son of God. But what He did on the cross, He did for the whole world! In this Gospel, John emphasizes the worldwide dimensions of the work of Christ. Without realizing it, Pilate wrote a "Gospel tract" when he prepared this title; for one of the thieves discovered that Jesus was King, and he asked entrance into His kingdom.

Jesus was crucified outside the city (Heb. 13:11-13) between two other victims, possibly associates of Barabbas. We do not know where our Saviour's cross stood. There have been so many changes in the topography of Jerusalem since A.D. 70 when Titus and the Romans destroyed it, that it is impossible to determine accurately either our Lord's route to the cross or where the cross stood. Pilgrims to the Holy Land today are shown both the Church of the Holy Sepulcher and "Gordon's Calvary" near the garden tomb.

The Hebrew word *Golgotha* means "cranium, skull"; Calvary is the Latin equivalent. We are not told why it had this peculiar name. Certainly Jewish people would not permit unclean skulls to be left at a place of public execution! For that matter, the bodies (with heads intact) were usually disposed of by burial (if the victims had friends) or by throwing them on the public garbage dump. "Gordon's Calvary" does resemble a skull, but did the terrain look like that 2,000 years ago?

That Jesus was crucified with two notorious thieves only added to the shame. But it also fulfilled Isaiah 53:12, "He was numbered with the transgressors." He was treated like a common criminal!

Modern executions are usually carried out in almost clinical privacy, but Jesus was nailed to a cross and hung up for everyone to see. It was Passover season and there were thousands of visitors in the city. The place of execution was outside the city where many people would pass. Jesus was a well-known figure, so His arrest and condemnation would be topics for discussion. It was natural for people to gather and watch the grim scene.

Of course, the soldiers had to be there; that was their job. At most Roman executions, a centurion would be assigned with four soldiers to assist him. Since Jesus was a popular teacher with many followers, Pilate may have assigned more guards to Golgotha. It was the privilege of the soldiers to share whatever personal belongings the victims had; so they divided up all that Jesus owned—His personal clothing. He would have had a turban, a pair of sandals, an undergarment (the seamless robe), an outer garment, and a girdle. The four men each took a piece of clothing, and then they gambled for the seamless robe. This fulfilled Psalm 22:18.

John does not record it, but the other Gospel writers tell us that some of the people passing by reviled Jesus, no doubt at the instigation of the chief priests and scribes (Mark 15:29-32). When you read Psalm 22, you see how David used the image of *animals* to describe the people who persecuted our Lord: bulls (Ps. 22:12), lions (Ps. 22:13, 21), and dogs (Ps. 22:16, 20). When men reject their Lord, they become like animals.

A group of women, along with the Apostle John, stood near the cross. (Later, they would move farther away and join other friends of Jesus [Matt. 27:55-56; Mark 15:40-41].) John specifies four women: Mary, the mother of Jesus; His mother's sister, Salome, the mother of James and John; Mary, the wife of Clopas (Cleophas); and Mary Magdalene. It took courage to stand there in the midst of such hatred and ridicule, but their being there must have encouraged our Lord.

The first time we meet Mary in the Gospel of John, she is attending a wedding (John 2:1-11); now she is preparing for a burial. The hour had come! She was experiencing "the sword" that had been predicted years before (Luke 2:35). Her silence is significant; for if anyone could have rescued Jesus, it was His mother. All she had to do was announce that His claims were false—but she said nothing! What a testimony to the deity of Christ.

Jesus assured her of His love, and He gave His choicest disciple, who rested on His bosom, to be her adopted son and to care for her. Whether that moment John took Mary away from the scene and took her home, we do not know. We do know that he cared for her and that she was among the believers in the Upper Room as they awaited Pentecost (Acts 1:14). Even while He was performing the great work of redemption, Jesus was faithful to His responsibilities as a son. What an honor it was for John to take his Lord's place in Mary's life!

Do not confuse Mary Magdalene with the "sinful woman" described in Luke 7:36ff. Jesus had delivered Mary Magdalene from demons (Mark 16:9; Luke 8:2), and she used her resources to assist Jesus in His ministry. Salome had asked Jesus for thrones for her two sons (Matt. 20:20-29), and He had denied her request. You wonder what she was thinking about as she stood there and beheld Jesus dying on the cross. The scene must have rebuked her selfishness.

Dead (John 19:28-30)

Our Lord knew what was going on; He was fully in control as He obeyed the Father's will. He had refused to drink the pain-deadening wine that was always offered to those about to be crucified (Matt. 27:34). In order to fulfill the Scriptures (Ps. 69:21), He said, "I thirst." He was enduring real physical suffering, for He had a real human body. He had just emerged from three hours of darkness when He felt the wrath of God and separation from God (Matt. 27:45-49). When you combine darkness, thirst, and isolation, you have—hell! There were physical reasons for His thirst (Ps. 22:15), but there were also spiritual reasons (Ps. 42:1-2).

One of the soldiers took pity on Jesus and moistened His lips with the cheap vinegar wine the soldiers drank. We must not imagine Jesus hanging many feet up in the air, almost inaccessible. His feet were perhaps three or four feet from the ground, so it would be easy for the man to put a sponge at the end of a reed and give Jesus a drink. You and I today can "give Jesus a drink" by sharing what we have with those in need (Matt. 25:34-40).

Psalm 69 has strong messianic overtones. Note Psalm 69:3, "My throat is dried." Psalm 69:4 is referred to by Jesus in John 15:25, and

Psalm 69:8 should be connected with John 7:3-5. Psalm 69:9 is quoted in John 2:17, and Psalm 69:21 is referred to in John 19:28-29. Note the emphasis on "reproach" (Ps. 69:7-10, 19-20) and the image of the "deep waters" (Ps. 69:14-15, and see Luke 12:50).

Our Lord made seven statements while He was on the cross; they are known as "the seven words from the cross." First, He thought of others: those who crucified Him (Luke 23:34), the believing thief (Luke 23:39-43), and His mother (John 19:25-27). The central word had to do with His relationship to the Father (Matt. 27:45-49); and the last three statements focused on Himself: His body (John 19:28-29), His soul (John 19:30; and see Isa. 53:10), and His spirit (Luke 23:46).

The drink of vinegar did not fully quench His thirst, but it did enable Him to utter that shout of triumph, in a loud voice, "It is finished!" In the Greek text, it is *tetelestai;* and it means, "It is finished, it stands finished, and it always will be finished!" While it is true that our Lord's sufferings were now finished, there is much more included in this dramatic word. Many of the Old Testament types and prophecies were now fulfilled, and the once-for-all sacrifice for sin had now been completed.

The word *tetelestai* is unfamiliar to us, but it was used by various people in everyday life in those days. A servant would use it when reporting to his or her master, "I have completed the work assigned to me" (see John 17:4). When a priest examined an animal sacrifice and found it faultless, this word would apply. Jesus, of course, is the perfect Lamb of God, without spot or blemish. When an artist completed a picture, or a writer a manuscript, he or she might say, "It is finished!" The death of Jesus on the cross "completes the picture" that God had been painting, the story that He had been writing, for centuries. Because of the cross, we understand the ceremonies and prophecies in the Old Testament.

Perhaps the most meaningful meaning of *tetelestia* was that used by the merchants: "The debt is paid in full!" When He gave Himself on the cross, Jesus fully met the righteous demands of a holy law; He paid our debt in full. None of the Old Testament sacrifices could take away sins; their blood only *covered* sin. But the Lamb of God shed His blood, and that blood can *take away* the sins of the world (John 1:29; Heb. 9:24-28).

There was once a rather eccentric evangelist named Alexander Wooten, who was approached by a flippant young man who asked, "What must I do to be saved?"

"It's too late!" Wooten replied, and went about his work.

The young man became alarmed. "Do you mean that it's too late for me to be saved?" he asked. "Is there nothing I can do?"

"Too late!" said Wooten. *"It's already been done!* The only thing you can do is believe."

The death of Jesus Christ is a major theme in the Gospel of John. It was announced by John the Baptist even before Jesus had officially begun His ministry (John 1:29, 35-36). Our Lord's first mention is in John 3:14, where the image is certainly that of crucifixion (and see John 8:28; 12:32). Jesus often spoke of "taking up the cross" (Matt. 10:38; 16:24). After Peter's confession of faith, Jesus clearly announced that He would be killed (Matt. 16:21), and later He told the disciples that He would be crucified (Matt. 20:17-19).

In John's Gospel, you find a number of pictures of our Lord's death: the slaying of the lamb (John 1:29); the destroying of the temple (John 2:19); the lifting up of the serpent (John 3:14); the shepherd laying down his life for the sheep (John 10:11-18); and the planting of the seed in the ground (John 12:20-25). These pictures make it clear that Jesus' death was not an accident; it was a divine appointment. He was not murdered in the strictest sense: He willingly gave His life for us. His death was an atonement, not just an example. He actually accomplished the work of redemption on the cross.

Some unbelievers have invented the idea that Jesus did not really die, that He only "swooned" on the cross and was then revived in the "cool tomb." But there are too many witnesses that Jesus Christ actually died: the centurion (Mark 15:44-45); all the Gospel writers; the angels (Matt. 28:5, 7); the Jews (Acts 5:28); Christ Himself (Luke 24:46; Rev. 1:18); and even the worshiping hosts in heaven (Rev. 5:9, 12). Of course, Paul, Peter, and John mention the death of Christ in their letters.

His death was voluntary: He willingly dismissed His spirit (John 19:30; and note 10:17-18). He "gave Himself" (Gal. 2:20). He offered Himself as a ransom (Mark 10:45), as a sacrifice to God (Eph. 5:2), and as a propitiation for sin (1 John 2:2). In Luke 9:31, His death is called a "decease," which in the Greek is "exodus," suggesting the Passover lamb and the deliverance from bondage. It will take eternity to reveal all that happened when Jesus Christ died on the cross.

Buried (John 19:31-42)

Two groups of people were involved in our Lord's burial: the Roman soldiers (John 19:31-37), and the Jewish believers (John 19:38-42). It was not unusual for victims to remain on the cross in a lingering death, so the Jewish religious leaders did all they could to hasten the death of Jesus and the two thieves. However, our Lord was in control; and He dismissed His spirit at "the ninth hour," which was 3 P.M. (see Matt. 27:45-50). The last three "words from the cross" were spoken within a short period of time just before He laid down His life.

It is remarkable that the Roman soldiers *did not do* what they were commanded to do—break the victims' legs—but they *did do* what they were not supposed to do—pierce the Saviour's side! In both matters, they fulfilled the very Word of God! The bones of the Passover lamb were not to be broken (Ex. 12:46; Num. 9:12; and note Ps. 34:20), so our Lord's bones were protected by the Lord. His side was to be pierced (Zech. 12:10; Rev. 1:7), so that was done by one of the soldiers.

John saw a special significance to the blood and water that came from the wound in the side. For one thing, it proved that Jesus had a real body (see 1 John 1:1-4) and experienced a real death. By the time John wrote this book, there were false teachers in the church claiming that Jesus did not have a truly human body. There may also be a symbolic meaning: the blood speaks of our justification, the water of our sanctification and cleansing. The blood takes care of the guilt of sin; the water deals with the stain of sin. Some students connect John 19:34 with 1 John 5:6, but perhaps the connection is weak. In 1 John 5, John deals with evidence that Jesus Christ is God come in the flesh; and he presents three witnesses: the Spirit, the water, and the blood (1 John 5:6, 8). The Spirit relates to Pentecost, the water to His baptism, and the blood to His crucifixion. In each of these events, God made it clear that Jesus Christ is what He claimed to be, God come in the flesh. In fact, in John 19:35, the apostle makes it clear that the water and blood should encourage his readers to believe that Jesus is the Christ (see John 20:31).

When the soldiers were through with their gruesome work, our Lord's friends took over; and from that point on, as far as the record is concerned, no unbelievers touched the body of Jesus. God had prepared two high-ranking men to prepare His body for burial and to place it in a proper tomb. Had Joseph and Nicodemus not been there, it is likely that the body of Jesus would have been "carried off to some obscure and accursed ditch," as James Stalker states in his classic *The Trial and Death of Jesus Christ.* If the friends of any victims appeared, the Romans were only too happy to give them the bodies and get them off their hands.

When you assemble the data available about Joseph of Arimathea, you learn that he was rich (Matt. 27:57), a prominent member of the Jewish council (Mark 15:43), a good and righteous man who had not consented to what the council did (Luke 23:50-51), a member of that "believing minority" of Jews who were praying for Messiah to come (Mark 15:43, and note Luke 2:25-38), and a disciple of Jesus Christ (John 19:38). It was he who asked for the body of Jesus and, with his friend Nicodemus, gave the Saviour a decent burial.

But there are some mysteries about Joseph that perplex us and invite closer investigation. Why did he have a tomb so near to a place of execution? Most pious Jews wanted to be buried in the Holy City, but a rich man like Joseph could certainly afford a better site for his final resting place. Imagine his relatives coming to pay their respects and having to listen to the curses and cries of criminals on crosses not far away! (Note John 19:41.)

Matthew, Luke, and John all tell us that the tomb was new and had never been used. It was "his [Joseph's] own new tomb" (Matt. 27:60); he had hewn it out for himself. *Or did he hew it out for Jesus?*

John informs us that Joseph was a "secret disciple for fear of the Jews." The Greek word translated "secretly" is a perfect passive participle and could be translated "having been secreted." In Matthew 13:35, this same verb form is translated "have been kept secret." In other words, Joseph was God's "secret agent" in the Sanhedrin! From the human standpoint, Joseph kept "under cover" because he feared the Jews (John 7:13; 9:22; 12:42); but from the divine standpoint, he was being protected so he could be available to bury the body of Jesus.

We have already met Nicodemus in our study of John 1–12. Note that each time he is named, he is identified as the man who came to Jesus by night (John 3:1ff; 7:50-53). But the man who started off with confusion at night (John 3) ended up with open confession in the daylight! Nicodemus came out of the dark and into the light and, with Joseph, was not ashamed to publicly identify with Jesus Christ. Of course, when the two men touched His dead body, they defiled themselves and could not participate in Passover. But, what difference did it make? They had found the Lamb of God!

It seems evident that Joseph and Nicodemus carefully planned their activities at Calvary. They certainly could not secure a tomb at the last minute, nor would they be able to purchase sixty-five pounds of costly spices so quickly during the Passover when many merchants would not be doing business. No sooner had Jesus died than Joseph went to Pilate and received permission to take the body. Nicodemus stayed at the cross to make sure nothing happened to his Lord's body. The two men might even have been waiting *in the new tomb,* with the spices and wrappings, ready for the moment when the Saviour would lay down His life.

Haste was important and the men worked quickly. They could not give Jesus' body the full ministry of washing and anointing that was traditional, but they did the best they could. It was important to get the body safely away from the Romans and the Jewish leaders. Of course, Mary of Bethany had already anointed His body for burial (Mark 14:8; John 12:1-8). Some of the other women watched the two men minister to Jesus, and they witnessed His burial (Matt. 27:61; Mark 15:47). They planned to return after the Sabbath and complete the burial procedures (Luke 23:55–24:1).

All of this raises the question, "How did Joseph and Nicodemus know to prepare for His burial?" What follows is only conjecture on my part but, to me, it seems reasonable.

When Nicodemus first visited Jesus, he was impressed with His miracles and His teachings; but he could not understand what it meant to be born again. Certainly after that interview, Nicodemus searched the Scriptures and asked God for guidance concerning these important spiritual matters.

At the critical council meeting recorded in John 7:45-53, Nicodemus boldly stood up and defended the Saviour! His associates ridiculed him for thinking that a prophet could come out of Galilee! "Search, and look!" they said—and that is exactly what Nicodemus did. It is likely that Joseph quietly joined him and revealed the fact that he too was more and more convinced that Jesus of Nazareth was indeed Israel's Messiah, the Son of God.

As Nicodemus and Joseph searched the Old Testament, they would find the messianic prophecies and discover that many of them had been fulfilled in Jesus Christ. Certainly they would see Him as the "Lamb of God" and conclude that He would be sacrificed at Passover. Jesus had already told Nicodemus that He would be "lifted up" (John 3:14), and this meant crucifixion. Since the Passover lambs were slain about 3 P.M., the two men could know almost the exact time when God's Lamb would die on the cross! Surely they would read Isaiah 53 and notice verse 9—"And He made His grave with the wicked, and with the rich in His death." Jesus would be buried in a rich man's tomb!

Joseph arranged to have the tomb hewn out, and the men assembled the cloths and spices needed for the burial. They may have been hiding in the tomb all during the six hours of our Lord's agony on the cross. When they heard, "It is finished! Father, into Thy hands I commend My spirit!" they knew that He was dead; and they went to work. They boldly identified with Jesus Christ at a time when He seemed like a failure and His cause hopelessly defeated. As far as we know, of all the disciples, only John was with them at the cross.

The Sabbath was about to dawn. Jesus had finished the work of the "new creation" (2 Cor. 5:17), and now He would rest.

CHAPTER TWENTY-TWO THE DAWNING OF A NEW DAY

John 20:1-18

If the Gospel of John were an ordinary biography, there would be no chapter 20. I am an incurable reader of biographies, and I notice that almost all of them conclude with the death and burial of the subject. I have yet to read one that describes the subject's resurrection from the dead! The fact that John continued his account and shared the excitement of the Resurrection miracle is proof that Jesus Christ is not like any other man. He is, indeed, the Son of God.

The Resurrection is an essential part of the Gospel message (1 Cor. 15:1-8) and a key doctrine in the Christian faith. It proves that Jesus Christ is the Son of God (Acts 2:32-36; Rom. 1:4) and that His atoning work on the cross has been completed and is effective (Rom. 4:24-25). The empty cross and the empty tomb are God's "receipts" telling us that the debt has been paid. Jesus Christ is not only the Saviour, but He is also the Sanctifier (Rom. 6:4-10) and the Intercessor (Rom. 8:34). One day He shall return as Judge (Acts 17:30-31).

From the very beginning, the enemies of the Lord tried to deny the historic fact of the Resurrection. The Jewish leaders claimed that the Lord's body had been stolen from the tomb. This statement is absurd, for if the body was stolen by His followers, how did they do it? The tomb was guarded by Roman soldiers and the stone sealed by an official Roman seal. Furthermore, His disciples *did not believe* that He was to be raised from the dead; it was His enemies who remembered His words (Matt. 27:62-66). *They* certainly would not have taken the body! The last thing they wanted was anyone believing that Jesus had indeed risen from the dead. If His friends *could not* steal the body, and His enemies *would not,* then who took it?

Perhaps the disciples had "visions" of the risen Lord and interpreted them as evidences for the Resurrection. But they did not *expect* to see Him, and that is not the kind of psychological preparation from which hallucinations are made. And how could more than 500 people have the same hallucination at the same time? (1 Cor. 15:6)

Did the followers of our Lord perhaps go to the wrong tomb? Not likely. They carefully watched where He was buried (Matt. 27:61; Mark 15:47; Luke 23:55-57). They loved the Master and were not likely to get confused about His resting place. In fact, as the women approached the tomb, they were worried about who would roll back the heavy stone (Mark 16:1-3); so they were acquainted with the situation.

As to the foolish argument that Jesus did not die, but only swooned and was later revived, little need be said. It was proved by many witnesses that Jesus was dead when His body was taken from the cross. Later, He was seen alive by dependable witnesses. The only logical conclusion is that He kept His promise and arose from the dead.

But the glorious truth of the Resurrection was not understood immediately by even His closest followers. It gradually dawned on these grieving people that their Master was not dead, but alive! And what a difference it made when the full realization of His resurrection took hold of them! For Mary Magdalene it meant moving from tears to joy (John 20:1-18); for the ten disciples it meant going from fear to courage (John 20:19-23); and for Thomas it meant moving from doubt to assurance (John 20:24-31). With Mary, the emphasis is on love; with the ten, the emphasis is on hope; and with Thomas, the emphasis is on faith.

As we consider Mary Magdalene's experience that Lord's Day morning, we can see three stages in her comprehension of the truth of the Resurrection. Peter and John are also a part of this experience.

Faith Eclipsed (John 20:1-2)

Mary Magdalene and several other women agreed to go to the tomb early on the first day of the week, so that they might show their love for Christ in completing the burial preparations. Joseph of Arimathea and Nicodemus had been forced by circumstances to prepare His body hastily, and the women wanted to finish the task. Their great concern was how to get into the tomb. Perhaps the Roman soldiers would take pity on them and give them a hand.

What they did not know was that an earthquake had occurred and the stone had been rolled back by an angel! It seems that Mary

Magdalene went ahead of the other women and got to the tomb first. When she saw the stone rolled away from the door of the tomb, she concluded that somebody had broken into the tomb and stolen the body of her Lord. We may criticize Mary for jumping to conclusions; but when you consider the circumstances, it is difficult to see how she would have reached any other conclusion. It was still dark, she was alone, and, like the other followers of Jesus, she did not believe that He would return from the dead.

She ran to give the news to Peter and John, who must have been living together at a place known to the other believers. Perhaps it was the Upper Room where they had met with Jesus. Mary's use of the pronoun "we" is interesting, for it included the other women who at that moment were discovering that Jesus was alive! (see Mark 16:1-8 and Luke 24:1-8) The women left the tomb and carried the angels' message to the other disciples.

It is significant that the first witnesses of the resurrection of Christ were *believing women.* Among the Jews in that day, the testimony of women was not held in high regard. "It is better that the words of the Law be burned," said the rabbis, "than be delivered to a woman." But these Christian women had a greater message than that of the Law, for they knew that their Saviour was alive.

Mary's faith was not extinguished; it was only eclipsed. The light was still there, but it was covered. Peter and John were in the same spiritual condition, but soon all three of them would move out of the shadows and into the light.

Faith Dawning (John 20:3-10)

John 20:3 suggests that Peter started off first to run to the tomb, but John 20:4 reports that John got there first. Perhaps John was a younger man in better physical condition, or perhaps John was just a better runner. It is tempting to "spiritualize" this footrace and relate it to Isaiah 40:31 and Hebrews 12:1-2. When a believer is out of fellowship with the Lord, it is difficult to run the race of faith. However, both men deserve credit for having the courage to run into enemy territory, not knowing what lay before them. The whole thing could have been a clever trap to catch the disciples.

When John arrived at the tomb, he cautiously remained outside and looked in. Perhaps he wanted Peter to be with him when he went into the burial chamber. What did John see? The graveclothes lying on the stone shelf without any evidence of violence or crime. *But the graveclothes were empty!* They lay there like an empty cocoon, still retaining the shape of Jesus' body.

Peter arrived and impulsively went into the tomb, just as we would expect him to do. He also saw the linen clothes lying there empty and the cloth for the head carefully rolled and lying by itself. Grave robbers do not carefully unwrap the corpse and then leave the graveclothes neatly behind. In fact, with the presence of the spices in the folds of the clothes, it would be almost impossible to unwrap a corpse without damaging the wrappings. The only way those linen clothes could be left in that condition would be if Jesus *passed through them* as He arose from the dead.

John then entered the tomb and looked at the evidence. "He saw, and believed."

When John wrote this account, he used three different Greek words for *seeing.* In John 20:5, the verb simply means "to glance in, to look in." In John 20:6, the word means "to look carefully, to observe." The word "saw" in John 20:8 means "to perceive with intelligent comprehension." Their Resurrection faith was now dawning!

It seems incredible that the followers of Jesus did not expect Him to come out of the tomb alive. After all, He had told them many times that He would be raised from the dead. Early in His ministry He had said, "Destroy this temple, and in three days I will raise it up" (John 2:19). After His resurrection, the disciples remembered that He had said this (John 2:22); however, His enemies remembered it too (Matt. 27:40, 63-64).

He compared Himself to Jonah (Matt. 12:40), and on two occasions clearly announced His resurrection after three days (Matt. 16:21; 20:19). On Thursday of His last week of ministry He again promised to be raised up and meet them in Galilee (Matt. 26:32, and see Luke 24:6-7).

What kind of faith did Peter and John have at that stage in their spiritual experience? They had faith based on evidence. They could see the graveclothes; they knew that the body of Jesus was not there. However, as good as evidence is to convince the mind, it can never change the life. Those of us who live centuries later cannot examine the evidence, for the material evidence (the tomb, the graveclothes) is no longer there for us to inspect.

But we have the record in the Word of God (John 20:9) and that record is true (John 19:35; 21:24). In fact, it is faith *in the Word* that the Lord really wanted to cultivate in His disciples (see John 2:22; 12:16; 14:26). Peter made it clear that the Word of God, not personal experiences, should be the basis for our faith (1 Peter 1:12-21).

The disciples had only the Old Testament Scriptures, so that is what is referred to in John 20:9. The early church used the Old Testament to prove to both Jews and Gentiles that Jesus is the Christ, that He died for sinners, and that He arose again (Acts 9:22; 13:16ff; 17:1-4; etc.). The Gospel includes "and that He arose again the third day according to the Scriptures" (1 Cor. 15:4). What Scriptures did Paul and John have in mind?

Paul saw the Resurrection in Psalm 2:7 (Acts 13:33). Peter saw it in Psalm 16:8-11 (Acts 2:23-36 and note 13:35). Peter also referred to Psalm 110:1 (Acts 2:34-35). The statement "He shall prolong His days" in Isaiah 53:10 is also interpreted as a prediction of Christ's resurrection. Jesus Himself used the Prophet Jonah to illustrate His own death, burial, and resurrection (Matt. 12:38-40); and this would include the "three days" part of the message. Paul saw in the Feast of Firstfruits a picture of the Resurrection (Lev. 23:9-14; 1 Cor. 15:20-23), and again, this would include "the third day." Some students see the Resurrection and "the third day" in Hosea 6:2.

After His resurrection, our Lord did not reveal Himself to everyone, but only to selected witnesses who would share the good news with others (Acts 10:39-43). This witness is now found in Scripture, the New Testament; and both the Old Testament and the New Testament agree in their witness. The Law, the Psalms, the Prophets, and the Apostles together bear witness that Jesus Christ is alive!

Peter and John saw the evidence and believed. Later, the Holy Spirit confirmed their faith through the Old Testament Scriptures. That evening, they would meet the Master personally! Faith that was eclipsed has now started to dawn, and the light will get brighter.

Faith Shining (John 20:11-18)

When I think of Mary Magdalene lingering alone in the garden, I recall Proverbs 8:17—"I love them that love Me; and those that seek Me early shall find Me." Mary loved her Lord and came early to the garden to express that love. Peter and John had gone home by the time Mary got back to the tomb, so they did not convey to her what conclusion they had reached from the evidence they had examined. Mary still thought that Jesus was dead. Another verse comes to mind—Psalm 30:5, "Weeping may endure for a night, but joy cometh in the morning."

Mary's weeping was the loud lamentation so characteristic of Jewish people when they express their sorrow (John 11:31, 33). There is certainly nothing wrong with sincere sorrow, because God made us to shed tears; and weeping is good therapy for broken hearts. The sorrow of the Christian, however, must be different from the hopeless sorrow of the world (1 Thes. 4:13-18), because we have been born again "unto a living hope by the resurrection of Jesus Christ from the dead" (1 Peter 1:3, NASB). We weep—not because our believing loved ones have gone to heaven—but because they have left us and we miss them.

When Mary looked into the sepulcher, she saw two men in white. Their position at either end of the shelf where the body had been lying makes us think of the cherubim on the mercy seat (Ex. 25:17-19). It is as though God is saying, "There is now a new mercy seat! My Son has paid the price for sin, and the way is open into the presence of God!" Mary apparently was not disturbed at seeing these men, and there is no evidence that she knew they were angels. The brief conversation neither dried her tears nor quieted her mind. She was determined to find the body of Jesus.

Why did Mary turn back and not continue her conversation with the two strangers? Did she hear a sound behind her? Or did the angels stand and recognize the presence of their Lord? Perhaps both of these speculations are true or neither is true. She was certain that the Lord's body was not in the tomb, so why linger there any longer?

Why did she not recognize the One for whom she was so earnestly searching? Jesus may have deliberately concealed Himself from her, as He would later do when He walked with the Emmaus disciples (Luke 24:13-32). It was still early and perhaps dark in that part of the garden. Her eyes were probably blinded by her tears as well.

Jesus asked her the same question that the angels had asked, "Why are you weeping?"

How tragic that she was weeping when she could have been praising, had she realized that her Lord was alive! Then He added, "Whom are you seeking?" (He had asked the mob the same question in the Garden—John 18:4.) It is encouraging to us to know that "Jesus knows all about our sorrows." The Saviour knew that Mary's heart was broken and that her mind was confused. He did not rebuke her; tenderly, He revealed Himself to her.

All He had to do was to speak her name, and Mary immediately recognized Him. His sheep hear [recognize] His voice and He calls them by name (John 10:3). Apparently Mary had turned away from Jesus, for when He spoke her name, she had to turn back to look at Him again. What a blessed surprise it was to see the face of her beloved Master!

All she could say was, "Rabboni—my Master, my Teacher." The title *Rabboni* is used in only one other place in the Gospels, Mark 10:51 (in the Greek text "Lord" is "Rabboni"). "Rabbi" and "Rabboni" were equivalent terms of respect. In later years, the Jews recognized three levels of teachers: rab (the lowest), rabbi, and rabboni (the highest).

Mary not only spoke to Him, but she grasped His feet and held on to Him. This was a natural gesture: now that she had found Him, she did not want to lose Him. She and the other believers still had a great deal to learn about His new state of glory; they still wanted to relate to Him as they had done during the years of His ministry before the cross.

Jesus permitted the other women to hold His feet (Matt. 28:9), and He did not forbid them. Why did He say to Mary, "Do not cling to Me"? One reason was that she would see Him again because He had not yet ascended to the Father. He remained on earth for forty days after His resurrection and often appeared to the believers to teach them spiritual truth (Acts 1:1-9). Mary had no need to panic; this was not her last and final meeting with the Lord.

A second reason is that she had a job to do—to go tell His brethren that He was alive and would ascend to the Father. "He is not ashamed to call them brethren" (Heb. 2:11). "I will declare Thy name unto My brethren" (Ps. 22:22). He had called His own *servants* (John 13:16) and *friends* (John 15:15), but now He called them *brethren.* This meant that they shared His resurrection power and glory.

Some students feel that Jesus did return to the Father on that morning, and that was the ascension He was referring to; but no other New Testament passage corroborates this interpretation. To say that He was fulfilling the symbolism of the Day of Atonement and presenting the blood to the Father is, I think, stretching a type too far (Lev. 16). For that matter, *He had no blood to present;* He had presented that on the cross when He was made sin for us. In His resurrection glory, Jesus was "flesh and bones" (Luke 24:39), not "flesh and blood." The Resurrection itself was proof that the work of redemption had been completed ("raised because of our justification"—Rom. 4:24-25, NASB). What more could He do?

Our Lord never used the phrases "our Father" or "our God." His relationship to the Father was different from that of the disciples, and He was careful to make that distinction. We say "our Father" and "our God" because all believers belong to the same family and have an equal standing before God. He reminded Mary and the other believers that God was their Father and that He would be with the Father in heaven after His ascension. In His Upper Room message, He had taught them that He would return to the Father so that the Spirit might come to them.

Though it was the same Jesus, only in a glorified body, it was not quite the same relationship. We must be careful not to relate to Christ "after the flesh" (1 Cor. 5:16), that is, relate to Him as though He were still in His state of humiliation. He is today the exalted Son of God in glory, and we must honor Him as such. The juvenile familiarity that some people display in public when they testify, pray, or sing only reveals that they have little understanding of Paul's words in 2 Corinthians 5:16. When John was with Jesus at the table, he leaned against His bosom (John 13:23); but when John saw Jesus on the Isle of Patmos, he fell at His feet as dead! (Rev. 1:17)

It would have been selfish and disobedient for Mary to have clung to Jesus and kept Him to herself. She arose and went to where the disciples were gathered and gave them the good news that she had seen Jesus alive. "I have seen the Lord!" (Note John 20:14, 18, 20, 25, 29.) Mark reports that these believers were mourning and weeping—and that they would not believe her! (Mark 16:9-11) Mary herself had been weeping, and Jesus had turned her sorrow into joy. If they had believed, their sorrow would also have turned to joy. Unbelief has a terribly deadening effect on a person. No wonder God warns us against "an evil heart of unbelief" (Heb. 3:12).

Mary not only shared the fact of His resurrection and that she had seen Him personally, but she also reported the words that He had spoken to her. Again, we see the importance of the Word of God. Mary could not transfer her experience over to them, but she could share the Word; and it is the Word that generates faith (Rom. 10:17). The living Christ shared His living Word (1 Peter 1:23-25).

It is good to have faith that is based on solid evidence, but the evidence should lead us to the Word, and the Word should lead us to the Saviour. It is one thing to accept a doctrine and defend it; it is something else to have a personal relationship to the living Lord. Peter and John believed that Jesus was alive, but it was not until that evening that they met the risen Christ in person along with the other disciples. (Jesus appeared to Peter sometime during the afternoon, Luke 24:34; 1 Cor. 15:5.) Evidence that does not lead to experience is nothing but dead dogma. The key is faith in the Word of God.

Dr. Robert W. Dale, one of Great Britain's leading Congregational pastors and theologians, was one day preparing an Easter sermon when a realization of the risen Lord struck him with new power.

"Christ is alive!" he said to himself. "Alive—alive—alive!" He paused, and then said, "Can that really be true? *Living* as really as I myself am?"

He got up from his desk and began to walk about the study, repeating, "Christ is living! Christ is living!"

Dr. Dale had known and believed this doctrine for years, but the reality of it overwhelmed him that day. From that time on, "the living Christ" was the theme of his preaching, and he had his congregation sing an Easter hymn every Sunday morning. "I want my people to get hold of the glorious fact that Christ is alive, and to rejoice over it; and Sunday, you know, is the day on which Christ left the dead."

Historical faith says, "Christ lives!"
Saving faith says, "Christ lives *in me!*"
Do you have saving faith?

CHAPTER TWENTY-THREE
THE POWER OF HIS RESURRECTION
John 20:19-31

The news that Jesus was alive began to spread among His followers, at first with hesitation, but then with enthusiasm. Even His disciples did not believe the first reports, and Thomas demanded proof. But wherever people were confronted with the reality of His resurrection, their lives were transformed. In fact, that same transforming experience can be yours today. As you see in John 20:19-31 the changes that took place in the lives of people, ask yourself, "Have I personally met the risen Christ? Has He changed *my* life?"

From Fear to Courage (John 20:19-25)
Our Lord rested in the tomb on the Sabbath and arose from the dead on the first day of the week. Many people sincerely call Sunday "the Christian Sabbath," but Sunday is not the Sabbath Day. The seventh day of the week, the Sabbath, commemorates God's finished work of Creation (Gen. 2:1-3). The Lord's Day commemorates Christ's finished work of redemption, the "new creation." God the Father worked for six days and then rested. God the Son suffered on the cross for six hours and then rested.

God gave the Sabbath to Israel as a special "sign" that they belonged to Him (Ex. 20:8-11; 31:13-17; Neh. 9:14). The nation was to use that day for physical rest and refreshment both for man and beast; but for Israel, it was not commanded as a special day of assembly and worship. Unfortunately, the scribes and Pharisees added all kinds of restrictions to the Sabbath observance until it became a day of bondage instead of a day of blessing. Jesus deliberately violated the Sabbath traditions, though He honored the Sabbath Day.

There were at least five Resurrection appearances of our Lord on that first day of the week: to Mary Magdalene (John 20:11-18), the other women (Matt. 28:9-10), Peter (1 Cor. 15:5 and Luke 24:34), the two Emmaus disciples (Luke 24:13-32), and the disciples minus Thomas (John 20:19-25). The next Sunday, the disciples met again and Thomas was with them (John 20:26-31). It would appear that the believers from the very first met together on Sunday evening, which came to be called "the Lord's Day" (Rev. 1:10). It appears that the early church met on the first day of the week to worship the Lord and commemorate His death and resurrection (Acts 20:7; 1 Cor. 16:1-2).

The Sabbath was over when Jesus arose from the dead (Mark 16:1). He arose on the first day of the week (Matt. 28:1; Luke 24:1; John 20:1). The change from the seventh day to the first day was not effected by some church decree; it was brought about from the beginning by the faith and witness of the first believers. For centuries, the Jewish Sabbath had been associated with Law: six days of work, and then you rest. But the Lord's Day, the first day of the week, is associated with grace: first there is faith in the living Christ, then there will be works.

There is no evidence in Scripture that God ever gave the original Sabbath command to the Gentiles, or that it was repeated for the church to obey. Nine of the Ten Commandments are repeated in the church epistles, but the Sabbath commandment is not repeated. However, Paul makes it clear that believers must not make "special days" a test of fellowship or spirituality (Rom. 14:5ff; Col. 2:16-23).

How did our Lord transform His disciples' fear into courage? For one thing, *He came to them.* We do not know where these ten frightened men met behind locked doors, but Jesus came to them and reassured them. In His resurrection body, He was able to enter the room without opening the doors! It was a solid body, for He asked them to touch Him—and He even ate some fish (Luke 24:41-43). But it was a different kind of body, one that was not limited by what we call "the laws of nature."

It is remarkable that these men were actually afraid. The women had reported to them that Jesus was alive, and the two Emmaus disciples had added their personal witness (Luke 24:33-35). It is likely that Jesus had appeared personally to Peter sometime that afternoon (Mark 16:7; Luke 24:34; 1 Cor. 15:5), though Peter's *public* restoration would not take place until later (John 21). No wonder Jesus reproached them at that time "with their unbelief and hardness of heart" (Mark 16:14).

But His first word to them was the traditional greeting, "Shalom—peace!" He could have rebuked them for their unfaithfulness and cowardice the previous weekend, but He did not. "He hath not dealt with us after our sins; nor rewarded us according to our iniquities" (Ps. 103:10). The work of the cross is peace (Rom. 5:1; Eph. 2:14-17), and the message they would carry would be the Gospel of peace (Rom. 10:15). Man had declared war on God (Ps. 2; Acts 4:23-30), but God would declare "Peace!" to those who would believe.

Not only did Jesus come to them, but *He reassured them.* He showed them His wounded hands and side and gave them opportunity to discover that it was indeed their Master, and that He was not a phantom. (The Gospels do not record wounds in His feet, but Psalm 22:16 indicates that His feet were also nailed to the cross.)

But the wounds meant more than identification; they also were evidence that the price for salvation had been paid and man indeed could have "peace with God." The basis for all our peace is found in the person and work of Jesus Christ. He died for us, He arose from the dead in victory, and now He lives for us. In our fears, we cannot lock Him out! He comes to us in grace and reassures us through His Word. "Faithful are the wounds of a friend" (Prov. 27:6).

When Jesus saw that the disciples' fear had now turned to joy, *He commissioned them:* "As My Father hath sent Me, even so send I you" (John 20:21). Keep in mind that the original disciples were not the only ones present; others, including the Emmaus disciples, were also in the room. This commission was not the "formal ordination" of a church order; rather, it was the dedication of His followers to the task of world evangelism. We are to take His place in this world (John 17:18). What a tremendous privilege and what a great responsibility! It is humbling to realize that Jesus loves us as the Father loves Him (John 15:9; 17:26), and that we are in the Father just as He is (John 17:21-22). It is equally as humbling to realize that He has sent us into the world just as the Father sent Him. As He was about to ascend to heaven, He again reminded them of their commission to take the message to the whole world (Matt. 28:18-20).

It must have given the men great joy to realize that, in spite of their many failures, their Lord was entrusting them with His Word and His work. They had forsaken Him and fled, but now He was sending them out to represent Him. Peter had denied Him three times; and yet in a few days, Peter would preach the Word (and accuse the Jews of denying Him—Acts 3:13-14!) and thousands would be saved.

Jesus came to them and reassured them; but He also *enabled them* through the Holy Spirit. John 20:22 reminds us of Genesis 2:7 when God breathed life into the first man. In both Hebrew and Greek, the word for "breath" also means "spirit." The breath of God in the first creation meant physical life, and the breath of Jesus Christ in the new creation meant spiritual life. The believers would receive the baptism of the Spirit at Pentecost and be empowered for ministry (Acts 1:4-5; 2:1-4). Apart from the filling of the Spirit, they could not go forth to witness effectively. The Spirit had dwelt *with* them in the person of Christ, but now the Spirit would be *in* them (John 14:17).

John 20:23 must not be interpreted to mean that Jesus gave to a select body of people the right to forgive sins and let people into heaven. Jesus had spoken similar words before (Matt. 16:19), but He was not setting aside the disciples (and their successors) as a "spiritual elite" to deal with the sins of the world. Remember, there were others in the room besides the disciples, and Thomas was missing!

A correct understanding of the Greek text helps us here. Some years ago, I corresponded with the eminent Greek scholar Dr. Julius R. Mantey (now deceased) about this verse, and he assured me that the correct translation both here and in Matthew 16:19 should be: "Whosoever sins you remit [forgive] shall have already been forgiven them, and whosoever sins you retain [do not forgive] shall have already not been forgiven them." In other words, the disciples did not provide forgiveness; they proclaimed forgiveness on the basis of the message of the Gospel. Another Greek scholar, Dr. Kenneth Wuest, translates it "they have been previously forgiven them."

As the early believers went forth into the world, they announced the good news of salvation. If sinners would repent and believe on Jesus Christ, their sins would be forgiven them! "Who can forgive sins but God only?" (Mark 2:7) All that the Christian can do is announce the message of forgiveness; God performs the miracle of forgiveness. If sinners will believe on Jesus Christ, we can authoritatively declare to them that their sins have been forgiven; but we are not the ones who provide the forgiveness.

By now, their fears had vanished. They were sure that the Lord was alive and that He was caring for them. They had both "peace with God" and the "peace of God" (Phil. 4:6-7). They had a high and holy commission and the power provided to accomplish it. And they had been given the great privilege of bearing the good news of forgiveness to the whole world. All they now had to do was tarry in Jerusalem until the Holy Spirit would be given.

From Unbelief to Confidence (John 20:26-28)

Why was Thomas not with the other disciples when they met on the evening of Resurrection Day? Was he so disappointed that he did not want to be with his friends? But when we are discouraged and defeated, we need our friends all the more! Solitude only feeds discouragement and helps it grow into self-pity, which is even worse.

Perhaps Thomas was afraid. But John 11:16 seems to indicate that he was basically a courageous man, willing to go to Judea and die with the Lord! John 14:5 reveals that Thomas was a spiritually minded man who wanted to know the truth and was not ashamed to ask questions. There seems to have been a "pessimistic" outlook in Thomas. We call him "Doubting Thomas," but Jesus did not rebuke him for his doubts. He rebuked him for unbelief: "Be not faithless, but believing." Doubt is often an intellectual problem: we want to believe, but the faith is overwhelmed by problems and questions. Unbelief is a moral problem; we simply will not believe.

What was it that Thomas would not believe? The reports of the other Christians that Jesus Christ was alive. The verb *said* in John 20:25 means that the disciples "kept saying to him" that they had seen the Lord Jesus Christ alive. No doubt the women and the Emmaus pilgrims also added their witness to this testimony. On the one hand, we admire Thomas for wanting *personal* experience; but on the other hand, we must fault him for laying down conditions for the Lord to meet.

Like most people in that day, he had two names: "Thomas" is Aramaic, "Didymus" is Greek, and they both mean "twin." Who was Thomas' twin? We do not know—but sometimes you and I feel as if we might be his twins! How often we have refused to believe and have insisted that God prove Himself to us!

Thomas is a good warning to all of us not to miss meeting with God's people on the Lord's Day (Heb. 10:22-25). Because Thomas was not there, he missed seeing Jesus Christ, hearing His words of peace, and receiving His commission and gift of spiritual life. He had to endure a week of fear and unbelief when he could have been experiencing joy and peace! Remember Thomas when you are tempted to stay home from church. You never know what special blessing you might miss!

But let's give him credit for showing up the next week. The other ten men had told Thomas that they had seen the Lord's hands and side (John 20:20), so Thomas made that the test. Thomas had been there when Jesus raised Lazarus, so why should he question our Lord's own resurrection? But, he still wanted proof; "seeing is believing."

Thomas' words help us to understand the difference between *doubt* and *unbelief.* Doubt says, "I cannot believe! There are too many problems!" Unbelief says, "I *will not* believe unless you give me the evidence I ask for!" In fact, in the Greek text, there is a double negative: "I positively will not believe!"

Jesus had heard Thomas' words; nobody had to report them to Him. So, the next Lord's Day, the Lord appeared in the room (again, the doors were locked) and dealt personally with Thomas and his unbelief. He still greeted them with "Shalom—peace!" Even Thomas' unbelief could not rob the other disciples of their peace and joy in the Lord.

How gracious our Lord is to stoop to our level of experience in order to lift us where we ought to be. The Lord granted Gideon the "tests of faith" that he requested (Jud. 6:36-40), and He granted Thomas his request as well. There is no record that Thomas ever accepted the Lord's invitation. When the time came to prove his faith, Thomas needed no more proof!

Our Lord's words translate literally, "Stop becoming faithless but become a believer." Jesus saw a dangerous process at work in Thomas' heart, and He wanted to put a stop to it. The best commentary on this is Hebrews 3, where God warns against "an evil heart of unbelief" (Heb. 3:12).

It is not easy to understand the psychology of doubt and unbelief. Perhaps it is linked to personality traits; some people are more trustful than others. Perhaps Thomas was so depressed that he was ready to quit, so he "threw out a challenge" and never really expected Jesus to accept it. At any rate, Thomas was faced with his own words, and he had to make a decision.

John 20:29 indicates that Thomas' testimony did not come from his *touching* Jesus, but from his *seeing* Jesus. "My Lord and my God!" is the last of the testimonies that John records to the deity of Jesus Christ. The others are: John the Baptist (John 1:34); Nathanael (John 1:49); Jesus Himself (John 5:25; 10:36); Peter (John 6:69); the healed blind man (John 9:35); Martha (John 11:27); and, of course, John himself (John 20:30-31).

It is an encouragement to us to know that the Lord had a personal interest in and concern for "Doubting Thomas." He wanted to strengthen his faith and include him in the blessings that lay in store for His followers. Thomas reminds us that unbelief robs us of blessings and opportunities. It may sound sophisticated and intellectual to question what Jesus did, but such questions are usually evidence of hard hearts, not of searching minds. Thomas represents the "scientific approach" to life—and it did not work! After all, when a skeptic says, "I will not believe unless—" he is already admitting that he does believe! He believes in the validity of the test or experiment that he has devised! If he can have faith in his own "scientific approach," why can he not have faith in what God has revealed?

We need to remind ourselves that everybody lives by faith. The difference is in the *object* of that faith. Christians put their faith in God and His Word, while unsaved people put their faith in themselves.

From Death to Life (John 20:29-31)

John could not end his book without bringing the Resurrection miracle to his own readers. We must not look at Thomas and the other disciples and envy them, as though the power of Christ's resurrection could never be experienced in our lives today. *That was why John wrote this Gospel*—so that people in *every* age could know that Jesus is God and that faith in Him brings everlasting life.

It is not necessary to "see" Jesus Christ in order to believe. Yes, it was a blessing for the early Christians to see their Lord and know that He was alive; but that is not what saved them. They were saved, not by seeing, but by believing. The emphasis throughout the Gospel of John is on *believing.* There are nearly 100 references in this Gospel to believing on Jesus Christ.

You and I today cannot see Christ, nor can we see Him perform the miracles (signs) that John wrote about in this book. But the record is there, and that is all that we need. "So then faith cometh by hearing, and hearing by the word of God" (Rom. 10:17; and note 1 John 5:9-13). As you read John's record, you come face to face with Jesus Christ, how He lived, what He said, and what He did. All of the evidence points to the conclusion that He is indeed God come in the flesh, the Saviour of the world.

The signs that John selected and described in this book are proof of the deity of Christ. They are important. But sinners are not saved by believing in miracles; they are saved by believing on Jesus Christ. Many of the Jews in Jerusalem believed on Jesus because of His miracles, but He did not believe in them! (John 2:23-25) Great crowds followed Him because of His miracles (John 6:2); but in the end, most of them left Him for good (John 6:66). Even the religious leaders who plotted His death believed that He did miracles, but this "faith" did not save them (John 11:47ff).

Faith in His miracles should lead to faith in His Word, and to personal faith in Jesus as Saviour and Lord. Jesus Himself pointed out that faith in His works (miracles) was but *the first step* toward faith in the Word of God (John 5:36-40). The sinner must "hear" the Word if he is to be saved (John 5:24).

There was no need for John to decribe every miracle that our Lord performed; in fact, he supposed that a complete record could never be written (John 21:25). The life and ministry of Jesus Christ were simply too rich and full for any writer, even an inspired one, to give a complete record. But a complete record is not necessary. All of the basic facts are here for us to read and consider. There is sufficient truth for any sinner to believe and be saved!

The *subject* of John's Gospel is "Jesus is the Christ, the Son of God." He presented a threefold proof of this thesis: our Lord's works, our Lord's walk, and our Lord's words. In this Gospel, you see Jesus performing miracles; you watch Him living a perfect life in the midst of His enemies; and you hear Him speaking words that nobody else could speak.

Either Jesus was a madman, or He was deluded, or He was all that He claimed to be. While some of His enemies did call Him deranged and deluded, the majority of people who watched Him and listened to Him concluded that He was unique, unlike anyone else they had ever known. How could a madman or a deluded man accomplish what Jesus accomplished? *When people trusted Him, their lives were transformed!* That does not happen when you trust a madman or a deceiver.

He claimed to be God come in the flesh, the Son of God, the Saviour of the world. That is what He is!

John was not content simply to explain a subject. He was an evangelist who wanted to achieve an object. He wanted his readers to believe in Jesus Christ and be saved! He was not writing a biography to entertain or a history to enlighten. He was writing an evangel to change men's lives.

"Life" is one of John's key words; he uses it at least thirty-six times. Jesus offers sinners abundant life and eternal life; and the only way they can get it is through personal faith in Him.

If sinners need life, then the implication is that they are *dead.* "And you hath He quickened [made alive, resurrected] who were dead in trespasses and sins" (Eph. 2:1). Salvation is not resuscitation; it is resurrection (John 5:24). The lost sinner is not sick or weak; *he is dead.*

This life comes "through His name." What is His name? In John's Gospel, the emphasis is on His name "I AM." Jesus makes seven great "I AM" statements in this Gospel, offering the lost sinner all that he needs.

Eternal life is not "endless time," for even lost people are going to live forever in hell. "Eternal life" means *the very life of God experienced today.* It is a quality of life, not a quantity of time. It is the spiritual experience of "heaven on earth" today. The Christian does not have to die to have this eternal life; he possesses it in Christ today.

The ten disciples were changed from fear to courage, and Thomas was changed from unbelief to confidence. Now, John invites *you* to trust Jesus Christ and be changed from death to eternal life.

If you have already made this life-changing decision, give thanks to God for the precious gift of eternal life.

If you have never made this decision, *do so right now.*

"He that believeth on the Son hath everlasting life; and he that believeth not the Son shall not see life, but the wrath of God abideth on him" (John 3:36).

CHAPTER TWENTY-FOUR TRANSFORMED TO SERVE
John 21

The average reader would conclude that John completed his book with the dramatic testimony of Thomas (John 20:28-31), and the reader would wonder why John added another chapter. The main reason is the Apostle Peter, John's close associate in ministry (Acts 3:1). John did not want to end his Gospel without telling his readers that Peter was restored to his apostleship. Apart from the information in this chapter, we would wonder why Peter was so prominent in the first twelve chapters of the Book of Acts.

John had another purpose in mind: he wanted to refute the foolish rumor that had spread among the believers that John would live until the return of the Lord (John 21:23). John made it clear that our Lord's words had been greatly misunderstood.

I think John may have had another purpose in mind: he wanted to teach us how to relate to the risen Christ. During the forty days between His resurrection and ascension, our Lord appeared and disappeared at will, visiting with the disciples and preparing them for the coming of the Spirit and their future ministries (Acts 1:1-9). They never knew when He would appear, so they had to stay alert! (The fact that He may return for His people *today* ought to keep us on our toes!) It was an important time for the disciples because they were about to take His place in the world and begin to carry the message to others.

I see in this chapter three pictures of the believer and a responsibility attached to each picture.

We Are Fishers of Men—Obey Him (John 21:1-8)

The Lord had instructed His disciples to meet Him in Galilee, which helps to explain why they were at the Sea of Galilee, or Sea of Tiberias (Matt. 26:32; 28:7-10; Mark 16:7). But John did not explain why Peter decided to go fishing, and Bible students are not in agreement in their suggestions. Some claim that he was perfectly within his rights, that he needed to pay his bills and the best way to get money was to go fishing. Why sit around idle? Get busy!

Others believe that Peter had been called *from* that kind of life (Luke 5:1-11) and that it was wrong for him to return. Furthermore, when he went fishing, Peter took six other men with him! If he was wrong, they were wrong too; and it is a sad thing when a believer leads others astray.

By the way, it is interesting that at least seven of the twelve disciples were probably fishermen. Why did Jesus call so many fishermen to follow Him? For one thing, fishermen are courageous, and Jesus needs brave people to follow Him. They are also dedicated to one thing and cannot easily be distracted. Fishermen do not quit! (We are thinking, of course, of professional fishermen, not idle people on vacation!) They know how to take orders, and they know how to work together.

Whether Peter and his friends were right or wrong we cannot prove—though I personally think that they were wrong—but we do know this: their efforts were in vain. Had they forgotten the Lord's words, "For without Me, ye can do nothing"? (John 15:5) They toiled all night and caught nothing. Certainly, Peter must have remembered what happened two years before, when Jesus called him into full-time discipleship (Luke 5:1-11). On that occasion, Peter had fished all night and caught nothing, but Jesus had turned his failure into success.

Perhaps Peter's impulsiveness and self-confidence were revealing themselves again. He was sincere, and he worked hard, but there were no results. How like some believers in the service of the Lord! They sincerely believe that they are doing God's will, but their labors are in vain. They are serving without direction from the Lord, so they cannot expect blessing from the Lord.

After His resurrection, our Lord was sometimes not recognized (Luke 24:16; John 20:14); so it was that His disciples did not recognize Him when, at dawning, He appeared on the shore. His question expected a negative reply: "You have not caught anything to eat, have you?" Their reply was brief and perhaps a bit embarrassed: "No."

It was time for Jesus to take over the situation, just as He did when He called Peter into discipleship. He told them where to cast the net; they obeyed, and they caught 153 fish! The difference between success and failure was the width of the ship! We are never far from success when we permit Jesus to give the orders, and we are usually closer to success than we realize.

It was John who first realized that the stranger on the shore was their own Lord and Master. It was John who leaned on the Lord's breast at the table (John 13:23) and who stood by the cross when his Lord suffered and died (John 19:26). It is love that recognizes the Lord and shares that good news with others: "It is the Lord!"

With characteristic impulsiveness, Peter quickly put on his outer garment ("naked" simply means "stripped for work") and dove into the water! He wanted to get to Jesus! This is in contrast to Luke 5:8 where Peter told the Lord to depart from him. The other six men followed in the boat, bringing the net full of fish. In the experience recorded in Luke 5, the nets began to break; but in this experience, the net held fast.

Perhaps we can see in these two "fishing miracles" an illustration of how the Lord helps His people fish for lost souls. All of our efforts are useless apart from His direction and blessing. During this present age, we do not know how many fish we have caught, and it often appears that the nets are breaking! But at the end of the age, when we see the Lord, not one fish will be lost and we will discover how many there are.

Jesus called the disciples and us to be "fishers of men." This phrase was not invented by Jesus; it had been used for years by Greek and Roman teachers. To be a "fisher of men" in that day meant to seek to persuade men and "catch" them with the truth. A fisherman catches living fish, but when he gets them, they die. A Christian witness seeks to catch "dead fish" (dead in their sins), and when he or she "catches" them, they are made alive in Christ!

Now we can understand why Jesus had so many fishermen in the disciple band. Fishermen know how to work. They have courage and faith to go out "into the deep." They have much patience and persistence, and they will not quit. They know how to cooperate with one another, and they are skilled in using the equipment and the boat. What examples for us to follow as we seek to "catch fish" for Jesus Christ!

We are indeed "fishers of men," and there are "fish" all around us. If we obey His directions, we will catch the fish.

We Are Shepherds—Love Him (John 21:9-18)

Jesus met His disciples on the beach where He had already prepared breakfast for them. This entire scene must have stirred Peter's memory and touched his conscience. Surely he was recalling that first catch of fish (Luke 5:1-11) and perhaps even the feeding of the 5,000 with bread and fish (John 6). It was at the close of the latter event that Peter had given his clear-cut witness of faith in Jesus Christ (John 6:66-71). The "fire of coals" would certainly remind him of the fire at which he denied the Lord (John 18:18). It is good for us to remember the past; we may have something to confess.

Three "invitations" stand out in John's Gospel: "Come and see" (John 1:39); "Come and drink" (John 7:37); and "Come and dine" (John 21:12). How loving of Jesus to feed Peter before He dealt with his spiritual needs. He gave Peter opportunity to dry off, get warm, satisfy his hunger, and enjoy personal fellowship. This is a good example for us to follow as we care for God's people. Certainly the spiritual is more important than the physical, but caring for the physical can prepare the way for spiritual ministry. Our Lord does not so emphasize "the soul" that He neglects the body.

Peter and his Lord had already met privately and no doubt taken care of Peter's sins (Luke 24:34; 1 Cor. 15:5), but since Peter had denied the Lord *publicly,* it was important that there be a public restoration. Sin should be dealt with only to the extent that it is known. Private sins should be confessed in private, public sins in public. Since Peter had denied his Lord three times, Jesus asked him three personal questions. He also encouraged him by giving a threefold commission that restored Peter to his ministry.

The key issue is Peter's love for the Lord Jesus, and that should be a key matter with us today. But what did the Lord mean by "more than these"? Was He asking, "Do you love Me more than you love these other men?" Not likely, because this had never been a problem among the disciples. They all loved the Lord Jesus supremely, even though they did not always obey Him completely. Perhaps Jesus meant, "Do you love Me more than you love these boats and nets and fish?" Again, this is not likely, for there is no evidence that Peter ever desired to go back permanently into the fishing business. Fishing did not seem to compete with the Saviour's love.

The question probably meant, "Do you love Me—as you claimed—more than these other disciples love Me?" Peter had boasted of his love for Christ and had even contrasted it with that of the other men. "I will lay down my life for Thy sake!" (John 13:37) "Though all men shall be offended because of Thee, yet will I never be offended!" (Matt. 26:33) There is more than a hint in these boastful statements that Peter believed that he loved the Lord more than did the other disciples.

Many commentaries point out that, in this conversation, two different words are used for "love." In His questions in John 21:15-16, our Lord used *agape,* which is the Greek word for the highest kind of love, sacrificing love, divine love. Peter always used *phileo,* which is the love of friend for friend, fondness for another. In John 21:17, Jesus and Peter both used *phileo.*

However, it is doubtful that we should make too much of an issue over this, because the two words are often used interchangeably in the Gospel of John. In John 3:16, God's love for man is *agape* love; but in John 16:27, it is *phileo* love. The Father's love for His Son is *agape* love in John 3:35 but *phileo* love in John 5:20. Christians are supposed to love one another. In John 13:34, this love is *agape* love; but in John 15:19, it is *phileo* love. It would appear that John used these two words as synonyms, whatever fine distinctions there might have been between them.

Before we judge Peter too severely, two other matters should be considered. When answering the first two questions, Peter did affirm his *agape* love when he said, "Yes, Lord!" The fact that Peter himself used *phileo* did not negate his wholehearted assent to the Lord's use of *agape.* Second, Peter and Jesus undoubtedly spoke in Aramaic, even though the Holy Spirit recorded the conversation in common Greek. It might be unwise for us to press the Greek too far in this case.

In spite of his faults and failures, Peter did indeed love the Lord, and he was not ashamed to admit it. The other men were certainly listening "over Peter's shoulder" and benefiting from the conversation, for they too had failed the Lord after boasting of their devotion. Peter had already confessed his sin and been forgiven. Now he was being restored to apostleship and leadership.

The image, however, changes from that of the fisherman to that of the shepherd. Peter was to minister both as an evangelist (catching the fish) and a pastor (shepherding the flock). It is unfortunate when we divorce these two because they should go together. Pastors ought to evangelize (2 Tim. 4:5) and then shepherd the people they have won so that they mature in the Lord.

Jesus gave three admonitions to Peter: "Feed My lambs," "Shepherd My sheep," and "Feed My sheep." Both the lambs and the more mature sheep need feeding and leading, and that is the task of the spiritual shepherd. It is an awesome responsibility to be a shepherd of God's flock! (1 Peter 5:2) There are enemies that want to destroy the flock, and the shepherd must be alert and courageous (Acts 20:28-35). By nature, sheep are ignorant and defenseless, and they need the protection and guidance of the shepherd.

While it is true that the Holy Spirit equips people to serve as shepherds, and gives these people to churches (Eph. 4:11ff), it is also true that each individual Christian must help to care for the flock. Each of us has a gift or gifts from the Lord, and we should use what He has given us to help protect and perfect the flock. Sheep are prone to wander, and we must look after each other and encourage each other.

Jesus Christ is the Good Shepherd (John 10:11), the Great Shepherd (Heb. 13:20-21), and the Chief Shepherd (1 Peter 5:4). Pastors are "under-shepherds" who must obey Him as they minister to the flock. *The most important thing the pastor can do is to love Jesus Christ.* If he truly loves Jesus Christ, the pastor will also love His sheep and tenderly care for them. The Greek word for "sheep" at the end of John 21:17 means "dear sheep." Our Lord's sheep are dear to Him and He wants His ministers to love them and care for them personally and lovingly. (See Ezek. 34 for God's indictment of unfaithful shepherds, the leaders of Judah.) A pastor who loves the flock will serve it faithfully, no matter what the cost.

We Are Disciples—Follow Him (John 21:19-25)

Jesus had just spoken about Peter's life and ministry, and now He talks about Peter's death. This must have been a shock to Peter, to have the Lord discuss his death in such an open manner. No doubt Peter was rejoicing that he had been restored to fellowship and apostleship. Why bring up martyrdom?

The first time Jesus spoke about His own death, Peter had opposed it (Matt. 16:21ff). Peter had even used his sword in the Garden in a futile attempt to protect his Lord. Yet Peter had boasted he would die for the Lord Jesus! But when the pressure was on, Peter failed miserably. (You and I probably would have done worse!) Anyone who yields himself to serve the Lord must honestly confront this matter of death.

When a person has settled the matter of death, then he is ready to live and to serve! Our Lord's own death is a repeated theme in John's Gospel: He knew that His "hour" would come, and He was prepared to obey the Father's will. We as His followers must yield ourselves—just as He yielded Himself for us—and be "living sacrifices" (Rom. 12:1-2) who are "ready to be offered" (2 Tim. 4:6-8) if it is the will of God.

Earlier that morning, Peter had "girded himself" and hurried to shore to meet Jesus (John 21:7). The day would come when another would take charge of Peter—and kill him (see 2 Peter 1:13-14). Tradition tells us that Peter was indeed crucified, but that he asked to be crucified upside down, because he was not worthy to die exactly as his Master had died.

But Peter's death would not be a tragedy; it would glorify God! The death of Lazarus glorified God (John 11:4, 40) and so did the death of Jesus (John 12:23ff). Paul's great concern was that he glorify God, whether by life or by death (Phil. 1:20-21). This should be our desire as well.

Our Lord's words, "Follow Me!" must have brought new joy and love to Peter's heart. Literally, Jesus said, "Keep on following Me." Immediately, Peter began to follow Jesus, just as he had done before his great denial. However, for a moment *Peter took his eyes off the Lord Jesus,* a mistake he had made at least two other times. After that first great catch of fish, Peter took his eyes off his Lord and looked at *himself.* "Depart from me; for I am a sinful man, O Lord!" (Luke 5:8) When he was walking on the stormy sea with Jesus, Peter looked away from the Lord and began to look at the wind and waves; and immediately he began to sink (Matt. 14:30). It is dangerous to look at the circumstances instead of looking to the Lord.

Why did Peter look away from his Lord and start to look back? He heard somebody walking behind him. It was the Apostle John who was also following Jesus Christ. Peter did a foolish thing and asked Jesus, "What shall this man do?" In other words, "Lord, you just told me what will happen to me; now, what will happen to John?"

The Lord rebuked Peter and reminded him that his job was to follow, not to meddle into the lives of other believers. Beware when you get your eyes off the Lord and start to look at other Christians! "Looking unto Jesus" should be the aim and practice of every believer (Heb. 12:1-2). To be distracted by ourselves, our circumstances, or by other Christians, is to disobey the Lord and possibly get detoured out of the will of God. Keep your eyes of faith on Him and on Him alone.

This does not mean that we ignore others, because we do have the responsibility of caring for one another (Phil. 2:1-4). Rather, it means that we must not permit our curiosity about others to distract us from following the Lord. God has His plan for us; He also has plans for our Christian friends and associates. How He works in their lives is His business. Our business is to follow Him as He leads us (see Rom. 14:1-13).

I recall a critical time in my own ministry when I was disturbed because other ministers were apparently getting God's "blessing" in abundance while I seemed to be reaping a meager harvest. I must confess that I envied them and wished that God had given their gifts to me. But the Lord tenderly rebuked me with, "What is that to thee? Follow thou Me." It was just the message I needed, and I have tried to heed it ever since.

Jesus did not say that John would live until His return, but that is the way some of the misguided believers understood it. More problems are caused by confused saints than by lost sinners! Misinterpreting the Word of God only creates misunderstanding about God's people and God's plans for His people.

However, there is a somewhat enigmatic quality to what the Lord said about John. Jesus did not say that John would live until He returned, nor did He say that John would die before He returned. As it was, John lived the longest of all the disciples and did witness the Lord's return when he saw the visions that he recorded in the Book of Revelation.

As John came to the close of his book, he affirmed again the credibility of his witness. (Remember, *witness* is a key theme in the Gospel of John. The word is used forty-seven times.) John witnessed these events himself and wrote them for us as he was led by the Holy Spirit. He could have included so much more, but he wrote only what the Spirit told him to write.

The book ends with Peter and John together following Jesus, and He led them right into the Book of Acts! What an exciting thing it was to receive the power of the Spirit and to bear witness of Jesus Christ! Had they not trusted Him, been transformed by Him, and followed Him, they would have remained successful fishermen on the Sea of Galilee; and the world would never have heard of them.

Jesus Christ is transforming lives today. Wherever He finds a believer who is willing to yield to His will, listen to His Word, and follow His way, He begins to transform that believer and accomplish remarkable things in that life. He also begins to do wonderful things through that life.

Peter and John have been off the scene (except for their books) for centuries, but you and I are still here. We are taking His place and taking their place. What a responsibility! What a privilege!

We can succeed only as we permit Him to transform us.

ACTS

OUTLINE

Key theme: The expansion of the church in the world
Key verse: Acts 1:8

I. **THE MINISTRY OF PETER—chapters 1–12**
Jerusalem the center
Ministry primarily to Israel
A. Peter and the Jews—1–7
B. Peter and the Samaritans—8
C. The conversion of Paul—9
D. Peter and the Gentiles—10–11
E. Peter's arrest and deliverance—12

II. **THE MINISTRY OF PAUL—chapters 13–28**
Syrian Antioch the center
Ministry primarily to the Gentiles
A. Paul's first missionary journey—13–14
B. The Jerusalem Conference—15
C. Paul's second missionary journey—16:1–18:22
D. Paul's third missionary journey—18:23–21:17
E. Paul's arrest and voyage to Rome—21:18–28:31

CONTENTS

CHAPTER ONE
THE FAITH OF THE FIRST CHRISTIANS
Acts 1

A famous Hollywood producer once said that for a movie to be successful, it must start with an earthquake and work up to a climax. Luke certainly didn't follow that formula when he wrote the Book of Acts. Except for the ascension of Jesus Christ, events recorded in Acts 1 are anything but dramatic. After all, what is exciting about a business meeting?

Then why record these events? Why didn't Luke just start with the story of Pentecost? For several reasons.

To begin with, Luke was writing volume two of a work that started with what we call the Gospel of Luke (see Luke 1:1-4); and he had to begin with the proper salutation and introduction. We don't know who Theophilus was or even if he was a believer; but Luke's salutation suggests that he may have been an important Roman official (see Acts 23:26; 24:3; 26:25). Likely Theophilus was a Christian or at least a seeker who was carefully studying the Christian faith. His name means "friend of God," and we hope he lived up to his name.

But even more important, Luke had to build a bridge between his Gospel and the Book of Acts (Luke 24:50-53). At the close of his Gospel, he had left the believers in the temple, praising God. Now he had to pick up the story and explain what happened next. Imagine how confused you would be if, in reading your New Testament, you turned the last page of the Gospel of John and discovered—Romans! "How did the church get to Rome?" you would ask yourself; and the answer is found in the Book of Acts.

The Book of Acts is also the account of the work of the Holy Spirit *in* and *through* the church. The Gospel of Luke records what Jesus "began both to do and teach" in His human body, and the Book of Acts tells us what Jesus *continued* to do and teach through His spiritual body, the church. Even today, congregations can learn much about church life and ministry from this book, and this even includes the business meetings!

In this chapter, we see the believers taking care of "unfinished business" and getting ready for Pentecost. What they said and did reveals to us the faith of the church. In what did they really believe?

They Believed in the Risen Christ (Acts 1:1-11)

After His resurrection, Jesus remained on earth for forty days and ministered to His disciples. He had already opened their minds to understand the Old Testament message about Himself (Luke 24:44-48), but there were other lessons they needed to learn before they could launch out in their new ministry. Jesus appeared and disappeared during those forty days, and the believers never knew when He might show up. It was excellent preparation for the church because the days were soon coming when He would no longer be on earth to instruct them personally. We believers today never know when our Lord may return, so our situation is somewhat similar to theirs.

The Lord taught them several important lessons during that time of special ministry.

The reality of His resurrection (v. 3a). Some of the believers may have had their doubts forty days before (Mark 16:9-14), but there could be no question now that Jesus had indeed been raised from the dead. To strengthen their faith, He gave them "many infallible proofs" which Luke did not explain. We know that when Jesus met His disciples, He invited them to touch His body, and He even ate before them (Luke 24:38-43). Whatever proofs He gave, they were convincing.

Faith in His resurrection was important to

the church because their own spiritual power depended on it. Also, the message of the Gospel involves the truth of the Resurrection (Rom. 10:9-10; 1 Cor. 15:1-8); and, if Jesus were dead, the church would be speechless. Finally, the official Jewish position was that the disciples had stolen Jesus' body from the tomb (Matt. 28:11-15), and the believers had to be able to refute this as they witnessed to the nation.

These believers were chosen to be special witnesses of Christ's resurrection, and that was the emphasis in their ministry (Acts 1:22; 2:32; 3:15; 5:30-32). Most of the people in Jerusalem knew that Jesus of Nazareth had been crucified, but they did not know that He had been raised from the dead. By their words, their walk, and their mighty works, the believers told the world that Jesus was alive. This was "the sign of Jonah" that Jesus had promised to the nation (Matt. 12:38-41)—His death, burial, and resurrection.

The coming of His kingdom (v. 3b). This refers to the reign of God over the hearts and lives of those who have trusted Him (see Matt. 6:33; Rom. 14:17; 1 John 3:1-9). When you read the four Gospels, you discover that the Apostles had a strongly political view of the kingdom and were especially concerned about their own positions and privileges. Being loyal Jews, they longed for the defeat of their enemies and the final establishment of the glorious kingdom under the rule of King Messiah. They did not realize that there must first be a spiritual change in the hearts of the people (see Luke 1:67-79).

Jesus did not rebuke them when they "kept asking" about the future Jewish kingdom (Acts 1:7). After all, He had opened their minds to understand the Scriptures (Luke 24:44), so they knew what they were asking. But God has not revealed His timetable to us and it is futile for us to speculate. The important thing is not to be curious about the future but to be busy in the present, sharing the message of God's *spiritual* kingdom. This is another emphasis in the Book of Acts (see Acts 8:12; 14:22; 20:25; 28:23, 31).

The power of His Holy Spirit (vv. 4-8). John the Baptist had announced a future baptism of the Holy Spirit (Matt. 3:11; Mark 1:8; Luke 3:16; John 1:33; and see Acts 11:16), and now that prophecy would be fulfilled. Jesus had also promised the coming of the Spirit (John 14:16-18, 26; 15:26-27; 16:7-15). It would be an enduement of power for the disciples so that they would be able to serve the Lord and accomplish His will (Luke 24:49). John had spoken about "the Holy Spirit and fire," but Jesus said nothing about fire. Why? Because the "baptism of fire" has to do with future judgment, when the nation of Israel will go through tribulation (Matt. 3:11-12). The appearing of "tongues of fire" at Pentecost (Acts 2:3) could not be termed a "baptism."

Acts 1:8 is a key verse. To begin with, it explains that the power of the church comes from the Holy Spirit and not from man (see Zech. 4:6). God's people experienced repeated fillings of the Spirit as they faced new opportunities and obstacles (Acts 2:4; 4:8, 31; 9:17; 13:9). Ordinary people were able to do extraordinary things because the Spirit of God was at work in their lives. The ministry of the Holy Spirit is not a luxury; it is an absolute necessity.

"Witness" is a key word in the Book of Acts and is used twenty-nine times as either a verb or a noun. A witness is somebody who tells what he has seen and heard (Acts 4:19-20). When you are on the witness stand in court, the judge is not interested in your ideas or opinions; he only wants to hear what you know. Our English word *martyr* comes from the Greek word translated "witness," and many of God's people have sealed their witness by laying down their lives.

We hear a great deal these days about "soul winning," and the emphasis is a good one. However, while *some* of God's people have a calling to evangelism (Eph. 4:11), *all* of God's people are expected to be witnesses and tell the lost about the Saviour. Not every Christian can bring a sinner to the place of faith and decision (though most of us could do better), but every Christian can bear faithful witness to the Saviour. "A true witness delivereth souls" (Prov. 14:25).

Acts 1:8 also gives us a general outline of the Book of Acts as it describes the geographical spread of the Gospel: from Jerusalem (Acts 1–7) to Judea and Samaria (Acts 8–9), and then to the Gentiles and to the ends of the earth (Acts 10–28). No matter where we live, as Christians we should begin our witness at home and then extend it "into all the world." As Dr. Oswald J. Smith used to say, "The light that shines the farthest will shine the brightest at home."

The assurance of His coming again (vv. 9-11). Our Lord's ascension into heaven was an important part of His ministry, for if He had not returned to the Father, He could not have sent the promised gift of the Holy Spirit (John 16:5-15). Also, in heaven today, the Saviour is our interceding High Priest, giving us the grace that we need for life and service (Heb. 4:14-16). He is also our Advocate before the Father, forgiving us when we confess our sins (1 John 1:9–2:2). The exalted and glorified Head of the church is now working with His people on earth and helping them accomplish His purposes (Mark 16:19-20).

As the believers watched Jesus being taken up to glory, two angels appeared and gently rebuked them. Angels play an important role in the ministry described in Acts, just as they do today, even though we cannot see them (see Acts 5:19-20; 8:26; 10:3-7; 12:7-10, 23; 27:23). The angels are the servants of the saints (Heb. 1:14).

The two messengers gave the believers assurance that Jesus Christ would come again, just as He had been taken from them. This seems to refer to His public "coming in clouds" (Matt. 24:30; 26:64; Rev. 1:7) rather than to His coming for His church "in a moment, in the twinkling of an eye" (1 Cor. 15:51-52; 1 Thes. 4:13-18). Regardless of what views different people may take of God's prophetic program, Christians agree that Jesus is coming again and that He can come at any time. This in itself is a great motivation for faithful Christian service (Luke 12:34-48).

They Believed in Each Other (Acts 1:12-14)

They obeyed their Lord's commandment and returned to Jerusalem "with great joy" (Luke 24:52). It is likely that the group met in the Upper Room where the last Passover had been celebrated, but they were also found at worship in the temple (Luke 24:53).

What a variety of people made up that first assembly of believers! There were men and women, apostles and "ordinary" people, and even members of the Lord's earthly family (see Matt. 13:55; Mark 6:3). His "brethren" had not believed in Him during His ministry (John 7:5), but they did come to trust Him after the Resurrection (Acts 1:14). Mary was there as a member of the assembly, participating in worship and prayer along with the others. The center of their fellowship was the risen Christ, and all of them adored and magnified Him.

How easy it would have been for someone to bring division into this beautiful assembly of humble people! The members of the Lord's family might have claimed special recognition, or Peter could have been criticized for his cowardly denial of the Saviour. Or perhaps Peter might have blamed John, because it was John who brought him into the high priest's house (John 18:15-16). John might well have reminded the others that *he* had faithfully stood at the cross, and had even been chosen by the Saviour to care for His mother. But there was none of this. In fact, nobody was even arguing over who among them was the greatest!

The key phrase is "with one accord," a phrase that is found six times in Acts (1:14; 2:1, 46; 4:24; 5:12; 15:25; and note also 2:44). There was among these believers a wonderful unity that bound them together in Christ (Ps. 133; Gal. 3:28), the kind of unity that Christians need today. "I do not want the walls of separation between different orders of Christians to be destroyed," said the godly British preacher Rowland Hill, "but only lowered, that we may shake hands a little easier over them!"

It is not enough for Christians to have faith in the Lord; they must also have faith in one another. To these 120 people (Acts 1:15) the Lord had given the solemn responsibility of bearing witness to a lost world, and none of them could do the job alone. They would experience severe persecution in the days ahead, and one of them, James, would lay down his life for Christ. It was not a time for asking, "Who is the greatest?" or, "Who committed the greatest sin?" It was a time for praying together and standing together in the Lord. As they waited and worshiped together, they were being better prepared for the work that lay before them.

They Believed in Prayer (Acts 1:15, 24-25)

Prayer plays a significant role in the story of the church as recorded in the Book of Acts. The believers prayed for guidance in making decisions (Acts 1:15-26) and for courage to witness for Christ (Acts 4:23-31). In fact, prayer was a normal part of their daily ministry (Acts 2:42-47; 3:1; 6:4). Stephen prayed as he was being stoned (Acts 7:55-60). Peter and John prayed for the Samaritans (Acts 8:14-17), and Saul of Tarsus prayed after his conversion (Acts 9:11). Peter prayed before he raised Dorcas from the dead (Acts 9:36-

43). Cornelius prayed that God would show him how to be saved (Acts 10:1-4), and Peter was on the housetop praying when God told him how to be the answer to Cornelius' prayers (Acts 10:9).

The believers in John Mark's house prayed for Peter when he was in prison, and the Lord delivered him both from prison and from death (Acts 12:1-11). The church at Antioch fasted and prayed before sending out Barnabas and Paul (Acts 13:1-3; and note 14:23). It was at a prayer meeting in Philippi that God opened Lydia's heart (Acts 16:13), and another prayer meeting in Philippi opened the prison doors (Acts 16:25ff). Paul prayed for his friends before leaving them (Acts 20:36; 21:5). In the midst of a storm, he prayed for God's blessing (Acts 27:35), and after a storm, he prayed that God would heal a sick man (Acts 28:8). In almost every chapter in Acts you find a reference to prayer, and the book makes it very clear that something happens when God's people pray.

This is certainly a good lesson for the church today. Prayer is both the thermometer and the thermostat of the local church; for the "spiritual temperature" either goes up or down, depending on how God's people pray. John Bunyan, author of *Pilgrim's Progress*, said, "Prayer is a shield to the soul, a sacrifice to God, and a scourge to Satan." In the Book of Acts, you see prayer accomplishing all of these things.

They Believed in God's Leading (Acts 1:16-23)

The Lord Jesus was no longer with them to give them personal directions, but they were not without the leading of the Lord, for they had the Word of God and prayer. In fact, the Word of God and prayer formed the foundation for the ministry of the church as recorded in the Book of Acts (Acts 6:4).

Peter has been criticized for taking charge, but I believe he was doing the will of God. Jesus had made it clear that Peter was to be their leader (Matt. 16:19; Luke 22:31-32; John 21:15-17). Peter was "first among equals," but he was their recognized leader. His name is mentioned first in each listing of the Apostles, including Acts 1:13.

But should Peter and the others have waited until the Spirit had been given? We must not forget that the Lord had previously "breathed" on them and imparted the Spirit to them (John 20:22). When the Spirit came at Pentecost, it was for the purpose of filling them with power and baptizing them into one body in Christ.

We must also remember that the Lord had opened up their minds to understand the Scriptures (Luke 24:45). When Peter referred to Psalms 69:25 and 109:8, he was not doing this on his own, but was being led by the Spirit of God. These people definitely believed in the divine inspiration of the Old Testament Scriptures (Acts 1:16; and see 3:18; 4:25), and they also believed that these Scriptures had a practical application to their situation.

A radio listener once wrote to ask me, "Why do you teach from the Old Testament? After all, it's ancient history and it's all been fulfilled by Jesus!" I explained that the only "Bible" the early church had was the Old Testament, and yet they were able to use it to discover the will of God. We need both the Old and the New; in fact, the New Testament writers often quote from the Old Testament to prove their point. St. Augustine said, "The New is in the Old concealed; the Old is by the New revealed."

Certainly we must interpret the Old by the New, but we must not think that God no longer speaks to His people through the Old Testament Scriptures. "*All* Scripture is given by inspiration of God, and is profitable" (2 Tim. 3:16, italics mine). "Man shall not live by bread alone, but by *every* word that proceedeth out of the mouth of God" (Matt. 4:4, italics mine). We must use the whole Bible and balance Scripture with Scripture as we seek to discover the mind of God.

"But it was wrong for them to select a new apostle," some claim, "because Paul was the one who was chosen by God to fill up the ranks. They chose Matthias and he was never heard of again!"

Except for Peter and John, *none of the original Twelve* are mentioned by name in the Book of Acts after 1:13! Paul could not have "filled up the ranks" because he could never have met the divine qualifications laid down in Acts 1:21-22. Paul was not baptized by John the Baptist; he did not travel with the Apostles when Jesus was with them on earth; and, though he saw the glorified Christ, Paul was not a witness of the Resurrection as were the original Apostles.

Paul made it clear that he was *not* to be classified with the Twelve (1 Cor. 15:8; Gal. 1:15-24), and the Twelve knew it. If the Twelve thought that Paul was supposed to be one of them, they certainly did not show it! In fact, they refused to admit Paul into the Jerusalem fellowship until Barnabas came to his rescue! (Acts 9:26-27) The 12 Apostles ministered primarily to the twelve tribes of Israel, while Paul was sent to the Gentiles (Gal. 2:1-10).

No, Paul was not meant to be the twelfth apostle. Peter and the other believers were in the will of God when they selected Matthias, and God gave His endorsement to Matthias by empowering him with the same Spirit that was given to the other men whom Jesus had personally selected (Acts 2:1-4, 14).

It was necessary that twelve men witness at Pentecost to the twelve tribes of Israel, and also that twelve men be prepared to sit on twelve thrones to judge the twelve tribes (Luke 22:28-30). From Acts 2–7, the witness was primarily to Israel, "to the Jew first" (see Rom. 1:16; Acts 3:26; 13:46). Once the message had gone to the Gentiles (Acts 10–11), this Jewish emphasis began to decline. When the Apostle James was martyred, he was not replaced (Acts 12). Why? Because the official witness to Israel was now completed and the message was going out to Jews and Gentiles alike. There was no more need for 12 Apostles to give witness to the twelve tribes of Israel.

Peter's account of the purchase of the land and the death of Judas appears to contradict the record in Matthew 27:3-10; but actually it complements it. Judas did not buy the field personally, but since it was his money that paid for it, in that sense, he was the buyer. And, since the thirty pieces of silver were considered "blood money," the field was called "the field of blood" (Matt. 27:8). It was not Judas' blood that gave the field its name, for the Jews would not use as a sacred cemetery a place that had been defiled by a suicide. Judas hanged himself, and apparently the rope broke and his body (possibly already distended) burst open when it hit the ground.

The believers prayed for God's guidance before they "voted," because they wanted to select the man that God had already chosen (Prov. 16:33). Their exalted Lord was working in them and through them from heaven. This is the last instance in the Bible of the casting of lots, and there is no reason why believers today should use this approach in determining God's will. While it is not always easy to discover what God wants us to do, if we are willing to obey Him, He will reveal His will to us (John 7:17). What is important is that we follow the example of the early church by emphasizing the Word of God and prayer.

Not all our Lord's followers were in the Upper Room, for there were only 120 present and 1 Corinthians 15:6 states that at least 500 persons saw the risen Christ at one time. Bible scholars do not agree on the size of the population of Palestine at that time, and their estimates run from 600,000 to 4 million. But regardless of what figure you select, the 120 believers were still a minority; yet they turned their world upside down for Christ!

What was their secret? The power of the Holy Spirit!

Dr. Luke explains this in Acts 2.

CHAPTER TWO
POWER FROM HEAVEN!
Acts 2

"We are not going to move this world by criticism of it nor conformity to it, but by the combustion within it of lives ignited by the Spirit of God."

Vance Havner made that statement and he was right. The early church had none of the things that we think are so essential for success today—buildings, money, political influence, social status—and yet the church won multitudes to Christ and saw many churches established throughout the Roman world. Why? Because the church had the power of the Holy Spirit energizing its ministry. They were a people who "were ignited by the Spirit of God."

That same Holy Spirit power is available to us today to make us more effective witnesses for Christ. The better we understand His working at Pentecost, the better we will be able to relate to Him and experience His power. The ministry of the Spirit is to glorify Christ in the life and witness of the believer (John 16:14), and that is what is important. Acts 2 helps us understand the Holy Spirit by recording four experiences in the life of the church.

The Church Waiting for the Spirit (Acts 2:1)

Pentecost means "fiftieth" because this feast was held fifty days after the Feast of Firstfruits (Lev. 23:15-22). The calendar of Jewish feasts in Leviticus 23 is an outline of the work of Jesus Christ. Passover pictures His death as the Lamb of God (John 1:29; 1 Cor. 5:7), and the Feast of Firstfruits pictures His resurrection from the dead (1 Cor. 15:20-23). Fifty days after Firstfruits is the Feast of Pentecost, which pictures the formation of the church. At Pentecost, the Jews celebrated the giving of the Law, but Christians celebrate it because of the giving of the Holy Spirit to the church.

The Feast of Firstfruits took place on the day after the Sabbath following Passover, which means it was always on the first day of the week. (The Sabbath is the seventh day.) Jesus arose from the dead on the first day of the week and "became the firstfruits of them that slept" (1 Cor. 15:20). Now, if Pentecost was fifty days later—seven weeks plus one day—then Pentecost also took place on the first day of the week. Christians assemble and worship on Sunday, the first day of the week, because on that day our Lord arose from the dead, but it was also the day on which the Holy Spirit was given to the church.

On the Feast of Firstfruits, the priest waved a sheaf of grain before the Lord; but on Pentecost, he presented two loaves of bread. Why? Because at Pentecost, the Holy Spirit baptized the believers and united them into one body. The Jewish believers received this baptism at Pentecost, and the Gentile believers in the home of Cornelius (Acts 10). This explains the presence of two loaves of bread (see 1 Cor. 10:17). The fact that there was leaven (yeast) in the loaves indicates the presence of sin in the church on earth. The church will not be perfect until it gets to heaven.

We must not conclude that this ten-day prayer meeting brought about the miracles of Pentecost, or that we today may pray as they did and experience "another Pentecost." Like our Lord's death at Calvary, Pentecost was a once-for-all event that will not be repeated. The church may experience new fillings of the Spirit, and certainly patient prayer is an essential element to spiritual power, but we would not ask for another Pentecost any more than we would ask for another Calvary.

The Church Worshiping the Lord (Acts 2:2-13)

As we study the events of Pentecost, it is important that we separate the accidentals from the essentials. The Spirit *came* and the people heard the sound of rushing wind and saw tongues of fire. The Spirit *baptized* and *filled* the believers, and then *spoke* as they praised God in various languages. The Spirit *empowered* Peter to preach, and then He *convicted* the listeners so that 3,000 of them trusted Christ and were saved. Let's consider these ministries one by one.

The Spirit came (vv. 2-3). The Holy Spirit had been active prior to Pentecost and had worked in Creation (Gen. 1:1-2), in Old Testament history (Jud. 6:34; 1 Sam. 16:13), and in the life and ministry of Jesus (Luke 1:30-37; 4:1, 14; Acts 10:38). However, now there would be two changes: the Spirit would dwell in people and not just come on them, and His presence would be permanent, not temporary (John 14:16-17). The Spirit could not have come sooner, for it was essential that Jesus die, be raised from the dead, and return to heaven before the Spirit could be given (John 7:37-39; 16:7ff). Remember the Jewish calendar in Leviticus 23: Passover, Firstfruits, and then Pentecost.

There were three startling signs that accompanied the coming of the Spirit: the sound of a rushing wind, tongues of fire, and the believers praising God in various languages. The word *Spirit* is the same as "wind" in both the Hebrew and the Greek (John 3:8). The people did not *feel* the wind; they heard *the sound* of a mighty wind. It is likely the believers were in the temple when this occurred (Luke 24:53). The word *house* in Acts 2:2 can refer to the temple (see Acts 7:47). The tongues of fire symbolized the powerful witness of the church to the people. Campbell Morgan reminds us that our tongues can be set on fire either by heaven or by hell! (James 3:5-6) Combine wind and fire and you have—a blaze!

The Spirit baptized (1:5). The Greek word *baptizo* has two meanings, one literal and the other figurative. The word literally means "to submerge," but the figurative meaning is "to be identified with." The baptism of the Spirit is that act of God by which He identified believers with the exalted Head of the church, Jesus Christ, and formed the spiritual body of Christ on earth (1 Cor. 12:12-14). Historically, this took place at Pentecost; today, it takes place whenever a sinner trusts Jesus Christ and is born again.

When you read about "baptism" in the New Testament, you must exercise discernment to determine whether the word is to be interpreted literally or symbolically. For example, in Romans 6:3-4 and Galatians 3:27-28, the reference is symbolic since water baptism cannot put a sinner into Jesus Christ. Only the Holy Spirit can do that (Rom. 8:9; 1 Cor. 12:13; see Acts 10:44-48). Water baptism is a public witness of the person's identification with Jesus Christ, while Spirit baptism is the personal and private experience that identifies the person with Christ.

It is important to note that historically, the baptism of the Spirit took place in two stages: the Jewish believers were baptized at Pentecost, and the Gentiles were baptized and added to the body in the home of Cornelius (Acts 10:44-48; 11:15-17; and see Eph. 2:11-22).

The Spirit filled (v. 4). The filling of the Spirit has to do with power for witness and service (Acts 1:8). We are not exhorted to be baptized by the Spirit, for this is something God does once and for all when we trust His Son. But we are commanded to be filled with the Spirit (Eph. 5:18), for we need His power constantly if we are to serve God effectively. At Pentecost, the Christians were filled with the Spirit and experienced the baptism of the Spirit; but after that, they experienced many fillings (Acts 4:8, 31; 9:17; 13:9) but no more baptisms.

Occasionally someone says, "What difference does it make what words we use? The important thing is that we have the experience!" I doubt that they would apply that same approach to any other area of life such as medicine, cooking, or mechanics. What difference does it make if the pharmacist uses arsenic or aspirin in the prescription, just so long as you get well? Or if the mechanic installs an alternator or a carburetor, just so long as the car works?

The Holy Spirit has revealed God's truth to us in *words* (1 Cor. 2:12-13), and these words have definite meanings that must not be changed. Regeneration must not be confused with justification, nor propitiation with adoption. Each of these words is important in God's plan of salvation and must be defined accurately and used carefully.

The baptism of the Spirit means that I belong to His body; the fullness of the Spirit means that my body belongs to Him. The baptism is final; the fullness is repeated as we trust God for new power to witness. The baptism involves all other believers, for it makes us one in the body of Christ (Eph. 4:1-6); while the fullness is personal and individual. These are two distinct experiences and they must not be confused.

The Spirit spoke (vv. 5-13). Note that the believers were praising God, not preaching the Gospel, and that they used known languages, not an "unknown tongue" (Acts 2:6, 8). Luke named fifteen different geographical locations and clearly stated that the citizens of those places heard Peter and the others declare God's wonderful works *in languages they could understand.* The Greek word translated "language" in Acts 2:6 and "tongue" in Acts 2:8 is *dialektos* and refers to a language or dialect of some country or district (Acts 21:40; 22:2; 26:14). Unless we are instructed otherwise in Scripture, we must assume that when "speaking in tongues" is mentioned elsewhere in Acts, or in 1 Corinthians, it refers to an identical experience: believers praising God in the Spirit in languages that are known.

Why did God do this? For one thing, Pentecost was a reversal of the judgment at the Tower of Babel when God confused man's language (Gen. 11:1-9). God's judgment at Babel scattered the people, but God's blessing at Pentecost united the believers in the Spirit. At Babel, the people were unable to understand each other; but at Pentecost, men heard God's praises and understood what was said. The Tower of Babel was a scheme designed to praise men and make a name for men, but Pentecost brought praise to God. The building of Babel was an act of rebellion, but Pentecost was a ministry of humble submission to God. What a contrast!

Another reason for this gift of tongues was to let the people know that the Gospel was for the whole world. God wants to speak to every person in his or her own language and give the saving message of salvation in Jesus Christ. The emphasis in the Book of Acts is on worldwide evangelization, "unto the uttermost part of the earth" (Acts 1:8). "The Spirit of Christ is the spirit of missions," said Henry Martyn, "and the nearer we get to Him, the more intensely missionary we must become."

Apparently the sound of the wind drew the people to the temple where the believers were gathered, but it was the praise by the believers that really captured their attention. The careless listeners mocked and accused the believers of being drunk, but others were sincerely concerned to find out what was going on. The people were perplexed (Acts 2:6), amazed (Acts 2:7, 12), and they marveled (Acts 2:7).

It is interesting that the mockers should accuse the believers of being drunk, for wine is associated with the Holy Spirit (Eph. 5:18). Paul relates the two *in contrast,* for when a man is filled with strong drink, he loses control of himself and ends up being ashamed; but when a person is filled with the Spirit, he has self-control and glorifies God. Strong drink can bring a temporary exhilaration, but the Spirit gives a deep satisfaction and a lasting joy.

The Church Witnessing to the Lost (Acts 2:14-41)

Peter did not preach in tongues; he addressed his audience in the everyday Aramaic that they understood. The message was given by a Jew, to Jews (Acts 2:14, 22, 29, 36), on a Jewish holy day, about the resurrection of the Jewish Messiah whom their nation had crucified. The Gentiles who were there were proselytes to the Jewish religion (Acts 2:10). Peter would not open the door of faith to the Gentiles until he visited Cornelius (Acts 10).

There are three explanations in Peter's sermon.

He explained what happened: the Spirit had come (vv. 14-21). The joyful worship of the believers was not the result of too much wine; it was the evidence of the arrival of God's Holy Spirit to dwell in His people. Orthodox Jews did not eat or drink before 9 A.M. on the Sabbath or on a holy day, nor did they usually drink wine except with meals.

Peter did not say that Pentecost was the *fulfillment* of the prophecy of Joel 2:28-32, because the signs and wonders predicted had not occurred. When you read Joel's prophecy in context, you see that it deals with the nation of Israel in the end times, in connection with "the Day of the Lord." However, Peter was led by the Spirit to see in the prophecy an application to the church. He said, "This is that same Holy Spirit that Joel wrote about. He is here!" Such an announcement would seem incredible to the Jews, because they thought God's Spirit was given only to a few select people (see Num. 11:28-29). But here were 120 of their fellow Jews, men and women, enjoying the blessing of the same Holy Spirit that had empowered Moses, David, and the prophets.

It was indeed the dawning of a new age, the "last days" in which God would bring to completion His plan of salvation for mankind. Jesus had finished the great work of redemption and nothing more had to be done except to share the Good News with the world, beginning with the nation of Israel. The invitation is, "Whosoever shall call on the name of the Lord shall be saved" (Acts 2:21).

He explained how it happened: Jesus was alive (vv. 22-35). News travels fast in the East; and probably most of the adults in Jerusalem, residents and visitors, knew about the arrest, trial, and crucifixion of Jesus of Nazareth. They also had heard rumors of an "official announcement" that His followers had stolen the body of Jesus just to make people think that He had kept His word and been raised from the dead.

But Peter told them the truth: Jesus of Nazareth had indeed been raised from the dead, and the Resurrection proves that He is the Messiah! Peter gave them four proofs of the resurrection of Jesus Christ of Nazareth, and then he called on them to believe on Christ and be saved.

His first proof was the person of Jesus Christ (vv. 22-24). Peter's audience knew that Jesus was a real Person from the town of Nazareth and that He had performed many signs and miracles. (On "Jesus of Nazareth," see Acts 2:22; 3:6; 4:10; 6:14; 10:38; 22:8; 26:9; also 24:5.) It was clear that God's hand was on Him. They had heard Him speak and had watched His life. They had even seen Him raise the dead, yet they could find no fault in Him—and these things were not "done in a corner"! (Acts 26:26)

It was incredible that such a Man should be defeated by death. From one point of view, the crucifixion of Jesus was a terrible crime (Acts 2:23), but from another point of view it was a wonderful victory (Acts 2:24). The word translated "pains" means "birth pangs," suggesting that the tomb was a "womb" out of which Jesus was "born" in Resurrection glory (see Acts 13:33).

Peter's second proof was the prophecy of David (vv. 25-31). He quoted Psalm 16:8-11, verses that obviously could not apply to David who was already dead and buried. Being a prophet of God, David wrote about the Messiah, that His soul would not remain in hades (the realm of the dead) or His body in the grave where it would decay.

The third proof was the witness of the believers (v. 33). After His resurrection, Jesus did not appear to the world at large, but to His own followers whom He had commissioned to give witness to others that He was alive (Acts 1:3, 22). But were these people dependable witnesses? Can we trust them? We certainly can! Prior to Christ's resurrection, the disciples did not even believe that He would be raised from the dead; and they themselves had to be convinced (Mark 16:9-14; Acts 1:3). They had nothing to gain by preaching a lie, because their message aroused official opposition and even led to the imprisonment and death of some of the believers. A few fanatics might be willing to believe and promote a lie for a time, but when thousands believe a message, and when that message is backed up by miracles, you cannot easily dismiss it. These witnesses were trustworthy.

Peter's fourth proof of the resurrection of Christ was the presence of the Holy Spirit (vv. 33-35). Follow his logic. If the Holy Spirit is in the world, then God must have sent Him. Joel promised that one day the Spirit would come, and Jesus Himself had promised to send the gift of the Holy Spirit to His people (Luke 24:49; John 14:26; 15:26; Acts 1:4). But if Jesus is dead, He cannot send the Spirit; therefore, He must be alive. Furthermore, He could not send the Spirit unless He had returned to heaven to the Father (John 16:7); so, Jesus has ascended to heaven! To back up this statement, Peter quoted Psalm 110:1, a verse that certainly could not be applied to David (note Matt. 22:41-46).

Peter's conclusion was both a declaration and an accusation: Jesus is your Messiah, *but you crucified Him!* (see Acts 2:23) Peter did not present the cross as the place where the Sinless Substitute died for the world, but where Israel killed her own Messiah! They committed the greatest crime in history! Was there any hope? Yes, for Peter gave a third explanation that was good news to their hearts.

He explained why it happened: to save sinners (vv. 36-41). The Holy Spirit took Peter's message and used it to convict the hearts of the listeners. (In Acts 5:33 and 7:54, a different Greek word is used that suggests anger rather than conviction for sin.) After all, if they were guilty of crucifying their Messiah, what might God do to them! Note that they addressed their question to the other Apostles as well as to Peter, for all twelve were involved in the witness that day, and Peter was only first among equals.

Peter told them how to be saved: they had to repent of their sins and believe on Jesus Christ. They would give proof of the sincerity of their repentance and faith by being baptized in the name of Jesus Christ, thus identifying themselves publicly with their Messiah and Saviour. Only by repenting and believing on Christ could they receive the gift of the Spirit (Gal. 3:2, 14), and this promise was for both the Jews and the "far off" Gentiles (Eph. 2:13-19).

It is unfortunate that the translation of Acts 2:38 in the *King James Version* suggests that people must be baptized in order to be saved, because this is not what the Bible teaches. The Greek word *eis* (which is translated "for" in the phrase "for the remission of sins") can mean "on account of" or "on the basis of." In Matthew 3:11 John the Baptist baptized on the basis that people had repented. Acts 2:38 should not be used to teach salvation by baptism. If baptism is essential for salvation, it seems strange that Peter said nothing about baptism in his other sermons (Acts 3:12-26; 5:29-32; 10:34-43). In fact, the people in the home of Cornelius received the Holy Spirit *before they were baptized!* (Acts 10:44-48) Since believers are commanded to be baptized, it is important that we have a clean conscience by obeying (1 Peter 3:21), but we must not think that baptism is a part of salvation. If so, then nobody in Hebrews 11 was saved because none of them was ever baptized.

Acts 2:40 indicates that the Apostles continued to share the Word and to urge the people to trust Jesus Christ. They looked on the nation of Israel as a "crooked generation" that was under condemnation (Matt. 16:4; 17:17; Phil. 2:15). Actually, the nation would have about forty years before Rome would come and destroy the city and the temple and scatter the people. History was repeating itself. During the forty years in the wilderness, the new generation "saved itself" from the older generation that rebelled against God. Now, God would give His people another forty years of grace; and on that day, 3,000 people repented, believed, and were saved.

The Church Walking in the Spirit (Acts 2:42-47)

The believers continued to use the temple for their place of assembly and ministry, but they also met in various homes. The 3,000 new converts needed instruction in the Word and fellowship with God's people if they were to grow and become effective witnesses. The early church did more than make converts; they also made *disciples* (Matt. 28:19-20).

Two phrases in Acts 2:42 may need explanation. "Breaking of bread" probably refers to their regular meals, but at the close of each meal, they probably paused to remember the Lord by observing what we call "the Lord's Supper." Bread and wine were the common fare at a Jewish table. The word *fellowship* means much more than "being together." It means "having in common" and probably refers to the sharing of material goods that was practiced in the early church. This was certainly not a form of modern communism, for the program was totally voluntary, temporary (Acts 11:27-30), and motivated by love.

The church was unified (Acts 2:44), magnified (Acts 2:47a), and multiplied (Acts 2:47b). It had a powerful testimony among the unsaved Jews, not only because of the miracles done by the Apostles (Acts 2:43), but also because of the way the members of the fellowship loved each other and served the Lord. The risen Lord continued to work with them (Mark 16:20) and people continued to be saved. What a church!

The Christians you meet in the Book of Acts were not content to meet once a week for "services as usual." They met daily (Acts 2:46), cared daily (Acts 6:1), won souls daily (Acts 2:47), searched the Scriptures daily (Acts 17:11), and increased in number daily (Acts 16:5). Their Christian faith was a day-to-day reality, not a once-a-week routine. Why? Because the risen Christ was a living reality to them, and His resurrection power was at work in their lives through the Spirit.

The promise is still good: "Whosoever shall call on the name of the Lord shall be saved" (Acts 2:21; Rom. 10:13). Have you called? Have you trusted Jesus Christ to save you?

CHAPTER THREE THE POWER OF HIS NAME

Acts 3:1–4:4

The emphasis in Acts 3 and 4 is on the name of the Lord Jesus (Acts 3:6, 16; 4:7, 10, 12, 17-18, 30). A name, of course, implies much more than identification; it carries with it authority, reputation, and power. When somebody says, "You can use my name!" you sincerely hope the name is worth using. If an order is given in the name of the President of the United States or the Prime Minister of Great Britain, those who receive the order know that they are obligated to obey. If I were to issue orders at the White House or at No. 10 Downing Street (even if I could get in), nobody would pay much attention because my name has no official authority behind it.

But the name of the Lord Jesus has *all authority* behind it, for He is the Son of God (Matt. 28:18). Because His name is "above every name" (Phil. 2:9-11), He deserves our worship and obedience. The great concern of the first Christians was that the name of Jesus Christ, God's Son, be glorified; and believers today should have that same concern.

As we study this section, we should note that the Jewish emphasis is very pronounced. Peter addressed Jewish men (Acts 3:12) and called them "children of the prophets and of the covenant" (Acts 3:25). He referred to the Jewish fathers (Acts 3:13) as well as to the prophets (Acts 3:18, 21-25). The phrase "times of restitution" (Acts 3:21) is definitely Jewish and refers to the messianic kingdom promised in the prophets. The message is still going out "to the Jew first" (Acts 3:26) and is presented in Jewish terms.

There are three stages in this event, and each stage reveals something wonderful about Jesus Christ.

Amazement: Jesus the Healer (Acts 3:1-10)

The believers were still attached to the temple and to the traditional hours of prayer (Ps. 55:17; Dan. 6:10; Acts 10:30). Keep in mind that Acts 1–10 describes a gradual transition from Israel to the Gentiles and from "Jewish

Christianity" (note Acts 21:20) to the "one body" made up of both Jews and Gentiles. It took several years before many of the Jewish believers really understood the place of the Gentiles in God's program, and this understanding did not come without its conflicts.

The contrast between Acts 2 and 3 is interesting: Peter the preacher—Peter the personal worker; multitudes—one poor man; ministry resulting in blessing—ministry resulting in arrest and persecution. The events in Acts 3 are an illustration of the last phrase in Acts 2:47, showing us how the Lord added to His church daily. While the Holy Spirit is not named in this chapter, He was certainly at work in and through the Apostles, performing His ministry of glorifying Jesus Christ (John 16:14).

Peter and John are often found together in Scripture. They were partners in the fishing business (Luke 5:10); they prepared the last Passover for Jesus (Luke 22:8); they ran to the tomb on the first Easter Sunday morning (John 20:3-4); and they ministered to the Samaritans who believed on Jesus Christ (Acts 8:14). Now that they were filled with the Holy Spirit, the Apostles were no longer competing for greatness, but were at last working faithfully together to build the church (Ps. 133).

That Peter noticed the lame beggar is another evidence of the Spirit's ministry. No doubt thousands of people were near the temple (Acts 4:4), and perhaps scores of beggars, but the Lord told Peter to heal a lame man lying at the Beautiful Gate. There were nine gates that led from the court of the Gentiles into the temple itself. Scholars are not agreed, but the Beautiful Gate was probably the "Eastern Gate" that led into the court of the women. Made of Corinthian bronze, the gate looked like gold; and it certainly was a choice place for a lame man to beg.

The giving of alms was an important part of the Jewish faith, so beggars found it profitable to be near the temple. Since the believers had pooled their resources (Acts 2:44-45), the two Apostles had no money to give; but money was not what the man needed most. He needed salvation for his soul and healing for his body, and money could provide neither. Through the power of the name of Jesus, the beggar was completely healed; and he was so happy and excited that he acted like a child, leaping and praising God.

It is easy to see in this man an illustration of what salvation is like. He was born lame, and all of us are born unable to walk so as to please God. Our father Adam had a fall and passed his lameness on to all of his descendants (Rom. 5:12-21). The man was also poor, and we as sinners are bankrupt before God, unable to pay the tremendous debt that we owe Him (Luke 7:36-50). He was "outside the temple," and all sinners are separated from God, no matter how near to the door they might be. The man was healed wholly by the grace of God, and the healing was immediate (Eph. 2:8-9). He gave evidence of what God had done by "walking, and leaping, and praising God" (Acts 3:8) and by publicly identifying himself with the Apostles, both in the temple (Acts 3:11) and in their arrest (Acts 4:14). Now that he could stand, there was no question *where* this man stood!

Indictment: Jesus, the Son of God (Acts 3:11-16)

The healing of the lame beggar drew a crowd around the three men. Solomon's Porch, on the east side of the temple, was a corridor where our Lord had ministered (John 10:23) and where the church worshiped (Acts 5:12).

In his sermon at Pentecost, Peter had to refute the accusation that the believers were drunk. In this sermon, he had to refute the notion that he and John had healed the man by their own power. (Paul and Barnabas would face a similar situation after healing a lame man. See Acts 14:8-18.) Peter immediately identified the source of the miracle—Jesus Christ, the Son of God. Wisely, Peter said that this was the God of their fathers, the God of Abraham, Isaac, and Jacob.

The Spirit certainly gave Peter boldness as he reminded the Jews of the way they had treated Jesus. They had denied Him and delivered Him up to be crucified. Even worse, they had asked for a guilty man, Barabbas, to be set free so that an innocent prisoner might be crucified! In order to convince them of their crimes, Peter used several different names and titles for our Lord: God's Son, Jesus, the Holy One, the Just One, the Prince (Pioneer) of life. This was no ordinary man that they had handed over to the Romans to crucify!

Calvary may have been man's last word, but the empty tomb was God's last word. He glorified His Son by raising Him from the dead and taking Him back to heaven. The enthroned Christ had sent His Holy Spirit and was working through His church. The healed beggar was proof that Jesus was alive. If ever a people were guilty, it was the people Peter addressed in the temple. They were guilty of killing their own Messiah!

This is probably not the kind of message we would give at an evangelistic meeting today, because it was designed especially for Peter's Jewish audience. As at Pentecost, Peter was addressing people who knew the Scriptures and were acquainted with the recent events in Jerusalem (see Luke 24:18). It was not a group of ignorant pagans with no religious background. Furthermore, the Jewish leaders had indeed perpetrated a great injustice when they arrested and condemned Jesus and asked Pilate to have Him crucified. How many citizens agreed with their decision, we do not know; but you can imagine the remorse of the people when they learned that they had betrayed and killed their own Messiah.

There must be conviction before a sinner can experience conversion. Unless a patient is convinced that he is sick, he will never accept the diagnosis or take the treatment. Peter turned the temple into a courtroom and laid all the evidence out for everybody to see. How could two ordinary fishermen perform such a great miracle unless God was with them? Nobody would dare deny the miracle because the beggar stood there before them all in "perfect soundness" (Acts 3:16; 4:14). To accept the miracle would have been to admit that Jesus Christ is indeed the living Son of God and that His name has power.

Encouragement: Jesus, the Saviour (Acts 3:17–4:4)

But Peter did not leave the people without hope. In fact, he almost seemed to defend them by pointing out that they had acted in ignorance (Acts 3:17) while at the same time they had fulfilled the Word of God (Acts 3:18).

In the Old Testament Law, there is a difference between deliberate sins and sins of ignorance (see Lev. 4–5; Num. 15:22-31). The person who sinned presumptuously was a rebel against God and was guilty of great sin. He was to be "cut off" from his people (Num. 15:30-31), which could mean excommunication and even death. The defiant "high-handed" sinner was condemned, but the person who sinned unwittingly and without deliberate intent was given opportunity to repent and seek God's forgiveness. Ignorance does not remove the sinner's guilt, but it does mitigate the circumstances.

Jesus had prayed, "Father, forgive them; for they know not what they do" (Luke 23:34); and God had answered that prayer. Instead of sending judgment, He sent the Holy Spirit to empower His church and to convict lost sinners. Israel's situation was something like that of the "manslayer" who killed his neighbor without prior malicious intent, and fled to the nearest city of refuge (Num. 35:9-34). So long as he remained in the city, he was safe, for then the avengers could not reach him and kill him. He was free to go home only after the death of the high priest. Peter invited these "murderers" to flee by faith to Jesus Christ and find refuge in Him (Heb. 6:18).

In his previous sermon, Peter had explained that the Cross was the meeting place of divine sovereignty and human responsibility (Acts 2:23); and he repeated this truth in this second sermon (Acts 3:17-18). There are mysteries here that the human mind cannot fully understand, so we must accept them by faith. God had a plan from all eternity, yet His plan did not force men to act against their own will. The prophets had foretold the sufferings and death of the Messiah, and the nation fulfilled these prophecies without realizing what they were doing. When God cannot rule, He overrules and always accomplishes His divine purposes and decrees.

Having announced the crime, presented the evidence, and explained the nature of their sin, Peter then offered them pardon! (Acts 3:19-26) What a strange thing for the prosecuting attorney to become the defense attorney and the pardoning judge! Peter's burden was to encourage his people to trust Christ and experience His gracious salvation.

What did he tell them to do? First of all, *they had to repent of their sins* (see Acts 2:38; 5:31; 17:30), which means to have a change of mind about themselves, their sin, and Jesus Christ. Repentance is much more than "feeling sorry for your sins." As the little Sunday School girl said, "It means feeling sorry enough to quit!" False sorrow for sin could be mere regret ("I'm sorry I got caught!") or remorse ("I feel terrible!"); and such feelings have a tendency to pass away. Repentance is not the same as "doing penance," as though we have to make a special sacrifice to God to prove that we are sincere. True repentance is admitting that what God says is true, and because it is true, to change our mind about our sins and about the Saviour.

The message of repentance was not new to the Jews, for John the Baptist had preached it and so had Jesus (Matt. 3:2; 4:17). In one sense, repentance is a gift from God (Acts 11:18); in another sense, it is the heart's response to the convicting ministry of the Spirit of God (Acts 26:20). The person who sincerely repents will have little problem putting his faith in the Saviour.

Second, they had to *be converted,* "to turn again" and exercise saving faith in Jesus Christ. The biblical message is "repentance toward God, and faith toward our Lord Jesus Christ" (Acts 20:21), and the two go together. Unless we turn from our sins, we cannot put saving faith in Jesus Christ. It is unfortunate that some preachers have so ignored the doctrine of repentance that their "converts" lack a true sense of conviction of sin. Balanced evangelism presents to the sinner both repentance and faith.

Peter announced what would happen if they repented and turned to Jesus Christ: "in order that your sins may be blotted out, in order that the times of refreshing may come from the presence of the Lord, in order that He may send Jesus Christ" (literal translation). There was a promise for the individual (sins forgiven) and a promise for the nation (times of spiritual refreshing). Peter was actually calling for *national repentance,* for the nation through its leaders had denied its Messiah and condemned Him to die. The declaration is that, if the nation repented and believed, the Messiah would return and establish the promised kingdom. The nation did not repent—and certainly God knew this would happen—so the message eventually moved from the Jews to the Samaritans (Acts 8) and to the Gentiles (Acts 10).

The emphasis in Acts 3:22-25 is on *the prophets* who had announced the coming of the Messiah. Peter quoted from Moses (Deut. 18:15, 18-19) and reminded his listeners that Moses had predicted the arrival of a Prophet, and this Prophet was the Messiah (see Luke 24:19; John 1:19-28; 6:14). Not to obey ("hear") this Prophet meant condemnation. But Moses was not the only one who foretold the coming of Jesus Christ, for all the prophets united in their witness to Him (see Luke 24:25-27, 44-48).

When Peter spoke about "these days," to what "days" was he referring? The days of the life and ministry of Jesus Christ, the days when God's Prophet would speak to His people and offer them salvation. The nation's rejection of Him made them especially guilty because the Jews were the privileged "sons of the prophets and of the covenant." They had sinned against a flood of light!

When God called Abraham, He made an unconditional covenant with him and his descendants that through them the nations of the world would be blessed (Gen. 12:1-3). This promise was fulfilled when Jesus Christ came into the world through the Jewish nation (Gal. 3:6-14). The Gospel message came "to the Jew first" because the Jews were God's chosen instrument through whom the Gentiles would be blessed (Acts 3:26; 13:46; Rom. 1:16). The first Christians were Jews and the first missionaries were Jews.

But notice that Peter did not permit the "national blessings" to overshadow the personal responsibility of the individuals listening to his message (Acts 3:26). God raised up Jesus Christ and sent Him to *each one* who would turn away from his iniquities (note Acts 3:20). National repentance depends on personal repentance, the response of individual sinners to the message of salvation. Peter was addressing a large crowd, but he still made the application personal.

His message produced two opposite results: (1) some 2,000 Jews believed the Word and were converted, and (2) the religious leaders of the nation rejected the message and tried to silence the Apostles. We have here the beginning of the persecution about which Jesus had already warned His followers (Matt. 10:17-18; Luke 21:12-15; John 15:18–16:4).

We would expect the Sadducees to oppose the message because they did not believe in the resurrection of the human body (Acts 23:6-8). Peter's fearless declaration that Jesus Christ had been raised from the dead ran contrary to their religious beliefs. If the common people questioned the theology of their spiritual leaders, it could undermine the authority of the whole Jewish council. Instead of honestly examining the evidence, the leaders arrested the Apostles and kept them in custody overnight, intending to try them the next day. However, the arrival of the temple guards could not prevent 2,000 men from trusting Jesus Christ and identifying themselves with the believers in Jerusalem.

As you review this section of Acts, you cannot help but be impressed with some practical truths that should encourage all of us in our witnessing for Christ.

1. God is long-suffering with lost sinners. The leaders of Israel had rejected the ministry of John the Baptist (Matt. 21:23-27) and the ministry of Jesus, and yet God gave them another opportunity to repent and be saved. They had denied and slain their own Messiah, and yet God patiently held back His judgment and sent His Spirit to deal with them. God's people today need patience as we witness to a lost world.

2. True witness involves the "bad news" of sin and guilt as well as the "good news" of salvation through faith in Jesus Christ. There can be no true faith in Christ unless first there is repentance from sin. It is the ministry of the Holy Spirit to convict lost sinners (John 16:7-11), and He will do this if we faithfully witness and use God's Word.

3. The way to reach the masses is by helping the individual sinner. Peter and John won the crippled beggar and his transformed life led to the conversion of 2,000 men! The servant of God who has no time for personal work with individual sinners will not be given many opportunities for ministering to great crowds. Like Jesus, the Apostles took time for individuals.

4. The best defense of the truth of the Christian faith is a changed life. The healed beggar was "Exhibit A" in Peter's defense of the resurrection of Jesus Christ. In his evangelistic ministries, the Methodist preacher Samuel Chadwick used to pray for "a Lazarus" in every campaign, some "great sinner" whose conversion would shock the community. He got the idea from John 12:9-11. God answered his prayers in meeting after meeting as infamous wicked men trusted Christ and became witnesses through their changed lives. Let's go after the "hard cases" and see what God can do!

5. Whenever God blesses, Satan shows up to oppose the work and silence the witness; and often he uses religious people to do his work. The same crowd that opposed the ministry of Jesus Christ also opposed the work of the Apostles, and they will oppose our ministry today. Expect it—but don't let it stop you! The important thing is not that we are comfortable, but that the name of the Lord is glorified through the preaching of the Gospel.

6. God has promised to bless and use His Word, so let's be faithful to witness. Jesus even prayed that our witness would have success (John 17:20), so we have every reason to be encouraged. There is power in the name of Jesus, so we need not fear to witness and call sinners to repent.

7. The name of Jesus Christ still has power! While we may not perform the same apostolic miracles today that were seen in the early church, we can still claim the authority of Jesus Christ as He has instructed us in the Word.

We can preach the "remission of sins" in His name (Luke 24:47) so that people might believe and have "life through His name" (John 20:31). We can give someone a cup of cold water in His name (Mark 9:41), and we can receive a child in His name (Matt. 18:5). These ministries may not seem as spectacular as healing a cripple, but they are still important to the work of God.

We can ask in His name as we pray (John 14:13-14; 15:16; 16:23-26). When we ask the Father for something "in the name of Jesus Christ," it is as though Jesus Himself were asking it. If we remember this, it will help to keep us from asking for things unworthy of His name.

Yes, the name of Jesus Christ still has authority and power. Let's go forth in His name and conquer!

CHAPTER FOUR
PERSECUTION, PRAYER, AND POWER
Acts 4:5-31

The early church had none of the "advantages" that some ministries boast of and depend on today. They did not have big budgets provided by wealthy donors. Their pastors lacked credentials from the accepted schools, nor did they have the endorsement of the influential political leaders of that day. Most of their ministers had jail records and would probably have a hard time today *joining* our churches, let alone *leading* them. What really was the secret of their success? This chapter provides the answer: the Christians of the early church knew how to pray so that God's hand could work in mighty power.

When asked to explain the secret of his

remarkable ministry, the noted British preacher Charles Haddon Spurgeon replied, "My people pray for me." St. Augustine said, "Pray as though everything depended on God, and work as though everything depended on you." Prayer is not an escape from responsibility; it is our *response* to God's *ability*. True prayer energizes us for service and battle.

Once again, the focus of attention is on the name of the Lord Jesus Christ (Acts 4:7, 10, 12, 17-18). In this chapter, we see what three groups of people do with His name.

The Apostles: Defending His Name (Acts 4:5-14)

The court (vv. 5-7). The court was essentially composed of the high priest's family. The Jewish religious system had become so corrupt that the offices were passed from one relative to another without regard for the Word of God. When Annas was deposed from the priesthood, Caiaphas his son-in-law was appointed. In fact, five of Annas' sons held the office at one time or another. Somebody has defined a "nepotist" as "a man who, being evil, knows how to give good gifts to his children." Annas certainly qualified.

This was an official meeting of the Sanhedrin (Acts 4:15), the same council that a few months before had condemned Jesus to die. In fact, these officials recognized Peter and John as the associates of Jesus (Acts 4:13). The Sanhedrin was charged with the responsibility of protecting the Jewish faith, and this meant that they had to examine every new teacher and teaching that appeared in the land (see Deut. 13). They certainly had the right to investigate what the church was doing, but they did not have the right to arrest innocent men and then refuse to honestly examine the evidence.

Their question was legal, but they did everything they could to avoid admitting that a miracle had taken place (Acts 4:14). They were evasive and merely referred to the miracle as "this." They were probably scornful as well, so that their question might be paraphrased, "Where did common people like you get the power and authority to do a thing like this?" It was once again the question of "By whose name?" After all, the Apostles might be in league with the devil! Even Satan can perform miracles!

The case (vv. 8-14). Peter spoke in the power of the Holy Spirit of God. Note that Peter was again filled with the Spirit (see Acts 2:4) and would experience another filling before the day ended (Acts 4:31). There is one baptism of the Spirit, and this is at conversion (1 Cor. 12:13), but there must be many fillings of the Spirit if the believer is to be an effective witness for Jesus Christ (Eph. 5:18ff).

Peter respectfully began with an explanation of how the miracle occurred. Certainly the members of the Sanhedrin had seen the crippled beggar many times, and perhaps they had even given alms to him and piously prayed for him. How was this well-known man healed? "By the name of Jesus Christ of Nazareth!" Those words must have pierced the hearts of the members of the council! They thought they had finished with the Prophet from Nazareth, and now His followers were telling everybody that Jesus was alive! Since the Sadducees did not believe in the resurrection of the dead, Peter's statement was almost a declaration of war!

But the Spirit was telling Peter what to say (see Luke 21:12-15), and the apostle quoted Psalm 118:22, definitely a messianic reference (see Matt. 21:42; 1 Peter 2:4-8). He made it clear that the members of the council were "the builders" and that they had rejected God's Stone, Jesus, the Son of God.

The image of "the stone" was not new to these men who were experts in the Old Testament Scriptures. They knew that the "rock" was a symbol of God (Deut. 32:4, 15, 18, 31; 2 Sam. 22:2; Ps. 18:2; Isa. 28:16), and that the Prophet Daniel had used the rock to picture Messiah and the coming of His kingdom on earth (Dan. 2:31-45). The Jews stumbled over the Rock (Rom. 9:32; 1 Cor. 1:23) and rejected Him, just as Psalm 118:22 had predicted. However, to those who have trusted Him, Jesus Christ is the precious Cornerstone (1 Peter 2:4-8) and the chief Cornerstone (Eph. 2:20).

Peter went on to explain that Jesus is not only the Stone, but He is also the Saviour (Acts 4:12). Peter saw in the healing of the beggar a picture of the spiritual healing that comes in salvation. "Made whole" in Acts 4:9 is a translation of the same Greek word that is translated "saved" in Acts 4:12, for salvation means wholeness and spiritual health. Jesus Christ is the Great Physician who alone can heal mankind's greatest malady, the sickness of sin (Mark 2:14-17). Of course, Peter also had "all the people of Israel" in mind as he spoke (see Acts 4:10) because the message was still going out exclusively to the Jews. Even Psalm 118, from which Peter quoted, speaks of a future national salvation for Israel.

The Council: Opposing His Name (Acts 4:15-22)

Their problem (vv. 13-14). They were in a dilemma; no matter which way they turned, they were "trapped." They could not deny the miracle, because the man was standing before them; and yet they could not explain how "uneducated and untrained men" (NASB) could perform such a mighty deed. Peter and John were ordinary fishermen, not professional scribes or authorized ministers of the Jewish religion. They were disciples of Jesus of Nazareth, but—He was dead! The council took notice of the courage and confidence of Peter and John, as well as the power of Peter's words; and it all added up to perplexity.

It is important to note that, of itself, the miracle was not proof of the resurrection of Christ or even of the truth of Peter's message. Satan can perform miracles (2 Thes. 2:9-10) and false prophets can do wonders (Deut. 13:1-5). The miracle and the message, *in the context of all that had been going on since Pentecost,* was one more evidence that Jesus Christ was alive and at work in the church by His Holy Spirit. In both sermons, Peter used the Old Testament to support and explain his claims, and this is one evidence of a true prophet of God (Deut. 13:1-5; Isa. 8:20). Miracles are not a substitute for the Word of God (Luke 16:27-31).

Their deliberation (vv. 15-18). The council did not seek for truth, but rather sought for some way to avoid the truth! Had they honestly considered the evidence and meekly listened to the message, they might have been saved, but their pride and hardness of heart stood in the way. Some of the chief priests and elders had experienced a similar dilemma during Passover when they had tried to trap Jesus in the temple (Matt. 21:23-27). Some people never learn! But their response is proof that miracles alone can never convict or convert the lost sinner. Only the Word of God can do that (see John 11:45-53; Acts 14:1-20).

Their conclusion. They wanted to "let the thing die a natural death." This meant threatening the Apostles and forbidding them to teach and preach in the name of Jesus. This official sentence shows how much the enemy fears the witness of the church, for Satan has been trying to silence God's people from the very beginning. Sad to say, he has succeeded with far too many Christians, the "silent witnesses" of the church. Even the existential philosopher Albert Camus said, "What the world expects of Christians is that Christians should speak out, loud and clear . . . in such a way that never a doubt, never the slightest doubt, could arise in the heart of the simplest man."

The council did not want the Gospel message to spread, and yet that is exactly what happened! From 120 praying men and women in Acts 1, the church increased to more than 3,000 on the Day of Pentecost; and now there were more than 5,000 disciples in the fellowship. In the days that followed, "believers were the more added to the Lord, multitudes both of men and women" (Acts 5:14; and see 6:1, 7). Satan's attempts to silence the church only led to a stronger witness for the Lord.

The failure of the council (vv. 19-22). This was evident when Peter refused to be intimidated by their threats. All of us need to follow Peter's example and make our decisions on the basis of "Is it right?" and not "Is it popular?" or "Is it safe?" However, we must be sure that we have the clear teaching of the Word of God on our side before we take a stand against the authority of the government. Peter knew what the Lord had commanded the believers to do (Acts 1:8), and he was going to obey Him at any cost.

It is popular today to promote various causes by defying the government, disobeying the law, and defending these actions on the basis of conscience. Since even some Christians are involved in this approach to social action, it is important to understand the kind of "civil disobedience" practiced by people in the Bible. Peter and John are not the only ones who disobeyed the authorities in order to serve God. A list of "dedicated conscientious objectors" would include, among others: the Jewish midwives (Ex. 1), Moses' parents (Heb. 11:23), Daniel (Dan. 1; 6), and the three Hebrew children (Dan. 3). When you examine the records, you discover the biblical principles by which they operated, principles that are not always followed today.

To begin with, each of these "objectors" had a message from God that could not be questioned. The midwives and Moses' parents knew that it was wrong to murder the babies. Daniel and his friends, and the three Hebrew men, knew that it was wrong to eat food offered to idols or to bow down to idols in worship. Peter and John knew that they were under orders from their Master to preach the Gospel to the ends of the earth, and that it would be wrong to obey the Sanhedrin. All of these people were faithfully obeying a clear word from God and not just following some selfish personal whim of their own.

Second, their convictions touched every area of their lives. In other words, they did everything "with conscience toward God" (1 Peter 2:19) because they belonged to God. The university student today whose conscience permits him to cheat on exams or drive while drunk, but not register for military service, does not convince me that he is really cultivating a healthy conscience. When a person's *total life* is under the direction of a godly conscience, then I find it easier to have confidence in his unpopular decisions.

Note also that our examples from the Bible acted with respect and courtesy, even when they defied the law. It is possible for Christians to respect authority and at the same time disobey the authorities (see Rom. 13; Titus 3:1-2; 1 Peter 2:13-25). Daniel tried to avoid getting his guard into trouble, and the Apostles used their arrests as opportunities for witness. This is quite a contrast to some of the modern "Christian objectors" who seem to major on denunciation and accusation rather than loving witness.

Of course, the greatest example of unjust suffering is that of Jesus Christ, and we must imitate Him (see 1 Peter 2:13-25). Jesus teaches us that righteous protest against injustice always involves sacrifice and suffering, and must be motivated by love. God's people must be careful not to clothe their prejudice in the garments of "righteous indignation" and pass themselves off as courageous soldiers of conscience. We must examine our own hearts honestly to make certain we are not conducting a "holy war" just to satisfy inner frustrations.

Because they had no real case to offer, the council could only threaten the men and let them go. After all, when you have a living miracle before you, as well as an approving public around you, you must be careful what you do!

The Church: Calling on His Name (Acts 4:23-31)

The greatest concentration of power in Jerusalem that day was in the prayer meeting that followed the trial. This is one of the truly great prayers recorded in the Bible, and it is a good example for us to follow.

To begin with, it was a prayer that was born out of witness and service for the Lord. Peter and John had just come in "from the trenches," and the church met to pray in order to defeat the enemy. Too often today, believers gather for prayer as though attending a concert or a party. There is little sense of urgency and danger because most of us are comfortable in our Christian walk. If more of God's people were witnessing for Christ in daily life, there would be more urgency and blessing when the church meets for prayer.

It was a united prayer meeting as they "lifted up their voice to God with one accord" (Acts 4:24; see 1:14). The people were of one heart and mind, and God was pleased to answer their requests. Division in the church always hinders prayer and robs the church of spiritual power.

Their praying was based solidly on the Word of God, in this case, Psalm 2. The Word of God and prayer must always go together (John 15:7). In His Word, God speaks to us and tells us what He wants to do. In prayer, we speak to Him and make ourselves available to accomplish His will. True prayer is not telling God what to do, but asking God to do His will in us and through us (1 John 5:14-15). It means getting God's will done on earth, not man's will done in heaven.

They did not pray to have their circumstances changed or their enemies put out of office. Rather, they asked God to empower them to make the best use of their circumstances and to accomplish what He had already determined (Acts 4:28). This was not "fatalism" but faith in the Lord of history who has a perfect plan and is always victorious. They asked for divine enablement, not escape; and God gave them the power that they needed.

"Do not pray for easy lives," wrote Phillips Brooks. "Pray to be stronger men and women. Do not pray for tasks equal to your powers. Pray for powers equal to your tasks." That is the way the early Christians prayed, and that is the way God's people should pray today.

They addressed God as "Sovereign Lord," the God who is in control of all things. The Greek word gives us our English word *despot,* a ruler who exercises absolute power, either benevolently or abusively. Simeon used this same title when he prayed in the temple (Luke 2:29). It is good to know the Sovereign Lord when you are experiencing persecution.

They also approached Him as the Creator, for, after all, if your Father is "Lord of heaven and earth," what have you to fear? (see Matt. 11:25-30) Nehemiah approached God on this same basis (Neh. 9:6), and so did the psalmist (see Ps. 145) and the Prophet Isaiah (Isa. 42). Years later, when he wrote his first epistle, Peter encouraged suffering saints to yield themselves to the faithful Creator (1 Peter 4:19).

Psalm 2 describes the revolt of the nations against the Lord and His Christ. The psalm originally grew out of the crowning of a new king in Israel, perhaps David; but its ultimate message points to the King of kings, Jesus Christ. Whenever a new king was enthroned, the vassal rulers around were required to come and submit to him; but some of them refused to do this. God only laughed at their revolt, for He knew that they could never stand up against His King.

The early believers applied the message of this psalm to their own situation and identified their adversaries as Herod, Pilate, the Romans, and the Jews. These enemies had "ganged up" against Jesus Christ and even crucified Him, yet God raised Him from the dead and enthroned Him in heaven. All of this was a part of God's perfect plan (see Acts 2:23; 3:18), so there was no need to fear.

The early church strongly believed in God's sovereignty and His perfect plan for His people. But note that they did not permit their faith in divine sovereignty to destroy human responsibility, for they were faithful to witness and pray. It is when God's people get out of balance and overemphasize either sovereignty or responsibility that the church loses power. Again, we are reminded of Augustine's wise words, "Pray as though everything depends on God, and work as though everything depended on you." Faith in a sovereign Lord is a tremendous encouragement for God's people to keep serving the Lord when the going is difficult.

They did not ask for protection; they asked for power. They did not ask for fire from heaven to destroy the enemy (see Luke 9:51-56), but for power from heaven to preach the Word and heal the sick (see Matt. 5:10-12, 43-48). Their great desire was for boldness in the face of opposition (see Acts 4:17). The emphasis is on the hand of God at work in the life of the church (Acts 4:28, 30), not the hand of man at work for God. Believing prayer releases God's power and enables God's hand to move (Isa. 50:2; 64:1-8).

Finally, note that they wanted to glorify God's Child (Servant) Jesus Christ (Acts 4:27, 30). It was His name that gave them power to minister the Word and to perform miracles, and His name alone deserved the glory. The glory of God, not the needs of men, is the highest purpose of answered prayer.

God's answer was to shake the place where they were meeting and to fill the people once again with the Spirit of God (Acts 4:31). This gave them the boldness that they needed to continue to serve God in spite of official opposition. This was not a "second Pentecost" because there cannot be another Pentecost any more than there can be another Calvary. It was a new filling of the Spirit to equip the believers to serve the Lord and minister to the people.

We will consider Acts 4:32-37 in our next study, but it is worth noting that the new fullness of the Spirit also created a deeper unity among the people (Acts 4:34) and a greater desire to sacrifice and share with one another. They enjoyed "great power" and "great grace," which ought to be the marks of a "great" church. This led to a great ingathering of souls for the Lord.

"Lord, Thou art God!" What a declaration of faith and what a practical application of good theology! However, if their lives had not been submitted to His control, they could not have prayed that way. Boldness in prayer is the result of faithfulness in life and service. The sovereignty of God is not an abstract doctrine that we accept and defend. It is a living truth that we act on and depend on for every need. When you are loyal to the Lord and put Him first (Acts 4:19), then you can trust Him to be faithful to you and see you through.

The name of Jesus Christ has not lost its power, but many of God's people have lost their power because they have stopped praying to the sovereign God. "Nothing lies beyond the reach of prayer except that which lies outside the will of God." I don't know who first said that, but the statement is absolutely true. Dr. R.A. Torrey, the noted evangelist and educator, said, "Pray for great things, expect great things, work for great things, but above all—pray."

The early church prayed, and God answered in mighty power.

CHAPTER FIVE
BEWARE OF THE SERPENT!
Acts 4:32–5:16

Satan had failed completely in his attempt to silence the witness of the church. However, the enemy never gives up; he simply changes his strategy. His first approach had been to attack the church from the outside, hoping that arrest and threats would frighten the leaders. When that failed, Satan decided to attack the church *from the inside* and use people who were a part of the fellowship.

We must face the fact that Satan is a clever foe. If he does not succeed as the "devouring lion" (1 Peter 5:8), then he attacks again as the "deceiving serpent" or an "angel of light" (2 Cor. 11:3, 13-14). Satan is both a murderer and a liar (John 8:44), and the church must be prepared for both attacks.

The Generosity of the Believers (Acts 4:32-37)

The believers had prayed and God's Spirit had filled them and given them new power. The church that depends on believing prayer will know the blessing of the Holy Spirit in its ministry. How can we tell when a local church is really filled with the Spirit? When you go back to the record of the first filling at Pentecost (Acts 2:44-47), you discover three outstanding characteristics of a Spirit-filled church.

It is unified (2:44, 46). This is a God-given spiritual unity, not a man-made organizational uniformity. The church is an organism that is held together by life, and that life comes through the Holy Spirit. Of course, the church must be organized; for if an organism is not organized, it will die. However, when the organization starts to hinder spiritual life and ministry, then the church becomes just another religious institution that exists to keep itself going. When the Holy Spirit is at work, God's people will be united in their doctrinal beliefs, as well as in fellowship, giving, and worship (Acts 4:42).

A Spirit-filled church is magnified and will have "favor with all the people" (2:47). In spite of the opposition of the rulers, the common people were drawn to the believers because something new and exciting was happening. When the religious leaders tried to silence the church, it was their fear of the people that restrained them (Acts 4:21; 5:26). Yes, a Spirit-filled church will have its enemies, but what the Lord is doing will attract the attention and the admiration of people who are hungry to know God.

A Spirit-filled church is multiplied, because the Lord will daily add new believers to the church (2:47). Evangelism will not be the work of a chosen few, but the daily delight and ministry of the whole congregation. In the early church, each member sought to be an effective witness for Jesus Christ, no matter where he happened to be. No wonder the church grew from 120 to over 5,000 in just a short time!

How did Satan's attack affect the spiritual condition of the church? Not at all! The fact that Peter and John were arrested, tried, and threatened had absolutely no effect on the spiritual life of the church, for the church was still unified (Acts 4:32), magnified (Acts 4:33), and multiplied! (Acts 4:32)

One evidence of the unity of the church was the way they sacrificed and shared with one another. When the Holy Spirit is at work, giving is a blessing and not a burden. We must keep in mind that this "Christian communism" was very unlike the political Communism of our day. What the believers did was purely voluntary (Acts 5:4) and was motivated by love. No doubt many of the new believers were visitors in Jerusalem, having come for the feasts; and they had to depend on their Christian friends to help meet their daily needs.

Nor should we think that every believer sold all his goods and brought the money to the Apostles. Acts 4:34 indicates that some of the members "from time to time" sold various pieces of property and donated to the common treasury. When the assembly had a need, the Spirit directed someone to sell something and meet the need.

While the early church's spirit of sacrifice and loving generosity is worthy of our emulation, believers today are not required to imitate these practices. The principles of Christian giving are outlined in the epistles, especially in 2 Corinthians 8–9; and nowhere are we instructed to bring our money and lay it at the pastor's feet (Acts 4:35), as though he were an apostle. It is the *spirit* of their giving that is important to us today and not the "letter" of their system.

Joseph, nicknamed "Barnabas" (son of encouragement), is introduced at this point for several reasons. First, he was a generous giver and illustrated the very thing Dr. Luke was describing. Second, his noble act apparently filled Ananias and Sapphira with envy so that they attempted to impress the church with their giving and ended up being killed. Third, Barnabas had a most important ministry in the church and is mentioned at least twenty-five times in the Book of Acts and another five times in the epistles. In fact, it is Barnabas who encouraged Paul in his early service for the Lord (Acts 9:26-27; 11:19-30; 13:1-5), and who gave his cousin John Mark the encouragement he needed after his failure (Acts 13:13; 15:36-41; Col. 4:10).

Levites were not permitted to own land, so it is difficult to understand how Barnabas acquired the property that he sold. Perhaps that particular law (Num. 18:20; Deut. 10:9) applied only in Palestine and the property was in Cyprus, or perhaps the corrupt religious leaders had become lax in enforcing the law. There is much we do not know about Joseph Barnabas, but this we do know: he was a Spirit-filled man who was an encouragement to the church because he gave his all to the Lord. Not every believer can be like Peter and John, but we can all be like Barnabas and have a ministry of encouragement.

The Hypocrisy of Ananias and Sapphira (Acts 5:1-11)

George MacDonald wrote, "Half of the misery in the world comes from trying to *look,* instead of trying to *be,* what one is not." The name that Jesus gave to this practice is "hypocrisy," which simply means "wearing a mask, playing the actor." We must not think that failure to reach our ideals is hypocrisy, because no believer lives up to all that he or she knows or has in the Lord. Hypocrisy is *deliberate* deception, trying to make people think we are more spiritual than we really are.

When I was pastoring my first church, the Lord led us to build a new sanctuary. We were not a wealthy congregation, so our plans had to be modest. At one point in the planning, I suggested to the architect that perhaps we could build a simple edifice with a more elaborate facade at the front to make it look more like an expensive church.

"Absolutely not!" he replied. "A church stands for truth and honesty, and any church I design will not have a facade! A building should tell the truth and not pretend to be what it isn't."

Years later, I ran across this poem, which is a sermon in itself:

> They build the front just like
> St. Mark's,
> Or like Westminster Abbey;
> And then, as if to cheat the Lord,
> They make the back parts shabby.

That was the sin of Ananias and Sapphira: putting on a lovely "front" in order to conceal the shabby sin in their lives, sin that cost them their lives.

Ananias means "God is gracious," but he learned that God is also holy; and Sapphira means "beautiful," but her heart was ugly with sin. No doubt some people are shocked when they read that God killed two people just because they lied about a business transaction and about their church giving. But when you consider the features connected with this sin, you have to agree that God did the right thing by judging them.

It is worth noting that the Lord judges sin severely *at the beginning of a new period in salvation history.* Just after the tabernacle was erected, God killed Nadab and Abihu for trying to present "false fire" to the Lord (Lev. 10). He also had Achan killed for disobeying orders after Israel had entered the Promised Land (Josh. 7). While God was certainly not responsible for their sins, He did use these judgments as warnings to the people, and even to us (1 Cor. 10:11-12).

To begin with, the sin of Ananias and Sapphira was *energized by Satan* (Acts 5:3); and that is a serious matter. If Satan cannot defeat the church by attacks from the outside, he will get on the inside and go to work (Acts 20:28-31). He knows how to lie to the minds and hearts of church members, even genuine Christians, and get them to follow his orders. We forget that the admonition about the spiritual armor (Eph. 6:10-18) was written to God's people, not to unbelievers, because it is the Christians who are in danger of being used by Satan to accomplish his evil purposes.

Oliver Wendell Holmes wrote, "Sin has many tools, but a lie is the handle which fits them all." Satan is a liar and a murderer (John 8:44). He lied *to* and *through* this couple, and the lie led to their deaths. When God judged

Ananias and Sapphira, He was also judging Satan. He was letting everybody know that He would not tolerate deception in His church.

Their sin was *motivated by pride,* and pride is a sin that God especially hates and judges (Prov. 8:13). No doubt the church was praising God for the generous offering that Barnabas had brought when Satan whispered to the couple, "You can also bask in this kind of glory! You can make others think that you are as spiritual as Barnabas!" Instead of resisting Satan's approaches, they yielded to him and planned their strategy.

Jesus made it very clear that we must be careful how we give, lest the glory that belongs to God should be given to us (Matt. 6:1-4, 19-34). The Pharisees were adept at calling attention to their gifts, and they received the praises of men—but that's all they received! Whatever we possess, God has given to us; we are stewards, not owners. We must use what He gives us for His glory alone (see John 5:44).

Daniel Defoe called pride "the first peer and president of hell." Indeed, it was pride that transformed Lucifer into Satan (Isa. 14:12-15), and it was pride ("Ye shall be as God!") that caused our first parents to sin (Gen. 3). Pride opens the door to every other sin, for once we are more concerned with our reputation than our character, there is no end to the things we will do just to make ourselves "look good" before others.

A third feature of their sin was especially wicked: their sin was *directed against God's church.* We have reason to believe that Ananias and Sapphira were believers. The spiritual level of the church at that time was so high that it is doubtful that a mere "professor" could have gotten into the fellowship without being detected. The fact that they were able to lie to the Spirit (Acts 5:3) and tempt the Spirit (Acts 5:9) would indicate that they had the Spirit of God living within.

God loves His church and is jealous over it, for the church was purchased by the blood of God's Son (Acts 20:28; Eph. 5:25) and has been put on earth to glorify Him and do His work. Satan wants to destroy the church, and the easiest way to do it is to use those who are within the fellowship. Had Peter not been discerning, Ananias and Sapphira would have become influential people in the church! Satan would have been working through them to accomplish his purposes!

The church is "the pillar and ground of the truth" (1 Tim. 3:15), and Satan attacks it with his lies. The church is God's temple in which He dwells (1 Cor. 3:16), and Satan wants to move in and dwell there too. The church is God's army (2 Tim. 2:1-4), and Satan seeks to get into the ranks as many traitors as he can. The church is safe so long as Satan is attacking from the outside, but when he gets on the inside, the church is in danger.

It is easy for us to condemn Ananias and Sapphira for their dishonesty, but we need to examine our own lives to see if our profession is backed up by our practice. Do we really mean everything we pray about in public? Do we sing the hymns and Gospel songs sincerely or routinely? "These people honor Me with their lips, but their hearts are far from Me" (Matt. 15:8, NIV). If God killed "religious deceivers" today, how many church members would be left?

What is described in this chapter is not a case of church discipline. Rather it is an example of God's personal judgment. "The Lord shall judge His people. It is a fearful thing to fall into the hands of the living God" (Heb. 10:30-31). Had Ananias and Sapphira judged their own sin, God would not have judged them (1 Cor. 11:31), but they agreed to lie, and God had to deal with them.

Ananias was dead and buried, and Sapphira did not even know it! Satan always keeps his servants in the dark, while God guides His servants in the light (John 15:15). Peter accused her of tempting God's Spirit, that is, deliberately disobeying God and seeing how far God would go (Ex. 17:2; Deut. 6:16). They were actually defying God and daring Him to act—and He acted, with swiftness and finality. "Thou shalt not tempt the Lord thy God" (Matt. 4:7).

We must keep in mind that their sin was not in robbing God of money but in lying to Him and robbing Him of glory. They were not required to sell the property; and, having sold it, they were not required to give any of the money to the church (Acts 5:4). Their lust for recognition conceived sin in their hearts (Acts 5:4, 9), and that sin eventually produced death (James 1:15).

The result was a wave of godly fear that swept over the church and over all those who heard the story (Acts 5:11). We have moved from "great power" and "great grace" (Acts 5:33) to "great fear," and all of these ought to be present in the church. "Let us have grace, whereby we may serve God acceptably with reverence and godly fear: for our God is a consuming fire" (Heb. 12:28-29).

The Ministry of the Apostles (Acts 5:12-16)

We have learned that the Spirit-filled church is unified, magnified, and multiplied. Satan wants to divide the church, disgrace the church, and decrease the church; and he will do it, if we let him.

But the church described here completely triumphed over the attacks of Satan! The people were still unified (Acts 5:12), magnified (Acts 5:13), and multiplied (Acts 5:14). Multitudes were added to the Lord, and for the first time, Luke mentions the salvation of women. Both in his Gospel and in Acts, Luke has a great deal to say about women and their relationship to Christ and the church. There are at least a dozen references in Acts to women, as Luke shows the key role women played in the apostolic church. This is a remarkable thing when you consider the general position of women in the culture of that day (see Gal. 3:26-28).

God gave the Apostles power to perform great miracles. While it is true that some of the ordinary members exercised miraculous powers (Acts 6:8), it was primarily the Apostles who did the miracles. These "signs and wonders" were God's way of authenticating their ministry (Rom. 15:18-19; 2 Cor. 12:12; Heb. 2:4).

Just as there were special judgments at the beginning of a new era, so there were also special miracles. We find no miracles performed in Genesis, but at the beginning of the age of Law, Moses performed great signs and wonders. Elijah and Elisha were miracle workers at the beginning of the great era of the Prophets, and Jesus and the Apostles performed signs and wonders when the Gospel Age was inaugurated. Each time God opened a new door, He called man's attention to it. It was His way of saying, "Follow these leaders, because I have sent them."

The mighty wonders performed by the Apostles were the fulfillment of the Lord's promise that they would do "greater works" in answer to believing prayer (John 14:13-14). When Jesus performed miracles during His ministry on earth, He had three purposes in mind: (1) to show compassion and meet human need; (2) to present His credentials as the Son of God; and (3) to convey spiritual truth. For example, when He fed the 5,000, the miracle met their physical need, revealed Him as the Son of God, and gave Him opportunity to preach a sermon about the Bread of Life (John 6).

The apostolic miracles followed a similar pattern. Peter and John healed the crippled beggar and met his need, but Peter used that miracle to preach a salvation sermon and to prove to the people and the council that he and John were indeed the servants of the living Christ. One of the qualifications for an apostle was that he had seen the risen Christ (Acts 1:22; 1 Cor. 9:1); and, since nobody can claim that experience today, there are no apostles in the church. The Apostles and prophets laid the foundation for the church (Eph. 2:20), and the pastors, teachers, and evangelists are building on it. If there are no apostles, there can be no "signs of an apostle" as are found in the Book of Acts (2 Cor. 12:12).

This certainly does not mean that God is limited and can no longer perform miracles for His people! But it does mean that the need for confirming miracles has passed away. We now have the completed Word of God and we test teachers by their message, not by miracles (1 John 2:18-29; 4:1-6). And we must keep in mind that Satan is a counterfeiter and well able to deceive the unwary. In the Old Testament, any prophet who performed miracles but, at the same time, led the people away from God's Word, was considered a false prophet and was killed (Deut. 13). The important thing was not the miracles, but whether his message was true to the Word of God.

A radio listener wrote me and wanted to debate this issue with me, insisting that there were instances today of people being raised from the dead. I wrote him a kind letter and asked him to send me the testimonies of the witnesses, the kind of evidence that could be presented in court. He wrote back and honestly admitted that that kind of evidence was not available, but he still believed it because he had heard a TV preacher say it was so. Most of the miracles recorded in the Bible were out in the open for everybody to see, and it would not be difficult to prove them in a court of law.

Peter and the other Apostles found themselves ministering as their Lord had ministered, with people coming from all over, bringing their sick and afflicted (Matt. 4:23-25; Mark 1:45; 2:8-12). The Twelve must have found it very difficult to walk down the street, for people crowded around them and laid before them sick people on their pallets. Some of the people even had the superstitious belief that there was healing in Peter's shadow.

It is significant that *all of these people were healed.* There were no failures and nobody was sent away because he or she "did not have faith to be healed." These were days of mighty power when God was speaking to Israel and telling them that Jesus of Nazareth was indeed their Messiah and Saviour. "For the Jews require a sign" (1 Cor. 1:22), and God gave signs to them. The important thing was not the healing of the afflicted, but the winning of lost souls, as multitudes were added to the fellowship. The Spirit gave them power for wonders and power for witness (Acts 1:8), for miracles apart from God's Word cannot save the lost.

The greatest miracle of all is the transformation of a lost sinner into a child of God by the grace of God. That is the miracle that meets the greatest need, lasts the longest, and costs the greatest price—the blood of God's Son.

And that is one miracle we can all participate in as we share the message of the Gospel, "the power of God unto salvation to every one that believeth" (Rom. 1:16).

CHAPTER SIX
TRUTH AND CONSEQUENCES
Acts 5:17-42

After Pentecost, the message of the resurrection of Jesus Christ spread rapidly in Jerusalem as Spirit-empowered witnesses shared the Gospel with the lost. Signs and wonders accompanied the preaching of the Word, and no one could deny that God was at work in a new way among His ancient people.

But not everybody was happy with the success of the church. The "religious establishment" that had opposed the ministry of Jesus, and then crucified Him, took the same hostile approach toward the Apostles. "If they persecuted Me, they will also persecute you," said Jesus. "They will put you out of the synagogues; yes, the time is coming that whoever kills you will think that he offers God service" (John 15:20; 16:2, NKJV). These words were beginning to be fulfilled.

It was the age-old conflict between living truth and dead tradition. The new wine could not be put into the old wineskins nor could the new cloth be sewn on the worn-out garments (Matt. 9:14-17). The English martyr Hugh Latimer said, "Whenever you see persecution, there is more than a probability that truth is on the persecuted side."

We see in this account four different responses to God's truth, responses we still see today.

The Council: Attacking the Truth (Acts 5:17-28)

The high priest and his associates had three reasons for arresting the Apostles (this time it was *all* of the Apostles) and bringing them to trial. To begin with, Peter and John had not obeyed the official orders to stop preaching in the name of Jesus Christ. They were guilty of defying the law of the nation. Second, the witness of the church was refuting the doctrines held by the Sadducees, giving every evidence that Jesus Christ was alive. Third, the religious leaders were filled with envy ("indignation") at the great success of these untrained and unauthorized men (see Matt. 27:18; Acts 13:45). The traditions of the fathers had not attracted that much attention or gained that many followers in such a short time. It is amazing how much envy can be hidden under the disguise of "defending the faith."

The Apostles did not resist arrest or organize a public protest. They quietly went along with the temple guard and actually spent a few hours in the public jail. But during the night, an angel set them free and told them to return to their witnessing in the temple. (The Sadducees, of course, did not believe in angels. See Acts 23:8.) In the Book of Acts, you will find several instances of angelic ministries as God cared for His people (Acts 8:26; 10:3, 7; 12:7-11, 23; 27:23). The angels are servants who minister to us as we serve the Lord (Heb. 1:14).

As in Peter's deliverance (Acts 12:7-11), neither the guards nor the leaders knew that the prisoners had been liberated. You are tempted to smile as you imagine the surprised looks on the faces of the guards when they discovered that their most important prisoners were gone. And just imagine the astonishment of the envious members of the Sanhedrin when they heard the report! Here they were trying to *stop* the miracles, but their actions only *multiplied* the miracles!

What a contrast between the Apostles and the members of the council. The council was educated, ordained, and approved, and yet they had no ministry of power. The Apostles were ordinary laymen, yet God's power was at work in their lives. The council was trying desperately to protect themselves and their dead traditions, while the Apostles were risking their lives to share the living Word of God. The dynamic church was enjoying the new; the dead council was defending the old.

You find a variety of emotions in this section: envy (Acts 5:17), bewilderment (Acts 5:24), and fear (Acts 5:26; see 4:21 and Matt. 21:26). Yet, when the Apostles came in, the high priest boldly accused them of defying the law and causing trouble. He would not even use the name of Jesus Christ, but instead said "this name" and "this Man's blood," lest by speaking His name he would defile his lips or bring down the wrath of God (see John 15:21).

But even this hateful indictment was an admission that the church was increasing and getting the job done! The wrath of man was bringing praise to the Lord (Ps. 76:10). The high priest realized that if the Apostles were right, then the Jewish leaders had been wrong in condemning Jesus Christ. Indeed, if the Apostles were right, then the council was guilty of His blood (Matt. 27:25; 1 Thes. 2:14-16). As this "trial" progressed, the Apostles became the judges and the council became the accused.

The Apostles: Affirming the Truth (Acts 5:29-32)

The Apostles did not change their convictions (Acts 4:19-20). They obeyed God and trusted Him to take care of the consequences. They could not serve two masters, and they had already declared whose side they were on. Had they been diplomats instead of ambassadors (2 Cor. 5:20), they could have pleased everybody and escaped a beating. But they stood firmly for the Lord, and He honored their courage and faith.

Neither did they change their message (Acts 5:30-32). Peter indicted the leaders for the death of Jesus (see Acts 3:13-14; 4:10), and boldly affirmed once again that Jesus Christ had been raised from the dead. Not only was Jesus raised from the dead, but He was also exalted by God to heaven. The work of the Holy Spirit in recent days was evidence that Jesus had returned to heaven and sent His Spirit as He promised. The Sadducees certainly did not rejoice to hear the Apostles speak about resurrection from the dead.

That Jesus Christ is at God's right hand is a key theme in the Scriptures. The right hand is, of course, the place of honor, power, and authority. Psalm 110:1 is the basic prophecy, but there are numerous references: Matthew 22:44; Mark 14:62; 16:19; Acts 2:33-34; 5:31; Romans 8:34; Ephesians 1:20; Colossians 3:1; Hebrews 1:3; 8:1; 10:12; 12:2; and 1 Peter 3:22. Soon, Stephen would see Jesus standing at God's right hand (Acts 7:55).

In his second sermon, Peter had called Jesus "the Prince of life" (Acts 3:15); and here he called Him "a Prince and a Saviour." The word *Prince* means "a pioneer, one who leads the way, an originator." The Sanhedrin was not interested in pioneering anything; all they wanted to do was protect their vested interests and keep things exactly as they were (see John 11:47-52). As the "Pioneer of life," Jesus saves us and leads us into exciting experiences as we walk "in newness of life" (Rom. 6:4). There are always new trails to blaze.

Hebrews 2:10 calls Him "the Pioneer [captain] of their salvation," for our salvation experience must never become static. The Christian life is not a parking lot; it is a launching pad! It is not enough just to be born again; we must also grow spiritually (2 Peter 3:18) and make progress in our walk. In Hebrews 12:2, Jesus is called "the Pioneer [author] . . . of our faith," which suggests that He leads us into new experiences that test our faith and help it to grow. One of the major themes of Hebrews is "let us press on to maturity" (Heb. 6:1, NASB), and we cannot mature unless we follow Christ, the Pioneer, into new areas of faith and ministry.

The title *Savior* was not new to the members of the council, for the word was used for physicians (who save people's lives), philosophers (who solve people's problems), and statesmen (who save people from danger and war). It was even applied to the Emperor. But only Jesus Christ is the true and living Saviour who rescues from sin, death, and judgment all who will trust Him.

Peter again called the nation to repentance (Acts 2:36; 3:19-26; 4:10-12) and promised that the gift of the Spirit would be given to all who "obey Him." This does not imply that the gift of the Spirit is a reward for obedience, for a gift can be received only by faith. The phrase "obey Him" is the same as "obedient to the faith" in Acts 6:7, and means "to obey God's call and trust God's Son." God does not *suggest* that sinners repent and believe; He *commands* it (Acts 17:30).

It was a bold witness that the Apostles gave before the highest Jewish religious court. The Spirit of God enabled them and they were not afraid. After all, Jesus had promised to be with them and, through His Holy Spirit, empower them for witness and service. They were His witnesses of His resurrection (Acts 1:22; 2:24, 32; 3:15, 26; 4:10), and He would see them through.

Gamaliel: Avoiding the Truth (Acts 5:33-39)

Gamaliel was a Pharisee who probably did not want to see the Sadducees win any victories. He was a scholar highly esteemed by the people, rather liberal in his applications of the Law, and apparently moderate in his approach to problems. "When Rabban Gamaliel the Elder died," said the Jews, "the glory of the Law ceased and purity and abstinence died." Paul was trained by Gamaliel (Acts 22:3). Gamaliel's "counsel" was unwise and dangerous, but God used it to save the Apostles from death. That the Sadducees would heed the words of a Pharisee shows how distinguished a man Gamaliel was.

In spite of the fact that Gamaliel tried to use cool logic rather than overheated emotions, his approach was still wrong. To begin with, he automatically classified Jesus with two rebels, which means *he had already rejected the evidence.* To him, this "Jesus of Nazareth" was just another zealous Jew, trying to set the nation free from Rome. But did Theudas or Judas ever do the things that Jesus did? Were they raised from the dead? With a clever twist of bad logic, Gamaliel convinced the council that there was really nothing to worry about! Troublemakers come and go, so be patient.

Furthermore, Gamaliel assumed that "history repeats itself." Theudas and Judas rebelled, were subdued, and their followers were scattered. Give these Galileans enough time and they too will disband, and you will never again hear about Jesus of Nazareth. While some students do claim to see "cycles" in history, these "cycles" are probably only in the eyes of the beholder. By selecting your evidence carefully, you can prove almost anything from history. The birth, life, death, and resurrection of Jesus Christ had never happened before and would never happen again. God had broken into history and visited this earth!

Gamaliel also had the mistaken idea that, if something is not of God, it must fail. But this idea does not take into consideration the sinful nature of man and the presence of Satan in the world. Mark Twain said that a lie runs around the world while truth is still putting on her shoes. In the end, God's truth will be victorious; but meanwhile, Satan can be very strong and influence multitudes of people.

Success is no test of truth, in spite of what the pragmatists say. False cults often grow faster than God's church. This world is a battlefield on which truth and error are in mortal combat, and often it looks as if truth is "on the scaffold" while wrong sits arrogantly on the throne. How long should the council wait to see if the new movement would survive? What tests would they use to determine whether or not it was successful? What is success? No matter how you look at it, Gamaliel's "wisdom" was foolish.

But the biggest weakness of his advice was his motive: he encouraged neutrality when the council was facing a life-and-death issue that demanded decision. "Wait and see!" is actually not neutrality; *it is a definite decision.* Gamaliel was voting "No!" but he was preaching "maybe someday."

There are many matters in life that do not demand a courageous decision of conscience. I had a friend in seminary who became emotionally disturbed because he tried to make every decision a matter of conscience, including the cereal he ate at breakfast and the route he took when he walked to the store. But when we face a serious matter of conscience, we had better examine the evidence carefully. This, Gamaliel refused to do. He lost an opportunity for salvation because he turned the meeting into a petty discussion about Jewish insurrectionists.

Jesus made it clear that it is impossible to be neutral about Him and His message. "He that is not with Me is against Me; and he that gathereth not with Me scattereth abroad" (Matt. 12:30). The members of the council knew the words of Elijah, "How long will you waver between two opinions?" (1 Kings 18:21, NIV) There are times when being neutral means making a quiet (and perhaps cowardly) decision to reject God's offer. It is significant that the first group named among those who go to hell is "the fearful" (Rev. 21:8), the people who knew the truth but were afraid to take their stand.

If Gamaliel was really afraid of fighting against God, why did he not honestly investigate the evidence, diligently search the Scriptures, listen to the witnesses, and ask God for wisdom? This was the opportunity of a lifetime! Daniel Defoe, author of *Robinson Crusoe,* claimed that nobody was born a coward. "Truth makes a man of courage," he wrote, "and guilt makes that man of courage a coward." What some men call caution, God would call cowardice. The Apostles were true ambassadors; Gamaliel was really only a "religious politician."

The Church: Announcing the Truth (Acts 5:40-42)

Part of the council wanted to kill the Apostles (Acts 5:33), but Gamaliel's speech tempered their violence. In a compromise move, the council decided to have the Apostles beaten; so the men were given thirty-nine strokes (see Deut. 25:1-3; 2 Cor. 11:24). Then the Apostles were commanded to stop speaking in the name of Jesus Christ lest something worse happen to them. (Review Acts 2:22; 3:6, 16; 4:10, 12, 17-18, 30.)

When people refuse to deal with disagreements on the basis of principle and truth, they often resort to verbal or physical violence, and sometimes both. The sad thing is that this violence often masquerades as patriotism or as religious zeal. When understanding fails, violence starts to take over; and people begin to destroy each other in the name of their nation or their God. It is tragic that even the history of religion is punctuated with accounts of persecutions and "holy wars." William Temple said that Christians are "called to the hardest of all tasks: to fight without hatred, to resist without bitterness, and in the end, if God grant it so, to triumph without vindictiveness."

How did the Apostles respond to this illegal treatment from their nation's religious leaders? They rejoiced! Jesus had told them to expect persecution and had instructed them to rejoice in it (Matt. 5:10-12). The opposition of men meant the approval of God, and it was actually a privilege to suffer for His name (Phil. 1:29).

To paraphrase Phillips Brooks, the purpose of life is to glorify God by the building of character through truth. The Sanhedrin thought that it had won a great victory, when actually the council had experienced a crushing defeat. No doubt they congratulated each other for doing such a good job of defending the faith! But it was the Apostles who were the winners, because they grew in godliness as they yielded to God's will and suffered for their Master. In later years, Peter would have much to say in his first epistle about the meaning of suffering in the life of the believer; but now he was learning the lessons.

Neither the threats nor the beatings stopped them from witnessing for Jesus Christ. If anything, this persecution only made them trust God more and seek greater power in their ministry. True believers are not "quitters." The Apostles had a commission to fulfill, and they intended to continue as long as their Lord enabled them. Acts 5:42 summarized the apostolic pattern for evangelism, an excellent pattern for us to follow.

To begin with, they witnessed "daily." This meant that they took advantage of witnessing opportunities no matter where they were (Eph. 5:15-16). *Every* Christian is a witness, either a good one or a bad one; and our witness either draws others to Christ or drives them away. It is a good practice to start each day asking the Lord for the wisdom and grace needed to be a loving witness for Christ that day. If we sincerely look for opportunities and expect God to give them to us, we will never lack for open doors.

D.L. Moody was fearless in his witness for Christ and sought to speak about spiritual matters to at least one soul each day. "How does your soul prosper today?" he would ask; or, "Do you love the Lord? Do you belong to Christ?" Some were offended by his blunt manner, but not a few were led to Christ then and there. "The more we use the means and opportunities we have," he said, "the more will our ability and our opportunities be increased." He also said, "I live for souls and for eternity; I want to win some soul to Christ." He was not satisfied only to address great crowds; he also felt constrained to speak to people personally and urge them to trust Jesus Christ.

The believers witnessed "in the temple." After all, that was where the "religious" people gathered, and it was easier to reach them there. For several years, the church was looked on as another "sect" of the Jewish faith, and both the temple and the many synagogues were open to believers. In his missionary journeys, Paul always went first to the local synagogue or Jewish place of prayer, and he witnessed there until he was thrown out.

My counsel to new Christians has usually been, "Go back to your home and church, be a loving witness for Christ, and stay until they ask you to leave" (see 1 Cor. 7:17-24). The Apostles did not abandon the Jewish temple, though they knew the old dispensation was ended and that one day the temple would be destroyed. They were not compromising; they were "buying up the opportunity" to reach more people for Christ.

While I was ministering at the Moody Church in Chicago, it was my joy to lead a pastor to Christ, a gifted man who ministered to a wealthy congregation. He went back to his church and began to share Christ, and numbers of his people were saved. Then the denominational leaders stepped in and started to threaten him with dismissal.

"What do I do?" he asked; and I said, "Stay there until they throw you out. Be loving and kind, but don't give in!" Eventually he was forced out of the church, but not before his witness had influenced many both in the church and in the community. Today, God is using him in a remarkable way to witness for Christ and to train others to witness. He is able to get into churches and groups that might never invite me!

The early Christians also witnessed "in every house." Unlike congregations today, these people had no buildings that were set aside for worship and fellowship. Believers would meet in different homes, worshiping the Lord, listening to teaching, and seeking to win the lost (see Acts 2:46). Paul referred to a number of "house fellowships" when he greeted the saints in Rome (Rom. 16:5, 10-11, 14). The early church took the Word right into the homes, and we should follow their example. This does not mean that it is wrong to have special buildings set aside for church ministry, but only that we must not confine the ministry to the four walls of a church building.

Their ministry went on without ceasing. The authorities had told them to stop witnessing, but they only witnessed all the more! Their motive was not defiance to the law but rather obedience to the Lord. It was not something they turned on and off, depending on the situation. They were "always at it" and they kept at it as long as God gave them opportunities.

The witness of the church included both teaching and preaching, and that is a good balance. The word translated "preach" gives us our English word *evangelize,* and this is the first of fifteen times it is used in Acts. It simply means "to preach the Gospel, to share the Good News of Jesus Christ." (See 1 Cor. 15:1-8 for the official statement of the Gospel message.)

However, proclamation must be balanced with instruction (see Acts 2:42) so that the sinners know *what* to believe and the new converts understand *why* they believed. The message cannot produce fruit unless the person understands it and can make an intelligent decision (Matt. 13:18-23). Believers cannot grow unless they are taught the Word of God (1 Peter 2:1-3).

Finally, it was Jesus Christ who was the center of their witness. That was the very name that the Sanhedrin had condemned! The early church did not go about arguing religion or condemning the establishment: they simply told people about Jesus Christ and urged them to trust in Him. "For we preach not ourselves, but Christ Jesus the Lord" (2 Cor. 4:5). "Ye shall be witnesses unto Me" (Acts 1:8).

It was my privilege to speak at a service celebrating the fortieth anniversary of a pastor friend whose ministry has blessed many. A number of his friends shared in the service and quite candidly expressed their love for him and their appreciation for his ministry. My friend became more and more embarrassed as the meeting progressed; and when it came time for me to bring the message, he leaned over and whispered in my ear, "Warren, please tell them about Jesus!"

In his clever and convicting book *The Gospel Blimp,* the late Joe Bayly wrote: "Jesus Christ didn't commit the Gospel to an advertising agency; He commissioned disciples."

That commission still stands.

In your life, is it commission—or omission?

CHAPTER SEVEN STEPHEN, THE MAN GOD CROWNED

Acts 6–7

There are two words for "crown" in the New Testament: *diadema,* which means "a royal crown" and gives us the English word "diadem"; and *stephanos,* the "victor's crown," which gives us the popular name Stephen. You can inherit a *diadema,* but the only way to get a *stephanos* is to earn it.

Acts 6 and 7 center on the ministry and martyrdom of Stephen, a Spirit-filled believer who was crowned by the Lord. "Be thou faithful unto death, and I will give thee a crown of life" (Rev. 2:10). He was faithful both in life and in death and therefore is a good example for us to follow.

These chapters present Stephen as a faithful believer in four different areas of ministry.

Stephen the Servant (Acts 6:1-7)

The church was experiencing "growing pains" and this was making it difficult for the Apostles to minister to everybody. The "Grecians" were the Greek-speaking Jews who had come to Palestine from other nations, and therefore may not have spoken Aramaic, while the "Hebrews" were Jewish residents of the land who spoke both Aramaic and Greek. The fact that the "outsiders" were being neglected created a situation that could have divided the church. However, the Apostles handled the problem with great wisdom and did not give Satan any foothold in the fellowship.

When a church faces a serious problem, this presents the leaders and the members with a number of opportunities. For one thing, problems give us the opportunity to examine our ministry and discover what changes must be made. In times of success, it is easy for us to maintain the *status quo,* but this is dangerous. Henry Ward Beecher called success "a last-year's nest from which the birds have flown." Any ministry or organization that thinks its success will go on automatically is heading for failure. We must regularly examine our lives and our ministries lest we start taking things for granted.

The Apostles studied the situation and concluded that *they* were to blame: they were so busy serving tables that they were neglecting prayer and the ministry of the Word of God. They had created their own problem because they were trying to do too much. Even today, some pastors are so busy with secondary tasks that they fail to spend adequate time in study and in prayer. This creates a "spiritual deficiency" in the church that makes it easy for problems to develop.

This is not to suggest that serving tables is a menial task, because *every* ministry in the church is important. But it is a matter of priorities; the Apostles were doing jobs that others could do just as well. D.L. Moody used to say that it was better to put ten men to work than to try to do the work of ten men. Certainly it is better for you, for the workers you enlist, and for the church as a whole.

Church problems also give us an opportunity to exercise our faith, not only faith in the Lord, but also faith in each other. The leaders suggested a solution, and all the members agreed with it. The assembly selected seven qualified men, and the Apostles set them apart for ministry. The church was not afraid to adjust their structure in order to make room for a growing ministry. When structure and ministry conflict, this gives us an opportunity to trust God for the solution. It is tragic when churches destroy ministry because they refuse to modify their structure. The Apostles were not afraid to share their authority and ministry with others.

Problems also give us the opportunity to express our love. The Hebrew leaders and the predominantly Hebrew members selected six men who were Hellenists and one man who was both a Gentile and a proselyte! What an illustration of Romans 12:10 and Philippians 2:1-4! When we solve church problems, we must think of others and not of ourselves only.

We commonly call these seven men of Acts 6 "deacons" because the Greek noun *diakonos* is used in Acts 6:1 ("ministration"), and the verb *diakoneo* ("serve") is used in Acts 6:2. However, this title is not given to them in this chapter, although you find deacons mentioned in Philippians 1:1 and their qualifications given in 1 Timothy 3:8-13. The word simply means "a servant." These seven men were humble servants of the church, men whose work made it possible for the Apostles to carry on their important ministries among the people.

Stephen was one of these men. The emphasis in Stephen's life is on *fullness*: he was full of the Holy Spirit and wisdom (Acts 6:3, 10), full of faith (Acts 6:5), and full of power (Acts 6:8). In Scripture, to be "full of" means "to be controlled by." This man was controlled by the Spirit, faith, wisdom, and power. He was a God-controlled man yielded to the Holy Spirit, a man who sought to lead people to Christ.

What was the result? The blessing of God continued and increased! The church was still unified (Acts 6:5), multiplied (Acts 6:7), and magnified (Acts 6:8). Acts 6:7 is one of several "summaries" found in the book, statements that let us know that the story has reached an important juncture (see Acts 2:41; 4:4; 5:12-16; 6:7; 9:31; 12:24; 16:5; 19:20; and 28:31). In Acts 6:7, Dr. Luke describes the climax of the ministry in Jerusalem, for the persecution following Stephen's death will take the Gospel to the Samaritans and then to the Gentiles. It has been estimated that there were 8,000 Jewish priests attached to the temple ministry in Jerusalem, and "a great company" of them trusted Jesus Christ as Saviour!

Stephen the Witness (Acts 6:8-15)

This Spirit-filled man did not limit his ministry to the serving of tables; he also won the lost and even did miracles. Up to this point, it was the Apostles who performed the miracles (Acts 2:43; 5:12), but now God gave this power to Stephen also. This was part of His plan to use Stephen to bear witness to the leaders of Israel. Stephen's powerful testimony would be the climax of the church's witness to the Jews. Then the message would go out to the Samaritans and then to the Gentiles.

Jews from many nations resided in Jerusalem in their own "quarters," and some of these ethnic groups had their own synagogues. The freedmen ("libertines") were the descendants of Jews who had previously been in bondage but had won their freedom from Rome. Since Paul came from Tarsus in Cilicia (Acts 21:39), it is possible that he heard Stephen in the synagogue and may have debated with him. However, nobody could match or resist Stephen's wisdom and power (see Luke 21:15). Their only alternative was to destroy him.

Their treatment of Stephen parallels the way the Jewish leaders treated Jesus. First, they hired false witnesses to testify against him. Then, they stirred up the people who accused him of attacking the Law of Moses and the temple. Finally, after listening to his witness, they executed him (see Matt. 26:59-62; John 2:19-22).

The Jews were jealous over their Law and could not understand how Christ had come to fulfill the Law and to bring in the new age. They were proud of their temple and refused to believe that God would permit it to be destroyed. Stephen faced the same spiritual blindness that Jeremiah faced in his ministry (see Jer. 7). The church faced the opposition of Jewish tradition for many years to come, from within its own ranks (Acts 15) and from false teachers coming in from the outside (Gal. 2:4).

The enemy surprised Stephen and arrested him while he was ministering ("having came upon him suddenly" is Wuest's translation of Acts 6:12); and they took him before the same council that had tried Jesus and the Apostles. It was not even necessary for Stephen to speak in order to give witness, for the very glow on his face told everybody that he was a servant of God. Certainly the members of the Sanhedrin would recall Moses' shining face (Ex. 34:29-30). It was as though God was saying, "This man is not against Moses! He is like Moses—he is My faithful servant!"

Stephen the Judge (Acts 7:1-53)

This is the longest address in the Book of Acts and one of the most important. In it, Stephen reviewed the history of Israel and the contributions made by their revered leaders: Abraham (Acts 7:2-8), Joseph (Acts 7:9-17), Moses (Acts 7:18-44), Joshua (Acts 7:45), and David and Solomon (Acts 7:46-50). But this address was more than a recitation of familiar facts; it was also a refutation of their indictments against Stephen and a revelation of their own national sins. Stephen proved from their own Scriptures that the Jewish nation was guilty of worse sins than those they had accused him of committing. What were these sins?

They misunderstood their own spiritual roots (vv. 1-8). Stephen's address opens with "the God of glory" and closes with the glory of God (Acts 7:55); and all the time he spoke, his face radiated that same glory! Why? Because Israel was the only nation privileged to have the glory of God as a part of its inheritance (Rom. 9:4). Alas, the glory of God had departed, first from the tabernacle (1 Sam. 4:19-22) and then from the temple (Ezek. 10:4, 18). God's glory had come in His

Son (John 1:14), but the nation had rejected Him.

Abraham was the founder of the Hebrew nation, and his relationship to God was one of *grace* and *faith.* God had graciously appeared to him and called him out of heathen darkness into the light of salvation, and Abraham had responded by faith. Abraham was saved by grace, through faith, and not because he was circumcised, kept a law, or worshiped in a temple. All of those things came afterward (see Rom. 4; Gal. 3). He believed the promises of God and it was this faith that saved him.

God promised the land to Abraham's descendants, and then told Abraham that his descendants would suffer in Egypt before they would enter and enjoy the land; and this took place just as God promised. From the very beginning, God had a wise plan for His people; and that plan would be fulfilled as long as they trusted His Word and obeyed His will.

The Jews greatly revered Abraham and prided themselves in being his "children." But they confused physical descent with spiritual experience and depended on their national heritage rather than their personal faith. John the Baptist had warned them about this sin (Matt. 3:7-12) and so had Jesus (John 8:33-59). The Jews were blind to the simple faith of Abraham and the patriarchs, and they had cluttered it with man-made traditions that made salvation a matter of good works, not faith. God has no grandchildren. Each of us must be born into the family of God through personal faith in Jesus Christ (John 1:11-13).

The Jews prided themselves in their circumcision, failing to understand that the rite was symbolic of an inner spiritual relationship with God (Deut. 10:16; Jer. 4:4; 6:10; Acts 7:51; Gal. 5:1-6; Phil. 3:3; Col. 2:11-12). Over the years, the fulfilling of ritual had taken the place of the enjoyment of reality. This happens in churches even today.

They rejected their God-sent deliverers (vv. 9-36). I have combined the sections dealing with Joseph and Moses because these two Jewish heroes have this in common: they were both rejected as deliverers the first time, but were accepted the second time. Joseph's brethren hated their brother and sold him into servitude, yet later he became their deliverer. They recognized Joseph "at the second time" (Acts 7:13) when they returned to Egypt for more food. Israel rejected Moses when he first tried to deliver them from Egyptian bondage, and he had to flee for his life (Ex. 2:11-22). But when Moses came to them the second time, the nation accepted him and he set them free (Acts 7:35).

These two events illustrate how Israel treated Jesus Christ. Israel rejected their Messiah when He came to them the first time (John 1:11), but when He comes again, they will recognize Him and receive Him (Zech. 12:10; Rev. 1:7). In spite of what they did to His Son, God has not cast away His people (Rom. 11:1-6). Israel today is suffering from a partial spiritual blindness that one day will be taken away (Rom. 11:25-32). Individual Jews are being saved, but the nation as a whole is blind to the truth about Jesus Christ.

Before leaving this section, we must deal with some seeming contradictions between Stephen's address and the Old Testament Scriptures.

Genesis 46:26-27 states that seventy people made up the household of Jacob, including Joseph's family already in Egypt; but Stephen claimed that there were seventy-five (Acts 7:14; and see Ex. 1:1-5). The Hebrew text has seventy in both Genesis and Exodus, but the Septuagint (Greek translation of the Old Testament) has seventy-five. Where did the number seventy-five come from in the Septuagint? In their count, the translators included Joseph's grandchildren (1 Chron. 7:14-15, 20-25). Being a Hellenistic Jew, Stephen would naturally use the Septuagint. There is no real contradiction; your total depends on the factors you include.

Acts 7:16 suggests that Jacob was buried at Shechem, but Genesis 50:13 states that he was buried in the cave of Machpelah at Hebron, along with Abraham, Isaac, and Sarah (Gen. 23:17). It was Joseph who was buried at Shechem (Josh. 24:32). It is likely that the Children of Israel carried out of Egypt the remains of all the sons of Jacob, and not just Joseph alone, and buried them together in Shechem. The "fathers" mentioned in Acts 7:15 would be the twelve sons of Jacob.

But who purchased the burial place in Shechem—Abraham or Jacob? Stephen seems to say that Abraham bought it, but the Old Testament record says that Jacob did (Gen. 33:18-20). Abraham purchased the cave of Machpelah (Gen. 23:14-20). The simplest explanation is that Abraham actually purchased *both* pieces of property and that Jacob later had to purchase the Shechem property again. Abraham moved around quite a bit and it would be very easy for the residents of the land to forget or ignore the transactions he had made.

They disobeyed their Law (vv. 37-43). Stephen's opponents had accused him of speaking against the sacred Law of Moses, but the history of Israel revealed that the nation had repeatedly *broken* that Law. God gave the Law to His congregation ("church") in the wilderness at Mount Sinai, His living Word through the mediation of angels (see Acts 7:53; Gal. 3:19). No sooner had the people received the Law than they disobeyed it by asking Aaron to make them an idol (Ex. 32), and thereby broke the first two of the Ten Commandments (Ex. 20:1-6).

The Jews had worshiped idols in Egypt (Josh. 24:14; Ezek. 20:7-8), and after their settlement in the Promised Land they gradually adopted the gods of the pagan nations around them. God repeatedly disciplined His people and sent them prophets to warn them, until finally He carried them off to Babylon where they were finally cured of idolatry.

Acts 7:42 should be compared with Romans 1:24-28, for all of these verses describe the judgment of God when He "takes His hands off" and permits sinners to have their own way. When Stephen quoted Amos 5:25-27, he revealed what the Jews had really been doing all those years: in outward form, they were worshiping Jehovah; but in their hearts, they were worshiping foreign gods! The form of the question in Acts 7:42 demands a negative reply: "No, you were not offering those sacrifices to the Lord!"

In this day of "pluralism" of religions and an emphasis on "toleration," we must understand why God hated the pagan religions and instructed Israel to destroy them. To begin with, these religions were unspeakably obscene in their worship of sex and their use of religious prostitutes. Their practices were also brutal, even to the point of offering children as sacrifices to their gods. It was basically demon worship, and it opened the way for all kinds of godless living on the part of the Jews. Had the nation turned from the true God and succumbed to idolatry, it could have meant the end of the godly remnant and the fulfillment of the promise of the Redeemer.

God's Law was given to the Jews to protect them from the pagan influence around them, and to enable them to enjoy the blessings of the land. It was the Law that made them a holy people, different from the other nations. When Israel broke down that wall of distinction by disobeying God's Law, they forfeited the blessing of God and had to be disciplined.

They despised their temple (vv. 44-50). The witnesses accused Stephen of seeking to destroy the temple, but that was exactly what the Jewish nation did! Moses built the tabernacle and God's glory graciously dwelt in the holy of holies (Ex. 40:34-38). Solomon built the temple, and once again God's glory came in (1 Kings 8:10-11). But over the years, the worship at the temple degenerated into mere religious formality, and eventually there were idols placed in the temple (2 Kings 21:1-9; Ezek. 8:7-12). Jeremiah warned people against their superstitious faith in the temple and told them that they had turned God's house into a den of thieves (Jer. 7:1-16).

Had the nation heeded their own prophets, they would have escaped the horrors of the Babylonian siege (see the Book of Lamentations) and the destruction of their city and temple. Even Solomon recognized the truth that God did not live in buildings (1 Kings 8:27), and the Prophet Isaiah made it even clearer (Isa. 66:1-2). We really make nothing for God, because everything comes from Him; and how can the Creator of the universe be contained in a man-made building? (Acts 17:24) The Jewish defense of their temple was both illogical and unscriptural.

They stubbornly resisted their God and His truth (vv. 51-53). This is the climax of Stephen's speech, the personal application that cut his hearers to the heart. Throughout the centuries, Israel had refused to submit to God and obey the truths He had revealed to them. Their ears did not hear the truth, their hearts did not receive the truth, and their necks did not bow to the truth. As a result, they killed their own Messiah!

The nation refused to accept the new truth that God was revealing from age to age. Instead of seeing God's truth as seed that produces fruit and more seed, the religious leaders "embalmed" the truth and refused to accept anything new. By the time Jesus came to earth, the truth of God was encrusted with so much tradition that the people could not recognize God's truth when He did present it. Man's dead traditions had replaced God's living truth (see Matt. 15:1-20).

Stephen the Martyr (Acts 7:54-60)

You wonder what kind of a world we live in when good and godly men like Stephen can be murdered by religious bigots! But we have similar problems in our "enlightened" age today: taking hostages, bombings that kill or maim innocent people, assassinations, and all in the name of politics or religion. The heart of man has not changed, nor can it be changed apart from the grace of God.

What were the results of Stephen's death? For Stephen, death meant *coronation* (Rev. 2:10). He saw the glory of God and the Son of God standing to receive him to heaven (see Luke 22:69). Our Lord sat down when He ascended to heaven (Ps. 110:1; Mark 16:19), but He stood up to welcome to glory the first Christian martyr (Luke 12:8). This is the last time the title "Son of man" is used in the Bible. It is definitely a messianic title (Dan. 7:13-14), and Stephen's use of it was one more witness that Jesus is indeed Israel's Messiah.

Stephen was not only tried in a manner similar to that of our Lord, but he also died with similar prayers on his lips (Luke 23:34, 46; Acts 7:59-60). A heckler once shouted to a street preacher, "Why didn't God do something for Stephen when they were stoning him?" The preacher replied, "God did do something for Stephen. He gave him the grace to forgive his murderers and to pray for them!" A perfect answer!

For Israel, Stephen's death meant *condemnation*. This was their third murder: they had *permitted* John the Baptist to be killed; they had *asked* for Jesus to be killed; and now they were killing Stephen themselves. When they allowed Herod to kill John, the Jews sinned against God the Father who had sent John (Matt. 21:28-32). When they asked Pilate to crucify Jesus, they sinned against God the Son (Matt. 21:33-46). When they stoned Stephen, Israel sinned against the Holy Spirit who was working in and through the Apostles (Matt. 10:1-8; Acts 7:51). Jesus said that this sin could never be forgiven (Matt. 12:31-32). Judgment finally came in A.D. 70 when Titus and the Roman armies destroyed Jerusalem and the temple.

For the church in Jerusalem, the death of Stephen meant *liberation*. They had been witnessing "to the Jew first" ever since Pentecost, but now they would be directed to take the message out of Jerusalem to the Samaritans (Acts 8) and even to the Gentiles (Acts 11:19-26). The opposition of the enemy helped prevent the church from becoming a Jewish "sect" and encouraged them to fulfill the commission of Acts 1:8 and Matthew 28:18-20.

Finally, as far as Saul (Acts 7:58) was concerned, the death of Stephen eventually meant *salvation*. He never forgot the event (Acts 22:17-21), and no doubt Stephen's message, prayers, and glorious death were used of the Spirit to prepare Saul for his own meeting with the Lord (Acts 9). God never wastes the blood of His saints. Saul would one day see the same glory that Stephen saw and would behold the Son of God and hear Him speak!

When Christians die, they "fall asleep" (John 11:11; 1 Thes. 4:13). The body sleeps and the spirit goes to be with the Lord in heaven (Acts 7:59; 2 Cor. 5:6-9; Phil. 1:23; Heb. 12:22-23). When Jesus returns, He will bring with Him the spirits of those who have died (1 Thes. 4:14), their bodies will be raised and glorified, and body and spirit will be united in glory to be "forever with the Lord." Even though we Christians weep at the death of a loved one (Acts 8:2), we do not sorrow hopelessly; for we know we shall meet again when we die or when the Lord returns.

God does not call all of us to be martyrs, but He does call us to be "living sacrifices" (Rom. 12:1-2). In some respects, it may be harder to *live* for Christ than to *die* for Him; but if we are living for Him, we will be prepared to die for Him if that is what God calls us to do.

In 1948, Auca martyr Jim Elliot wrote in his journal, "I seek not a long life, but a full one, like You, Lord Jesus." Two years later, he wrote: "I must not think it strange if God takes in youth those whom I would have kept on earth till they were older. God is peopling Eternity, and I must not restrict Him to old men and women."

Like Stephen, Jim Elliot and his four comrades were called on January 8, 1956, to "people Eternity" as they were slain by the people they were seeking to reach. What has happened to the Aucas since then is proof that the blood of the martyrs is indeed the seed of the church. Many Aucas are now Christians.

"Be thou faithful unto death, and I will give thee a crown of life" (Rev. 2:10).

CHAPTER EIGHT
A CHURCH ON THE MOVE
Acts 8

"There is one thing stronger than all the armies in the world," wrote Victor Hugo, "and that is an idea whose time has come."

The Gospel of Jesus Christ is much more than an idea. The Gospel is "the power of God to salvation for everyone who believes" (Rom. 1:16, NKJV). It is God's "dynamite" for breaking down sin's barriers and setting the prisoners free. Its time had come and the church was on the move. The "salt" was now leaving the "Jerusalem saltshaker" to be spread over all Judea and Samaria, just as the Lord had commanded (Acts 1:8).

The events in Acts 8 center around four different men.

A Zealous Persecutor—Saul (Acts 8:1-3)

The Book of Acts and the epistles give sufficient data for a sketch of Saul's early life. He was born in Tarsus in Cilicia (Acts 22:3), a "Hebrew of the Hebrews" (see 2 Cor. 11:22; Phil. 3:5), the "son of a Pharisee" (Acts 23:6), and a Roman citizen (Acts 16:37; 22:25-28). He was educated in Jerusalem by Gamaliel (Acts 22:3) and became a devoted Pharisee (Acts 26:4-5; Phil. 3:5). Measured by the Law, his life was blameless (Phil. 3:6). He was one of the most promising young Pharisees in Jerusalem, well on his way to becoming a great leader for the Jewish faith (Gal. 1:14).

Saul's zeal for the Law was displayed most vividly in his persecution of the church (Gal. 1:13-14; Phil. 3:6). He really thought that persecuting the believers was one way of serving God, so he did it with a clear conscience (2 Tim. 1:3). He obeyed the light that he had and, when God gave him more light, he obeyed that and became a Christian!

In what ways did Saul persecute the church? He "made havoc of the church," and the verb here describes a wild animal mangling its prey. When Christ spoke to Saul on the Damascus road, He compared him to a beast! (Acts 9:5) The stoning of Stephen, which Saul approved, shows the lengths to which he would go to achieve his purpose. He persecuted both men and women "unto the death" (Acts 22:4), entering both houses and synagogues (Acts 22:19). He had the believers imprisoned and beaten (Acts 22:19; 26:9-11). If they renounced their faith in Jesus Christ ("compelling them to blaspheme"—Acts 26:11), they were set free; if they did not recant, they could be killed.

In later years, Paul described himself as "exceedingly mad against them" (Acts 26:11), "a blasphemer [he denounced Jesus Christ], and a persecutor, and injurious [violent]" (1 Tim. 1:13). He was a man with great authority whose devotion to Moses completely controlled his life, and almost destroyed his life. He did it "ignorantly in unbelief" (1 Tim. 1:13), and God showed him mercy and saved him. Saul of Tarsus is the last person in Jerusalem you would have chosen to be the great apostle to the Gentiles!

A Faithful Preacher—Philip (Acts 8:4-8)

Persecution does to the church what wind does to seed: it scatters it and only produces a greater harvest. The word translated "scattered" (*diaspeiro,* Acts 8:1, 4) means "to scatter seed." The believers in Jerusalem were God's seed and the persecution was used of God to plant them in new soil so they could bear fruit (Matt. 13:37-38). Some went throughout Judea and Samaria (see Acts 1:8), and others went to more distant fields (Acts 11:19ff).

The Samaritans were a "half-breed" people, a mixture of Jew and Gentile. The nation originated when the Assyrians captured the ten northern tribes in 732 B.C., deported many of the people, and then imported others who intermarried with the Jews. The Samaritans had their own temple and priesthood and openly opposed fraternization with the Jews (John 4:9).

We have no reason to believe that God permitted this persecution because His people were negligent and had to be "forced" to leave Jerusalem. The fact that Saul persecuted believers "even unto strange [foreign] cities" (Acts 26:11) would suggest that their witness was bearing fruit even beyond Jerusalem. Nor should we criticize the Apostles for remaining in the city. If anything, we should commend them for their courage and devotion to duty. After all, somebody had to remain there to care for the church.

Because of the witness and death of Stephen, it is possible that the focus of the persecution was against the Hellenistic Jews rather than the "native" Jews. It would be easier for Saul and his helpers to identify the Hellenistic believers since many of the "native" Jews were still very Jewish and very much attached to the temple. Peter was still keeping a "kosher home" when he was sent to evangelize the household of Cornelius (Acts 10:9-16).

Philip was chosen as a deacon (Acts 6:5) but, like Stephen, he grew in his ministry and became an effective evangelist (see Acts 21:8). God directed him to evangelize in Samaria, an area that had been prohibited to the Apostles (Matt. 10:5-6). Both John the Baptist and Jesus had ministered there (John 3:23; 4:1ff), so Philip entered into their labors (John 4:36-38).

The word for preaching in Acts 8:4 means "to preach the Gospel, to evangelize"; while the word in Acts 8:5 means "to announce as a herald." Philip was God's commissioned herald to deliver His message to the people of Samaria. To reject the messenger would mean to reject the message and rebel against the authority behind the herald, Almighty God. How people respond to God's messenger and God's message is serious business.

Philip not only declared God's Word, but he also demonstrated God's power by performing miracles. It was the Apostles who had majored on miracles (Acts 2:43; 5:12), yet both Stephen and Philip did signs and wonders by the power of God (Acts 6:8). However, the emphasis here is on the Word of God: the people gave heed to the Word because they saw the miracles, and by believing the Word, they were saved. Nobody was ever saved simply because of miracles (John 2:23-25; 12:37-41).

Great persecution (Acts 8:1) plus the preaching of the Gospel resulted in great joy! Both in his Gospel and in the Book of Acts, Luke emphasizes the joy of salvation (Luke 2:10; 15:7, 10; 24:52; Acts 8:8; 13:52; 15:3). The people of Samaria who heard the Gospel and believed were delivered from physical affliction, demonic control, and, most important, from their sins. No wonder there was great joy!

The Gospel had now moved from "Jewish territory" into Samaria where the people were part Jew and part Gentile. God in His grace had built a bridge between two estranged peoples and made the believers one in Christ, and soon He would extend that bridge to the Gentiles and include them as well. Even today, we need "bridge builders" like Philip, men and women who will carry the Gospel into pioneer territory and dare to challenge ancient prejudices. "Into all the world . . . the Gospel to every creature" is still God's commission to us.

A Clever Deceiver—Simon the Sorcerer (Acts 8:9-25)

It is a basic principle in Scripture that wherever God sows His true believers, Satan will eventually sow his counterfeits (Matt. 13:24-30, 36-43). This was true of the ministry of John the Baptist (Matt. 3:7ff) and Jesus (Matt. 23:15, 33; John 8:44), and it would be true of Paul's ministry also (Acts 13:6ff; 2 Cor. 11:1-4, 13-15). The enemy comes as a lion to devour, and when that approach fails, he comes as a serpent to deceive. Satan's tool in this case was a sorcerer named Simon.

The word translated "bewitched" in Acts 8:9 and 11 simply means "astounded, confounded." It is translated "wondered" in Acts 8:13. The people were amazed at the things that Simon did and, therefore, they believed the things that he said. They considered him "the great power of God." Simon's sorcery was energized by Satan (2 Thes. 2:1-12) and was used to magnify himself, while Philip's miracles were empowered by God and were used to glorify Christ. Simon started to lose his following as the Samaritans listened to Philip's messages, believed on Jesus Christ, were born again, and were baptized.

What does it mean that "Simon himself believed"? (Acts 8:13) We can answer that question best by asking another one: What was the basis of his "faith"? His faith was not in the Word of God, but in the miracles he saw Philip perform; and there is no indication that Simon repented of his sins. He certainly did not believe with *all* his heart (Acts 8:37). His faith was like that of the people of Jerusalem who witnessed our Lord's miracles (John 2:23-25), or even like that of the demons (James 2:19). Simon continued with Philip, not to hear the Word and learn more about Jesus Christ, but to witness the miracles and perhaps learn how they were done.

It is important to note that the Samaritans did not receive the gift of the Holy Spirit when they believed. It was necessary for two of the Apostles, Peter and John, to come from Jerusalem, put their hands on the converts, and impart to them the gift of the Spirit. Why?

Because God wanted to unite the Samaritan believers with the original Jewish church in Jerusalem. He did not want two churches that would perpetuate the division and conflict that had existed for centuries. Jesus had given Peter the "keys of the kingdom of heaven" (Matt. 16:13-20), which meant that Peter had the privilege of "opening the door of faith" to others. He opened the door to the Jews at Pentecost, and now he opened the door to the Samaritans. Later, he would open the door of faith to the Gentiles (Acts 10).

Remember too that the first ten chapters of Acts record a period of transition, from the Jew to the Samaritan to the Gentile. God's pattern for today is given in Acts 10: the sinner hears the Gospel, believes, receives the gift of the Spirit, and then is baptized. It is dangerous to base any doctrine or practice *only* on what is recorded in Acts 1–10, for you might be building on that which was temporary and transitional. Those who claim we must be baptized to receive the gift of the Spirit (Acts 2:38) have a hard time explaining what happened to the Samaritans; and those who claim we must have "the laying on of hands" to receive the Spirit have a difficult time with Acts 10. Once you accept Acts 1–10 as a transitional period in God's plan, with Acts 10 being the climax, the problems are solved.

The wickedness of Simon's heart was fully revealed by the ministry of the two apostles. Simon not only wanted to perform miracles, but he also wanted the power to convey the gift of the Holy Spirit to others—and he was quite willing to pay for this power! It is this passage that gives us the word *simony,* which means "the buying and selling of church offices or privileges."

As you study the Book of Acts, you will often find the Gospel in conflict with money and "big business." Ananias and Sapphira lost their lives because they lied about their gift (Acts 5:1-11). Paul put a fortune-teller out of business in Philippi and ended up in jail (Acts 16:16-24). He also gave the silversmiths trouble in Ephesus and helped cause a riot (Acts 19:23-41). The early church had its priorities straight: it was more important to preach the Word than to win the support of the wealthy and influential people of the world.

Peter's words to Simon give every indication that the sorcerer was not a converted man. "Thy money perish with thee!" is pretty strong language to use with a believer. He had neither "part or lot in this matter" ("this word") and his heart was not right before God. While it is not out of place for believers to repent (see Rev. 2–3), the command to repent is usually given to unbelievers. The word *thought* in Acts 8:22 means "plot or scheme" and is used in a bad sense. The fact that Simon was "in the gall of bitterness" (Deut. 29:18; Heb. 12:15) and "the bond of iniquity" would indicate that he had never truly been born again.

Simon's response to these severe words of warning was not at all encouraging. He was more concerned about avoiding judgment than getting right with God! There is no evidence that he repented and sought forgiveness. A sinner who wants the prayers of others but who will not pray himself is not going to enter God's kingdom.

This episode only shows how close a person can come to salvation and still not be converted. Simon heard the Gospel, saw the miracles, gave a profession of faith in Christ, and was baptized; and yet he was never born again. He was one of Satan's clever counterfeits; and, had Peter not exposed the wickedness of his heart, Simon would have been accepted as a member of the Samaritan congregation!

Even though the persecution was still going on, Peter and John returned to Jerusalem, preaching the Gospel in "many villages of the Samaritans" as they went their way. They lost no opportunity to share the Good News with others now that the doors were open in Samaria.

A Concerned Seeker—an Ethiopian (Acts 8:26-40)

Philip was not only a faithful preacher; he was also an obedient personal worker. Like his Master, he was willing to leave the crowds and deal with one lost soul. The angel could have told this Ethiopian official how to be saved, but God has not given the commission to angels: He has given it to His people. Angels have never personally experienced God's grace; therefore, they can never bear witness of what it means to be saved.

D.L. Moody once asked a man about his soul, and the man replied, "It's none of your business!"

"Oh, yes, it is my business!" Moody said; and the man immediately exclaimed, "Then you must be D.L. Moody!" It is every Christian's business to share the Gospel with others, and to do it without fear or apology.

Philip's experience ought to encourage us in our own personal witness for the Lord. To begin with, God directed Philip to the right person at the right time. You and I are not likely to have angels instruct us, but we can know the guidance of the Holy Spirit in our witnessing, if we are walking in the Spirit and praying for God's direction.

Late one afternoon, I was completing my pastoral calling and I felt impressed to make one more visit to see a woman who was faithfully attending church but was not a professed Christian. At first, I told myself that it was foolish to visit her that late in the day, since she was probably preparing a meal for her family. But I went anyway and discovered that she had been burdened about her sins all that day! Within minutes, she opened her heart to Christ and was born again. Believe me, I was glad I obeyed the leading of the Spirit!

This court official did not come from what we know today as Ethiopia; his home was in ancient Nubia, located south of Egypt. Since he was a eunuch, he could not become a full Jewish proselyte (Deut. 23:1); but he was permitted to become a "God fearer" or "a proselyte of the gate." He was concerned enough about his spiritual life to travel over 200 miles to Jerusalem to worship God; but his heart was still not satisfied.

This Ethiopian represents many people today who are religious, read the Scriptures, and seek the truth, yet do not have saving faith in Jesus Christ. They are sincere, but they are lost! They need someone to show them the way.

As Philip drew near to the chariot, he heard the man reading from the Prophet Isaiah. (It was customary in those days for students to read out loud.) God had already prepared the man's heart to receive Philip's witness! If we obey the Lord's leading, we can be sure that God will go before us and open the way for our witness.

Isaiah 53 was the passage he was reading, the prophecy of God's Suffering Servant. Isaiah 53 describes our Lord Jesus Christ in His birth (Isa. 53:1-2), life and ministry (Isa. 53:3), substitutionary death (Isa. 53:4-9), and victorious resurrection (Isa. 53:10-12). Isaiah 53:4 should be connected with 1 Peter 2:24; Isaiah 53:7 with Matthew 26:62-63; Isaiah 53:9 with Matthew 27:57-60; and Isaiah 53:12 with Luke 23:34, 37.

The Ethiopian focused on Isaiah 53:7-8, which describes our Lord as the willing Sacrifice for sinners, even to the point of losing His human rights. As Philip explained the verses to him, the Ethiopian began to understand the Gospel because the Spirit of God was opening his mind to God's truth. It is not enough for the lost sinner to desire salvation; he must also understand God's plan of salvation. It is the heart that understands the Word that eventually bears fruit (Matt. 13:23).

The idea of substitutionary sacrifice is one that is found from the beginning of the Bible to the end. God killed animals so that He might clothe Adam and Eve (Gen. 3:21). He provided a ram to die in the place of Isaac (Gen. 22:13). At Passover, innocent lambs died for the people of Israel (Ex. 12); and the entire Jewish religious system was based on the shedding of blood (Lev. 17, especially v. 11). Jesus Christ is the fulfillment of both the Old Testament types and the prophecies (John 1:29; Rev. 5).

"Faith cometh by hearing, and hearing by the Word of God" (Rom. 10:17). The Ethiopian believed on Jesus Christ and was born again! So real was his experience that he insisted on stopping the caravan and being baptized immediately! He was no "closet Christian"; he wanted everybody to know what the Lord had done for him.

How did he know that believers were supposed to be baptized? Perhaps Philip had included this in his witness to him, or perhaps he had even seen people baptized while he was in Jerusalem. We know that Gentiles were baptized when they became Jewish proselytes. Throughout the Book of Acts, baptism is an important part of the believer's commitment to Christ and witness for Christ.

While Acts 8:37 is not found in all the New Testament manuscripts, there is certainly nothing in it that is unbiblical (Rom. 10:9-10). In the days of the early church, converts were not baptized unless they first gave a clear testimony of their faith in Jesus Christ. And keep in mind that the Ethiopian was speaking not only to Philip but also to those in the caravan who were near his chariot. He was an important man, and you can be sure that his attendants were paying close attention.

Philip was caught away to minister elsewhere (compare 1 Kings 18:12), but the treasurer "went on his way rejoicing" (see Acts 8:8). God did not permit Philip to do the necessary discipling of this new believer, but surely He provided for it when the man arrived home. Even though he was a eunuch, the Ethiopian was accepted by God! (see Isa. 56:3-5)

Philip ended up at Azotus, about twenty miles from Gaza; and then made his way to Caesarea, a journey of about sixty miles. Like Peter and John, Philip "preached his way home" (Acts 8:25) as he told others about the Saviour. Twenty years later, we find Philip living in Caesarea and still serving God as an evangelist (Acts 21:8ff).

As you trace the expansion of the Gospel during this transition period (Acts 2–10), you see how the Holy Spirit reaches out to the whole world. In Acts 8, the Ethiopian who was converted was a descendant of Ham (Gen. 10:6, where "Cush" refers to Ethiopia). In Acts 9, Saul of Tarsus will be saved, a Jew and therefore a descendant of Shem (Gen. 10:21ff). In Acts 10, the Gentiles find Christ, and they are the descendants of Japheth (Gen. 10:2-5). The whole world was peopled by Shem, Ham, and Japheth (Gen. 10:1); and God wants the whole world—all of their descendants—to hear the message of the Gospel (Matt. 28:18-20; Mark 16:15).

In October 1857, J. Hudson Taylor began to minister in Ningpo, China, and he led a Mr. Nyi to Christ. The man was overjoyed and wanted to share his faith with others.

"How long have you had the good tidings in England?" Mr. Nyi asked Hudson Taylor one day. Taylor acknowledged that England had known the Gospel for many centuries.

"My father died seeking the truth," said Mr. Nyi. "Why didn't you come sooner?"

Taylor had no answer to that penetrating question.

How long have *you* known the Gospel?

How far have you shared it personally?

CHAPTER NINE
GOD ARRESTS SAUL
Acts 9:1-31

The conversion of Saul of Tarsus, the leading persecutor of the Christians, was perhaps the greatest event in church history after the coming of the Spirit at Pentecost. The next great event would be the conversion of the Gentiles (Acts 10), and Saul (Paul) would become the apostle to the Gentiles. God was continuing to work out His plan to bring the Gospel to the whole world.

"Paul was a great man," said Charles Spurgeon, "and I have no doubt that on the way to Damascus he rode a very high horse. But a few seconds sufficed to alter the man. How soon God brought him down!"

The account of the conversion of Saul of Tarsus is given three times in Acts, in chapters 9, 22, and 26. According to the record before us, Saul experienced four meetings that together transformed his life.

He Met Jesus Christ (Acts 9:1-9)

When you look at Saul *on the road* (Acts 9:1-2), you see a very zealous man who actually thought he was doing God a service by persecuting the church. Had you stopped him and asked for his reasons, he might have said something like this:

"Jesus of Nazareth is dead. Do you expect me to believe that a crucified nobody is the promised Messiah? According to our Law, anybody who is hung on a tree is cursed [Deut. 21:23]. Would God take a cursed false prophet and make him the Messiah? No! His followers are preaching that Jesus is both alive and doing miracles through them. But their power comes from Satan, not God. This is a dangerous sect, and I intend to eliminate it before it destroys our historic Jewish faith!"

In spite of his great learning (Acts 26:24), Saul was spiritually blind (2 Cor. 3:12-18) and did not understand what the Old Testament really taught about the Messiah. Like many others of his countrymen, he stumbled over the Cross (1 Cor. 1:23) because he depended on his own righteousness and not on the righteousness of God (Rom. 9:30–10:13; Phil. 3:1-10). Many self-righteous religious people today do not see their need for a Saviour and resent it if you tell them they are sinners.

Saul's attitude was that of an angry animal whose very breath was dangerous! (see Acts 8:3) Like many other rabbis, he believed that the Law had to be obeyed before Messiah could come; and yet these "heretics" were preaching against the Law, the temple, and the traditions of the fathers (Acts 6:11-13). Saul wasted the churches in Judea (Gal. 1:23) and then got authority from the high priest to go as far as Damascus to hunt down the disciples of Jesus. This was no insignificant enterprise, for the authority of the highest Jewish council was behind him (Acts 22:5).

Damascus had a large Jewish population, and it has been estimated that there could well have been thirty to forty synagogues in the city. The fact that there were already believers there indicates how effective the church had been in getting out the message. Some of the believers may have fled the persecution in Jerusalem, which explains why Saul wanted authority to bring them back. Believers were still identified with the Jewish synagogues, for the break with Judaism would not come for a few years. (See James 2:2, where "assembly" is "synagogue" in the original Greek.)

Saul suddenly found himself *on the ground!* (Acts 9:4) It was not a heat stroke or an attack of epilepsy that put him there, but a personal meeting with Jesus Christ. At midday (Acts 22:6), he saw a bright light from heaven and heard a voice speaking his name (Acts 22:6-11). The men with him also fell to the earth (Acts 26:14) and heard the sound, but they could not understand the words spoken from heaven. They stood to their feet in bewilderment (Acts 9:7), hearing Saul address someone, but not knowing what was happening.

Saul of Tarsus made some wonderful discoveries that day. To begin with, he discovered to his surprise that Jesus of Nazareth was actually *alive!* Of course, the believers had been constantly affirming this (Acts 2:32; 3:15; 5:30-32), but Saul had refused to accept their testimony. If Jesus was alive, then Saul had to change his mind about Jesus and His message. He had to repent, a difficult thing for a self-righteous Pharisee to do.

Saul also discovered that he was a lost sinner who was in danger of the judgment of God. "I am Jesus, whom you are persecuting" (Acts 9:5, NKJV). Saul thought he had been serving God, when in reality he had been persecuting the Messiah! When measured by the holiness of Jesus Christ, Saul's good works and legalistic self-righteousness looked like filthy rags (Isa. 64:6; Phil. 3:6-8). All of his values changed. He was a new person because he trusted Jesus Christ.

The Lord had a special work for Saul to do (Acts 26:16-18). The Hebrew of the Hebrews would become the apostle to the Gentiles; the persecutor would become a preacher; and the legalistic Pharisee would become the great proclaimer of the grace of God. Up to now, Saul had been like a wild animal, fighting against the goads; but now he would become a vessel of honor, the Lord's "tool," to preach the Gospel in the regions beyond. What a transformation!

Some thirty years later, Paul wrote that Christ had "apprehended him" on the Damascus road (Phil. 3:12). Saul was out to arrest others when the Lord arrested him. He had to lose his religion before he could gain the righteousness of Christ. His conversion experience is unique, because sinners today certainly do not hear God's voice or see blinding heavenly lights. However, Paul's experience is an example of how Israel will be saved when Jesus Christ returns and reveals Himself to them (Zech. 12:10; Matt. 24:29ff; 1 Tim. 1:12-16). His salvation is certainly a great encouragement to any lost sinner, for if "the chief of sinners" could be saved, surely anybody can be saved!

It is worth noting that the men who were with Saul saw the light, but did not see the Lord; and they heard the sound, but did not hear the voice speaking the words (note John 12:27-29). We wonder if any of them later trusted in Christ because of Saul's testimony. He definitely saw the glorified Lord Jesus Christ (1 Cor. 15:7-10).

The men led Saul *into the city* (Acts 9:8-9), for the angry bull (Acts 9:1) had now become a docile lamb! The leader had to be led because the vision had left him blind. His spiritual eyes had been opened, but his physical eyes were closed. God was thoroughly humbling Saul and preparing him for the ministry of Ananias. He fasted and prayed (Acts 9:11) for three days, during which time he no doubt started to "sort out" what he believed. He had been saved by grace, not by Law, through faith in the living Christ. God began to instruct Saul and show him the relationship between the Gospel of the grace of God and the traditional Mosaic religion that he had practiced all his life.

He Met Ananias (Acts 9:10-19)

Ananias was a devout Jew (Acts 22:12) who was a believer in Jesus Christ. He knew what kind of reputation Saul had and that he was coming to Damascus to arrest believers. It was up to a week's journey from Jerusalem to Damascus, but some of the Jerusalem Christians had gotten to the city first in order to warn the saints.

It is interesting to note in Acts 9 the different names used for God's people: disciples (Acts 9:1, 10, 19, 25-26, 36, 38), those of the way (Acts 9:2), saints (Acts 9:13, 32, 41), all that call on God's name (Acts 9:14, 21), and brethren (Acts 9:17, 30). We use the word *Christian* most frequently, and yet that name did not appear on the scene until later (Acts 11:26). "Disciples" is the name that is used most in the Book of Acts, but you do not find it used in the epistles. There the name "saints" is the most frequently used title for God's people.

Ananias was available to do God's will, but he certainly was not anxious to obey! The fact that Saul was "praying" instead of "preying" should have encouraged Ananias. "Prayer is the autograph of the Holy Ghost upon the renewed heart," said Charles Spurgeon (Rom. 8:9, 14-16). Instead of trusting himself, Saul was now trusting the Lord and waiting for Him to show him what to do. In fact, Saul had already seen a vision of a man named Ananias (Hananiah = "the Lord is gracious") coming to minister to him; so, how could Ananias refuse to obey?

Acts 9:15 is a good summary of Paul's life and ministry. It was all of grace, for he did not choose God; it was God who chose him (1 Tim. 1:14). He was God's vessel (2 Tim. 2:20-21), and God would work in and through him to accomplish His purposes (Eph. 2:10; Phil. 2:12-13). God's name would be glorified as His servant would take the Gospel to Jews and Gentiles, kings and commoners, and as he would suffer for Christ's sake. This is the first reference in the Book of Acts to the Gospel going to the Gentiles (see also Acts 22:21; 26:17).

Once convinced, Ananias lost no time going to the house of Judas and ministering to waiting Saul. The fact that he called him "brother" must have brought joy to the heart of the blinded Pharisee. Saul not only heard Ananias' voice, but he felt his hands (Acts 9:12, 17). By the power of God, his eyes were opened and he could see! He was also filled with the Holy Spirit and baptized, and then he ate some food.

The *King James Version* of Acts 22:16 conveys the impression that it was necessary for Saul to be baptized in order to be saved, but that was not the case. Saul washed away his sins by "calling on the Lord" (Acts 2:21; Rom. 10:13). Kenneth Wuest translates Acts 22:16, "Having arisen, be baptized and wash away your sins, having previously called upon His name." In the Greek, it is not a present participle ("calling"), but an aorist participle ("having called"). His calling on the Lord preceded his baptism.

Saul tarried with the believers in Damascus and no doubt learned from them. Imagine what it would be like to disciple the great Apostle Paul! He discovered that they were loving people, undeserving of the persecution he had inflicted on them; and that they knew the truth of God's Word and only wanted to share it with others.

Before we leave this section, we should emphasize some practical lessons that all believers ought to learn.

To begin with, *God can use even the most obscure saint.* Were it not for the conversion of Saul, we would never have heard of Ananias; and yet Ananias had an important part to play in the ongoing work of the church. Behind many well-known servants of God are lesser-known believers who have influenced them. God keeps the books and will see to it that each servant will get a just reward. The important thing is not fame but faithfulness (1 Cor. 4:1-5).

The experience of Ananias also reminds us that we *should never be afraid to obey God's will.* Ananias at first argued with the Lord and gave some good reasons why he should not visit Saul. But the Lord had everything under control, and Ananias obeyed by faith. When God commands, we must remember that He is working "at both ends of the line," and that His perfect will is always the best.

There is a third encouragement: *God's works are always balanced.* God balanced a great public miracle with a quiet meeting in the house of Judas. The bright light and the voice from heaven were dramatic events, but the visit of Ananias was somewhat ordinary. The hand of God pushed Saul from his "high horse," but God used the hand of a man to bring Saul what he most needed. God spoke from heaven, but He also spoke through an obedient disciple who gave the message to Saul. The "ordinary" events were just as much a part of the miracle as were the extraordinary.

Finally, *we must never underestimate the value of one person brought to Christ.* Peter was ministering to thousands in Jerusalem, and Philip had seen a great harvest among the Samaritan people, but Ananias was sent to only one man. Yet what a man! Saul of Tarsus became Paul the apostle, and his life and ministry have influenced people and nations ever since. Even secular historians confess that Paul is one of the significant figures in world history.

On April 21, 1855, Edward Kimball led one of his Sunday School boys to faith in Christ. Little did he realize that Dwight L. Moody would one day become the world's leading evangelist. The ministry of Norman B. Harrison in an obscure Bible conference was used of God to bring Theodore Epp to faith in Christ, and God used Theodore Epp to build the Back to the Bible ministry around the world. Our task is to lead men and women to Christ; God's task is to use them for His glory; and every person is important to God.

He Met the Opposition (Acts 9:20-25)

Saul immediately began to proclaim the Christ that he had persecuted, declaring boldly that Jesus is the Son of God. This is the only place in Acts that you find this title, but Paul used it in his epistles at least fifteen times. It was a major emphasis in his ministry. The dramatic change in Saul's life was a source of wonder to the Jews at Damascus. Every new convert's witness for Christ ought to begin right where he is, so Saul began his ministry first in Damascus (Acts 26:20).

It is likely that Saul's visit to Arabia (Gal. 1:17) took place about this time. Had Dr. Luke included it in his account, he would have placed it between Acts 9:21 and 22. We do not know how long he remained in Arabia, but we do know that after three years, Saul was back in Jerusalem (Gal. 1:18).

Why did he go to Arabia? Probably because the Lord instructed him to get alone so that He might teach Saul His Word. There were many things that would have to be clarified in Saul's mind before he could minister effectively as an apostle of Jesus Christ. If Saul went to the area near Mount Sinai (Gal. 4:25), it took considerable courage and strength for such a journey. Perhaps it was then that he experienced "perils of robbers" and "perils in the wilderness" (2 Cor. 11:26). It is also possible that he did some evangelizing while in Arabia, because when he returned to Damascus, he was already a marked man.

The important thing about this Arabian sojourn is the fact that Saul did not "confer with flesh and blood" but received his message and mandate directly from the Lord (see Gal. 1:10-24). He did not borrow anything from the Apostles in Jerusalem, because he did not even meet them until three years after his conversion.

When Saul returned to Damascus, he began his witness afresh, and the Jews sought to silence him. Now he would discover what it meant to be the hunted instead of the hunter! This was but the beginning of the "great things" he would suffer for the name of Christ (Acts 9:16). How humiliating it must have been for Saul to be led into Damascus as a blind man and then smuggled out like a common criminal (see 2 Cor. 11:32-33).

Throughout his life, the great apostle was hated, hunted, and plotted against by both Jews and Gentiles ("in perils of my own countrymen, in perils of the Gentiles"—2 Cor. 11:26, NKJV). As you read the Book of Acts, you see how the opposition and persecution increase, until the apostle ends up a prisoner in Rome (Acts 13:45, 50; 14:19; 17:5, 13; 18:12; 20:3, 19; 21:10-11, 27ff). But he counted it a privilege to suffer for the sake of Christ, and so should we. "Yea, and all that will live godly in Christ Jesus shall suffer persecution" (2 Tim. 3:12).

He Met the Jerusalem Believers (Acts 9:26-31)

There were two stages in Saul's experience with the church in Jerusalem.

Saul rejected (v. 26). At first, the believers in the Jerusalem church were afraid of him. Saul "kept trying" (literal Greek) to get into their fellowship, but they would not accept him. For one thing, they were afraid of him and probably thought that his new attitude of friendliness was only a trick to get into their fellowship so he could have them arrested. They did not believe that he was even a disciple of Jesus Christ, let alone an apostle who had seen the risen Saviour.

Their attitude seems strange to us, for surely the Damascus saints had gotten word to the church in Jerusalem that Saul had been converted and was now preaching the Word. Perhaps Saul's "disappearance" for almost three years gave an air of suspicion to his testimony. Where had he been? What was he doing? Why had he waited so long to contact the Jerusalem elders? Furthermore, what right did he have to call himself an apostle when he had not been selected by Jesus Christ? There were many unanswered questions that helped create an atmosphere of suspicion and fear.

Saul accepted (vv. 27-31). It was Barnabas who helped the Jerusalem church accept Saul. We met Joseph, the "son of encouragement," in Acts 4:36-37, and we will meet him again as we continue to study Acts. Barnabas "took hold" of Saul, brought him to the church leaders, and convinced them that Saul was both a believer and a chosen apostle. He had indeed seen the risen Christ (1 Cor. 9:1). It is not necessary to invent some "hidden reason" why Barnabas befriended Saul. This was just the nature of the man: he was an encouragement to others.

There seems to be a contradiction between Acts 9:27 and Galatians 1:18-19. How could Barnabas introduce Saul to "the apostles" (plural) if Peter was the only apostle Saul met? Dr. Luke is obviously using the word "apostle" in the wider sense of "spiritual leader." Even Galatians 1:19 calls James, the brother of the Lord, an apostle; and Barnabas is called an apostle in Acts 14:4 and 14. In his epistles, Paul sometimes used "apostle" to designate a special messenger or agent of the church (Rom. 16:7; 2 Cor. 8:23; Phil. 2:25, original Greek). So, there really is no contradiction; it is the leaders of the Jerusalem church that Saul met.

Saul began to witness to the Greek-speaking Jews, the Hellenists that had engineered the trial and death of Stephen (Acts 6:9-15). Saul was one of them, having been born and raised in Tarsus; and no doubt he felt an obligation to take up the mantle left by Stephen (Acts 22:20). The Hellenistic Jews were not about to permit this kind of witness, so they plotted to kill him.

At this point, we must read Acts 22:17-21. God spoke to Saul in the temple and reminded him of his commission to take the message to the Gentiles (Acts 9:15). Note the urgency of God's command: "Quick! Leave Jerusalem immediately, because they will not accept your testimony about Me" (Acts 22:18, NIV). Saul shared this message with the church leaders, and they assisted him in returning to his native city, Tarsus. The fact that they believed Saul's testimony about the vision is proof that he had been fully accepted by the church.

We will not meet Saul again until Acts 11:25, when once more it is Barnabas who finds him and brings him to the church at Antioch where they ministered together. That took place about seven years after Saul left Jerusalem, about ten years after his conversion. We have every reason to believe that Saul used Tarsus as his headquarters for taking the Gospel to the Gentiles in that part of the Roman Empire. He ministered "in the regions of Syria and Cilicia" (Gal. 1:21) and established churches there (Acts 15:41). Some Bible scholars believe that the Galatian churches were founded at this time.

It is likely that some of the trials listed in 2 Corinthians 11:24-26 occurred during this period. Only one Roman beating is recorded in Acts (16:22), which leaves two not accounted for. Likewise, the five Jewish beatings are not recorded either in Acts or the epistles. Luke tells us about only one shipwreck (Acts 27), but we have no record of the other two. Anyone who thinks that the apostle was taking a vacation during those years is certainly in error!

Acts 9:31 is another of Luke's summaries that he regularly dropped into the book (Acts 2:46-47; 4:4, 32; 5:12-14). Note that the geographic locations parallel those given in Acts 1:8. Luke is telling us that the message was going out just as the Lord had commanded. Soon, the center would be Antioch, not Jerusalem, and the key leader Paul, not Peter; and the Gospel would be taken to the uttermost part of the earth.

It was a time of "peace" for the churches, but not a time of complacency, for they grew both spiritually and numerically. They seized the opportunity to repair and strengthen their sails before the next storm began to blow! The door of faith had been opened to the Jews (Acts 2) and to the Samaritans (Acts 8), and soon it would be opened to the Gentiles (Acts 10). Saul has moved off the scene, and Peter now returns. Soon, Peter will move off the scene (except for a brief mention in Acts 15) and Paul will fill the pages of the Book of Acts.

God changes His workmen, but His work goes on.

And you and I are privileged to be a part of that work today!

CHAPTER TEN
PETER'S MIRACLE MINISTRY
Acts 9:32–10:48

What is the greatest miracle that God can do for us? Some would call the healing of the body God's greatest miracle, while others would vote for the raising of the dead. However, I think that the greatest miracle of all is the salvation of a lost sinner. Why? Because salvation costs the greatest price, it produces the greatest results, and it brings the greatest glory to God.

In this section, we find Peter participating in all three miracles: he heals Aeneas, he raises Dorcas from the dead, and he brings the message of salvation to Cornelius and his household.

A Great Miracle—Healing the Body (Acts 9:32-35)

The Apostle Peter had been engaged in an itinerant ministry (Acts 8:25) when he found himself visiting the saints in Lydda, a largely Gentile city about twenty-five miles from Jerusalem. It is possible that the area had first been evangelized by people converted at Pentecost, or perhaps by faithful believers who had been scattered far and wide during the great persecution. No doubt Philip the evangelist had also ministered there (Acts 8:40).

We know very little about Aeneas. How old was he? Did he believe on Jesus Christ? Was he a Jew or a Gentile? All that Dr. Luke tells us is the man had been palsied for eight years, which meant he was crippled and helpless. He was a burden to himself and a burden to others, and there was no prospect that he would ever get well.

Peter's first miracle had been the healing of a crippled man (Acts 3), and now that miracle was repeated. As you read the Book of Acts, you will see parallels between the ministries of Peter and Paul. Both healed cripples. Both were arrested and put into jail and were miraculously delivered. Both were treated like gods (Acts 10:25-26; 14:8-18), and both gave a bold witness before the authorities. Both had to confront false prophets (Acts 8:9-24; 13:6-12). No one reading the Book of Acts could end up saying, "I am for Paul!" or "I am for Peter!" (1 Cor. 1:12) "But it is the same God which worketh all in all" (1 Cor. 12:6).

The resurrected Christ, by the authority of His name, brought perfect soundness to Aeneas (see Acts 3:6, 16; 4:10). The healing was instantaneous, and the man was able to get up and make his bed. He became a walking miracle! Acts 9:35 does not suggest that the entire population of Lydda and Sharon were saved, but only all those who had contact with Aeneas. Just seeing him walk around convinced them that Jesus was alive and they needed to trust in Him. (See John 12:10-11 for a similar instance.)

You can be sure that Peter did much more in Lydda than heal Aeneas, as great and helpful as that miracle was. He evangelized, taught and encouraged the believers, and sought to establish the church in the faith. Jesus had commissioned Peter to care for the sheep (John 21:15-17), and Peter was faithful to fulfill that commission.

A Greater Miracle—Raising the Dead (Acts 9:36-43)

Joppa, the modern Jaffa, is located on the seacoast, some ten miles beyond Lydda. The city is important in Bible history as the place from which the Prophet Jonah embarked when he tried to flee from God (Jonah 1:1-3). Jonah went to Joppa to avoid going to the Gentiles, but Peter in Joppa received his call to go to the Gentiles! Because Jonah disobeyed God, the Lord sent a storm that caused the Gentile sailors to fear. Because Peter obeyed the Lord, God sent the "wind of the Spirit" to the Gentiles and they experienced great joy and peace. What a contrast!

It seemed so tragic that a useful and beloved saint like Dorcas (Tabitha = gazelle) should die when she was so greatly needed by the church. This often happens in local churches and it is a hard blow to take. In my own pastoral ministry, I have experienced the loss of choice saints who were difficult to replace in the church; yet, all we can say is, "The Lord gave, and the Lord hath taken away; blessed be the name of the Lord" (Job 1:21).

The believers in Joppa heard that Peter was in the area, and they sent for him immediately. There is no record in Acts that any of the Apostles had raised the dead, so their sending for Peter was an evidence of their faith in the power of the risen Christ. When our Lord ministered on earth, He raised the dead; so why would He not be able to raise the dead from His exalted throne in glory?

We usually think of the Apostles as leaders who told other people what to do, but often the people commanded them! (For Peter's "philosophy of ministry" read 1 Peter 5.) Peter was a leader who served the people and was ready to respond to their call. Peter had the power to heal, and he used the power to glorify God and help people, not to promote himself.

It was a Jewish custom first to wash the dead body, and then to anoint it with spices for burial. When Peter arrived in the upper room where Dorcas lay in state, he found a group of weeping widows who had been helped by her ministry. Keep in mind that there was no "government aid" in those days for either widows or orphans, and needy people had to depend on their "network" for assistance. The church has an obligation to help people who are truly in need (1 Tim. 5:3-16; James 1:27).

The account of Peter's raising of Dorcas should be compared with the account of our Lord's raising of Jairus' daughter (Mark 5:34-43). In both cases, the mourning people were put out of the room; and the words spoken are almost identical: "*talitha cumi*: little girl, arise; *Tabitha cumi*: Tabitha, arise." Jesus took the girl by the hand before He spoke to her, for He was not afraid of becoming ceremonially defiled; and Peter took Dorcas by the hand after she had come to life. In both instances, it was the power of God that raised the person from the dead, for the dead person certainly could not exercise faith.

As with the healing of Aeneas, the raising of Dorcas attracted great attention and resulted in many people trusting Jesus Christ. During the "many days" that he tarried in Joppa, Peter took the opportunity to ground these new believers in the truth of the Word, for faith built on miracles alone is not substantial.

It was a good thing Peter tarried in Joppa, because God met with him there in a thrilling new way. God's servants need not always be "on the go." They should take time to be alone with God, to reflect and meditate and pray, especially after experiencing great blessings. Yes, there were plenty of sick people Peter might have visited and healed, but God had other plans. He deliberately detained His servant in Joppa to prepare him for his third use of "the keys."

It is significant that Peter stayed in the home of a tanner, because tanners were considered "unclean" by the Jewish rabbis (see Lev. 11:35-40). God was moving Peter a step at a time from Jewish legalism into the freedom of His wonderful grace.

The Greatest Miracle—Winning Lost Sinners (Acts 10:1-48)

Chapter 10 is pivotal in the Book of Acts, for it records the salvation of the Gentiles. We see Peter using "the keys of the kingdom" for the third and last time. He had opened the door of faith for the Jews (Acts 2) and also for the Samaritans (Acts 8), and now he would be used of God to bring the Gentiles into the church (see Gal. 3:27-28; Eph. 2:11-22).

This event took place about ten years after Pentecost. Why did the Apostles wait so long before going to the lost Gentiles? After all, in His Great Commission (Matt. 28:19-20), Jesus had told them to go into *all* the world; and it would seem logical for them to go to their Gentile neighbors as soon as possible. But God has His times as well as His plans, and the transition from the Jews to the Samaritans to the Gentiles was a gradual one.

The stoning of Stephen and the subsequent persecution of the church marked the climax of the Apostles' witness to the Jews. Then the Gospel moved to the Samaritans. When God saved Saul of Tarsus, He got hold of His special envoy to the Gentiles. Now was the time to open the door of faith (Acts 14:27) to the Gentiles and bring them into the family of God.

There were four acts to this wonderful drama.

Preparation (vv. 1-22). Before He could save the Gentiles, God had to prepare Peter to bring the message and Cornelius to hear the message. Salvation is a divine work of grace, but God works through human channels. Angels can deliver God's messages to lost men, but they cannot preach the Gospel to them. That is our privilege—and responsibility.

Caesarea is sixty-five miles northwest of Jerusalem and thirty miles north of Joppa (Jaffa). At that time, Caesarea was the Roman capital of Judea and boasted of many beautiful public buildings. In that city lived Cornelius, the Roman centurion, whose heart had tired of pagan myths and empty religious rituals, and who had turned to Judaism in hopes he could find salvation. Cornelius was as close to Judaism as he could get without becoming a proselyte. There were many "God fearers" like him in the ancient world (Acts 13:16) and they proved to be a ready field for spiritual harvest.

It is interesting to see how religious a person can be and still not be saved. Certainly, Cornelius was sincere in his obedience to God's Law, his fasting, and his generosity to the Jewish people (compare this to Luke 7:1-10). He was not permitted to offer sacrifices in the temple, so he presented his prayers to God as his sacrifices (Ps. 141:1-2). In every way, he was a model of religious respectability—and yet he was not a saved man.

The difference between Cornelius and many religious people today is this: he knew that his religious devotion was not sufficient to save him. Many religious people today are satisfied that their character and good works will get them to heaven, and they have no concept either of their own sin or of God's grace. In his prayers, Cornelius was asking God to show him the way of salvation (Acts 11:13-14).

In many respects, John Wesley was like Cornelius. He was a religious man, a church member, a minister, and the son of a minister. He belonged to a "religious club" at Oxford, the purpose of which was the perfecting of the Christian life. Wesley served as a foreign missionary, but even as he preached to others, he had no assurance of his own personal salvation.

On May 24, 1738, Wesley reluctantly attended a small meeting in London where someone was reading aloud from Martin Luther's commentary on Romans. "About a quarter before nine," Wesley wrote in his journal, "while he was describing the change which God works in the heart through faith in Christ, I felt my heart strangely warmed, I felt I did trust in Christ, Christ alone for salvation; and an assurance was given me that He had taken away my sins, even mine, and saved me from the law of sin and death." The result was the great Wesleyan revival that not only swept many into the kingdom, but also helped transform British society through Christian social action.

God sent an angel to instruct Cornelius and, in true military fashion, Cornelius immediately obeyed. But why send for Peter, who was thirty miles away in Joppa, when Philip the evangelist was already in Caesarea? (Acts 8:40) Because it was Peter, not Philip, who had been given the "keys." God not only works at the right time, but He also works through the right servant; and both are essential.

Peter also had to be prepared for this event since he had lived as an orthodox Jew all of his life (Acts 10:14). The Law of Moses was a wall between the Jews and the Gentiles, and this wall had been broken down at the cross (Eph. 2:14-18). The Gentiles were considered aliens and strangers as far as the Jewish covenants and promises were concerned (Eph. 2:11-13). But now, all of that would change, and God would declare that, as far as the Jew and the Gentile were concerned, "There is no difference" either in condemnation (Rom. 3:22-23) or in salvation (Rom. 10:12-13).

Why did God use a vision about food to teach Peter that the Gentiles were not unclean? For one thing, Peter was hungry, and a vision about food would certainly "speak to his condition," as the Quakers say. Second, the distinction between "clean and unclean foods" was a major problem between the Jews and the Gentiles in that day. In fact, Peter's Christian friends criticized him for eating with the Gentiles! (Acts 11:1-3) God used this centuries-old regulation (Lev. 11) to teach Peter an important spiritual lesson.

A third reason goes back to something Jesus had taught Peter and the other disciples when He was ministering on earth (Mark 7:1-23). At that time, Peter did not fully understand what Jesus was saying, but now it would all come together. God was not simply changing Peter's diet; He was changing His entire program! The Jew was not "clean" and the Gentile "unclean," but *both Jew and Gentile were "unclean" before God!* "For God hath concluded them all in unbelief, that He might have mercy on all" (Rom. 11:32). This meant that a Gentile did not have to become a Jew in order to become a Christian.

Even though Peter's refusal was in the most polite terms, it was still wrong. Dr. W. Graham Scroggie wrote, "You can say 'No,' and you can say 'Lord'; but you cannot say 'No, Lord!' " If He is truly our Lord, then we can only say "Yes!" to Him and obey His commands.

God's timing is always perfect, and the three men from Caesarea arrived at the door just as Peter was pondering the meaning of the vision. The Spirit commanded Peter to meet the men and go with them. The phrase "nothing doubting" (Acts 10:20) means "making no distinctions." You find it again in Acts

11:12, and a similar word is used in Acts 11:2 ("contended with him" = "made a difference"). Peter was no longer to make any distinctions between the Jews and the Gentiles.

Explanation (vv. 23-33). The fact that Peter allowed the Gentiles to lodge with him is another indication that the walls were coming down. Peter selected six Jewish believers to go along as witnesses (Acts 11:12), three times the official number needed. It would take at least two days to cover the thirty miles between Joppa and Caesarea. When Peter arrived, he discovered that Cornelius had gathered relatives and friends to hear the message of life. He was a witness even before he became a Christian!

How easy it would have been for Peter to accept honor and use the situation to promote himself; but Peter was a servant, not a celebrity (1 Peter 5:1-6). When he announced that he did not consider the Gentiles unclean, this must have amazed and rejoiced the hearts of his listeners. For centuries the Jews, on the basis of Old Testament Law, had declared the Gentiles to be unclean, and some Jews even referred to the Gentiles as "dogs."

The remarkable thing in this section is Peter's question, "I ask, therefore, for what intent ye have sent for me?" (Acts 10:29) Didn't Peter know that he had been summoned there to preach the Gospel? Had he forgotten the Acts 1:8 commission to go to "the uttermost part of the earth"? Today, we can look back at developing events in the church and understand what God was doing, but it might not have been that easy had we been living in the midst of those events. In fact, the Jerusalem church questioned Peter about his actions (Acts 11:1-18), and later called a conference to deal with the place of the Gentiles in the church (Acts 15).

Cornelius rehearsed his experience with the angel and then told Peter why he had been summoned: to tell him, his family, and his friends how they could be saved (Acts 11:14). They were not interested Gentiles asking for a lecture on Jewish religion. They were lost sinners begging to be told how to be saved.

Before we leave this section, some important truths must be emphasized. First, the idea that "one religion is as good as another" is completely false. Those who tell us that we should worship "the God of many names" and not "change other people's religions" are going contrary to Scripture. "Salvation is of the Jews" (John 4:22), and there can be no salvation apart from faith in Jesus Christ, who was born a Jew. Cornelius had piety and morality, but he did not have salvation. Some might say, "Leave Cornelius alone! His religion is a part of his culture, and it's a shame to change his culture!" God does not see it that way. Apart from hearing the message of the Gospel and trusting Christ, Cornelius had no hope.

Second, the seeking Saviour (Luke 19:10) will find the seeking sinner (Jer. 29:13). Wherever there is a searching heart, God responds. This is why it is essential that we as God's children obey His will and share His Word. You never know when your witness for Christ is exactly what somebody has been waiting and praying for.

Third, Peter certainly was privileged to minister to a model congregation (Acts 10:33). They were all present, they wanted to hear the Word, and they listened, believed, and obeyed. What more could a preacher ask?

Proclamation (vv. 34-43). There can be no faith apart from the Word (Rom. 10:17), and Peter preached that Word. God is no respecter of persons as far as nationality and race are concerned. When it comes to sin and salvation, "there is no difference" (Rom. 2:11; 3:22-23; 10:1-13). All men have the same Creator (Acts 17:26), and all men need the same Saviour (Acts 4:12). Acts 10:35 does not teach that we are saved by works, otherwise Peter would be contradicting himself (Acts 10:43). To "fear God and work righteousness" is a description of the Christian life. To fear God is to reverence and trust Him (Micah 6:8). The evidence of this faith is a righteous walk.

Peter then summarized the story of the life, death, and resurrection of Jesus Christ. Cornelius and his friends knew about Christ's life and death, for "this thing was not done in a corner" (Acts 26:26). Peter made it clear that Israel was God's instrument for accomplishing His work (Acts 10:36), but that Jesus is "Lord of all," and not just Lord of Israel. From the very founding of the nation of Israel, God made it clear that the blessing would be from Israel to the whole world (Gen. 12:1-3).

The public at large knew about Christ's life, ministry, and death, but only the Apostles and other believers were witnesses of His resurrection. As in his previous sermons, Peter laid the blame for the Crucifixion on the Jewish leaders (Acts 3:15; 4:10; 5:30), as did Stephen (Acts 7:52). Paul would pick up this same emphasis (1 Thes. 2:14-16).

Having finished this recitation of the historical basis for the Gospel message, Christ's death and resurrection, Peter then announced the good news: "Whosoever believeth in Him shall receive remission of sin" (Acts 10:43; see 2:21). His hearers laid hold of that word "whosoever," applied it to themselves, believed on Jesus Christ and were saved.

Vindication (vv. 44-48). Peter was just getting started in his message when his congregation believed and the Holy Spirit interrupted the meeting (Acts 11:15). God the Father interrupted Peter on the Mount of Transfiguration (Matt. 17:4-5), and God the Son interrupted him in the matter of the temple tax (Matt. 17:24-27). Now, God the Spirit interrupted him—and Peter never was able to finish his sermon! Would that preachers today had interruptions of this kind!

The Holy Spirit was giving witness to the six Jews who were present that these Gentiles were truly born again. After all, these men had not seen the vision with Peter and come to understand that the Gentiles were now on an equal footing with the Jews. This does not suggest that every new believer gives evidence of salvation by speaking in tongues, though every true believer will certainly use his or her tongue to glorify God (Rom. 10:9-10). This was an event parallel to Pentecost: the same Spirit who had come on the Jewish believers had now come on the Gentiles (Acts 11:15-17; 15:7-9). No wonder the men were astonished!

With this event, the period of transition in the early history of the church comes to an end. Believers among the Jews, Samaritans, and Gentiles have all received the Spirit of God and are united in the body of Christ (1 Cor. 12:13; Gal. 3:27).

These Gentiles were not saved by being baptized; they were baptized because they gave evidence of being saved. To use Acts 2:38 to teach salvation by baptism, or Acts 8:14-16 to teach salvation by the laying on of hands, is to ignore the transitional character of God's program. Sinners have always been saved by faith; that is one principle God has never changed. But God does change His methods of operation, and this is clearly seen in Acts 1–10. The experience of Cornelius and his household makes it very clear that baptism is not essential for salvation. From now on, the order will be: hear the Word, believe on Christ, and receive the Spirit, and then be baptized and unite with other believers in the church to serve and worship God.

Peter tarried in Caesarea and helped to ground these new believers in the truth of the Word. Perhaps Philip assisted him. This entire experience is an illustration of the commission of Matthew 28:19-20. Peter went where God sent him and made disciples ("teach") of the Gentiles. Then he baptized them and taught them the Word.

That same commission applies to the church today. Are we fulfilling it as we should?

CHAPTER ELEVEN
MAKING ROOM FOR THE GENTILES
Acts 11

Acts 11 describes how the church in Jerusalem related to "the saints below," the Gentiles in Caesarea and Antioch who had trusted Jesus Christ as their Saviour and Lord. Having fellowship with the Gentiles was a new experience for these Jewish Christians, who all their lives had looked on the Gentiles as pagans and outsiders. Tradition said that a Gentile had to "become a Jew" in order to be accepted; but now Jews and Gentiles were united in the church through faith in Jesus Christ (Gal. 3:26-28).

Acts 11 describes three responses of the Jewish believers to the Gentile Christians. As you study these responses, you will better understand how Christians today ought to relate to one another.

They Accepted the Gentiles (Acts 11:1-18)

Peter no sooner returned to Jerusalem when he was met by members of the strong legalistic party in the church of Judea ("they that were of the circumcision") who rebuked him for fellowshipping with Gentiles and eating with them. Keep in mind that these Jewish believers did not yet understand the relationship between Law and grace, Jews and Gentiles, and Israel and the church. Most Christians today understand these truths; but, after all, we have Romans, Galatians, Ephesians, and Hebrews! There were many converted priests in the church who would be zealous for the Law (Acts 6:7), and even the ordinary Jewish believer would have a difficult time making the transition (Acts 21:20). It was not only a matter of religion, but also of culture; and cultural habits are very hard to break.

The phrase "contended with him" comes from the same word translated "doubting nothing" in Acts 10:20 and 11:12. It means "to make a difference." These legalists were making a difference between the Gentiles and the Jews after Peter had demonstrated that "there is no difference!" God had declared the Gentiles "clean," that is, accepted before God on the same basis as the Jews—through faith in Jesus Christ.

Peter had nothing to fear. After all, he had only followed orders from the Lord; and the Spirit had clearly confirmed the salvation of the Gentiles. Peter reviewed the entire experience from beginning to end; and, when he was finished, the Jewish legalists dropped their charges and glorified God for the salvation of the Gentiles (Acts 11:18). However, this did not end the matter completely, for this same legalistic party later debated with Paul about the salvation of the Gentiles (Acts 14:26–15:2). Even after the Jerusalem Conference, legalistic teachers continued to attack Paul and invade the churches he founded. They wanted to woo the believers into a life of obedience to the Law (Gal. 1:6ff; Phil. 3:1-3, 17-21). It is possible that many of these legalists were genuine believers, but they did not understand their freedom in Jesus Christ (Gal. 5:1ff).

In his personal defense in Acts 11, Peter presented three pieces of evidence: the vision from God (Acts 11:5-11), the witness of the Spirit (Acts 11:12-15, 17), and the witness of the Word (Acts 11:16). Of course, none of these men had seen the vision, but they trusted Peter's report, for they knew that he had been as orthodox as they in his personal life (Acts 10:14). He was not likely to go to the Gentiles on his own and then invent a story to back it up.

The witness of the Spirit was crucial, for this was God's own testimony that He had indeed saved the Gentiles. It is interesting that Peter had to go *all the way back to Pentecost* to find an example of what happened in the home of Cornelius! This suggests that a dramatic "baptism of the Spirit" (Acts 11:16), accompanied by speaking in tongues, was not an everyday occurrence in the early church. Peter could not use the experience of the Samaritans as his example, because the Samaritans received the gift of the Spirit through the laying on of the Apostles' hands (Acts 8:14-17). Cornelius and his household received the Spirit the moment they trusted Christ. This is the pattern for today.

"What was I, that I could withstand God?" asked Peter; and to this question, the legalists had no answer. From beginning to end, the conversion of the Gentiles was God's gracious work. He gave them the gift of repentance and the gift of salvation when they believed. In later years, God would use the letters of Paul to explain the "one body," how believing Jews and believing Gentiles are united in Christ (Eph. 2:11–3:12). But at that time, this "mystery" was still hidden; so we must not be too hard on those saints who were uneasy about the place of the Gentiles in the church.

Christians are to receive one another and not dispute over cultural differences or minor matters of personal conviction (Rom. 14–15). Some of the Jewish Christians in the early church wanted the Gentiles to become Jews, and some of the Gentile believers wanted the Jews to stop being Jews and become Gentiles! This attitude can create serious division in the church even today, so it is important that we follow the example of Acts 11:18 and the admonition of Romans 14:1, and receive those whom God has also received.

They Encouraged the Gentiles (Acts 11:19-26)

When the saints were scattered abroad during Saul's persecution of the church (Acts 8:1), some of them ended up in Antioch, the capital of Syria, 300 miles north of Jerusalem. (Don't confuse this city with Antioch in Pisidia, Acts 13:14.) There were at least sixteen Antiochs in the ancient world, but this one was the greatest.

With a population of half a million, Antioch ranked as the third largest city in the Roman Empire, following Rome and Alexandria. Its magnificent buildings helped give it the name "Antioch the Golden, Queen of the East." The main street was more than four miles long, paved with marble, and lined on both sides by marble colonnades. It was the only city in the ancient world at that time that had its streets lighted at night.

A busy port and a center for luxury and culture, Antioch attracted all kinds of people, including wealthy retired Roman officials who spent their days chatting in the baths or gambling at the races. With its large cosmopolitan population and its great commercial and political power, Antioch presented to the church an exciting opportunity for evangelism.

Antioch was a wicked city, perhaps second only to Corinth. Though all the Greek, Roman, and Syrian deities were honored, the local shrine was dedicated to Daphne, whose worship included immoral practices. "Antioch was to the Roman world what New York City is to ours," writes James A. Kelso in *An Archaeologist Follows the Apostle Paul.* "Here where all the gods of antiquity were worshiped, Christ must be exalted." Not only was an effective church built in Antioch, but it became the church that sent Paul out to win the Gentile world for Christ.

When the persecuted believers arrived in Antioch, they did not at all feel intimidated by the magnificence of the buildings or the pride of the citizens. The Word of God was on their lips and the hand of God was on their witness, and "a great number" of sinners repented and believed. It was a thrilling work of God's wonderful grace.

The church leaders in Jerusalem had a responsibility to "shepherd" the scattered flock, which now included Gentile congregations as far away as Syria. Apparently the Apostles were ministering away from Jerusalem at the time, so the elders commissioned Barnabas to go to Antioch to find out what was going on among the Gentiles. This proved to be a wise choice, for Barnabas lived up to his nickname, "son of encouragement" (Acts 4:36).

Acts 11:24 gives us a "spiritual profile" of Barnabas, and he appears to be the kind of Christian all of us would do well to emulate. He was a righteous man who obeyed the Word in daily life so that his character was above reproach. He was filled with the Spirit, which explains the effectiveness of his ministry. That he was a man of faith is evident from the way he encouraged the church and then encouraged Saul. New Christians and new churches need people like Barnabas to encourage them in their growth and ministry.

How did Barnabas encourage these new Gentile believers? For one thing, he rejoiced at what he saw. Worshiping with Gentiles was a new experience for him, but he approached it positively and did not look for things to criticize. It was a work of God, and Barnabas gave thanks for God's grace.

He emphasized dedication of the heart as he taught the people the Word of God. The phrase "cleave [cling] to the Lord" does not suggest that they were to "keep themselves saved." The same grace that saves us can also keep us (1 Cor. 15:10; Heb. 13:9). The phrase reminds us of Joshua's admonition to Israel in Joshua 22:5. To "cleave to the Lord" includes loving the Lord, walking in His ways, obeying His Word, and serving Him wholeheartedly. It means that we belong to Him alone and that we cultivate our devotion to Him. "No man can serve two masters" (Matt. 6:24).

There were two wonderful results from Barnabas' work in Antioch. First, the church's witness made a great impact on the city so that "many people were added to the Lord" (Acts 11:24). When the saints are grounded in the Word, they will have a strong witness to the lost, and there will be a balance in the church between edification and evangelism, worship and witness, teaching and testifying.

Second, the growth of the church meant that Barnabas needed help; so he went to Tarsus and enlisted Saul. But why go so far away just to find an assistant? Why not send to Jerusalem and ask the deacon Nicolas who was from Antioch? (Acts 6:5) Because Barnabas knew that God had commissioned Saul to minister to the Gentiles (Acts 9:15; 22:21; 26:17). You recall that Barnabas befriended Saul in Jerusalem (Acts 9:26-27), and no doubt the two of them often talked about Saul's special call from God.

Saul had been converted about ten years when Barnabas brought him to Antioch. The New Testament does not tell us what Saul did back home in Tarsus after he left Jerusalem (Acts 9:28-30), but it is likely he was busy evangelizing both Jews and Gentiles. It may have been during this period that he founded the churches in Cilicia (Acts 15:23, 41; Gal. 1:21), and that he experienced some of the sufferings listed in 2 Corinthians 11:23-28. As he witnessed in the synagogues, you can be sure he would not have an easy time of it!

What Barnabas did for Saul needs to be practiced in our churches today. Mature believers need to enlist others and encourage them in their service for the Lord. It was one of D.L. Moody's policies that each new Christian be given a task soon after conversion. At first, it might be only passing out hymnals or ushering people to their seats, but each convert had to be busy. As previously mentioned, he said, "It is better to put ten men to work than to do the work of ten men." Many of Mr. Moody's "assistants" became effective Christian workers in their own right and this multiplied the witness.

It was at Antioch that the name *Christian* was first applied to the disciples of Jesus Christ. The Latin suffix *ian* means "belonging to the party of." In derision, some of the pagan citizens of Antioch joined this Latin suffix to the Hebrew name "Christ" and came up with *Christian.* The name is found only three times in the entire New Testament: Acts 11:26; 26:28; 1 Peter 4:16.

Unfortunately, the word *Christian* has lost a great deal of significance over the centuries and no longer means "one who has turned from sin, trusted Jesus Christ, and received salvation by grace" (Acts 11:21-23). Many people who have never been born again consider themselves "Christians" simply because they say they are not "pagans." After all, they may belong to a church, attend services somewhat regularly, and even occasionally give to the work of the church! But it takes more than that for a sinner to become a child of God. It takes repentance from sin and faith in Jesus Christ, who died for our sins on the cross and rose again to give us eternal life.

The believers in the early church *suffered* because they were Christians (1 Peter 4:16). Dr. David Otis Fuller has asked, "If you were arrested for being a Christian, would there be enough evidence to convict you?" A good question! And the answer is a matter of life or death!

They Received Help from the Gentiles (Acts 11:27-30)

The foundation for the church was laid by the Apostles and prophets (Eph. 2:20), and then both eventually moved off the scene. After all, you don't keep laying the foundation! The New Testament prophets received their messages from the Lord by the Holy Spirit, and delivered them to the people, sometimes in a tongue. The message would then have to be interpreted, after which the people would evaluate the message to make sure it came from God (note 1 Cor. 12:10; 14:27-33; 1 Thes. 5:19-21).

The New Testament prophets received their messages from the Lord *immediately,* but ministers and teachers today get their messages *mediately* through the Scriptures. We today have the completed Word of God from which the Holy Spirit teaches and guides us. First Corinthians 12:10 ties together the gifts of prophecy, discernment, and tongues and the interpretation of tongues. Of course, the Spirit is sovereign and can give to a believer any gift He desires (1 Cor. 12:11), but the passing of Apostles and prophets from the scene, and the completing of God's revelation in the Word, suggest that a change has taken place.

There are people today who claim to receive special "words of revelation" or "words of wisdom" from the Lord, but such revelations are suspect and even dangerous. "To the law and to the testimony; if they speak not according to this word, it is because there is no light in them" (Isa. 8:20). "Hearken not unto the words of the prophets that prophesy unto you," warned Jeremiah. "They make you vain [fill you with false hopes]; they speak a vision of their own heart, and not out of the mouth of the Lord" (Jer. 23:16).

The Spirit told Agabus (see Acts 21:10-11) that a great famine was soon to come, and it did come during the reign of Claudius Caesar (A.D. 41–54) when crops were poor for many years. Ancient writers mention at least four famines: two in Rome, one in Greece, and one in Judea. The famine in Judea was especially severe, and the Jewish historian Josephus records that many people died for lack of money to buy what little food was available.

Agabus delivered his message to the Antioch believers; and they determined to help their fellow Christians in Judea. The purpose of true prophecy is not to satisfy our curiosity about the future but to stir up our hearts to do the will of God. The believers could not stop the famine from coming, but they could send relief to those in need.

An important spiritual principle is illustrated in this passage: if people have been a spiritual blessing to us, we should minister to them out of our material possessions. "Let him who is taught in the word share in all good things with him who teaches" (Gal. 6:6, NKJV). The Jewish believers in Jerusalem had brought the Gospel to Antioch. Then they had sent Barnabas to encourage the new believers. It was only right that the Gentiles in Antioch reciprocate and send material help to their Jewish brothers and sisters in Judea. Some years later, Paul would gather a similar offering from the Gentile churches and take it to the saints in Jerusalem (Acts 24:17; and see Rom. 15:23-28).

It is important to note that a change had

taken place in the Jerusalem church. At one time, nobody in the church had any need (Acts 4:34), nor was it necessary to ask others for help. Those early years were "days of heaven on earth" as God richly blessed His people and used them as witnesses to the unbelieving nation. They were "times of refreshing" from the Lord (Acts 3:19). But when the message moved from the Jews to the Samaritans and the Gentiles, the Jerusalem "sharing program" gradually faded away and things became more normal.

The pattern for Christian giving today is not Acts 2:44-45 and 4:31-35, but Acts 11:29, "every man according to his ability." It is this pattern that Paul taught in 2 Corinthians 8–9. The practice of "Christian communism" was found only in Jerusalem and was a temporary measure while the message was going "to the Jew first." Like God's care of the Jews in the wilderness, it was a living exhibition of the blessings God would bestow if the nation would repent and believe.

The fact that the church elected Barnabas and Saul to take the relief offering to Jerusalem is evidence that they had confidence in them. The men had been working together in the teaching of the Word, and now they joined hands in the practical ministry of relieving the wants of the Jerusalem believers. No doubt they also ministered the Word along the way as they made the long journey from Antioch to Jerusalem. In a short time, the Spirit would call these two friends to join forces and take the Gospel to the Gentiles in other lands (Acts 13:1ff), and they would travel many miles together.

Another significant result from this ministry was the addition of John Mark to their "team" (Acts 12:25). It is likely that Mark was converted through the ministry of Peter (1 Peter 5:13). His mother's house was a gathering place for the Jerusalem believers (Acts 12:12), and she and Barnabas were related (Col. 4:10). Even though John Mark failed in his first "term" as a missionary (Acts 13:13), and helped cause a rift between Barnabas and Paul (Acts 15:38-40), he later became an effective assistant to Paul (2 Tim. 4:11) and was used of God to write the Gospel of Mark.

The word *elders* in Acts 11:30 has not been used before in Acts, except to refer to the Jewish leaders (Acts 4:5, 23; 6:12). In the church, the elders were mature believers who had the spiritual oversight of the ministry (1 Peter 5:1; 2 John 1). When you compare Acts 20:17 and 28, and Titus 1:5 and 7, you learn that "elder" and "bishop" [overseer] are equivalent titles. The elders/bishops were the "pastors" of the flocks, assisted by the deacons; and the qualifications for both are found in 1 Timothy 3.

Wherever Paul established churches, he saw to it that qualified elders were ordained to give leadership to the assemblies (Acts 14:23; Titus 1:5). In the Jerusalem church, the Apostles and elders gave spiritual oversight (Acts 15:2, 4, 6, 22). The delegation from the Antioch church did not ignore the spiritual leaders in Jerusalem, but delivered the gift to them for distribution to the needy members. This is an important principle and should be heeded in this day when so many organizations want to get support from local churches.

Was it a humbling experience for the Jewish believers to receive help from the Gentiles? Perhaps, but it was also a beautiful demonstration of love and a wonderful testimony of unity. Sir Winston Churchill said, "We make a living by what we get, but we make a life by what we give." It was an enriching experience for the churches in Jerusalem and in Antioch, for there is blessing both in giving and receiving when God's grace is in control.

It is unfortunate when individual Christians and local churches forget those who have been a spiritual blessing to them. The church at Antioch is a splendid example of how we as believers ought to show gratitude in a practical way to those who have helped us in our Christian life. Phillips Brooks was asked what he would do to revive a dead church, and he replied, "I would take up a missionary offering!"

Sincerely thinking of others is still the best formula for a happy and useful Christian life, both for individuals and for churches.

CHAPTER TWELVE
WAKE UP TO A MIRACLE!
Acts 12

Imagine waking up to a miracle and having an angel for your alarm clock!

That's what happened to Peter when he was in prison for the third time, awaiting trial and certain death. Years later, when he wrote his first epistle, Peter may have had this miraculous experience in mind when he quoted Psalm 34:15-16, "For the eyes of the Lord are over the righteous, and His ears are open unto their prayers; but the face of the Lord is against them that do evil" (1 Peter 3:12). That quotation certainly summarizes what God did for Peter, and it reveals to us three wonderful assurances to encourage us in the difficult days of life.

God Sees Our Trials (Acts 12:1-4)

"The eyes of the Lord are over the righteous" (1 Peter 3:12).

God watched and noted what Herod Agrippa I was doing to His people. This evil man was the grandson of Herod the Great, who ordered the Bethlehem children to be murdered, and the nephew of Herod Antipas, who had John the Baptist beheaded. A scheming and murderous family, the Herods were despised by the Jews, who resented having Edomites ruling over them. Of course, Herod knew this; so he persecuted the church to convince the Jewish people of his loyalty to the traditions of the fathers. Now that the Gentiles were openly a part of the church, Herod's plan was even more agreeable to the nationalistic Jews who had no place for "pagans."

Herod had several believers arrested, among them James, the brother of John, whom he beheaded. Thus James became the first of the Apostles to be martyred. When you ponder his death in the light of Matthew 20:20-28, it takes on special significance. James and John, with their mother, had asked for thrones, but Jesus made it clear that there can be no glory apart from suffering. "Are ye able to drink of the cup that I shall drink of, and to be baptized with the baptism that I am baptized with?" He asked (Matt. 20:22). Their bold reply was, "We are able."

Of course, they did not know what they were saying, but they eventually discovered the high cost of winning a throne of glory: James was arrested and killed, and John became an exile on the Isle of Patmos, a prisoner of Rome (Rev. 1:9). Indeed, they did drink of the cup and share in the baptism of suffering that their Lord had experienced!

If it pleased the Jews when James was killed, just think how delighted they would be if Peter were slain! God permitted Herod to arrest Peter and put him under heavy guard in prison. Sixteen soldiers, four for each watch, kept guard over the apostle, with two soldiers chained to the prisoner and two watching the doors. After all, the last time Peter was arrested, he mysteriously got out of jail, and Herod was not about to let that happen again.

Why was James allowed to die while Peter was rescued? After all, both were dedicated servants of God, needed by the church. The only answer is *the sovereign will of God,* the very thing Peter and the church had prayed about after their second experience of persecution (Acts 4:24-30). Herod had "stretched forth" his hand to destroy the church, but God would stretch forth His hand to perform signs and wonders and glorify His Son (Acts 4:28-30). God allowed Herod to kill James, but He kept him from harming Peter. It was the throne in heaven that was in control, not the throne on earth.

Please note that the Jerusalem church did not replace James as they had replaced Judas (Acts 1:15-26). As long as the Gospel was going "to the Jew first," it was necessary to have the full complement of 12 Apostles to witness to the twelve tribes of Israel. The stoning of Stephen ended that special witness to Israel, so the number of official witnesses was no longer important.

It is good to know that, no matter how difficult the trials or how disappointing the news, God is still on the throne and has everything under control. We may not always understand His ways, but we know His sovereign will is best.

God Hears Our Prayers (Acts 12:5-17)

"And His ears are open unto their prayers" (1 Peter 3:12).

The phrase "but prayer" is the turning point in the story. Never underestimate the power of a praying church! "The angel fetched Peter out of prison," said the Puritan preacher Thomas Watson, "but it was prayer that fetched the angel." Follow the scenes in this exciting drama in Acts 12.

Peter sleeping (vv. 5-6). If you were chained to two Roman soldiers and facing the possibility of being executed the next day, would you sleep very soundly? Probably not, but Peter did. In fact, Peter was so sound asleep that the angel had to strike him on the side to wake him up!

The fact that Peter had been a prisoner twice before is not what gave him his calm heart. For that matter, this prison experience was different from the other two. This time, he was alone, and the deliverance did not come right away. The other two times, he was able to witness; but this time, no special witnessing opportunities appeared. Peter's previous arrests had taken place after great victories, but this one followed the death of James, his dear friend and colleague. It was a new situation altogether.

What gave Peter such confidence and peace? To begin with, many believers were praying for him (Acts 12:12), and kept it up day and night for a week; and this helped to bring him peace (Phil. 4:6-7). Prayer has a way of reminding us of the promises of God's Word, such as, "I will both lay me down in peace, and sleep; for Thou, Lord, only makest me to dwell in safety" (Ps. 4:8). Or, "Fear thou not, for I am with thee. Be not dismayed, for I am thy God. I will strengthen thee; yea, I will help thee; yea, I will uphold thee with the right hand of My righteousness" (Isa. 41:10).

But the main cause of Peter's peace was the knowledge that Herod could not kill him. Jesus had promised Peter that he would live to be an old man and end his life crucified on a Roman cross (John 21:18-19). Peter simply laid hold of that promise and committed the entire situation to the Lord, and God gave him peace and rest. He did not know how or when God would deliver him, but he did know that deliverance was coming.

Peter obeying (vv. 7-11). Once again we behold the ministry of angels (Acts 5:19; 8:26; 10:3, 7) and are reminded that the angels care for God's children (Ps. 34:7). The angel brought light and liberty into the prison cell, but the guards had no idea that anything was going on. However, if Peter was going to be delivered, he had to obey what the angel commanded. He probably thought it was a dream or a vision, but he arose and followed the angel out of the prison and into the street. Only then did he come to himself and realize that he had been a part of another miracle.

The angel commanded Peter to bind his garments with his girdle, and then to put on his sandals. These were certainly ordinary tasks to do while a miracle is taking place! But God often joins the miraculous with the ordinary just to encourage us to keep in balance. Jesus multiplied the loaves and fishes, but then commanded His disciples to gather up the leftovers. He raised Jairus' daughter from the dead, then told her parents to give her something to eat. Even in miracles, God is always practical.

God alone can do the extraordinary, but His people must do the ordinary. Jesus raised Lazarus from the dead, but the men had to roll the stone from the tomb. The same angel that removed the chains from Peter's hands could have put the shoes on Peter's feet, but he told Peter to do it. God never wastes miracles.

Peter had to stoop before he could walk. It was a good lesson in humility and obedience. In fact, from that night on, every time Peter put on his shoes, it must have reminded him of the prison miracle and encouraged him to trust the Lord.

This deliverance took place at Passover season, the time of year when the Jews celebrated their Exodus from Egypt. The word "delivered" in Acts 12:11 is the same word Stephen used when he spoke about the Jewish Exodus (Acts 7:34). Peter experienced a new kind of "exodus" in answer to the prayers of God's people.

Peter knocking (vv. 12-16). As Peter followed the angel, God opened the way; and when Peter was free, the angel vanished. His work was done and now it was up to Peter to trust the Lord and use his common sense in taking the next step. Since it was the prayers of God's people that had helped to set him free, Peter decided that the best place for him would be in that prayer meeting at Mary's house. Furthermore, he wanted to report the good news that God had answered their prayers. So Peter headed for the house of Mary, mother of John Mark.

When you remember that (a) many people were praying, (b) they were praying earnestly, (c) they prayed night and day for perhaps as long as a week, and (d) their prayers were centered specifically on Peter's deliverance, then the scene that is described here is almost comical. The answer to their prayers is standing at the door, but they don't have faith enough to open the door and let him in! God could get Peter out of a prison, but Peter can't get himself into a prayer meeting!

Of course, the knock at the door might have been that of Herod's soldiers, coming to arrest more believers. It took courage for the maid Rhoda ("rose") to go to the door; but imagine her surprise when she recognized Peter's voice! She was so overcome that she forgot to open the door! Poor Peter had to keep knocking and calling while the "believers" in the prayer meeting decided what to do! And the longer he stood at the gate, the more dangerous his situation became.

The exclamation, "It is his angel!" (Acts 12:15) reveals their belief in "guardian angels" (Matt. 18:10; Heb. 1:14). Of course, the logical question is, "Why would an angel bother to knock?" All he had to do was simply walk right in! Sad to say, good theology plus unbelief often leads to fear and confusion.

We must face the fact that even in the most fervent prayer meetings there is sometimes a spirit of doubt and unbelief. We are like the father who cried to Jesus, "Lord, I believe; help Thou mine unbelief!" (Mark 9:24) These Jerusalem saints believed that God could answer their prayers, so they kept at it night and day. But, when the answer came right to their door, they refused to believe it. God graciously honors even the weakest faith, but how much more He would do if only we would trust Him.

Note the plural pronouns in Acts 12:16: "They . . . opened the door and . . . they were astonished." I get the impression that, for safety's sake, they decided to open the door *together* and face *together* whatever might be on the other side. Rhoda would have done it by herself, but she was too overcome with joy. It is commendable that a lowly servant girl recognized Peter's voice and rejoiced that he was free. Rhoda surely was a believer who knew Peter as a friend.

Peter declaring (v. 17). Apparently everybody began to speak at once and Peter had to silence them. He quickly gave an account of the miracle of his deliverance and no doubt thanked them for their prayer help. He instructed them to get the word to James, the half brother of the Lord, who was the leader of the Jerusalem assembly (Matt. 13:55; Acts 15:13ff; Gal. 1:19). James was also the author of the Epistle of James.

Where Peter went when he left the meeting, nobody knows to this day! It certainly was a well-kept secret. Except for a brief appearance in Acts 15, Peter walks off the pages of the Book of Acts to make room for Paul and the story of his ministry among the Gentiles. First Corinthians 9:5 tells us that Peter traveled in ministry with his wife, and 1 Corinthians 1:12 suggests that he visited Corinth. There is no evidence in Scripture that Peter ever visited Rome. In fact, if Peter had founded the church in Rome, it is unlikely that Paul would have gone there, for his policy was to work where other Apostles had not labored (Rom. 15:18-22). Also, he certainly would have said something to or about Peter when he wrote his letter to the Romans.

Before we leave this section, it would be profitable to consider how Christians can best pray for those in prison; for even today there are many people in prison only because they are Christians. "Remember them that are in bonds, as bound with them" commands Hebrews 13:3. In other words, pray for them as you would want them to pray for you if your situations were reversed.

We ought to pray that God will give them grace to bear with suffering so that they might have a triumphant witness for the Lord. We should ask the Spirit to minister the Word to them and bring it to their remembrance. It is right to ask God to protect His own and to give them wisdom as they must day after day deal with a difficult enemy. We must ask God that, if it is His will, they be delivered from their bondage and suffering and reunited with their loved ones.

God Deals with Our Enemies (Acts 12:18-25)

"But the face of the Lord is against them that do evil" (1 Peter 3:12).

If the account had ended with Peter's departure, we would find ourselves wondering, "What happened to the prison guards and to Herod?" We do not know at what time the angel delivered Peter, but when the next quaternion arrived at the cell, imagine their consternation when they discovered that the guards were there but the prisoner was gone! If the new watch awakened the old watch, it was certainly a rude awakening for them! If the old watch was already awake and alert, they must have had a difficult time explaining the situation to the new watch. How could a chained prisoner escape when there were four guards present and the doors were locked?

If a guard permitted a prisoner to escape, Roman law required that he receive the same punishment that the prisoner would have received, even if it was death (see Acts 16:27; 27:42). This law did not strictly apply in Herod's jurisdiction, so the king was not forced to kill the guards; but, being a Herod, he did it anyway. Instead of killing one man to please the Jews, he killed four and perhaps hoped it would please them more.

"The righteous is delivered out of trouble, and the wicked cometh in his stead" (Prov. 11:8). This truth is illustrated in the death of Herod. While God does not always bring retribution this quickly, we can be sure that the Judge of all the earth will do what is right (Gen. 18:25; Rev. 6:9-11).

The people of Tyre and Sidon, who depended on the Jews for food (see Ezra 3:7), had in some way displeased King Herod and were in danger of losing this assistance. In true political fashion, they bribed Blastus, who was in charge of the king's bed chamber, and thus a trusted official; he in turn convinced the king to meet the delegation. It was an opportunity for the proud king to display his authority and glory, and for the delegates to please him with their flattery.

The Jewish historian Josephus said that this scene took place during a festival honoring Claudius Caesar, and that the king wore a beautiful silver garment in honor of the occasion. We do not know what Herod said in his oration, but we do know why he said it: he wanted to impress the people. And he did! They played on his Herodian ego and told him he was a god, and he loved every minute of it.

But he did not give the glory to the Lord, so this whole scene was nothing but idolatry. "I am the Lord: that is My name: and My glory will I not give to another" (Isa. 42:8; see 48:11). Instead of Peter being killed by Herod, it was Herod who was killed by Peter's God! Perhaps the same angel who delivered Peter also smote the king. Herod contracted some affliction in his bowels and died five days later, according to Josephus. This was in A.D. 44.

This event is more than a slice of ancient history, because it typifies the world and its people today. The citizens of Tyre and Sidon were concerned about one thing only—getting sufficient food to feed their stomachs. To be sure, food is essential to life, but when we pay any price to get that food, we are doing wrong. By flattering the king and calling him a god, the delegation knew they could get what they wanted.

I cannot help but see in King Herod an illustration of the future "man of sin" who will one day rule the world and persecute God's people (2 Thes. 2; Rev. 13). This "man of sin" (or Antichrist) will make himself god and will command the worship of the whole world. But Jesus Christ will return and judge him and those who follow him (Rev. 19:11-21).

The world still lives for praise and pleasure. Man has made himself his own god (Rom. 1:25). The world still lives on the physical and ignores the spiritual (see 1 John 2:15-17). It lives by force and flattery instead of faith and truth, and one day it will be judged.

The church today, like Israel of old, suffers because of people like Herod who use their authority to oppose the truth. Beginning with Pharaoh in Egypt, God's people have often suffered under despotic rulers and governments, and God has always preserved His witness in the world. God has not always judged evil officials as He judged Herod, but He has always watched over His people and seen to it that they did not suffer and die in vain. Our freedom today was purchased by their bondage.

The early church had no "political clout" or friends in high places to "pull strings" for them. Instead, they went to the highest throne of all, the throne of grace. They were a praying people, for they knew that God could solve their problems. God's glorious throne was greater than the throne of Herod, and God's heavenly army could handle Herod's weak soldiers any day or night! The believers did not need to bribe anyone at court. They simply took their case to the highest court and left it with the Lord!

And what was the result? "But the word of God grew and multiplied" (Acts 12:24). This is another of Luke's summaries, or "progress reports," that started with Acts 6:7 (see 9:31; 16:5; 19:20; 28:31). Luke is accomplishing the purpose of his book and showing us how the church spread throughout the Roman world from its small beginnings in Jerusalem. What an encouragement to us today!

At the beginning of Acts 12, Herod seemed to be in control and the church was losing the battle. But at the end of the chapter, Herod is dead and the church—very much alive—is growing rapidly!

The secret? A praying church!

Missionary Isobel Kuhn used to pray when in trouble, "If this obstacle is from Thee, Lord, I accept it; but if it is from Satan, I refuse him and all his works in the name of Calvary!" And Dr. Alan Redpath has often said, "Let's keep our chins up and our knees down—we're on the victory side!"

God works when churches pray, and Satan still trembles "when he sees the weakest saint upon his knees."

CHAPTER THIRTEEN GOD OPENS THE DOORS

Acts 13–14

We usually identify the preaching of the Gospel with the quiet rural villages of Palestine where the Lord Jesus ministered. For this reason, many Christians are surprised to learn that the church in the Book of Acts was almost entirely *urban*. Historian Wayne A. Meeks writes that "within a decade of the crucifixion of Jesus, the village culture of Palestine had been left behind, and the Greco-Roman city became the dominant environment of the Christian movement" (*The First Urban Christians*, p. 11).

The church began in Jerusalem, and then spread to other cities, including Samaria, Damascus, Caesarea, and Antioch in Syria. At least forty different cities are named in Acts. From Antioch, Paul and his helpers carried the Gospel throughout the then-known world. In fact, the record given in Acts 13–28 is almost a review of ancient geography. About the year 56, the Apostle Paul was able to write, "So that from Jerusalem, and round about unto Illyricum, I have fully preached the Gospel of Christ" (Rom. 15:19). What a record!

In these two chapters, Dr. Luke described Paul's ministry in six different cities, beginning and ending at Antioch.

Antioch in Syria—Decision (Acts 13:1-5)

That sainted missionary to India and Persia, Henry Martyn, once said, "The Spirit of Christ is the spirit of missions, and the nearer we get to Him, the more intensely missionary we must become." Paul (Saul) and Barnabas had that experience as they ministered in Antioch and were called by the Spirit to take the Gospel to the Roman world.

Until now, Jerusalem had been the center of ministry, and Peter had been the key apostle. But from this point on, Antioch in Syria would become the new center (Acts 11:19ff), and Paul the new leader. The Gospel was on the move!

Luke listed five different men who were ministering in the church: *Barnabas,* whom we have already met (Acts 4:36-37; 9:27; 11:22-26); *Simeon,* who may have been from Africa since he was nicknamed "Black"; *Lucius,* who came from Cyrene and may have been one of the founders of the church in Antioch (Acts 11:20); *Manaen,* who was an intimate friend (or perhaps an adopted foster brother) of Herod Antipas, who had killed John the Baptist; and *Saul* (Paul), last on the list but soon to become first.

These men were serving as "prophets and teachers" in a local church. The prophets helped lay the foundation for the church as they proclaimed the Word of God (Eph. 2:20; 1 Cor. 14:29-32). They were more "forth-tellers" than "foretellers," though at times the prophets did announce things to come (Acts 11:27-30). The teachers helped to ground the converts in the doctrines of the faith (2 Tim. 2:2).

God had already called Paul to minister to the Gentiles (Acts 9:15; 21:17-21), and now He summoned Barnabas to labor with him. The church confirmed their calling, commissioned the men, and sent them forth. It is the ministry of the Holy Spirit, working through the local church, to equip and enlist believers to go forth and serve. The modern mission board is only a "sending agency" that expedites the work authorized by the local church.

Barnabas and Paul took John Mark with them as their assistant. He was a cousin to Barnabas (Col. 4:10), and his mother's home in Jerusalem was a gathering place for the believers (Acts 12:12). It is likely that it was Peter who led John Mark to faith in Christ (1 Peter 5:13). John Mark no doubt helped Barnabas and Paul in numerous ways, relieving them of tasks and details that would have interfered with their important ministry of the Word.

Paphos—Deception (Acts 13:6-12)
It was logical to go first to Cyprus, for this was the home of Barnabas (Acts 4:36). Luke gives us no details of the ministry in Salamis, the great commercial center at the east end of the island. We trust that some people did believe the Gospel and that a local assembly was formed. The men then moved ninety miles to Paphos on the west end of the island, and there they met their first opposition.

Paphos was the capital of Cyprus, and the chief Roman official there was Sergius Paulus, "an understanding man" who wanted to hear the Word of God. He was opposed by a Jewish false prophet named "Son of Jesus [Joshua]." It is unusual to find a *Jewish* false prophet and sorcerer, for the Jews traditionally shunned such demonic activities. The name *Elymas* means "sorcerer" or "wise man" (cf. the "wise men" of Matt. 2).

This event is an illustration of the lesson that Jesus taught in the Parable of the Tares (Matt. 13:24-30, 36-43): wherever the Lord sows His true children (the wheat), Satan comes along and sows a counterfeit (the tares), a child of the devil. Paul recognized that Elymas was a child of the devil (John 8:44), and he inflicted blindness on the false prophet as a judgment from God. This miracle was also evidence to Sergius Paulus that Paul and Barnabas were servants of the true God and preached the true message of salvation (Heb. 2:4). The Roman official believed and was saved.

Acts 13:9 is the first place you find the familiar name *Paul* in the New Testament. As a Jewish Roman citizen, the apostle's full name was probably "Saul Paulus," for many Jews had both Jewish and Roman names.

Perga—Desertion (Acts 13:13)
Why did John Mark desert his friends and return to Jerusalem? Perhaps he was just plain homesick, or he may have become unhappy because Paul had begun to take over the leadership from Mark's cousin Barnabas (note "Paul and his company" in Acts 13:13). Mark was a devoted Jew, and he may have felt uncomfortable with the saved Gentiles. Some students think that John Mark's return to Jerusalem helped start the opposition of the legalistic Judaizers who later opposed Paul (see Acts 15 and the Epistle to the Galatians).

Another possibility is the fear of danger as the party moved into new and difficult areas. But whatever the cause of his defection, John Mark did something so serious that Paul did not want him back on his "team" again! (Acts 15:36ff) Later, Paul would enlist Timothy to take John Mark's place (Acts 16:1-5). John Mark did redeem himself and was eventually accepted and approved by Paul (2 Tim. 4:11).

During my years of ministry as a pastor and as a member of several mission boards, I have seen first-term workers do what John Mark did; and it has always been heartbreaking. But I have also seen some of them restored to missionary service, thanks to the prayers and encouragement of God's people. A.T. Robertson said that Mark "flickered in the crisis," but the light did not completely go out. This is an encouragement to all of us.

Antioch in Pisidia—Disputation (Acts 13:14-52)
Paul and Barnabas traveled 100 miles north and about 3,600 feet up to get to this important city on the Roman road. As you follow Paul's journeys in Acts, you will notice that he selected strategic cities, planted churches in them, and went on from the churches to evangelize the surrounding areas. You will also notice that, where it was possible, he started his ministry in the local synagogue, for he had a great burden for his people (Rom. 9:1-5; 10:1), and he found in the synagogue both Jews and Gentiles ready to hear the Word of God.

This is the first of Paul's sermons recorded in the Book of Acts, and it may be divided into three parts, each of which is introduced by the phrase "men and brethren."

Preparation (vv. 16-25). In this section, Paul reviewed the history of Israel, climaxing with the ministry of John the Baptist and the coming of their Messiah. He made it clear that it was God who was at work in and for Israel, preparing the way for the coming of the promised Messiah. He also reminded his hearers that the nation had not always been faithful to the Lord and the covenant, but had often rebelled. Every pious Jew knew that the Messiah would come from David's family, and that a prophet would announce His coming beforehand. John the Baptist was that prophet.

Declaration (vv. 26-37). As Paul addressed both the Jews and the Gentile "God-fearers" in the congregation, he changed his approach from third person ("they") to second person ("you"). He explained to them why their leaders in Jerusalem rejected and crucified the nation's Messiah. It was not because they had not read or heard the message of the prophets, but because they did not understand the message. Furthermore, the crucifixion of Jesus of Nazareth was even promised in the prophets. (Peter took this same approach in his second message, Acts 3:12-18.)

It was the resurrection of Jesus Christ that was the crucial event: "But God raised Him from the dead" (Acts 13:30). (See Acts 13:33-34, 37, and note that "raised" in Acts 13:22-23 means "brought.") Paul has declared the Gospel to them, "the word of this salvation" (Acts 13:26) and "the glad tidings" (Acts 13:32). Christ died, He was buried, and He arose again!

Since Paul was addressing a synagogue congregation, he used the Old Testament Scriptures to support his argument. In Acts 13:33, Psalm 2:7 is quoted; and note that it refers to the *resurrection* of Christ, not to the birth of Christ. The "virgin tomb" (John 19:41) was like a "womb" that gave birth to Jesus Christ in resurrection glory.

Then he quoted Isaiah 55:3, referring to the covenant that God made with David, "the sure mercies of David." God had promised David that from him the Messiah would come (2 Sam. 7:12-17). This was an "everlasting covenant" with a throne to be established forever (2 Sam. 7:13, 16). If Jesus is the Messiah, and He died and remained dead, this covenant could never be fulfilled. Therefore, Jesus had to be raised from the dead or the covenant would prove false.

His third quotation was from Psalm 16:10, the same passage Peter quoted in his message at Pentecost (Acts 2:24-28). The Jews considered Psalm 16 to be a messianic psalm, and it was clear that this promise did not apply to David, who was dead, buried, and decayed. It had to apply to Jesus Christ, the Messiah.

Application (vv. 38-52). Paul had declared the Good News to them (Acts 13:32), and now all that remained was to make the personal application and "draw the net." He told them that through faith in Jesus Christ, they could have two blessings that the Law could never provide: the forgiveness of their sins and justification before the throne of God.

Justification is the act of God whereby He declares the believing sinner righteous in Jesus Christ. It has to do with the believer's standing before the throne of God. The Jews were taught that God justified the righteous and punished the wicked (2 Chron. 6:22-23). But God justifies the ungodly who will put their faith in Jesus Christ (Rom. 4:1-8).

The Law cannot justify the sinner; it can only condemn him (Rom. 3:19-20; Gal. 2:16). God not only forgives our sins, but He also gives us the very righteousness of Christ and puts it on our account! This was certainly good news delivered by Paul to that searching congregation of Jews and Gentiles who had no peace in their hearts, even though they were religious.

Paul closed his message with a note of warning taken from Habakkuk 1:5 (and see Isa. 29:14). In Habakkuk's day, the "unbelievable work" God was doing was the raising up of the Chaldeans to chasten His people, a work so remarkable that nobody would believe it. After all, why would God use an evil pagan nation to punish His own chosen people, sinful though they might be? God was using Gentiles to punish Jews! But the "wonderful work" in Paul's day was that God was using the Jews to save the Gentiles!

What was the result? Many Jews and Gentile proselytes believed and associated with Paul and Barnabas. The Gentiles were especially excited about Paul's message and wanted him to tell them more, which he did the next Sabbath. The people had done a good job of spreading the news, because a great crowd gathered. They were probably predominantly Gentiles, which made the Jews envious and angry.

Paul's final message in the synagogue declared that God had sent the Word to the Jews first (Acts 3:26; Rom. 1:16), but they had now rejected it. Therefore, Paul would now take the Good News to the Gentiles; and he quoted Isaiah 49:6 to back up his decision. (Note also Luke 2:29-32.) He was ready to go to the ends of the earth to win souls to Christ!

Acts 13:48 gives us the divine side of evangelism, for God has His elect people (Eph. 1:4). The word translated *ordained* means "enrolled," and indicates that God's people have their names written in God's book (Luke 10:20; Phil. 4:3). But Acts 13:49 is the human side of evangelism: if we do not preach the Word, then nobody can believe and be saved. It takes both (see 2 Thes. 2:13-14 and Rom. 10:13-15).

The unbelieving Jews were not going to sit back and let Paul and Barnabas take over.

First, they disputed with them, and then brought legal action against them and expelled them from their borders. The missionaries were not discouraged: they shook off the dust of their feet against them (Luke 9:5; 10:11) and went to the next town, leaving behind them a group of joyful disciples.

Iconium—Division (Acts 14:1-7)

This city, more Greek than Roman, was in the Roman province of Galatia. Paul's ministry in the synagogue was singularly blessed and a multitude of Jews and Gentiles believed. Once again, the unbelieving Jews stirred up hatred and opposition, but the missionaries stayed on and witnessed boldly for Christ. (Note the "therefore" in Acts 14:3.)

God also enabled the men to perform signs and wonders as their "credentials" that they were indeed the servants of the true God (see Acts 15:12; Gal. 3:5; Heb. 2:4). Faith is not based on miracles (Luke 16:27-31; John 2:23-25), but faith can be bolstered by miracles. The important thing is "the word of His grace" that performs the work of His grace (Acts 14:26).

The result? The city was divided and the Christians were threatened with public disgrace and stoning. Obedient to their Lord's counsel in Matthew 10:23, they fled from that area into a different Roman district and continued to minister the Word of God.

Lystra—Delusion (Acts 14:8-20)

Lystra was in the Roman province of Galatia, about eighteen miles southwest of Iconium. This was the first of three visits Paul made to this city, and an eventful visit it was! On his second missionary journey, Paul enlisted Timothy in Lystra (Acts 16:1-5); and he made a visit to this church on his third journey as well (Acts 18:23). We should note four different responses during this visit.

The crippled man's response to the Word (vv. 8-10). Both Peter and Paul healed men who were lame from birth (Acts 3). Had their lameness been caused by disease or accident, the cure might have been attributed to a sudden change in their health. As it was, the cure was obviously miraculous.

The word translated "speak" in Acts 14:9 means ordinary conversation, though it can refer to formal speaking. It is likely that Paul was simply conversing with some of the citizens in the marketplace, telling them about Jesus, and the lame man overheard what he said. The Word produced faith (Rom. 10:17) and faith brought healing.

The crowd's response to the crippled man (vv. 11-13). Miracles by themselves do not produce either conviction or faith. They must be accompanied by the Word (Acts 14:3). This was a superstitious crowd that interpreted events in the light of their own mythology. They identified Barnabas as Jupiter (Zeus), the chief of the gods; and Paul, the speaker, they identified with Mercury (Hermes), the messenger of the gods. Jupiter was the patron deity of the city, so this was a great opportunity for the priest of Jupiter to become very important and lead the people in honoring their god.

The Apostles' response to the crowd (vv. 14-19). How easy it would have been to accept this worship and try to use the honor as a basis for teaching the people the truth, but that is not the way God's true servants minister (2 Cor. 4:1-2; 1 Thes. 2:1-5). Paul and Barnabas opposed what they were doing and boldly told the people that the gods of Lystra were "vanities."

Paul's message was not based on the Old Testament, because this was a pagan Gentile audience. He started with the witness of God in creation (see Acts 17:22ff). He made it clear that there is but one God who is the living God, the giving God, and the forgiving God. And He has been patient with the sinning nations (Acts 17:30) and has not judged them for their sins as they deserve.

The crowd quieted down, but when some troublemaking Jews arrived from Antioch and Iconium, the crowd followed their lead and stoned Paul. One minute, Paul was a god to be worshiped; the next minute, he was a criminal to be slain! Emerson called a mob "a society of bodies voluntarily bereaving themselves of reason." Often this is true.

The disciples' response to Paul (v. 20). There were new believers in Lystra, and this was a crisis situation for them. They were a minority, their leader had been stoned, and their future looked very bleak. But they stood by Paul! It is likely that they joined hearts and prayed for him, and this is one reason God raised him up. Was Paul dead? We are not told. This is the only stoning he ever experienced (2 Cor. 11:25), but from it came glory to God. It may have been this event that especially touched Timothy and eventually led to his association with Paul (2 Tim. 3:10).

Antioch in Syria—Declaration (Acts 14:21-28)

On their return trip to Antioch, the missionaries were engaged in several important ministries.

First, they preached the Gospel and made disciples ("taught many"). It is difficult to understand how they got back into the cities from which they had been expelled, but the Lord opened the doors.

Second, they strengthened ("confirmed") the believers in the things of Christ and encouraged ("exhorted") them to continue in the faith. Continuance is a proof of true faith in Jesus Christ (John 8:31-32; Acts 2:42). Paul made it very clear that living the Christian life was not an easy thing and that they would all have to expect trials and sufferings before they would see the Lord in glory.

Third, they organized the churches (Acts 14:23-25). The local church is both an organism and an organization, for if an organism is not organized, it will die! Paul and Barnabas ordained spiritual leaders and gave them the responsibility of caring for the flock. If you compare Titus 1:5 and 7, you will see that "elder" and "bishop" (overseer) refer to the same office, and both are equivalent to "pastor" (shepherd).

The word translated *ordained* means "to elect by a show of hands." It is possible that Paul chose the men and the congregation voted its approval, or that the people selected them by vote and Paul ordained them (see Acts 6:1-6).

Finally, they reported to their "sending church" on the work God had done (Acts 14:26-28). They had been gone at least a year, and it must have been exciting for them and for the church when they arrived back home. They had, by the grace of God, fulfilled the work God had given them to do; and they joyfully reported the blessings to the church family.

This is perhaps the first "missionary conference" in church history, and what a conference it must have been! A church officer once said to me, "I don't care how much money you want for missions, I'll give it; but *just don't make me listen to missionaries speak!"* I felt sorry for him that his spiritual temperature was so low that he could not listen to reports of what God was doing in the difficult corners of the harvest field.

As you review Paul's first missionary journey, you can see the principles by which he operated, principles that are still applicable today.

He worked primarily in the key cities and challenged the believers to take the message out to the more remote areas. The Gospel works in the population centers, and we must carry it there.

He used one approach with the synagogue congregations and another with the Gentiles. He referred the Jews and Jewish proselytes to the Old Testament Scriptures; but when preaching to the Gentiles, he emphasized the God of creation and His goodness to the nations. His starting point was different, but his finishing point was the same: faith in the Lord Jesus Christ.

He majored on establishing and organizing local churches. Jesus had the local church in mind when He gave what we call "The Great Commission" (Matt. 28:19-20). After we make disciples ("teach"), we must baptize them (the responsibility primarily of a local church) and then teach them the Word of God. Merely winning people to Christ is but fulfilling one-third of the Commission! It takes the local assembly of believers to help us fulfill all of what Jesus commanded us to do.

He grounded the believers in the Word of God. This is the only source of strength and stability when persecution comes, as it inevitably does come. Paul did not preach a popular "success Gospel" that painted a picture of an easy Christian life.

The amazing thing is that Paul and his associates did all of this without the modern means of transportation and communication that we possess today. Dr. Bob Pierce used to say to us in Youth For Christ, "Others have done so much with so little, while we have done so little with so much!" The wasted wealth of American believers alone, if invested in world evangelization, might lead to the salvation of millions of lost people.

Paul and Barnabas announced that the "door of faith" had been opened to the Gentiles.

That door is still open, to Jews and Gentiles alike—to a whole world! Walk through that open door and help take the Gospel to others.

Be daring!

CHAPTER FOURTEEN
DON'T CLOSE THE DOORS!
Acts 15:1-35

The progress of the Gospel has often been hindered by people with closed minds who stand in front of open doors and block the way for others.

In 1786, when William Carey laid the burden of world missions before a ministerial meeting in Northampton, England, the eminent Dr. Ryland said to him, "Young man, sit down! When God pleases to convert the heathen, He will do it without your aid or mine!" More than one Spirit-filled servant of God has had to enter open doors of opportunity without the support of churches and religious leaders.

Paul and his associates faced this same challenge at the Jerusalem Conference about twenty years after Pentecost. Courageously, they defended both the truth of the Gospel and the missionary outreach of the church. There were three stages in this event.

The Dispute (Acts 15:1-5)

It all started when some legalistic Jewish teachers came to Antioch and taught that the Gentiles, in order to be saved, had to be circumcised and obey the Law of Moses. These men were associated with the Jerusalem congregation but not authorized by it (Acts 15:24). Identified with the Pharisees (Acts 15:5), these teachers were "false brethren" who wanted to rob both Jewish and Gentile believers of their liberty in Christ (Gal. 2:1-10; 5:1ff).

It is not surprising that there were people in the Jerusalem church who were strong advocates of the Law of Moses but ignorant of the relationship between Law and grace. These people were Jews who had been trained to respect and obey the Law of Moses; and, after all, Romans, Galatians, and Hebrews had not yet been written! There was a large group of priests in the Jerusalem assembly (Acts 6:7), as well as people who still followed some of the Old Testament practices (see Acts 21:20-26). It was a time of transition, and such times are always difficult.

What were these legalists actually doing and why were they so dangerous? They were attempting to mix Law and grace and to pour the new wine into the ancient brittle wineskins (Luke 5:36-39). They were stitching up the rent veil (Luke 23:45) and blocking the new and living way to God that Jesus had opened when He died on the cross (Heb. 10:19-25). They were rebuilding the wall between Jews and Gentiles that Jesus had torn down on the cross (Eph. 2:14-16). They were putting the heavy Jewish yoke on Gentile shoulders (Acts 15:10; Gal. 5:1) and asking the church to move out of the sunlight into the shadows (Col. 2:16-17; Heb. 10:1). They were saying, "A Gentile must first become a Jew before he can become a Christian! It is not sufficient for them simply to trust Jesus Christ. They must also obey Moses!"

Several important issues are involved here, not the least of which is the work of Christ on the cross as declared in the message of the Gospel (1 Cor. 15:1-8; Heb. 10:1-18). God pronounces a solemn anathema on anyone who preaches any other Gospel than the Gospel of the grace of God found in Jesus Christ His Son (Gal. 1:1-9). When any religious leader says, "Unless you belong to our group, you cannot be saved!" or, "Unless you participate in our ceremonies and keep our rules, you cannot be saved!" he is adding to the Gospel and denying the finished work of Jesus Christ. Paul wrote his Epistle to the Galatians to make it clear that salvation is wholly by God's grace, through faith in Christ, *plus nothing!*

Another issue involved was the nature of the church's missionary program. If these legalists (we call them "the Judaizers") were correct, then Paul and Barnabas had been all wrong in their ministry. Along with preaching the Gospel, they should have been teaching the Gentiles how to live as good Jews. No wonder Paul and Barnabas debated and disputed with these false teachers! (Acts 15:2, 7) The Antioch believers were being "troubled" and "subverted" (Acts 15:24), and this same confusion and disruption would soon spread to the Gentile churches Paul and Barnabas had founded. This was a declaration of war that Paul and Barnabas could not ignore.

God gave Paul a revelation instructing him to take the whole matter to the Jerusalem church leaders (Gal. 2:2), and to this the Antioch assembly agreed ("they" in Acts 15:2). The gathering was not a "church council" in the denominational sense, but rather a meeting of the leaders who heard the various groups and then made their decision. Though the "mother church" in Jerusalem did have great influence, each local church was autonomous.

The Defense (Acts 15:6-18)

It appears that at least four different meetings were involved in this strategic conference: (1) a public welcome to Paul and his associates, Acts 15:4; (2) a private meeting of Paul and the key leaders, Galatians 2:2; (3) a second public meeting at which the Judaizers presented their case, Acts 15:5-6 and Galatians 2:3-5; and (4) the public discussion described in Acts 15:6ff. In this public discussion, four key leaders presented the case for keeping the doors of grace open to the lost Gentiles.

Peter reviewed the past (vv. 6-11). We get the impression that Peter sat patiently while the disputing ("questioning") was going on, waiting for the Spirit to direct him. "He who answers a matter before he hears it, it is folly and shame to him" (Prov. 18:13, NKJV). Peter reminded the church of four important ministries that God had performed for the Gentiles, ministries in which he had played an important part.

First, God made a choice that Peter should preach the Gospel to the Gentiles (Acts 15:7). Jesus had given the keys of the kingdom to Peter (Matt. 16:19), and he had used them to open the door of faith to the Jews (Acts 2), the Samaritans (Acts 8:14-17), and the Gentiles (Acts 10). The Apostles and brethren in Judea had censured Peter for visiting the Gentiles and eating with them, but he had satisfactorily defended himself (Acts 11:1-18). Note that Peter made it clear that Cornelius and his household were saved by hearing and believing, not by obeying the Law of Moses.

Second, God gave the Holy Spirit to the Gentiles to bear witness that they truly were born again (Acts 15:8). Only God can see the human heart; so, if these people had not been saved, God would never have given them the Spirit (Rom. 8:9). But they did not receive the Spirit by keeping the Law, but by believing God's Word (Acts 10:43-46; see Gal. 3:2). Peter's message was "whoever believes in Him will receive remission of sins" (Acts 10:43, NKJV), not "whoever believes and obeys the Law of Moses."

Third, God erased a difference (Acts 15:9, 11). For centuries, God had put a difference between Jews and Gentiles, and it was the task of the Jewish religious leaders to protect and maintain that difference (Lev. 10:10; Ezek. 22:26; 44:23). Jesus taught that the Jewish dietary laws had nothing to do with inner holiness (Mark 7:1-23), and Peter had learned that lesson again when he had that vision on the housetop in Joppa (Acts 10:1ff).

Ever since the work of Christ on Calvary, God has made no difference between Jews and Gentiles as far as sin (Rom. 3:9, 22) or salvation (Rom. 10:9-13) are concerned. Sinners can have their hearts purified only by faith in Christ; salvation is not by keeping the Law (Acts 15:9). We would expect Peter to conclude his defense by saying, "They [the Gentiles] shall be saved even as we Jews," but he said just the reverse! "We [Jews] shall be saved, even as they!"

God's fourth ministry—and this was Peter's strongest statement—was the removing of the yoke of the Law (Acts 15:10). The Law was indeed a yoke that burdened the Jewish nation, but that yoke has been taken away by Jesus Christ (see Matt. 11:28-30; Gal. 5:1ff; Col. 2:14-17). After all, the Law was given to the Jewish nation to protect them from the evils of the Gentile world and prepare them to bring the Messiah into the world (Gal. 4:1-7). The Law cannot purify the sinner's heart (Gal. 2:21), impart the gift of the Holy Spirit (Gal. 3:2), or give eternal life (Gal. 3:21). What the Law could not do, God did through His own Son (Rom. 8:1-4). Those who have trusted Christ have the righteousness of God's Law in their hearts and, through the Spirit, obey His will. They are not motivated by fear, but by love, for "love is the fulfilling of the Law" (Rom. 13:8-10).

Paul and Barnabas reported on the present (v. 12). Peter's witness made a great impact on the congregation because they sat in silence after he was finished. Then Paul and Barnabas stood up and told the group what God had done among the Gentiles through their witness. Dr. Luke devoted only one summary sentence to their report since he had already given it in detail in Acts 13–14. Paul and Barnabas were greatly respected by the church (see Acts 15:25-26) and their testimony carried a great deal of weight.

Their emphasis was on the miracles that God had enabled them to perform among the Gentiles. These miracles were proof that God was working with them (Mark 16:20; Acts 15:4) and that they were God's chosen messengers (Rom. 15:18-19; Heb. 2:2-4). "Does God give you His Spirit and work miracles among you because you observe the Law, or because you believe what you heard?" (Gal. 3:5, NIV) They had preached grace, not Law; and God had honored this message.

If you will review the record of the first missionary journey (Acts 13–14), you will see that the emphasis is on what God did in response to men's faith. See Acts 13:8, 12, 39, 41, 48; 14:1, 22-23, 27. Note also the emphasis on grace (Acts 13:43; 14:3, 26). God opened for the Gentiles "the door of faith," not "the door of Law." For that matter the Antioch church, which commissioned Paul and Barnabas, was founded by people who "believed and turned unto the Lord" (Acts 11:21) and experienced the grace of God (Acts 11:23). They were saved the same way sinners are saved today, "by grace, through faith" (Eph. 2:8-9).

Both Peter and Paul received from God special visions directing them to go to the Gentiles (Acts 10:1ff; 22:21). However, it was Paul whom God set apart as the apostle to the Gentiles (Rom. 11:13; Gal. 2:6-10; Eph. 3:1-12). If Gentile sinners had to obey the Law of Moses in order to be saved, then why did God give Paul the Gospel of grace and send him off to the Gentiles? God could just as well have sent Peter!

Peter reviewed God's ministries to the Gentiles in the past, and Paul and Barnabas reported on God's work among the Gentiles in that present day. James was the final speaker and he focused on the future.

James related it all to the future (vv. 13-18). James was a brother to Jesus (Matt. 13:55; Gal. 1:19) and the writer of the Epistle of James. He and his brethren were not believers in Christ until after the Resurrection (John 7:5; 1 Cor. 15:7; Acts 1:14). James had strong leanings toward the Law (there are at least ten references to law in his epistle), so he was most acceptable to the legalistic party in the Jerusalem church.

The key idea in James' speech is *agreement.* First, he expressed his full agreement with Peter that God was saving the Gentiles by grace. It must have startled the Judaizers when James called these saved Gentiles "a people for His [God's] name," because for centuries the Jews had carried that honorable title (see Deut. 7:6; 14:2; 28:10). Today, God is graciously calling out a people, the church, from both Jews and Gentiles. In fact, the Greek word for "church" (*ekklesia*) means "a called out assembly" (*kaleo* = to call; *ek* = out). But if they are called out, then their salvation is all of grace and not through the keeping of the Law!

The Judaizers did not understand how the Gentiles and the Jews related to each other in the church, or how the church fit into God's promise to establish a kingdom for Israel. The Old Testament declared both the salvation of the Gentiles (Isa. 2:2; 11:10) and the future establishing of a glorious kingdom for Israel (Isa. 11–12; 35; 60), but it did not explain how they related to each other. The legalists in the church were jealous for both the future glory of Israel and the past glory of Moses and the Law. It seemed to them that their acceptance of the Gentiles as "spiritual equals" jeopardized the future of Israel.

We today have a better grasp of this truth because Paul explained it in Ephesians 2–3 and Romans 9–11. Saved Jews and Gentiles are both members of the same body and "one in Christ Jesus" (Gal. 3:28). The truth about the church, the body of Christ, was a "mystery" (a sacred secret) hidden in past ages and revealed to the church by the Spirit. God's "mystery program" for the church does not cancel His great "prophecy program" for Israel. Paul makes it clear in Romans 9–11 that there is a future for Israel and that God will keep His "kingdom promises" to His people.

James stated that the prophets also agreed with this conclusion, and he cited Amos 9:11-12 to prove his point. Note that he did not state that what Peter, Paul, and Barnabas had said was a *fulfillment* of this prophecy. He said that what Amos wrote *agreed with their testimony.* A careful reading of Amos 9:8-15 reveals that the prophet is describing events in the end times, when God will regather His people Israel to their land and bless them abundantly. If we "spiritualize" these promises, we rob them of their plain meaning and James' argument falls apart.

Amos also prophesied that the fallen house ("tent") of David would be raised up and God would fulfill His covenant with David that a king would sit on his throne (see 2 Sam. 7:25-29). This future King, of course, will be Jesus Christ, the Son of David (2 Sam. 7:13, 16; Isa. 9:6-7; Luke 1:32) who will reign over Israel during the kingdom. In fact, the only Jew alive today who can prove His genealogy and defend His kingship is Jesus Christ!

God revealed these truths gradually to His people, but His plan had been settled from the beginning. Neither the Cross nor the church were afterthoughts with God (Acts 2:23; 4:27-28; Eph. 1:4). The Judaizers thought that Israel had to "rise" in her glorious kingdom before the Gentiles could be saved, but God revealed that it was through Israel's "fall" that the Gentiles would find salvation (Rom. 11:11-16). At the time of the Jerusalem Conference, David's house and throne indeed were fallen; but they would be restored one day and the kingdom established.

The Decision (Acts 15:19-35)

The leaders and the whole church (Acts 15:22), directed by the Holy Spirit (Acts 15:28), made a twofold decision; a doctrinal decision about salvation, and a practical decision about how to live the Christian life.

The doctrinal decision we have already examined. The church concluded that Jews and Gentiles are all sinners before God and can be saved only by faith in Jesus Christ. There is one need, and there is but one Gospel to meet that need (Gal. 1:6-12). God has today but one program: He is calling out a people for His name. Israel is set aside but not cast away (Rom. 11:1ff); and when God's program for the church is completed, He will begin to fulfill His kingdom promises to the Jews.

But all doctrine must lead to duty. James emphasized this in his epistle (James 2:14-26), and so did Paul in his letters. It is not enough for us simply to accept a biblical truth; we must apply it personally in everyday life. Church problems are not solved by passing resolutions, but by practicing the revelations God gives us from His Word.

James advised the church to write to the Gentile believers and share the decisions of the conference. This letter asked for obedience to two *commands* and a willingness to agree to two personal *concessions*. The two commands were that the believers avoid idolatry and immorality, sins that were especially prevalent among the Gentiles (see 1 Cor. 8–10). The two concessions were that they willingly abstain from eating blood and meat from animals that had died by strangulation. The two commands do not create any special problems, for idolatry and immorality have always been wrong in God's sight, both for Jews and Gentiles. But what about the two concessions concerning food?

Keep in mind that the early church did a great deal of eating together and practicing of hospitality. Most churches met in homes, and some assemblies held a "love feast" in conjunction with the Lord's Supper (1 Cor. 11:17-34). It was probably not much different from our own potluck dinners. If the Gentile believers ate food that the Jewish believers considered "unclean," this would cause division in the church. Paul dealt clearly with this whole problem in Romans 14–15.

The prohibition against eating blood was actually given by God before the time of the Law (Gen. 9:4), and it was repeated by Moses (Lev. 17:11-14; Deut. 12:23). If an animal is killed by strangulation, some of the blood will remain in the body and make the meat unfit for Jews to eat. Hence, the admonition against strangulation. "Kosher" meat is meat that comes from clean animals that have been killed properly so that the blood has been totally drained from the body.

It is beautiful to see that this letter expressed the loving unity of people who had once been debating with each other and defending opposing views. The legalistic Jews willingly gave up insisting that the Gentiles had to be circumcised to be saved, and the Gentiles willingly accepted a change in their eating habits. It was a loving compromise that did not in any way affect the truth of the Gospel. As every married person and parent knows, there are times in a home when compromise is wrong, but there are also times when compromise is right. Wise Samuel Johnson said, "Life cannot subsist in society but by reciprocal concessions." The person who is always right, and who insists on having his or her own way, is difficult to live with happily.

What did this decision accomplish in a practical way? At least three things. First, it strengthened the unity of the church and kept it from splitting into two extreme "Law" and "grace" groups. President Eisenhower called the right kind of compromise "all of the usable surface. The extremes, right or left, are in the gutters." Again, this is not *doctrinal* compromise, for that is always wrong (Jude 3). Rather, it is learning to give and take in the practical arrangements of life so that people can live and work together in love and harmony.

Second, this decision made it possible for the church to present a united witness to the lost Jews (Acts 15:21). For the most part, the church was still identified with the Jewish synagogue; and it is likely that in some cities, entire synagogue congregations believed on Jesus Christ—Jews, Gentile proselytes, and Gentile "God-fearers" together. If the Gentile believers abused their freedom in Christ and ate meat containing blood, this would offend both the saved Jews and their unsaved friends whom they were trying to win to Christ. It was simply a matter of not being a stumbling block to the weak or to the lost (Rom. 14:13-21).

Third, this decision brought blessing as the letter was shared with the various Gentile congregations. Paul and Barnabas, along with Judas and Silas, took the good news to Antioch; and the church rejoiced and was encouraged because they did not have to carry the burdensome yoke of the Law (Acts 15:30-31). On his second missionary journey, Paul shared the letter with the churches he had founded on his first missionary journey. The result was a strengthening of the churches' faith and an increase of their number (Acts 16:5).

We today can learn a great deal from this difficult experience of the early church. To begin with, problems and differences are opportunities for growth just as much as temptations for dissension and division. Churches need to work together and take time to listen, love, and learn. How many hurtful fights and splits could have been avoided if only some of God's people had given the Spirit time to speak and to work.

Most divisions are caused by "followers" and "leaders." A powerful leader gets a following, refuses to give in on even the smallest matter, and before long there is a split. Most church problems are not caused by doctrinal differences but by different viewpoints on practical matters. What color shall we paint the church kitchen? Can we change the order of the service? I heard of one church that almost split over whether the organ or the piano should be on the right side of the platform!

Christians need to learn the art of loving compromise. They need to have their priorities in order so they know when to fight for what is really important in the church. It is sinful to follow some impressive member of the church who is fighting to get his or her way on some minor issue that is not worth fighting about. Every congregation needs a regular dose of the love described in 1 Corinthians 13 to prevent division and dissension.

As we deal with our differences, we must ask, "How will our decisions affect the united witness of the church to the lost?" Jesus prayed that His people might be united so that the world might believe on Him (John 17:20-21). Unity is not uniformity, for unity is based on love and not law. There is a great need in the church for diversity in unity (Eph. 4:1-17), for that is the only way the body can mature and do its work in the world.

God has opened a wonderful door of opportunity for us to take the Gospel of God's grace to a condemned world. But there are forces in the church even today that want to close that door. There are people who are preaching "another gospel" that is not the Gospel of Jesus Christ.

Help keep that door open—and reach as many as you can!

Be daring!

CHAPTER FIFTEEN MORE OPEN DOORS

Acts 15:36–16:40

For the Apostle Paul, the church at Antioch was not a parking lot: it was a launching pad. He could never settle down to a "comfortable ministry" anywhere as long as there were open doors for the preaching of the Gospel.

Paul would have agreed enthusiastically with the words of Robertson McQuilken from his book *The Great Omission*: "In a world in which nine out of every ten people are lost, three out of four have never heard the way out, and one of every two cannot hear, the church sleeps on. Could it be we think there must be some other way? Or perhaps we don't really care that much." Paul cared—and so should we.

There were several new elements in this second journey that indicated that God was still at work, in spite of the seeming obstacles and personal difficulties that arose.

A New Partner (Acts 15:36-41)

Paul and Barnabas agreed on the importance of the trip, but they could not agree on the composition of the "team." Here were two dedicated men who had just helped bring unity to the church, and yet they could not settle their own disagreements! Disturbing and painful as these conflicts are, they are often found in church history; and yet God is able to overrule them and accomplish His purposes.

That Barnabas would champion John Mark is certainly no surprise. He and Mark were cousins (Col. 4:10, NASB), and the family ties would be strong. But even more, Barnabas was the kind of man who eagerly tried to help others, which is why the early church named him "son of encouragement" (Acts 4:36). He was ready to give John Mark an opportunity to serve the Lord and to prove himself. Barnabas "kept on insisting" (WUEST) that they take Mark along.

But Paul was just as adamant that they *not* take Mark! After all, on the first missionary journey, John Mark had deserted them to return home (Acts 13:13); and this was a mark of weakness. The ministry was too important, and the work too demanding, to enlist someone who might prove unreliable.

As the discussion continued, it turned into a real argument (the word *paroxysm* comes from the word translated "contention"); and it seemed like the only solution was for the friends to divide the territory and separate. Barnabas took Mark and went to his native Cyprus, and Paul took Silas and headed for Syria and Celicia (note Acts 15:23).

Who was right? It really doesn't make much difference. Perhaps both men were right on some things and wrong on other things. We know that John Mark ultimately did succeed in the ministry and that Paul came to love and appreciate him (see Col. 4:10; 2 Tim. 4:11; Phile. 23-24). Good and godly people in the church do disagree; this is one of the painful facts of life that we must accept. Paul looked at people and asked, "What can they do for God's work?" while Barnabas looked at people and asked, "What can God's work do for them?" Both questions are important to the Lord's work, and sometimes it is difficult to keep things balanced.

Paul selected a new partner, Silas, a chief man in the church, a prophet (Acts 15:22, 32), and one chosen to take the Jerusalem Conference decrees to the churches (Acts 15:27). "Silas" is probably a Greek version of the name *Saul.* He was coauthor with Paul of the Thessalonian epistles, and he was the secretary for Peter's first epistle (1 Peter 5:12). Like Paul, he was a Roman citizen (Acts 16:37).

God changes His workmen, but His work goes right on. Now there were *two* missionary teams instead of one! If God had to depend on perfect people to accomplish His work, He would never ever get anything done. Our limitations and imperfections are good reasons for us to depend on the grace of God, for our sufficiency is from Him alone (2 Cor. 3:5).

A New Helper (Acts 16:1-5)

Paul and Silas approached their destination from the east, so they came first to Derbe and then to Lystra, just the reverse of the first journey (Acts 14:6-20). The preachers went from church to church, delivering the decrees and helping establish the believers in the faith. The result was fruit from the witness of the believers so that the churches increased in number daily (see Acts 2:47). It was certainly a most successful tour, but I wonder if any of the believers asked about Barnabas? And what did Paul tell them?

Perhaps the best thing that happened at Lystra was the enlistment of Timothy to replace John Mark as Paul's special assistant. Timothy was probably converted through Paul's ministry when the apostle first visited Lystra, for Paul called him "my beloved son" (1 Cor. 4:17) and "my own son in the faith" (1 Tim. 1:2). Timothy's mother and grandmother had prepared the way for his decision by being the first in the family to trust Christ (2 Tim. 1:5). Young Timothy undoubtedly witnessed Paul's sufferings in Lystra (Acts 14:19-20; 2 Tim. 3:10-11) and was drawn by the Lord to the apostle. Timothy was Paul's favorite companion and coworker (Phil. 2:19-23), perhaps the son Paul never had but always wanted.

Because he had a good report from the churches (1 Tim. 3:7), Timothy was ordained by Paul and added to his "team" (1 Tim. 4:14; 2 Tim. 1:6). Paul's next step was to have Timothy circumcised, an action that seems to contradict the decision of the Jerusalem Conference. However, there was an important spiritual principle behind Paul's decision.

The decision at the Jerusalem Conference was that it was not necessary to be circumcised *in order to be saved.* Paul did not allow Titus to be circumcised lest the enemy think he was promoting their cause (Gal. 2:1-5). The battle in Jerusalem was over the truth of the Gospel, not over the fitness of a man to serve. Paul's concern with Timothy was not his salvation but his fitness for service.

Timothy would be working with both Jews and Gentiles in the churches, and it was essential that he not offend them. That was why Paul had Timothy circumcised (see 1 Cor.

9:19-23). Again, it was not a matter of Timothy's salvation or personal character, but rather of avoiding serious problems that would surely become stumbling blocks as the men sought to serve the Lord (Rom. 14:13-15). It is a wise spiritual leader who knows how and when to apply the principles of the Word of God, when to stand firm and when to yield.

In the years that followed, Timothy played an important part in the expansion and strengthening of the churches. He traveled with Paul and was often his special ambassador to the "trouble spots" in the work, such as Corinth. He became shepherd of the church in Ephesus (1 Tim. 1:3) and probably joined Paul in Rome shortly before the apostle was martyred (2 Tim. 4:21).

A New Vision (Acts 16:6-40)

In this section, we see three wonderful "openings."

God opened the way (vv. 6-12). After visiting the churches he had founded, Paul tried to enter new territory for the Lord by traveling east into Asia Minor and Bythinia, but the Lord closed the door. We don't know how God revealed His will in this matter, but we can well imagine that Paul was disappointed and perhaps a bit discouraged. Everything had been going so smoothly on this second journey that these closed doors must have come as a great surprise. However, it is comforting to know that even apostles were not always clear as to God's will for their ministries! God planned for the message to get there another time (Acts 18:19–19:41; see 1 Peter 1:1).

In His sovereign grace, God led Paul west into Europe, not east into Asia. It is interesting to speculate how world history might have been changed had Paul been sent to Asia instead of to Europe. At Troas, Paul was called to Macedonia by a man whom he saw in a night vision. "Nothing makes a man strong like a call for help," wrote George MacDonald, and Paul was quick to respond to the vision (compare Acts 26:19).

Note the pronoun *we* in Acts 16:10, for Dr. Luke, who wrote the Book of Acts, joined Paul and his party at Troas. There are three "we sections" in Acts: 16:10-17; 20:5-15; and 27:1–28:16. Luke changed from "we" to "they" in Acts 17:1, which suggests that he may have remained in Philippi to pastor the church after Paul left. The next "we section" begins in Acts 20:5 in connection with Paul's trip from Macedonia. Luke devoted a good deal of space to Paul's ministry in Philippi, so perhaps he was a resident of that city. Some students think Luke may have been the man Paul saw in the vision.

From Troas to Neapolis, the port of Philippi was a distance of about 150 miles, and it took them two days to make the journey. Later, the trip in the opposite direction would take five days, apparently because of contrary winds (Acts 20:6). Philippi lay ten miles inland from Neapolis, and the way Luke described the city would suggest that he was indeed one of its proudest citizens.

Philippi was a Roman colony, which meant that it was a "Rome away from Rome." The emperor organized "colonies" by ordering Roman citizens, especially retired military people, to live in selected places so there would be strong pro-Roman cities in these strategic areas. Though living on foreign soil, the citizens were expected to be loyal to Rome, to obey the laws of Rome, and to give honor to the Roman emperor. In return, they were given certain political privileges, not the least of which was exemption from taxes. This was their reward for leaving their homes in Italy and relocating elsewhere.

God opened Lydia's heart (vv. 13-15). Paul and his friends did not plunge immediately into evangelizing the city, even though they knew God had called them there. No doubt they needed to rest and pray and make their plans together. It is not enough to know *where* God wants us to work; we must also know *when* and *how* He wants us to work.

The Jewish population in Philippi must have been very small since there was no synagogue there, only a place of prayer by the river outside the city. (It required ten men for the founding of a synagogue.) Paul had seen a *man* in the vision at Troas, but here he was ministering to a group of *women!* "It is better that the words of the Law be burned than be delivered to a woman!" said the rabbis; but that was no longer Paul's philosophy. He had been obedient and the Lord had gone before to prepare the way.

Lydia was a successful businesswoman from Thyatira, a city renowned for its purple dye. She probably was in charge of a branch office of her guild in Philippi. God brought her all the way to Greece so that she might hear the Gospel and be converted. She was "a worshiper of God," a Gentile who was not a full Jewish proselyte but who openly worshiped with the Jews. She was seeking truth.

Paul shared the Word ("spoken" in Acts 16:14 means personal conversation, not preaching), God opened her heart to the truth, and she believed and was saved. She boldly identified herself with Christ by being baptized, and she insisted that the missionaries stay at her house. All of her household had been converted, so this was a good opportunity for Paul and his associates to teach them the Word and establish a local church. (We will deal with "household salvation" when we get to Acts 16:31.)

We must not conclude that because *God* opened Lydia's heart, Lydia's part in her conversion was entirely passive. She listened attentively to the Word, and it is the Word that brings the sinner to the Saviour (John 5:24). The same God who ordained the end, Lydia's salvation, also ordained the *means to the end,* Paul's witness of Jesus Christ. This is a beautiful illustration of 2 Thessalonians 2:13-14.

God opened the prison doors (vv. 16-40). No sooner are lost people saved than Satan begins to hinder the work. In this case, he used a demonized girl who had made her masters wealthy by telling fortunes. As Paul and his "team" went regularly to the place of prayer, still witnessing to the lost, this girl repeatedly shouted after them, "These men are the servants of the Most High God, who show us the way of salvation!" Paul did not want either the Gospel or the name of God to be "promoted" by one of Satan's slaves, so he cast out the demon. After all, Satan may speak the truth one minute and the next minute tell a lie; and the unsaved would not know the difference.

The owners had no concern for the girl; they were interested only in the income she provided, and now that income was gone. (The conflict between money and ministry appears often in Acts: 5:1-11; 8:18-24; 19:23ff; 20:33-34.) Their only recourse was the Roman law, and they thought they had a pretty good case because the missionaries were Jewish and were propagating a religion not approved by Rome. Moved by both religious and racial prejudices, the magistrates acted rashly and did not investigate the matter fully. This neglect on their part later brought them embarrassment.

Why didn't Paul and Silas plead their Roman citizenship? (see Acts 22:25-29; 25:11-12) Perhaps there was not time, or perhaps Paul was saving that weapon for better use later on. He and Silas were stripped and beaten (see 2 Cor. 11:23, 25) and put in the city prison. It looked like the end of their witness in Philippi, but God had other plans.

Instead of complaining or calling on God to judge their enemies, the two men prayed and praised God. When you are in pain, the midnight hour is not the easiest time for a sacred concert, but God gives "songs in the night" (Job 35:10; also see Ps. 42:8). "Any fool can sing in the day," said Charles Haddon Spurgeon. "It is easy to sing when we can read the notes by daylight; but the skillful singer is he who can sing when there is not a ray of light to read by. . . . Songs in the night come only from God; they are not in the power of men."

Prayer and praise are powerful weapons (2 Chron. 20:1-22; Acts 4:23-37). God responded by shaking the foundations of the prison, opening all the doors, and loosening the prisoners' bonds. They could have fled to freedom, but instead they remained right where they were. For one thing, Paul immediately took command; and, no doubt, the fear of God was on these pagan men. The prisoners must have realized that there was something very special about those two Jewish preachers!

Paul's attention was fixed on the jailer, the man he really wanted to win to Christ. It was a Roman law that if a guard lost a prisoner, he was given the same punishment the prisoner would have received; so there must have been some men in the prison who had committed capital crimes. The jailer would rather commit suicide than face shame and execution. A hard-hearted person seeking vengeance would have let the cruel jailer kill himself, but Paul was not that kind of a man (see Matt. 5:10-12, 43-48). It was the jailer who was the prisoner, not Paul; and Paul not only saved the man's life, but pointed him to eternal life in Christ.

"What must I do to be saved?" is the cry of lost people worldwide, and we had better be able to give them the right answer. The legalists in the church would have replied, "Unless you are circumcised according to the custom of Moses, you cannot be saved" (Acts 15:1, NKJV). But Paul knew the right answer—faith in Jesus Christ. In the Book of Acts, the emphasis is on faith in Jesus Christ alone (Acts 2:38-39; 4:12; 8:12, 37; 10:10-43; 13:38-39).

The phrase "and thy house" does not mean that the faith of the jailer would automatically bring salvation to his family. Each sinner must trust Christ personally in order to be born again, for we cannot be saved "by proxy." The phrase means "and your household will be saved if they will also believe." We must not read into this statement the salvation of infants (with or without baptism) because it is clear that Paul was dealing with people old enough to hear the Word (Acts 16:32), to believe, and to rejoice (Acts 16:34).

So-called "household salvation" has no basis in the Word of God—that is, that the decision of the head of the household brings salvation to the members of the household. The people in the household of Cornelius were old enough to respond to his call (Acts 10:24) and to understand the Word and believe (Acts 10:44; 11:15-17; 15:7-9). The household of Crispus was composed of people old enough to hear and believe God's Word (Acts 18:8). There is no suggestion here that the adults made decisions for infants or children.

It is touching to see the change in the attitude of the jailer as he washed the wounds of these two prisoners who were now his brothers in Christ. One of the evidences of true repentance is a loving desire to make restitution and reparation wherever we have hurt others. We should not only wash one another's feet (John 13:14-15), but we should also cleanse the wounds we have given to others.

What about the other prisoners? Luke doesn't give us the details, but it is possible that some of them were also born again through the witness of Paul and Silas and the jailer. Some of these prisoners may have been waiting for execution, so imagine their joy at hearing a message of salvation! Paul and Silas thought nothing of their own pains as they rejoiced in what God did in that Philippian jail! No doubt the jailer later joined with Lydia in the assembly.

The city officials knew that they had no convincing case against Paul and Silas, so they sent word to the jailer to release them. Paul, however, was unwilling to "sneak out of town," for that kind of exit would have left the new church under a cloud of suspicion. People would have asked, "Who were those men? Were they guilty of some crime? Why did they leave so quickly? What do their followers believe?" Paul and his associates wanted to leave behind a strong witness of their own integrity as well as a good testimony for the infant church in Philippi.

It was then that Paul made use of his Roman citizenship and boldly challenged the officials on the legality of their treatment. This was not personal revenge but a desire to give protection and respect for the church. While the record does not say that the magistrates officially and publicly apologized, it does state that they respectfully came to Paul and Silas, escorted them out of the prison, and politely asked them to leave town. Paul and Silas remained in Philippi long enough to visit the new believers and encourage them in the Lord.

As you review this chapter, you can see that the work of the Lord progresses through difficulties and challenges. Sometimes the workers have problems with each other, and sometimes the problems come from the outside. It is also worth noting that not every sinner comes to Christ in exactly the same manner. Timothy was saved partly through the influence of a godly mother and grandmother. Lydia was converted through a quiet conversation with Paul at a Jewish prayer meeting, while the jailer's conversion was dramatic. One minute he was a potential suicide, and the next minute he was a child of God!

Different people with different experiences, and yet all of them changed by the grace of God.

Others just like them are waiting to be told God's simple plan of salvation.

Will you help them hear?

In your own witness for Christ, will you be daring?

CHAPTER SIXTEEN
RESPONDING TO GOD'S WORD
Acts 17

This chapter describes Paul's ministry in three cities and how some of the people in those cities responded to the Word of God. These pictures are snapshots, not murals, for Dr. Luke did not give us many details. However, as we study these three different responses, we can certainly see our modern world and better understand what to expect as we seek to witness for Christ today.

Thessalonica—Resisting the Word (Acts 17:1-9)

Following the famous Egnatian Way, Paul and Silas went 100 miles from Philippi to Thessalonica. (Timothy is not mentioned again until Acts 17:14, so he may have remained in Philippi.) As far as we can tell, they did not pause to minister in either Amphipolis or Apollonia. Perhaps there were no synagogues in those cities, and Paul certainly expected the new believers in Philippi to carry the message to their neighbors. It was Paul's policy to minister in the larger cities and make them centers for evangelizing a whole district (see Acts 19:10, 26; and 1 Thes. 1:8).

Paul knew that Thessalonica (our modern Salonika) was a strategic city for the work of the Lord. Not only was it the capital of Macedonia, but it was also a center for business, rivaled only by Corinth. It was located on several important trade routes, and it boasted an excellent harbor. The city was predominantly Greek, even though it was controlled by Rome. Thessalonica was a "free city," which meant that it had an elected citizens' assembly, it could mint its own coins, and it had no Roman garrison within its walls.

Paul labored at his tentmaking trade (Acts 18:3; 1 Thes. 2:9; 2 Thes. 3:7-10), but on the Sabbath ministered in the Jewish synagogue where he knew he would find both devout Jews and Gentiles, "God-seekers" and proselytes. This witness went on for only three Sabbaths; then he had to minister outside the synagogue. We do not know exactly how long Paul remained in Thessalonica, but it was long enough to receive financial help twice from the church in Philippi (Phil. 4:15-16). Read 1 Thessalonians 1 to learn how God blessed Paul's ministry and how the message spread from Thessalonica to other places. It was not a long ministry, but it was an effective one.

Four key words in Acts 17:2-3 describe Paul's approach to the synagogue congregation. First, he *reasoned,* which means he dialogued with them through questions and answers. He *explained* ("opening") the Scriptures to them and *proved* ("alleging") that Jesus is indeed the Messiah. The word translated "alleging" means "to lay down alongside, to prove by presenting the evidence." The apostle set before them one Old Testament proof after another that Jesus of Nazareth is Messiah God.

Paul was careful to *announce* ("preach") the death and resurrection of Jesus Christ, which is the message of the Gospel (1 Cor. 15:1ff). In the sermons in Acts, you will find an emphasis on the Resurrection, for the believers were called to be witnesses of His resurrection (Acts 1:21-22; 2:32; 3:15; 5:32). "Christianity is in its very essence a resurrection religion," says Dr. John R.W. Stott. "The concept of resurrection lies at its heart. If you remove it, Christianity is destroyed."

As the result of three weeks' ministry, Paul saw a large number of people believe, especially Greek proselytes and influential women. Among the men were Aristarchus and Secundus, who later traveled with Paul (Acts 20:4). Luke's phrase "not a few" (Acts 17:4, 12) is one way of saying, "It was a big crowd!"

But these results did not bring joy to everybody. The unbelieving Jews envied Paul's success and were grieved to see the Gentiles and the influential women leaving the synagogue. Paul hoped that the salvation of the Gentiles would "provoke" the Jews into studying the Scriptures and discovering their promised Messiah (Rom. 11:13-14), but in this case, it only provoked them into persecuting the infant church.

The Jews wanted to drag the missionaries before their city assembly ("the people," Acts 17:5; see 19:30), so they manufactured a riot to get the attention of the magistrates. Unable to find the missionaries, the mob seized Jason, host to Paul and his friends, and took him and some of the believers instead. The Jews' accusations were similar to the ones used at the trial of Jesus: disturbing the peace and promoting treason (Luke 23:2). Their crime was that of "saying that there is another king, one Jesus."

The Greek word translated "another" means "another of a different kind," that is, a king unlike Caesar. When you read Paul's two Thessalonian letters, you see the strong emphasis he gave in Thessalonica on the kingship of Christ and the promise of His return. Of course, our Lord's kingdom is neither political nor "of this world" (John 18:36-37), but we cannot expect unsaved pagans to understand this.

The kingship of Jesus Christ is unlike that of the rulers of this world. He conquers with ambassadors, not armies; and His weapons are truth and love. He brings men peace by upsetting the peace and turning things upside down! He conquers through His cross where He died for a world of lost sinners. He even died for His enemies! (Rom. 5:6-10)

The mob was agitated because they could not find Paul and Silas, so they settled for second best and obtained a peace bond against them. Jason had to put up the money and guarantee that Paul and Silas would leave the city and not return. It is possible that Jason was a relative of Paul's, which would make the transaction even more meaningful (Rom. 16:21). Paul saw this prohibition as a device of Satan to hinder the work (1 Thes. 2:18), but it certainly did not hinder the Thessalonian church from "sounding out the word" and winning the lost (1 Thes. 1:6-9).

Berea—Receiving the Word (Acts 17:10-15)

Under cover of night, Paul and Silas left the city and headed for Berea, about forty-five miles away. It does not appear that Timothy was with them, as he was probably working in Philippi. Later, he would join Paul in Athens (Acts 17:15) and then be sent to Thessalonica to encourage the church in its time of persecution (1 Thes. 3:1ff). Since Timothy was a Gentile, and had not been present when the trouble erupted, he could minister in the city freely. The peace bond could keep Paul out, but it would not apply to Paul's young assistant.

Paul went into the synagogue and there discovered a group of people keenly interested in the study of the Old Testament Scriptures. In fact, they met *daily* to search the Scriptures to determine whether or not what Paul was saying was true. Paul had been overjoyed at the way the people in Thessalonica had received the Word (1 Thes. 2:13), so these "noble Bereans" must have really encouraged his heart. All of us should imitate these Bereans by faithfully studying God's Word daily, discussing it, and testing the messages that we hear.

God used His Word so that many people trusted Christ. One of the men who was converted was Sopater, who later assisted Paul (Acts 20:4). He may be the same man (Sosipater) who later sent greetings to the Christians in Rome (Rom. 16:21).

Once again, Satan brought the enemy to the field as the unbelieving Jews from Thessalonica came to Berea and stirred up the people (note 1 Thes. 2:13-20). How did these men hear that Paul and Silas were ministering in Berea? Perhaps the growing witness of the Berean believers reached as far as Thessalonica, or it may be that some troublemaker took the message to his friends in Thessalonica. Satan also has his "missionaries" and they are busy (2 Cor. 11:13-15).

The believers in Berea outwitted the enemy by taking Paul to the sea and putting him on a ship bound for Athens. Once more, Paul had to leave a place of rich ministry and break away from dear people he had come to love. Silas and Timothy later joined Paul in Athens, and then Timothy was sent to Thessalonica to help the saints there (1 Thes. 3:1-6). Silas was also sent on a special mission somewhere in Macedonia (Philippi?), and later both men met Paul in Corinth (Acts 18:1-5).

Athens—Ridiculing the Word (Acts 17:16-34)

Paul arrived in the great city of Athens, not as a sightseer, but as a soul-winner. The late Noel O. Lyons, for many years director of the Greater Europe Mission, used to say, "Europe is looked over by millions of visitors and is overlooked by millions of Christians." Europe needs the Gospel today just as it did in Paul's day, and we dare not miss our opportunities. Like Paul, we must have open eyes and broken hearts.

The city. Athens was in a period of decline at this time, though still recognized as a center of culture and education. The glory of its politics and commerce had long since faded. It had a famous university and numerous beautiful buildings, but it was not the influential city it once had been. The city was given over to a "cultured paganism" that was nourished by idolatry, novelty (Acts 17:21), and philosophy.

"The Greek religion was a mere deification of human attributes and the powers of nature," wrote Conybeare and Howson in their classic *Life and Epistles of St. Paul.* "It was a religion which ministered to art and amusement, and was entirely destitute of moral power" (pp. 280–281). The Greek myths spoke of gods and goddesses that, in their own rivalries and ambitions, acted more like humans than gods; and there were plenty of deities to choose from! One wit jested that in Athens it was easier to find a god than a man. Paul saw that the city was "wholly given to idolatry," and it broke his heart.

We today admire Greek sculpture and architecture as beautiful works of art, but in Paul's day, much of this was directly associated with their religion. Paul knew that idolatry was demonic (1 Cor. 10:14-23) and that the many gods of the Greeks were only characters in stories who were unable to change men's lives (1 Cor. 8:1-6). With all of their culture and wisdom, the Greeks did not know the true God (1 Cor. 1:18-25).

As for novelty, it was the chief pursuit of both the citizens and the visitors (Acts 17:21). Their leisure time was spent telling or hearing "some new thing." Eric Hoffer wrote that "the fear of becoming a 'has been' keeps some people from becoming anything." The person who chases the new and ignores the old soon discovers that he has no deep roots to nourish his life. He also discovers that nothing is really new; it's just that our memories are poor (Ecc. 1:8-11).

The city was also devoted to philosophy. When you think of Greece, you automatically think of Socrates and Aristotle and a host of other thinkers whose works are still read and studied today. Newspaper columnist Franklin P. Adams once defined philosophy as "unintelligible answers to insoluble problems," but the Greeks would not have agreed with him. They would have followed Aristotle who called philosophy "the science which considers truth."

Paul had to confront two opposing philosophies as he witnessed in Athens, those of the Epicureans and the Stoics. We today associate the word *Epicurean* with the pursuit of pleasure and the love of "fine living," especially fine food. But the Epicurean philosophy involved much more than that. In one sense, the founder Epicurus was an "existentialist" in that he sought truth by means of personal experience and not through reasoning. The Epicureans were materialists and atheists, and their goal in life was pleasure. To some, "pleasure" meant that which was grossly physical; but to others, it meant a life of refined serenity, free from pain and anxiety. The true Epicurean avoided extremes and sought to enjoy life by keeping things in balance, but pleasure was still his number one goal.

The Stoics rejected the idolatry of pagan worship and taught that there was one "World God." They were pantheists, and their emphasis was on personal discipline and self-control. Pleasure was not good and pain was not evil. The most important thing in life was to follow one's reason and be self-sufficient, unmoved by inner feelings or outward circumstances. Of course, such a philosophy only fanned the flames of pride and taught men that they did not need the help of God. It is interesting that the first two leaders of the Stoic school committed suicide.

The Epicureans said "Enjoy life!" and the Stoics said "Endure life!" but it remained for Paul to explain how they could enter into life through faith in God's risen Son.

The witness. "Left at Athens alone" (1 Thes. 3:1), Paul viewed the idolatrous city and his spirit was "stirred" (same word as "contention" in Acts 15:39—"paroxysm"). Therefore, he used what opportunities were available to share the Good News of the Gospel. As was his custom, he "dialogued" in the synagogue with the Jews, but he also witnessed in the marketplace (*agora*) to the Greeks. Anyone who was willing to talk was welcomed by Paul to his daily "classes."

It did not take long for the philosophers to hear about this "new thing" that was going on in the *agora,* and they came and listened to Paul and probably debated with him. As they listened, they gave two different responses. One group ridiculed Paul and his teachings and called him a "babbler." The word literally means "birds picking up seed," and it refers to someone who collects various ideas and teaches as his own the secondhand thoughts he borrows from others. It was not a very flattering description of the church's greatest missionary and theologian.

The second group was confused but interested. They thought Paul believed as they themselves did in many gods, because he was preaching "Jesus and Anastasis" (the Greek word for "resurrection"). The word translated "preached" in Acts 17:18 means "to preach the Gospel." Those who say that Paul modified his evangelistic tactics in Athens, hoping to appeal to the intellectuals, have missed the point. He preached the Gospel as boldly in Athens as he did in Berea and would do in Corinth.

The defense. The Council of the Aeropagus was responsible to watch over both religion and education in the city, so it was natural for them to investigate the "new doctrine" Paul was teaching. They courteously invited Paul to present his doctrine at what appears to have been an informal meeting of the council on Mars' Hill. Paul was not on trial; the council members only wanted him to explain what he had been telling the people in the *agora.* After all, life in Athens consisted in hearing and telling new things, and Paul had something new!

Paul's message is a masterpiece of communication. He started where the people were by referring to their altar dedicated to an unknown god. Having aroused their interest, he then explained who that God is and what He is like. He concluded the message with a personal application that left each council member facing a moral decision, and some of them decided for Jesus Christ.

Paul opened his address with a compliment: "I see that in every way you are very religious" (Acts 17:22, NIV). They were so religious, in fact, that they even had an altar to "the unknown god," lest some beneficent deity be neglected. If they did not know this god, how could they worship him? Or how could he help them? It was this God that Paul declared.

In this message, which is similar to his sermon at Lystra (Acts 14:15-17), Paul shared four basic truths about God.

The greatness of God: He is Creator (v. 24). Every thinking person asks, "Where did I come from? Why am I here? Where am I going?" Science attempts to answer the first question, and philosophy wrestles with the second; but only the Christian faith has a satisfactory answer to all three. The Epicureans, who were atheists, said that all was matter and matter always was. The Stoics said that everything was God, "the Spirit of the Universe." God did not create anything; He only organized matter and impressed on it some "law and order."

But Paul boldly affirmed, "In the beginning, God!" God made the world and everything in it, and He is Lord of all that He has made. He is not a distant God, divorced from His creation; nor is He an imprisoned God, locked in creation. He is too great to be housed in man-made temples (1 Kings 8:27; Isa. 66:1-2; Acts 7:48-50), but He is not too great to be concerned about man's needs (Acts 17:25). We wonder how the Council members reacted to Paul's statement about temples, for right there on the Acropolis were several shrines dedicated to Athena.

The goodness of God; He is Provider (v. 25). Men may pride themselves in serving God, but it is God who serves man. If God is God, then He is self-sufficient and needs nothing that man can supply. Not only do the temples not contain God, but the services in the temples add nothing to God! In two brief statements, Paul completely wiped out the entire religious system of Greece!

It is God who gives to us what we need: "life, and breath, and all things." God is the source of every good and perfect gift (James 1:17). He gave us life and He sustains that life by His goodness (Matt. 5:45). It is the goodness of God that should lead men to repentance (Rom. 2:4). But instead of worshiping the Creator and glorifying Him, men worship His creation and glorify themselves (Rom. 1:18-25).

The government of God: He is Ruler (vv. 26-29). The gods of the Greeks were distant beings who had no concern for the problems and needs of men. But the God of Creation is also the God of history and geography! He created mankind "from one man" (Acts 17:36, NIV) so that all nations are made of the same stuff and have the same blood. The Greeks felt that they were a special race, different from other nations; but Paul affirmed otherwise. Even their precious land that they revered came as a gift from God. It is not the power of man, but the government of God, that determines the rise and fall of nations (Dan. 4:35).

God is not a distant deity; "He [is] not far from every one of us" (Acts 17:27). Therefore, men ought to seek God and come to know Him in truth. Here Paul quoted from the poet Epimenides: "For in Him we live, and move, and have our being." Then he added a quotation from two poets, Aratus and Cleanthes, "For we are also His offspring." Paul was not saying that all people on earth are the spiritual children of God, for sinners become God's children only by faith in Jesus Christ (John 1:11-13). Rather, he was affirming the "Fatherhood of God" in a *natural* sense, for man was created in the image of God (Gen. 1:26). In this sense, Adam was a "son of God" (Luke 3:38).

This led to Paul's logical conclusion: God made us in His image, so it is foolish for us to make gods in our own image! Greek religion was nothing but the manufacture and worship of gods who were patterned after men and who acted like men. Paul not only showed the folly of temples and the temple rituals, but also the folly of all idolatry.

The grace of God: He is Saviour (vv. 30-34). As he brought his message to a close, Paul summarized the clear evidences of God's grace. For centuries, God was patient with man's sin and ignorance (see Acts 14:16; Rom. 3:25). This does not mean that men were not guilty (Rom. 1:19-20), but only that God held back divine wrath. In due time, God sent a Saviour, and now He commands all men to repent of their foolish ways. This Saviour was killed and then raised from the dead, and one day, He will return to judge the world. The proof that He will judge is that He was raised from the dead.

It was the doctrine of the Resurrection that most of the members of the Council could not accept. To a Greek, the body was only a prison; and the sooner a person left his body, the happier he would be. Why raise a dead body and live in it again? And why would God bother with a personal judgment of each man? This kind of teaching was definitely incompatible with Greek philosophy. They believed in immortality, but not in resurrection.

There were three different responses to the message. Some laughed and mocked and did not take Paul's message seriously. Others were interested but wanted to hear more. A small group accepted what Paul preached, believed on Jesus Christ, and were saved. We wonder if the others who postponed their decision eventually trusted Christ. We hope they did.

When you contrast the seeming meager results in Athens with the great harvests in Thessalonica and Berea, you are tempted to conclude that Paul's ministry there was a dismal failure. If you do, you might find yourself drawing a hasty and erroneous conclusion. Paul was not told to leave, so we assume he lingered in Athens and continued to minister to both believers and unbelievers. Proud, sophisticated, wise Athens would not take easily to Paul's humbling message of the Gospel, especially when he summarized all of Greek history in the phrase "the times of this ignorance." The soil here was not deep and it contained many weeds, but there was a small harvest.

And, after all, one soul is worth the whole world!

We still need witnesses who will invade the "halls of academe" and present Christ to people who are wise in this world but ignorant of the true wisdom of the world to come. "Not many wise men after the flesh, not many mighty, not many noble are called" (1 Cor. 1:26); but some *are* called, and God may use you to call them.

Take the Gospel to your "Athens."

CHAPTER SEVENTEEN
IT'S ALWAYS TOO SOON TO QUIT
Acts 18:1-22

A man was shoveling snow from his driveway when two boys carrying snow shovels approached him.

"Shovel your snow, Mister?" one of them asked. "Only two dollars!"

Puzzled, the man replied, "Can't you see that I'm doing it myself?"

"Sure," said the enterprising lad; "that's why we asked. We get most of our business from people who are half through and feel like quitting!"

Dr. V. Raymond Edman used to say to the students at Wheaton (Illinois) College, "It's always too soon to quit!" And Charles Spurgeon reminded his London congregation, "By perseverance, the snail reached the ark."

Corinth, with its 200,000 people, would not be the easiest city in which to start a church, and yet that's where Paul went after leaving Athens. And he went alone! The going was tough, but the apostle did not give up.

Corinth's reputation for wickedness was known all over the Roman Empire. (Rom. 1:18-32 was written in Corinth!) Thanks to its location, the city was a center for both trade and travel. Money and vice, along with strange philosophies and new religions, came to Corinth and found a home there. Corinth was the capital of Achaia and one of the two most important cities Paul visited. The other was Ephesus.

When God opens doors, the enemy tries to close them, and there are times when we close the doors on ourselves because we get discouraged and quit. As Paul ministered in Corinth, the Lord gave him just the encouragements that he needed to keep him going, and these same encouragements are available to us today.

Devoted Helpers (Acts 18:1-5)

Paul came to Corinth following his ministry to the philosophers in Greece; and he determined to magnify Jesus Christ and the Cross, to depend on the Holy Spirit, and to present the Gospel in simplicity (1 Cor. 2:1-5). There were many philosophers and itinerant teachers in Corinth, preying on the ignorant and superstitious population; and Paul's message and ministry could easily be misunderstood.

One way Paul separated himself from the "religious hucksters" was by supporting himself as a tentmaker. By the providence of God, he met a Jewish couple, Aquila and Priscilla ("Prisca," 2 Tim. 4:19), who were workers in leather as was Paul. Jewish rabbis did not accept money from their students but earned their way by practicing a trade. All Jewish boys were expected to learn a trade, no matter what profession they might enter. "He who does not teach his son to work, teaches him to steal!" said the rabbis; so Saul of Tarsus learned to make leather tents and to support himself in his ministry (see Acts 18:3; 1 Cor. 9:6-15; 2 Cor. 11:6-10).

Were Aquila and Priscilla Christian believers at that time? We don't know for certain, but it's likely that they were. Perhaps they were even founding members of the church in Rome. We do know that this dedicated couple served most faithfully and even risked their lives for Paul (Rom. 16:3-4). They assisted him in Ephesus (Acts 18:18-28) where they even hosted a church in their home (1 Cor. 16:19). Aquila and Priscilla were an important part of Paul's "team" and he thanked God for them. They are a good example of how "lay ministers" can help to further the work of the Lord. Every pastor and missionary thanks God for people like Aquila and Priscilla, people with hands, hearts, and homes dedicated to the work of the Lord.

Paul lived and worked with Aquila and Priscilla, but on the Sabbath days witnessed boldly in the synagogue. After all, that was why he had come to Corinth. When Silas and Timothy arrived from Macedonia (Acts 17:14-15; 18:5), they brought financial aid (2 Cor. 11:9), and this enabled Paul to devote his full time to the preaching of the Gospel. What a joy it must have been for Paul to see his friends and to hear from them the good news of the steadfastness of the Christians in the churches they had planted together (1 Thes. 3).

Everyone agrees that Paul was a great Christian and a great missionary evangelist, but how much would Paul have accomplished *alone?* Friends like Aquila and Priscilla, Silas and Timothy, and the generous believers in Macedonia, made it possible for Paul to serve the Lord effectively. His Christian friends, new and old, encouraged him at a time when he needed it the most.

Of course, this reminds us that we should encourage our friends in the work of the Lord. Ralph Waldo Emerson wrote, "God evidently does not intend us all to be rich or powerful or great, but He does intend us all to be friends." "Bear ye one another's burdens, and so fulfill the law of Christ" is the way Paul expressed it (Gal. 6:2). Humanly speaking, there would have been no church in Corinth were it not for the devotion and service of many different people.

Opposition (Acts 18:6-8)

Whenever God is blessing a ministry, you can expect increased opposition as well as increased opportunities. "For a great and effective door has opened to me, and there are many adversaries" (1 Cor. 16:9, NKJV). After all, the enemy gets angry when we invade his territory and liberate his slaves. As in Thessalonica and Berea (Acts 17:5-13), the unbelieving Jews who rejected the Word stirred up trouble for Paul and his friends (see 1 Thes. 2:14-16). Such opposition is usually proof that God is at work, and this ought to encourage us. Spurgeon used to say that the devil never kicks a dead horse!

Jewish opposition had forced Paul to leave Thessalonica and Berea, but in Corinth, it only made him determined to stay there and get the job done. It is always too soon to quit! Like the undaunted Christopher Columbus, Paul could write in his journal, "Today we sailed on!"

Two interesting Old Testament images are found in Acts 18:6. To shake out one's garments was an act of judgment that said, "You have had your opportunity, but now it's over!" Today we might say that we were washing our hands of a situation. (See Neh. 5:13, and compare Acts 13:51 and Matt. 10:14.) While Paul never ceased witnessing to the Jews, his primary calling was to evangelize the Gentiles (Acts 13:46-48; 28:28).

To have blood *on your hands* means that you bear the responsibility for another's death because you were not faithful to warn him. The image comes from the watchman on the city walls whose task it was to stay alert and warn of coming danger (see Ezek. 3:17-21; 33:1-9). But to have blood *on your head* means that you are to blame for your own judgment. You had the opportunity to be saved, but you turned it down (see Josh. 2:19). Paul's hands were clean (Acts 20:26) because he had been faithful to declare the message of the Gospel. The Jews had their own blood on their own heads because they rejected God's truth.

At just the right time, God brought another friend into Paul's life—Gentile, God-fearing Titus Justus. Some Bible students think his full name was Gaius Titus Justus and that he was the "Gaius my host" referred to in Romans 16:23. The connection between Gaius and Crispus in Acts 18:7-8 and 1 Corinthians 1:14 is certainly significant.

Paul departed from the synagogue and began using the house of Titus Justus as his preaching station, right next to the synagogue! This was certainly a wise decision on Paul's part, because it gave him continued contact with the Jews and Gentile proselytes; and as a result, even the chief ruler of the synagogue was converted! It was the ruler's job to see to it that the synagogue building was cared for and that the services were held in a regular and orderly manner. We have here another instance of an entire family turning to the Lord (Acts 10:24, 44; 16:15, 34). How that must have stirred the Jewish population in Corinth!

When you examine Paul's ministry in Corinth, you will see that he was fulfilling the Lord's commission given in Matthew 28:19-20. Paul came to Corinth ("Go"), he won sinners to Christ ("make disciples"), he baptized, and he taught them (note Acts 18:11). He even experienced the assurance of the Lord's "Lo, I am with thee always!" (Acts 18:9-10)

Paul's associates baptized most of the new converts (1 Cor. 1:11-17), just as our Lord's disciples did when He ministered on earth (John 4:1-2; and note Acts 10:46-48). The important thing is the believer's obedience to the Lord and not the name of the minister who does the baptizing. When I became senior pastor at the Moody Church in Chicago, an older member boastfully said to me, "I was baptized by Dr. Ironside!" He was surprised that I was not impressed. I was sure that Dr. Ironside would have lovingly rebuked him for speaking like that, for Dr. Ironside was a humble man who wanted Christ's name exalted, not his own.

To walk by faith means to see opportunities even in the midst of opposition. A pessimist sees only the problems; an optimist sees only the potential; but a realist sees the potential in the problems. Paul did not close his eyes to the many dangers and difficulties in the situation at Corinth, but he did look at them from the divine point of view.

Faith simply means obeying God's will in spite of feelings, circumstances, or consequences. There never was an easy place to serve God; and if there is an easy place, it is possible that something is wrong. Paul reminded Timothy, "Yes, and all who desire to live godly in Christ Jesus will suffer persecution" (2 Tim. 3:12, NKJV).

"Prosperity is the blessing of the Old Testament," wrote Francis Bacon; "adversity is the blessing of the New." Paul did not allow adversity to keep him from serving God.

The Word of Assurance (Acts 18:9-17)

The conversion of Crispus, an important Jewish leader, opened up more opportunities for evangelism and brought more opposition from the enemy! The Jewish community in Corinth was no doubt furious at Paul's success and did everything possible to silence him and get rid of him. Dr. Luke does not give us the details, but I get the impression that between Acts 18:8 and 9, the situation became especially difficult and dangerous. Paul may have been thinking about leaving the city when the Lord came to him and gave him the assurance that he needed.

It is just like our Lord to speak to us when we need Him the most. His tender "Fear not!" can calm the storm in our hearts regardless of the circumstances around us. This is the way He assured Abraham (Gen. 15:1), Isaac (Gen. 26:24), and Jacob (Gen. 46:3), as well as Jehoshaphat (2 Chron. 20:15-17), Daniel (Dan. 10:12, 19), Mary (Luke 1:30), and Peter (Luke 5:10). The next time you feel alone and defeated, meditate on Hebrews 13:5 and Isaiah 41:10 and 43:1-7, and claim by faith the presence of the Lord. He is with you!

When he was a young man, the famous British preacher G. Campbell Morgan used to read the Bible each week to two elderly women. One evening, when he finished reading the closing words of Matthew 28, Morgan said to the ladies, "Isn't that a wonderful promise!" and one of them replied, "Young man, that is not a promise—it is a certainty!"

Jesus had already appeared to Paul on the Damascus road (Acts 9:1-6; 26:12-18) and also in the temple (Acts 22:17-18). Paul would be encouraged by Him again when he was imprisoned in Jerusalem (Acts 23:11) and later in Rome (2 Tim. 4:16-17). Our Lord's angel would also appear to Paul in the midst of the storm and give him a word of assurance for the passengers and crew (Acts 27:23-25). One of our Lord's names is "Immanuel—God with us" (Matt. 1:23), and He lives up to His name.

Paul was encouraged not only by the presence of the Lord, but also by His promises. Jesus assured Paul that no one would hurt him and that he would bring many sinners to the Saviour. The statement "I have many people in this city" implies the doctrine of divine election, for "the Lord knows those who are His" (2 Tim. 2:19, NKJV). God's church is made up of people who were "chosen . . . in Him [Christ] before the foundation of the world" (Eph. 1:4; and see Acts 13:48).

Please note that divine sovereignty in election is not a deterrent to human responsibility in evangelism. Quite the opposite is true! Divine election is one of the greatest encouragements to the preaching of the Gospel. Because Paul knew that God already had people set apart for salvation, he stayed where he was and preached the Gospel with faith and courage. Paul's responsibility was to obey the commission; God's responsibility was to save sinners. If salvation depends on sinful man, then all of our efforts are futile; but if "salvation is of the Lord" (Jonah 2:9), then we can expect Him to bless His Word and save souls.

"Scripture nowhere dispels the mystery of election," writes John Stott in *God's New Society* (InterVarsity, p. 37), "and we should beware of any who try to systematize it too precisely or rigidly. It is not likely that we shall discover a simple solution to a problem which has baffled the best brains of Christendom for centuries."

The important thing is that we accept God's truth and act on it. Paul did not spend his time speculating about divine sovereignty and human responsibility, the way some ivory-tower Christians do today. *He got busy and tried to win souls to Christ!* You and I do not know who God's elect are, so we take the Gospel to every creature and let God do the rest. And we certainly do not discuss election with the lost! D.L. Moody once told some unconverted people, "You have no more to do with the doctrine of election than you have with the government of China!"

Before leaving this theme, we should note that it is our personal responsibility to make sure that we are among God's elect. "Therefore, brethren, be even more diligent to make your calling and election sure" (2 Peter 1:10, NKJV). To the inquisitive theorist who asked about the number of the elect, Jesus replied, "Strive to enter in at the narrow gate!" (Luke 13:23-24) In other words, "What you need is salvation for yourself, not speculation about others! Be sure you are saved yourself; then we can talk about these wonderful truths."

Paul continued in Corinth, knowing that God was with Him and that people would be saved. During those eighteen months of witness, Paul saw many victories in spite of Satan's opposition. The church was not made up of many mighty and noble people (1 Cor. 1:26-31), but of sinners whose lives were transformed by the grace of God (1 Cor. 6:9-11).

Dr. Luke shared only one example of divine protection during Paul's ministry in Corinth (Acts 18:12-17), but it is a significant one. The arrival of a new proconsul gave the unbelieving Jews hope that Rome might declare this new "Christian sect" illegal. They broke the law by attacking Paul and forcing him to go to court. This was not the first time that fanatical Jews had tried to prove that Paul was breaking the Roman law (Acts 16:19-24; 17:6-7).

Being a Roman citizen, Paul was prepared to defend himself; but this turned out to be unnecessary because Gallio defended Paul! The proconsul immediately saw that the real issue was not the application of the Roman law but the interpretation of the Jewish religion, so he refused to try the case!

But that was not the end of the matter. The Greeks who were witnessing the scene got hold of Sosthenes, the man who replaced Crispus as ruler of the synagogue, and beat him right before the eyes of the proconsul! It was certainly a flagrant display of anti-Semitism, but Gallio looked the other way. If this is the same Sosthenes mentioned by Paul in 1 Corinthians 1:1, then he too got converted; and the Jews had to find another ruler for their synagogue! It would be interesting to know exactly how it happened. Did Paul and some of the believers visit Sosthenes and minister to him? Perhaps his predecessor Crispus helped "wash the wounds" (Acts 16:33) and used this as an opportunity to share the love of Christ.

How strange and wonderful are the providences of God! The Jews tried to force the Roman proconsul to declare the Christian faith illegal, but Gallio ended up doing just the opposite. By refusing to try the case, Gallio made it clear that Rome would not get involved in cases involving Jewish religious disputes. As far as he was concerned, Paul and his disciples had as much right as the Jews to practice their religion and share it with others.

In the Book of Acts, Luke emphasizes the relationship between the Roman government and the Christian church. While it was true that the *Jewish* council prohibited the Apostles to preach (Acts 4:17-21; 5:40), there is no evidence in Acts that Rome ever did so. In fact, in Philippi (Acts 16:35-40), Corinth, and Ephesus (Acts 19:31), the Roman officials were not only tolerant but almost cooperative. Paul knew how to use his Roman citizenship wisely so that the government worked for him and not against him, and he was careful not to accuse the government or try to escape its authority (Acts 25:10-12).

God's Will (Acts 18:18-22)

"If God will" (Acts 18:21) was more than a religious slogan with Paul; it was one of the strengths and encouragements of his life and ministry. Knowing and doing God's will is one of the blessings of the Christian life (Acts 22:14). In some of his letters, Paul identified himself as "an apostle of Jesus Christ by the will of God" (1 Cor. 1:1; 2 Cor. 1:1; Eph. 1:1; Col. 1:1; 2 Tim. 1:1). At a most critical time in his life and ministry, Paul found courage in affirming, "The will of the Lord be done!" (Acts 21:14)

After eighteen months of ministry, Paul decided that it was God's will for him to leave Corinth and return to his home church in Antioch. His friends Priscilla and Aquila (note how Luke varies the order of their names) accompanied him to Ephesus and remained there when he departed for Caesarea. In Acts 18:24, we will pick up the story of the church in Ephesus and the important part played by Aquila and Priscilla.

Cenchraea was the seaport for Corinth, and there was a Christian congregation there (Rom. 16:1). Here Paul had his head shorn, "for he had a vow." This probably refers to the Nazarite vow described in Numbers 6. Since the Nazarite vow was purely voluntary, Paul was not abandoning grace for law when he undertook it. The vow was not a matter of salvation but of personal devotion to the Lord. He allowed his hair to grow for a specific length of time and then cut it when the vow was completed. He also abstained from using the fruit of the vine in any form.

We are not told why Paul took this vow. Perhaps it was a part of his special dedication to God during the difficult days of the early ministry in Corinth. Or perhaps the vow was an expression of gratitude to God for all that He had done for him and his associates. According to Jewish law, the Nazarite vow had to be completed in Jerusalem with the offering of the proper sacrifices. The hair was shorn at the completion of the vow, not at the beginning; and it was not necessary for one to be in Jerusalem to make the vow.

Luke does not tell us how long Paul was in Ephesus, but the time was evidently very short. The Jews there were much more receptive to the Gospel and wanted Paul to stay; but he wanted to get to Jerusalem to complete his vow, and then to Antioch to report to the church. However, he did promise to return, and he kept that promise (Acts 19:1).

The statement "I must by all means keep this feast that cometh in Jerusalem" (Acts 18:21) must not be interpreted to mean that Paul and the early Christians felt obligated to observe the Jewish feasts (see Acts 20:16). Being in Jerusalem during the important feasts (in this case, Passover) would give Paul opportunity to meet and witness to key Jewish leaders from throughout the Roman Empire. He would also be able to minister to Christian Jews who returned to their homeland.

Paul taught clearly that the observing of religious feasts was neither a means of salvation nor an essential for sanctification (Gal. 4:1-11). Christians are at liberty to follow their own conscience so long as they do not judge others or cause others to stumble (Rom. 14:1–15:7). Also, keep in mind Paul's personal policy with regard to these matters of Jewish practice (1 Cor. 9:19-23).

Arriving at Caesarea, Paul went up to Jerusalem and greeted the believers there. He then went to Antioch and reported to his home church all that God had done on this second missionary journey. He had been gone from Antioch perhaps two years or more, and the saints were no doubt overjoyed to see him and hear about the work of God among the Gentiles.

There's no proof, but likely Paul kept reminding the believers in Antioch, "It's always too soon to quit!"

That's a good reminder for us to heed today.

CHAPTER EIGHTEEN
EXCITEMENT IN EPHESUS
Acts 18:23–19:41

We don't know how long Paul remained in Antioch before leaving on his third missionary journey, but perhaps it was as long as a year. As in his second journey, he visited the churches and strengthened the believers. Luke does not describe this journey in detail because his main purpose is to get Paul to Ephesus. He wants to share with his readers the marvelous ministry God gave to Paul in that strategic city so steeped in idolatry and the occult.

Ephesus, with its 300,000 inhabitants, was the capital city of the Roman province of Asia and its most important commercial center. Thanks to a large harbor, Ephesus grew wealthy on trade; and, thanks to the temple of Diana, it attracted hosts of visitors who wanted to see this building that was one of the seven wonders of the world.

The temple was probably four centuries old in Paul's day. It measured 418 feet by 239 feet, and boasted of 100 columns that stood over 50 feet high. In the sacred enclosure of the temple stood the "sacred image" of Artemis (Diana) that was supposed to have fallen from heaven (Acts 19:35). It was probably a meteorite. Since Artemis was a fertility goddess, cultic prostitution was an important part of her worship, and hundreds of "priestesses" were available in the temple.

Paul's three years in Ephesus (Acts 20:31)—the longest he stayed in any city—were certainly exciting and fruitful. Let's meet some of the people who were involved.

A Man with an Incomplete Message (Acts 18:23-28)

When Paul departed from Ephesus for Jerusalem, he left his friends Aquila and Priscilla behind to carry on the witness in the synagogue. Imagine their surprise one Sabbath to hear a visiting Jewish teacher named Apollos preach many of the truths that they themselves believed and taught!

Apollos was certainly an exceptional man in many ways. He came from Alexandria, the second most important city in the Roman Empire. A center for education and philosophy, the city was founded by (and named after) Alexander the Great, and it boasted a university with a library of almost 700,000 volumes. The population of Alexandria (about 600,000) was quite cosmopolitan, being made up of Egyptians, Romans, Greeks, and Jews. At least a quarter of the population was Jewish, and the Jewish community was very influential.

Apollos knew the Old Testament Scriptures well and was able to teach them with eloquence and power. He was fervent ("boiling") in his spirit and diligent in his presentation of the message. He was bold enough to enter the synagogue and preach to the Jews. The only problem was that this enthusiastic man was declaring an incomplete Gospel. His message got as far as John the Baptist and then stopped! He knew nothing about Calvary, the resurrection of Christ, or the coming of the Holy Spirit at Pentecost. He had zeal, but he lacked spiritual knowledge (Rom. 10:1-4).

The ministry of John the Baptist was an important part of God's redemptive plan. God sent John to prepare the nation of Israel for their Messiah (John 1:15-34). John's baptism was a baptism of repentance; those who were baptized looked forward to the coming Messiah (Acts 19:4). John also announced a future baptism of the Holy Spirit (Matt. 3:11; Mark 1:8) which took place on the Day of Pentecost (Acts 1:5). Apollos knew about the promises, but he did not know about their fulfillment.

Where did Apollos get his message to begin with? Since Alexandria was a famous center for learning, it is possible that some of John the Baptist's disciples (Matt. 14:12; Luke 11:1) had gone there while Christ was still ministering on earth, and shared with the Jews as much as they knew. The word *instructed* in Acts 18:25 means "catechized" and suggests that Apollos had personal formal training in the Scriptures. However, that training was limited to the facts about the ministry of John the Baptist. Apollos' message was not inaccurate or insincere; it was just incomplete.

When I travel in conference ministry, I depend on my wife to plan the routes and do the navigating. (I can get lost in a parking lot!) On one particular trip, we got confused because we could not find a certain road. Then we discovered that our map was out of date! We quickly obtained a new map and everything was fine. Apollos had an old map that had been accurate in its day, but he desperately needed a new one. That new map was supplied by Aquila and Priscilla.

Aquila and Priscilla did not instruct him in public because that would have only confused the Jews. They took him home to a Sabbath dinner and then told him about Jesus Christ and the coming of the Holy Spirit. They led him into a deeper knowledge of Christ; and the next Sabbath, Apollos returned to the synagogue and gave the Jews the rest of the story! In fact, so effective was his ministry that the believers in Ephesus highly recommended him to the churches in Achaia. Here Apollos not only strengthened the saints, but he also debated with the unbelieving Jews and convinced many of them that Jesus is the Messiah.

Apollos ministered for a time to the church in Corinth (Acts 19:1), where his learning and eloquence attracted attention (1 Cor. 1:12; 3:4-6, 22; 4:6). It is unfortunate that a clique gathered around him and helped bring division to the church, because he was definitely one of Paul's friends and a trusted helper (1 Cor. 16:12; Titus 3:13).

Twelve Men with an Inconsistent Witness (Acts 19:1-10)

When Paul arrived back in Ephesus, he met twelve men who professed to be Christian "disciples" but whose lives gave evidence that something was lacking. Paul asked them, "Did you receive the Holy Spirit when you believed?" (Acts 19:2, NIV, NASB, NKJV) The question was important because *the witness of the Spirit is the one indispensable proof that a person is truly born again* (Rom. 8:9, 16; 1 John 5:9-13), and you receive the Spirit when you believe on Jesus Christ (Eph. 1:13).

Their reply revealed the vagueness and uncertainty of their faith, for they did not even know that the Holy Spirit had been given! As disciples of John the Baptist, they knew that there was a Holy Spirit, and that the Spirit would one day baptize God's people (Matt. 3:11; Luke 3:16; John 1:32-33). It is possible that these men were Apollos' early "converts" and therefore did not fully understand what Christ had done.

Why did Paul ask about their baptism? Because in the Book of Acts, a person's baptismal experience is an indication of his or her spiritual experience. Acts 1–10 records a transition period in the history of the church, from the Apostles' ministry to the Jews to their ministry to the Gentiles. During this transition period, Peter used "the keys of the kingdom" (Matt. 16:19) and opened the door of faith to the Jews (Acts 2), the Samaritans (Acts 8:14ff), and finally to the Gentiles (Acts 10).

It is important to note that God's pattern for today is given in Acts 10:43-48: sinners hear the Word, they believe on Jesus Christ, they *immediately* receive the Spirit, and then they are baptized. The Gentiles in Acts 10 did not receive the Spirit by means of water baptism or by the laying on of the Apostles' hands (Acts 8:14-17).

The fact that these men did not have the Spirit dwelling within was proof that they had never truly been born again. But they had been baptized by John's baptism, the same baptism that the Apostles had received! (see Acts 1:21-22) What was wrong with them?

Some people say that these men were already saved, but they lacked the fullness of the Spirit in their lives. So Paul explained how to be "baptized in the Spirit," and this led to a new life of victory. But that's not what the record says. Paul sensed that these men did not have the witness of the Spirit in their lives, and therefore they were not converted men. He certainly would not discuss the fullness of the Spirit with unsaved people! No, these twelve men had been baptized and were seeking to be religious, but something was missing. Alas, we have people just like them in our churches today!

Paul explained to them that John's baptism was a baptism of repentance that *looked forward* to the coming of the promised Messiah, while Christian baptism is a baptism that *looks back* to the finished work of Christ on the cross and His victorious resurrection. John's baptism was on "the other side" of Calvary and Pentecost. It was correct for its day, but now that day was ended.

Keep in mind that John the Baptist was a prophet who ministered under the old dispensation (Matt. 11:7-14). The Old Covenant was ended, not by John at the Jordan, but by Jesus Christ at Calvary (Heb. 10:1-18). The baptism of John was important to the Jews of that time (Matt. 21:23-32), but it is no longer valid for the church today. In a very real sense, these twelve men were like "Old Testament believers" who were anticipating the coming of the Messiah. Certainly Paul explained to the men many basic truths that Luke did not record. Then he baptized them, for their first "baptism" was not truly Christian baptism.

Why was it necessary for Paul to lay hands on these men before they could receive the Spirit? Didn't this contradict the experience of Peter recorded in Acts 10:44-48? Not if you keep in mind that this was a special group of men who would help form the nucleus of a great church in Ephesus. By using Paul to convey the gift of the Spirit, God affirmed Paul's apostolic authority and united the Ephesian church to the other churches as well as to the "mother church" in Jerusalem. When Peter and John laid hands on the believing Samaritans, it united them to the Jerusalem church and healed a breach between Jews and Samaritans that had existed for centuries.

What God did through Paul for these twelve men was not normative for the church today. How do we know? Because it was not repeated. The people who were converted in Ephesus under Paul's ministry all received the gift of the Holy Spirit *when they trusted the Saviour.* Paul makes this clear in Ephesians 1:13-14, and this is the pattern for us today.

In Acts 19:6, we have the last instance of the gift of tongues in the Book of Acts. The believers spoke in tongues at Pentecost and praised God, and their listeners recognized these tongues as known languages (Acts 2:4-11) and not as some "heavenly speech." The Gentile believers in the house of Cornelius also spoke in tongues (Acts 10:44-46), and their experience was identical to that of the Jews in Acts 2 (see Acts 11:15). This was of historic significance since the Spirit was baptizing Jews (Acts 2) and Gentiles (Acts 10) into the body of Christ (see 1 Cor. 12:13).

Today, the gift of tongues is not an evidence of the baptism of the Spirit or the fullness of the Spirit. Paul asked, "Do all speak with tongues?" (1 Cor. 12:30) and the Greek construction demands no as an answer. When Paul wrote to his Ephesian friends about the filling of the Holy Spirit, he said nothing about tongues (Eph. 5:18ff). Nowhere in Scripture are we admonished to seek a baptism of the Holy Spirit, or to speak in tongues, but we are commanded to be filled with the Spirit. Read Paul's letter to the Ephesian church and note the many references to the Holy Spirit of God and His work in the believer.

Seven Men with Inadequate Power (Acts 19:11-20)

It is remarkable that Paul was able to witness in the synagogue for three months before he had to leave. No doubt the faithful ministry of Aquila and Priscilla played an important part in this success. However, hardness of heart set in (Heb. 3:7ff), so Paul left the synagogue and moved his ministry to a schoolroom, taking his disciples with him. He probably used the room during the "off hours" each day (11 A.M. to 4 P.M.), when many people would be resting. Paul ministered in this way for about two years and "all they who dwelt in Asia heard the word of the Lord Jesus, both Jews and Greeks" (Acts 19:10).

What a victorious ministry! It appears that everybody knew what Paul was saying and doing! (see Acts 19:17, 20) Even Paul's enemies had to admit that the Word was spreading and people were being saved (Acts 19:26). Two factors made this possible: the witness of the believers as they went from place to place, and the "special miracles" that God enabled Paul to perform in Ephesus (Acts 19:11).

In Bible history, you will find three special periods of miracles: (1) the time of Moses; (2) the time of Elijah and Elisha; and (3) the time of Jesus and His Apostles. Each period was less than 100 years. Depending on how some of these events are classified, the total number of miracles for all three periods is less than 100. Of course, not all the miracles were recorded (see John 20:30-31).

When our Lord performed miracles, He usually had at least three purposes in mind: (1) to show His compassion and meet human needs; (2) to teach a spiritual truth; and (3) to present His credentials as the Messiah. The Apostles followed this same pattern in their miracles. In fact, the ability to do miracles was one of the proofs of apostolic authority (Mark 16:20; Rom. 15:18-19; 2 Cor. 12:12; Heb. 2:1-4). Miracles *of themselves* do not save lost sinners (Luke 16:27-31; John 2:23-25). Miracles must be tied to the message of the Word of God.

God enabled Paul to perform "special miracles" because Ephesus was a center for the occult (Acts 19:18-19), and Paul was demonstrating God's power right in Satan's territory. But keep in mind that wherever God's people minister the truth, Satan sends a counterfeit to oppose the work. Jesus taught this truth in His Parable of the Tares (Matt. 13:24-30, 36-43); Peter experienced it in Samaria (Acts 8:9ff); and Paul experienced it at Paphos (Acts 13:4-12). Satan imitates whatever God's people are doing, because he knows that the unsaved world cannot tell the difference (2 Cor. 11:13-15).

It was not unusual for Jewish priests to seek to cast out demons (Luke 11:19), but it was unusual for them to use the name of Jesus Christ. Since these men had no personal relationship with the Saviour, they had to invoke the name of Paul as well; but their scheme did not work. The demon said, "Jesus I recognize, and Paul I am acquainted with; but who are you?" (literal translation) The demonized man then attacked the seven priests and drove them from the house.

Had this exorcism succeeded, it would have discredited the name of Jesus Christ and the ministry of the church in Ephesus. (Paul faced a similar situation in Philippi. See Acts 16:16ff.) However, God used the scheme to defeat Satan and to bring conviction to the believers who were still involved in magical arts. Instead of disgracing the name of Jesus, the event magnified His name and caused the Word of God to spread even more rapidly.

The tense of the verbs in Acts 19:18 indicates that the people "kept coming . . . kept confessing . . . kept showing." These believers apparently had not made a clean break with sin and were still practicing their magic, but the Lord had dealt with them. The total value of the magical books and spells that they burned was equivalent to the total salaries of 150 men working for a whole year! These people did not count the cost but repented and turned from their sins.

A Mob of Indignant Citizens (Acts 19:21-41)

In Acts 19:21, we have the first mention of Paul's plan to go to Rome. The fulfilling of this plan will be described in the last third of the Book of Acts. Paul would soon write to the saints in Rome and express this desire to them (Rom. 1:13-15; 15:22-29). But first he had to visit the churches in Macedonia and Achaia in order to complete the "love offering" that he was taking for the poor saints in Jerusalem (Acts 24:17; Rom. 15:25-33; 1 Cor. 16:3-7). While he remained in Ephesus (1 Cor. 16:8-9), he sent Timothy to help him finish the job (1 Cor. 4:17; 16:10-11).

It was at this point that Satan attacked again, not as the deceiver (2 Cor. 11:3-4), but as the destroyer (1 Peter 5:8), and the murderer (John 8:44). Satan incited the guild of silversmiths to stage a public protest against Paul and the Gospel. Paul may have been referring to this riot when he wrote, "I have fought with beasts at Ephesus" (1 Cor. 15:32). The enemy had been repeatedly defeated throughout Paul's three years of ministry in Ephesus. It would have been a master stroke on Satan's part to climax that ministry with a city-wide attack that could result in Paul's arrest, or even his death.

Wherever the Gospel is preached in power, it will be opposed by people who make money from superstition and sin. Paul did not arouse the opposition of the silversmiths by picketing the temple of Diana or staging anti-idolatry rallies. All he did was teach the truth daily and send out his converts to witness to the lost people in the city. As more and more people got converted, fewer and fewer customers were available.

"For the love of money is a root of all kinds of evil" (1 Tim. 6:10, NKJV). Demetrius and his silversmiths were promoting idolatry and immorality in order to make a living, while Paul was declaring the true God and pointing people to cleansing and purity through the free grace of God. The silversmiths were really more concerned about their jobs and their income than they were about Diana and her temple, but they were wise enough not to make this known.

Benjamin Franklin said that a mob was "a monster with heads enough, but no brains." How sad it is when people permit themselves to be led by a few selfish leaders who know the art of manipulation. Demetrius made use of the two things the Ephesians loved the most: the honor of their city and the greatness of their goddess and her temple. Without the help of radio, TV, or newspaper, he got his propaganda machine going and soon had the whole city in an uproar.

Max Lerner wrote in *The Unfinished Country*, "Every mob, in its ignorance and blindness and bewilderment, is a League of Frightened Men that seeks reassurance in collective action." It was a "religious mob" that shouted "Crucify Him! Crucify Him!" to Pilate, and eventually got its way. Had this Ephesian mob succeeded in its plans, Paul would have been arrested and executed before the law could have stepped in to protect him.

The confused crowd, some 25,000 shouting people, finally filled up the amphitheater; most of them did not know what was happening or why they were there. Since the mob could not find Paul, they seized two of his helpers, Gaius (*not* the Gaius of Acts 20:4; Rom. 16:23;

1 Cor. 1:14) and Aristarchus (Acts 20:4). Paul wanted to enter the theater—what an opportunity for preaching the Gospel!—but the believers and some of the city leaders wisely counseled him to stay away (Acts 19:30-31).

Before long, race prejudice entered the picture, when a Jew named Alexander tried to address the crowd (Acts 19:33-34). No doubt he wanted to explain to them that the Jews living in Ephesus did not endorse Paul's message or ministry, and, therefore, must not be made scapegoats just to satisfy the crowd. But his very presence only aroused the mob even more, and they shouted for two more hours, "Great is Diana of the Ephesians!" The crowd knew that the Jews did not approve of idols and would not honor Diana. The only thing that protected the Jews was the Roman law that gave them freedom of religion.

It was the city clerk who finally got matters under control, and he did it primarily for political reasons. Ephesus was permitted by Rome to exist as a "free city" with its own elected assembly, but the Romans would have rejoiced to find an excuse for removing these privileges (Acts 19:40). The same tactics that the silversmiths used to arouse the mob, the clerk used to quiet and reassure them—the greatness of their city and of their goddess.

Luke records the official statement that the believers were innocent of any crime, either public (Acts 19:37) or private (Acts 19:38). Paul had this same kind of "official approval" in Philippi (Acts 16:35-40) and in Corinth (Acts 18:12-17); and he would receive it again after his arrest in Jerusalem. Throughout the Book of Acts, Luke makes it clear that the persecution of the Christian church was incited by the unbelieving Jews and not by the Romans. If anything, Paul used his Roman citizenship to protect himself, his friends, and the local assemblies.

The crowd was dismissed, and no doubt the people went home congratulating themselves that they had succeeded in defending their great city and their famous goddess. It is doubtful that many of them questioned the truthfulness of their religion or determined to investigate what Paul had been preaching for three years. It is much easier to believe a lie and follow the crowd.

But Ephesus is gone, and so is the worldwide worship of Diana of the Ephesians. The city and the temple are gone, and the silversmiths' guild is gone. Ephesus is a place visited primarily by archeologists and people on Holy Land tours. Yet the Gospel of God's grace and the church of Jesus Christ are still here! We have four inspired letters that were sent to the saints in Ephesus—Ephesians, 1 and 2 Timothy, and Revelation 2:1-7. The name of Paul is honored, but the name of Demetrius is forgotten. (Were it not for Paul, we would not have met Demetrius in the first place!)

The church ministers by persuasion, not propaganda. We share God's truth, not man's religious lies. Our motive is love, not anger; and the glory of God, not the praise of men. This is why the church goes on, and we must keep it so.

CHAPTER NINETEEN A MINISTER'S FAREWELL

Acts 20

In the final third of the Book of Acts, Dr. Luke records Paul's journey to Jerusalem, his arrest there, and his voyage to Rome. The Gospel of Luke follows a similar pattern as Luke describes Christ's journey to Jerusalem to die (Luke 9:53; 13:33; 18:31; 19:11, 28). Much as Jesus set His face "like a flint" to do the Father's will (Isa. 50:7; Luke 9:51), so Paul determined to finish his course with joy, no matter what the cost might be (Acts 20:24).

This chapter describes three "farewell events" as Paul closed his ministry in Macedonia, Achaia, and Asia.

A Farewell Journey (Acts 20:1-5)

"I do not expect to visit this country again!" D.L. Moody spoke those words in 1867 when he made his first trip to England. He was so seasick during the voyage that he decided he would never sail again, but he made five more visits to England, seasickness notwithstanding.

Paul was ready for another journey. He wanted to make at least one more visit to the churches the Lord had helped him to found, because Paul was a man with a concerned heart. "The care of all the churches" was his greatest joy as well as his heaviest burden (2 Cor. 11:23-28).

After the riot, Paul left Ephesus and headed toward Macedonia and Achaia (see Acts 19:21). He expected to meet Titus at Troas and get a report on the problems in Corinth, but Titus did not come (2 Cor. 2:12-13). The men finally met in Macedonia and Paul rejoiced over the good news Titus brought (2 Cor. 7:5-7). Paul had originally planned to make two visits to Corinth (2 Cor. 1:15-16), but instead he made one visit that lasted three months (Acts 20:3; 1 Cor. 16:5-6). During that visit, he wrote his Epistle to the Romans.

Paul had two goals in mind as he visited the various churches. His main purpose was to encourage and strengthen the saints so that they might stand true to the Lord and be effective witnesses. His second purpose was to finish taking up the collection for the needy believers in Jerusalem (Rom. 15:25-27; 1 Cor. 16:1-9; 2 Cor. 8–9). The men who accompanied him (Acts 20:4) were representatives of the churches, appointed to travel with Paul and help handle the funds (2 Cor. 8:18-24).

Once again, Paul had to change his plans, this time because of a Jewish plot to kill him at sea. Instead of sailing from Corinth, he traveled overland through Achaia and Macedonia, sailing from Philippi to Troas, where his "team" agreed to rendezvous. As a person who dislikes travel and changes in plans, I admire Paul for his courage, stamina, and adaptability. In spite of the complications and delays in travel today, we have a much easier time than Paul did—and we complain! He kept going!

A Farewell Service (Acts 20:6-12)

Paul was not able to make it to Jerusalem for the annual Passover celebration, so now his goal was to arrive there at least by Pentecost (Acts 20:16). Note the pronoun change to "us" and "we," for Dr. Luke has now joined the party (see Acts 16:17). He had probably been ministering at Philippi where he joined Paul for the last leg of the journey. Paul must have rejoiced to have Luke, Titus, and Timothy at his side again. The men remained at Troas a week so that they might fellowship with the believers there. Perhaps they were also waiting for the departure of the next ship.

Luke gives us a brief report of a local church service in Troas, and from it we learn something of how they met and worshiped the Lord. Consider the elements involved.

The Lord's Day. To begin with, they met on the first day of the week and not on the seventh day which was the Sabbath (see also 1 Cor. 16:1-2). The first day came to be called "the Lord's Day" because on it the Lord Jesus Christ arose from the dead (Rev. 1:10). We should also remember that the church was born on the first day of the week when the Spirit came at Pentecost. During the early years of the church, the believers did maintain some of the Jewish traditions, such as the hours of prayer (Acts 3:1). But as time went on, they moved away from the Mosaic calendar and developed their own pattern of worship as the Spirit taught them.

The Lord's people. The church met in the evening because Sunday was not a holiday during which people were free from daily employment. Some of the believers would no doubt be slaves, unable to come to the assembly until their work was done. The believers met in an upper room because they had no church buildings in which to gather. This room may have been in the private home of one of the believers. The assembly would have been a cosmopolitan group, but their social and national distinctions made no difference: they were "all one in Christ Jesus" (Gal. 3:28).

The Lord's Supper. The early church shared a "potluck" meal called the "love feast" (*agape*), after which they would observe the Lord's Supper (Acts 2:42; 1 Cor. 11:17-34). The "breaking of bread" in Acts 20:7 refers to the Lord's Supper, whereas in Acts 20:11 it describes a regular meal. By sharing and eating with one another, the church enjoyed fellowship and also gave witness of their oneness in Christ. Slaves would actually eat at the same table with their masters, something unheard of in that day.

It is likely that the church observed the Lord's Supper each Lord's Day when they met for fellowship and worship. In fact, some believers probably ended many of their regular meals at home by taking the bread and wine and remembering the Lord's death. While Scripture does not give us specific instructions in the matter ("as often," 1 Cor. 11:26), the example of the early church would encourage us to meet at the Lord's table often. However, the Communion must not become routine, causing us to fail to receive the blessings involved.

The Lord's message. The Word of God was always declared in the Christian assemblies, and this included the public reading of the Old Testament Scriptures (1 Tim. 4:13) as well as whatever apostolic letters had been received (Col. 4:16). It is sad to see how the Word is neglected in church services today. Knowing that this would probably be his last meeting with the saints at Troas, Paul preached a long sermon, after which he ate and conversed with the people until morning. It's doubtful that anybody complained. How we today wish we could have been there to hear the Apostle Paul preach!

The Word of God is important to the people of God, and the preaching and teaching of the Word must be emphasized. The church meets for edification as well as for celebration, and that edification comes through the Word. "Preach the Word!" is still God's admonition to spiritual leaders (2 Tim. 4:2). According to Dr. D. Martyn Lloyd-Jones, "the decadent periods and eras in the history of the church have always been those periods when preaching has declined" (*Preachers and Preaching*, Zondervan, p. 24).

The Lord's power. Whether it was the lateness of the hour or the stuffiness of the room (surely not the dullness of Paul's sermon!), Eutychus ("Fortunate") fell asleep and then fell out the window, and was killed by the fall. However, Paul raised him from the dead and left him and the church comforted. God's power was present to work for His people.

How old was Eutychus? The Greek word *neanias* in Acts 20:9 means a man from twenty-four to forty years of age. The word *pais* in Acts 20:12 means a young child or youth. Dr. Howard Marshall, an eminent Greek scholar, says he was a "young lad of eight to fourteen years. Since the word *pais* can mean "a servant," Eutychus may have been a young man who was also a servant. He may have worked hard that day and was weary. No wonder he fell asleep during the lengthy sermon!

Let's not be too hard on Eutychus. At least he was there for the service, and he did try to keep awake. He sat near ventilation, and he must have tried to fight off the sleep that finally conquered him. The tense of the Greek verb indicates that he was gradually overcome, not suddenly.

Also, let's not be too hard on Paul. After all, he was preaching his farewell sermon to this assembly, and he had a great deal to tell them for their own good. Those sitting near should have been watching Eutychus; but, of course, they were engrossed in what Paul was saying. Paul did interrupt his sermon to rush downstairs to bring the young man back to life. His approach reminds us of Elijah (1 Kings 17:21-22) and Elisha (2 Kings 4:34-35).

Perhaps each of us should ask ourselves, "What really keeps me awake?" Christians who slumber during one hour in church somehow manage to stay awake during early-morning fishing trips, lengthy sporting events and concerts, or late-night TV specials. Also, we need to prepare ourselves physically for public worship to make sure we are at our best. "Remember," said Spurgeon, "if we go to sleep during the sermon and die, there are no apostles to restore us!"

A Farewell Message (Acts 20:13-38)

Paul chose to walk from Troas to Assos, a distance of about twenty miles. Why? For one thing, it enabled him to stay longer with the saints in Troas while he sent Luke and the party on ahead (Acts 20:13). It would take the ship at least a day to sail from Troas to Assos, and Paul could probably walk it in ten hours or less. Also, Paul probably wanted time alone to commune with the Lord about his trip to Jerusalem. The apostle must have sensed already that difficult days lay ahead of him. He may also have been pondering the message he would give to the Ephesian elders. Finally, the exercise was certainly beneficial! Even inspired apostles need to care for their bodies. I personally would prefer walking to sailing!

There were fifty days between Passover (Acts 20:6) and Pentecost (Acts 20:16), and Paul's trip from Philippi to Troas had already consumed twelve of them (Acts 20:6). It took another four days to get to Miletus, so Paul decided not to go to Ephesus lest he lose any more valuable time. Instead, he invited the leaders of the Ephesian church to travel about thirty miles and meet him at Miletus, where the ship was waiting to unload cargo and take on more. Paul was not one to waste time or to lose opportunities.

In the Book of Acts, Luke reports eight messages given by the Apostle Paul to various people: a Jewish synagogue congregation (Acts 13:14-43); Gentiles (Acts 14:14-18; 17:22-34); church leaders (Acts 20:17-38); a Jewish mob (Acts 22:1-21); the Jewish council (Acts 23:1-10); and various government officials (Acts 24:10-21; 26:1-32). His address to the Ephesian elders is unique in that it reveals Paul the pastor rather than Paul the evangelist or Paul the defender of the faith. The message enables us to get a glimpse of how Paul ministered in Ephesus for three years.

The word "elder" is *presbutos* in the Greek ("presbyter") and refers to a mature person who has been selected to serve in office (Acts 14:23). These same people are called "overseers" in Acts 20:28, which is *episkopos* or "bishop." They were chosen to "feed the church" (Acts 20:28), which means "to shepherd." Paul called the local church "a flock, (Acts 20:28-29), so these men were also pastors. (The word *pastor* means "shepherd.") Thus in the New Testament churches, the three titles *elder, bishop,* and *pastor* were synonymous. The qualifications for this office are given in 1 Timothy 3:1-7 and Titus 1:5-9.

There were three parts to Paul's farewell message. First he reviewed the past (Acts 20:18-21); then he discussed the present (Acts 20:22-27); and finally, he spoke about the future (Acts 20:28-35). In the first part, he emphasized his faithfulness to the Lord and to the church as he ministered for three years in Ephesus. The second section reveals Paul's personal feelings in view of both the past and the future. In the third part, he warned them of the dangers that the churches faced.

A review of the past (vv. 18-21). Paul was not one to work into his ministry gradually like a diplomat feeling his way. "From the first day" he gave himself unsparingly to the work of the Lord in Ephesus, for Paul was an ambassador and not a diplomat.

The *motive* for Paul's ministry is found in the phrase "serving the Lord" (Acts 20:19). He was not interested in making money (Acts 20:33) or in enjoying an easy life (Acts 20:34-35), for he was the bondslave of Jesus Christ (Acts 20:24; Rom. 1:1). Paul was careful to let people know that his motives for ministry were spiritual and not selfish (1 Thes. 2:1-13).

The *manner* of his ministry was exemplary (Acts 20:18-19). He lived a consistent life which anybody could inspect, for he had nothing to hide. He served in humility and not as a "religious celebrity" demanding that others serve him. But his humility was not a sign of weakness, for he had the courage to face trials and dangers without quitting. Paul was not ashamed to admit to his friends that there had also been times of tears (see also Acts 20:31, 37; Rom. 9:1-2; 2 Cor. 2:4; Phil. 3:18).

The *message* of his ministry (Acts 20:20-21) was also widely known, because he announced it and taught it publicly (Acts 19:9) as well as in the various house churches of the fellowship. He told sinners to repent of their sins and believe in Jesus Christ. This message was "the Gospel of the grace of God" (Acts 20:24), and it is the *only* message that can save the sinner (1 Cor. 15:1-8; Gal. 1:6-12).

Furthermore, Paul reminded them that, in his ministry, he had not held back anything that was profitable to them. He declared to them "all the counsel of God" (Acts 20:27). His was a balanced message that included the doctrines and duties, as well as the privileges and responsibilities, that belonged to the Christian life. In his preaching, he neither compromised nor went to extremes, but kept things in balance. Paul also kept his outlook and congregation balanced, witnessing both to Jews and to Gentiles.

A testimony of the present (vv. 22-27). The phrase "And now, behold" shifts the emphasis from the past to the present as Paul opens his heart and tells his friends just how he feels. He did not hide from them the fact that he was bound in his spirit (Acts 19:21) to go to Jerusalem, even though he knew that danger and possible death awaited him there. The Holy Spirit had witnessed this message to him in city after city. A lesser man would have found some way to escape, but not Paul. He was too gripped by his calling and his devotion to Jesus Christ to look for some safe and easy way out. In his testimony, Paul used six graphic pictures of his ministry to explain why he would not quit but would go to Jerusalem to die for Jesus Christ if necessary. Paul could say, "None of these things move me!" because he knew what he was as a minister of Jesus Christ.

Paul saw himself as *an accountant* (Acts 20:24) who had examined his assets and liabilities and decided to put Jesus Christ ahead of everything else. He had faced this kind of reckoning early in his ministry and had willingly made the spiritual the number one priority in his life (Phil. 3:1-11).

He also saw himself as a *runner* who wanted to finish his course in joyful victory (Phil. 3:12-14; 2 Tim. 4:8). The three phrases "my life, my course, the ministry" are the key. Paul realized that his life was God's gift to him, and that God had a special plan for his life that would be fulfilled in his ministry. Paul was devoted to a great Person ("serving the Lord") and motivated by a great purpose, the building of the church.

Paul's third picture is that of the *steward,*

for his ministry was something that he had "received of the Lord." The steward owns little or nothing, but he possesses all things. His sole purpose is to serve his master and please him. "Moreover it is required in stewards that one be found faithful" (1 Cor. 4:2, NKJV). The steward must one day give an account of his ministry, and Paul was ready for that day.

The next picture is that of the *witness*, "testifying of the Gospel of the grace of God" (Acts 20:24, and note v. 21). The word means "to solemnly give witness," and it reminds us of the seriousness of the message and of the ministry. As we share the Gospel with others, it is a matter of life or death (2 Cor. 2:15-16). Paul was a faithful witness both in the life that he lived (Acts 20:18) and the message that he preached.

Picture number five is the *herald* (Acts 20:25). The word *preaching* means "to declare a message as the herald of the king." The witness tells what has happened to him, but the herald tells what the king tells him to declare. He is a man commissioned and sent with a message, and he must not change that message in any way. And since he is sent by the king, the people who listen had better be careful how they treat both the messenger and the message.

The final picture, and perhaps the most dramatic, is that of the *watchman* (Acts 20:26). As in Acts 18:6, this is a reference to the "watchman on the walls" in Ezekiel 3:17-21; 33:1-9. What a serious calling it was to be a watchman! He had to stay awake and alert, ready to sound the alarm if he saw danger approaching. He had to be faithful, not fearful, because the safety of many people rested with him. Paul had been a faithful watchman (Acts 20:31), for he had declared to sinners and saints all the counsel of God. Unfortunately, we have today many unfaithful watchmen who think only of themselves (Isa. 56:10-13).

A group of servicemen asked their new chaplain if he believed in a real hell for lost sinners, and he smiled and told them that he did not. "Then you are wasting your time," the men replied. "If there is no hell, we don't need you; and if there is a hell, you are leading us astray. Either way, we're better off without you!"

A warning about the future (vv. 28-38). Paul brought his farewell message to a close by warning the leaders of the dangers they had to recognize and deal with if they were to protect and lead the church. Never underestimate the great importance of the church. The church is important to God the Father because His name is on it—"the church of God." It is important to the Son because He shed His blood for it; and it is important to the Holy Spirit because He is calling and equipping people to minister to the church. It is a serious thing to be a spiritual leader in the church of the living God.

To begin with, there are dangers *around us*, "wolves" that want to ravage the flock (Acts 20:29). Paul was referring to false teachers, the counterfeits who exploit the church for personal gain (Matt. 7:15-23; 10:16; Luke 10:3; 2 Peter 2:1-3). How important it is that believers know the Word of God and be able to detect and defeat these religious racketeers.

But there are also dangers *among us* (Acts 20:30), because of people within the church who are ambitious for position and power. Church history, ancient and modern, is filled with accounts of people like Diotrephes who love to have the preeminence (3 John 9-11). It is shocking to realize that more than one false prophet got his or her start within the Christian church family! Read 1 John 2:18-19 and take heed.

There are also dangers *within us* (Acts 20:31-35), and this seems to be where Paul put the greatest emphasis. "Take heed, therefore, unto yourselves" (Acts 20:28). He names five sins that are especially destructive to the life and ministry of spiritual leaders in the church.

The first is *carelessness* (Acts 20:31), failing to stay alert and forgetting the price that others have paid so that we might have God's truth. "Watch and remember!" are words we had better heed. It is so easy for us today to forget the toil and tears of those who labored before us (Heb. 13:7). Paul's warning and weeping should be constant reminders to us to take our spiritual responsibilities seriously.

The second sin is *shallowness* (Acts 20:32). We cannot build the church unless God is building our lives daily. There is a balance here between prayer ("I commend you to God") and the Word of God ("the word of His grace"), because these two must always work together (1 Sam. 12:23; John 15:7; Acts 6:4). The Word of God alone is able to edify and enrich us, and the spiritual leader must spend time daily in the Word of God and prayer.

Covetousness is the third sin we must avoid

(Acts 20:33). It means a consuming and controlling desire for what others have and for more of what we ourselves already have. "Thou shalt not covet" is the last of the Ten Commandments, but if we do covet, we will end up breaking all the other nine! Those who covet will steal, lie, and murder to get what they want, and even dishonor their own parents. Covetousness is idolatry (Eph. 5:5; Col. 3:5). In the qualifications for an elder, it is expressly stated that he must not be guilty of the sin of covetousness (1 Tim. 3:3).

Paul also mentioned *laziness* (Acts 20:34). Paul earned his own way as a tentmaker, even though he could have used his apostolic authority to demand support and thereby have an easier life. It is not wrong for Christian workers to receive salaries, for "the laborer is worthy of his hire" (Luke 10:7; 1 Tim. 5:18). But they should be certain that they are really *earning* those salaries! (Read Prov. 24:30-34.)

Finally, Paul warned about *selfishness* (Acts 20:35). True ministry means giving, not getting; it means following the example of the Lord Jesus Christ. Dr. Earl V. Pierce used to call this "the supreme beatitude" because, unlike the other beatitudes, it tells us how to be *more* blessed! These words of Jesus are not found anywhere in the Gospels, but they were a part of the oral tradition, and Paul memorized them.

This beatitude does not suggest that people who receive are "less blessed" than people who give. (The beggar in Acts 3 would argue about that!) It could be paraphrased, "It's better to share with others than to keep what you have and collect more." In other words, the blessing does not come in accumulating wealth, but in sharing it. After all, Jesus became poor that we might become rich (2 Cor. 8:9). One of the best commentaries on this statement is Luke 12:16-31.

Paul closed this memorable occasion by kneeling down and praying for his friends, and then they all wept together. It is a difficult thing to say good-bye, especially when you know you will not see your friends again in this life. But we have the blessed assurance that we will one day see our Christian friends and loved ones in heaven, when Jesus Christ returns (1 Thes. 4:13-18).

Meanwhile, there is a job to be done—so, let's do it!

CHAPTER TWENTY THE MISUNDERSTOOD MISSIONARY

Acts 21:1–22:29

Is it so bad, then, to be misunderstood?" asked Ralph Waldo Emerson. "Pythagoras was misunderstood, and Socrates, and Jesus, and Luther, and Copernicus, and Galileo, and Newton. . . . To be great is to be misunderstood."

Emerson might have added that the Apostle Paul was misunderstood, by friends and foes alike. Three of these misunderstandings—and their consequences—are recorded in these chapters.

Paul's Friends Misunderstood His Plans (Acts 21:1-17)

Paul had to tear himself away from the Ephesian elders, so great was his love for them. He and his party sailed from Miletus to Cos, then to Rhodes, and then to Patera, a total of three days' journey. But Paul was uncomfortable with a "local coastal" ship that stopped at every port; so when he found a boat going directly to Phoenicia, he and his friends boarded it. It would be a voyage of about 400 miles.

Tyre (vv. 3-6). This would have been Paul's first contact with the believers in Tyre, though it is likely that his persecution of the Jerusalem believers helped to get this church started (Acts 11:19). The men had to seek out the believers, so it must not have been a large assembly; and apparently there was no synagogue in the town. They stayed a week with the saints while their ship unloaded its cargo and took on new cargo.

Paul had devoted a good part of his third missionary journey to taking up a love gift for the Jews in Judea. It was a practical way for the Gentiles to show their oneness with their Jewish brothers and sisters, and to repay them for sharing the Gospel with the Gentiles (Rom. 15:25-27). There was in the church a constant threat of division, for the Jewish extremists (the Judaizers) wanted the Gentiles to live like Jews and follow the Law of Moses (Acts 15:1ff). Wherever Paul ministered, these extremists tried to hinder his work and steal his converts. Paul hoped that his visit to Jerusalem with the offering would help to strengthen the fellowship between Jews and Gentiles.

Now, Paul began to get messages from his friends that his visit to Jerusalem would be difficult and dangerous. Of course, he had already suspected this, knowing how the false teachers operated (Rom. 15:30-31); but these messages were very personal and powerful. In Tyre, the believers "kept on saying to him" (literal Greek) that he should not set foot in Jerusalem.

After a week in Tyre, Paul and his party departed. It is touching to see how the believers had come to love Paul, though they had known him only a week. The first stop was Ptolemais, where they visited the believers for a day; and then they sailed to Caesarea, their final destination.

Caesarea (vv. 7-14). The men stayed with Philip, one of the original deacons (Acts 6:1-6) who also served as an evangelist (Acts 8:5ff). It was now some twenty years since he had come to Caesarea and made it his headquarters (Acts 8:40). Since Philip had been an associate of Stephen, and Paul had taken part in Stephen's death, this must have been an interesting meeting.

While Paul rested in Caesarea, the Prophet Agabus came to give him a second warning message from the Lord. Some fifteen years before, Paul and Agabus had worked together in a famine relief program for Judea (Acts 11:27-30), so they were not strangers. Agabus delivered his message in a dramatic way as he bound his own hands and feet with Paul's girdle and told the apostle that he would be bound in Jerusalem.

As did the saints in Tyre, so the believers in Caesarea begged Paul not to go to Jerusalem. Surely the men chosen by the churches could deliver the love offering to James and the Jerusalem elders, and it would not be necessary for Paul to go personally. But Paul silenced them and told them that he was prepared ("ready") not only to be bound, but also to die if necessary for the name of the Lord Jesus Christ.

Now we must pause to consider whether Paul was right or wrong in making that trip to Jerusalem. If it seems improper, or even blasphemous, so to examine the actions of an apostle, keep in mind that he was a human being like anyone else. His epistles were inspired, but this does not necessarily mean that everything he did was perfect. Whether he was right or wrong, we can certainly learn from his experience.

On the *con* side, these repeated messages do sound like warnings to Paul to stay out of Jerusalem. For that matter, over twenty years before, the Lord had commanded Paul to get out of Jerusalem because the Jews would not receive his testimony (Acts 22:18). Paul had already written to the Romans about the dangers in Judea (Acts 15:30-31), and he had shared these same feelings with the Ephesian elders (Acts 20:22-23); so he was fully aware of the problems involved.

On the *pro* side, the prophetic utterances can be taken as warnings ("Get ready!") rather than as prohibitions ("You must not go!"). The statement in Acts 21:4 does not use the Greek negative *ou*, which means absolute prohibition, but *me*, used "where one *thinks* a thing is not" (*Manual Greek Lexicon of the New Testament*, by G. Abbott-Smith, p. 289). Agabus did not forbid Paul to go to Jerusalem; he only told him what to expect if he did go. As for the Lord's command in Acts 22:18, it applied to that particular time and need not be interpreted as a prohibition governing the rest of Paul's life. While it is true that Paul avoided Jerusalem, it is also true that he returned there on other occasions: with famine relief (Acts 11:27-30); to attend the Jerusalem Conference (Acts 15:1ff); and after his second missionary journey (Acts 18:22—"going up to greet the church" refers to Jerusalem).

In view of Paul's statement in Acts 23:1, and the Lord's encouraging words in Acts 23:11, it is difficult to believe that the apostle deliberately disobeyed the revealed will of God. God's prophecy to Ananias (Acts 9:15) certainly came true in the months that followed as Paul had opportunity to witness for Christ.

Instead of accusing Paul of compromise, we ought to applaud him for his courage. Why? Because in going to Jerusalem, he took his life in his hands in order to try to solve the most pressing problem in the church: the growing division between the "far right" legalistic Jews and the believing Gentiles. Ever since the Jerusalem Conference (Acts 15), trouble had been brewing; and the legalists had been following Paul and seeking to capture his converts. It was a serious situation, and Paul knew that he was a part of the answer as well as a part of the problem. But he could not solve the problem by remote control through representatives; he had to go to Jerusalem personally.

Jerusalem (vv. 15-17). A company of believers left Caesarea and traveled with Paul to Jerusalem, probably to celebrate the feast. It was a journey of sixty-five miles that took at least three days by foot—two days if they had animals. What fellowship they must have enjoyed as they recounted what God had done in and through them! What a great encouragement it was for Paul to have these friends at his side as he faced the challenge of Jerusalem.

The city would be crowded with pilgrims, but Paul and his party planned to live with Mnason, "an early disciple," who lived in Jerusalem and had been visiting Caesarea. Was he perhaps converted under Peter's preaching at Pentecost? Or did his fellow Cypriot Barnabas win him to Christ? (Acts 4:36) We are not told; but we do know that Mnason was a man given to hospitality, and his ministry helped Paul at a strategic time in the apostle's ministry.

We could wish that Dr. Luke had told us more about that first meeting with the church leaders in Jerusalem. James and the other leaders did receive them gladly, but how did they respond to the gift from the Gentiles? Nothing is said about it. Were some of them perhaps a bit suspicious? A few years later, the Roman writer Martial would say, "Gifts are like hooks!" and perhaps some of the Jerusalem elders felt that way about this gift. Certainly the legalistic wing of the church would question anything that Paul said or did.

The Jerusalem Church Misunderstood His Message (Acts 21:18-26)

Apparently that first meeting was devoted primarily to fellowship and personal matters, because the second meeting was given over to Paul's personal report of his ministry to the Gentiles. The Jerusalem leaders had agreed years before that Paul should minister to the Gentiles (Gal. 2:7-10), and the elders rejoiced at what they heard. The phrase "declared particularly" means "reported in detail, item by item." Paul gave a full and accurate account, not of what he had done, but of what the Lord had done through his ministry (see 1 Cor. 15:10).

You get the impression that the legalists had been working behind the scenes. No sooner had Paul finished his report than the elders brought up the rumors that were then being circulated about Paul among the Jewish Christians. It has well been said that, though a rumor doesn't have a leg to stand on, it travels mighty fast!

What were his enemies saying about Paul? Almost the same things they said about Jesus and Stephen: he was teaching the Jews to forsake the laws and customs given by Moses and the fathers. They were not worried about what Paul taught the Gentile believers, because the relationship of the Gentiles to the Law had been settled at the Jerusalem Conference (Acts 15). In fact, the elders carefully rehearsed the matter (Acts 21:25), probably for the sake of Paul's Gentile companions. The leaders were especially concerned that Paul's presence in the city not cause division or disruption among the "thousands of Jews . . . zealous of the Law" (Acts 21:20).

But, why were so many believing Jews still clinging to the Law of Moses? Had they not read Romans and Galatians? Probably not, and even if they had, old customs are difficult to change. In fact, one day God would have to send a special letter to the Jews, the Epistle to the Hebrews, to explain the relationship between the Old and New Covenants. As Dr. Donald Grey Barnhouse used to say, "The Book of Hebrews was written to the Hebrews to tell them to stop being Hebrews!" It was not until the city and the temple were destroyed in A.D. 70 that traditional Jewish worship ceased.

Paul did warn the Gentiles not to get involved in the old Jewish religion (Gal. 4:1-11); but he nowhere told the Jews that it was wrong for them to practice their customs, *so long as they did not trust in ceremony or make their customs a test of fellowship* (Rom. 14:1–15:7). There was freedom to observe special days and diets, and believers were not to judge or condemn one another. The same grace that gave the Gentiles freedom to abstain also gave the Jews freedom to observe. All God asked was that they receive one another and not create problems or divisions.

It seems incredible that Paul's enemies would accuse him of these things, for all the evidence was against them. Paul had Timothy circumcised before taking him along on that second missionary journey (Acts 16:1-3). Paul had taken a Jewish vow while in Corinth (Acts 18:18), and it was his custom not to offend the Jews in any way by deliberately violating their customs or the Law of Moses (1 Cor. 9:19-

23). However, rumors are not usually based on fact, but thrive on half-truths, prejudices, and outright lies.

The leaders suggested that Paul demonstrate publicly his reverence for the Jewish Law. All they asked was that he identify himself with four men under a Nazarite vow (Num. 6), pay for their sacrifices, and be with them in the temple for their time of purification. He agreed to do it. If it had been a matter involving somebody's personal salvation, you can be sure that Paul would never have cooperated; for that would have compromised his message of salvation by grace, through faith. But this was a matter of personal conviction on the part of Jewish believers who were given the freedom to accept or reject the customs.

Paul reported to the priest the next day and shared in the purification ceremony, but he himself did not take any vows. He and the men had to wait seven days and then offer the prescribed sacrifices. The whole plan appeared to be safe and wise, but it did not work. Instead of bringing peace, it caused an uproar; and Paul ended up a prisoner.

The Jews Misunderstood Paul's Ministry (Acts 21:27–22:29)

In the temple, separating the court of the Gentiles from the other courts, stood a wall beyond which no Gentile was allowed to go (note Eph. 2:14). On the wall was this solemn inscription: "No foreigner may enter within the barricade which surrounds the sanctuary and enclosure. Anyone who is caught so doing will have himself to blame for his ensuing death." The Romans had granted the Jewish religious leaders authority to deal with anybody who broke this law, and this included the right of execution. This law plays an important role in what happened to Paul a week after he and the four Nazarites began their purification ceremonies.

Some Jews from Asia saw Paul in the temple and jumped to the conclusion that he had polluted their sacred building by bringing Gentiles past the barricade. It is likely that these Jews came from Ephesus, because they recognized Paul's friend Trophimus, who came from Ephesus. With their emotions running at full speed, and their brains in neutral, these men argued: (1) wherever Paul went, his Gentile friends went; (2) Paul was seen in the temple; therefore, his friends had been in the temple too! Such is the logic of prejudice.

They seized Paul and would have killed him had the Roman guards not intervened in the nick of time. (At least 1,000 soldiers were stationed in the Antonia Fortress at the northwest corner of the temple area.) The temple crowd was in an uproar, completely ignorant of what was going on. The scene reminds you of the riot in Ephesus. Compare Acts 21:30 with Acts 19:29, and Acts 21:34 with Acts 19:32. It required the chief captain (Claudius Lysias, Acts 23:26), 2 centurions, and perhaps 200 soldiers to get the mob under control and to rescue Paul. The captain actually thought Paul was an Egyptian rebel who was wanted by the Romans for inciting a revolt (Acts 21:38). This explains why he had Paul bound with two chains (see Acts 21:11).

When Claudius interrogated the people, they could not explain what caused the riot because they did not really know. The original troublemakers must have escaped during the great excitement, knowing that they could not actually substantiate their charges. Since Claudius could get no help from the people in the temple, he decided to interrogate Paul; so his soldiers carried Paul from the court of the Gentiles up the stairs into the barracks. As Paul was borne away, the crowd shouted angrily, "Away with him!" This again reminds us of our Lord's arrest and trial (Luke 23:18, 21; John 19:15).

At this point, Paul decided it was time to speak up; and the captain was amazed that his dangerous prisoner could speak Greek. When Paul asked for permission to address the Jews, Claudius consented, hoping that perhaps he would get enough information for an official report. He never did (see Acts 23:23-30). Paul spoke to the Jews in their native Aramaic, and this helped quiet them down. He was never able to finish his speech, but he did get to explain three important aspects of his life and ministry.

His early conduct (vv. 3-5). Paul had been a leading rabbi in his day (Gal. 1:13-14), so he was certainly known to some of the people in the crowd. Note how Paul piled up his Jewish credentials: he was a Jew, a native of Tarsus, brought up in Jerusalem, trained by Gamaliel, a follower of the Law, a zealous persecutor of the church, and a representative of the Sanhedrin. How could his countrymen not respectfully listen to a man with that kind of record!

Instead of accusing them of participating in a riot, he commended them for being "zealous toward God." (He had used a similar approach with the Athenians; Acts 17:22.) He admitted that he too had been guilty of having people arrested and bound, and even killed. The Christian faith was known as "the way" (Acts 9:2; 19:9, 23; 24:14, 22), probably a reference to our Lord's statement, "I am the way" (John 14:6).

His wonderful conversion (vv. 6-16). Luke recorded Paul's conversion experience in Acts 9, and Paul would repeat the account later for Felix and Agrippa (Acts 26:1-32). It is difficult to imagine a comparable crowd today quietly listening to that kind of a testimony. However, people in that day expected miraculous things to happen and were no doubt fascinated by Paul's story (see Acts 23:9). Also, Paul was on official Sanhedrin business when these events took place, which at least gave it some aura of authority.

In his testimony, Paul affirmed that Jesus of Nazareth was alive. Paul saw His glory and heard His voice. The people listening in the temple courts knew the official Jewish position that Jesus of Nazareth was an impostor who had been crucified and His body stolen from the tomb by His disciples who then started the rumor that Jesus had been raised from the dead. Of course, Paul himself had believed this story when he was persecuting the church.

The men with Paul saw the bright light, but were not blinded as he was; and they heard a sound, but could not understand what was being said (Acts 9:7). Imagine Paul's amazement to discover that Jesus was alive! Instantly, he had to change his whole way of thinking (repentance) and let the risen Lord have control.

Note Paul's wisdom as he identified himself with Ananias, a devout Jew who kept the Law and who called him "brother." Note also that Ananias attributed Paul's great experience to "the God of our fathers." In quoting Ananias, Paul gave reason for his listeners to accept his salvation experience and his call to service. Paul had seen "the Just [Righteous] One," which was a title for Messiah (see Acts 3:14; 7:52). Paul was now commissioned by God to take His message to "all men." This would include the Gentiles, but Paul did not say so until later.

Acts 22:16 in the *King James Version* seems to suggest that baptism is required for the washing away of our sins, but such is not the case. In his *Expanded Translation of the New Testament*, Greek scholar Kenneth Wuest puts it, "Having arisen, be baptized and wash away your sins, having previously called upon His Name." We are saved by calling on the Lord by faith (Acts 2:21; 9:14), and we give evidence of that faith by being baptized. According to Acts 9:17, Paul was filled with the Spirit *before* he was baptized; and this would indicate that he was already born again. It is the "calling," not the baptizing, that effects the cleansing.

Certainly many of Paul's listeners knew about the new "Christian sect" that had sprung up, the baptisms that had taken place, the stoning of Stephen, and the miracles that these "people of the way" had wrought. Paul was not speaking to ignorant people, because these things had not been "done in a corner" (Acts 26:26).

His special calling (vv. 17-29). After his conversion, Paul had ministered in Damascus and then had gone to Arabia, perhaps to evangelize and to meditate on God's Word (Acts 9:19-25; Gal. 1:16-17). When Paul did return to Jerusalem, the church leaders did not accept him until Barnabas interceded and got him in (Acts 9:26-29). Note how Paul again emphasized the Jewish elements in his experience, for the Jews would be impressed with a man who prayed in the temple and had a vision from God.

The Lord told Paul to leave Jerusalem quickly, because the people would not receive his witness. By obeying this command, Paul saved his life, because the Hellenistic Jews had plotted to kill him (Acts 9:29-30). But first, Paul debated with the Lord! He wanted to show the Jews that he was a new person and tell them that Jesus was the Messiah, and He was alive. If Paul won some of them to the Lord, it would perhaps help to compensate for all the damage he had done, especially in the killing of Stephen.

The Lord's command was, "Depart, for I will send you far from here to the Gentiles!" (Acts 22:21, NKJV) Paul was about to explain why he was involved with the Gentiles, but the Jews in the temple courts would not permit him to go on. No devout Jew would have anything to do with the Gentiles! Had Paul not uttered that one word, he might have later been released; *and perhaps he knew this.* However, he had to be faithful in his witness, no matter what it cost him. Paul would rather be a prisoner than give up his burden for lost souls and for missions! We could use more Christians like that today.

When Claudius saw that the riot was starting again, he took Paul into the barracks for "examination by torture." The apostle had already mentioned that he was born in Tarsus, but he had not told them that his citizenship was Roman. It was unlawful for a Roman citizen to be scourged. We do not know how people proved their citizenship in those days; perhaps they carried the first-century equivalent of an ID card.

Claudius must have been shocked that this little Jewish troublemaker who spoke Aramaic and Greek was actually a Roman citizen. "With great sum I obtained this freedom," Claudius boasted, indicating that he had gotten his citizenship by bribing the Roman officials, for it could not be actually purchased. But Paul was ahead of the Roman captain, for he had been born into freedom and Roman citizenship, thanks to his father. How Paul's father obtained his freedom, we do not know. We do know that Paul knew how to make use of his Roman citizenship for the cause of Christ.

The soldiers had made two mistakes, and they were quick to undo them: they had bound Paul and had planned to scourge him. No doubt Claudius and his men were especially kind to Paul now that they knew he was a Roman citizen. God was using the great power of the Empire to protect His servant and eventually get him to Rome.

Paul's entire time in Jerusalem was one filled with serious misunderstandings, but he pressed on. Perhaps at this point some of his friends were saying, "We told him so! We warned him!" For Paul and his associates, it may have looked like the end of the road, but God had other plans for them. Paul would witness again and again, and to people he could never have met had he not been a Roman prisoner. God's missionary did get to Rome—and the Romans paid the bill!

That's what happens when God's people are willing to be daring!

CHAPTER TWENTY-ONE
PAUL THE PRISONER
Acts 22:30–23:35

I was once called to be a character witness in a child custody case involving a man who had served time in prison. This was a new experience for me, and I was completely unprepared for the first question the attorney asked me: "Reverend, do you think that a man who has been a prisoner is fit to raise a child?"

"That depends on the man," I replied bravely. "Some of the greatest men in history have been prisoners—John the Baptist, John Bunyan, and even the Apostle Paul."

"Simply answer yes or no!" said the judge curtly, and that was the end of my sermon.

"Paul the prisoner" (Acts 23:18) was the name the Roman soldiers used for the apostle, a designation he himself often used (Eph. 3:1; 4:1; 2 Tim. 1:8; Phile. 1, 9). Paul was under "military custody," which meant he was bound to a Roman soldier who was responsible for him. Prisoners under "public custody" were put in the common jail, a horrible place for any human being to suffer (Acts 16:19-24).

Paul's friends could visit him and help meet his personal needs. It is sad that we don't read, "And prayer was made fervently by the church for Paul" (see Acts 12:5). There is no record that the Jerusalem church took any steps to assist him, either in Jerusalem or during his two years in Caesarea.

This is an exciting chapter, and in it we read of three confrontations that Paul experienced.

Paul and the Jewish Council (Acts 22:30–23:10)

Having discovered that Paul was a Roman citizen, the Roman captain now had two serious problems to solve. First, he needed to let the prisoner know what the official charges were against him, since that was Paul's right as a Roman citizen. Second, he also needed to have some official charges for his own records and to share with his superiors. He was sure that Paul had done something notorious, otherwise why would so many people want to do away with him? Yet nobody seemed to know what Paul's crimes were. What a plight for a Roman official to be in!

The logical thing was to let Paul's own people try him, so the captain arranged for a special meeting of the Jewish council (Sanhedrin). This group was composed of seventy (or seventy-one) of the leading Jewish teachers, with the high priest presiding. It was their responsibility to interpret and apply the sacred Jewish Law to the affairs of the nation, and to try those who violated that Law. The Romans gave the council permission to impose capital punishment where the offense deserved it.

The captain and his guard (Acts 23:10) brought Paul into the council chamber and stepped aside to watch the proceedings. Knowing how the Jews in the temple had treated Paul, Claudius remained there on guard lest his prisoner be taken from him and killed. No Roman soldier could afford to lose a prisoner, for that might mean the forfeiting of his own life. The loss of a prisoner against whom the charges were nebulous would be especially embarrassing for any Roman officer.

As Paul faced the council and examined it carefully, he decided to start with a personal approach. "Men and brethren" immediately identified him as a Jew and no doubt helped win the attention of his countrymen.

The Greek word translated "lived" means "to live as a citizen." It gives us the English word *politics*. Paul affirmed that he was a loyal Jew who had lived as a good Jewish citizen and had not broken the Law. His conscience did not condemn him even though the Jews had condemned him.

"Conscience" is one of Paul's favorite words; he used it twice in Acts (23:1; 24:16) and twenty-one times in his letters. The word means "to know with, to know together." Conscience is the inner "judge" or "witness" that approves when we do right and disapproves when we do wrong (Rom. 2:15). Conscience does not *set* the standard; it only *applies* it. The conscience of a thief would bother him if he told the truth about his fellow crooks just as much as a Christian's conscience would convict him if he told a lie about his friends. Conscience does not make the standards; it only applies the standards of the person, whether they are good or bad, right or wrong.

Conscience may be compared to a window that lets in the light. God's Law is the light; and the cleaner the window is, the more the light shines in. As the window gets dirty, the light gets dimmer; and finally the light becomes darkness. A good conscience, or pure conscience (1 Tim. 3:9), is one that lets in God's light so that we are properly convicted if we do wrong and encouraged if we do right. A defiled conscience (1 Cor. 8:7) is one that has been sinned against so much that it is no longer dependable. If a person continues to sin against his conscience, he may end up with an evil conscience (Heb. 10:22) or a seared conscience (1 Tim. 4:2). Then he would feel convicted if he did what was *right* rather than what was wrong!

Paul had persecuted the church and had even caused innocent people to die, so how could he claim to have a good conscience? *He had lived up to the light that he had,* and that is all that a good conscience requires. After he became a Christian and the bright light of God's glory shone into his heart (2 Cor. 4:6), Paul then saw things differently and realized that he was "the chief of sinners" (1 Tim. 1:15).

Ananias the high priest (not to be confused with Annas in Acts 4:6) was so incensed at Paul's saying that he had "lived in all good conscience" that he ordered the nearest Jewish council members to slap Paul across the mouth. (Jesus had been treated in a similar way—John 18:22.) This was, of course, illegal and inhumane; for, after all, Paul had not even been proven guilty of anything. Certainly the high priest would be expected to show honesty and fairness, if not compassion and concern (Lev. 19:15; Heb. 5:2).

Paul responded with what appears to me to be justified anger, though many disagree about this. When called to account for what he had said, Paul did not apologize. Rather, he showed respect for the *office* but not for the *man.* Ananias was indeed one of the most corrupt men ever to be named high priest. He stole tithes from the other priests and did all he could to increase his authority. He was known as a brutal man who cared more for Rome's favor than for Israel's welfare.

In calling the high priest a "whited wall," Paul was simply saying that the man was a hypocrite (Matt. 23:27; see Ezek. 13:10-12). Paul spoke prophetically, because God did indeed smite this wicked man. When the Jews revolted against Rome in the year 66, Ananias had to flee for his life because of his known sympathies with Rome. The Jewish guerrillas found him hiding in an aqueduct at Herod's palace, and they killed him. It was an ignominious death for a despicable man.

Paul's reply in Acts 23:5 has been variously interpreted. Some say that Paul did not know who the high priest was. Or perhaps Paul was speaking in holy sarcasm: "Could such a man actually be the high priest?" Since this was an informal meeting of the council, perhaps the high priest was not wearing his traditional garments and sitting in his usual place. For that matter, Paul had been away from the Jewish religious scene for many years and probably did not know many people in the council.

The quoting of Exodus 22:28 would indicate that Paul may not have known that it was the high priest who ordered him to be smitten. Again, note that Paul showed respect for the office, but not for the man who held the office. There is a difference.

Having failed in his personal approach, Paul then used a doctrinal approach. He declared that the real issue was his faith in the doctrine of the Resurrection, a doctrine over which the Pharisees and Sadducees violently disagreed. Paul knew that by defending this important doctrine, he would divide the council and soon have the members disputing among themselves, which is exactly what happened. So violent was the response that Claudius and his men had to rush down to the floor of the council chamber and rescue their prisoner for the second time!

Was Paul "playing politics" when he took this approach? I don't think so. After his unfortunate clash with the high priest, Paul realized that he could never get a fair trial before the Sanhedrin. If the trial had continued, he might well have been condemned and taken out and stoned as a blasphemer. The Asian Jews, if given opportunity to testify, could well have added fuel to the fire with their false witness. No, the wisest thing to do was to end the hearing as soon as possible and trust God to use the Roman legions to protect him from the Jews.

There is a second consideration: Paul was absolutely right when he said that the real issue was the doctrine of the Resurrection, not "the resurrection" in general, but the resurrection of Jesus Christ (see Acts 24:21; 26:6-8; 28:20). Had he been given the opportunity, Paul would have declared the Gospel of "Jesus Christ and the Resurrection" just as he had declared it before Jewish congregations in many parts of the Empire. The witness in Acts centers on the Resurrection (see Acts 1:22; 2:32; 3:15).

Jesus had stood trial before the Sanhedrin, and so had His Apostles; and now Paul had witnessed to them. What great opportunities the council had and yet they would not believe!

Paul and the Lord Jesus (Acts 23:11)

A few years after Paul's conversion, when Paul's life was in danger in Jerusalem, Jesus appeared to him in the temple and told him what to do (Acts 22:17-21). When Paul was discouraged in Corinth and contemplated going elsewhere, Jesus appeared to him and encouraged him to stay (Acts 18:9-10). Now, when Paul was certainly at "low ebb" in his ministry, Jesus appeared once again to encourage and instruct him. Paul would later receive encouragement during the storm (Acts 27:22-25) and during his trial in Rome (2 Tim. 4:16-17). "Lo, I am with you always" is a great assurance for every situation (Matt. 28:20).

The Lord's message to Paul was one of *courage*. "Be of good cheer!" simply means "Take courage!" Jesus often spoke these words during His earthly ministry. He spoke them to the palsied man (Matt. 9:2) and to the woman who suffered with the hemorrhage (Matt. 9:22). He shouted them to the disciples in the storm (Matt. 14:27), and repeated them in the Upper Room (John 16:33). As God's people, we can always take courage in times of difficulty because the Lord is with us and will see us through.

It was also a message of *commendation*. The Lord did not rebuke Paul for going to Jerusalem. Rather, He commended him for the witness he had given, even though that witness had not been received. When you read the account of Paul's days in Jerusalem, you get the impression that everything Paul did failed miserably. His attempt to win over the legalistic Jews only helped cause a riot in the temple, and his witness before the Sanhedrin left the council in confusion. But the Lord was pleased with Paul's testimony, and that's what really counts.

Finally, it was a message of *confidence*: Paul would go to Rome! This had been Paul's desire for months (Acts 19:21; Rom. 15:22-29), but events in Jerusalem had made it look as though that desire would not be fulfilled. What encouragement this promise gave to Paul in the weeks that followed, difficult weeks when leaders lied about him, when fanatics tried to kill him, and when government officials ignored him. In all of this, the Lord was with him and fulfilling His perfect plan to get His faithful servant to Rome.

Paul and the Jewish Conspirators (Acts 23:12-35)

Paul's life had been in danger from the very beginning of his ministry, when he witnessed for Christ in Damascus (Acts 9:22-25). During his first visit to Jerusalem after his conversion, the Hellenistic Jews tried to kill him (Acts 9:29). The Jews drove him out of Antioch in Pisidia (Acts 13:50-51) and threatened to stone him in Iconium (Acts 14:5). Paul was stoned in Lystra (Acts 14:19-20); and in Corinth, the Jews tried to get him arrested (Acts 18:12-17). In Ephesus, the Jews had a plot to kill him (Acts 20:19), and they even planned to kill him at sea (Acts 20:3). Paul's words in 1 Thessalonians 2:14-16 take on special meaning when you consider all that Paul suffered at the hands of his own countrymen.

Perhaps it was the Asian Jews who conspired to kill Paul (Acts 21:27-29). Certain of the chief priests and elders agreed to cooperate with them and try to influence Claudius. It was a natural thing for the council to want further information from Paul, and it would have been an easy thing to ambush Paul's party and kill the apostle. If this got the captain in trouble with his superiors, the high priest could protect him. The Romans and the Jews had cooperated this way before (Matt. 28:11-15).

But the forty fasting men and the scheming religious leaders had forgotten that Paul was an apostle of Jesus Christ, and that the exalted Lord was watching from heaven. At Paul's conversion, the Lord had told him that he would suffer, but He had also promised that He would deliver him from his enemies (Acts 9:15-16; 26:16-17). Paul held on to that promise all of his life, and God was faithful.

We know nothing about Paul's sister and nephew except what is recorded here. Philippians 3:8 suggests that Paul lost his family when he became a Christian, but we do not know if any of his relatives were converted later. (The word "kinsman" in Rom. 16:7 and 11 means "fellow Jew," as in Rom. 9:3.) Since Paul's family had long been connected with the Pharisees (Acts 23:6), his sister was no doubt in touch with the "powers that be" and able to pick up the news that was passed along. Wives do chat with each other, and a secret is something you tell one person at a time!

It is not likely that either the sister or the nephew were believers, for that certainly would have shut them out of the official religious circle in Jerusalem. But they were devout Jews and knew that the plot was evil (Ex. 23:2). It was in the providence of God that they were able to hear the news and convey it privately to Claudius. St. Augustine said, "Trust the past to the mercy of God, the present to His love, and the future to His providence."

We certainly must admire the integrity and courage of Claudius Lysias, the captain. How did he know the boy was even telling the truth? Paul had already caused Claudius so much trouble that it might be a relief to get rid of him! The Jews did not know that Claudius was aware of their plot, so he could have used his "inside knowledge" for his own profit. No Roman soldier could afford to lose a prisoner, but there were always ways to work things out.

Throughout the Book of Acts, Dr. Luke speaks favorably of the Roman military officers, beginning with Cornelius in Acts 10 and ending with Julius (Acts 27:1, 3, 43). There is no record in Acts of *official* Roman persecution against the church; the opposition was instigated by the unbelieving Jews. While the Empire had its share of corrupt political opportunists, for the most part, the military leaders were men of quality who respected the Roman law.

Claudius' plan was simple and wise. He knew that he had to get Paul out of Jerusalem or there would be one murderous plot after another, and one of them just might succeed. He also knew that he had better determine the charges against Paul or he might be accused of illegally holding a Roman citizen. He could solve both problems by sending Paul to Caesarea and putting him under the authority of Felix, the Roman governor.

If Paul had been a private citizen, attempting to travel from Jerusalem to Caesarea (about sixty-five miles), he would have been an easy target for the conspirators. But God arranged for 470 Roman soldiers to protect him, almost half of the men in the temple garrison! Once again in his career, Paul was smuggled out of a city under cover of night (Acts 9:25; 17:10).

The captain's official letter is most interesting. Of course, Claudius put himself and his men in the best light, which is to be expected. While it is true they prevented Paul from being killed, it was not because they knew he was a Roman. Claudius thought Paul was an Egyptian and almost had him scourged!

Acts 23:29 is another of Luke's "official

statements" from Roman officials, proving that Christians were not considered criminals. The officials in Philippi had almost apologized to Paul (Acts 16:35-40), and Gallio in Corinth had refused to try him (Acts 18:14-15). In Ephesus, the town clerk told 25,000 people that the Christians were innocent of any crime (Acts 19:40), and now the Roman captain from the temple fortress was writing the same thing. Later, Festus (Acts 25:24-25) and Herod Agrippa (Acts 26:31-32) would also affirm that Paul should have been set free. Even the Jewish leaders in Rome had to confess that they had had no official news against Paul (Acts 28:21).

Leaving at 9 o'clock that night, Paul and his escort went from Jerusalem to Antiparis, about thirty-seven miles away. This must have been an all-night forced march for that many people to cover that much ground in that short a time. The cavalry then continued with Paul while the 200 soldiers returned to the barracks, since the dangerous part of the trip was now over. They traveled another twenty-seven miles to Caesarea where Paul was officially turned over to Felix. Paul was safe from the Jewish plotters, but was he safe from Felix?

Antonius Felix was governor (procurator) of Judea. He was married to Drusilla, a Jewess who was daughter of Herod Agrippa I (Acts 12:1) and who left her husband to become Felix's third wife. She was sister of Herod Agrippa II (Acts 25:13ff). The Roman historian Tacitus said that Felix "exercised the power of a king in the spirit of a slave." Felix was called "a vulgar ruffian" and lived up to the name.

Not only was Paul protected by an escort fit for a king, but he was put, not in the common prison, but in the palace built by Herod the Great, where the governor had his official headquarters. We wonder if any of the believers in Caesarea knew about Paul's presence and sought to bring him personal aid and encouragement. They would certainly remember the visit of Agabus and realize that his dire prophecy had been fulfilled (Acts 21:10-14).

As you review the events recorded in this chapter, you cannot help but be impressed with the commitment of the Apostle Paul to his calling. "None of these things move me!" (Acts 20:24) If ever a man dared to follow Christ, come what may, he was that man. Paul did not look for the easy way but for the way that would most honor the Lord and win the lost. He was even willing to become a prisoner if that would further the work of the Gospel.

You are also impressed with the amazing providence of God in caring for His servant. "The angel of the Lord encamps all around those who fear Him, and delivers them" (Ps. 34:7, NKJV). "Let us trust in God, and be very courageous for the Gospel," wrote Charles Spurgeon, "and the Lord Himself will screen us from all harm."

God's people can afford to be daring, in the will of God, because they know their Saviour will be dependable and work out His perfect will. Paul was alone—but not alone! His Lord was with him and he had nothing to fear.

CHAPTER TWENTY-TWO
PAUL THE WITNESS
Acts 24

"Law was the most characteristic and lasting expression of the Roman spirit," wrote historian Will Durant in *Caesar and Christ.* "The first person in Roman law was the citizen." In other words, it was the responsibility of the court to protect the citizen from the State; but too often various kinds of corruption infected the system and made justice difficult for the common man. Paul would soon discover how corrupt a Roman governor could be.

"The secret of Roman government was the principle of indirect rule," wrote Arnold Toynbee. This meant that the real burden of administration was left pretty much on the shoulders of the local authorities. Imperial Rome got involved only if there was danger from without or if the local governing units were at odds with one another.

In this chapter we see the Roman legal system at work and three men each making his contribution.

Tertullus: False Accusations (Acts 24:1-9)

In the Bible record, when people go *to* Jerusalem, they always go up; but when they go *from* Jerusalem, they always go down. This explains why the official Jewish party "descended" when they came to Caesarea. With Ananias the high priest were some of the Jewish elders as well as a lawyer to present the case and defend their charges. Roman law was as complex as our modern law, and it took an expert to understand it and know how to apply it successfully to his client's case.

Tertullus began with the customary *flattery*, a normal part of the judicial routine. After all, before you can win your case, you must win over your judge. Tacitus, the Roman orator and politician, called flatterers "those worst of enemies"; and Solomon wrote that "a flattering mouth works ruin" (Prov. 26:28, NKJV).

The lawyer complimented Felix because the governor's many reforms had brought quietness to the land. (Question: Why did it require nearly 500 soldiers to protect one man in transit from Jerusalem to Caesarea?) It was true that Felix had put down some revolts, but he had certainly not brought peace to the land. In fact, during the time Felix was suppressing robbers in his realm, he was also hiring robbers to murder the high priest Jonathan! So much for his reforms.

But the prosecutor's accusations against Paul were no more truthful than his flattery. He brought three charges: a personal charge ("he is a pestilent fellow"), a political charge (sedition and leading an illegal religion), and a doctrinal charge (profaning the temple).

As for Paul being "a pest," it all depends on one's point of view. The Jews wanted to maintain their ancient traditions, and Paul was advocating something new. The Romans were afraid of anything that upset their delicate "peace" in the Empire, and Paul's record of causing trouble was long and consistent. As Vance Havner used to say, "Wherever Paul went, there was either a riot or a revival!"

This personal charge was based on the Jews' conflicts with Paul in different parts of the Roman world. I have already pointed out that it was his own countrymen, not the Roman authorities, who caused Paul trouble from city to city. The Jews from Asia (Acts 21:27) would certainly have stories to tell about Lystra, Corinth, and Ephesus! This first accusation reminds us of the charges brought against the Lord Jesus at His trial (Luke 23:1-2, 5).

The political charge was much more serious, because no Roman official wanted to be guilty of permitting illegal activities that would upset the "Pax Romana" (Roman Peace). Rome had given the Jews freedom to practice their religion, but the Roman officials kept their eyes on them lest they use their privileges to weaken the Empire. When Tertullus called Paul "an instigator of insurrections among all the Jews throughout the Roman Empire" (WUEST), he immediately got the attention of the governor. Of course, his statement was an exaggeration, but how many court cases have been won by somebody stretching the truth?

Tertullus knew that there was some basis for this charge because Paul had preached to the Jews that Jesus Christ was their King and Lord. To the Romans and the unbelieving Jews, this message sounded like treason against Caesar (Acts 16:20-21; 17:5-9). Furthermore, it was illegal to establish a new religion in Rome without the approval of the authorities. If Paul indeed was a "ringleader of the sect of the Nazarenes," then his enemies could easily build a case against him.

At that time, the Christian faith was still identified with the Jews, and they were permitted by the Romans to practice their religion. There had been Gentile seekers and God-fearers in the synagogues, so the presence of Gentiles in the churches did not create legal problems. Later, when the number of Gentile believers increased and more of the congregations separated from the Jewish synagogues, then Rome saw the difference between Jews and Christians and trouble began. Rome did not want a rival religion thriving in the Empire and creating problems.

Tertullus' third accusation had to be handled with care because it implicated a Roman officer who had saved a man's life. For the most part, Roman officials like Felix did not want anything to do with cases involving Jewish Law (John 18:28-31; Acts 16:35-40; 18:12-17). The fewer Jews who ended up in Roman courts, the better it would be for the Empire. Tertullus had to present this third charge in a way that made the Jews look good without making the Romans look too bad, and he did a good job.

To begin with, he softened the charge. The accusation given by the Asian Jews was that Paul had polluted the temple (Acts 21:28), but Tertullus said, "He even tried to profane the temple" (Acts 24:6, NKJV). Why the change? For at least two good reasons. To begin with, Paul's accusers realized that the original charge could never be substantiated if the facts were investigated. But even more, the Asian Jews who started the story seemed to have vanished from the scene! If there were no witnesses, there could be no evidence or conviction.

When you compare Luke's account of Paul's arrest (Acts 21:27-40) with the captain's account (Acts 23:25-30) and the lawyer's account (Acts 24:6-8), you can well understand why judges and juries can get confused. Tertullus gave the impression that Paul had actually been guilty of profaning the temple, that the Jews had been within their rights in seizing him, and that the captain had stepped out of line by interfering. It was Claudius, not the Jews, who was guilty of treating a Roman citizen with violence! But Felix had the official letter before him and was more likely to believe his captain than a paid Hellenistic Jewish lawyer.

Tertullus knew that the Jews had authority from Rome to arrest and prosecute those who violated Jewish Law. True, the Romans thought that the Jews' devotion to their traditions was excessive and superstitious; yet Rome wisely let them have their way. The Jews were even permitted to execute guilty offenders in capital cases, such as Paul's "offense" of permitting Gentiles to cross the protective barricade in the temple (Acts 21:28-29). Tertullus argued that if Claudius had not interfered, the Jews would have tried Paul themselves, and this would have saved Felix and Rome a great deal of trouble and expense.

In closing his argument, Tertullus hinted that Claudius Lysias should have been there personally and had not just sent the Jewish leaders to present the case. Why was he absent? Could he not defend his case? Was he trying to "pass the buck" to others? As far as we know, during the two years Paul was detained in Caesarea, Claudius never did show up to tell his side of the story. We wonder why.

But Paul was there and Felix could get the truth out of him! "If you examine Paul," the clever lawyer said, "you will find that what I am saying is true." The other members of the Jewish delegation united in agreeing with their lawyer, which was no surprise to anybody.

Paul: Faithful Answers (Acts 24:10-21)

But the governor did not examine Paul. He merely nodded his head as a signal that it was now Paul's turn to speak. Paul did not flatter Felix (see 1 Thes. 2:1-6); he merely acknowledged that the governor was a man of experience and therefore a man of knowledge. After this brief but honest introduction, Paul then proceeded to answer the charges of Tertullus (Acts 24:10-16), the Asian Jews (Acts 24:17-19) and the Jewish council (Acts 24:20-21).

As far as the temple charge was concerned, Paul was in the temple to worship and not to lead a disturbance. In fact, the temple records would show that Paul was registered to pay the costs for four Jews who had taken a Nazarite vow. Paul had not preached in the temple or the synagogues, nor had he preached anywhere in the city. (Years before, Paul had made an agreement with Peter and the Jerusalem elders that he would not evangelize the Jews in Jerusalem. See Gal. 2:7-10.) Nobody could prove that he was guilty of leading any kind of rebellion against the Jews or the Romans.

Furthermore, since he had been in Jerusalem only a week (the twelve days of Acts 24:11, minus the five days of Acts 24:1), there had hardly been time to organize and lead an assault on the temple! While students of Paul's life do not agree on every detail, the order of events was probably something like this:

Day 1 —Paul arrived in Jerusalem (21:17)
Day 2 —Met with James and the elders (21:18)
Day 3 —In the temple with the Nazarites (21:26)
Day 4 —In the temple
Day 5 —In the temple
Day 6 —Arrested in the temple (21:27)
Day 7 —Met with the Jewish council (23:1-10)
Day 8 —Threatened; taken to Caesarea (23:12, 23)
Day 9 —Arrived in Caesarea (23:33)
Day 10—Waited (Felix sent for the Jewish leaders)
Day 11—Waited for the Jewish leaders to arrive
Day 12—Waited—they arrived—hearing scheduled
Day 13—The hearing conducted

The four men who had taken the Nazarite vow were evidently already involved in their temple duties when James suggested that Paul pay their costs (Acts 21:24). If they had started the day before Paul arrived in Jerusalem, then the day of Paul's arrest would have been the seventh day of their obligations (Acts 21:27). The *New American Standard Bible* translates Acts 21:27, "And when the seven days were almost over." This implies that the events occurred on the seventh day of their schedule, Paul's sixth day in the city.

It would probably take two days for the official Roman messenger to get from Caesarea to Jerusalem, and another two days for Ananias and his associates to make it to Caesarea. They were not likely to linger; the case was too important.

Having disposed of the temple charges, Paul then dealt with the charges of sedition and heresy. Even though the high priest was a Sadducee, there were certainly Pharisees in the official Jewish delegation, so Paul appealed once again to their religious roots in the Scriptures. The fact that Paul was a Christian did not mean that he worshiped a different God from the God of his fathers. It only meant he worshiped the God of his fathers in a new and living way, for the only acceptable way to worship the Father is through Jesus Christ (John 5:23). His faith was still founded on the Old Testament Scriptures, and they bore witness to Jesus Christ.

The Sadducees accepted the five Books of Moses (the Law), but not the rest of the Old Testament. They rejected the doctrine of the Resurrection because they said it could not be found anywhere in what Moses wrote. (Jesus had refuted that argument, but they chose to ignore it. See Matt. 22:23-33.) By declaring his personal faith in the Resurrection, Paul affirmed his orthodox convictions and identified himself with the Pharisees. Once again, the Pharisees were caught on the horns of a dilemma, for if Paul's faith was that of a heretic, then they were heretics too!

Paul and the early Christians did not see themselves as "former Jews" but as "fulfilled Jews." The Old Testament was a new book to them because they had found their Messiah. They knew that they no longer needed the rituals of the Jewish Law in order to please God, but they saw in these ceremonies and ordinances a revelation of the Saviour. Both as a Pharisee and a Christian, Paul had "taken pains" always to have a good conscience and to seek to please the Lord.

Having replied to the false charges of Tertullus, Paul then proceeded to answer the false accusation of the Asian Jews that he had profaned the temple (Acts 24:17-19). He had not come to Jerusalem to defile the temple but to bring needed help to the Jewish people and to present his own offerings to the Lord. (This is the only mention in Acts of the special offering.) When the Asians saw him in the temple, he was with four men who were fulfilling their Nazarite vows. How could Paul possibly be *worshiping* God and *profaning* God's house at the same time? A Jewish priest was in charge of Paul's temple activities; so, if the holy temple was defiled, the priest was responsible. Paul was only obeying the Law.

Now Paul reached the heart of his defense, for it was required by Roman law that the accusers face the accused at the trial, or else the charges would be dropped. Ananias had wisely not brought any of the Hellenistic Jews with him, for he was sure that their witness would fall down under official examination. These men were good at inciting riots; they were not good at producing facts.

Paul closed his defense by replying to the members of the Jewish council (Acts 24:20-21). Instead of giving him a fair hearing, the high priest and the Sanhedrin had abused him and refused to hear him out. Ananias was no doubt grateful that Paul said nothing about his slap in the face, for it was not legal for a Roman citizen to be treated that way.

Do we detect a bit of holy sarcasm in Paul's closing statement? We might paraphrase it, "If I have done anything evil, it is probably this: I reminded the Jewish council of our great Jewish doctrine of the Resurrection." Remember, the Book of Acts is a record of the early church's witness to the resurrection of Jesus Christ (Acts 1:22). The Sadducees had long abandoned the doctrine, and the Pharisees did not give it the practical importance it deserved. Of course, Paul would have related this doctrine to the resurrection of Jesus Christ, and the Sanhedrin did not want that.

They had accused Paul of being anti-Jewish and anti-Roman, but they could not prove their charges. If the Jewish leaders had further pursued any of these charges, their case would have collapsed. But there was enough circumstantial evidence to plant doubts in the minds of the Roman officials, and perhaps there was enough race prejudice in them to water that seed and encourage it to grow. After all, had not the Emperor Claudius expelled the Jews from Rome? (Acts 18:2) Perhaps Paul would bear watching.

Felix: Foolish Attitudes (Acts 24:22-27)

If ever a man failed both personally and officially, that man was Felix, procurator of Judea. He certainly could not plead ignorance of the facts, because he was "well acquainted with the Way" (Acts 24:22, NIV). His wife, Drusilla, was a Jewess and perhaps kept him informed of the activities among her people, and as a Roman official, he would carefully (if privately) investigate these things. He saw the light, but he preferred to live in the darkness.

Felix saw to it that Paul was comfortably cared for while at the same time safely guarded. "Liberty" in Acts 24:23 means that he was not put in the common jail or kept in close confinement. He had limited freedom in the palace, chained to a soldier. (The guards were changed every six hours, a perfect captive congregation!) Paul's friends were permitted to minister to him (Greek: "wait on him as personal servants"), so people could come and go to meet his needs. What Paul's ministry was during those two years in Caesarea, we do not know, but we can be sure he gave a faithful witness for the Lord.

The record of one such witness is given by Luke, and it makes Felix's guilt even greater. Not only was Felix's mind informed, but his heart was moved by fear, and yet he would not obey the truth. It is not enough for a person to know the facts about Christ, or to have an emotional response to a message. He or she must willingly repent of sin and trust the Saviour. "But you are not willing to come to Me that you may have life" (John 5:40, NKJV).

It must have been the curiosity of his wife, Drusilla, that prompted Felix to give Paul another hearing. She wanted to hear Paul; for, after all, her family had been involved with "the Way" on several occasions. Her great-grandfather tried to kill Jesus in Bethlehem (Matt. 2); her great-uncle killed John the Baptist and mocked Jesus (Luke 23:6-12); and Acts 12:1-2 tells of her father killing the Apostle James.

Dr. Luke has given us only the three points of Paul's sermon to this infamous couple: righteousness, self-control, and the judgment to come. But what an outline! Paul gave them three compelling reasons why they should repent and believe on Jesus Christ.

First, they had to do something about *yesterday's sin* ("righteousness"). In 1973, Dr. Karl Menninger, one of the world's leading psychiatrists, published a startling book, *Whatever Became of Sin?* He pointed out that the very word *sin* has gradually dropped out of our vocabulary, "the word, along with the notion." We talk about mistakes, weaknesses, inherited tendencies, faults, and even errors; but we do not face up to the fact of sin.

"People are no longer sinful," said Phyllis McGinley, noted American writer and poet. "They are only immature or underprivileged or frightened or, more particularly, sick." But a holy God demands righteousness; that's the bad news. Yet the good news is that this same holy God *provides* His own righteousness to those who trust Jesus Christ (Rom. 3:21-26). We can never be saved by our own righteousness of good works. We can be saved only through Christ's righteousness made available by His finished work of salvation on the cross.

The second point in Paul's sermon dealt with self-control: we must do something about *today's temptations*. Man can control almost everything but himself. Here were Felix and Drusilla, prime illustrations of lack of self-control. She divorced her husband to become Felix's third wife, and though a Jewess, she lived as though God had never given the Ten Commandments at Sinai. Felix was an unscrupulous official who did not hesitate to lie, or even to murder, in order to get rid of his enemies and promote himself. Self-control was something neither of them knew much about.

Paul's third point was the clincher: "judgment to come." *We must do something about tomorrow's judgment.* Perhaps Paul told Felix and Drusilla what he told the Greek philosophers: God has "appointed a day, in which He will judge the world in righteousness" by the Lord Jesus Christ (Acts 17:31). Jesus Christ is either your Saviour or your Judge. How do we know that Jesus Christ is the Judge? "He has given assurance of this to all by raising Him from the dead" (Acts 17:31, NKJV). Once again, the Resurrection!

"Felix trembled" (Acts 24:25), which literally means, "Felix became terrified." Roman leaders prided themselves in their ability to be stoical and restrain their emotions under all circumstances, but a conviction from God gripped Felix's heart, and he could not hide it. Paul had diagnosed the case and offered the remedy. It was up to Felix to receive it.

What did Felix do? *He procrastinated!* "When I have a convenient time, I will call for you," he told the apostle. "Procrastination is the thief of time," wrote Edward Young. Perhaps he was thinking about the English proverb, "One of these days is none of these days." Procrastination is also the thief of souls. The most "convenient season" for a lost sinner to be saved is *right now.* "Behold, now is the accepted time; behold, now is the day of salvation" (2 Cor. 6:2).

"I think there's a special time for each person to be saved," a man argued to whom I was witnessing. "I can't get saved until that time comes."

"What are the signals that your special time has come?" I asked.

"Well," he drawled, "I don't rightly know."

"Then how will you know when you are supposed to be saved?" I asked. But the stupidity of his position never bothered him. I do hope he was saved before he died.

Consider Felix's foolish attitudes. He had a foolish attitude toward God's Word, thinking that he could "take it or leave it." But God "now *commands* all men everywhere to repent" (Acts 17:30, NKJV, italics mine). When God speaks, men and women had better listen and obey.

Felix had a foolish attitude toward his sins. He knew he was a sinner, yet he refused to break with his sins and obey the Lord. He had a foolish attitude toward God's grace. The Lord had been long-suffering toward Felix, yet the governor would not surrender. Felix was not sure of another day's life, yet he foolishly procrastinated. "Do not boast about tomorrow, for you do not know what a day may bring forth" (Prov. 27:1, NIV).

Instead of listening to Paul, Felix tried to "use" Paul as a political pawn, either to get money from the church or to gain favor with the Jews. The fact that Felix had further discussions with Paul is no indication that his heart was interested in spiritual things. Paul's friends were coming and going, and perhaps some of them had access to the large offering sent by the Gentile churches. Certainly Paul gave further witness to the governor, but to no avail. When Felix was replaced, he left Paul a prisoner, but it was Felix who was really the prisoner.

The governor's mind was enlightened (Acts 24:22), his emotions were stirred (Acts 24:25), but his will would not yield. He tried to gain the world, but, as far as we know, he lost his soul. He procrastinated himself into hell.

Dr. Clarence Macartney told a story about a meeting in hell. Satan called his four leading demons together and commanded them to think up a new lie that would trap more souls.

"I have it!" one demon said. "I'll go to earth and tell people there is no God."

"It will never work," said Satan. "People can look around them and see that there is a God."

"I'll go and tell them there is no heaven!" suggested a second demon, but Satan rejected that idea. "Everybody knows there is life after death and they want to go to heaven."

"Let's tell them there is no hell!" said a third demon.

"No, conscience tells them their sins will be judged," said the devil. "We need a better lie than that."

Quietly, the fourth demon spoke. "I think I've solved your problem," he said. "I'll go to earth and tell everybody *there is no hurry.*"

The best time to trust Jesus Christ is—*now!*

And the best time to tell others the Good News of the Gospel is—*now!*

CHAPTER TWENTY-THREE
PAUL THE DEFENDER
Acts 25–26

The new governor, Porcius Festus, was a better man than his predecessor and took up his duties with the intention of doing what was right. However, he soon discovered that Jewish politics was not easy to handle, especially the two-year-old case of the Apostle Paul, a prisoner with no official charges against him. Paul was a Jew whose countrymen wanted to kill him, and he was a Roman whose government did not know what to do with him.

What a dilemma! If Festus released Paul, the Jews would cause trouble, and that was something the new governor dared not risk. However, if he held Paul prisoner, Festus would have to explain why a Roman citizen was being held without definite official charges. Festus knew that it was smart for him to act quickly and take advantage of the fact that he was a newcomer on the scene. To delay would only make the problem worse, and it was bad enough already.

These two chapters present Festus in three

different situations, each of which related to the Apostle Paul.

Conciliation: Festus and the Jewish Leaders (Acts 25:1-12)

Knowing how important it was for him to get along well with the Jewish leaders, Festus lost no time in visiting the holy city and paying his respects; and the leaders lost no time in bringing up Paul's case. The new high priest was Ishmael; he had replaced Jonathan who had been killed by Felix. Ishmael wanted to resurrect the plot of two years before and remove Paul once and for all (Acts 23:12-15).

It is not likely that the new governor knew anything about the original plot or even suspected that the Jewish religious leaders were out for blood. Since a Roman court could meet in Jerusalem as well as in Caesarea, transferring Paul would be a normal procedure. Festus would probably not demand that a large retinue go with him, so an ambush would be easy. Finally, since it was a matter involving a Jewish prisoner and the Jewish law, the logical place to meet would be Jerusalem.

"Kill Paul!" had been the cry of the unbelieving Jews ever since Paul had arrived in Jerusalem (Acts 21:27-31; 22:22; 23:10-15; 25:3); however, Festus knew nothing of this. Paul had been warned of this danger, but he had also been assured that the Lord would protect him, use his witness and then take him safely to Rome (Acts 23:11; 26:17). The situation was growing more serious, for now it was the council itself, and not a group of outsiders, that was plotting Paul's death. You would think that their anger would have subsided after two years, but it had not. Satan the murderer was hard at work (John 8:44).

Festus was wise not to cooperate with their scheme, but he did invite the leaders to accompany him to Caesarea and face Paul once again. This would give Festus opportunity to review the case and get more facts. The Jews agreed, but the hearing brought out nothing new. The Jewish delegation (this time without their lawyer) only repeated the same unfounded and unproved accusations, hoping that the governor would agree with them and put Paul to death (Acts 25:15-16).

What did Paul do? He once again affirmed that he was innocent of any crime against the Jewish law, the temple, or the Roman government. Festus saw that no progress was being made, so he asked Paul if he would be willing to be tried in Jerusalem. He did this to please the Jews and probably did not realize that he was jeopardizing the life of his famous prisoner. But a Roman judge could not move a case to another court without the consent of the accused, *and Paul refused to go!* Instead, he claimed the right of every Roman citizen to appeal to Caesar.

What led Paul to make that wise decision? For one thing, he knew that his destination was Rome, not Jerusalem; and the fastest way to get there was to appeal to Caesar. Paul also knew that the Jews had not given up their hopes of killing him, so he was wise to stay under the protection of Rome. By appealing to Caesar, Paul forced the Romans to guard him and take him to Rome. Finally, Paul realized that he could never have a fair trial in Jerusalem anyway, so why go?

It must have infuriated the Jewish leaders when Paul, by one statement, took the case completely out of their hands. He made it clear that he was willing to die *if* he could be proved guilty of a capital crime, but first they had to find him guilty. Festus met with his official council, and they agreed to send Paul to Nero for trial. No doubt the new governor was somewhat embarrassed that he had handled one of his first cases so badly that the prisoner was forced to appeal to Caesar; and to Caesar he must go!

Consultation: Festus and Agrippa (Acts 25:13-22)

But the new governor's problems were not over. He had managed not to offend the Jews, but he had not determined the legal charges against his prisoner. How could he send such a notable prisoner to the emperor and not have the man's crimes listed against him?

About that time, Festus had a state visit from Herod Agrippa II and Herod's sister, Bernice. This youthful king, the last of the Herodians to rule, was the great-grandson of the Herod who killed the Bethlehem babes, and the son of the Herod who killed the Apostle James (Acts 12). The fact that his sister lived with him created a great deal of suspicion on the part of the Jewish people, for their Law clearly condemned incest (Lev. 18:1-18; 20:11-21). Rome had given Herod Agrippa II legal jurisdiction over the temple in Jerusalem, so it was logical that Festus share Paul's case with him.

Festus was smart enough to understand that the Jewish case against Paul had nothing to do with civil law. It was purely a matter of "religious questions" (Acts 18:14-15; 23:29) which the Romans were unprepared to handle, especially the doctrine of the Resurrection. Acts 25:19 proves that Paul was defending much more than the resurrection in general. He was declaring and defending the resurrection of Jesus Christ. As we have noted in our studies, this is the key emphasis of the witness of the church in the Book of Acts.

Festus gave the impression that he wanted to move the trial to Jerusalem because the "Jewish questions" could be settled only by Jewish people in Jewish territory (Acts 25:20). It was a pure fabrication, of course, because his real reason was to please the Jewish leaders, most of whom King Herod knew. Festus needed something definite to send to the Emperor Nero, and perhaps Agrippa could supply it. ("Augustus" in Acts 25:21, 25 is a title, "the august one," and not a proper name.)

The king was an expert in Jewish matters (Acts 26:2-3) and certainly would be keenly interested in knowing more about this man who caused a riot in the temple. Perhaps Herod could assist Festus in finding out the real charges against Paul, and perhaps Festus could assist Herod in learning more about Jewish affairs in the holy city.

Confrontation: Festus, Agrippa, and Paul (Acts 25:23–26:32)

It seems incredible that all of this pomp and ceremony was because of one little Jewish man who preached the Gospel of Jesus Christ! But the Lord had promised Paul he would bear witness before "Gentiles and kings" (Acts 9:15), and that promise was being fulfilled again. Once Paul was finished with his witness, all his hearers would know how to be saved and would be without excuse.

They met in an "audience room" in the palace, and the key military men and officers of the Roman government were there. Paul's case had probably been discussed by various official people many times over the past two years, so very few of those present were ignorant of the affair.

Festus was certainly exaggerating when he said that "all the multitude of the Jews" had pressed charges against Paul, but that kind of statement would make the Jews present feel much better. Acts 25:25 gives us the second of Luke's "official statements" declaring Paul's innocence (see Acts 23:29); and there will be others before his book is completed.

In his flowery speech before Agrippa, Festus indicated that he wanted the king to examine Paul (Acts 25:26), but there is no record that he did. In fact, before the session ended, Paul became the judge, and Festus, King Agrippa, and Bernice became the defendants! Paul was indeed defending himself (Acts 26:24, NKJV), but at the same time, he was presenting the truth of the Gospel and witnessing to the difference Jesus Christ can make in a person's life. This is the longest of Paul's speeches found in Acts.

King Agrippa was in charge and told Paul that he was free to speak. In his brief introduction, Paul sincerely gave thanks that Agrippa was hearing his case, because he knew the king was an expert in Jewish religious matters. Paul did not mention it then, but he also knew that the king believed the Old Testament prophets (Acts 26:27). Paul also hinted that his speech might be a long one and that he would appreciate the king's patience in hearing him out.

Five key statements summarize Paul's defense.

"I lived a Pharisee" (vv. 4-11). Paul's early life in Jerusalem was known to the Jews, so there was no need to go into great detail. He was a devout Pharisee (Phil. 3:5) and the son of a Pharisee (Acts 23:6), and his peers had likely realized he would accomplish great things as a rabbi (Gal. 1:13-14, NIV). It was because of his convictions about the Resurrection and "the hope of Israel" that he was now a prisoner (see Acts 23:6; 24:15). Once again, Paul appealed to Jewish orthodoxy and loyalty to the Hebrew tradition.

It is worth noting that Paul mentioned "our twelve tribes" (Acts 26:7). While it is true that the ten northern tribes (Israel) were conquered by Assyria in 722 B.C. and assimilated to some extent, it is not true that these ten tribes were "lost" or annihilated. Jesus spoke about all twelve tribes (Matt. 19:28), and so did James (James 1:1) and the Apostle John (Rev. 7:4-8; 21:12). God knows where His chosen people are, and He will fulfill the promises He has made to them.

The pronoun *you* in Acts 26:8 is plural, so Paul must have looked around at the entire audience as he spoke. The Greeks and Romans, of course, would not believe in the doctrine of the Resurrection (Acts 17:31-32), nor would the Sadducees who were present (Acts 23:8). To Paul, this was a crucial doctrine, for if there is no Resurrection, then Jesus Christ was not raised and Paul had no Gospel to preach. (For Paul's argument about the Resurrection and the Gospel, see 1 Cor. 15).

Paul was not only a Pharisee, but he had also been a zealous persecutor of the church. He had punished the believers and tried to force them to deny Jesus Christ, and some of them he had helped send to their death. The phrase "gave my voice" (Acts 26:10) literally means "registered my vote." This suggests that Paul had been an official member of the Sanhedrin, but surely if that were true, seemingly he would have mentioned it in one of his speeches. The phrase probably means nothing more than he "voted against them" as a special representative of the high priest (Acts 9:2, 14).

In the early days of the church, the Jewish believers continued to meet in the synagogues, and that was where Paul found them and punished them (Matt. 10:17; 23:34). What Paul in his early years looked on as "religious zeal" (Gal. 1:13-14), in his later years he considered to be "madness" (Acts 26:11). Like a wild animal, he had "made havoc of the church" (Acts 8:3), "breathing out threatenings and slaughter" (Acts 9:1).

"I saw a light" (vv. 12-13). Not content to limit his work to Jerusalem, Paul had asked for authority to visit the synagogues in distant cities. His zeal had driven out many of the believers and they had taken their message to Jews in other communities (Acts 8:4).

Paul considered himself an enlightened man; for, after all, he was a Jew (Rom. 9:4-5), a scholar (Acts 22:3), and a Pharisee. In reality, Paul had lived in gross spiritual darkness. He knew the Law in his preconversion days, but he had not realized that the purpose of the Law was to bring him to Christ (Gal. 3:24). He had been a self-righteous Pharisee who needed to discover that his good works and respectable character could never save him and take him to heaven (Phil. 3:1-11).

The light that Paul saw was supernatural, for it was the glory of God revealed from heaven (compare Acts 7:2, 55-56). It actually had blinded Paul for three days (Acts 9:8-9), but his spiritual eyes had been opened to behold the living Christ (2 Cor. 4:3-6). But seeing a light was not enough; he also had to hear the Word of God.

"I heard a voice" (vv. 14-18). Paul's companions had seen the light, but not the Lord; and they had heard a sound, but they could not understand the words. They all fell to the earth, but only Paul remained there (Acts 9:7). Jesus Christ spoke to Paul in the familiar Aramaic tongue of the Jews, called him by name, and told him it was futile for him to continue fighting the Lord. In that moment, Paul had made two surprising discoveries: Jesus of Nazareth was alive, and He was so united to His people that their suffering was His suffering! Paul was persecuting not only the church, but also his own Messiah!

How encouraging it is to know that God in His grace speaks to those who are His enemies. God had been dealing with Paul, but Paul had been resisting Him, kicking against the "goads." What were these "goads"? Certainly the testimony and death of Stephen (Acts 22:20), plus the faithful witness of the other saints who had suffered because of Paul. Perhaps Paul had also struggled with the emptiness and weakness of Judaism and his own inability to meet the demands of the Law. Even though he could now say he was "blameless" in conduct and conscience (Acts 23:1; Phil. 3:6), yet within his own heart, he certainly knew how far short he came of meeting God's holy standards (Rom. 7:7-16).

The word *minister* in Acts 26:16 means "an under-rower" and refers to a lowly servant on a galley ship. Paul had been accustomed to being an honored leader, but after his conversion he became a subordinate worker; and Jesus Christ became his Master. The Lord had promised to be with Paul and protect him; and He also promised to reveal Himself to him. Paul saw the Lord on the Damascus road, and again three years later while in the temple (Acts 22:17-21). Later, the Lord appeared to him in Corinth (Acts 18:9) and in Jerusalem (Acts 23:11), and He would appear to him again.

No doubt it was a surprise to Paul after his conversion to hear that the Lord was sending him to the Gentiles. He had a great love for his own people and would gladly have lived and died to win them to Christ (Rom. 9:1-3), but that was not God's plan. Paul would always be "the apostle to the Gentiles."

Acts 26:18 describes both the spiritual condition of the lost and the gracious provision of Christ for those who will believe. You will find parallels in Isaiah 35:5; 42:6ff; and 61:1. The lost sinner is like a blind prisoner in a dark dungeon, and only Christ can open his eyes and give him light and freedom (2 Cor. 4:3-6). But even after he is set free, what about his court record and his guilt? The Lord forgives his sins and wipes the record clean! He then takes him into His own family as His own child and shares His inheritance with him!

What must the sinner do? He must trust Jesus Christ ("faith that is in Me"—Acts 26:18). Paul had to lose his religion to gain salvation! He discovered in a moment of time that all of his righteousnesses were but filthy rags in God's sight, and that he needed the righteousness of Christ (Isa. 64:6).

"I was not disobedient" (vv. 19-21). When Paul had asked, "Lord, what wilt Thou have me to do?" (Acts 9:6) he meant it sincerely; and when the Lord told him, he obeyed orders immediately. He began right at Damascus and it almost cost him his life (Acts 9:20-25). Likewise, when he had witnessed to the Jews in Jerusalem, they attempted to kill him (Acts 9:29-30). In spite of repeated discouragements and dangers, Paul had remained obedient to the call and the vision that Jesus Christ gave him. Nothing moved him! (Acts 20:24)

In Acts 26:21, Paul clearly explained to Agrippa and Festus what had really happened in the temple and why it had happened. It was "on account of these things" that Paul had been attacked and almost killed: his declaration that Jesus of Nazareth was alive and was Israel's Messiah, his ministry to the Gentiles, and his offer of God's covenant blessings to both Jews and Gentiles *on the same terms of repentance and faith* (see Acts 20:21). The proud nationalistic Israelites would have nothing to do with a Jew who treated Gentiles like Jews!

"I continue unto this day" (vv. 22-32). It is one thing to have a great beginning, with visions and voices, but quite another thing to keep on going, especially when the going is tough. The fact that Paul continued was proof of his conversion and evidence of the faithfulness of God. He was saved by God's grace and enabled to serve by God's grace (1 Cor. 15:10).

The one word that best summarizes Paul's life and ministry is "witnessing" (see Acts 26:16). He simply shared with others what he had learned and experienced as a follower of Jesus Christ. His message was not something he manufactured, for it was based solidly on the Old Testament Scriptures. We must remind ourselves that Paul and the other apostles did not have the New Testament, but used the Old Testament to lead sinners to Christ and to nurture the new believers.

Acts 26:23 is a summary of the Gospel (1 Cor. 15:3-4), and each part can be backed up from the Old Testament. See, for example, Isaiah 52:13–53:12 and Psalm 16:8-11. Paul could even defend his call to the Gentiles from Isaiah 49:6 (see also Acts 13:47). Jesus was not the first person to be raised from the dead, but He was the first one to be raised and never die again. He is "the firstfruits of them that slept" (1 Cor. 15:20).

In his message in the temple, when Paul got to the word *Gentiles*, the crowd exploded (Acts 22:21-22). That is the word Paul spoke when Festus responded and loudly accused Paul of being mad. How strange that Festus did not think Paul was mad when he was persecuting the church! (Acts 26:11) Nobody called D.L. Moody crazy when he was energetically selling shoes and making money, but when he started winning souls, people gave him the nickname "Crazy Moody." This was not the first time Paul had been called "crazy" (2 Cor. 5:13), and he was only following in the footsteps of his Master (Mark 3:20-21; John 10:20).

Paul had been addressing King Agrippa, but the emotional interruption of the governor forced him to reply. He reminded Festus that the facts about the ministry of Jesus Christ, including His death and resurrection, were public knowledge and "not done in a corner." The Jewish Sanhedrin was involved and so was the Roman governor, Pilate. Jesus of Nazareth had been a famous public figure for at least three years, and huge crowds had followed Him. How then could the governor plead ignorance?

Festus had not interrupted because he really thought Paul was mad. Had that been the case, he would have treated Paul gently and ordered some of his guards to escort him to a place of rest and safety. Furthermore, what official would send a raving madman to be tried before the emperor? No, the governor was only giving evidence of conviction in his heart. Paul's words had found their mark, and Festus was trying to escape.

But Paul did not forget King Agrippa, a Jew who was an expert in these matters. When Paul asked if Agrippa believed the prophets, he was forcing him to take a stand. Certainly the king would not repudiate what every Jew believed! But Agrippa knew that if he affirmed his faith in the prophets, he must then face the question, "Is Jesus of Nazareth the one about whom the prophets wrote?"

Festus avoided decision by accusing Paul of

being mad. King Agrippa eluded Paul's question (and the dilemma it presented) by adopting a superior attitude and belittling Paul's witness. His reply in Acts 26:28 can be stated, "Do you think that in such a short time, with such few words, you can persuade *me* to become a Christian?" Perhaps he spoke with a smirk on his face and a sneer in his voice. But he certainly spoke his own death warrant (John 3:18-21, 36).

Paul was polite in his reply. "I would to God, that whether in a short or long time, not only you, but also all who hear me this day, might become such as I am, except for these chains" (Acts 26:29, NASB). Festus and Agrippa knew that their prisoner had a compassionate concern for them, and they could not easily escape his challenge. The best thing to do was to end the hearing, so the king stood up; and this told everybody that the audience was over.

Both Agrippa and Festus declared that Paul was innocent of any crime deserving of death. Luke continues to accumulate these official statements so that his readers will understand that Paul was an innocent man (see Acts 16:35-40; 18:12-17; 23:29; 25:25). In fact, Paul might have been set free, had he not appealed to Caesar. Was he foolish in making his appeal? No, he was not, for it was the appeal to Caesar that finally ended the repeated accusations of the Jewish leaders. They knew they could not successfully fight against Rome.

What Agrippa and Festus did not understand was that *Paul* had been the judge and *they* had been the prisoners on trial. They had been shown the light and the way to freedom, but they had deliberately closed their eyes and returned to their sins. Perhaps they felt relieved that Paul would go to Rome and trouble them no more. The trial was over, but their sentence was still to come; and come it would.

What a wonderful thing is the opportunity to trust Jesus Christ and be saved! What a terrible thing is wasting that opportunity and perhaps never having another.

CHAPTER TWENTY-FOUR PAUL ARRIVES IN ROME

Acts 27–28

I must also see Rome!" Those were Paul's words during his ministry in Ephesus (Acts 19:21), and little did he realize all that would happen to him before he would arrive in the Imperial city: illegal arrest, Roman and Jewish trials, confinement, and even shipwreck. He had long wanted to preach the Gospel in Rome (Rom. 1:14-16) and then go on into Spain (Rom. 15:28), but he had not planned to travel as a prisoner. Through it all, Paul trusted God's promise that he would witness in Rome (Acts 23:11); and the Lord saw him through.

Why would Luke devote such a long section of his book to a description of a voyage and shipwreck? Surely he could have summarized the account for us! But Luke was a skilled writer, inspired by the Spirit of God, and he knew what he was doing. For one thing, this exciting report balances the speeches that we have been reading and brings more drama into the account. Also, Luke was an accurate historian who presented the important facts about his hero and his voyage to Rome.

But perhaps the major purpose Luke had in mind was the presenting of Paul as the courageous leader who could take command of a difficult situation in a time of great crisis. Future generations would love and appreciate Paul all the more for what he did en route to Rome.

Since ancient times, writers have pictured life as a journey or a voyage. *Pilgrim's Progress* by John Bunyan is based on this theme, and so is Homer's *Odyssey*. We sometimes use the "voyage" metaphor in everyday conversation: "Smooth sailing!" or "Don't make shipwreck!" or "Sink or swim!" When a Christian dies, we might say, "She has reached the other shore." Dr. Luke was certainly not writing an allegory, but he did use this exciting event to show how one man's faith can make a big difference for him and others "in the storms of life." What an encouragement to our own faith!

In Paul's journey to Rome, we see the great apostle in four important roles.

Paul the Counselor (Acts 27:1-20)
Luke had not included himself since Acts 21:18, but now he joined Paul and Aristarchus (Acts 19:29; 20:2, 4) for the voyage to Rome. It is possible that Luke was allowed to go as Paul's physician and Aristarchus as Paul's personal attendant. How Paul must have thanked God for his faithful friends who gave up their liberty, and even risked their lives, that he might have the help he needed. There is no evidence that either of these men had been arrested, yet Paul referred to Aristarchus as a "fellow prisoner" (Col. 4:10). This could refer to a voluntary imprisonment on his part in order to assist Paul.

Paul was not the only prisoner that Julius and his men were taking to Rome, for there were "certain other prisoners" with them. The Greek word means "others of a different kind" and may suggest that, unlike Paul, these men were going to Rome to die and not to stand trial. What mercy that they met Paul who could tell them how to go to heaven when they died!

The centurion found a coastal ship leaving Caesarea, so they embarked and covered the eighty miles from Caesarea to Sidon in one day. In Sidon, Paul was permitted to visit his friends and put together the things needed for the long trip. Luke records the kindness of a Roman officer to the Apostle Paul (Acts 24:23), as well as the encouragement of the anonymous believers in Sidon. Their names are in God's book and they shall be rewarded one day (Phil. 4:3).

From Sidon to Myra, the voyage became difficult because of the westerly winds. At Myra, Julius, a Roman officer, found a ship going to Italy; so he abandoned the slower coastal ship and put Paul and the others on board this large grain ship from Egypt that carried 276 passengers (Acts 27:37-38). Rome depended on Egypt for much of its grain supply, and the Roman government gave special consideration to those who ran these ships.

The strong winds again hindered their progress so that "many days" were required to cover the 130 miles from Myra to Cnidus. The pilot then steered south-southwest to Crete, passing Salmone and finally struggling into Fair Havens. It had been a most difficult voyage, a portent of things to come.

The centurion now had to decide whether to winter at Fair Havens or set sail and try to reach the port of Phoenix (Phoenicia, Acts 27:12) on the southern coast of Crete, about forty miles away. His approach to making this decision is a classic illustration of how *not* to determine the will of God.

Paul admonished them to stay in Fair Havens. They had already encountered adverse winds, and it was now the start of the stormy season. "The fast" refers to the Day of Atonement, which fell in September/October; and every sailor knew that sailing was difficult from mid-September to mid-November, and impossible from mid-November to February.

Acts 27:10 sounds so much like a prophecy that we are prone to believe God gave Paul a premonition of danger. Paul had already experienced three shipwrecks (2 Cor. 11:25), so he was certainly speaking from experience. (The Greek word translated "perceive" in Acts 27:10 means "to perceive from past experience.") However, the men in charge gave little value to Paul's warning, an attitude they lived to regret.

What were the factors that governed Julius' decision? To begin with, Fair Havens was not a comfortable place to settle down because it was too open to the winter storms. Phoenix had a more sheltered harbor. Julius also listened to the "expert advice" of the pilot and captain ("master and owner") of the ship. They advised that the ship head for Phoenix as fast as possible. Surely they could cover forty miles safely, and already they had lost too much time (Acts 27:9). When Julius added up the votes, it was three to one that the ship set sail. After all, the majority cannot be wrong, especially when it includes the experts!

But the clinching argument came with an encouraging change in the weather, for the south wind began to blow gently, and that was just what they needed. As the ship left the harbor, perhaps Julius, the pilot, and the captain smiled tolerantly at Paul and his two friends as if to say, "See, you were wrong!"

However, it was not long before Paul was proved right, for the "soft wind" became a stormy wind. The word translated "tempestuous" gives us the English word "typhoon." Sailors called this special wind *Euroclydon,* a hybrid Greek and Latin word that means "a northeasterner." The crew had to let the ship drift because it was impossible to steer it, and the wind drove it twenty-three miles to the south, to the island of Cauda. Here the sailors pulled in the small boat that was towed behind larger ships, lest they lose it or it be driven against the ship and cause damage.

As the storm grew worse, the crew did all it could to keep the ship afloat. They wrapped ropes (or chains) around the hull so the boat would not come apart, and they took down some of the sails. The second day, they started throwing some of the wheat overboard, and the third day they jettisoned the furnishings. (Note Luke's use of "we" in Acts 27:19.) Because of the storm, they could not see the sun or the stars, so it was impossible to determine their position. The situation seemed hopeless, and it all happened because one man would not listen to God's messenger.

Sometimes we get ourselves into storms for the same reasons: impatience (Acts 27:9), accepting expert advice that is contrary to God's will, following the majority, and trusting "ideal" conditions (Acts 27:13). "He that believeth shall not make haste" (Isa. 28:16). It pays to listen to God's Word.

Paul the Encourager (Acts 27:21-44)

"Paul began as a prisoner," said Joseph Parker; "he ended as the captain." Paul "took over" the situation when it was obvious that nobody else knew what to do. A crisis does not make a person; a crisis shows what a person is made of, and it tends to bring true leadership to the fore. Paul gently rebuked the centurion, pilot, and captain for ignoring his warning. Soon they would discover that God had spared all of them only because of Paul.

Consider Paul's four ministries of encouragement to the passengers and crew.

He shared God's Word with them (vv. 22-26). A messenger from the Lord had visited Paul and told him that the ship and cargo would be lost, but that all the passengers would be spared and cast on an island. Once again, the Lord gave him a special word of encouragement at the right time (Acts 18:9-10; 23:11). Today, we are not likely to have visions, but we do have the promises in His Word to encourage us (Isa. 41:10; 43:1-5; Rom. 15:4). It was for Paul's sake that God did this, and it was Paul's faith that God honored. What a testimony he was to the people on that storm-tossed ship!

He warned them (vv. 27-32). During the two weeks they had been at sea, the ship had been driven over 500 miles off course and was now adrift in the Adrian Sea. (It is now called the Ionian Sea and must not be confused with the Adriatic Sea.) As the crew took soundings, they discovered that the water was getting shallower (from 120 feet to 90 feet), indicating that land was near. From the roar of the waves, it appeared that the ship was headed for the rocks.

In order to keep the prow headed toward shore, some of the crew dropped four anchors from the stern. But others of the crew tried to escape from the ship in the dinghy that had been brought on board (Acts 27:16). This was not only an act of selfishness and revolt on their part, but it was also an act of unbelief. Paul had told everybody God's promise that He would keep all those safe who sailed with him on the voyage (Acts 27:24). For the men to abandon ship was to take their lives in their own hands and threaten the lives of others. Whether the soldiers acted wisely in cutting the boat free, it is difficult to determine; but in an emergency, you take emergency measures.

He set a good example before them (vv. 33-38). What a difference it makes when a person has faith in God! Instead of vainly wishing for a change (Acts 27:29) or selfishly trying to escape (Acts 27:30), Paul got ready for the demands that would come at daybreak. It is not difficult to understand why everyone had fasted those two weeks, but now it was time to eat. Caring for one's health is an important part of the Christian life, and even an apostle must not abuse his body.

Paul took the bread and openly prayed and gave thanks to God. (This is a good example for us to follow when we are eating in public places.) His example encouraged the others to join him, and before long, everybody felt better. There are times when one dedicated believer can change the whole atmosphere of a situation simply by trusting God and making that faith visible.

He rescued them (vv. 39-44). When it was day, the pilot saw where they were and made every effort to get the ship to shore. But it was all futile; the ship was grounded and the waves began to beat the stern to pieces. The only thing the passengers could do was jump into the water and make for land.

The soldiers, of course, were concerned about their prisoners; for if a prisoner escaped, the soldier was held accountable and could be killed. Once again, it was Paul whose presence saved their lives. Just as the Lord promised, all of them made it safely to shore, and not one was lost. I have a feeling that Paul had been sharing the Gospel with his fellow passengers and that some of them had trusted in the Lord as a result of this experience. Luke does not give us the details, but would you expect Paul to do otherwise?

Before leaving this exciting section of Acts, we should note some practical lessons that it teaches us. First of all, storms often come when we disobey the will of God. (Jonah is a good example of this truth.) However, it was not Paul who was at fault, but the centurion in charge of the ship. We sometimes suffer because of the unbelief of others.

Second, storms have a way of revealing character. Some of the sailors selfishly tried to escape, others could only hope for the best; but Paul trusted God and obeyed His will.

Third, even the worst storms cannot hide the face of God or hinder the purposes of God. Paul received the word of assurance that they needed, and God overruled so that His servant arrived safely in Rome.

Finally, storms can give us opportunities to serve others and bear witness to Jesus Christ. Paul was the most valuable man on that ship! He knew how to pray, he had faith in God, and he was in touch with the Almighty.

Paul the Helper (Acts 28:1-10)

God had brought them to the Isle of Malta (which means "refuge"), where the native people welcomed all 276 of them and did their best to make them comfortable. To the Greeks, anybody who did not speak Greek was a "barbarian." These people proved to be kind and sympathetic. The storm abated, but the weather was cold; so the natives built a fire.

After all he had done for the passengers, Paul could well have requested a throne and insisted that everybody serve him! Instead, he did his share of the work and helped gather fuel for the fire. No task is too small for the servant of God who has "the mind of Christ" (Phil. 2:1-13).

One rainy day, a man accompanied by two women arrived at Northfield, hoping to enroll his daughter in D.L. Moody's school for young women. The three needed help in getting their luggage from the railway depot to the hotel, so the visitor "drafted" a rather common-looking man with a horse and wagon, assuming he was a local cabby. The "cabby" said he was waiting for students, but the visitor ordered him to take them to the hotel. The visitor was shocked when the "cabby" did not charge him, and was even more shocked to discover that the "cabby" was D.L. Moody himself! Moody was a leader because he knew how to be a servant.

The episode of the viper reminds us of Paul's experience in Lystra (Acts 14:6-18). First, the people thought that Justice, one of their goddesses, had caught up with this notorious prisoner who was supposed to drown in the sea but had somehow escaped. (If only they knew!) When Paul failed to swell up and die, they decided that he must be a god himself! Such are the reasonings of people who judge by appearances.

Was the viper a weapon of Satan to get Paul out of the way? The storm did not drown him, but a hidden trap might catch him. As Christians, we must constantly be alert, for either the serpent or the lion will attack us (2 Cor. 11:3; 1 Peter 5:8). We should also keep in mind that we are being watched, and we must use every opportunity to magnify Christ.

Paul and the party remained on Malta for three months; and, thanks to Paul, they were treated graciously and sent on their way with generous gifts. Since they had lost everything in the shipwreck, the passengers were grateful to have their needs supplied. Luke says nothing about evangelism on the island, but we must believe that Paul shared the Gospel with anybody who would listen. His miraculous deliverance from the sea and from the viper, and his power to heal, would certainly arouse the interest of the people; and Paul would want to give the glory to the Lord (Matt. 5:16).

Paul the Preacher (Acts 28:11-31)

Whether all 276 people boarded the Alexandrian ship, or just Julius and his guard and prisoners, we do not know; nor do we know why Luke took such care to identify the ship. In Greek mythology, "Castor and Pollux" were the names of the twin sons of Zeus and were revered as the protectors of men on the sea. Many Roman ships bore their image as a plea for safety. It was 80 miles to Syracuse, another 70 to Rhegium, and about 180 to Puteoli, the port of Naples. This time the "south wind" was exactly what they needed in order to make the voyage quickly and safely.

In Puteoli, Paul and his friends, along with Julius and the other prisoners and guards, were urged by the believers to stay and rest for a week; and Julius gave his consent. The centurion knew that Paul had saved their lives, and perhaps he was even getting interested in what these Christians had to offer.

Word had gotten to Rome that Paul was coming; how, we do not know. Perhaps Aristarchus did not go with Paul and Luke on the grain ship, but made his way instead overland to Rome where he met Paul's friends. (At least twenty-six are named in Rom. 16.) Or, perhaps a delegation from Caesarea headed for Rome as soon as Paul appealed to Caesar.

Julius and his party took the famous Appian Way and traveled 125 miles from Puteoli to Rome. The first group of Christians met Paul at the Forum of Appius, about 43 miles from Rome; and the second group met him at the Three Taverns, 10 miles nearer to the city. (Some saints will go farther than others!) Paul was greatly encouraged when he met them, as well he might be. Now he could fellowship with the saints and they could be a blessing to one another.

Paul's greatest concern was his witness to the Jews in Rome. They had received no special word about Paul, but they did know that the "Christian sect" was being spoken against in many places (Acts 28:21-22). When you read Paul's letter to the Romans, you get the impression that the Jews in Rome had misunderstood some of his teachings (Rom. 3:8; 14:1ff). The apostle made it clear that his appeal to Caesar must not be interpreted as an indictment against his nation. Actually, he was a prisoner *on behalf of* his nation and "the hope of Israel."

On the day appointed, Paul spent "from morning till evening" explaining the Scriptures and revealing Christ in the Law and the Prophets. He had "dialogued" this way with the Jews in one synagogue after another, and now he was sharing the Word with the leaders of many synagogues in Rome.

The result? Some were persuaded and some were not. When the Jewish leaders left Paul's house, they were still arguing among themselves! But Paul had faithfully given his witness to the Jews in Rome, and now he would turn to the Gentiles.

Paul quoted the words of Isaiah to these men (Isa. 6:9-10), words that described their tragic spiritual condition. Jesus had used this passage in connection with His parables of the kingdom (Matt. 13:13-15; Mark 4:12; Luke 8:10). The Apostle John in his Gospel applied them to Israel (John 12:39-40), and Paul quoted them in his Roman epistle (Rom. 11:7-8). It is one thing to *listen* and quite something else to *hear,* and there is a great difference between *seeing* and *perceiving.* If anybody should have possessed spiritual understanding, it was these Jewish leaders, but their hearts were dull and hard. Too often those who enjoy the most spiritual privileges are not ready when they must make spiritual decisions.

But their unbelief did not put an end to Paul's ministry of the Gospel! He announced that the Gospel some of the Jews had rejected would be proclaimed to the Gentiles, "and they will hear it!" This is one of the major themes of Acts, how the Gospel moved from the Jews to the Gentiles and from Jerusalem to Rome. Without the Book of Acts, we would turn in the New Testament from the Gospel of John to Romans and ask, "How did the Gospel ever get from the Jews in Jerusalem to the Gentiles in Rome?"

Paul kept "open house" and received anybody who wanted to discuss the things of the kingdom of God. He was chained to a guard who was relieved every six hours, but who was forced to listen as Paul preached and taught and prayed. No wonder some of them were saved! (Phil. 1:12-14; 4:22)

During these two years in Rome, Paul wrote Philippians, Ephesians, Colossians, and Philemon. He expected to be released (Phil. 1:23-27; 2:24; Phile. 22) and most students agree that he was. During this time, he had Timothy with him (Phil. 1:1; 2:19; Col. 1:1), as well as John Mark, Luke, Aristarchus, Epaphras, Justus, and Demas (Col. 4:10-14; Phile. 24). He also met Philemon's runaway slave Onesimus and led him to faith in Christ (Phile. 10-21). Epaphroditus brought a gift to him from the Philippian church and almost died ministering to Paul (Phil. 2:25-30; 4:18). Tychicus was Paul's "mailman" who delivered Ephesians (Eph. 6:21), Colossians, and Philemon (Col. 4:7-9).

Dr. Luke ended his book before Paul's case had been heard, so he could not give us the results of the trial. We have every reason to believe that Paul was indeed released and that he resumed his ministry, probably traveling as far as Spain (Rom. 15:24, 28). During this period (A.D. 63–66/67), he wrote letters to Timothy and Titus. He left Titus in Crete (Titus 1:5), Trophimus sick in Miletus (2 Tim. 4:20), and Timothy in Ephesus (1 Tim. 1:3). He planned to meet some of his helpers at Nicopolis (Titus 3:12-13) after he had visited some of the churches he had established. Wherever he went, he sought to bring Jews and Gentiles to faith in Jesus Christ.

He was arrested again, probably about the year 67, and this time his situation was changed drastically. He did not live in a house, but was chained in a prison and treated like a criminal (2 Tim. 1:16; 2:9). Winter was coming, and he asked Timothy to bring him his cloak (2 Tim. 4:13). But the saddest thing about this second imprisonment was his being forsaken by the believers in Rome (2 Tim. 4:16-17). The great apostle to the Gentiles was abandoned by the very people he came to assist.

Even Demas forsook him, and only Luke was with him (2 Tim. 4:10-11). The family of Onesiphorus ministered to his needs (2 Tim. 1:16-18), but he longed for Timothy and Mark to come to be at his side (2 Tim. 1:4; 4:9, 21). Paul knew that the end was coming (2 Tim. 4:6-8). Tradition tells us that he was beheaded at Rome in A.D. 67/68.

Luke did not write his book simply to record ancient history. He wrote to encourage the church in every age to be faithful to the Lord and carry the Gospel to the ends of the earth. "What was begun with so much heroism ought to be continued with ardent zeal," said Charles Spurgeon, "since we are assured that the same Lord is mighty still to carry on His heavenly designs."

"Lo, I am with you always!"

ROMANS

OUTLINE

Key theme: The righteousness of God
Key verse: Romans 1:17

I. INTRODUCTION—1:1-17

II. SIN—RIGHTEOUSNESS DEMANDED—1:18–3:20
A. The Gentiles guilty—1:18-32
B. The Jews guilty—2:1–3:8
C. The whole world guilty—3:9-20

III. SALVATION—RIGHTEOUSNESS DECLARED—3:21–5:21
A. Justification stated—3:21-31
B. Justification illustrated in Abraham—4
C. Justification explained in Adam—5

IV. SANCTIFICATION—RIGHTEOUSNESS DEFENDED—chapters 6–8
A. Victory—the flesh—6
B. Liberty—the Law—7
C. Security—the Spirit—8

V. SOVEREIGNTY—RIGHTEOUSNESS DECLINED—chapters 9–11
A. Israel's past riches—9
B. Israel's present rejection—10
C. Israel's future restoration—11

VI. SERVICE—RIGHTEOUSNESS DEMONSTRATED—12:1–15:7
A. In the church body—12
B. In society—13
C. Toward the weaker believer—14:1–15:7

VII. CONCLUSION—15:8–16:27

CONTENTS

CHAPTER ONE
READY FOR ROME
Romans 1:1-17

On May 24, 1738, a discouraged missionary went "very unwillingly" to a religious meeting in London. There a miracle took place. "About a quarter before nine," he wrote in his journal, "I felt my heart strangely warmed. I felt I did trust in Christ, Christ alone, for salvation; and an assurance was given me that He had taken away my sins, even mine, and saved me from the law of sin and death."

That missionary was John Wesley. The message he heard that evening was the preface to Martin Luther's commentary on Romans. Just a few months before, John Wesley had written in his journal: "I went to America to convert the Indians; but Oh! who shall convert me?" That evening in Aldersgate Street, his question was answered. And the result was the great Wesleyan Revival that swept England and transformed the nation.

Paul's Epistle to the Romans is still transforming people's lives, just the way it transformed Martin Luther and John Wesley. The one Scripture above all others that brought Luther out of mere religion into the joy of salvation by grace, through faith, was Romans 1:17: "The just shall live by faith." The Protestant Reformation and the Wesleyan Revival were both the fruit of this wonderful letter written by Paul from Corinth about the year A.D. 56. The letter was carried to the Christians at Rome by one of the deaconesses of the church at Cenchrea, Sister Phebe (Rom. 16:1).

Imagine! You and I can read and study the same inspired letter that brought life and power to Luther and Wesley! And the same Holy Spirit who taught them can teach us! You and I can experience revival in our hearts, homes, and churches if the message of this letter grips us as it has gripped men of faith in centuries past.

In the opening verses of the letter, Paul introduces himself to the believers in Rome. Some of them must have known him personally, since he greets them in the final chapter; but many of them he had never met. So, in these first seventeen verses, Paul seeks to link himself to his Roman readers in three ways.

He Presented His Credentials (Rom. 1:1-7)

In ancient days, the writer of a letter always opened with his name. But there would be many men named Paul in that day, so the writer had to further identify himself and convince the readers that he had a right to send the letter. What were Paul's credentials?

He was a servant of Jesus Christ (v. 1a). The word Paul used for *servant* would be meaningful to the Romans, because it is the word *slave.* There were an estimated 60 million slaves in the Roman Empire; and a slave was looked on as a piece of property, not a person. In loving devotion, Paul had enslaved himself to Christ, to be His servant and obey His will.

He was an apostle (v. 1b). This word means "one who is sent by authority with a commission." It was applied in that day to the representatives of the emperor or the emissaries of a king. One of the requirements for an apostle was the experience of seeing the risen Christ (1 Cor. 9:1-2). Paul saw Christ when he was on the road to Damascus (Acts 9:1-9), and it was then that Christ called him to be His apostle to the Gentiles. Paul received from Christ divine revelations that he was to share with the churches.

He was a preacher of the Gospel (vv. 1c-4). When he was a Jewish rabbi, Paul was separated as a Pharisee to the laws and traditions of the Jews. But when he yielded to Christ, he was separated to the Gospel and its ministry. *Gospel* means "the Good News." It is the message that Christ died for our sins, was buried and rose again, and now is able to save all who trust Him (1 Cor. 15:1-4). It is "the Gospel of God" (Rom. 1:1) because it originates with God; it was not invented by man. It is "the Gospel of Christ" (Rom. 1:16) because it centers in Christ, the Saviour. Paul also calls it "the Gospel of His Son" (Rom. 1:9), which indicates that *Jesus Christ is God!* In Romans 16:25-26, Paul called it "my Gospel." By this he meant the special emphasis he gave in his ministry to the doctrine of the church and the place of the Gentiles in the plan of God.

The Gospel is not a new message; it was promised in the Old Testament, beginning in Genesis 3:15. The Prophet Isaiah certainly preached the Gospel in passages such as Isaiah 1:18, and chapters 53 and 55. The salvation we enjoy today was promised by the prophets, though they did not fully understand all that they were preaching and writing (1 Peter 1:10-12).

Jesus Christ is the center of the Gospel message. Paul identified Him as a man, a Jew, and the Son of God. He was born of a virgin (Isa. 7:14; Matt. 1:18-25) into the family of David, which gave Him the right to David's throne. He died for the sins of the world, and then was raised from the dead. It is this miraculous event of substitutionary death and victorious resurrection that constitutes the Gospel; and it was this Gospel that Paul preached.

He was a missionary to the Gentiles (vv. 5-7). *Missionary* is the Latin form of "apostle—one who is sent." There were probably several assemblies of believers in Rome and not just one church, since in Romans 16 Paul greets a number of "home church" groups (Rom. 16:5, 10-11, 14). We do not know for certain how these churches began, but it is likely that believers from Rome who were at Pentecost established the assemblies on their return to Rome (Acts 2:10). There were both Jews and Gentiles in these fellowships, because Paul addresses both in this letter. (Jews: Rom. 2:17-29; 4:1; 7:1. Gentiles: Rom. 1:13; 11:13-24; 15:15-21.) The churches in Rome were not founded by Peter or any other apostle. If they had been, Paul would not have planned to visit Rome, because his policy was to minister only where no other apostle had gone (Rom. 15:20-21).

Note the repetition of the word *called:* Paul was called to be an apostle; the believers were the called of Jesus Christ; and they were also called saints. (Not "to be" saints; they already were saints! A saint is a set-apart one, and the person who trusts Jesus Christ is set apart and is a saint.) Salvation is not something that we do for God; it is God who calls us in His grace (2 Thes. 2:13-14). When you trust Christ, you are saved by His grace and you experience His peace.

Paul's special commission was to take the Gospel to the Gentiles (the word *nations* means Gentiles), and this is why he was planning to go to Rome, the very capital of the empire. He was a preacher of the Gospel, and the Gospel was for all nations. In fact, Paul was anxious to go to Spain with the message of Christ (Rom. 15:28).

Having presented his credentials, Paul proceeded to forge a second link between himself and the believers in Rome.

He Expressed His Concern (Rom. 1:8-15)

We can well understand Paul's concern for the churches that *he* founded, but why would he be concerned about the believers at Rome? He was unknown to many of them, yet he wanted to assure them that he was deeply concerned about their welfare. Note the evidences of Paul's concern.

He was thankful for them (v. 8). "The whole world"—meaning the whole Roman Empire—knew of the faith of the Christians at Rome. Travel was relatively common in that day and "all roads led to Rome." It is no wonder that the testimony of the church spread abroad, and this growing witness made Paul's ministry easier as he went from place to place, and was able to point to this testimony going out from the heart of the Roman Empire.

He prayed for them (vv. 9-10). They did not know of Paul's prayer support, but the Lord knew about it and honored it. (I wonder how many of us know the people who are praying for us?) One of the burdens of Paul's prayer was that God would permit him to visit Rome and minister to the churches there. He would have visited them sooner, but his missionary work had kept him busy (Rom. 15:15-33). He was about to leave Corinth for Jerusalem to deliver the special offering received from the Gentile churches for the poor Jewish saints. He hoped he would be able to travel from Jerusalem to Rome, and then on to Spain; and he was hoping for a prosperous journey.

Actually, Paul had a very perilous journey; and he arrived in Rome a prisoner as well as a preacher. In Jerusalem he was arrested in the temple, falsely accused by the Jewish authorities and eventually sent to Rome as the Emperor's prisoner to be tried before Caesar. When Paul wrote this letter, he had no idea that he would go through imprisonment and even shipwreck before arriving in Rome! At the close of the letter (Rom. 15:30-33), he asked the believers in Rome to pray for him as he contemplated this trip; and it is a good thing that they did pray!

He loved them (vv. 11-12). "I long to see you!" This is the pastor's heart in Paul the great missionary. Some of the saints in Rome were very dear to Paul, such as Priscilla and Aquila (Rom. 16:3-4), who risked their lives for him; "the beloved Persis" (Rom. 16:12); and others who had labored and suffered with Paul. But he also loved the believers that he did not know, and he longed to be able to share some spiritual gift with them. He was looking forward to a time of mutual blessing in the love of Christ.

He was in debt to them (vv. 13-14). As the apostle to the Gentiles, Paul had an obligation to minister in Rome. He would have fulfilled that obligation sooner, but his other labors had hindered him. Sometimes Paul was hindered because of the work of Satan (1 Thes. 2:17-20); but in this case he was hindered because of the work of the Lord. There was so much to do in Asia Minor and Greece that he could not immediately spare time for Rome. But Paul had to pay his debt; he was under orders from the Lord.

The Greeks considered every non-Greek a barbarian. Steeped in centuries of philosophy, the Greeks saw themselves as wise and everyone else as foolish. But Paul felt an obligation to *all* men, just as we need to feel a burden for the whole world. Paul could not be free from his debt until he had told as many people as possible the Good News of salvation in Christ.

He was eager to visit them (v. 15). Two different Greek words are translated "ready" in the *King James Version.* One means "prepared," as in Acts 21:13. "I am ready . . . to die at Jerusalem for the name of the Lord Jesus." The other one, used in Romans 1:15, means "eager, with a ready mind." Paul was not eager to die, though he was prepared to die. But he was eager to visit Rome that he might minister to the believers there. It was not the eagerness of a sightseer, but the eagerness of a soul-winner.

After reading these five evidences of Paul's concern for the Christians at Rome, these saints could not but give thanks to God for the Apostle Paul and his burden to come and minister to them. Actually, the Epistle to the Romans in which Paul explained the Gospel he preached, was his letter of introduction that prepared the believers for his visit. No doubt the false teachers had already gotten to Rome and were seeking to poison the Christians against Paul (see Rom. 3:8). Some would accuse him of being anti-Law; others would say he was a traitor to the Jewish nation. Still others would twist his teaching about grace and try to prove that he taught loose living. No wonder Paul was eager to get to Rome! He wanted to share with them the fullness of the Gospel of Christ.

But would the Gospel of Christ work in the great city of Rome as it had in other places? Would Paul succeed there, or would he fail? The apostle no doubt felt these objections and raised these questions in his own mind, which is why he forged a third link between himself and his readers.

He Affirmed His Confidence (Rom. 1:16-17)

What a testimony: "I am debtor! I am eager! I am not ashamed!" Why would Paul even be tempted to be ashamed of the Gospel as he contemplated his trip to Rome? For one thing, the Gospel was identified with a poor Jewish carpenter who was crucified. The Romans had no special appreciation for the Jews, and crucifixion was the lowest form of execution given a criminal. Why put your faith in a Jew who was crucified?

Rome was a proud city, and the Gospel came from Jerusalem, the capital city of one of the little nations that Rome had conquered. The Christians in that day were not among the elite of society; they were common people and even slaves. Rome had known many great philosophers and philosophies; why pay any attention to a fable about a Jew who arose from the dead? (1 Cor. 1:18-25) Christians looked on each other as brothers and sisters, all one in Christ, which went against the grain of Roman pride and dignity. To think of a little Jewish tentmaker, going to Rome to preach such a message, is almost humorous.

But Paul was not ashamed of the Gospel. He had confidence in his message, and he gave us several reasons that explain why he was not ashamed.

The origin of the Gospel: it is the Gospel of Christ (v. 16a). Any message that was handed down from Caesar would immediately get the attention of the Romans. But the message of the Gospel is from and about the very Son of God! In his opening sentence, Paul called this message "the Gospel of God" (Rom. 1:1). How could Paul be ashamed of such a message, when it came from God and centered in His Son, Jesus Christ?

During my years in high school, I was chosen to be an office monitor. The other hall monitors sat at various stations around the building, but I was privileged to sit right outside the door of the main high school office. I was entrusted with important messages that I had to deliver to different teachers and staff members, and on occasion even to other schools. Believe me, it was fun to walk into a classroom and even interrupt a lesson! No teacher ever scolded me, because all of them knew I carried messages from the principal. I never had to be afraid or ashamed, because I knew where my messages came from.

The operation of the Gospel: it is the power of God (v. 16b). Why be ashamed of power? Power is the one thing that Rome boasted of the most. Greece might have its philosophy, but Rome had its power. The fear of Rome hovered over the empire like a cloud. Were they not the conquerors? Were not the Roman legions stationed all over the known world? But with all of her military power, Rome was still a weak nation. The philosopher Seneca called the city of Rome "a cesspool of iniquity"; and the writer Juvenal called it a "filthy sewer into which the dregs of the empire flood."

No wonder Paul was not ashamed: he was taking to sinful Rome the one message that had the power to change men's lives! He had seen the Gospel work in other wicked cities such as Corinth and Ephesus; and he was confident that it would work in Rome. It had transformed his own life, and he knew it could transform the lives of others. There was a third reason why Paul was not ashamed.

The outcome of the Gospel: it is the power of God unto salvation (v. 16c). That word "salvation" carried tremendous meaning in Paul's day. Its basic meaning is "deliverance," and it was applied to personal and national deliverance. The emperor was looked on as a savior, as was the physician who healed you of illness. The Gospel delivers sinners from the penalty and power of sin. "Salvation" is a major theme in this letter; salvation is the great need of the human race (see Rom. 10:1, 9-10). If men and women are to be saved, it must be through faith in Jesus Christ as proclaimed in the Gospel.

The outreach of the Gospel: "to everyone that believeth" (vv. 16d-17). This was not an exclusive message for either the Jew or the Gentile; it was for all men, *because all men need to be saved.* "Go ye into all the world and preach the Gospel," was Christ's commission (Mark 16:15). "To the Jew first" does not suggest that the Jew is better than the Gentile; for there is "no difference" in condemnation or in salvation (Rom. 2:6-11; 10:9-13). The Gospel came "to the Jew first" in the ministry of Jesus Christ (Matt. 10:5-7) and the Apostles (Acts 3:26). How marvelous it is to have a message of power that can be taken to *all* people!

God does not ask men to *behave* in order to be saved, but to *believe.* It is faith in Christ that saves the sinner. Eternal life in Christ is one gift that is suitable for all people, no matter what their need may be or what their station in life.

Romans 1:17 is the key verse of the letter. In it Paul announces the theme: "the righteousness of God." The word "righteousness" is used in one way or another over sixty times in this letter (righteous, just, and justified). God's righteousness is revealed in the Gospel; for in the death of Christ, God revealed His righteousness by punishing sin; and in the resurrection of Christ, He revealed His righteousness by making salvation available to the believing sinner. The problem "How can a holy God ever forgive sinners and still be holy?" is answered in the Gospel. Through the death and resurrection of Christ, God is seen to be "both just and justifier" (Rom. 3:26).

The Gospel reveals a righteousness that is *by faith.* In the Old Testament, righteousness was *by* works, but sinners soon discovered they could not obey God's Law and meet His righteous demands. Here Paul refers to Habakkuk 2:4: "The just shall live by his faith." This verse is quoted three times in the New Testament: Romans 1:17; Galatians 3:11; and Hebrews 10:38. Romans explains "the just"; Galatians explains "shall live"; and Hebrews explains "by faith." There are more than sixty references to faith or unbelief in Romans.

When you study Romans, you walk into a courtroom. First, Paul called Jews and Gentiles to the stand and found both guilty before God. Then he explained God's marvelous way of salvation—justification by faith. At this point, he answered his accusers and defended God's salvation. "This plan of salvation will encourage people to sin!" they cry. "It is against the very Law of God!" But Paul refuted them, and in so doing explained how the Christian can experience victory, liberty, and security.

Chapters 9–11 are not a parenthesis or a detour. There were Jewish believers in the Roman assemblies and they would naturally ask, "What about Israel? How does God's righteousness relate to them in this new age of the church?" In these three chapters, Paul gave a complete history of Israel, past, present, and future.

Then he concluded with the practical outworking of God's righteousness in the life of the believer. This begins with dedication to God (Rom. 12:1-2), continues with ministry in the church (Rom. 12:3-21), and then obedience to the government (Rom. 13:1-14). He also told Jews and Gentiles, strong and weak, how to live together in harmony and joy. In the closing section (Rom. 15:14–16:27), Paul explained his plans and greeted his friends.

When you sum it all up, the Book of Romans is saying to us—*"Be right!"* Be right with God, with yourself, and with others! The righteousness of God received by faith makes it possible for us to live right lives. Rome needed this message, and we need it today: *Be right!*

CHAPTER TWO
WHEN GOD GIVES UP
Romans 1:18–3:20

"Hear ye! Hear ye! Court is now in session!" Paul could have used those awesome words at this point in his letter, because Romans 1:18 is the door that leads us into God's courtroom. The theme of Romans is the righteousness of God, but Paul had to begin with the *un*righteousness of man. Until man knows he is a sinner, he cannot appreciate the gracious salvation God offers in Jesus Christ. Paul followed the basic Bible pattern: first Law and condemnation; then grace and salvation.

In this section, God makes three declarations that together prove that all men are sinners and need Jesus Christ.

The Gentile World Is Guilty! (Rom. 1:18-32)

The picture Paul paints here is an ugly one. I confess that there are some neighborhoods that I dislike driving through, and I avoid them if I can. My avoiding them does not change them or eliminate them. God's description of sinners is not a pretty one, but we cannot avoid it. This section does not teach evolution (that man started low and climbed high), but *devolution:* he started high and, because of sin, sank lower than the beasts. Four stages mark man's tragic devolution.

Intelligence (vv. 18-20). Human history began with man knowing God. Human history is not the story of a beast that worshiped idols, and then evolved into a man worshiping one God. Human history is just the opposite: man began knowing God, but turned from the truth and rejected God. God revealed Himself to man through creation, the things that He made. From the world around him, man knew that there was a God who had the wisdom to plan and the power to create. Man realized too that this Creator was eternal . . . "His eternal power and Godhead" (Rom. 1:20), since God could not be created if He is the Creator. These facts about God are not hidden in creation; they are "clearly seen" (Rom. 1:20). "The heavens declare the glory of God, and the firmament showeth His handiwork" (Ps. 19:1).

The word translated "hold" in Rom. 1:18 can also be translated "hold down, suppress." Men knew the truth about God, but they did not allow this truth to work in their lives. They suppressed it in order that they might live their own lives and not be convicted by God's truth. The result, of course, was refusing the truth (Rom. 1:21-22), and then turning the truth into a lie (Rom. 1:25). Finally, man so abandoned the truth that he became like a beast in his thinking and in his living.

Ignorance (vv. 21-23). Man knew God; this is clear. But man did not *want* to know God or honor Him as God. Instead of being thankful for all that God had given him, man refused to thank God or give Him the glory He deserves. Man was willing to use God's gifts, but he was not willing to worship and praise God for His gifts. The result was an empty mind and a darkened heart. Man the worshiper became man the philosopher, but his empty wisdom only revealed his foolishness. Paul summarized all of Greek history in one dramatic statement: "the times of this ignorance" (Acts 17:30). First Corinthians 1:18-31 is worth reading at this point.

Having held down God's truth and refusing to acknowledge God's glory, man was left without a god; and man is so constituted that he must worship something. If he will not worship the true God, he will worship a false god, *even if he has to manufacture it himself!* This fact about man accounts for his propensity to idolatry. Man exchanged the glory of the true God for substitute gods that he himself made. He exchanged glory for shame, incorruption for corruption, truth for lies.

Note that first on the list of false gods is *man.* This fulfilled Satan's purpose when he told Eve, "Ye shall be as God!" (Gen. 3:5, NASB) "Glory to man in the highest!" Satan encouraged man to say. Instead of man being made in God's image, man made gods in his own image—and then descended so low as to worship birds, beasts, and bugs!

Indulgence (vv. 24-27). From idolatry to immorality is just one short step. If man is his own god, then he can do whatever he pleases and fulfill his desires without fear of judgment. We reach the climax of man's battle with God's truth when man exchanges the truth of God for "the lie" and abandons truth completely. "The lie" is that man is his own god, and he should worship and serve himself and not the Creator. It was "the lie" Satan used in the Garden to lead Eve into sin: "Ye shall be as God!" Satan has always wanted the worship that belongs only to God (Isa. 14:12-15; Matt. 4:8-10); and in idolatry, he receives that worship (1 Cor. 10:19-21).

The result of this self-deification was self-indulgence; and here Paul mentions a vile sin that was rampant in that day and has become increasingly prevalent in our own day; homosexuality. This sin is repeatedly condemned in Scripture (Gen. 18:20ff; 1 Cor. 6:9-10; Jude 7). Paul characterizes it as "vile" and "unnatural," as well as "against nature." Not only were the men guilty, but "even the women."

Because of their sin "God gave them up" (Rom. 1:24, 26) which means that He permitted them to go on in their sins and reap the sad consequences. They received "in their own persons the due penalty of their error" (Rom. 1:27, NASB). This is the meaning of Romans 1:18, "The wrath of God is being revealed from heaven" (literal translation). God revealed His wrath, not by sending fire from heaven, but by abandoning sinful men to their lustful ways. But there was one more stage.

Impenitence (vv. 28-32). When man began to feel the tragic consequences of his sins, you would think he would repent and seek God; but just the opposite was true. Because he was abandoned by God, he could only become worse. Man did not even want to retain God in his knowledge! So, "God gave them over" this time to a "depraved mind" (Rom. 1:28, NASB), which means a mind that cannot form right judgments. They now abandoned themselves to sin. Paul names twenty-four specific sins, all of which are with us today. (For other lists, see Mark 7:20-23; Gal. 5:19-21; 1 Tim. 1:9-10; and 2 Tim. 3:2-5.)

But the worst is yet to come. Men not only committed these sins in open defiance of God, but encouraged others and applauded them when they sinned. How far man fell! He began glorifying God but ended exchanging that glory for idols. He began knowing God but ended refusing to keep the knowledge of God in his mind and heart. He began as the highest of God's creatures, made in the image of God; but he ended lower than the beasts and insects, because he worshiped them as his gods. The verdict? "They are without excuse!" (Rom. 1:20)

This portion of Scripture gives ample proof that the heathen are lost. Dan Crawford, British missionary to Africa, said: "The heathen are sinning against a flood of light." There is a desperate need for us to carry the Gospel to all men, for this is the only way they can be saved.

The Jewish World Is Guilty! (Rom. 2:1–3:8)

Bible scholars do not agree on whom Paul was addressing in Romans 2:1-16. Some think he was dealing with the moral pagan who did not commit the sins named in Romans 1:18-32, but who sought to live a moral life. But it seems to me that Paul was addressing his Jewish readers in this section. To begin with, his discussion of the Law in Romans 2:12-16 would have been more meaningful to a Jew than to a Gentile. And in Romans 2:17, he openly addressed his reader as "a Jew." This would be a strange form of address if in the first half of the chapter he were addressing Gentiles.

It would not be an easy task to find the Jews guilty, since disobedience to God was one sin they did not want to confess. The Old Testament prophets were persecuted for indicting Israel for her sins, and Jesus was crucified for the same reason. Paul summoned four witnesses to prove the guilt of the Jewish nation.

The Gentiles (vv. 1-3). Certainly the Jews would applaud Paul's condemnation of the Gentiles in Romans 1:18-32. In fact, Jewish national and religious pride encouraged them to despise the "Gentile dogs" and have nothing to do with them. Paul used this judgmental attitude to prove the guilt of the Jews; *for the very things they condemned in the Gentiles, they themselves were practicing!* They thought that they were free from judgment because they were God's chosen people. But Paul affirmed that God's election of the Jews made their responsibility and accountability even greater.

God's judgment is according to truth. He does not have one standard for the Jews and another for the Gentiles. One who reads the list of sins in Romans 1:29-32 cannot escape the fact that each person is guilty of at least one of them. There are "sins of the flesh and of the spirit" (2 Cor. 7:1); there are "prodigal sons" and "elder brothers" (Luke 15:11-32). In condemning the Gentiles for their sins, the Jews were really condemning themselves. As the old saying puts it, "When you point your finger at somebody else, the other three are pointing at you."

God's blessing (vv. 4-11). Instead of giving the Jews special treatment from God, the blessings they received from Him gave them greater responsibility to obey Him and glorify Him. In His goodness, God had given Israel great material and spiritual riches: a wonderful land, a righteous Law, a temple and priesthood, God's providential care, and many more blessings. God had patiently endured Israel's many sins and rebellions, and had even sent them His Son to be their Messiah. Even after Israel crucified Christ, God gave the nation nearly forty more years of grace and withheld His judgment. It is not the *judgment* of God that leads men to repentance, but the *goodness* of God; but Israel did not repent.

In Romans 2:6-11, Paul was not teaching salvation by character or good deeds. He was explaining another basic principle of God's judgment: God judges according to deeds, just as He judges according to truth. Paul was dealing here with the consistent actions of a person's life, the total impact of his character and conduct. For example, David committed some terrible sins; but the total emphasis of his life was obedience to God. Judas confessed his sin and supplied the money for buying a cemetery for strangers; yet the total emphasis of his life was disobedience and unbelief.

True saving faith results in obedience and godly living, even though there may be occasional falls. When God measured the deeds of the Jews, He found them to be as wicked as those of the Gentiles. The fact that the Jews occasionally celebrated a feast or even regularly honored the Sabbath Day did not change the fact that their consistent daily life was one of disobedience to God. God's blessings did not lead them to repentance.

God's Law (vv. 12-24). Paul's statement in Romans 2:11, "For there is no respect of persons with God" would shock the Jew, for he considered himself deserving of special treatment because he was chosen by God. But Paul explained that the Jewish Law only made the guilt of Israel that much greater! God did not give the Law to the Gentiles, so they would not be judged by the Law. Actually, the Gentiles had "the work of the Law written in their hearts" (Rom. 2:15). Wherever you go, you find people with an inner sense of right and wrong; and this inner judge, the Bible calls "conscience." You find among all cultures a sense of sin, a fear of judgment, and an attempt to atone for sins and appease whatever gods are feared.

The Jew boasted in the Law. He was different from his pagan neighbors who worshiped idols! But Paul made it clear that it was not the *possession* of the Law that counted, but the *practice* of the Law. The Jews looked on the Gentiles as blind, in the dark, foolish, immature, and ignorant! But if God found the "deprived" Gentiles guilty, how much more guilty were the "privileged" Jews! God not only judges according to truth (Rom. 2:2), and according to men's deeds (Rom. 2:6); but He also judges "the secrets of men" (Rom. 2:16). He sees what is in the heart!

The Jewish people had a religion of outward action, not inward attitude. They may have been moral on the outside, but what about the heart? Our Lord's indictment of the Pharisees in Matthew 23 illustrates the principle perfectly. God not only sees the deeds but He also sees the "thoughts and intents of the heart" (Heb. 4:12). It is possible for a Jew to be guilty of theft, adultery, and idolatry (Rom. 2:21-22) even if no one saw him commit these sins outwardly. In the Sermon on the Mount we are told that such sins can be committed in the heart.

Instead of glorifying God among the Gentiles, the Jews were dishonoring God; and Paul quoted Isaiah 52:5 to prove his point. The pagan Gentiles had daily contact with the Jews in business and other activities, and they were not fooled by the Jews' devotion to the Law. The very Law that the Jews claimed to obey only indicted them!

Circumcision (vv. 25-29). This was the

great mark of the covenant, and it had its beginning with Abraham, the father of the Jewish nation (Gen. 17). To the Jews, the Gentiles were "uncircumcised dogs." The tragedy is that the Jews depended on this physical mark instead of the spiritual reality it represented (Deut. 10:16; Jer. 9:26; Ezek. 44:9). A true Jew is one who has had an *inward* spiritual experience in the heart, and not merely an outward physical operation. People today make this same mistake with reference to baptism or the Lord's Supper, or even church membership.

God judges according to "the secrets of the heart" (Rom. 2:16), so that He is not impressed with mere outward formalities. An obedient Gentile with no circumcision would be more acceptable than a disobedient Jew with circumcision. In fact, a disobedient Jew turns his circumcision into *un*circumcision in God's sight, for God looks at the heart. The Jews praised each other for their obedience to the Law, but the important thing is the "praise of God" and not the praise of men (Rom. 2:29). When you recall that the name "Jew" comes from "Judah" which means "praise," this statement takes on new meaning (Gen. 29:35; 49:8).

Paul's summation (vv. 1-8). All of Paul's four witnesses agreed: the Jews were guilty before God. In Romans 3:1-8, Paul summed up the argument and refuted those Jews who tried to debate with him. They raised three questions. (1) "What advantage is it to be a Jew?" Reply: Every advantage, especially possessing the Word of God. (2) "Will Jewish unbelief cancel God's faithfulness?" Reply: Absolutely not—it establishes it. (3) "If our sin commends His righteousness, how can He judge us?" Reply: We do not do evil that good may come of it. God judges the world righteously.

The Whole World Is Guilty! (Rom. 3:9-20)

The third declaration was obvious, for Paul had already proved (charged) both Jews and Gentiles to be guilty before God. Next he declared that all men were sinners, and proved it with several quotations from the Old Testament. Note the repetition of the words "none" and "all," which in themselves assert the universality of human guilt.

His first quotation was from Psalm 14:1-3. This psalm begins with, "The fool hath said in his heart, 'There is no God.' " The words "there is" are in italics, meaning they were added by the translators; so you can read the sentence, "The fool hath said in his heart, 'No, God!' " This parallels the description of man's devolution given in Romans 1:18-32, for it all started with man saying no to God.

These verses indicate that the whole of man's inner being is controlled by sin: his *mind* ("none that understandeth"), his *heart* ("none that seeketh after God"), and his *will* ("none that doeth good"). Measured by God's perfect righteousness, no human being is sinless. No sinner seeks after God. Therefore, God must seek the sinner (Gen. 3:8-10; Luke 19:10). Man has gone astray, and has become unprofitable both to himself and to God. Our Lord's parables in Luke 15 illustrate this perfectly.

In Romans 3:13-18, Paul gave us an X-ray study of the lost sinner, from head to foot. His quotations are as follows: verse 13a—Psalm 5:9; verse 13b—Psalm 140:3; verse 14—Psalm 10:7; verses 15-17—Isaiah 59:7-8; verse 18—Psalm 36:1. These verses need to be read in their contexts for the full impact.

Romans 3:13 and 14 emphasize human speech—the throat, tongue, lips, and mouth. The connection between words and character is seen in Matthew 12:34: "For out of the abundance of the heart the mouth speaketh." The sinner is spiritually dead by nature (Eph. 2:1-3), therefore only death can come out of his mouth. The condemned mouth can become a converted mouth and acknowledge that "Jesus Christ is Lord" (Rom. 10:9-10). "For by thy words thou shalt be justified, and by thy words thou shalt be condemned" (Matt. 12:37).

In Romans 3:15 and 16, Paul pictured the sinner's feet. Just as his words are deceitful, so his ways are destructive. The Christians' feet are shod with the Gospel of peace (Eph. 6:15); but the lost sinner brings death, destruction, and misery wherever he goes. These tragedies may not occur immediately, but they will come inevitably. The lost sinner is on the broad road that leads to destruction (Matt. 7:13-14); he needs to repent, trust Jesus Christ, and get on the narrow road that leads to life.

Romans 3:17 deals with the sinner's mind: he does not know the way of God's peace. This is what caused Jesus to weep over Jerusalem (Luke 19:41-44). The sinner does not want to know God's truth (Rom. 1:21, 25, 28); he prefers to believe Satan's lie. God's way of peace is through Jesus Christ: "Therefore being justified by faith, we have peace with God through our Lord Jesus Christ" (Rom. 5:1).

In Romans 3:18, which cites Psalm 36:1, the sinner's arrogant pride is prescribed: "There is no fear of God before their eyes." The entire psalm should be read to get the full picture. The ignorance mentioned in Romans 3:17 is caused by the pride of verse 18; for it is "the fear of the Lord" that is the beginning of knowledge (Prov. 1:7).

These quotations from God's Law, the Old Testament Scriptures, lead to one conclusion: *the whole world is guilty before God!* There may be those who want to argue, but every mouth is stopped. There is no debate or defense. The whole world is guilty, Jews and Gentiles. The Jews stand condemned by the Law of which they boast, and the Gentiles stand condemned on the basis of creation and conscience.

The word "therefore" in Romans 3:20 carries the meaning of "because," and gives the reason why the whole world is guilty. No flesh can obey God's Law and be justified (declared righteous) in His sight. It is true that "the doers of the Law shall be justified" (Rom. 2:13), but *nobody can do what the Law demands!* This inability is one way that men know they are sinners. When they try to obey the Law, they fail miserably and need to cry out for God's mercy. Neither Jew nor Gentile can obey God's Law; therefore God must save sinners by some other means. The explanation of that means by which man can be saved occupied Paul for the rest of his letter.

The best way to close this section would be to ask a simple question: Has your mouth ever been stopped? Are you boasting of your own self-righteousness and defending yourself before God? If so, then perhaps you have never been saved by God's grace. It is only when we stand silent before Him as sinners that He can save us. As long as we defend ourselves and commend ourselves, we cannot be saved by God's grace. The whole world is guilty before God—and that includes you and me!

CHAPTER THREE
FATHER ABRAHAM
Romans 3:21–4:25

Paul's theme in the second section of his letter was *Salvation—Righteousness Declared.* He had proved that all men are sinners; next he was to explain how sinners can be saved. The theological term for this salvation is *justification by faith.* Justification is the act of God whereby He declares the believing sinner righteous in Christ on the basis of the finished work of Christ on the cross. Each part of this definition is important, so we must consider it carefully.

To begin with, justification is an *act,* not a process. There are no degrees of justification; each believer has the same right standing before God. Also, justification is something *God* does, not man. No sinner can justify himself before God. Most important, justification does not mean that God *makes* us righteous, but that He *declares* us righteous. Justification is a legal matter. God puts the righteousness of Christ on our record in the place of our own sinfulness. And nobody can change this record.

Do not confuse justification and sanctification. Sanctification is the process whereby God makes the believer more and more like Christ. Sanctification may change from day to day. Justification never changes. When the sinner trusts Christ, God declares him righteous, and that declaration will never be repealed. God looks on us and deals with us as though we had never sinned at all!

But, how can the holy God declare sinners righteous? Is justification merely a "fictional idea" that has no real foundation? In this section of Romans, Paul answered these questions in two ways. First, he explained justification by faith (Rom. 3:21-31); then he illustrated justification by faith from the life of Abraham (Rom. 4:1-25).

Justification Explained (Rom. 3:21-31)
"But now the righteousness of God . . . has been manifested" (Rom. 3:21, literal translation). God had revealed His righteousness in many ways before the full revelation of the Gospel: His Law, His judgments against sin, His appeals through the prophets, His blessing

on the obedient. But in the Gospel, a new kind of righteousness has been revealed (Rom. 1:16-17); and the characteristics of this righteousness are spelled out in this section.

Apart from the Law (v. 21). Under the Old Testament Law, righteousness came by man *behaving;* but under the Gospel, righteousness comes by *believing.* The Law itself reveals the righteousness of God, because the Law is "holy and just and good" (Rom. 7:12). Furthermore, the Law bore witness to this Gospel righteousness even though it could not provide it. Beginning at Genesis 3:15, and continuing through the entire Old Testament, witness is given to salvation by faith in Christ. The Old Testament sacrifices, the prophecies, the types, and the great "Gospel Scriptures" (such as Isa. 53) all bore witness to this truth. The Law could witness to God's righteousness, but it could not provide it for sinful man. Only Jesus Christ could do that (see Gal. 2:21).

Through faith in Christ (v. 22a). Faith is only as good as its object. All men trust something, if only themselves; but the Christian trusts Christ. Law righteousness is a reward for works. Gospel righteousness is a gift through faith. Many people say, "I trust in God!" But this is not what saves us. It is personal, individual faith in Jesus Christ that saves and justifies the lost sinner. Even the demons from hell believe in God and tremble, yet this does not save them (James 2:19).

For all men (vv. 22b-23). God gave His Law to the Jews, not to the Gentiles; but the Good News of salvation through Christ is offered to all men. All men need to be saved. There is no difference between the Jew and the Gentile when it comes to condemnation. "All have sinned, and are coming short of the glory of God" (Rom. 3:23, literal translation). God declared all men guilty so that He might offer to all men His free gift of salvation.

By grace (v. 24). God has two kinds of attributes: *absolute* (what He is in Himself), and *relative* (how He relates to the world and men). One of His absolute attributes is love: "God is love" (1 John 4:8). When God relates that love to you and me, it becomes *grace* and *mercy.* God in His mercy does not give us what we do deserve, and God in grace gives us what we do not deserve. The Greek word translated "freely" is translated in John 15:25 as "without a cause." We are justified *without a cause!* There is no cause in us that would merit the salvation of God! It is all of grace!

At great cost to God (vv. 24b-25). Salvation is free, but it is not cheap. Three words express the price God paid for our salvation: propitiation, redemption, and blood. In human terms, "propitiation" means appeasing someone who is angry, usually by a gift. But this is not what it means in the Bible. "Propitiation" means the satisfying of God's holy Law, the meeting of its just demands, so that God can freely forgive those who come to Christ. The word "blood" tells us what the price was. Jesus had to die on the cross in order to satisfy the Law and justify lost sinners.

The best illustration of this truth is the Jewish Day of Atonement described in Leviticus 16. Two goats were presented at the altar, and one of them was chosen for a sacrifice. The goat was slain and its blood taken into the holy of holies and sprinkled on the mercy seat, that golden cover on the ark of the covenant. This sprinkled blood covered the two tablets of the Law inside the ark. The shed blood met (temporarily) the righteous demands of the holy God.

The priest then put his hands on the head of the other goat and confessed the sins of the people. Then the goat was taken out into the wilderness and set free to symbolize the carrying away of sins. "As far as the east is from the west, so far hath He removed our transgressions from us" (Ps. 103:12). In the Old Testament period, the blood of animals could never take away sin; it could only cover it until the time when Jesus would come and purchase a finished salvation. God had "passed over" the sins that were past (Rom. 3:25, literal translation), knowing that His Son would come and finish the work. Because of His death and resurrection, there would be "redemption"—a purchasing of the sinner and setting him free.

Dr. G. Campbell Morgan was trying to explain "free salvation" to a coal miner, but the man was unable to understand it. "I have to pay for it," he kept arguing. With a flash of divine insight, Dr. Morgan asked, "How did you get down into the mine this morning?" "Why, it was easy," the man replied. "I just got on the elevator and went down."

Then Morgan asked, "Wasn't that too easy? Didn't it cost you something?"

The man laughed. "No, it didn't cost me anything; but it must have cost the company plenty to install that elevator." Then the man saw the truth: "It doesn't cost *me* anything to be saved, but it cost *God* the life of His Son."

In perfect justice (vv. 25a-26). God must be perfectly consistent with Himself. He cannot break His own Law or violate His own nature. "God is love" (1 John 4:8), and "God is light" (1 John 1:5). A God of love wants to forgive sinners, but a God of holiness must punish sin and uphold His righteous Law. How can God be both "just and the justifier"? The answer is in Jesus Christ. When Jesus suffered the wrath of God on the cross for the sins of the world, He fully met the demands of God's Law, *and also fully expressed the love of God's heart.* The animal sacrifices in the Old Testament never took away sin; but when Jesus died, He reached all the way back to Adam and took care of those sins. No one (including Satan) could accuse God of being unjust or unfair because of His seeming passing over of sins in the Old Testament time.

To establish the Law (vv. 27-31). Because of his Jewish readers, Paul wanted to say more about the relationship of the Gospel to the Law. The doctrine of justification by faith is not against the Law, because it establishes the Law. God obeyed His own Law in working out the plan of salvation. Jesus in His life and death completely fulfilled the demands of the Law. God does not have two ways of salvation, one for the Jews and one for the Gentiles; for He is one God. He is consistent with His own nature and His own Law. If salvation is through the Law, then men can boast; but the principle of faith makes it impossible for men to boast. The swimmer, when he is saved from drowning, does not brag because he trusted the lifeguard. What else could he do? When a believing sinner is justified by faith, he cannot boast of his faith, but he can boast in a wonderful Saviour.

In Romans 4–8, Paul explained how God's great plan of salvation was in complete harmony with the Old Testament Scriptures. He began first with the father of the Jewish nation, Abraham.

Justification Illustrated (Rom. 4:1-25)

The Jewish Christians in Rome would immediately have asked, "How does this doctrine of justification by faith relate to our history? Paul, you say that this doctrine is witnessed to by the Law and the Prophets. Well, what about Abraham?"

Paul accepted the challenge and explained how Abraham was saved. Abraham was called "our father," referring primarily to the Jews' natural and physical descent from Abraham. But in Romans 4:11, Abraham was also called "the father of all them that believe," meaning, all who have trusted Christ (see Gal. 3:1-18). Paul stated three important facts about Abraham's salvation that prove that the patriarch's spiritual experience was like that of believers today.

He was justified by faith, not works (vv. 1-8). Paul called two witnesses to prove that statement: Moses (Gen. 15:6) and David (Ps. 32:1-2). In Romans 4:1-3, Paul examined the experience of Abraham as recorded in Genesis 15. Abraham had defeated the kings (Gen. 14) and was wondering if they would return to fight again. God appeared to him and assured him that He was his shield and "exceeding great reward." But the thing that Abraham wanted most was a son and heir. God had promised him a son, but as yet the promise had not been fulfilled.

It was then that God told him to look at the stars. "So shall thy seed [descendants] be!" God promised; *and Abraham believed God's promise.* The Hebrew word translated *believed* means "to say amen." God gave a promise, and Abraham responded with "Amen!" It was this faith that was counted for righteousness.

The word *counted* in Romans 4:3 is a Greek word that means "to put to one's account." It is a banking term. This same word is used eleven times in this chapter, translated "reckoned" (Rom. 4:4, 9-10) and "imputed" (Rom. 4:6, 8, 11, 21-24), as well as "counted." When a man works, he earns a salary and this money is put to his account. But Abraham did not work for his salvation; he simply trusted God's Word. It was Jesus Christ who did the work on the cross, and His righteousness was put on Abraham's account.

Romans 4:5 makes a startling statement: God justifies *the ungodly!* The Law said, "I will not justify the wicked" (Ex. 23:7). The Old Testament judge was commanded to "justify the righteous, and condemn the wicked" (Deut. 25:1). When Solomon dedicated the temple, he asked God to condemn the wicked and justify the righteous! (1 Kings 8:31-32) But God justifies the ungodly—*because there are no godly for Him to justify!* He put our sins on Christ's account that He might put Christ's righteousness on our account.

In Romans 4:6-8, Paul used David as a witness, quoting from one of David's psalms of confession after his terrible sin with Bathsheba (Ps. 32:1-2). David made two amazing statements: (1) God forgives sins and imputes righteousness apart from works; (2) God does not impute our sins. In other words, once we are justified, our record contains Christ's perfect righteousness *and can never again contain our sins.* Christians do sin, and these sins need to be forgiven if we are to have fellowship with God (1 John 1:5-7); *but these sins are not held against us.* God does keep a record of our works, so that He might reward us when Jesus comes; but He is not keeping a record of our sins.

He was justified by grace, not Law (vv. 9-17). As we have seen, the Jews gloried in circumcision and the Law. If a Jew was to become righteous before God, he would have to be circumcised and obey the Law. Paul had already made it clear in Romans 2:12-29 that there must be an *inward* obedience to the Law, and a "circumcision of the heart." Mere external observances can never save the lost sinner.

But Abraham was declared righteous when he was in the state of uncircumcision. From the Jewish point of view, Abraham was a Gentile. Abraham was ninety-nine years old when he was circumcised (Gen. 17:23-27). This was more than fourteen years after the events in Genesis 15. The conclusion is obvious: circumcision had nothing to do with his justification.

Then why was circumcision given? It was a sign and a seal (Rom. 4:11). As a sign, it was evidence that he belonged to God and believed His promise. As a seal, it was a reminder to him that God had given the promise and would keep it. Believers today are sealed by the Holy Spirit of God (Eph. 1:13-14). They have also experienced a spiritual circumcision in the heart (Col. 2:10-12), not just a minor physical operation, but the putting off of the old nature through the death and resurrection of Christ. Circumcision did not add to Abraham's salvation; it merely attested to it.

But Abraham was also justified before the Law was given, and this fact Paul discusses in Romans 4:13-17. The key word here is "promise." Abraham was justified by believing God's promise, not by obeying God's Law; for God's Law through Moses had not yet been given. The promise to Abraham was given purely through God's grace. Abraham did not earn it or merit it. So today, God justifies the ungodly because they believe His gracious promise, not because they obey His Law. The Law was not given to save men, but to show men that they need to be saved (Rom. 4:15).

The fact that Abraham was justified by grace and not Law proves that salvation is for all men. Abraham is the father of all believers, both Jews and Gentiles (Rom. 4:16; Gal. 3:7, 29). Instead of the Jew complaining because Abraham was not saved by Law, he ought to rejoice that God's salvation is available to all men, and that Abraham has a spiritual family (all true believers) as well as a physical family (the nation of Israel). Paul saw this as a fulfillment of Genesis 17:5: "I have made thee a father of many nations."

He was justified by Resurrection power, not human effort (vv. 18-25). These verses are an expansion of one phrase in Romans 4:17: "who quickeneth the dead." Paul saw the rejuvenation of Abraham's body as a picture of resurrection from the dead; and then he related it to the resurrection of Christ.

One reason why God delayed in sending Abraham and Sarah a son was to permit all their natural strength to decline and then disappear. It was unthinkable that a man ninety-nine years old could beget a child in the womb of his wife who was eighty-nine years old! From a reproductive point of view, both of them were dead.

But Abraham did not walk by sight; he walked by faith. What God promises, He performs. All we need do is believe. Abraham's initial faith in God as recorded in Genesis 15 did not diminish in the years that followed. In Genesis 17–18, Abraham was "strong in faith." It was this faith that gave him strength to beget a son in his old age.

The application to salvation is clear: God must wait until the sinner is "dead" and unable to help himself before He can release His saving power. As long as the lost sinner thinks he is strong enough to do anything to please God, he cannot be saved by grace. It was when Abraham admitted that he was "dead" that God's power went to work in his body. It is when the lost sinner confesses that he is spiritually dead and unable to help himself that God can save him.

The Gospel is "the power of God unto salvation" (Rom. 1:16) because of the resurrection of Jesus Christ from the dead. Romans 4:24 and Romans 10:9-10 parallel each other. Jesus Christ was "delivered up to die on account of our offenses, and was raised up because of our justification" (Rom. 4:25, literal translation). This means that the resurrection of Christ is the proof that God accepted His Son's sacrifice, and that now sinners can be justified without God violating His own Law or contradicting His own nature.

The key, of course, is "if we believe" (Rom. 4:24). There are over sixty references to faith or unbelief in Romans. God's saving power is experienced by those who believe in Christ (Rom. 1:16). His righteousness is given to those who believe (Rom. 3:22). We are justified by faith (Rom. 5:1). The object of our faith is Jesus Christ who died for us and rose again.

All of these facts make Abraham's faith that much more wonderful. He did not have a Bible to read; he had only the simple promise of God. He was almost alone as a believer, surrounded by heathen unbelievers. He could not look back at a long record of faith; in fact, he was helping to write that record. Yet Abraham believed God. People today have a complete Bible to read and study. They have a church fellowship, and can look back at centuries of faith as recorded in church history and the Bible. Yet many refuse to believe!

Dr. Harry Ironside, for eighteen years pastor of the Moody Church in Chicago, told of visiting a Sunday School class while on vacation. The teacher asked, "How were people saved in Old Testament times?"

After a pause, one man replied, "By keeping the Law."

"That's right," said the teacher.

But Dr. Ironside interrupted: "My Bible says that by the deeds of the Law shall no flesh be justified."

The teacher was a bit embarrassed, so he said, "Well, does somebody else have an idea?"

Another student replied, "They were saved by bringing sacrifices to God."

"Yes, that's right!" the teacher said, and tried to go on with the lesson.

But Dr. Ironside interrupted, "My Bible says that the blood of bulls and goats cannot take away sin."

By this time the unprepared teacher was sure the visitor knew more about the Bible than he did, so he said, "Well, *you* tell us how people were saved in the Old Testament!"

And Dr. Ironside explained that they were saved by faith—the same way people are saved today! Twenty-one times in Hebrews 11 you find the same words "by faith."

If you are a Jew, you are a child of Abraham physically; but are you a child of Abraham *spiritually?* Abraham is the father of all who believe on Jesus Christ and are justified by faith. If you are a Gentile, you can never be a natural descendant of Abraham; but you can be one of his *spiritual* descendants. Abraham "believed God and it was counted unto him for righteousness."

CHAPTER FOUR
LIVE LIKE A KING!
Romans 5

Since Romans is a book of logic, it is a book of "therefores." We have the "therefore" of *condemnation* in Romans 3:20, *justification* in Romans 5:1, *no condemnation* in Romans 8:1, and *dedication* in Romans 12:1. In presenting his case, Paul has proved that the whole world is guilty before God, and that no one can be saved by religious deeds, such as keeping the Law. He has explained that God's way of salvation has always been "by grace, through faith" (Eph. 2:8-9), and he has used Abraham as his illustration. If a reader of the letter stopped at this point, he would know that he *needed* to and *could* be saved.

But there is much more the sinner needs to know about justification by faith. Can he be sure that it will last? How is it possible for God to save a sinner through the death of Christ on the cross? Romans 5 is Paul's explanation of the last two words in Romans 4: "our justification." He explained two basic truths: the blessings of our justification (Rom. 5:1-11), and the basis for our justification (Rom. 5:12-21).

The Blessings of Our Justification (Rom. 5:1-11)

In listing these blessings, Paul accomplished two purposes. First, he told how wonderful it is to be a Christian. Our justification is not simply a guarantee of heaven, as thrilling as that is, but it is also the source of tremendous blessings that we enjoy here and now.

His second purpose was to assure his readers that justification is a lasting thing. His Jewish readers in particular would ask, "Can this spiritual experience last if it does not require obedience to the Law? What about the trials and sufferings of life? What about the coming judgment?" When God declared us righteous in Jesus Christ, He gave to us seven spiritual blessings that assure us that we cannot be lost.

Peace with God (v. 1). The unsaved person is at "enmity with God" (Rom. 5:10; 8:7) because he cannot obey God's Law or fulfill God's will. Two verses from Isaiah make the matter clear: "There is no peace, saith the Lord, unto the wicked" (Isa. 48:22); "And the work of righteousness shall be peace" (Isa. 32:17). Condemnation means that God declares us *sinners,* which is a declaration of *war.* Justification means that God declares us *righteous,* which is a declaration of *peace,* made possible by Christ's death on the cross. "Mercy and truth are met together; righteousness and peace have kissed each other" (Ps. 85:10). "Because the Law worketh wrath" (Rom. 4:15), nobody condemned by the Law can enjoy peace with God. But when you are justified by faith, you are declared righteous, and the Law cannot condemn you or declare war!

Access to God (v. 2a). The Jew was kept from God's presence by the veil in the temple; and the Gentile was kept out by a wall in the temple with a warning on it that any Gentile who went beyond would be killed. But when Jesus died, He tore the veil (Luke 23:45) and broke down the wall (Eph. 2:14). In Christ, believing Jews and Gentiles have access to God (Eph. 2:18; Heb. 10:19-25); and they can draw on the inexhaustible riches of the grace of God (Eph. 1:7; 2:4; 3:8). We stand "in grace" and not "in Law." Justification has to do with our standing; sanctification has to do with our state. The child of a king can enter his father's presence no matter how the child looks. The word "access" here means "entrance to the king through the favor of another."

Glorious hope (v. 2b). "Peace with God" takes care of the past: He will no longer hold our sins against us. "Access to God" takes care of the present: we can come to Him at any time for the help we need. "Hope of the glory of God" takes care of the future: one day we shall share in His glory! The word "rejoice" can be translated "boast," not only in Romans 5:2, but also in Romans 5:3 and 11 ("joy"). When we were sinners, there was nothing to boast about (Rom. 3:27), because we fell short of the glory of God (Rom. 3:23). But in Christ, we boast in *His* righteousness and glory! Paul will amplify this in Romans 8:18-30.

Christian character (vv. 3-4). Justification is no escape from the trials of life. "In this world ye shall have tribulation" (John 16:33). But for the believer, trials work *for* him and not *against* him. No amount of suffering can separate us from the Lord (Rom. 8:35-39); instead, trials bring us closer to the Lord and make us more like the Lord. Suffering builds Christian character. The word "experience" in Romans 5:4 means "character that has been proved." The sequence is: tribulation—patience—proven character—hope. Our English word "tribulation" comes from a Latin word *tribulum.* In Paul's day, a *tribulum* was a heavy piece of timber with spikes in it, used for threshing the grain. The *tribulum* was drawn over the grain and it separated the wheat from the chaff. As we go through tribulations, and depend on God's grace, the trials only purify us and help to get rid of the chaff.

God's love within (vv. 5-8). "Hope deferred maketh the heart sick" (Prov. 13:12). But as we wait for this hope to be fulfilled, the love of God is "poured out into our hearts" (literal translation). Note how the first three of the "fruit of the Spirit" are experienced: love (Rom. 5:5), joy (Rom. 5:2), and peace (Rom. 5:1). Before we were saved, God proved His love by sending Christ to die for us. Now that we are His children, surely He will love us more. It is the inner experience of this love through the Spirit that sustains us as we go through tribulations.

For many months I visited a young man in a hospital who had almost burned to death. I do not know how many operations and skin grafts he had during those months, or how many specialists visited him. But the thing that sustained him during those difficult months was not the explanations of the doctors but the promises they gave him that he would recover. That was his hope. And the thing that sustained his hope was the love of his family and many friends as they stood by him. The love of God was channeled through them to him. He did recover and today gives glory to God.

Faith (Rom. 5:1), hope (Rom. 5:2), and love (Rom. 5:5) all combine to give the believer patience in the trials of life. And patience makes it possible for the believer to grow in character and become a mature child of God (James 1:1-4).

Salvation from future wrath (vv. 9-10). Paul argued from the lesser to the greater. If God saved us when we were enemies, surely He will keep on saving us now that we are His children. There is a "wrath to come," but no true believer will experience it (1 Thes. 1:9-10; 5:8-10). Paul further argued that if Christ's *death* accomplished so much for us, how much more will He do for us in His *life* as He intercedes for us in heaven! "Saved by His life" refers to Romans 4:25: "raised again for [on account of] our justification." Because He lives, we are eternally saved (Heb. 7:23-25).

A will is of no effect until the death of the one who wrote it. Then an executor takes over and sees to it that the will is obeyed and the inheritance distributed. But suppose the executor is unscrupulous and wants to get the inheritance for himself? He may figure out many devious ways to circumvent the law and steal the inheritance.

Jesus Christ wrote us into His will, and He wrote the will with His blood. "This cup is the new testament in My blood, which is shed for you" (Luke 22:20). He died so that the will would be in force; but then He arose from the dead and returned to heaven that He might enforce the will Himself and distribute the inheritance. Thus, we are "saved by His life."

Reconciliation with God (v. 11). The word *atonement* means "reconciliation, brought back into fellowship with God." The term is mentioned also in Romans 5:10. In Romans 1:18-32, Paul explained how men declared war on God and, because of this, deserved to be condemned eternally. But God did not declare war on man. Instead, He sent His Son as the Peacemaker (Eph. 2:11-18) that men might be reconciled to God.

A review of these seven blessings of justification shows how certain our salvation is in Christ. Totally apart from Law, and purely by grace, we have a salvation that takes care of the past, the present, and the future. Christ died for us; Christ lives for us; Christ is coming for us! Hallelujah, what a Saviour!

The Basis of Our Justification (Rom. 5:12-21)

How is it possible for God to save sinners in the person of Jesus Christ? We understand that somehow Christ took our place on the cross, but how was such a substitution possible?

Paul answered the question in this section, and these verses are the very heart of the letter. To understand these verses a few general truths about this section need to be understood. First, note the repetition of the little word *one.* It is used eleven times. The key idea here is our identification with Adam and with Christ. Second, note the repetition of the word *reign* which is used five times. Paul saw two men—Adam and Christ—each of them reigning over a kingdom. Finally, note that the phrase *much more* is repeated five times. This means that in Jesus Christ we have gained much more than we ever lost in Adam!

In short, this section is a contrast of Adam and Christ. Adam was given dominion over the old creation, he sinned, and he lost his kingdom. Because of Adam's sin, all mankind is under condemnation and death. Christ came as the King over a new creation (2 Cor. 5:17). By His obedience on the cross, He brought in righteousness and justification. Christ not only undid all the damage that Adam's sin effected, but He accomplished "much more" by making us the very sons of God. Some of this "much more" Paul has already explained in Romans 5:1-11.

Skeptics sometimes ask, "Was it fair for God to condemn the whole world just because of one man's disobedience?" The answer, of course, is that it was not only fair; but it was also wise and gracious. To begin with, if God had tested each human being individually, the result would have been the same: disobedience. But even more important, by condemning the human race through one man (Adam), God was then *able to save the human race through one Man* (Jesus Christ)! Each of us is racially united to Adam, so that his deed affects us. (See Heb. 7:9-10 for an example of this racial headship.) The fallen angels cannot be saved because they are not a race. They sinned individually and were judged individually. There can be no representative to take their judgment for them and save them. But because you and I were lost in Adam, our *racial* head, we can be saved in Christ, the Head of the new creation. God's plan was both gracious and wise.

Our final question must be answered: how do we *know* that we are racially united to Adam? The answer is in Romans 5:12-14, and the argument runs like this: We know that all men die. But death is the result of disobeying the Law. There was no Law from Adam to Moses, but men still died. A general result demands a general cause. What is that cause? It can be only one thing: the disobedience of

Adam. When Adam sinned, he ultimately died. All of his descendants died (Gen. 5), yet the Law had not yet been given. Conclusion: they died because of Adam's sin. "For that all have sinned" (Rom. 5:12) means "all have sinned *in Adam's sin.*" Men do not die because of their own acts of sin; otherwise, babies would not die (Rom. 9:11). Men die because they are united racially to Adam, and "in Adam all men die" (1 Cor. 15:22).

Having understood these general truths about the passage, we may now examine the contrasts that Paul gives between Adam and Christ and between Adam's sin and Christ's act of obedience on the cross.

Adam's offense is contrasted with Christ's free gift (v. 15). Because of Adam's trespass, many died; because of Christ's obedience the grace of God abounds to many bringing life. The word "many" (literally "the many") means the same as "all men" in Romans 5:12 and 18. Note the "much more"; for the grace of Christ brings not only physical life, but also spiritual life and abundant life. Christ did conquer death and one day will raise the bodies of all who have died "in Christ." If He stopped there, He would only reverse the effects of Adam's sin; but He went on to do "much more." He gives eternal life abundantly to all who trust Him (John 10:10).

The effect of Adam's sin is contrasted with the effect of Christ's obedience (v. 16). Adam's sin brought judgment and condemnation; but Christ's work on the cross brings justification. When Adam sinned, he was declared unrighteous and condemned. When a sinner trusts Christ, he is justified—declared righteous in Christ.

The two "reigns" are contrasted (v. 17). Because of Adam's disobedience, death reigned. Read the "book of the generations of Adam" in Genesis 5, and note the solemn repetition of the phrase "and he died." In Romans 5:14, Paul argued that men did not die "from Adam to Moses" for the same reason that Adam died—breaking a revealed law of God—for the Law had not yet been given. "The wages of sin is death" (Rom. 6:23). Because *sin* was reigning in men's lives (Rom. 5:21), *death* was also reigning (Rom. 5:14, 17).

But in Jesus Christ we enter a new kingdom: "For the kingdom of God is not meat and drink; but *righteousness,* and *peace,* and *joy* in the Holy Ghost" (Rom. 14:17). "Therefore being justified by faith" we are declared *righteous,* we have *peace* with God, and we *rejoice* in the hope of the glory of God. Note that it is *we* who reign! "Much more they . . . shall reign in life by one, Jesus Christ." In Adam we lost our kingship, but in Jesus Christ we reign as kings. And we reign "much more"! Our spiritual reign is far greater than Adam's earthly reign, for we share "abundance of grace and of the gift of righteousness" (Rom. 5:17).

The two "one acts" are contrasted (vv. 18-19). Adam did not have to commit a series of sins. In one act God tested Adam, and he failed. It is termed an "offense" and an act of "disobedience." The word *offense* means "trespass—crossing over the line." God told Adam how far he could go, and Adam decided to go beyond the appointed limit. "Of every tree of the Garden thou mayest freely eat: but of the tree of the knowledge of good and evil, thou shalt not eat of it: for in the day that thou eatest thereof, thou shalt surely die" (Gen. 2:16-17).

In contrast to "the trespass of one" is "the righteousness of one," meaning the righteous work of Christ on the cross. In Romans 5:19 Paul calls it "the obedience of One" (see Phil. 2:5-12). Christ's sacrifice on the cross not only made possible "justification," but also "justification *of life*" (italics mine). Justification is not merely a legal term that describes our position before God ("just as if I'd never sinned"); but it results in a certain kind of life. "Justification of life" in Romans 5:18 is parallel to "be made righteous" in Romans 5:19. In other words, our justification is the result of a living union with Christ. And this union ought to result in a new kind of life, a righteous life of obedience to God. Our union with Adam made us sinners; our union with Christ enables us to "reign in life."

Law and grace are contrasted (vv. 20-21). "Then Law crept in" (WMS); or, "Then the Law came in beside" (literal translation). Grace was not an addition to God's plan; grace was a part of God's plan from the very beginning. God dealt with Adam and Eve in grace; He dealt with the patriarchs in grace; and He dealt with the nation of Israel in grace. He gave the Law through Moses, not to replace His grace, but to reveal man's need for grace. Law was temporary, but grace is eternal.

But as the Law made man's sins increase, God's grace abounded even more. God's grace was more than adequate to deal with man's sins. Even though sin and death still reign in this world, God's grace is also reigning through the righteousness of Christ. The Christian's body is subject to death and his old nature tempts him to sin; but in Jesus Christ, he can "reign in life" because he is a part of the gracious kingdom of Christ.

An Old Testament story helps us understand the conflict between these two "reigns" in the world today. God rejected Saul as the king of Israel, and anointed David. Those who trusted David eventually shared his kingdom of peace and joy. Those who trusted Saul ended in shame and defeat.

Like David, Jesus Christ is God's anointed King. Like Saul, Satan is still free to work in this world and seek to win men's allegiance. Sin and death are reigning in the "old creation" over which Adam was the head, but grace and righteousness are reigning in "the new creation" over which Christ is the Head. And as we yield to Him, we "reign in life."

In Romans 5:14, Adam is called "the figure of Him that was to come." Adam was a type, or picture, of Jesus Christ. Adam came from the earth, but Jesus is the Lord from heaven (1 Cor. 15:47). Adam was tested in a Garden, surrounded by beauty and love; Jesus was tempted in a wilderness, and He died on a cruel cross surrounded by hatred and ugliness. Adam was a thief, and was cast out of Paradise; but Jesus Christ turned to a thief and said, "Today shalt thou be with Me in Paradise" (Luke 23:43). The Old Testament is "the book of the generations of Adam" (Gen. 5:1) and it ends with "a curse" (Mal. 4:6). The New Testament is "The book of the generation of Jesus Christ" (Matt. 1:1) and it ends with "no more curse" (Rev. 22:3).

You cannot help *being* "in Adam," for this came by your first birth over which you had no control. But you can help *staying* "in Adam," for you can experience a second birth—a new birth from above—that will put you "in Christ." This is why Jesus said, "Ye must be born again" (John 3:7).

CHAPTER FIVE
DYING TO LIVE
Romans 6

During a court session, an attorney will often rise to his feet and say, "Your Honor, I object!" Some of the Roman Christians must have felt like objecting as they heard Paul's letter being read, and Paul seemed to anticipate their thinking. In Romans 6–8 Paul defended his doctrine of justification by faith. He anticipated three objections: (1) "If God's grace abounds when we sin, then let's continue sinning so we might experience more grace" (Rom. 6:1-14); (2) "If we are no longer under the Law, then we are free to live as we please" (Rom. 6:15–7:6); and (3) "You have made God's Law sinful" (Rom. 7:7-25).

These objections prove that the readers did not understand either Law or grace. They were going to extremes: legalism on the one hand and license on the other. So as Paul defended justification he also explained sanctification. He told how we can live lives of *victory* (Rom. 6), *liberty* (Rom. 7), and *security* (Rom. 8). He explained our relationship to the flesh, the Law, and the Holy Spirit. In Romans 6, Paul gave three instructions for attaining victory over sin.

Know (Rom. 6:1-10)

The repetition of the word "know" in Romans 6:1, 6, and 9 indicates that Paul wanted us to understand a basic doctrine. Christian living depends on Christian learning; duty is always founded on doctrine. If Satan can keep a Christian ignorant, he can keep him impotent.

The basic truth Paul was teaching is the believer's identification with Christ in death, burial, and resurrection. Just as we are identified with Adam in sin and condemnation, so we are now identified with Christ in righteousness and justification. At Romans 5:12, Paul made a transition from discussing "sins" to discussing "sin"—from the actions to the principle, from the fruit to the root. Jesus Christ not only died for our sins, but He also died unto sin, and we died with Him. Perhaps a chart will explain the contrasts better.

Romans 3:21–5:21	*Romans 6–8*
Substitution: He died for me	Identification: I died with Him
He died *for* my sins	He died *unto* sin
He paid sin's penalty	He broke sin's power
Justification: righteousness imputed (put to my account)	Sanctification: righteousness imparted (made a part of my life)
Saved by His death	Saved by His life

In other words, justification by faith is not simply a legal matter between me and God; it is a living relationship. It is "a justification which brings life" (Rom. 5:18, literal translation). I am in Christ and identified with Him. Therefore, whatever happened to Christ has happened to me. When He died, I died. When He arose, I arose in Him. I am now seated with Him in the heavenlies! (see Eph. 2:1-10; Col. 3:1-3) Because of this living union with Christ, the believer has a totally new relationship to sin.

He is dead to sin (vv. 2-5). Paul's illustration is baptism. The Greek word has two basic meanings: (1) a literal meaning—to dip or immerse; and (2) a figurative meaning—to be identified with. An example of the latter would be 1 Corinthians 10:2: "And were all baptized unto Moses in the cloud and in the sea." The nation of Israel was identified with Moses as their leader when they crossed the Red Sea.

It appears that Paul had both the literal and the figurative in mind in this paragraph, for he used the readers' experience of water baptism to remind them of their identification with Christ through the baptism of the Holy Spirit. To be "baptized into Jesus Christ" (Rom. 6:3) is the same as "For by one Spirit are we all baptized into one body" (1 Cor. 12:13). There is a difference between water baptism and the baptism of the Spirit (John 1:33). When a sinner trusts Christ, he is immediately born into the family of God and receives the gift of the Holy Spirit. A good illustration of this is the household of Cornelius when they heard Peter preach (Acts 10:34-48). When these people believed on Christ, they immediately received the Holy Spirit. After that, they were baptized. Peter's words, "Whosoever believeth in Him shall receive remission of sins" gave to them the promise that they needed. They believed—and they were saved!

Historians agree that the mode of baptism in the early church was immersion. The believer was "buried" in the water and brought up again as a picture of death, burial, and resurrection. Baptism by immersion (which is the illustration Paul is using in Rom. 6) pictures the believer's identification with Christ in His death, burial, and resurrection. It is an outward symbol of an inward experience. Paul is not saying that their immersion in water put them "into Jesus Christ," for that was accomplished by the Spirit when they believed. Their immersion was a picture of what the Spirit did: the Holy Spirit identified them with Christ in His death, burial, and resurrection.

This means that the believer has a new relationship to sin. He is "dead to sin." "I am crucified with Christ" (Gal. 2:20). If a drunk dies, he can no longer be tempted by alcohol because his body is dead to all physical senses. He cannot see the alcohol, smell it, taste it, or desire it. In Jesus Christ we have died to sin so that we no longer want to "continue in sin." But we are not only dead to sin; we are also alive in Christ. We have been raised from the dead and now walk in the power of His resurrection. We walk in "newness of life" because we share His life. "I am crucified with Christ, nevertheless I live" (Gal. 2:20).

This tremendous spiritual truth is illustrated in the miracle of the resurrection of Lazarus (John 11). When Jesus arrived at Bethany, Lazarus had been in the tomb four days; so there was no question about his death. By the power of His word ("Lazarus, come forth!") Jesus raised His friend from the dead. But when Lazarus appeared at the door of the tomb, he was wrapped in graveclothes. So Jesus commanded, "Loose him, and let him go!" He had been raised to walk "in newness of life." In John 12, Lazarus was seated with Christ at the table, in fellowship with Him. Dead—raised from the dead—set free to walk in newness of life—seated with Christ: all of these facts illustrate the spiritual truths of our identification with Christ as given in Ephesians 2:1-10.

Too many Christians are "betweeners": they live between Egypt and Canaan, saved but never satisfied; or they live between Good Friday and Easter, believing in the Cross but not entering into the power and glory of the Resurrection. Romans 6:5 indicates that our union with Christ assures our future resurrection should we die. But Romans 6:4 teaches that we share His resurrection power *today*. "Since, then, you have been raised with

Christ, set your hearts on things above. . . . For you died, and your life is now hidden with Christ in God" (Col. 3:1, 3, NIV).

It is clear, then, that the believer cannot deliberately live in sin since he has a new relationship to sin because of his identification with Christ. The believer has died to the old life; he has been raised to enjoy a new life. The believer does not want to go back into sin any more than Lazarus wanted to go back into the tomb dressed again in his graveclothes! Then Paul introduced a second fact:

He should not serve sin (vv. 6-10). Sin is a terrible master, and it finds a willing servant in the human body. The body is not sinful; the body is neutral. It can be controlled either by sin or by God. But man's fallen nature, which is not changed at conversion, gives sin a beachhead from which it can attack and then control. Paul expressed the problem: "For I know that in me (that is, in my flesh) dwelleth no good thing: for to will is present with me; but how to perform that which is good I find not" (Rom. 7:18).

A tremendous fact is introduced here: the old man (the old ego, self) was crucified with Christ so that the body need not be controlled by sin. The word "destroyed" in Romans 6:6 does not mean annihilated; it means "rendered inactive, made of no effect." The same Greek word is translated "loosed" in Romans 7:2. If a woman's husband dies, she is "loosed" from the law of her husband and is free to marry again. There is a change in relationship. The law is still there, but it has no authority over the woman because her husband is dead.

Sin wants to be our master. It finds a foothold in the old nature, and through the old nature seeks to control the members of the body. But in Jesus Christ, we died to sin; and the old nature was crucified so that the old life is rendered inoperative. Paul was not describing an experience; he was stating a fact. The practical experience was to come later. It is a fact of history that Jesus Christ died on the cross. It is also a fact of history that the believer died with Him; and "he that is dead is freed from sin" (Rom. 6:7). Not "free *to* sin" as Paul's accusers falsely stated; but "freed from sin."

Sin and death have no dominion over Christ. We are "in Christ"; therefore, sin and death have no dominion over us. Jesus Christ not only died "for sin," but He also died "unto sin." That is, He not only paid the penalty for sin, but He broke the power of sin. This idea of dominion takes us back to Romans 5:12-21 where Paul dealt with the "reigns" of sin, death, and grace. Through Christ we "reign in life" (Rom. 5:17) so that sin no longer controls our lives.

The big question now is, "I believe the facts of history; but how do I make this work in daily experience?" This leads to Paul's second instruction.

Reckon (Rom. 6:11)

In some parts of the United States, "to reckon" means "to think" or "to guess." "I reckon" is also the equivalent of "I suppose." But none of these popular meanings can apply to this verse. The word *reckon* is a translation of a Greek word that is used forty-one times in the New Testament—nineteen times in Romans alone. It appears in Romans 4 where it is translated as "count, reckon, impute." It means "to take into account, to calculate, to estimate." The word *impute*—"to put to one's account"—is perhaps the best translation.

To reckon means "to put to one's account." It simply means to believe that what God says in His Word is really true in your life.

Paul didn't tell his readers to *feel* as if they were dead to sin, or even to *understand* it fully, but to act on God's Word and claim it for themselves. Reckoning is a matter of faith that issues in action. It is like endorsing a check: if we really believe that the money is in the checking account, we will sign our name and collect the money. Reckoning is not claiming a promise, but acting on a fact. God does not command us to become dead to sin. He tells us that we *are* dead to sin and alive unto God, and then commands us to act on it. Even if we do not act on it, the facts are still true.

Paul's first instruction ("know") centered in the *mind,* and this second instruction ("reckon") focuses on the *heart.* His third instruction touches the *will.*

Yield (Rom. 6:12-23)

The word *yield* is found five times in this section (Rom. 6:13, 16, and 19), and means "to place at one's disposal, to present, to offer as a sacrifice." According to Romans 12:1, the believer's body should be presented to the Lord as "a living sacrifice" for His glory. The Old Testament sacrifices were dead sacrifices. The Lord may ask some of us to die for Him, but He asks all of us to *live* for Him.

How we are to yield (vv. 12-13). This is an act of the will based on the knowledge we have of what Christ has done for us. It is an intelligent act—not the impulsive decision of the moment based on some emotional stirring. It is important to notice the tenses of the verbs in these verses. A literal translation is: "Do not constantly allow sin to reign in your mortal body so that you are constantly obeying its lusts. Neither constantly yield your members of your body as weapons [or tools] of unrighteousness to sin; but once and for all yield yourselves to God." That once-and-for-all surrender is described in Romans 12:1.

There must be in the believer's life that final and complete surrender of the body to Jesus Christ. This does not mean there will be no further steps of surrender, because there will be. The longer we walk with Christ, the deeper the fellowship must become. But there can be no subsequent steps without that first step. The tense of the verb in Romans 12:1 corresponds with that in Romans 6:13—a once-and-for-all yielding to the Lord. To be sure, we daily surrender afresh to Him; but even that is based on a final and complete surrender.

Why does the Lord want your body? To begin with, the believer's body is God's temple, and He wants to use it for His glory (1 Cor. 6:19-20; Phil. 1:20-21). But Paul wrote that the body is also God's tool and God's weapon (Rom. 6:13). God wants to use the members of the body as tools for building His kingdom and weapons for fighting His enemies.

The Bible tells of people who permitted God to take and use their bodies for the fulfilling of His purposes. God used the rod in Moses' hand and conquered Egypt. He used the sling in David's hand to defeat the Philistines. He used the mouths and tongues of the prophets. Paul's dedicated feet carried him from city to city as he proclaimed the Gospel. The Apostle John's eyes saw visions of the future, his ears heard God's message, and his fingers wrote it all down in a book that we can read.

But you can also read in the Bible accounts of the members of the body being used for sinful purposes. David's eyes looked on his neighbor's wife; his mind plotted a wicked scheme; his hand signed a cowardly order for the woman's husband to be killed. As you read Psalm 51, you see that his whole body was affected by sin: his eyes (Ps. 51:3), mind (Ps. 51:6), ears (Ps. 51:8), heart (Ps. 51:10), and lips and mouth (Ps. 51:14-15). No wonder he prayed for a *thorough* cleansing! (Ps. 51:2)

Why we are to yield (vv. 14-23). Three words summarize the reasons for our yielding: *favor* (Rom. 6:14-15), *freedom* (Rom. 6:16-20), and *fruit* (Rom. 6:21-23).

Favor (vv. 14-15). It is because of God's grace that we yield ourselves to Him. Paul has proved that we are not saved by the Law and that we do not live under the Law. The fact that we are saved by grace does not give us an excuse to sin; but it does give us a reason to obey. Sin and Law go together. "The sting of death is sin; and the strength of sin is the Law" (1 Cor. 15:56). Since we are not under Law, but under grace, sin is robbed of its strength.

Freedom (vv. 16-20). The illustration of the master and servant is obvious. Whatever you yield to becomes your master. Before you were saved, you were the slave of sin. Now that you belong to Christ, you are freed from that old slavery and made the servant of Christ. Romans 6:19 suggests that the Christian ought to be as enthusiastic in yielding to the Lord as he was in yielding to sin. A friend once said to me, "I want to be as good a saint as I was a sinner!" I knew what he meant because in his unconverted days he was almost "the chief of sinners."

The unsaved person is free—free *from* righteousness (Rom. 6:20). But his bondage to sin only leads him deeper into slavery so that it becomes harder and harder to do what is right. The Prodigal Son is an example of this (Luke 15:11-24). When he was at home, he decided he wanted his freedom, so he left home to find himself and enjoy himself. But his rebellion only led him deeper into slavery. He was the slave of wrong desires, then the slave of wrong deeds; and finally he became a literal slave when he took care of the pigs. He wanted to find himself, but he lost himself! What he thought was freedom turned out to be the worst kind of slavery. It was only when he returned home and *yielded to his father* that he found true freedom.

Fruit (vv. 21-23). If you serve a master, you can expect to receive wages. Sin pays wages—death! God also pays wages—holiness and everlasting life. In the old life, we produced fruit that made us ashamed. In the new life in Christ, we produce fruit that glorifies God and brings joy to our lives. We usually apply Romans 6:23 to the lost, and certainly it does apply; but it also has a warning for the saved. (After all, it was written to Christians.) "There is a sin unto death" (1 John 5:17).

"For this reason many among you are weak and sick, and a number sleep" (1 Cor. 11:30, NASB). Samson, for example, would not yield himself to God, but preferred to yield to the lusts of the flesh, and the result was death (Jud. 16). If the believer refuses to surrender his body to the Lord, but uses its members for sinful purposes, then he is in danger of being disciplined by the Father, and this could mean death. (See Heb. 12:5-11, and note the end of v. 9 in particular.)

These three instructions need to be heeded each day that we live. KNOW that you have been crucified with Christ and are dead to sin. RECKON this fact to be true in your own life. YIELD your body to the Lord to be used for His glory.

Now that you KNOW these truths, RECKON them to be true in *your* life, and then YIELD yourself to God.

CHAPTER SIX CHRISTIANS AND THE LAW

Romans 7

Something in human nature makes us want to go to extremes, a weakness from which Christians are not wholly free. "Since we are saved by grace," some argue, "we are free to live as we please," which is the extreme of *license.*

"But we cannot ignore God's Law," others argue. "We are saved by grace, to be sure; but we must live under Law if we are to please God." This is the extreme expression of *legalism.*

Paul answered the first group in Romans 6; the second group he answered in Romans 7. The word *law* is used twenty-three times in this chapter. In Romans 6, Paul told us how to stop doing bad things; in Romans 7 he told how *not* to do good things. "You were not justified by keeping the Law," he argued, "and you cannot be sanctified by keeping the Law."

Every growing Christian understands the experience of Romans 6 and 7. Once we learn how to "know, reckon, and yield," we start getting victory over the habits of the flesh, and we feel we are becoming more spiritual. We set high standards and ideals for ourselves and for a while seem to attain them. *Then everything collapses!* We start to see deeper into our own hearts and we discover sins that we did not know were there. God's holy Law takes on a new power, and we wonder if we can ever do anything good! Without realizing it, we have moved into "legalism" and have learned the truth about sin, the Law, and ourselves.

What really is "legalism"? It is the belief that I can become holy and please God by obeying laws. It is measuring spirituality by a list of do's and don'ts. The weakness of legalism is that it sees *sins* (plural) but not *sin* (the root of the trouble). It judges by the outward and not the inward. Furthermore, the legalist fails to understand the real purpose of God's Law and the relationship between Law and grace.

In my pastoral experience, I have counseled many people who have suffered severe emotional and spiritual damage because they have tried to live holy lives on the basis of a high standard. I have seen the consequences of these attempts: either the person becomes a pretender, or he suffers a complete collapse and abandons his desires for godly living. I have seen too that many legalists are extremely hard on other people—critical, unloving, unforgiving. Paul wanted to spare his readers this difficult and dangerous experience. In Romans 7, he discussed three topics, which, if understood and applied, will deliver us from legalism.

The Authority of the Law (Rom. 7:1-6)

These verses actually continue the discussion that Paul began in Romans 6:15, answering the question, "Shall we sin because we are not under the Law, but under grace?" He used the illustration of a master and servant to explain how the Christian should yield himself to God. In this passage he used the illustration of a husband and wife to show that the believer has a new relationship to the Law because of his union with Jesus Christ.

The illustration is a simple one, but it has a profound application. When a man and woman marry, they are united for life. Marriage is a physical union ("They two shall be one flesh" Gen. 2:24) and can only be broken by a physical cause. One such cause is *death.* (Matt. 5:31-34; 19:1-12 indicate that unfaithfulness also breaks the marriage bond, but Paul does not bring this up. He is not discussing marriage and divorce; he is using marriage to illustrate a point.)

As long as they live, the husband and wife are under the authority of the law of marriage. If the woman leaves the man and marries another man, she commits adultery. But if the husband dies, she is free to remarry because she is no longer a wife. It is death that has broken the marriage relationship and set her free.

Paul's *application* in Romans 7:4-6 clinches the argument. He states two marvelous facts that explain the believer's relationship to the Law.

We died to the Law (vv. 4-5). It appears that Paul has confused his illustration, but he has not. When we were unsaved ("in the flesh," Rom. 7:5), we were under the authority of God's Law. We were condemned by that Law. When we trusted Christ and were united to Him, *we died to the Law* just as we died to the flesh (Rom. 6:1-10). The Law did not die; *we* died.

But in Paul's illustration from marriage, it was the *husband* who died and the wife who married again. If you and I are represented by the wife, and the Law is represented by the husband, then the application does not follow the illustration. If the wife died in the illustration, the only way she could marry again would be to come back from the dead. But that is exactly what Paul wants to teach! When we trusted Christ, we died to the Law; but in Christ, we arose from the dead and now are "married" (united) to Christ to live a new kind of life!

The Law did not die, because God's Law still rules over men. We died to the Law, and it no longer has dominion over us. But we are not "lawless"; we are united to Christ, sharing His life, and thus walking "in newness of life." Romans 8:4 climaxes the argument: "That the righteousness of the Law might be fulfilled in us, who walk not after the flesh but after the Spirit." In the old life of sin, we brought forth fruit "unto death," but in the new life of grace, we "bring forth fruit unto God." To be "dead to the Law" does not mean that we lead lawless lives. It simply means that the *motivation* and *dynamic* of our lives does not come from the Law: it comes from God's grace through our union with Christ.

We are delivered from Law (v. 6). This is the logical conclusion: the Law cannot exercise authority over a dead person. The *Authorized Version* reads as though the Law died; but Paul wrote, "We having died to that wherein we were held." Death means deliverance (note Rom. 6:9-10). But we were delivered that we might serve. The Christian life is not one of independence and rebellion. We died to the Law that we might be "married to Christ." We were delivered from the Law that we might serve Christ. This truth refutes the false accusation that Paul taught lawlessness.

What is different about Christian service as opposed to our old life of sin? To begin with, the Holy Spirit of God energizes us as we seek to obey and serve the Lord. (The word spirit ought to be capitalized in Romans 7:6—"newness of Spirit.") Under Law, no enablement was given. God's commandments were written on stones and read to the people. But under grace, God's Word is written in our hearts (2 Cor. 3:1-3). We "walk in newness of life" (Rom. 6:4) and serve "in newness of Spirit." The believer, then, is no longer under the authority of the Law.

The Ministry of the Law (Rom. 7:7-13)

Paul's objectors were ready! "What good is the Law if we don't need it anymore? Why, a teaching such as yours turns the Law into sin!" In answering that objection, Paul explained the ministries of the Law, ministries that function even today.

The Law reveals sin (v. 7). "By the Law is the knowledge of sin" (Rom. 3:20). "Where no Law is, there is no transgression" (Rom. 4:15). The Law is a mirror that reveals the inner man and shows us how dirty we are (James 1:22-25). Note that Paul did not use murder, stealing, or adultery in his discussion; he uses *coveting*. This is the last of the Ten Commandments, and it differs from the other nine in that it is an inward attitude, not an outward action. Covetousness leads to the breaking of the other commandments! It is an insidious sin that most people never recognize in their own lives, but God's Law reveals it.

The rich ruler in Mark 10:17-27 is a good example of the use of the Law to reveal sin and show a man his need for a Saviour. The young man was very moral outwardly, but he had never faced the sins within. Jesus did not tell him about the Law because the Law would save him; He told him about the Law because the young man did not realize his own sinfulness. True, he had never committed adultery, robbed anyone, given false witness, or dishonored his parents; but what about covetousness? When Jesus told him to sell his goods and give to the poor, the man went away in great sorrow. The commandment, "Thou shalt not covet," had revealed to him what a sinner he really was! Instead of admitting his sin, he rejected Christ and went away unconverted.

The Law arouses sin (vv. 8-9). Since Paul was a devout Pharisee, seeking to obey the Law before his conversion, it is easier to understand these verses. (Read Phil. 3:1-11 and Gal. 1 for other autobiographical data on Paul's relationship to the Law in his unconverted days.) Keep in mind too that "the strength of sin is the Law" (1 Cor. 15:56). Since we have a sinful nature, the Law is bound to arouse that nature the way a magnet draws steel.

Something in human nature wants to rebel whenever a law is given. I was standing in Lincoln Park in Chicago, looking at the newly painted benches; and I noticed a sign on each bench: "Do Not Touch." As I watched, I saw numbers of people deliberately reach out and touch the wet paint! Why? Because the sign told them not to! Instruct a child not to go near the water, and that is the very thing he will do! Why? "Because the carnal mind is enmity against God: for it is not subject to the law of God, neither indeed can be" (Rom. 8:7).

Believers who try to live by rules and regulations discover that their legalistic system only arouses more sin and creates more problems. The churches in Galatia were very legalistic, and they experienced all kinds of trouble. "But if ye bite and devour one another, take heed that ye be not consumed one of another" (Gal. 5:15). Their legalism did not make them more spiritual; it made them more sinful! Why? Because the Law arouses sin in our nature.

The Law kills (vv. 10-11). "For if there had been a law given which could have given life, verily righteousness should have been by the Law" (Gal. 3:21). But the Law cannot give life: it can only show the sinner that he is guilty and condemned. This explains why legalistic Christians and churches do not grow and bear spiritual fruit. They are living by Law, and the Law always kills. Few things are more dead than an orthodox church that is proud of its "high standards" and tries to live up to them in its own energy. Often the members of such a church start to judge and condemn one another, and the sad result is a church fight and then a church split that leaves members—or former members—angry and bitter.

As the new Christian grows, he comes into contact with various philosophies of the Christian life. He can read books, attend seminars, listen to tapes, and get a great deal of information. If he is not careful, he will start following a human leader and accept his teachings as Law. This practice is a very subtle form of legalism, and it kills spiritual growth. No human teacher can take the place of Christ; no book can take the place of the Bible. Men can give us information, but only the Spirit can give us illumination and help us understand spiritual truths. The Spirit enlightens us and enables us; no human leader can do that.

The Law shows the sinfulness of sin (vv. 12-13). Unsaved people know that there is such a thing as sin; but they do not realize the sinfulness of sin. Many Christians do not realize the true nature of sin. We excuse our sins with words like "mistakes" or "weaknesses"; but God condemns our sins and tries to get us to see that they are "exceedingly sinful." Until we realize how wicked sin really is, we will never want to oppose it and live in victory.

Paul's argument here is tremendous: (1) the Law is not sinful—it is holy, just, and good; (2) but the Law reveals sin, arouses sin, and then uses sin to slay us; if something as good as the Law accomplishes these results, then something is radically wrong somewhere; (3) conclusion: see how sinful sin is when it can use something good like the Law to produce such tragic results. Sin is indeed "exceedingly sinful." The problem is not with the Law; the problem is with my sinful nature. This prepares the way for the third topic in this chapter.

The Inability of the Law (Rom. 7:14-25)

Having explained what the Law is supposed to do, Paul now explains what the Law cannot do.

The Law cannot change you (v. 14). The character of the Law is described in four words: holy, just, good, and spiritual. That the Law is holy and just, nobody can deny, because it came from the holy God who is perfectly just in all that He says and does. The Law is good. It reveals God's holiness to us and helps us to see our need for a Saviour.

What does it mean that the Law is "spiritual"? It means that the Law deals with the inner man, the spiritual part of man, as well as with the outer actions. In the original giving of the Law in Exodus, the emphasis was on the outward actions. But when Moses restated the Law in Deuteronomy, he emphasized the inner quality of the Law as it relates to man's heart. This spiritual emphasis is stated clearly in Deuteronomy 10:12-13. The repetition of the word "love" in Deuteronomy also shows that the deeper interpretation of the Law relates to the inner man (Deut. 4:37; 6:4-6; 10:12; 11:1; 30:6, 16, 20).

Our nature is carnal (fleshly); but the Law's nature is spiritual. This explains why the old nature responds as it does to the Law. It has well been said, "The old nature knows no Law, the new nature needs no Law." The Law cannot transform the old nature; it can only reveal how sinful that old nature is. The believer who tries to live under Law will only *activate* the old nature; he will not eradicate it.

The Law cannot enable you to do good (vv. 15-21). Three times in this passage Paul stated that sin dwells in us (Rom. 7:14, 18, 20). He was referring, of course, to the old nature. It is also true that the Holy Spirit dwells in us; and in Romans 8, Paul explained how the Spirit of God enables us to live in victory, something the Law cannot help us do.

The many pronouns in this section indicate that the writer is having a problem with *self.* This is not to say that the Christian is a split personality, because he is not. Salvation makes a man whole. But it does indicate that the believer's mind, will, and body can be controlled either by the old nature or the new nature, either by the flesh or the Spirit. The statements here indicate that the believer has two serious problems: (1) he cannot do the good he wants to do, and (2) he does the evil that he does not want to do.

Does this mean that Paul could not stop himself from breaking God's Law, that he was a liar and thief and murderer? Of course not! Paul was saying that of *himself* he could not obey God's Law; and that even when he did, evil was still present with him. No matter what he did, his deeds were tainted by sin. Even after he had done his best, he had to admit that he was "an unprofitable servant" (Luke 17:10). "So I find this law at work: when I want to do good, evil is right there with me" (Rom. 7:21, NIV). This, of course, is a different problem from that in Romans 6. The problem there was, "How can I stop doing bad things?" while the problem here is, "How can I ever do anything good?"

The legalist says, "Obey the Law and you will do good and live a good life." But the Law only reveals and arouses sin, showing how sinful it is! It is impossible for me to obey the Law because I have a sinful nature that rebels against the Law. Even if I think I have done good, I know that evil is present. The Law is good, but by nature, I am bad! So, the legalist is wrong: the Law cannot enable us to do good.

The Law cannot set you free (vv. 21-25). The believer has an old nature that wants to keep him in bondage; "I will get free from these old sins!" the Christian says to himself. "I determine here and now that I will not do this any longer." What happens? He exerts all his willpower and energy, and for a time succeeds; but then when he least expects it, he falls again. Why? Because he tried to overcome his old nature with Law, and the Law cannot deliver us from the old nature. When you move under the Law, you are only making the old nature stronger; because "the strength of sin is the Law" (1 Cor. 15:56). Instead of being a dynamo that gives us power to overcome, the Law is a magnet that draws out of us all kinds of sin and corruption. The inward man may delight in the Law of God (Ps. 119:35), but the old nature delights in breaking the Law of God. No wonder the believer under Law becomes tired and discouraged, and eventually gives up! He is a captive, and his condition is "wretched." (The Greek word indicates a person who is exhausted after a battle.) What could be more wretched than exerting all your energy to try to live a good life, only to discover that the best you do is still not good enough!

Is there any deliverance? Of course! "I thank God that there is Someone who shall deliver me—Jesus Christ our Lord!" Because the believer is united to Christ, he is dead to the Law and no longer under its authority. But he is alive to God and able to draw on the power of the Holy Spirit. The explanation of this victory is given in Romans 8.

The final sentence in the chapter does not teach that the believer lives a divided life: sinning with his flesh but serving God with his mind. This would mean that his body was being used in two different ways *at the same time,* and this is impossible. The believer realizes that there is a struggle within him between the flesh and the Spirit (Gal. 5:16-18), but he knows that one or the other must be in control.

By "the mind" Paul meant "the inward man" (Rom. 7:22) as opposed to "the flesh" (Rom. 7:18). He amplified this thought in Romans 8:5-8. The old nature cannot do anything good. Everything the Bible says about the old nature is negative: "no good thing" (Rom. 7:18); "the flesh profiteth nothing" (John 6:63); "no confidence in the flesh" (Phil. 3:3). If we depend on the energy of the flesh, we cannot serve God, please God, or do any good thing. But if we yield to the Holy Spirit, then we have the power needed to obey His will. The flesh will never serve the Law of God because the flesh is at war with God. But the Spirit can only obey the Law of God! Therefore, the secret of doing good is to yield to the Holy Spirit.

Paul hinted at this in the early verses of this chapter when he wrote, "That we should bring forth fruit unto God" (Rom. 7:4). Just as we are dead to the old nature, so we are dead to the Law. But we are united to Christ and alive in Christ, and therefore can bring forth fruit unto God. It is our union with Christ that enables us to serve God acceptably. "For it is God which worketh in you, both to will and to do of His good pleasure" (Phil. 2:13). That solved Paul's problem in Romans 7:18: "For to will is present with me; but how to perform that which is good I find not."

The old nature knows no law and the new nature needs no law. Legalism makes a believer wretched because it grieves the new nature and aggravates the old nature! The legalist becomes a Pharisee whose outward actions are acceptable, but whose inward attitudes are despicable. No wonder Jesus called them "whited sepulchres, which indeed appear beautiful outward, but are within full of dead men's bones, and of all uncleanness" (Matt. 23:27). How wretched can you get!

The best is yet to come! Romans 8 explains the work of the Holy Spirit in overcoming the bad and producing the good.

CHAPTER SEVEN
FREEDOM AND FULFILLMENT
Romans 8

On January 6, 1941, President Franklin Delano Roosevelt addressed Congress on the state of the war in Europe. Much of what he said that day has been forgotten. But at the close of his address, he said that he looked forward "to a world founded upon four essential human freedoms." He named them: freedom of speech, freedom of worship, freedom from want, and freedom from fear. These words are still remembered, even though their ideals have not yet been realized everywhere in the world.

Romans 8 is the Christian's "Declaration of Freedom," for in it Paul declares the four spiritual freedoms we enjoy because of our union with Jesus Christ. A study of this chapter shows the emphasis on the Holy Spirit, who is mentioned nineteen times. "Where the Spirit of the Lord is, there is liberty" (2 Cor. 3:17).

Freedom from Judgment—No Condemnation (Rom. 8:1-4)

Romans 3:20 shows the "therefore" of condemnation; but Romans 8:1 gives the "therefore" of *no* condemnation—a tremendous truth and the conclusion of a marvelous argument. (The words "who walk not . . . etc." do not belong here according to the best manuscripts. There are no conditions for us to meet.) The basis for this wonderful assurance is the phrase "in Christ Jesus." In Adam, we were condemned. In Christ, there is no condemnation!

The verse does not say "no mistakes" or "no failures," or even "no sins." Christians *do* fail and make mistakes, and they do sin. Abraham lied about his wife; David committed adultery; Peter tried to kill a man with his sword. To be sure, they suffered consequences because of their sins, but they did not suffer condemnation.

The Law condemns; but the believer has a new relationship to the Law, and therefore he cannot be condemned. Paul made three statements about the believer and the Law, and together they add up to: *no condemnation.*

The Law cannot claim you (v. 2). You

have been made free from the law of sin and death. You now have life in the Spirit. You have moved into a whole new sphere of life in Christ. "The law of sin and death" is what Paul described in Romans 7:7-25. "The law of the Spirit of life" is described in Romans 8. The Law no longer has any jurisdiction over you: you are dead to the Law (Rom. 7:4) and free from the Law (Rom. 8:2).

The Law cannot condemn you (v. 3). Why? Because Christ has already suffered that condemnation for you on the cross. The Law could not save; it can only condemn. But God sent His Son to save us and do what the Law could not do. Jesus did not come as an angel; He came as a man. He did not come "in sinful flesh," for that would have made Him a sinner. He came *in the likeness* of sinful flesh, as a man. He bore our sins in His body on the cross.

The "law of double jeopardy" states that a man cannot be tried twice for the same crime. Since Jesus Christ paid the penalty for your sins, and since you are "in Christ," God will not condemn you.

The Law cannot control you (v. 4). The believer lives a righteous life, not in the power of the Law, but in the power of the Holy Spirit. The Law does not have the power to produce holiness; it can only reveal and condemn sin. But the indwelling Holy Spirit enables you to walk in obedience to God's will. The righteousness that God demands in His Law is fulfilled in you through the Spirit's power. In the Holy Spirit, you have life and liberty (Rom. 8:2) and "the pursuit of happiness" (Rom. 8:4).

The legalist tries to obey God in his own strength and fails to measure up to the righteousness that God demands. The Spirit-led Christian, as he yields to the Lord, experiences the sanctifying work of the Spirit in his life. "For it is God that worketh in you, both to will and to do of His good pleasure" (Phil. 2:13). It is this fact that leads to the second freedom we enjoy as Christians.

Freedom from Defeat—No Obligation (Rom. 8:5-17)

"Therefore, brethren, we are debtors, not to the flesh, to live after the flesh" (Rom. 8:12). There is no obligation to the old nature. The believer can live in victory. In this section, Paul described life on three different levels; and he encouraged his readers to live on the highest level.

"You have not the Spirit" (vv. 5-8). Paul is not describing two kinds of Christians, one carnal and one spiritual. He is contrasting the saved and the unsaved. There are four contrasts.

In the flesh—in the Spirit (v. 5). The unsaved person does not have the Spirit of God (Rom. 8:9) and lives *in* the flesh and *for* the flesh. His mind is centered on the things that satisfy the flesh. But the Christian has the Spirit of God within and lives in an entirely new and different sphere. His mind is fixed on the things of the Spirit. This does not mean that the unsaved person never does anything good, or that the believer never does anything bad. It means that the bent of their lives is different. One lives for the flesh, the other lives for the Spirit.

Death—life (v. 6). The unsaved person is alive physically, but dead spiritually. The inner man is dead toward God and does not respond to the things of the Spirit. He may be moral, and even religious; but he lacks spiritual life. He needs "the Spirit of life in Christ Jesus" (Rom. 8:2).

War with God—peace with God (vv. 6-7). In our study of Romans 7, we have seen that the old nature rebels against God and will not submit to God's Law. Those who have trusted Christ enjoy "peace with God" (Rom. 5:1), while the unsaved are at war with God. " 'There is no peace,' saith the Lord, 'unto the wicked' " (Isa. 48:22).

Pleasing self—pleasing God (v. 8). To be "in the flesh" means to be lost, outside Christ. The unsaved person lives to please himself and rarely if ever thinks about pleasing God. The root of sin is selfishness—"I will" and not "Thy will."

To be unsaved and not have the Spirit is the lowest level of life. But a person need not stay on that level. By faith in Christ he can move to the second level.

"You have the Spirit" (vv. 9-11). "But ye are not in the flesh, but in the Spirit, if so be that the Spirit of God dwell in you" (Rom. 8:9). The evidence of conversion is the presence of the Holy Spirit within, witnessing that you are a child of God (Rom. 8:16). Your body becomes the very temple of the Holy Spirit (1 Cor. 6:19-20). Even though the body is destined to die because of sin (unless, of course, the Lord returns), the Spirit gives life to that body today so that we may serve God. If we should die, the body will one day be raised from the dead, because the Holy Spirit has sealed each believer (Eph. 1:13-14).

What a difference it makes in your body when the Holy Spirit lives within. You experience new life, and even your physical faculties take on a new dimension of experience. When evangelist D.L. Moody described his conversion experience, he said: "I was in a new world. The next morning the sun shone brighter and the birds sang sweeter . . . the old elms waved their branches for joy, and all nature was at peace." Life in Christ is abundant life.

But there is a third level of experience for which the other two are preparation.

"The Spirit has you!" (vv. 12-17) It is not enough for us to have the Spirit; the Spirit must have us! Only then can He share with us the abundant, victorious life that can be ours in Christ. We have no obligation to the flesh, because the flesh has only brought trouble into our lives. We do have an obligation to the Holy Spirit, for it is the Spirit who convicted us, revealed Christ to us, and imparted eternal life to us when we trusted Christ. Because He is "the Spirit of Life," He can empower us to obey Christ, and He can enable us to be more like Christ.

But He is also the Spirit of death. He can enable us to "put to death" (mortify) the sinful deeds of the body. As we yield the members of our body to the Spirit (Rom. 6:12-17), He applies to us and in us the death and resurrection of Christ. He puts to death the things of the flesh, and He reproduces the things of the Spirit.

The Holy Spirit is also "the Spirit of adoption" (Rom. 8:14-17). The word *adoption* in the New Testament means "being placed as an adult son." We come into God's family by birth. But the instant we are born into the family, God adopts us and gives us the position of an adult son. A baby cannot walk, speak, make decisions, or draw on the family wealth. But the believer can do all of these the instant he is born again.

He can walk and be "led of the Spirit" (Rom. 8:14). The verb here means "willingly led." We yield to the Spirit, and He guides us by His Word day by day. We are not under bondage to Law and afraid to act. We have the liberty of the Spirit and are free to follow Christ. The believer can also speak: "We cry, Abba, Father" (Rom. 8:15). Would it not be amazing if a newborn baby looked up and greeted his father! First, the Spirit says, "Abba, Father" to us (Gal. 4:6), and then we say it to God. ("Abba" means "papa"—a term of endearment.)

A baby cannot sign checks, but the child of God by faith can draw on his spiritual wealth because he is an heir of God and a joint-heir with Christ (Rom. 8:17). The Spirit teaches us from the Word, and then we receive God's wealth by faith. What a thrilling thing it is to have "the Spirit of adoption" at work in our lives!

There is no need for the believer to be defeated. He can yield his body to the Spirit and by faith overcome the old nature. The Spirit of life will empower him. The Spirit of death will enable him to overcome the flesh. And the Spirit of adoption will enrich him and lead him into the will of God.

Freedom from Discouragement—No Frustration (Rom. 8:18-30)

Paul in this section dealt with the very real problem of suffering and pain. Perhaps the best way to understand this section is to note the three "groans" that are discussed.

Creation groans (vv. 18-22). When God finished His Creation, it was a good Creation (Gen. 1:31); but today it is a groaning Creation. There is suffering and death; there is pain, all of which is, of course, the result of Adam's sin. It is not the fault of creation. Note the words that Paul used to describe the plight of creation: suffering (Rom. 8:18), vanity (Rom. 8:20), bondage (Rom. 8:21), decay (Rom. 8:21), and pain (Rom. 8:22). However, this groaning is not a useless thing: Paul compared it to a woman in travail. There is pain, but the pain will end when the child is delivered. One day creation will be delivered, and the groaning creation will become a glorious creation! The believer does not focus on today's sufferings; he looks forward to tomorrow's glory (Rom. 8:18; 2 Cor. 4:15-18). Today's groaning bondage will be exchanged for tomorrow's glorious liberty!

We believers groan (vv. 23-25). The reason we groan is because we have experienced "the firstfruits of the Spirit," a foretaste of the glory to come. Just as the nation of Israel tasted the firstfruits of Canaan when the spies returned (Num. 13:23-27), so we Christians have tasted of the blessings of heaven through the ministry of the Spirit. This makes us want to see the Lord, receive a new body, and live with Him and serve Him forever. We are waiting for "the adoption," which is the redemption of the body when Christ returns

(Phil. 3:20-21). This is the thrilling climax to "the adoption" that took place at conversion when "the Spirit of adoption" gave us an adult standing in God's family. When Christ returns, we shall enter into our full inheritance.

Meanwhile, we wait and hope. "For we are saved by that hope" (Rom. 8:24, literal translation). What hope? "That blessed hope and the glorious appearing of the great God and our Saviour Jesus Christ" (Titus 2:13). The best is yet to come! The believer does not get frustrated as he sees and experiences suffering and pain in this world. He knows that the temporary suffering will one day give way to eternal glory.

The Holy Spirit groans (vv. 25-30). God is concerned about the trials of His people. When He was ministering on earth, Jesus groaned when He saw what sin was doing to mankind (Mark 7:34; John 11:33, 38). Today the Holy Spirit groans with us and feels the burdens of our weaknesses and suffering. But the Spirit does more than groan. He prays for us in His groaning so that we might be led into the will of God. We do not always know God's will. We do not always know how to pray, but the Spirit intercedes so that we might live in the will of God in spite of suffering. The Spirit "shares the burden."

The believer never need faint in times of suffering and trial because he knows that God is at work in the world (Rom. 8:28), and that He has a perfect plan (Rom. 8:29). God has two purposes in that plan: our good and His glory. Ultimately, He will make us like Jesus Christ! Best of all, God's plan is going to succeed! It started in eternity past when He chose us in Christ (Eph. 1:4-5). He predetermined that one day we would be like His Son. Predestination applies only to saved people. Nowhere are we taught that God predestines people to be eternally condemned. If they are condemned, it is because of their refusal to trust Christ (John 3:18-21). Those whom He chose, He called (see 2 Thes. 2:13-14); when they responded to His call, He justified them, and He also glorified them. This means that the believer has already been glorified in Christ (John 17:22); the revelation of this glory awaits the coming of the Lord (Rom. 8:21-23).

How can we Christians ever be discouraged and frustrated when we already share the glory of God? Our suffering today only guarantees that much more glory when Jesus Christ returns!

Freedom from Fear—No Separation (Rom. 8:31-39)

There is no condemnation because we share the righteousness of God and the Law cannot condemn us. There is no obligation because we have the Spirit of God who enables us to overcome the flesh and live for God. There is no frustration because we share the glory of God, the blessed hope of Christ's return. There is no separation because we experience the love of God: "What shall separate us from the love of Christ?" (Rom. 8:35)

The emphasis in this final section is on the security of the believer. We do not need to fear the past, present, or future because we are secure in the love of Christ. Paul presented five arguments to prove that there could be no separation between the believer and the Lord.

God is for us (v. 31). *The Father* is for us and proved it by giving His Son (Rom. 8:32). *The Son* is for us (Rom. 8:34) and so is *the Spirit* (Rom. 8:26). God is making all things work for us (Rom. 8:28). In His person and His providence, God is for us. Sometimes, like Jacob, we lament, "All these things are against me" (Gen. 42:36), when actually everything is working for us. The conclusion is obvious: "If God be for us, who can be against us?"

The believer needs to enter into each new day realizing that God is for him. There is no need to fear, for his loving Father desires only the best for His children, even if they must go through trials to receive His best. " 'For I know the plans that I have for you,' declares the Lord, 'plans for welfare and not for calamity to give you a future and a hope' " (Jer. 29:11, NASB).

Christ died for us (v. 32). The argument here is from the lesser to the greater. If when we were sinners, God gave us His best, now that we are God's children, will He not give us all that we need? Jesus used this same argument when He tried to convince people that it was foolish to worry and fear. God cares for the birds and sheep, and even for the lilies; surely He will care for you! God is dealing with His own on the basis of Calvary grace, not on the basis of Law. God freely gives all things to His own!

God has justified us (v. 33). This means that He has declared us righteous in Christ. Satan would like to accuse us (Zech. 3:1-7; Rev. 12:10), but we stand righteous in Jesus Christ. We are God's elect—chosen in Christ and accepted in Christ. God will certainly not accuse us since it is He who has justified us. For Him to accuse us would mean that His salvation was a failure and we are still in our sins.

Understanding the meaning of justification brings peace to our hearts. When God declares the believing sinner righteous in Christ, that declaration never changes. Our Christian experience changes from day to day, but justification never changes. We may accuse ourselves, and men may accuse us; but God will never take us to court and accuse us. Jesus has already paid the penalty and we are secure in Him.

Christ intercedes for us (v. 34). A dual intercession keeps the believer secure in Christ: the Spirit intercedes (Rom. 8:26-27) and the Son of God intercedes (Rom. 8:34). The same Saviour who died for us is now interceding for us in heaven. As our High Priest, He can give us the grace we need to overcome temptation and defeat the enemy (Heb. 4:14-16). As our Advocate, He can forgive our sins and restore our fellowship with God (1 John 1:9–2:2). Intercession means that Jesus Christ represents us before the throne of God and we do not have to represent ourselves.

Paul hinted at this ministry of intercession in Romans 5:9-10. We are not only saved by His death, but we are also saved by His life. "Therefore He is able to save completely those who come to God through Him, because He always lives to intercede for them" (Heb. 7:25, NIV). Peter sinned against the Lord, but he was forgiven and restored to fellowship because of Jesus Christ. "Simon, Simon, listen! Satan has asked permission to sift all of you like wheat, but I have prayed especially for you that your own faith may not utterly fail" (Luke 22:31-32, WMS). He is interceding for each of us, a ministry that assures us that we are secure.

Christ loves us (vv. 35-39). In Romans 8:31-34 Paul proved that God cannot fail us, but is it possible that we can fail Him? Suppose some great trial or temptation comes, and we fail? Then what? Paul deals with that problem in this final section and explains that nothing can separate us from the love of Jesus Christ.

To begin with, God does not shelter us from the difficulties of life because we need them for our spiritual growth (Rom. 5:3-5). In Romans 8:28 God assures us that the difficulties of life are working *for* us and not *against* us. God permits trials to come that we might use them for our good and His glory. We endure trials for His sake (Rom. 8:36), and since we do, do you think that He will desert us? Of course not! Instead, He is closer to us when we go through the difficulties of life.

Furthermore, He gives us the power to conquer (Rom. 8:37). We are "more than conquerors," literally, "we are superconquerors" through Jesus Christ! He gives us victory and more victory! We need not fear life or death, things present or things to come, because Jesus Christ loves us and gives us the victory. This is not a promise with conditions attached: "If you do this, God will do that." This security in Christ is an established fact, and we claim it for ourselves because we are in Christ. Nothing can separate you from His love! Believe it—and rejoice in it!

A review of this wonderful chapter shows that the Christian is completely victorious. We are free from judgment because Christ died for us and we have His righteousness. We are free from defeat because Christ lives in us by His Spirit and we share His life. We are free from discouragement because Christ is coming for us and we shall share His glory. We are free from fear because Christ intercedes for us and we cannot be separated from His love.

No condemnation! No obligation! No frustration! No separation!

If God be for us, who can be against us!

CHAPTER EIGHT
DID GOD MAKE A MISTAKE?
Romans 9

It seems strange that Paul would interrupt his discussion of salvation and devote a long section of three chapters to the nation of Israel. Why didn't he move from the doctrinal teaching of Romans 8 to the practical duties given in Romans 12–15? A careful study of Romans 9–11 reveals that this section is not an interruption at all; it is a necessary part of Paul's argument for justification by faith.

To begin with, Paul was considered a traitor to the Jewish nation. He ministered to Gentiles and he taught freedom from the Law of Moses. He had preached in many synagogues and caused trouble, and no doubt many of the Jewish believers in Rome had heard of his questionable reputation. In these chapters, Paul showed his love for Israel and his desire for their welfare. This is the personal reason for this discussion.

But there was a doctrinal reason. Paul had argued in Romans 8 that the believer is secure in Jesus Christ and that God's election would stand (Rom. 8:28-30). But someone might ask, "What about the Jews? They were chosen by God, and yet now you tell us they are set aside and God is building His church. Did God fail to keep His promises to Israel?" In other words, the very character of God was at stake. If God was not faithful to the Jews, how do we know He will be faithful to the church?

The emphasis in Romans 9 is on Israel's past election, in Romans 10 on Israel's present rejection, and in Romans 11 on Israel's future restoration. Israel is the only nation in the world with a complete history—past, present, and future. In Romans 9, Paul defended the character of God by showing that Israel's past history actually magnified the attributes of God. He specifically named four attributes of God: His faithfulness (Rom. 9:1-13), righteousness (Rom. 9:14-18), justice (Rom. 9:19-29), and grace (Rom. 9:30-33). You will note that these divisions correspond with Paul's three questions: "Is there unrighteousness with God?" (Rom. 9:14) "Why doth He find fault?" (Rom. 9:19) and "What shall we say then?" (Rom. 9:30)

God's Faithfulness (Rom. 9:1-13)

It is remarkable how Paul moved from the joy of Romans 8 into the sorrow and burden of Romans 9. When he looked at Christ, he rejoiced; but when he looked at the lost people of Israel, he wept. Like Moses (Ex. 32:30-35), he was willing to be cursed and separated from Christ if it would mean the salvation of Israel. What a man this Paul was! He was willing to stay out of heaven for the sake of the saved (Phil. 1:22-24), and willing to go to hell for the sake of the lost.

His theme was God's election of Israel; and the first thing he dealt with was the blessing of their election (Rom. 9:4-5). Israel was adopted by God as His own people (Ex. 4:22-23). He gave them His glory in the tabernacle and the temple (Ex. 40:34-38; 1 Kings 8:10-11). The glory Moses beheld on Mount Sinai came to dwell with Israel (Ex. 24:16-17). God gave Israel His covenants, the first to Abraham, and then additional covenants to Moses and to David. He also gave them His Law to govern their political, social, and religious life, and to guarantee His blessing if they obeyed. He gave them "the service of God," referring to the ministry in the tabernacle and the temple. He gave them the promises and the patriarchs ("the fathers" in Rom. 9:5). The purpose of all of this blessing was that Jesus Christ, through Israel, might come into the world. (Note that Rom. 9:5 affirms that Jesus Christ is God.) All of these blessings were given freely to Israel and to no other nation.

But in spite of these blessings, Israel failed. When the Messiah appeared, Israel rejected Him and crucified Him. No one knew this better than Paul, because in his early days he had persecuted the church. Does Israel's failure mean that God's Word has failed? (The Greek word translated "taken none effect" pictures a ship going off its course.) The answer is, "No! God is faithful no matter what men may do with His Word." Here Paul explains the basis for Israel's election.

It was not of natural descent (vv. 6-10). As we saw in Romans 2:25-29, there is a difference between the natural seed of Abraham and the spiritual children of Abraham. Abraham actually had two sons, Ishmael (by Hagar) and Isaac (by Sarah). Since Ishmael was the firstborn, he should have been chosen, but it was Isaac that God chose. Isaac and Rebecca had twin sons, Esau and Jacob. As the firstborn, Esau should have been chosen, but it was Jacob that God chose. And Esau and Jacob had the same father and mother, unlike Ishmael and Isaac who had the same father but different mothers. God did not base His election on the physical. Therefore, if the nation of Israel—Abraham's physical descendants—has rejected God's Word, this does not nullify God's elective purposes at all.

It is not of human merit (vv. 11-13). God chose Jacob before the babies were born. The two boys had done neither good nor evil, so God's choice was not based on their character or conduct. Romans 9:13 is a reference to Malachi 1:2-3 and refers to nations (Israel and Edom) and not individual sinners. God does not hate sinners. John 3:16 makes it clear that He loves sinners. The statement here has to do with national election, not individual. Since God's election of Israel does not depend on human merit, their disobedience cannot nullify the elective purposes of God. God is faithful even though His people are unfaithful.

God's Righteousness (Rom. 9:14-18)
The fact that God chose one and not the other seems to indicate that He is unrighteous. "Is there unrighteousness with God?" Paul asked; and then he replied, "God forbid!" It is unthinkable that the holy God should ever commit an unrighteous act. Election is always totally a matter of grace. If God acted only on the basis of righteousness, nobody would ever be saved. Paul quoted Exodus 33:19 to show that God's mercy and compassion are extended according to God's will and not man's will. All of us deserve condemnation—not mercy. The reference in Exodus 33 deals with Israel's idolatry while Moses was on the mount receiving the Law. The whole nation deserved to be destroyed, yet God killed only 3,000 people—not because they were more wicked or less godly, but purely because of His grace and mercy.

Paul then quoted Exodus 9:16, using Pharaoh as an illustration. Moses was a Jew, Pharaoh was a Gentile; yet both were sinners. In fact, both were murderers! Both saw God's wonders. Yet Moses was saved and Pharaoh was lost. God raised up Pharaoh that He might reveal His glory and power; and He had mercy on Moses that He might use him to deliver the people of Israel. Pharaoh was a ruler, and Moses was a slave; yet it was Moses who experienced the mercy and compassion of God—because God willed it that way. God is sovereign in His work and acts according to His own will and purposes. So it was not a matter of righteousness but of the sovereign will of God.

God is holy and must punish sin; but God is loving and desires to save sinners. If everybody is saved, it would deny His holiness; but if everybody is lost, it would deny His love. The solution to the problem is God's sovereign election.

A seminary professor once said to me, "Try to explain election, and you may lose your mind; but explain it away and you will lose your soul!"

God chose Israel and condemned Egypt, because this was His sovereign purpose. Nobody can condemn God for the way He extends His mercy, because God is righteous.

Before leaving this section, we need to discuss the "hardening" of Pharaoh (Rom. 9:18). This hardening process is referred to at least fifteen times in Exodus 7–14. Sometimes we are told that Pharaoh hardened his heart (Ex. 8:15, 19, 32), and other times that God hardened Pharaoh's heart (Ex. 9:12; 10:1, 20, 27). By declaring His Word and revealing His power, God gave Pharaoh opportunity to repent; but instead, Pharaoh resisted God and hardened his heart. The fault lay not with God but Pharaoh. The same sunlight that melts the ice also hardens the clay. God was not unrighteous in His dealings with Pharaoh because He gave him many opportunities to repent and believe.

God's Justice (Rom. 9:19-29)
But this fact of God's sovereign will only seems to create a new problem. "If God is sovereign, then who can resist Him? And if one does resist Him, what right does He have to judge?" It is the age-old question of the justice of God as He works in human history.

I recall sharing in a street meeting in Chicago and passing out tracts at the corner of Madison and Kedzie. Most of the people graciously accepted the tracts, but one man took the tract and with a snarl crumpled it up and threw it in the gutter. The name of the tract was "Four Things God Wants You to Know."

"There are a few things I would like God to know!" the man said. "Why is there so much sorrow and tragedy in this world? Why do the innocent suffer while the rich go free? Bah! Don't tell me there's a God! If there is, then God is the biggest sinner that ever lived!" And he turned away with a sneer and was lost in the crowd.

We know that God by nature is perfectly just. "Shall not the Judge of all the earth do right?" (Gen. 18:25) It is unthinkable that God would will an unjust purpose or perform an unjust act. But at times it seems that He does just that. He had mercy on Moses but condemned Pharaoh. Is this just? He elected Israel and rejected the other nations. Is this just? Paul gives three answers to this charge.

Who are we to argue with God? (vv. 19-21) This is a logical argument. God is the Potter and we are the clay. God is wiser than we are and we are foolish to question His will or to resist it. (The reference here is to Isa. 45:9.) To be sure, the clay has no life and is passive in the potter's hand. We have feelings, intellect, and willpower, and we can resist

Him if we choose. (See Jer. 18 where this thought is developed.) But it is God who determines whether a man will be a Moses or a Pharaoh. Neither Moses, nor Pharaoh, nor anyone else, could choose his parents, his genetic structure, or his time and place of birth. We have to believe that these matters are in the hands of God.

However, this does not excuse us from responsibility. Pharaoh had great opportunities to learn about the true God and trust Him, and yet he chose to rebel. Paul did not develop this aspect of truth because his theme was divine sovereignty, not human responsibility. The one does not deny the other, even though our finite minds may not fully grasp them both.

God has His purposes (vv. 22-24). We must never think that God enjoyed watching a tyrant like Pharaoh. He endured it. God said to Moses, "I have surely seen the affliction of My people . . . and have heard their cry . . . for I know their sorrows" (Ex. 3:7). The fact that God was long-suffering indicates that He gave Pharaoh opportunities to be saved (see 2 Peter 3:9). The word "fitted" in Romans 9:22 does not suggest that *God* made Pharaoh a "vessel of wrath." The verb is in what the Greek grammarians call the middle voice, making it a reflexive action verb. So, it should read: *"fitted himself* for destruction." God prepares men for glory (Rom. 9:23), but sinners prepare themselves for judgment. In Moses and Israel God revealed the riches of His mercy; in Pharaoh and Egypt He revealed His power and wrath. Since neither deserved any mercy, God cannot be charged with injustice.

Ultimately, of course, God's purpose was to form His church from both Jews and Gentiles (Rom. 9:24). Believers today are, by God's grace, "vessels of mercy" which He is preparing for glory, a truth that reminds us of Romans 8:29-30.

All of this was prophesied (vv. 25-29). First Paul quoted Hosea 2:23, a statement declaring that God would turn from the Jews and call the Gentiles. Then he cited Hosea 1:10 to prove that this new people being called would be God's people and "children of the living God." He then quoted Isaiah 10:22-23 to show that only a remnant of Israel would be saved, while the greater part of the nation would suffer judgment. Romans 9:28 probably refers to God's work of judgment during the Tribulation, when the nation of Israel will be persecuted and judged, and only a small remnant left to enter into the kingdom when Jesus Christ returns to earth. But the application for today is clear: only a remnant of Jews is believing; and they, together with the Gentiles, are the "called of God" (Rom. 9:24). The final quotation from Isaiah 1:9 emphasized the grace of God in sparing the believing remnant.

Now, what does all of this prove? That God was not unjust in saving some and judging others, because He was only fulfilling the Old Testament prophecies given centuries ago. He would be unjust if He did not keep His own Word. But even more than that, these prophecies show that God's election has made possible the salvation of the Gentiles. This is the grace of God. At the Exodus, God rejected the Gentiles and chose the Jews, so that, through the Jews, He might save the Gentiles. The nation of Israel rejected His will, but this did not defeat His purposes. A remnant of Jews does believe and God's Word has been fulfilled.

So far, Paul had defended the character of God by showing His faithfulness, His righteousness, and His justice. Israel's rejection had not canceled God's election; it had only proved that He was true to His character and His purposes.

God's Grace (Rom. 9:30-33)

Paul moved next from divine sovereignty to human responsibility. Note that Paul did not say "elect" and "nonelect," but rather emphasized faith. Here is a paradox: the Jews sought for righteousness but did not find it, while the Gentiles, who were not searching for it, found it! The reason? Israel tried to be saved by works and not by faith. They rejected "grace righteousness" and tried to please God with "Law righteousness." The Jews thought that the Gentiles had to *come up* to Israel's level to be saved; when actually the Jews had to *go down* to the level of the Gentiles to be saved. "For there is no difference: for all have sinned and come short of the glory of God" (Rom. 3:22-23). Instead of permitting their religious privileges (Rom. 9:1-5) to lead them to Christ, they used these privileges as a substitute for Christ.

But see the grace of God: Israel's rejection means the Gentiles' salvation! Paul's final quotation was from Isaiah 28:16. It referred to Christ, God's Stone of salvation (see Ps. 118:22). God gave Christ to be a Foundation Stone, but Israel rejected Him and He became a stumbling stone. Instead of "rising" on this Stone, Israel fell (Rom. 11:11); but, as we shall see, their fall made possible the salvation of the Gentiles by the grace of God.

We need to decide what kind of righteousness we are seeking, whether we are depending on good works and character, or trusting Christ alone for salvation. God does not save people on the basis of birth or behavior. He saves them "by grace, through faith" (Eph. 2:8-9). It is not a question of whether or not we are among God's elect. That is a mystery known only to God. He offers us His salvation by faith. The offer is made to "whosoever will" (Rev. 22:17). After we have trusted Christ, then we have the witness and evidence that we are among His elect (Eph. 1:4-14; 1 Thes. 1:1-10). But first we must trust Him and receive by faith His righteousness which alone can guarantee heaven.

No one will deny that there are many mysteries connected with divine sovereignty and human responsibility. Nowhere does God ask us to choose between these two truths, because they both come from God and are a part of God's plan. They do not compete; they cooperate. The fact that we cannot fully understand *how* they work together does not deny the fact that they do. When a man asked Charles Spurgeon how he reconciled divine sovereignty and human responsibility, Spurgeon replied: "I never try to reconcile friends!"

But the main thrust of this chapter is clear: Israel's rejection of Christ does not deny the faithfulness of God. Romans 9 does not negate Romans 8. God is still faithful, righteous, just, and gracious, and He can be depended on to accomplish His purposes and keep His promises.

CHAPTER NINE
THE WRONG RIGHTEOUSNESS
Romans 10

The theme of this chapter is Israel's present rejection. Paul moved from divine sovereignty (Rom. 9) to human responsibility. He continued the theme of righteousness introduced at the end of the previous chapter (Rom. 9:30-33) and explains three aspects of Israel's rejection.

The Reasons for Their Rejection (Rom. 10:1-13)

You would think that Israel as a nation would have been eagerly expecting the arrival of their Messiah and been prepared to receive Him. For centuries they had known the Old Testament prophecies and had practiced the Law, which was "a schoolmaster" to lead them to Christ (Gal. 3:24). God had sought to prepare the nation, but when Jesus Christ came, they rejected Him. "He came unto His own [world] and His own [people] received Him not" (John 1:11). To be sure, there was a faithful remnant in the nation that looked for His arrival, such as Simeon and Anna (Luke 2:25-38); but the majority of the people were not ready when He came.

How do we explain this tragic event? Paul gives several reasons why Israel rejected their Messiah.

They did not feel a need for salvation (v. 1). There was a time when Paul would have agreed with his people, for he himself opposed the Gospel and considered Jesus Christ an impostor. Israel considered the Gentiles in need of salvation, but certainly not the Jews. In several of His parables, Jesus pointed out this wrong attitude: the elder brother (Luke 15:11-32) and the Pharisee (Luke 18:9-14) are two examples. Israel would have been happy for political salvation from Rome, but she did not feel she needed spiritual salvation from her own sin.

They were zealous for God (v. 2). Ever since Israel returned to their land from Babylonian Captivity, the nation had been cured of idolatry. In the temple and the local synagogues, only the true God was worshiped and served, and only the true Law was taught. So zealous were the Jews that they even "improved upon God's Law" and added their own traditions, making them equal to the Law. Paul himself had been zealous for the Law and the traditions (Acts 26:1-11; Gal. 1:13-14).

But their zeal was not based on knowledge; it was heat without light. Sad to say, many religious people today are making the same mistake. They think that their good works and religious deeds will save them, when actually these practices are keeping them from being saved. Certainly many of them are sincere and devout, but sincerity and devotion will never save the soul. "Therefore by the deeds of the Law there shall no flesh be justified in His sight" (Rom. 3:20).

They were proud and self-righteous (v. 3). Israel was ignorant of God's righteousness, not because they had never been told, but because they refused to learn. There is an ignorance that comes from lack of opportunity, but Israel had had many opportunities to be saved. In their case, it was an ignorance that stemmed from willful, stubborn resistance to the truth. They would not submit to God. They were proud of their own good works and religious self-righteousness, and would not admit their sins and trust the Saviour. Paul had made the same mistake before he met the Lord (Phil. 3:1-11).

The godly Presbyterian preacher, Robert Murray McCheyne, was passing out tracts one day and handed one to a well-dressed lady. She gave him a haughty look and said, "Sir, you must not know who I am!"

In his kind way, McCheyne replied, "Madam, there is coming a day of judgment, and on that day it will not make any difference who you are!"

They misunderstood their own Law (vv. 4-13). Everything about the Jewish religion pointed to the coming Messiah—their sacrifices, priesthood, temple services, religious festivals, and covenants. Their Law told them they were sinners in need of a Saviour. But instead of letting the Law bring them to Christ (Gal. 3:24), they worshiped their Law and rejected their Saviour. The Law was a signpost, pointing the way. But it could never take them to their destination. The Law cannot give righteousness; it only leads the sinner to the Saviour who can give righteousness.

Christ is "the end of the Law" in the sense that through His death and resurrection, He has terminated the ministry of the Law for those who believe. The Law is ended as far as Christians are concerned. The righteousness of the Law is being fulfilled in the life of the believer through the power of the Spirit (Rom. 8:4); but the reign of the Law has ended (see Eph. 2:15; Col. 2:14). "For ye are not under the Law, but under grace" (Rom. 6:14).

Paul quoted from the Old Testament to prove to his readers that they did not even understand their own Law. He began with Leviticus 18:5 which states the purpose of the Law: if you obey it, you live.

"But we did obey it!" they would argue.

"You may have obeyed it *outwardly,*" Paul would reply, "but you did not believe it from your heart." He then quoted Deuteronomy 30:12-14 and gave the passage a deeper spiritual meaning. The theme of Moses' message was "the commandment" (Deut. 30:11), referring to the Word of God. Moses argued that the Jews had no reason to disobey the Word of God because it had been clearly explained to them and it was not far from them. In fact, Moses urged them to receive the Word in their hearts (see Deut. 5:29; 6:5-12; 13:3; 30:6). The emphasis in Deuteronomy is on the heart, the inner spiritual condition and not mere outward acts of obedience.

Paul gave us the spiritual understanding of this admonition. He saw "the commandment" or "the Word" as meaning "Christ, God's Word." So, he substituted "Christ" for "the commandment." He told us that God's way of salvation was not difficult and complicated. We do not have to go to heaven to find Christ, or into the world of the dead. He is near to us. In other words, the Gospel of Christ—the Word of faith—is available and accessible. The sinner need not perform difficult works in order to be saved. All he has to do is trust Christ. The very Word on the lips of the religious Jews was the Word of faith. The very Law that they read and recited pointed to Christ.

At this point Paul quoted Isaiah 28:16 to show that salvation is *by faith:* "Whosoever believeth on Him shall not be ashamed." He quoted this verse before in Romans 9:33. He made it clear in Romans 10:9-10 that salvation is *by faith*—we believe in the heart, receive God's righteousness, and then confess Christ openly and without shame.

Paul's final quotation was from Joel 2:32, to prove that this salvation is open to everyone: "For whosoever shall call upon the name of the Lord shall be saved." Paul had already proved that "there is no difference" in condemnation (Rom. 3:20-23); now he affirms that "there is no difference" in salvation. Instead of the Jew having a special righteousness of his own through the Law, he was declared to be as much a sinner as the Gentile he condemned.

This entire section emphasizes the difference between "Law righteousness" and "faith righteousness." The contrasts are seen in the following summary.

Law Righteousness	*Faith Righteousness*
Only for the Jew	For "whosoever"
Based on works	Comes by faith alone
Self-righteousness	God's righteousness
Cannot save	Brings salvation
Obey the Lord	Call on the Lord
Leads to pride	Glorifies God

Having explained the reasons for Israel's rejection of God's righteousness, Paul moves into the next aspect of the subject.

The Remedy for Their Rejection (Rom. 10:14-17)

This passage is often used as the basis for the church's missionary program, and rightly so, but its first application is to the nation of Israel. The only way unbelieving Jews can be saved is by calling on the Lord. But before they can call on Him, they must believe. For the Jew, this meant believing that Jesus Christ of Nazareth truly is the Son of God and the Messiah of Israel. It also meant believing in His death and resurrection (Rom. 10:9-10). But in order to believe, they must hear the Word, for it is the Word that creates faith in the heart of the hearer (Rom. 10:17). This meant that a herald of the Word must be sent, and it is the Lord who does the sending. At this point, Paul could well have been remembering his own call to preach the Word to the Gentiles (Acts 13:1-3).

The quotation in Romans 10:15 is found in Isaiah 52:7 and Nahum 1:15. The Nahum reference had to do with the destruction of the Assyrian Empire, the hated enemies of the Jews. Nineveh was their key city, a wicked city to which God had sent Jonah some 150 years before Nahum wrote. God had patiently dealt with Nineveh, but now His judgment was going to fall. It was this "good news" that the messenger brought to the Jews, and this is what made his feet so beautiful.

Isaiah used this statement for a *future* event—the return of Christ and the establishing of His glorious kingdom. "Thy God reigneth!" (Read Isa. 52:7-10.) The messenger with the beautiful feet announced that God had defeated Israel's enemies and that Messiah was reigning from Jerusalem.

But Paul used the quotation in a *present* application: the messengers of the Gospel taking the Good News to Israel today. The "peace" spoken of is "peace with God" (Rom. 5:1) and the peace Christ has effected between Jews and Gentiles by forming the one body, the church (Eph. 2:13-17). The remedy for Israel's rejection is in hearing the Word of the Gospel and believing on Jesus Christ.

Isaiah 53:1 was Paul's next quotation, proving that not all of Israel would obey His Word. This verse introduced one of the greatest messianic chapters in the Old Testament. Traditionally, Jewish scholars have applied Isaiah 53 to the nation of Israel rather than to Messiah; but many ancient rabbis saw in it a picture of a suffering Messiah bearing the sins of His people (see Acts 8:26-40). In Isaiah's day, the people did not believe God's Word, nor do they believe it today. John 12:37-41 cites Isaiah 53:1 to explain how the nation saw Christ's miracles and still refused to believe. Because they would not believe, judgment came on them and they could not believe.

Note that trusting Christ is not only a matter of believing, but also obeying. Not to believe on Christ is to disobey God. God "commandeth all men everywhere to repent" (Acts 17:30). Romans 6:17 also equates "believing" and "obeying." True faith must touch the will and result in a changed life.

We must never minimize the missionary outreach of the church. While this passage relates primarily to Israel, it applies to all lost souls around the world. They cannot be saved unless they call on the Lord Jesus Christ. But they cannot call unless they believe. Faith comes by hearing, so they must hear the message. How will they hear? A messenger must go to them with the message. But this means that God must call the messenger and the messenger must be sent. What a privilege it is to be one of His messengers and have beautiful feet!

As I was writing this chapter, my phone rang and one of the businessmen in our city reported another soul led to Christ. My caller had had serious spiritual problems a few years ago and I was able to help him. Since that time, he has led many to Christ, including some in his office. His phone call was to give me the good news that one of his associates had led a friend to Christ, another miracle in a spiritual chain reaction that has been going on for three years now. My friend has beautiful feet, and wherever he goes he shares the Good News of the Gospel.

Some of us share the news here at home, but others are sent to distant places. In spite of some closed doors, there are still more open doors for the Gospel than ever before; and we have better tools to work with. My friend, the late Dr. E. Meyers Harrison, veteran missionary and professor of missions, says that there are four reasons why the church must send out missionaries: (1) *the command from above*—"go ye into all the world" (Mark 16:15); (2) *the cry from beneath*—"send him to my father's house" (Luke 16:27); (3) *the call from without*—"come over and help us" (Acts 16:9); and (4) *the constraint from within*—"the love of Christ constraineth us" (2 Cor. 5:14).

There remains a third aspect of Israel's rejection for Paul to discuss.

The Results of Their Rejection (Rom. 10:18-21)

There are three results, and each of them is supported by a quotation from the Old Testament.

Israel is guilty (v. 18). Someone might have argued with Paul: "But how do you know that Israel really heard?" His reply would have been Psalm 19:4, a psalm that emphasizes the revelation of God in the world. God reveals Himself in creation (Ps. 19:1-6) and in His Word (Ps. 19:7-11). The "Book of Nature" and the "Book of Revelation" go together and proclaim the glory of God. Israel had the benefit of both books, for she saw God at work in nature and she received God's written Word. Israel heard, but she would not *heed.* No wonder Jesus often had to say to the crowds, "He that hath ears to hear, let him hear!"

The message goes to the Gentiles (vv. 19-20). What marvelous grace! When Israel rejected her Messiah, God sent the Gospel to the Gentiles that they might be saved. This was predicted by Moses in Deuteronomy 32:21. Paul had mentioned this truth before in Romans 9:22-26. One reason why God sent the Gospel to the Gentiles was that they might provoke the Jews to jealousy (Rom. 10:19; 11:11). It was an act of grace both to the Jews and to the Gentiles. The Prophet Isaiah predicted too that God would save the Gentiles (Isa. 65:1).

As you study the New Testament, you discover that "to the Jew first" is a ruling principle of operation. Jesus began His ministry with the Jews. He forbad His disciples to preach to the Gentiles or the Samaritans when He sent them on their first tour of ministry (Matt. 10:1-6). After His resurrection, He commanded them to wait in Jerusalem and to start their ministry there (Luke 24:46-49; Acts 1:8). In the first seven chapters of Acts, the ministry is to Jews and to Gentiles who were Jewish proselytes. But when the nation stoned Stephen and persecution broke loose, God sent the Gospel to the Samaritans (Acts 8:1-8), and then to the Gentiles (Acts 10).

The Jewish believers were shocked when Peter went to the Gentiles (Acts 11:1-18). But he explained that it was God who sent him and that it was clear to him that Jews and Gentiles were both saved the same way—by faith in Christ. But the opposition of the legalistic Jews was so great that the churches had to call a council to discuss the issue. The record of this council is given in Acts 15. Their conclusion was that Jews and Gentiles were all saved by faith in Christ, and that a Gentile did not have to become a Jewish proselyte before he could become a Christian.

God still yearns over His people (v. 21). This quotation is from Isaiah 65:2. "All day long" certainly refers to this present "day of salvation" or day of grace in which we live. While Israel as a nation has been set aside, individual Jewish people can be saved and are being saved. The phrase "all day long" makes us think of Paul's ministry to the Jews in Rome when he arrived there as a prisoner. "From morning till evening" Paul expounded the Scriptures to them and sought to convince them that Jesus is the Messiah (Acts 28:23). Through Paul, God was stretching out His arms of love to His disobedient people, yearning over them, and asking them to return. God's favor to the Gentiles did not change His love for the Jews.

God wants to use us to share the Gospel with both Jews and Gentiles. God can use our feet and our arms just as He used Paul's. Jesus Christ wept over Jerusalem and longed to gather His people in His arms! Instead, those arms were stretched out on a cross where He willingly died for Jews and Gentiles alike. God is long-suffering and patient "not willing that any should perish, but that all should come to repentance" (2 Peter 3:9).

Will God's patience with Israel wear out? Is

there any future for the nation? Yes, there is, as the next chapter will show.

CHAPTER TEN
GOD IS NOT THROUGH WITH ISRAEL!
Romans 11

For centuries people have been puzzled by the nation of Israel. The Roman government recognized the Jewish religion, but it still called the nation *secta nefaria*—"a nefarious sect." The great historian Arnold Toynbee classified Israel as "a fossil civilization" and did not know what to do with it. For some reason, the nation did not fit into his historical theories.

Paul devoted all of Romans 11 to presenting proof that God is not through with Israel. We must not apply this chapter to the church today, because Paul is discussing a literal future for a literal nation. He called five witnesses to prove there was a future in God's plan for the Jews.

Paul Himself (Rom. 11:1)

"Hath God cast away His people? God forbid! For I also am an Israelite!" If God has cast away His people, then how can the conversion of the Apostle Paul be explained? The fact that his conversion is presented three times in the Book of Acts is significant (Rom. 9, 22, 26). Certainly Dr. Luke did not write these chapters and repeat the story just to exalt Paul. No, they were written to show Paul's conversion as an illustration of the future conversion of the nation of Israel. Paul called himself "one born out of due time" (1 Cor. 15:8). In 1 Timothy 1:16 he stated that God saved him "that in me first Jesus Christ might show forth all long-suffering, for a pattern to them which should hereafter believe on Him to life everlasting."

The accounts of Paul's conversion tell very little that parallels our salvation experience today. Certainly none of us has seen Christ in glory or actually heard Him speak from heaven. We were neither blinded by the light of heaven nor thrown to the ground. In what way, then, is Paul's conversion "a pattern"? It is a picture of how the nation of Israel will be saved when Jesus Christ returns to establish His kingdom on earth. The details of Israel's future restoration and salvation are given in Zechariah 12:10–13:1. The nation shall see Him as He returns (Zech. 14:4; Acts 1:11; Rev. 1:7), recognize Him as their Messiah, repent, and receive Him. It will be an experience similar to that of Saul of Tarsus when he was on his way to Damascus to persecute Christians (Acts 9).

This is why Paul used himself as the first witness. The *fact* that he was saved does not prove that there is a future for Israel. Rather, what is important is the *way* he was saved.

The Prophet Elijah (Rom. 11:2-10)

Israel is God's elect nation; He foreknew them, or chose them, and they are His. The fact that most of the nation has rejected Christ is no proof that God has finished with His people. In his day, Elijah thought that the nation had totally departed from God (see 1 Kings 19). But Elijah discovered that there was yet a remnant of true believers. He thought he was the only faithful Jew left and discovered that there were 7,000 more.

Paul referred to this "remnant" in Romans 9:27, a quotation from Isaiah 10:22-23. At no time has the entire nation of Israel been true to the Lord. God makes a distinction between Abraham's natural children and his spiritual children (Rom. 2:25-29). The fact that the Jews shared in the covenant by being circumcised did not guarantee their salvation. Like Abraham, they had to believe God in order to receive His righteousness (Rom. 4:1-5).

Note that this remnant is saved by grace and not by works (Rom. 11:5-6). Note also the parallel in Romans 9:30-33. It is impossible to mix grace and works, for the one cancels the other. Israel's main concern had always been in trying to please God with good works (Rom. 9:30–10:4). The nation refused to submit to Christ's righteousness, just as religious, self-righteous people refuse to submit today.

If a remnant had been saved, thus proving that God was not through with His people, then what had happened to the rest of the nation? They had been hardened (a better translation than "blinded" in Rom. 11:7). This was the result of their resisting the truth, just as Pharaoh's heart was hardened because he resisted the truth. Paul quoted Isaiah 29:10 to support his statement, and also referred to Deuteronomy 29:4. We would expect a pagan ruler to harden himself against the Lord, but we do not expect God's people to do so.

Romans 11:9-10 are cited from Psalm 69:22-23. This psalm is one of the most important of the messianic psalms and is referred to several times in the New Testament. Note especially Romans 11:4, 9, 21-22. Their "table to become a snare" means that their blessings turn into burdens and judgments. This is what happened to Israel: their spiritual blessings should have led them to Christ, but instead they became a snare that kept them from Christ. Their very religious practices and observances became substitutes for the real experience of salvation. Sad to say, this same mistake is made today when people depend on religious rituals and practices instead of trusting in the Christ who is pictured in these activities.

Paul made it clear that the hardening of Israel is neither total nor final, and this is proof that God has a future for the nation. "Hardness in part is happened to Israel, until the fullness of the Gentiles be come in" (Rom. 11:25). The existence of the believing Jewish remnant today, as in Elijah's day, is evidence that God still has a plan for His people. Paul did not imitate Elijah's mistake and say, "I only am left!" He knew that there was a remnant of Israel in this world who trusted God.

The Gentiles (Rom. 11:11-15)

In Romans 2:1-3 Paul used the Gentiles to prove the Jews guilty of sin, but here he used the Gentiles to assure Israel of a future restoration. His logic here is beautiful. When the Jews rejected the Gospel, God sent it to the Gentiles and they believed and were saved. Three tragedies occurred in Israel: the nation *fell* (Rom. 11:11), was *lost* (Rom. 11:12, "diminished"), and was *cast away* (Rom. 11:15). None of these words suggests a *final* judgment on Israel. But the amazing thing is that through Israel's fall, salvation came to the Gentiles. God promised that the Gentiles would be saved (Rom. 9:25-26) and He kept His promise. Will He not also keep His promise to the Jews?

It is important to understand that the Old Testament promises to the Gentiles were linked to Israel's "rise"—her entering into her kingdom. Prophecies like Isaiah 11 and Isaiah 60 make it clear that the Gentiles will share in Israel's kingdom. But Israel did not "rise"; *she fell!* What would God then do with the Gentiles? God introduced a new factor—the church—in which believing Jews and Gentiles are one in Christ (Eph. 2:11-22). In Ephesians 3, Paul called this new program "the mystery," meaning "the sacred secret" that was not revealed in the Old Testament. Does this mean that God has abandoned His kingdom program for Israel? Of course not! Israel is merely set aside until the time comes for God's plans for Israel to be fulfilled.

Paul stated that the Gentiles had a vital ministry to Israel. Today, the saved Gentiles provoke Israel "to jealousy" (see Rom. 10:19) because of the spiritual riches they have in Christ. Israel today is spiritually bankrupt, while Christians have "all spiritual blessings" in Christ (Eph. 1:3). (If an unsaved Jew visited the average church service, would he be provoked *to jealousy* and wish he had what we have—or would he just be provoked?)

There is a future for Israel. Paul calls it "their fullness" (Rom. 11:12) and their "receiving" (Rom. 11:15). Today, Israel is fallen spiritually, but when Christ returns, the nation will rise again. Today, Israel is cast away from God, but one day they shall be received again. God will never break His covenant with His people, and He has promised to restore them. (See Jer. 31:35-37 where God links His promises to Israel to the sun, moon, and stars.)

The Patriarchs (Rom. 11:16-24)

From looking at the future, Paul next looked to the past to show Israel's spiritual heritage. From the beginning, Israel was a special people, set apart by God. Paul used two illustrations to prove his argument that God was not finished with the Jews.

The lump of dough (v. 16a). The reference here is to Numbers 15:17-21. The first part of the dough was to be offered up to God as a symbol that the entire lump belonged to Him. The same idea was involved in the Feast of Firstfruits, when the priest offered a sheaf to the Lord as a token that the entire harvest was His (Lev. 23:9-14). The basic idea is that when God accepts the part He sanctifies the whole.

Applying this to the history of Israel, we understand Paul's argument. God accepted the founder of the nation, Abraham, and in so doing set apart his descendants as well. God also accepted the other patriarchs, Isaac and Jacob, in spite of their sins or failings. This means that God must accept the "rest of the lump"—the nation of Israel.

The olive tree (vv. 16b-24). This is a symbol of the nation of Israel (Jer. 11:16-17; Hosea 14:4-6). Please keep in mind that Paul was not discussing the relationship of individual believers to God, but the place of Israel in the plan of God. The roots of the tree support the tree; again, this was a symbol of the patriarchs who founded the nation. God made His covenants with Abraham, Isaac, and Jacob, and He cannot deny them or change them. Thus, it is God's promise to Abraham that sustains Israel even today.

Many of the Jewish people did not believe. Paul pictured them as branches broken off the tree. But he saw an amazing thing taking place: other branches were grafted into the tree to share in the life of the tree. These branches were the Gentiles. In Romans 11:24, Paul described this "grafting in" as "contrary to nature." Usually a cultivated branch is grafted into a wild tree and shares its life without producing its poor fruit. But in this case, it was the "wild branch" (the Gentiles) that was grafted into the good tree! "Salvation is of the Jews" (John 4:22).

To say that the olive tree, with its natural and grafted branches, is a picture of the church would be a great mistake. In the church, "there is no difference"; believers are "all one in Christ Jesus" (Gal. 3:28). God does not look on the members of Christ's body and see them as Jews or Gentiles. The olive tree illustrates the relationship between Jew and Gentile in the program of God. The "breaking off of the branches" is the equivalent of "the fall" (Rom. 11:11), "the diminishing" (Rom. 11:12), and "the casting away" (Rom. 11:15). To read into this illustration the matter of the eternal destiny of the individual believer is to abuse the truth Paul was seeking to communicate.

Paul warned the Gentiles that they were obligated to Israel, and therefore they dared not boast of their new spiritual position (Rom. 11:18-21). The Gentiles entered into God's plan because of faith, and not because of anything good they had done. Paul was discussing the Gentiles collectively, and not the individual experience of one believer or another.

It is worth noting that, according to Bible prophecy, the professing Gentile church will be "cut off" because of apostasy. First Timothy 4 and 2 Timothy 3, along with 2 Thessalonians 2, all indicate that the professing church in the last days will depart from the faith. *There is no hope for the apostate church, but there is hope for apostate Israel!* Why? Because of the roots of the olive tree. God will keep His promises to the patriarchs, but God will break off the Gentiles because of their unbelief.

No matter how far Israel may stray from the truth of God, the roots are still good. God is still the "God of Abraham, and the God of Isaac, and the God of Jacob" (Ex. 3:6; Matt. 22:23). He will keep His promises to these patriarchs. This means that the olive tree will flourish again!

God Himself (Rom. 11:25-36)

Paul saved his best witness for the last. He proved that the very character and work of God were involved in the future of Israel. Men may dispute about prophecy and differ in their interpretations, but let every man realize that he is dealing with *God's people,* Israel.

God's timing (v. 25). What has happened to Israel is all a part of God's plan, and He knows what He is doing. The blinding (or hardening, Rom. 11:7) of Israel as a nation is neither total nor final: it is partial and temporary. How long will it last? "Until the fullness of the Gentiles be come in" (Rom. 11:25). There is a "fullness" for Israel (Rom. 11:12) and for the Gentiles. Today, God in His grace is visiting the Gentiles and taking out a people for His name (Acts 15:12-14). Individual Jews are being saved, of course; but this present age is primarily a time when God is visiting the Gentiles and building His church. When this present age has run its course, and the fullness of the Gentiles has come in, then God will once more deal with the nation of Israel.

Romans 11:25 is one of several *"until* verses" in the Bible, all of which are important. Read Matthew 23:32-39; Luke 21:24; and Psalm 110:1 for other references. It is reassuring that God knows what time it is and that He is never late in fulfilling His will.

God's promise (v. 26). The reference here is Isaiah 59:20-21; and you ought to read Isaiah 60 to complete the picture. God has promised to save His people, and He will keep His promise. There are those who interpret this as meaning salvation to individuals through the Gospel, but it is my conviction that the prophet has national conversion in mind. "All Israel shall be saved" does not mean that every Jew who has ever lived will be converted, but that the Jews living when the Redeemer returns will see Him, receive

Him, and be saved. Zechariah 12–13 give the details. It seems to me that there are too many details in these Old Testament prophecies of national restoration for Israel for us to spiritualize them and apply them to the church today.

God's covenant (vv. 27-28). This is, of course, a continuation of the quotation from Isaiah 59; but the emphasis is on the covenant of God with Israel. God chose Israel in His grace and not because of any merit in her (Deut. 7:6-11; 9:1-6). If the nation was not chosen because of its goodness, can it be rejected because of its sin? "Election" means grace, not merit. The Jewish people are "enemies" to the believing Gentiles because of their hostile attitude toward the Gospel. But to God, the Jewish people are "beloved for the fathers' sakes." God will not break His covenant with Abraham, Isaac, and Jacob.

God's nature (v. 29). "I am the Lord, I change not" (Mal. 3:6). "God is not a man that He should lie; neither the son of man, that He should repent" (Num. 23:19). God's gifts to Israel, and God's calling of Israel, cannot be taken back or changed, or God would cease to be true to His own perfect nature. The fact that Israel may not enjoy her gifts, or live up to her privileges as an elect nation, does not affect this fact one bit. God will be consistent with Himself and true to His Word no matter what men may do. "Shall their unbelief make the faithfulness of God without effect?" (Rom. 3:3, literal translation)

God's grace (vv. 30-32). "Because of the unbelief of the Jews, you Gentiles were saved," said Paul. "Now, may it be that through your salvation Israel will come to know Christ." Note that Paul repeatedly reminded the saved Gentiles that they had a spiritual obligation to Israel to "provoke them to jealousy" (Rom. 10:19; 11:11, 14). Israel's hardness is only "in part" (Rom. 11:25), which means that individual Jews can be saved. God has included "all in unbelief"—Jews and Gentiles—so that *all* might have the opportunity to be saved by grace. "There is no difference." If God can save Jews by His grace and mercy today, why can He not save them in the future?

We must remember that God chose the Jews so that the Gentiles might be saved. "In thee shall all families of the earth be blessed," was God's promise to Abraham (Gen. 12:1-3). The tragedy was that Israel became exclusive and failed to share the truth with the Gentiles. They thought that the Gentiles had to become Jews in order to be saved. But God declared both Jews and Gentiles to be lost and condemned. This meant that He could have mercy on all because of the sacrifice of Christ on the cross.

God's wisdom (vv. 33-36). Having contemplated God's great plan of salvation for Jews and Gentiles, all Paul could do was sing a hymn of praise. As someone has remarked, "Theology becomes doxology!" Only a God as wise as our God could take the fall of Israel and turn it into salvation for the world! His plans will not be aborted nor will His purposes lack fulfillment. No human being can fully know the mind of the Lord; and the more we study His ways, the more we offer Him praise. Are we to conclude that God does *not* know what He is doing, and that the nation of Israel completely ruined His plans? Of course not! God is too wise to make plans that will not be fulfilled. Israel did not allow Him to rule, so He overruled!

Paul summoned five witnesses, and they all agreed: there is a future for Israel. When Israel recovers from her "fall" and enters into her "fullness," the world will experience the riches of God's grace as never before. When Jesus Christ returns and sits on David's throne to reign over His kingdom, then Israel will be "reconciled" and "received," and it will be like a resurrection!

CHAPTER ELEVEN
RIGHT RELATIONSHIPS MEAN RIGHT LIVING
Romans 12–13

In all of his letters, Paul concluded with a list of practical duties that were based on the doctrines he had discussed. In the Christian life, doctrine and duty always go together. What we believe helps to determine how we behave. It is not enough for us to understand Paul's doctrinal explanations. We must translate our *learning* into *living* and show by our daily lives that we trust God's Word.

The key idea in this section is *relationships*. The term "relational theology" is a relatively new one, but the idea is not new. If we have a right relationship to God, we will have a right relationship to the people who are a part of our lives. "If a man say, I love God, and hateth his brother, he is a liar" (1 John 4:20).

Our Relationship to God (Rom. 12:1-2)
This is the fourth "therefore" in the letter. Romans 3:20 is the "therefore" of condemnation, declaring that the whole world is guilty before God. Romans 5:1 is the "therefore" of justification, and Romans 8:1 the "therefore" of assurance. In Romans 12:1, we have the "therefore" of dedication, and it is this dedication that is the basis for the other relationships that Paul discussed in this section.

What is true dedication? As Paul described it here, Christian dedication involves three steps.

You give God your body (v. 1). Before we trusted Christ, we used our body for sinful pleasures and purposes, but now that we belong to Him, we want to use our body for His glory. The Christian's body is God's temple (1 Cor. 6:19-20) because the Spirit of God dwells within him (Rom. 8:9). It is our privilege to glorify Christ in our body and magnify Christ in our body (Phil. 1:20-21).

Just as Jesus Christ had to take on Himself a body in order to accomplish God's will on earth, so we must yield our bodies to Christ that He might continue God's work through us. We must yield the members of the body as "instruments of righteousness" (Rom. 6:13) for the Holy Spirit to use in the doing of God's work. The Old Testament sacrifices were dead sacrifices, but we are to be living sacrifices.

There are two "living sacrifices" in the Bible and they help us understand what this really means. The first is Isaac (Gen. 22); the second is our Lord Jesus Christ. Isaac willingly put himself on the altar and would have died in obedience to God's will, but the Lord sent a ram to take his place. Isaac "died" just the same—he died to self and willingly yielded himself to the will of God. When he got off that altar, Isaac was a "living sacrifice" to the glory of God.

Of course, our Lord Jesus Christ is the perfect illustration of a "living sacrifice," because He actually died as a sacrifice, in obedience to His Father's will. But He arose again. And today He is in heaven as a "living sacrifice," bearing in His body the wounds of Calvary. He is our High Priest (Heb. 4:14-16) and our Advocate (1 John 2:1) before the throne of God.

The verb "present" in this verse means "present once and for all." It commands a definite commitment of the body to the Lord, just as a bride and groom in their wedding service commit themselves to each other. It is this once-for-all commitment that determines what they do with their bodies. Paul gives us two reasons for this commitment: (1) it is the right response to all that God has done for us—"I beseech you *therefore,* brethren, *by the mercies of God*" (italics mine); and (2) this commitment is "our reasonable service" or "our spiritual worship." This means that every day is a worship experience when your body is yielded to the Lord.

You give Him your mind (v. 2a). The world wants to control your mind, but God wants to transform your mind (see Eph. 4:17-24; Col. 3:1-11). This word *transform* is the same as *transfigure* in Matthew 17:2. It has come into our English language as the word "metamorphosis." It describes a change from within. The world wants to change your mind, so it exerts pressure from without. But the Holy Spirit changes your mind by releasing power from within. If the world controls your thinking, you are a *conformer;* if God controls your thinking, you are a *transformer.*

God transforms our minds and makes us spiritually minded by using His Word. As you spend time meditating on God's Word, memorizing it, and making it a part of your inner man, God will gradually make your mind more spiritual (see 2 Cor. 3:18).

You give Him your will (v. 2b). Your mind controls your body, and your will controls your mind. Many people think they can control their will by "willpower," but usually they fail. (This was Paul's experience as recorded in Rom. 7:15-21). It is only when we yield the will to God that His power can take over and give us the willpower (and the won't power!) that we need to be victorious Christians.

We surrender our wills to God through disciplined prayer. As we spend time in prayer, we surrender our will to God and pray, with the Lord, "Not my will, but Thy will be done." We must pray about everything, and let God have His way in everything.

For many years I have tried to begin each day by surrendering my body to the Lord.

Then I spend time with His Word and let Him transform my mind and prepare my thinking for that new day. Then I pray, and I yield the plans of the day to Him and let Him work as He sees best. I especially pray about those tasks that upset or worry me—and He always sees me through. To have a right relationship with God, we must start the day by yielding to Him our bodies, minds, and wills.

Relationship to Other Believers (Rom. 12:3-16)

Paul was writing to Christians who were members of local churches in Rome. He described their relationship to each other in terms of the members of a body. (He used this same picture in 1 Cor. 12; Eph. 4:7-16.) The basic idea is that each believer is a living part of Christ's body, and each one has a spiritual function to perform. Each believer has a gift (or gifts) to be used for the building up of the body and the perfecting of the other members of the body. In short, we belong to each other, we minister to each other, and we need each other. What are the essentials for spiritual ministry and growth in the body of Christ?

Honest evaluation (v. 3). Each Christian must know what his spiritual gifts are and what ministry (or ministries) he is to have in the local church. It is not wrong for a Christian to recognize gifts in his own life and in the lives of others. What *is* wrong is the tendency to have a false evaluation of ourselves. Nothing causes more damage in a local church than a believer who overrates himself and tries to perform a ministry that he cannot do. (Sometimes the opposite is true, and people undervalue themselves. Both attitudes are wrong.)

The gifts that we have came because of God's grace. They must be accepted and exercised by faith. We were saved "by grace, through faith" (Eph. 2:8-9), and we must live and serve "by grace through faith." Since our gifts are from God, we cannot take the credit for them. All we can do is accept them and use them to honor His name. (See 1 Cor. 15:10 for Paul's personal testimony about gifts.)

I once ministered with two men who had opposite attitudes toward their gifts: the one man constantly belittled his gifts and would not use them, and the other man constantly boasted about gifts that he did not possess. Actually, both of them were guilty of pride, because both of them refused to acknowledge God's grace and let Him have the glory. Moses made a similar mistake when God called him (Ex. 4:1-13). When the individual believers in a church know their gifts, accept them by faith, and use them for God's glory, then God can bless in a wonderful way.

Faithful cooperation (vv. 4-8). Each believer has a different gift, and God has bestowed these gifts so the local body can grow in a balanced way. But each Christian must exercise his or her gift by faith. We may not see the result of our ministry, but the Lord sees it and He blesses. Note that "exhortation" (encouragement) is just as much a spiritual ministry as preaching or teaching. Giving and showing mercy are also important gifts. To some people, God has given the ability to rule, or to administer the various functions of the church. Whatever gift we have must be dedicated to God and used for the good of the whole church.

It is tragic when any one gift is emphasized in a local church beyond all the other gifts. "Are all apostles? are all prophets? are all teachers? are all workers of miracles? have all the gifts of healing? do all speak with tongues? do all interpret?" (1 Cor. 12:29-30) The answer to all these questions is no! And for a Christian to minimize the other gifts while he emphasizes his own gift is to deny the very purpose for which gifts are given: the benefit of the whole body of Christ. "Now to each man the manifestation of the Spirit is given for the common good" (1 Cor. 12:7, NIV).

Spiritual gifts are tools to build with, not toys to play with or weapons to fight with. In the church at Corinth, the believers were tearing down the ministry because they were abusing spiritual gifts. They were using their gifts as ends in themselves and not as a means toward the end of building up the church. They so emphasized their spiritual gifts that they lost their spiritual graces! They had the gifts of the Spirit but were lacking in the fruit of the spirit—love, joy, peace, etc. (Gal. 5:22-23).

Loving participation (vv. 9-16). Here the emphasis is on the attitudes of those who exercise the spiritual gifts. It is possible to use a spiritual gift in an unspiritual way. Paul makes this same point in 1 Corinthians 13, the great "love chapter" of the New Testament. Love is the circulatory system of the spiritual body, which enables all the members to function in a healthy, harmonious way. This must be an honest love, not a hypocritical love (Rom. 11:9); and it must be humble, not proud (Rom. 11:10). "Preferring one another" means treating others as more important than ourselves (Phil. 2:1-4).

Serving Christ usually means satanic opposition and days of discouragement. Paul admonished his readers to maintain their spiritual zeal because they were serving the Lord and not men. When life becomes difficult, the Christian cannot permit his zeal to grow cold. "Be joyful in hope, patient in affliction, faithful in prayer" (Rom. 12:12, NIV).

Finally, Paul reminded them that they must enter into the feelings of others. Christian fellowship is much more than a pat on the back and a handshake. It means sharing the burdens and the blessings of others so that we all grow together and glorify the Lord. If Christians cannot get along with one another, how can they ever face their enemies? A humble attitude and a willingness to share are the marks of a Christian who truly ministers to the body. Our Lord ministered to the common people, and they heard Him gladly (Mark 12:37). When a local church decides it wants only a certain "high class" of people, it departs from the Christian ideal for ministry.

Our Relationship to Our Enemies (Rom. 12:17-21)

The believer who seeks to obey God is going to have his enemies. When our Lord was ministering on earth, He had enemies. No matter where Paul and the other apostles traveled, there were enemies who opposed their work. Jesus warned His disciples that their worst enemies might be those of their own household (Matt. 10:36). Unfortunately, some believers have enemies because they lack love and patience, and not because they are faithful in their witness. There is a difference between sharing in "the offense of the cross" (Gal. 5:11; 6:12-15) and being an offensive Christian!

The Christian must not play God and try to avenge himself. Returning evil for evil, or good for good, is the way most people live. But the Christian must live on a higher level and return good for evil. Of course, this requires *love,* because our first inclination is to fight back. It also requires *faith,* believing that God can work and accomplish His will in our lives and in the lives of those who hurt us. We must give place to "the wrath"—the wrath of God (Deut. 32:35).

A friend of mine once heard a preacher criticize him over the radio and tell things that were not only unkind, but also untrue. My friend became very angry and was planning to fight back, when a godly preacher said, "Don't do it. If you defend yourself, then the Lord can't defend you. Leave it in His hands." My friend followed that wise counsel, and the Lord vindicated him.

The admonition in Romans 12:20 reminds us of Christ's words in Matthew 5:44-48. These words are easy to read but difficult to practice. Surely we need to pray and ask God for love as we try to show kindness to our enemies. Will they take advantage of us? Will they hate us more? Only the Lord knows. Our task is not to protect ourselves but to obey the Lord and leave the results with Him. Paul referred to Proverbs 25:21-22 as he urged us to return good for evil in the name of the Lord. The "coals of fire" refer perhaps to the feeling of shame our enemies will experience when we return good for evil.

As children of God, we must live on the highest level—returning good for evil. Anyone can return good for good and evil for evil. The only way to overcome evil is with good. If we return evil for evil, we only add fuel to the fire. And even if our enemy is not converted, we have still experienced the love of God in our own hearts and have grown in grace.

Our Relationship to the State (Rom. 13:1-14)

God has established three institutions: the home (Gen. 2:18-25), government (Gen. 9:1-17), and the church (Acts 2). Paul was writing to believers at the very heart of the Roman Empire. As yet, the great persecutions had not started, but were on the way. Christianity was still considered a Jewish sect, and the Jewish religion was approved by Rome. But the day would come when it would be very difficult, if not impossible, for a Christian to be loyal to the emperor. He could not drop incense on the altar and affirm, "Caesar is god!"

In our own day, we have people who teach riot and rebellion *in the name of Christ!* They would have us believe that the Christian thing to do is to disobey the law, rebel against the authorities, and permit every man to do that which is right in his own eyes. Paul refuted this position in this chapter by explaining four reasons why the Christian must be in subjection to the laws of the State.

For wrath's sake (vv. 1-4). It is God who has established the governments of the world (see Acts 17:24-28). This does not mean that He is responsible for the sins of tyrants, but only that the authority to rule comes originally from God. It was this lesson that Nebuchadnezzar had to learn the hard way. (See Dan. 4, and especially vv. 17, 25, and 32.) To resist the law is to resist the God who established government in the world, and this means inviting punishment.

Rulers must bear the sword; that is, they have the power to afflict punishment and even to take life. God established human government because man is a sinner and must have some kind of authority over him. God has given the sword to rulers, and with it the authority to punish and even to execute. Capital punishment was ordained in Genesis 9:5-6, and it has not been abolished. Even though we cannot always respect the man in office, we must respect the office, for government was ordained by God.

On more than one occasion in his ministry, Paul used the Roman law to protect his life and to extend his work. The centurions mentioned in the Book of Acts appear to be men of character and high ideals. Even though government officials are not believers, they are still the "ministers of God" because He established the authority of the State.

For conscience's sake (vv. 5-7). We move a bit higher in our motivation now. Any citizen can obey the law because of fear of punishment, but a Christian ought to obey because of conscience. Of course, if the government interferes with conscience, then the Christian must obey God rather than men (Acts 5:29). But when the law is right, the Christian must obey it if he is to maintain a good conscience (1 Tim. 1:5, 19; 3:9; 4:2; Acts 24:16).

The United States Government maintains a "Conscience Fund" for people who want to pay their debts to the Government and yet remain anonymous. Some city governments have a similar fund. I read about a city that had investigated some tax frauds and announced that several citizens were going to be indicted. They did not release the names of the culprits. That week, a number of people visited the City Hall to "straighten out their taxes"—and many of them were not on the indictment list. When conscience begins to work, we cannot live with ourselves until we have made things right.

Romans 13:7 commands us to pay what we owe: taxes, revenue, respect, honor. If we do not pay our taxes, we show disrespect to the law, the officials, and the Lord. And this cannot but affect the conscience of the believer. We may not agree with all that is done with the money we pay in taxes, but we dare not violate our conscience by refusing to pay.

For love's sake (vv. 8-10). Paul enlarged the circle of responsibility by including other people besides government officials. "Love one another" is the basic principle of the Christian life. It is the "new commandment" that Christ gave to us (John 13:34). When we practice love, there is no need for any other laws, because love covers it all! If we love others, we will not sin against them. This explained why the Ten Commandments were not referred to often in the New Testament. In fact, the Sabbath commandment is not quoted at all in any of the epistles. As believers, we do not live under the Law; we live under grace. Our motive for obeying God and helping others is the love of Christ in our hearts.

Does "Owe no man anything" refer also to the Christian's financial practices? Some people believe that it does, and that it is a sin to have a debt. J. Hudson Taylor, the godly missionary to China, would never incur a debt, basing his conviction on this verse. Charles Spurgeon, the great Baptist preacher, had the same conviction. However, the Bible does not forbid borrowing or legal financial transactions that involve interest. What the Bible does forbid is the charging of high interest, robbing the brethren, and failing to pay honest debts (see Ex. 22:25-27; Neh. 5:1-11). Matthew 25:27 and Luke 19:23 indicate that banking and investing for gain are not wrong. Certainly no one should get into unnecessary debt, or sign contracts he cannot maintain. "Thou shalt not steal." But to make Romans 13:8 apply to all kinds of legal obligations involving money is, to me, stretching a point.

In this section, Paul has centered on the very heart of the problem—the human heart. Because the heart of man is sinful, God established government. But laws cannot change the heart; man's heart is still selfish and can be changed only by the grace of God.

For Jesus' sake (vv. 11-14). We have come a long way in our reasons for obeying the law: from fear to conscience to love to our devotion to Jesus Christ! The emphasis is on the imminent return of Christ. As His servants, we want to be found faithful when He returns. The completion of our salvation is near! The light is dawning! Therefore, be ready!

Paul gave several admonitions in the light of the Lord's soon return. The first is, "Wake up!" Relate this with 1 Thessalonians 5:1-11, and also Matthew 25:1-13. The second is, "Clean up!" We do not want to be found dressed in dirty garments when the Lord returns (1 John 2:28–3:3). The Christian wears the armor of light, not the deeds of darkness. He has no reason to get involved in the sinful pleasures of the world. Finally, Paul admonished, "Grow up!" (Rom. 13:14) To "put on" the Lord Jesus Christ means to become more like Him, to receive by faith all that He is for our daily living. We grow on the basis of the food we eat. This is why God warns us not to make provisions for the flesh. If we feed the flesh, we will fail; but if we feed the inner man the nourishing things of the Spirit, we will succeed.

In other words, a Christian citizen ought to be the best citizen. Christians may not always agree on politics or parties, but they can all agree on their attitude toward human government.

CHAPTER TWELVE
WHEN CHRISTIANS DISAGREE
Romans 14:1–15:7

Disunity has always been a major problem with God's people. Even the Old Testament records the civil wars and family fights among the people of Israel, and almost every local church mentioned in the New Testament had divisions to contend with. The Corinthians were divided over human leaders, and some of the members were even suing each other (1 Cor. 1:10-13; 6:1-8). The Galatian saints were "biting and devouring" one another (Gal. 5:15), and the saints in Ephesus and Colossae had to be reminded of the importance of Christian unity (Eph. 4:1-3; Col. 2:1-2). In the church at Philippi, two women were at odds with each other and, as a result, were splitting the church (Phil. 4:1-3). No wonder the psalmist wrote, "Behold, how good and how pleasant it is for brethren to dwell together in unity" (Ps. 133:1).

Some of these problems stemmed from the backgrounds of the believers in the churches. The Jews, for example, were saved out of a strict legalistic background that would be difficult to forget. The Gentiles never had to worry about diets and days. The first church council in history debated the issue of the relationship of the Christian to the Law (Acts 15).

The believers in Rome were divided over special diets and special days. Some of the members thought it was a sin to eat meat, so they ate only vegetables. Other members thought it a sin not to observe the Jewish holy days. If each Christian had kept his convictions to himself, there would have been no problem, but they began to criticize and judge one another. The one group was sure the other group was not at all spiritual.

Unfortunately, we have similar problems today with many "gray areas" of life that are not clearly right or wrong to every believer. Some activities we know are wrong, because the Bible clearly condemns them. Other activities we know are right, because the Bible clearly commands them. But when it comes to areas that are not clearly defined in Scripture, we find ourselves needing some other kind of guidance. Paul gave principles of this guidance. He explained how believers could disagree on nonessentials and still maintain unity in the church. He gave his readers three important admonitions.

Receive One Another (Rom. 14:1-12)

You will note that this section begins and ends with this admonition (Rom. 15:7). Paul was addressing those who were "strong in the faith," that is, those who understood their spiritual liberty in Christ and were not enslaved to diets or holy days. The "weak in faith" were immature believers who felt obligated to obey legalistic rules concerning what they ate and when they worshiped. Many people have the idea that the Christians who follow strict rules are the most mature, but this is not necessarily the case. In the Roman assemblies, the weak Christians were those who clung to the Law and did not enjoy their freedom in the Lord. The weak Christians were judging and condemning the strong Christians, and the strong Christians were despising the weak Christians.

"Welcome one another!" was Paul's first admonition; and he gave four reasons why they should.

God has received us (vv. 1-3). It is not

our responsibility to decide the requirements for Christian fellowship in a church; only the Lord can do this. To set up man-made restrictions on the basis of personal prejudices (or even convictions) is to go beyond the Word of God. Because God has received us, we must receive one another. We must not argue over these matters, nor must we judge or despise one another. Perhaps St. Augustine put the matter best: "In essentials, unity; in nonessentials, liberty; in all things, charity."

When God sent Peter to take the Gospel to the Gentiles, the church criticized Peter because he ate with these new Christians (Acts 11:1-3). But God had clearly revealed His acceptance of the Gentiles by giving them the same Holy Spirit that He bestowed on the Jewish believers at Pentecost (Acts 10:44-48; 11:15-18). Peter did not obey this truth consistently, for later on he refused to fellowship with the Gentile Christians in Antioch, and Paul had to rebuke him (Gal. 2:11-13). God showed both Peter and Paul that Christian fellowship was not to be based on food or religious calendars.

In every church there are weak and strong believers. The strong understand spiritual truth and practice it, but the weak have not yet grown into that level of maturity and liberty. The weak must not condemn the strong and call them unspiritual. The strong must not despise the weak and call them immature. God has received both the weak and the strong; therefore, they should receive one another.

God sustains His own (v. 4). The strong Christian was judged by the weak Christian, and this Paul condemned because it was wrong for the weak Christian to take the place of God in the life of the strong Christian. God is the Master; the Christian is the servant. It is wrong for anyone to interfere with this relationship.

It is encouraging to know that our success in the Christian life does not depend on the opinions or attitudes of other Christians. God is the Judge, and He is able to make us stand. The word "servant" here suggests that Christians ought to be busy working for the Lord; then they will not have the time or inclination to judge or condemn other Christians. People who are busy winning souls to Christ have more important things to do than to investigate the lives of the saints!

Jesus Christ is Lord (vv. 5-9). The word "Lord" is found eight times in these verses. No Christian has the right to "play God" in another Christian's life. We can pray, advise, and even admonish, but we cannot take the place of God. What is it that makes a dish of food "holy" or a day "holy"? It is the fact that we relate it to the Lord. The person who treats a special day as "holy" does so "unto the Lord." The person who treats every day as sacred, does so "unto the Lord." The Christian who eats meat gives thanks to the Lord, and the Christian who abstains from meat abstains "unto the Lord." To be "fully persuaded—or assured—in his own mind" (Rom. 14:5) means: Let every man see to it that he is really doing what he does for the Lord's sake, and not merely on the basis of some prejudice or whim.

Some standards and practices in our local churches are traditional but not necessarily scriptural. Some of us can remember when dedicated Christians opposed Christian radio "because Satan was the prince of the power of the air!" Some people even make Bible translations a test of orthodoxy. The church is divided and weakened because Christians will not allow Jesus Christ to be Lord.

An interesting illustration of this truth is given in John 21:15-25. Jesus had restored Peter to his place as an apostle, and once again He told him, "Follow Me." Peter began to follow Christ, but then he heard someone walking behind him. It was the Apostle John.

Then Peter asked Jesus, "Lord, what shall this man do?"

Notice the Lord's reply: "What is that to thee? Follow thou Me!" In other words, "Peter, you make sure you have made Me Lord of your life. Let Me worry about John." Whenever I hear believers condemning other Christians because of something they disagree with, something that is not essential or forbidden in the Word, I feel like saying, "What is that to thee? Follow Christ! Let Him be the Lord!"

Paul emphasized the believer's union with Christ: "Whether we live, therefore, or whether we die, we are the Lord's" (Rom. 14:8). Our first responsibility is to the Lord. If Christians would go to the Lord in prayer instead of going to their brother with criticism, there would be stronger fellowship in our churches.

Jesus Christ is Judge (vv. 10-12). Paul asked the weak Christian, "Why are you judging your brother?" Then he asked the strong Christian, "Why are you despising your brother?" Both strong and weak must stand at the Judgment Seat of Christ, and they will not judge each other—they will be judged by the Lord.

The Judgment Seat of Christ is that place where Christians will have their works judged by the Lord. It has nothing to do with our sins, since Christ has paid for them and they can be held against us no more (Rom. 8:1). The word for "judgment seat" in the Greek is *bema,* meaning the place where the judges stood at the athletic games. If during the games they saw an athlete break the rules, they immediately disqualified him. At the end of the contests, the judges gave out the rewards (see 1 Cor. 9:24-27). First Corinthians 3:10-15 gives another picture of the Judgment Seat of Christ. Paul compared our ministries with the building of a temple. If we build with cheap materials, the fire will burn them up. If we use precious, lasting materials, our works will last. If our works pass the test, we receive a reward. If they are burned up, we lose the reward, but we are still saved "yet so as by fire."

How does the Christian prepare for the Judgment Seat of Christ? By making Jesus Lord of his life and faithfully obeying Him. Instead of judging other Christians, we had better judge our own lives and make sure we are ready to meet Christ at the bema (see Luke 12:41-48; Heb. 13:17; and 1 John 2:28).

The fact that our sins will never be brought up against us should not encourage us to disobey God. Sin in our lives keeps us from serving Christ as we should, and this means loss of reward. Lot is a good example of this truth (Gen. 18–19). Lot was not walking with the Lord as was his uncle, Abraham, and as a result, he lost his testimony even with his own family. When the judgment finally came, Lot was spared the fire and brimstone, but everything he lived for was burned up. He was saved "yet so as by fire."

Paul explained that they did not have to give an account for anyone else but themselves. So they were to make sure that their account would be a good one. He was stressing the principle of lordship—make Jesus Christ the Lord of your life, and let Him be the Lord in the lives of other Christians as well.

Two of the most famous Christians in the Victorian Era in England were Charles Spurgeon and Joseph Parker, both of them mighty preachers of the Gospel. Early in their ministries they fellowshipped and even exchanged pulpits. Then they had a disagreement, and the reports even got into the newspapers. Spurgeon accused Parker of being unspiritual because he attended the theater. Interestingly enough, Spurgeon smoked cigars, a practice many believers would condemn. Who was right? Who was wrong? Perhaps *both* of them were wrong! When it comes to questionable matters in the Christian life, cannot dedicated believers disagree without being disagreeable? "I have learned that God blesses people I disagree with!" a friend of mine told me one day, and I have learned the same thing. When Jesus Christ is Lord, we permit Him to deal with His own servants as He wishes.

Edify One Another (Rom. 14:13-23)

If we stopped with the first admonition, it might give the impression that Christians were to leave each other alone and let the weak remain weak. But this second admonition explains things further. The emphasis is not on "master-servant" but on "brother." It is the principle of brotherly love. If we love each other, we will seek to edify each other, build each other up in the faith. Paul shared several facts to help his readers help their brethren.

Christians affect each other (vv. 13-15). Note the possible ways we can affect each other. We can cause others to stumble, grieve others, or even destroy others. Paul was speaking of the way the strong Christian affected the weak Christian. Paul dealt with a similar problem in 1 Corinthians 8–9, where the question was, "Should Christians eat meat that has been offered to idols in heathen temples?" There he pointed out that knowledge and love must work together. "Knowledge puffs up, but love builds up" (1 Cor. 8:1, NIV). The strong Christian has spiritual knowledge, but if he does not practice love, his knowledge will hurt the weak Christian. Knowledge must be balanced by love.

Often little children are afraid of the dark and think there is something hiding in the closet. Of course, Mother knows that the child is safe; but her knowledge alone cannot assure or comfort the child. You can never argue a child into losing fear. When the mother sits at the bedside, talks lovingly to the child, and assures him that everything is secure, then the child can go to sleep without fear. Knowledge plus love helps the weak person grow strong.

"There is nothing unclean of itself," Paul wrote (Rom. 14:14). No foods are unclean, no days are unclean, no people are unclean. (Read Acts 10 to see how Peter learned this lesson.) What something *does* to a person determines its quality. One man may be able to read certain books and not be bothered by them, while a weaker Christian reading the same books might be tempted to sin. But the issue is not, "How does it affect me?" so much as, "If I do this, how will it affect my brother?" Will it make him stumble? Will it grieve him or even destroy him by encouraging him to sin? Is it really worth it to harm a brother just so I can enjoy some food? No!

Christians must have priorities (vv. 16-18). Like the Pharisees of old, we Christians have a way of majoring in the minor (Matt. 23:23-24). I have seen churches divided over matters that were really insignificant when compared with the vital things of the Christian faith. I have heard of churches being split over such minor matters as the location of the piano in the auditorium and the serving of meals on Sundays. "The kingdom of God is not meat and drink" (Rom. 14:17). "But food does not bring us near to God; we are no worse if we do not eat, and no better if we do" (1 Cor. 8:8, NIV)

Not the externals, but the eternals must be first in our lives: righteousness, peace, and joy. Where do they come from? The Holy Spirit of God at work in our lives (see Rom. 5:1-2). If each believer would yield to the Spirit and major in a godly life, we would not have Christians fighting with each other over minor matters. Spiritual priorities are essential to harmony in the church.

Christians must help each other grow (vv. 19-21). Both the strong believer and the weak believer need to grow. The strong believer needs to grow in *love;* the weak believer needs to grow in *knowledge.* So long as a brother is weak in the faith, we must lovingly deal with him in his immaturity. But if we really love him, we will help him to grow. It is wrong for a Christian to remain immature, having a weak conscience.

An illustration from the home might help us better understand what is involved. When a child comes into a home, everything has to change. Mother and Father are careful not to leave the scissors on the chair or anything dangerous within reach. But as the child matures, it is possible for the parents to adjust the rules of the house and deal with him in a more adult fashion. It is natural for a child to stumble when he is learning to walk. But if an adult constantly stumbles, we know something is wrong.

Young Christians need the kind of fellowship that will protect them and encourage them to grow. But we cannot treat them like "babies" all their lives! The older Christians must exercise love and patience and be careful not to cause them to stumble. But the younger Christians must "grow in grace and in the knowledge of our Lord and Saviour Jesus Christ" (2 Peter 3:18). As they mature in the faith, they can help other believers to grow. To gear the ministry of a Sunday School class or local church only to the baby Christians is to hinder their growth as well as the ministry of the more mature saints. The weak must learn from the strong, and the strong must love the weak. The result will be peace and maturity to the glory of God.

Christians must not force their opinions on others (vv. 22-23) There are certain truths that all Christians must accept because they are the foundation for the faith. But areas of honest disagreement must not be made a test of fellowship. If you have a sincere conviction from God about a matter, keep it to yourself and do not try to force everybody else to accept it. No Christian can "borrow" another Christian's convictions and be honest in his Christian life. Unless he can hold them and practice them "by faith," he is sinning. Even if a person's convictions are immature, he must never violate his conscience. This would do great damage to his spiritual life. For example, the mature Christian knows that an idol is nothing. But a young Christian, just converted out of pagan idolatry, would still have fears about idols. If the strong believer forced the new Christian to eat meat sacrificed to an idol, the younger Christian would experience problems in his conscience that would only further weaken it (see 1 Cor. 8–9).

Conscience is strengthened by knowledge. But knowledge must be balanced by love; otherwise it tears down instead of building up. The truth that "all foods are clean" (Rom. 14:14, 20) will not of itself make a Christian grow. When this truth is taught in an atmosphere of love, then the younger Christian can grow and develop a strong conscience. Believers may hold different convictions about many matters, but they must hold them in love.

Please One Another (Rom. 15:1-7)

Paul classified himself with the strong saints as he dealt with a basic problem—*selfishness.* True Christian love is not selfish; rather, it seeks to share with others and make others happy. It is even willing to carry the younger Christians, to help them along in their spiritual development. We do not endure them. We encourage them!

Of course, the great example in this is our Lord Jesus Christ. He paid a tremendous price in order to minister to us. Paul quoted Psalm 69:9 to prove his point. Does a strong Christian think he is making a great sacrifice by giving up some food or drink? Then let him measure his sacrifice by the sacrifice of Christ. No sacrifice we could ever make could match Calvary.

A person's spiritual maturity is revealed by his discernment. He is willing to give up his rights that others might be helped. He does this, not as a burden, but as a blessing. Just as loving parents make sacrifices for their children, so the mature believer sacrifices to help younger Christians grow in the faith.

Paul shared the two sources of spiritual power from which we must draw if we are to live to please others: the Word of God (Rom. 15:4) and prayer (Rom. 15:5-6). We must confess that we sometimes get impatient with younger Christians, just as parents become impatient with their children. But the Word of God can give us the "patience and encouragement" that we need. Paul closed this section praying for his readers, that they might experience from God that spiritual unity that He alone can give.

This suggests to us that the local church must major in the Word of God and prayer. The first real danger to the unity of the church came because the Apostles were too busy to minister God's Word and pray (Acts 6:1-7). When they found others to share their burdens, they returned to their proper ministry, and the church experienced harmony and growth.

The result of this is, of course, glory to God (Rom. 15:7). Disunity and disagreement do not glorify God; they rob Him of glory. Abraham's words to Lot are applicable to today: "Let there be no strife, I pray thee, between me and thee . . . for we be brethren" (Gen. 13:8). The neighbors were watching! Abraham wanted them to see that he and Lot were different from them because they worshiped the true God. In His prayer in John 17, Jesus prayed for the unity of the church to the glory of God (John 17:20-26).

Receive one another; edify one another; and please one another—all to the glory of God.

CHAPTER THIRTEEN
MAN ON THE MOVE

Romans 15:8–16:27

One of the key words in the closing chapters of Romans is "ministry." In fact, Paul used three different Greek words to discuss the theme. In Romans 15:8, 25, 31; and 16:1, it is the simple word for a servant or service. Our English word "deacon" comes from this word. In Romans 15:16 and 27 (the word "minister"), he used the ordinary word for service in public office or in the temple. In Romans 15:16 he used a word that is found nowhere else in the Greek New Testament; and it means "to perform sacred rites, to minister in a priestly service."

In this section, Paul explained four different ministries.

The Ministry of Jesus Christ to the Gentiles (Rom. 15:8-13)

The supreme example of ministry must always be Jesus Christ. "But I am among you as he that serveth" (Luke 22:27). He came first of all to minister to the Jews, that through Israel He might be able to minister to the Gentiles. "To the Jew first" is a principle that was followed in the earthly ministry of Christ and in the early ministry of the church.

For example, John the Baptist came to minister to the nation of Israel to prepare them for their Messiah. When Jesus began His ministry, it was only to the people of Israel. When He sent out the Apostles on their first evangelistic mission, He ordered them, "Go not into the way of the Gentiles, and into any city of the Samaritans enter ye not; but go rather to the lost sheep of the house of Israel" (Matt. 10:5-6). This does not mean that He ignored individual Gentiles, because He did minister to a few (Matt. 8:5-13; 15:21-28); but His major emphasis was on Israel.

After His resurrection, He commanded the Apostles to remain in Jerusalem and begin their ministry there (Luke 24:44-49). The period covered by Acts 1–7 is characterized by a ministry only to Jews or Jewish proselytes. It was not until Acts 8 that the Gospel went to the Samaritans; in Acts 10 it went to the Gentiles. Then, through the ministry of Paul, it went throughout the Roman Empire (Acts 13:1-3).

When He came and died, Jesus Christ confirmed the promises that God made to Abraham and the other "fathers" of the Jewish nation (see Luke 1:30-33, 46-55, and 67-80). Some of these promises have already been fulfilled, but many await fulfillment when He returns to earth to establish His kingdom.

Was it selfish of God to emphasize the Jews? No, because through the Jews, He would send the Good News of salvation to the Gentiles. The first Christians were Jewish believers! "Salvation is of the Jews" (John 4:22). In the Old Testament period, God chose Israel to be a minister to the Gentiles; but instead, Israel copied the idolatrous ways of the Gentiles and had to be chastened. In the New Testament period, God chose Jewish believers to carry the Good News to the Gentiles, and they obeyed Him.

There is a beautiful progression in the promises that Paul quoted in Romans 15:9-12.

- The Jews glorify God *among* the Gentiles (Rom. 15:9, quoting Ps. 18:49)
- The Gentiles rejoice *with* the Jews (Rom. 15:10, quoting Deut. 32:43)
- All the Jews and Gentiles *together* praise God (Rom. 15:11, quoting Ps. 117:1)
- Christ shall reign over Jews and Gentiles (Rom. 15:12, quoting Isa. 11:10)

Romans 15:8 covers the period of the Gospels and Acts 1–7. Romans 15:9 describes the ministry of Paul as he witnessed among the Gentiles. Romans 15:10 could be applied to the church council in Acts 15 when the Gentiles were given equal status "with His people." Today, Jews and Gentiles in the church are praising God together.

The word "trust" at the end of Romans 15:12 is actually the word "hope." At one time the Gentiles were "without hope" (Eph. 2:12, NIV), but now in Christ they have hope. Not only do believers have hope, but they also have joy and peace and power (Rom. 15:13). The Holy Spirit of God shares these blessings with them as they yield to Him.

Because the Jewish Christians were faithful to take the Gospel to the Gentiles, the nations of the world today have the opportunity to trust Christ as Saviour.

Paul's Ministry to the Gentiles (Rom. 15:14-24)

Unless we understand the distinctive ministry of Paul, we will not fully appreciate the message of God's grace. Paul explained the characteristics of his ministry.

It was received by grace (vv. 14-15). When he was Saul of Tarsus, the crusading rabbi, Paul knew little of the grace of God. He persecuted the church and sought to destroy it. When Paul met Jesus Christ on the Damascus road (Acts 9), he experienced the grace of God. It was God's grace that saved him, and it was God's grace that called him and made him an apostle (1 Cor. 15:8-11). "We have received grace and apostleship, for obedience to the faith among all nations, for His name" (Rom. 1:5). In Ephesians 3, Paul explained his ministry to the Gentiles in greater detail.

It was centered in the Gospel (v. 16). As mentioned before, Paul used two different words for *minister* in this verse, but the emphasis is on priestly service. Paul looked on himself as a priest at the altar, offering up to God the Gentiles he had won to Christ. They were a "spiritual sacrifice" to the glory of God (see 1 Peter 2:5). Even his preaching of the Gospel was a "priestly duty" (NIV). This insight into ministry certainly adds dignity and responsibility to our service. It was important that the priests offer to God only that which was the best (see Mal. 1:6-14).

Note the involvement of the Trinity in the ministry of the Word. Paul was the minister of Jesus Christ; he preached "the Gospel of God"; and he served in the power of the Holy Spirit of God who sanctified his ministry. What a privilege, and yet what a responsibility, to be the servant of the Triune God, winning the lost to Jesus Christ! We must remember that soul-winning is a priestly ministry, a sacred obligation. And we must serve the Lord with dedication and devotion just as the priest in the temple.

It was done for God's glory (v. 17). "Therefore I glory in Christ Jesus in my service to God" (NIV). The word translated "glory" carries the idea of "boast, take pride in." Paul used it before in Romans 2:17, 23; 5:2-3, 11 ("joy"); 3:27; and 4:2. Paul was not bragging about his ministry. He was boasting in what the Lord had done. The apostle did not serve and suffer as he did just to make a name for himself, for he had a much higher purpose in mind. He wanted to bring glory to Jesus Christ. "That in all things He might have the preeminence" (Col. 1:18).

It was done by God's power (vv. 18-19). The Holy Spirit empowered Paul to minister, and enabled him to perform mighty signs and wonders. The miracles God gave Paul to do were "signs" in that they came from God and revealed Him to others. And they were "wonders" in that they aroused the wonder of the people. But their purpose was always to open the way for the preaching of the Gospel. Miracles were given to authenticate the messenger and the message (Heb. 2:1-4). Miracles *by themselves* can never save the lost. When Paul healed the crippled man at Lystra (Acts 14), the immediate response was pagan: the people called Paul and Barnabas gods and tried to worship them! When Paul shared the Gospel with them, they did not respond so enthusiastically. Finally, the people stoned Paul and left him for dead outside the city walls.

The Spirit of God empowered Paul to share the Word, and the purpose was to "make the Gentiles obedient" (Rom. 15:18). It was "by word and deed" that the apostle shared the Good News.

We may not be able to perform miracles today, since this was a special apostolic gift. But "by word and deed" we can share the love of God with the lost around us. Changes in conduct and character are just as much miracles as the healing of the sick.

It was according to God's plan (vv. 20-24). God had a special plan for Paul to follow: he was not to preach where any other apostle had ministered. (This is one evidence that Peter had not founded the churches at Rome, or had been to Rome; for this would have prevented Paul from going there.) "From Jerusalem and round about unto Illyricum" (Rom. 15:19) covers about 1,400 miles! When you consider the slowness of travel and the dangers involved (2 Cor. 11:26-27), you can appreciate the tremendous achievement of Paul's missionary ministry. While it is not wrong to enter into another man's labors (John 4:38), it is also good to have a pioneer ministry and take the Gospel to new territory. Paul cited Isaiah 52:15 as the divine approval for this kind of ministry.

The vast area of opportunity in other parts of the empire kept Paul from visiting Rome sooner. He was not hindered from going to Rome by satanic opposition or physical obstacles, but by the challenge of completing his work right where he was. He was so faithful in his evangelistic outreach that he was able to say that he had no more place to minister in those parts. This did not mean that Paul personally witnessed to every person in that area, but that he took the Gospel and left behind witnessing churches and Christians who would carry on the work. Paul finished one job before he started another one, a good example for our evangelistic ministry today.

Paul's desire for many years had been to visit Rome and then move on to Spain, but there is no record that he ever did. Tradition says that he did go to Spain, and possibly to Britain, after he was released, but church tradition is not always to be trusted.

The Gentiles' Ministry to the Jews (Rom. 15:25-33)

Paul and his associates had received a special offering from the Gentile churches in Greece for the suffering Jewish saints in Jerusalem. Details about this collection are recorded in 2 Corinthians 8–9. There were several purposes behind this special offering. To begin with, it was an expression of love on the part of the Gentiles toward their Jewish brethren. Second, it meant practical relief at a time when the poor Jewish believers needed it the most. Third, it helped to unite Jews and Gentiles in the church. It was a bond that brought them closer together.

Paul looked on this offering as the paying of a debt. The Gentiles had received *spiritual* wealth from the Jews. They now returned *material* wealth, paying their debt. Paul considered himself a "debtor" to the whole world (Rom. 1:14). He also considered the Gentile Christians debtors to the Jews, for it was the Jews who gave to the Gentiles the Word of God and the Son of God. We Christians ought to feel an obligation to Israel, and to pay that debt by praying for Israel, sharing the Gospel, and helping in a material way. Anti-Semitism has no place in the life of a dedicated Christian.

Not only was this offering a payment of a debt, but it was also "fruit" (Rom. 15:28). It was not "loot" that Paul stole from the churches! It was fruit—the natural result of their walk with the Lord (see John 15:1-8).

When the life of the Spirit flows through a church, giving is no problem. Paul, in 2 Corinthians 8:1-5, described the miracle of grace that occurred in the churches of Macedonia.

Paul was anxious that this offering be received by the Jewish believers and be acceptable to them. He wanted to bring about, under God, a closer bond between the mother church at Jerusalem and the daughter churches in other parts of the empire. Unfortunately, there were still Jews who opposed the message of grace to the Gentiles and who wanted the Gentiles to become Jews and accept the Jewish Law. (Bible students call these people "Judaizers." They followed Paul wherever he went and tried to steal his churches from him. The Epistle to the Galatians was written to combat their evil works.)

The words "strive together" in Romans 15:30 suggest an athlete giving his best in the contest. Perhaps the words "wrestling together" better express the idea. This same term is used of the praying of Epaphras in Colossians 4:12. This verse does not mean that we must fight with God to get what we need. Rather, it means our praying must not be a casual experience that has no heart or earnestness. We should put as much fervor into our praying as a wrestler does into his wrestling!

The Believers' Ministry to Paul (Rom. 16:1-27)

What a remarkable chapter! In it Paul greeted at least twenty-six people by name, as well as two unnamed saints; and he also greeted several churches that were meeting in homes. He closed with greetings from nine believers who were with him in Corinth when he wrote the letter. What is the significance of this? It shows that Paul was a friend maker as well as a soul winner. He did not try to live an isolated life; he had friends in the Lord, and he appreciated them. They were a help to him personally and to his ministry. In my own reading of Christian biography, I have discovered that the servants whom God has used the most were people who could make friends. They multiplied themselves in the lives of their friends and associates in the ministry. While there may be a place for the secluded saint who lives alone with God, it is my conviction that most of us need each other. We are sheep, and sheep flock together.

Some friends to greet (vv. 1-16). He began with Phebe, a member of the church at Cenchrea, and the lady who carried the letter to the saints at Rome. Never did a messenger carry a more important letter! Cenchrea was the seaport of Corinth, so Phebe was probably won to Christ during Paul's year and a half of ministry in Corinth. The word "servant" is the feminine of *deacon,* and some students believe she was a "deaconess" in the church. This is possible, because there were women in the early church who served by visiting the sick, assisting the young women, and helping the poor. Paul confessed that Phebe had been a helper (literally "protectress") of himself and other Christians. And he encouraged the church to care for her.

How we wish we had the details of the stories behind each of these names! We have met Priscilla and Aquila in the Book of Acts (18:1-3, 18-19, 26). Where and when they risked their lives for Paul, we do not know, but we are glad they did it! (see also 1 Cor. 16:19; 2 Tim 4:19) At the time of this writing, they were in Rome and a church met in their house. In this chapter, Paul greeted a number of such assemblies (Rom. 16:10-11, 14-15).

Four persons are called "beloved" by Paul: Epenetus (Rom. 16:5), Amplias (Rom. 16:8), Stachys (Rom. 16:9), and Persis (Rom. 16:12). Paul would remember Epenetus in particular, for he was the first of the converts in Asia. Apparently he belonged to the household of Stephanas, for in 1 Corinthians 16:15 these people are also called "the firstfruits of Achaia."

Andronicus and Junias are called "kinsmen," which may mean blood relatives of Paul, or only that they too were Jewish, possibly of the tribe of Benjamin like Paul. At one time they had been in prison with Paul. The word "apostle" here does not imply that they held the same office as Paul, but rather that they were "messengers" of the Lord. The word "apostle" has both a narrow and a broad meaning.

The Rufus mentioned in Romans 16:13 may be the same as the one named in Mark 15:21, but we cannot be certain. If so, then Simon's experience at Calvary led to his conversion and that of his household. Paul and Rufus were not related. "His mother and mine" means only that Rufus' mother had been like a mother to Paul (see Mark 10:30).

This list shows the parts that people played in Paul's ministry and the ministry of the churches. Phebe was a "succourer" of many. Priscilla and Aquila were "helpers" and "laid down their own necks" for Paul. The conversion of Epenetus led to the salvation of others in Asia. Mary "bestowed much labor."

Andronicus and Junias went to prison with Paul. One can only give thanks for these devoted saints who fulfilled their ministries to the glory of God. May we follow in their train!

Some foes to avoid (vv. 17-20). Not everyone was working with Paul for the spreading of the Gospel. There were some who, for selfish reasons, were dividing the churches by teaching false doctrine. These people were probably the same Judaizers who had given Paul trouble in other churches (see Phil. 3:17-21). Instead of preaching the truth, these men spread their own religious propaganda, using deceit and clever speeches. We have the same problem today, and Christians must beware of false teachers. They come to your front door with magazines, books, and tapes, trying to convince you that they are teaching the truth. Paul gives two instructions: mark them (identify them), and avoid them.

It is a matter of obedience to the Lord and testimony to others. The issue is not making or keeping friends, but pleasing the Lord and maintaining a consistent testimony. Romans 16:20 suggests that these false teachers really come from Satan, and one day even he shall be completely defeated.

Some faithful servants to honor (vv. 21-27). What a roll call of heroes! Timothy was mentioned often in the Book of Acts and the Epistles. He was Paul's "son in the faith" and labored with Paul in many difficult places (see Phil. 2:19-24). Lucius was a fellow Jew, as were Jason and Sosipater. We have no proof that this is the same Jason who protected Paul in Thessalonica (Acts 17:1-9). That Jason was probably a Gentile.

Tertius was the secretary who wrote the letter as Paul dictated it. Gaius was the man in whose home Paul was residing at Corinth. First Corinthians 1:14 told how Paul won Gaius to Christ and baptized him when he founded the church in Corinth. Apparently there was an assembly of believers meeting in his house. Erastus held a high office in the city, probably the treasurer. The Gospel reached into high places in Corinth as well as into low places (1 Cor. 1:26-31; 6:9-11).

Romans 16:24 was probably written by Paul's own hand, since this was his "official seal" in every letter (see 2 Thes. 3:17-18).

The closing benediction is the longest one Paul ever wrote. It reflects his special ministry to the Gentiles. "The mystery" has to do with God's program of uniting believing Jews and Gentiles in the one body, the church (see Eph. 3). This was Paul's special message. It was because of this message that the Judaizers persecuted Paul, because they wanted to maintain Jewish privileges. Both Jews and Gentiles in the Roman churches needed to know what God's program was. Some of this Paul had explained in Romans 9–11.

Christians are established by the truth, which explains why Paul wrote this letter: to explain God's plan of salvation to Christians so they would be established, and so they would share the truth with the lost. After all, we cannot really share with others something we do not have ourselves.

This means that our own study of Romans should make us more stable in the faith, and more excited to share Christ with others. And the result: "To God only wise, be glory through Jesus Christ forever!"

1 CORINTHIANS

OUTLINE

Key theme: God's wisdom
Key verses: 1 Corinthians 2:6-8

I. **GREETING—1:1-3**

II. **REPROOF: THE REPORT OF SIN IN THE CHURCH—1:4–6:20**
   A. Divisions in the church—1:4–4:21
   B. Discipline in the church—5
   C. Disputes in the courts—6:1-8
   D. Defilement in the world—6:9-20

III. **INSTRUCTION: THE REPLY TO THEIR QUESTIONS—7:1–16:12**
   A. Marriage—7
   B. Food offered to idols—8–10
   C. Church ordinances—11
   D. Spiritual gifts—12:1–14:40
   E. The Resurrection—15
   F. The offering—16:1-12

IV. **CONCLUSION—16:13-24**

CONTENTS

CHAPTER ONE
BE WISE ABOUT... THE CHRISTIAN'S CALLING
1 Corinthians 1

"Jesus, yes! The church, no!"

Remember when that slogan was popular among young people in the '60s? They certainly could have used it with sincerity in Corinth back in A.D. 56, because the local church there was in serious trouble. Sad to say, the problems did not stay within the church family; they were known by the unbelievers outside the church.

To begin with, the church at Corinth was a *defiled* church. Some of its members were guilty of sexual immorality; others got drunk; still others were using the grace of God to excuse worldly living. It was also a *divided* church, with at least four different groups competing for leadership (1 Cor. 1:12). This meant it was a *disgraced* church. Instead of glorifying God, it was hindering the progress of the Gospel.

How did this happen? The members of the church permitted the sins of the city to get into the local assembly. Corinth was a polluted city, filled with every kind of vice and worldly pleasure. About the lowest accusation you could make against a man in that day would be to call him "a Corinthian." People would know what you were talking about.

Corinth was also a proud, philosophical city, with many itinerant teachers promoting their speculations. Unfortunately, this philosophical approach was applied to the Gospel by some members of the church, and this fostered division. The congregation was made up of different "schools of thought" instead of being united behind the Gospel message.

If you want to know what Corinth was like, read Romans 1:18-32. Paul wrote the Roman epistle while in Corinth, and he could have looked out the window and seen the very sins that he listed!

Of course, when you have proud people, depending on human wisdom, adopting the lifestyle of the world, you are going to have problems. In order to help them solve their problems, Paul opened his letter by reminding them of their *calling in Christ.* He pointed out three important aspects of this calling.

Called to Be Holy (1 Cor. 1:1-9)

Paul first attacked the serious problem of defilement in the church, yet he said nothing about the problem itself. Instead, he took the positive approach and reminded the believers of their high and holy position in Jesus Christ. In 1 Corinthians 1:1-9, he described the church that God sees; in 1 Corinthians 1:10-31, he described the church that men see. What we are in Jesus Christ *positionally* ought to be what we practice in daily life, but often we fail.

Note the characteristics of the church because of our holy calling in Jesus Christ.

Set apart by God (vv. 1-3). The word *church* in the Greek language means "a called-out people." Each church has two addresses: a geographic address ("at Corinth") and a spiritual address ("in Christ Jesus"). The church is made up of saints, that is, people who have been "sanctified" or "set apart" by God. A saint is not a dead person who has been honored by men because of his or her holy life. No, Paul wrote to *living* saints, people who, through faith in Jesus Christ, had been set apart for God's special enjoyment and use.

In other words, every true believer is a saint because every true believer has been set apart by God and for God.

A Christian photographer friend told me about a lovely wedding that he "covered." The bride and groom came out of the church, heading for the limousine, when the bride suddenly left her husband and ran to a car parked across the street! The motor was running and a man was at the wheel, and off they drove, leaving the bridegroom speechless. The driver of the "get-away car" turned out to be an old boyfriend of the bride, a man who had boasted that "he could get her anytime he wanted her." Needless to say, the husband had the marriage annulled.

When a man and woman pledge their love to each other, they are set apart for each other; and any other relationship outside of marriage is sinful. Just so, the Christian belongs completely to Jesus Christ; he is set apart for Him and Him alone. But he is also a part of a worldwide fellowship, the church, "all that in every place call upon the name of Jesus Christ" (1 Cor. 1:2). A defiled and unfaithful believer not only sins against the Lord, but he also sins against his fellow Christians.

Enriched by God's grace (vv. 4-6). Salvation is a gracious gift from God; but when you are saved, you are also given spiritual gifts. (Paul explained this in detail in 1 Cor. 12–14.) The Greek word translated "enriched" gives us our English word *plutocrat,* "a very wealthy person." The Corinthians were especially rich in spiritual gifts (2 Cor. 8:7), but were not using these gifts in a spiritual manner. The fact that God has called us, set us apart, and enriched us ought to encourage us to live holy lives.

Expecting Jesus to return (v. 7). Paul will have a great deal to say about this truth in 1 Corinthians 15. Christians who are looking for their Saviour will want to keep their lives above reproach (1 John 2:28–3:3).

Depending on God's faithfulness (vv. 8-9). The work of God was confirmed *in* them (1 Cor. 1:6), but it was also confirmed *to* them in the Word. This is a legal term that refers to the guarantee that settles a transaction. We have the witness of the Spirit within us and the witness of the Word before us, guaranteeing that God will keep His "contract" with us and save us to the very end. This guarantee is certainly not an excuse for sin! Rather, it is the basis for a growing relationship of love, trust, and obedience.

Now, in the light of these great truths, how could the people in the Corinthian assembly get involved in the sins of the world and the flesh? They were an elect people, an enriched people, and an established people. They were saints, set apart for the glory of God! Alas, their practice was not in accord with their position.

When Paul mentioned the word *fellowship* in 1 Corinthians 1:9, he introduced a second aspect of the Christian's calling.

Called into Fellowship (1 Cor. 1:10-25)

Having mentioned the problem of defilement in the church, now Paul turned to the matter of division in the church. Division has always been a problem among God's people, and almost every New Testament epistle deals with this topic or mentions it in one way or another. Even the 12 Apostles did not always get along with each other.

In 1 Corinthians 1:13, Paul asked his readers three important questions, and these three questions are the key to this long paragraph.

Is Christ divided? (vv. 10-13a) The verb means, "Has Christ been divided and different parts handed out to different people?" The very idea is grotesque and must be rejected. Paul did not preach one Christ, Apollos another, and Peter another. There is but one Saviour and one Gospel (Gal. 1:6-9). How, then, did the Corinthians create this four-way division? Why were there quarrels ("contentions") among them?

One answer is that they were looking at the Gospel from a philosophical point of view. Corinth was a city filled with teachers and philosophers, all of whom wanted to share their "wisdom."

Another answer is that human nature enjoys following human leaders. We tend to identify more with spiritual leaders who help us and whose ministry we understand and enjoy. Instead of emphasizing the *message* of the Word, the Corinthians emphasized the *messenger.* They got their eyes off the Lord and on the Lord's servants, and this led to competition.

Paul will point out in 1 Corinthians 3 that there can be no competition among true servants of God. It is sinful for church members to compare pastors, or for believers to follow human leaders as disciples of men and not disciples of Jesus Christ. The "personality cults" in the church today are in direct disobedience to the Word of God. Only Jesus Christ should have the place of preeminence (Col. 1:18).

Paul used several key words in this section to emphasize the unity of the saints in Christ. He called his readers *brethren,* reminding them that they belonged to one family. The phrase "perfectly joined together" is a medical term that describes the unity of the human body *knit together.* So, they had a *loving* union as members of the body. They were also identified by the name of Jesus Christ. This was probably a reference to their baptism.

We do not know who the people were who belonged to "the house of Chloe," but we commend them for their courage and devotion. They did not try to hide the problems. They were burdened about them; they went to the right person with them; and they were not afraid to be mentioned by Paul. This was not the kind of "cloak and dagger" affair that we often see in churches—activities that usually make the problem worse and not better.

Paul was the minister who founded the church, so most of the members would have been converted through his ministry. Apollos followed Paul (Acts 18:24-28) and had an effective ministry. We have no record that Peter (Cephas) ever visited Corinth, unless 1 Corinthians 9:5 records it. Each of these men had a different personality and a different approach to the ministry of the Word; *yet they were one* (1 Cor. 3:3-8; 4:6).

Were you baptized in the name of Paul? (vv. 13b-17) Keep in mind that baptism was an important matter in the New Testament church. When a sinner trusted Christ and was baptized, he cut himself off from his old life and often was rejected by his family and friends. It cost something to be baptized in that day.

Just as Jesus did not baptize people (John 4:1-2), so both Peter (Acts 10:48) and Paul allowed their associates to baptize the new converts. Until the church grew in Corinth, Paul did some of the baptizing; but that was not his main ministry. In this section, Paul was not minimizing baptism, but rather was putting it into its proper perspective, because the Corinthians were making too much of it. "I was baptized by Apollos!" one would boast, while another would say, "Oh, but I was baptized by Paul!"

It is wrong to identify any man's name with your baptism other than the name of Jesus Christ. To do so is to create division. I have read accounts about people who had to be baptized by a certain preacher, using special water (usually from the Jordan River), on a special day, as though these are the matters that are important! Instead of honoring the Lord Jesus Christ and promoting the unity of the church, these people exalt men and create disunity.

Crispus had been the ruler of the synagogue in Corinth (Acts 18:8); and Gaius was probably the man Paul lived with when he wrote Romans (Rom. 16:23). "The household of Stephanas" (1 Cor. 1:16) is probably described in part in 1 Corinthians 16:15-18. Apparently Paul did not carry with him a record of the names of all the people he baptized. It was sufficient that they were written in God's book.

Was Paul crucified for you? (vv. 18-25) The mention of the cross in 1 Corinthians 1:17 introduced this long section on the power of the Gospel versus the weakness of man's wisdom. It is interesting to see how Paul approached this problem of division in the church. First, he pointed to the unity of Christ: there is one Saviour and one body. Then he reminded them of their baptism, a picture of their spiritual baptism into Christ's body (1 Cor. 12:13). Then he took them to the cross.

Crucifixion was not only a horrible death; it was a shameful death. It was illegal to crucify a Roman citizen. Crucifixion was never mentioned in polite society, any more than we today would discuss over dinner the gas chamber or the electric chair.

The key word in this paragraph is *wisdom*; it is used eight times. The key idea that Paul expressed is that we dare not mix man's wisdom with God's revealed message. The entire section on wisdom (1 Cor. 1:17–2:16) presents a number of contrasts between the revealed Word of God and the wisdom of men.

God's wisdom is revealed primarily in the cross of Jesus Christ, but not everybody sees this. Paul pointed out that there are three different attitudes toward the cross.

Some stumble at the cross (v. 23a). This was the attitude of the Jews, because their emphasis is on miraculous signs and the cross appears to be weakness. Jewish history is filled with miraculous events, from the Exodus out of Egypt to the days of Elijah and Elisha. When Jesus was ministering on earth, the Jewish leaders repeatedly asked Him to perform a sign from heaven; but He refused.

The Jewish nation did not understand their own sacred Scriptures. They looked for a Messiah who would come like a mighty conqueror and defeat all their enemies. He would then set up His kingdom and return the glory to Israel. The question of the Apostles in Acts 1:6 shows how strong this hope was among the Jews.

At the same time, their scribes noticed in the Old Testament that the Messiah would suffer and die. Passages like Psalm 22 and Isaiah 53 pointed toward a different kind of Messiah, and the scholars could not reconcile these two seemingly contradictory prophetic images. They did not understand that their Messiah had to suffer and die before He could enter into His glory (see Luke 24:13-35), and that the future messianic kingdom was to be preceded by the age of the church.

Because the Jews were looking for power and great glory, they stumbled at the weakness of the cross. How could anybody put faith in an unemployed carpenter from Nazareth who died the shameful death of a common criminal? But the Gospel of Jesus Christ is "the power of God unto salvation" (Rom.

1:16). Rather than a testimony of weakness, the cross is a tremendous instrument of power! After all, the "weakness of God [in the cross] is stronger than men" (1 Cor. 1:25).

Some laugh at the cross (v. 23b). This was the response of the Greeks. To them, the cross was foolishness. The Greeks emphasized wisdom; we still study the profound writings of the Greek philosophers. But they saw no wisdom in the cross, for they looked at the cross from a human point of view. Had they seen it from God's viewpoint, they would have discerned the wisdom of God's great plan of salvation.

Paul called on three men to bear witness: the wise (the expert), the scribe (the interpreter and writer), and the disputer (the philosopher and debater). He asked them one question: Through your studies into man's wisdom, have you come to know God in a personal way? They all must answer no! The fact that they laugh at the cross and consider it foolishness is evidence that they are perishing.

Paul quoted Isaiah 29:14 in 1 Corinthians 1:19, proving that God has written a big "0—Failure!"—over the wisdom of men. In his address on Mars' Hill, Paul dared to tell the philosophers that Greek and Roman history were but "times of this ignorance" (Acts 17:30). He was not suggesting that they knew nothing, because Paul knew too well that the Greek thinkers had made some achievements. However, their wisdom did not enable them to find God and experience salvation.

Some believe and experience the power and the wisdom of the cross (v. 24). Paul did not alter his message when he turned from a Jewish audience to a Greek one: he preached Christ crucified. "The foolishness of preaching" (1 Cor. 1:21) does not mean that the *act* of preaching is foolish, but rather the content of the message. The *New International Version* states it, "Through the foolishness of what was preached," and this is correct.

Those who have been called by God's grace, and who have responded by faith (see 2 Thes. 2:13-14), realize that Christ is God's power and God's wisdom. Not the Christ of the manger, or the temple, or the marketplace—but the Christ of the cross. It is in the death of Christ that God has revealed the foolishness of man's wisdom and the weakness of man's power.

We are called into fellowship because of our union with Jesus Christ: He died for us; we were baptized in His name; we are identified with His cross. What a wonderful basis for spiritual unity!

Called to Glorify God (1 Cor. 1:26-31)

The Corinthians had a tendency to be "puffed up" with pride (1 Cor. 4:6, 18-19; 5:2). But the Gospel of God's grace leaves no room for personal boasting. God is not impressed with our looks, our social position, our achievements, our natural heritage, or our financial status. Note that Paul wrote *many,* not *any.* In the New Testament, we do meet some believers with "high social standing," but there are not many of them. The description Paul gave of the converts was certainly not a flattering one (1 Cor. 6:9-11).

Paul reminded them of what they were (v. 26). They were not wise, mighty, or noble. God called them, not *because* of what they were, but *in spite of* what they were! The Corinthian church was composed primarily of ordinary people who were terrible sinners. Before his conversion, Paul had been very self-righteous; he had to give up his religion in order to go to heaven! The Corinthians were at the other end of the spectrum, and yet they were not too sinful for God to reach and save them.

Paul reminded the Corinthians of why God called them (vv. 27-29). God chose the foolish, the weak, the base ("low born"), and the despised to show the proud world their need and His grace. The lost world admires birth, social status, financial success, power, and recognition. But none of these things can guarantee eternal life.

The message and miracle of God's grace in Jesus Christ utterly confounds ("puts to shame") the high and mighty people of this world. The wise of this world cannot understand how God changes sinners into saints, and the mighty of this world are helpless to duplicate the miracle. God's "foolishness" confounds the wise; God's "weakness" confounds the mighty!

The annals of church history are filled with the accounts of great sinners whose lives were transformed by the power of the Gospel. In my own ministry, as in the ministry of most pastors and preachers, I have seen amazing things take place that the lawyers and psychologists could not understand. We have seen delinquent teenagers become successful students and useful citizens. We have seen marriages restored and homes reclaimed, much to the amazement of the courts.

And why does God reveal the foolishness and the weakness of this present world system, even with its philosophy and religion? "That no flesh should glory in His presence" (1 Cor. 1:29). Salvation must be wholly of grace; otherwise, God cannot get the glory.

It is this truth that Paul wanted to get across to the Corinthians, because they were guilty of glorying in men (1 Cor. 3:21). If we glory in men—even godly men like Peter and Paul and Apollos—we are robbing God of the glory that He alone deserves. It was this sinful attitude of pride that was helping to cause division in the church.

Finally, Paul reminded the Corinthians of all they had in Jesus Christ (vv. 30-31). Since every believer is "in Christ," and he has all that he needs, why compete with each other or compare yourselves with each other? It is the Lord who has done it all! "He that glorieth, let him glory in the Lord" (1 Cor. 1:31, a quotation from Jer. 9:24, quoted again in 2 Cor. 10:17).

The spiritual blessings that we need are not abstractions that elude our grasp; they are all in a Person, Jesus Christ. He is our wisdom (Col. 2:3), our righteousness (2 Cor. 5:21), our sanctification (John 17:19), and our redemption (Rom. 3:24).

Actually, the emphasis here is that God shows His wisdom by means of the righteousness, sanctification, and redemption that we have in Christ. Each of these theological words carries a special meaning for Christians. *Righteousness* has to do with our standing before God. We are justified: God declares us righteous in Jesus Christ. But we are also *sanctified,* set apart to belong to God and to serve Him. *Redemption* emphasizes the fact that we are set free because Jesus Christ paid the price for us on the cross. This will lead to complete redemption when Christ returns.

So, in one sense, we have the three tenses of salvation given here: we *have been saved* from the penalty of sin (righteousness); we *are being saved* from the power of sin (sanctification); and we *shall be saved* from the presence of sin (redemption). And every believer has all of these blessings in Jesus Christ!

Therefore, why glory in men? What does Paul have that you do not have? Does Peter have more of Jesus Christ than you do? (It was likely that Jesus Christ had more of Peter, but that is another matter!) We should glory in the Lord and not in ourselves or our spiritual leaders.

As you review this chapter, you can see the mistakes that the Corinthians were making, mistakes that helped to create problems in their church. They were not living up to their holy calling, but were instead following the standards of the world. They ignored the fact that they were called into a wonderful spiritual fellowship with the Lord and with each other. Instead, they were identifying with human leaders and creating divisions in the church. Instead of glorifying God and His grace, they were pleasing themselves and boasting about men.

They were a defiled church, a divided church, a disgraced church!

But, before we pass judgment on them, we should examine our own churches and our own lives. We have been called to be holy, called into fellowship, and called to glorify God.

Are we living up to this calling?

CHAPTER TWO
BE WISE ABOUT... THE CHRISTIAN MESSAGE
1 Corinthians 2

My wife was at the wheel of our car as we drove to Chicago, and I was in the copilot's seat reading the page proofs of another author's book that a publisher had asked me to review. Occasionally I would utter a grunt, and then a groan, and finally I shook my head and said, "Oh, no! I can't believe it!"

"I take it you don't like the book," she said. "Something wrong with it?"

"You bet there is!" I replied. "Just about everything is wrong with it, because this man does not know what the message of the Gospel really is!"

There was a time, however, when that author had been faithful to the Gospel. But over the years, he had begun to take a philosophical (and, I fear, political) approach to the Gospel. The result was a hybrid message that was no Gospel at all.

It is worth noting that when Paul ministered in Corinth, he obeyed our Lord's commission and preached the Gospel. There is a beautiful parallel between Matthew 28:18-20 and Acts 18:1-11.

Christ's Commission (Matt. 28:18-20)	*Paul's Ministry* (Acts 18:1-11)
"Go ye therefore" (v. 19)	Paul came to Corinth (v. 1)
"make disciples" [teach] (v. 19)	many heard and believed (v. 8)
"baptizing them" (v. 19)	and were baptized (v. 8)
"teaching them" (v. 20)	for a year and six months he taught the Word (v. 11)
"Lo, I am with you" (v. 20)	"For I am with thee" (v. 10)

What had happened at Corinth is happening in churches today: men are mixing philosophy (man's wisdom) with God's revealed message, and this is causing confusion and division. Different preachers have their own "interpretation" to God's message, and some even invent their own vocabulary!

Paul explained the three fundamentals of the Gospel message and urged his readers to return to these fundamentals.

The Gospel Centers in the Death of Christ (1 Cor. 2:1-5)

Paul reminded the Corinthians of his approach (vv. 1-2). The opening words, "And I," can be translated "Accordingly," on the basis of 1 Corinthians 1:31—the glory of God. Paul had not come to Corinth to glorify himself or to start a religious "fan club." He had come to glorify God.

The itinerant philosophers and teachers depended on their wisdom and eloquence to gain followers. The city of Corinth was filled with such "spellbinders." Paul did not depend on eloquent speech or clever arguments; he simply declared God's Word in the power of the Spirit. He was an ambassador, not a "Christian salesman."

Had he used spectacular speech and philosophy, Paul would have exalted himself and hidden the very Christ he came to proclaim! God had sent him to preach the Gospel "not with wisdom of words, lest the cross of Christ should be made of no effect" (1 Cor. 1:17).

A certain church had a beautiful stained-glass window just behind the pulpit. It depicted Jesus Christ on the cross. One Sunday there was a guest minister who was much smaller than the regular pastor. A little girl listened to the guest for a time, then turned to her mother and asked, "Where is the man who usually stands there so we can't see Jesus?"

Too many preachers of the Word so magnify themselves and their gifts that they fail to reveal the glory of Jesus Christ. Paul gloried in the cross of Christ (Gal. 6:14) and made it the center of his message.

Then Paul reminded the Corinthians of his attitude (vv. 3-4). Though he was an apostle, Paul came to them as a humble servant. He did not depend on himself; he became nothing that Christ might be everything. In later years, Paul brought this up again and contrasted himself to the false teachers that had invaded Corinth (2 Cor. 10:1-12). Paul had learned that when he was weak, then God made him strong.

Paul depended on the power of the Holy Spirit. It was not his experience or ability that gave his ministry its power; it was the work of the Spirit of God. His preaching was a "demonstration," not a "performance." The word translated *demonstration* means "legal proof presented in court." The Holy Spirit used Paul's preaching to change lives, and that was all the proof Paul needed that his message was from God. Wicked sinners were transformed by the power of God! (1 Cor. 6:9-11)

However, we must note that Paul is not telling ministers deliberately to preach poorly, or to avoid using the gifts God gave them. Men like Charles Spurgeon and George Whitefield were gifted orators whose words carried power, *but they did not depend on their natural talents.* They trusted the Spirit of God to work in the hearts of their hearers, and He did. Those who minister the Word must prepare and use every gift God has given them—but they must not put their confidence in themselves (see 2 Cor. 3:5).

Finally, Paul reminded them of his aim (v. 5). He wanted them to trust in God and not in the messenger God sent. Had he depended on human wisdom and presented the plan of salvation as a philosophical system, then the Corinthians would have put their trust in an *explanation.* Because Paul declared the Word of God in the power of God, his converts put their faith in a *demonstration*: they experienced God at work in their own lives.

Years ago, a wise Christian said to me, "When you are leading people to Christ, never tell them that they are saved because they have done this or that. It is the job of the Holy Spirit to witness to people that they are saved. Unless He is at work, there can be no salvation." Wise counsel, indeed!

I recall a fine professional man who faithfully attended a church I pastored—a man who was unsaved, but not antagonistic to the Gospel. Many of us prayed for him as he continued to listen to the Word. One day a Christian friend of his decided to win him to Christ, or else! He spent several hours presenting argument after argument, and finally the man "prayed the sinner's prayer." Then he stopped attending church! Why? Because he had been "talked into" something that was not real, and he knew he could not follow through. Later on, he *did* trust Christ and, through the Spirit, have the assurance of salvation. Up to that point, if anybody asked him if he were saved, he would reply, "Sure—Tom told me I was saved!" What a difference when the Spirit gives the assurance!

The Gospel is still God's power to change men's lives (Rom. 1:16). Effectiveness in evangelism does not depend on our arguments or persuasive gimmicks, but on the power of the Spirit of God at work in our lives and through the Word that we share.

The Gospel Is Part of the Father's Eternal Plan (1 Cor. 2:6-9)

Salvation was purchased by the Son, but it was planned by the Father. Those who talk about "the simple Gospel" are both right and wrong. Yes, the message of the Gospel is simple enough for an illiterate pagan to understand, believe, and be saved. But it is also so profound that the most brilliant theologian cannot fathom its depths.

There is a "wisdom of God" in the Gospel that challenges the keenest intellect. However, this wisdom is not for the masses of lost sinners, nor is it for the immature believers. It is for the mature believers who are growing in their understanding of the Word of God. (The word *perfect* in 1 Cor. 2:6 means "mature." See 1 Cor. 3:1-4.) Perhaps here Paul was answering those in the church who were promoting Apollos, who was an eloquent and profound preacher (Acts 18:24-28).

Let's notice the characteristics of this wisdom.

This wisdom comes from God, not man (v. 7). This wisdom tells the mature saint about the vast eternal plan that God has for His people and His creation. The wisest of the "princes of this world [age]" could not invent or discover this marvelous wisdom that Paul shared from God.

This wisdom has been hidden (v. 7). That is why it is called a mystery, for in the New Testament, a mystery is a "sacred secret," a truth hidden in past ages but now revealed to the people of God. It was Paul whom God used in a special way to share the various "mysteries" that are related to the Gospel (see Eph. 3); but note the repetition of the pronoun "we." Paul did not leave out the other apostles.

This wisdom involves God's ordination (v. 7). This means that God made the plan, set it in motion, and will see to it that it will succeed. The great plan of redemption was not a hasty afterthought on the part of God after He saw what man had done. Though all of this boggles our minds, we must accept the Bible truth of divine election and predestination. Even the death of Jesus Christ was ordained of God (Acts 2:22-23; 1 Peter 1:18-20), though men were held responsible for the wicked deed. One of the secrets of an effective prayer life is to lay hold of God's purposes by faith (Acts 4:23-31).

This wisdom results in the glory of God's people (v. 7). One of the greatest expositions of this "plan of the ages" is in Ephesians 1. Three times in that passage, Paul explains that all of this is done for God's glory (Eph. 1:6, 12, 14). It is a staggering thought that we shall one day share in the very glory of God! (see John 17:22-24; Rom. 8:28-30)

This wisdom is hidden from the unsaved world (v. 8). Who are "the princes of this world [age]" that Paul mentions? Certainly the men who were in charge of government when Jesus was on earth did not know who He was (Acts 3:17; 4:25-28). When Jesus on the cross prayed "Father, forgive them: for they know not what they do" (Luke 23:34), He was echoing this truth. Their ignorance did not *excuse* their sin, of course, because every evidence had been given by the Lord and they should have believed.

But there is another possibility. Paul may have been referring to the *spiritual and demonic rulers of this present age* (Rom. 8:38; Col. 2:15; Eph. 6:12ff). This would make more sense in 1 Corinthians 2:6, for certainly

Pilate, Herod, and the other rulers were not recognized for any special wisdom. The wisdom of this age has its origin in the rulers of this age, of which Satan is the prince (John 12:31; 14:30; 16:11). Of course, the spiritual rulers would have to work in and through the human rulers. So perhaps we must not press the distinction (John 13:2, 27).

But if this interpretation is true, then it opens up a challenging area of consideration. The satanic forces, including Satan himself, did not understand God's great eternal plan! They could understand from the Old Testament Scriptures that the Son of God would be born and die, but they could not grasp the full significance of the cross because these truths were hidden by God. In fact, it is now, through the church, that these truths are being revealed to the principalities and powers (Eph. 3:10).

Satan thought that Calvary was God's great defeat; but it turned out to be God's greatest victory and *Satan's defeat!* (Col. 2:15) From the time of our Lord's birth into this world, Satan had tried to kill Him, because Satan did not fully understand the vast results of Christ's death and resurrection. Had the demonic rulers known, they would not have "engineered" the death of Christ. (Of course, all of this was part of God's eternal plan. It was God who was in control, not Satan.)

Finally, this wisdom applies to the believer's life today (v. 9). This verse is often used at funerals and applied to heaven, but the basic application is to the Christian's life *today*. The next verse makes it clear that God is revealing these things to us here and now.

This verse is a quotation (with adaptation) from Isaiah 64:4. The immediate context relates it to Israel in captivity, awaiting God's deliverance. The nation had sinned and had been sent to Babylon for chastening. They cried out to God that He would come down to deliver them, and He did answer their prayer after seventy years of their exile. God had plans for His people and they did not have to be afraid (Jer. 29:11).

Paul applied this principle to the church. Our future is secure in Jesus Christ no matter what our circumstances may be. In fact, God's plans for His own are so wonderful that our minds cannot begin to conceive of them or comprehend them! God has ordained this for our glory (1 Cor. 2:7). It is glory all the way from earth to heaven!

For those who love God, every day is a good day (Rom. 8:28). It may not *look* like a good day, or *feel* like it; but when God is working His plan, we can be sure of the best. It is when we fail to trust Him or obey Him, when our love for Him grows cold, that life takes on a somber hue. If we walk in God's wisdom, we will enjoy His blessings.

We have considered two fundamental truths of the Gospel: this message centers in the death of Christ, and it is part of the Father's vast eternal plan. The believers at Corinth had forgotten the cost of their salvation; they had gotten their eyes off of the cross. They were also involved in minor matters—"baby toys"—because they had lost the wonder of the greatness of God's plan for them. They needed to return to the ministry of the Holy Spirit, and this would be Paul's next point.

The Gospel Is Revealed by the Spirit through the Word (1 Cor. 2:10-16)

Our salvation involves all three Persons in the Godhead (Eph. 1:3-14; 1 Peter 1:2). You cannot be saved apart from the Father's electing grace, the Son's loving sacrifice, and the Spirit's ministry of conviction and regeneration. It is not enough to say, "I believe in God." What God? Unless it is "the God and Father of our Lord Jesus Christ" (Eph. 1:3), there can be no salvation.

This trinitarian aspect of our salvation helps us to understand better some of the mysteries of our salvation. Many people get confused (or frightened) when they hear about election and predestination. As far as the Father is concerned, I was saved when He chose me in Christ before the foundation of the world (Eph. 1:4); but I knew nothing about that the night I was saved! It was a hidden part of God's wonderful eternal plan.

As far as God the Son is concerned, I was saved when He died for me on the cross. He died for the sins of the whole world, yet the whole world is not saved. This is where the Spirit comes in: as far as the Spirit is concerned, I was saved in May 1945 at a Youth for Christ rally where I heard Billy Graham (then a young evangelist) preach the Gospel. It was then that the Holy Spirit applied the Word to my heart, I believed, and God saved me.

Paul pointed out four important ministries of the Holy Spirit of God.

The Spirit indwells believers (v. 12). The very moment you trusted Jesus Christ, the Spirit of God entered your body and made it His temple (1 Cor. 6:19-20). He baptized you (identified you) into the body of Christ (1 Cor. 12:13). He sealed you (Eph. 1:13-14) and will remain with you (John 14:16). He is God's gift to you.

The Holy Spirit is the Spirit of liberty (2 Cor. 3:17). We have not received the "spirit of the world" because we have been called out of this world and no longer belong to it (John 17:14, 16). We are no longer under the authority of Satan and his world system.

Nor have we received a "spirit of bondage again to fear" (Rom. 8:15). The Holy Spirit ministers to us and makes the Father real to us. This ties in with 2 Timothy 1:7—"For God hath not given us the spirit of fear; but of power, and of love, and of a sound [disciplined] mind." We have a wealth of spiritual resources because the Spirit lives within us!

The Spirit searches (vv. 10-11). I cannot know what is going on within your personality, but your human spirit within you knows. Neither can I know "the deep things of God" unless somehow I can enter into God's personality. I cannot do that—but by His Spirit, God has entered into my personality. Through the Holy Spirit, each believer becomes a sharer of the very life of God.

The Holy Spirit knows "the deep things of God" and reveals them to us. First Corinthians 2:10 makes it clear that "the deep things of God" is another description of "the things which God hath prepared for them that love Him" (1 Cor. 2:9). God wants us to know *today* all the blessings of His grace that He has planned for us.

The Spirit teaches (v. 13). Jesus promised that the Spirit would teach us (John 14:26) and guide us into truth (John 16:13). But we must note carefully the sequence here: the Spirit taught Paul from the Word, and Paul then taught the believers. The truth of God is found in the Word of God. And it is very important to note that these spiritual truths are given in specific *words*. In the Bible, we have much more than inspired thoughts; we have inspired *words*. "For I have given unto them the words which Thou gavest Me" (John 17:8).

Each of our four children has a different vocation. We have a pastor, a nurse, an electronics designer, and a secretary in a commercial real estate firm. Each of the children had to learn a specialized vocabulary in order to succeed. The only one I really understand is the pastor.

The successful Christian learns the vocabulary of the Spirit and makes use of it. He knows the meaning of justification, sanctification, adoption, propitiation, election, inspiration, and so forth. In understanding God's vocabulary, we come to understand God's Word and God's will for our lives. If the engineering student can grasp the technical terms of chemistry, physics, or electronics, why should it be difficult for Christians, taught by the Spirit, to grasp the vocabulary of Christian truth?

Yet I hear church members say, "Don't preach doctrine. Just give us heartwarming sermons that will encourage us!" Sermons based on what? If they are not based on doctrine, they will accomplish nothing! "But doctrine is so dull!" people complain. Not if it is presented the way the Bible presents it. Doctrine to me is exciting! What a thrill to be able to study the Bible and let the Spirit teach us "the deep things of God" (1 Cor. 2:10).

How does the Spirit teach the believer? He compares "spiritual things with spiritual." He reminds us of what He has taught us (John 14:26), relates that truth to something new, and then leads us into new truth and new applications of old truth. What a joy it is to sit before the pages of the Bible and let the Spirit reveal God's truth. The trouble is, many Christians are too busy for this kind of quiet meditation. What enrichment they are missing!

The Holy Spirit is like a householder who "bringeth forth out of his treasure things new and old" (Matt. 13:52). The new always comes out of the old and helps us better understand the old. God gives us new insights into old truths as we compare one part of Scripture with another. Jesus based His teaching on the Old Testament, yet people were amazed at what He taught because it was so fresh and exciting.

I suggest that you make time every day to read the Word and meditate on it. Follow a regular schedule in your reading and give yourself time to pray, think, and meditate. Let the Spirit of God search the Word and teach you. The study and application of basic Bible doctrine can transform your life.

The Spirit matures the believer (vv. 14-16). The contrast here is between the saved person (called "spiritual" because he is indwelt by the Spirit) and the unsaved person (called "natural" because he does not have the Spirit within). In 1 Corinthians 3:1-4, Paul will introduce a third kind of person, the "carnal man." He is the immature Christian, the one who lives on a childhood level because he will not feed on the Word and grow.

At one time, every Christian was "natural," having only the things of nature. When we trusted the Saviour, the Spirit came in and we moved into the plane of "spiritual"—able to live in the realm of the Spirit. *Then we had to grow!* The unsaved man cannot receive the things of the Spirit because he does not believe in them and cannot understand them. But as the Christian day by day receives the things of the Spirit, he grows and matures.

One of the marks of maturity is discernment—the ability to penetrate beneath the surface of life and see things as they really are. Unsaved people "walk by sight" and really see nothing. They are spiritually blind. The maturing Christian grows in his spiritual discernment and develops the ability (with the Spirit's help) to understand more and more of the will and mind of God. The Corinthians lacked this discernment; they were spiritually ignorant.

To "have the mind of Christ" does not mean we are infallible and start playing God in the lives of other people. Nobody instructs God! (Paul quoted Isa. 40:13. Also see Rom. 11:33-36.) To "have the mind of Christ" means to look at life from the Saviour's point of view, having His values and desires in mind. It means to think God's thoughts and not think as the world thinks.

The unsaved person does not understand the Christian; they live in two different worlds. But the Christian understands the unsaved person. First Corinthians 2:15 does not suggest that unsaved people cannot point out flaws in the believer's life (they often do), but that the unsaved man really cannot penetrate into the full understanding of what the Christian's life is all about. I like the *New American Standard Bible's* translation: "But he who is spiritual appraises all things, yet he himself is appraised by no man." That "no man" includes other Christians as well. We must be very careful not to become spiritual dictators in the lives of God's people (2 Cor. 1:24).

The Corinthian Christians were so wrapped up in the miraculous gifts of the Spirit that they were neglecting the basic ministries of the Spirit. And in their emphasis on the Spirit, they were also neglecting the Father and the Son.

Blessed are the balanced! And blessed are they who understand and share "all the counsel of God" (Acts 20:27).

CHAPTER THREE
BE WISE ABOUT . . . THE LOCAL CHURCH
1 Corinthians 3

British Bible teacher Dr. G. Campbell Morgan had four sons; all became ministers. Someone asked one of the grandsons if he also would become a minister, and he replied, "No, I plan to work for a living."

What is a pastor supposed to do? What really is "the work of the ministry"? If we don't know, we will never know how to evaluate the minister's work. Perhaps no issue creates more problems in the local church than this one: how do we know when the pastor and church leaders are really doing their job?

Paul painted three pictures of the church in this chapter and, using these pictures, pointed out what the ministry is supposed to accomplish. The church is a *family* and the goal is *maturity* (1 Cor. 3:1-4). The church is a *field* and the goal is *quantity* (1 Cor. 3:5-9a). The church is a *temple* and the goal is *quality* (1 Cor. 3:9b-23).

The Family—Maturity (1 Cor. 3:1-4)

Paul already explained that there are two kinds of people in the world—natural (unsaved) and spiritual (saved). But now he explained that there are two kinds of saved people: mature and immature (carnal). A Christian matures by allowing the Spirit to teach him and direct him by feeding on the Word. The immature Christian lives for the things of the flesh (*carnal* means "flesh") and has little interest in the things of the Spirit. Of course, some believers are immature because they have been saved only a short time, but that is not what Paul is discussing here.

Paul was the "spiritual father" who brought this family into being (1 Cor. 4:15). During the eighteen months he ministered in Corinth, Paul had tried to feed his spiritual children and help them mature in the faith. Just as in a human family, everybody helps the new baby grow and mature, so in the family of God we must encourage spiritual maturity.

What are the marks of maturity? For one thing, you can tell the mature person by *his diet.* As I write this chapter, we are watching our grandson and our granddaughter grow up. Becky is still being nursed by her mother, but Jonathan now sits at the table and uses his little cup and (with varying degrees of success) his tableware. As children grow, they learn to eat different food. They graduate (to use Paul's words) from milk to meat.

What is the difference? The usual answer is that "milk" represents the easy things in the Word, while "meat" represents the hard doctrines. But I disagree with that traditional explanation, and my proof is Hebrews 5:10-14. That passage seems to teach that "milk" represents what Jesus Christ did on earth, while "meat" concerns what He is doing now in heaven. The writer of Hebrews wanted to teach his readers about the present heavenly priesthood of Jesus Christ, but his readers were so immature, he could not do it (note Heb. 6:1-4).

The Word of God is our spiritual food: milk (1 Peter 2:2), bread (Matt. 4:4), meat (Heb. 5:11-14), and even honey (Ps. 119:103). Just as the physical man needs a balanced diet if his body is to be healthy, so the inner man needs a balanced diet of spiritual food. The baby begins with milk, but as he grows and his teeth develop, he needs solid food.

It is not difficult to determine a believer's spiritual maturity, or immaturity, if you discover what kind of "diet" he enjoys. The immature believer knows little about the present ministry of Christ in heaven. He knows the *facts* about our Lord's life and ministry on earth, but not the *truths* about His present ministry in heaven. He lives on "Bible stories" and not Bible doctrines. He has no understanding of 1 Corinthians 2:6-7.

In my itinerant ministry, I have preached in hundreds of churches and conferences; and I have always been grateful for congregations that wanted to be enlightened and edified, not entertained. It is important that we preach the Gospel to the lost; but it is also important that we *interpret* the Gospel to the saved. The entire New Testament is an interpretation and application of the Gospel. Paul did not write Romans, for example, to tell the Romans how to be saved—for they were already saints. He wrote to explain to them what was really involved in their salvation. It was an explanation of the "deep things of God" and how they applied to daily life.

There is another way to determine maturity: the mature Christian practices love and seeks to get along with others. Children like to disagree and fuss. And children like to identify with heroes, whether sports heroes or Hollywood heroes. The "babes" in Corinth were fighting over which preacher was the greatest—Paul, Apollos, or Peter. It sounded like children on the playground: "My father can fight better than your father! My father makes more money than your father!"

When immature Christians, without spiritual discernment, get into places of leadership in the church, the results will be disastrous. More than one brokenhearted pastor has phoned me, or written me, asking what to do with church officers who talk big but live small. (In all fairness, I should say that sometimes it is the *officers* who write asking what to do with an immature pastor!)

The work of the pastor is to help the church grow spiritually and mature in the Lord. This is done by the steady, balanced ministry of the Word. Ephesians 4:1-16 explains how this is done: It is necessary for each member of the body to make his own contribution. God gives spiritual gifts to His people, and then He gives these gifted people to the various churches to build up the saints. As the believers grow, they build the church.

Paul will have more to say about spiritual gifts in 1 Corinthians 12–14, but this should be said now: A mature Christian uses his gifts as tools to build with, while an immature believer uses gifts as toys to play with or trophies to boast about. Many of the members of the Corinthian church enjoyed "showing off" their gifts, but they were not interested in serving one another and edifying the church.

What is the ministry all about? It involves loving, feeding, and disciplining God's family so that His children mature in the faith and become more like Jesus Christ.

The Field—Quantity (1 Cor. 3:5-9a)

Paul was fond of agricultural images and often used them in his letters. "Ye are God's husbandry" simply means, "You are God's cultivated field, God's garden." In the Parable of the Sower, Jesus compared the human heart to soil and the Word of God to seed (Matt. 13:1-9, 18-23). Paul took this *individual* image and made it *collective:* the local church is a field that ought to bear fruit. The task of the ministry is the sowing of the seed, the cultivating of the soil, the watering of the plants, and the harvesting of the fruit.

How did this image of the church as a "field" apply to the special problems of the Corinthians? To begin with, the emphasis must be on *God* and not on the laborers. Paul and Apollos were only servants who did their assigned tasks. It was God who gave life to their efforts. Even the faith of the believers was a gift from God (1 Cor. 3:5). It is wrong to center attention on the servants. Look instead to the Lord of the harvest, the source of all blessing.

Note the emphasis in this paragraph on *increase* or *growth*. Why compare preachers or statistics? God is the source of the growth; no man can take the credit. Furthermore, no one man can do *all* the necessary work. Paul planted the seed, Apollos watered it, but only God could make it grow (1 Cor. 3:6).

Three main lessons appear from this image.

First, diversity of ministry. One laborer plows the soil, another sows the seed, a third waters the seed. As time passes, the plants grow, the fruit appears, and other laborers enjoy reaping the harvest. This emphasis on diversity will also show up when Paul compares the church to a body with many different parts.

Second, unity of purpose. No matter what work a person is doing for the Lord, he is still a part of the harvest. "Now he that planteth and he that watereth are one" (1 Cor. 3:8). Paul, Apollos, and Peter were not competing with each other. Rather, each was doing his assigned task under the lordship of Jesus Christ. Even though there is diversity of ministry, there is unity of purpose; and there ought to be unity of spirit.

Third, humility of spirit. It is not the human laborers that produce the harvest, but the Lord of the harvest. "God gave the increase. . . . God that giveth the increase" (1 Cor. 3:6-7). Granted, God has ordained that human beings should be His ministers on earth; but their efforts apart from God's blessing would be failures. The Corinthians were proud of their church, and various groups in the assembly were proud of their leaders. But this attitude of being "puffed up" was dividing the church because God was not receiving the glory.

Jesus expressed the same idea as recorded in John 4:34-38. The sower and the reaper not only work together, but one day they shall rejoice together and receive their own rewards. There can be no such thing as isolated ministry, because each worker enters into the labors of others. I have had the privilege of leading people to Christ who were total strangers to me, but others had sown the seed and watered it with their love and prayers.

"And every man shall receive his own reward according to his own labor" (1 Cor. 3:8). What men may think of our ministry is not important; what God may think is of supreme importance. Our reward must not be the praise of men, but the "Well done!" of the Lord of the harvest.

God wants to see increase in His field. He wants each local church to produce the fruit of the Spirit (Gal. 5:22-23), holiness (Rom. 6:22), giving (Rom. 15:26), good works (Col. 1:10), praise to the Lord (Heb. 13:15), and souls won to Christ (Rom. 1:13). Along with spiritual growth, there should be a measure of numerical growth. *Fruit has in it the seed for more fruit.* If the fruit of our ministry is genuine, it will eventually produce "more fruit . . . much fruit" to the glory of God (John 15:1-8).

Those who serve in ministry must constantly be caring for the "soil" of the church. It requires diligence and hard work to produce a harvest. The lazy preacher or Sunday School teacher is like the slothful farmer Solomon wrote about in Proverbs 24:30-34. Satan is busy sowing discord, lies, and sin; and we must be busy cultivating the soil and planting the good seed of the Word of God.

The Temple—Quality (1 Cor. 3:9b-23)

The usual explanation of this passage is that it describes the building of the Christian life. We all build on Christ, but some people use good materials while others use poor materials. The kind of material you use determines the kind of reward you will get.

While this may be a valid *application* of this passage, it is not the basic *interpretation.* Paul is discussing the building of the local church, the temple of God. (In 1 Cor. 6:19-20 the individual believer is God's temple; but here it is the local assembly that is in view. In Eph. 2:19-22, the whole church is compared to a temple of God.) Paul points out that one day God will judge our labors as related to the local assembly. "The fire will test the quality of each man's work" (1 Cor. 3:13, NIV).

God is concerned that we build with quality.

The church does not belong to the preacher or to the congregation. It is *God's* church. "Ye are God's building" (1 Cor. 3:9). If we are going to build the local church the way God wants it built, we must meet certain conditions.

First, we must build on the right foundation (vv. 10-11). That foundation is Jesus Christ. When Paul came to Corinth, he determined to preach only Christ and Him crucified (1 Cor. 2:1-2). He laid the only foundation that would last. In more than thirty years of ministry, I have seen "churches" try to build on a famous preacher or a special method or a doctrinal emphasis they felt was important; but these ministries simply did not last. The Corinthians were emphasizing personalities—Paul, Peter, Apollos—when they should have been glorifying Christ.

The foundation is laid by the proclaiming of the Gospel of Jesus Christ. The foundation is the most important part of the building, because it determines the size, shape, and strength of the superstructure. A ministry may seem to be successful for a time, but if it is not founded on Christ, it will eventually collapse and disappear.

I am thinking now of a pastor who "discovered a great truth" in the Bible (actually, he read it in some books) and decided to build his church on the promotion of that "great truth." He split his church and took a group with him who were "devoted to the truth" he had discovered. But the new church never succeeded. Now his group is scattered and he goes from church to church, trying to get converts to his cause. He built on the wrong foundation.

Second, we must build with the right materials (vv. 12-17). Paul described two opposite kinds of materials, as the chart reveals.

Gold, Silver, Precious Stones	*Wood, Hay, Stubble*
Permanent Beautiful Valuable Hard to obtain	Passing, temporary Ordinary, even ugly Cheap Easy to obtain

What did Paul want to symbolize by his choice of materials? He is not talking about *people,* because Christians are the "living stones" that make up God's temple (1 Peter 2:5). I personally believe Paul is referring to the *doctrines of the Word of God.* In each section of this chapter, the Word is symbolized in a way that fits the image of the church Paul used. The Word is food for the family, seed for the field, and materials for the temple.

The Book of Proverbs presents the wisdom of the Word of God as treasure to be sought, protected, and invested in daily life. Consider these passages:

> Happy is the man that findeth wisdom, and the man that getteth understanding. For the merchandise of it is better than the merchandise of silver, and the gain thereof than fine gold. She is more precious than rubies (3:13-15a).

> My son, if thou wilt receive my words, and hide my commandments with thee; so that thou incline thine ear unto wisdom, and apply thine heart to understanding; yea, if thou criest after knowledge, and liftest up thy voice for understanding; if thou seekest her as silver, and searchest for her as for hid treasures; then shalt thou understand the fear of the Lord, and find the knowledge of God (2:1-5).

> Receive my instruction, and not silver; and knowledge rather than choice gold. For wisdom is better than rubies; and all the things that may be desired are not to be compared to it (8:10-11).

When you remember that Paul has been writing about *wisdom* in these first three chapters, you can easily see the connection. The Corinthians were trying to build their church by man's wisdom, the wisdom of this world, when they should have been depending on the wisdom of God as found in the Word.

This says to me that ministers of the Word must dig deep into the Scriptures and mine out the precious gold, silver, and jewels, and then build these truths into the lives of the people. D.L. Moody used to say that converts should be weighed as well as counted. God is interested in *quality* as well as *quantity,* and Paul makes it clear that it is possible to have both. The faithful minister can work in the field and see increase, and he can build with the Word of God and see beauty and lasting blessings.

It is a serious thing to be a part of the building of God's temple. First Corinthians 3:16-17 warn us that, if we destroy ("defile")

God's temple by using cheap materials, God will destroy us! This does not mean eternal condemnation, of course, because 1 Corinthians 3:15 assures us that each worker will be saved, even if he loses a reward. I think Paul is saying that each of us builds into the church *what we build into our own lives.* Veteran missionary to India, Amy Carmichael, used to say, "The work will never go deeper than we have gone ourselves." So we end up tearing down our own lives if we fail to build into the church the values that will last. We may look very successful to men, but "the day shall declare it" and on that day, some ministers will go up in smoke.

It is unwise to compare and contrast ministries. Paul warned in 1 Corinthians 4:5, "Therefore, judge nothing before the time."

Young ministers often asked Dr. Campbell Morgan the secret of his pulpit success. Morgan replied, "I always say to them the same thing—work; hard work; and again, work!" Morgan was in his study at 6 o'clock each morning, digging treasures out of the Bible. You can find wood, hay, and stubble in your backyard, and it will not take too much effort to pick it up. But if you want gold, silver, and jewels, *you have to dig for them.* Lazy preachers and Sunday School teachers will have much to answer for at the Judgment Seat of Christ—and so will preachers and teachers who *steal* materials from others instead of studying and making it their own.

Third, we must build according to the right plan (vv. 18-20). It comes as a shock to some church members that you cannot manage a local church the same way you run a business. This does not mean we should not follow good business principles, but the operation is totally different. There is a wisdom of this world that works for the world, but it will not work for the church.

The world depends on promotion, prestige, and the influence of money and important people. The church depends on prayer, the power of the Spirit, humility, sacrifice, and service. The church that imitates the world may seem to succeed in time, but it will turn to ashes in eternity. The church in the Book of Acts had none of the "secrets of success" that seem to be important today. They owned no property; they had no influence in government; they had no treasury ("Silver and gold have I none," said Peter); their leaders were ordinary men without special education in the accepted schools; they held no attendance contests; they brought in no celebrities; and yet they turned the world upside down!

God has a specific plan for each local church (Phil. 2:12-13). Each pastor and church leader must seek the mind of God for His wisdom. First Corinthians 3:19 warns that man's wisdom will only trap him (a quotation from Job 5:13); and 1 Corinthians 3:20 warns that man's wisdom only leads to vanity and futility (a quotation from Ps. 94:11). Though the church must be identified with the *needs* of the world, it must not imitate the *wisdom* of the world.

Finally, we must build with the right motive (vv. 21-23). That motive is the glory of God. The members of the Corinthian church were glorying in men, and this was wrong. They were comparing men (1 Cor. 4:6) and dividing the church by such carnal deeds. Had they been seeking to glorify God alone, there would have been harmony in the assembly.

Paul closed this appeal by pointing out that each believer possesses all things in Christ. Each one of God's servants belongs to *each* believer. No member of the church should say, "I belong to Paul!" or "I like Peter!" because each servant belongs to each member equally. Perhaps we cannot help but have our personal preferences when it comes to the way different men minister the Word. But we must not permit our personal preferences to become divisive prejudices. In fact, the preacher I may enjoy the least may be the one I need the most!

"All are yours"—the world, life, death, things present, things to come! How rich we are in Christ! If all things belong to all believers, then why should there be competition and rivalry? "Get your eyes off of men!" Paul admonished. "Keep your eyes on Christ, and work with Him in building the church!"

"Ye are Christ's"—this balances things. I have all things in Jesus Christ, but I must not become careless or use my freedom unwisely. "All things are yours"—that is Christian *liberty.* "And ye are Christ's"—that is Christian *responsibility.* We need both if we are to build a church that will not turn to ashes when the fire falls.

How we need to pray for ministers of the Word! They must feed the family and bring the children to maturity. They must sow the seed in the field and pray for an increase. They must mine the treasures of the Word and build these treasures into the temple.

No wonder Paul cried, "And who is sufficient for these things?" But he also gave the answer: "Our sufficiency is of God" (2 Cor. 2:16; 3:5).

CHAPTER FOUR
BE WISE ABOUT . . . THE CHRISTIAN MINISTRY
1 Corinthians 4

In 1 Corinthians 3, Paul presented three pictures of the local church. Now he presents three pictures of the minister—a steward (1 Cor. 4:1-6), a spectacle (1 Cor. 4:7-13), and a father (1 Cor. 4:14-21). He wanted his readers to understand how God measured and evaluated a Christian's service. First Corinthians 4:6 explains Paul's purpose: "That no one of you be puffed up for one against another."

We must avoid extremes when it comes to evaluating men and their ministries. On the one hand, we can be so indifferent that we accept anybody who comes along. But the other extreme is to be so hypercritical that Paul himself would fail the test. It is important that we "try the spirits" (1 John 4:1-6; and note 2 John), but we must be careful not to grieve the Spirit as we do so.

In these three pictures of ministry, Paul presented three characteristics of a true minister of Jesus Christ.

Faithfulness—The Steward (1 Cor. 4:1-6)

Paul answered the leaders of the various factions in the church when he called himself, Peter, and Apollos "ministers of Christ." The word translated *ministers* is literally "under-rowers." It described the slaves who rowed the huge Roman galleys. "We are not the captains of the ship," said Paul, "but only the galley slaves who are under orders. Now, is one slave greater than another?"

Then Paul explained the image of the *steward.* A steward is a servant who manages everything for his master, but who himself owns nothing. Joseph was a chief steward in Potiphar's household (Gen. 39). The church is the "household of faith" (Gal. 6:10), and the ministers are stewards who share God's wealth with the family (Matt. 13:52). Paul called this spiritual wealth "the mysteries of God." We met this important word *mystery* in 1 Corinthians 2:7, so you may want to review it.

The responsibility of the steward is to be *faithful to his master.* A steward may not please the members of the household; he may not even please some of the other servants; but if he pleases his own master, he is a good steward. This same idea is expressed in Romans 14:4.

So, the main issue is not, "Is Paul popular?" or, "Is Apollos a better preacher than Paul?" The main issue is, "Have Paul, Apollos, and Peter been faithful to do the work God assigned to them?" Jesus had this same test in mind when He told the parable recorded in Luke 12:41-48. If a servant of God is faithful in his personal life, in his home, and in his ministry of the Word, then he is a good steward and will be adequately rewarded.

But a servant is constantly being judged. There is always somebody criticizing something he does. Paul pointed out that there are three judgments in the life of the steward.

There is man's judgment (v. 3a). Paul did not get upset when people criticized him, for he knew that his Master's judgment was far more important. The phrase *man's judgment* is literally "man's day." This is in contrast to *God's* day of judgment yet to come (1 Cor. 1:8; 3:13).

There is the servant's own self-judgment (vv. 3b-4a). Paul knew nothing that was amiss in his life and ministry, but even that did not excuse him. Sometimes we do not really know ourselves. There can be a fine line between a clear conscience and a self-righteous attitude, so we must beware.

The most important judgment is God's judgment (v. 4b). Certainly God judges us today through His Word (Heb. 4:12) and by the ministry of the Spirit. Sometimes He uses the ministry of a loving friend to help us face and confess sin (Matt. 18:15-17). But the main reference here is to the final evaluation when each Christian stands at the Judgment Seat of Christ (Rom. 14:10; 2 Cor. 5:10). Then the true facts will be revealed and the faithful servants rewarded.

These verses must not be used to cultivate a self-righteous independence of people. The local church is a family, and members of the family must help each other to grow. There is a place for honest, loving criticism (Eph. 4:15). If the critic is right, then he has helped us. If he is wrong, then we can help him. Either way, the truth is strengthened.

Paul's "therefore" in 1 Corinthians 4:5 alerts us that he is about to make a personal application of the truths just discussed. He closed this section with a threefold rebuke.

First, "you are judging God's servants at the wrong time" (v. 5). It is when the Lord returns that He will evaluate their lives and ministries, so wait until then. In fact, you cannot see into men's hearts; you cannot begin to judge their motives. Only God can do that. "Man looketh on the outward appearance, but the Lord looketh on the heart" (1 Sam. 16:7).

The Corinthians who were passing judgment on Paul were actually "playing God" and assuming to themselves the privileges that only God has. How often in my own ministry I have made this mistake! How easy it is to misread a situation and misjudge a person.

Second, "you are judging by the wrong standard" (v. 6a). The Corinthians were measuring different men by their own personal preferences and prejudices. They were even comparing ministers with one another. The only true basis for evaluation is "that which is written"—the Word of God.

The Bible clearly reveals what kind of life and service is required of God's ministers. There is no need for us to devise new standards. Often I receive letters from churches seeking pastors, asking if I could recommend candidates to them. Too often their "requirements" have gone beyond what God requires in His Word. Again, it is the problem Paul discussed in 1 Corinthians 1 and 2—the wisdom of men versus the wisdom of God.

Third, "you are judging with the wrong motive" (v. 6b). Each group in the church was tearing down the other preachers in order to build up the man they liked. Their motive was not at all spiritual. They were promoting division in the church by being partisan to one man as opposed to the others. They needed to examine their own hearts and get rid of the pride that was destroying the church.

God's servants are stewards of His truth, and the key test is: *Have they been faithful to obey and to teach the Word of God?* Not just faithful *preaching,* but faithful *practicing* as well. The testimony of Samuel (1 Sam. 12:1-5) and Paul (Acts 20:17ff) will bear witness to this truth.

Humbleness—The Spectacle (1 Cor. 4:7-13)

When Paul called himself and other apostles "a spectacle unto the world" (1 Cor. 4:9), he was using an image familiar to people in the Roman Empire. The government kept the people pacified by presenting entertainments in the different cities. The amphitheaters would be filled with citizens, eager to see men compete in the games and prisoners fight with the beasts. (In fact, the Greek word translated *spectacle* gives us our English word "theater.") The Colosseum at Rome became the center for these "entertainments."

When the "main events" were ended, then the poorest and weakest prisoners were brought in to fight with the beasts. Nobody expected too much from their performance.

What a picture of the Apostles of Jesus Christ! But it forms the background for a series of contrasts that Paul presents for the purpose of trying to humble the Corinthians.

Kings—prisoners (vv. 7-9). The questions in 1 Corinthians 4:7 ought to make all of us stop and think. I like the *New American Standard Bible's* translation of the first question: "Who regards you as superior?" A young preacher once said to a friend of mine, "Please pray that I will stay humble." My friend replied, "Tell me, what do you have to be proud about?" Why would anybody regard us as superior? Perhaps it is our own biased opinion that makes us feel so important. The best commentary on 1 Corinthians 4:7 is the witness of John the Baptist, "A man can receive nothing, except it be given him from heaven. . . . He [Christ] must increase, but I must decrease" (John 3:27, 30).

Paul used a bit of sanctified sarcasm in 1 Corinthians 4:8 when he described the Corinthians as kings. "I wish I could reign with you and be important!" he wrote. "But instead, I must go into the arena and suffer for the Lord Jesus Christ. You are first in men's eyes, but we apostles are last." In the eyes of God, the apostles were first (1 Cor. 12:28), but in the eyes of men they were last.

There is no place for pride in the ministry. If a truly great leader like Paul considered himself "on exhibition last in the program," where does this leave the rest of us? Church members are wrong when they measure ministers other than by the standards God has given. They are also wrong when they boast about their favorite preachers. This is not to say that faithful servants cannot be recognized and honored, but in all things, God must be glorified (1 Thes. 5:12-13).

Wise men—fools (v. 10a). Paul was a fool according to the standards of men. Had he remained a Jewish rabbi, he could have attained great heights in the Jewish religion (Gal. 1:14). Or had he sided with the Jewish legalists in the Jerusalem church and not ministered to the Gentiles, he could have avoided a great deal of persecution (Acts 15; 21:17ff). But when Paul asked the Lord, "What wilt Thou have me to do?" (Acts 9:6) he really meant it.

The Corinthians were wise in their own eyes, but they were actually fools in the sight of God. By depending on the wisdom and the standards of the world, they were acting like fools. The way to be spiritually wise is to become a fool in the eyes of the world (1 Cor. 3:18). I often find myself quoting those words of martyred Jim Elliot: "He is no fool who gives what he cannot keep to gain what he cannot lose."

Strong men—weak (v. 10b). There was a time when Paul gloried in his strengths; but then he met Jesus Christ and discovered that what he thought were assets were really liabilities (Phil. 3). It was through his own personal suffering that Paul discovered that his spiritual strength was the result of personal weakness (2 Cor. 12:7-10). Strength that knows itself to be strength is weakness; but weakness that knows itself to be weakness becomes strength.

The Corinthians were proud of their spiritual achievements. The factions in the church were proud of their human leaders and favorite preachers. But all of this was only weakness. There is strength only when God gets the glory. "My strength is made perfect in weakness" (2 Cor. 12:9).

Honorable—despised (vv. 10c-13). This was the crux of the whole matter: the Christians in Corinth wanted the honor that comes from men, not the honor that comes from God. They were trying to "borrow" glory by associating themselves with "great men." Paul answered, "If you associate with us, you had better be ready for suffering. We apostles are not held in honor—we are despised!"

Paul then described the privations and sufferings that he had to endure as a servant of God. The fact that he worked with his own hands as a tentmaker would have lowered him in the eyes of many, because the Greeks despised manual labor.

Paul also described how he responded to the way people treated him; and this, in itself, helped to make him great. What life does to us depends on what life finds in us. When Paul was reviled, he blessed—just as Jesus commanded (Matt. 5:44). When persecuted, he endured it by the grace of God and did not retaliate. When he was slandered, Paul tried to conciliate. In all things, he sought to respond in love.

What was the result? Men treated him "as the filth of the world . . . the offscouring of all things" (1 Cor. 4:13). "Away with such a fellow from the earth! For it is not fit that he should live!" (Acts 22:22) Paul and the other apostles were treated just as their Lord was treated; but God vindicated them and brought glory to His name.

Faithfulness in service and humbleness of mind: these are two important characteristics of a minister of Jesus Christ. He must be willing to work and willing to suffer. It is one thing to be faithful and quite another to be popular. But there is a third characteristic that helps to balance the others.

Tenderness—The Father (1 Cor. 4:14-21)

Paul had already compared the local church to a family (1 Cor. 3:1-4). But now the emphasis is on the minister as a "spiritual father." In none of his letters did Paul ever call himself "father." He was mindful of the Lord's teaching in Matthew 23:8-12. But in comparing himself to a "spiritual father," Paul reminded the church of the important ministries he had performed on their behalf.

First, Paul had founded the family (vv. 14-15). The Corinthians were Paul's beloved children in the faith. Whenever we share the Gospel with someone and have the joy of leading him to faith in Christ, we become a "spiritual parent" in his life. This does not give us any special authority over his faith (2 Cor. 1:24), but it *does* create a special relationship that God can use to help him grow. The local church is God's family for helping the newborn Christians develop.

It is important to note that Paul did not take the "credit" for their conversion. Their spiritual birth was *in Christ* and *through the Gospel.*

Sinners are born again through the ministry of the Spirit of God and the Word of God (John 3:6; 1 Peter 1:23-25). Paul was the "father" who stood by and assisted at their birth.

A child may have many guardians and teachers, but he can have only one father. He has a special relationship to his father that must not be preempted by anyone else. There had been no church in Corinth before Paul came, so that even the second-generation believers in the church were the results of Paul's effective ministry.

Paul founded the church and Apollos followed him and taught the people. In some way that is not made clear in the Scriptures, Peter also ministered at Corinth. (Perhaps he had not been there personally, but other teachers from Jerusalem had ministered in Corinth as "representatives" of Peter.) God's children need the ministry of different teachers, but they must never forget the "spiritual father" who brought them to Christ.

Second, Paul was an example to the family (vv. 16-17). Children have a way of imitating their parents, either for good or for ill. Researchers tell us that teenagers learn to drink at home and not from their peers. My guess is that other bad habits are learned the same way.

The word *followers* literally is "mimics." Paul gave the same admonition in Philippians 3:17, but we must not think that he was exalting himself. Little children learn first by example, then by explanation. When Paul pastored the church in Corinth, he set the example before them in love, devotion to Christ, sacrifice, and service. "Be ye followers of me, even as I also am of Christ" (1 Cor. 11:1). Paul was a good example because he was following the greatest Example of all, Jesus Christ.

But Paul was also a good teacher. It takes both example and instruction to bring a child to maturity. Paul sent Timothy (also one of his spiritual children) to remind the church of the doctrines and practices that Paul always taught. Timothy did not carry the letter to the church (1 Cor. 16:10), but apparently went ahead to prepare the way for the letter.

God does not have one standard for one church and a different standard for another church. He may work out His will in different ways (Phil. 2:12-13), but the basic doctrines and principles are the same. Because churches have gotten away from God's wisdom and have substituted man's wisdom, we have serious doctrinal differences among various churches. Men have gone beyond "that which is written" (1 Cor. 4:6) and this has brought division into the church.

Third, Paul was faithful to discipline the family (vv. 18-21). A child's will must be broken, but not destroyed. Until a colt is broken, it is dangerous and useless; but once it learns to obey, it becomes gentle and useful. Pride is a terrible thing in the Christian life and in the church. The yeast of sin (leaven, 1 Cor. 5:6-8) had made the Corinthians "puffed up," even to the point of saying, "Paul will not come to us! His bark is worse than his bite!" (2 Cor. 10:8-11)

Paul had been patient with their disobedience, but now he warned them that the time had come for discipline. Paul was not like the tolerant modern mother who shouted at her spoiled son, "This is the last time I'm going to tell you for the last time!"

A faithful parent must discipline his children. It is not enough to teach them and be an example before them; he must also punish them when they rebel and refuse to obey. Paul would have preferred to come with meekness and deal with their sins in a gentle manner, but their own attitude made this difficult. They were puffed up—and even proud of their disobedience! (1 Cor. 5:1-2)

The contrast in this paragraph is between *speech* and *power,* words and deeds. The arrogant Corinthians had no problem "talking big," the way children often will do; but they could not back up their talk with their "walk." Their religion was only in words. Paul was prepared to back up his "talk" with power, with deeds that would reveal their sins and God's holiness.

This section prepared the way for the next two chapters that deal with discipline in the local church. There was much sin in the Corinthian congregation and Paul was prepared to deal with it. He had already written them a letter about the matter (1 Cor. 5:9), but the congregation had not obeyed him. It was then that some of the more spiritual members contacted Paul (1 Cor. 1:11; 16:17) and shared the burdens with him. Some of the church leaders had written Paul for counsel (1 Cor. 7:1), and Paul prayed that they might obey the counsel he wrote to them.

It is a principle of life that those who will not govern themselves must be governed. Insurance companies and medical authorities urge drivers to wear seat belts, but many of them refuse. So the government must pass a law *requiring* drivers to wear seat belts. If you fail to obey, you will be punished.

Paul gave the Corinthian church opportunity to set their household in order. In the following chapters, he explains how the local church ought to be governed in the will of God. Unfortunately, the church did not immediately obey. Paul had to make a quick visit to Corinth and his experience during that visit was very painful (2 Cor. 2:1; 12:14; 13:1). He then had to write them a very strong letter (1 Cor. 7:8-12); possibly it was carried by Titus.

To the glory of God, the matters did get settled for the most part. There was still some "mopping up" to do (2 Cor. 12:20–13:5), but the crisis was now over.

It is not an easy thing to be a minister of Jesus Christ. As a steward, you must be faithful to your Master no matter what men may say to you or do to you. You will be treated as refuse by the people of the world. Your own spiritual children may break your heart and have to be disciplined.

God's faithful servants deserve our love, respect, obedience, and prayer support.

CHAPTER FIVE
BE WISE ABOUT... CHURCH DISCIPLINE
1 Corinthians 5–6

The church at Corinth was not only a divided church, but it was also a disgraced church. There was sin in the assembly and, sad to say, everybody knew about it. But the church was slow to *do* anything about it.

No church is perfect, but human imperfection must never be an excuse for sin. Just as parents must discipline their children in love, so local churches must exercise discipline over the members of the assembly. Church discipline is not a group of "pious policemen" out to catch a criminal. Rather, it is a group of brokenhearted brothers and sisters seeking to restore an erring member of the family.

Since some of the members at Corinth did not want to face the situation and change it, Paul presented to the church three important considerations.

Consider the Church (1 Cor. 5:1-13)

"What will this sin do to the church?" is certainly an important consideration. Christians are "called to be saints" (1 Cor. 1:2), and this means holy living to the glory of God. If a Christian loves his church, he will not stand by and permit sin to weaken it and perhaps ruin its testimony.

How should we respond? Paul gave three specific instructions for the church to follow.

Mourn over the sin (vv. 1-2). This is the word used for mourning over the dead, which is perhaps the deepest and most painful kind of personal sorrow possible. Instead of mourning, the people at Corinth were puffed up. They were boasting of the fact that their church was so "open-minded" that even fornicators could be members in good standing!

The sin in question was a form of incest: a professed Christian (and a member of the church) was living with his stepmother in a permanent alliance. Since Paul does not pass judgment on the woman (1 Cor. 5:9-13), we assume that she was not a member of the assembly and probably not even a Christian. This kind of sin was condemned by the Old Testament Law (Lev. 18:6-8; 20:11) as well as by the laws of the Gentile nations. Paul shamed the church by saying, "Even the unsaved Gentiles don't practice this kind of sin!"

While it is true that the Christian life is a feast (1 Cor. 5:8), there are times when it becomes a funeral. Whenever a Christian brother or sister sins, it is time for the family to mourn and to seek to help the fallen believer (Gal. 6:1-2). The offending brother in Corinth was "dead" as far as the things of the Lord were concerned. He was out of fellowship with the Lord and with those in the church who were living separated lives.

Judge the sin (vv. 3-5). While Christians are not to judge one another's motives (Matt. 7:1-5) or ministries (1 Cor. 4:5), we are certainly expected to be honest about each other's conduct. In my own pastoral ministry, I have never enjoyed having to initiate church discipline; but since it is commanded in the Scriptures, we must obey God and set personal feelings aside.

Paul described here an official church meeting at which the offender was dealt with according to divine instructions. Public sin must be publicly judged and condemned. (For our Lord's instructions about discipline, study Matt. 18:15-20.) The sin was not to be "swept under the rug"; for, after all, it was known far and wide even among the unsaved who were outside the church.

The church was to gather together and expel the offender. Note the strong words that Paul used to instruct them: "taken away from among you" (1 Cor. 5:2), "deliver such an one unto Satan" (1 Cor. 5:5), "purge out" (1 Cor. 5:7), and "put away" (1 Cor. 5:13). Paul did not suggest that they handle the offender gently. Of course, we assume that first the spiritual leaders of the church sought to restore the man personally.

This was to be done by the authority of Jesus Christ—in His name—and not simply on the authority of the local church. Church membership is a serious thing and must not be treated carelessly or lightly.

What does it mean to deliver a Christian "unto Satan"? It does not mean to deprive him of salvation, since it is not the church that grants salvation to begin with. When a Christian is in fellowship with the Lord and with the local church, he enjoys a special protection from Satan. But when he is out of fellowship with God and excommunicated from the local church, he is "fair game" for the enemy. God could permit Satan to attack the offender's body so that the sinning believer would repent and return to the Lord.

Purge the sin (vv. 6-13). The image here is that of the Passover supper (Ex. 12). Jesus is the Lamb of God who shed His blood to deliver us from sin (John 1:29; 1 Peter 1:18-25). The Jews in Egypt were delivered from death by the application of the blood of the lamb. Following the application of the blood, the Jewish families ate the Passover supper. One of the requirements was that no yeast (leaven) be found anywhere in their dwellings. Even the bread at the feast was to be unleavened.

Leaven is a picture of sin. It is small but powerful; it works secretly; it "puffs up" the dough; it spreads. The sinning church member in Corinth was like a piece of yeast: he was defiling the entire loaf of bread (the congregation). It was like a cancer in the body that needed to be removed by drastic surgery.

The church must purge itself of "old leaven"—the things that belong to the "old life" before we trusted Christ. We must also get rid of malice and wickedness (there was a great deal of hard feelings between members of the Corinthian church) and replace them with sincerity and truth. As a loaf of bread (1 Cor. 10:17), the local church must be as pure as possible.

However, the church must not judge and condemn those who are *outside* the faith. That judgment is future, and God will take care of it. In 1 Corinthians 5:9-13, Paul emphasized once again the importance of separation from the world. Christians are not to be *isolated,* but separated. We cannot avoid contact with sinners, but we can avoid contamination by sinners.

If a professed Christian is guilty of the sins named here, the church must deal with him. Individual members are not to "company" with him (1 Cor. 5:9—"get mixed up with, associate intimately"). They are not to *eat* with him, which could refer to private hospitality or more likely the public observance of the Lord's Supper (see 1 Cor. 11:23-34).

Church discipline is not easy or popular, but it is important. If it is done properly, God can use it to convict and restore an erring believer. Second Corinthians 2:1-11 indicates that this man did repent and was restored to fellowship.

Consider Lost Sinners (1 Cor. 6:1-8)

The church at Corinth was rapidly losing its testimony in the city. Not only did the unsaved know about the immorality in the assembly, but they were also aware of the lawsuits involving members of the church. Not only were there sins of the flesh, but also sins of the spirit (2 Cor. 7:1).

The Greeks in general, and the Athenians in particular, were known for their involvement in the courts. The Greek playwright Aristophanes has one of his characters look at a map and ask where Greece is located. When it is pointed out to him, he replies that there must be some mistake—because he cannot see any lawsuits going on! However, the United States is rapidly getting a similar reputation: over 200,000 civil suits were filed in the federal courts in one recent twelve-month period. Nearly 1 million lawyers (their number is increasing) are handling them. In one year, more than 12 million suits were filed in the state courts.

Paul detected three tragedies in this situation. First, *the believers were presenting a poor testimony to the lost.* Even the unbelieving Jews dealt with their civil cases in their own synagogue courts. To take the problems of Christians and discuss them before the "unjust" and "unbelievers" was to weaken the testimony of the Gospel.

Second, *the congregation had failed to live up to its full position in Christ.* Since the saints will one day participate in the judgment of the world and even of fallen angels, they ought to be able to settle their differences here on earth. The Corinthians boasted of their great spiritual gifts. Why, then, did they not use them in solving their problems?

Bible students are not agreed on the meaning of Paul's statement in 1 Corinthians 6:4. Some think he is using a bit of sarcasm: "You are better off asking the weakest member of your church to settle the matter, than to go before the most qualified unsaved judge!" Others take the phrase "who are least esteemed in [or 'by'] the church" to refer to the pagan judges. Or it may be that Paul is saying that God can use even the least member of the church to discern His will. The result is still the same: It is wrong for Christians to take their civil suits to court.

Sometimes there are "friendly suits" that are required by law to settle certain issues. That is not what Paul was referring to. It seems that the church members were "at each other's throats," trying to get their way in the courts. I am happy to see that there is a trend in our churches today for Christian lawyers to act as arbitrators in civil cases, and help to settle these matters out of court.

There was a third tragedy: *the members suing each other had already lost.* Even if some of them won their cases, they had incurred a far greater loss in their disobedience to the Word of God. "Now, therefore, there is utterly a fault among you" (1 Cor. 6:7) can be translated, "It is already a complete defeat for you." Paul was certainly referring to our Lord's teaching in Matthew 5:39-42. Better to lose money or possessions than to lose a brother and lose your testimony as well.

Over the years of my own ministry, I have seen the sad results of churches and church members trying to solve personal problems in court. Nobody really wins—except the devil! The Corinthians who were going to court were disgracing the name of the Lord and the church just as much as the man who was guilty of incest, and they needed to be disciplined.

I recall a ministerial student who phoned me to tell me he was going to sue his school. Apparently the administration would not allow him to do something he felt was very necessary to his education. I advised him to "cool off," talk to his faculty counselor, and get the idea out of his mind. He took my advice and in so doing not only avoided a bad testimony, but grew spiritually through the experience.

Consider the Lord (1 Cor. 6:9-20)

There was a great deal of sexual laxness in the city of Corinth. It was a permissive society with a philosophy similar to that which the world has today: Sex is a normal physical function, so why not use it as you please? Paul pointed out that God created sex when He made the first man and woman, and therefore He has the right to tell us how to use it. The Bible is the "owner's manual" and it must be obeyed.

God condemns sexual sins; Paul named some of them in 1 Corinthians 6:9. In that day, idolatry and sensuality went together. "Effeminate" and "abusers" describe the passive and active partners in a homosexual relationship. (Paul dealt with this and with lesbianism in Rom. 1:26-27.) In 1 Corinthians 6:10, Paul pointed his finger at the members guilty of sins of the spirit, those suing each other because of their covetous attitude.

But God can also cleanse sexual sins and make sinners into new creatures in Christ. "Ye are washed, but ye are sanctified, but ye are justified" (1 Cor. 6:11). The tenses of these verbs indicate a completed transaction. Now, because of all that God had done for them, they had an obligation to God to use their bodies for His service and His glory.

Consider God the Father (vv. 12-14). He created our bodies and one day He will resurrect them in glory. (More about the resurrection in 1 Cor. 15.) In view of the fact that our bodies have such a wonderful origin, and an even more wonderful future, how can we use them for such evil purposes?

The Corinthians had two arguments to defend their sensuality. First, "All things are lawful unto me" (1 Cor. 6:12). This was a popular phrase in Corinth, based on a false view of Christian freedom. We have not been set free so that we can enter into a new kind of bondage! As Christians, we must ask ourselves, "Will this enslave me? Is this activity really profitable for my spiritual life?"

Their second argument was, "Meats for the

belly, and the belly for meats" (1 Cor. 6:13). They treated sex as an appetite to be satisfied and not as a gift to be cherished and used carefully. Sensuality is to sex what gluttony is to eating; both are sinful and both bring disastrous consequences. Just because we have certain normal desires, given by God at Creation, does not mean that we must give in to them and always satisfy them. Sex outside of marriage is destructive, while sex in marriage can be creative and beautiful.

There may be excitement and enjoyment in sexual experience outside of marriage, *but there is not enrichment.* Sex outside of marriage is like a man robbing a bank: he gets something, but it is not his and he will one day pay for it. Sex within marriage can be like a person putting money into a bank: there is safety, security, and he will collect dividends. Sex within marriage can build a relationship that brings joys in the future; but sex apart from marriage has a way of weakening future relationships, as every Christian marriage counselor will tell you.

Consider God the Son (vv. 15-18). The believer's body is a member of Christ (see 1 Cor. 12:12ff). How can we be joined to Christ and joined to sin at the same time? Such a thought astounds us. Yet some of the Corinthians saw no harm in visiting the temple prostitutes (there were 1,000 of them at the temple of Aphrodite) and committing fornication.

Jesus Christ bought us with a price (1 Cor. 6:20), and therefore our bodies belong to Him. We are one spirit with the Lord and we must yield our bodies to Him as living sacrifices (Rom. 12:1-2). If you begin each day by surrendering your body to Christ, it will make a great deal of difference in what you do with your body during the day.

Paul referred to the Creation account (Gen. 2:24) to explain the seriousness of sexual sin. When a man and woman join their bodies, *the entire personality is involved.* There is a much deeper experience, a "oneness" that brings with it deep and lasting consequences. Paul warned that sexual sin is the most serious sin a person can commit against his body, for it involves the whole person (1 Cor. 6:18). Sex is not just a part of the body. Being "male" and "female" involves the total person. Therefore, sexual experience affects the total personality.

Paul did not suggest that being joined to a harlot was the equivalent of marriage, for marriage also involves *commitment.* The man and woman leave the parental home to begin a new home. This helps us to understand why sex *within marriage* can be an enriching experience of growth, because it is based on commitment. When two people pledge their love and faithfulness to each other, they lay a strong foundation on which to build. Marriage protects sex and enables the couple, committed to each other, to grow in this wonderful experience.

Consider God the Holy Spirit (vv. 19-20). God the Father created our bodies; God the Son redeemed them and made them part of His body; and God the Spirit indwells our bodies and makes them the very temple of God. How can we defile God's temple by using our bodies for immorality?

The word *your* is plural, but the words *body* and *temple* are singular (1 Cor. 6:19). It may be that Paul is here describing not only the individual believer, but also the local church. Each local assembly is a "body" of people united to Jesus Christ. The conduct of individual members affects the spiritual life of the entire church.

In both cases, the lesson is clear: "Glorify God in your body!" The Holy Spirit was given for the purpose of glorifying Jesus Christ (John 16:14). The Spirit can use our bodies to glorify Him and to magnify Him (Phil. 1:20-21). Our special relationship to the Holy Spirit brings with it a special responsibility.

So God the Father, God the Son, and God the Holy Spirit are all involved in what we do with our bodies. If we break God's laws, then we must pay the penalty (Rom. 1:24-27).

As you review this section, you will see that sexual sins affect the entire personality. They affect the *emotions,* leading to slavery (1 Cor. 6:12b). It is frightening to see how sensuality can get ahold of a person and defile his entire life, enslaving him to habits that destroy. It also affects a person *physically* (1 Cor. 6:18). The fornicator and adulterer, as well as the homosexual, may forget their sins, *but their sins will not forget them.*

In my pastoral counseling, I have had to help married couples whose relationship was falling apart because of the consequences of *pre*marital sex, as well as *extra*marital sex. The harvest of sowing to the flesh is sometimes delayed, but it is certain (Gal. 6:7-8). How sad it is to live with the consequences of *forgiven* sin.

Having said all this, we must also realize that there are *eternal* consequences for people who practice sexual sins. In 1 Corinthians 6:9-10, Paul *twice* states that people who *practice* such sins will not inherit God's kingdom. A Christian may fall into these sins and be forgiven, as was David; but no Christian would *practice* such sins (1 John 3:1-10).

Finally, in all fairness, we must note that there are other sins besides sexual sins. For some reason, the church has often majored on condemning the sins of the prodigal son and has forgotten the sins of the elder brother (see Luke 15:11-32). There are sins of the spirit as well as sins of the flesh—Paul names some of them in 1 Corinthians 6:10. Covetousness can send a man to hell just as easily as can adultery.

We must remember that the grace of God can change the sinner's life. "And such *were* some of you" (1 Cor. 6:11). It is wonderful how faith in Christ makes a sinner into a "new creation" (2 Cor. 5:17, 21). And it is important that we *live* like those who are a part of God's new creation. We are not our own. We belong to the Father who made us, the Son who redeemed us, and the Spirit who indwells us. We also belong to the people of God, the church, and our sins can weaken the testimony and infect the fellowship.

"Be ye holy, for I am holy" (1 Peter 1:16).

CHAPTER SIX
BE WISE ABOUT... CHRISTIAN MARRIAGE
1 Corinthians 7

Up to this point, Paul had been dealing with the sins reported to be known in the Corinthian congregation. Now he takes up the questions about which they had written to him: marriage (1 Cor. 7:1, 25), food offered to idols (1 Cor. 8:1), spiritual gifts (1 Cor. 12:1), the resurrection of the dead (1 Cor. 15:1), and the missionary offering for the Jews (1 Cor. 16:1).

As you study 1 Corinthians 7, please keep in mind that Paul is replying to definite questions. He is not spelling out a complete "theology of marriage" in one chapter. It is necessary to consider as well what the rest of the Bible has to say about this important subject.

Some liberal critics have accused Paul of being against both marriage and women. These accusations are not true, of course. Nor is it true that in 1 Corinthians 7:6, 10, 12, and 25 Paul is disclaiming divine inspiration for what he wrote. Rather, he is referring to what Jesus taught when He was on earth (Matt. 5:31-32; 19:1-12; Mark 10:1-12; Luke 16:18). Paul had to answer some questions that Jesus never discussed; but when a question arose that the Lord had dealt with, Paul referred to His words. Instead of disclaiming inspiration, Paul claimed that what he wrote was equal in authority to what Christ taught.

Paul explained God's will concerning Christian marriage, and he addressed his counsel to three different groups of believers.

Christians Married to Christians (1 Cor. 7:1-11)

Apparently one of the questions the church asked was, "Is celibacy [remaining unmarried] more spiritual than marriage?" Paul replied that it is good for a man or a woman to have the gift of celibacy, but the celibate state is not better than marriage, nor is it the best state for everybody. Dr. Kenneth Wuest translates Paul's reply, "It is perfectly proper, honorable, morally befitting for a man to live in strict celibacy."

First Corinthians 7:6 makes it clear that celibacy is permitted, but it is not commanded; and 1 Corinthians 7:7 informs us that not everybody has the gift of remaining celibate. This ties in with our Lord's teaching in Matthew 19:10-12, where "eunuchs" refers to those who abstain from marriage. "It is not good that the man should be alone" (Gen. 2:18) is generally true for most people; but some have been called to a life of singleness for one reason or another. Their singleness is not "subspiritual" or "superspiritual." It all depends on the will of God.

One purpose for marriage is "to avoid fornication." First Corinthians 7:2 makes it clear that God does not approve either of polygamy or homosexual "marriages." One man married to one woman has been God's pattern from the first. However, the husband and wife must not abuse the privilege of sexual love that is a normal part of marriage. The wife's body belongs to the husband, and the husband's body to the wife; and each must be considerate of the other. Sexual love is a beautiful tool to build with, not a weapon to fight with. To refuse each other is to commit robbery (see 1 Thes. 4:6) and to invite Satan to tempt the partners to seek their satisfaction elsewhere.

As in all things, the spiritual must govern the physical; for our bodies are God's temples. The husband and wife may abstain in order to devote their full interest to prayer and fasting (1 Cor. 7:5); but they must not use this as an excuse for prolonged separation. Paul is encouraging Christian partners to be "in tune" with each other in matters both spiritual and physical.

In 1 Corinthians 7:8-9, Paul applied the principle stated in 1 Corinthians 7:1 to single believers and widows: If you cannot control yourself, then marry.

Not only did the church ask about celibacy, but they also asked Paul about divorce. Since Jesus had dealt with this question, Paul cited His teaching: Husbands and wives are not to divorce each other (see also 1 Cor. 7:39). If divorce does occur, the parties should remain unmarried or seek reconciliation.

This is, of course, the ideal for marriage. Jesus did make one exception: If one party was guilty of fornication, this could be grounds for divorce. Far better that there be confession, forgiveness, and reconciliation; but if these are out of the question, then the innocent party may get a divorce. However, divorce is the last option; first, every means available should be used to restore the marriage.

It has been my experience as a pastor that when a husband and wife are yielded to the Lord, and when they seek to please each other in the marriage relationship, the marriage will be so satisfying that neither partner would think of looking elsewhere for fulfillment. "There are no sex problems in marriage," a Christian counselor once told me, "only personality problems with sex as one of the symptoms." The present frightening trend of increased divorces among Christians (and even among the clergy) must break the heart of God.

Christians Married to Non-Christians (1 Cor. 7:12-24)

Some of the members of the Corinthian church were saved after they had been married, but their mates had not yet been converted. No doubt, some of these believers were having a difficult time at home; and they asked Paul, "Must we remain married to unsaved partners? Doesn't our conversion alter things?"

Paul replied that they were to remain with their unconverted mates so long as their mates were willing to live with them. Salvation does not alter the marriage state; if anything, it ought to enhance the marriage relationship. (Note Peter's counsel to wives with unsaved husbands in 1 Peter 3:1-6.) Since marriage is basically a physical relationship ("they shall be one flesh"—Gen. 2:24), it can only be broken by a physical cause. Adultery and death would be two such causes (1 Cor. 7:39).

It is an act of disobedience for a Christian knowingly to marry an unsaved person (note "only in the Lord" in 1 Cor. 7:39; 2 Cor. 6:14). But if a person becomes a Christian after marriage, he should not use that as an excuse to break up the marriage just to avoid problems. In fact, Paul emphasized the fact that the Christian partner could have a spiritual influence on the unsaved mate. First Corinthians 7:14 does not teach that the unsaved partner is *saved* because of the believing mate, since each person must individually decide for Christ. Rather, it means that the believer exerts a spiritual influence in the home that can lead to the salvation of the lost partner.

What about the children? Again, the emphasis is on the influence of the godly partner. The believing husband or wife must not give up. In my own ministry, I have seen devoted Christians live for Christ in divided homes and eventually see their loved ones trust the Saviour.

Salvation does not change the marriage state. If the wife's becoming a Christian annulled the marriage, then the children in the home would become illegitimate ("unclean" in 1 Cor. 7:14). Instead, these children may one day be saved if the Christian mate is faithful to the Lord.

It is difficult for us who are "accustomed" to the Christian faith to realize the impact that this new doctrine had on the Roman world. Here was a teaching for every person, regardless of race or social status. The church was perhaps the only assembly in the Roman Empire where slaves and freemen, men and women, rich and poor, could fellowship on an equal basis (Gal. 3:28). However, this new equality also brought with it some misunderstandings and problems; and some of these Paul dealt with in 1 Corinthians 7:17-24.

The principle that Paul laid down was this: Even though Christians are all one in Christ, each believer should remain in the same calling he was in when the Lord saved him. Jewish believers should not try to become Gentiles (by erasing the physical mark of the covenant), and Gentiles should not try to become Jews (by being circumcised). Slaves should not *demand* freedom from their Christian masters, just because of their equality in Christ. However, Paul *did* advise Christian slaves to secure their freedom if at all possible, probably by purchase. This same principle would apply to Christians married to unsaved mates.

But suppose the unsaved mate leaves the home? First Corinthians 7:15 gives the answer: the Christian partner is not obligated to keep the home together. We are called to peace, and we should do all we can to live in peace (Rom. 12:18); but there comes a time in some situations where peace is impossible. If the unsaved mate separates from his or her partner, there is little the Christian can do except to pray and continue faithful to the Lord.

Does separation then give the Christian mate the right to divorce and remarriage? Paul did not say so. What if the unconverted mate ends up living with another partner? That would constitute adultery and give grounds for divorce. But even then, 1 Corinthians 7:10-11 would encourage forgiveness and restoration. Paul did not deal with every possible situation. He laid down spiritual principles, not a list of rules.

We are prone to think that a change in circumstances is always the answer to a problem. But the problem is usually *within* us and not *around* us. The heart of every problem is the problem in the heart. I have watched couples go through divorce and seek happiness in new circumstances, only to discover that they carried their problems with them. A Christian lawyer once told me, "About the only people who profit from divorces are the attorneys!"

Unmarried Christians (1 Cor. 7:25-40)

Paul had already addressed a brief word to this group in 1 Corinthians 7:8-9, but in this closing section of the chapter, he went into greater detail. Their question was, "*Must* a Christian get married? What about the unmarried women in the church who are not getting any younger?" (see 1 Cor. 7:36) Perhaps Paul addressed this section primarily to the parents of marriageable girls. Since Jesus did not give any special teaching on this topic, Paul gave his counsel as one taught of the Lord. He asked them to consider several factors when they made their decision about marriage.

First, consider the present circumstances (vv. 25-31). It was a time of distress (1 Cor. 7:26) when society was going through change (1 Cor. 7:31). There was not much time left for serving the Lord (1 Cor. 7:29). It is possible that there were political and economic pressures in Corinth about which we have no information. In view of the difficulties, it would be better for a person to be unmarried. However, this did not mean that married people should seek a divorce (1 Cor. 7:27). Paul's counsel was to the unmarried.

This did not mean that *nobody* should get married; but those who do marry must be ready to accept the trials that will accompany it (1 Cor. 7:28). In fact, the situation might become so difficult that even those already married will have to live as though they were not married (1 Cor. 7:29). Perhaps Paul was referring to husbands and wives being separated from each other because of economic distress or persecution.

To consider the circumstances is good counsel for engaged people today. The average age for first-time brides and grooms is climbing, which suggests that couples are waiting longer to get married. In my pastoral premarital counseling, I used to remind couples that the cheapest thing in a wedding was the marriage license. From then on, the prices would go up!

Second, face the responsibilities honestly (vv. 32-35). The emphasis in this paragraph is on the word *care,* which means "to be anxious, to be pulled in different directions." It is impossible for two people to live together without burdens of one kind or another, but there is no need to rush into marriage and create more problems. Marriage requires a measure of maturity, and age is no guarantee of maturity.

Once again, Paul emphasized living for the Lord. He did not suggest that it was impossible for a man or a woman to be married and serve God acceptably, because we know too many people who have done it. But the married servant of God must consider his or her mate, as well as the children God may give them; and this could lead to distraction. It is a fact of history that both John Wesley and George Whitefield might have been better off had they remained single—Wesley's wife finally left him, and Whitefield traveled so much that his wife was often alone for long periods of time.

It is possible to please both the Lord and your mate, if you are yielded to Christ and obeying the Word. Many of us have discovered that a happy home and satisfying marriage are a wonderful encouragement in the difficulties of Christian service. A well-known Scottish preacher was experiencing a great deal of public criticism because of a stand he took on a certain issue, and almost every day there was a negative report in the newspapers. A friend met him one day and asked, "How are you able to carry on in the face of this opposition?" The man replied quietly, "I am happy at home."

Unmarried believers who feel a call to serve God should examine their own hearts to see if marriage will help or hinder their ministry. They must also be careful to wed mates who feel a like call to serve God. Each person has his own gift and calling from God and must be obedient to His Word.

Third, each situation is unique (vv. 36-38). Paul addressed here the fathers of the unmarried girls. In that day, it was the parents who arranged the marriages, the father in particular (2 Cor. 11:2). Paul had already said in 1 Corinthians 7:35 that he was not laying down an ironclad rule for everybody to follow, regardless of circumstances. Now he made it clear that the father had freedom of choice whether or not he would give his daughter in marriage.

I have noticed that often in churches marriages come in "packs." One couple gets engaged and before long four couples are engaged. If all of these engagements are in the will of God, it can be a very exciting and wonderful experience; but I fear that some couples get engaged just to keep up with the crowd. Sometimes in Christian schools, couples get what I call "senior panic" and rush out of engagement and into marriage immediately after graduation, lest they be left "waiting at the church." Sad to say, not all of these marriages are successful.

Even though our modern approach to dating and marriage was completely foreign to the Corinthians, the counsel Paul gave them still applies today. It is a wise thing for couples to counsel with their parents and with their Christian leaders in the church, lest they rush into something which afterward they regret.

Paul hit on a key problem in 1 Corinthians 7:36 when he mentioned "the flower of her age." This is a delicate phrase that simply means the girl is getting older. Dr. Kenneth Wuest translates it "past the bloom of her youth." She is starting to become one of the "unclaimed blessings" in the church. The danger, of course, is that she rush into marriage just to avoid becoming a spinster, and she might make a mistake. A pastor friend of mine likes to say to couples, "Better to live in single loneliness than in married cussedness!"

Each situation is unique, and parents and children must seek the Lord's will. It takes more than two Christian people to make a happy marriage. Not every marriage that is scriptural is necessarily sensible.

Finally, remember that marriage is for life (vv. 39-40). It is God's will that the marriage union be permanent, a lifetime commitment. There is no place in Christian marriage for a "trial marriage," nor is there any room for the "escape hatch" attitude: "If the marriage doesn't work, we can always get a divorce."

For this reason, marriage must be built on something sturdier than good looks, money, romantic excitement, and social acceptance. There must be Christian commitment, character, and maturity. There must be a willingness to grow, to learn from each other, to forgive and forget, to minister to one another. The kind of love Paul described in 1 Corinthians 13 is what is needed to cement two lives together.

Paul closed the section by telling the widows that they were free to marry, but "only in the Lord" (1 Cor. 7:39). This means that they must not only marry believers, but marry in the will of God. Paul's counsel (for the reasons already given) was that they remain single, but he left the decision to them.

God has put "walls" around marriage, not to make it a prison, but to make it a safe fortress. The person who considers marriage a prison should not get married. When two people are lovingly and joyfully committed to each other—and to their Lord—the experience of marriage is one of enrichment and enlargement. They grow together and discover the richness of serving the Lord as a "team" in their home and church.

As you review this chapter, you cannot help

but be impressed with the seriousness of marriage. Paul's counsel makes it clear that God takes marriage seriously, and that we cannot disobey God's Word without suffering painful consequences. While both Paul and Jesus leave room for divorce under certain conditions, this can never be God's first choice for a couple. God hates divorce (Mal. 2:14-16) and certainly no believer should consider divorce until *all* avenues of reconciliation have been patiently explored.

While a person's marital failure may hinder him from serving as a pastor or deacon (1 Tim. 3:2, 12), it need not keep him from ministering in other ways. Some of the best personal soul winners I have known have been men who, before their conversion, had the unfortunate experience of divorce. A man does not have to hold an office in order to have a ministry.

In summary, each person must ask himself or herself the following questions if marriage is being contemplated:

1. What is my gift from God?
2. Am I marrying a believer?
3. Are the circumstances such that marriage is right?
4. How will marriage affect my service for Christ?
5. Am I prepared to enter into this union for life?

CHAPTER SEVEN
BE WISE ABOUT . . . CHRISTIAN LIBERTY
1 Corinthians 8; 10

After answering their questions about marriage, Paul turned to one of the most controversial subjects in the letter he received from the Corinthian church: "Can Christians eat meat that has been sacrificed to idols?" The immediate question does not interest believers today since we do not face that problem. But the wider issue of "Christian liberty" *does* apply to us, because we face questions that Paul never faced. Is it right for Christians to attend the theater? Should a believer have a television set in his home? To what extent can a Christian get involved in politics?

In 1 Corinthians 8–10, Paul enunciated four basic principles that would guide believers in making personal decisions about those "questionable" areas of the Christian life. The four principles are:

KNOWLEDGE MUST BE BALANCED BY LOVE (1 COR. 8)
AUTHORITY MUST BE BALANCED BY DISCIPLINE (1 COR. 9)
EXPERIENCE MUST BE BALANCED BY CAUTION (1 COR. 10:1-22)
FREEDOM MUST BE BALANCED BY RESPONSIBILITY (1 COR. 10:23-33)

As you can see, Paul addressed himself primarily to the strong Christians in the church, believers who had spiritual knowledge and experience and who understood their authority and freedom in Christ. It is the strong who must care for the weak (Rom. 14–15).

The question of meats offered to idols is dealt with in 1 Corinthians 8; 10, so we will examine it in this chapter. In 1 Corinthians 9, Paul illustrated this principle of the right use of authority by explaining his own financial policy; so we will consider that in our next study.

Knowledge Must Be Balanced by Love (1 Cor. 8:1-13)

There were two sources of meat in the ancient world: the regular market (where the prices were higher) and the local temples (where meat from the sacrifices was always available). The strong members of the church realized that idols could not contaminate food, so they saved money by purchasing the cheaper meat available from the temples. Furthermore, if unconverted friends invited them to a feast at which sacrificial meat was served, the strong Christians attended it whether at the temple or in the home.

All of this offended the weaker Christians. Many of them had been saved out of pagan idolatry and they could not understand why their fellow believers would want to have anything to do with meat sacrificed to idols. (In Rom. 14–15, the weak Christians had problems over diets and holy days, but it was the same basic issue.) There was a potential division in the church, so the leaders asked Paul for counsel.

Paul called to their attention three important factors.

Knowledge (vv. 1-2). The Corinthians were enriched in spiritual knowledge (1 Cor. 1:5) and were, in fact, rather proud of their achievements. They knew that an idol was nothing, merely the representation of a false god who existed only in the darkened minds of those who worshiped it. The presence of an idol in a temple was no solid proof that the god existed. (Later, Paul would point out that idolatry was basically the worship of demons.) So the conclusion was logical: A nonexistent god could not contaminate food offered on his altar.

So far, it is the strong Christians who are ahead. Why, then, are the weak Christians upset with them when their position is so logical? Because you don't always solve every problem with logic. The little child who is afraid of the dark will not be assured by arguments, especially if the adult (or older brother) adopts a superior attitude. Knowledge can be a weapon to fight with or a tool to build with, depending on how it is used. If it "puffs up" then it cannot "build up [edify]."

A know-it-all attitude is only an evidence of ignorance. The person who really knows truth is only too conscious of how much he does not know. Furthermore, it is one thing to know *doctrine* and quite something else to know *God.* It is possible to grow in Bible knowledge and yet not grow in grace or in one's personal relationship with God. The test is *love,* which is the second factor Paul discussed.

Love (vv. 3-6). Love and knowledge must go together; "speaking the truth in love" (Eph. 4:15). It has well been said, "Truth without love is brutality, but love without truth is hypocrisy." Knowledge is power and it must be used in love. But love must always be controlled by knowledge (see Paul's prayer in Phil. 1:9-11). The strong believers in the church had knowledge, but they were not using their knowledge in love. Instead of building up the weak saints, the strong Christians were only puffing up themselves.

Paul's great concern was that the strong saints help the weaker saints to grow and to stop being weak saints. Some people have the false notion that the *strong* Christians are the ones who live by rules and regulations and who get offended when others exercise their freedom in Christ; but such is not the case. It is the *weak* Christians who must have the security of law and who are afraid to use their freedom in Christ. It is the weak Christians who are prone to judge and criticize stronger believers and to stumble over what they do. This, of course, makes it difficult for the strong saints to minister to their weaker brothers and sisters.

It is here that love enters the picture, for "love builds up" and puts others first. When spiritual knowledge is used in love, the stronger Christian can take the hand of the weaker Christian and help him to stand and walk so as to enjoy his freedom in Christ. *You cannot force-feed immature believers and transform them into giants.* Knowledge must be mixed with love; otherwise, the saints will end up with "big heads" instead of enlarged hearts. A famous preacher used to say, "Some Christians grow; others just swell."

Knowledge and love are two important factors, for knowledge must be balanced by love if we are to use our Christian freedom in the right way. But there is a third factor.

Conscience (vv. 7-13). The word *conscience* simply means "to know with," and it is used thirty-two times in the New Testament. Conscience is that internal court where our actions are judged and are either approved or condemned (Rom. 2:14-15). Conscience is not the law; it bears witness to God's moral law. But the important thing is this: *conscience depends on knowledge.* The more spiritual knowledge we know *and act on,* the stronger the conscience will become.

Some Christians have weak consciences because they have been saved only a short time and have not had opportunity to grow. Like little babes in the home, they must be guarded carefully. Other saints have weak consciences because they *will* not grow. They ignore their Bibles and Christian fellowship and remain in a state of infancy (1 Cor. 3:1-4; Heb. 5:11-14). But some believers remain weak because they are afraid of freedom. They are like a child old enough to go to school, who is afraid to leave home and must be taken to school each day.

The conscience of a weak Christian is easily defiled (1 Cor. 8:7), wounded (1 Cor. 8:12), and offended (1 Cor. 8:13). For this reason, the stronger saints must defer to the weaker saints and do nothing that would harm them. It might not harm the mature saint to share a feast in an idolatrous temple, but it might harm his weaker brother. First Corinthians 8:10 warns that the immature believer might decide to imitate his stronger brother and thus be led into sin.

It is important to note that the stronger believer defers to the weaker believer in love *only that he might help him to mature.* He does not "pamper" him; he seeks to edify him, to help him grow. Otherwise, *both* will become weak.

We are free in Christ, but we must take care that our spiritual knowledge is tempered by love, and that we do not tempt the weaker Christian to run ahead of his conscience. Where knowledge is balanced by love, the strong Christian will have a ministry to the weak Christian, and the weak Christian will grow and become strong.

Experience Must Be Balanced by Caution (1 Cor. 10:1-22)

Paul reminded the experienced believers who were strong in the faith that they had better not grow overconfident in their ability to overcome temptation. "Wherefore let him that thinketh he standeth take heed lest he fall" (1 Cor. 10:12). Paul used the nation of Israel as his example to warn the mature believers that their experience must be balanced by caution. He gave three warnings.

First, he warned that privileges were no guarantee of success (vv. 1-4). Israel had been delivered from Egypt by the power of God, just as the Christian believer has been redeemed from sin. (In 1 Cor. 5:7-8, Paul had already related Passover to salvation.) Israel was identified with Moses in their Red Sea "baptism," just as the Corinthians had been identified with Christ in their Christian baptism. Israel ate the manna from heaven and drank the water God provided, just as Christians nourish themselves on the spiritual sustenance God supplies (John 6:63, 68; 7:37-39). However, these spiritual privileges did not prevent the Jews from falling into sin.

There are dangers to maturity as well as to immaturity, and one of them is overconfidence. When we think we are strong, we discover that we are weak. The strong believer who eats in the temple may find himself struggling with an enemy who is too strong for him.

Paul did not suggest in 1 Corinthians 10:4 that an actual rock accompanied the Jews throughout their wilderness journey, though some Jewish rabbis taught this idea. It was a *spiritual* rock that supplied what they needed, and that Rock was Christ. Sometimes the water came from a rock (Ex. 17:1-7; Num. 20:7-11) and at other times from a well (Num. 21:16-18). God provided the water.

Paul issued a second warning: good beginnings do not guarantee good endings (vv. 5-12). The Jews experienced God's miracles, and yet they failed when they were tested in the wilderness. Experience must always be balanced with caution, for we never come to the place in our Christian walk where we are free from temptation and potential failure. All of the Jews twenty years old and upward who were rescued from Egypt, except for Joshua and Caleb, died in the wilderness during their years of wandering (Num. 14:26ff).

We can hear some of the "strong" Corinthians asking, "But what does that have to do with us?" Paul then pointed out that the Corinthian church was guilty of the same sins that the Jews committed. Because of their lust for evil things, the Corinthians were guilty of immorality (1 Cor. 6), idolatry (1 Cor. 8; 10), and murmuring against God (2 Cor. 12:20-21). Like the nation of Israel, they were tempting God and just "daring Him" to act.

Paul certainly knew his Old Testament, and his readers would recognize the events referred to. The "lusting" is found in Numbers 11:4ff, the idolatry in Exodus 32, and the fornication in Numbers 25. The Israelites often tempted God, but perhaps Numbers 21:4-6 was the reference Paul had in mind. For their complaining, see Numbers 14 and 16.

This kind of sin is serious and God must judge it. Not only did some of these rebels immediately die (see 1 Cor. 11:29-31), but those who remained were not permitted to enter the Promised Land. They were saved from Egypt but were not privileged to claim their rich inheritance. Paul was not suggesting that his readers might lose their salvation, but he was afraid that some of them would be "castaways" (1 Cor. 9:27), disapproved of God and unable to receive any reward.

I heard about a pastor who gave a series of sermons on "The Sins of the Saints." One member of the church, apparently under conviction, disapproved of the series and told the pastor so. "After all," she said, "sin in the life of a Christian is different from sin in the life of an unsaved person."

"Yes, it is," the pastor replied. *"It's worse!"*

We must not think that because the Jews were under the Law that their sins were worse than ours and therefore dealt with more severely. Sin in the church today is far more serious, because we have Israel's example to learn from, and we are living "at the end of the ages." To sin against the Law is one thing; to sin against grace is quite something else.

Paul's third warning was that God can enable us to overcome temptation if we heed His Word (vv. 13-22). God permits us to be tempted because He knows how much we can take; and He always provides a way to escape if we will trust Him and take advantage of it. The believer who thinks he can stand, may fall; but the believer who flees will be able to stand.

Paul had already told his readers to "flee fornication" (1 Cor. 6:18); and now his warning is, "Flee from idolatry" (1 Cor. 10:14). He explained the reason why: the idol itself is nothing, but it can be used by Satan to lead you into sin. Idolatry is demonic (Deut. 32:17; Ps. 106:37). To sit at an idol's table could mean fellowship ("communion, partakers") with demons. Paul was again enforcing the important doctrine of separation from sin (2 Cor. 6:14–7:1).

He used the Lord's Supper as an illustration. When the believer partakes of the cup and loaf at the Lord's table, he is, in a spiritual way, having fellowship with the body and blood of Christ. By remembering Christ's death, the believer enters into a communion with the risen Lord. In 1 Corinthians 10:18, Paul pointed to the temple altar and sacrifices as another illustration of this truth. The application is clear: A believer cannot partake of the Lord's food (the Old Testament sacrifice, the New Testament supper) and the devil's food (the idol's table) without exposing himself to danger and provoking the Lord.

"Are we stronger than He?" (1 Cor. 10:22) is directed at the strong Christian who was sure he could enjoy his liberty in the pagan temple and not be harmed. "You may be stronger than your weaker brother," Paul intimated, "but you are not stronger than God!" It is dangerous to play with sin and tempt God.

Freedom Must Be Balanced by Responsibility (1 Cor. 10:23-33)

At no time did Paul deny the freedom of the mature Christian to enjoy his privileges in Christ. "All things are lawful"—BUT not everything is profitable, and some things lead to slavery (1 Cor. 6:12). "All things are profitable"—BUT some activities can cause your weaker brother to stumble (1 Cor. 8:11-13). In other words, it is a mark of maturity when we balance our freedom with responsibility; otherwise, it ceases to be freedom and becomes anarchy, lawlessness.

To begin with, we have a responsibility to our fellow Christians in the church (1 Cor. 10:23-30). We are responsible to build others up in the faith and to seek their advantage. Philippians 2:1-4 gives the same admonition. While we do have freedom in Christ, we are not free to harm another believer.

Paul applied this truth to the impending question of meat offered to idols. He had already warned against a believer *publicly* participating in pagan feasts (1 Cor. 8:9-13), so now he dealt with *private* meals. In 1 Corinthians 10:25-26, he instructed the believers to ask no questions about the meat purchased at the market for use in their own homes. After all, everything comes from God (he quoted Ps. 24:1) and all food is permissible to the believer (see Mark 7:14-23; Acts 10:9-16, 28; 1 Tim. 4:3-5). The mature believer can enjoy in his own home even meat sacrificed to idols. Even if meat purchased at the regular market originally came from the temple (which was often the case), he would not be harmed.

But what about those times when the believer is the guest in the home of an unbeliever? Paul handled that problem in 1 Corinthians 10:27-30. If the Christian feels disposed to go (Paul did not make this decision a matter of great import), he should eat whatever is set before him and ask no questions (see Luke 10:8; 1 Tim. 6:17). However, there may be present at the meal one of the weaker brothers or sisters who wants to avoid meat offered to idols, and who has done some investigating. If this weaker saint informs the stronger Christian that the meat indeed has been offered to idols, then the stronger saint must not eat it. If he did, he would cause the weaker believer to stumble and possibly to sin.

Paul anticipated the objections. "Why should I not enjoy food for which I give thanks? Why should my liberty be curtailed because of another person's weak conscience?" His reply introduced the second responsibility we have: *We are responsible to glorify God in all things* (1 Cor. 10:31). We cannot glorify God by causing another Christian to stumble. To be sure, our own conscience may be strong enough for us to participate in some activity and not be harmed. But we dare not use our freedom in Christ in any way that will injure a fellow Christian.

But there is a third responsibility that ties in with the first two: *We are responsible to seek to win the lost* (1 Cor. 10:32-33). We must not make it difficult either for Jews or Gentiles to trust the Lord, or for other members of the church to witness for the Lord. We must not live to seek our own benefit ("profit"), but also the benefit of others, that they might be saved.

When Paul wrote, "I please all men in all things" (1 Cor. 10:33), he was not suggesting that he was a compromiser or a man-pleaser (see Gal. 1:10). He was affirming the fact that his life and ministry were centered on helping others rather than on promoting himself and his own desires.

Before we leave this important section, we ought to note the fact that Paul probably appeared inconsistent to those who did not understand his principles of Christian living. At times, he would eat what the Gentiles were eating. At other times, he would eat only "kosher" food with the Jews. But instead of being inconsistent, he was actually living *consistently* by the principles he laid down in these chapters. A weather vane seems inconsistent, first pointing in one direction and then in another. But a weather vane is always consistent: it always points toward the direction where the wind is blowing. That is what makes it useful.

Are there some things that a mature Christian can do in the privacy of his own home that he would not do in public? Yes, provided they do not harm him personally and he does not tempt the Lord. I know a couple who, when their children were small, eliminated all games from their home that used either cards or dice. When their children were more mature, they were permitted to play those games.

As Christians, we *do* have freedom. This freedom was purchased for us by Jesus Christ, so it is very precious. Freedom comes from knowledge: "And ye shall know the truth, and the truth shall make you free" (John 8:32). The more we understand about the atom, for example, the more freedom we have to use it wisely. However, knowledge must be balanced by love; otherwise, it will tear down instead of build up.

The strong Christian not only has knowledge, but he also has experience. He can look back and see how the Lord has dealt with him through the years. But he must be careful, for experience must be balanced with caution. Take heed, lest you fall!

The strong Christian knows that he has this freedom, but he also knows that freedom involves responsibility. I have the freedom, for example, to take my car out of the garage and drive it on the highway; *but I must drive it responsibly.* I am not free to drive at any speed on my street; nor am I free to ignore the traffic signs along the way.

Out of these chapters come several "tests" we may apply to our own decisions and activities.

"All things are lawful," BUT—

1. Will they lead to freedom or slavery? (1 Cor. 6:12)
2. Will they make me a stumbling block or a stepping-stone? (1 Cor. 8:13)
3. Will they build me up or tear me down? (1 Cor. 10:23)
4. Will they only please me, or will they glorify Christ? (1 Cor. 10:31)
5. Will they help to win the lost to Christ or turn them away? (1 Cor. 10:33)

The way we use our freedom and relate to others indicates whether we are mature in Christ. Strong and weak Christians need to work together in love to edify one another and glorify Jesus Christ.

CHAPTER EIGHT
BE WISE ABOUT… PERSONAL PRIORITIES
1 Corinthians 9

This chapter deals with Paul's policy of financial support, and it appears to be an interruption to his discussion of "meats offered to idols." Actually, it is not an interruption; it is an illustration of the very principles that he presents in 1 Corinthians 8 and 10. Paul used himself as an illustration of the mature use of liberty: he was free to receive financial support from the Corinthian church, yet he set aside that right in order to achieve a higher goal.

Keep in mind that, for the most part, the Greeks despised manual labor. They had slaves to do manual labor so that the citizens could enjoy sports, philosophy, and leisure. The Jews, of course, magnified honest labor. Even the learned rabbis each practiced a trade, and they taught the people, "He who does not teach his son to work, teaches him to be a thief." Paul was trained as a tentmaker, a worker in leather.

In order to illustrate the Christian use of personal rights, Paul presented a twofold defense of his financial policy as a servant of Christ.

He Defended His Right to Receive Support (1 Cor. 9:1-14)

In this first half of the chapter, Paul proved that he had the right to receive financial support from the church at Corinth. He gave five arguments to support this contention.

His apostleship (vv. 1-6). The word *apostle* means "one sent under commission," and refers primarily to the 12 Apostles and Paul. These men had a special commission, along with the New Testament prophets, to lay the foundation of the church (Eph. 2:20). One of the qualifications for being an apostle was a personal experience of seeing the resurrected Christ (Acts 1:21-22). Paul saw the Lord when he was traveling to Damascus to arrest Christians (Acts 9:1-9). The Apostles were to be witnesses of Christ's resurrection (Acts 2:32; 3:15; 5:32; 10:39-43).

The Apostles also were given the ability to perform special signs and wonders to attest the message that they preached (Heb. 2:4). Paul had performed such miracles during his ministry in Corinth (2 Cor. 12:12). In fact, Paul considered the Corinthian church a very special "seal" of his ministry as an apostle. Corinth was a difficult city to minister in, and yet Paul accomplished a great work because of the Lord's enablement (see Acts 18:1-17).

Therefore, as an apostle, Paul had the right to receive support from the people to whom he ministered. (The word *power* is used six times in this chapter, and means "authority, right.") The apostle was the representative of Christ; he deserved to be welcomed and cared for. Paul was unmarried; but if he'd had a wife, she too would have had the right to be supported by the church. Peter was a married man (Mark 1:30), and his wife traveled with him. Paul had the same right, but he did not use it.

Paul also had the right to devote his full time to the ministry of the Word. He did not have to make tents. The other Apostles did not work to support themselves because they gave themselves completely to the ministry of the Word. However, both Paul and Barnabas labored with their own hands to support not only themselves, but also the men who labored with them.

Human experience (v. 7). Everyday experience teaches us that a workman deserves some reward for his labors. If a man is drafted to be a soldier, the government pays his wages and provides a certain amount of supplies for him. The man who plants a vineyard gets to eat the fruit, just as the shepherd or herdsman has the right to use the milk from the animals.

Perhaps in the "back of his mind," Paul was comparing the church to an army, a vineyard, and a flock. As an apostle, Paul was in the very front line of the battle. He had already compared the church at Corinth to a cultivated field (1 Cor. 3:6-9), and the Lord Himself had used the image of the vine and branches (John 15) as well as the flock (John 10). The lesson was clear: The Christian worker has the right to expect benefits for his labors. If this is true in the "secular" realm, it is also true in the spiritual realm.

The Old Testament Law (vv. 8-12). The Old Testament was the "Bible" of the early church, since the New Testament was in the process of being written. The first believers found guidance in the spiritual principles of the Law, even though they had been liberated from obeying the commandments of the Law. St. Augustine said, "The New is in the Old concealed; the Old is by the New revealed."

Paul quoted Deuteronomy 25:4 to prove his point. (He quoted this same verse when he wrote to Timothy and encouraged the church to pay their ministers adequately, 1 Tim. 5:17-18.) Since oxen cannot read, this verse was not written for them. Nor was it written only for the farmer who was using the labors of the ox. It would be cruel for the farmer to bind the mouth of the ox and prevent him from eating the available grain. After all, the ox was doing the work.

Paul correctly saw a spiritual principle in this commandment: The laborer has the right to share in the bounties. The ox had plowed the soil in preparation for sowing, and now he was treading out the grain that had been harvested. Paul had plowed the soil in Corinth.

He had seen a harvest from the seed he had planted. It was only right that he enjoyed some of the fruits of that harvest.

First Corinthians 9:11 enunciates a basic principle of the Christian life: If we receive *spiritual* blessings, we should in turn share *material* blessings. For example, the Jews gave spiritual blessings to the Gentiles; so the Gentiles had an obligation to share materially with the Jews (Rom. 15:25-27). Those who teach us the Word have the right to expect us to support them (Gal. 6:6-10).

We have reason to believe that Paul did accept financial support from other churches. The Philippian believers sent him two gifts when he went to Thessalonica (Phil. 4:15-16). "I robbed other churches, taking wages of them, to do you service," Paul reminded the Corinthians (2 Cor. 11:8). Apparently other ministers had accepted support at Corinth (1 Cor. 9:12), but Paul preferred to remain independent "lest we should hinder the Gospel of Christ." He wanted to be the best example possible to other believers (2 Thes. 3:6-9).

Old Testament practice (v. 13). The priests and Levites lived off of the sacrifices and offerings that were brought to the temple. The regulations governing their part of the offerings, and the special tithes they received also are found in Numbers 18:8-32; Leviticus 6:14–7:36; and 27:6-33. The application is clear: If the Old Testament ministers under Law were supported by the people to whom they ministered, should not God's servants who minister under grace also be supported?

The teaching of Jesus (v. 14). Paul was no doubt referring to our Lord's words recorded in Luke 10:7-8 and Matthew 10:10. The Corinthians did not have a copy of either Gospel to refer to, but the Lord's teaching would have been given to them as a part of the oral tradition shared by the Apostles. *The laborer is worthy of his hire* is a fundamental principle that the church dare not neglect.

Paul certainly proved his point. His five arguments proved conclusively that he had the right to expect the Corinthian believers to support him in his ministry when he was with them. Yet he had deliberately refused their support. Why? This he explained in the second part of his defense.

He Defended His Right to Refuse Support (1 Cor. 9:15-27)

Paul had the authority (right) to receive material support, but being a mature Christian, he balanced his authority with discipline. He did not have the right to give up his liberty in Christ, but he did have the liberty to give up his rights. Now we understand why he wrote as he did: he gave the Corinthian believers a living example of the very principles he was writing about. Should not the stronger believers in the church be able to set aside their rights for the sake of the weaker saints? Was eating meat more important than edifying the church?

Paul was talking about *priorities,* the things that are really important to us in our lives. It is unfortunate that some Christians have their personal priorities confused and, as a result, are hindering the work of Christ. If each believer were practicing Matthew 6:33, there would be plenty of money for missions, plenty of manpower for service, and the work of the Lord would prosper. But not every Christian is practicing Matthew 6:33.

A lady sent a gift to a ministry and explained that it was money she had saved because she had turned off the hot water tank in her house. She also did without a daily paper so that she might have more to give to the Lord's work. When she took a bath, she heated the water on the stove, "just the way we did it when we were kids." The Lord may not call all of us to this kind of sacrifice, but her example is worthy of respect.

Paul gave three reasons that explained why he had refused support from the Corinthian church.

For the Gospel's sake (vv. 15-18). Paul did not want to "hinder the Gospel of Christ" (1 Cor. 9:12). In that day, the Greek cities were filled with all kinds of itinerant teachers and preachers, most of whom were out to make money. Not only had Paul refused to use the kind of oratory and arguments that these teachers used (1 Cor. 2:1-5), but he also refused to accept money from those to whom he ministered. He wanted the message of the Gospel to be free from any obstacles or hindrances in the minds of lost sinners.

For that matter, when Paul added "neither have I written these things" (1 Cor. 9:15), he was making sure that his readers did not get the idea that he was "hinting" that they should support him!

Paul could not claim any credit for preaching the Gospel, because he had been called of God to preach. "Necessity is laid upon me; yea, woe is unto me, if I preach not the Gospel!" (1 Cor. 9:16) God had given him a divine stewardship ("dispensation"), and "it is required in stewards, that a man be found faithful" (1 Cor. 4:2). God would see to it that Paul would receive his wages (*reward*—same word translated "hire" in Luke 10:7).

What was Paul's reward? The joy of preaching the Gospel without charge! This meant that no man could accuse him of underhanded motives or methods as he shared the Good News of Jesus Christ.

It is unfortunate when the ministry of the Gospel is sometimes hindered by an overemphasis on money. The unsaved world is convinced that most preachers and missionaries are only involved in "religious rackets" to take money from innocent people. No doubt there are religious "racketeers" in the world today (1 Tim. 6:3-16), people who "use" religion to exploit others and control them. We would certainly not agree with their purposes or their practices. We must make sure that nothing we do in our own ministry gives the impression that we are of their number.

A wrong attitude toward money has hindered the Gospel from the earliest days of the church. Ananias and Sapphira loved money more than they loved the truth, and God killed them (Acts 5). Simon the magician thought he could buy the gift of the Spirit with money (Acts 8:18-24). His name is now in the dictionary. *Simony* is the practice of buying and selling religious offices and privileges.

For eighteen fruitful years, Dr. H.A. Ironside pastored the Moody Church in Chicago. I recall the first time I heard him announce an offering. He said, "We ask God's people to give generously. If you are not a believer in Jesus Christ, we do not ask you to give. We have a gift for you—eternal life through faith in Christ!" He made it clear that the offering was for believers, lest the unsaved in the congregation stumble over money and then reject the Gospel.

For the sinners' sake (vv. 19-23). What a paradox: free from all men, yet the servant of all men! "Ourselves your servants for Jesus' sake" (2 Cor. 4:5). Because he was free, Paul was able to serve others and to set aside his own rights for their sake.

It is unfortunate that the phrase "all things to all men" (1 Cor. 9:22) has been used and abused by the world and made to mean what Paul did not intend for it to mean. Paul was not a chameleon who changed his message and methods with each new situation. Nor was Paul a compromiser who adjusted his message to please his audience. He was an ambassador, not a politician!

Paul was a Jew who had a great burden for his own people (Rom. 9:1-3; 10:1). But his special calling was to minister to the Gentiles (Eph. 3:8). Whenever he went into a new city (and he always went where the Gospel had not yet been preached—Rom. 15:20), he headed straight for the synagogue, if there was one, and boldly shared the Gospel. If he was rejected by the Jews, then he turned to the Gentiles.

What separated Jews and Gentiles in that day? The Law and the covenants (Eph. 2:11-15). In his personal life, Paul so lived that he did not offend either the Jews or the Gentiles. He did not parade his liberty before the Jews, nor did he impose the Law on the Gentiles.

Was Paul behaving in an inconsistent manner? Of course not. He simply adapted his approach to different groups. When you read his sermons in the Book of Acts, you see this wise adaptation. When he preached to Jews, he started with the Old Testament patriarchs; but when he preached to Gentiles, he began with the God of Creation. Paul did not have a "stock sermon" for all occasions.

It is worth noting that our Lord followed the same approach. To the highborn Jew, Nicodemus, He talked about spiritual birth (John 3); but to the Samaritan woman, He spoke about living water (John 4). Jesus was flexible and adaptable, and Paul followed His example. Neither Jesus nor Paul had an inflexible "evangelistic formula" that was used in every situation.

It takes tact to have contact. When the people I witness to tell me about their experience of confirmation, I tell them that I too was confirmed. I express my appreciation for the pastor who taught me and prayed for me. Then I tell them, "A year after I was confirmed, I met Jesus Christ personally and was born again." A good witness tries to build bridges, not walls.

To immature people, Paul's lifestyle probably looked inconsistent. In reality, he was very consistent, for his overriding purpose was to win people to Jesus Christ. Consistency can become a very legalistic thing, and a man can become so bound by man-made rules and standards that he has no freedom to minister. He is like young David trying to battle in Saul's armor.

Paul had the right to eat whatever pleased him, but he gave up that right so that he might win the Jews. Paul revered the Law (see Rom. 7:12), but set that aside so that he might reach the lost Gentiles. He even identified himself with the legalistic weak Christians so that he might help them to grow. It was not compromise, but rather total abandonment to the higher law of love. Paul followed the example of the Saviour and humbled himself to become the servant of all.

For his own sake (vv. 24-27). Paul was fond of athletic images and used them often in his letters. The Corinthians would have been familiar with the Greek Olympic Games as well as their own local Isthmian Games. Knowing this, Paul used a metaphor very close to their experience.

An athlete must be disciplined if he is to win the prize. Discipline means giving up the good and the better for the best. The athlete must watch his diet as well as his hours. He must smile and say "No, thank you" when people offer him fattening desserts or invite him to late-night parties. There is nothing wrong with food or fun, but if they interfere with your highest goals, then they are hindrances and not helps.

The Christian does not run the race in order to get to heaven. He is in the race because he has been saved through faith in Jesus Christ. Only Greek citizens were allowed to participate in the games, and they had to obey the rules both in their training and in their performing. Any contestant found breaking the training rules was automatically disqualified.

In order to give up his rights and have the joy of winning lost souls, Paul had to discipline himself. That is the emphasis of this entire chapter: Authority (rights) must be balanced by discipline. If we want to serve the Lord and win His reward and approval, we must pay the price.

The word *castaway* (1 Cor. 9:27) is a technical word familiar to those who knew the Greek games. It means "disapproved, disqualified." At the Greek games, there was a herald who announced the rules of the contest, the names of the contestants, and the names and cities of the winners. He would also announce the names of any contestants who were disqualified.

Paul saw himself as both a "herald" and a "runner." He was concerned lest he get so busy trying to help others in the race that he ignore himself and find himself disqualified. Again, it was not a matter of losing personal salvation. (The disqualified Greek athlete did not lose his citizenship, only his opportunity to win a prize.) The whole emphasis is on *rewards,* and Paul did not want to lose his reward.

Only one runner could win the olive-wreath crown in the Greek games, but *every* believer can win an incorruptible crown when he stands before the Judgment Seat of Christ. This crown is given to those who discipline themselves for the sake of serving Christ and winning lost souls. They keep their bodies under control and keep their eyes on the goal.

In recent years, evangelical Christians have rediscovered the importance of personal discipline and the relationship between a disciplined body and a Spirit-filled life. We must, of course, avoid extremes. On the one hand, religious asceticism is unhealthy and of no value spiritually (Col. 2:18-23). But on the other hand, there is something to be said for disciplined eating, exercising, and resting, and a Spirit-directed balanced life. We smugly congratulate ourselves that we do not smoke or use alcohol, but what about our overeating and overweight? And many Christians cannot discipline their time so as to have a consistent devotional life or Bible-study program.

Paul had one great goal in life: to glorify the Lord by winning the lost and building up the saints. To reach this goal, he was willing to pay any price. *He was willing even to give up his personal rights!* He sacrificed immediate gains for eternal rewards, immediate pleasures for eternal joys.

CHAPTER NINE
BE WISE ABOUT... CHURCH ORDER
1 Corinthians 11

Since Paul had some negative things to say to the church later in this section, he opened it on a positive note by praising the church. Two matters in particular merited praise: the church remembered Paul and appreciated him, and the church was faithful to keep the teaching that had been given them. The word *ordinances* simply means "traditions," teachings that were passed on from one person to another (2 Tim. 2:2). The traditions of men should be avoided (Matt. 15:2-3; Col. 2:8), but the traditions that are given in the Word of God must be observed.

One of the biggest problems in the Corinthian church was disorder in the public meetings. Some of the women were assuming more freedom than they should have; there was disorder at the Lord's Supper; and there was confusion in the use of the spiritual gifts. The church had been greatly enriched with spiritual *gifts,* but they were sadly lacking in spiritual *graces.*

Paul could have tried to solve these problems by issuing apostolic edicts, but instead he patiently explained the spiritual principles that supported the teachings he had given the church. He founded his arguments on the Word of God.

Paul dealt with three particular areas of confusion in their public worship.

Women Praying and Prophesying (1 Cor. 11:3-16)

The Christian faith brought freedom and hope to women, children, and slaves. It taught that all people, regardless of race or sex, were equal before their Creator, and that all believers were one in Jesus Christ (Gal. 3:28). As we have noted before, the local church was perhaps the only fellowship in the Roman Empire that welcomed all people, regardless of nationality, social status, sex, or economic position.

It was to be expected that there would be some who would carry this newfound freedom to excess. A new movement always suffers more from its disciples than from its enemies, and this was true in Corinth. Some of the women flaunted their "freedom" in the public meetings by refusing to cover their heads when they participated.

Paul did not forbid the women to pray or to prophesy. (Prophesying is not quite the same as our "preaching" or "expounding the Word." A person with the gift of prophecy proclaimed God's message as it was given to him *immediately* by the Spirit. The modern preacher studies the Word and prepares his message.) While the New Testament does not seem to permit women elders (1 Tim. 3:2), women in the early church who had the gift of prophecy were allowed to exercise it. They were also permitted to pray in the public meetings. However, they were not permitted to usurp authority over the men (1 Tim. 2:11-15) or to judge the messages of the other prophets (1 Cor. 14:27-35). If they had any questions, they were to ask their husbands (or other men) outside of the church meeting.

Eastern society at that time was very jealous over its women. Except for the temple prostitutes, the women wore long hair and, in public, wore a covering over their heads. (Paul did not use the word *veil,* i.e., a covering over the face. The woman put the regular shawl over her head, and this covering symbolized her submission and purity.) For the Christian women in the church to appear in public without the covering, let alone to pray and share the Word, was both daring and blasphemous.

Paul sought to restore order by reminding the Corinthians that God had made a difference between men and women, that each had a proper place in God's economy. There were also appropriate customs that symbolized these relationships and reminded both men and women of their correct places in the divine scheme. Paul did not say, or even hint, that *difference* meant *inequality* or *inferiority.* If there is to be peace in the church (1 Cor. 15:33), then there must be some kind of order; and order of necessity involves rank. However, *rank* and *quality* are two different things. The captain has a higher rank than the private, but the private may be a better man.

God's order in the church is based on three fundamentals that Paul considered to be self-evident.

Redemption (vv. 3-7). There is a definite order of "headship" in the church: the Father is the Head over Christ, Christ is the Head of the man, and the man is the head of the woman. Some interpret *head* to mean "origin," but this would mean that the Father originated Christ—something we cannot accept. In His redemptive ministry, the Son was subject to the Father even though He is equal to the Father (John 10:30; 14:28). Likewise, the woman is subject to the man even though in Christ she is equal to the man (1 Cor. 3:21-23; Gal. 3:28; Eph. 5:21-33).

Keep in mind that Paul was writing about the relationship *within the local assembly,* not in the world at large. It is God's plan that in the home and in the local church, the men should exercise headship under the authority of Jesus Christ.

The important fact is this: both women and men must honor the Lord by respecting the symbols of this headship—hair and the head-covering. Whenever a woman prays or prophesies in the assembly, she must have long hair and must wear a covering. The man should have short hair and not wear any covering. (This would be a change for Paul, for devout Jewish men always wore a cap when they prayed.) The man honors his Head (Christ) by being uncovered, while the woman honors her head (the man) by being covered. She is showing her submission both to God and to the man.

The Corinthian women who appeared in the assembly without the head-covering were actually putting themselves on the low level of the temple prostitutes. The prostitutes wore their hair very short, and they did not wear a head-covering in public. Their hairstyle and manner announced to others just what they were and what they were offering. "If you are going to abandon the covering," wrote Paul, "then why not go all the way and cut your hair?"

In Jewish law, a woman proved guilty of adultery had her hair cut off (Num. 5:11-31). Paul used two different words in 1 Corinthians 11:5-6: *shaved* means exactly that, all the hair shaved off; *shorn* means "cut short." Either one would be a disgrace to a woman.

Both man and woman are made in the image of God and for the glory of God; but since the woman was made from the man (Gen. 2:18-25), she is also the "glory of the man." She glorifies God and brings glory to the man by submitting to God's order and keeping her head covered in public worship. Thus, Paul tied together both local custom and biblical truth, the one pointing to the other.

Creation (vv. 8-12). We have already touched briefly on this truth. God's order is based on the fact that man was created first (1 Tim. 2:13), and that the woman was created for the man. Again, priority does not imply inferiority; for Paul made it clear in 1 Corinthians 11:11-12 that there is *partnership* as well as headship in God's creation. The man and the woman are spiritually one in the Lord (Gal. 3:28) and one cannot do without the other. Furthermore, the woman may have come from the man at the beginning, but today, it is the man who is born of the woman. Man and woman belong to each other and need each other.

Why did Paul bring up the angels in 1 Corinthians 11:10? He was arguing from the facts of Creation, and the angels were a part of that Creation. The angels also know their place and show respect when they worship God, for they cover their faces (Isa. 6:2). Finally, in some special way, the angels share in the public worship of the church and learn from the church (Eph. 3:10; 1 Peter 1:12). Public worship is a serious thing, for the angels are present; and we ought to conduct ourselves *as if we were in heaven.*

Nature (vv. 13-16). In a general way, it is true that nature gives women longer hair and men shorter hair. The Romans, Greeks, and Jews (except for the Nazarites) pretty much followed this custom. Nowhere does the Bible tell us how long our hair should be. It simply states that there ought to be a noticeable difference between the length of the men's hair and the women's hair so that there be no confusion of the sexes. (This principle eliminates the so-called "unisex" styles.) It is shameful for the man to look like a woman or the woman to look like a man.

The woman's long hair is her glory, and it is given to her "*instead of* a covering" (literal translation). In other words, if local custom does not dictate a head-covering, her long hair can be that covering. I do not think that Paul meant for all women in every culture to wear a shawl for a head-covering; but he did expect them to use their long hair as a covering and as a symbol of their submission to God's order. This is something that every woman can do.

In my ministry in different parts of the world, I have noticed that the basic principle of headship applies in every culture; but the means of demonstrating it differs from place to place. The important thing is the submission of the heart to the Lord and the public manifestation of obedience to God's order.

Selfishness at the "Love Feasts" (1 Cor. 11:17-22)

Since the beginning of the church, it was customary for the believers to eat together (Acts 2:42, 46). It was an opportunity for fellowship and for sharing with those who were less privileged. No doubt they climaxed this meal by observing the Lord's Supper. They called this meal "the love feast" since its main emphasis was showing love for the saints by sharing with one another.

The "agape feast" (from the Greek word for "love") was part of the worship at Corinth, but some serious abuses had crept in. As a result, the love feasts were doing more harm than good to the church. For one thing, there were various cliques in the church and people ate with their own "crowd" instead of fellowshipping with the whole church family. While Paul condemned this selfish practice, he did take a positive view of the results: at least God would use this to reveal those who were true believers.

Another fault was selfishness: the rich people brought a great deal of food for themselves while the poorer members went hungry. The original idea of the "agape feast" was sharing, but that idea had been lost. Some of the members were even getting drunk. It is likely that the weekly "agape feast" was the only decent meal some of the poorer members regularly had; and to be treated so scornfully by the richer members not only hurt their stomachs, but also their pride.

Of course, the divisions at the dinner were but evidence of the deeper problems in the church. The Corinthians thought they were advanced believers, when in reality they were but little children. Paul did not suggest that they abandon the feast, but rather that they restore its proper meaning. "Let the rich eat at home if they are hungry. When you abuse believers who are less fortunate than you are, then you are actually despising the church!" The "agape feast" should have been an opportunity for edification, but they were using it as a time for embarrassment.

I recall an incident at a Sunday School picnic when I was just a teenager. The person in charge of the games set up a relay that involved various people throwing eggs to each other as they backed farther and farther apart. Of course, the farther the teams went from each other, the harder the participants had to throw the eggs, and the results were hilarious.

However, some of us noticed two Sunday School children watching the eggs with great fascination. They came from a poor family that probably rarely ate eggs because they could not afford them. The little girl went to the lady leading the games and asked, "If there are any eggs left over, can my brother and I take them home?" Wisely, the lady stopped the game before it was really over, awarded the prizes, and gave all the eggs to the two children. She knew that it was wrong for some of the saints to have a good time at the expense of others.

A drinking party is hardly the best way to prepare for the Lord's Supper. Scorning others is certainly not the way to remember the Saviour who died for all sinners, rich and poor. How important it is that we prepare our hearts when we come to the Lord's Table!

Abuses at the Lord's Supper (1 Cor. 11:23-34)

Evangelical churches recognize two ordinances established by Jesus Christ for His people to observe: baptism and the Lord's Supper. (The Supper is also called *The Communion* as in 1 Corinthians 10:16, and *The Eucharist* which means "the giving of thanks.") Jesus Christ took the cup and the loaf—the ingredients of a common meal in that day—and transformed them into a meaningful spiritual experience for believers. However, the value of the experience depends on the condition of the hearts of those who participate; and this was the problem at Corinth.

It is a serious thing to come to the Communion with an unprepared heart. It is also a serious thing to receive the Supper in a careless manner. Because the Corinthians had been sinning in their observing of the Lord's Supper, God had disciplined them. "For this cause many are weak and sickly among you, and many sleep [have died]" (1 Cor. 11:30).

The Lord's Supper gives us an opportunity for spiritual growth and blessings if we approach it in the right attitude. What, then, must we do if the Supper is to bring blessing and not chastening?

First, we should look back (vv. 23-26a). The broken bread reminds us of Christ's body, given for us; and the cup reminds us of His shed blood. It is a remarkable thing that Jesus wants His followers to remember His *death.* Most of us try to forget how those we love died, but Jesus wants us to remember how He died. Why? Because everything we have as Christians centers in that death.

We must remember *that* He died, because this is a part of the Gospel message: "Christ died . . . and was buried" (1 Cor. 15:3-4). It is not the life of our Lord, or His teachings, that will save sinners—but His death. Therefore, we also remember *why* He died: Christ died for our sins; He was our substitute (Isa. 53:6; 1 Peter 2:24), paying the debt that we could not pay.

We should also remember *how* He died: willingly, meekly, showing forth His love for us (Rom. 5:8). He gave His body into the hands of wicked men, and He bore on His body the sins of the world.

However, this "remembering" is not simply the recalling of historical facts. It is a participation in spiritual realities. At the Lord's Table, we do not walk around a monument and admire it. We have fellowship with a living Saviour as our hearts reach out by faith.

Second, we should look ahead (v. 26b). We observe the Supper "till He comes." The return of Jesus Christ is the blessed hope of the church and the individual Christian. Jesus not only died for us, but He arose again and ascended to heaven; and one day He shall return to take us to heaven. Today, we are not all that we should be; but when we see Him, "we shall be like Him" (1 John 3:2).

Third, we should look within (vv. 27-28, 31-32). Paul did not say that we had to be *worthy* to partake of the Supper, but only that we should partake *in a worthy manner.* At a Communion service in Scotland, the pastor noted that a woman in the congregation did not accept the bread and cup from the elder, but instead sat weeping. The pastor left the table and went to her side and said, "Take it, my dear, *it's for sinners!*" And, indeed, it is; but sinners saved by God's grace must not treat the Supper in a sinful manner.

If we are to participate in a worthy manner, we must examine our own hearts, judge our sins, and confess them to the Lord. To come to the table with unconfessed sin in our lives is to be guilty of Christ's body and blood, for it was sin that nailed Him to the cross. If we will not judge our own sins, then God will judge us and chasten us until we do confess and forsake our sins.

The Corinthians neglected to examine themselves, but they were experts at examining everybody else. When the church gathers together, we must be careful not to become "religious detectives" who watch others, but who fail to acknowledge our own sins. If we eat and drink in an unworthy manner, we eat and drink judgment (chastening) to ourselves, and that is nothing to take lightly.

Chastening is God's loving way of dealing with His sons and daughters to encourage them to mature (Heb. 12:1-11). It is not a judge condemning a criminal, but a loving Father punishing His disobedient (and perhaps stubborn) children. Chastening proves God's love for us, and chastening can, if we cooperate, perfect God's life in us.

Finally, we should look around (vv. 33-34). We should not look around in order to criticize other believers, but in order to discern the Lord's body (1 Cor. 11:29). This perhaps has a dual meaning: we should discern His body in the loaf, but also in the church around us—for the church is the body of Christ. "For we being many are one bread, and one body" (1 Cor. 10:17). The Supper should be a demonstration of the unity of the church—but there was not much unity in the Corinthian church. In fact, their celebration of the Lord's Supper was only a demonstration of their disunity.

The Lord's Supper is a family meal, and the Lord of the family desires that His children love one another and care for one another. It is impossible for a true Christian to get closer to his Lord while at the same time he is separated from his fellow believers. How can we remember the Lord's death and not love one another? "Beloved, if God so loved us, we ought also to love one another" (1 John 4:11).

No one ought to come to the table who is not a true believer. Nor should a true believer come to the table if his heart is not right with God and with his fellow Christians. This is why many churches have a time of spiritual preparation before they observe the Lord's Supper, lest any of the participants bring chastening on themselves. I recall one church member who approached me and shared with me a personal defeat that had not only hurt him spiritually, but had been "advertised" by others and was about to bring reproach on him and the church.

"What can I do to make this right?" he asked, convincing me that he had indeed judged the sin and confessed it. I reminded him that the next week we were going to observe the Lord's Supper, and I suggested that he ask the Lord for direction. The evening of the Supper, I opened the service in a way I had not done before. "Is there anyone here who has anything to share with the church?" I asked, and my repentant friend stood to his feet and walked forward, meeting me at the table. In a quiet, concise manner, he admitted that he had sinned, and he asked the church's forgiveness. We felt a wave of Spirit-given love sweep over the congregation and people began to weep openly. At that observance of the Supper, we truly discerned the Lord's body.

The Communion is not supposed to be a time of "spiritual autopsy" and grief, even though confession of sin is important. It should be a time of thanksgiving and joyful anticipation of seeing the Lord! Jesus gave thanks, even though He was about to suffer and die. Let us give thanks also.

CHAPTER TEN
BE WISE ABOUT... THE CHURCH BODY
1 Corinthians 12–13

One of the marks of an individual's maturity is a growing understanding of, and appreciation for, his own body. There is a parallel in the spiritual life: as we mature in Christ, we gain a better understanding of the church, which is Christ's body. The emphasis in recent years on "body life" has been a good one. It has helped to counteract the wrong emphasis on "individual Christianity" that can lead to isolation from the local church.

Of course, the image of the "body" is not the only one Paul used in discussing the church, and we must be careful not to press it too far. The church is also a family, an army, a temple, and even a bride; and each image has important lessons to teach us. However, in three of his letters, Paul gave emphasis to the church as a body; and, in each of these passages, he brought out the same three important truths: unity, diversity, and maturity. The chart below makes this clear.

It is impossible to discuss the body without also discussing the ministry of the Holy Spirit.

	Unity	*Diversity*	*Maturity*
1 Corinthians	12:1-13	12:14-31	13:1-13
Romans	12:1-5	12:6-8	12:9-21
Ephesians	4:1-6	4:7-12	4:13-16

It was the Spirit who gave birth to the body at Pentecost and who ministers in and through the body. In the Corinthian church, unfortunately, the members were grieving the Holy Spirit by the carnal ways in which they were using spiritual gifts. They were like children with toys instead of adults with valuable tools, and they needed to mature.

Unity: The Gift of the Spirit (1 Cor. 12:1-13)

Since there was division in the Corinthian church, Paul began with an emphasis on the oneness of the church. He pointed out four wonderful bonds of spiritual unity.

We confess the same Lord (vv. 1-3). Paul contrasted their experience as unconverted idolaters with their present experience as Christians. They had worshiped dead idols, but now they belonged to the living God. Their idols never spoke to them, but God spoke to them by His Spirit, and He even spoke *through* them in the gift of prophecy. When they were lost, they were under the control of the demons (1 Cor. 10:20) and were led astray ("carried away," 1 Cor. 12:2). But now the Spirit of God lived in them and directed them.

It is only through the Spirit that a person can *honestly* say, "Jesus is Lord." A sneering sinner may mouth the words, but he is not giving a true confession. (Perhaps Paul was referring to things they had said when influenced by the demons prior to conversion.) It is important to note that the believer is always in control of himself when the Holy Spirit is at work (1 Cor. 14:32) because Jesus Christ *the Lord* is in charge. Any so-called "Spirit manifestation" that robs a person of self-control is not of God; for "the fruit of the Spirit is . . . self-control" (Gal. 5:22-23, NASB).

If Jesus Christ truly is Lord in our lives, then there should be unity in the church. Division and dissension among God's people only weakens their united testimony to a lost world (John 17:20-21).

We depend on the same God (vv. 4-6). There is a trinitarian emphasis here: "the same Spirit . . . the same Lord . . . the same God." We individually may have different gifts, ministries, and ways of working, but "it is God which worketh in you both to will and to do of His good pleasure" (Phil. 2:13). The source of the gift is God; the sphere for administering the gift is from God; and the energy to use the gift is from God. Why, then, glorify men?

Why compete with one another?

We minister to the same body (vv. 7-11). The gifts are given for the good of the whole church. They are not for individual enjoyment, but for corporate employment. The Corinthians especially needed this reminder, because they were using their spiritual gifts selfishly to promote themselves and not to prosper the church. When we accept our gifts with humility, then we use them to promote harmony, and this helps the whole church.

The various gifts are named in 1 Corinthians 12:8-10 and 28, and also in Ephesians 4:11 and Romans 12:6-8. When you combine the lists, you end up with nineteen different gifts and offices. Since the listing in Romans is not identical with the listing in 1 Corinthians, we may assume that Paul was not attempting to exhaust the subject in either passage. While the gifts named are adequate for the ministry of the church, God is not limited to these lists. He may give other gifts as He pleases.

We have already discussed *apostles* (1 Cor. 9:1-6). *Prophets* were New Testament spokesmen for God whose messages came immediately from God by the Spirit. Their ministry was to edify, encourage, and comfort (1 Cor. 14:3). Their messages were tested by the listeners to determine whether they were truly from God (1 Cor. 14:29; 1 Thes. 5:19-21). Ephesians 2:20 makes it clear that apostles and prophets worked together to lay the foundation of the church, and we may assume that they were no longer needed once that foundation was completed.

Teachers (also pastor-teacher) instructed converts in the doctrinal truths of the Christian life. They taught from the Word and from the teachings of the Apostles (tradition). Unlike the prophets, they did not get their messages immediately by the Spirit, though the Spirit helped them in their teaching. James 3:1 indicates that this is a serious calling.

The *evangelist* majored on sharing the Good News of salvation with the lost. All ministers should do the work of an evangelist (2 Tim. 4:5) and seek to win souls, but some men have been given evangelism as a special calling.

In the early church, *miracles* were a part of the credentials of God's servants (Heb. 2:1-4). In fact, miracles, healings, and tongues all belong to what theologians call "the sign gifts" and belonged in a special way to the infancy of the church. The Book of Acts, as well as church history, indicates that these miraculous gifts passed off the scene.

Helps and *governments* have to do with the serving of others and the guiding of the church. Without spiritual leadership, the church flounders. *Ministry* (Rom. 12:7) and *ruling* belong to this same category. In my three pastorates, I was grateful for people with the gifts of helps and leadership.

There were several "speaking gifts": *tongues* and the *interpretation of tongues* (about which more will be said later), the *word of wisdom* and the *word of knowledge* (the ability to understand and apply God's truth to a definite situation), and *exhortation* (encouragement, rebuke if necessary).

Giving and *showing mercy* relate to sharing material aid with those in need, as well as supporting God's servants in ministry. The gift of *faith* has to do with believing God for what He wants to accomplish in the church's ministry, that He will lead and provide. The *discerning of spirits* was important in the early church since Satan tried to counterfeit the work of God and the Word of God. Today, the Spirit especially uses the written Word to give us discernment (1 John 2:18-24; 4:1-6). Since there are no prophets in the church today, we need not worry about false prophets; but we do have to beware of false *teachers* (2 Peter 2:1).

Some students have categorized the various gifts as the speaking gifts, the sign gifts, and the serving gifts. However, we should not be so fascinated by the individual gifts that we forget the main reason why Paul listed them: to remind us that they unite us in our ministries to the one body. The Holy Spirit bestows these gifts "as He will" (1 Cor. 12:11), not as we will. No Christian should complain about his or her gifts, nor should any believer boast about his or her gifts. We are many members in one body, ministering to each other.

We have experienced the same baptism (vv. 12-13). It is unfortunate that the term "baptism of the Spirit" has been divorced from its original New Testament meaning. God has spoken to us in Spirit-given *words* which we must not confuse (1 Cor. 2:12-13). The baptism of the Spirit occurs at conversion when the Spirit enters the believing sinner, gives him new life, and makes his body the temple of God. *All* believers have experienced this once-for-all baptism (1 Cor. 12:13). Nowhere does the Scripture command us to *seek* this baptism, because we have already experienced it and it need not be repeated.

The "filling of the Spirit" (Eph. 5:18ff) has to do with the Spirit's control of our lives. (In Scripture, to be *filled by* something means "to be controlled by.") We are *commanded* to be filled, and we can be if we yield all to Christ and ask Him for the Spirit's filling. This is a repeated experience, for we constantly need to be filled with spiritual power if we are to glorify Christ. To be baptized by the Spirit means that we belong to *Christ's body.* To be filled with the Spirit means that *our bodies* belong to Christ.

The evidence of the Spirit's baptism at conversion is the witness of the Spirit within (Rom. 8:14-16). It is not "speaking in tongues." *All* of the believers in the Corinthian assembly had been baptized by the Spirit, but not all of them spoke in tongues (1 Cor. 12:30). The evidences of the Spirit's filling are: power for witnessing (Acts 1:8), joyfulness and submission (Eph. 5:19ff), Christlikeness (Gal. 5:22-26), and a growing understanding of the Word (John 16:12-15).

Because of the gift of the Spirit, which is received at conversion, we are all members of the body of Christ. Race, social status, wealth, or even sex (Gal. 3:28) are neither advantages nor handicaps as we fellowship and serve the Lord.

Diversity: The Gifts of the Spirit (1 Cor. 12:14-31)

Unity without diversity would produce uniformity, and uniformity tends to produce death. Life is a balance between unity and diversity. As a human body weakens, its "systems" slow down and everything tends to become uniform. The ultimate, of course, is that the body itself turns to dust.

This helps to explain why some churches (and other Christian ministries) have weakened and died: there was not sufficient diversity to keep unity from becoming uniformity. Dr. Vance Havner has expressed it, "First there is a man, then a movement, then a machine, and then a monument." Many ministries that began as a protest against "dead orthodoxy" became dead themselves; because in their desire to remain pure and doctrinally sound, they stifled creativity and new ideas.

However, if diversity is not kept under control, it could destroy unity; and then you have anarchy. We shall discover in 1 Corinthians 13 that it is *maturity* that balances unity and diversity. The tension in the body between individual members and the total organism can only be solved by maturity.

Using the human body as his illustration, Paul explained three important facts about diversity in the body of Christ. Why are there different members?

The body needs different functions if it is to live, grow, and serve (vv. 14-20). No member should compare or contrast itself with any other member, because each one is different and each one is important. I suppose I could learn to walk on my hands, but I prefer to use my feet, even though I have not yet learned to type or to eat with my feet. The ear cannot see and the eye cannot hear, yet each organ has an important ministry. And have you ever tried to smell through your ears?

There is a tendency today for some people to magnify the "sensational" gifts. Some believers feel very guilty because they possess gifts that do not put them into the limelight. It is this attitude that Paul opposed and refuted in this paragraph. Diversity does not suggest inferiority. Are we to believe that the sovereign Lord made a mistake when He bestowed the gifts?

The members promote unity as they discover their dependence on one another (vv. 21-26). Diversity in the body is an evidence of the wisdom of God. Each member needs the other members, and no member can afford to become independent. When a part of the human body becomes independent, you have a serious problem that could lead to sickness and even death. In a healthy human body, the various members cooperate with each other and even compensate for each other when a crisis occurs. The instant any part of the body says to any other part, "I don't need you!" it begins to weaken and die and create problems for the whole body.

A famous preacher was speaking at a ministers' meeting, and he took time before and after the meeting to shake hands with the pastors and chat with them. A friend asked him, "Why take time for a group of men you may never see again?" The world-renowned preacher smiled and said, "Well, I may be where I am because of them! Anyway, if I didn't need them on the way up, I might need them on the way down!" No Christian servant can say to any other servant, "My ministry can get along without you!"

Paul may be referring to the private parts of the body in 1 Corinthians 12:23-24. If so, then to "bestow honor" on them refers to the use of attractive clothing. The more beautiful parts of the body need no special help.

God's desire is that there be no division ("schism") in the church. Diversity leads to disunity when the members compete with one another; but diversity leads to unity when the members care for one another. How do the members care for each other? By each one functioning according to God's will and helping the other members to function. If one member suffers, it affects every member. If one member is healthy, it helps the others to be strong.

Diversity of members fulfills the will of God in the body (vv. 27-31). It is God who bestows the gifts and assigns the offices. He has a perfect plan, not only for the church as a whole, but also for each local congregation. We have no reason to believe that each congregation in the New Testament possessed all of the gifts. The church at Corinth was an especially gifted assembly (1 Cor. 1:4-7; 2 Cor. 8:7). However, God gives to each congregation just the gifts it needs when they are needed.

In this paragraph, Paul pointed out that there is a "priority list" for the gifts, that some have more significance than others. But this fact does not contradict the lesson already shared—that each gift is important and each individual believer is important. Even in the human body, there are some parts that we can do without, even though their absence might handicap us a bit.

The Apostles and prophets, of course, appeared first on the scene because they had a foundational ministry (Eph. 2:20). Teachers were needed to help establish believers in the faith. The other gifts were needed from time to time to help individual believers and to build the church.

The construction of the Greek in 1 Corinthians 12:29-30 demands *no* as the answer to each of these questions. No individual believer possesses all the spiritual gifts. Each believer has the gift (or gifts) assigned to him by the Lord and needed at that time.

The word translated *best* in 1 Corinthians 12:31 simply means "greater." Some spiritual gifts are greater in significance than others, and it is proper for the believer to desire these gifts (1 Cor. 14:1). Paul put a high value on prophecy, but the Corinthians valued the gift of tongues. Paul put tongues at the end of the list.

Unity and diversity must be balanced by maturity, and that maturity comes with love. It is not enough to have the *gift* of the Spirit and *gifts* from the Spirit. We must also have the *graces* of the Spirit as we use our gifts to serve one another.

Maturity: The Graces of the Spirit (1 Cor. 13:1-13)

It was Jonathan Swift, the satirical author of *Gulliver's Travels,* who said, "We have just enough religion to make us hate, but not enough to make us love one another." Spiritual gifts, no matter how exciting and wonderful, are useless and even destructive if they are not ministered in love. In all three of the "body" passages in Paul's letters, there is an emphasis on love. The main evidence of maturity in the Christian life is a growing love for God and for God's people, as well as a love for lost souls. It has well been said that love is the "circulatory system" of the body of Christ.

Few chapters in the Bible have suffered more misinterpretation and misapplication than 1 Corinthians 13. Divorced from its context, it becomes "a hymn to love" or a sentimental sermon on Christian brotherhood. Many people fail to see that Paul was still dealing with the Corinthians' problems when he wrote these words: the abuse of the gift of tongues, division in the church, envy of others' gifts, selfishness (remember the lawsuits?), impatience with one another in the public meetings, and behavior that was disgracing the Lord.

The only way spiritual gifts can be used creatively is when Christians are motivated by love. Paul explained three characteristics of Christian love that show why it is so important in ministry.

Love is enriching (vv. 1-3). Paul named five spiritual gifts: tongues, prophecy, knowledge, faith, and giving (sacrifice). He pointed out that, without love, the exercise of these gifts is *nothing.* Tongues apart from love is just a lot of noise! It is love that enriches the gift and that gives it value. Ministry without love cheapens both the minister and those who are touched by it; but ministry with love enriches the whole church. "Speaking the truth in love" (Eph. 4:15).

Christians are "taught of God to love one another" (1 Thes. 4:9). God the Father taught us to love by sending His Son (1 John 4:19), and God the Son taught us to love by giving His life and by commanding us to love each other (John 13:34-35). The Holy Spirit teaches us to love one another by pouring out God's love in our hearts (Rom. 5:5). The most important lesson in the school of faith is to love one another. Love enriches all that it touches.

Love is edifying (vv. 4-7). "Knowledge puffeth up, but love edifieth [builds up]" (1 Cor. 8:1). The purpose of spiritual gifts is the edification of the church (1 Cor. 12:7; 14:3, 5, 12, 17, 26). This means we must not think of ourselves, but of others; and this demands love.

The Corinthians were impatient in the public meetings (1 Cor. 14:29-32), but love would make them long-suffering. They were envying each other's gifts, but love would remove that envy. They were "puffed up" with pride (1 Cor. 4:6, 18-19; 5:2), but love would remove pride and self-vaunting and replace it with a desire to promote others. "Be kindly affectioned one to another with brotherly love, in honor preferring one another" (Rom. 12:10).

At the "love feast" and the Lord's Table, the Corinthians were behaving in a very unseemly manner. If they had known the meaning of real love, they would have behaved themselves in a manner pleasing to the Lord. They were even suing one another! But love "seeketh not [its] own, is not easily provoked, thinketh no evil" (1 Cor. 13:5). The phrase *thinketh no evil* means "does not keep any record of wrongs." One of the most miserable men I ever met was a professed Christian who actually kept in a notebook a list of the wrongs he felt others had committed against him. Forgiveness means that we wipe the record clean and never hold things against people (Eph. 4:26, 32).

Love does not rejoice in iniquity, yet the Corinthians were boasting about sin in their church (1 Cor. 5). Love "shall cover the multitude of sins" (1 Peter 4:8). Like Noah's sons, we should seek to hide the sins of others, and then help them make things right (Gen. 9:20-23).

Read 1 Corinthians 13:4-7 carefully and compare this with the fruit of the Spirit listed in Galatians 5:22-23. You will see that all of the characteristics of love show up in that fruit. This is why love edifies: it releases the power of the Spirit in our lives and churches.

Love is enduring (vv. 8-13). Prophecy, knowledge, and tongues were not permanent gifts. (*Knowledge* does not mean "education," but the immediate imparting of spiritual truth to the mind.) These three gifts went together. God would impart knowledge to the prophet, and he would give the message in a tongue. Then an interpreter (sometimes the prophet himself) would explain the message. These were gifts that some of the Corinthians prized, especially the gift of tongues.

These gifts will fail (be abolished) and cease, but love will endure forever; for "God is love" (1 John 4:8, 16). The Corinthians were like children playing with toys that would one day disappear. You expect a child to think, understand, and speak like a child; but you also expect the child to mature and start thinking and speaking like an adult. The day comes when he must "put away childish things" (1 Cor. 13:11).

In the New Testament (which at that time was not completed) we have a complete revelation, but our understanding of it is partial. (Review 1 Cor. 8:1-3 if you think otherwise.) There is a maturing process for the church as a whole (Eph. 4:11-16) and also for the individual believer (1 Cor. 14:20; 2 Peter 3:18). We will not be fully completed until Jesus returns, but we ought to be growing and maturing now. Children live for the temporary; adults live for the permanent. Love is enduring, and what it produces will endure.

Note that all three of the Christian graces will endure, even though "faith will become sight and hope will be fulfilled." But the greatest of these graces is love; because when you love someone, you will trust him and will always be anticipating new joys. Faith, hope, and love go together, but it is love that energizes faith and hope.

Unfortunately, some of the emphasis today on the Holy Spirit has not been *holy* (because it has ignored Scripture) and has not been *spiritual* (because it has appealed to the carnal nature). We must not tell other believers what gifts they should have or how they can obtain them. This matter is in the sovereign will of God. We must not minimize gifts, but neither should we neglect the *graces* of the Spirit. In my itinerant ministry, I have run across too many local church problems created by people who were zealous for the gifts, but careless of the graces.

Unity—diversity—maturity; and maturity comes through love.

CHAPTER ELEVEN
BE WISE ABOUT . . . USING SPIRITUAL GIFTS
1 Corinthians 14

Paul had discussed the gift of the Spirit, the gifts of the Spirit, and the graces of the Spirit; and now he concluded this section by explaining the government of the Spirit in the public worship services of the church. Apparently there was a tendency for some of the Corinthians to lose control of themselves as they exercised their gifts, and Paul had to remind them of the fundamental principles that ought to govern the public meetings of the church. There are three principles: edification, understanding, and order.

Edification (1 Cor. 14:1-5, 26b)

This was one of Paul's favorite words, borrowed, of course, from architecture. *To edify* means "to build up." This concept is not alien to the "body" image of the church; even today, we speak about "bodybuilding exercises." There is an overlapping of images here, for the body of Christ is also the temple of the living God. Paul's choice of the word *edify* was a wise one.

The mistake the Corinthians were making was to emphasize their own personal edification to the neglect of the church. They wanted to build themselves up, but they did not want to build up their fellow believers. This attitude, of course, not only hurt the other Christians, but it also hurt the believers who were practicing it. After all, if we are all members of the same body, the way we relate to the other members must ultimately affect us personally. "The eye cannot say unto the hand, I have no need of thee" (1 Cor. 12:21). If one member of the body is weak or infected, it will affect the other members.

Paul detected that the church was neglecting prophecy and giving a wrong emphasis to tongues. We must not think of a New Testament prophet as a person who foretold the future, for even the Old Testament prophets did more than that. Prophets received God's message immediately, through the Holy Spirit, and communicated that message to the church, usually in a tongue, but not always. Prophecy was not the same as our modern-day "preaching," because today's preachers study the Bible and prepare their messages. No preacher today should claim that he has immediate inspiration from God.

Paul explained the supreme value of prophecy over tongues by contrasting the two gifts.

Prophecy speaks to men, tongues to God (vv. 1-3). "If you are zealous for spiritual gifts, at least desire the best gifts," was Paul's counsel. Prophecy was best because it built up the church. It gave the listeners encouragement and comfort—something that everybody needs.

It is unfortunate that our translators inserted *unknown* in 1 Corinthians 14:2, because the New Testament knows nothing of an "unknown tongue." From the very beginning of the church, tongues were *known* languages, recognized by the listeners (Acts 2:4, 6, 8, 11). The tongue would be unknown *to the speaker* and to the listeners, but it was not unknown in the world (1 Cor. 14:10-11, 21).

It is also unfortunate that people have the idea that tongues were used to preach the Gospel to the lost. Quite the contrary was true: Paul was afraid that the excessive tongues-speaking in the church would convince the lost that the Christians were crazy! (1 Cor. 14:23) At Pentecost, the believers extolled "the wonderful works of God," but Peter preached the Gospel in the Aramaic language his listeners could all understand.

The believer who speaks in a tongue speaks to God in praise and worship; but the believer who prophesies shares the Word with the church and helps those who listen. This leads to the second contrast.

Prophecy edifies the church, tongues edify only the speaker (vv. 4-5). Paul did not deny the value of tongues to the speaker, but he did place a greater value on building up the church. "Greater is he that prophesieth than he that speaketh with tongues" (1 Cor. 14:5). Unless the tongues are interpreted (1 Cor. 12:10, 30), the message can do the church no good. Paul pointed out that an interpreter must be present before the gift of tongues may be exercised (1 Cor. 14:28).

Keep in mind that the members of the Corinthian church did not sit in the services with Bibles on their laps. The New Testament was being written and the Old Testament scrolls were expensive and not available to most believers. God spoke to His people directly through the prophets, and the message was sometimes given in a tongue. The three gifts of knowledge, prophecy, and tongues worked together to convey truth to the people (1 Cor. 13:1-2, 8-11).

Paul emphasized the importance of doctrinal teaching in the church. Our worship must be based on truth, or it may become superstitious emotionalism. Christians need to know what they believe and why they believe it. The prophet shared truth with the church, and thereby edified the assembly. The person speaking in tongues (unless there is an interpreter) is enjoying his worship of God, but he is not edifying the church.

In my own ministry, I have shared in many local church services and conferences, and I have always tried to communicate biblical truth to the people. Sometimes the music has not been edifying, and at other times, the music communicated the Word of God in a powerful way. Whenever all of us as ministers have aimed at edification, and not entertainment, God has blessed and the people have been helped. A ministry that does not build up will tear down, no matter how "spiritual" it may seem. When we explain and apply the Word of God to individual lives, we have a ministry of edification.

Understanding (1 Cor. 14:6-25)

Eight times in this section, Paul used the word *understanding.* It is not enough for the minister to impart information to people; the people must *receive* it if it is to do them any good. The seed that is received in the good ground is the seed that bears fruit, but this means that there must be an *understanding* of the Word of God (Matt. 13:23). If a believer wants to be edified, he must prepare his heart to receive the Word (1 Thes. 2:13). Not everybody who *listens* really *hears.*

The famous Congregationalist minister, Dr. Joseph Parker, preached at an important meeting and afterward was approached by a man who pointed out an error in the sermon. Parker listened patiently to the man's criticism, and then asked, "And what *else* did you get from the message?" This remark simply withered the critic, who then disappeared into the crowd. Too often we are quick to judge the sermon instead of allowing the Word of God to judge us.

Illustration (vv. 6-11). Paul used three simple illustrations to prove his point that there must be understanding if there is to be an edifying spiritual ministry: musical instruments, a bugle call in battle, and daily conversation.

If a musical instrument does not give a clear and distinct sound, nobody will recognize the music being played. Everyone knows how uncomfortable one feels when a performer *almost* plays the right note because the instrument is defective or out of tune. Large pipe organs must be constantly serviced lest their reeds fail to perform properly. I was in a church service one evening during which the organ pitch gradually changed because of atmospheric conditions, and by the close of the service, the organ could not be played with the piano because of the radical change that had occurred.

If the bugler is not sure whether he is calling "Retreat!" or "Charge!" you can be sure none of the soldiers will know what to do either. Half of them will rush forward, while the other half will run back! The call must be a clear one if it is to be understood.

But this fact is also true in everyday conversation. I recall the first time my wife and I visited Great Britain and were confronted with the variety of local dialects there. We asked directions of a friendly gentleman in London and, quite frankly, could understand very little of what he said. (Perhaps he had a difficult time understanding us!)

First Corinthians 14:10 gives us good reason to believe that, when Paul wrote about tongues, he was referring to known languages and not some "heavenly" language. Each language is different and yet each language has its own meaning. No matter how sincere a speaker may be, if I do not understand his language, he cannot communicate with me. To the Greeks, a *barbarian* was the lowest person on the social or national ladder. In fact, anybody who was not a Greek was considered a barbarian.

The musician, the bugler, and the everyday conversationalist cannot be understood unless their messages are communicated in a manner that is meaningful to the listener. Having illustrated the principle of understanding, Paul then applied it to three different persons.

Application (vv. 12-25). Paul first applied the principle of understanding to the speaker himself (1 Cor. 14:12-15). Again, he reminded the Corinthians that it is better to be a blessing to the church than to experience some kind of personal "spiritual excitement."

If the believer speaks in a tongue, his spirit (inner person) may share in the experience, but his mind is not a part of the experience. It is not wrong to pray or sing "in the spirit," but it is better to include the mind and understand what you are praying or singing. (Note that the word *spirit* in 1 Cor. 14:14-15 does not refer to the Holy Spirit, but to the inner person, as in 1 Cor. 2:11.) If the speaker is to be edified, he must understand what he is saying.

What, then, is the speaker to do? He must ask God for the interpretation of the message. Paul assumed that an interpreter would be present (1 Cor. 14:27-28) or that the speaker himself had the gift of interpreting. Of course, all of this discussion emphasized once again the superiority of prophecy over tongues: prophecy needs no interpretation and can therefore be a blessing to everybody.

Paul then applied the principle to other believers in the assembly (1 Cor. 14:16-20). He assumed that they would listen to the message and respond to it. But if they did not understand the message, how could they respond? (Apparently, saying *Amen!* in church was not frowned on in those days.) The "unlearned" person was probably a new believer, or possibly an interested "seeker." He could not be edified unless he understood what was being said.

Again, it was a matter of priorities. While Paul did not oppose the ministry of tongues, he did try to put it into a right perspective. The issue was not quantity of words, but quality of communication. The Corinthians were acting like children playing with toys. When it came to knowing about sin, Paul wanted them to be "babes"; but when it came to spiritual understanding, he wanted them to be mature men (1 Cor. 3:1-4; 13:11-13).

Some people have the idea that speaking in a tongue is an evidence of spiritual maturity, but Paul taught that it is possible to exercise the gift in an unspiritual and immature manner.

Paul's final application was to the unsaved person who happened to come into the assembly during a time of worship (1 Cor. 14:21-25). Paul made here another point for the superiority of prophecy over tongues: a message in tongues (unless interpreted) could never bring conviction to the heart of a lost sinner. In fact, the unsaved person might leave the service before the interpretation was given, thinking that the whole assembly was crazy. Tongues were not used for evangelism, neither at Pentecost nor in the meetings of the early church.

However, tongues did have a "message" for the lost Jews in particular: they were a sign of God's judgment. Paul quoted Isaiah 28:11-12, a reference to the invading Assyrian army whose "barbaric" language the Jews would not understand. The presence of this "tongue" was evidence of God's judgment on the nation. God would rather speak to His people in clear language they could understand, but their repeated sins made this impossible. He *had* spoken to them through His messengers in their own tongue, and the nation would not repent. Now He had to speak in a foreign tongue, and this meant judgment.

As a nation, the Jews were always seeking a sign (Matt. 12:38; 1 Cor. 1:22). At Pentecost, the fact that the Apostles spoke in tongues was a sign to the unbelieving Jews who were there celebrating the feast. The miracle of tongues aroused their interest, but it did not convict their hearts. It took Peter's preaching (in Aramaic, which the people all understood) to bring them to the place of conviction and conversion.

The principle of *edification* encourages us to major on sharing the Word of God so that the church will be strengthened and grow. The principle of *understanding* reminds us that what we share must be understood if it is to do any good. The private use of spiritual gifts may edify the user, but it will not edify the church; and Paul admonished us to "excel to the edifying of the church" (1 Cor. 14:12).

But a third principle must be applied: the principle of order.

Order (1 Cor. 14:26-40)

Two statements in this section go together: "Let all things be done unto edifying" (1 Cor. 14:26), and, "Let all things be done decently and in order" (1 Cor. 14:40). When a building is constructed, there must be a plan, or everything will be in chaos. I know of a church that had terrible problems building their parsonage, until someone discovered that the lumberyard had a different set of plans from that of the contractor. It was no wonder that the materials shipped to the site did not fit into the building!

The Corinthian church was having special problems with disorders in their public meetings (1 Cor. 11:17-23). The reason is not difficult to determine: they were using their spiritual gifts to please themselves and not to help their brethren. The key word was not *edification,* but *exhibition.* If you think that *your* contribution to the service is more important than your brother's contribution, then you will either be impatient until he finishes, or you will interrupt him. Add to this problem the difficulties caused by the "liberated women" in the assembly, and you can understand why the church experienced carnal confusion.

First Corinthians 14:26 gives us a cameo picture of worship in the early church. Each member was invited to participate as the Lord directed. One would want to sing a psalm (Eph. 5:19; Col. 3:16). Another would be led to share a doctrine. Someone might have a revelation that would be given in a tongue and then interpreted. Apart from some kind of God-given order, there could never be edification.

Note that the tongues speakers were the ones causing the most trouble, so Paul addressed himself to them and gave several instructions for the church to obey in their public meetings.

First, speaking and interpreting, along with judging (evaluating the message) must be done in an orderly manner (1 Cor. 14:27-33). There must not be more than three speakers at any one meeting, and each message must be interpreted and evaluated in order. If no interpreter was present, then the tongues speaker must keep silent. Paul's admonitions to the Thessalonian congregation would apply here: "Quench not the Spirit. Despise not prophesyings. Prove all things; hold fast that which is good" (1 Thes. 5:19-21).

Why were the messages evaluated? To determine whether the speaker had truly communicated the Word of God through the Holy Spirit. It was possible for a speaker, under the control of his own emotions, to imagine that God was speaking to him and through him. It was even possible for Satan to counterfeit a prophetic message (see 2 Cor. 11:13-14). The listeners would test the message, then, by Old Testament Scriptures, apostolic tradition, and the personal guidance of the Spirit ("discerning of spirits," 1 Cor. 12:10).

If while a person is speaking, God gives a revelation to another person, the speaker must be silent while the new revelation is shared. If God is in charge, there can be no *competition* or *contradiction* in the messages. If, however, the various speakers are "manufacturing" their messages, there will be confusion and contradiction.

When the Holy Spirit is in charge, the various ministers will have self-control; for self-control is one fruit of the Spirit (Gal. 5:23). I once shared a Bible conference with a speaker who had "poor terminal facilities." He often went fifteen to twenty minutes past his deadline, which meant, of course, that I had to condense my messages at the last minute. He excused himself to me by saying, "You know, when the Holy Spirit takes over, you can't worry about clocks!" My reply was to quote 1 Corinthians 14:32: "And the spirits of the prophets are subject to the prophets."

Our own self-control is one of the evidences that the Spirit is indeed at work in the meeting. One of the ministries of the Spirit is to bring order out of chaos (Gen. 1). Confusion comes from Satan, not from God (James 3:13-18). When the Spirit is leading, the participants are able to minister "one by one" so that the total impact of God's message may be received by the church.

How do we apply this instruction to the church today since we do not have New Testament prophets, but we do have the completed Scripture? For one thing, we must use the Word of God to test every message that we hear, asking the Spirit to guide us. There are false teachers in the world and we must beware (2 Peter 2; 1 John 4:1-6). But even true teachers and preachers do not know everything and sometimes make mistakes (1 Cor. 13:9, 12; James 3:1). Each listener must evaluate the message and apply it to his own heart.

Our public meetings today are more formal than those of the early church, so it is not likely that we need to worry about the order of the service. But in our more informal meetings, we need to consider one another and maintain order. I recall being in a testimony meeting where a woman took forty minutes telling a boring experience and, as a result, destroyed the spirit of the meeting.

Evangelist D.L. Moody was leading a service and asked a man to pray. Taking advantage of his opportunity, the man prayed on and on. Sensing that the prayer was killing the meeting instead of blessing it, Moody spoke up and said, "While our brother finishes his prayer, let us sing a hymn!" Those who are in charge of public meetings need to have discernment—and courage.

Second, the women in the meeting were not to speak (1 Cor. 14:34-35). Paul had already permitted the women to pray and prophesy (1 Cor. 11:5), so this instruction must apply to the immediate context of evaluating the prophetic messages. It would appear that the major responsibility for doctrinal purity in the early church rested on the shoulders of the men, the elders in particular (1 Tim. 2:11-12).

The context of this prohibition would indicate that some of the women in the assembly were creating problems by asking questions and perhaps even generating arguments. Paul reminded the married women to be submitted to their husbands and to get their questions answered at home. (We assume that the unmarried women could counsel with the elders or with other men in their own families.) Sad to say, in too many Christian homes today, it is the wife who has to answer the questions for the husband because she is better taught in the Word.

What "law" was Paul referring to in 1 Corinthians 14:34? Probably Genesis 3:16. (The word *law* was a synonym for the Old Testament Scriptures, especially the first five books.) In 1 Corinthians 11, Paul had discussed the relationship of men and women in the church, so there was no need to go into detail.

Third, participants must beware of "new revelations" that go beyond the Word of God (1 Cor. 14:36-40). "To the law and to the testimony; if they speak not according to this word, it is because there is no light in them" (Isa. 8:20). The church had the Old Testament as well as the oral tradition given by the Apostles (2 Tim. 2:2), and this was the standard by which all revelations would be tested. We today have the completed Scriptures as well as the accumulated teachings of centuries of church history to help us discern the truth. The historic evangelical creeds, while not inspired, do embody orthodox theology that can direct us.

In these verses, Paul was answering the church member who might say, "We don't need Paul's help! The Spirit speaks to us. We have received new and wonderful revelations from God!" This is a dangerous attitude, because it is the first step toward rejecting God's Word and accepting counterfeit revelations, including the doctrines of demons (1 Tim. 4:1ff). "The Word did not originate in your congregation!" Paul replied. "One of the marks of a true prophet is his obedience to apostolic teaching." In this statement, Paul claimed that what he wrote was actually inspired Scripture, "the commandments of the Lord" (1 Cor. 14:37).

First Corinthians 14:38 does not suggest that Paul wanted people to remain ignorant; otherwise, he would not have written this letter and answered their questions. The *New International Version* translates it, "If he ignores this [Paul's apostolic authority], he himself will be ignored [by Paul and the churches]." Fellowship is based on the Word, and those who willfully reject the Word automatically break the fellowship (1 John 2:18-19).

Paul summarized the main teachings of 1 Corinthians 14 in verses 39-40. Prophecy is more important than tongues, but the church should not prohibit the correct exercise of the gift of tongues. The purpose of spiritual gifts is the edification of the whole church, and therefore, gifts must be exercised in an orderly manner. Public worship must be carried on "in a seemly manner," that is, with beauty, order, and spiritual motivation and content.

Before leaving this chapter, it might be helpful to summarize what Paul wrote about the gift of tongues. It is the God-given ability to speak in a known language with which the speaker was not previously acquainted. The purpose was not to win the lost, but to edify the saved. Not every believer had this gift, nor was this gift an evidence of spirituality or the result of a "baptism of the Spirit."

Only three persons were permitted to speak in tongues in any one meeting, and they had to do so in order and with interpretation. If there was no interpreter, they had to keep silent. Prophecy is the superior gift, but tongues were not to be despised if they were exercised according to Scripture.

When the foundational work of the Apostles and prophets ended, it would seem that the gifts of knowledge, prophecy, and tongues would no longer be needed. "Whether there be tongues, they shall cease" (1 Cor. 13:8). Certainly God could give this gift today if He pleased, but I am not prepared to believe that every instance of tongues is divinely energized. Nor would I go so far as to say that all instances of tongues are either satanic or self-induced.

It is unfortunate when believers make tongues a test of fellowship or spirituality. That in itself would alert me that the Spirit would not be at work. Let's keep our priorities straight and major on winning the lost and building the church.

CHAPTER TWELVE
BE WISE ABOUT . . . THE RESURRECTION
1 Corinthians 15

Corinth was a Greek city, and the Greeks did not believe in the resurrection of the dead. When Paul had preached at Athens and declared the fact of Christ's resurrection, some of his listeners actually laughed at him (Acts 17:32). Most Greek philosophers considered the human body a prison, and they welcomed death as deliverance from bondage.

This skeptical attitude had somehow invaded the church and Paul had to face it head-on. The truth of the resurrection had doctrinal and practical implications for life that were too important to ignore. Paul dealt with the subject by answering four basic questions.

Are the Dead Raised? (1 Cor. 15:1-19)

It is important to note that the believers at Corinth did believe in the resurrection of Jesus Christ; so Paul started his argument with that fundamental truth. He presented three proofs to assure his readers that Jesus Christ indeed had been raised from the dead.

Proof #1—their salvation (vv. 1-2). Paul had come to Corinth and preached the message of the Gospel, and their faith had transformed their lives. But an integral part of the Gospel message was the fact of Christ's resurrection. After all, a dead Saviour cannot save anybody. Paul's readers had received the Word, trusted Christ, been saved, and were now standing on that Word as the assurance of their salvation. The fact that they were standing firm was proof that their faith was genuine and not empty.

Proof #2—the Old Testament Scriptures (vv. 3-4). *First of all* means "of first importance." The Gospel is the most important message that the church ever proclaims. While it is good to be involved in social action and the betterment of mankind, there is no reason why these ministries should preempt the Gospel. "Christ died . . . He was buried . . . He rose again . . . He was seen" are the basic historical *facts* on which the Gospel stands (1 Cor. 15:3-5). "Christ died *for our sins*" (author's italics) is the theological explanation of the historical facts. Many people were crucified by the Romans, but only one "victim" ever died for the sins of the world.

When Paul wrote "according to the Scriptures" (1 Cor. 15:3) he was referring to the Old Testament Scriptures. Much of the sacrificial system in the Old Testament pointed to the sacrifice of Christ as our substitute and Saviour. The annual Day of Atonement (Lev. 16) and prophecies like Isaiah 53 would also come to mind.

But where does the Old Testament declare His resurrection on the third day? Jesus pointed to the experience of Jonah (Matt. 12:38-41). Paul also compared Christ's resurrection to the "firstfruits," and the firstfruits were presented to God on the day following the Sabbath after Passover (Lev. 23:9-14; 1 Cor. 15:23). Since the Sabbath must always be the seventh day, the day after Sabbath must be the *first* day of the week, or Sunday, the day of our Lord's resurrection. This covers three days on the Jewish calendar. Apart from the Feast of Firstfruits, there were other prophecies of Messiah's resurrection in the Old Testament: Psalm 16:8-11 (see Acts 2:25-28); Psalm 22:22ff (see Heb. 2:12); Isaiah 53:10-12; and Psalm 2:7 (see Acts 13:32-33).

Proof #3—Christ was seen by witnesses (vv. 5-11). On the cross, Jesus was exposed to the eyes of unbelievers; but after the Resurrection, He was seen by believers who could be witnesses of His resurrection (Acts 1:22; 2:32; 3:15; 5:32). Peter saw Him and so did the disciples collectively. James was a half brother of the Lord who became a believer after the Lord appeared to him (John 7:5; Acts 1:14). The 500 *plus* brethren all saw Him at the same time (1 Cor. 15:6), so it could not have been a hallucination or a deception. This event may have been just before His ascension (Matt. 28:16ff).

But one of the greatest witnesses of the Resurrection was Paul himself, for as an unbeliever he was soundly convinced that Jesus was dead. The radical change in his life—a change which brought him persecution and suffering—is certainly evidence that the Lord had indeed been raised from the dead. Paul made it clear that his salvation was purely an act of God's grace; but that grace worked in and through him as he served the Lord. "Born out of due time" probably refers to the future salvation of Israel when they, like Paul, see the Messiah in glory (Zech. 12:10–13:6; 1 Tim. 1:16).

At this point, Paul's readers would say, "Yes, we agree that *Jesus* was raised from the dead." Then Paul would reply, "If you believe that, then you must believe in the resurrection of *all* the dead!" Christ came as a man, truly human, and experienced all that we experienced, except that He never sinned. If there is no resurrection, then Christ was not raised. If He was not raised, there is no Gospel to preach. If there is no Gospel, then you have believed in vain and you are still in your sins! If there is no resurrection, then believers who have died have no hope. We shall never see them again!

The conclusion is obvious: Why be a Christian if we have only suffering in this life and no future glory to anticipate? (In 1 Cor. 15:29-34, Paul expanded this idea.) The Resurrection is not just important; it is "of first importance," because all that we believe hinges on it.

When Are the Dead Raised? (1 Cor. 15:20-28)

Paul used three images to answer this question.

Firstfruits (vv. 20, 23). We have already noted this reference to the Old Testament feast (Lev. 23:9-14). As the Lamb of God, Jesus died on Passover. As the sheaf of firstfruits, He arose from the dead three days later on the first day of the week. When the priest waved the sheaf of the firstfruits before the Lord, it was a sign that the entire harvest belonged to Him. When Jesus was raised from the dead, it was God's assurance to us that we shall also be raised one day as part of that future harvest. To believers, death is only "sleep." The body sleeps, but the soul is at home with the Lord (2 Cor. 5:1-8; Phil. 1:21-23). At the resurrection, the body will be "awakened" and glorified.

Adam (vv. 21-22). Paul saw in Adam a type of Jesus Christ *by the way of contrast* (see also Rom. 5:12-21). The first Adam was made from the earth, but the Last Adam (Christ, 1 Cor. 15:45-47) came from heaven. The first Adam disobeyed God and brought sin and death into the world, but the Last Adam obeyed the Father and brought righteousness and life.

The word *order* in 1 Corinthians 15:23 originally referred to military rank. God has an order, a sequence, in the resurrection. Passages like John 5:25-29 and Revelation 20 indicate that there is no such thing taught in Scripture as a "general resurrection." When Jesus Christ returns in the air, He will take His church to heaven and at that time raise from the dead all who have trusted Him and have died in the faith (1 Thes. 4:13-18). Jesus called this "the resurrection of life" (John 5:29). When Jesus returns to the earth in judgment, then the lost will be raised in "the resurrection of damnation" (John 5:29; Rev. 20:11-15). Nobody in the first resurrection will be lost, but nobody in the second resurrection will be saved.

The kingdom (vv. 24-28). When Jesus Christ comes to the earth to judge, He will banish sin for a thousand years and establish His kingdom (Rev. 20:1-6). Believers will reign with Him and share His glory and authority. This kingdom, prophesied in the Old Testament, is called "the Millennium" by prophetic teachers. The word comes from the Latin: *mille*—thousand, *annum*—year.

But even after the Millennium, there will be one final rebellion against God (Rev. 20:7-10) which Jesus Christ will put down by His power. The lost will then be raised, judged, and cast into the lake of fire. Then death itself shall be cast into hell, and the last enemy shall be destroyed. Jesus Christ will have put all things under His feet! He will then turn the kingdom over to the Father and then the eternal state—the new heavens and new earth—shall be ushered in (Rev. 21–22).

Good and godly students of the Word have not always agreed on the details of God's prophetic program, but the major truths seem to be clear. Jesus Christ reigns in heaven today, and all authority is "under His feet" (Ps. 110; Eph. 1:15-23). Satan and man are still able to exercise choice, but God is sovereignly in control. Jesus Christ is enthroned in heaven today (Ps. 2). The resurrection of the saved has not yet taken place, nor the resurrection of the lost (2 Tim. 2:17-18).

When will Jesus Christ return for His church? Nobody knows; but when it occurs, it will be "in a moment, in the twinkling of an eye" (1 Cor. 15:52). It behooves us to be ready (1 John 2:28–3:3).

Why Are the Dead Raised? (1 Cor. 15:29-34, 49-58)

The resurrection of the human body is a future event that has compelling implications for our personal lives. If the resurrection is not true, then we can forget about the future and live as we please! But the resurrection *is* true! Jesus *is* coming again! Even if we die before He comes, we shall be raised at His coming and stand before Him in a glorified body.

Paul cited four areas of Christian experience that are touched by the fact of the resurrection.

Evangelism (v. 29). What does it mean to be "baptized for the dead"? Some take this to mean "proxy baptism," where a believer is baptized on behalf of a dead relative; but we find no such teaching in the New Testament. In the second century, there were some heretical groups that practiced "vicarious baptism," but the church at large has never accepted the practice. To begin with, salvation is a personal matter that each must decide for himself; and, second, nobody needs to be baptized to be saved.

The phrase probably means "baptized to take the place of those who have died." In other words, if there is no resurrection, why bother to witness and win others to Christ? Why reach sinners who are then baptized and take the place of those who have died? If the Christian life is only a "dead-end street," get off of it!

Each responsible person on earth will share in either the resurrection of life and go to heaven, or the resurrection of judgment and go to hell (John 5:28-29). We weep for believers who have died, but we ought also to weep for unbelievers who still have opportunity to be saved! The reality of the resurrection is a motivation for evangelism.

Suffering (vv. 30-32). *I die daily* does not refer to "dying to self," as in Romans 6, but to the physical dangers Paul faced as a servant of Christ (2 Cor. 4:8–5:10; 11:23-28). He was in constant jeopardy from his enemies and on more than one occasion had been close to death. Why endure suffering and danger if death ends it all? "Let us eat and drink, for tomorrow we shall die" (Isa. 22:13).

What we do in the body in this life comes up for review at the Judgment Seat of Christ (2 Cor. 5:10). God deals with the *whole* person, not just with the "soul." The body shares in salvation (Rom. 8:18-23). The suffering endured in the body will result in glory at the resurrection (2 Cor. 4:7-18). If there is no future for the body, then why suffer and die for the cause of Christ?

Separation from sin (vv. 33-34). If there is no resurrection, then what we do with our bodies will have no bearing on our future. Immorality was a way of life in Corinth, and some of the believers rejected the resurrection in order to rationalize their sin. "Evil company corrupts good morals" is a quotation from the Greek poet Menander, a saying no doubt familiar to Paul's readers. The believer's body is the temple of God and must be kept separated from the sins of the world (2 Cor. 6:14–7:1). To fellowship with the "unfruitful works of darkness" (Eph. 5:6-17) is only to corrupt God's temple.

It was time for the Corinthians to *wake up* and *clean up* (see 1 Thes. 5:4-11). The believer who is compromising with sin has no witness to the lost around him, those who "have not the knowledge of God." What a shameful thing to be selfishly living in sin while multitudes die without Christ!

Death (vv. 49-57). The heavenly kingdom is not made for the kind of bodies we now have, bodies of flesh and blood. So when Jesus returns, the bodies of living believers will instantly be transformed to be like His body (1 John 3:1-3), and the dead believers shall be raised with new glorified bodies. Our new bodies will not be subject to decay or death.

Sigmund Freud, the founder of psychiatry, wrote: "And finally there is the painful riddle of death, for which no remedy at all has yet been found, nor probably ever will be." Christians have victory *in* death and *over* death! Why? Because of the victory of Jesus Christ in His own resurrection. Jesus said, "Because I live, ye shall also" (John 14:19).

Sin, death, and the Law go together. The Law reveals sin, and the "wages of sin is death" (Rom. 6:23). Jesus bore our sins on the cross (1 Peter 2:24), and also bore the curse of the Law (Gal. 3:13). It is through Him that we have this victory, and we share the victory *today.* The literal translation of 1 Corinthians 15:57 is, "But thanks be to God who *keeps on giving us the victory* through our Lord Jesus Christ." We experience "the power of His resurrection" in our lives as we yield to Him (Phil. 3:10).

First Corinthians 15:58 is Paul's hymn of praise to the Lord as well as his closing admonition to the church. Because of the assurance of Christ's victory over death, we know that nothing we do for Him will ever be wasted or lost. We can be steadfast in our service, unmovable in suffering, abounding in ministry to others, because we know our labor is not in vain. First Corinthians 15:58 is the answer to Ecclesiastes, where thirty-eight times Solomon used the sad word *vanity*. "Vanity of vanities, all is vanity!" wept Solomon; but Paul sang a song of victory!

How Are the Dead Raised? (1 Cor. 15:35-48)

Being philosophers, the Greeks reasoned that the resurrection of the human body was an impossibility. After all, when the body turned to dust, it became soil from which other bodies derived nourishment. In short, the food that we eat is a part of the elements of the bodies of generations long gone. When the body of the founder of Rhode Island, Roger Williams, was disinterred, it was discovered that the roots of a nearby apple tree had grown through the coffin. To some degree, the people who ate the apples partook of his body. At the resurrection, then, who will claim the various elements?

Paul's reply to this kind of reasoning was very blunt: "You fool!" Then he made the important point that *resurrection is not reconstruction*. Nowhere does the Bible teach that, at the resurrection, God will "put together the pieces" and return to us our former bodies. There is *continuity* (it is *our* body), but there is not *identity* (it is not the *same* body).

Paul knew that such miracles cannot be explained, so he used three analogies to make the doctrine clear.

Seeds (vv. 35-38, 42-48). When you sow seed, you do not expect that same seed to come up at the harvest. The seed dies, but from that death there comes life. (See John 12:23-28 for our Lord's use of this same analogy.) You may sow a few grains of wheat, but you will have many grains when the plant matures. Are they the same grains that were planted? No, but there is still continuity. You do not sow wheat and harvest barley.

Furthermore, what comes up at the harvest is usually more beautiful than what was planted. This is especially true of tulips. Few things are as ugly as a tulip bulb, yet it produces a beautiful flower. If at the resurrection, all God did was to put us back together again, there would be no improvement. Furthermore, flesh and blood cannot inherit God's kingdom. The only way we can enjoy the glory of heaven is to have a body suited to that environment.

Paul discussed the details of this marvelous change in 1 Corinthians 15:42-48. The body is sown (in burial) in corruption, because it is going to decay; but it is raised with such a nature that it cannot decay. There is no decay or death in heaven. It is buried in humility (in spite of the cosmetic skill of the mortician); but it is raised in glory. In burial, the body is weak; but in resurrection, the body has power. We shall be like Jesus Christ!

Today, we have a "natural body," that is, a body suited to an earthly environment. We received this body from our first parent, Adam: he was made of dust, and so are we (Gen. 2:7). But the resurrection body is suited to a spiritual environment. In His resurrection body, Jesus was able to move quickly from place to place, and even walk through locked doors; yet He was also able to eat food, and His disciples were able to touch Him and feel Him (Luke 24:33-43; John 20:19-29).

The point Paul was making was simply this: The resurrection body completes the work of redemption and gives to us the image of the Saviour. We are made in the image of God as far as personality is concerned, but in the image of Adam as far as the body is concerned. One day we shall bear the image of the Saviour when we share in His glory.

First Corinthians 15:46 states an important biblical principle: first the "natural" (earthly), and then the "spiritual" (heavenly). The first birth gives us that which is natural, but the second birth gives us that which is spiritual. God rejects the first birth, the natural, and says, "You must be born again!" He rejected Cain and chose Abel. He rejected Abraham's firstborn, Ishmael, and chose Isaac, the second-born. He rejected Esau and chose Jacob. If we depend on our first birth, we shall be condemned forever; but if we experience the new birth, we shall be blessed forever.

Flesh (v. 39). Paul anticipated here the discovery of science that the cell structure of different kinds of animals is different; and therefore, you cannot breed various species indiscriminately. The human body has a nature of one kind, while animals, birds, and fish have their own particular kind of flesh. The conclusion is this: If God is able to make different kinds of bodies for men, animals, birds, and fish, why can He not make a different kind of body for us at the resurrection? (Pet lovers take note: Paul did not teach here that animals will be resurrected. He only used them as an example.)

Heavenly bodies (vv. 40-41). Not only are there earthly bodies, but there are also heavenly bodies; and they differ from one another. In fact, the heavenly bodies differ from each other in glory as far as the human eye is concerned. Paul is suggesting here that believer may differ from believer in glory, even though all Christians will have glorified bodies. Every cup in heaven will be filled, but some cups will be bigger than others, because of the faithfulness and sacrifice of those saints when they were on earth.

These illustrations may not answer every question that we have about the resurrection body, but they do give us the assurances that we need. God will give to us a glorified body suited to the new life in heaven. It will be as unlike our present body in quality as the glory of the sun is unlike a mushroom in the cellar. We will use this new body to serve and glorify God for all eternity.

We must remember that this discussion was not written by Paul merely to satisfy the curiosity of believers. He had some practical points to get across, and he made them very clear in 1 Corinthians 15:29-34. If we really believe in the resurrection of the body, then we will use our bodies today to the glory of God (1 Cor. 6:9-14).

Finally, the lost will be given bodies suited to their environment in hell. They will suffer forever in darkness and pain (Matt. 25:41; 2 Thes. 1:7-10; Rev. 20:11-15). It behooves us who are saved to seek to rescue them from judgment! "Knowing therefore the terror of the Lord, we persuade men" (2 Cor. 5:11).

If you have never trusted the Saviour, do so now—before it is too late!

CHAPTER THIRTEEN
BE WISE ABOUT... CHRISTIAN STEWARDSHIP
1 Corinthians 16

It is to the credit of the believers at Corinth that, when they wrote their questions to Paul, they asked him about the collection he was taking for the poor saints in Jerusalem. Paul answered their question and then closed the letter by informing the church of his personal travel plans and also the plans for his associates in the ministry.

This chapter may seem unrelated to our needs today, but actually it deals in a very helpful way with three areas of stewardship: money (1 Cor. 16:1-4), opportunities (1 Cor. 16:5-9), and people (1 Cor. 16:10-24). These are probably the greatest resources the church has today, and they must not be wasted.

Money (1 Cor. 16:1-4)

One of the most important ministries Paul had during his third journey was the gathering of a special "relief offering" for the poor believers in Jerusalem. He wanted to achieve several purposes in this offering. For one thing, the Gentiles owed material help to the Jews in return for the spiritual blessings the Jews had given them (Rom. 15:25-27). At the Jerusalem Conference years before, Paul had agreed to "remember the poor," so he was keeping his pledge (Gal. 2:10). Paul not only preached the Gospel, but he also tried to assist those who had physical and material needs.

Why was there such a great need in the Jerusalem church? It is likely that many of the believers had been visiting Jerusalem at Pentecost when they heard the Word and were saved. This meant that they were strangers, without employment, and the church would have to care for them. In the early days of the church, the members had gladly shared with each other (Acts 2:41-47; 4:33-37); but even their resources were limited. There had also been a famine (Acts 11:27-30) and the relief sent at that time could not last for too long a time.

Apart from keeping his promise and meeting a great need, Paul's greatest motive for taking up the offering was to help unite Jewish and Gentile believers. Paul was a missionary to the Gentiles, and this bothered some of the Jewish believers (Acts 17:21-25). Paul hoped that this expression of Gentile love would help to heal some wounds and build some bridges between the churches. (For more information about this offering, read 2 Cor. 8–9.)

Even though this was a special missionary offering, from Paul's instructions we may learn some basic principles that relate to Christian stewardship.

Giving is an act of worship. Each member was to come to the Lord's Day gathering prepared to give his share for that week. The early church met on the first day of the week in commemoration of the resurrection of Jesus Christ. (The Holy Spirit came on the church at Pentecost on the first day of the week.) It is tragic when church members give only as a duty and forget that our offerings are to be "spiritual sacrifices" presented to the Lord (Phil. 4:18). Giving should be an act of worship to the resurrected and ascended Saviour.

Giving should be systematic. Some students have suggested that many people were paid on the first day of the week during that time in history. But even if they were not, each believer was to set aside his offering at home and then bring it to the assembly on the first day. Paul did not want to have to take up a number of collections when he arrived in Corinth. He wanted the whole contribution to be ready. If today's church members were as systematic in their giving as they are in handling their other financial matters, the work of the Lord would not suffer as it sometimes does.

Giving was personal and individual. Paul expected each member to share in the offering, the rich and poor alike. Anyone who had an income was privileged to share and to help those in need. He wanted all to share in the blessing.

Giving is to be proportionate. "As God hath prospered him" (1 Cor. 16:2) suggests that believers who have more should give more. The Jewish believers in the church would have been accustomed to the tithe, but Paul did not mention any special proportion. Certainly the tithe (10 percent of one's income) is a good place to *begin* our stewardship, but we must not remain at that level. As the Lord gives us more, we should plan to give more.

The trouble is, too many saints, as they earn more, involve themselves in more and more financial obligations; and then they do not have more to give to the Lord. Instead of finding a suitable "level" and remaining there, they keep trying to "go higher," and their income is *spent* rather than *invested.* As the old saying goes, "When your outgo exceeds your income, then your upkeep is your downfall."

Paul made it clear in 2 Corinthians 8–9 that Christian giving is a *grace,* the outflow of the grace of God in our lives and not the result of promotion or pressure. An open heart cannot maintain a closed hand. If we appreciate the grace of God extended to us, we will want to express that grace by sharing with others.

Money is to be handled honestly. The various churches involved in this special offering appointed delegates to help Paul manage it and take it safely to Jerusalem. (See 2 Cor. 8:16-24 for more information on the "finance committee" that assisted Paul.) It is unfortunate when Christian ministries lose their testimony because they mismanage funds entrusted to them. Every ministry ought to be businesslike in its financial affairs. Paul was very careful not to allow anything to happen that would give his enemies opportunity to accuse him of stealing funds (2 Cor. 8:20-21).

This explains why Paul encouraged the *churches* to share in the offering and to select dependable representatives to help manage it. Paul was not against *individuals* giving personally; in this chapter, as well as in Romans 16, he named various individuals who assisted him personally. This no doubt included helping him with his financial needs. But generally speaking, Christian giving is church-centered. Many churches encourage their members to give designated gifts through the church budget.

It is interesting that Paul mentioned the offering just after his discussion about the resurrection. There were no "chapter breaks" in the original manuscripts, so the readers would go right from Paul's hymn of victory into his discussion about money. Doctrine and duty go together; so do worship and works. Our giving is "not in vain" because our Lord is alive. It is His resurrection power that motivates us to give and to serve.

Opportunities (1 Cor. 16:5-9)

"Be very careful, then, how you live—not as unwise but as wise, making the most of every opportunity, because the days are evil" (Eph. 5:15-16, NIV). Paul was as careful in his use of time as he was in his use of money. Someone has said that killing time is the chief occupation of modern society, but no Christian can afford to kill time or waste opportunities.

Paul informed his friends at Corinth of his plans for future travel and ministry. It is worth noting that his statements were very tentative: "It may be suitable . . . it may be . . . wherever I go . . . but I trust." Of course, the entire plan was dependent on God's providential leading: "if the Lord permit." Paul's attitude toward his future plans agreed with the injunctions in James 4:13-17.

Paul was at Ephesus when he wrote this letter. His plan was to travel to Macedonia for a time of ministry (*pass through* in 1 Cor. 16:5 means "travel in a systematic ministry"), winter at Corinth, and then go to Judea with the collection. From November to February, it was impossible to travel by ship; so it would have been convenient for Paul to stay at Corinth and be with his friends. There were some problems to solve in the church and Paul had promised to come to help the leaders (1 Cor. 11:34).

However, various circumstances forced Paul to revise his plans at least twice. His "Plan B" was to visit Corinth, then travel through Macedonia, passing through Corinth a second time on his way to Judea (2 Cor. 1:15-16). Instead of one long visit, he planned two shorter visits; but even this plan did not materialize. "Plan C" turned out to be a quick and painful visit to Corinth, after which he returned to Ephesus. He then went to Troas to wait for Titus (who had been sent to Corinth, 2 Cor. 2:12-13; 7:5ff), visited Macedonia, and then went to Judea. He did not spend as much time at Corinth as he had hoped or as they had expected.

What do we learn from this difficult experience of Paul's? For one thing, a Christian must use his common sense, pray, study the situation, and seek the best he can to determine the will of God. Proverbs 3:5-6 ("lean not unto thine own understanding") must not be interpreted to mean, "Put your brain in neutral and don't think!" God gave us our minds and He expects us to think, but He does not want us to *depend* only on our own reasoning. We must pray, meditate on the Word, and even seek the counsel of mature Christian friends.

Second, our decisions may not always be in the will of God. We may make promises that we cannot keep and plans that we cannot fulfill. Does this mean that we are liars or failures? (Some of the believers at Corinth thought Paul was deceptive and not to be trusted. See 2 Cor. 1:12—2:13.) In my own ministry, I have had to change my plans and alter my schedule because of situations over which I had no control. Did this mean I had been out of the will of God in making my plans? Not necessarily. Even an apostle (who had been to heaven and back) occasionally had to revise his datebook.

There are two extremes we must avoid in this important matter of seeking God's will. One is to be so frightened at making a mistake that we make no decisions at all. The other is to make impulsive decisions and rush ahead, without taking time to wait on the Lord. After we have done all we can to determine the leading of the Lord, we must decide and act, and leave the rest to the Lord. If we are in some way out of His will, He will so work that we will finally have His guidance. The important thing is that we sincerely *want* to do His will (John 7:17). After all, He guides us "for His name's sake" (Ps. 23:3), and it is *His* reputation that is at stake.

Paul had an open door of ministry in Ephesus, and this was important to him. He wanted to win the lost in Ephesus, not go to Corinth to pamper the saved. (On "open doors," see Acts 14:27; 2 Cor. 2:12; Col. 4:3; Rev. 3:8.) Paul was neither an optimist nor a pessimist; he was a realist. He saw both the opportunities and the obstacles. God had opened "a great door for effective work" and Paul wanted to seize the opportunities while they were still there.

An ancient Roman proverb says, "While we stop to think, we often miss our opportunity." Once we know what to do, we must do it and not delay. We can usually think of many reasons (or excuses) not to act. Even though Paul was in danger in Ephesus (1 Cor. 15:32), he planned to remain there while the door was open. Like a wise merchant, he had to "buy up the opportunity" before it vanished and would never return.

The stewardship of opportunity is important. The individual believer, and the church family, must constantly ask, *What opportunities is God giving us today?* Instead of complaining about the obstacles, we must take advantage of the opportunities, and leave the results with the Lord.

People (1 Cor. 16:10-24)

Often at the close of his letters, Paul named various people who were a part of his life and his ministry; and what a variety they were! He was not only a soul winner, but he was a friend maker; and many of his friends found their way into dedicated service for the Lord. Evangelist Dwight L. Moody possessed this same gift of making friends and then enlisting them for the Lord's service. Some of the greatest preachers and musicians of the late nineteenth and early twentieth centuries were "found" by Moody, including Ira Sankey, G. Campbell Morgan, Henry Drummond, and F.B. Meyer.

Money and opportunities are valueless without people. The church's greatest asset is people, and yet too often the church takes people for granted. Jesus did not give His disciples money, but He did invest three years training them for service so they might seize the opportunities He would present them. If *people* are prepared, then God will supply both the *opportunities* and the *money* so that His work will be accomplished.

Timothy (vv. 10-11). Timothy along with Titus, was one of Paul's special assistants, usually sent to the most difficult places. Timothy had been brought up in a godly home (2 Tim. 1:5), but it was Paul who had led the young man to Christ. Paul usually referred to him as "my own son in the faith" (1 Tim. 1:2). When John Mark abandoned Paul and returned to Jerusalem, it was Timothy who was called to work as Paul's assistant (Acts 16:1-5).

Timothy learned his lessons well and made great progress in Christian life and service (Phil. 2:20-22). Eventually, Timothy took Paul's place at Ephesus, a most difficult place to minister. (It would not be easy to be Paul's successor!) At one point, Timothy wanted to leave the city, but Paul encouraged him to stay (1 Tim. 1:3).

The advice Paul gave the Corinthians about Timothy (1 Cor. 16:10) would suggest that the young man had some physical and emotional problems (1 Tim. 5:23; 2 Tim. 1:4). He needed all the encouragement he could get. The important thing was that he was doing God's work and laboring with God's servant. A church should not expect every servant of God to be an Apostle Paul. Young men starting out in service have great potential, and the church should encourage them. "Let no man despise thee!"

Apollos (vv. 12-14). Apollos was an eloquent Jew who was brought into the full understanding of the Gospel by Priscilla and Aquila (Acts 18:24-28). He had ministered with great power at Corinth, and there was a segment of the church there that felt attached to him (1 Cor. 1:12; 3:4-8). It is unlikely that Apollos promoted this division, for his great concern seemed to be to preach Christ. In spite of the division ("The Apollos Fan Club"), Paul did not hesitate to encourage Apollos to return to Corinth for further ministry. It is clear that there was no envy on Paul's part or sense of competition on the part of Apollos.

Paul did not have the authority to place men against their will. Apollos did not feel he should go to Corinth at that time, and Paul had to concur with his decision. It is wonderful the way these different men worked together.

Perhaps it was in the light of the divisions in the church that Paul gave the admonitions in 1 Corinthians 16:13-14. *Watch* simply means "Be alert! Be vigilant!" The enemy is always at hand, and we are never safe from attack. Satan would certainly attack the church and try to hinder the ministry of Timothy or Apollos.

To *stand fast in the faith* means to have mature stability. Paul had already warned them that they were immature children who needed to grow up (1 Cor. 3:1ff). No wonder Paul added, *Quit you like men* which means, "Act like men, not children." (The word *quit* is short for "acquit"—to perform or act.) It was a call to courageous manliness at an hour when mature leadership was needed.

But even manliness needs to be balanced with love, lest leadership become dictatorship. Paul had expounded the value and virtues of love in 1 Corinthians 13. Carl Sandburg, when addressing the United States Congress, said that Abraham Lincoln was a man of "velvet steel." That is a good image for the Christian to borrow, for true manliness does not exclude tenderness.

Stephanas and his household (vv. 15-18). These were the first people to be won to Christ in Achaia, and Paul had baptized them himself, instead of leaving it to one of his helpers (1 Cor. 1:16). They became important leaders in the church, for they "devoted themselves" to Christ's service. The verb means "they appointed themselves," but it does not suggest that they pushed their way into leadership. Rather, whenever they saw a need, they went to work to meet it without waiting to be asked. They were Paul's helpers, and they labored ("toiled to the point of exhaustion") for the Lord. What a wonderful thing it is when an entire family serves the Lord faithfully in the local church.

Stephanas was joined by Fortunatus and Achaicus as an official committee sent from Corinth to Ephesus to confer with Paul about church problems. Paul saw in them a representation of the entire church; their love to Paul compensated for Paul's absence from Corinth. But these men did more than share problems with Paul; they also refreshed his spirit and brought him blessing.

This is a good place to encourage church members to refresh and encourage their pastor. Too often, believers share only problems and burdens with their spiritual leaders, and rarely share the blessings. Who is the pastor's pastor? To whom does the pastor turn for spiritual refreshment and encouragement? Every church member, if he will, can help refresh the pastor and make his burdens lighter.

Paul encouraged the church to honor this very special family and submit to their spiritual leadership. It is right to honor faithful Christians if God gets the glory.

Aquila and Priscilla (vv. 19-20). These two were a dedicated husband-and-wife team whose lives and ministries intersected and intertwined with Paul's. The apostle met them at Corinth because, like Paul, they were tentmakers (Acts 18:1-3). This godly couple had been expelled from Rome because Aquila was a Jew; but that was only part of God's providence to get them to Corinth where they could assist Paul.

Priscilla must have been a remarkable woman. This couple's names occur in the New Testament six times, and in four of these instances, Priscilla's name stands first. (The best texts put Priscilla first in Acts 18:26.) We get the impression that she was the stronger of the two, a devoted leader and witness. They worked together in serving the Lord and helping Paul.

When Paul moved from Corinth to Ephesus, Aquila and Priscilla packed up and moved their business with him and assisted in founding the church in that needy city (Acts 18:18ff). So capable were they that Paul left them to oversee the ministry while he returned to Antioch. It was while they were at Ephesus that they assisted Apollos in better understanding the truth of the Gospel.

Every local church can be thankful for husbands and wives like Aquila and Priscilla, people who work together in serving the Lord and helping the preacher. The fact that his wife was a better leader did not hinder Aquila from standing with her in their united ministry. (I am sure that Priscilla submitted to her husband and did not try to act important.) One of the Ephesian assemblies met in their house, which shows they were people given to hospitality. Romans 16:4 states that, at one time, this dedicated couple risked their own lives to help save Paul. (See Acts 19:29-30; 20:19 for possible situations where this rescue might have occurred.)

But Priscilla and Aquila did not remain in Ephesus; for when Paul wrote to the saints at Rome, he greeted this couple there (Rom. 16:3). Once again, they had a church meeting in their house (Rom. 16:5). In my itinerant ministry, I have more than once preached to an assembly that had been founded in somebody's living room.

In Paul's last letter, he sent greetings to Prisca (alternate spelling) and Aquila by way of Timothy, who was then overseeing the work in Ephesus (2 Tim. 4:19). This remarkable couple had left Rome and were now back in Ephesus, this time to assist Timothy as they had assisted Paul.

How many couples today would move as often as did Priscilla and Aquila, just to be able to serve the Lord better? And whenever they moved, they had to move their business as well. People with this kind of dedication and sacrifice are not easy to find, but they are great assets to the local church.

Paul's closing words need not detain us. The "holy kiss" (1 Cor. 16:20) was a common mode of greeting, the men kissing the men and the women kissing the women (Rom. 16:16; 2 Cor. 13:12; 1 Thes. 5:26; 1 Peter 5:14). If Paul were writing to Western churches, he would say, "Shake hands with one another."

Paul usually dictated his letters and then took the pen and added his signature. He also added his "benediction of grace" as a mark that the letter was authentic (see Gal. 6:11; 2 Thes. 3:17).

The word *anathema* is Aramaic and means "accursed" (see 1 Cor. 12:3). Not to love Christ means not to believe in Him, and unbelievers are accursed (John 3:16-21). The word *maranatha* is Greek and means "our Lord comes" or (as a prayer) "our Lord, come!" (see Rev. 22:20) If a person loves Jesus Christ, he will also love His appearing (2 Tim. 4:8).

Paul had been stern with the Corinthian believers, but he closed his letter by assuring them of his love. After all, "Faithful are the wounds of a friend" (Prov. 27:6).

Paul has shared a great deal of spiritual wisdom with us. May we receive it with meekness and put it into practice to the glory of God!

2 CORINTHIANS

OUTLINE

Key theme: God's encouragement
Key verses: 2 Corinthians 4:1, 6

I. PAUL EXPLAINS HIS MINISTRY—chapters 1–7
A. Triumphant—1–2
B. Glorious—3
C. Sincere—4
D. Believing—5
E. Loving—6–7

II. PAUL ENCOURAGES THEIR GENEROSITY—chapters 8–9
(He was receiving an offering for the Jewish saints.)
A. Principles of "grace giving"—8
B. Promises for "grace givers"—9

III. PAUL ENFORCES HIS AUTHORITY—chapters 10–13
A. The warrior, attacking the opposition—10
B. The spiritual father, protecting the church—11:1-15
C. The "fool," boasting of suffering—11:16–12:10
D. The apostle, exercising loving authority—12:11–13:14

CONTENTS

CHAPTER ONE
DOWN—BUT NOT OUT!
2 Corinthians 1:1-11

"You seem to imagine that I have no ups and downs, but just a level and lofty stretch of spiritual attainment with unbroken joy and equanimity. By no means! I am often perfectly wretched and everything appears most murky."

So wrote the man who was called in his day "The Greatest Preacher in the English-speaking World"—Dr. John Henry Jowett. He pastored leading churches, preached to huge congregations, and wrote books that were best-sellers.

"I am the subject of depressions of spirit so fearful that I hope none of you ever get to such extremes of wretchedness as I go to."

Those words were spoken in a sermon by Charles Haddon Spurgeon whose marvelous ministry in London made him perhaps the greatest preacher England ever produced.

Discouragement is no respecter of persons. In fact, discouragement seems to attack the successful far more than the unsuccessful; for the higher we climb, the farther down we can fall. We are not surprised then when we read that the great Apostle Paul was "pressed out of measure" and "despaired even of life" (2 Cor. 1:8). Great as he was in character and ministry, Paul was human just like the rest of us.

Paul could have escaped these burdens except that he had a call from God (2 Cor. 1:1) and a concern to help people. He had founded the church at Corinth and had ministered there for a year and a half (Acts 18:1-18). When serious problems arose in the church after his departure, he sent Timothy to deal with them (1 Cor. 4:17) and then wrote the letter that we call 1 Corinthians.

Unfortunately, matters grew worse and Paul had to make a "painful visit" to Corinth to confront the troublemakers (2 Cor. 2:1ff). Still, no solution. He then wrote "a severe letter" which was delivered by his associate, Titus (2 Cor. 2:4-9; 7:8-12). After a great deal of distress, Paul finally met Titus and got the good report that the problem had been solved. It was then that he wrote the letter we call 2 Corinthians.

He wrote the letter for several reasons. First, he wanted to encourage the church to forgive and restore the member who had caused all the trouble (2 Cor. 2:6-11). He also wanted to explain his change in plans (2 Cor. 1:15-22) and enforce his authority as an apostle (2 Cor. 4:1-2; 10–12). Finally, he wanted to encourage the church to share in the special "relief offering" he was taking up for the needy saints in Judea (2 Cor. 8–9).

One of the key words in this letter is *comfort* or *encouragement.* The Greek word means "called to one's side to help." The verb is used eighteen times in this letter, and the noun eleven times. In spite of all the trials he experienced, Paul was able (by the grace of God) to write a letter saturated with encouragement.

What was Paul's secret of victory when he was experiencing pressures and trials? His secret was *God.* When you find yourself discouraged and ready to quit, get your attention off of yourself and focus it on God. Out of his own difficult experience, Paul tells us how we can find encouragement in God. He gives us three simple reminders.

Remember What God Is to You (2 Cor. 1:3)

Paul began his letter with a doxology. He certainly could not sing about his circumstances, but he could sing about the God who is in control of all circumstances. Paul had learned that praise is an important factor in achieving victory over discouragement and depression. "Praise changes things" just as much as "Prayer changes things."

Praise Him because He is God! You find this phrase "blessed be God" in two other places in the New Testament, in Ephesians 1:3 and 1 Peter 1:3. In Ephesians 1:3 Paul praised God for what He did *in the past,* when He "chose us in [Christ]" (Eph. 1:4) and blessed us "with all spiritual blessings" (NASB). In 1 Peter 1:3 Peter praised God for *future* blessings and "a living hope" (NASB). But in 2 Corinthians Paul praised God for *present* blessings, for what God was accomplishing then and there.

During the horrors of the Thirty Years' War, Pastor Martin Rinkart faithfully served the people in Eilenburg, Saxony. He conducted as many as 40 funerals a day, a total of over 4,000 during his ministry. Yet out of this devastating experience, he wrote a "table grace" for his children which today we use as a hymn of thanksgiving:

Now thank we all our God,
With heart and hands and voices,
Who wondrous things hath done,
In whom His world rejoices!

Praise Him because He is the Father of our Lord Jesus Christ! It is because of Jesus Christ that we can call God "Father" and even approach Him as His children. God sees us in His Son and loves us as He loves His Son (John 17:23). We are "beloved of God" (Rom. 1:7) because we are "accepted in the beloved" (Eph. 1:6).

Whatever the Father did for Jesus when He was ministering on earth, He is able to do for us today. We are dear to the Father because His Son is dear to Him and we are citizens of "the kingdom of His dear Son [the Son of His love]" (Col. 1:13). We are precious to the Father, and He will see to it that the pressures of life will not destroy us.

Praise Him because He is the Father of mercies! To the Jewish people, the phrase *father of* means "originator of." Satan is the father of lies (John 8:44) because lies originated with him. According to Genesis 4:21, Jubal was the father of musical instruments because he originated the pipe and the harp. God is the Father of mercies because all mercy originates with Him and can be secured only from Him.

God in His grace gives us what we do not deserve, and in His mercy He does not give us what we do deserve. "It is of the Lord's mercies that we are not consumed" (Lam. 3:22). God's mercy is *manifold* (Neh. 9:19), *tender* (Ps. 25:6), and *great* (Num. 14:19). The Bible frequently speaks of the "multitude of God's mercies" so inexhaustible is the supply (Pss. 5:7; 51:1; 69:13, 16; 106:7, 45; Lam. 3:32).

Praise Him because He is the God of all comfort! The words *comfort* or *consolation* (same root word in the Greek) are repeated ten times in 2 Corinthians 1:1-11. We must not think of *comfort* in terms of "sympathy," because sympathy can weaken us instead of strengthen us. God does not pat us on the head and give us a piece of candy or a toy to distract our attention from our troubles. No, He puts strength into our hearts so we can face our trials and triumph over them. Our English word *comfort* comes from two Latin words meaning "with strength." The Greek word means "to come alongside and help." It is the same word used for the Holy Spirit ("the Comforter") in John 14–16.

God can encourage us by His Word and through His Spirit, but sometimes He uses other believers to give us the encouragement we need (2 Cor. 2:7-8; 7:6-7). How wonderful it would be if all of us had the nickname "Barnabas—son of encouragement"! (Acts 4:36)

When you find yourself discouraged because of difficult circumstances, it is easy to look at yourself and your feelings, or to focus on the problems around you. But the first step we must take is to look by faith to the Lord and realize all that God is to us. "I will lift up mine eyes unto the hills, from whence cometh my help. My help cometh from the Lord, which made heaven and earth" (Ps. 121:1-2).

Remember What God Does for You (2 Cor. 1:4a, 8-11)

He permits the trials to come. There are ten basic words for suffering in the Greek language, and Paul used five of them in this letter. The most frequently used word is *thlipsis,* which means "narrow, confined, under pressure," and in this letter is translated *affliction* (2 Cor. 2:4; 4:17), *tribulation* (2 Cor. 1:4), and *trouble* (2 Cor. 1:4, 8). Paul felt hemmed in by difficult circumstances, and the only way he could look was up.

In 2 Corinthians 1:5-6, Paul used the word *pathēma,* "suffering," which was also used for the sufferings of our Saviour (1 Peter 1:11; 5:1). There are some sufferings that we endure simply because we are human and subject to pain; but there are other sufferings that come because we are God's people and want to serve Him.

We must never think that trouble is an accident. For the believer, everything is a divine appointment. There are only three possible outlooks a person can take when it comes to the trials of life. If our trials are the products of "fate" or "chance," then our only recourse is to give up. Nobody can control fate or chance. If *we* have to control everything ourselves, then the situation is equally as hopeless. But if *God* is in control, and we trust Him, then we can overcome circumstances with His help.

God encourages us in all our tribulations by teaching us from His Word that it is He who permits trials to come.

He is in control of trials (v. 8). "We were under great pressure, far beyond our ability to endure, so that we despaired even of life" (NIV). Paul was weighed down like a beast of burden with a load too heavy to bear. But God knew just how much Paul could take and He kept the situation in control.

We do not know what the specific "trouble" was, but it was great enough to make Paul think he was going to die. Whether it was peril from his many enemies (see Acts 19:21ff; 1 Cor. 15:30-32), serious illness, or special satanic attack, we do not know; but we do know that God controlled the circumstances and protected His servant. When God puts His children into the furnace, He keeps His hand on the thermostat and His eye on the thermometer (1 Cor. 10:13; 1 Peter 1:6-7). Paul may have despaired of life, but God did not despair of Paul.

God enables us to bear our trials (v. 9). The first thing He must do is show us how weak we are in ourselves. Paul was a gifted and experienced servant of God, who had been through many different kinds of trials (see 2 Cor. 4:8-12; 11:23ff). Surely all of this experience would be sufficient for him to face these new difficulties and overcome them.

But God wants us to trust *Him*—not our gifts or abilities, our experience, or our "spiritual reserves." Just about the time we feel self-confident and able to meet the enemy, we fail miserably. "For when I am weak, then am I strong" (2 Cor. 12:10).

When you and I die to self, then God's resurrection power can go to work. It was when Abraham and Sarah were as good as dead physically that God's resurrection power enabled them to have the promised son (Rom. 4:16-25). However, "dying to self" does not mean idle complacency, doing nothing and expecting God to do everything. You can be sure that Paul prayed, searched the Scriptures, consulted with his associates, and trusted God to work. The God who raises the dead is sufficient for *any* difficulty of life! He is able, but we must be available.

Paul did not deny the way he felt, nor does God want us to deny our emotions. "We were troubled on every side; without were fightings, within were fears" (2 Cor. 7:5). The phrase "sentence of death" in 2 Corinthians 1:9 could refer to an official verdict, perhaps an order for Paul's arrest and execution. Keep in mind that the unbelieving Jews hounded Paul's trail and wanted to eliminate him (Acts 20:19). "Perils by my own countrymen" must not be overlooked in the list of dangers (2 Cor. 11:26).

God delivers us from our trials (v. 10). Paul saw God's hand of deliverance whether he looked back, around, or ahead. The word Paul used means "to help out of distress, to save and protect." God does not always deliver us immediately, nor in the same way. James was beheaded, yet Peter was delivered from prison (Acts 12). *Both* were delivered, but in different ways. Sometimes God delivers us *from* our trials, and at other times He delivers us *in* our trials.

God's deliverance was in response to Paul's faith, as well as to the faith of praying people in Corinth (2 Cor. 1:11). "This poor man cried, and the Lord heard him, and saved him out of all his troubles" (Ps. 34:6).

God is glorified through our trials (v. 11). When Paul reported what God had done for him, a great chorus of praise and thanksgiving went up from the saints to the throne of God. The highest service you and I can render on earth is to bring glory to God, and sometimes that service involves suffering. "The gift bestowed" refers to Paul's deliverance from death, a wonderful gift indeed!

Paul was never ashamed to ask Christians to pray for him. In at least seven of his letters, he mentioned his great need for prayer support (Rom. 15:30-32; Eph. 6:18-19; Phil. 1:19; Col. 4:3; 1 Thes. 5:25; 2 Thes. 3:1; Phile. 22). Paul and the believers in Corinth were helping each other (2 Cor. 1:11, 24).

A missionary friend told me about the miraculous deliverance of his daughter from what was diagnosed as a fatal disease. At the very time the girl was so ill, several friends in the United States were praying for the family; and God answered prayer and healed the girl. The greatest help we can give to God's servants is "helping together by prayer."

The word *sunupourgeō* translated "helping together" is used only here in the Greek New Testament and is composed of three words: with, under, work. It is a picture of laborers under the burden, working together to get the job accomplished. It is encouraging to know that the Holy Spirit also assists us in our praying and helps to carry the load (Rom. 8:26).

God works out His purposes in the trials of life, if we yield to Him, trust Him, and obey what He tells us to do. Difficulties can increase our faith and strengthen our prayer lives. Difficulties can draw us closer to other Christians as they share the burdens with us. Difficulties can be used to glorify God. So, when you find yourself in the trials of life, remember what God is to you and what God does for you.

Remember What God Does through You (2 Cor. 1:4b-7)

In times of suffering, most of us are prone to think only of ourselves and to forget others. We become cisterns instead of channels. Yet one reason for trials is so that you and I might learn to be channels of blessing to comfort and encourage others. Because God has encouraged us, we can encourage them.

One of my favorite preachers is Dr. George W. Truett, who pastored the First Baptist Church of Dallas, Texas for nearly 50 years. In one of his sermons, he told about an unbelieving couple whose baby died suddenly. Dr. Truett conducted the funeral and later had the joy of seeing them both trust Jesus Christ.

Many months later, a young mother lost her baby; and again, Dr. Truett was called to bring her comfort. But nothing he shared with her seemed to help her. But at the funeral service, the newly converted mother stepped to the girl's side and said, "I passed through this, and I know what you are passing through. God called me, and through the darkness I came to Him. He has comforted me, and He will comfort you!"

Dr. Truett said, "The first mother did more for the second mother than I could have done, maybe in days and months; for the first young mother had traveled the road of suffering herself."

However, Paul made it clear that we do not need to experience *exactly* the same trials in order to be able to share God's encouragement. If we have experienced God's comfort, then we can "comfort them which are in any trouble" (2 Cor. 1:4b). Of course, if we have experienced similar tribulations, they can help us identify better with others and know better how they feel; but our experiences cannot alter the comfort of God. That remains sufficient and efficient no matter what our own experiences may have been.

Later in 2 Corinthians 12, Paul will give us an example of this principle. He was given a thorn in the flesh—some kind of physical suffering that constantly buffeted him. We do not know what this "thorn in the flesh" was, nor do we need to know. What we do know is that Paul experienced the grace of God and then shared that encouragement with us. No matter what your trial may be, "My grace is sufficient for thee" (2 Cor. 12:9) is a promise you can claim. We would not have that promise if Paul had not suffered.

The subject of human suffering is not easy to understand, for there are mysteries to the working of God that we will never grasp until we get to heaven. Sometimes we suffer because of our own sin and rebellion, as did Jonah. Sometimes we suffer to keep us from sinning, as was the case with Paul (2 Cor. 12:7). Suffering can perfect our character (Rom. 5:1-5) and help us to share the character of God (Heb. 12:1-11).

But suffering can also help us to minister to others. In every church, there are mature saints of God who have suffered and experienced God's grace, and they are the great "encouragers" in the congregation. Paul experienced trouble, not as punishment for something he had done, but as preparation for something he was yet *going to do*—minister to others in need. Just think of the trials that King David had to endure in order to give us the great encouragement that we find in the Psalms.

Second Corinthians 1:7 makes it clear that there was always the possibility that the situation might be reversed: the Corinthian believers might go through trials and receive God's grace so that they might encourage others. God sometimes calls a church family to experience special trials in order that He might bestow on them special abundant grace.

God's gracious encouragement helps us *if we learn to endure*. "Patient endurance" is an evidence of faith. If we become bitter or critical of God, if we rebel instead of submit, then our trials will work *against* us instead of *for* us. The ability to endure difficulties patiently, without giving up, is a mark of spiritual maturity (Heb. 12:1-7).

God has to work *in* us before He can work *through* us. It is much easier for us to grow in knowledge than to grow in grace (2 Peter 3:18). Learning God's truth and getting it into our heads is one thing, but living God's truth and getting it into our character is quite something else. God put young Joseph through thirteen years of tribulation before He made him second ruler of Egypt, and what a great man Joseph turned out to be! God always prepares us for what He is preparing for us, and a part of that preparation is suffering.

In this light, 2 Corinthians 1:5 is very important: even our Lord Jesus Christ had to suffer! When we suffer in the will of God, we are sharing the sufferings of the Saviour. This does not refer to His "vicarious sufferings" on the cross, for only He could die as a sinless substitute for us (1 Peter 2:21-25). Paul was referring here to "the fellowship of His sufferings" (Phil. 3:10), the trials that we endure because, like Christ, we are faithfully doing the Father's will. This is suffering "for righteousness' sake" (Matt. 5:10-12).

But as the sufferings increase, so does the supply of God's grace. The word *abound* suggests the picture of a river overflowing. "But He giveth more grace" (James 4:6). This is an important principle to grasp: God has ample grace for our every need, *but He will not bestow it in advance.* We come by faith to the throne of grace "that we may obtain mercy, and find grace to help in time of need" (Heb. 4:16). The Greek word means "help when you need it, timely help."

I read about a devoted believer who was arrested for his faith and condemned to be burned at the stake. The night before the execution, he wondered if he would have enough grace to become a human torch; so he tested his courage by putting his finger into the flame of the candle. Of course, it burned him and he pulled his hand back in pain. He was certain that he would never be able to face martyrdom without failing. But the next day, God gave him the grace he needed, and he had a joyful and triumphant witness before his enemies.

Now we can better understand 2 Corinthians 1:9; for, if we could store up God's grace for emergency use, we would be prone to trust ourselves and not "the God of all grace" (1 Peter 5:10). All the resources God gives us may be kept for future use—money, food, knowledge, etc.—but the grace of God cannot be stored away.

Rather, as we experience the grace of God in our daily lives, it is *invested into our lives as godly character* (see Rom. 5:1-5). This investment pays dividends when new troubles come our way, for godly character enables us to endure tribulation to the glory of God.

There is a "companionship" to suffering: it can draw us closer to Christ and to His people. But if we start to wallow in self-pity, suffering will create isolation instead of involvement. We will build walls and not bridges.

The important thing is to fix your attention on God and not on yourself. Remember *what God is to you*—"the Father of our Lord Jesus Christ, the Father of mercies, and the God of all comfort" (2 Cor. 1:3). Remember *what God does for you*—that He is able to handle your trials and make them work out for your good and His glory. Finally, remember *what God does through you*—and let Him use you to be an encouragement to others.

CHAPTER TWO
YOU DON'T HAVE TO FAIL!
2 Corinthians 1:12–2:17

In his book, *Profiles in Courage,* John F. Kennedy wrote, "Great crises produce great men and great deeds of courage."

While it is true that a crisis helps to make a person, it is also true that a crisis helps to reveal what a person is made of. Pilate faced a great crisis, but his handling of it did not give him either courage or greatness. How we handle the difficulties of life will depend largely on what kind of character we have; for what life does to us depends on what life finds in us.

In this very personal letter, Paul opened his heart to the Corinthians (and to us) and revealed the trials he had experienced. To begin with, he had been severely criticized by some of the people in Corinth because he had changed his plans and apparently not kept his promise. When Christians misunderstand each other, the wounds can go very deep. Then, there was the problem of opposition to his apostolic authority in the church. One of the members—possibly a leader—had to be disciplined, and this gave Paul great sorrow. Finally, there were the difficult circumstances Paul had to endure in Asia (2 Cor. 1:8-11), a trial so severe that he despaired of life.

What kept Paul from failing? Other people, facing these same crises, would have collapsed! Yet Paul not only triumphed over the circumstances, but out of them produced a great letter that even today is helping God's people experience victory. What were the spiritual resources that kept Paul going?

A Clear Conscience (2 Cor. 1:12-24)

Our English word *conscience* comes from two Latin words: *com,* meaning "with," and *scire,* meaning "to know." Conscience is that inner faculty that "knows with" our spirit and approves when we do right, but accuses when we do wrong. Conscience is not the Law of God, but it bears witness to that Law. It is the window that lets in the light; and if the window gets dirty because we disobey, then the light becomes dimmer and dimmer (see Matt. 6:22-23; Rom. 2:14-16).

Paul used the word *conscience* twenty-three times in his letters and spoken ministry as given in Acts. "And herein do I exercise myself, to have always a conscience void of offense toward God, and toward men" (Acts 24:16). When a person has a good conscience, he has integrity, not duplicity; and he can be trusted.

Why were the Corinthians accusing Paul of deception and carelessness? Because he had been forced to change his plans. He had originally promised to spend the winter in Corinth "if the Lord permit" (1 Cor. 16:2-8). Paul wanted to gather the offerings that the Corinthians collected for the poor Jewish believers and give the church the privilege of sending him and his associates on their way to Jerusalem.

Much to Paul's regret and embarrassment, he had to change those plans. I sympathize with him, for in my own limited ministry I have sometimes had to change plans and even cancel meetings—and without benefit of apostolic authority! "Plans get you into things," said Will Rogers, "but you have to work your way out." Paul now planned to make *two* visits to Corinth, one on his way into Macedonia, and the other on his way from Macedonia. He would then add the Corinthian collection to that of the Macedonian churches and go on his way to Jerusalem.

Alas, even Plan B had to be scrapped. Why? Because his own loving heart could not endure another "painful visit" (2 Cor. 1:23; 2:1-3). Paul had informed the church about his change in plans, but even this did not silence the opposition. They accused him of following "fleshly wisdom" (2 Cor. 1:12), of being careless with the will of God (2 Cor. 1:17), and of making plans just to please himself. They were saying, "If Paul says or writes one thing, he really means another! His yes is no, and his no is yes."

Misunderstandings among God's people are often very difficult to untangle, because one misunderstanding often leads to another. Once we start to question the integrity of others or distrust their words, the door is opened to all kinds of problems. But, no matter what his accusers might say, Paul stood firm because he had a clear conscience. What he wrote, what he said, and what he lived were all in agreement. And, after all, he had added to his original plan "if the Lord permit" (1 Cor. 16:7, and note James 4:13-17).

When you have a clear conscience, you will live in the light of the return of Jesus Christ (2 Cor. 1:14). "The day of Jesus Christ" refers to that time when Christ appears and takes His church to heaven. Paul was certain that, at the Judgment Seat of Christ, he would rejoice over the Corinthian believers and they would rejoice over him. Whatever misunderstandings there may be today, when we stand before Jesus Christ, all will be forgiven, forgotten, and transformed into glory, to the praise of Jesus Christ.

When you have a clear conscience, you will be serious about the will of God (2 Cor. 1:15-18). Paul did not make his plans carelessly or haphazardly; he sought the leading of the Lord. Sometimes he was not sure what God wanted him to do (Acts 16:6-10), but he knew how to wait on the Lord. His motives were sincere: he was seeking to please the Lord and not men. When we stop to consider how difficult both transportation and communication were in that day, we can marvel that Paul did not have *more* problems with his busy schedule.

Jesus instructed us to mean what we say. "Say just a simple, 'Yes, I will' or 'No, I won't.' Your word is enough. To strengthen your promise with a vow shows that something is wrong" (Matt. 5:37, TLB). Only a person with bad character uses extra words to strengthen his yes or no. The Corinthians knew that Paul was a man of true character, because he was a man with a clear conscience. During his eighteen months of ministry among them, Paul had proved himself faithful; and he had not changed.

When you have a clear conscience, you glorify Jesus Christ (2 Cor. 1:19-20). You cannot glorify Christ and practice deception at the same time. If you do, you will violate your conscience and erode your character; but eventually the truth will come out. The Corinthians were saved because Paul and his friends preached Jesus Christ to them. How could God reveal truth *through false instruments?* The witness and the walk of the minister must go together, for the work that we do flows out of the lives that we live.

There is no yes and no about Jesus Christ. He is God's "eternal yes" to those who trust Him. "For no matter how many promises God has made, they are yes in Christ. And so through Him the Amen is spoken by us to the glory of God" (2 Cor. 1:20, NIV). Jesus Christ reveals the promises, fulfills the promises, and enables us to claim the promises! One of the blessings of a good conscience is that we are not afraid to face God or men, or to claim the promises God gives in His Word. Paul was not guilty of "manipulating" the Word of God in order to support his own sinful practices (see 2 Cor. 4:2).

Finally, when you have a clear conscience, you will be on good terms with the Spirit of God (2 Cor. 1:21-24). The word *established* is a business term and refers to the guarantee of the fulfilling of a contract. It was the assurance that the seller gave to the buyer that the product was as advertised, or that the service would be rendered as promised.

The Holy Spirit is God's guarantee that He is dependable and will accomplish all that He has promised. Paul was careful not to grieve the Holy Spirit; and, because the Spirit was not convicting him, he knew that his motives were pure and his conscience was clear.

All Christians have been anointed by the Spirit (2 Cor. 1:21). In the Old Testament, the only persons who were anointed by God were prophets, priests, and kings. Their anointing equipped them for service. As we yield to the Spirit, He enables us to serve God and to live godly lives. He gives us the special spiritual discernment that we need to serve God acceptably (1 John 2:20, 27).

The Spirit has also sealed us (2 Cor. 1:22; Eph. 1:13) so that we belong to Christ and are claimed by Him. The witness of the Spirit within guarantees that we are authentic children of God and not counterfeit (Rom. 5:5; 8:9). The Spirit also assures us that He will protect us, because we are His property.

Finally, the Holy Spirit enables us to serve others (2 Cor. 1:23-24), not as "spiritual dictators" who tell others what to do, but as servants who seek to help others grow. The false teachers who invaded the Corinthian church were guilty of being dictators (see 2 Cor. 11), and this had turned the hearts of the people away from Paul, who had sacrificed so much for them.

The Spirit is God's "earnest" (down payment, guarantee, security) that one day we shall be with Him in heaven and possess glorified bodies (see Eph. 1:14). He enables us to enjoy the blessings of heaven in our hearts today! Because of the indwelling Holy Spirit, Paul was able to have a clear conscience and face misunderstandings with love and patience. If you live to please people, misunderstandings will depress you; but if you live to please God, you can face misunderstandings with faith and courage.

A Compassionate Heart (2 Cor. 2:1-11)

One of the members of the Corinthian church caused Paul a great deal of pain. We are not sure if this is the same man Paul wrote about in 1 Corinthians 5, the man who was living in open fornication, or if it was another person, someone who publicly challenged Paul's apostolic authority. Paul had made a quick visit to Corinth to deal with this problem (2 Cor. 12:14; 13:1) and had also written a painful letter to them about the situation. In all of this, he revealed a compassionate heart. Note the evidences of Paul's love.

Love puts others first (vv. 1-4). He did not think of his own feelings, but of the feelings of others. In Christian ministry, those who bring us great joy can also create for us great sorrow; and this was what Paul was experiencing. He wrote them a stern letter, born out of the anguish of his own heart, and bathed in Christian love. His great desire was that the church might obey the Word, discipline the offender, and bring purity and peace to the congregation.

"Faithful are the wounds of a friend, but the kisses of an enemy are deceitful" (Prov. 27:6). Paul knew that his words would wound those he loved, and this brought pain to his heart. But he also knew (as every loving parent knows) that there is a big difference between *hurting* someone and *harming* him. Sometimes those who love us must hurt us in order to keep us from harming ourselves.

Paul could have exercised his apostolic authority and commanded the people to respect him and obey him; but he preferred to minister with patience and love. God knew that Paul's change in plans had as its motive the sparing of the church from further pain (2 Cor. 1:23-24). Love always considers the feelings of others and seeks to put their good ahead of everything else.

Love also seeks to help others grow (vv. 5-6). It is worth noting that Paul did not mention the name of the man who had opposed him and divided the church family. However, Paul did tell the church to discipline this man *for his own good.* If the person referred to is the fornicator mentioned in 1 Corinthians 5, then these verses indicate that the church did hold a meeting and discipline the man, and that he repented of his sins and was restored.

True discipline is an evidence of love (see Heb. 12). Some young parents with "modern views" of how to raise children refuse to discipline their disobedient offspring because these parents claim they love their children too much. But if they really loved their children, they would chasten them.

Church discipline is not a popular subject or a widespread practice. Too many churches sweep such things "under the rug" instead of obeying the Scriptures and confronting the situation boldly by "speaking the truth in love" (Eph. 4:15). "Peace at any price" is not a biblical principle, for there cannot be true spiritual peace without purity (James 3:13-18). Problems that are "swept under the rug" have a way of multiplying and creating even worse problems later on.

The man whom Paul confronted, and whom the church disciplined, was helped by this kind of loving attention. When I was a child, I didn't always appreciate the discipline that my parents gave me, though I must confess that I deserved far more than I received. But now that I look back, I can thank God that they loved me enough to hurt me and hinder me from harming myself. Now I understand what they really meant when they said, "This hurts us more than it hurts you."

Love forgives and encourages (vv. 7-11). Paul urged the church family to forgive the man, and he gave solid reasons to back up this admonition. To begin with, they were to forgive him *for his own sake,* "lest [he] be swallowed up with overmuch sorrow" (2 Cor. 2:7-8). Forgiveness is the medicine that helps to heal broken hearts. It was important that the church assure this repentant member of their love.

In my own pastoral ministry, I have shared in meetings where disciplined members have been forgiven and restored to fellowship; and they have been high and holy hours in my life. When a church family assures a forgiven brother or sister that the sin is forgotten and the fellowship restored, there is a sense of the Lord's presence that is wonderful to experience. Every parent who disciplines a child must follow that discipline with assurance of love and forgiveness, or the discipline will do more harm than good.

They should confirm their love to the forgiven brother *for the Lord's sake* (2 Cor. 2:9-10). After all, discipline is as much a matter of obedience to the Lord as it is obligation to a brother. The problem was not simply between a sinning brother and a grieving apostle: it was also between a sinning brother and a grieving Saviour. The man had sinned against Paul and the church, but he had most of all sinned against the Lord. When timid church leaders try to "whitewash" situations instead of facing them honestly, they are grieving the heart of the Lord.

Paul gave a third reason: they must forgive the offender *for the church's sake* (2 Cor. 2:11). When there is an unforgiving spirit in a congregation because sin has not been dealt with in a biblical manner, it gives Satan a "beachhead" from which he can operate in the congregation. We grieve the Holy Spirit and "give place to the devil" when we harbor an unforgiving spirit (Eph. 4:27-32).

One of Satan's "devices" is to accuse believers who have sinned so that they feel their case is hopeless. I have had people write me or phone me to ask for help because they have been under satanic oppression and accusation. The Holy Spirit convicts us of sin so that we will confess it and turn to Christ for cleansing; but Satan accuses us of sin so that we will despair and give up.

When an offending brother or sister is disciplined according to the Bible, and repents, then the church family must forgive and restore the member, and the matter must be forgotten and never brought up again. If the church family—or any person in the family—carries an unforgiving spirit, then Satan will use that attitude as a beachhead for new assaults against the church.

Paul was able to overcome the problems that he faced because he had a clear conscience and a compassionate heart. But there was a third spiritual resource that gave him victory.

A Conquering Faith (2 Cor. 2:12-17)

It appeared in Asia that Paul's plans had completely fallen apart. Where was Titus? What was going on at Corinth? Paul had open doors of ministry at Troas, but he had no peace in his heart to walk through those doors. Humanly speaking, it looked like the end of the battle, with Satan as the victor.

Except for one thing: Paul had a conquering faith! He was able to break out in praise and write, "Thanks be unto God!" (2 Cor. 2:14) This song of praise was born out of the assurances Paul had because he trusted the Lord.

Paul was sure that God was leading him (v. 14a). The circumstances were not comfortable, and Paul could not explain the detours and disappointments, but he was sure that God was in control. The believer can always be sure that God is working everything together for good, so long as we love Him and seek to obey His will (Rom. 8:28). This promise is not an excuse for carelessness, but it is an encouragement for confidence.

A friend of mine was to meet a Christian leader behind the Iron Curtain and arrange for the publishing of a certain book, but all the arrangements fell through. My friend was alone in a dangerous place wondering what to do next, when he "chanced" to make contact with a stranger—who took him right to the very leaders he wanted to reach! It was the providence of God at work, the fulfilling of Romans 8:28.

Paul was also sure that God was leading him in triumph (v. 14b). The picture here is that of the "Roman Triumph," the special tribute that Rome gave to their conquering generals. It was their equivalent of the American "ticker-tape parade."

If a commander in chief won a complete victory over the enemy on foreign soil, and if he killed at least 5,000 enemy soldiers and gained new territory for the Emperor, then that commander in chief was entitled to a Roman Triumph. The processional would include the commander riding in a golden chariot, surrounded by his officers. The parade would also include a display of the spoils of battle, as well as the captive enemy soldiers. The Roman priests would also be in the parade, carrying burning incense to pay tribute to the victorious army.

The procession would follow a special route through the city and would end at the Circus Maximus where the helpless captives would entertain the people by fighting wild beasts. It was a very special day in Rome when the citizens were treated to a full-scale "Roman Triumph."

How does this piece of history apply to the burdened believer today? Jesus Christ, our great Commander in chief, came to foreign soil (this earth) and completely defeated the enemy (Satan). Instead of killing 5,000 persons, He gave life to more than 5,000 persons—to 3,000 plus at Pentecost and to another 2,000 plus shortly after Pentecost (Acts 2:41; 4:4). Jesus Christ claimed the spoils of battle—lost souls who had been in bondage to sin and Satan (Luke 11:14-22; Eph. 4:8; Col. 2:15). What a splendid victory!

The victorious general's sons would walk behind their father's chariot, sharing in his victory; and that is where believers are today—following in Christ's triumph. We do not fight *for* victory; we fight *from* victory. Neither in Asia nor in Corinth did the situation look like victory to Paul, but he believed God—and God turned defeat into victory.

Paul was sure that God was using him as He was leading him (vv. 14c-17). As the Roman priests burned the incense in the parade, that odor affected different people in different ways. To the triumphant soldiers, it meant life and victory; but to the conquered enemy, it meant defeat and death. They were on their way to be killed by the beasts.

Using this image of the incense, Paul pictured the Christian ministry. He saw believers as incense, giving forth the fragrance of Jesus Christ in their lives and labors. To God, believers are the very fragrance of Jesus Christ. To other believers, we are the fragrance of life; but to unbelievers, we are the fragrance of death. In other words, the Christian life and ministry are matters of life and death. The way we live and work can mean life or death to a lost world around us.

No wonder Paul cried out, "And who is sufficient for these things?" (2 Cor. 2:16) He gave his answer in the next chapter: "our sufficiency is of God" (2 Cor. 3:5). He reminded the Corinthians that his heart was pure and his motives sincere. After all, there was no need to be clever and "peddle" the Word of God, when he was following in the triumphant train of the victorious Saviour! They might misunderstand him, but God knew his heart.

We don't have to fail! Circumstances may discourage us, and people may oppose us and misunderstand us; but we have in Christ the spiritual resources to win the battle: a clear conscience, a compassionate heart, and a conquering faith.

"If God be for us, who can be against us? . . . Nay, in all these things we are more than conquerors through Him that loved us" (Rom. 8:31, 37).

CHAPTER THREE
FROM GLORY TO GLORY
2 Corinthians 3

Wherever you find the genuine, you will find somebody promoting the counterfeit. Even art critics have been fooled by fake "masterpieces," and sincere publishers have purchased "valuable manuscripts," only to discover them to be forgeries. Henry Ward Beecher was right when he said, "A lie always needs a truth for a handle to it."

No sooner did the Gospel of God's grace begin to spread among the Gentiles than a counterfeit "gospel" appeared, a mixture of Law and grace. It was carried by a zealous group of people that we have come to call "the Judaizers." Paul wrote his letter to the Galatians to refute their doctrines, and you will find him referring to them several times in 2 Corinthians.

Their major emphasis was that salvation was by faith in Christ *plus* the keeping of the Law (see Acts 15:1ff). They also taught that the believer is perfected in his faith by obeying the Law of Moses. Their "gospel of legalism" was very popular, since human nature enjoys achieving religious goals instead of simply trusting Christ and allowing the Holy Spirit to work. It is much easier to measure "religion" than true righteousness.

Paul looked on these false teachers as "peddlers" of the Word of God (see 2 Cor. 2:17, NIV), "religious racketeers" who preyed on ignorant people. He rejected their devious methods of teaching the Bible (2 Cor. 4:2), and despised their tendency to boast about their converts (2 Cor. 10:12-18). One reason why the Corinthians were behind in their contribution to the special offering was that the Judaizers had "robbed" the church (2 Cor. 11:7-12, 20; 12:14).

How did Paul refute the doctrines and practices of these legalistic false teachers? By showing the surpassing glory of the ministry of the Gospel of the grace of God. In 2 Corinthians 3, Paul contrasted the ministry of the Old Covenant (Law) with the ministry of the New Covenant (grace), and he proved the superiority of the New Covenant ministry. Note the contrasts that he presented.

Tablets of Stone—Human Hearts (2 Cor. 3:1-3)

The Judaizers boasted that they carried "letters of recommendation" (2 Cor. 3:1, NIV) from the "important people" in the Jerusalem church, and they pointed out that Paul had no such credentials. It is a sad thing when a person measures his worth by what people say about him instead of by what God knows about him. Paul needed no credentials from church leaders: his life and ministry were the only recommendations needed.

When God gave the Law, He wrote it on tablets of stone, and those tablets were placed in the ark of the covenant. Even if the Israelites could read the two tablets, this experience would not change their lives. The Law is an external thing, and people need an *internal* power if their lives are to be transformed. The legalist can admonish us with his "Do this!" or "Don't do that!" but he cannot give us the power to obey. If we do obey, often it is not from the heart—and we end up worse than before!

The ministry of grace changes the heart. The Spirit of God uses the Word of God and writes it on the heart. The Corinthians were wicked sinners when Paul came to them, but his ministry of the Gospel of God's grace completely changed their lives (see 1 Cor. 6:9-11). Their experience of God's grace certainly meant more to them than the letters of commendation carried by the false teachers. The Corinthian believers were lovingly written on Paul's heart, and the Spirit of God had written the truth on their hearts, making them "living epistles of Christ."

The test of ministry is changed lives, not press releases or statistics. It is much easier for the legalist to boast, because he can "measure" his ministry by external standards. The believer who patiently ministers by the Spirit of God must leave the results with the Lord. How tragic that the Corinthians followed the boastful Judaizers and broke the heart of the man who had rescued them from judgment.

Death—Life (2 Cor. 3:4-6)

Paul was quick to give the glory to God and not to himself. His confidence ("trust") was in God, and his sufficiency came from God. Paul was a brilliant and well-educated man; yet he did not depend on his own adequacy. He depended on the Lord.

The legalists, of course, told people that any person could obey the Law and become spiritual. A legalistic ministry has a way of inflating the egos of people. When you emphasize the grace of God, you must tell people that they are lost sinners who cannot save themselves. Paul's testimony was, "But by the grace of God I am what I am" (1 Cor. 15:10). No one is sufficient of himself to minister to the hearts of people. That sufficiency can only come from God.

As you read this chapter, note the different names that Paul used for the Old Covenant and the New Covenant as he contrasted them. In 2 Corinthians 3:6, "the letter" refers to the Old Covenant Law, while "the spirit" refers to the New Covenant message of grace. Paul was not contrasting two approaches to the Bible, a "literal interpretation" and a "spiritual interpretation." He was reminding his readers that the Old Covenant Law could not give life; it was a ministry of death (see Gal. 3:21). The Gospel gives life to those who believe because of the work of Jesus Christ on the cross.

Paul was not suggesting that the Law was a mistake or that its ministry was unimportant. Far from it! Paul knew that the lost sinner must be slain by the Law and left helplessly condemned before he can be saved by God's grace. John the Baptist came with a message of judgment, preparing the way for Jesus and His message of saving grace.

A legalistic ministry brings death. Preachers who major on rules and regulations keep their congregations under a dark cloud of guilt, and this kills their joy, power, and effective witness for Christ. Christians who are constantly measuring each other, comparing "results," and competing with each other, soon discover that they are depending on the flesh and not the power of the Spirit. There never was a standard that could transform a person's life, and that includes the Ten Commandments. Only the grace of God, ministered by the Spirit of God, can transform lost sinners into living epistles that glorify Jesus Christ.

Paul's doctrine of the New Covenant was not something that he invented for the occasion. As a profound student of the Scriptures, Paul certainly had read Jeremiah 31:27-34, as well as Ezekiel 11:14-21. In the New Testament, Hebrews 8–10 is the key passage to study. The Old Covenant Law, with its emphasis on external obedience, was preparation for the New Covenant message of grace and the emphasis on internal transformation of the heart.

Fading Glory—Increasing Glory (2 Cor. 3:7-11)

This paragraph is the heart of the chapter, and it should be studied in connection with Exodus 34:29-35. Paul did not deny the glory of the Old Covenant Law, because in the giving of the Law and the maintaining of the tabernacle and temple services, there certainly was glory. What he affirmed, however, was that the glory of the New Covenant of grace was far superior, and he gave several reasons to support his affirmation.

The New Covenant glory means spiritual life, not death (vv. 7-8). When Moses descended from the mountain, after conversing with God, his face shone with the glory of God. This was a part of the glory of the giving of the Law, and it certainly impressed the people. Paul then argued from the lesser to the greater: if there was glory in the giving of a Law which brought death, how much more glory is there in a ministry that brings life!

Legalists like the Judaizers like to magnify the glory of the Law and minimize its weaknesses. In his letter to the Galatian churches, Paul pointed out the deficiencies of the Law: the Law cannot justify the lost sinner (Gal. 2:16), give a sinner righteousness (Gal. 2:21), give the Holy Spirit (Gal. 3:2), give an inheritance (Gal. 3:18), give life (Gal. 3:21), or give freedom (Gal. 4:8-10). The glory of the Law is really the glory of a ministry of death.

The New Covenant glory means righteousness, not condemnation (vv. 9-10). The Law was not given for the purpose of salvation, for there is no salvation through obedience to the Law. The Law produces condemnation, and is the mirror that reveals how dirty our faces really are. But we cannot wash our faces in the mirror.

The ministry of the New Covenant produces righteousness and changes lives to the glory of God. Man's greatest need is righteousness, and God's greatest gift is righteousness through faith in Jesus Christ. "For if righteousness [comes] by the Law, then Christ is dead in vain" (Gal. 2:21). The person who tries to live under the Law will find himself feeling more and more guilty, and this can produce a feeling of hopelessness and rejection. It is when we trust Christ, and live by faith in God's grace, that we experience acceptance and joy.

Second Corinthians 3:10 states that the Law really "lost its glory" when compared to the surpassing glory of the ministry of God's grace. There simply is no comparison. Sad to say, there are some people who cannot "feel spiritual" unless they carry a weight of guilt. The Law produces guilt and condemnation, for it is like a bond of indebtedness (Col. 2:14), a guardian who disciplines us (Gal. 4:1-5), and a yoke too heavy to bear (Gal. 5:1; Acts 15:10).

The New Covenant glory is permanent, not temporary (v. 11). The tense of the verb here is very important: "that which is passing away." Paul wrote at a period in history when the ages were overlapping. The New Covenant of grace had come in, but the temple services were still being carried on and the nation of Israel was still living under Law. In A.D. 70, the city of Jerusalem and the temple would be destroyed by the Romans, and that would mark the end of the Jewish religious system.

The Judaizers wanted the Corinthian believers to go back under the Law, to "mix" the two Covenants. "Why go back to that which is temporary and fading away?" Paul asked. "Live in the glory of the New Covenant, which is getting greater and greater." The glory of the Law is but the glory of past history, while the glory of the New Covenant is the glory of present experience. As believers, we can be "changed . . . from glory to glory" (2 Cor. 3:18), something that the Law can never accomplish.

The glory of the Law was fading in Paul's day, and today that glory is found only in the records in the Bible. The nation of Israel has no temple or priesthood. If they did build a temple, there would be no Shekinah glory dwelling in the holy of holies. The Law of Moses is a religion with a most glorious past, but it has no glory today. The light is gone; all that remain are shadows (Col. 2:16-17).

Paul has pointed out that the ministry of grace is internal (2 Cor. 3:1-3), it brings life (2 Cor. 3:4-6), and it involves increasing glory (2 Cor. 3:7-11). He presented one final contrast to prove the superiority of the New Covenant ministry of grace.

Concealment—Openness (2 Cor. 3:12-18)

The Bible is basically a "picture book," because it uses symbols, similes, metaphors, and other literary devices to get its message across. In this paragraph, Paul used the experience of Moses and his veil to illustrate the glorious freedom and openness of the Christian life under grace. Paul saw in Moses' experience a deeper spiritual meaning than you and I would have seen as we read Exodus 34:29-35.

The historical event (vv. 12-13). When you are a part of a ministry of increasing glory, you can be bold in what you say; and Paul did not hide his boldness. Unlike Moses, Paul had nothing to conceal.

When Moses came down from communing with God, his face shone, reflecting the glory of God. When he spoke to the people, they could see the glory on his face, and they were impressed by it. But Moses knew that the glory would fade away; so, when he finished teaching the people, he put on a veil. This prevented them from seeing the glory disappear; for, after all, who wants to follow a leader who is losing his glory?

The word translated *end* in 2 Corinthians 3:13 has two meanings: "purpose" and "finish." The veil prevented the people from seeing the "finish" of the glory as it faded away. But the veil also prevented them from understanding the "purpose" behind the fading glory. The Law had just been instituted, and the people were not ready to be told that this glorious system was only temporary. The truth that the covenant of Law was a preparation for something greater was not yet made known to them.

The national application (vv. 14-17). Paul had a special love for Israel and a burden to see his people saved (Rom. 9:1-3). Why were the Jewish people rejecting their Christ? As the missionary to the Gentiles, Paul was seeing many Gentiles trust the Lord, but the Jews—his own people—were rejecting the truth and persecuting Paul and the church.

The reason? There was a "spiritual veil" over their minds and hearts. Their "spiritual eyes" were blinded, so that when they read the Old Testament Scriptures, they did not see the truth about their own Messiah. Even though the Scriptures were read systematically in the synagogues, the Jewish people did not grasp the spiritual message God had given to them. They were blinded by their own religion.

Is there any hope for the lost Children of Israel? Yes, there is! "Nevertheless, when it [the heart] shall turn to the Lord [by trusting Jesus Christ], the veil shall be taken away" (2 Cor. 3:16).

In each of the three churches I have pastored, it has been my joy to baptize Jewish people who have trusted Jesus Christ. It is amazing how their minds open to the Scriptures after they have been born again. One man told me, "It's like scales falling from your eyes. You wonder why everybody doesn't see what you see!" The veil is removed by the Spirit of God and they receive spiritual vision.

But no sinner—Jew or Gentile—can turn to Christ apart from the ministry of the Holy Spirit of God. "Now the Lord is that Spirit" (2 Cor. 3:17). This statement is a bold declaration of the deity of the Holy Spirit: He is God. The Judaizers who had invaded the church at Corinth were depending on the Law to change men's lives, but only the Spirit of God can bring about spiritual transformation. The Law can bring only bondage, but the Spirit introduces us into a life of liberty. "For ye have not received the spirit of bondage again to fear; but ye have received the Spirit of adoption, whereby we cry, 'Abba, Father' " (Rom. 8:15).

As a nation, Israel today is spiritually blind; but this does not mean that individual Jews cannot be saved. The church today needs to recover its lost burden for Israel. We are their debtors, because all the spiritual blessings we have came through Israel. "Salvation is of the Jews" (John 4:22). The only way we can "pay off" this debt is by sharing the Gospel with them and praying that they might be saved (Rom. 10:1).

The personal application (v. 18). "But we all, with open face beholding as in a glass the glory of the Lord, are changed into the same image from glory to glory, even as by the Spirit of the Lord." This verse is the climax of the chapter, and it presents a truth so exciting that I marvel so many believers have missed it—or ignored it. You and I can share the image of Jesus Christ and go "from glory to glory" through the ministry of the Spirit of God!

Under the Old Covenant, only Moses ascended the mountain and had fellowship with God; but under the New Covenant, all believers have the privilege of communion with Him. Through Jesus Christ, we may enter into the very holy of holies (Heb. 10:19-20)—and we don't have to climb a mountain!

The "mirror" is a symbol of the Word of God (James 1:22-25). As we look into God's Word and see God's Son, the Spirit transforms us into the very image of God. It is important, however, that we hide nothing from God. We must be open and honest with Him and not "wear a veil."

The word translated *changed* is the same word translated *transfigured* in the accounts of our Lord's transfiguration (Matt. 17; Mark 9). It describes a change on the outside that comes from the inside. Our English word *metamorphosis* is a transliteration of this Greek word. Metamorphosis describes the process that changes an insect from a larva into a pupa and then into a mature insect. The changes come from within.

Moses *reflected* the glory of God, but you and I may *radiate* the glory of God. When we meditate on God's Word and in it see God's Son, then the Spirit transforms us! We become more like the Lord Jesus Christ as we grow "from glory to glory." *This wonderful process cannot be achieved by keeping the Law.* The glory of the Law faded away, but the glory of God's grace continues to increase in our lives.

Keep in mind that Paul was contrasting, not only the Old Covenant with the New, but also the Old Covenant *ministry* with the ministry of grace. The goal of Old Covenant ministry is obedience to an external standard, but this obedience cannot change human character. The goal of New Covenant ministry is likeness to Jesus Christ. Law can bring us to Christ (Gal. 3:24), but only grace can make us like Christ. Legalistic preachers and teachers may get their listeners to conform to some standard, but they can never transform them to be like the Son of God.

The means for Old Covenant ministry is the Law, but the means for New Covenant ministry is the Spirit of God using the Word of God. (By "the Law" I do not mean the Old Testament, but rather the whole legal system given by Moses. Certainly, the Spirit can use both the Old and New Testaments to reveal Jesus Christ to us.) Since the Holy Spirit wrote the Word, He can teach it to us. Even more, because the Spirit lives in us, He can enable us to obey the Word from our hearts. This is not legal obedience, born of fear, but filial obedience born of love.

Finally, the result of Old Covenant ministry is bondage; but the result of New Covenant ministry is freedom in the Spirit. Legalism keeps a person immature and immature people must live by rules and regulations (see Gal. 4:1-7). God wants His children to obey, not because of an external code (the Law), but because of internal character. Christians do not live under the Law, but this does not mean that we are lawless! The Spirit of God writes the Word of God on our hearts, and we obey our Father because of the new life He has given us within.

The lure of legalism is still with us. False cults prey on professed Christians and church members, as did the Judaizers in Paul's day. We must learn to recognize false cults and reject their teachings. But there are also Gospel-preaching churches that have legalistic tendencies and keep their members immature, guilty, and afraid. They spend a great deal of time dealing with the externals, and they neglect the cultivation of the inner life. They exalt standards and they denounce sin, but they fail to magnify the Lord Jesus Christ. Sad to say, in some New Testament churches we have an Old Testament ministry.

Paul has now explained two aspects of his own ministry: it is triumphant (2 Cor. 1–2) and it is glorious (2 Cor. 3). The two go together: "Therefore seeing we have this [kind of] ministry, as we have received mercy, we faint not" (2 Cor. 4:1).

When your ministry involves the glory of God—you cannot quit!

CHAPTER FOUR
COURAGE FOR THE CONFLICT
2 Corinthians 4:1–5:8

The key theme of this section is repeated in 1 Corinthians 4:1 and 16: "We faint not!" Literally, Paul said, "We do not lose heart!" There were certainly plenty of reasons for discouragement in Paul's situation, yet the great apostle did not quit. What was it that kept him from fainting in the conflicts of life? *He knew what he possessed in Jesus Christ!* Instead of complaining about what he did not have, Paul rejoiced in what he did have; and you and I can do the same thing.

We Have a Glorious Ministry (2 Cor. 4:1-6)

"Therefore, seeing we have *this kind* of ministry" is the literal translation of what Paul wrote. What kind of ministry? The kind described in the previous chapter: a glorious ministry that brings men life, salvation, and righteousness; a ministry that is able to transform men's lives. This ministry is a gift—we receive it from God. It is given to us because of God's mercy, not because of anything we are or we have done (see 1 Tim. 1:12-17).

The way you look at your ministry helps to determine how you will fulfill it. If you look on serving Christ as a burden instead of a privilege, you will be a drudge and do only what is required of you. Some people even look on service as a punishment from God. When Paul considered the fact that he was a minister of Jesus Christ, he was overwhelmed by the grace and mercy of God. His positive attitude toward the ministry had some practical consequences in his life.

It kept him from being a quitter (v. 1). He confessed to the Corinthians that his trials in Asia had almost brought him to despair (2 Cor. 1:8). In spite of his great gifts and vast experience, Paul was human and subject to human frailties. But how could he lose heart when he was involved in such a wonderful ministry? Would God have entrusted this ministry to him so that he might fail? Of course not! With the divine calling came the divine enabling; he knew that God would see him through.

A discouraged Methodist preacher wrote to the great Scottish preacher, Alexander Whyte, to ask his counsel. Should he leave the ministry? "Never think of giving up preaching!" Whyte wrote to him. "The angels around the throne envy you your great work!" That was the kind of reply Paul would have written, the kind of reply all of us need to ponder whenever we feel our work is in vain.

It kept him from being a deceiver (vv. 2-4). "But we have renounced the things hidden because of shame, not walking in craftiness or adulterating the Word of God, but by the manifestation of the truth commending ourselves to every man's conscience in the sight of God" (2 Cor. 4:2, NASB). Paul was certainly alluding to the Judaizers when he wrote these words. Many false teachers today claim to base their doctrine on the Word of God, but false teachers handle God's Word in deceptive ways. You can prove anything by the Bible, provided you twist the Scriptures out of context and reject the witness of your own conscience. The Bible is a book of literature and it must be interpreted according to the fundamental rules of interpretation. If people treated other books the way they treat the Bible, they would never learn anything.

Paul had nothing to hide, either in his personal life or in his preaching of the Word. Everything was open and honest; there was no deception or distortion of the Word. The Judaizers were guilty of twisting the Scriptures to fit their own preconceived interpretations, and ignorant people were willing to follow them.

If Paul was such a faithful teacher of the Word, then why did not more people believe his message? Why were the false teachers so successful in winning converts? Because the mind of the lost sinner is blinded by Satan, and fallen man finds it easier to believe lies than to believe truth. The Gospel "is hid to them that are lost: in whom the god of this world hath blinded the minds of them which believe not, lest the light of the glorious Gospel of Christ, who is the image of God, should shine unto them" (2 Cor. 4:3-4).

Paul had already explained that the minds of the Jews were "veiled" because of the blindness of their hearts (Rom. 11:25; 2 Cor. 3:14-16). The minds of the Gentiles are also blinded! Those who are lost ("perishing") cannot understand the message of the Gospel. Satan does not want the glorious light of salvation to shine into their hearts. As the god of this age and the prince of this world (John 12:31), Satan keeps lost sinners in the dark. The sad thing is that Satan uses *religious* teachers (like the Judaizers) to deceive people. Many of the people who today belong to cults were originally members of Christian churches.

It kept him from being a self-promoter (vv. 5-6). The awesome fact that Paul had received this ministry from Christ kept him from being a quitter and a deceiver; but it also kept him from being a self-promoter (2 Cor. 4:5-6). "We preach not ourselves!" (2 Cor. 4:5) The Judaizers enjoyed preaching about themselves and glorying in their achievements (2 Cor. 10:12-18). They were not servants who tried to help people; they were dictators who exploited people.

Paul was certainly a man who practiced genuine humility. He did not trust in himself (2 Cor. 1:9) or commend himself (2 Cor. 3:1-5) or preach himself (2 Cor. 4:5). He sought only to lead people to Jesus Christ and to build them up in the faith. It would have been easy for Paul to build a "fan club" for himself and take advantage of weak people who thrive on associating with great men. The Judaizers operated in that way, but Paul rejected that kind of ministry.

What happens when you share Jesus Christ with lost sinners? The light begins to shine! Paul compared conversion to Creation as described in Genesis 1:3. Like the earth of Genesis 1:2, the lost sinner is formless and empty; but when he trusts Christ, he becomes a new creation (2 Cor. 5:17). God then begins to *form* and *fill* the life of the person who trusts Christ, and he begins to be fruitful for the Lord. God's, "Let there be light!" makes everything new.

We Have a Valuable Treasure (2 Cor. 4:7-12)

From the glory of the new creation, Paul moved to the humility of the clay vessel. The believer is simply a "jar of clay"; it is the treasure *within the vessel* that gives the vessel its value. The image of the vessel is a recurring one in Scripture, and from it we can learn many lessons.

To begin with, God has made us the way we are so that we can do the work He wants us to do. God said of Paul, "He is a chosen vessel unto Me, to bear My name before the Gentiles" (Acts 9:15). No Christian should ever complain to God because of his lack of gifts or abilities, or because of his limitations or handicaps. Psalm 139:13-16 indicates that our very genetic structure is in the hands of God. Each of us must accept himself and be himself.

The important thing about a vessel is that it be clean, empty, and available for service. Each of us must seek to become "a vessel unto honor, sanctified [set apart], and meet for the master's use, and prepared unto every good work" (2 Tim. 2:21). We are vessels so that God might use us. We are *earthen* vessels so that we might depend on God's power and not our own.

We must focus on the treasure and not on the vessel. Paul was not afraid of suffering or trial, because he knew that God would guard the vessel so long as Paul was guarding the treasure (see 1 Tim. 1:11; 6:20). God permits trials, God controls trials, and God uses trials for His own glory. *God is glorified through weak vessels.* The missionary who opened inland China to the Gospel, J. Hudson Taylor, used to say, "All God's giants have been weak men who did great things for God because they reckoned on Him being with them."

Sometimes God permits our vessels to be

jarred so that some of the treasure will spill out and enrich others. Suffering reveals not only the weakness of man but also the glory of God. Paul presented a series of paradoxes in this paragraph: earthen vessels—power of God; the dying of Jesus—the life of Jesus; death working—life working. The natural mind cannot understand this kind of spiritual truth and therefore cannot understand why Christians triumph over suffering.

Not only must we focus on the treasure and not on the vessel, but we must also focus on the Master and not on the servant. If we suffer, it is for Jesus' sake. If we die to self, it is so that the life of Christ might be revealed in us. If we go through trials, it is so that Christ might be glorified. And all of this is for the sake of others. As we serve Christ, death works in us—but life works in those to whom we minister.

Dr. John Henry Jowett said, "Ministry that costs nothing, accomplishes nothing." He was right. A pastor friend and I once heard a young man preach an eloquent sermon, but it lacked something. "There was something missing," I said to my friend; and he replied, "Yes, and it won't be there until his heart is broken. After he has suffered awhile, he will have a message worth listening to."

The Judaizers did not suffer. Instead of winning lost souls, they stole converts from Paul's churches. Instead of sacrificing for the people, they made the people sacrifice for them (2 Cor. 11:20). The false teachers did not have a treasure to share. All they had were some museum pieces from the Old Covenant, faded antiques that could never enrich a person's life.

It has been my experience that many churches are ignorant of the price a pastor pays to be faithful to the Lord in serving His people. This section is one of three sections in 2 Corinthians devoted to a listing of Paul's sufferings. The other two are 6:1-10 and 11:16–12:10. The test of a true ministry is not stars, but scars. "From henceforth let no man trouble me: for I bear in my body the marks [brands] of the Lord Jesus" (Gal. 6:17).

How can we keep from giving up? By remembering that we are privileged to have the treasure of the Gospel in our vessels of clay!

We Have a Confident Faith (2 Cor. 4:13-18)

The phrase *spirit of faith* means "attitude or outlook of faith." Paul was not referring to a special gift of faith (1 Cor. 12:9), but rather to that attitude of faith that ought to belong to every believer. He saw himself identified with the believer who wrote Psalm 116:10, "I believed, and therefore have I spoken." True witness for God is based on faith in God, and this faith comes from God's Word (Rom. 10:17). Nothing closes a believer's mouth like unbelief (see Luke 1:20).

Of what was Paul so confident? That he had nothing to fear from life or death! He had just listed some of the trials that were a part of his life and ministry, and now he was affirming that his faith gave him victory over all of them. Note the assurances that he had because of his faith.

He was sure of ultimate victory (v. 14). If Jesus Christ has conquered death, the last enemy, then why fear anything else? Men do everything they can to penetrate the meaning of death and prepare for it, yet the world has no answer to death. Until a person is prepared to die, he is not really prepared to live. The joyful message of the early church was the victory of Christ over death, and we need to return to that victorious emphasis. Note too that Paul saw a future reunion of God's people when he wrote, "and shall present us with you." Death is the great divider, but in Jesus Christ there is assurance that His people shall be reunited in His presence (1 Thes. 4:13-18).

He was sure God would be glorified (v. 15). This verse parallels Romans 8:28 and gives us the assurance that our sufferings are not wasted: God uses them to minister to others and also to bring glory to His name. How is God glorified in our trials? By giving us the "abundant grace" we need to maintain joy and strength when the going gets difficult. Whatever begins with grace, leads to glory (see Ps. 84:11; 1 Peter 5:10).

He was sure his trials were working for him, not against him (vv. 16-17). "We faint not" (see 2 Cor. 4:1) was Paul's confident testimony. What does it matter if the "outward person" is perishing, so long as the "inward person" is experiencing daily spiritual renewal? Paul was not suggesting that the body is not important, or that we should ignore its warnings and needs. Since our bodies are the temples of God, we must care for them; but we cannot control the natural deterioration of human nature. When we consider all the physical trials that Paul endured, it is no wonder he wrote as he did.

As Christians, we must live a day at a time. No person, no matter how wealthy or gifted, can live two days at a time. God provides for us "day by day" as we pray to Him (Luke 11:3). He gives us the strength that we need according to our daily requirements (Deut. 33:25). We must not make the mistake of trying to "store up grace" for future emergencies, because God gives us the grace that we need when we need it (Heb. 4:16). When we learn to live a day at a time, confident of God's care, it takes a great deal of pressure off of our lives.

Yard by yard, life is hard!
Inch by inch, life's a cinch!

When you live by faith in Christ, you get the right perspective on suffering. Note the contrasts Paul presented in 2 Corinthians 4:17: light affliction—weight of glory; momentary—eternal; working against us—working for us. Paul was writing with eternity's values in view. He was weighing the present trials against the future glory, and he discovered that his trials were actually working *for him* (see Rom. 8:18).

We must not misunderstand this principle and think that a Christian can live any way he pleases and expect everything to turn into glory in the end. Paul was writing about trials experienced in the will of God as he was doing the work of God. God can and does turn suffering into glory, but He cannot turn sin into glory. Sin must be judged, because there is no glory in sin.

Second Corinthians 4:16 should be related to 3:18, because both verses have to do with the spiritual renewal of the child of God. Of itself, suffering will not make us holier men and women. Unless we yield to the Lord, turn to His Word, and trust Him to work, our suffering could make us far worse Christians. In my own pastoral ministry, I have seen some of God's people grow critical and bitter, and go from bad to worse instead of "from glory to glory." We need that "spirit of faith" that Paul mentioned in 2 Corinthians 4:13.

He was sure the invisible world was real (v. 18). Dr. A.W. Tozer used to remind us that the invisible world described in the Bible was the only "real world." If we would only see the visible world the way God wants us to see it, we would never be attracted by what it offers (1 John 2:15-17). The great men and women of faith, mentioned in Hebrews 11, achieved what they did because they "saw the invisible" (Heb. 11:10, 13-14, 27).

The things of this world seem so real because we can see them and feel them; but they are all temporal and destined to pass away. Only the eternal things of the spiritual life will last. Again, we must not press this truth into extremes and think that "material" and "spiritual" oppose each other. When we use the material in God's will, He transforms it into the spiritual, and this becomes a part of our treasure in heaven. (More on this in 2 Cor. 8–9.) We value the material *because* it can be used to promote the spiritual, and not for what it is in itself.

How can you look at things that are invisible? By faith, when you read the Word of God. We have never seen Christ or heaven, yet we know they are real because the Word of God tells us so. Faith is "the evidence of things not seen" (Heb. 11:1). Because Abraham looked for the heavenly city, he separated himself from Sodom; but Lot chose Sodom because he walked by sight and not by faith (Gen. 13; Heb. 11:10).

Of course, the unsaved world thinks we are odd—perhaps even crazy—because we insist on the reality of the invisible world of spiritual blessing. Yet Christians are content to govern their lives by eternal values, not temporal prices.

We Have a Future Hope (2 Cor. 5:1-8)

"We have this ministry. . . . We have this treasure. . . . We [have] the same spirit of faith. . . . We have a building of God" (2 Cor. 4:1, 7, 13; 5:1). What a testimony Paul gave to the reality of the Christian faith!

This "building of God" is not the believer's heavenly home, promised in John 14:1-6. It is his glorified body. Paul was a tentmaker (Acts 18:1-3) and here he used a tent as a picture of our present earthly bodies. A tent is a weak, temporary structure, without much beauty; but the glorified body we shall receive will be eternal, beautiful, and never show signs of weakness or decay (see Phil. 3:20-21). Paul saw the human body as an earthen vessel (2 Cor. 4:7) and a temporary tent; but he knew that believers would one day receive a wonderful glorified body, suited to the glorious environment of heaven.

It is interesting to trace Paul's testimony in this paragraph.

We know (v. 1). How do we know? Because we trust the Word of God. No Christian has to consult a fortune-teller, a Ouija board, a spiritist, or a deck of cards to find out what the future holds or what lies on the other side of death. God has told us all that we need to know in the pages of His Word. Paul's "we know" connects with his "knowing" in 2 Corinthians 4:14, and this relates to the resurrection of Jesus Christ. We know that He is alive; therefore, we know that death cannot claim us. "Because I live, ye shall live also" (John 14:19).

If our tent is "taken down" ("dissolved"), we need not fear. The body is only the house we live in. When a believer dies, the body goes to the grave, but the spirit goes to be with Christ (Phil. 1:20-25). When Jesus Christ returns for His own, He will raise the dead bodies in glory, and body and spirit shall be joined together for a glorious eternity in heaven (1 Cor. 15:35-58; 1 Thes. 4:13-18).

We groan (vv. 2-5). Paul was not expressing a morbid desire for death. In fact, his statement is just the opposite: he was eager for Jesus Christ to return so that he would be "clothed upon" with the glorified body. He presented three possibilities, using the image of the body as a tent: (1) *alive*—residing in the tent; (2) *dead*—unclothed, out of the tent, "naked"; (3) *clothed upon*—the transformation of the body at the return of Christ. Paul was hoping that he would be alive and on the earth at the return of Christ, so that he might not have to go through the experience of death. Paul used a similar picture in 1 Corinthians 15:51–58, and he used the idea of "groaning" in Romans 8:22-26.

The glorified body is called "a building of God, a house not made with hands" in 2 Corinthians 5:1, and "our house which is from heaven" in 2 Corinthians 5:2. This is in contrast to our mortal bodies which came from the dust of the earth. "And as we have borne the image of the earthy, we shall also bear the image of the heavenly" (1 Cor. 15:49). It is important to note that Paul was not groaning because he was in a human body, but because he longed to see Jesus Christ and receive a glorified body. He was groaning for glory!

This explains why death holds no terrors for the Christian. Paul called his death a "departure" (2 Tim. 4:6). One meaning of this Greek word is "to take down one's tent and move on." But how can we be sure that we shall one day have new bodies like the glorified body of our Saviour? We can be sure because the Spirit lives within us. Paul mentioned the sealing and the earnest of the Spirit in 2 Corinthians 1:22 (see also Eph. 1:13-14). The Holy Spirit dwelling in the believer's body is the "down payment" that guarantees the future inheritance, including a glorified body. In modern Greek, the word translated "earnest" means "engagement ring." The church is engaged to Jesus Christ and is waiting for the Bridegroom to come to take her to the wedding.

We are always confident (vv. 6-8). The people of God can be found in one of two places: either in heaven or on earth (Eph. 3:15). None of them is in the grave, in hell, or in any "intermediate place" between earth and heaven. Believers on earth are "at home in the body," while believers who have died are "absent from the body." Believers on earth are "absent from the Lord," while believers in heaven are "present with the Lord."

Because he had this kind of confidence, Paul was not afraid of suffering and trials, or even of dangers. This is not to suggest that he tempted the Lord by taking unnecessary risks, but it does mean that he was willing to "lose his life" for the sake of Christ and the ministry of the Gospel. He walked by faith and not by sight. He looked at the eternal unseen, not the temporal seen (2 Cor. 4:18). Heaven was not simply a *destination* for Paul: it was a *motivation.* Like the heroes of faith in Hebrews 11, he looked for the heavenly city and governed his life by eternal values.

As we review this section of 2 Corinthians, we can see how Paul had courage for the conflict and would not lose heart. He had a glorious ministry that transformed lives. He had a valuable treasure in the earthen vessel of his body, and he wanted to share that treasure with a bankrupt world. He had a confident faith that conquered fear, and he had a future hope that was both a destination and a motivation.

No wonder Paul was "more than conqueror"! (Rom. 8:37)

Every believer in Jesus Christ has these same marvelous possessions and can find through them courage for the conflict.

CHAPTER FIVE
MOTIVES FOR MINISTRY
2 Corinthians 5:9-21

What we believe and how we behave must always go together. Paul usually connected *duty* and *doctrine,* because what God has done for us must motivate us to do something for God. Phillips Brooks said, "Christianity knows no truth which is not the child of love and the parent of duty."

"You would have preached a marvelous sermon," a woman said to her pastor, "except for all those 'therefores' at the end!"

Paul would have agreed with the pastor, for he usually used "therefores" and "wherefores" liberally in his letters. In fact, you find them in this section of 2 Corinthians 5 in verses 9, 11, 16-17. Paul has moved from explanation to application, and his theme is *motivation for ministry.* His enemies had accused him of using the ministry of the Gospel for his own selfish purposes, when in reality *they* were the ones who were "merchandising" the Gospel (see 2 Cor. 2:17; 4:2).

What is the ministry of the Christian? To persuade sinners to be reconciled to God (2 Cor. 5:11, 20). We must never force people to trust Christ, or coerce them by some devious approach. "Our message to you is true, our motives are pure, our conduct is absolutely aboveboard" (1 Thes. 2:3, PH). The Christian worker must have the right motive for ministry as well as the right message.

In this section, Paul stated three acceptable motives for ministry.

The Fear of the Lord (2 Cor. 5:9-13)

"Knowing, therefore, the terror [fear] of the Lord" (2 Cor. 5:11). This kind of attitude is often lacking in ministry. The famous Bible scholar, B.F. Westcott, once wrote, "Every year makes me tremble at the daring with which people speak of spiritual things." Phillips Brooks used to warn about "clerical jesters" whose jesting about the Bible robbed that inspired Book of some of its glory and power. Too often there is a sad absence of reverence in the public meetings of the church, so that it is no surprise that the younger generation is not taking the things of God seriously.

Paul explained this motive by sharing his own testimony in three powerful statements.

We labor (v. 9). This means "we are ambitious." There is an ambition that is selfish and worldly, but there is also a holy ambition that honors the Lord. Paul's great ambition was to be well-pleasing to Jesus Christ. The Judaizers ministered to please men and enlisted them in their cause; but Paul ministered to please Jesus Christ alone (Gal. 1:10). A man-pleasing ministry is a carnal, compromising ministry; and God cannot bless it.

The word translated "accepted" ("well-pleasing") is used in several other places in the New Testament, and each of these references helps us better understand what it is that pleases the Lord. It is well-pleasing to Him when we present our bodies to Him as living sacrifices (Rom. 12:1), and when we live so as to help others and avoid causing them to stumble (Rom. 14:18). God is well-pleased when His children separate themselves from the evil around them (Eph. 5:10), as well as when they bring their offerings to Him (Phil. 4:18). He is pleased with children who submit to their parents (Col. 3:20), as well as with saints who permit Jesus Christ to work out His perfect will in their lives (Heb. 13:20-21).

There is nothing wrong with godly ambition. "Yea, so have I strived [been ambitious] to preach the Gospel," was Paul's testimony in Romans 15:20; it was this godly ambition that compelled him to take the message where it had never been heard. Paul commanded the Thessalonian believers to "study [be ambitious] to be quiet" (1 Thes. 4:11). If, led by the Spirit, believers would put as much drive into Christian living and service as they do athletics or business, the Gospel would make a greater impact on the lost world. "I want to be as zealous for God as I was for the devil!" a new Christian told me, and his life was greatly used of God.

We must all appear (v. 10). Not every believer is ambitious for the Lord, but every believer is going to appear before the Lord; and now is the time to prepare. The Judgment Seat of Christ is that future event when God's people will stand before the Saviour as their works are judged and rewarded (see Rom. 14:8-10). Paul was ambitious for the Lord because he wanted to meet Him with confidence and not shame (1 John 2:28).

The term "judgment seat" comes from the Greek word *bema,* which was the platform in

Greek towns where orations were made or decisions handed down by rulers (see Matt. 27:19; Acts 12:21; 18:12). It was also the place where the awards were given out to the winners in the annual Olympic Games. This "judgment seat" must not be confused with the Great White Throne from which Christ will judge the wicked (Rev. 20:11-15). Because of the gracious work of Christ on the cross, believers will not face their sins (John 5:24; Rom. 8:1); but we will have to give an account of our works and service for the Lord.

The Judgment Seat of Christ will be a place of *revelation;* for the word *appear* means "be revealed." As we live and work here on earth, it is relatively easy for us to hide things and pretend; but the true character of our works will be exposed before the searching eyes of the Saviour. He will reveal whether our works have been good or bad ("worthless"). The character of our service will be revealed (1 Cor. 3:13) as well as the motives that impelled us (1 Cor. 4:5).

It will also be a place of *reckoning* as we give an account of our ministries (Rom. 14:10-12). If we have been faithful it will be a place of *reward* and *recognition* (1 Cor. 3:10-15; 4:1-6). For those of us who have been faithful, it will be a time of *rejoicing* as we glorify the Lord by giving our rewards back to Him in worship and in praise.

Is the desire for reward a proper motive for service? The fact that God does promise rewards is proof that the motive is not a sinful one, even though it may not be the highest motive. Just as parents are happy when their children achieve recognition, so our Lord is pleased when His people are *worthy* of recognition and reward. The important thing is not the reward itself, but the joy of pleasing Christ and honoring Him.

We persuade men (vv. 11-13). If God judges His own people, then what will happen to the lost? "And if the righteous scarcely be saved, where shall the ungodly and the sinner appear?" (1 Peter 4:18) The word *terror* does not mean fright, dread, or horror. After all, we are going to see our Saviour—and He loves us. But Paul did not minimize the awesomeness of the occasion. We shall stand before Christ, "and there is no respect of persons" (Col. 3:23-25). Christ has commanded us to spread the Gospel to all nations, and we must be obedient. Someone asked the Duke of Wellington what he thought of foreign missions, and his reply was, "What are your marching orders?"

How can the Christian prepare for the Judgment Seat of Christ? To begin with, he must maintain a clear conscience (2 Cor. 5:11). No doubt some of the enemies at Corinth were saying, "Just wait until Paul stands before the Lord!" But Paul was not afraid, because he knew that his conscience was clear (see 2 Cor. 1:12). The truth about each one of us shall be revealed and Jesus Christ will commend us for those things that have pleased Him.

Second, we must take care not to depend on the praise of men (2 Cor. 5:12). This verse relates to 2 Cor. 3:1, where Paul referred to the "letters of commendation" that the Judaizers prized so highly. If we live only for the praise of men, we will not win the praise of God at the Judgment Seat of Christ. To live for man's praise is to exalt reputation over character, and it is character that will count when we see Christ. Actually, the Corinthians should have commended Paul! Instead, they were "promoting" the Judaizers who gloried in appearance (see 2 Cor. 11:18), but were unspiritual in heart.

Finally, we must ignore the criticisms of men (2 Cor. 5:13). Paul's enemies said that he was crazy. Paul said that he was "mad" when he was persecuting the church (Acts 26:11), but his enemies said he was "mad" since he had become a believer himself (Acts 26:24). But people said that our Lord was mad, so Paul was in good company (see Mark 3:21). "If I am mad," Paul was saying, "it is for your good and the glory of God—so that makes it worthwhile!"

When Dwight L. Moody was ministering at his large Sunday School and church in Chicago, people often called him "Crazy Moody." In the eyes of the unsaved world, Moody was "crazy" to have given up a successful business career to become a Sunday School worker and evangelist; but time has proved his decision to be a wise one. Today, we don't know the names of the people who laughed at him, but we do know—and honor—the name of D.L. Moody.

It behooves every Christian to examine his own life regularly to see if he is ready for the Judgment Seat of Christ. Wanting to give a good account before Christ is a worthy motive for Christian service.

The Love of Christ (2 Cor. 5:14-17)

How can such opposite emotions as fear and love dwell in the same heart? Certainly they are found in the hearts of children who love their parents and yet respect them and their authority. "Serve the Lord with fear, and rejoice with trembling" (Ps. 2:11).

The phrase "the love of Christ" means His love for us as seen in His sacrificial death. "We love Him, because He first loved us" (1 John 4:19). He loved us when we were unlovely; in fact, He loved us when we were ungodly, sinners, and enemies (see Rom. 5:6-10). When He died on the cross, Christ proved His love for the world (John 3:16), the church (Eph. 5:25), and individual sinners (Gal. 2:20). When you consider the reasons why Christ died, you cannot help but love Him.

He died that we might die (v. 14). The tense of the verb gives the meaning "then all died." This truth is explained in detail in Romans 6, the believer's identification with Christ. When Christ died, we died in Him and with Him. Therefore, the old life should have no hold on us today. "I am crucified with Christ" (Gal. 2:20).

He died that we might live (vv. 15-17). This is the positive aspect of our identification with Christ: we not only died with Him, but we also were raised with Him that we might "walk in newness of life" (Rom. 6:4). Because we have died with Christ, we can overcome sin; and because we live with Christ, we can bear fruit for God's glory (Rom. 7:4).

He died that we might live *through* Him: "God sent His only begotten Son into the world, that we might live through Him" (1 John 4:9). This is our experience of salvation, eternal life through faith in Jesus Christ. But He also died that we might live *for* Him, and not live unto ourselves (2 Cor. 5:15). This is our experience of service. It has well been said, "Christ died our death for us that we might live His life for Him." If a lost sinner has been to the cross and been saved, how can he spend the rest of his life in selfishness?

In 1858, Frances Ridley Havergal visited Germany with her father who was getting treatment for his afflicted eyes. While in a pastor's home, she saw a picture of the Crucifixion on the wall, with the words under it: "I did this for thee. What hast thou done for Me?" Quickly she took a piece of paper and wrote a poem based on that motto; but she was not satisfied with it, so she threw the paper into the fireplace. The paper came out unharmed! Later, her father encouraged her to publish it; and we sing it today to a tune composed by Philip P. Bliss.

I gave My life for thee,
My precious blood I shed,
That thou might'st ransomed be,
And quickened from the dead;
I gave, I gave My life for thee,
What hast thou given for Me?

Christ died that we might live *through* Him and *for* Him, and that we might live *with* Him. "Who died for us, that, whether we wake or sleep, we should live together with Him" (1 Thes. 5:10). Because of Calvary, believers are going to heaven to live with Christ forever!

He died that we might die, and He died that we might live. But He also died that we might *share in the new creation* (2 Cor. 5:16-17). Our new relationship to Christ has brought about a new relationship to the world and the people around us. *We no longer look at life the way we used to.* To know Christ "after the flesh" means to evaluate Him from a human point of view. But "the days of His flesh" are ended (Heb. 5:7) because He has ascended to heaven and is now glorified at the Father's right hand.

Adam was the head of the old creation, and Christ (the Last Adam, 1 Cor. 15:45) is the Head of the new creation. The old creation was plunged into sin and condemnation because of the disobedience of Adam. The new creation means righteousness and salvation because of the obedience of Jesus Christ. (See Rom. 5:12-21 for the explanation of the "two Adams.") Because we are a part of the new creation, everything has become new.

For one thing, we have a new view of Christ. It is unfortunate that too great an emphasis is given in music and art on Christ "after the flesh." The facts about the earthly life of Jesus are important, because the Christian message is grounded in history. But we must interpret the manger by the throne. We do not worship a Babe in a manger; we worship a glorified Saviour on the throne.

Because "all things are become new," we also have a new view of people around us. We see them as sinners for whom Christ died. We no longer see them as friends or enemies, customers or coworkers; we see them the way Christ sees them, as lost sheep who need a shepherd. When you are constrained by the love of Christ, you want to share His love with others.

During an especially controversial presidential election, a church officer came into a Sunday School class wearing a large pin that promoted one of the candidates. The pastor stopped him and advised him to take it off until he was out of church.

"Why take it off?" he argued. "He's a perfectly good candidate!"

"But suppose the pin is seen by an unsaved man of the other party?" the pastor replied. "Will it upset him and maybe keep him from hearing the Word and getting saved?"

Sullenly, the man removed the pin; and then he smiled and said, "I guess I should remember that people aren't Republicans or Democrats. They're sinners who need a Saviour—and that's more important than winning an election."

But we should also look at other Christians as a part of the new creation, and not evaluate them on the bases of education, race, finances, or position in society. "There is neither Jew nor Greek, there is neither bond nor free, there is neither male nor female: for ye are all one in Christ Jesus" (Gal. 3:28).

The Commission of Christ (2 Cor. 5:18-21)

The key idea in this paragraph is *reconciliation.* Because of his rebellion, man was the enemy of God and out of fellowship with Him. Through the work of the Cross, Jesus Christ has brought man and God together again. God has been reconciled and has turned His face in love toward the lost world. The basic meaning of the word *reconcile* is "to change thoroughly." It refers to a changed relationship between God and the lost world.

God does not have to be reconciled to man, because that was accomplished by Christ on the cross. It is sinful man who must be reconciled to God. "Religion" is man's feeble effort to be reconciled to God, efforts that are bound to fail. The Person who reconciles us to God is Jesus Christ, and the place where He reconciles us is His cross.

Another key idea in this section is *imputation.* This is a word borrowed from banking; it simply means "to put to one's account." When you deposit money in the bank, the computer (or the clerk) puts that amount to your account, or to your credit. When Jesus died on the cross, all of our sins were imputed to Him—put to His account. He was treated by God as though He had actually committed those sins.

The result? All of those sins have been paid for and God no longer holds them against us, because we have trusted Christ as our Saviour. But even more: God has put to our account the very righteousness of Christ! "For He hath made Him [Christ] to be sin for us, who knew no sin; that we might be made the righteousness of God in Him" (2 Cor. 5:21).

Reconciliation is based on imputation: because the demands of God's holy Law have been fully met on the cross, God can be reconciled to sinners. Those who believe on Jesus Christ as their Saviour will never have their sins imputed against them again (Ps. 32:1-2; Rom. 4:1-8). As far as their records are concerned, they share the righteousness of Jesus Christ!

There is a lovely illustration of this truth in the little letter Paul wrote to his friend Philemon. Philemon's slave, Onesimus, stole from his master and then fled to Rome. Because of his crimes, he could have been crucified. But in the providence of God, Onesimus met Paul and was converted. Paul wrote the Letter to Philemon to encourage his friend to forgive Onesimus and receive him home. "Receive him as myself," wrote Paul (Phile. 17); "if he . . . oweth thee aught, put that on mine account" (Phile. 18). Paul was willing to pay the bill (imputation) so that Onesimus and Philemon could be reconciled.

How does this wonderful doctrine of reconciliation motivate us to serve Christ? We are ambassadors with a message. God has committed to us the ministry and the word of reconciliation (2 Cor. 5:18-19).

In the Roman Empire, there were two kinds of provinces: senatorial provinces and imperial provinces. The senatorial provinces were made up of people who were peaceful and not at war with Rome. They had surrendered and submitted. But the imperial provinces were not peaceful; they were dangerous because they would rebel against Rome if they could. It was necessary for Rome to send ambassadors to the imperial provinces to make sure that rebellion did not break out.

Since Christians in this world are the ambassadors of Christ, this means that the world is in rebellion against God. This world is an "imperial province" as far as God is concerned. He has sent His ambassadors into the world to declare peace, not war. "Be ye reconciled to God!" We represent Jesus Christ

(John 20:21; 2 Cor. 4:5). If sinners reject us and our message, it is Jesus Christ who is actually rejected. What a great privilege it is to be heaven's ambassadors to the rebellious sinners of this world!

When I was a young pastor, it used to embarrass me somewhat to make visits and confront people with the claims of Christ. Then it came to me that I was a privileged person, an ambassador of the King of kings! There was nothing to be embarrassed about. In fact, the people I visited should have been grateful that one of Christ's ambassadors came to see them.

God has not declared war on the world; at the cross He declared peace. But one day, He *will* declare war; and then it will be too late for those who have rejected the Saviour (2 Thes. 1:3-10). Satan is seeking to tear everything apart in this world, but Christ and His church are involved in the ministry of reconciliation, bringing things back together again, and back to God.

Ministry is not easy. If we are to succeed, we must be motivated by the fear of the Lord, the love of Christ, and the commission that He has given to us. What a privilege it is to serve Him!

CHAPTER SIX
HEART TO HEART
2 Corinthians 6–7

These two chapters bring to a heartfelt conclusion Paul's explanation of his ministry. He has told his readers that, in spite of trials, his was a triumphant ministry (2 Cor. 1–2) and a glorious ministry (2 Cor. 3), and that he could not ever think of quitting. His enemies had accused him of using the ministry for personal gain, but he had proved his ministry to be sincere (2 Cor. 4) and based on faith in God (2 Cor. 5). All that remained now was to challenge the hearts of the Corinthians and assure them of his love; and this he did by presenting them with three loving appeals.

An Appeal for Appreciation (2 Cor. 6:1-10)

Principles of Psychology by William James has been a classic text and certainly was a pioneer work in that field. But the author admitted that there was "an immense omission" in the book. "The deepest principle of human nature is the craving to be appreciated," he wrote; and yet he had not dealt with this principle in his book.

As you read 2 Corinthians, you get the strong impression that the church did not really appreciate Paul and the work he had done among them. They should have been defending Paul and not forcing him to defend himself. The Corinthians were boasting about the Judaizers who had invaded the church, and yet the Judaizers had done nothing for them. So Paul reminded them of the ministry God had given him at Corinth.

Paul the evangelist (vv. 1-2). It was Paul who had gone to Corinth with the Good News of the Gospel; and through his ministry, the church had been founded. He had fulfilled the work of the "ambassador" described in 2 Corinthians 5:18-21. It was not the Judaizers who had won them to Christ; it was Paul.

But even now, Paul was not certain that everybody in the church who professed to be saved was truly a child of God (see 2 Cor. 13:5). He quoted Isaiah 49:8 as his appeal for them to receive God's grace. Because of the reconciling work of Christ on the cross (2 Cor. 5:18-19), today is indeed "the day of salvation." There is no guarantee that any sinner will have the opportunity to be saved *tomorrow.* "Seek ye the Lord while He may be found" (Isa. 55:6).

A pastor was dealing with a young lady who was arguing that she had plenty of time to decide for Jesus Christ. He handed her a piece of paper and said, "Would you sign a statement that you would be willing to postpone salvation for a year?" No, she would not do that. Six months? No again. One month? She hesitated, but said no. Then she began to see the folly of her argument because she had assurance of opportunity *only for today;* and she trusted Christ without delay.

Paul the example (vv. 3-10). One of the greatest obstacles to the progress of the Gospel is the bad example of people who profess to be Christians. Unsaved people like to use the inconsistencies of the saints—especially preachers—as an excuse for rejecting Jesus Christ. Paul was careful not to do anything that would put a stumbling block in the way of either sinners or saints (see Rom. 14). He did not want the ministry to be discredited ("blamed") in any way because of his life.

Paul reminded his readers of *the trials he had endured for them* (2 Cor. 6:4-5). He had been a man of endurance ("patience") and had not quit when things were tough. *Afflictions* are trials under pressure, when you are pressed down by circumstances. *Necessities* are the everyday hardships of life, and *distresses* refer to experiences that push us into a corner where there seems to be no escape. The Greek word means "a narrow place."

But even unsaved people go through those experiences, so Paul then listed a few of the trials he endured because of the opposition of people: stripes, imprisonments, and tumults (riots). These he experienced because he was faithfully serving the Lord. He then named some of the sacrifices he made voluntarily for the sake of the ministry: labors (work resulting in weariness), watchings (sleepless nights), fastings (willingly going without food). Of course, Paul had not announced these things publicly. The only reason he mentioned them in this letter was to assure the Corinthians of his love for them.

He further reminded them of the tools he had used in his ministry (2 Cor. 6:6-7). *Pureness* means "chastity" (see 2 Cor. 11:2). Paul kept himself morally clean. *Long-suffering* refers to patience with difficult people, while *patience* (2 Cor. 6:4) refers to endurance in difficult circumstances. Paul depended on the power of the Spirit so that he might manifest the fruit of the Spirit, such as kindness and sincere love. He used the Word of God to convey spiritual knowledge, and he wore the armor of God (see Eph. 6:10ff) to protect him from satanic attacks.

Finally, he reminded them of *the testimony that he bore* (2 Cor. 6:8-10). Paul listed a series of paradoxes, because he knew that not everybody really understood him and his ministry. Paul's enemies gave an evil report of him as a man who was a dishonorable deceiver. But God gave a good report of Paul as a man who was honorable and true. Paul was well known and yet, at the same time, unknown.

What a price Paul paid to be faithful in his ministry! And yet how little the Corinthians really appreciated all he did for them. They brought sorrow to his heart, yet he was "always rejoicing" in Jesus Christ. He became poor that they might become rich (see 1 Cor. 1:5; 2 Cor. 8:9). The word translated *poor* means "the complete destitution of a beggar."

Was Paul wrong in appealing for their appreciation? I don't think so. Too many churches are prone to take for granted the sacrificial ministry of pastors, missionaries, and faithful church officers. Paul was not begging for praise, but he was reminding his friends in Corinth that his ministry to them had cost him dearly.

Of course, in all of this personal testimony, Paul was refuting the malicious accusations of the Judaizers. How much had *they* suffered for the people at Corinth? What price did *they* pay for their ministry? Like most "cultists" today, these false teachers stole another man's converts; they did not seek to win the lost themselves.

It has well been said, "If you want to find gratitude, look in the dictionary." Are we showing gratitude to those who have ministered to us?

An Appeal for Separation (2 Cor. 6:11–7:1)

In spite of all the problems and heartaches the church had caused him, Paul still loved the believers at Corinth very much. He had spoken honestly and lovingly to them; now he tenderly asked them to open their hearts to him. He felt like a father whose children were robbing him of the love that he deserved (see 1 Cor. 4:15).

Why were they withholding their love? Because they had divided hearts. The false teachers had stolen their hearts, and now they were cool toward Paul. They were like a daughter engaged to be married, but being seduced by an unworthy suitor (see 2 Cor. 11:1-3). The Corinthians were compromising with the world, so Paul appealed to them to separate themselves to God, the way a faithful wife is separated to her husband.

It is unfortunate that the important doctrine of separation has been misunderstood and abused in recent years, for it is an essential truth. Some sincerely zealous Christians have turned separation into isolation, until their fellowship has become so narrow that they cannot even get along with themselves. In reaction to this extreme position, other believers have torn down all the walls and will fellowship with anybody, regardless of what he believes or how he lives. While we applaud their desire to practice Christian love, we want to remind them that even Christian love must exercise discernment (Phil. 1:9-11).

Paul presented three arguments to try to convince these believers that they must separate themselves from that which is contrary to God's will.

The nature of the believer (vv. 14-16). It is nature that determines association. Because a pig has a pig's nature, it associates with other pigs in the mud hole. Because a sheep has a sheep's nature, it munches grass with the flock in the pasture. The Christian possesses a divine nature (2 Peter 1:3-4), and therefore he should want to associate himself only with that which pleases the Lord.

The concept of the "unequal yoke" comes from Deuteronomy 22:10, "Thou shalt not plow with an ox and an ass together." The ox was a clean animal to the Jews, but the ass was not (Deut. 14:1-8); and it would be wrong to yoke them together. Furthermore, they have two opposite natures and would not even work well together. It would be cruel to bind them to each other. In the same way, it is wrong for believers to be yoked together with unbelievers.

Note the nouns that Paul used: *fellowship, communion, concord* (harmony), *part, agreement.* Each of these words speaks of having something in common. The word *concord* gives us our English word "symphony," and it speaks of beautiful music that comes when the players are reading the same score and obeying the same leader. What chaos we would have if each instrumentalist played his own tune in his own way!

God's desires for His people are seen in these words. He wants us to *share* with each other (fellowship) and *have in common* (communion) the blessings of the Christian life. He wants us to enjoy *harmony* and *agreement* as we live and work together. When we try to walk with the world and with the Lord at the same time, we break this spiritual fellowship and create discord and division.

Paul saw believers and unbelievers in stark contrast to each other: righteousness—unrighteousness, light—darkness, Christ—Belial (Satan), belief—infidelity (unbelief), God's temple—idols. How could you possibly bring these opposites together? The very nature of the Christian demands that he be separated from that which is unholy. When a saved person marries an unsaved partner, it sets up an impossible situation; and the same thing applies to business partnerships and religious "fellowship."

Note that the word *ye* is plural in 2 Corinthians 6:16. Paul is here referring to the local church as a whole, and not to the individual believer only, as in 1 Corinthians 6:19-20. The local church is the dwelling place of God because believers are the people of God (see Ex. 6:7; 25:8; Lev. 26:12; Ezek. 37:26-27). For a local church to compromise its testimony is like a holy temple being defiled.

The command of Scripture (v. 17). The major part of this quotation is from Isaiah 52:11, but there are also echoes in it of Ezekiel 20:34, 41. The reference in Isaiah is to the captive nation leaving Babylon and returning to their own land, but the spiritual application is to the separation of the people of God today.

God commands His people to "come out," which implies a definite act on their part. "Be ye separate" suggests devotion to God for a special purpose. Separation is not just a negative act of departure; it is also a positive act of dedication to God. We must separate *from* sin and *unto* God. "Touch not the unclean thing" is a warning against defilement. The Old Testament Jew was defiled if he touched a dead body or the issue from a festering sore. Of course, Christians today do not contract spiritual defilement by touch, but the principle is the same: we must not associate with that which will compromise our testimony or lead us into disobedience.

God's command of separation is found throughout Scripture. He warned Israel not to mingle with the pagan nations in the land of Canaan (Num. 33:50-56); yet they repeatedly disobeyed His Word and were punished because of it. The prophets repeatedly pled with the people to forsake their heathen idols and devote themselves wholly to the Lord. Finally, God had to send Israel into Assyrian captivity and Judah into Babylonian Captivity. Our Lord rejected the false "separation" of the Pharisees, but He did warn His disciples against the leaven (false doctrine) of the Pharisees and Sadducees, and He prayed that they would be kept from the defilement of the world (Matt. 16:6, 11; John 17:14-17).

The apostles in their letters to the churches also emphasized doctrinal and personal purity. The believer was *in* the world, but he must be careful not to become like the world. The church must also separate itself from those who reject the doctrine given by Christ and the apostles (Rom. 12:1-2; 16:17-20; Col. 3:1-2; 1 Tim. 6:10-11; Titus 2:14; 1 Peter 4:3-6; 1 John 4:6). Even in the Book of Revelation, there is an emphasis on God's people being separated from that which is false and contrary to holy living (Rev. 2:14-16, 20-24; 18:4ff).

In our desire for doctrinal and personal purity, we must not become so self-centered that we ignore the needy world around us. Our Lord was "holy, harmless, undefiled, separate from sinners" (Heb. 7:26), and yet He was "a friend of publicans and sinners" (Luke 7:34). Like a skillful physician, we must practice "contact without contamination." Otherwise, we will isolate ourselves from the people who need our ministry the most.

The promise of God's blessing (v. 17–7:1). God becomes our Father when we trust Jesus Christ as our Saviour, but He cannot *be to us* a Father unless we obey Him and fellowship with Him. He longs to receive us in love and treat us as His precious sons and daughters. Salvation means we share the Father's life, but separation means that we enter fully into the Father's love. Jesus promised this "deeper love" in John 14:21-23.

God blesses those who separate themselves from sin and unto the Lord. Abraham separated himself from Ur of the Chaldees and God blessed him. When Abraham compromised and went to Egypt, God had to chasten him (Gen. 11:31–12:20). As long as Israel was separated from the sinful nations in Canaan, God blessed them; but when they began to mingle with the heathen, God had to discipline them. Both Ezra and Nehemiah had to teach the people again the meaning of separation (Ezra 9–10; Neh. 9:2; 10:28; 13:1-9, 23-31).

Because of God's gracious promises, we have some spiritual responsibilities (2 Cor. 7:1). We must cleanse ourselves once and for all of anything that defiles us. It is not enough to ask God to cleanse us; we must clean up our own lives and get rid of those things that make it easy for us to sin. No believer can legislate for any other believer; each one knows the problems of his own heart and life.

Too often Christians deal with symptoms and not causes. We keep confessing the same sins because we have not gotten to the root of the trouble and "cleansed ourselves." Perhaps there is "filthiness of the flesh," some pet sin that "feeds" the old nature (Rom. 13:14). Or it may be "filthiness of the spirit," an attitude that is sinful. The Prodigal Son was guilty of sins of the flesh, but his "moral" elder brother was guilty of sins of the spirit. He could not even get along with his own father (see Luke 15:11-21).

But cleansing ourselves is only half of the responsibility; we must also be "perfecting holiness in the fear of God" (2 Cor. 7:1). This is a constant process as we grow in grace and knowledge (2 Peter 3:18). It is important to be balanced. The Pharisees were keen on putting away sin, but they neglected to perfect holiness. But it is foolish to try to perfect holiness if there is known sin in our lives.

Paul had appealed for appreciation and for separation. He gave one final appeal in his attempt to regain the love and devotion of the believers in Corinth.

An Appeal for Reconciliation (2 Cor. 7:2-16)

"Open wide your hearts to us!" (2 Cor. 6:13) "Receive us!" (2 Cor. 7:2) "Can two walk together, except they be agreed?" (Amos 3:3) If the Corinthians would only cleanse their lives and their church fellowship, God would receive them (2 Cor. 6:17) and they could again have close fellowship with Paul.

The emphasis in this section is on the way God encouraged Paul after he had experienced such great trials in Asia and Troas (see 2 Cor. 1:8-10; 2:12-13). There is actually a threefold encouragement recorded in these verses.

Paul encouraged the church (vv. 2-4). The church had received Titus; now they should receive Paul (2 Cor. 7:13). Paul asked them to trust him, for he had never done anything to wrong them. This is certainly a reference to the false teachers who had accused Paul, especially the use of the word *defrauded* ("exploits"—see 2 Cor. 11:20, NIV). "Paul is taking up this missionary offering so he can use the money himself!" they were saying.

Why is it so difficult to assure people of our love? What more could Paul do to convince them? He was willing to die for them if necessary, for they were in his heart (see 2 Cor. 3:1ff; 6:11-13). He was boasting of them to others ("glorying of you"), but they were criticizing him.

But, in spite of these problems, Paul had good reason to encourage the church because the visit of Titus had been successful; and now there was opportunity to "mend the fences" and restore fellowship. This leads to the second encouragement.

Titus encouraged Paul (vv. 5-10). The first encouragement Paul received was the coming of Titus after they had been separated from each other. It was not easy to communicate or to travel in those days, and Paul had to depend on the providence of God for his plans to work out regarding the visit of Titus to Corinth. (Even with our modern means of transportation and communication, we still need to depend on God's providence.)

But Paul was encouraged by the report that Titus gave of his reception at Corinth. They had read Paul's "painful letter" and had repented of their sins and disciplined the members who had created the problems. It is unfortunate that the *King James Version* translates two different Greek words as "repent," for they have different meanings. The word *repent* in 2 Corinthians 7:8 means "regret," and *repented* in 2 Corinthians 7:10 means "to be regretted."

Paul had written them a stern letter, and then had regretted it. But the letter achieved its purpose and the Corinthians repented, and this made Paul rejoice. Their repentance was not merely a passing "regret"; it was a true godly sorrow for sin. "Godly sorrow brings repentance that leads to salvation and leaves no regret, but worldly sorrow brings death" (2 Cor. 7:10, NIV). The difference is seen in Judas and Peter. Judas "repented himself" (was full of regret) and went and committed suicide, while Peter wept and repented of his fall (Matt. 26:75–27:5).

Do Christians need to repent? Jesus said that we do (Luke 17:3-4), and Paul agreed with Him (2 Cor. 12:21). Four of the seven churches of Asia Minor, listed in Revelation 2–3, were commanded to repent. To repent simply means "to change one's mind," and disobedient Christians need to repent, not in order to be saved, but in order to restore their close fellowship with God.

The Corinthians encouraged Titus (vv. 11-16). They went to great lengths to do the will of God. First of all, they received Titus and refreshed him by their fellowship (2 Cor. 7:13). They rejoiced his heart as they proved to be all that Paul boasted that they were. They accepted his message from Paul and acted on it.

In 2 Corinthians 7:11, Paul spelled out their handling of the matter of discipline. "For behold what earnestness this very thing, this godly sorrow, has produced in you; what vindication of yourselves, what indignation, what fear, what longing, what zeal, what avenging of wrong! In everything you demonstrated yourselves to be innocent in the matter" (NASB). Paul was encouraged when Titus told him of the way they repented and showed concern and zeal to do what was right. Paul assured them that the purpose of his letter was not only to rebuke the offender and help the offended, but to prove his love for the church. Paul had suffered a great deal because of this situation, but his suffering was worth it all now that the problem was solved.

One of the most difficult things to do is to rebuild a shattered relationship. This Paul tried to do in 2 Corinthians, and especially in chapters 6 and 7. Unfortunately, there are many shattered relationships today—in homes, churches, and ministries—and they can be repaired and strengthened only when people face problems honestly, deal with them biblically and lovingly, and seek to get right with God.

As you and I examine our own lives, we must determine to be a part of the answer and not a part of the problem. We must show appreciation, practice separation, and encourage reconciliation if God is to use us to restore broken relationships.

CHAPTER SEVEN
THE GRACE OF GIVING—PART 1
2 Corinthians 8

One of the major ministries of Paul's third missionary journey was the taking up of a special "relief offering" for the poor Christians in Judea. Once before Paul had assisted in this way (Acts 11:27-30), and he was happy to do it again. It is significant that it was Paul who remembered the "forgotten beatitude" of our Lord: "It is more blessed to give than to receive" (Acts 20:35).

But Paul had other blessings in mind besides the material assisting of the poor. He wanted this offering to strengthen the unity of the church as the Gentile churches shared with the Jewish congregations across the sea. Paul saw the Gentiles as "debtors" to the Jews (Rom. 15:25-28), and the special collection was one way to pay that debt.

This offering was also evidence to the Jewish believers (some of whom were still zealous for the Law) that Paul was not the enemy of the Jews or of Moses (Acts 20:17ff). Early in his ministry, Paul had promised to remember the poor (Gal. 2:6-10), and he labored to keep that promise; but at the same time, he hoped that the generosity of the Gentiles would silence the jealousy of the Jews.

Unfortunately, the Corinthians were not doing their part. Like many people, they had made promises, but they failed to keep them. In fact, an entire year had been wasted (2 Cor. 8:10). What was the cause of this serious delay? The low spiritual level of the church. When a church is not spiritual, it is not generous. Another factor was the invasion of the Judaizers, who probably siphoned off as much money as they could (2 Cor. 11:7-12, 20; 12:14).

Paul knew that it would be difficult to get the Corinthians to participate, so he lifted his appeal to the highest spiritual level possible: he taught them that giving was an act of grace. Paul used nine different words to refer to the offering, but the one he used the most was *grace*. Giving is truly a *ministry* and *fellowship* (2 Cor. 8:4) that helps others, but the motivation must be from the grace of God in the heart. Paul knew that this collection was a *debt* owed by the Gentiles (Rom. 15:27) and *fruit* from their Christian lives (Rom. 15:28); but it was even more: it was the working of the grace of God in human hearts.

It is a wonderful thing when Christians enter into the grace of giving, when they really believe that giving is more blessed than receiving. How can we tell when we are practicing "grace giving"? Paul indicated that there were a number of evidences that appear when our giving is motivated by grace.

When We Give in Spite of Circumstances (2 Cor. 8:1-2)

The Macedonian churches that Paul was using as an example had experienced severe difficulties, and yet they had given generously. They had not simply gone through "affliction"; they had experienced a "great trial of affliction" (2 Cor. 8:2). They were in *deep poverty*, which means "rock-bottom destitution." The word describes a beggar who has absolutely nothing and has no hope of getting anything. Their difficult situation may have been caused in part by their Christian faith, for they may have lost their jobs or been excluded from the trade guilds because they refused to have anything to do with idolatry.

But their circumstances did not hinder them from giving. In fact, they gave joyfully and liberally! No computer could analyze this amazing formula: great affliction and deep poverty *plus grace* = abundant joy and abounding liberality! It reminds us of the paradox in Paul's ministry: "as poor, yet making many rich" (2 Cor. 6:10). It also reminds us of the generous offerings that were taken at the building of the tabernacle (Ex. 35:5-6) and the temple (1 Chron. 29:6-9).

When you have experienced the grace of God in your life, you will not use difficult circumstances as an excuse for not giving. For that matter, are circumstances *ever* an encouragement to giving? In my first pastorate, we had a great need for a new church building; but some of the people opposed a building program because of the "economic situation." Apparently the steel mills were planning to go on strike, and the refineries were going to shut down, and the railroads were having problems . . . and it seemed like a risky time to build. But there were enough people who believed in "grace giving" so that the church did erect a new sanctuary—in spite of the strikes, shutdowns, layoffs, and other economic problems. Grace giving means giving in spite of circumstances.

When We Give Enthusiastically (2 Cor. 8:3-4)

It is possible to give generously but not give enthusiastically. "The preacher says I should give until it hurts," said a miserly church member, "but for me, it hurts just to think about giving!" The Macedonian churches needed no prompting or reminding, as did the church at Corinth. They were more than willing to share in the collection. In fact, *they begged to be included!* (2 Cor. 8:4) How many times have you heard a Christian *beg* for somebody to take an offering?

Their giving was voluntary and spontaneous. It was of grace, not pressure. They gave because they wanted to give and because they had experienced the grace of God. Grace not only frees us from our sins, but it frees us from ourselves. The grace of God will open your heart *and your hand*. Your giving is not the result of cold calculation, but of warm-hearted jubilation!

When We Give as Jesus Gave (2 Cor. 8:5-9)

Jesus Christ is always the preeminent example for the believer to follow, whether in service, suffering, or sacrifice. Like Jesus Christ, the Macedonian Christians *gave themselves to God and to others* (2 Cor. 8:5). If we give ourselves to God, we will have little problem giving our substance to God. If we give ourselves to God, we will also give of ourselves for others. It is impossible to love God and ignore the needs of your neighbor. Jesus Christ gave Himself for us (Gal. 1:4; 2:20). Should we not give ourselves to Him? He died so that we might not live for ourselves, but for Him and for others (2 Cor. 5:15).

The Macedonians' giving was, like Christ's, *motivated by love* (2 Cor. 8:7-8). What a rebuke to the Corinthians who were so enriched with spiritual blessings (1 Cor. 1:4-5). They were so wrapped up in the *gifts* of the Spirit that they had neglected the *graces* of the Spirit, including the grace of giving. The Macedonian churches had an "abundance of deep poverty" (2 Cor. 8:2), and yet they abounded in their liberality. The Corinthians had an abundance of spiritual gifts, yet they were lax in keeping their promise and sharing in the collection.

We must never argue that the ministry of our spiritual gifts is a substitute for generous giving. "I teach a Sunday School class, so I don't have to give!" is not an explanation—it's an excuse. The Christian who remembers that his gifts are *gifts* will be motivated to give to others and not "hide" behind his ministry for the Lord. I have met pastors and missionaries who have argued that, since they devote their whole time in serving the Lord, they are not obligated to give. Paul argued just the opposite: since you are wonderfully gifted from God, you ought to want to give even more!

Paul was careful that they understood that he was not *ordering* them to give. Actually, he was contrasting the attitude of the Macedonians with that of the Corinthians. He was pointing out that the Macedonians were following the example of the Lord: they were poor, yet they gave. The Corinthians said that they loved Paul; now he asked them to prove that love by sharing in the offering. Grace giving is an evidence of love—love for Christ, love for God's servants who have ministered to us, and love for those who have special needs that we are able to help meet.

Finally, *their giving was sacrificial* (2 Cor. 8:9). In what ways was Jesus rich? Certainly He was rich in His person, for He is eternal God. He is rich in His possessions and in His position as King of kings and Lord of lords. He is rich in His power, for He can do anything. Yet, in spite of the fact that He had all these riches—and more—*He became poor.*

The tense of the verb indicates that it is His incarnation, His birth at Bethlehem, that is meant here. He united Himself to mankind and took on Himself a human body. He left the throne to become a servant. He laid aside all His possessions so that He did not even have a place to lay His head. His ultimate experience of poverty was when He was made sin for us on the cross. Hell is eternal poverty, and on the cross Jesus Christ became the poorest of the poor.

Why did He do it? That we might become rich! This suggests that we were poor before we met Jesus Christ, and we were—totally bankrupt. But now that we have trusted Him, we share in all of His riches! We are now the children of God, "heirs of God, and joint-heirs with Jesus Christ" (Rom. 8:17). Since this is true, *how can we refuse to give to others?* He became poor to make us rich! Can we not follow His example, as did the Macedonian churches, who out of their deep poverty abounded in liberality?

When We Give Willingly (2 Cor. 8:10-12)

There is a great difference between *promise* and *performance.* The Corinthians had boasted to Titus a year before that they would share in the special collection (2 Cor. 8:6), but they did not keep their promise. Note that in 2 Corinthians 8:10-12 Paul emphasized *willingness.* Grace giving must come from a willing heart; it cannot be coerced or forced.

During my years of ministry, I have endured many offering appeals. I have listened to pathetic tales about unbelievable needs. I have forced myself to laugh at old jokes that were supposed to make it easier for me to part with my money. I have been scolded, shamed, and almost threatened, and I must confess that none of these approaches has ever stirred me to give more than I planned to give. In fact, more than once I gave *less* because I was so disgusted with the worldly approach. (However, I have never gotten like Mark Twain, who said that he was so sickened by the long appeal that he not only did not give what he planned to give, but he took a bill out of the plate!)

We must be careful here not to confuse *willing* with *doing,* because the two must go together. If the willing is sincere and in the will of God, then there must be "a performance also" (2 Cor. 8:11; Phil. 2:12-13). Paul did not say that *willing* was a substitute for *doing,* because it is not. But if our giving is motivated by grace, we will give willingly, and not because we have been forced to give.

God sees the "heart gift" and not the "hand gift." If the heart wanted to give more, but was unable to do so, God sees it and records it accordingly. But if the hand gives more than the heart wants to give, God records what is in the heart, no matter how big the offering in the hand might be.

A friend of mine was leaving for a business trip, and his wife reminded him before church that she needed some extra money for household expenses. Just before the offering, he slipped some money into her hand; and she, thinking it was their weekly offering, put it all in the plate. It was the expense money for the week.

"Well," said my friend, "we gave it to the Lord and He keeps the records."

"How much did you *intend* to give?" asked their pastor, and my friend gave an amount. "Then that's what God recorded," said the pastor, "because He saw the intent of your heart!"

God sees, not the portion, but the proportion. If we could have given more, and did not, God notes it. If we wanted to give more, and could not, God also notes that. When we give willingly, according to what we have, we are practicing grace giving.

When We Give by Faith (2 Cor. 8:13-24)

Paul did not suggest that the rich become poor so that the poor might become rich. It would be unwise for a Christian to go into debt in order to relieve somebody else's debt, unless, of course, he was able to handle the responsibility of paying the debt back. Paul saw an "equality" in the whole procedure: the Gentiles were enriched spiritually by the Jews, so the Jews should be enriched materially by the Gentiles (see Rom. 15:25-28). Furthermore, the Gentile churches at that time were enjoying some measure of material wealth, while the believers in Judea were suffering. That situation could one day be reversed. There might come a time when the Jewish believers would be assisting the Gentiles.

Who does the equalizing? God does. Paul used the miracle of the manna as an illustration of the principle (Ex. 16:18). No matter how much manna the Jews gathered each day, they always had what they needed. Those who tried to hoard the manna discovered that it was impossible, because the manna would decay and smell (Ex. 16:20). The lesson is clear: gather what you need, share what you can, and don't try to hoard God's blessings. God will see to it that you will not be in need if you trust Him and obey His Word.

Our *motive* for giving is God's spiritual blessing in our lives, but our *measure* for giving is God's material blessing. Paul made this clear when he wrote to the Corinthians in his first letter, "Let every one of you lay by him in store, as God hath prospered him" (1 Cor. 16:2). Paul did not lay down any mathematical formula, because grace giving is not limited by a tithe (10 percent). Grace giving is systematic, but it is not legalistic. It is not satisfied with only the minimum, whatever that minimum might be.

Since it is God who does the "balancing of the books," we cannot accuse Paul of teaching some form of communism. In fact, 2 Corinthians 8:13 is a direct statement against communism. The so-called "communism" of the early church (Acts 2:44-47; 4:32-37) has no relationship to the communistic political and economic systems that are promoted today. The early Christians (like many Christians today) *voluntarily* shared what they had, but did not force people to participate. The entire program was temporary; and the fact that Paul had to take up a special collection to relieve their needs is proof that the program was never meant to be imitated by later generations of Christians.

Grace giving is a matter of faith: we obey God and believe that He will meet our needs as we help to meet the needs of others. As the Jews gathered the manna each day, so we must depend on God to "give us this day our daily bread" (Matt. 6:11). We must not waste or squander what God gives us, neither must we hoard it. In the will of God, it is right to save. (The Jews saved Friday's manna to eat on the Sabbath, and the manna did not decay [Ex. 16:22-26].) But out of God's will, the wealth that we hoard will harm us rather than help us (see James 5:1-6).

Beginning in 2 Corinthians 8:16, Paul suddenly turned from a profound spiritual principle to some practical counsel on how the special collection would be handled. While it is true that grace giving means giving by faith, it is also true that grace giving does not mean giving by chance. The Christian who shares with others must be sure that what he gives is managed honestly and faithfully.

Over the years, I have tried to encourage God's people to support ministries that could be trusted. On more than one occasion, I have warned a church member not to give to an unworthy organization, only to discover that he gave anyway. Then he would come to me a few months later and say, "I sent a check to that outfit, and now I discover that it's a fake!"

"I warned you not to give anything," I would reply very gently.

"Well, the Lord knows my heart," he would argue. "Even though the money was wasted, I got credit for the gift in heaven!"

Grace giving is not foolish giving. Even in a local church, the people who handle the funds must possess certain qualifications. Paul was very careful how he handled money entrusted to him, because he did not want to get the reputation of being a "religious thief." The churches that contributed to the collection chose certain representatives to travel with Paul, so that everything would be done honestly, decently, and in order.

I noted in one of our Sunday School classes in a church I pastored that *one* young man was taking up the offering, counting it, recording it, and then taking it to the Sunday School office. In a nonthreatening way, I suggested that he was putting himself in a dangerous position if anybody accused him of anything, because he could not prove that he was handling the money honestly. "I trust you," I said, "but I don't trust the people who may be watching you and looking for something to criticize." Instead of following my suggestion, he became very angry and left the church.

The men and women in every Christian ministry—a local church, a missionary organization, an evangelistic meeting—should possess the following qualifications if they are to handle God's money.

A God-given desire to serve (vv. 16-17). Paul did not "draft" Titus; the young man had a desire in his heart to assist in the gathering of the special offering. Too often in local churches, men and women are put on the Finance Committee who do not have a sincere desire to serve God in this way. Above all else, a person who handles the Lord's money must have a heart that is right with God.

A burden for lost souls (v. 18). We do not know who this brother was, but we thank God he had a testimony that he shared the Gospel. Perhaps he was an evangelist; at least he was known to the churches as a man burdened for souls. Local church nominating committees put the good "soul winners" on the Evangelism Committee or on the Missions Committee, which is fine; but some of them also ought to be on the Finance Committee or the Board of Trustees. Why? *To keep the priorities straight.* I have seen committees approve large sums for buildings and equipment who would not release funds for a soul-winning ministry.

A discouraged young pastor sought my counsel one day. "My Finance Committee is running scared," he said. "The economic situation has made them so tightfisted, they won't spend any money—and we have a big surplus in the bank!" I had never met his committee, but I knew one thing about them: they needed a burden for lost souls.

A desire to honor God (v. 19). Too often, financial reports glorify the church, or a group of special donors, and do not glorify God. There is no such thing in the church as "secular and sacred," "business and ministry." All that we do is "sacred business" and ministry for the Lord. When the church constitution says that the deacons (or elders) handle the "spiritual affairs" of the church, and the trustees handle the "material and financial affairs," it is making an unbiblical distinction. *The most spiritual thing a church can do is use its money wisely for spiritual ministry.*

We glorify God by using what He gives us the way He wants it used. If the people who manage church finances are not burdened to glorify God, they will soon be using those funds in ways that dishonor God.

A reputation for honesty (vv. 20-22). Paul made it clear that he welcomed the representatives from the cooperating churches. He wanted to avoid any blame. It is not enough to say, "Well, the Lord sees what we're doing!" We should make certain that *men* can see what we are doing. I like the way J.B. Phillips translates 2 Corinthians 8:21: "Naturally we want to avoid the slightest breath of criticism in the distribution of their gifts, and to be absolutely aboveboard not only in the sight of God but in the eyes of men."

Personally, I would not support a missionary or Christian worker who was not identified in some way with a reputable committee or board, or a reputable organization. Nor would I give support to any ministry that did not have its books audited and the report available to the donors. I am not saying that all "free-lance" Christian workers are irresponsible; but I would have more confidence in their ministries if they were attached to a board or an organization that supervised their financial support.

Note the emphasis in 2 Corinthians 8:22 on *diligence.* If there is one quality that is needed when handling finances, it is diligence. I have heard of church treasurers who did not keep up-to-date accurate records of income and expenditures, and who handed in careless annual reports with the excuse that they were "too busy to keep up with the books." Then they should not have taken the office!

A cooperative spirit (vv. 23-24). Titus not only had a heart for this ministry (2 Cor. 8:16), but he knew how to be a good "team member." Paul called him his "partner" and "fellow helper." Titus was not like the committee member I heard about who said at the first meeting, "As long as I am on this committee, there will be no unanimous votes!"

Finance committee members do not *own* the money; it belongs to the Lord. The committee is but a steward, managing the money honestly and carefully for the service of the Lord. Note too that Paul saw the committee as special servants of the *churches.* The raising of this special "relief fund" was a cooperative effort of the Gentile churches, and Paul and the representatives were but "messengers" of the churches. The Greek word is *apostolos,* from which we get "apostle—one sent with a special commission." These dedicated Christians felt an obligation to the churches to do their work honestly and successfully.

Grace giving is an exciting adventure! When you learn to give "by grace, through faith" (just the way you were saved—Eph. 2:8-9), you start to experience a wonderful liberation from things and from circumstances. Instead of *things* possessing you, you start to control them; you develop a new set of values and priorities. You no longer measure life or other people on the basis of money or possessions. If money is the best test of success, then Jesus was a failure, because He was a poor Man!

Grace giving enriches you as you enrich others.

Grace giving makes you more like Jesus Christ.

Have you discovered the thrill of grace giving?

CHAPTER EIGHT
THE GRACE OF GIVING—PART 2
2 Corinthians 9

It seems strange that we Christians need encouragements to give, when God has given so much to us. God had enriched the Corinthians in a wonderful way, and yet they were hesitant to share what they had with others. They were not accustomed to *grace* giving, so Paul had to explain it to them. Having explained grace giving to them, Paul then tried to motivate them to get involved in the special offering; he did this by sharing five encouragements that relate to grace giving.

Your Giving Will Provoke Others (2 Cor. 9:1-5)

While Christians must not compete with each other in their service for Christ, they ought to "consider one another to provoke unto love and to good works" (Heb. 10:24). When we see what God is doing in and through the lives of others, we ought to strive to serve Him better ourselves. There is a fine line between fleshly imitation and spiritual emulation, and we must be careful in this regard. But a zealous Christian can be the means of stirring up a church and motivating people to pray, work, witness, and give.

The interesting thing is this: Paul had used the zeal of the Corinthians to challenge the Macedonians; but now he was using the Macedonians to challenge the Corinthians! A year before, the Corinthians had enthusiastically boasted that they would share in the offering, but then they had done nothing. The Macedonians had followed through on their promise, and Paul was afraid that his boasting would be in vain.

Paul sent Titus and the other brothers to Corinth to stir them up to share in the offering. Far more important than the money itself was the spiritual benefit that would come to the church as they shared in response to God's grace in their lives. Paul had written to the church before to tell them how to take up the contributions (1 Cor. 16:1-4), so there was no excuse for their delay. Paul wanted the entire contribution to be ready when he and his "finance committee" arrived, so that there might not be any last-minute collections that might appear to be forced on the church.

What did Paul want to avoid? Embarrassment to himself and to the church if the offering was not ready. For, after all, there were several representatives from the Macedonian churches on the special committee (see Acts 20:4). Paul had boasted to the Macedonians about Corinth, and now he feared that his boasting might be in vain.

Apparently, Paul did not see anything wrong or unspiritual about asking people to promise to give. He did not tell them *how much* they had to promise, but he did expect them to keep their promise. When a person signs up for a telephone, he promises to pay a certain amount each month. If it is acceptable to make financial commitments for things like telephones, cars, and credit cards, certainly it ought to be acceptable to make commitments for the work of the Lord.

Notice the words that Paul used as he wrote about the collection. It was "ministering to the saints," a service to fellow believers. It was also a "bounty" (2 Cor. 9:5), which means "a generous gift." Was Paul perhaps hinting that the Corinthians give more than they had planned?

However, Paul was careful not to put on any pressure. He wanted their gift to be "a matter of bounty [generosity], and not as of covetousness [something squeezed out of them]." High-pressure offering appeals do not belong to grace giving.

Our greatest encouragement for giving is that it pleases the Lord, but there is nothing wrong with practicing the kind of giving that provokes others to give. This does not mean that we should advertise what we do as individuals, because that kind of practice would violate one of the basic principles of giving: give secretly to the Lord (Matt. 6:1-4). However, Paul was writing to *churches;* and it is not wrong for congregations to announce what they have given collectively. If our motive is to boast, then we are not practicing grace giving. But if our desire is to provoke others to share, then God's grace can work through us to help others.

Your Giving Will Bless You (2 Cor. 9:6-11)

"Give, and it shall be given unto you," was our Lord's promise; and it still holds true (Luke 6:38). The "good measure" He gives back to us is not always money or material goods, but it is always worth far more than we gave. Giving is not something we *do,* but something we *are.* Giving is a way of life for the Christian who understands the grace of God. The world simply does not understand a statement like Proverbs 11:24: "There is that scattereth, and yet increaseth; and there is that withholdeth more than is meet, but it tendeth to poverty." In grace giving, our motive is not "to get something," but receiving God's blessing is one of the fringe benefits.

If our giving is to bless us and build us up, we must be careful to follow the principles that Paul explained in this section.

The principle of increase: we reap in measure as we sow (v. 6). This principle needs little explanation, because we see it operating in everyday life. The farmer who sows much seed will have a better chance for a bigger harvest. The investor who puts a large sum of money in the bank will certainly collect more dividends. The more we invest in the work of the Lord, the more "fruit" will abound to our account (Phil. 4:10-20).

Whenever we are tempted to forget this principle, we need to remind ourselves that God was unsparing in His giving. "He that spared not His own Son, but delivered Him up for us all, how shall He not with Him also freely give us all things?" (Rom. 8:32) In both nature and grace, God is a generous Giver; and he who would be godly must follow the divine example.

The principle of intent: we reap as we sow with right motives (v. 7). Motive makes absolutely no difference to the farmer! If he sows good seed and has good weather, he will reap a harvest whether he is working for profit, pleasure, or pride. It makes no difference how he plans to use the money that he earns, the harvest will probably come just the same.

But not so with the Christian: motive in giving (or in any other activity) is vitally important. Our giving must come from the heart, and the motive in the heart must please God. We must not be "sad givers" who give grudgingly, or "mad givers" who give because we have to ("of necessity"); but we should be "glad givers" who cheerfully share what we have because we have experienced the grace of God. "He that hath a bountiful eye shall be blessed" (Prov. 22:9).

If we cannot give joyfully (the Greek word gives us our English word *hilarious*), then we must open our hearts to the Lord and ask Him to grant us His grace. Certainly God can bless a gift that is given out of a sense of duty, but God cannot bless the giver unless his heart is right. Grace giving means that God blesses the giver as well as the gift, and that the giver is a blessing to others.

The principle of immediacy: we reap even while we are sowing (vv. 8-11). The farmer has to wait for his harvest, but the believer who practices grace giving begins to reap the harvest immediately. To be sure, there are long-range benefits from our giving, but there are also immediate blessings.

To begin with, we start to share God's abundant grace (2 Cor. 9:8). The "universals" in this verse are staggering: *all* grace; *always*; *all* sufficiency; *every* good work. This does not mean that God makes every Christian wealthy in material things; but it does mean that the Christian who practices grace giving will always have what he needs when he needs it. Furthermore, the grace of God enriches him morally and spiritually so that he grows in Christian character. In his walk and his work, he depends wholly on the sufficiency of God.

It is disturbing to see how many Christians today are totally dependent on others for their spiritual resources. Preachers cannot get sermons unless they borrow them from a book or a cassette. Church officers are bewildered about what to do with a problem unless they phone two or three well-known preachers for advice. Far too many church members have to consult with the pastor once a week or they fall apart spiritually.

The word *sufficiency* means "adequate resources within" (see Phil. 4:11). Through Jesus Christ, we can have the adequacy to meet the demands of life. As Christians, we do need to help and encourage one another; but we must not depend on one another. Our dependence must be on the Lord. He alone can give us that "well of water" in the heart that makes us sufficient for life (John 4:14).

We not only share God's grace, but we also share His righteousness (2 Cor. 9:9). Paul quoted Psalm 112:9 to prove his point. That psalm describes the righteous man who has no fears because his heart is sincere and obedient to the Lord. Paul did not suggest that we *earn* righteousness by our giving, because the only way to get righteousness is by faith in Jesus Christ. However, if our hearts are right, our giving will be used by God to make our characters righteous. Grace giving builds Christian character.

We reap as we sow, and we share God's miracle multiplication of what we give and do (2 Cor. 9:10). The farmer has to decide how much seed he will keep for food, and how much he will plant. If the harvest has been lean, there is less seed available both for eating and planting. But the Christian who believes in grace giving never has to worry about this decision: God supplies all that he needs. There is always spiritual and material "bread" for the eating and spiritual and material "seed" for the sowing.

Paul referred here to Isaiah 55:10-11, a passage that uses "seed" and "bread" to refer to both the Word of God and to the literal harvest in the field. There is no such thing as "secular" and "sacred" in the Christian life. The giving of money is just as spiritual an act as the singing of a hymn or the handing out of a Gospel tract. *Money is seed.* If we give it according to the principles of grace, it will multiply to the glory of God and meet many needs. If we use it in ways other than God desires, the harvest will be poor.

Finally, as we sow, we are enriched and we enrich others (2 Cor. 9:11). The farmer reaps immediate physical benefits as he works in his field, but he has to wait for the harvest. The Christian who is motivated by grace reaps the blessings of personal enrichment in his or her own life and character, and this enrichment benefits others. The final result is glory to God as others give thanks to Him. Paul was careful to point out that grace giving does not bring credit to us; it brings thanksgiving to God. We are but channels through whom God works to meet the needs of others.

But 2 Corinthians 9:11 teaches another truth: God enriches us so that we may give even more bountifully. One of the joys of grace giving is the joy of giving more and more. Everything we have—not just our income—belongs to God, is given to God, and is used by God to accomplish His work. We are enriched in everything because we share everything with Him and with others.

As a pastor, I have watched young Christians lay hold of these principles of grace giving and start to grow. It has been a great joy to see them trust God as their giving is motivated by grace. At the same time, I have seen other believers smile at these principles and gradually impoverish themselves. Some of them "prospered" financially, but their income was their downfall: it did not enrich them. They had their reward, but they lost their opportunities for spiritual enrichment.

Grace giving means that we really believe that God is the great giver, and we use our material and spiritual resources accordingly. You simply cannot outgive God!

Your Giving Will Meet Needs (2 Cor. 9:12)

Paul introduced a new word for the offering: *service.* It means "priestly service," so once again, Paul lifted the offering to the highest level possible. He saw this collection as a "spiritual sacrifice" presented to God, the way a priest presents a costly sacrifice on the altar.

Christians no longer bring animals as sacrifices to God, because the work of Christ on the cross has ended the levitical system (Heb. 10:1-14). But the material gifts we bring to the Lord become "spiritual sacrifices," if they are given in the name of Jesus (Phil. 4:10-20; Heb. 13:15-16; 1 Peter 2:5).

But the emphasis in 2 Corinthians 9:12 is on the fact that their offering would meet the needs of poor saints in Judea. "For the administration of this service not only supplieth the want of the saints, but is abundant also by many thanksgivings unto God" (2 Cor. 9:12). The Gentile believers could have given a number of excuses for not giving. "It's not our fault that they had a famine and are poor!" might have been one of them. Or, "The churches closer to Judea ought to give them help." Or, "We believe in giving, but we think we should first take care of our own."

When a Christian starts to think of excuses for not giving, he automatically moves out of the sphere of grace giving. *Grace never looks for a reason; it only looks for an opportunity.* If there is a need to be met, the grace-controlled Christian will do what he can to meet it.

"As we have therefore opportunity, let us do good unto all men, especially unto them who are of the household of faith" (Gal. 6:10). Paul admonished the wealthy Christians "that they do good, that they be rich in good works, ready to distribute, willing to communicate [share]" (1 Tim. 6:18). Most of us would not consider ourselves "wealthy," but the rest of the world does.

However, *we* are not the ones who get the glory; it is the Lord who is glorified (Matt. 5:16). Many people will give thanksgiving to God because of our sharing in the meeting of their needs. We may not hear that thanksgiving on earth today, but we will hear it in heaven when the church is gathered together.

It might be profitable here to notice Paul's use of the concept of *abundance* as he wrote this letter. He opened the letter with abundant suffering that was matched by abundant comfort (2 Cor. 1:5). He also mentioned abundant grace (2 Cor. 4:15) and abundant joy and liberality (2 Cor. 8:2). Because of God's abundant grace, we can abound always in every good work (2 Cor. 9:8). The apostle saw the Christian life as one of abundance, for Jesus Christ can make us adequate for every situation.

Our giving ought to provide for necessities, not subsidize luxuries. There are needs to be met and our limited resources must not be squandered. It is true that the need itself is not the only reason for giving, for there are always more needs than any one Christian or church can meet; but the need is important. Some needs are greater than others, and some needs are more strategic than others. We need accurate information as well as spiritual illumination as we seek to meet the many needs that are pressing on us today.

Your Giving Will Glorify God (2 Cor. 9:13)

"Let your light so shine before men," said our Lord, "that they may see your good works, and glorify your Father which is in heaven" (Matt. 5:16). This is one of the beauties of church giving: no individual gets the glory that belongs only to God.

For what would the grateful Jewish believers give thanks? Of course, they would praise God for the generosity of the Gentile churches in meeting their physical and material needs. But they would also praise God for the spiritual submission of the Gentiles, their obedience to the Spirit of God who gave them the desire to give. They would say, "Those Gentiles not only preach the Gospel, but they also practice it!"

The little phrase *and unto all men* at the end of this verse (2 Cor. 9:13) is significant. The Jewish believers would give thanks that *others* were also being assisted by the Gentile churches. Each little congregation that received aid would be thankful for that aid and for the aid being given to others. Instead of saying, "Why didn't *we* get more?" they would be praising God that others in need were also being helped. That is the way grace giving works.

It might be good for our churches to take inventory to see if anybody is giving thanks to God for our obedience and generosity. No amount of evangelistic zeal or worship activity can compensate for lost opportunities in serving others and meeting their practical needs. It is not a matter of choosing one and ignoring the other. There must be a balance of sharing the Gospel and meeting practical needs, if our light is to shine brightly and steadily. It has well been said that it is difficult to preach the Gospel to a hungry man (see James 2:15-16).

I recall reading about a wealthy Christian who daily, at family devotions, prayed for the needs of the missionaries that his church supported. One morning, after he had concluded family prayers, his little boy said, "Dad, if I had your checkbook, I could answer your prayers!" A discerning lad, indeed!

Your Giving Will Unite God's People (2 Cor. 9:14-15)

This, of course, was one of the major purposes that Paul had on his heart when he challenged the Gentile churches to assist the Jewish believers. The extreme legalists in the church had accused Paul of being anti-Jewish and even anti-Law. The Gentile churches were removed from the "mother church" in Jerusalem both by distance and culture. Paul wanted to prevent a division in the church, and the "relief offering" was a part of that prevention program.

In what ways would this offering bind the Jewish and Gentile congregations more closely? For one thing, the offering was an expression of love. The Gentiles were not obligated to share (though Paul did see the offering as the payment of a "spiritual debt," Rom. 15:25-27), but they did so because of the grace of God. The Jews, in turn, would feel themselves bound to their Gentile brothers and sisters.

Another spiritual bond would be prayer. "And in their prayers for you their hearts will go out to you, because of the surpassing grace God has given you" (2 Cor. 9:14, NIV). Were the Gentile churches "buying" the prayer support of the Jewish churches? Not in the least! Paul envisioned a spontaneous expression of love, praise, and prayer as he shared the offering in Judea.

I have had the experience of visiting several mission fields and hearing believers there say, "We are praying for you." I recall chatting with a fine Christian from eastern Europe, who said, "We are praying for you in the United States, because in some ways, you have a more difficult time being spiritual Christians than we do." When I asked him to explain, he smiled and said, "You have relatively easy lives, and comfort is an enemy of the spiritual life. In eastern Europe, we know who our enemies are, and we know who our friends are. Where you live, it is easy to be fooled. Yes, we are praying for you!"

Both the Jewish and the Gentile churches would be drawn closer to Jesus Christ. "Thanks [grace] be unto God for His unspeakable [indescribable] gift" (2 Cor. 9:15). In Jesus Christ, all human distinctions are erased, and we no longer see each other as Jews or Gentiles, rich or poor, givers or recipients. "For ye are all one in Christ Jesus" (Gal. 3:28).

It is sad when our giving becomes a substitute for our living. A church officer once complained to me, "I'll give any amount of money you want for missions. Just don't make me listen to a missionary speak!" When a Christian practices grace giving, his money is not a substitute for either his concern or his service. He first gives himself to the Lord (2 Cor. 8:5) and then he gives what he has. His gift is a symbol, as it were, of the surrender of his heart. You cannot separate the gift and the giver when your giving is motivated by God's grace.

I suggest you read 2 Corinthians 8 and 9 again, and that you note the emphasis on the grace of God. If our churches and other ministries would get back to grace giving, there would be fewer high-pressure offering appeals, fewer gimmicks to raise funds, and fewer complaints from the people of God. Instead, there would be plenty of money available for the ministries that truly magnify the grace of God. And I think that the unsaved people in the world would sit up and take notice!

You and I are saved because God believed in grace giving.

How much do *we* believe in grace giving?

CHAPTER NINE MINISTERIAL MISUNDERSTANDINGS

2 Corinthians 10

Whenever I receive a critical letter from a reader or a radio listener, I usually set it aside in a special file until I feel I am really ready to answer it. On a few occasions, I have replied to letters too quickly, and I have regretted it. By waiting, I give myself time to think and pray, to "read between the lines," and to prepare a reply that would do the most good and the least damage.

The Spirit led Paul to use a wise approach as he wrote to the Corinthians. He was writing to a divided church (1 Cor. 1:11ff), a church that was resisting his authority, and a church that was being seduced by false teachers. So, first he explained his ministry so that they would no longer doubt his sincerity. He then encouraged them to share in the offering, for he knew that this challenge would help them grow in their spiritual lives. Grace giving and grace living go together.

Now, in the last section of the letter, Paul challenged the rebels in the church—including the false teachers—and enforced his apostolic ministry. As you read 2 Corinthians 10–13, you will find Paul referring directly to his accusers (2 Cor. 10:7, 10-12; 11:4, 20-23, for example) and answering their false charges. He does not hide the fact that the Judaizers in the church are ministers of Satan who want to destroy the work of God (2 Cor. 11:12-15).

Paul used one word twenty times in 2 Corinthians 10–13, the word translated *boast* or *glory.* When you first read these chapters, you get the impression that Paul was bragging about himself; but such was not the case. Paul "gloried in Jesus Christ" and not in himself or his achievements (Rom. 5:11; Gal. 6:14; Phil. 3:3). He boasted to others about the Corinthians, but it seemed that his boasting might be in vain (2 Cor. 7:4, 14; 8:24).

Keep in mind that Paul was not defending himself personally; he was defending his ministry and his apostolic authority. He was not involved in a "personality contest" with other ministers. His enemies did not hesitate to accuse him falsely, nor did they hesitate to promote themselves (2 Cor. 11:12). It was the worldly attitude of the Corinthians that *forced* Paul to defend himself by reminding them of his life and ministry. Paul never hesitated to talk about Jesus Christ, but he did refuse to talk about himself, unless there was good reason to do so.

Finally, when Paul did *boast,* he limited himself to the ministry God had given him (2 Cor. 10:13), and then he emphasized his *sufferings,* not his successes. When this letter was read in the Corinthian assembly, it must have brought shame to the hearts of those who had criticized Paul—and it must have made the Judaizers look foolish.

Paul's first step in enforcing his ministry was to correct the misunderstandings that existed in the minds of the people with reference to his work. They did not understand three important areas of ministry.

How to Wage Spiritual Warfare (2 Cor. 10:1-6)

The accusation (vv. 1-2). This is not difficult to find. The rebels in the church (led by the Judaizers) said that Paul was very courageous when he wrote letters from a distance, but very timid and even weak when he was present with the Corinthians (see also 2 Cor. 10:9-11). The Judaizers, of course, were consistently overbearing in their attitudes—and the people loved them (2 Cor. 11:20). Paul's "inconsistent" manner of life paralleled his "yes and no" approach to making promises (2 Cor. 1:15-20).

When Paul founded the church at Corinth, his purpose was to exalt Christ and not himself (1 Cor. 2:1-5). Christians usually grow the way they are born. If they are born in an atmosphere of dictatorial leadership, they grow up depending on man's wisdom and strength. If they are born in an atmosphere of humility and love, they learn to depend on the Lord. Paul wanted his converts to trust the Lord, and not the servant; so he deliberately "played down" his own authority and ability.

How ignorant the Corinthians were, even after all that Paul had taught them. They failed to realize that true spiritual power is in "meekness and gentleness" (2 Cor. 10:1), not in "throwing weight around." Paul's very attitude in these opening verses disarmed his opponents. (In fact, his use of his own name is significant; for *Paul* means "little.") If Paul was a weakling, then so was Jesus Christ; for Jesus exhibited meekness and gentleness (Matt. 11:29). However, our Lord could also be stern and even angry when the occasion demanded it (see Matt. 15:1-2; 23:13-33; Mark 11:15-17; John 2:13-16). Paul was warning them in a loving way, "Please don't force me to come and show how bold I can be!"

The answer (vv. 3-6). This reveals what spiritual warfare is all about. Because the Corinthians (led by the false teachers) judged Paul's ministry by the outward appearance, they completely missed the power that was there. They were evaluating things "according to the flesh" (2 Cor. 10:2) and not according to the Spirit. The Judaizers, like some "great religious personalities" today, impressed the people with their overpowering abilities, their oratorical powers, and their "commendations" from church leaders.

Paul took a different approach; for, though he was as human as anyone else, he did not depend on the human but on the divine, the spiritual weapons provided by the Lord. His warfare was not according to the flesh, because he was not fighting against flesh and blood (see Eph. 6:10ff). You cannot fight spiritual battles with carnal weapons.

The word *warfare* in 2 Corinthians 10:4 means "campaign." Paul was not simply fighting a little skirmish in Corinth; the attack of the enemy there was part of a large satanic campaign. The powers of hell are still trying to destroy the work of God (Matt. 16:18), and it is important that we not yield any ground to the enemy, not even one church!

There are walls of resistance in the minds of people, and these walls (like the walls of Jericho) must be pulled down. What are these "mental walls"? Reasonings that are opposed to the truth of God's Word. Pride of intelligence that exalts itself. Paul was not attacking intelligence, but intellectualism, the high-minded attitude that makes people think they know more than they really do (Rom. 12:16). Paul had faced this "wisdom of men" when he founded the church (1 Cor. 1:18ff), and it had surfaced again with the coming of the Judaizers.

Paul's attitude of humility was actually one of his strongest weapons, for pride plays right into the hands of Satan. The meek Son of God had far more power than Pilate (see John 19:11), and He proved it. Paul used spiritual weapons to tear down the opposition—prayer, the Word of God, love, the power of the Spirit at work in his life. He did not depend on personality, human abilities, or even the authority he had as an apostle. However, he was ready to punish the offenders, if necessary, once the congregation had submitted to the Lord.

Many believers today do not realize that the church is involved in warfare, and those who do understand the seriousness of the Christian battle do not always know how to fight the battle. They try to use human methods to defeat demonic forces, and these methods are doomed to fail. When Joshua and his army marched around Jericho for a week, the spectators thought they were mad. When the Jews trusted God and obeyed orders, they brought down the high walls and conquered the enemy (Josh. 6:1-20).

When I was pastoring in Chicago, I met weekly with three pastor friends, and together we united in "warfare praying." We claimed God's promise to cast down the wrong thinking that was keeping people from surrendering to God; and God did great things in the lives of many people for whom we interceded. Once the walls in the mind have been torn down, the door to the heart can be opened.

How to Use Spiritual Authority (2 Cor. 10:7-11)

One of the most difficult lessons Christ's disciples had to learn was that, in the kingdom of God, position and power were no evidence of authority. Jesus warned His followers not to pattern their leadership after that of the Gentiles who loved to "lord it over" others and to act important (see Mark 10:35-45). The example we must follow is that of Jesus Christ who came as a servant and ministered to others. Paul followed that example.

But the Corinthians were not spiritually minded enough to discern what Paul was doing. They contrasted his meekness with the "personality power" of the Judaizers, and they concluded that Paul had no authority at all. To be sure, he wrote powerful letters; but his physical appearance was weak, and his speech "unimpressive." They were judging by the outward appearance and were not exercising spiritual discernment.

Some friends and I once listened to a man preach whose entire sermon was made up of impressive "big words," an occasional quotation from the Bible (usually taken out of context), and many references to world events and "the signs of the times." As we left the meeting, one of my friends said, "First Kings

19:11 describes that performance perfectly: 'The Lord was not in the wind.' " Yet people around us were saying that it was "the most wonderful sermon" they had ever heard. I seriously doubt that ten minutes later, they were able to recall one concrete thing that the preacher had said.

Paul did not deny that he had authority, but he did refuse to exercise that authority in an unspiritual manner. The purpose for his authority was to build them up, not tear them down; and it requires much more skill to build than to destroy. Furthermore, it takes love to build up (1 Cor. 8:1); and the Corinthians interpreted Paul's love and meekness as a sign of weakness.

The difference between Paul and the Judaizers was this: Paul used his authority to build up the church, while the Judaizers used the church to build up their authority.

In my many years of pastoral and itinerant ministry, I have never ceased to be amazed at how some local churches treat their pastors. If a man shows love and true humility, they resist his leadership and break his heart. The next pastor will be a "dictator" who "runs the church"—and he gets just what he wants. And the people love him and brag about him! Our Lord was treated the same way, so perhaps we should not be surprised.

The opponents in the church were accusing Paul of not being a true apostle; for, if he were a true apostle, he would show it by using his authority. On the other hand, if Paul *had* "thrown his weight around," they would have found fault with that. No matter what course Paul took, they were bound to condemn him. This is what always happens when church members are not spiritually minded, but evaluate ministry from a worldly viewpoint.

But their accusation backfired. If Paul was not an apostle, then he was a counterfeit and not even a believer. But if that were true, then the church at Corinth was not a true church. Paul had already made it clear that nobody could separate his ministry and his personal life (2 Cor. 1:12-14). If he were a deceiver, then the Corinthians were the deceived!

Paul also pointed out that there was no contradiction between his preaching and his writing. He was bold in his letters because that was what was needed at the time. How much more would he have enjoyed being able to write with gentleness. But it would not have achieved the desired purpose. And, even when he wrote "weighty and powerful" letters, he wrote from a heart of love. "You had better prepare for my next visit," he was saying, "because if it is necessary, I will show you how powerful I can be."

How a Christian uses authority is an evidence of his spiritual maturity and character. An immature person *swells* as he uses his authority, but a mature person *grows* in the use of authority, and others grow with him. The wise pastor, like the wise parent, knows when to wait in loving patience and when to act with determined power. It takes more power to wait than to strike. A mature person does not use authority to *demand* respect, but to *command* respect. Mature leaders suffer while they wait to act, while immature leaders act impetuously and make others suffer.

The false teachers depended on "letters of recommendation" for their authority, but Paul had a divine commission from heaven. The life that he lived and the work that he did were "credentials" enough, for it was evident that the hand of God was on his life. Paul could dare to write, "From henceforth let no man trouble me; for I bear in my body the marks of the Lord Jesus" (Gal. 6:17).

When my wife and I have ministered in England, we have always tried to arrange our schedule so that we might visit in London. We especially enjoy shopping in Selfridge's and Harrod's, London's two leading department stores. H. Gordon Selfridge, who built the great store that bears his name, always claimed that he was a success because he was a leader and not a "boss." The leader says, "Let's go!" while the boss says, "Go!" The boss *knows* how it is done, but the leader *shows* how it is done. The boss inspires fear; the leader inspires enthusiasm based on respect and goodwill. The boss fixes the *blame* for the breakdown, while the true leader fixes the breakdown. The boss keeps saying, "I" while the leader says, "We." Mr. Selfridge's philosophy of management would certainly agree with the Apostle Paul's philosophy of leadership.

How to Measure Spiritual Ministry (2 Cor. 10:12-18)

I suppose more problems have been caused by people "measuring the ministry" than by any other activity in the church. If the work of the church is the work of God, and if the work of God is a miracle, how do we go about measuring a miracle? In His personal examination of the seven churches named in Revelation 2–3, the Lord Jesus measured them far differently than they measured themselves. The church that thought it was poor, He considered to be rich; and the church that boasted of its wealth, He declared to be poor (Rev. 2:8-11; 3:14-22).

Some people measure ministry only by statistics. While it is true that the early church did take note of numbers (Acts 2:41; 4:4), it is also true that uniting with the church at that time was a much more difficult (and dangerous) thing (see Acts 5:13). Some years ago, one of America's large denominations had as its theme, "A Million More in '64, and Every One a Tither!" I heard one of their leading preachers comment, "If we get a million more like the last million, God help us!" Quantity is no guarantee of quality.

False measurement (v. 12). The Judaizers were great on measuring their ministry, because a religion of external activities is much easier to measure than one of internal transformation. The legalist can measure what he does and what he does not do, but the Lord is the only One who can see spiritual growth in a believer's heart. Sometimes those who are growing the most feel like they are less than the least.

In a sense, the Judaizers belonged to a "mutual admiration society" that set up its own standards and measured everybody by them. Of course, those inside the group were successful; those outside were failures. Paul was one of the outsiders, so he was considered a failure. Unfortunately, they did not measure themselves by Jesus Christ (see Eph. 4:12-16). If they had, it would have made a difference.

True measurement (vv. 13-18). Paul suggests three questions we may ask ourselves as we seek to measure our ministries by the will of God.

Am I where God wants me to be? (vv. 13-14) God "assigned a field" in which Paul was to work: he was the apostle to the Gentiles (Acts 9:15; 22:21; Eph. 3). He was also to go where no other apostle had ministered; he was to be a "pioneer preacher" to the Gentiles.

Paul used a bit of sanctified sarcasm in his defense. "The area God assigned to me included even you Corinthians!" (see 2 Cor. 10:13) It was not the Judaizers who had come to Corinth with the Gospel. They, like the cultists today, arrived on the scene only after the church had already been established (see Rom. 15:15-22).

Churches and ministers are not competing with each other; they are competing with themselves. God is not going to measure us on the basis of the gifts and opportunities that He gave to Charles Spurgeon or Billy Sunday. He will measure my work by what He assigned to me. God requires faithfulness above everything else (1 Cor. 4:2).

There is something intimidating about attending a pastors' conference or a denominational convention, because the people on the program are usually the "front-runners" with the best records. Young pastors and older men in narrow places often go home carrying feelings of guilt because their faithful work does not seem to produce as much fruit. Some of these discouraged men then try all kinds of programs and promotions, only to have more disappointment; and then they contemplate leaving the ministry. If only they would realize that God measures their ministries on the basis of where He has put them, and not on the basis of what is going on in some other city, it would encourage them to stay on the job and keep being faithful.

Is God glorified by my ministry? (vv. 15-17) This is another jibe at the Judaizers who stole other men's converts and claimed them as their own. Paul would not boast about another man's work, nor would he invade another man's territory. Whatever work he did, God did through him, and God alone should receive the glory.

I once listened to a man give a lecture on how to build a large Sunday School. Everything in the lecture was correct and certainly had worked in some of the large ministries in the United States. The only problem was, *the man had never built a large Sunday School himself!* He had visited many of the large ministries, interviewed the pastors and staff members, and developed his lecture. After he finished his lecture, people flocked to his side to ask questions and get autographs. I happened to be standing next to a pastor who had built one of the finest churches—and one of the largest—in America.

"Those people ought to be talking to you," I said to him. "You've done it and you know more about Sunday School work than he does!"

"Let him enjoy himself," said my friend with a kind smile. "We're all doing the same work, and all that counts is that God is glorified."

Paul added another bit of "holy irony" when he told the Corinthians that the only thing that had kept him from going to "the regions beyond" them was their own lack of faith. Had they been submissive to his leadership and obedient to the Word, he could have reached other lost souls; but they created so many problems for him, that he had to take time from missionary evangelism to solve the problems in the church. "I would have better statistics to report," he was saying, "but you hindered me."

Paul quoted Jeremiah 9:24 in 2 Corinthians 10:17, a statement he had also quoted in 1 Corinthians 1:31. The Corinthians were prone to glory in men, especially now that the Judaizers had taken over in the church. When the Corinthians heard the "reports" of what these teachers had done, and when they saw the "letters of recommendation" that they carried, the church was quite carried away with them. As a result, Paul and his ministry looked small and unsuccessful.

But the final test is not when the reports are published for the annual meeting. The final test comes at the Judgment Seat of Christ, "and then shall every man have praise of God" (1 Cor. 4:5). If men get the glory, then God cannot be glorified. "I am the Lord: that is My name: and My glory will I not give to another" (Isa. 42:8).

This is not to suggest that well-known ministers with flourishing works are robbing God of glory. As we grow and bear "much fruit," we bring glory to the Father (John 15:1-8). But we must be careful that it is "fruit" that comes from spiritual life and not "results" that appear when we manipulate people and manufacture statistics.

Can the Lord commend my work? (v. 18) We may commend ourselves or be commended by others, and still not deserve the commendation of God. How does God approve our work? By testing it. The word *approved* in 2 Corinthians 10:18 means "to approve by testing." There is a future testing at the Judgment Seat of Christ (1 Cor. 3:10ff), but there is also a present testing of the work that we do. God permits difficulties to come to local churches in order that the work might be tested and approved.

Over the years, I have seen ministries tested by financial losses, the invasion of false doctrine, the emergence of proud leaders who want to "run the church," and the challenge of change. Some of the churches have fallen apart and almost died, because the work was not spiritual. Other ministries have grown because of the trials and have become purer and stronger; and, through it all, God was glorified.

Certainly our ministries must keep records and issue reports, but we must not fall into the "snare of statistics" and think that numbers are the only measurement of ministry. Each situation is unique, and no ministry can honestly be evaluated on the basis of some other ministry. The important thing is that we are where God wants us to be, doing what He wants us to do so that He might be glorified. Motive is as much a part of God's measurement of our work as is growth. If we are seeking to glorify and please God alone, and if we are not afraid of His evaluation of our hearts and lives, then we need not fear the estimates of men or their criticisms.

"But he that glorieth, let him glory in the Lord" (2 Cor. 10:17).

CHAPTER TEN
FATHER KNOWS BEST
2 Corinthians 11

If you were a Christian minister, how would you go about convincing the people in your congregation that you really loved them?

This was the problem Paul faced as he wrote this epistle. If he reminded the people of the work he did among them, they would only reply, "Paul is bragging!" If he said nothing about his ministry at Corinth, the Judaizers would say, "See, we told you Paul didn't accomplish anything!"

So what did Paul do? He was led by the Spirit of God to use a beautiful image—a comparison—that was certain to reach the hearts of the believers at Corinth. He compared himself to a "spiritual father" caring for his family. He had used this image before to remind the Corinthians that, as a "father" he had begotten them through the Gospel, and that he could discipline them if he felt it was necessary (1 Cor. 4:14-21). They were his beloved spiritual children, and he wanted the very best for them.

Paul gave them three evidences of his fatherly love for them.

His Jealousy over the Church (2 Cor. 11:1-6, 13-15)

True love is never envious, but it has a right to be jealous over those who are loved. A husband is jealous over his wife and rightfully resents and resists any rivalry that threatens their love for each other. A true patriot has every right to be jealous over his freedom and will fight to protect it. Likewise, a father (or a mother) is jealous over his or her children and seeks to protect them from anything that will harm them.

The *picture* here is that of a loving father who has a daughter engaged to be married. He feels it is his privilege and duty to keep her pure, so that he can present her to her husband with joy and not with sorrow. Paul saw the local church as a bride, engaged to be married to Jesus Christ (see Eph. 5:22ff and Rom. 7:4). That marriage will not take place until Jesus Christ has come for His bride (Rev. 19:1-9). Meanwhile, the church—and this means individual Christians—must keep herself pure as she prepares to meet her Beloved.

The *peril,* then, is that of unfaithfulness to her fiancé. The engaged woman owes her love and allegiance to but one—her betrothed. If she shares herself with any other man, she is guilty of unfaithfulness. The word translated "simplicity" in 2 Corinthians 11:3 means "sincerity, singleness of devotion." A divided heart leads to a defiled life and a destroyed relationship.

The image of love and marriage, and the need for faithfulness, is often used in the Bible. The Prophet Jeremiah saw the people of Judah losing their love for God, and he warned them. "Thus saith the Lord; 'I remember thee, the kindness of thy youth, the love of thine espousals' " (Jer. 2:2). The nation of Judah had lost its "honeymoon love" and was guilty of worshiping idols. Jesus used the same image when He warned the church at Ephesus: "Nevertheless I have somewhat against thee, because thou hast left thy first love" (Rev. 2:4).

The *person behind the peril* was Satan, pictured here as the serpent. The reference is to Genesis 3. It is worth noting that Paul had a great deal to say about our adversary, the devil, when he wrote this letter to the Corinthians. He warned that Satan had several devices for attacking believers. He can burden the consciences of believers who have sinned (2 Cor. 2:10-11), blind the minds of unbelievers (2 Cor. 4:4) or beguile the minds of believers (2 Cor. 11:3), and even buffet the bodies of God's ministers (2 Cor. 12:7).

The focus here is on the mind, for Satan is a liar and tries to get us to listen to his lies, ponder them, and then believe them. This is what he did with Eve. First, he *questioned* God's word ("Yea, hath God said?"), then he *denied* God's word ("Ye shall not surely die!"), and then he *substituted his own lie* ("Ye shall be as gods") (see Gen. 3:1, 4-5).

Satan, of course, is crafty. He knows that believers will not immediately accept a lie, so the enemy has to "bait the hook" and make it easy for us to accept what he has to offer. Basically, Satan is an imitator: he copies what God does and then tries to convince us that his offer is better than God's. How does he do this? By using counterfeit ministers who pretend to serve God, but who are really the servants of Satan.

Satan has a counterfeit gospel (Gal. 1:6-12) that involves a different savior and a different spirit. Unfortunately, the Corinthians had "welcomed" this "new gospel," which was a mixture of Law and grace and not a true gospel at all. There is only one Gospel and, therefore, there can be only one Saviour (1 Cor. 15:1ff). When you trust the Saviour, you receive the Holy Spirit of God within, and there is only one Holy Spirit.

The *preachers* of this false gospel (and they are with us yet today) are described in 2 Corinthians 11:13-15. They claimed to have divine authority as God's servants, but their authority was bogus. They claimed that the true servants of God were all impostors; in Paul's day, they said this about him. They even claimed to be "super-apostles," on a much higher level than Paul. With their clever oratory, they mesmerized the ignorant believers, while at the same time they pointed out that Paul was not a very gifted speaker (2 Cor. 11:6; 10:10). How tragic it is when unstable believers are swayed by the "fair speech" of Satan's ministers, instead of standing firm on the basic truths of the Gospel taught to them by faithful pastors and teachers.

"They are not 'super-apostles' at all!" warned Paul. "They are *pseudo* apostles—false apostles! Their motive is not to glorify God, but to get personal gain by capturing converts. Their methods are deceitful" (2 Cor. 2:17; 4:2). The basic idea here is that of using bait to catch fish. They offer church members a Christian life that is "superior" to that described in the New Testament, a life that is an unbiblical mixture of Law and grace.

Instead of being empowered by the Spirit, these ministers are energized by Satan. Three times, Paul used the word *transform* in referring to their work (see 2 Cor. 11:13-15). This Greek word simply means "to disguise, to masquerade." There is a change on the outside, but there is no change on the inside. Satan's workers, like Satan himself, never appear in their true character; they always wear a disguise and hide behind a mask.

As I was writing this book, several of Satan's "masquerading ministers" appeared at my front door. One of them, an attractive young lady, tried to tell me she was working for world peace; but when I confronted her, she admitted that she belonged to a cult. Two well-dressed young men introduced themselves with, "We are here representing Jesus Christ!" I quickly informed them that I knew what group they represented, and I closed the door. I did not even say, "Good-bye." If you think I was unkind, read 2 John 5-11—and obey it.

Paul proved his love for the church by protecting it from the attacks of false teachers; and yet the members of the church "fell for" the Judaizers and let them come in. The Corinthians had "left their first love" and were no longer giving single-hearted devotion to Jesus Christ. It was not only that they had turned against Paul, but they had turned away from Christ; and that was far more serious.

His Generosity to the Church (2 Cor. 11:7-12)

A loving parent provides for the needs of the family, and Paul sacrificed that he might minister to the church at Corinth. While Paul was there, he labored with his own hands as a tentmaker (Acts 18:1-3) and even received gifts from other churches so that he might evangelize Corinth. In other words, it had cost the Corinthians nothing to benefit from the apostolic ministry of this great man of God.

Did the Corinthians appreciate the sacrifices that Paul made for them? No, most of them did not. In fact, the Judaizers even used Paul's financial policy as "proof" that he was not a true apostle. After all, if he *were* a true apostle, he would accept financial support.

Paul had already explained his policy in a previous letter (1 Cor. 9). He had pointed out that he *was* a true apostle because he had seen the risen Christ and had been commissioned by Him. Paul had the right to ask for financial support, just as God's faithful servants do today; but he had deliberately given up that right so that nobody could accuse him of using the Gospel simply as a means of making money. He gave up his "financial rights" for the Gospel's sake and for the sake of lost sinners who might stumble over anything that gave the impression of being "religious business."

On the other hand, it was the Judaizers who were guilty of "peddling the Gospel" for personal profit. Paul had preached the Gospel to them *freely* (2 Cor. 11:7, literally "without charge, for nothing"), but the false teachers were preaching a *false* gospel—and robbing the church (2 Cor. 11:20). Paul used a bit of irony in 2 Corinthians 11:8: "Yes, I have been a 'robber.' I 'robbed' other churches so I would not have to 'rob' you!" And now the Judaizers were *really* robbing them.

A loving father does not lay his burdens on his children. Instead, he sacrifices so that the children might have what they need. It is a difficult thing to teach children the difference between "prices" and "values." Children seem to have no idea what it means for parents to go to work and earn the money that provides what the family needs. When one of my nephews was very young, he heard his parents discussing the purchase of some major appliance, and he could not understand why they did not just go out and buy it. "Why don't you just write one of those pieces of paper?" he asked, pointing to his father's checkbook. He did not understand that there has to be money in the bank to back up what you write on those "pieces of paper."

Paul did not bring up this matter of money in order to boast about himself. Rather, he was using every means possible to silence the boasting of the Judaizers. Paul knew that not a single person could accuse him of covetousness or selfishness (see Acts 20:33-35, Paul's testimony to the Ephesian church). His hands were clean. He wanted to "cut off" any opportunity for his enemies to accuse him.

The word *chargeable* in 2 Corinthians 11:9 is worth considering in a special way (see also 2 Cor. 12:13-14). In the Greek, it literally means "to grow numb." The word comes from the image of the electric eel numbing its victim with its shock. A numbed part of the body would be a burden to the victim. Paul had not used any devious tricks to catch the believers by surprise, attack them, or rob them. Both in his preaching of the Gospel and his handling of finances, he was open and honest.

In my own travels, I have seen situations in local churches that have broken my heart. I have seen congregations show little or no appreciation to faithful pastors who were laboring sacrificially to see the church grow. Some of these men were underpaid and overworked, yet the churches seemed to have no love for them. However, their successors were treated like kings! Certainly at the Judgment Seat of Christ, the books will be balanced.

I once heard Dr. W.A. Criswell tell about the faithful missionary couple who returned to the United States on the same ship that brought Teddy Roosevelt home from a safari in Africa. Many reporters and photographers were on the dock, waiting to see Roosevelt and interview him and take pictures; but nobody was on hand to welcome home the veteran missionaries who had spent their lives serving Christ in Africa.

That evening, in their modest hotel room, the couple reviewed their arrival in New York City; and the husband was somewhat bitter.

"It isn't fair," he said to his wife. "Mr. Roosevelt comes home from a hunting trip, and the whole country is out to meet him. We get home after years of service, and nobody was there to greet us."

But his wife had the right answer: "Honey, *we aren't home yet.*"

Paul has presented two pieces of evidence to prove his love for the Corinthians: his jealousy over the church—protecting them from "spiritual unfaithfulness," and his generosity to the church—refusing to accept support from them. He shared a third piece of evidence.

His Anxiety for the Church (2 Cor. 11:16-33)

The key to this long section is 2 Corinthians 11:28, which could be paraphrased: "Yes, I have been through many trials, but the greatest trial of all, the heaviest burden of all, is my concern for the churches!" The word translated *care* means "pressure, stress, anxiety." The other experiences were external ("without") and occasional, but the burden of the churches was internal and constant.

"We never know the love of our parents for us till we have become parents," said Henry Ward Beecher, and he was right. When our older son was a tot, he pushed a toy into the electric socket and was "zapped" across the room. (We didn't have the word *zap* in those days, but that's still what happened.) One day recently he discovered his own little son playing with the socket, and father's explosive response nearly frightened the child out of a year's growth. "Now I know how you and Mom felt when I was a kid," he told me over the phone. "Being a parent has its fears as well as its joys."

Before listing the various kinds of trials he had experienced, Paul was careful to explain why he was "boasting" in this way. Paul never had any problem boasting about Christ and telling of His sufferings, but he was always hesitant to speak of his own painful experiences as a servant of God. Paul and John the Baptist would have agreed: "He [Christ] must increase, but I must decrease" (John 3:30). "But he that glorieth, let him glory in the Lord" (2 Cor. 10:17).

It was the immature and unspiritual attitude of the Corinthians that forced Paul to write about himself and "glory" (boast) in these experiences. He had begun this section (2 Cor. 11:1) by apologizing for his boasting, and he repeated this sentiment in 2 Corinthians 11:16. In 2 Corinthians 11:17, Paul was not denying the inspiration of his words; rather, he was admitting that, by boasting, he was being very unlike the Lord (see 2 Cor. 10:1). However, he had to do it to prove his love for the Corinthians and protect them from those who would lead them astray.

To begin with, the false teachers were not ashamed to boast, and the Corinthians were not afraid to accept their boasting. "Since boasting is the 'in thing' in your fellowship," Paul seemed to be saying, "then I will boast." Paul may have had the principle of Proverbs 26:5 in mind: "Answer a fool according to his folly, lest he be wise in his own conceit."

Furthermore, Paul was boasting so that he might *help* the church, while the false teachers boasted so that they might "help themselves" to what they could get out of the church. Paul's motive was pure; theirs was selfish. Second Corinthains 11:20 lists the various ways the Judaizers had taken advantage of the church:

Bondage: They taught a doctrine of legalism that was contrary to the Gospel of grace.

Devour: They "ate up" all they could get in the church; they took advantage of their privilege of receiving financial support.

Take of you: "Take you in," fool you. The image is that of a bird caught in a snare or a fish caught on a hook. "They baited you and caught you!"

Exalt: They exalted themselves, not the Lord Jesus Christ; they loved to be honored and treated as great leaders.

Smite you: This probably refers to verbal attacks rather than physical violence; the Judaizers did not hesitate to "slap them in the face" and embarrass them in public.

Paul ended this exposure of the unspiritual attitudes and actions of the Judaizers by bringing in some more "inspired irony": "To my shame I admit that we were too weak for that!" (2 Cor. 11:21, NIV) The Corinthians thought that Paul's meekness was weakness, when it was really strength. And they thought that the Judaizers' arrogance was power. How ignorant the saints can sometimes be.

When it came to their Jewish heritage, the false teachers were equal to Paul; but when it came to ministry for Christ, it was Paul who was the "super-apostle" and not the Judaizers. Consider what Paul endured for the cause of Christ and the care of the churches.

Sufferings for Christ (vv. 23-25a). Had Paul not been an apostle, he would not have experienced these trials. He received "stripes above measure" from both the Gentiles and from the Jews. Three times the Gentiles beat him with rods, and five times he was given thirty-nine lashes by the Jews. Only one beating is recorded in the Book of Acts (16:22), as well as the one stoning (Acts 14:19).

Paul knew from the outset of his ministry that he would suffer for Jesus' sake (Acts 9:15-16), and God reaffirmed this to him as his ministry continued (Acts 20:23). He who caused others to suffer for their faith, himself had to suffer for his faith.

Natural hardships (vv. 25b-33). Almost any traveler in that day could have experienced some of these hardships; yet we cannot help but believe that they were caused by the enemy in an attempt to hinder the work of the Lord. Acts 27 records one of the three shipwrecks; we know nothing about the other two. We wonder how many of his precious personal possessions Paul lost in this way.

Because he was constantly on the move, Paul was exposed to the perils of travel. The Judaizers visited the safe places; Paul journeyed to the difficult places. But Paul was no ordinary traveler: he was a marked man. He had enemies among both the Jews and the Gentiles, and some would like to have killed him.

Second Corinthians 11:27 describes the personal consequences of all this difficult travel. In my own limited itinerant ministry, I have had the convenience of automobiles and planes, and yet I must confess that travel wears me out. How much more difficult it was for Paul! No wonder he was filled with weariness and pain. He often had to go without food, drink, and sleep; and sometimes he lacked sufficient clothing to keep himself warm.

While any other traveler could have suffered these things, Paul endured them because of his love for Christ and the church. His greatest burden was not *around* him, but *within* him: the care of all the churches. Why did he care so much? Because he identified with the believers (2 Cor. 11:29). Whatever happened to "his children" touched his own heart and he could not abandon them.

Paul climaxed this narration of his sufferings by telling of his humiliating experience at Damascus, when he—the great apostle—was smuggled out of the city in a basket let over the wall! (2 Cor. 11:32-33) Would any of the Judaizers ever tell a story like that? Of course not! Even when Paul did narrate his sufferings, he was careful that Christ was glorified, and not Paul.

We cannot read these verses without admiring the courage and devotion of the Apostle Paul. Each trial left its mark on his life, and yet he kept moving on, serving the Lord. "But none of these things move me, neither count I my life dear unto myself" (Acts 20:24).

Paul certainly proved his love for the church.

Now the church had to prove its love for Paul.

May we never take for granted the sacrifices that others have made so that we might enjoy the blessings of the Gospel today.

CHAPTER ELEVEN A PREACHER IN PARADISE
2 Corinthians 12:1-10

This section is the climax of Paul's defense of his apostleship and his love for the believers at Corinth. He was reticent to write about these personal experiences, but there was no other way to solve the problem. In fact, to avoid exalting himself, Paul described his experience in the third person rather than the first person. He shared with his readers three experiences from God.

Glory: God Honored Him (2 Cor. 12:1-6)
The Judaizers were anxious to receive honors, and they boasted about their "letters of recommendation" (2 Cor. 3:1ff). But Paul did not look for honor from men; he let God honor him, for that alone is the honor that really counts.

First, God honored Paul by giving him visions and revelations. Paul saw the glorified Christ on the very day he was converted (Acts 9:3; 22:6). He saw a vision of Ananias coming to minister to him (Acts 9:12), and he also had a vision from God when he was called to minister to the Gentiles (Acts 22:17).

During his ministry, he had visions from God to guide him and encourage him. It was by a vision that he was called to Macedonia (Acts 16:9). When the ministry was difficult in Corinth, God encouraged Paul by a vision (Acts 18:9-10). After his arrest in Jerusalem, Paul was again encouraged by a vision from God (Acts 23:11). An angel appeared to him in the midst of the storm and assured him that he and the passengers would be saved (Acts 27:23).

Along with these special visions that related to his call and ministry, spiritual revelations of divine truth were also communicated to Paul (see Eph. 3:1-6). God gave him a profound understanding of the plan of God for this present age. Certainly Paul understood the mysteries of God.

God also honored Paul by taking him to heaven, and then sending him back to the earth again. This marvelous experience had taken place fourteen years before the writing of this letter, which would place the experience in about the year A.D. 43. This would be the period in Paul's life between his departure for Tarsus (Acts 9:30) and his visit from Barnabas (Acts 11:25-26). There is no record of the details of this event, and it is useless for us to speculate.

Jewish rabbis were accustomed to speaking about themselves in the third person, and Paul adopted that approach as he unfolded this experience to his friends (and enemies) at Corinth. So wonderful was this experience that Paul was not quite sure whether God had taken him bodily to heaven, or whether his spirit had left his body. (There is quite a contrast between being "let down" in a basket and being "caught up" to the third heaven!) Paul affirmed here the reality of heaven and the ability of God to take people there. The *third heaven* is the same as "paradise," the heaven of heavens where God dwells in glory. Thanks to modern science, men today have visited the heaven of the clouds (we fly above the clouds) and the heaven of the planets (men have walked on the moon), but man cannot get to God's heaven without God's help.

The interesting thing is that Paul kept quiet about this experience for fourteen years! During those years, he was buffeted by his "thorn in the flesh," and perhaps people wondered why he had such a burdensome affliction. The Judaizers may have adopted the views of Job's comforters and said, "This affliction is a punishment from God." (Actually, it was a *gift* from God.) Some of Paul's good friends may have tried to encourage him by saying, "Cheer up, Paul. One day you'll be in heaven!" Paul could have replied, "That's why I have this thorn—I went to heaven!"

God honored Paul by granting him visions and revelations, and by taking him to heaven; but He honored him further by permitting him to hear "unspeakable words" while he was in heaven. He overheard the divine secrets that are shared only in heaven. These things could be spoken by God and by beings in heaven, but they could not be spoken by men.

Could the Judaizers relate any experiences that were like this one? Even Moses, who was intimate with God, met the Lord on the mountaintop; but Paul met the Lord in paradise. Paul had exercised great spiritual discipline during those fourteen years, for he had told this experience to no one. There is no doubt that this vision of God's glory was one of the sustaining powers in Paul's life and ministry. No matter where he was—in prison, in the deep, in dangerous travels—he knew that God was with him and that all was well.

You and I are not going to heaven till we die or till our Lord returns. But we have a marvelous encouragement in the fact that we are *today* seated with Christ in the heavenly places (Eph. 2:6). We have a position of authority and victory "far above all" (Eph. 2:21-22). While we have not seen God's glory as Paul did, we do share God's glory now (John 17:22) and one day we shall enter into heaven and behold the glory of Christ (John 17:24).

Such an honor as this would have made most people very proud. Instead of keeping quiet for fourteen years, they would have immediately told the world and become famous. But Paul did not become proud. He simply told the truth—it was not empty boasting—and let the facts speak for themselves. His great concern was that nobody rob God of the glory and give it to Paul. He wanted others to have an honest estimate of him and his work (see Rom. 12:3).

How could Paul have such a great experience and still remain humble? Because of the second experience that God brought to his life.

Goodness: God Humbled Him (2 Cor. 12:7-8)

The Lord knows how to balance our lives. If we have only blessings, we may become proud; so He permits us to have burdens as well. Paul's great experience in heaven could have ruined his ministry on earth; so God, in His goodness, permitted Satan to buffet Paul in order to keep him from becoming proud.

The mystery of human suffering will not be solved completely in this life. Sometimes we suffer simply because we are human. Our bodies change as we grow older, and we are susceptible to the normal problems of life. The same body that can bring us pleasures can also bring us pains. The same family members and friends that delight us can also break our hearts. This is a part of the "human comedy," and the only way to escape it is to be less than human. But nobody wants to take that route.

Sometimes we suffer because we are foolish and disobedient to the Lord. Our own rebellion may afflict us, or the Lord may see fit to chasten us in His love (Heb. 12:3ff). King David suffered greatly because of his sin; the consequences were painful and so was the discipline of God (see 2 Sam. 12:1-22; Ps. 51). In His grace, God forgives our sins; but in His government, He must permit us to reap what we sow.

Suffering also is a tool God uses for building godly character (Rom. 5:1-5). Certainly Paul was a man of rich Christian character because he permitted God to mold and make him in the painful experiences of his life. When you walk along the shore of the ocean, you notice that the rocks are sharp in the quiet coves, but polished in those places where the waves beat against them. God can use the "waves and billows" of life to polish us, if we will let Him.

Paul's thorn in the flesh was given to him to keep him from sinning. Exciting spiritual experiences—like going to heaven and back—have a way of inflating the human ego; and pride leads to a multitude of temptations to sin. Had Paul's heart been filled with pride, those next fourteen years would have been filled with failure instead of success.

We do not know what Paul's thorn in the flesh was. The word translated *thorn* means "a sharp stake used for torturing or impaling someone." It was a physical affliction of some kind that brought pain and distress to Paul. Some Bible students think that Paul had an eye affliction (see Gal. 6:11); but we cannot know for sure. It is a good thing that we do not know, because no matter what our sufferings may be, we are able to apply the lessons Paul learned and get encouragement.

God permitted Satan to afflict Paul, just as He permitted Satan to afflict Job (see Job 1–2). While we do not fully understand the origin of evil in this universe, or all the purposes God had in mind when He permitted evil to come, we do know that God controls evil and can use it even for His own glory. Satan cannot work against a believer without the permission of God. Everything that the enemy did to Job and Paul was permitted by the will of God.

Satan was permitted to *buffet* Paul. The word means "to beat, to strike with the fist." The tense of the verb indicates that this pain was either constant or recurring. When you stop to think that Paul had letters to write, trips to take, sermons to preach, churches to visit, and dangers to face as he ministered, you can understand that this was a serious matter. No wonder he prayed three times (as his Lord had done in the Garden [Mark 14:32-41]) that the affliction might be removed from him (2 Cor. 12:8).

When God permits suffering to come to our lives, there are several ways we can deal with it. Some people become bitter and blame God for robbing them of freedom and pleasure. Others just "give up" and fail to get any blessing out of the experience because they will not put any courage into the experience. Still others grit their teeth and put on a brave front, determined to "endure to the very end." While this is a courageous response, it usually drains them of the strength needed for daily living; and after a time, they may collapse.

Was Paul sinning when he prayed to be delivered from Satan's buffeting? I don't think so. It is certainly a normal thing for a Christian to ask God for deliverance from sickness and pain. God has not *obligated* Himself to heal every believer whenever he prays; but He has encouraged us to bring our burdens and needs to Him. Paul did not know whether this "thorn in the flesh" was a temporary testing from God, or a permanent experience he would have to learn to live with.

There are those who want us to believe that an afflicted Christian is a disgrace to God. "If you are obeying the Lord and claiming all that you have in Christ," they say, "then you will never be sick." I have never found that teaching in the Bible. It is true that God promised the Jews special blessing and protection under the Old Covenant (Deut. 7:12ff) but He never promised the New Testament believers freedom from sickness or suffering. If Paul had access to "instant healing" because of his relationship to Christ, then why didn't he make use of it for himself and for others, such as Epaphroditus? (Phil. 2:25ff)

What a contrast between Paul's two experiences! Paul went from paradise to pain, from glory to suffering. He tasted the blessing of God in heaven and then felt the buffeting of Satan on earth. He went from ecstasy to agony, and yet the two experiences belong together. His one experience of glory prepared him for the constant experience of suffering, for he knew that God was able to meet his need. Paul had gone to heaven—but then he learned that heaven could come to him.

Grace: God Helped Him (2 Cor. 12:9-10)

Two messages were involved in this painful experience. The thorn in the flesh was Satan's message to Paul, but God had another message for him, a message of grace. The tense of the verb in 2 Corinthians 12:9 is important: "And He [God] has once-for-all said to me." God gave Paul a message that stayed with him. The words Paul heard while in heaven, he was not permitted to share with us; but he did share the words God gave him on earth—and what an encouragement they are.

It was a message of *grace.* What is grace? It is God's provision for our every need when we need it. It has well been said that God in His grace gives us what we do not deserve, and in His mercy He does not give us what we do deserve. Someone has made an acrostic of the word *grace:* **G**od's **R**iches **A**vailable at **C**hrist's **E**xpense. "And of His [Christ's] fullness have all we received, and grace for grace" (John 1:16).

It was a message of *sufficient grace.* There is never a shortage of grace. God is sufficient for our spiritual ministries (2 Cor. 3:4-6) and our material needs (2 Cor. 9:8) as well as our physical needs (2 Cor. 12:9). If God's grace is sufficient to save us, surely it is sufficient to keep us and strengthen us in our times of suffering.

It was a message of *strengthening grace.* God permits us to become weak so that we might receive His strength. This is a continuous process: "My power is [being] made perfect in [your] weakness" (2 Cor. 12:9, NIV). Strength that knows itself to be strength is actually weakness, but weakness that knows itself to be weakness is actually strength.

In the Christian life, we get many of our blessings through *transformation,* not *substitution.* When Paul prayed three times for the removal of his pain, he was asking God for a substitution: "Give me health instead of sickness, deliverance instead of pain and weakness." Sometimes God does meet the need by substitution; but other times He meets the need by transformation. He does not remove the affliction, but He gives us His grace so that the affliction works *for* us and not *against* us.

As Paul prayed about his problem, God gave him a deeper insight into what He was doing. Paul learned that his thorn in the flesh was *a gift from God.* What a strange gift! There was only one thing for Paul to do: accept the gift from God and allow God to accomplish His purposes. God wanted to keep Paul from being "exalted above measure," and this was His way of accomplishing it.

When Paul accepted his affliction as the gift of God, this made it possible for God's grace to go to work in his life. It was then that God spoke to Paul and gave him the assurance of

His grace. Whenever you are going through suffering, spend extra time in the Word of God; and you can be sure God will speak to you. He always has a special message for His children when they are afflicted.

God did not give Paul any explanations; instead, He gave him a promise: "My grace is sufficient for thee." *We do not live on explanations; we live on promises.* Our feelings change, but God's promises never change. Promises generate faith, and faith strengthens hope.

Paul claimed God's promise and drew on the grace that was offered to him; this turned seeming tragedy into triumph. God did not change the situation by removing the affliction; He changed it by adding a new ingredient: grace. Our God is "the God of all grace" (1 Peter 5:10), and His throne is a "throne of grace" (Heb. 4:16). The Word of God is "the word of His grace" (Acts 20:32), and the promise is that "He giveth more grace" (James 4:6). No matter how we look at it, God is adequate for every need that we have.

But God does not give us His grace simply that we might "endure" our sufferings. Even unconverted people can manifest great endurance. God's grace should enable us to *rise above* our circumstances and feelings and cause our afflictions to work *for us* in accomplishing positive good. God wants to build our character so that we are more like our Saviour. God's grace enabled Paul not only to accept his afflictions, but to glory in them. His suffering was not a tyrant that controlled him, but a servant that worked for him.

What benefits did Paul receive because of his suffering? For one thing, he experienced the power of Christ in his life. God transformed Paul's weakness into strength. The word translated *rest* means "to spread a tent over." Paul saw his body as a frail tent (2 Cor. 5:1ff), but the glory of God had come into that tent and transformed it into a holy tabernacle.

Something else happened to Paul: he was able to glory in his infirmities. This does not mean that he preferred pain to health, but rather that he knew how to turn his infirmities into assets. What made the difference? The grace of God *and* the glory of God. He "took pleasure" in these trials and problems, not because he was psychologically unbalanced and enjoyed pain, but because he was suffering for the sake of Jesus Christ. He was glorifying God by the way he accepted and handled the difficult experiences of life.

"It is a greater thing to pray for pain's conversion than its removal," wrote P.T. Forsyth, and this is true. Paul won the victory, not by substitution, but by transformation. He discovered the sufficiency of the grace of God.

From Paul's experience, we may learn several practical lessons.

1. The spiritual is far more important to the dedicated believer than the physical. This is not to suggest that we ignore the physical, because our bodies are the temples of the Spirit of God. But it does mean that we try not to make our bodies an end in themselves. They are God's tools for accomplishing His work in this world. What God does in developing our Christian character is far more valuable than physical healing without character.

2. God knows how to balance burdens and blessings, suffering and glory. Life is something like a prescription: the individual ingredients might hurt us, but when properly blended, they help us.

3. Not all sickness is caused by sin. The argument of Job's comforters was that Job had sinned, and that was why he was suffering. But their argument was wrong in Job's case, as well as in Paul's case. There are times when God permits Satan to afflict us so that God might accomplish a great purpose in our lives.

4. There is something worse than sickness, and that is sin; and the worst sin of all is pride. The healthy person who is rebelling against God is in worse shape than the suffering person who is submitting to God and enjoying God's grace. It is a paradox—and an evidence of the sovereignty of God—that God used Satan, the proudest of all beings, to help keep Paul humble.

5. Physical affliction need not be a barrier to effective Christian service. Today's saints are too prone to pamper themselves and use every little ache or pain as an excuse to stay home from church or refuse to accept opportunities for service. Paul did not permit his thorn in the flesh to become a stumbling block. In fact, he let God turn that thorn into a stepping-stone.

6. We can always rest in God's Word. He always has a message of encouragement for us in times of trial and suffering.

The great French mystic, Madame Guyon, once wrote to a suffering friend, "Ah, if you knew what power there is in an accepted sorrow!"

Paul knew about that power, because he

trusted the will of God and depended on the grace of God.

That same power can be yours today.

CHAPTER TWELVE
THREE TO GET READY!
2 Corinthians 12:11–13:14

As Paul brought his letter to a close, his great love for the Corinthians constrained him to make one last appeal. He did not want his third visit to their church to be another painful experience for them and for him. He had opened his heart to them, explained his ministry, answered their accusations, and urged them to submit to the Word of God and obey the Lord. What more could he say or do?

In this closing section of the letter, Paul used three approaches in his attempt to motivate the Corinthians toward obedience and submission.

He Shamed Them (2 Cor. 12:11-21)

When we were children, how many times did we hear, "Shame on you!" from a parent or a neighbor? It is a good thing when people can be ashamed of their bad actions or attitudes. It is evidence of a hard heart and a calloused conscience when a guilty person no longer feels shame. "Were they ashamed when they had committed abomination? Nay, they were not at all ashamed, neither could they blush" (Jer. 6:15).

First, Paul shamed the Corinthians for their *lack of commendation* (2 Cor. 12:11-13). They should have been boasting about him instead of compelling him to boast. Instead, the Corinthians were boasting about the "super-apostles," the Judaizers who had won their affection and were now running their church.

Was Paul inferior to these men? In no way! The Corinthians had seen Paul in action; in fact, they owed their very souls to him. He had done among them the miraculous signs that proved his apostleship (Heb. 2:1-4). He had persevered in his ministry at Corinth in spite of external persecution and internal problems. He had cost the church nothing. Paul used his subtle irony again when he wrote, "How were you inferior to the other churches, except that I was never a burden to you? Forgive me this wrong!" (2 Cor. 12:13, NIV)

One of the dangers of the Christian life is that of getting accustomed to our blessings. A godly pastor or Sunday School teacher can do so much for us that we begin to take the ministry for granted. (To be fair, I must admit that pastors are sometimes guilty of taking their church members for granted.) This attitude led Paul to shame them for their *lack of appreciation* (2 Cor. 12:14-18).

In spite of the difficulties involved, Paul had been faithful to visit the Corinthians; and now he was about to make his third visit (see 2 Cor. 13:1). Instead of being grateful, the Corinthians criticized Paul for changing his plans. Paul had taken no support from the church, but rather had given sacrificially for the church; yet they were unwilling to show their appreciation by sharing with others. It seemed that the more Paul loved them, the less they loved Paul! Why? Because they did not have a sincere love for Christ (2 Cor. 11:3). Paul was willing to "spend and expend" in order to help the church.

The Judaizers had used crafty methods in order to exploit the church (see 2 Cor. 4:2), but Paul had been open and without guile. The only "trick" Paul had played on them was his refusal to receive financial support. In this, he disarmed them so that they could never accuse him of being interested only in money. None of the associates that Paul sent to them exploited them in any way or took advantage of them.

It is a tragic thing when children do not appreciate what their parents do for them. It is also a tragedy when God's children fail to appreciate what their "spiritual parents" do for them. What is the cause of this *lack of appreciation?* Paul dealt with it in the next paragraph: *lack of consecration* (2 Cor. 12:19-21). There were terrible sins in the church, and Paul wanted them judged and put away before he came for his visit. Otherwise, his visit would just be another painful experience.

Some of the church members were probably saying, "If Paul visits us again, he will just create more problems!" Paul made it clear that his desire was to *solve* problems and strengthen the church. Sins in the church must be faced honestly and dealt with courageously. To "sweep them under the rug" is to make matters worse. Sin in the church is like cancer in the human body: it must be cut out.

Consider the sins that the church was guilty of, sins that should have been confessed and put away. They were guilty of quarreling (debates) because they envied one another. They had sudden explosions of anger (wraths). They promoted carnal intrigues and plots in the church (strifes), which involved backbitings and whisperings. All of this was born out of pride and an exaggerated sense of importance (swellings) and resulted in disorder in the church (tumults) (2 Cor. 12:20). If you will compare this list of sins with 1 Corinthians 13, you will see that there was a lack of love in the congregation.

Along with these "sins of the spirit" (2 Cor. 7:1), there were also gross sins of the flesh—fornication and lasciviousness (debauchery). Paul had dealt with these sins in 1 Corinthians 5–6, but some of the offenders had persisted in their disobedience. They were permitting their old life to take over again (1 Cor. 6:9-11), instead of yielding to the new life.

Paul did not eagerly anticipate this third visit. He feared that he would not find the church as he wanted it to be, and that they would not find him as they wanted him to be. But Paul promised them that, though he would be humbled and grieved (the word means "to grieve for the dead"), he would still use his authority to straighten things out. His love for them was too great for him to ignore these problems and permit them to continue to weaken the church.

The Corinthians should have been ashamed, but they were not. To assure that he would get his message across, Paul used a second approach.

He Warned Them (2 Cor. 13:1-8)

There are two warnings here.

"Prepare yourselves!" (vv. 1-4) In dealing with sin in a local church, we must have facts and not rumors. Paul quoted Deuteronomy 19:15, and we find parallels in Numbers 35:30 and Matthew 18:16, as well as 1 Timothy 5:19. The presence of witnesses would help to guarantee the truth about a matter, especially when the church members were at such variance with one another.

Had the church members followed the instructions given by Jesus in Matthew 18:15-20, they would have solved most of their problems themselves. I have seen small disagreements in a church grow into large and complicated problems, only because the believers did not obey our Lord's directions. The pastor and congregation must not get involved in a matter until the individuals involved have sincerely sought a solution.

The Judaizers in the church had accused Paul of being a weak man (see 2 Cor. 10:7-11). Their approach to ministry was heavy-handed and dictatorial, while Paul's was gentle and humble (see 2 Cor. 1:24). Now Paul assured them that he would show them how strong he could be—*if* that is what it took to solve the problems. "I will not spare!" was his warning, and he used a word that means "to spare in battle." In short, Paul was declaring war on anybody who opposed the authority of God's Word.

"Let Paul prove he is a true apostle!" said his opponents. Paul's reply was, "Like Jesus Christ, I am strong when it appears I am weak." On the cross, Jesus Christ manifested weakness; but the cross is still "the power of God" (1 Cor. 1:18). Paul had already explained his method of spiritual warfare (2 Cor. 10:1-6) and had cautioned his readers not to look on the surface of things, but to look deeper.

By the standards of the world, both Jesus and Paul were weak; but by the standards of the Lord, both were strong. It is a wise and mature worker who knows when to be "weak" and when to be "strong" as he deals with the discipline problems in the local church.

A pastor friend of mine, now in heaven, had a quiet manner of delivery in the pulpit, and a similar approach in his personal ministry. After hearing him preach, a visitor said, "I kept waiting for him to start preaching!" She was accustomed to hearing a loud preacher who generated more heat than light. But my friend built a strong church because he knew the true standards for ministry. He knew how to be "weak in Christ" and also how to be "strong."

How do people measure the ministry today? By powerful oratory or biblical content? By Christian character or what the press releases say? Too many Christians follow the world's standards when they evaluate ministries, and they need to pay attention to God's standards.

"Examine yourselves!" (vv. 5-8) This paragraph is an application of the word *proof* that Paul used in 2 Corinthians 13:3. "You have been examining me," wrote Paul, "but why don't you take time to examine yourselves?" I have noticed in my ministry that those who are quick to examine and condemn others are often guilty of worse sins themselves. In fact, one way to make yourself look better is to condemn somebody else.

To begin with, Paul told the Corinthians that they should examine their hearts to see if they were really born again and members of the family of God. Do you have the witness of the Holy Spirit in your heart? (Rom. 8:9, 16) Do you love the brethren? (1 John 3:14) Do you practice righteousness? (1 John 2:29; 3:9) Have you overcome the world so that you are living a life of godly separation? (1 John 5:4) These are just a few of the tests we can apply to our own lives to be certain that we are the children of God.

In one of the churches I pastored, we had a teenager who was the center of every problem in the youth group. He was a gifted musician and a member of the church, but nevertheless he was a problem. One summer when he went off to our church youth camp, the youth leaders and church officers and I agreed together to pray for him daily. At one of the meetings, he got up and announced that he had been saved that week! His Christian profession up to that time had been counterfeit. He experienced a dramatic change in his life, and today he is serving the Lord faithfully.

No doubt many of the problems in the church at Corinth were caused by people who professed to be saved, but who had never repented and trusted Jesus Christ. Our churches are filled with such people today. Paul called such people *reprobate,* which means "counterfeit, discredited after a test." Paul used this word again in 2 Corinthians 13:6-7, emphasizing the fact that it is important for a person to know for sure that he is saved and going to heaven (see 1 John 5:11-13).

In 2 Corinthians 13:7, Paul made it clear that he did not want the Corinthians to fail the test just to prove that he was right. Nor did he want them to live godly lives just so he could boast about them. He did not mind being despised and criticized for their sakes, so long as they were obeying the Lord. He was not concerned about his own reputation, for the Lord knew his heart; but he was concerned about their Christian character.

The important thing is the truth of the Gospel and the Word of God (2 Cor. 13:8). Paul did not state here that it is impossible to attack the truth or hinder the truth, for these things were going on at that time in the Corinthian church. He was affirming that he and his associates wanted the truth to prevail, come what may, and that they were determined to further the truth, not obstruct it. In the end, God's truth will prevail, so why try to oppose it? "There is no wisdom nor understanding nor counsel against the Lord" (Prov. 21:30).

He Encouraged Them (2 Cor. 13:9-14)

To begin with, Paul encouraged the Corinthians by his personal prayers on their behalf (2 Cor. 13:9). The word translated "wish" in the *King James Version* carries the meaning of "pray." Paul prayed for their *perfection,* which does not mean absolute sinless perfection, but "spiritual maturity." The word is part of a word family in the Greek that means "to be fitted out, to be equipped." As a medical term, it means "to set a broken bone, to adjust a twisted limb." It also means "to outfit a ship for a voyage" and "to equip an army for battle." In Matthew 4:21, it is translated "mending nets."

One of the ministries of our risen Lord is that of perfecting His people (Heb. 13:20-21). He uses the Word of God (2 Tim. 3:16-17) in the fellowship of the local church (Eph. 4:11-16) to equip His people for life and service. He also uses suffering as a tool to equip us (1 Peter 5:10). As Christians pray for one another (1 Thes. 3:10) and personally assist one another (Gal. 6:1, where "restore" is this same word *perfect*), the exalted Lord ministers to His church and makes them fit for ministry.

Balanced Christian growth and ministry is impossible in isolation. Someone has said that you can no more raise one Christian than you can raise one bee. Christians belong to each other and need each other. A baby must grow up in a loving family if it is to be balanced and normal. The emphasis today on the "individual Christian," as apart from his place in a local assembly, is wrong and very dangerous. We are sheep, and we must flock together. We are members of the same body, and we must minister to one another.

In 2 Corinthians 13:10, Paul gave the Corinthians a second encouragement—the Word of God. Paul wrote this letter to meet the immediate needs of a local congregation, but we today benefit from it because it is a part of the inspired Word of God. This letter carries the same authority as the presence of the apostle himself. Paul's great desire was that the congregation's obedience to the letter solve their problems, so that he would not have to exercise authority when he visited them.

Sometimes the minister of the Word must tear down before he can build up (see Jer. 1:7-10). The farmer must pull up the weeds before he can plant the seeds and get a good crop. Paul had to tear down the wrong thinking in the minds of the Corinthians (2 Cor. 10:4-6) before he could build up the truth in their hearts and minds. The negative attitude of the Corinthians made it necessary for Paul to *destroy,* but his great desire was to *build.*

In my own ministry, I have been through two building programs and two remodeling programs and, in spite of all their demands, building programs to me are much easier. It is much simpler and less expensive to build a new structure on unimproved land than to tear down walls and try to remodel an old building. Likewise, it is much easier to take a new believer and teach him the Word than it is to try to change the wrong thinking of an older saint. Wrong ideas can "hold out" against the truth for a long time, until the Spirit of God demolishes the walls in the mind.

Paul encouraged the saints *to cultivate grace, love, and peace* (2 Cor. 13:11-12). The word translated *farewell* means "grace," a common form of greeting in that day. It can also be translated *rejoice.* The command *be perfect* relates to Paul's prayer in 2 Corinthians 13:9 and carries the idea "be mature, be restored and fitted for life." *Be of good comfort* means "be encouraged." In spite of all their sins and problems, they had every right to be encouraged.

Live in peace was a needed admonition, for there were divisions and dissensions in the church (see 2 Cor. 12:20). If they practiced love and sought to be of one mind, the wars would cease and they would enjoy peace in their fellowship. To *be of one mind* does not mean that we all agree on everything, but that we agree not to disagree over matters that are not essential.

Our God is the "God of love and peace" (2 Cor. 13:11). Can the outside world tell that from the way we live and the way we conduct the business of the church? "Behold how they love one another!" was what the lost world said about the early church, but it has been a long time since the church has earned that kind of commendation.

Since ancient times, the kiss has been a form of greeting and a gesture of love and fellowship. However, it was usually exchanged between members of the same sex. The early church used the *kiss of peace* and *kiss of love* as evidences of their affection and concern for one another. It was a "holy kiss," sanctified because of their devotion to Jesus Christ. Members of the early church often kissed new believers after their baptism and thus welcomed them into the fellowship.

The everyday fellowship of God's people is important to the church. We must greet each other in other places as well as the fellowship of the assembly, and we must show concern for each other. In giving this admonition in 2 Corinthians 13:12, Paul was certainly hitting hard at one of the most serious problems in the church: their division and lack of concern for one another.

The closing benediction in 2 Corinthians 13:14 is one of the most beloved used in the church. It emphasizes the Trinity (see Matt. 28:19) and the blessings we can receive because we belong to God. *The grace of our Lord Jesus Christ* reminds us of His birth, when He became poor in order to make us rich (see 2 Cor. 8:9). The *love of God* takes us to Calvary where God gave His Son as the sacrifice for our sins (John 3:16). The *communion of the Holy Ghost* reminds us of Pentecost, when the Spirit of God came and formed the church (Acts 2).

The Corinthian believers then, and all believers now, desperately needed the blessings of grace, love, and communion. The Judaizers then, and the cultists today, emphasize Law instead of grace, exclusiveness instead of love, and independence rather than communion (fellowship). The competition in the Corinthian church, resulting in divisions, would have been solved if the people had only lived by God's grace and love.

The church is a miracle, and it can be sustained only by the miracle ministry of God. No amount of human skill, talents, or programs can make the church what it ought to be. Only God can do that. If each believer is depending on the grace of God, walking in the love of God, and participating in the fellowship of the Spirit, not walking in the flesh, then he will be a part of the answer and not a part of the problem. He will be *living* this benediction—and being a benediction to others!

Ask God to make you that kind of Christian.

Be encouraged—and then encourage others.

GALATIANS

OUTLINE

Key theme: Christian liberty in the grace of God
Key verse: Galatians 5:1

I. PERSONAL: GRACE AND THE GOSPEL—chapters 1–2
A. Grace declared in Paul's message—1:1-10
B. Grace demonstrated in Paul's life—1:11-24
C. Grace defended in Paul's ministry—2:1-21
1. Before the church collectively—2:1-10
2. Before Peter personally—2:11-21

II. DOCTRINAL: GRACE AND THE LAW—chapters 3–4
A. The personal argument—3:1-5
B. The scriptural argument—3:6-14
C. The logical argument—3:15-29
D. The historical argument—4:1-11
E. The sentimental argument—4:12-18
F. The allegorical argument—4:19-31

III. PRACTICAL: GRACE AND THE CHRISTIAN LIFE—chapters 5–6
A. Liberty, not bondage—5:1-12
B. The Spirit, not the flesh—5:13-26
C. Others, not self—6:1-10
D. God's glory, not man's praise—6:11-18

CONTENTS

CHAPTER ONE
BAD NEWS ABOUT THE GOOD NEWS
Galatians 1:1-10

The lad at my front door was trying to sell me a subscription to a weekly newspaper, and he was very persuasive. "It only costs a quarter a week," he said, "and the best thing about this newspaper is that it prints only the good news!"

In a world filled with trouble, it is becoming more and more difficult to find any "good news," so perhaps the newspaper was a bargain after all. To the person who has trusted Christ as Saviour, the real "Good News" is the Gospel: "Christ died for our sins according to the Scriptures . . . He was buried, and . . . He rose again the third day according to the Scriptures" (1 Cor. 15:3-4). It is the Good News that sinners can be forgiven and go to heaven because of what Jesus Christ did on the cross. The Good News of salvation through faith in Christ is the most important message in the world.

This message had changed Paul's life and, through him, the lives of others. But now this message was being attacked, and Paul was out to defend the truth of the Gospel. Some false teachers had invaded the churches of Galatia—churches Paul had founded—and were teaching a different message from that which Paul had taught.

As you begin to read Paul's letter to the Galatian Christians, you can tell immediately that something is radically wrong, because he does not open his letter with his usual praise to God and prayer for the saints. He has no time! Paul is about to engage in a battle for the truth of the Gospel and the liberty of the Christian life. False teachers are spreading a false "gospel" which is a mixture of Law and grace, and Paul is not going to stand by and do nothing.

How does Paul approach the Galatian Christians in his attempt to teach them the truth about the Gospel? In these opening verses, the apostle takes three definite steps as he prepares to fight this battle.

He Explains His Authority (Gal. 1:1-5)

Later on in his letter, Paul will deal with the Galatians on the basis of affection (Gal. 4:12-20); but at the outset he is careful to let them know the authority he has from the Lord. He has three sources of authority.

His ministry (vv. 1-2). "Paul, an apostle." In the early days of the church, God called special men to do special tasks. Among them were the *apostles.* The word means "one who is sent with a commission." While He was ministering on earth, Jesus had many *disciples* ("learners"), and from these He selected 12 *Apostles* (Mark 3:13-19). Later, one of the requirements for an apostle was that he have witnessed the Resurrection (Acts 1:21-22; 2:32; 3:15). Of course, Paul himself was neither a disciple nor an apostle during Christ's earthly ministry, but he had seen the risen Lord and been commissioned by Him (Acts 9:1-18; 1 Cor. 9:1).

Paul's miraculous conversion and call to apostleship created some problems. From the very beginning, he was apart from the original Apostles. His enemies said that he was not a true apostle for this reason. Paul is careful to point out that he had been made an apostle by Jesus Christ just as much as had the original Twelve. His apostleship was not from human selection and approval, but by divine appointment. Therefore, he had the authority to deal with the problems in the Galatian churches.

But in his ministry, Paul had a second basis for authority: *he had founded the churches in Galatia.* He was not writing to them as a stranger, but as the one who had brought them the message of life in the beginning! This letter reveals Paul's affection for these believers (see Gal. 4:12-19). Unfortunately, this affection was not being returned to him.

This matter of the founding of the Galatian churches has kept serious Bible students at work for many years. The problem stems from the meaning of the word *Galatia.* Several hundred years before the birth of Christ, some fierce tribes migrated from Gaul (modern France) into Asia Minor, and founded Galatia, which simply means "the country of the Gauls." When the Romans reorganized the ancient world, they made Galatia a part of a larger province that included several other areas, and they called the entire province Galatia. So, back in Paul's day, when a person talked about Galatia, you could not be sure whether he meant the smaller country of Galatia or the larger Roman province.

Bible students are divided over whether Paul wrote to churches in the *country* of Galatia or in the *province* of Galatia. The former view is called the "north Galatian theory" and the latter the "south Galatian theory." The matter is not finally settled, but the evidence seems to indicate that Paul wrote to churches in the southern part of the province of Galatia—Antioch, Iconium, Lystra, Derbe—churches he founded on his first missionary journey (Acts 13–14).

Paul always had a loving concern for his converts and a deep desire to see the churches he had founded glorify Christ (see Acts 15:36; 2 Cor. 11:28). He was not content to lead men and women to Christ and then abandon them. (For an example of his "after-care," read 1 Thes. 2.)

When Paul heard that false teachers had begun to capture his converts and lead them astray, he was greatly concerned—and rightly so. After all, teaching new Christians how to live for Christ is as much a part of Christ's commission as winning them (Matt. 28:19-20). Sad to say, many of the Galatian Christians had turned away from Paul, their "spiritual father" in the Lord, and were now following legalistic teachers who were mixing Old Testament Law with the Gospel of God's grace. (We call these false teachers "Judaizers" because they were trying to entice Christians back into the Jewish religious system.)

So, Paul had a ministry as an apostle, and specifically as the founder of the Galatian churches. As such, he had the authority to deal with the problems in the churches. But there was a second source of authority.

His message (vv. 3-4). From the very beginning, Paul clearly states the message of the Gospel, because it was this message that the Judaizers were changing. The Gospel centers in a *Person*—Jesus Christ, the Son of God. This Person paid *a price*—He gave Himself to die on the cross. (You will discover that the cross is important in the Galatian letter, see 2:19-21; 3:1, 13; 4:5; 5:11, 24; 6:12-14.) Christ paid the price that He might achieve a *purpose*—delivering sinners from bondage.

"Liberty in Christ" is the dominant theme of Galatians. (Check the word *bondage* in 2:4; 4:3, 9, 24-25; 5:1.) The Judaizers wanted to lead the Christians out of the liberty of grace into the bondage of Law. Paul knew that bondage was not a part of the message of the Gospel, for Christ had died to set men free.

Paul's ministry and message were sources of spiritual authority.

His motive (v. 5). "To whom be glory forever and ever!" The false teachers were not ministering for the glory of Christ, but for their own glory (see Gal. 6:12-14). Like false teachers today, the Judaizers were not busy winning lost people to Christ. Rather, they were stealing other men's converts and bragging about their statistics. But Paul's motive was pure and godly: he wanted to glorify Jesus Christ (see 1 Cor. 6:19-20; 10:31-33).

Paul has now explained his authority. He is ready for a second step as he begins this battle for the liberty of the Christian.

He Expresses His Anxiety (Gal. 1:6-7)

"I am amazed that you are so quickly moving away!" This is the first reason for Paul's anxiety: the Galatians were *deserting the grace of God.* (The verb indicates they were in the process of deserting and had not fully turned away.)

Paul strikes while the iron is hot. God had called them in His grace, and saved them from their sins. Now they are moving from grace back into Law. They are abandoning liberty for legalism! And they are doing it so quickly, without consulting Paul, their "spiritual father," or giving time for the Holy Spirit to teach them. They have become infatuated with the religion of the Judaizers, just the way little children follow a stranger because he offers them candy.

"The grace of God" is a basic theme in this letter (Gal. 1:3, 6, 15; 2:9, 21; 5:4; 6:18). Grace is simply God's favor to undeserving sinners. The words "grace" and "gift" go together, because salvation is the gift of God through His grace (Eph. 2:8-10). The Galatian believers were not simply "changing religions" or "changing churches" but were actually abandoning the very grace of God! To make matters worse, they were deserting the very God of grace! God had called them and saved them; now they were deserting Him for human leaders who would bring them into bondage.

We must never forget that the Christian life is a living relationship with God through Jesus Christ. A man does not become a Christian merely by agreeing to a set of doctrines; he becomes a Christian by submitting to Christ and trusting Him (Rom. 11:6). You cannot mix grace and works, because the one excludes the other. Salvation is the gift of God's grace, purchased for us by Jesus Christ on the cross. To turn from grace to Law is to desert the God who saved us.

But they were guilty of another sin that gave Paul great anxiety: *they were perverting the Gospel of God.* The Judaizers claimed to be preaching "the Gospel," but there cannot be two gospels, one centered in works and the other centered in grace. "They are not preaching another gospel," writes Paul, "but a *different* message—one so different from the true Gospel that it is no gospel at all." Like the cultists today, the Judaizers would say, "We believe in Jesus Christ—*but* we have something wonderful *to add* to what you already believe." As if any man could "add" something better to the grace of God!

The word translated "pervert" in Galatians 1:7 is used only three times in the New Testament (Acts 2:20; Gal. 1:7; James 4:9). It means "to turn about, to change into an opposite character." The word could be translated "to reverse." In other words, the Judaizers had reversed the Gospel—they had turned it around and taken it back into the Law! Later in this letter, Paul explains how the Law was preparation for the coming of Christ, but the Judaizers had a different interpretation. To them, the Law and the Gospel went together. "Except ye be circumcised after the manner [Law] of Moses, ye cannot be saved" (Acts 15:1).

What was this "deserting and perverting" doing to the Galatian Christians? It was troubling them (Gal. 1:7). This verb "trouble" carries with it the idea of perplexity, confusion, and unrest. You get some idea of the force of this word when you see how it is used in other places. "Trouble" describes the feelings of the disciples in the ship during the storm (Matt. 14:26). It also describes the feelings of King Herod when he heard that a new King had been born (Matt. 2:3). No wonder Paul was anxious for his converts: they were going through great agitation because of the false doctrines that had been brought to the churches. Grace always leads to peace (see Gal. 1:3), but the believers had deserted grace and therefore had no peace in their hearts.

Keep in mind that God's grace involves something more than man's salvation. We not only are saved by grace, but we are to live by grace (1 Cor. 15:10). We stand in grace; it is the foundation for the Christian life (Rom. 5:1-2). Grace gives us the strength we need to be victorious soldiers (2 Tim. 2:1-4). Grace enables us to suffer without complaining, and even to use that suffering for God's glory (2 Cor. 12:1-10). When a Christian turns away from living by God's grace, he must depend on his own power. This leads to failure and disappointment. This is what Paul means by "fallen from grace" (Gal. 5:4)—moving out of the sphere of grace into the sphere of Law, ceasing to depend on God's resources and depending on our own resources.

No wonder Paul was anxious. His friends in Christ were deserting the God of grace, perverting the grace of God, and reverting to living by the flesh and their own resources. They had begun their Christian lives in the Spirit, but now they were going to try to continue in the power of the flesh (Gal. 3:3).

Having explained his authority and expressed his anxiety, Paul now takes the third step.

He Exposes His Adversaries (Gal. 1:8-10)

"Make love, not war!" may have been a popular slogan, but it is not always feasible. Doctors must make war against disease and death; sanitary engineers must war against filth and pollution; legislators must war against injustice and crime. And they all fight *because of something they love!*

"Ye that love the Lord, hate evil" (Ps. 97:10). "Abhor that which is evil; cleave to that which is good" (Rom. 12:9). Paul waged war against the false teachers because he loved the truth, and because he loved those whom he had led to Christ. Like a loving father who guards his daughter until she is married, Paul watched over his converts lest they be seduced into sin (2 Cor. 11:1-4).

The Judaizers are identified by *the false gospel that they preached.* The test of a man's ministry is not popularity (Matt. 24:11), or miraculous signs and wonders (Matt. 24:23-24), but his faithfulness to the Word of God (see Isa. 8:20; 1 Tim. 4; 1 John 4:1-6; and note that 2 John 5-11 warns us not to encourage those who bring false doctrine). Christ had committed the Gospel to Paul (1 Cor. 15:1-8), and he, in turn, had committed it to other faithful servants (1 Tim. 1:11; 6:20; 2 Tim. 1:13; 2:2). But the Judaizers had come along and substituted their false gospel for the true Gospel, and for this sin, Paul pronounced them accursed. The word he uses is *anathema,* which means "dedicated to destruction."

(Read Acts 23:14 for a forceful illustration of the meaning of this word.) No matter who the preacher may be—an angel from heaven or even Paul himself—if he preaches any other gospel, he is accursed!

But there is a second characteristic of Paul's adversaries: *the false motives that they practiced.* His enemies accused Paul of being a compromiser and "adjusting" the Gospel to fit the Gentiles. Perhaps they twisted the meaning of Paul's statement, "I am made all things to all men, that I might by all means save some" (1 Cor. 9:22). They said, "When Paul is with the Jews, he lives like a Jew; but when he is with the Gentiles, he lives like the Gentiles. He is a man-pleaser, and therefore you cannot trust him!"

But in reality, it was the false teacher who was the man-pleaser. "These men are paying you special attention, but not sincerely," Paul wrote (Gal. 4:17). "They want to shut you off from me, so that you may keep on paying them special attention" (WMS). Later, Paul also exposes the false teachers as the compromisers, going back to Old Testament practices so that they would not be persecuted by the Jewish people (Gal. 6:12-15). Paul was definitely *not* a man-pleaser. His *ministry* did not come from man (Gal. 1:1), nor did his *message* come from man (Gal. 1:12). Why, then, should he be afraid of men? Why should he seek to please men? His heart's desire was to please Christ.

When Verdi produced his first opera in Florence, the composer stood by himself in the shadows and kept his eye on the face of one man in the audience—the great Rossini. It mattered not to Verdi whether the people in the hall were cheering him or jeering him; all he wanted was a smile of approval from the master musician. So it was with Paul. He knew what it was to suffer for the Gospel, but the approval or disapproval of men did not move him. "Therefore also we have as our ambition . . . to be pleasing to Him" (2 Cor. 5:9, NASB). Paul wanted the approval of Christ.

The servant of God is constantly tempted to compromise in order to attract and please men. When D.L. Moody was preaching in England, a worker came to him on the platform and told him that a very important nobleman had come into the hall. "May the meeting be a blessing to him!" was Moody's reply, and he preached just as before, without trying to impress anybody.

Paul was not a politician; he was an ambassador. His task was not to "play politics" but to proclaim a message. These Judaizers, on the other hand, were cowardly compromisers who mixed Law and grace, hoping to please both Jews and Gentiles, but never asking whether or not they were pleasing God.

We have noted three steps Paul took toward engaging these false teachers in battle: he explained his authority, expressed his anxiety, and exposed his adversaries. But how is he going to attack his enemies? What approach will he use to convince the Galatian believers that all they need is faith in God's grace? A quick survey of the entire letter shows that Paul is a master defender of the Gospel. Take time to read the entire letter at one sitting, and, as you read, note the three approaches that Paul takes.

His first approach is *personal* (Gal. 1–2). He reviews his own personal experience with Jesus Christ and the message of the Gospel. He points out that he had received the Gospel independently, from the Lord and not from the 12 Apostles (Gal. 1:11-24), but that they had approved his message and his ministry (Gal. 2:1-10). Furthermore, Paul had even defended the Gospel when Peter, the leading apostle, had compromised his earlier stand (Gal. 2:11-21). The autobiographical section of the letter proves that Paul was not a "counterfeit apostle," but that his message and ministry were true to the faith.

Galatians 3 and 4 are *doctrinal,* and in them Paul presents several arguments to establish that sinners are saved by faith and grace, not by works and Law. First he appeals to their own experiences (Gal. 3:1-5). Then he goes back to the Old Testament Law in Galatians 3:6-14 to show that even Abraham and the prophets understood salvation as being by grace through faith. Having mentioned the Law, Paul now explains why the Law was given originally (Gal. 3:15–4:18). He then uses the story of Sarah and Hagar to illustrate the relationship between Law and grace (Gal. 4:19-31).

The final two chapters of the letter are *practical* in emphasis, as Paul turns from argument to application. The Judaizers accused Paul of promoting lawlessness because he preached the Gospel of the grace of God; so in this section, Paul explains the relationship between the grace of God and practical Christian living. He shows that living by grace means liberty, not bondage (Gal. 5:1-12); depending on the Spirit, not the flesh (Gal. 5:13-26); living for others, not for self (Gal. 6:1-10); and living for the glory of God, not for man's approval (Gal. 6:11-18). It is either one series of actions or the other—Law or grace—but it cannot be both.

CHAPTER TWO
BORN FREE!
Galatians 1:11-24

"Whoso would be a man must be a nonconformist." So wrote Emerson, and many a thinker agrees with him.

The English art critic John Ruskin said, "I fear uniformity. You cannot manufacture great men any more than you can manufacture gold."

The German philosopher Schopenhauer wrote, "We forfeit three-fourths of ourselves in order to be like other people."

Francis Asbury, first bishop of the Methodist Church in the United States, once prayed at a deacon ordination, "O Lord, grant that these brethren may never want to be like other people."

Of course, there is a wrong kind of individualism that destroys instead of fulfills; but in a society accustomed to interchanging parts, it is good to meet a man like Paul who dared to be himself in the will of God. But his freedom in Christ was a threat to those who found safety in conformity.

Paul's enemies pointed to his nonconformity as proof that his message and ministry were not really of God. "He claims to be an apostle," they argued, "but he does not stand in the apostolic tradition." It is this misrepresentation that Paul answers in this section of Galatians. His nonconformity was divinely deliberate. God had chosen to reveal Himself in a different way to Paul.

In Galatians 1:11-12, Paul states his theme: his message and ministry are of divine origin. He did not invent the Gospel, nor did he receive it from men; but he received the Gospel from Jesus Christ. Both his message and his apostolic ministry were divinely given. Therefore, anybody who added anything to Paul's Gospel was in danger of divine judgment, because that Gospel was given by Jesus Christ from heaven (1 Cor. 15:1-11).

The best way for Paul to prove his point is to reach into his past and remind the Galatian Christians of the way God had dealt with him. Paul states that his past life was already known to his readers (Gal. 1:13), but it was obvious that they did not fully understand what those experiences meant. So, Paul flashes on the screen three pictures from his past as evidence that his apostleship and his Gospel are truly of God.

The Persecutor (Gal. 1:13-14)

Paul begins with his past conduct as an unconverted Jewish rabbi. (For a vivid account of these years from Paul's own lips, read Acts 22 and 26, as well as Acts 9.) In this historical flashback, Paul points out his relationship to the church (Gal. 1:13) and to the religion of the Jews (Gal. 1:14). He was persecuting the church and profiting and progressing in the Jewish religion. Everything was "going his way" and he was rapidly being recognized as a spiritual leader in Israel.

It is interesting to note the words that are used to describe Paul's activities when he was "Saul of Tarsus" persecuting the church. He "consented" to the murder of Stephen (see Acts 8:1), and then proceeded to "make havoc of the church" (see Acts 8:3) by breaking up families and putting believers in prison. The very atmosphere that he breathed was "threatening and slaughter" (Acts 9:1). So bent on destroying the church was Paul that he voted to kill the believers (Acts 22:4-5; 26:9-11). He mentions these facts in his letters (1 Cor. 15:9; Phil. 3:6; 1 Tim. 1:13), marveling that God could save such a sinner as he.

Paul actually thought that Jesus was an impostor and His message of salvation a lie. He was sure that God had spoken through Moses, but how could he be sure that God had spoken through Jesus of Nazareth? Steeped in Jewish tradition, young Saul of Tarsus championed his faith. His reputation as a zealous persecutor of "the sect of the Nazarenes" became known far and wide (see Acts 9:13-14). Everybody knew that this brilliant student of Rabbi Gamaliel (Acts 22:3) was well on his way to becoming an influential leader of the Jewish faith. His personal religious life, his scholarship (Acts 26:24), and his zeal in opposing alien religious faiths, all combined to make him the most respected young rabbi of his day.

Then something happened: Saul of Tarsus, the persecutor of the church, became Paul the Apostle, the preacher of the Gospel. This change was not gradual; it happened suddenly and without warning (Acts 9:1-9). Saul was on his way to Damascus to persecute the Christians; a few days later he was in Damascus preaching to the Jews that the Christians are right. How could the Judaizers explain this sudden transformation?

Was Saul's remarkable "about-face" caused by his own people, the Jews? Unthinkable! The Jews were encouraging Saul in his program of persecution, and his conversion was an embarrassment to them.

Was Saul's change caused by the Christians he was persecuting? Certainly the believers prayed for him, and no doubt the death of Stephen—and especially the glorious testimony he had given—affected Paul deeply (Acts 22:19-20). But the Christians ran from Paul (Acts 8:1, 4; 9:10-16), and, as far as we know, they had no idea that the young rabbi would ever become a Christian.

But if the amazing change in Paul was not caused by the Jews or the church, *then who caused it?* It had to come from God!

No matter how you look at it, the conversion of Paul was a spiritual miracle. It was humanly impossible for Rabbi Saul to become the Apostle Paul apart from the miracle of God's grace. And the same God who saved Paul also called him to be an apostle, and gave him the message of the Gospel. *For the Judaizers to deny Paul's apostleship and Gospel was the same as denying his conversion!* Certainly Paul was preaching the same message that he himself had believed—the truth that had changed him. But no mere human message could effect such a change. Paul's argument is conclusive: his past conduct as a persecutor of the church plus the dramatic change that he experienced prove that his message and ministry are from God.

The Believer (Gal. 1:15-16b, 24)

Having discussed his past character and conduct, Paul now explains his conversion; for, after all, this was the crucial thing in his life. "What I preach to others, I have experienced myself," he is saying to his accusers. "This is the true Gospel. Any other Gospel is counterfeit." In these verses Paul explains the characteristics of his conversion experience.

God did it (vv. 15a, 16a). "It pleased God . . . to reveal His Son in me." Whenever Paul spoke or wrote about his conversion, it was always with emphasis on the fact that God did the work. "Salvation is of the Lord!" (Jonah 2:9)

God did it by grace (v. 15b). Paul's experience reminds us of young Jeremiah (Jer. 1:4-10) and also of John the Baptist (Luke 1:5-17). Salvation is by God's grace, not man's efforts or character. *Grace* and *called* (Gal. 1:15b) go together, for whomever God chooses in His grace He calls through His Word (1 Thes. 1:4-5). The mysteries of God's sovereign will and man's responsibility to obey are not fully revealed to us. We do know that God is "not willing that any should perish" (2 Peter 3:9), and that those who do trust Christ discover they have been "chosen . . . in Him before the foundation of the world" (Eph. 1:4).

God did it through Christ (v. 16a). In another letter Paul makes it clear that he had plenty to boast about when he was an unconverted man (Phil. 3). He had religion and self-righteousness, as well as reputation and recognition; *but he did not have Christ!* When on the Damascus Road, Paul saw his own self-righteous rags contrasted to the righteousness of Christ, he realized what he was missing. "But what things were gain to me, those I counted loss for Christ" (Phil. 3:7).

God revealed Christ *to* Paul, *in* Paul, and *through* Paul. The "Jews' religion" (Gal. 1:14) had been an experience of outward rituals and practices; but faith in Christ brought about an inward experience of reality with the Lord. This "inwardness" of Christ is a major truth with Paul (Gal. 2:20; 4:19).

God did it for the sake of others (v. 16b). God chose Paul, not only to save him, but also to use him to win others. In the Bible, the doctrine of election is never taught with a view to producing pride or selfishness. Election involves responsibility. God chose Paul to preach among the Gentiles the same grace that he had experienced. This, in itself, was evidence that Paul's conversion was of God; for certainly a prejudiced Jewish rabbi would never decide of himself to minister to the despised Gentiles! (See Acts 9:15; 15:12; 22:21-22; Eph. 3:1, 8.)

God did it for His glory (v. 24). As a fanatical rabbi, Paul had all the glory a man could want; but what he was doing did not glorify God. Man was *created* to glorify God

(Isa. 43:7) and man is *saved* to glorify God (1 Cor. 6:19-20). Bringing glory to God was ever a compelling motive in Paul's life and ministry (Rom. 11:36; 16:27; 1 Cor. 10:31; Eph. 1:6; 3:20-21; Phil. 4:20). The Judaizers were interested in their own glory (Gal. 6:11-18). That is why they were stealing Paul's converts and leading them astray. If Paul had been interested in glorifying himself, he could have remained a Jewish rabbi and perhaps become Gamaliel's successor. But it was the glory of God that motivated Paul, and this ought to motivate our lives as well.

When Charles Haddon Spurgeon was a young preacher, his father, the Rev. John Spurgeon, suggested that Charles go to college to gain prominence. It was arranged for him to meet Dr. Joseph Angus, the principal of Stepney College, London. They were to meet at Mr. Macmillan's home in Cambridge, and Spurgeon was there at the appointed hour. He waited for two hours, but the learned doctor never appeared. When Spurgeon finally inquired about the man, he discovered that Dr. Angus had been waiting in another room and, because of another appointment, had already departed. Disappointed, Spurgeon left for a preaching engagement. While he was walking along, he heard a voice clearly say to him, "Seekest thou great things for thyself? Seek them not!" (see Jer. 45:5) From that moment, Spurgeon determined to do the will of God for the glory of God; and God blessed him in an exceptional way.

Paul has pictured himself as a persecutor, and has reviewed his character and conduct. He has also pictured himself as a believer, reviewing his conversion. He now presents a third picture.

The Preacher (Gal. 1:16c-23)

What were Paul's contacts with other believers after he was converted? This is a question vital to his defense. Paul had no personal contacts with the Apostles right after his conversion experience on the Damascus Road. "Immediately I conferred not with flesh and blood" (Gal. 1:16c). The logical thing for Paul to have done after his conversion was to introduce himself to the church at Jerusalem and profit from the spiritual instruction of those who had been "in Christ" before him. But this he did not do—and his decision was led of the Lord. For if he had gone to Jerusalem, his ministry might have been identified with that of the Apostles—all Jews—and this could have been a hindrance to his work among the Gentiles.

At this point we need to remind ourselves that the message of the Gospel came "to the Jew first" (Acts 3:26; Rom. 1:16). Our Lord's ministry was to the nation of Israel, and so was the ministry of the Apostles for the first few years (see Acts 1–7). The death of Stephen was a turning point. As the believers were scattered, they took the Good News with them to other places (Acts 8:4; 11:19ff). Philip took the message to the Samaritans (Acts 8), and then God directed Peter to introduce it to the Gentiles (Acts 10). However, it remained for Paul to carry the Gospel to the Gentile masses (Acts 22:21-22; Eph. 3:1, 8), and for this reason God kept him separated from the predominantly Jewish ministry being conducted by the Apostles in Jerusalem.

Paul did not immediately go to Jerusalem. Where did he go? He reviews his contacts and shows that there was no opportunity for him to receive either his message or his apostolic calling from any of the leaders of the church. (Compare this section with Acts 9:10-31, and keep in mind that even the best biblical scholars are not agreed on the chronology of Paul's life. Fortunately, the details of history do not affect the understanding of what Paul has written: we can disagree on chronology and yet agree on theology!)

He went to Arabia (v. 17b). This was after his initial ministry in Damascus (Acts 9:19-20). Instead of "conferring with flesh and blood," Paul gave himself to study, prayer, and meditation, and met with the Lord alone. He may have spent the greater part of three years in Arabia (Gal. 1:18), and no doubt was involved in evangelism as well as personal spiritual growth. The Apostles had received three years of teaching from the Lord Jesus, and now Paul was going to have his own opportunity to be taught of the Lord.

He went back to Damascus (v. 17c). It would have been logical to visit Jerusalem at this point, but the Lord directed otherwise. Certainly it was a risky thing for Paul to go back to the city that knew he had become a Christian. The Jewish leaders who had looked to him as their champion against Christianity would definitely be after his blood. Apparently the "basket incident" of Acts 9:23-25 (see 2 Cor. 11:32-33) took place at this time. The return to Damascus and the danger it brought to Paul's life are further proof that the Jewish leaders considered Paul an enemy, and therefore that his experience with Christ was a valid one.

He finally visited Jerusalem (vv. 18-20). This was three years after his conversion, and his main purpose was to visit Peter. But Paul had a tough time getting into the church fellowship! (Acts 9:26-28) If his message and ministry had been from the Apostles, this would never have happened; but because Paul's experience had been with the Lord Jesus alone, the Apostles were suspicious of him. He stayed in Jerusalem only fifteen days, and he saw only Peter and James (the Lord's brother). Thus he received neither his message nor his apostleship from the Jerusalem church. There simply was not the time nor the opportunity. He had already received them both directly from Christ.

He returned home to Tarsus (vv. 21-23). Again, the record in Acts explains why: his life was in danger in Jerusalem, just as it had been in Damascus (Acts 9:28-30). As Paul went through Syria, he preached the Word, and when he arrived in Cilicia, his home province (Acts 21:39; 22:3), he began to evangelize (see Acts 15:23). Historians have concluded that he remained there perhaps seven years, until Barnabas recruited him for the work in Antioch (Acts 11:19-26). A few believers in Jerusalem knew Paul, but the believers in the churches of Judea did not know him, though they heard that he was now preaching the very faith he had once tried to destroy.

In the light of Paul's conduct, his conversion, and his contacts, how could anybody accuse him of borrowing or inventing either his message or his ministry? Certainly he *did* receive his Gospel by a revelation from Jesus Christ. Therefore, we must be careful what we do with this Gospel, for it is not the invention of men, but the very truth of God.

Some critical scholars have accused Paul of "corrupting the simple Gospel," but the evidence is against this accusation. *The same Christ who taught on earth also taught through Paul from heaven.* Paul did not invent his teaching; he "received" it (Rom. 1:5; 1 Cor. 11:23; 15:3). At the time of Paul's conversion, God said He would appear to him in the future (Acts 26:16), apparently for the purpose of revealing His truths to him. This means that the Christ of the four Gospels and the Christ of the epistles is the same Person; there is no conflict between Christ and Paul. When Paul wrote his letters to the churches, he put his own teaching on the same level with that of Jesus Christ (2 Thes. 3:3-15). The Apostle Peter even calls Paul's letters "Scripture" (2 Peter 3:15-16).

Modern-day "Judaizers," like their ancient counterparts, reject the authority of Paul and try to undermine the Gospel which he preached. In Paul's day, their message was "the Gospel *plus* Moses." In our day it is "the Gospel *plus*" any number of religious leaders, religious books, or religious organizations. "You cannot be saved unless . . ." is their message (Acts 15:1); and that "unless" usually includes joining their group and obeying their rules. If you dare to mention the Gospel of grace as preached by Jesus, Paul, and the other Apostles, they reply, "But God has given us a new revelation!"

Paul has the answer for them: "If any man preach any other gospel unto you than that ye have received, let him be accursed!" (Gal. 1:9) When a sinner trusts Christ and is born again (John 3:1-18), he is "born free." He has been redeemed—purchased by Christ and set free. He is no longer in bondage to sin or Satan, nor should he be in bondage to human religious systems (Gal. 4:1-11; 5:1). "If the Son therefore shall make you free, ye shall be free indeed" (John 8:36).

CHAPTER THREE
THE FREEDOM FIGHTER, PART I
Galatians 2:1-10

"This will remain the land of the free only so long as it is the home of the brave."

So wrote veteran news analyst Elmer Davis in his book *But We Were Born Free,* and his convictions would certainly be echoed by the Apostle Paul. To Paul, his spiritual liberty in Christ was worth far more than popularity or even security. He was willing to fight for that liberty.

Paul's first fight for Christian liberty was at the Jerusalem Council (Acts 15:1-35; Gal. 2:1-10); his second was at a private meeting with Peter (Gal. 2:11-21). Had Paul been unwilling to wage this spiritual warfare, the church in the first century might have become only a Jewish sect, preaching a mixture of Law and grace. But because of Paul's courage, the Gospel was kept free from legalism, and it was carried to the Gentiles with great blessing.

Before we look at the three acts in the first drama, the Council at Jerusalem, we must get acquainted with the participants. *Paul,* of course, we know as the great apostle to the Gentiles.

Barnabas was one of Paul's closest friends. In fact, when Paul tried to get into the fellowship of the Jerusalem church, it was Barnabas who opened the way for him (Acts 9:26-28).

The name *Barnabas* means "son of encouragement," and you will always find Barnabas encouraging somebody. When the Gospel came to the Gentiles in Antioch, it was Barnabas who was sent to encourage them in their faith (Acts 11:19-24).

Thus, from the earliest days, Barnabas was associated with the Gentile believers. It was Barnabas who enlisted Paul to help minister at the church in Antioch (Acts 11:25-26), and the two of them worked together, not only in teaching, but also in helping the poor (Acts 11:27-30).

Barnabas accompanied Paul on the first missionary trip (Acts 13:1–14:28) and had seen God's blessings on the Gospel that they preached. It is worth noting that it was Barnabas who encouraged young John Mark after he had "dropped out" of the ministry and incurred the displeasure of Paul (Acts 13:13; 15:36-41). In later years, Paul was able to commend Mark and benefit from his friendship (Col. 4:10; 2 Tim. 4:11).

Titus was a Gentile believer who worked with Paul and apparently was won to Christ through the apostle's ministry (Titus 1:4). He was a "product" of the apostle's ministry among the Gentiles, and was taken to the Jerusalem conference as "exhibit A" from the Gentile churches. In later years, Titus assisted Paul by going to some of the most difficult churches to help them solve their problems (2 Cor. 7; Titus 1:5).

Three men were the "pillars" of the church in Jerusalem: Peter, John, and James, the brother of the Lord (who must not be confused with the Apostle James, who was killed by Herod, Acts 12:1-2). *Peter* we know from his prominent part in the accounts in the Gospels as well as in the first half of the Book of Acts. It was to Peter that Jesus gave "the keys," so that it was he who was involved in opening the door of faith to the Jews (Acts 2), the Samaritans (Acts 8), and the Gentiles (Acts 10). *John* we also know from the Gospel records as one of Christ's "inner three" apostles, associated with Peter in the ministry of the Word (Acts 3:1ff).

It is *James* who perhaps needs more introduction. The Gospel record indicates that Mary and Joseph had other children, and James was among them (Matt. 13:55; Mark 6:3). (Of course, Jesus was born by the power of the Spirit, and not through natural generation; Matt. 1:18-25; Luke 1:26-38.) Our Lord's brothers and sisters did not believe in Him during His earthly ministry (John 7:1-5). Yet we find "His brethren" associated with the believers in the early church (Acts 1:13-14). Paul informs us that the risen Christ appeared to James, and this was the turning point in his life (1 Cor. 15:5-7). James was the leader of the early church in Jerusalem (Acts 15; see also 21:18). He was also the writer of the Epistle of James; and that letter, plus Acts 21:18, would suggest that he was very Jewish in his thinking.

Along with these men, and the "Apostles and elders" (Acts 15:4, 6), were a group of "false brethren" who infiltrated the meetings and tried to rob the believers of their liberty in Christ (Gal. 2:4). Undoubtedly these were some of the Judaizers who had followed Paul in church after church and had tried to capture his converts. The fact that Paul calls them "false brethren" indicates that they were not true Christians, but were only masquerading as such so they could capture the conference for themselves.

This, then, is the cast of characters. Acts 15 should be read along with Galatians 2:1-10 to get the full story of the event.

Act 1—The Private Consultation (Gal. 2:1-2)

Paul and Barnabas had returned to Antioch from their first missionary journey, excited about the way God had "opened the door of faith unto the Gentiles" (Acts 14:27). But the Jewish legalists in Jerusalem were upset with their report; so they came to Antioch and taught, in effect, that a Gentile had to become a Jew before he could become a Christian (Acts 15:1).

Circumcision, which they demanded of the Gentiles, was an important Jewish rite, handed down from the days of Abraham (Gen. 17).

Submitting to circumcision meant accepting and obeying the whole Jewish Law. Actually, the Jewish people had forgotten the inner, spiritual meaning of the rite (Deut. 10:16; Jer. 4:1-4; Rom. 2:25-29), just as some churches today have lost the spiritual meaning of baptism and have turned it into an external ritual. The true Christian has experienced an inner circumcision of the heart (Col. 2:10-11) and does not need to submit to any physical operation (Phil. 3:1-3).

When Paul and Barnabas confronted these men with the truth of the Gospel, the result was a heated argument (Acts 15:2). It was decided that the best place to settle the question was before the church leaders in Jerusalem. We should not think that this "Jerusalem Conference" was a representative meeting from all the churches, such as a denominational conference; it was not. Paul, Barnabas, Titus, and certain other men from Antioch represented the Gentile Christians who had been saved totally apart from Jewish Law; but there were no representatives from the churches Paul had established in Gentile territory.

When the deputation arrived in Jerusalem, they met privately with the church leaders. Paul did not go to Jerusalem because the church sent him; he "went up by revelation" —that is, the Lord sent him (compare Gal. 2:1 and 1:12). And the Lord gave him the wisdom to meet with the leaders first so that they would be able to present a united front at the public meetings.

"Lest by any means I should run, or had run, in vain" (Gal. 2:2) does not mean that Paul was unsure either of his message or his ministry. His conduct on the way to the conference indicates that he had no doubts (Acts 15:3). What he was concerned about was the future of the Gospel among the Gentiles, because this was his specific ministry from Christ. If the "pillars" sided with the Judaizers, or tried to compromise, then Paul's ministry would be in jeopardy. He wanted to get their approval *before* he faced the whole assembly; otherwise a three-way division could result.

What was the result of this private consultation? *The Apostles and elders approved Paul's Gospel.* They added nothing to it (Gal. 2:6b) and thereby declared the Judaizers to be wrong. But this private meeting was only the beginning.

Act 2—The Public Convocation (Gal. 2:3-5)

The historical account of the Council of Jerusalem is recorded by Luke (Acts 15:6-21). Several witnesses presented the case for the Gospel of the grace of God, beginning with Peter (Acts 15:7-11). It was he who had been chosen by God to take the Gospel to the Gentiles originally (Acts 10); and he reminds the assembly that God gave the Holy Spirit to the believing Gentiles just as He did to the Jews, so that there was "no difference."

This had been a difficult lesson for the early Christians to learn, because for centuries there had been a difference between Jews and Gentiles (Lev. 11:43-47; 20:22-27). In His death on the cross, Jesus had broken down the barriers between Jews and Gentiles (Eph. 2:11-22), so that in Christ there are no racial differences (Gal. 3:28). In his speech to the conference, Peter makes it clear that there is but one way of salvation: faith in Jesus Christ.

Then Paul and Barnabas told the assembly what God had done among the Gentiles (Acts 15:12), and what a "missionary report" that must have been! The "false brethren" who were there must have debated with Paul and Barnabas, but the two soldiers of the Cross would not yield. Paul wanted the "truth of the Gospel" to continue among the Gentiles (Gal. 2:5).

It seems that Titus became a "test case" at this point. He was a Gentile Christian who had never submitted to circumcision. Yet it was clear to all that he was genuinely saved. Now, if the Judaizers were right ("Except you be circumcised after the manner of Moses, you cannot be saved," Acts 15:1), *then Titus was not a saved man.* But he *was* a saved man, and gave evidence of having the Holy Spirit; therefore, the Judaizers were wrong.

At this point, it might be helpful if we considered another associate of Paul—Timothy (see Acts 16:1-3). Was Paul being inconsistent by refusing to circumcise Titus, yet agreeing to circumcise Timothy? No, because two different issues were involved. In the case of Timothy, Paul was not submitting to Jewish Law in order to win him to Christ. Timothy was part Jew, part Gentile, and his lack of circumcision would have hindered his ministry among the people of Israel. Titus was a full Gentile, and for him to have submitted would have indicated that he was missing something in his Christian experience. To have circumcised Titus would have been cowardice and compromise; *not* to have circumcised Timothy would have been to create unnecessary problems in his ministry.

James, the leader of the church, gave the summation of the arguments and the conclusion of the matter (Acts 15:13-21). As Jewish as he was, he made it clear that a Gentile does *not* have to become a Jew in order to become a Christian. God's program for this day is to "take out of the Gentiles a people for His name." Jews and Gentiles are saved the same way: through faith in Jesus Christ. James then asked that the assembly counsel the Gentiles to do nothing that would offend unbelieving Jews, lest they hinder them from being saved. Paul won the battle.

His view prevailed in the private meeting when the leaders approved his Gospel and in the public meeting when the group agreed with Paul and opposed the Judaizers.

Echoes of the Jerusalem Conference are heard repeatedly in Paul's Letter to the Galatians. Paul mentions the "yoke of bondage" (Gal. 5:1), reminding us of Peter's similar warning (Acts 15:10). The themes of liberty and bondage are repeated often (Gal. 2:4; 4:3, 9, 21-31; 5:1), as is the idea of circumcision (Gal. 2:3; 5:3-4; 6:12-13).

Centuries later, today's Christians need to appreciate afresh the courageous stand Paul and his associates took for the liberty of the Gospel. Paul's concern was "the truth of the Gospel" (Gal. 2:5, 14), not the "peace of the church." The wisdom that God sends from above is "first pure, then peaceable" (James 3:17). "Peace at any price" was not Paul's philosophy of ministry, nor should it be ours.

Ever since Paul's time, the enemies of grace have been trying to add something to the simple Gospel of the grace of God. They tell us that a man is saved by faith in Christ *plus* something—good works, the Ten Commandments, baptism, church membership, religious ritual—and Paul makes it clear that these teachers are wrong. In fact, Paul pronounces a curse on any person (man or angel) who preaches any other gospel than the Gospel of the grace of God, centered in Jesus Christ (Gal. 1:6-9; see 1 Cor. 15:1-7 for a definition of the Gospel). It is a serious thing to tamper with the Gospel.

Act 3—The Personal Confirmation (Gal. 2:6-10)

The Judaizers had hoped to get the leaders of the Jerusalem church to disagree with Paul. By contrast, Paul makes it clear that he himself was not impressed either by the persons or the positions of the church leaders. He respected them, of course. Otherwise he would not have consulted with them privately. But he did not fear them or seek to buy their influence. All he wanted them to do was recognize "the grace of God" at work in his life and ministry (Gal. 2:9), and this they did.

Not only did the assembly approve Paul's Gospel, and oppose Paul's enemies, but they encouraged Paul's ministry and recognized publicly that God had committed the Gentile aspect of His work into Paul's hands. They could add nothing to Paul's message or ministry, and they dared not take anything away. There was agreement and unity: one Gospel would be preached to Jews and to Gentiles.

However, the leaders recognized that God had assigned different areas of ministry to different men. Apart from his visit to the household of Cornelius (Acts 10) and to the Samaritans (Acts 8), Peter had centered his ministry primarily among the Jews. Paul had been called as God's special ambassador to the Gentiles. So, it was agreed that each man would minister in the sphere assigned to him by God.

"The Gospel of the circumcision" and "the Gospel of the uncircumcision" are not two different messages; it had already been agreed that there is only one Gospel. Rather, we have here two different spheres of ministry, one to the Jews and the other to the Gentiles. Peter and Paul would both preach the same Gospel, and the same Lord would be at work in and through them (Gal. 2:8), but they would minister to different peoples.

This does not mean that Paul would never seek to win the Jews. To the contrary, he had a great burden on his heart for his people (Rom. 9:1-3). In fact, when Paul came to a city, he would first go to the Jewish synagogue, if there was one, and start his work among his own people. Nor was Peter excluded from ministering to the Gentiles. But each man would concentrate his work in his own sphere assigned to him by the Holy Spirit. James, Peter, and John would go to the Jews; Paul would go to the Gentiles (Gal. 2:9b, where the word *heathen* means "Gentile nations").

The Jerusalem Conference began with a great possibility for division and dissension; yet it ended with cooperation and agreement. "Behold, how good and how pleasant it is for brethren to dwell together in unity" (Ps. 133:1). Perhaps we need to practice some of this same cooperation today.

We need to recognize the fact that God calls people to different ministries in different places; yet we all preach the same Gospel and are seeking to work together to build His church. Among those who know and love Christ, there can be no such thing as "competition." Peter was a great man, and perhaps the leading apostle; yet he gladly yielded to Paul—a newcomer—and permitted him to carry on his ministry as the Lord led him. Previously, Paul explained his *independence* from the Apostles (Gal. 1); now in Galatians 2 he points out his *interdependence* with the Apostles. He was free, and yet he was willingly in fellowship with them in the ministry of the Gospel.

We move next from the theological to the practical—helping the poor (Gal. 2:10). Certainly these things go together. Correct doctrine is never a substitute for Christian duty (James 2:14-26). Too often our church meetings discuss problems, but they fail to result in practical help for the needy world. Paul had always been interested in helping the poor (Acts 11:27-30), so he was glad to follow the leaders' suggestion.

Even though the conference ended with Paul and the leaders in agreement, it did not permanently solve the problem. The Judaizers did not give up, but persisted in interfering with Paul's work and invading the churches he founded. Paul carried the good news of the council's decision to the churches in Antioch, Syria, and Cilicia (Acts 15:23) and in the other areas where he had ministered (Acts 16:4). But the Judaizers followed at his heels (like yelping dogs—see Phil. 3:1-3), starting at Antioch where they even swayed Peter to their cause (see Gal. 2:11ff).

There is little question that the Judaizers went to the churches of Galatia to sow their seeds of discord, and for this reason Paul had to write the letter we are now studying. It may have been written from Antioch shortly after the Council of Jerusalem, though some scholars date it later and have Paul writing from either Ephesus or Corinth. These historical details are important, but they are not vital to an understanding of the letter itself. Suffice it to say that this is probably Paul's earliest letter, and in it we find every major doctrine that Paul believed, preached, and wrote about in his subsequent ministry.

The curtain falls on this drama, but it will go up to reveal another. Once again God's "freedom fighter" will have to defend the truth of the Gospel, this time before Peter.

CHAPTER FOUR
THE FREEDOM FIGHTER, PART II
Galatians 2:11-21

"Eternal vigilance is the price of liberty!"

Wendell Phillips said that at a Massachusetts antislavery meeting in 1852, but its sentiment is valid today—not only in the realm of the political, but even more so in the realm of the spiritual. Paul had risked his life to carry the Gospel of God's grace to the regions beyond, and he was not willing for the enemy to rob him or his churches of their liberty in Christ. It was this "spiritual vigilance" that led Paul into another dramatic encounter, this time with the Apostle Peter, Barnabas, and some of the friends of James. Again, the drama is in three acts.

Peter's Relapse (Gal. 2:11-13)

Apparently, sometime after the important conference described in Acts 15, Peter came from Jerusalem to Antioch. The first thing to note is *Peter's freedom* then. He enjoyed fellowship with *all* the believers, Jews and Gentiles alike. To "eat with the Gentiles" meant to accept them, to put Jews and Gentiles on the same level as one family in Christ.

Raised as an orthodox Jew, Peter had a difficult time learning this lesson. Jesus had taught it while He was with Peter before the Crucifixion (Matt. 15:1-20). The Holy Spirit had reemphasized it when He sent Peter to the home of Cornelius, the Roman centurion (Acts 10). Furthermore, the truth had been accepted and approved by the conference of leaders at Jerusalem (Acts 15). Peter had been one of the key witnesses at that time.

Before we criticize Peter, perhaps we had better examine our own lives to see how many familiar Bible doctrines *we* are actually obeying. As you examine church history, you see that, even with a complete Bible, believers through the years have been slow to believe and practice the truths of the Christian faith. When we think of the persecution and discrimination that have been practiced in the name of Christ, it embarrasses us. It is one thing for us to defend a doctrine in a church meeting, and quite something else to put it into practice in everyday life.

Peter's freedom was threatened by *Peter's fear.* While he was in Antioch, the church was visited by some of the associates of James. (You will remember that James was a strict Jew even though he was a Christian believer.) Paul does not suggest that James sent these men to investigate Peter, or even that they were officials of the Jerusalem church. No doubt they belonged to the "circumcision party" (Acts 15:1, 5) and wanted to lead the Antioch church into religious legalism.

After his experience with Cornelius, Peter had been "called on the carpet" and had ably defended himself (Acts 11). But now, he became afraid. Peter had not been afraid to obey the Spirit when He sent him to Cornelius, nor was he afraid to give his witness at the Jerusalem Conference. But now, with the arrival of some members of "the opposition," Peter lost his courage. "The fear of man bringeth a snare" (Prov. 29:25).

How do we account for this fear? For one thing, we know that Peter was an impulsive man. He could show amazing faith and courage one minute and fail completely the next. He walked on the waves to go to Jesus, but then became frightened and began to sink. He boasted in the Upper Room that he would willingly die with Jesus, and then denied his Lord three times. Peter in the Book of Acts is certainly more consistent than in the four Gospels, but he was not perfect—*nor are we!* Peter's fear led to Peter's *fall.* He ceased to enjoy the "love feast" with the Gentile believers and separated himself from them.

There are two tragedies to Peter's fall. First, it made him a hypocrite (which is the meaning of the word *dissembled*). Peter pretended that his actions were motivated by faithfulness, when they were really motivated by fear. How easy it is to use "Bible doctrine" to cover up our disobedience.

The second tragedy is that *Peter led others astray with him.* Even Barnabas was involved. Barnabas had been one of the spiritual leaders of the church in Antioch (Acts 11:19-26), so his disobedience would have a tremendous influence on the others in the fellowship.

Suppose Peter and Barnabas had won the day and led the church into legalism? What might the results have been? Would Antioch have continued to be the great missionary church that sent out Paul and Barnabas? (Acts 13) Would they, instead, have sent out the "missionaries" of the circumcision party and either captured or divided the churches Paul had already founded? You can see that this problem was not a matter of personality or party; it was a question of "the truth of the Gospel." And Paul was prepared to fight for it.

Paul's Rebuke (Gal. 2:14-21)

Bible students are not sure just where Paul's conversation with Peter ends and where his letter to the Galatians continues in the passage. It does not really matter since the entire section deals with the same topic: our liberty in Jesus Christ. We will assume that the entire section represents Paul's rebuke of Peter. It is interesting to note that Paul builds the entire rebuke on doctrine. There are five basic Christian doctrines that were being denied by Peter because of his separation from the Gentiles.

The unity of the church (v. 14). Peter was a Jew, but through his faith in Christ he had become a Christian. Because he was a Christian, he was part of the church, and in the church there are no racial distinctions (Gal. 3:28). We have seen how the Lord taught Peter this important lesson, first in the house of Cornelius and then at the Jerusalem Conference.

Paul's words must have stung Peter: "You are a Jew, yet you have been living like a Gentile. Now you want the Gentiles to live like Jews. What kind of inconsistency is that?"

Peter himself had stated at the Jerusalem Conference that God had "put no difference between us and them" (Acts 15:9). But now *Peter* was putting a difference. God's people are one people, even though they may be divided into various groups. Any practice on our part that violates the Scripture and separates brother from brother is a denial of the unity of the body of Christ.

Justification by faith (vv. 15-16). This is the first appearance of the important word *justification* in this letter, and probably in Paul's writings (if, as we believe, Galatians was the first letter he wrote). "Justification by faith" was the watchword of the Reformation, and it is important that we understand this doctrine.

"How should [a] man be just with God?" (Job 9:2) was a vital question, because the answer determined eternal consequences. "The just shall live by his faith" (Hab. 2:4) is God's answer; and it was this truth that liberated Martin Luther from religious bondage and fear. So important is this concept that three New Testament books explain it to us: Romans (see 1:17), Galatians (see 3:11), and Hebrews (see 10:38). Romans explains the meaning of "the just"; Galatians explains "shall live"; and Hebrews explains "by faith."

But what is justification? *Justification is the act of God whereby He declares the believing sinner righteous in Jesus Christ.* Every word of this definition is important. Justification is *an act* and not a process. No Christian is "more justified" than another Christian. "Having therefore been once-and-for-all justified by faith, we have peace with God" (Rom. 5:1, literal translation). Since we are justified by faith, it is an instant and immediate transaction between the believing sinner and God. If we were justified by works, then it would have to be a gradual process.

Furthermore, justification is an act *of God;* it is not the result of man's character or works. "It is God that justifieth" (Rom. 8:33). It is not by doing the "works of the Law" that the sinner gets a right standing before God, but by putting his faith in Jesus Christ. As Paul will explain later in this letter, the Law was given to reveal sin and not to redeem from sin (see Rom. 3:20). God in His grace has put our sins on Christ—and Christ's righteousness has been put to our account (see 2 Cor. 5:21).

In justification, God *declares* the believing sinner righteous; He does not *make* him righteous. (Of course, real justification leads to a changed life, which is what James 2 is all about.) Before the sinner trusts Christ, he stands GUILTY before God; but the moment he trusts Christ, he is declared NOT GUILTY and he can never be called GUILTY again!

Justification is not simply "forgiveness," because a person could be forgiven and then go out and sin and become guilty. Once you have been "justified by faith" you can never be held guilty before God.

Justification is also different from "pardon," because a pardoned criminal still has a record. When the sinner is justified by faith, *his past sins are remembered against him no more,* and God no longer puts his sins on record (see Ps. 32:1-2; Rom. 4:1-8).

Finally, God justifies *sinners,* not "good people." Paul declares that God justifies "the ungodly" (Rom. 4:5). The reason most sinners are not justified is because they will not admit they are sinners! And sinners are the only kind of people Jesus Christ can save (Matt. 9:9-13; Luke 18:9-14).

When Peter separated himself from the Gentiles, he was denying the truth of justification by faith, because he was saying, "We Jews are different from—and better than—the Gentiles." Yet both Jews and Gentiles are sinners (Rom. 3:22-23) and can be saved only by faith in Christ.

Freedom from the Law (vv. 17-18). At the Jerusalem Conference, Peter had compared the Mosaic Law to a burdensome yoke (Acts 15:10; see Gal. 5:1). Now he had put himself under that impossible yoke.

Paul's argument goes like this: "Peter, you and I did not find salvation through the Law; we found it through faith in Christ. But now, after being saved, you go back into the Law! This means that Christ alone did not save you; otherwise you would not have needed the Law. So, Christ actually made you a sinner!

"Furthermore, you have preached the Gospel of God's grace to Jews and Gentiles, and have told them they are saved by faith and not by keeping the Law. By going back into legalism, you are building up what you tore down! This means that you sinned by tearing it down to begin with!"

In other words, Paul is arguing from Peter's own experience of the grace of God. To go back to Moses is to deny everything that God had done for him and through him.

The very Gospel itself (vv. 19-20). If a man is justified by the works of the Law, then why did Jesus Christ die? His death, burial, and resurrection are the key truths of the Gospel (1 Cor. 15:1-8). We are *saved* by faith in Christ (He died for us), and we *live* by faith in Christ (He lives in us). Furthermore, we are so identified with Christ by the Spirit that *we died with Him* (see Rom. 6). This means that we are dead to the Law. To go back to Moses is to return to the graveyard! We have been "raised to walk in newness of life" (Rom. 6:4); and since we live by His resurrection power, we do not need the "help" of the Law.

The grace of God (v. 21). The Judaizers wanted to mix Law and grace, but Paul tells us that this is impossible. To go back to the Law means to "set aside" the grace of God.

Peter had experienced God's grace in his own salvation, and he had proclaimed God's grace in his own ministry. But when he withdrew from the Gentile Christian fellowship, he openly denied the grace of God.

Grace says, "There is no difference! All are sinners, and all can be saved through faith in Christ!"

But Peter's actions had said, "There *is* a difference! The grace of God is not sufficient; we also need the Law."

Returning to the Law nullifies the Cross: "If righteousness came by the Law, then Christ is dead in vain" (Gal. 2:21). Law says DO! Grace says DONE! "It is finished!" was Christ's victory cry (John 19:30). "For by grace are ye saved through faith" (Eph. 2:8).

We have no record of Peter's reply to Paul's rebuke, but Scripture would indicate that he admitted his sin and was restored to the fellowship once again. Certainly when you read his two letters (1 and 2 Peter) you detect no deviation from the Gospel of the grace of God. In fact, the theme of 1 Peter is "the true grace of God" (1 Peter 5:12); and the word *grace* is used in every chapter of the letter. Peter is careful to point out that he and Paul were in complete agreement, lest anyone try to "rob Peter to pay Paul" (2 Peter 3:15-16).

So end the two acts of this exciting drama. But the curtain has not come down yet, for there is a third act which involves you and me.

The Believer's Response

We know what Peter's response was when he was challenged to live up to the truth of the Gospel: fear and failure. And we know what Paul's response was when he saw the truth of the Gospel being diluted: courage and defense. But the important question *today* is: what is *my* response to the "truth of the Gospel"? Perhaps this is a good place to take inventory of ourselves before we proceed into the doctrinal chapters of this letter. Let me suggest some questions for each of us to answer.

Have I been saved by the grace of God? The only Gospel that saves is the Gospel of the grace of God as revealed in Jesus Christ. Any other Gospel is a false gospel and is under a curse (Gal. 1:6-9). Am I trusting in *myself* for salvation—*my* morality, *my* good works, even *my* religion? If so, then I am not a Christian, for a true Christian is one who has trusted Christ *alone.* "For by grace are ye saved through faith; and that not of yourselves: it is the gift of God: not of works, lest any man should boast" (Eph. 2:8-9).

Am I trying to mix Law and grace? Law means I must do something to please God, while grace means that God has finished the work for me and all I need do is believe on Christ. Salvation is not by faith in Christ *plus* something: it is by faith in Christ *alone.* While church membership and religious activities are good in their place as expressions of faith in Christ, they can never be added to faith in Christ in order to secure eternal life. "And if by grace, then is it no more of works: otherwise grace is no more grace. But if it be of works, then it is no more grace: otherwise work is no more work" (Rom. 11:6).

Am I rejoicing in the fact that I am justified by faith in Christ? It has often been said that "justified" means "just as if I'd never sinned" and this is correct. It brings great peace to the heart to know that one has a right standing before God (Rom. 5:1). Just think: the righteousness of Christ has been put to our account! God has not only declared that we are righteous in Christ, but He deals with us as though we had never sinned at all! We need never fear judgment because our sins have already been judged in Christ on the cross (Rom. 8:1).

Am I walking in the liberty of grace? Liberty does not mean license; rather, it means the freedom in Christ to enjoy Him and to become what He has determined for us to become (Eph. 2:10). It is not only "freedom to *do*" but also "freedom *not* to do." We are no longer in bondage to sin and the Law. As Paul will explain in the practical section of this letter (Gal. 5–6), we obey God because of love and not because of Law. Christians enjoy a wonderful liberty in Christ. Am I enjoying it?

Am I willing to defend the truth of the Gospel? This does not mean that we become evangelical detectives investigating every church and Sunday School class in town. But it does mean that we do not fear men when they deny the truths that have brought us eternal life in Christ. "Do I seek to please men? For if I yet pleased men, I should not be the servant of Christ" (Gal. 1:10).

Many people with whom we come in contact actually believe that people are saved by faith in Christ plus "doing good works . . . keeping the Ten Commandments . . . obeying the Sermon on the Mount," and any number of other "religious *plusses.*" We may not have the same apostolic authority that Paul exercised, but we do have the Word of God to proclaim; and it is our obligation to share the truth.

Am I "walking uprightly according to the truth of the Gospel"? The best way to defend the truth is to live the truth. My verbal defense of the Gospel will accomplish very little if my life contradicts what I say. Paul is going to explain to us how to live in liberty by the grace of God, and it is important that we obey what he says.

A new employee was instructed how to measure valve parts to make sure they were ready for the final assembly. But after a few hours, his foreman was receiving complaints that the parts he was approving were faulty. "What are you doing?" the foreman asked. "I showed you how to use that micrometer. You're sending through parts that are oversize!"

The employee replied, "Oh, most of the parts I was measuring were too large, so I opened up the micrometer a bit."

Changing the standards will never make for success, either in manufacturing or ministry. Paul maintained the standards of "the truth of the Gospel"—and so should we.

CHAPTER FIVE
BEWITCHED AND BOTHERED
Galatians 3:1-14

The sixty verses that make up Galatians 3 and 4 are some of the strongest writing that Paul ever penned. But, after all, he was in a battle! He was out to prove that salvation is by grace alone, and not by the works of the Law. His opponents had used every possible means to try to capture the churches of Galatia, and Paul was not going to fight them halfheartedly. The apostle was no amateur when it came to debate, and in these two chapters he certainly proves his abilities. His logic is unassailable.

Paul uses six different arguments to prove that God saves sinners through faith in Christ and not by the works of the Law. He begins with the *personal argument* (Gal. 3:1-5) in which he asks the Galatians to recall their personal experience with Christ when they were saved. Then he moves into the *scriptural argument* (Gal. 3:6-14), in which he quotes six Old Testament passages to prove his point. In the *logical argument* (Gal. 3:15-29) he reasons with his readers on the basis of what a covenant is and how a covenant works. He then presents the *historical argument* (Gal. 4:1-11), explaining the place of Law in the history of Israel.

At this point, Paul's love for his converts comes to the surface. The result is a *sentimental argument* (Gal. 4:12-18) as the apostle appeals to them to remember his love and their happy relationship in days past. But then Paul goes right back to his close reasoning, and concludes with the *allegorical argument* (Gal. 4:19-31), based on the life of Abraham and his relationships with Sarah and Hagar. Practical application of his doctrinal argument follows in the last two chapters.

The Personal Argument (Gal. 3:1-5)

The key to this section is in the word *suffered* (Gal. 3:4), which can be translated "experienced." Paul asks, "Have you experienced so many things in vain?" The argument from Christian experience was a wise one with which to begin, because Paul had been with them when they had trusted Christ. Of course, to argue from experience can be dangerous, because experiences can be counterfeited and they can be misunderstood. Subjective experience must be balanced with objective evidence, because experiences can change, but truth never changes. Paul balances the subjective experience of the Galatian Christians with the objective teaching of the unchanging Word of God (Gal. 3:6-14).

It was obvious that these people had experienced something in their lives when Paul had first visited them; but the Judaizers had come along and convinced them that their experience was not complete. They needed something else, and that "something else" was obedience to the Law of Moses. These false teachers had bewitched them and turned them into fools. In calling them "fools" Paul is not violating Christ's words in the Sermon on the Mount (Matt. 5:22), because two different words are used and two different ideas are expressed. *Foolish* in Galatians 3:1 means "spiritually dull" (see Luke 24:25), while the word Jesus used carries the idea of "a godless person." Paul is declaring a fact; Jesus is warning against verbal abuse.

Paul reminds them that they had truly experienced a meeting with God.

They saw God the Son (v. 1). It was "Christ and Him crucified" that Paul had preached in Galatia, and with such effectiveness that the people could almost see Jesus crucified for them on the cross. The words *evidently set forth* translate a Greek word that means "publicly portrayed, or announced on a poster." Just as we put important information on a poster and display it in a public place, so Paul openly presented Christ to the Galatians, with great emphasis on His death for sinners on the cross. They heard this truth, believed it, and obeyed it; and as a result, were born into the family of God.

They received God the Holy Spirit (vv. 2-4). The Holy Spirit is mentioned eighteen times in this epistle and plays an important part in Paul's defense of the Gospel of the grace of God. The only real evidence of conversion is the presence of the Holy Spirit in the life of the believer (see Rom. 8:9). Paul asks an important question: did they receive the Spirit by faith in the Word of God, or by doing the works of the Law? Of course, there could be but one answer: the Spirit came into their lives because they trusted Jesus Christ.

It is important that we understand the work of the Spirit in salvation and Christian living. The Holy Spirit *convicts* the lost sinner and reveals Christ to him (John 16:7-11). The sinner can resist the Spirit (Acts 7:51) or yield to the Spirit and trust Jesus Christ. When the sinner believes in Christ, he is then *born of the Spirit* (John 3:1-8) and receives new life. He is also *baptized by the Spirit* so that he becomes a part of the spiritual body of Christ (1 Cor. 12:12-14). The believer is *sealed by the Spirit* (Eph. 1:13-14) as a guarantee that he will one day share in the glory of Christ.

Since the Holy Spirit does so much for the believer, this means that the believer has a responsibility to the Holy Spirit, who lives within his body (1 Cor. 6:19-20). The Christian should *walk in the Spirit* (Gal. 5:16, 25) by reading the Word, praying, and obeying God's will. If he disobeys God, then he is *grieving the Spirit* (Eph. 4:30), and if he persists in doing this, he may *quench the Spirit* (1 Thes. 5:19). This does not mean that the Holy Spirit will leave him, because Jesus has promised that the Spirit abides forever (John 14:16). But it does mean that the Spirit cannot give him the joy and power that he needs for daily Christian living. Believers should be *filled with the Spirit* (Eph. 5:18-21), which simply means "controlled by the Spirit." This is a continuous experience, like drinking water from a fresh stream (John 7:37-39).

So, in their conversion experience, the believers in Galatia had received the Spirit by faith and not by the works of the Law. This leads Paul to another question: "If you did not *begin* with the Law, why bring it in anyway? If you began with the Spirit, can you go on to maturity without the Spirit, depending on the flesh?" The word *flesh* here does not refer to the human body, but rather to the believer's old nature. Whatever the Bible says about "flesh" is usually negative (see Gen. 6:1-7; John 6:63; Rom. 7:18; Phil. 3:3). Since we were saved through the Spirit, and not the flesh, through faith and not Law, then it is reasonable that we should continue that way.

The illustration of human birth is appropriate here. Two human parents are required for a child to be conceived and born, and two *spiritual* parents are required for a child to be born into God's family: the Spirit of God and the Word of God (John 3:1-8; 1 Peter 1:22-25). When a normal child is born, he has all that he needs for life; nothing need be added. When the child of God is born into God's family, he has all that he needs spiritually; *nothing need be added!* All that is necessary is that the child have food, exercise, and cleansing that he might grow into maturity. It would be strange if the parents had to take the child to the doctor at one month to receive ears, at two months to receive toes, and so on.

"You have begun in the Spirit," writes Paul. "Nothing need be added! Walk in the Spirit and you will grow in the Lord."

They experienced miracles from God the Father (v. 5). The *He* in this verse refers to the Father as the One who ministers the Spirit and "worketh miracles among [them]." The same Holy Spirit who came into the believer at conversion continues to work in him and through him so that the whole body is built up (see Eph. 4:16; Col. 2:19). The Father continues to supply the Spirit in power and blessing, and this is done by faith and not by the works of the Law. The phrase *among you* can also be translated *within you.* These miracles would therefore include wonderful changes *within* the lives of the Christians, as well as signs and wonders within the church fellowship.

"Do you really believe the miracles in the Bible?" a skeptic asked a new Christian who had been a terrible drinker.

"Of course I do!" the believer replied.

The skeptic laughed. "Do you mean that you really believe that Jesus could turn water into wine?" he asked.

"I sure do! In my home He turned wine into food and clothing and furniture!"

The Scriptural Argument (Gal. 3:6-14)

Paul turns now from subjective experience to the objective evidence of the Word of God. We never judge the Scriptures by our experience; we test our experience by the Word of God. In the first section, Paul asked six questions; in this section he will quote six Old Testament statements to prove that salvation is by faith in Christ and not by the works of the Law. Since the Judaizers wanted to take the believers back into the Law, Paul quotes the Law! And, since they magnified the place of Abraham in their religion, Paul uses Abraham as one of his witnesses!

Abraham was saved by faith (vv. 6-7). Paul begins by quoting Moses to show that God's righteousness was placed to Abraham's account only because he believed God's promise (Gen. 15:6). The words *accounted* in Galatians 3:6 and *counted* in Genesis 15:6 mean the same as *imputed* in Romans 4:11, 22-24. The Greek word means "to put to one's account." When the sinner trusts Christ, God's righteousness is put to his account. More than this, the believer's sins are no longer put to his account (see Rom. 4:1-8). This means that the record is always clean before God, and therefore the believer can never be brought into judgment for his sins.

The Jewish people were very proud of their relationship with Abraham. The trouble was, they thought that this relationship guaranteed them eternal salvation. John the Baptist warned them that their *physical* descent did not guarantee *spiritual* life (Matt. 3:9). Jesus made a clear distinction between "Abraham's seed" physically and "Abraham's children" spiritually (John 8:33-47). Some people today still imagine that salvation is inherited. Because mother and father were godly people, the children are automatically saved. But this is not true. It has well been said, "God has no grandchildren."

This salvation is for the Gentiles (vv. 8-9). The word *heathen* (Gal. 3:8), as used here, simply means Gentiles. Paul's quotation of Moses (Gen. 12:3) proves that, from the very beginning of Abraham's relationship with God, the blessing of salvation was promised to all the nations of the world. God preached the "Good News" to Abraham centuries ago, and Paul brought that same Good News to the Galatians: sinners are justified through faith and not by keeping the Law. The logic here is evident: if God promised to save the Gentiles by faith, then the Judaizers are wrong in wanting to take the Gentile believers back into Law. The true "children of Abraham" are not the Jews by physical descent, but Jews and Gentiles who have believed in Jesus Christ. All those who are "of faith" (believers) are blessed with "believing Abraham."

When you read God's great covenant with Abraham in Genesis 12:1-3, you discover that many different blessings were promised—some personal, some national and political, and some universal and spiritual. Certainly God did make Abraham's name great; he is revered not only by Jews, but also by Christians, Muslims, and many others. God did multiply his descendants, and God did bless those who blessed Abraham. He also judged those who cursed his descendants (Egypt, Babylon, and Rome are cases in point). But the greatest blessings that God sent through Abraham and the Jewish nation have to do with our eternal salvation. Jesus Christ is that promised "'Seed," through whom all the nations have been blessed (Gal. 3:16).

This salvation is by faith, not Law (vv. 10-12). Salvation could never come by obedience to Law because the Law brings a curse, not a blessing. Here Paul quotes from Deuteronomy 27:26. Law demands obedience, and this means obedience in *all things*. The Law is not a "religious cafeteria" where people can pick and choose (see James 2:10-11). Paul next quotes Habakkuk, "The just shall live by his faith" (Hab. 2:4). This statement is so important that the Holy Spirit inspired three New Testament books to explain it as mentioned before. *Romans* explains "the just" and tells how the sinner can be justified before God (see Rom. 1:17). *Galatians* explains how the just "shall live"; and *Hebrews* discusses "by faith" (see Heb. 10:38). Nobody could ever live "by Law" because the Law kills and shows the sinner he is guilty before God (Rom. 3:20; 7:7-11).

But someone might argue that it takes faith even to obey the Law; so Paul quotes Leviticus to prove that it is *doing* the Law, not believing it, that God requires (Lev. 18:5). Law says, "Do and live!" but grace says, "Believe and live!" Paul's own experience (Phil. 3:1-10), as well as the history of Israel (Rom. 10:1-10), proves that works righteousness can never save the sinner; only faith righteousness can do that.

The Judaizers wanted to seduce the Galatians into a religion of legal works, while Paul wanted them to enjoy a relationship of love and life by faith in Christ. For the Christian to abandon faith and grace for Law and works is to lose everything exciting that the Christian can experience in his daily fellowship with the Lord. The Law cannot justify the sinner (Gal. 2:16); neither can it give him righteousness (Gal. 2:21). The Law cannot give the gift of the Spirit (Gal. 3:2), nor can it guarantee that spiritual inheritance that belongs to God's children (Gal. 3:18). The Law cannot give life (Gal. 3:21), and the Law cannot give liberty (Gal. 4:8-10). Why, then, go back into the Law?

This salvation comes through Christ (vv. 13-14). These two verses beautifully summarize all that Paul has been saying in this section. Does the Law put sinners under a curse? Then Christ has redeemed us from that curse! Do you want the blessing of Abraham? It comes through Christ! Do you want the gift of the Spirit, but you are a Gentile? This gift is given through Christ to the Gentiles! All that you need is in Christ! There is no reason to go back to Moses.

Paul quotes Deuteronomy again, "He that is hanged is accursed of God" (Deut. 21:33, NKJV). The Jews did not crucify criminals; they stoned them to death. But in cases of shameful violation of the Law, the body was hung on a tree and exposed for all to see. This was a great humiliation, because the Jewish people were very careful in their treatment of a dead body. After the body had been exposed for a time, it was taken down and buried (see Josh. 8:29; 10:26; 2 Sam. 4:12).

Of course, Paul's reference to a "tree" relates to the cross on which Jesus died (Acts 5:30; 1 Peter 2:24). He was not stoned and then His dead body exposed; He was nailed alive to a tree and left there to die. But by dying on the cross, Jesus Christ bore the curse of the Law for us; so that now the believer is no longer under the Law and its awful curse. "The blessing of Abraham" (justification by faith and the gift of the Spirit) is now ours through faith in Jesus Christ.

The word *redeemed* in Galatians 3:13 means to purchase a slave for the purpose of setting him free. It is possible to purchase a slave and keep him as a slave, but this is not what Christ did. By shedding His blood on the cross, He purchased us that we might be set free. The Judaizers wanted to lead the Christians into slavery, but Christ died to set them free. Salvation is not exchanging one form of bondage for another. Salvation is being set free from the bondage of sin and the Law *into* the liberty of God's grace through Christ.

This raises an interesting question: how could these Judaizers ever convince the Galatian Christians that the way of Law was better than the way of grace? Why would any believer deliberately want to choose bondage instead of liberty? Perhaps part of the answer is found in the word *bewitched* that Paul uses in Galatians 3:1. The word means "to cast a spell, to fascinate." What is there about legalism that can so fascinate the Christian that he will turn from grace to Law?

For one thing, legalism appeals to the flesh. The flesh loves to be "religious"—to obey laws, to observe holy occasions, even to fast (see Gal. 4:10). Certainly there is nothing wrong with obedience, fasting, or solemn times of spiritual worship, *provided that the Holy Spirit does the motivating and the empowering.* The flesh loves to boast about its religious achievements—how many prayers were offered, or how many gifts were given (see Luke 18:9-14; Phil. 3:1-10).

Another characteristic of religious legalism that fascinates people is the appeal to the senses. Instead of worshiping God "in spirit and in truth" (John 4:24), the legalist invents his own system that satisfies his senses. He cannot walk by faith; he has to walk by sight and hearing and tasting and smelling and feeling. To be sure, true Spirit-led worship does not deny the five senses. We see other believers; we sing and hear the hymns; we taste and feel the elements of the Lord's Supper. But these external things are but windows through which faith perceives the eternal. They are not ends in themselves.

The person who depends on religion can measure himself and compare himself with others. This is another fascination to legalism. But the true believer measures himself with Christ, not other Christians (Eph. 4:11ff). There is no room for pride in the spiritual walk of the Christian who lives by grace; but the legalist constantly boasts about his achievements and his converts (Gal. 6:13-14).

Yes, there is a fascination to the Law, but it

is only bait that leads to a trap; and once the believer takes the bait, he finds himself in bondage. Far better to take God at His Word and rest on His grace. We were saved "by grace, through faith" and we must live "by grace, through faith." This is the way to blessing. The other way is the way to bondage.

CHAPTER SIX THE LOGIC OF LAW

Galatians 3:15-29

The Judaizers had Paul in a corner. He had just finished proving from the Old Testament that God's plan of salvation left no room for the works of the Law. But the fact that Paul quoted six times from the Old Testament raised a serious problem: If salvation does not involve the Law, then why was the Law given in the first place? Paul quoted from the Law to prove the insignificance of the Law. If the Law is now set aside, then his very arguments are worthless, because they are taken from the Law.

Our faith is a logical faith and can be defended on rational grounds. While there are divine mysteries in the faith that no man can fully explain, there are also divine reasons that any sincere person can understand. Paul was trained as a Jewish rabbi and was fully equipped to argue his case. In this section, he makes four statements that help us understand the relationship between *promise* and *Law.*

The Law Cannot Change the Promise (Gal. 3:15-18)

The word *promise* is used eight times in these verses, referring to God's promise to Abraham that in him all the nations of the earth would be blessed (Gen. 12:1-3). This promise involved being justified by faith and having all the blessings of salvation (Gal. 3:6-9). It is obvious that the promise to Abraham (and, through Christ, to us today), given about 2000 B.C., preceded by centuries the Law of Moses (about 1450 B.C.). The Judaizers implied that the giving of the Law *changed* that original covenant of promise. Paul argues that it did not.

To begin with, once two parties conclude an agreement, a third party cannot come along years later and change that agreement. The only persons who can change an original agreement are the persons who made it. To add anything to it or take anything from it would be illegal.

If this is true among sinful men, how much more does it apply to the holy God? Note that Abraham did not make a covenant with God; *God made a covenant with Abraham!* God did not lay down any conditions for Abraham to meet. In fact, when the covenant was ratified *Abraham was asleep!* (see Gen. 15) It was a covenant of grace: God made promises to Abraham; Abraham did not make promises to God.

But Paul reveals another wonderful truth: God made this promise, not only to Abraham, but also to Christ. "And to thy Seed, which is Christ" (Gal. 3:16).

The Bible concept of "the seed" goes back to Genesis 3:15, after the Fall of man. God states that there will be a conflict in the world between Satan's seed (children of the devil, see John 8:33-44) and the woman's seed (God's children, and, ultimately, God's Son). The Scriptures show this conflict: Cain versus Abel (see 1 John 3:10-12); Israel versus the nations; John the Baptist and Jesus versus the Pharisees (Matt. 3:7-9; 23:29-33); the true believer versus the counterfeit (see the Parable of the Tares, Matt. 13:24-30, 36-43). Satan's goal in the Old Testament was to keep the Seed (Christ) from being born into the world, for Satan knew that God's Son would one day crush his head.

In the final analysis, God made this covenant of promise with Abraham *through Christ,* so that the only two parties who can make any changes are God the Father and God the Son. *Moses cannot alter this covenant!* He can add nothing to it; he can take nothing from it. The Judaizers wanted to add to God's grace (as though anything could be added to grace!) and take from God's promises. They had no right to do this since they were not parties in the original covenant.

The 430 years of Galatians 3:17 has puzzled Bible students for many years. From Abraham's call (Gen. 12) to Jacob's arrival in Egypt (Gen. 46) is 215 years. (This may be computed as follows: Abraham was 75 years old when God called him and 100 when Isaac was born, Gen. 12:4; 21:5. This gives us 25 years. Isaac was 60 when Jacob was born, Gen. 25:26; and Jacob was 130 years old when he arrived in Egypt, Gen. 47:9. Thus, 25 + 60 + 130 = 215 years.) But Moses tells us that Israel sojourned in Egypt 430 years (Ex. 12:40); so the total number of years from Abraham's call to the giving of the Law is 645 years, not 430. The length of the stay in Egypt is recorded also in Genesis 15:13 and Acts 7:6, where the round figure of 400 years is used.

Several solutions have been offered to this puzzle, but perhaps the most satisfying is this: Paul is counting from the time Jacob went into Egypt, when God appeared to him and *reaffirmed* the covenant (Gen. 46:1-4). The 430 years is the time from God's confirmation of His promise to Jacob until the giving of the Law at Sinai.

Regardless of what solution to the dating question we may choose, the basic argument is clear: a law given centuries later cannot change a covenant made by other parties. But suppose the later revelation, such as the Law of Moses, was greater and more glorious than the earlier? What then? Paul makes a second statement.

The Law Is Not Greater Than the Promise (Gal. 3:19-20)

The account of the giving of the Law is impressive (Ex. 19). There were thunders and lightnings, and the people were trembling with fear. Even Moses was shaking in his sandals (Heb. 12:18-21). It was a dramatic event in comparison with the giving of the covenant to Abraham (Gen. 15), and, of course, the Judaizers were impressed with these emotional externals. But Paul points out that the Law is inferior to the covenant of promise in two ways.

The Law was temporary (v. 19a). "It was added . . . until the Seed should come." Now it is obvious that a temporary law cannot be greater than a permanent covenant. When you read God's covenant with Abraham, you find no "ifs" in His words. Nothing was conditional; all was of grace. But the blessings of the Law were dependent on the meeting of certain conditions. Furthermore, the Law had a terminus point: "until the Seed [Christ] should come." With the death and resurrection of Christ, the Law was done away and now its righteous demands are fulfilled in us through the Spirit (Rom. 7:4; 8:1-4).

The Law required a mediator (vv. 19b-20). When God gave the Law to Israel, He did it by means of angels and through the mediation of Moses. Israel "received the Law by the disposition of angels" (Acts 7:53). This means that the nation received the Law third-hand: from God to angels to Moses. But when God made His covenant with Abraham, He did it personally, without a mediator. God was revealing to Abraham all that He would do for him and his descendants. A mediator stands between two parties and helps them to agree; but there was no need for a mediator in Abraham's case since God was entering into a covenant with him, not Abraham with God. "God is one" (Gal. 3:20), therefore there was no need for a go-between.

The Judaizers were impressed by the *incidentals* of the Law—glory, thunder, lightning, angels, and other externals. But Paul looked beyond incidentals to the *essentials.* The Law was temporary, and required a mediator. The covenant of promise was permanent, and no mediator was required. There could be but one conclusion: the covenant was greater than the Law.

The Law Is Not Contrary to the Promise (Gal. 3:21-26)

You can almost hear the Judaizers shouting the question in Galatians 3:21: "Is the Law then *against* the promises of God?" Is God contradicting Himself? Does His right hand not know what His left hand is doing? As he replies to this question, Paul reveals his deep insight into the ways and purposes of God. He does not say that the Law *contradicts* the promise, but rather that it *cooperates* with the promise in fulfilling the purposes of God. While *Law* and *grace* seem to be contrary to one another, if you go deep enough, you will discover that they actually *complement* one another. Why, then, was the Law given?

The Law was not given to provide life (v. 21). Certainly the Law of Moses regulated the lives of the Jewish people, but it did not and could not provide *spiritual* life to the people. (Gal. 3:21 should be matched with 2:21.) If life and righteousness could have come through the Law, then Jesus Christ would never have died on the cross. But Jesus did die; therefore, the Law could never give the sinner life and righteousness. It was "worship of the Law" that led Israel into a self-righteous religion of works, the result of which was the rejection of Christ (Rom. 9:30–10:13).

The Law was given to reveal sin (vv. 19a, 22). It is here that we see the way that Law and grace cooperate in bringing the lost sinner to Jesus Christ. Law shows the sinner his guilt, and grace shows him the forgiveness he can have in Christ. The Law is "holy, and just, and good" (Rom. 7:12), but we are unholy, unjust, and bad. The Law does not *make* us sinners; it reveals to us that we already *are* sinners (see Rom. 3:20). The Law is a mirror that helps us see our "dirty faces" (James 1:22-25)—*but you do not wash your face with the mirror!* It is grace that provides the cleansing through the blood of Jesus Christ (see 1 John 1:7b).

There is a lawful use of the Law, and there is an unlawful use (1 Tim. 1:8-11). The lawful use is to reveal sin and cause men to see their need of a Saviour. The unlawful use is to try to achieve salvation by the keeping of the Law. When people claim they are saved by "keeping the Ten Commandments," they are revealing their ignorance of the true meaning of the Law. The Law concludes "all [men] under sin" (Gal. 3:22), Jews and Gentiles alike. But since *all* are under sin, then *all* may be saved by grace! God does not have two ways of salvation; He has but one—faith in Jesus Christ.

The Law was given to prepare the way for Christ (vv. 23-26). Here Paul uses an illustration that was familiar to all his readers—the child guardian. In many Roman and Greek households, well-educated slaves took the children to and from school and watched over them during the day. Sometimes they would teach the children, sometimes they would protect and prohibit, and sometimes they would even discipline. This is what Paul means by *schoolmaster* (Gal. 3:24); but please do not read into this word our modern idea of a schoolteacher. The transliteration of the Greek would give us our word *pedagogue,* which literally means "a child conductor."

By using this illustration, Paul is saying several things about the Jews and their Law. First, he is saying that the Jews were not *born* through the Law, but rather were *brought up* by the Law. The slave was not the child's father; he was the child's guardian and disciplinarian. So, the Law did not *give* life to Israel; it *regulated* life. The Judaizers taught that the Law was necessary for life and righteousness, and Paul's argument shows their error.

But the second thing Paul says is even more important: *the work of the guardian was preparation for the child's maturity.* Once the child came of age, he no longer needed the guardian. So the Law was a preparation for the nation of Israel until the coming of the promised Seed, Jesus Christ. The ultimate goal in God's program was His coming (Gal. 3:22), but "before this faith [Christ] came" (Gal. 3:23, NIV), the nation was "imprisoned by the Law" (literal translation).

The Law separated Israel from the Gentile nations (Eph. 2:12-18); it governed every aspect of their lives. During the centuries of Jewish history, the Law was preparing for the coming of Christ. The *demands* of the Law reminded the people that they needed a Saviour. The *types* and *symbols* in the Law were pictures of the coming Messiah (see Luke 24:27).

A good example of this purpose of the Law is in the account of the rich young ruler (Matt. 19:16ff). This young man had everything anybody could desire, but he was not satisfied. He had tried to keep the commandments all his life, but still something was missing. *But these commandments brought him to Christ!* This is one of the purposes of the Law, to create in lost sinners a sense of guilt and need. The sad thing is that the young man was not honest as he looked into the mirror of the Law, for the last commandment ("Thou shalt not covet") escaped him; and he went away without eternal life.

The Law has performed its purpose: the Saviour has come and the "guardian" is no longer needed. It is tragic that the nation of Israel did not recognize their Messiah when He appeared. God finally had to destroy the temple and scatter the nation, so that today it is impossible for a devoted Jew to practice the faith of his fathers. He has no altar, no priesthood, no sacrifice, no temple, no king (Hosea 3:4). All of these have been fulfilled in Christ, so that any man—Jew or Gentile—who trusts Christ becomes a child of God.

The Law cannot change the promise, and the Law is not greater than the promise. But the Law is not contrary to the promise: they work together to bring sinners to the Saviour.

The Law Cannot Do What the Promise Can Do (Gal. 3:27-29)

With the coming of Jesus Christ, the nation of Israel moved out of childhood into adulthood. The long period of preparation was over. While there was a certain amount of glory to the Law, there was a greater glory in the gracious salvation of God as found in Christ. The Law could reveal sin and, to a certain extent, control behavior, but the Law could not do for the sinner what Jesus Christ can do.

To begin with, the Law could never justify the guilty sinner. "I will not justify the wicked," said the Lord (Ex. 23:7); yet Paul states that God "justifies the ungodly" (Rom. 4:5). King Solomon, at the dedication of the temple, reminded God to condemn the wicked and justify the righteous (1 Kings 8:32); and this was a proper request in light of the holiness of God. The trouble is, nobody was righteous! It is only through faith in Jesus Christ that the sinner is justified—declared righteous—before God.

Furthermore, the Law could never give a person a oneness with God; it separated man from God. There was a fence around the tabernacle and a veil between the holy place and the holy of holies.

Faith in Jesus baptizes us "into Christ" (Gal. 3:27). This baptism of the Spirit identifies the believer with Christ and makes him part of His body (1 Cor. 12:12-14). Water baptism is an outward picture of this inner work of the Holy Spirit (see Acts 10:44-48).

The phrase *put on Christ* (Gal. 3:27) refers to a change of garments. The believer has laid aside the dirty garments of sin (Isa. 64:6) and, by faith, received the robes of righteousness in Christ (see Col. 3:8-15). But to the Galatians, this idea of "changing clothes" would have an additional meaning. When the Roman child came of age, he took off the childhood garments and put on the toga of the adult citizen. The believer in Christ is not just a "child of God"; he is also a "son of God" (see Gal. 3:26, where *children* ought to be translated "adult sons"). The believer has an adult status before God—so why go back into the childhood of the Law?

"All one in Christ Jesus"—what a tremendous claim! The Law created differences and distinctions, not only between individuals and nations, but also between various kinds of foods and animals. Jesus Christ came, not to divide, but to unite.

This must have been glorious news for the Galatian Christians, for in their society slaves were considered to be only pieces of property; women were kept confined and disrespected; and Gentiles were constantly sneered at by the Jews.

The Pharisee would pray each morning, "I thank Thee, God, that I am a Jew, not a Gentile; a man, not a woman; and a freeman, and not a slave." Yet all these distinctions are removed "in Christ."

This does not mean that our race, political status, or sex is changed at conversion; but it does mean that these things are of no value or handicap when it comes to our spiritual relationship to God through Christ. The Law perpetuated these distinctions, but God in His grace has declared *all men* to be on the same level that He might have mercy on *all men* (Rom. 11:25-32).

Finally, the Law could never make us heirs of God (Gal. 3:29). God made the promise to "Abraham's Seed" (singular, Gal. 3:16), and that Seed is Christ. If we are "in Christ" by faith, then we too are "Abraham's seed" spiritually speaking. This means we are heirs of the spiritual blessings God promised to Abraham. This does not mean that the material and national blessings promised to Israel are set aside, but that Christians today are enriched spiritually because of God's promise to Abraham (see Rom. 11:13ff).

This section of Galatians is valuable to us as we read the Old Testament Scriptures. It shows us that the spiritual lessons of the Old Testament are not for the Jews only but have application to Christians today (see Rom. 15:4; 1 Cor. 10:11-12). In the Old Testament we have *preparation for Christ;* in the Gospels, the *presentation of Christ;* and in the Acts through Revelation, the *appropriation of Christ.*

Your Christian life ought to take on new wonder and meaning as you realize all that you have in Christ. And all of this is by grace—not by Law! You are an adult son in God's family, an heir of God. Are you drawing on your inheritance? This will be Paul's theme in the next section.

CHAPTER SEVEN
IT'S TIME TO GROW UP!
Galatians 4:1-18

One of the tragedies of legalism is that it gives the appearance of spiritual maturity when, in reality, it leads the believer back into a "second childhood" of Christian experience. The Galatian Christians, like most believers, wanted to grow and go forward for Christ; but they were going about it in the wrong way. Their experience is not too different from that of Christians today who get involved in various legalistic movements, hoping to become better Christians. Their motives may be right, but their methods are wrong.

This is the truth Paul is trying to get across to his beloved converts in Galatia. The Judaizers had bewitched them into thinking that the Law would make them better Christians. Their old nature felt an attraction for the Law because the Law enabled them to *do* things and measure external results. As they measured themselves and their achievements, they felt a sense of accomplishment, and, no doubt, a little bit of pride. They thought they were going forward when actually they were regressing.

Such people are in a situation similar to the airplane passengers who heard their pilot announce: "Our navigator has lost our position, folks, and we have been flying rather aimlessly for over an hour. That's the bad news. But the good news is that we are making very good time."

Paul takes three approaches in this section as he seeks to convince the Galatians that they do not need legalism in order to live the Christian life. They have all they need in Jesus Christ.

He Explains Their Adoption (Gal. 4:1-7)

Among the blessings of the Christian experience is *adoption* (Gal. 4:5; Eph. 1:5). We do not *enter* God's family by adoption, the way a homeless child would enter a loving family in our own society. The only way to get into God's family is by *regeneration,* being "born again" (John 3:3).

The New Testament word for *adoption* means "to place as an adult son." It has to do with our *standing* in the family of God: we are not little children but adult sons with all of the privileges of sonship.

It is unfortunate that many translations of the New Testament do not make a distinction between *children of God* and *sons of God.* We are the children of God by faith in Christ, born into God's family. But every child of God is automatically placed into the family as a *son,* and as a son he has all the legal rights and privileges of a son. When a sinner trusts Christ and is saved, as far as his *condition* is concerned, he is a "spiritual babe" who needs to grow (1 Peter 2:2-3); but as far as his *position* is concerned, he is an adult son who can draw on the Father's wealth and who can exercise all the wonderful privileges of sonship.

We *enter* God's family by regeneration, but we *enjoy* God's family by adoption. The Christian does not have to wait to begin enjoying the spiritual riches he has in Christ. "If a son, then an heir of God through Christ" (Gal. 4:7). Now follows Paul's discussion about adoption. He reminds his readers of three facts.

What we were: children in bondage (vv. 1-3). No matter how wealthy a father may be, his infant son or toddling child cannot really enjoy that wealth. In the Roman world, the children of wealthy people were cared for by slaves. No matter who his father was, the child was still a child, under the supervision of a servant. In fact, the child himself was not much different from the servant who guarded him. The servant was commanded by the master of the house, and the child was commanded by the servant.

This was the spiritual condition of the Jews under the age of the Law. The Law, you recall, was the "guardian" that disciplined the nation and prepared the people for the coming of Christ (Gal. 3:23-25). So, when the Judaizers led the Galatians back into legalism, they were leading them not only into religious bondage, but also into moral and spiritual infancy and immaturity.

Paul states that the Jews were, like little children, in bondage to "the elements of the world." This word *elements* means *the basic principles, the ABCs.* For some fifteen centuries, Israel had been in kindergarten and grade school, learning their "spiritual ABCs," so that they would be ready when Christ would come. Then they would get the full revelation, for Jesus Christ is "the Alpha and the Omega"

(Rev. 22:13); He encompasses *all* the alphabet of God's revelation to man. He is God's last Word (Heb. 1:1-3).

Legalism, then, is not a step toward maturity; it is a step back into childhood. The Law was not God's final revelation; it was but the preparation for that final revelation in Christ. It is important that a person know his ABCs, because they are the foundation for understanding all of the language. But the man who sits in a library and recites the ABCs instead of reading the great literature that is around him, is showing that he is immature and ignorant, not mature and wise. Under the Law, the Jews were children in bondage, not sons enjoying liberty.

What God did: redeemed us (vv. 4-5). The expression *the fullness of the time* (Gal. 4:4) refers to that time when the world was providentially ready for the birth of the Saviour. Historians tell us that the Roman world was in great expectation, waiting for a Deliverer, at the time when Jesus was born. The old religions were dying; the old philosophies were empty and powerless to change men's lives. Strange new mystery religions were invading the empire. Religious bankruptcy and spiritual hunger were everywhere. God was preparing the world for the arrival of His Son.

From the historical point of view, the Roman Empire itself helped prepare the world for the birth of the Saviour. Roads connected city with city, and all cities ultimately with Rome. Roman laws protected the rights of citizens, and Roman soldiers guarded the peace. Thanks to both the Greek and Roman conquests, Latin and Greek were known across the empire. Christ's birth at Bethlehem was not an accident; it was an appointment: Jesus came in "the fullness of the time." (And, it is worth noting, that He will come again when the time is ready.)

Paul is careful to point out the dual nature of Jesus Christ (Gal. 4:4), that He is both God and man. As God, Jesus "came forth" (John 16:28); but as man, He was "made of a woman." The ancient promise said that the Redeemer would be of "the woman's seed" (Gen. 3:15); and Jesus fulfilled that promise (Isa. 7:14; Matt. 1:18-25).

Paul has told us *who* came—God's Son; he has told us *when* He came and *how* He came. Now he explains *why* He came: "to redeem them that were under the Law" (Gal. 4:5). *Redeem* is the same word Paul used earlier (Gal. 3:13); it means "to set free by paying a price." A man could purchase a slave in any Roman city (there were about 60 million slaves in the empire), either to keep the slave for himself or to set him free. Jesus came to set us free. So, to go back into the Law is to undo the very work of Christ on the cross. He did not purchase us to make us slaves, but *sons!* Under Law, the Jews were mere children, but under grace, the believer is a son of God with an adult standing in God's family.

Perhaps at this point a chart will help us understand better the contrast between being a "child of God" and a "son of God."

The Child	*The Son*
by regeneration	by adoption
entering the family	enjoying the family
under guardians	the liberty of an adult
cannot inherit	an heir of the Father

What we are: sons and heirs (vv. 6-7). Once again, the entire Trinity is involved in our spiritual experience: God the Father sent the Son to die for us, and God the Son sent His Spirit to live in us. The contrast here is not between immature children and adult sons, but between *servants* and *sons.* Like the Prodigal Son, the Galatians wanted their Father to accept them as servants, when they really were sons (Luke 15:18-19). The contrasts are easy to see. For example:

The son has the same nature as the father, but the servant does not. When we trust Christ, the Holy Spirit comes to live within us; and this means we are "partakers of the divine nature" (2 Peter 1:4). The Law could never give a person God's nature within. All it could do was reveal to the person his desperate need for God's nature. So, when the believer goes back into Law, he is denying the very divine nature within, and he is giving the old nature (the flesh) opportunity to go to work.

The son has a father, while the servant has a master. No servant could ever say "Father" to his master. When the sinner trusts Christ, he receives the Holy Spirit within, and the Spirit tells him that he is a child of the Father (Rom. 8:15-16). It is natural for a baby to cry, but not for a baby to talk to his father. When the Spirit enters the heart, He says, "Abba, Father" (Gal. 4:6); and, in response, the believer cries, "Abba, Father!" (Rom. 8:15) The word *Abba* is an Aramaic word that is the equivalent of our English word "papa." This shows the closeness of the child to the Father. No servant has this.

The son obeys out of love, while the servant obeys out of fear. The Spirit works in the *heart* of the believer to quicken and increase his love for God. "The fruit of the Spirit is love" (Gal. 5:22). "The love of God is shed abroad in our hearts by the Holy [Spirit]" (Rom. 5:5). The Judaizers told the Galatians that they would become better Christians by submitting to the Law, but the Law can never produce obedience. Only love can do that. "If ye love Me, keep My commandments" (John 14:15).

The son is rich, while the servant is poor. We are both "sons and heirs." And since we are adopted—placed as adult sons in the family—we may begin drawing on our inheritance right now. God has made available to us the riches of His grace (Eph. 1:7; 2:7), the riches of His glory (Phil. 4:19), the riches of His goodness (Rom. 2:4), and the riches of His wisdom (Rom. 11:33ff)—and all of the riches of God are found in Christ (Col. 1:19; 2:3).

The son has a future, while the servant does not. While many kind masters did provide for their slaves in old age, it was not required of them. The father always provides for the son (2 Cor. 12:14).

In one sense, our adoption is not yet final, because we are awaiting the return of Christ and the redemption of our bodies (Rom. 8:23). Some scholars think that this second stage in our adoption corresponds to the Roman practice when a man adopted someone outside his family to be his son. First there was a *private* ceremony at which the son was purchased; then there was a *public* ceremony at which the adoption was declared openly before the officials.

Christians have experienced the first stage: we have been purchased by Christ and indwelt by the Spirit. We are awaiting the second stage: the public declaration at the return of Christ when "we shall be like Him" (1 John 3:1-3). We are "sons and heirs," and the best part of our inheritance is yet to come (see 1 Peter 1:1-5).

He Laments Their Regression (Gal. 4:8-11)

What really happened when the Galatians turned from grace to Law? To begin with, they abandoned liberty for bondage. When they were ignorant sinners, they had served their false gods and had experienced the tragedy of such pagan slavery. But then they had trusted Christ and been delivered from superstition and slavery. Now they were abandoning their liberty in Christ and going back into bondage. They were "dropping out" of the school of grace and enrolling in the kindergarten of Law! They were destroying all the good work the Lord had done in them through Paul's ministry.

The phrase *weak and beggarly elements* tells us the extent of their regression. They were giving up the power of the Gospel for the weakness of Law, and the wealth of the Gospel for the poverty of Law. The Law never made anybody rich or powerful; on the contrary, the Law could only reveal man's weakness and spiritual bankruptcy. No wonder Paul weeps over these believers, as he sees them abandon liberty for bondage, power for weakness, and wealth for poverty.

How were they doing this? By adopting the Old Testament system of religion with its special observations of "days, and months, and times, and years" (Gal. 4:10).

Does this mean that it is wrong for Christians to set aside one day a year to remember the birth of Christ? Or that a special observance of the coming of the Spirit at Pentecost, or the blessing of the harvest in autumn, is a sin?

Not necessarily. If we observe special days like slaves, hoping to gain some spiritual merit, then we are sinning. But if in the observance, we express our liberty in Christ and let the Spirit enrich us with His grace, then the observance can be a spiritual blessing.

The New Testament makes it clear that Christians are not to legislate religious observances for each other (Rom. 14:4-13). We are not to praise the man who celebrates the day, nor are we to condemn the man who does not celebrate. But if a man thinks he is saving his soul, or automatically growing in grace, because of a religious observance, then he is guilty of legalism.

Our evangelical churches have many different kinds of observances, and it is wrong for us to go beyond the Word of God in comparing, criticizing, or condemning. But all of us must beware of that legalistic spirit that caters to the flesh, leads to pride, and makes the outward event a substitute for the inward experience.

He Seeks Their Affection (Gal. 4:12-18)

Paul was a wonderful spiritual father; he knew just how to balance rebuke with love. Now he turns from "spanking" to "embracing" as he reminds the believers of their love for him and his love for them. At one point they were willing to sacrifice anything for Paul, so great was their love; but now he had become their enemy. The Judaizers had come in and stolen their affection.

Bible students wish Paul had been more explicit here, because we are not sure just what events he is talking about. When Paul had originally visited them, he was suffering from some physical affliction. If, as noted in Galatians 1, Paul wrote this letter to the churches of South Galatia, then he is referring to his first missionary journey, recorded in Acts 13–14. Apparently Paul had not intended to visit these cities, but was forced to do so because of some bodily infirmity. We can only speculate as to what this was. Some have suggested malaria; others, an affliction of the eyes (see Gal. 4:15). Whatever it was, it must have made Paul somewhat repulsive in appearance, because he commends the Galatians for the way they received him in spite of the way he looked. To them, he was an angel of God. It is a wonderful thing when people accept God's servants, not because of their outward appearance, but because they represent the Lord and bring His message.

Now Paul asks them: "What has happened to that love? What has happened to the blessedness—the happiness—you experienced when you heard the Gospel and trusted Christ?" Of course, Paul knew what had happened: the Judaizers had come in and stolen their hearts.

One of the marks of a false teacher is that he tries to attract other men's converts to himself, and not simply to the truth of the Word or to the person of Jesus Christ. It was not the Judaizers who originally came to Galatia and led them to Christ; it was Paul. Like the cultists today, these false teachers were not winning lost sinners to Christ, but were stealing converts from those who were truly serving the Lord. Paul had proved to be their loving friend. He had "become as they were" by identifying himself with them (Gal. 4:12). Now they were turning away from Paul and following false shepherds.

Paul told them the truth, but the Judaizers told them lies. Paul sought to glorify Christ, but the Judaizers glorified themselves and their converts. "Those people are zealous to win you over, but for no good. What they want is to alienate you from us, so that you may be zealous for them" (Gal. 4:17, NIV).

A true servant of God does not "use people" to build himself up or his work; he ministers in love to help people know Christ better and glorify Him. Beware of that religious worker who wants your exclusive allegiance because he is the only one who is right. He will use you as long as he can and then drop you for somebody else—and your fall will be a painful one. The task of the spiritual leader is to get people to love and follow Christ, not to promote himself and his ministry.

"Faithful are the wounds of a friend, but the kisses of an enemy are deceitful" (Prov. 27:6). Paul had proved his love to the Galatians by telling them the truth; but they would not accept it. They were enjoying the "kisses" of the Judaizers, not realizing that these kisses were leading them into bondage and sorrow. Christ had made them sons and heirs, but they were rapidly becoming slaves and beggars.

They had not lost the *experience* of salvation—they were still Christians; but they were losing the *enjoyment* of their salvation and finding satisfaction in their works instead. Sad to say, *they did not realize their losses.* They actually thought they were becoming better Christians by substituting Law for grace, and the religious deeds of the flesh for the fruit of the Spirit.

Is *your* Christian life moving forward into liberty or backward into bondage? Think carefully before you answer.

CHAPTER EIGHT
MEET YOUR MOTHER
Galatians 4:19-31

We parents never seem to outgrow our children. "'When they're little, they're a handful; but when they're grown, they're a heartful!" I remember hearing my mother say, "When they're little, they step on your toes; but when they're grown, they step on your heart."

This is what Paul was experiencing as he tried to help the Galatian believers with their confused spiritual lives. When he had first come to them with the Gospel, he had "travailed" spiritually to see them turn to the Lord. But, after all, the Lord Jesus had travailed on the cross to make possible their salvation (Isa. 53:11), and Paul's travail was nothing in comparison. But now the Galatian Christians were falling back into legalism and a "second childhood" experience; and Paul had to travail over them again. He longed to see Christ formed in them, just as we parents long to see our children mature in the will of God.

Since the Judaizers appealed to the Law, Paul accepts their challenge and uses the Law to prove that Christians are not under the Law. He takes the familiar story of Ishmael and Isaac (Gen. 16–21) and draws from it basic truths about the Christian's relationship to the Law of Moses.

The events described actually happened, but Paul uses them as an allegory, which is a narrative that has a deeper meaning behind it. Perhaps the most famous allegory in the English language is John Bunyan's *A Pilgrim's Progress,* in which Bunyan traces Christian's experiences from the City of Destruction to heaven. In an allegory, persons and actions represent hidden meanings, so that the narrative can be read on two levels: the literal and the symbolic.

Paul's use of Genesis in this section does not give us license to find "hidden meanings" in all the events of the Old Testament. If we take that approach to the Bible, we can make it mean almost anything we please. This is the way many false teachings arise. The Holy Spirit inspired Paul to discern the hidden meaning of the Genesis story. We must always interpret the Old Testament in the light of the New Testament, and where the New Testament gives us permission, we may search for hidden meanings. Otherwise, we must accept the plain statements of Scripture and not try to "spiritualize" everything.

The Historical Facts (Gal. 4:19-23)

Perhaps the easiest way to grasp the historical account is to trace briefly Abraham's experiences as recorded in Genesis 12 through 21. Using his age as our guide, we will trace the events on which Paul is basing his argument for Christian liberty.

75—Abraham is called by God to go to Canaan; and God promises him many descendants (Gen. 12:1-9). Both Abraham and his wife, Sarah, wanted children, but Sarah was barren. God was waiting until both of them were "as good as dead" before He would perform the miracle of sending them a son (Rom. 4:16-25).

85—The promised son has not yet arrived, and Sarah becomes impatient. She suggests that Abraham marry Hagar, her maid, and try to have a son by her. This act was legal in that society, but it was not in the will of God. Abraham followed her suggestion and married Hagar (Gen. 16:1-3).

86—Hagar gets pregnant and Sarah gets jealous! Things are so difficult in the home that Sarah throws Hagar out. But the Lord intervenes, sends Hagar back, and promises to take care of her and her son. When Abraham is 86, the son is born, and he calls him Ishmael (Gen. 16:4-16).

99—God speaks to Abraham and promises again that he will have a son by Sarah and says to call his name Isaac. Later, God appears again and reaffirms the promise to Sarah as well (see Gen. 17–18).

100—The son is born (Gen. 21:1-7). They name him Isaac ("laughter") as commanded by God. But the arrival of Isaac creates a new problem in the home: Ishmael has a rival. For fourteen years, Ishmael has been his father's only son, very dear to his heart. How will Ishmael respond to the presence of a rival?

103—It was customary for the Jews to wean their children at about the age of three, and to make a great occasion of it. At the feast, Ishmael starts to mock Isaac (Gen. 21:8ff) and to create trouble in the home. There is only one solution to the problem, and a costly one at that: Hagar and her son have to go. With a broken heart, Abraham sends his son away, because this is what the Lord tells him to do (Gen. 21:9-14).

On the surface, this story appears to be nothing more than a tale of a family problem, but beneath the surface are meanings that carry tremendous spiritual power. Abraham, the two wives, and the two sons represent spiritual realities; and their relationships teach us important lessons.

The Spiritual Truths (Gal. 4:24-29)

Paul now explains the meanings that lie behind these historical events; perhaps they are best classified as shown in the chart at the top of page 710.

Paul begins with the two sons, Ishmael and Isaac (Gal. 4:22-23), and explains that they illustrate our two births: the physical birth that makes us sinners and the spiritual birth that makes us the children of God. As you think about this, and read Genesis 21:1-12, you discover some wonderful spiritual truths about your salvation.

The Old Covenant	*The New Covenant*
Law	Grace
Hagar the slave	Sarah the freewoman
Ishmael, conceived after the flesh	Isaac, conceived miraculously
Earthly Jerusalem in bondage	Heavenly Jerusalem, which is free

Isaac illustrates the believer in several particulars.

He was born by God's power. In fact, God deliberately waited twenty-five years before He granted Abraham and Sarah their son. Isaac was "born after the Spirit" (Gal. 4:29), and, of course, the Christian is "born of the Spirit" (John 3:1-7). Isaac came into the world through Abraham (who represents faith, Gal. 3:9) and Sarah (who represents grace); so that he was born "by grace . . . through faith" as is every true Christian (Eph. 2:8-9).

He brought joy. His name means "laughter," and certainly he brought joy to his aged parents. Salvation is an experience of joy, not only to the believer himself, but also to those around him.

He grew and was weaned (Gen. 21:8). Salvation is the beginning, not the ending. After we are born, we must grow (1 Peter 2:2; 2 Peter 3:18). Along with maturity comes weaning: we must lay aside "childish things" (1 Cor. 13:11). How easy it is for us to hold the "toys" of our earlier Christian days and fail to lay hold of the "tools" of the mature believer. The child does not enjoy being weaned, but he can never become a man until it happens. (Read Ps. 131 at this point.)

He was persecuted (Gen. 21:9). Ishmael (the flesh) caused problems for Isaac, just as our old nature causes problems for us. (Paul will discuss this in detail in Gal. 5:16ff.) Ishmael created no problems in the home until Isaac was born, just as our old nature creates no problems for us until the new nature enters when we trust Christ. In Abraham's home we see the same basic conflicts that we Christians face today:

Hagar versus Sarah = Law versus grace
Ishmael versus Isaac = flesh versus Spirit

It is important to note that *you cannot separate these four factors.* The Judaizers taught that Law made the believer more spiritual, but Paul makes it clear that Law only releases the opposition of the flesh and a conflict within the believer ensues (see Rom. 7:19). There was no Law strong enough either to change or to control Ishmael, *but Isaac never needed any Law.* It has well been said, "The old nature knows no Law and the new nature needs no Law."

Having explained the significance of the two sons, Paul now turns to an explanation of the two wives, Sarah and Hagar. He is illustrating the contrasts between Law and grace and is proving that the believer is not under Law but is under the loving freedom that comes through God's grace. Notice, then, the facts about Hagar that prove that the Law no longer has power over the Christian.

Hagar was Abraham's second wife. God did not *begin* with Hagar; He began with Sarah.

As far as God's dealings with men are concerned, *God began with grace.* In Eden, God provided for Adam and Eve by grace. Even after they sinned, in His grace He provided them with coats of skins for a covering (Gen. 3:21). He did not give them laws to obey as a way of redemption; instead, He gave them a gracious promise to believe: the promise of a victorious Redeemer (Gen. 3:15).

In His relationship with Israel also, God first operated on the basis of grace, not Law. His covenant with Abraham (Gen. 15) was all of grace, because Abraham was in a deep sleep when the covenant was established. When God delivered Israel from Egypt, it was on the basis of grace and not Law, for the Law had not yet been given. Like Hagar, Abraham's second wife, the Law was "added" (Gal. 3:19). Hagar performed a function temporarily, and then moved off the scene, just as the Law performed a special function and then was taken away (Gal. 3:24-25).

Hagar was a slave. Five times in this section she is called a "bondmaid" or "bondwoman" (Gal. 4:22-23, 30-31). Sarah was a freewoman, and therefore her position was one of liberty; but Hagar, even though married to Abraham, was still a servant. Likewise, the Law was given *as a servant.* "Wherefore then serveth the Law?" (Gal. 3:19) It served as a *mirror* to reveal men's sins (Rom. 3:20) and as a *monitor* to control men and ultimately lead them to Christ (Gal. 3:23-25); but the Law was never meant to be *a mother!*

Hagar was not meant to bear a child. Abraham's marriage to Hagar was out of the will of God; it was the result of Sarah's and Abraham's unbelief and impatience. Hagar was trying to do what only Sarah could do, and it failed. The Law cannot give life (Gal. 3:21), or righteousness (Gal. 2:21), or the gift of the Spirit (Gal. 3:2), or a spiritual inheritance (Gal. 3:18). Isaac was born Abraham's heir (Gen. 21:10), but Ishmael could not share in this inheritance. The Judaizers were trying to make Hagar a mother again, while Paul was in spiritual travail for his converts that they might become more like Christ. No amount of religion or legislation can give the dead sinner life. Only Christ can do that through the Gospel.

Hagar gave birth to a slave. Ishmael was "a wild man" (Gen. 16:12), and even though he was a slave, nobody could control him, including his mother. Like Ishmael, the old nature (the flesh) is at war with God, and the Law cannot change or control it. By nature, the Spirit and the flesh are "contrary the one to the other" (Gal. 5:17), and no amount of religious activity is going to change the picture. Whoever chooses Hagar (Law) for his mother is going to experience bondage (Gal. 4:8-11, 22-25, 30-31; 5:1). But whoever chooses Sarah (grace) for his mother is going to enjoy liberty in Christ. God wants His children to be free (Gal. 5:1).

Hagar was cast out. It was Sarah who gave the order: "Cast out this bondwoman and her son" (Gen. 21:9-10), and God subsequently approved it (Gen. 21:12). Ishmael had been in the home for at least seventeen years, but his stay was not to be permanent; eventually he had to be cast out. There was not room in the household for Hagar and Ishmael with Sarah and Isaac; one pair had to go.

It is impossible for Law and grace, the flesh and the Spirit, to compromise and stay together. God did not ask Hagar and Ishmael to make occasional visits to the home; the break was permanent. The Judaizers in Paul's day—and in our own day—are trying to reconcile Sarah and Hagar, and Isaac and Ishmael; such reconciliation is contrary to the Word of God. It is impossible to mix Law and grace, faith and works, God's gift of righteousness and man's attempts to earn righteousness.

Hagar was not married again. God never gave the Law to any other nation or people, including His church. For the Judaizers to impose the Law on the Galatian Christians was to oppose the very plan of God. In Paul's day, the nation of Israel was under bondage to the Law, while the church was enjoying liberty under the gracious rule of the "Jerusalem which is above" (Gal. 4:26). The Judaizers wanted to "wed" Mt. Sinai and the heavenly Mt. Zion (Heb. 12:22), but to do this would be to deny what Jesus did on Mt. Calvary (Gal. 2:21). Hagar is not to be married again.

From the human point of view, it might seem cruel that God should command Abraham to send away his own son Ishmael, whom he loved very much. But it was the only solution to the problem, for "the wild man" could never live with the child of promise. In a deeper sense, however, think of what it cost God when He gave His Son to bear the curse of the Law to set us free. Abraham's broken heart meant Isaac's liberty; God's giving of His Son means our liberty in Christ.

The Practical Blessings (Gal. 4:30-31)

We Christians, like Isaac, are the children of promise by grace. The covenant of grace, pictured by Sarah, is our spiritual mother. The Law and the old nature (Hagar and Ishmael) want to persecute us and bring us into bondage. How are we to solve this problem?

We can try to change them. This must fail, for we cannot change either the Law or the old nature. "That which is born of the flesh is flesh" (John 3:6), and, we might add, *it always will be flesh.* God did not try to change Ishmael and Hagar, either by force or by education; neither can you and I change the old nature and the Law.

We can try to compromise with them. This did not work in Abraham's home, and neither will it work in our lives. The Galatians were trying to effect such a compromise, but it was only leading them gradually into bondage. False teachers today tell us, "Don't abandon Christ; simply move into a deeper Christian life by practicing the Law along with your faith in Christ." Invite Hagar and Ishmael back home again. But this is a path back into slavery: "How turn ye again to the weak and beggarly elements, whereunto ye desire again to be in bondage?" (Gal. 4:9)

We can cast them out. This is what we are supposed to do. First, Paul applies this to the nation of Israel (Gal. 4:25-27); then he applies it to the individual Christian. The nation of Israel had been in bondage under the Law, but this was a temporary thing, preparing them for the coming of Christ. Now that Christ had come, Law had to go. Jesus Christ, like Isaac, was a child of promise, born by the miraculous power of God. Once He had come and died for the people, the Law had to go.

Paul quotes Isaiah 54:1, applying his words to Sarah who was barren before the birth of Isaac; but also applying it to the church (Gal. 4:27). Note the contrasts.

Israel	*The Church*
earthly Jerusalem	heavenly Jerusalem
bondage	freedom
barren legalism	fruitful grace

Sarah had been barren, and she tried to become fruitful by having Abraham marry Hagar. This failed and brought only trouble. *The Law cannot give life or fruitfulness; legalism is barren.* For the early church to go back into bondage would mean barrenness and disobedience to the Word of God. Because it held fast to grace, the church spread across the world in fruitfulness.

But individual churches and Christians can make the same mistake the Galatians were making: they can fail to cast out Hagar and Ishmael. *Legalism* is one of the major problems among Christians today. We must keep in mind that *legalism* does not mean the setting of spiritual standards; it means worshiping these standards and thinking that we are spiritual because we obey them. It also means judging other believers on the basis of these standards. A person can refrain from smoking, drinking, and attending theaters, for example, *and still not be spiritual.* The Pharisees had high standards; yet they crucified Jesus.

The old nature loves legalism, because it gives the old nature a chance to "look good." It costs very little for Ishmael not to do certain bad things, or to do certain religious deeds, just so long as he can remain Ishmael. For seventeen years Ishmael caused no trouble in the home; and then Isaac came along, and there was conflict. Legalism caters to Ishmael. The Christian who claims to be spiritual because of what he doesn't do is only fooling himself. It takes more than negations to make a positive, fruitful spiritual life.

No doubt the Judaizers were attractive people. They carried credentials from religious authorities (2 Cor. 3:1). They had high standards and were careful in what they ate and drank. They were effective in making converts and liked to advertise their accomplishments (Gal. 4:17-18; 6:12-14). They had rules and standards to cover every area of life, making it easy for their followers to know who was "spiritual" and who was not. But the Judaizers were leading the people into bondage and defeat, not liberty and victory, *and the people did not know the difference.*

In the closing chapters of this letter, Paul will point out the greatest tragedy of legalism: it gives opportunity for the flesh to work. The old nature cannot be controlled by Law; eventually it has to break out—and when it does, watch out! This explains why legalistic religious groups often have fights and divisions ("ye fight and devour one another," Gal. 5:15), and often are plagued with the defiling sins of the flesh (Gal. 5:19ff). While every church has its share of these problems, it is especially prominent in those groups where there is an atmosphere of legalism. When you invite Hagar and Ishmael to live with Sarah and Isaac, you are inviting trouble.

Thank God, the Christian is set free from the curse of the Law and the control of the Law. "Cast out the bondwoman and her son." It may pain us deeply, as it did Abraham; but it must be done. To attempt to mix Law and grace is to attempt the impossible. It makes for a frustrated, barren Christian life. But to live by grace, through faith, gives one a free and fulfilling Christian life.

What is the secret? The Holy Spirit. And it is this secret that Paul will share in the closing "practical" chapters of the letter. Meanwhile, you and I need to beware lest Ishmael and Hagar have crept back into our lives. If they have—let us cast them out.

CHAPTER NINE
STOP! THIEF!
Galatians 5:1-12

"Paul's doctrine of grace is dangerous!" cried the Judaizers. "It replaces Law with license. Why, if we do away with our rules and abandon our high standards, the churches will fall apart."

First-century Judaizers are not the only ones afraid to depend on God's grace. Legalists in our churches today warn that we dare not teach people about the liberty we have in Christ lest it result in religious anarchy. These people misunderstand Paul's teaching about grace, and it is to correct such misunderstanding that Paul wrote the final section of his letter (Gal. 5–6).

Paul turns now from argument to application, from the doctrinal to the practical. The Christian who lives by faith is not going to become a rebel. Quite the contrary, he is going to experience the *inner discipline* of God that is far better than the outer discipline of man-made rules. No man could become a rebel who depends on God's grace, yields to God's Spirit, lives for others, and seeks to glorify God. The *legalist* is the one who eventually rebels, because he is living in bondage, depending on the flesh, living for self, and seeking the praise of men and not the glory of God.

No, Paul's doctrine of Christian liberty through grace is not the dangerous doctrine. It is *legalism* that is the dangerous doctrine, because *legalism* attempts to do the impossible: change the old nature and make it obey the Laws of God. Legalism succeeds for a short time, and then the flesh begins to rebel. The surrendered Christian who depends on the power of the Spirit is not *denying* the Law of God, or rebelling against it. Rather, that Law is *being fulfilled in him* through the Spirit (Rom. 8:1-4). It is easy to see the sequence of thought in these closing chapters:

1. I have been set free by Christ. I am no longer under bondage to the Law (Gal. 5:1-12).
2. But I need something—Someone—to control my life from within. That Someone is the Holy Spirit (Gal. 5:13-26).
3. Through the Spirit's love, I have a desire to live for others, not for self (Gal. 6:1-10).
4. This life of liberty is so wonderful, I want to live it to the glory of God; for He is the One making it possible (Gal. 6:11-18).

Now, contrast this with the experience of the person who chooses to live under Law, under the discipline of some religious leader.

1. If I obey these rules, I will become a more spiritual person. I am a great admirer of this religious leader, so I now submit myself to his system.
2. I believe I have the strength to obey and improve myself. I do what I am told, and measure up to the standards set for me.
3. I'm making progress. I don't do some of the things I used to do. Other people compliment me on my obedience and discipline. I can see that I am better than others in my fellowship. How wonderful to be so spiritual.
4. If only others were like me! God is certainly fortunate that I am His. I have a desire to share this with others so they can be as I am. Our group is growing and we have a fine reputation. Too bad other groups are not as spiritual as we are.

No matter how you look at it, legalism is an insidious, dangerous enemy. *When you abandon grace for Law, you always lose.* In this first section (Gal. 5:1-12), Paul explains what the believer loses when he turns from God's grace to man-made rules and regulations.

The Slave—You Lose Your Liberty (Gal. 5:1)

Paul has used two comparisons to show his readers what the Law is really like: a schoolmaster or guardian (Gal. 3:24; 4:2), and a bondwoman (Gal. 4:22ff). Now he compares it to a yoke of slavery. You will recall that Peter used this same image at the famous Conference in Jerusalem (see Acts 15:10).

The image of the yoke is not difficult to understand. It usually represents slavery, service, and control by someone else over your life; it may also represent willing service and submission to someone else. When God delivered Israel from Egyptian servitude, it was the breaking of a yoke (Lev. 26:13). The farmer uses the yoke to control and guide his oxen, because they would not willingly serve if they were free.

When the believers in Galatia trusted Christ, they lost the yoke of servitude to sin and put on the yoke of Christ (Matt. 11:28-30). The yoke of religion is hard, and the burdens heavy; Christ's yoke is "easy" and His burden is "light." That word *easy* in the Greek means "kind, gracious." The yoke of Christ *frees* us to fulfill His will, while the yoke of the Law *enslaves* us. The unsaved person wears a yoke of sin (Lam. 1:14); the religious legalist wears the yoke of bondage (Gal. 5:1); but the Christian who depends on God's grace wears the liberating yoke of Christ.

It is Christ who has made us free from the bondage of the Law. He freed us from the curse of the Law by dying for us on the tree (Gal. 3:13). The believer is no longer under Law; he is under grace (Rom. 6:14). This does not mean that we are outlaws and rebels. It simply means that we no longer need the *external* force of Law to keep us in God's will, because we have the *internal* leading of the Holy Spirit of God (Rom. 8:1-4). Christ died to set us free, not to make us slaves. To go back to Law is to become entangled in a maze of "do's and don'ts" and to abandon spiritual adulthood for a "second childhood."

Sad to say, there are some people who feel very insecure with liberty. They would rather be under the tyranny of some leader than to make their own decisions freely. There are some believers who are frightened by the liberty they have in God's grace; so they seek out a fellowship that is legalistic and dictatorial, where they can let others make their decisions for them. This is comparable to an adult climbing back into the crib. The way of Christian liberty is the way of fulfillment in Christ. No wonder Paul issues that ultimatum: "Do not be entangled again in the yoke of bondage. Take your stand for liberty."

The Debtor—You Lose Your Wealth (Gal. 5:2-6)

Paul uses three phrases to describe the losses the Christian incurs when he turns from grace to Law: "Christ shall profit you nothing" (Gal. 5:2); "a debtor to do the whole Law" (Gal. 5:3); "Christ is become of no effect unto you" (Gal. 5:4). This leads to the sad conclusion in Galatians 5:4: "Ye are fallen from grace." It is bad enough that legalism robs the believer of his liberty, but it also robs him of his spiritual wealth in Christ. The believer living under Law becomes a bankrupt slave.

God's Word teaches that when we were unsaved, we owed God a debt we could not pay. Jesus makes this clear in His Parable of the Two Debtors (Luke 7:36-50). Two men owed money to a creditor, the one owing ten times as much as the other. But neither was able to pay, so the creditor "graciously forgave them both" (literal translation). No matter how much morality a man may have, he still comes short of the glory of God. Even if his sin debt is one tenth that of others, he stands unable to pay, bankrupt at the judgment bar of God. God in His grace, because of the work of Christ on the cross, is able to forgive sinners, no matter how large their debt may be.

Thus when we trust Christ, *we become spiritually rich.* We now share in the riches of God's grace (Eph. 1:7), the riches of His glory (Eph. 1:18; Phil. 4:19), the riches of His wisdom (Rom. 11:33), and the "unsearchable riches of Christ" (Eph. 3:8). In Christ we have "all the treasures of wisdom and knowledge" (Col. 2:3), and we are "complete in Him" (Col. 2:10). Once a person is "in Christ," he has all that he needs to live the kind of Christian life God wants him to live.

The Judaizers, however, want us to believe that we are "missing something," that we would be more "spiritual" if we practiced the Law with its demands and disciplines. But Paul makes it clear that *the Law adds nothing—because nothing can be added!* Instead, the Law comes in as a thief and robs the believer of the spiritual riches he has in Christ. It puts him back into bankruptcy, responsible for a debt he is unable to pay.

To live by grace means to depend on God's abundant supply of every need. To live by Law means to depend on my own strength—the flesh—and be left to get by without God's supply. Paul warns the Galatians that to submit to circumcision in these circumstances would rob them of all the benefits they have in Christ (though circumcision itself is an indifferent matter—Gal. 5:6; 6:15). Furthermore, to submit would put them under obligation to obey *the whole Law.*

It is at this point that legalists reveal their hypocrisy, for they fail to keep the *whole* Law. They look on the Old Testament Law the way a customer surveys the food in a cafeteria: they choose what they want and leave the rest. But this is not honest. To teach that a Christian today should, for example, keep the Sabbath but not the Passover, is to dismember God's Law. The same Lawgiver who gave the one commandment also gave the other (James 2:9-11). Earlier, Paul had quoted Moses to prove that the curse of the Law is on everyone who fails to keep *all* the Law (Gal. 3:10; see Deut. 27:26).

Imagine a motorist driving down a city street and deliberately driving through a red light. He is pulled over by a policeman who asks to see his driver's license. Immediately the driver begins to defend himself. "Officer, I know I ran that red light—but I have never robbed anybody. I've never committed adultery. I've never cheated on my income tax."

The policeman smiles as he writes out the ticket, because he knows that *no amount of obedience can make up for one act of disobedience.* It is one Law, and the same Law that protects the obedient man punishes the offender. To boast about keeping part of the Law while at the same time breaking another part is to confess that I am worthy of punishment.

Now we can better understand what Paul

means by "fallen from grace" (Gal. 5:4). Certainly he is not suggesting that the Galatians had "lost their salvation," because throughout this letter he deals with them *as believers.* At least nine times he calls them *brethren,* and he also uses the pronoun *we* (Gal. 4:28, 31). This Paul would never do if his readers were lost. He boldly states, "And because ye are sons, God hath sent forth the Spirit of His Son into your hearts, crying, 'Abba, Father' " (Gal. 4:6). If his readers were unsaved, Paul could never write those words.

No, to be "fallen from grace" does not mean to lose salvation. Rather, it means "fallen out of the sphere of God's grace." You cannot mix grace and Law. If you decide to live in the sphere of Law, then you cannot live in the sphere of grace. The believers in Galatia had been *bewitched* by the false teachers (Gal. 3:1) and thus were *disobeying* the truth. They had *removed* toward another gospel (Gal. 1:6-9), and had *turned back* to the elementary things of the old religion (Gal. 4:9). As a result, they had become *entangled* with the yoke of bondage, and this led to their present position: "fallen from grace." And the tragedy of this fall is that they had robbed themselves of all the good things Jesus Christ could do for them.

Paul next presents the life of the believer in the sphere of grace (Gal. 5:5-6). This enables us to contrast the two ways of life. When you live by grace, you depend on the power of the Spirit; but under Law, you must depend on yourself and your own efforts. Faith is not dead; faith *works* (see James 2:14-26). But the efforts of the flesh can never accomplish what faith can accomplish through the Spirit. And faith works *through love*—love for God and love for others. Unfortunately, flesh does not manufacture love; too often it produces selfishness and rivalry (see Gal. 5:15). No wonder Paul pictures the life of legalism as a fall!

When the believer walks by faith, depending on the Spirit of God, he lives in the sphere of God's grace; and all his needs are provided. He experiences the riches of God's grace. And, he always has something to look forward to (Gal. 5:5): one day Jesus shall return to make us like Himself in perfect righteousness. The Law gives no promise for perfect righteousness in the future. The Law prepared the way for the first coming of Christ (Gal. 3:23–4:7), but it cannot prepare the way for the second coming of Christ.

So, the believer who chooses legalism robs himself of spiritual liberty and spiritual wealth. He deliberately puts himself into bondage and bankruptcy.

The Runner—You Lose Your Direction (Gal. 5:7-12)

Paul was fond of athletic illustrations and used them often in his letters. His readers were familiar with the Olympic games as well as other Greek athletic contests that always included foot races. It is important to note that Paul never uses the image of the race to tell people how to be saved. He is always talking to Christians about how to live the Christian life. *A contestant in the Greek games had to be a citizen before he could compete.* We become citizens of heaven through faith in Christ; then the Lord puts us on our course and we run to win the prize (see Phil. 3:12-21). We do not run to be saved; we run because we are already saved and want to fulfill God's will in our lives (Acts 20:24).

"You did run well." When Paul first came to them, they received him "as an angel of God" (Gal. 4:14). They accepted the Word, trusted the Lord Jesus Christ, and received the Holy Spirit. They had a deep joy that was evident to all, and were willing to make any sacrifice to accommodate Paul (Gal. 4:15). But now, Paul was their enemy. What had happened?

A literal translation of Galatians 5:7 gives us the answer: "You were running well. Who cut in on you so that you stopped obeying the truth?" In the races, each runner was to stay in his assigned lane, but some runners would cut in on their competitors to try to get them off course. This is what the Judaizers had done to the Galatian believers: they cut in on them and forced them to change direction and go on a "spiritual detour." It was not God who did this, because He had called them to run faithfully in the lane marked "Grace."

His explanation changes the figure of speech from athletics to cooking, for Paul introduces the idea of yeast (leaven). In the Old Testament, leaven is generally pictured as a symbol of evil. During Passover, for example, no yeast was allowed in the house (Ex. 12:15-19; 13:7). Worshipers were not permitted to mingle leaven with sacrifices (Ex. 34:25), though there were some exceptions to this rule. Jesus used leaven as a picture of sin when He warned against the "leaven of the Pharisees" (Matt. 16:6-12); and Paul used leaven as a symbol of sin in the church at Corinth (1 Cor. 5).

Yeast is really a good illustration of sin: it is small, but if left alone it grows and permeates the whole. The false doctrine of the Judaizers was introduced to the Galatian churches in a small way, but, before long, the "yeast" grew and eventually took over.

The spirit of legalism does not suddenly overpower a church. Like leaven, it is introduced secretly, it grows, and before long poisons the whole assembly. In most cases, the *motives* that encourage legalism are good ("We want to have a more spiritual church"), but the *methods* are not scriptural.

It is not wrong to have standards in a church, but we should never think that the standards will make anybody spiritual, or that the keeping of the standards is an evidence of spirituality. How easy it is for the yeast to grow. Before long, we become proud of our spirituality ("puffed up" is the way Paul puts it, 1 Cor. 5:2, and that is exactly what yeast does: it puffs up), and then critical of everybody else's lack of spirituality. This, of course, only feeds the flesh and grieves the Spirit, but we go on our way thinking we are glorifying God.

Every Christian has the responsibility to watch for the *beginnings* of legalism, that first bit of yeast that infects the fellowship and eventually grows into a serious problem. No wonder Paul is so vehement as he denounces the false teachers: "I am suffering persecution because I preach the Cross, but these false teachers are popular celebrities because they preach a religion that pampers the flesh and feeds the ego. Do they want to circumcise you? I wish that they themselves were *cut off!*" (Gal. 5:11-12, literal translation)

Since the death and resurrection of Christ, there is no spiritual value to circumcision; it is only a physical operation. Paul wished that the false teachers would *operate on themselves*—"castrate themselves"—so that they could not produce any more "children of slavery."

The believer who lives in the sphere of God's grace is free, rich, and running in the lane that leads to reward and fulfillment. The believer who abandons grace for Law is a slave, a pauper, and a runner on a detour. In short, he is a loser. And the only way to become a winner is to "purge out the leaven," the false doctrine that mixes Law and grace, and yield to the Spirit of God.

God's grace is sufficient for every demand of life. We are saved by grace (Eph. 2:8-10), and we serve by grace (1 Cor. 15:9-10). Grace enables us to endure suffering (2 Cor. 12:9). It is grace that strengthens us (2 Tim. 2:1), so that we can be victorious soldiers. Our God is the God of *all* grace (1 Peter 5:10). We can come to the throne of grace and find grace to help in every need (Heb. 4:16). As we read the Bible, which is "the Word of His grace" (Acts 20:32), the Spirit of grace (Heb. 10:29) reveals to us how rich we are in Christ.

"And of His fullness have all we received, and grace for grace" (John 1:16).

How rich we are!

CHAPTER TEN
THE FIFTH FREEDOM
Galatians 5:13-26

At the close of an important speech to Congress on January 6, 1941, President Franklin D. Roosevelt shared his vision of the kind of world he wanted to see after the war was over. He envisioned four basic freedoms enjoyed by all people: freedom of speech, freedom of worship, freedom from want, and freedom from fear. To some degree, these freedoms have been achieved on a wider scale than in 1941, but our world still needs another freedom, a fifth freedom. Man needs to be free from himself and the tyranny of his sinful nature.

The legalists thought they had the answer to the problem in laws and threats, but Paul has explained that no amount of legislation can change man's basic sinful nature. It is not law on the *outside,* but love on the *inside* that makes the difference. We need another power within, and that power comes from the Holy Spirit of God.

There are at least fourteen references to the Holy Spirit in Galatians. When we believe on Christ, the Spirit comes to dwell within us (Gal. 3:2). We are "born after the Spirit" as was Isaac (Gal. 4:29). It is the Holy Spirit in the heart who gives assurance of salvation (Gal. 4:6); and it is the Holy Spirit who enables us to live for Christ and glorify Him. The Holy Spirit is not simply a "divine influence"; He is a divine Person, just as are the Father and the Son. What God the Father *planned* for you, and God the Son *purchased* for you on the cross, God the Spirit *personalizes* for you and applies to your life as you yield to Him.

This paragraph is perhaps the most crucial in the entire closing section of Galatians; for in it Paul explains three ministries of the Holy Spirit that enable the believer to enjoy liberty in Christ.

The Spirit Enables Us to Fulfill the Law of Love (Gal. 5:13-15)

We are prone to go to extremes. One believer interprets *liberty* as *license* and thinks he can do whatever he wants to do. Another believer, seeing this error, goes to an opposite extreme and imposes Law on everybody. Somewhere between *license* on the one hand and *legalism* on the other hand is true Christian liberty.

So, Paul begins by explaining *our calling:* we are called to liberty. The Christian is a free man. He is free from the *guilt* of sin because he has experienced God's forgiveness. He is free from the *penalty* of sin because Christ died for him on the cross. And he is, through the Spirit, free from the *power* of sin in his daily life. He is also free from the *Law* with its demands and threats. Christ bore the curse of the Law and ended its tyranny once and for all. We are "called unto liberty" because we are "called into the grace of Christ" (Gal. 1:6). *Grace* and *liberty* go together.

Having explained our calling, Paul then issues *a caution:* "Don't allow your liberty to degenerate into license!"

This, of course, is the fear of all people who do not understand the true meaning of the grace of God. "If you do away with rules and regulations," they say, "you will create chaos and anarchy."

Of course, that danger is real, not because God's grace fails, but because men fail of the grace of God (Heb. 12:15). If there is a "true grace of God" (1 Peter 5:12), then there is also a *false* grace of God; and there are false teachers who "change the grace of our God into a license for immorality" (Jude 4, NIV). So, Paul's caution is a valid one. Christian liberty is not a license to sin but an opportunity to serve.

This leads to *a commandment:* "By love serve one another" (Gal. 5:13). The key word, of course, is *love.* The formula looks something like this:

liberty + love = service to others
liberty — love = license (slavery to sin)

"I have an extra day off this week," Carl told his wife as he walked into the kitchen. "I think I'll use it to fix Donna's bike and then take Larry on that museum trip he's been talking about."

"Fixing a bike and visiting a museum hardly sound like exciting ways to spend a day off," his wife replied.

"It's exciting *if you love your kids!*"

The amazing thing about love is that it takes the place of all the laws God ever gave. "Thou shalt love thy neighbor as thyself" solves every problem in human relations (see Rom. 13:8-14). If you love people (because you love Christ), you will not steal from them, lie about them, envy them, or try in any way to hurt them. Love in the heart is God's substitute for laws and threats.

When our children were small, we lived next to a busy highway, and the children knew they would be spanked if they went near the road. As they grew older, they discovered that obedience brought rewards. They learned to obey not only to escape pain but to gain pleasure. Today they live in different metropolitan areas and all of them drive. But we neither threaten nor bribe them in order to keep them safe. They have a built-in discipline of love that regulates their lives, and they would not deliberately hurt themselves, their parents, or other people. Love has replaced law.

On a much higher level, the Holy Spirit within gives us the love that we need (Rom. 5:5; Gal. 5:6, 22). Apparently the Galatian believers were lacking in this kind of love because they were "biting and devouring one another" and were in danger of destroying one another (Gal. 5:15). The picture here is of wild animals attacking each other. This in itself is proof that law cannot force people to get along with each other. No matter how many rules or standards a church may adopt, they are no guarantee of spirituality. Unless the Holy Spirit of God is permitted to fill hearts with His love, selfishness and competition will reign. Both extremes in the Galatian churches —the legalists and the libertines—were actually destroying the fellowship.

The Holy Spirit does not work in a vacuum. He uses the Word of God, prayer, worship, and the fellowship of believers to build us up in Christ. The believer who spends time daily in the Word and prayer, and who yields to the Spirit's working, is going to enjoy liberty and will help build up the church. Read 2 Corinthians 3 for Paul's explanation of the difference between a spiritual ministry of grace and a carnal ministry of Law.

The Spirit Enables Us to Overcome the Flesh (Gal. 5:16-21, 24)

The conflict (vv. 16-17). Just as Isaac and Ishmael were unable to get along, so the Spirit and the flesh (the old nature) are at war with each other. By "the flesh," of course, Paul does not mean "the body." The human body is not sinful; it is neutral. If the Holy Spirit controls the body, then we walk in the Spirit; but if the flesh controls the body, then we walk in the lusts (desires) of the flesh. The Spirit and the flesh have different appetites, and this is what creates the conflict.

These opposite appetites are illustrated in the Bible in different ways. For example, the sheep is a clean animal and avoids garbage, while the pig is an unclean animal and enjoys wallowing in filth (2 Peter 2:19-22). After the rain ceased and the ark settled, Noah released a raven which never came back (Gen. 8:6-7). The raven is a carrion-eating bird and found plenty to feed on. But when Noah released the dove (a clean bird), it came back (Gen. 8:8-12). The last time he released the dove and it did not return, he knew that it had found a clean place to settle down; therefore the waters had receded.

Our old nature is like the pig and the raven, always looking for something unclean on which to feed. Our new nature is like the sheep and the dove, yearning for that which is clean and holy. No wonder a struggle goes on within the life of the believer! The unsaved man knows nothing of this battle because he does not have the Holy Spirit (Rom. 8:9).

Note that the Christian cannot simply *will* to overcome the flesh: "These two are opposed to each other, so that you cannot do anything you please" (Gal. 5:17, WMS). It is this very problem that Paul discusses in Romans: "I do not know what I am doing. For what I want to do I do not do, but what I hate I do. . . . For what I do is not the good I want to do; no, the evil I do not want to do—this I keep on doing" (Rom. 7:15, 19, NIV). Paul is not denying that there is victory. He is simply pointing out that we cannot win this victory in our own strength and by our own will.

The conquest (v. 18). The solution is not to pit our will against the flesh, but to surrender our will to the Holy Spirit. This verse literally means, "But if you are *willingly led* by the Spirit, then you are not under the Law." The Holy Spirit writes God's Law on our hearts (Heb. 10:14-17; see 2 Cor. 3) so that we *desire* to obey Him in love. "I delight to do Thy will, O my God: yea, Thy Law is within my heart" (Ps. 40:8). Being "'led of the Spirit" and "walking in the Spirit" are the opposites of yielding to the desires of the flesh.

The crucifixion (vv. 19-21, 24). Paul now lists some of the ugly "works of the flesh." (You will find similar lists in Mark 7:20-23; Rom. 1:29-32; 1 Tim. 1:9-10; 2 Tim. 3:2-5.) The flesh is able to manufacture sin but it can never produce the righteousness of God. "The heart is deceitful above all things, and desperately wicked" (Jer. 17:9). This list in Galatians can be divided into three major categories:

The sensual sins (vv. 19, 21b). Adultery is illicit sex between married people, while *fornication* generally refers to the same sin among unmarried people. *Uncleanness* means just that: a filthiness of heart and mind that makes the person defiled. The unclean person sees dirt in everything (see Titus 1:15). *Lasciviousness* is close to our word debauchery. It speaks of a wanton appetite that knows no shame. It goes without saying that all of these sins were rampant in the Roman Empire. *Drunkenness* and *revellings* (orgies) need no explanation.

The superstitious sins (v. 20a). Idolatry, like the sins named above, is with us today. Idolatry is simply putting things ahead of God and people. We are to worship God, love people, and use things, but too often we use people, love self, and worship things, leaving God out of the picture completely. Jesus tells us that whatever we worship, we serve (Matt. 4:10). The Christian who devotes more of himself to his car, house, or boat than he does to serving Christ may be in danger of idolatry (Col. 3:5).

The word *witchcraft* is from the Greek word *pharmakeia,* which means "the use of drugs." Our English word *pharmacy* is derived from this word. Magicians in Paul's day often used drugs to bring about their evil effects. Of course, sorcery is forbidden in the Bible as are all activities of the occult (Deut. 18:9-22).

The social sins (vv. 20b-21a). Hatred means "enmity," the attitude of mind that defies and challenges others. This attitude leads to variance, which is strife, the outworking of enmity. *Emulations* means jealousies or rivalries. How tragic when Christians compete with one another and try to make one another look bad in the eyes of others. *Wrath* means outbursts of anger, and *strife* carries with it the idea of "self-seeking, selfish ambition," that creates divisions in the church.

Seditions and *heresies* are kindred terms. The first suggests division, and the second cliques caused by a party spirit. *Divisions and factions* would be a fair translation. These are the result of church leaders promoting themselves and insisting that the people follow them, not the Lord. (The word *heresy* in the Greek means "to make a choice.") *Envyings* suggests the carrying of grudges, the deep desire for what another has (see Prov. 14:30). *Murders* and *drunkenness* need no elucidation.

The person who *practices* these sins shall not inherit the kingdom of God. Paul is not talking about an *act* of sin, but a *habit* of sin. There is a false assurance of salvation that is not based on the Word of God. The fact that the believer is not under Law, but under grace, is no excuse for sin (Rom. 6:15). If anything, it is an encouragement to live in obedience to the Lord.

But how does the believer handle the old nature when it is capable of producing such horrible sins? The Law cannot *change* or *control* the old nature.

The old nature must be crucified (v. 24). Paul explains that the believer is identified with Christ in His death, burial, and resurrection (Rom. 6). Christ not only died *for* me, but *I died with Christ.* Christ died for me to remove the *penalty* of my sin, but I died with Christ to break sin's *power.*

Paul has mentioned this already in Galatians (see 2:19-20), and he will mention it again (6:14). He does not tell *us* to crucify ourselves, because this is impossible. (Crucifixion is one death a man cannot inflict on himself.) He tells us that the flesh has already been crucified. It is our responsibility to *believe* this and *act on it.* (Paul calls this "reckoning" in Rom. 6; you have the same truth presented in Col. 3:5ff).

You and I are not debtors to the flesh, but to the Spirit (Rom. 8:12-14). We must accept what God says about the old nature and not try to make it something that it is not. We must not make "provision for the flesh" (Rom. 13:14) by feeding it the things that it enjoys. In the flesh dwells no good thing (Rom. 7:18), so we should put no confidence in the flesh (Phil. 3:3). The flesh is not subject to God's Law (Rom. 8:7) and it cannot please God (Rom. 8:8). Only through the Holy Spirit can we "put to death" the deeds that the flesh would do through our body (Rom. 8:13). The Holy Spirit is not only the Spirit of life (Rom. 8:2; Gal. 5:25), but He is also the Spirit of death: He helps us to reckon ourselves dead to sin.

We have seen two ministries of the Spirit of God: He enables us to fulfill the Law, and He enables us to overcome the flesh. He has a third ministry as well.

The Spirit Enables Us to Produce Fruit (Gal. 5:22-23, 25-26)

It is one thing to overcome the flesh and *not do* evil things, but quite something else *to do* good things. The legalist might be able to boast that he is not guilty of adultery or murder (but see Matt. 5:21-32), but can anyone see the beautiful graces of the Spirit in his life? Negative goodness is not enough in a life; there must be positive qualities as well.

The contrast between *works* and *fruit* is important. A machine in a factory *works,* and turns out a product, but it could never manufacture fruit. Fruit must grow out of life, and, in the case of the believer, it is the life of the Spirit (Gal. 5:25). When you think of "works" you think of effort, labor, strain, and toil; when you think of "fruit" you think of beauty, quietness, the unfolding of life. The flesh produces "dead works" (Heb. 9:14), but the Spirit produces living fruit. And this fruit has in it the seed for still more fruit (Gen. 1:11). Love begets more love! Joy helps to produce more joy! Jesus is concerned that we produce "fruit . . . more fruit . . . much fruit" (John 15:2, 5), because this is the way we glorify Him. The old nature cannot produce fruit; only the new nature can do that.

The New Testament speaks of several different kinds of "fruit": people won to Christ (Rom. 1:13), holy living (Rom. 6:22), gifts brought to God (Rom. 15:26-28), good works (Col. 1:10), and praise (Heb. 13:15). The "fruit of the Spirit" listed in our passage has to do with *character* (Gal. 5:22-23). It is important that we distinguish the *gift* of the Spirit, which is salvation (Acts 2:38; 11:17), and the *gifts* of the Spirit, which have to do with service (1 Cor. 12), from the *graces* of the Spirit, which relate to Christian character. It is unfortunate that an overemphasis on gifts has led some Christians to neglect the graces of the Spirit. Building Christian character must take precedence over displaying special abilities.

The characteristics that God wants in our

lives are seen in the ninefold fruit of the Spirit. Paul begins with *love* because all of the other fruit is really an outgrowth of love. Compare these eight qualities with the characteristics of love given to the Corinthians (see 1 Cor. 13:4-8). This word for love is *agape,* which means divine love. (The Greek word *eros,* meaning "sensual love," is never used in the New Testament.) This divine love is God's gift to us (Rom. 5:5), and we must cultivate it and pray that it will increase (Phil. 1:9).

When a person lives in the sphere of love, then he experiences *joy*—that inward peace and sufficiency that is not affected by outward circumstances. (A case in point is Paul's experience recorded in Phil. 4:10-20.) This "holy optimism" keeps him going in spite of difficulties. Love and joy together produce *peace,* "the peace of God, which passeth all understanding" (Phil. 4:7). These first three qualities express the *Godward* aspect of the Christian life.

The next three express the *manward* aspect of the Christian life: *long-suffering* (courageous endurance without quitting), *gentleness* (kindness), and *goodness* (love in action). The Christian who is long-suffering will not avenge himself or wish difficulties on those who oppose him. He will be kind and gentle, even with the most offensive, and will sow goodness where others sow evil. Human nature can never do this on its own; only the Holy Spirit can.

The final three qualities are *selfward: faith* (faithfulness, dependability); *meekness* (the right use of power and authority, power under control); and *temperance* (self-control). Meekness is not weakness. Jesus said, "I am meek and lowly in heart" (Matt. 11:29), and Moses was "very meek" (Num. 12:3); yet no one could accuse either of them of being weak. The meek Christian does not throw his weight around or assert himself. Just as wisdom is the right use of knowledge, so meekness is the right use of authority and power.

It is possible for the old nature to *counterfeit* some of the fruit of the Spirit, but the flesh can never *produce* the fruit of the Spirit. One difference is this: when the Spirit produces fruit, God gets the glory and the Christian is not conscious of his spirituality; but when the flesh is at work, the person is inwardly proud of himself and is pleased when others compliment him. The work of the Spirit is to make us more like Christ for His glory, not for the praise of men.

The cultivation of the fruit is important. Paul warns that there must be a right atmosphere before the fruit will grow (Gal. 5:25-26). Just as fruit cannot grow in every climate, so the fruit of the Spirit cannot grow in every individual's life or in every church.

Fruit grows in a climate blessed with an abundance of the Spirit and the Word. "Walk in the Spirit" (Gal. 5:25) means "keep in step with the Spirit"—not to run ahead and not to lag behind. This involves the Word, prayer, worship, praise, and fellowship with God's people. It also means "pulling out the weeds" so that the seed of the Word can take root and bear fruit. The Judaizers were anxious for praise and "vainglory," and this led to competition and division. Fruit can never grow in that kind of an atmosphere.

We must remember that this fruit is produced *to be eaten,* not to be admired and put on display. People around us are starving for love, joy, peace, and all the other graces of the Spirit. When they find them in our lives, they know that we have something they lack. We do not bear fruit for our own consumption; we bear fruit that others might be fed and helped, and that Christ might be glorified. The flesh may manufacture "results" that bring praise to us, but the flesh cannot bear fruit that brings glory to God. It takes patience, an atmosphere of the Spirit, walking in the light, the seed of the Word of God, and a sincere desire to honor Christ.

In short, the secret is the Holy Spirit. He alone can give us that "fifth freedom"—freedom from sin and self. He enables us to fulfill the law of love, to overcome the flesh, and to bear fruit.

Will you yield to Him and let Him work?

CHAPTER ELEVEN
THE LIBERTY OF LOVE
Galatians 6:1-10

The story has often been told about the message the founder of the Salvation Army sent to their international convention. General William Booth was unable to attend personally because of ill health, so he cabled the delegates a message containing one word: "OTHERS!"

In the popular comic strip "Peanuts," Lucy asks Charlie Brown, "Why are we here on earth?" He replies, "To make others happy." She ponders this for a moment and then asks, "Then why are the others here?"

"One another" is one of the key phrases in the Christian's vocabulary. "Love one another" is found at least a dozen times in the New Testament, along with "pray one for another" (James 5:16), "edify one another" (1 Thes. 5:11), prefer one another (Rom. 12:10), "use hospitality one to another" (1 Peter 4:9), and many other like admonitions.

In the section before us, Paul adds another phrase: "Bear ye one another's burdens" (Gal. 6:2). The Spirit-led Christian thinks of others and how he can minister to them. In this section, Paul describes two important ministries that we ought to share with one another.

Bearing Burdens (Gal. 6:1-5)

The legalist is not interested in bearing burdens. Instead, he *adds* to the burdens of others (Acts 15:10). This was one of the sins of the Pharisees in Jesus' day: "For they bind heavy burdens and grievous to be borne, and lay them on men's shoulders; but they themselves will not move them with one of their fingers" (Matt. 23:4). The legalist is always harder on other people than he is on himself, but the Spirit-led Christian demands more of himself than he does of others *that he might be able to help others.*

Paul presents a hypothetical case of a believer who is suddenly tripped up and falls into sin. The word *overtaken* carries the idea of being surprised, so it is not a case of deliberate disobedience. Why does Paul use this illustration? *Because nothing reveals the wickedness of legalism better than the way the legalists treat those who have sinned.* Call to mind the Pharisees who dragged a woman taken in adultery before Jesus (John 8). Or that Jewish mob that almost killed Paul because they *thought* he had defiled the temple by bringing in Gentiles (Acts 21:27ff). (Legalists do not need facts and proof; they need only suspicions and rumors. Their self-righteous imaginations will do the rest.) So, in this paragraph, Paul is really contrasting the way the legalist would deal with the erring brother, and the way the spiritual man would deal with him.

A contrast in aim. The spiritual man would seek to restore the brother in love, while the legalist would exploit the brother. The word *restore* means "to mend, as a net, or to restore a broken bone." If you have ever had a broken bone, you know how painful it is to have it set. The sinning believer is like a broken bone in the body, and he needs to be restored. The believer who is led by the Spirit and living in the liberty of grace will seek to help the erring brother, for "the fruit of the Spirit is love" (Gal. 5:22). "By love serve one another" (Gal. 5:13). When Jesus sought to be a physician to the sinful, He was severely criticized by the Pharisees (Mark 2:13-17), and so the spiritual believer today will be criticized by the legalists.

Instead of trying to restore the erring brother, the legalist will condemn him and then *use the brother to make himself look good.* This is what the Pharisee did in the Parable of the Pharisee and the Publican (Luke 18:9-14). "[Love] shall cover the multitude of sins" (1 Peter 4:8). The legalist rejoices when a brother falls, and often gives the matter wide publicity, because then he can boast about his own goodness and how much better his group is than the group to which the fallen brother belongs.

This is why Paul admonishes us, "Let us not be desirous of vainglory, provoking one another, envying one another" (Gal. 5:26). The word *provoke* means "to challenge to a contest, to compete with." The believer who walks in the Spirit is not *competing* with other Christians or challenging them to become "as good as he is." However, the legalist lives by competition and comparison, and tries to make himself look good by making the other fellow look bad.

A contrast in attitude. The Spirit-led believer approaches the matter in a spirit of meekness and love, while the legalist has an attitude of pride and condemnation. The legalist does not need to "consider himself" because he pretends he could never commit such a sin. But the believer living by grace realizes that no man is immune from falling. "Let him that thinketh he standeth take heed lest he fall" (1 Cor. 10:12). He has an attitude of humility because he realizes his own weaknesses.

But there is a second contrast: he knows the love of Christ in his own heart. "The law of Christ" is: "Love one another" (John 13:34; 15:12). Paul has already discussed the "law of love" (Gal. 5:13-15), and now he is applying it. "Tender loving care" is not a modern invention, because Paul is urging it on believers in this passage. How much we appreciate it when the doctor uses tenderness as he sets a broken bone. And how much more should we use "tender loving care" when we seek to restore a broken life.

It takes a great deal of love and courage for us to approach an erring brother and seek to help him. Jesus compares this to eye surgery (Matt. 7:1-5)—and how many of us feel qualified for that?

Paul probably has in mind here our Lord's instructions on reconciliation (Matt. 18:15-35). If your brother sins against you, go talk to him privately, *not* for the purpose of winning an argument, but for the purpose of winning your brother. (That word *gained* is the same word Paul uses in 1 Cor. 9:19-22 to refer to winning the lost to Christ. It is important to win the lost, but it is also important to win the saved.) If he hears you, then the matter is settled. But if he will not agree, then ask one or two spiritual people to go with you. If he will still not settle the matter, then the whole church must be informed and take steps of discipline. But Jesus goes on to point out that the church must practice prayer (Matt. 18:19-20) and forgiveness (Matt. 18:21-35), or discipline will not be effective.

The legalist, of course, has no time for this kind of spiritual "soul-winning." When he hears that his brother has sinned, instead of going to the brother, he shares the sad news with others ("so you can pray more intelligently about it") and then condemns the brother for not being more spiritual.

Remember, the legalist makes himself look better by making his brother look worse. Thus Paul's warnings here (Gal. 6:3-4). The Judaizers were guilty of boasting about themselves, their achievements, and their converts (Gal. 6:12-14). They usually did this by comparing themselves with others (see 2 Cor. 10:11). But such comparisons are sinful and deceptive. It is easy to find somebody worse off than we are, so that our comparison makes us look better than we really are. Christian love would lead us not to expose a brother's failures or weaknesses, no matter how much better it would make us look.

A man should "prove his own work" (Gal. 6:4) in the light of God's will and not in the shadows of somebody else's achievements. "Each man should test his own actions. Then he can take pride in himself, without comparing himself to somebody else, for each man should carry his own load" (Gal. 6:4-5, NIV). There is no place for competition in the work of God, unless we are competing against sin and Satan. When we see words like "best, fastest-growing, biggest, finest" applied to Christian ministries, we wonder who is getting the glory.

This does not mean that it is wrong to keep records. Charles Haddon Spurgeon used to say, "Those who criticize statistics usually have none to report." But we must be careful that we are not making others look bad just to make ourselves look good. And we should be able to rejoice at the achievements and blessings of others just as if they were our own (Rom. 12:10). After all, if one member of the body is blessed, it blesses the whole body.

There is no contradiction between Galatians 6:2 and 5, because two different Greek words for *burden* are used. In Galatians 6:2 it is a word meaning "a heavy burden," while in Galatians 6:5 it describes "a soldier's pack." We should help each other bear the heavy burdens of life, but there are personal responsibilities that each man must bear for himself. "Each soldier must bear his own pack." If my car breaks down, my neighbor can help drive my children to school, but he cannot assume the responsibilities that only belong to me as their father. That is the difference. It is wrong for me to expect somebody else to be the father in our family; that is a burden (and a privilege) that I alone can bear.

Sharing Blessings (Gal. 6:6-10)

Just as *one another* is a key phrase in the Christian vocabulary, so is the word *fellowship* (translated "communicate" in Gal. 6:6). From the very beginning of the church, *sharing* was one of the marks of Christian experience (Acts 2:41-47). The Greek word has now worked its way into our English vocabulary, and we see the word *koinonia* here and there in religious publications. It simply means "to have in common," and refers to our common fellowship in Christ (Gal. 2:9), our common faith (Jude 3), and even our sharing in the sufferings of Christ (Phil. 3:10). But often in the New Testament, *koinonia* refers to the sharing of material blessings with one another (Acts 2:42; 2 Cor. 8:4; Heb. 13:16 [Greek text]). It is this that Paul has in mind in these verses.

He begins with *a precept* (Gal. 6:6), urging us to share with one another. The teacher of the Word shares spiritual treasures, and those who are taught ought to share material treasures. (Paul uses a similar approach when he explains why the Gentile churches ought to give an offering to the Jewish believers—Rom. 15:27.) We must remember that what we do with *material* things is an evidence of how we value *spiritual* things. "For where your treasure is, there will your heart be also" (Matt. 6:21).

Because the Apostle Paul did not want money to become a stumbling block to the unsaved, he earned his own living (see 1 Cor. 9), but he repeatedly taught that the spiritual leader in the church was to be supported by the gifts of the people. Jesus said, "The laborer is worthy of his hire" (Luke 10:7), and Paul echoes this statement (1 Cor. 9:11, 14).

But we must realize the spiritual *principle* that lies behind this precept. God does not command believers to give simply that pastors and teachers (and missionaries, Phil. 4:10-19) might have their material needs met, *but that the givers might get a greater blessing* (Gal. 6:7-8). The basic principle of sowing and reaping is found throughout the entire Bible. God has ordained that we *reap what we sow.* Were it not for this law, the whole principle of "cause and effect" would fail. The farmer who sows wheat can expect to reap wheat. If it were otherwise, there would be chaos in our world.

But God has also told us to be careful *where we sow,* and it is this principle that Paul deals with here. He looks on our material possessions as seed, and he sees two possible kinds of soil: the flesh and the Spirit. We can use our material goods to promote the flesh, or to promote the things of the Spirit. But once we have finished sowing, *we cannot change the harvest.*

Money sown to the flesh will bring a harvest of corruption (see Gal. 5:19-21). That money is gone and can never be reclaimed. Money sown to the Spirit (such as sharing with those who teach the Word) will produce life, and in that harvest will be seeds that can be planted again for another harvest, and on and on into eternity. If every believer only looked on his material wealth as seed, and planted it properly, there would be no lack in the work of the Lord. Sad to say, much seed is wasted on carnal things and can never bring glory to God.

Of course, there is a much wider application of the principle to our lives; because all that we do is either an investment in the flesh or the Spirit. We shall reap whatever we have sown, and we shall reap *in proportion* as we have sown. "He which soweth sparingly shall reap also sparingly; and he which soweth bountifully shall reap also bountifully" (2 Cor. 9:6). The believer who walks in the Spirit and "sows" in the Spirit is going to reap a spiritual harvest. If his sowing has been generous, the harvest will be bountiful, if not in this life, certainly in the life to come.

Paul's enemies, the Judaizers, did not have this spiritual attitude toward giving and receiving. Paul sacrificed and labored that he might not be a burden to the churches, but the false teachers used the churches to promote their own schemes and fill their own coffers. This is also what happened in the Corinthian church, and Paul had to write them: "In fact, you even put up with anyone who enslaves you or exploits you or takes advantage of you or pushes himself forward or slaps you in the face" (2 Cor. 11:20, NIV).

How many times we have seen the sacrificing godly pastor persecuted and driven out, while the arrogant promoter is honored and gets everything he wants. The carnal believer thrives under the "spiritual dictatorship" of a legalistic promoter-pastor, because it makes him feel secure, successful, and spiritual. The carnal believer will sacrifice what he has to make the work more successful, only to discover that he is sowing to the flesh and not to the Spirit.

Having given us the precept (Gal. 6:6) and the principle behind the precept (Gal. 6:7-8), Paul now gives us *a promise* (Gal. 6:9): "In due season we shall reap if we faint not." Behind this promise is a peril: getting weary in the work of the Lord, and then eventually fainting, and stopping our ministry.

Sometimes spiritual fainting is caused by a lack of devotion to the Lord. It is interesting to contrast two churches that are commended for "work, labor, and patience" (1 Thes. 1:3; Rev. 2:2). The church at Ephesus had actually left its first love and was backslidden (Rev. 2:4-5). Why? The answer is seen in the commendation to the Thessalonian church: "Work of faith, labor of love, patience of hope." Not just work, labor, and patience, but the proper motivation: "faith, love, and hope." How easy it is for us to work for the Lord, but permit the spiritual motivation to die. Like the priests of Israel that Malachi addressed, we serve the Lord but complain, "Behold, what a weariness is it" (Mal. 1:13).

Sometimes we faint because of lack of prayer. "Men ought always to pray, and not to faint" (Luke 18:1). Prayer is to the spiritual life what breathing is to the physical life, and if you stop breathing, you will faint. It is also possible to faint because of lack of nourishment. "Man shall not live by bread alone, but by every word that proceedeth out of the mouth of God" (Matt. 4:4). If we try to keep going without proper food and rest, we will faint. How important it is to "wait upon the Lord" to get the strength we need for each day (Isa. 40:28-31).

But the promise Paul gives us will help to keep us going: "In due season we shall reap." The seed that is planted does not bear fruit immediately. There are seasons to the soul just as there are seasons to nature, and we must give the seed time to take root and bear fruit. How wonderful it is when the plowman overtakes the reaper (Amos 9:13). Each day we ought to sow the seed so that one day we will be able to reap (Ps. 126:5-6). But we must remember that the Lord of the harvest is in charge, and not the laborers.

Sharing blessings involves much more than teaching the Word and giving of our material substance. It also involves doing good "unto all men" (Gal. 6:10). There are those in this world who do evil (Ps. 34:16); in fact, there are those who return evil for good (Ps. 35:12). Most of the people in the world return good for good and evil for evil (see Luke 6:32-35; 1 Thes. 5:15). But the Christian is supposed to return good for evil (Rom. 12:18-21) and to do this in a spirit of Christian love. Actually, the Christian's good works are a spiritual sacrifice that he gives to the Lord (Heb. 13:16).

We are to "do good unto all men." This is how we let our light shine and glorify our Father in heaven (Matt. 5:16). It is not only by *words* that we witness to the lost, but also by our *works*. In fact, our works pave the way for our verbal witness; they win us the right to be heard. It is not a question of asking, "Does this person deserve my good works?" Did we deserve what God did for us in Christ? Nor should we be like the defensive lawyer who tried to argue, "Who is my neighbor?" (Luke 10:25-37) Jesus made it very clear that the question is not "Who is my neighbor?" but "To whom can I be a neighbor?"

As we "do good unto all men," we must give priority to "the household of faith," the fellowship of believers. This does not mean that the local church should become an exclusive clique with the members isolated from the world around them and doing nothing to help the lost. Rather, it is a matter of balance. Certainly the believers in Paul's day would have greater needs than would the outsiders, since many of the believers suffered for their faith (see Heb. 10:32-34). Furthermore, a man always cares for his own family before he cares for the neighborhood (1 Tim. 5:8).

We must remember, however, that we share with other Christians so that all of us might be able to share with a needy world. The Christian in the household of faith is a receiver that he might become a transmitter. As we abound in love for one another, we overflow in love for all men (1 Thes. 3:12).

This is how it was meant to be.

CHAPTER TWELVE THE MARKS OF FREEDOM

Galatians 6:11-18

It was Paul's custom, after dictating a letter, to take the pen and write his own farewell. His standard signature was, "The grace of our Lord Jesus Christ be with you" (1 Thes. 5:28; see 2 Thes. 3:17-18). But so concerned is Paul that the Galatians get the message of this letter that he takes the pen and writes *an entire concluding paragraph* with his own hand. "Look at the large letters I write with my own hand!"

Why did Paul write this paragraph, and why did he use such large letters? The Holy Spirit inspired him to add these closing words to give one more contrast between the legalists and the Spirit-led Christians, to show that the Spirit-led believer lives for the glory of God, not the praise of man. And he wrote in large letters for emphasis: "DON'T MISS THIS!"

Some Bible students believe that Paul's thorn in the flesh (2 Cor. 12:7-10; Gal. 4:14-15) was some kind of eye trouble. This would mean that he would have to write in large letters so that he himself would be able to read what he had written. Whether or not that is true, Paul is making it clear that he has something important to write in conclusion, that he is not simply going to end the letter in some conventional manner. If he did have eye trouble, his willingness to write this closing paragraph with his own hand would certainly appeal to the hearts of the readers.

He has shown them that the believer living under Law and the believer living under grace are diametrically opposed to each other. It is not just a matter of "different doctrine," but a matter of two different ways of life. They had to choose between bondage or liberty (Gal. 5:1-12), the flesh or the Spirit (Gal. 5:13-26), and living for self or living for others (Gal. 6:1-10).

Now he presents a fourth contrast: living for the praise of men or the glory of God (Gal. 6:11-18). He is dealing with *motive,* and there is no greater need in our churches today than for an examination of the motives for our ministries. We know *what* we are doing, but do we know *why* we are doing it? A good work is spoiled by a bad motive.

Paul approaches this delicate subject in an interesting way. The legalists wanted to subject the Galatian believers to circumcision, so Paul takes this up and relates it to the work of Christ on the cross, and also to his own ministry. In this paragraph Paul presents three "marked men"—the legalist (Gal. 6:12-13), the Lord Jesus Christ (Gal. 6:14-16), and the Apostle Paul himself (Gal. 6:17-18).

The Legalist (Gal. 6:12-13)

Paul does not have anything good to say about the legalist. He describes him and his kind in four ways.

They are braggarts (vv. 12a, 13b). Their main purpose was not to win people to Christ, or even to help the believers grow in grace. Their chief purpose was to win more converts so they could brag about them. They wanted to "make a fine impression outwardly" even though they did no good inwardly. Their work was not done for the good of the church or for the glory of God; it was done for their own glory.

While it is certainly not wrong to want to win people to Christ, or to see the work of the Lord increase, it is definitely wrong to want these blessings for the glory of man. We want to see more people sharing in our ministries, not so that we can count people, but because people count. But we must be careful not to "use people" to further our own selfish programs for our own glorification.

I receive a number of local church newsletters and newspapers. I was shocked to find an article in one of them in which the pastor named several other churches and proceeded to explain how his church was much better. Some of the churches he mentioned were not evangelical in belief, and I wondered what those members would think of Christ and the Gospel if they read his boastful critique. No doubt it made it difficult for the believers to witness to these other people once this pastor had condemned their churches.

They are compromisers (v. 12b). Why did they preach and practice circumcision and all that went with it? *To escape persecution.* Because Paul preached the grace of God and salvation apart from the works of the Law, he was persecuted (Gal. 5:11). The Judaizers tried to make the Christians think that they too were Christians, and they tried to make the followers of the Mosaic Law think that they too obeyed the Law. Consequently, they escaped being persecuted by the legalistic group for their identification with the cross of Christ and its devastating effect on the Law.

We are prone to look at the cross (and crucifixion) in a sentimental way. We wear crosses on our lapels or on chains around our necks. But to the first-century citizen, the cross was not a beautiful piece of jewelry; it was the lowest form of death and the ultimate in humiliation. The proper Roman citizen would never mention the cross in polite conversation. It stood for rejection and shame.

When Paul trusted Christ, he identified himself with the cross and took the consequences. To the Jew the cross was a stumbling block, and to the Gentile it was foolishness (1 Cor. 1:18-31). The legalists, emphasizing circumcision rather than crucifixion, won many converts. Theirs was a popular religion because it avoided the shame of the cross.

They are persuaders (v. 12a). The word *constrain* carries with it the idea of strong persuasion and even force. It is translated "compel" in Galatians 2:14. While it does not mean "to force against one's will," it is still a strong word. It indicates that the Judaizers were great persuaders; they had a "sales talk" that convinced the Galatian believers that legalism was the way for them. Whenever Paul presented the Word, it was in truth and sincerity, and he used no oratorical tricks or debater's skills. (See 1 Cor. 2:1-5 and 2 Cor. 4:1-5 to see how Paul presented the Word to his listeners. Paul was not a politician; he was an ambassador.)

They are hypocrites (v. 13). "They want you to submit to the Law, but they themselves do not obey the Law." The legalists belonged to the same group as the Pharisees about whom Jesus said, "They say and do not" (Matt. 23:3). Of course, Paul is not suggesting that the Judaizers *should* keep the Law, because keeping the Law is neither possible nor necessary. Rather, he is condemning them for their dishonesty; they had no intention of keeping the Law, even if they could. Their reverence for the Law was only a mask to cover their real goal: winning more converts to their cause. They wanted to report more statistics and get more glory.

Yes, the legalist is a marked man; so when you detect him, avoid him.

Jesus Christ (Gal. 6:14-16)

Paul keeps coming back to the cross (Gal. 2:20-21; 3:13; 4:5; 5:11, 24; 6:12). "If righteousness come by the Law, then Christ is dead in vain" (Gal. 2:21). The wounds of Calvary certainly make Christ a "marked Man," for those wounds mean liberty to those who will trust Him. The Judaizers boasted in circumcision; but Paul boasted in a crucified and risen Saviour. He gloried in the Cross. Certainly this does not mean that he gloried in the brutality or suffering of the cross. He was not looking at the cross as a piece of wood on which a criminal died. He was looking at the cross of *Christ* and glorying in it. Why would Paul glory in the Cross?

He knew the Person of the Cross. Jesus Christ is mentioned at least forty-five times in the Galatian letter, which means that one third of the verses contain some reference to Him. The person of Jesus Christ captivated Paul, and it was Christ who made the Cross glorious to him. In his early years as a Jewish rabbi, Paul had much to glory in (Gal. 1:13-14; Phil. 3:1-10); but after he met Christ, all his self-glory turned to mere refuse. The legalists did not glory in the cross of Christ *because they did not glory in Christ.* It was Moses—and themselves—who got the glory. They did not really know the Person of the Cross.

He knew the power of the Cross. To Saul, the learned Jewish rabbi, a doctrine of sacrifice on a cross was utterly preposterous. That the Messiah would come, he had no doubt, but that He would come to die—and to die *on a cursed cross*—well, there was no place for this in Saul's theology. The cross in that day was the ultimate example of weakness and shame. Yet Saul of Tarsus experienced the power of the Cross and became Paul the apostle. The cross ceased to be a stumbling block to him and became, instead, the very foundation stone of his message: "Christ died for our sins."

For Paul, the Cross meant *liberty:* from self (Gal. 2:20), the flesh (Gal. 5:24), and the world (Gal. 6:14). In the death and resurrection of Christ the power of God is released to give believers deliverance and victory. It is no longer *we* who live; it is Christ who lives in us and through us. As we yield to Him, we have victory over the world and the flesh. There is certainly no power in the Law to give a man victory over self, the flesh, and the Law. Quite the contrary, the Law *appeals* to the human ego ("I can do something to please God"), and encourages the flesh to work. And the world does not care if we are "religious" just so long as the Cross is left out. In fact, the world approves of religion—apart from the Gospel of Jesus Christ. So, the legalist inflates the ego, flatters the flesh, and pleases the world; the true Christian crucifies all three.

He knew the purpose of the Cross. It was to bring into the world a new "people of God." For centuries, the nation of Israel had been the people of God, and the Law had been their way of life. All of this was preparation for the coming of Jesus Christ (Gal. 4:1-7). Now that Christ had come and finished His great work of redemption, God had set aside the nation of Israel and brought into the world a "new creation" and a new nation, "the Israel of God." This does not mean that God is finished with the nation of Israel. Today, God is calling out from both Jews and Gentiles "a people for His name" (Acts 15:14), and in Christ there are no racial or national distinctions (Gal. 3:27-29). Paul clearly teaches, however, that there is a future in God's plan for the Jewish nation (Rom. 11).

One purpose of the cross was to bring in *a new creation* (Gal. 6:15, NIV). This "new creation" is the church, the body of Christ. The "old creation" was headed by Adam, and it ended in failure. The new creation is headed by Christ, and it is going to succeed.

To the Romans, Paul explained the doctrine of the two Adams—Adam and Christ (Rom. 5:12-21). The first Adam disobeyed God and brought into the world sin, death, and judgment. The Last Adam (1 Cor. 15:45) obeyed God and brought life, righteousness, and salvation. Adam committed one sin and plunged all of creation into judgment. Christ performed one act of obedience in His death on the cross, and paid for all the sins of the world. Because of Adam's sin, death reigns in this world. Because of Christ's victory, *we can "reign in life"* through Jesus Christ (Rom. 5:17). In other words, the believer belongs to a "new creation," a spiritual creation, that knows nothing of the defects and limitations of the "old creation" (see 2 Cor. 5:17).

Another purpose of the cross was to create *a new nation,* "the Israel of God" (Gal. 6:16). This is one of many names for the church found in the New Testament. Jesus said to the Jewish leaders, "The kingdom of God shall be taken from you, and given to a nation bringing forth the fruits thereof" (Matt. 21:43). Peter identifies that nation as the family of God: "But ye are a chosen generation, a royal priesthood, an holy nation" (1 Peter 2:9).

As mentioned previously, this does not mean that the church has permanently replaced the nation of Israel in the program of God, but only that the church is "the people of God" on earth today just as Israel was in centuries past.

What a rebuke to the Judaizers. They wanted to take the church back into Old Testament Law, when that Law could not even be kept by the nation of Israel! That nation was set aside to make way for God's new people, the church!

Believers today may not be "Abraham's children" in the flesh, but they are "Abraham's seed" through faith in Jesus Christ (Gal. 4:28-29). They have experienced a circumcision of the heart that is far more effective than physical circumcision (Rom. 2:29; Phil. 3:3; Col. 2:11). For this reason, neither circumcision nor the lack of it is of any consequence to God (Gal. 6:15; see also Gal. 5:6).

The Apostle Paul (Gal. 6:17-18)

There was a time when Paul was proud of his mark of circumcision (Phil. 3:4-6), but after he became a believer, he became a "marked man" in a different way. He now gloried in the scars he had received and in the suffering he had endured in the service of Jesus Christ.

The contrast with the legalists is plain to see: "The Judaizers want to mark your flesh and brag about you, but I bear in my body the brands of the Lord Jesus Christ—for His glory." What a rebuke! "If your religious celebrities have any scars to show for the glory of Christ, then let them be shown. Otherwise—stop bothering me!"

Paul is not claiming that he bore the five wounds of Calvary on his body. Rather he is affirming that he has suffered for Christ's sake (something the legalists never did), and he had on his body the scars to prove it. When you read 2 Corinthians 11:18-33, you have no difficulty understanding this claim of his, for in many ways and in many places Paul suffered physically for Christ.

In Paul's day, it was not unusual for the follower of some heathen god or goddess to be branded with the mark of that idol. He was proud of his god and wanted others to know it. In the same way, Paul was "branded" for Jesus Christ. It was not a temporary mark that could be removed, but a permanent mark that he would take to his grave. Nor did he receive his brands in an easy way: he had to suffer repeatedly to become a marked man for Christ.

It was also the practice in that day to brand slaves, so that everyone would know who the owner was. Paul was the slave of Jesus Christ, and he wore His mark to prove it.

It is worth noting that *sin brands a person.* It may mark his mind, his personality, even his body. Few people are proud of the sin marks they bear, and conversion does not change them. (Thank God, those changes will come when Jesus returns!) How much better it is to love Christ and live for Him and be "branded" for His glory.

Believers today need to remember that it is the Christian leader who has *suffered* for Christ who has something to offer. The Judaizers in Paul's day knew nothing of suffering. They may have been persecuted in some small way for belonging to a religious group, but this is far different from "the fellowship of His [Christ's] sufferings" (Phil. 3:10).

Beware of that religious leader who lives in his ivory tower and knows nothing of battling against the world, the flesh, and the devil, who has no "marks" to show for his obedience to Christ. Paul was no armchair general; he was out in the front lines, waging war against sin, and taking his share of suffering.

So, Paul comes to the end of his letter; and he closes just the way he began: GRACE! Not "the Law of Moses," but THE GRACE OF OUR LORD JESUS CHRIST!

No more need be said, because that says it all.